SCRIBNER LIBRARY OF DAILY LIFE

ENCYCLOPEDIA OF
FOOD
AND CULTURE

EDITORIAL BOARD

Central Europe Market hall in Wrocław, Poland. The new market hall, shown here, replaced the old hall, which was destroyed during World War II. Photo by André Baranowski.

SCRIBNER LIBRARY OF DAILY LIFE

ENCYCLOPEDIA OF
FOOD
AND CULTURE

VOLUME 2:
Food Production to Nuts

Solomon H. Katz, Editor in Chief

William Woys Weaver, Associate Editor

CHARLES SCRIBNER'S SONS®

THOMSON

GALE

New York • Detroit • San Diego • San Francisco • Cleveland • New Haven, Conn. • Waterville, Maine • London • Munich

Encyclopedia of Food and Culture

Solomon H. Katz, Editor in Chief

William Woys Weaver, Associate Editor

© 2003 by Charles Scribner's Sons

Charles Scribner's Sons is an imprint of The Gale Group, Inc., a division of Thomson Learning, Inc.

Charles Scribner's Sons® and Thomson Learning™ are trademarks used herein under license.

For more information, contact
Charles Scribner's Sons
An imprint of the Gale Group
300 Park Avenue South
New York, NY 10010

For permission to use material from this product, submit your request via Web at http://www.gale-edit.com/permissions, or you may download our Permissions Request form and submit your request by fax or mail to:

Permissions Department
The Gale Group, Inc.
27500 Drake Rd.
Farmington Hills, MI 48331-3535
Permissions Hotline:
248-699-8006 or 800-877-4253, ext. 8006
Fax: 248-699-8074 or 800-762-4058

LIBRARY OF CONGRESS CATALOGING-IN-PUBLICATION DATA

Encyclopedia of food and culture / Solomon H. Katz, editor in chief ;
William Woys Weaver, associate editor.
    p. cm.
Includes bibliographical references and index.
    ISBN 0-684-80568-5 (set : alk. paper) — ISBN 0-684-80565-0 (v. 1) —
ISBN 0-684-80566-9 (v. 2) — ISBN 0-684-80567-7 (v. 3)
    1. Food habits—Encyclopedias. 2. Food—Encyclopedias. I. Katz, Solomon H., 1939-
II. Weaver, William Woys, 1947-   III. Title.
GT2850 .E53 2003
394.1'2'097303—dc21   2002014607

Printed in the United States of America
10 9 8 7 6 5 4

ENCYCLOPEDIA OF
FOOD
AND CULTURE

FOOD PRODUCTION, HISTORY OF.

Ensuring sufficient food supplies is one of the most basic challenges facing any human society. Organized and efficient food production supports population growth and the development of cities and towns, trade, and other essential elements of human progress.

For many thousands of years, people collected their food from the wild or hunted animals large and small. The teamwork required to bring down a mastodon may have been the first type of collective enterprise in which humans engaged. The "hunter-gatherer" mode was sufficient for small groups in favorable environments, but as population grew and people pushed into areas less endowed with easily obtainable food, they sought more reliable sources of nutrition.

Scientists believe that agriculture was established first in the Fertile Crescent of the Middle East about ten or eleven thousand years B.C.E. The region was home to a variety of edible and easily cultivated crops: wheat and barley among the cereal crops, and lentils, peas, and chickpeas among the vegetables. Also, the region was endowed with wild goats, sheep, pigs, and cattle, all of which were domesticated and became important sources of food. Cattle are also useful work animals, and all these animals produce manure for fertilizer. Thus, a complete agricultural package was available, and it helped give rise to the civilizations in the Middle East. The need for common facilities to thresh and store grain was a major impetus for settlements; the wall of Jericho dates from around 8000 B.C.E. and was presumably built to protect its food supply.

Agriculture developed independently in the part of Mexico and Central America known as Mesoamerica; in the Andean highlands of Peru; in the American Midwest; in north and south China; and in Africa. But the Fertile Crescent had a long head start and the most favorable combination of plants and animals, and this eventually translated into a significant cultural advantage for Europe.

In the ancient world, the Mediterranean Sea was crisscrossed with ships carrying spices from the Middle East and ultimately India, wine and olive oil from Greece, and grain from Egypt. The city of Rome came to depend on wheat from Egypt and North Africa to supply the grain (and, later, bread) that was distributed free of charge to its plebeians. The *annona* (the distribution of free or reduced-price grain or bread) reached impressive dimensions: by 350 B.C.E., an estimated 120,000 people received six half-pound loaves per day provided by 274 public bakeries. It was one of the world's first examples of mass production of a specific food product.

Roman agriculture was otherwise centered on the *villa rustica*, a type of large estate with diversified production of grain, vegetables, fruits, nuts, and livestock. After the Roman Empire collapsed, these estates became the model of the medieval fief, the property held by a lord and worked by serfs who were legally bound to the land. The serfs had to work the lord's land but also had the right to work strips of their own, plus small kitchen gardens. In the early feudal period, peasant families could gather game in the forests, but eventually these were reserved to the aristocracy and the peasants got by on little more than bread and gruel.

Technology, as simple as it was in the Middle Ages, played a role in increasing food production. The development of a heavy plow capable of breaking the dense,

Professional trade journals from the past provide rich source material for the history of food production. ROUGHWOOD COLLECTION.

1

This Australian photograph from the early 1890s records an old method of hand grading and packing apples. © BETTMANN/ CORBIS.

wet soils of northern Europe reached Germany by the eighth century, and opened up a major new grain source for the rest of the continent. Grist mills powered by wind or water popped up all over Europe beginning in the eleventh century, providing large-scale processing of grain into flour.

Medieval European crop farmers had few options for increasing production. The usual practice was to rotate fields between grain and pasture so that they would be refreshed by animal manure between crops, a practice called "fallows." In the later Middle Ages, the revitalizing power of legumes, which supply nitrogen to the soil, a technique lost since Roman times, was rediscovered. Rotating fields through grain, legumes, and fallows boosted productivity by at least a third and added peas, beans, chickpeas, lentils, and other vegetables to the European diet.

China, often thought of as a land of rice, also depended heavily on millet, wheat, and soybeans. Rice production increased significantly in the eleventh century when new strains were imported from Southeast Asia. Chinese fishermen also gathered fish from the ocean, lakes, and rivers, and sold them in vast central markets, which supplied networks of cookshops, restaurants, banqueting halls, and other eating places.

The Arab world also had a varied and sophisticated system of food production, with water-powered mills grinding grain full-time in North Africa and fishermen packing Mediterranean tuna in salt. The Arabs introduced citrus, rice, and sugarcane to Europe and controlled the lucrative spice trade with India. European

interest in breaking the Arab hold on the spice trade led to the voyages of discovery of Vasco da Gama and Columbus.

Discovery of the New World touched off the greatest and most rapid spread of new crops the world had seen. The Americas contributed maize (corn), potatoes, tomatoes, and peppers to Europe, while the Europeans brought wheat and other staple crops, and sugarcane, which was very successful in Brazil and later the Caribbean region. Sugarcane cultivation created a demand for labor that was met by the African slave trade. The "Columbian Exchange" thus laid the basis for much of the subsequent economic and political history of the New World.

In the Old World, the decline of feudalism and the rise of cities and towns helped move agriculture from subsistence to a market orientation. Land that had been held in common and used mainly for grazing was consolidated under the control of individual landowners, which greatly increased production of both crops and animals. The draining of marshy land, especially in England and the Low Countries, was accelerated. All these trends supported the more intensive cultivation of the available land and the production of more and cheaper food for growing and more urban populations. By 1700, European agriculture could provide approximately two-and-a-half times the yield per input of seed that had been normal in the Middle Ages (Roberts, 1997).

Science and technology played an increasingly important role in food production in the eighteenth and nineteenth centuries. The development of mineral and then chemical fertilizers freed farmers from reliance on manure and fallows as ways of renewing the soil. New equipment, such the mechanical seed drill, made for more efficient planting. The mechanization of agriculture advanced rapidly in the nineteenth century with mechanical reapers, the tractor, and electric milking machines, among other innovations. Scientists also developed a better understanding of the nutritional components of food, which led to an emphasis on a balanced diet and, by the twentieth century, resulted in the improvement of food with the addition of vitamins and minerals to products such as bread and breakfast food.

Preserving food for later consumption has always been a challenge, especially in countries with long winters when little fresh food was available. Grain kept well if kept dry, but meat and fish had to be salted, and a monotonous diet of bread, dried peas, and salted fish sustained many Europeans through the winter until the early modern period. The preservation of food by heating it and sealing it in jars or cans began in the early nineteenth century, followed by pasteurization of wine and later milk to kill spoilage organisms. (The great chemist Louis Pasteur developed the process that bears his name to save the French wine industry, not its dairy farmers.) Canning and pasteurization made a wider variety of foods available to urban populations

With the development of steamships and refrigeration in the nineteenth century, the international food trade was transformed. Beef could be shipped from Argentina to England and bananas from Central America to New York. Worldwide food exports went from 4 million tons in the 1850s to 18 million tons thirty years later and 40 million tons by 1914 (Ponting, 1992). Chicago became the center of the U.S. meatpacking industry when refrigerated rail cars allowed packers to ship butchered meat virtually nationwide.

Agriculture, fisheries, and livestock and poultry production are now so efficient in Europe, North America, Australia, Argentina, Brazil, Japan, and other advanced countries that production can easily overwhelm demand, resulting in low prices and financial losses for producers. Governments all over the world subsidize their farmers and attempt to protect them from foreign competition, which keeps farmers in business but raises the cost of food to consumers. In the United States, for example, sugar costs twice what it does on the world market because of the protection of domestic producers.

Some of the benefits of Western agriculture and food production have been modified and transferred to the developing world. The use of high-yield wheat and rice, along with large doses of fertilizer—the so-called "Green Revolution"—has transformed the food picture in many countries. Wheat production in India nearly tripled from 1965 to 1980 while rice production increased 60 percent with the new strains and new methods. During the 1970s alone, rice production rose 37 percent in Indonesia and 40 percent in the Philippines.

Food today is often highly processed before being sold to consumers. Conversely, "pure," "organic," "all-natural" foods are becoming more popular. While dwarfed by the mainstream food industry, organic production can be profitable and viable. Governments seek to encourage this type of production, with strict regulations (effective 2003) on what can be labeled "organic" in the United States and programs such as "Label Rouge" ("red label"), which recognizes organic-style production, in France.

With rapid advances in biotechnology, genetic manipulation of crops accelerated in the 1990s and is expected to have a significant impact on food production. Maize, for example, is bioengineered to resist insect pests, and soybeans are modified to shrug off a common herbicide that keeps the fields free of weeds. These traits are advantageous to producers but not directly beneficial to consumers. The next level of genetic modification will be to insert traits actually beneficial to humans into food plants, such as rice fortified with extra vitamins that ward off blindness. Genetic modification of food plants is controversial and closely regulated by government but is felt by many to be the next frontier in food production.

See also **Agriculture, Origins of; Agriculture since the Industrial Revolution; Agronomy; Food Supply and the Global Food Market; Food Supply, Food Shortages; Green Revolution; High-Technology Farming; Horticulture; Packaging and Canning; Pasteur, Louis.**

BIBLIOGRAPHY

Diamond, Jared. *Guns, Germs, and Steel: The Fates of Human Societies.* New York: Norton, 1997.

Flandrin, Jean-Louis, and Massimo Montanari, eds. *Food: A Culinary History.* New York: Penguin, 2000.

Ponting, Clive. *A Green History of the World: The Environment and the Collapse of Great Civilizations.* New York: St. Martin's, 1992.

Riera-Melis, Antoni. "Society, Food and Feudalism," in *Food: A Culinary History,* Jean-Louis Flandrin, and Massimo Montanari, eds. New York: Penguin Books, 2000.

Roberts, J. M. *A History of Europe.* New York: Allen Lane/ Penguin, 1997.

Solbrig, Otto T., and Dorothy J. Solbrig. *So Shall You Reap: Farming and Crops in Human Affairs.* Washington, D.C.: Island Press, 1994.

Tannahill, Reay. *Food in History.* New York: Three Rivers Press, 1989.

Thomas, Hugh. *World History: The Story of Mankind from Prehistory to the Present.* New York: HarperCollins, 1996.

Richard L. Lobb

FOOD RIOTS. A food riot can be defined as any gathering, whether planned or spontaneous, that may begin peacefully (a "food protest") but evolves into disorder, leading to loss of control, violence, bodily harm, or damage to property. "Food riot" and "food protest" can be understood and discussed together as "food disturbances" (Gilje, p. 4). Food disturbances occur and have occurred for obvious reasons: When people feel their sense of entitlement to an adequate supply of food is being breached by those controlling the food supply, they will go to extreme measures to get the kind, quantity, and quality of food they feel they need for themselves and their families.

Historical and archaeological evidence documents the existence of food riots for several thousands of years and in all parts of the world, with periods of greater and lesser activity (Newman). Food riots occurred most frequently in the modern era (sixteenth through eighteenth centuries), declined through the nineteenth and twentieth centuries, and increased again toward the end of the twentieth century, primarily in developing countries.

Types of Food Riots

Since it is such a strong component and shaper of identity, food is deeply enmeshed in a collective as well as an individual sense of identity. How and why foods accrue special meaning—what makes them unique to particular groups of people—can vary widely: method of preparation, long-held tradition, particular "flavor principles,"

A political power struggle in Haiti resulted in massive food riots and looting in Port-au-Prince in 1994. © PETER TURNLEY/ CORBIS.

perception of purity, religious, cultural, or political significance, signification of wealth or status, or any combination of factors. The restriction in availability of foods imbued with distinctive meaning, then, whether through government manipulation or the vicissitudes of a "free market" economy, can function as a catalyst for collective protest. This is true not only in relatively isolated communities in the past, but in the ever-changing global villages of the twenty-first century.

A major subfield in social history, a rich body of scholarly work both documents and theorizes about food disturbances. European social historians especially have set the standard for scholarship in the field. While no two riots are ever exactly the same, and each contains a multiplicity of circumstances, historians have generalized that in the past food riots have fallen into three main categories: First, a blockage or entrave, where protesters blocked shipments of grain or other foodstuffs shipped from one region to another; second, the price riot or *taxation populaire*, where peasants seized the goods from a retail shop whose prices were deemed too high, which would then be sold for a "just price," and often the money paid to the merchant. The final form of food riots, the market riot, was simply looting stores and supply depots to protest high prices or the lack of goods (Thompson; Gilje; Walton and Seddon).

Modern-day riots tend to conform to the latter category of market riots, as looting and destroying property are common factors. In addition are the more calculated, less volatile, demonstrations where the food at issue is ceremoniously dumped on the grounds of, for example, the local government headquarters. The boycotting of food, also a common means of protest in the twentieth century, can be effective, especially when centered on one item such as milk, beer, bread, or grapes, or on a single manufacturer (Linden). Boycotts, however, can evolve into full-fledged food riots if participants harass or vio-

lently attack those choosing to purchase a targeted item or frequent a targeted store.

Theories of Food Rioting

Why do people riot over food? The obvious answer, that they riot because they are hungry, does not begin to answer the question since most who are poor and hungry do not riot. What intervening variables determine who eventually riots over which foods? Historians have analyzed and explained food riots in a variety of ways, including as collective action representing the "moral economy" of an era, as part of a so-called "female consciousness," and as an exhibition of nationalism/patriotism. In his 1971 article, "The Moral Economy of the English Crowd in the Eighteenth Century," eminent British historian E. P. Thompson sets about to provide a "thick description" of food rioters' motives in preindustrial England, an era when subsistence riots happened with great frequency. Thompson argues that English peasant bread riots were symptomatic of a society caught between changing economic and political forces, of an England in the midst of moving from a looser collection of landed gentry to a stronger state, and from a mercantilist, feudal economic system to one of laissez-faire market capitalism. Peasants under the feudal system were used to bread sold at "just prices"—an amount reduced for the poor as part of the communal moral ethos. In the shift to an emerging market economy that abandoned the notion of the just price, peasants understandably clung to the older "moral economy." Viewing inexpensive bread prices as an entitlement, when peasants felt the long-held social pact was not being honored under the new system, they rioted in response. People, argues Thompson, were thus not just rioting because they were hungry, but also out of a sense of injustice. As the peasantry evolved into the industrialized working class, conflicts over food were absorbed into and displaced by organized labor strikes. This explains why the number of food riots diminished considerably in the nineteenth century and beyond. Scholars have taken issue with Thompson's moral economy theory, but few if any reject his theory outright.

Since women as well as men participated in food riots, often in unique ways, in recent years historians have employed gender as a category of analysis. While not disagreeing with the moral economists, historians such as Temma Kaplan point out that, although the number of food riots decreased in the nineteenth century, food disturbances nevertheless continued. Moreover, they argue, food rioting took on a noticeably female persona, in part because labor unions, the new locus of collective action, largely excluded women. Studying early-twentieth-century food riots in Barcelona, Kaplan argues that women participated in food riots as an extension of their role in the sexual division of labor: caring for home and family, which included food procurement and preparation. Women who accepted the traditional division of labor, argues Kaplan, could be radicalized to action in the public sphere if they were prevented from fulfilling their obligation, especially the feeding and care of their families.

Food riots can also be examined in light of cultural meanings of consumption and their connection to nationalism. Historian Timothy Breen explores the relation between the growth of national consciousness and the American colonial rejection of British manufactured goods, including foodstuffs. Manufactured goods imported from Britain, readily available to so many people, Breen argues, resulted in a standardization of taste that transcended (to some extent) class boundaries. Consumer goods became politicized in the decades leading up to the American Revolution, providing a "shared language of consumption" that colonists of all regions and classes could understand and identify with, hence providing a common experience and knowledge base that united them enough to wage war against the mother country. While Breen does not limit his analysis to food but explores the meaning of consumer goods of all kinds, he focuses on the struggle over tea and its culminating food protest, the Boston Tea Party.

Modern-Day Food Rioting
While food riots and protests have occurred in the nineteenth and twentieth centuries, the recent wave of food riots and protests are directly tied to strict economic austerity plans forced on developing countries by the International Monetary Fund (IMF) and other international banks. Governments attempting to repay bank loans must enact draconian measures, including abandoning the long tradition of subsidizing staple foods such as bread, rice, and cooking oil. The resulting high prices, deflated wages, scarce resources, shrinking food supplies, and empty bellies has led to a series of food riots, including the looting and pillaging of stores, fast-food restaurants, and supply depots, the blockading of farm and supply trucks, and protests in town squares that have erupted into mayhem and violence. Often the protests and riots have centered on one food item, usually a staple or key ingredient (often with a tradition of subsidization by the government) integral to the culture's cuisine and consumed by rich and poor alike: rice, tortillas, onions, bread. The item, so central to their food habits, has functioned as a symbol of people's intense frustration and anger at being trapped in a global economic web in which they seem to have no agency. Social scientists John Walton and David Seddon note similarities between these recent austerity riots and those of the preindustrial European peasantry. Each era of food rioting, they argue, includes a context of burgeoning urban metropolises, severe economic hardship, and populations with a strong sense of moral economy that regards subsidized food prices as a government obligation.

See also **Consumer Protests; Food as a Weapon of War; Food Supply, Food Shortages; Hunger, Physiology of; Hunger Strikes; Malnutrition; Political Economy.**

BIBLIOGRAPHY

Breen, T. H. "Baubles of Britain: The American and Consumer Revolutions of the Eighteenth Century." *Past and Present* 119 (1988): 73–104.

Gilje, Paul A. *Rioting in America*. Bloomington: Indiana University Press, 1996.

Kaplan, Temma. "Female Consciousness and Collective Action: The Case of Barcelona, 1910–1918." *Signs* 7 (1982): 545–566.

Linden, Marcel van der. "Working-Class Consumer Power." *International Labor and Working-Class History* 46 (1994): 109–121.

Newman, Lucile F., Alan Boegehold, David Herlihy, Robert W. Kates, and Kurt Raaflaub. "Agricultural Intensification, Urbanization, and Hierarchy." *Hunger in History: Food Shortage, Poverty, and Deprivation*, edited by L. Newman et al. Oxford, England, and Cambridge, Mass.: Blackwell, 1990.

Thompson, E. P. "The Moral Economy of the English Crowd in the Eighteenth Century." *Past and Present* 50 (1971): 76–136.

Walton, John, and David Seddon. *Free Markets and Food Riots: The Politics of Global Adjustment*. Oxford, England, and Cambridge, Mass.: Blackwell, 1994.

Amy Bentley

FOOD SAFETY. Food safety is a matter that affects anyone who eats food. Whether or not a person consciously thinks about food safety before eating a meal, a host of other people have thought about the safety of that food, from farmers to scientists to company presidents to federal government officials and public health officials. Ensuring the safety of food is a shared responsibility among producers, industry, government, and consumers. Safe food is food that is free not only from toxins, pesticides, and chemical and physical contaminants, but also from microbiological pathogens such as bacteria, parasites, and viruses that can cause illness.

Those working in the field of food safety are most concerned about microbial foodborne illness, a widespread but often unrecognized sickness that affects most people at one time or another. At least four factors are necessary for foodborne illness to occur: (1) a pathogen; (2) a food vehicle; (3) conditions that allow the pathogen to survive, reproduce, or produce a toxin; and (4) a susceptible person who ingests enough of the pathogen or its toxin to cause illness. The symptoms often are similar to those associated with the flu—nausea, vomiting, diarrhea, abdominal pain, fever, headache. Most people have experienced foodborne illness, even though they might not recognize it as such, instead blaming it on the stomach flu or a twenty-four-hour bug. Usually symptoms disappear within a few days, but in some cases there can be more long-lasting effects such as joint inflammation or kidney failure. In the most severe cases people die from foodborne illness.

Current estimates of foodborne illness in the United States are 76 million cases, 325,000 hospitalizations, and 5,194 deaths from foodborne pathogens per year. In cases when the pathogen is identified, bacteria cause 30 percent of foodborne illnesses, parasites 3 percent, and viruses 67 percent. But as far as deaths are concerned, bacterial pathogens are the leading cause of death, with 72 percent of total foodborne illness deaths attributable to bacteria. Fatality rates for two bacteria are particularly high; for *Listeria* 20 percent of the people may die, and for *Vibrio vulnificus* 39 percent. Just six pathogens account for over 90 percent of the deaths associated with foodborne illness: *Salmonella* (31 percent), *Listeria* (28 percent), Toxoplasma (21 percent), Norwalk-like viruses (7 percent), *Campylobacter* (5 percent), and *Escherichia coli* (3 percent). According to FoodNet data from 1996–1997, each person in the United States suffers 1.4 episodes of diarrhea per year. With a U.S. population of 267.7 million persons, that works out to 375 million episodes per year, many of them related to eating unsafe food. Factors that contributed the most to foodborne illness are improper holding temperatures, inadequate cooking, contaminated equipment, food from unsafe sources, and poor personal hygiene.

Factors Influencing the Safety of Food

Stories of foodborne illness have become much more prevalent throughout the world. Is food less safe than it used to be, and if so, what factors account for this? News travels fast these days, both electronically and through the news media. What were once isolated events and stories, now reach millions within hours. Diagnostic techniques are constantly improving, allowing for identification of diseases, foodborne and otherwise, that would have been of unknown origin in the past. But even considering these facts, public-health officials believe that the risk of foodborne illness has increased over the past twenty years (GAO, 1996). Some threats to food safety have been around since ancient times, while others are newer, the result of changing demographics and lifestyles, production practices, and even evolution of microorganisms themselves.

Demographics

The proportion of the population at serious risk of foodborne illness is increasing as the population ages and the number of people with weakened immune systems grows. People who are at higher risk of becoming seriously ill include infants, young children, the elderly, pregnant women, those taking certain medications, and those with diseases such as acquired immunodeficiency syndrome (AIDS), cancer, and diabetes that weaken their immune systems. Demographers predict that the proportion of people over sixty years old in industrialized countries such as the United States will rise from the current 17 percent of the population to 25 percent by 2025 (Kaferstein, 1999). In one survey, 89 percent of deaths with diarrhea as an underlying cause were adults fifty-five and over or children under the age of five (Morris, 1997).

While anybody can get sick from eating contaminated food, the severity of the illness depends on a number of factors. Most important among these are age, amount of contamination consumed, and health status of the individual. The body has a number of defenses to protect itself against harmful bacteria. The acidic gastric juices of the stomach are one of the first defenses against foodborne pathogens, as many bacteria cannot survive in an acidic environment. Very young infants and aging adults produce fewer, or less acidic, gastric juices than younger, healthy adults. The normal bacteria present in the gastrointestinal system form another protective barrier against foodborne illness by preventing harmful bacteria from colonizing the gut. Use of antibiotics, which destroy the protective bacteria normally present in the gastrointestinal tract as well as their target bacteria, make it easier for pathogenic bacteria to invade and cause illness. Finally, the human immune system, not fully developed at birth, gradually reaches maturity in puberty and then slowly begins to decline after about fifty years of age.

Consumer Lifestyles and Demand

As the pace of life quickens, we often eat meals on the run, and spend less time on food preparation, preferring instead restaurants, convenience foods, or already prepared meals. This means that by the time you eat your food, it may have been transported, cooked, cooled, stored, transported again, reheated, and touched by numerous individuals. Each processing step introduces new hazards that could allow for the survival and growth of pathogens. In the United States, two out of three people ate their main meal away from home at least once a week in 1998. The typical consumer over eight years of age ate food away from home at least four times per week (Collins, 1997). Americans spend fifty cents of every food dollar on food prepared outside the home—from supermarkets, restaurants, or institutions.

Add to this the mishandling of food that occurs after a consumer purchases food and takes it home, and the likelihood of illness increases. Approximately 20 percent of reported foodborne illness cases occur from food cooked at home. Experts believe that this number is actually much higher, but that most people do not report cases of illness caused by foods cooked at home (Knabel, 1995; Doyle, 2000). As people cook less, they pass on less knowledge of cooking to their children, who are nevertheless increasingly responsible for preparing meals. This has grave implications for the future of food safety. In a survey of consumer food safety knowledge and practices, 86 percent of respondents knew that they should wash their hands before preparing food, but only 66 percent reported actually doing so. Only 67 percent of respondents reported washing or changing cutting boards after cutting raw meat or poultry. Older adults practiced safe behaviors more often than did younger adults (Altekruse, 1995). In an Australian study in which researchers asked people about their food safety and kitchen habits, and then filmed them preparing food, there were large differences in what people said they did and what they actually did. Almost half the people who said they washed their hands after handling raw meat did not, and when they did it was often without soap. Nineteen percent of the households that claimed to have soap in the kitchen did not (Jay, 1999).

Consumers are increasingly demanding fresh and natural products, prepared with fewer preservatives. Without the traditional preservatives and processing methods that prevent microbial growth, modern all-natural and fresh products are more perishable. Food processing, mainly canning, freezing, and pasteurizing, not only extends the shelf-life of foods, but also inhibits bacterial growth, making food safer. As an example, fresh apple cider has been associated with several foodborne disease outbreaks. An outbreak of *Escherichia coli* O157:H7 in which a child died was associated with raw unpasteurized apple juice from a company that built its reputation on the naturalness of its products.

As the role of fresh fruits and vegetables in a nutritious diet has become evident, people are including them in their diet more. In 1993 Americans ate 27 percent more fresh produce than they did in 1973. An increase in the number of foodborne illness outbreaks associated with fresh produce has accompanied this increase in consumption. In the last twenty years of the twentieth century, the number of identifiable outbreaks in which produce was the food vehicle doubled (Tauxe et al., 1997). Most produce only grows in the United States in certain seasons, yet this seasonal availability has almost disappeared from our supermarkets as consumers demand year-round availability of produce. From 1996 to 1998 *Cyclospora cayetanensis* sickened more than 2,400 people throughout twenty states and Canada. The only common food vehicle among these individuals was raspberries imported from Guatemala. Smaller outbreaks of *Cyclospora* have been traced to basil and mesclun lettuce grown in the United States.

Food Production and Economics
In the past, outbreaks of foodborne illness were relatively small and local. Illness could be traced back to local events such as weddings, church dinners, and other gatherings where a large number of people ate the same food. Today's food is produced in vastly different ways from those of even several decades ago. Food used to be grown, produced, and distributed on a local basis. Food production is now centralized and on a larger scale than in the past. Products made in a single processing plant in mass quantities are shipped all over the country, sometimes throughout the world. A mistake made in the processing will be felt nationwide instead of just locally. In 1994 an estimated 224,000 people throughout the nation became ill from *Salmonella enteritidis* after eating ice cream produced at one ice cream processing facility in Minnesota,

but shipped around the country (Hennessy, 1996). Recalls from processing plants are on a larger and larger scale. In 1998 Sara Lee recalled 35 million pounds of hot dogs and lunch meat due to the presence of *Listeria*. This is food contamination on a scale unprecedented a generation ago.

Even the manner in which farmers raise animals can contribute to an increase in food safety problems. A large number of animals are often crowded together, increasing their stress levels and weakening their immune systems. This crowding also facilitates the spread of disease from one animal to another. In the old days a sick animal would be fairly isolated and if it became sick it would not pass on illness to the rest of the flock or herd. But with closer animal-to-animal contact, disease can quickly spread throughout the whole group.

New and Evolving Pathogens
As recently as fifty years ago scientists had identified four foodborne pathogens. Today five times that number are on the list. Twenty years ago scientists did not even recognize three of the four pathogens that the Centers for Disease Control considers the most important in causing foodborne illness—*Campylobacter jejuni*, *Listeria monocytogenes*, and *E. coli* O157:H7. *C. cayetanensis* first appeared in 1979 and is still not well understood. It is likely that scientists will discover new foodborne pathogens as laboratory techniques improve.

As living organisms, pathogens are constantly evolving. With better ability to trace outbreaks, scientists are discovering that some bacteria survive in environments previously thought safe. For example, *E. coli* O157:H7, originally called "hamburger disease" because of its presence in undercooked ground beef, has shown up in foods as diverse as salami, apple cider, raw milk, and lettuce. It also survives in lower pH conditions than originally thought, leading to the outbreaks in acidic foods such as salami and apple cider. It is now known that *Yersinia enterocolitica* and *L. monocytogenes* can survive and multiply at refrigeration temperatures.

Some foods long considered safe have recently been implicated in foodborne outbreaks. For years scientists believed the inside of an egg was sterile and that *Salmonella enteritidis* was not of concern. Now however, they know that chickens infected with *Salmonella* pass this infection along in their eggs, so that the bacteria can be found inside the raw egg, making it unsafe to eat raw or undercooked eggs. This was not known until 1989. Knowledge of this fact caused food safety experts to advise people to cook eggs thoroughly or to use liquid pasteurized eggs.

Bacteria have long been capable of evolving to thwart attempts to eliminate them. Some pathogens are now becoming resistant to common antimicrobial agents. It is thought that the resistance may be related to the subtherapeutic use of these antibiotics in animals. We are seeing this same adaptability in foodborne bacteria. *Salmonella typhimurium* DT104 is widely distributed in wild and farm animals, especially in Europe, and is resistant to several common antibiotics. There has been a parallel increase with people getting sick from this type of drug-resistant *Salmonella*.

History of Food Safety
Very little about foodborne illness or food safety is found in historical records. Scientists did not begin to understand bacteria, and their relationship to disease, until the late nineteenth century. People did recognize that food spoils, but the reasons for that and the potential for becoming ill from food were not known. The history of food safety is really the history of the numerous discoveries, inventions, and regulations that all led to the present knowledge.

Food preservation methods such as drying, smoking, freezing, marinating, salting, and pickling have their beginnings thousands of years ago. Whether these methods were employed solely to keep food for later use, to improve flavor, or for other reasons is not known; but for whatever reason they were developed, they also had the effect of keeping food safer. Even cooking can be viewed as an ancient method of making food safer. The Chinese Confucian Analects of 500 B.C.E. warned against consumption of sour rice, spoiled fish or flesh, food kept too long, or insufficiently cooked food. The Chinese disliked eating uncooked food, believing that anything boiled or cooked cannot be poisonous. It is possible that the practice of drinking tea originated because tea required using hot water, which would make it safer than using unheated contaminated water (Trager, 1995). Doubtless other cultures in antiquity, while oblivious to the causes or prevention of foodborne disease, experienced it and prescribed methods to avoid it.

Much of the present knowledge about pathogens and foodborne illness is built on a foundation of scientific discoveries spanning back over three centuries. Italians Francisco Redi and Lazzaro Spallanzani performed experiments that dispelled the theory of spontaneous generation of organisms. The discovery of bacteria in the late nineteenth century, the increased understanding of bacteria's role in disease, and the realization that there is a connection between human diseases and animal diseases led to the ideas that cleanliness is important and that unsanitary conditions can contribute to disease. A leader in this effort was Hungarian physician Ignaz Semmelweiss, who in 1847 required hospital doctors to wash their hands before delivering babies. As a result, maternal death rates plummeted from 10 to 1.5 percent. His colleagues greeted his theory that doctors were carrying disease from person to person with ridicule. Instead they attributed maternal deaths to a phenomenon arising from the combustible nature of pregnant women. Lack of personal hygiene remains one of the main causes of foodborne illness 150 years later.

Louis Pasteur further elucidated the link between spoilage, disease, and microorganisms with his work on fermentation and pasteurization in the 1860s and 1870s. In 1872 German scientist Ferdinand Julius Cohn published a three-volume treatise on bacteria, essentially founding the science of bacteriology. But this new field of bacteriology needed bacteria on which to conduct experiments and study. It took Robert Koch in the 1880s to perfect the process of growing pure strains of bacteria in the laboratory. At first he used flat glass slides to grow the bacteria. His assistant, Julius Richard Petri, suggested using shallow glass dishes with covers, now commonly called Petri dishes. Koch also established strict criteria for showing that a specific microbe causes a specific disease. These are now known as Koch's Postulates. Using these criteria scientists can identify bacteria that cause a number of diseases, including foodborne diseases. In 1947 Joshua Lederberg and Edward Lawrie Tatum discovered that bacteria reproduce sexually, opening up a whole new field of bacterial genetics (Asimov, 1972).

Even though Antonie van Leeuwenhoek, a Dutch biologist and microscopist, had improved the microscope to the degree that small microscopic organisms could be seen as far back as 1673, the discovery of foodborne disease causing microorganisms developed slowly. Although James Paget and Richard Owen described the parasite *Trichinella spiralis* for the first time in 1835, and German pathologists Friedrich Albert von Zenker and Rudolph Virchow noted the clinical symptoms of trichinosis in 1860, the association between trichinosis and the parasite *Trichinella spiralis* was not realized until much later. The English scientist William Taylor showed in 1857 that milk can transmit typhoid fever. In 1885, United States Department of Agriculture (USDA) veterinarian Daniel Salmon described a microorganism that caused gastroenteritis with fever when ingested in contaminated food. The bacteria was eventually named Salmonella (Asimov, 1972). August Gärtner, a German scientist, was the first to isolate *Bacillus enteritidis* from a patient with food poisoning, in 1888. The case was the result of a cow with diarrhea slaughtered for meat; fifty-seven people who ate the meat become ill (Satin, 1999). Emilie Pierre-Mare van Ermengem, a Belgian bacteriologist, was the first to isolate the bacteria that causes botulism, *Clostridium botulinum*, in 1895. The case concerned an uncooked, salted ham served at a wake in Belgium. Twenty-three people became ill, and three died. In a perhaps overzealous use of the scientific method, M. A. Barber demonstrated that *Staphylococcus aureus* causes food poisoning. After each of three visits to a particular farm in the Philippines in 1914, he became ill. Suspecting cream from a cow with an udder infection, Barber took home two bottles of cream, let them sit out for five hours, drank some of the cream, and became ill two hours later with the same symptoms as on the farm. He isolated a bacterium from the milk, placed it in a germ-free container of milk, waited awhile, and then convinced two hapless volunteers to drink the milk with him. Sure enough, they all became ill with the same symptoms (Asimov, 1972). In 1945 *Clostridium perfringens* was first recognized as a cause of foodborne illness. It was not until the years 1975 to 1985 that scientists first recognized some of today's major foodborne pathogens—*C. jejuni, Y. enterocolitica, E. coli* O157:H7, and *Vibrio cholerae*.

Food Safety Regulations

The earliest food safety regulations in the United States were motivated not by a desire to provide safe food to consumers, but rather out of foreign trade concerns. In 1641 Massachusetts passed the Meat and Fish Inspection Law to assure foreign trading partners that the colony produced high-quality food products. Until the late nineteenth and early twentieth century state and local governments regulated food. Most food was grown and produced locally, so local laws were adequate to deal with problems. As the population changed from rural to urban, and people no longer had a personal connection with food producers, the food supply became more national in scope and distribution. This national scope necessitated national regulation.

The year 1906 was an important one for federal food safety regulation with the passage of both the Pure Food and Drug Act and the Federal Meat Inspection Act. The public was fed up with shocking disclosures of unsanitary conditions in meatpacking plants and the use of poisonous preservatives and dyes in foods. In *A Popular Treatise on the Extent and Character of Food Adulterations* consumers read that almost every food they purchased was adulterated or mislabeled. The Poison Squad, a group of USDA chemists formed in 1902 to study preservatives used in food products by eating the foods themselves, revealed that many of the chemicals used in food production were harmful to human health. Upton Sinclair's 1906 novel, *The Jungle*, highlighted the horrible working conditions of the nation's working class by describing in lurid detail the filthy conditions and adulteration of meat that was common in the Chicago meat industry. The public was more horrified at the thought of rats and other undesirables mixed in with their sausage than of the poor treatment of workers. Sinclair later wrote, "I aimed at the public's heart and by accident hit it in the stomach." Meat sales dropped by half within weeks after the book's publication.

The Federal Meat Inspection Act protected consumers by "assuring that meat and meat food products are wholesome, not adulterated, and properly marked, labeled, and packaged." The act established sanitary standards and mandated continuous inspection of cattle, sheep, goats, and equines before, during, and after slaughter. The 1906 Pure Food and Drug Act forbade the adulteration of foods, drinks, and drugs in interstate commerce. Foods were considered misbranded if they were labeled so as to deceive the public, if the contents in terms of weights and measures were either incorrect or not present on the package, or if the label contained any false or misleading statement concerning the ingredients of a food.

Although it was a good start, the Pure Food and Drug Act had some very large flaws. Since it did not set standards as to what exactly should be in a particular food, it was almost impossible to prove adulteration of a food. For example, without knowing how much strawberry was supposed to be in strawberry jam, federal lawyers could not prove that a product with almost no strawberry in it was not strawberry jam. The act required the government to prove that offenders intended to deceive or poison consumers with their product. When brought to court defendants pleaded ignorance of the results of their actions. These deficiencies led to a renewed push for regulatory reform in the 1930s.

In 1933 Arthur Kallet and F. J. Schlink published the immensely popular book *100,000,000 Guinea Pigs: Dangers in Everyday Foods, Drugs and Cosmetics*. Written in true muckraking style, it stirred the public's ire at the condition of the food they were eating. The basic premise of the book was that the federal government was unable to protect consumers from bad food and drugs, both due to incompetence and to the lack of adequate laws.

As with passage of the 1906 act, public opinion played a strong role in sending the message to Congress that reform was needed. Since much of the media sided with the food manufacturing industry against reform, the Food and Drug Administration (FDA) took its message directly to the people, speaking at women's clubs, to civic organizations, and on the radio. The FDA collected hundreds of products (both food and drug) that had injured or cheated consumers, emphasizing that the 1906 act did not regulate these products enough to prevent such occurrences. The exhibits were photographed and converted into posters to illustrate the need for new laws. They were displayed at FDA talks and at a museum in FDA headquarters. The exhibit was christened the "Chamber of Horrors," leading to the publication of *The American Chamber of Horrors* by the FDA's Chief Educational Officer, Ruth deForest Lamb, in 1936. Ms. Lamb recounted some of the little-known, and sickeningly lurid, behind-the-scenes details of the food industry. In arguing the need for a new food and drug law, she noted that the 1906 laws were outdated due to new modes of living, new kinds of products, new methods of manufacturing and selling, new tricks of sophistication, and new scientific discoveries, all demanding a more modern method of control.

Finally, in 1938, Congress passed the Federal Food, Drug, and Cosmetic Act (FDCA). This act, with a number of adjustments and amendments, is still the major force regulating foods. It continued with many of the intentions of the 1906 act, but broadened the scope of federal regulation and plugged many of the loopholes. For the first time the law defined adulteration to include bacteria or chemicals that are potentially harmful; allowed the FDA to inspect food manufacturing and processing facilities; required ingredients of nonstandard foods to be listed on labels; prohibited the sale of food prepared under unsanitary conditions; gave the FDA the authority to monitor animal drugs, feeds, and veterinary devices; and authorized mandatory standards for foods. Few laws have as great an impact on the life and health of Americans as does the Food, Drug, and Cosmetic Act. The overall function of the law was to prevent the distribution of harmful or deceptive food and drug products.

Seafood regulation came about on a voluntary basis with the Seafood Inspection Act of 1934. In the early 1930s, canned shrimp processors found that the FDA was seizing increasingly large amounts of their product because of decomposition. Poor fishing practices and poorly supervised packing operations contributed greatly to the spoilage of shrimp products. As the canners could not themselves influence fishermen and packers to improve their handling of the product, they requested that Congress enact an inspection law. Packers of any seafood product could request an inspector to examine the premises, equipment, methods, containers, and materials used. If the inspection was favorable, they could use that information on their label. The new seafood inspection program had an almost immediate favorable effect on the canned seafood industry. Product quality improved and the industry was able to regain consumer confidence in its product.

In August 1996, Congress signed into law the Food Quality Protection Act (FQPA), fundamentally changing the way the Environmental Protection Agency (EPA) regulates pesticides used in the production of food. The FQPA sets special provisions concerning pesticide ingestion for infants and children. Because little data exist on pesticide intake for children, an additional safety factor of up to tenfold, if necessary, is to be used. All existing tolerances are to be reviewed within ten years, and consideration of children's special sensitivity and exposure to pesticide chemicals must be taken into account when setting tolerance levels. The EPA is now required to periodically review pesticide registrations, with a goal of establishing a fifteen-year cycle, to ensure that all pesticides meet updated safety standards. Most importantly, the new law establishes a health-based safety standard for pesticide residues in all foods. It uses "a reasonable certainty that no harm" will result from all combined sources of exposure, including drinking water, as the general safety standard. This last facet of the FQPA is perhaps the most important because it eliminates the Delaney Clause of the Food, Drug, and Cosmetic Act, which prohibited the addition of any cancer-causing substance, no matter how small the amount, from being added to foods.

Hazard Analysis and Critical Control Points (HACCP)

In 1996 USDA issued its Pathogen Reduction: Hazard Analysis and Critical Control Points (HACCP) System rule. This rule requires that all 6,500 meat and poultry processing plants in the United States operate under a HACCP system. The FDA began its own HACCP regulations with a 1995 rule that mandated seafood processing facilities must have in place a HACCP plan by 1997. The 1999 FDA Food Code incorporates HACCP principles and in 2001 the FDA mandated that all producers of fruit and vegetable juices use HACCP principles by 2004.

Since the passage of the Meat Inspection Act in 1906, inspectors had visually examined and smelled meat to determine if it was safe or not. Such methods are not effective against the main threat to the safety of food today—bacteria so small that they cannot be seen or smelled. The failure of inspection methods in the United States came to the fore in 1993 when an outbreak of *E. coli* O157:H7 in hamburgers in the northwestern United States sickened over five hundred people and killed four. This provided the final push needed for the U.S. Department of Agriculture (USDA) to issue the Pathogen Reduction: Hazard Analysis and Critical Control Points (HACCP) System rule in 1996. Under HACCP regulations, the food processing industry assumes primary responsibility for the safety of the food it produces. The government's role is to verify that the industry is carrying out its responsibility, and to initiate appropriate regulatory action if necessary.

HACCP started from a National Aeronautics and Space Administration (NASA) food safety program in the 1960s. NASA needed to come as close as possible to 100 percent assurance that the foods astronauts consumed while on space missions would be free of bacterial or viral pathogens. NASA, the U.S. Army Natick Laboratories, and the Pillsbury Company began to develop these first space foods. While Pillsbury researchers struggled with problems such as how to keep food from crumbling in zero gravity, they also realized that traditional food quality control programs would not provide the degree of safety desired. To produce the safest food possible, they needed to have control over their production process, the raw materials, the environment, and their employees. To provide this level of control, in 1971 they introduced the HACCP system.

A typical HACCP system identifies critical points during food processing where contamination is likely to occur. Then, controls can be put in place to focus on these critical areas. Traditionally, industry and regulators depended on spot-checks of manufacturing conditions and random sampling of final products to ensure safe food. This approach, however, tends to be reactive, rather than preventive. HACCP is a preventive, systematic approach to food safety, rather than a reactive method. One key advantage of HAACP is that it focuses on identifying and preventing hazards that may contaminate food, thereby allowing control to be exerted in the manufacturing phase, rather than after food is produced. HAACP permits more efficient and effective government regulation, primarily because record keeping allows investigators to see how well a firm is complying with food safety laws over a given extended period rather than only on a given day. HACCP has achieved international recognition as the most effective means of controlling foodborne disease. The National Academy of Sciences, the joint Food and Agriculture Organization/World Health Organization Codex Alimentarius Commission, and the U.S. National Advisory Committee on Microbiological Criteria for Foods (NACMCF) all endorse the use of HACCP.

HACCP involves seven principles:

1. Analyze potential hazards (biological, such as a microbe; chemical, such as a toxin; or physical, such as ground glass or metal fragments) associated with a food and determine measures to control those hazards.

2. Identify critical control points in the production of a food—from its raw state through processing and shipping to consumption—at which it is possible to control or eliminate the potential hazard. Examples are cooking, cooling, packaging, and metal detection.

3. Establish preventive measures with critical limits for each control point. For a cooked food, this might include setting the minimum cooking temperature and time required to ensure elimination of harmful microbes.

4. Establish procedures—such as how cooking time and temperature should be checked, and by whom—to monitor critical control points.

5. Establish corrective actions to be taken when monitoring shows that a critical limit has not been met—for example, reprocessing or disposing of food if the minimum cooking temperature is has not been attained.

6. Establish procedures to verify that the system is working properly—for example, testing time and temperature recording devices to make sure that a cooking device is working properly.

7. Establish effective record keeping to document that the HAACP system is working properly, by maintaining records of hazards, methods to control them, monitoring to ensure safety requirements are met, and actions taken to control potential problems.

To protect the public from foodborne illness, more and more of the U.S. food industry is operating under voluntary or mandatory HACCP controls. The Food and Drug Administration issued HACCP regulations requiring seafood processing facilities to have a HACCP plan in place by 1997. The 1999 FDA Food Code incorporated HACCP principles, and much of the retail food industry is moving toward implementation of HACCP requirements. In 2001, the FDA implemented HACCP regulations for fruit and vegetable juices after several high-profile foodborne illness outbreaks from the consumption of contaminated juice. The dairy industry is also moving toward adopting a HACCP systems, as are other sectors of the food industry

Food Safety at the International Level

Several international organizations interact to improve the safety of the world's food supply. The Food and Agricultural Organization (FAO) was founded as part of the United Nations in 1945 to raise levels of nutrition and standards of living, to improve agricultural productivity, and to better the condition of people in rural areas. Food safety is an important part of FAO's mission since foodborne disease is one of the most widespread threats to human health, as well as an important cause of reduced economic productivity. The World Health Organization (WHO), founded in 1948, has as its mission to set global standards of health and to aid governments in strengthening national health programs. WHO recognizes that protecting consumers from contaminants and preventing foodborne diseases are two of the most important strategies for overcoming malnutrition in the world. WHO's activity in food safety issues centers around development of national food safety policies and infrastructures, food legislation and enforcement, food safety education, promotion of food technologies, food safety in urban settings and in tourism, surveillance of foodborne diseases, and monitoring of chemical contaminants in food. FAO and WHO collaborate on many food safety issues as joint FAO/WHO committees and conferences.

One of the most important joint FAO/WHO commissions is the Codex Alimentarius Commission. This body has as its task the development of uniform food standards that can be used by governments throughout the world. This food code is known as the Codex Alimentarius. The Codex Alimentarius consists of food standards for commodities, codes of practice for hygiene and technology, pesticide evaluations and limits for pesticide residues, evaluations of food additives, guidelines for contaminants, and evaluations of veterinary drugs. Although the main goal of the Codex is to set uniform regulatory standards in the interests of international trade, it has also served to raise food safety standards in many countries. One hundred forty member nations accept its standards and follow its codes of practice.

See also **Codex Alimentarius; FAO (Food and Agriculture Organization); Government Agencies, U.S.; International Agencies; Labeling, Food; Pesticides.**

BIBLIOGRAPHY

Acheson, David W. K., and Robin K. Levinson. *Safe Eating.* New York: Dell, 1998.

Altekruse, S. F., D. A. Street, et al. "Consumer Knowledge of Foodborne Microbial Hazards and Food-Handling Practices." *Journal of Food Protection* 59, 3 (1995): 287–294.

Asimov, Isaac. *Asimov's Biographical Encyclopedia of Science and Technology: The Lives and Achievements of 1195 Great Scientists From Ancient Times to the Present.* Rev. ed. Garden City, N.Y.: Doubleday, 1972.

Centers for Disease Control and Prevention. "Preliminary FoodNet Data on the Incidence of Foodborne Illnesses—Selected Sites, United States, 2001." *Morbidity and Mortality Weekly Report*. Vol. 51, 15 (19 April 2002): 325–329. Available at http://www.cdc.gov/mmwr/preview/mmwr html/mm5115a3.htm

Cliver, Dean O. *Eating Safely: Avoiding Foodborne Illness*. 2d ed. New York: American Council on Science and Health, 1999. Available at http://www.acsh.org/publications/book lets/eatsaf.html.

Collins, J. E. "Impact of Changing Consumer Lifestyles on the Emergence/Reemergence of Foodborne Pathogens." *Emerging Infectious Diseases* 3, 4 (1997): 471–479.

Doyle, Michael P., et al. "Reducing Transmission of Infectious Agents in the Home." *Dairy, Food and Environmental Sanitation* 96, 1 (June 2000): 330–337.

Food and Agriculture Organization of the United Nations. *Understanding the Codex Alimentarius*. Rome: FAO/WHO, 1999. Available at http://www.fao.org/docrep/w9114e/w9114e00.htm

Hennessy, T. W., C. W. Hedberg, et al. "A National Outbreak of *Salmonella enteritidis* Infections from Ice Cream." *New England Journal of Medicine* 334, 20 (1996): 1281–1286.

Hutt, Peter Barton, and Peter Barton Hutt II. "A History of Government Regulation of Adulteration and Misbranding of Food." *Food Drug Cosmetic Law Journal* 39 (1984): 2–73.

Jay, L. S., D. Comar, and L. D. Govenlock. "A Video Study of Australian Domestic Food-Handling Practices." *Journal of Food Protection* 62, 11 (1999): 1285–1296.

Kaferstein, F. K., and M. Abdussalam. "Food Safety in the 21st Century." *Dairy, Food and Environmental Sanitation* 19 (1999): 760–763.

Knabel, S. J. "Foodborne Illness: Role of Home Food Handling Practices." *Food Technology* 49 (1995): 119–131.

MacKenzie, W. R., N. J. Hoxie, et al. "A Massive Outbreak in Milwaukee of *Cryptosporidium* Infection Transmitted through the Public Water Supply." *New England Journal of Medicine* 331, 3 (1994): 161–167.

Mead, Paul S., Laurence Slutsker, et al. "Food-Related Illness and Death in the United States." *Emerging Infectious Diseases*. Vol. 5, 5 (1999): 607–625. Available at http://www.cdc.gov/ncidod/eid/vol5no5/mead.htm

Morris, J. Glenn Jr., and Morris Potter. "Emergence of New Pathogens as a Function of Changes in Host Susceptibility." *Emerging Infectious Diseases*. 3, 4 (October–December 1997): 435–441.

National Research Council. *Ensuring Safe Food: From Production to Consumption*. Washington, D.C.: National Academy Press, 1998.

Olsen, Sonja J., Linda C. MacKinon, et al. "Surveillance for Foodborne-Disease Outbreaks—United States, 1993–1997." *Morbidity and Mortality Weekly Report*. 49 (17 March 2000): 1–62. Available at http://www.cdc.gov/epo/mmwr/preview/mmwrhtml/ss4901a1.htm

Proceedings of the Fourth ASEPT International Conference, Laval, France, 1996. Edited by A. Amgar, pp. 185–195.

Rawson, Jean M., and Donna U. Vogt. *Food Safety Agencies and Authorities: A Primer*. Congressional Research Service Report for Congress; 98-91 ENR. Washington, D.C.: Congressional Research Service, 1998. Available at http://www.cnie.org/NLE/CRSreports/Agriculture/ag-40.html.

Satin, Morton. *Food Alert! The Ultimate Sourcebook for Food Safety*. New York: Facts on File, 1999.

Tauxe, R. V. "Emerging Foodborne Diseases: An Evolving Public Health Challenge." *Emerging Infectious Diseases* 3, 4 (1997): 425–433.

United States Food and Drug Administration. *Food Safety: A Team Approach*. Washington, D.C.: Dept. of Health and Human Services, 24 September 1998. Available at http://vm.cfsan.fda.gov/lrd/foodteam.html.

United States General Accounting Office. *Food Safety: Information on Foodborne Illnesses*. Washington, D.C.: General Accounting Office, May 1996.

United States Food and Drug Administration. "The Story of the Laws behind the Labels. Part I: 1906 Food and Drugs Act." *FDA Consumer* June 1981. Available at http://vm.cfsan.fda.gov/lrd/history1.html

Vetter, James L. *Food Laws and Regulations*. Manhattan, Kans.: American Institute of Baking, 1996.

Cynthia A. Roberts

FOOD SECURITY. Most people are familiar with the terms "national security" or "home security," but relatively few are familiar with the term "food security." These terms convey a sense of an absence of or lowered risk; a home is less likely to be burglarized, a nation's state secrets are less likely to fall into the hands of unfriendly nations. Food security has similar connotations in relation to food. According to the 1996 World Food Summit, food security exists "when every person has physical and economic access at all times to healthy and nutritious food in sufficient quantity to cover the needs of their daily ration and food preferences, in order to live a healthy and active life."

In its simplest form, food security means that all people have enough to eat at all times to be healthy and active, and do not have to fear that the situation will change in the future. As a concept it can be applied at many levels—global, national, household, and individual.

There are three fundamental pillars in achieving food security. The first is food availability. At the global level this is the key factor—sufficient food must be grown to ensure that everyone can be adequately fed. In the early 1970s several political missteps, combined with droughts, raised concerns about whether this could be attained. Indeed the crises of the early 1970s which resulted in high world grain prices led to an international conference in 1974 and the founding of the International Fund for Agricultural Development (IFAD), the World Food Council, and the FAO Committee on World Food Security. Today the world is food secure from the perspective of food availability, and global grain prices are less costly in real terms than at any time in recent decades.

The next pillar of food security is access to food—economic and physical. This pillar is critical at the national and household levels. At the national level, if a country does not produce all the food it consumes then it must import food. A number of countries are too poor to purchase food on the international market and thus have a structural food deficit. International food aid must make up the shortfall. At local and household levels the market distribution system needs to be adequate to ensure that food is available at all marketplaces.

At the household level, sufficient levels of food must be grown, or purchased at the marketplace, or some combination of the two. Thus poverty plays the major role in food insecurity. Generally, if there is too little food it is the result of inadequate food demand driven by poverty rather than of market failure.

The third pillar of food security is food utilization, important at the household level and critical at the individual level, which brings together both the quality of the food and other complementary factors such as safe water that underpin good nutritional outcomes. This is the pillar that ensures the nutritional outcomes of every individual in the household are adequate. This is a very complex pillar. First, the household must be able to obtain, through production or purchase, the right types of food for all household members. Inadequate dietary diversity, which results in mineral and micronutrient deficiencies, increases the incidence of sickness, which sets up a vicious cycle of malnutrition. Second, unsafe water and poor sanitation increase the likelihood of frequent illness, which affects nutritional outcomes. Third, mothers need to have sufficient time to care for small children who require frequent feeding. In the developing world many poor mothers face excessive time burdens given the absence of electricity, or running water, or labor-saving food preparation devices. Many hours can be spent fetching firewood and water, growing food, processing it, and finally cooking it. Fourth, food must be available to all household members according to their needs. In some areas of the world, notably south Asia, girls and women in poor households often receive less food than they need even though the household has sufficient amounts. They are also less likely to receive health care when they become sick. In 1995 more than 6 million children died of causes associated with being underweight. Today the growth of one in three children five years old and younger is stunted, that is, they are too short for their age, a stark testimony to a life of too little food and too much sickness.

International concerns with regard to food security have shifted in the last three decades. In the 1960s and early 1970s, with rising world grain prices, fears arose that the world would run out of food in the future as its population grew ever larger. Major improvements in agricultural productivity, particularly the impact of the "Green Revolution" on wheat and rice, have removed that fear despite a population that increased from 1.6 bil-

FAMINES

Famines, the worst manifestations of food insecurity, occur in specific areas when widespread and extreme hunger result in drastic weight loss and a rising death rate. They generally occur in rural areas and are the result of a complex interaction of factors such as drought, civil unrest, floods, and economic disruptions. Today, famines are rare and should be confined to the past. There is more than enough food in the world to feed everyone. Global information systems enable policymakers to predict when famine is likely, either as a result of crop failure due to drought or pest or because of civil unrest and war. Famine in today's world is testimony to policy failure, not the absence of food. Food insecurity, on the other hand, is a fact of life today for many people. Today, 815 million people go to bed at night not knowing whether they will have enough to eat tomorrow. Each year, more than 6 million children do not live to see their fifth birthday. They die silently of causes associated with hunger and malnutrition, absent the widespread media attention that famine attracts.

lion in 1900 to 6.1 billion by 2000. Today the expectation is that new advances in agriculture, particularly in biotechnology, will increase agricultural productivity sufficiently to feed a world population expected to stabilize at about 9.3 billion. This expectation, together with abundant global grain supplies at record low prices, has removed the specter of food insecurity from the agenda of most policymakers.

Today, the focus of the international development community and many policymakers is on the AIDS crisis in Africa, which is finally attracting enormous attention and with it the promise of more economic assistance. AIDS kills about 6 million people a minute, a tragedy by any definition. Yet this tragedy pales in significance when compared to the 12 million people a day who die of causes related to malnutrition, the ultimate outcome of food insecurity. The 1996 World Food Summit called for the number of undernourished people in the world to be cut in half by 2015—a not insurmountable goal given current world food supplies and their predicted trend. Reducing hunger and food insecurity today is a matter of political will. However, past performance indicates the goal is unlikely to be met. Despite falling food prices during the 1990s, the number of undernourished fell by only 40 million, with the average rate of decline slowing to just 6 million per year by the end of the decade. Achievement of the WFS target requires that at least 22 million people a year are removed from the ranks of the food insecure.

Recognition that food supplies are adequate but political will lacking has led to a new emphasis on food as a human right. The plan of action emanating from the 1996 WFS highlighted the need to implement Article 11 of the International Covenant on Economic, Social and Cultural Rights and called on countries, United Nations agencies, and intergovernmental agencies to better implement and realize the fundamental right of everyone to be free from hunger. In 2001 the international food security community has a double focus with a delicate balance—how to engage sufficient political will to secure food as a human right today, while maintaining a commitment to increasing agricultural productivity that will be required if we are to feed a more than 50 percent larger population by midcentury without further damaging the environment in the future.

See also **Food Supply and the Global Food Market**; **Food Supply, Food Shortages**.

BIBLIOGRAPHY

Bread for the World Institute. *Hunger 1999: The Changing Politics of World Hunger*. Silver Spring, Md.: Bread for the World Institute, 1998.

Food and Agriculture Organization of the United Nations. *The State of Food Insecurity in the World: When People Live with Hunger and Fear Starvation*. 3rd ed. Rome: Food and Agriculture Organization of the United Nations, 2001.

Food and Agriculture Organization of the United Nations. *World Food Summit: Five Years Later*. 2002. Available at www.fao.org

Narayan Deepa, Raj Patel, et al. *Can Anyone Hear Us? Voices of the Poor*. New York: Oxford University Press for the World Bank, 2000.

Pinstrup-Andersen, Per, and Rajul Pandya-Lorch, eds. *The Unfinished Agenda. Perspectives on Overcoming Hunger, Poverty, and Environmental Degradation*. Washington, D.C.: International Food Policy Research Institute, 2001

Wiebe, Keith, Nicole Ballenger, and Per Pinstrup-Andersen, eds. *Who Will Be Fed in the 21st Century: Challenges for Science and Policy*. Washington, D.C.: International Food Policy Research Institute, 2001.

World Bank. *World Development Report 2000/2001: Attacking Poverty*. New York: Oxford University Press, 2000. Available at http://www.worldbank.org/poverty/wdrpoverty/

Lynn Brown

FOOD STAMPS. The Food Stamp Program (FSP) is intended to help low-income individuals and families meet their basic nutritional needs. Although the first food stamps were issued to needy families in 1939, the FSP was not authorized as an official food-assistance program until 1964. In 1974, all states were required to offer food stamps, and in 1977 participation increased when eligible persons no longer had to buy food stamps with cash. Participation in the FSP continued to increase through the mid-1990s, until the Personal Responsibility and Work Opportunity Reconciliation Act (PRWORA, also known as "welfare reform") of 1996 reduced the number of people who were eligible.

In the early twenty-first century, the FSP remained the largest of the fifteen federal food-assistance programs, providing aid to an estimated 17.3 million individuals in 2001. An analysis of participants in 2000 showed that 51 percent were children (eighteen years or younger), 39 percent were nonelderly adults, and 10 percent were elderly adults. About 70 percent of participating adults were women. The majority (89 percent) of FSP households included a child, or elderly or disabled person. Of the households with children, 68 percent were headed by a single adult. Average gross monthly income per household was $620, with 89 percent of households having gross monthly incomes below 100 percent, and 58 percent having gross monthly incomes below 75 percent, of the federal poverty guideline. In 2000, 40 percent of participants were white, 36 percent were non-Hispanic African Americans, 18 percent were Hispanic, and 6 percent were of another race or ethnicity.

The total cost of the FSP in 2001 was approximately $17.8 billion, of which $15.5 billion was distributed in the form of food stamps. These numbers are noticeably lower than in 1994, when expenditures peaked at $24.5 billion and the number of participants also peaked, at 27.5 million (see Table 1). Trends in FSP participation and expenditures parallel trends in poverty and reduced unemployment. They also reflect changes in FSP policy and lack of information about such changes—the most likely reason why the participation rate among persons who remained eligible decreased from 74 percent in 1994 to 57 percent in 1999.

The FSP is administered at the federal level by the Food and Nutrition Service of the U.S. Department of Agriculture, but eligibility and distribution of benefits are administered by state and local agencies. In 2002, a household qualified for Food Stamps if its gross income was less than 130 percent of the federal poverty guideline (for example, $1,585 per month for a three-person household as of 1 October 2001), if net income after certain deductions (such as for child care) was less than 100 percent of the poverty guideline (for example, $1,220 per month for a three-person household as of the same date), and if countable assets (such as a bank account, but not a home or lot) were less than $2,000 (or less than $3,000 if the household had an elderly member). After the PRWORA took effect in 1997, legal permanent-resident aliens not employed in the United States for the past ten years could no longer receive FSP assistance, and most adults who were able-bodied, nonworking, and childless could receive only three months of aid in any thirty-six months. In addition, the maximum FSP benefit amounted to 100 percent of the

TABLE 1

Food Stamp Program Participation and Costs

Fiscal Year	Average Participation Thousands	Average Benefit Per Person Dollars	Total Benefits	All Other Costs Millions of Dollars	Total Costs
1969	2,87	86.63	228.8	21.7	250.5
1970	4,340	10.55	549.7	27.2	576.9
1975	17,064	21.40	4,385.5	233.2	4,618.7
1980	21,082	34.47	8,720.9	485.6	9,206.5
1985	19,899	44.99	10,743.6	959.6	11,703.2
1990	20,067	58.92	14,186.7	1,304.4	15,491.1
1995	26,619	71.26	22,764.1	1,855.5	24,619.6
2000	17,158	72.78	14,984.8	2,073.3	17,058.1
2001 (P)	17,316	74.77	15,536.1	2,253.9	17,790.0

Data as of 25 April 2002. Fiscal Year (FY) 2001 data are preliminary; all data are subject to revision. "Average Benefit per Person" represents average monthly benefit. "All Other Costs" includes the Federal share of state administrative expenses and employment and training programs. It also includes other Federal costs (such as printing and processing of stamps, antifraud funding, and program valuation). Puerto Rico initiated Food Stamp operations during FY 1975 and participated through June of FY 1982. A separate Nutrition Assistance Grant was begun in July 1982.

Thrifty Food Plan (TFP) allowance (reduced from the 103 percent issued in 1988). The TFP identifies types and quantities of foods for twelve age-gender groups that would meet the respective 1989 Recommended Dietary Allowances (RDAs), the 1995 Dietary Guidelines for Americans, and the U.S. Department of Agriculture's Food Guide Pyramid serving recommendations, according to data from the 1989–1991 Continuing Survey of Food Intake by Individuals (CSFII) and according to national average food prices. Eligibility for the FSP has changed constantly, however, as demonstrated by the decision in 1998 to restore Food Stamp benefits to children, elderly, and disabled individuals who were legal permanent residents in the United States. The U.S. Department of Agriculture maintains a toll-free telephone number to answer questions about current policies of the FSP.

In 2001, FSP participants received an average of $75 per person monthly in the form of paper coupons in denominations of $1, $5, and $10, or as electronic benefit transfers (EBTs). The computer-based EBT system employs a plastic card that functions like a bank debit card, allowing items to be purchased without the exchange of cash or coupons. The implementation of the EBT system was intended to make Food Stamp fraud (such as the exchange of cash for coupons at a lower value) more difficult. As of October 2001, thirty-seven states and Washington, D.C. issued all Food Stamp benefits in the form of EBTs. The PRWORA of 1996 mandates that all states use EBTs by October 2002.

Food Stamp coupons or EBTs can be used to buy foods such as breads and cereals, fruits and vegetables, meats, fish and poultry, and dairy products, and to buy seeds and plants that produce food, from an estimated 155,000 authorized stores in the United States. But coupons or EBTs cannot be used to buy beer, wine, liquor, cigarettes or other forms of tobacco; nonfood items like pet foods, household supplies, or toiletries; foods that can be eaten in the store; or hot foods. Food Stamps also cannot be used to buy dietary supplements, including vitamins and minerals, a controversial policy that has undergone much scrutiny.

Evaluation of the impact of the FSP on the diets of participants is mixed. Using data from the 1996–1997 National Food Stamp Program Survey (NFSPS), average nutrient intakes of FSP participants exceeded the RDA, but a substantial number of households had folic acid and iron intakes below the respective RDAs. Data from the 1994 to 1996 CSFII and the Third National Health and Nutrition Examination Survey (NHANES III) show that FSP participants had higher intakes of most nutrients than other adults, but that median intakes of vitamin E, calcium, and zinc still fell below the respective RDAs. Within population subgroups, Food Stamps have been associated with improved nutrient intakes in children but not among the elderly. Interestingly, Food Stamp participants are more likely to be food-insecure, meaning their household does not have enough food to eat at all times. However, this counterintuitive finding is credible because people who are food-insecure are more likely than others to apply for and receive Food Stamps. The dietary quality and food security of Food Stamp participants after the implementation of the PRWORA of 1996 and subsequent changes in FSP policy are of keen interest.

See also **Class, Social; Government Agencies, U.S.; Poverty; School Meals; Soup Kitchens; WIC (Women, Infants, and Childrens) Program**.

BIBLIOGRAPHY

Center for Nutrition Policy and Promotion. *The Thrifty Food Plan: Executive Summary*. CNPP-7A. Available at http://www.usda.gov/cnpp/FoodPlans/TFP99/Index.htm.

Cohen, B., J. Ohls, M. Andrews, M. Ponza, L. Moreno, A. Zambrowski, and R. Cohen. *Food Stamp Participants' Food Security and Nutrient Availability*. Princeton, N.J.: Mathematica Policy Research, July 1999.

Gundersen, C., and V. Oliveira. "The Food Stamp Program and Food Insufficiency." *American Journal of Agricultural Economics* 83 (2001): 875–887.

Guthrie, J., and C. Olander. "The Adequacy of Vitamin and Mineral Intakes among Low-income Adults." In *The Use of Food Stamps to Purchase Vitamin and Mineral Supplements*. Washington, D.C.: U.S. Government Printing Office, September 1999.

Lee, J. S., and E. A. Frongillo. "Understanding Needs Is Important for Assessing the Impact of Food Assistance Program Participation on Nutritional and Health Status in U.S. Elderly Persons." *Journal of Nutrition* 131 (2000): 765–773.

Oliveira, V., and J. W. Levedahl. "All Food Stamp Benefits to Be Issued Electronically." *Food Review* 21 (1998): 35–39.

Perez-Escamilla, R., A. M. Ferris, L. Drake, L. Haldeman, J. Peranick, M. Campbell, Y. K. Peng, G. Burke, and B. Bernstein. "Food Stamps Are Associated with Food Security and Dietary Intake of Inner-city Preschoolers from Hartford, Connecticut." *Journal of Nutrition* 130 (2000): 2711–2717.

Rose, D., J. P. Habicht, and B. Devaney. "Household Participation in the Food Stamp and WIC Programs Increases the Nutrient Intakes of Preschool Children." *Journal of Nutrition* 128 (1998): 548–555.

United States Department of Agriculture, Economic Research Service. Food and Nutrition Assistance Programs: Food Stamp Program. *Graphs and Source Data: Food Stamp Participants, Persons in Poverty and Unemployed Persons, 1980–1999*. Available at http://www.ers.usda.gov/briefing/FoodNutrtion Assistance/gallery/foodstamp1.htm.

United States Department of Agriculture, Economic Research Service. *Food Assistance Landscape*. Available at http://www.ers.usda.gov/.

United States Department of Agriculture, Food and Nutrition Service. *Food Stamp Program*. Available at http://www.fns.usda.gov/fsp/.

United States Department of Agriculture, Food and Nutrition Service. *The Use of Food Stamps to Purchase Vitamin and Mineral Supplements*. Washington, D.C.; U.S. Government Printing Office, September 1999.

United States Department of Agriculture, Food and Nutrition Service, Office of Analysis, Nutrition, and Evaluation. *Characteristics of Food Stamp Households: Fiscal Year 2000*. Alexandria, Va.: Karen Cunnyngham, Mathematica Policy Research, October 2001.

United States Department of Agriculture, Food and Nutrition Service, Office of Analysis, Nutrition, and Evaluation. *Trends in Food Stamp Program Participation Rates: 1994 to 1999*. Washington, D.C.: Randy Rosso, Mathematica Policy Research, October 2001.

Weimer, J. "Factors Affecting Nutrient Intake of the Elderly." U.S. Department of Agriculture, Economic Research Service, Agricultural Economic Report No. 769. Washington, D.C.: U.S. Government Printing Office, October 1998.

L. Beth Dixon

FOOD STUDIES. Although accounts of food and eating habits date to the earliest written records, the designation of more scholarly investigations of food as food studies is a modern development. In the 1990s researchers began applying this term to descriptions and analyses relying upon every conceivable method for studying the historical, cultural, behavioral, biological, and socioeconomic determinants and consequences of food production and consumption. The idea that such investigations might collectively constitute a legitimate field of study in its own right derived from earlier explorations of food practices within traditional academic disciplines. In the 1960s, for example, the folklorist Don Yoder popularized the term "foodways" to describe the entire range of food habits, behaviors, customs, and cultural practices associated with food consumption.

In the 1990s Boston University established a master's program in gastronomy focused on the cultural and culinary aspects of food consumption. In 1996 the Department of Nutrition and Food Studies at New York University began admitting students to undergraduate, master's, and doctoral programs in food studies, thereby formalizing this emerging field as a state-accredited academic entity. The NYU programs emphasize the ways individuals, communities, and societies relate to food within a cultural and historical context. In this view, food studies is an umbrella term that includes foodways, gastronomy, and culinary history as well as historical, cultural, political, economic, and geographic examinations of food production and consumption. Any field defined so broadly immediately raises questions, in this case related to the scope, methods, and acceptance of food studies as a distinct academic entity.

An Inclusive, Interdisciplinary Field

Because the concept of food studies is new, scholars investigating food topics have not yet reached complete agreement on what it should and should not include. Anthropologists, folklorists, and sociologists always have examined the relationships of individuals and populations to their food. In the era of economic globalization, with its food inequities and scarcities, precarious and often tainted food supply, concerns about diet and health, and fears of genetically modified foods and food bioterrorism, food is recognized as a "lens" through which to view, explore, analyze, and interpret society in the present as well as in the past. The breadth of this approach means that food studies can also include applied disciplines that deal with the fundamental properties of food—culinary arts, food science, and nutrition, for example—as well as food history and culinary history, agriculture and food production, and descriptive and economic analyses of food systems and the food industry.

By its very nature, food studies is interdisciplinary and must rely on methods, approaches, and themes derived from other disciplines. In this sense it is developing in much the same manner as other interdisciplinary fields, such as American studies, women's studies, and performance studies, that emerged a generation ago. Food studies may be unusual, however, in the breadth of the disciplines on which it draws. Economists, historians, psychologists, nutritionists, agronomists, geologists, geographers, archaeologists, environmental scientists, legal scholars, political scientists, and historians—culinary and otherwise—all bring distinct methods of research and analysis to bear on food themes.

Multiple Methods and Approaches

Traditional academic disciplines are often defined by the distinct methods used by scholars in conducting research. Certain areas of inquiry, for example, use surveys, participant observations, or analyses of texts, historical documents, social interactions, and self-reports. Because food studies emerged from the humanities and social sciences, researchers typically rely on ethnography, case studies, and historical investigations. Throughout the twentieth century, for example, anthropologists debated whether culture is rooted in tangible and concrete artifacts—the implements and debris of hunting, gathering, and cooking—or in ideas and belief systems. They asked why people chose certain foods and used them in certain ways. They examined how religious beliefs, practices, and rituals influenced dietary practices, and they compared those influences to the effects of the environment or evolutionary biology. Claude Lévi-Strauss, for example, used a classic anthropological approach in his study of the symbolic use of food in culture, *The Raw and the Cooked* (1979). In contrast, the anthropologist Sidney Mintz produced a quintessential example of food studies research in his book *Sweetness and Power* (1985), in which he traced the ways a single food substance, in this case sugar, transformed modern history and culture. Anthropologists have further expanded the scope of their investigations to include the nutritional implications of dietary practices.

Scholars in other fields also examine food themes from the perspectives of their traditional disciplines. Food historians investigate the ways in which foods have influenced world events in the past and present. Culinary historians focus on recipes and cooking techniques, exploring when, where, and how specific foods or ingredients might have been grown, produced, prepared, and consumed in different periods. Food sociologists focus on issues of hunger, malnutrition, and inequities of the global food supply as well as on societal determinants of diet-related conditions, such as obesity or heart disease. Psychologists often investigate how and why people make food choices or such matters as eating disorders, food phobias, and the psychological connections between eating and taste, pleasure, and disgust. Scholars trained in literature or languages examine how novels, poems, and essays are enriched with food imagery or the ways in which travel writing and memoirs use food themes to express ideas or points of view. Because food studies draws on many such disciplines, encyclopedias of food history or culture necessarily include examples of many different scholarly approaches to the study of food.

The Food Studies "Movement"

As participants in an emerging field, food studies researchers are not constrained by the methods and approaches of any one discipline, and they enjoy the freedom to study what they like in whatever way seems most appropriate. Because food studies is inherently interdisciplinary, its scholars must define their own research agendas based on elements incorporated from traditional disciplines. Because this flexibility may be perceived as unfamiliar or lacking in rigor no matter how excellent the quality of the work, the academic study of food itself, as opposed to studying food within a traditional discipline, is established in only a few universities. The field appears to be expanding, however. In the United States, culinary schools are broadening their offerings to include courses in food history and culture, and universities in France, Mexico, and Australia have established degree programs that emphasize food. To scholars writing about food, such developments constitute the food studies "movement." As further evidence for this movement, they cite the series of books on food and culture established by university presses, such as those of Columbia University, Northwestern University, and the University of California; the breadth and depth of the culinary history and food studies collections of the Schlesinger Library at Radcliffe College and the Fales Library at NYU; and the proliferation of encyclopedias on food history and culture, such as those cited in the bibliography.

In part, the growing acceptance and legitimacy of food studies as a discrete field reflects increasing recognition that innovative scholarship often crosses disciplinary boundaries. In the academic environment, the identification of food studies as a separate field may not matter much. The very existence of the food studies movement encourages students and faculty in traditional academic disciplines to conduct research on food themes and facilitates the publication of scholarly work related to the role of food in society, culture, and commerce.

See also **Anthropology and Food**; **Chef, The**; **Cuisine, Evolution of**; **Education about Food**; **Foodways**; **Gastronomy**.

BIBLIOGRAPHY

Davidson, Alan. *The Oxford Companion to Food*. Oxford: Oxford University Press, 1999.

Flandrin, Jean-Louis, and Massimo Montanari, eds. *Food: A Culinary History from Antiquity to the Present*. English edition by Albert Sonnenfeld. Translated by Clarissa Botsford et al. New York: Columbia University Press, 1999.

Kiple, Kenneth F., and Kriemhild Coneè Ornelas, eds. *The Cambridge World History of Food*, vols. 1 and 2. Cambridge, U.K.: Cambridge University Press, 2000.

Lévi-Strauss, Claude. *The Raw and the Cooked*. Translated by John Weightman and Doreen Weightman. New York: Octagon Books, 1979.

Mintz, Sidney W. *Sweetness and Power: The Place of Sugar in Modern History*. New York: Viking, 1985.

Jennifer Berg
Marion Nestle
Amy Bentley

FOOD SUPPLY AND THE GLOBAL FOOD MARKET.

Worldwide, the food supply available to people depends on a variety of environmental, technical, and sociopolitical factors, the relative importance of which have varied considerably in time as well as geographically. Environmental factors have governed food production and availability throughout history, and this remains so for many societies. However, in a world where food is abundant as never before, food supply is extremely vulnerable to economic and political interests, as well as technical factors, such as transportation and communications.

Food Supply through the Ages

Before the advent of agriculture and the domestication of animals (c. 10,000 B.C.E.), hunting, fishing, and gathering provided enough food for small groups of people such as bands of wanderers. Along with agriculture came a sedentary way of life, and self-sufficient agricultural settlements appeared in every region of the world. In this type of environment, food supply was direct and immediate. Careful management of produce ensured the survival of every household member until the next harvest. Except for times of warfare or environmental calamities, the balance between food demand and food supply remained fairly stable. Though hunting and gathering societies are almost extinct today, agricultural villages still endure in many parts of the world.

As some of these villages grew into towns, however, things began to change. Societies became more complex as certain groups of people ceased to be directly involved in the production of food. Food supply and distribution became dependent on an increasingly complex set of relations among groups of different professions and ranks. Surplus food (mainly grains) was traded with neighboring settlements. Concentrated in a few hands, food became a means to political power.

The growth of empires is associated with the emergence of a professional specialist, the merchant, who ventured into new territories exchanging food and other goods across borders, often between far-off places. Food began to be regarded as a commodity subject to the rationale of profit, and it eventually became the responsibility of the state to ensure an adequate food supply for its citizens.

The Industrial Revolution of the late eighteenth century was also an agricultural revolution that dramatically changed the way food was to be produced, distributed, and used in most of the world. Farming, fishing, and other food-production activities became large-scale enterprises, organized according to the principles of maximum productivity and maximum profit. Capital-intensive agriculture produced surpluses of a magnitude never before possible. The modernization of transport and communications, and the emergence of food-processing and food-packaging industries, made it possible to extend food trade on a global scale. In urban centers, supermarkets can offer not only frozen and packaged food, but also fresh produce year-round from all over the world. For some this increased food supply has created a sense of plenty, albeit a localized and exclusive one.

Food Supply as a Political Weapon

In the twentieth century, food supply came under the rules of a new political and economic order. Large food stocks have proved to be one of the main geopolitical assets of rich nations. Most affluent countries are or have been large exporters of food, and they control the global food market to their advantage. Food prices are set at the major stock exchange institutions in North America, Europe, and Japan. In competing for the hegemony of the global food market, the United States, the world's main food exporter, has been engaged in "food wars" with Japan and the European Union. International organizations, such as the recently formed WTO (World Trade Organization), have been created to defuse these conflicts, as well as to balance the "market distortions" that affect less powerful nations.

The global food market is dominated by the most affluent countries, which, on average, have controlled almost 70 percent of the total value of imports and over 62 percent of the total value of exports of all agricultural products in the world since 1961 (see Table 1). During the last quarter of the twentieth century, these countries have been reducing the value of their imports while expanding the value of their exports. Food imports by these countries typically concentrate on specialized agricultural items, such as tropical fruits and selected vegetables, as well as coffee, tobacco, sugar, and tea, none of which is a staple in its place of origin. In order to meet the domestic demand for staples, many of the exporting countries of such products have to import large quantities of basic staples in exchange. From 1961 to 2000, the countries of Africa and Latin America increased more than eight times their imports of cereals, those of Asia more than four times, and those of Oceania more than five times.

TABLE 1

Main importers and exporters of total agricultural products, 1961–2000

(Value of imports/exports in US$1,000)

Imports

Countries	\	\	Years	\	\	Decadal average
	1961	1970	1980	1990	2000	
Germany	4,191,324	7,214,668	27,890,046	38,652,300	34,488,729	22,487,413
United States of America	3,836,796	6,301,029	18,410,350	27,088,094	44,949,426	20,117,139
Japan	2,022,576	4,140,227	17,747,335	28,659,121	36,153,814	17,744,615
United Kingdom	5,362,951	5,776,370	16,309,835	22,952,289	25,877,168	15,255,723
France	2,125,596	3,262,917	14,867,182	22,613,082	23,224,627	13,218,681
Italy	1,450,729	3,386,200	14,856,545	23,651,782	21,608,095	12,990,670
Netherlands	949,437	2,121,927	11,637,467	17,962,752	16,218,531	9,778,023
USSR	1,380,364	2,478,054	17,643,338	19,714,301	0	8,243,211
Belgium-Luxembourg	823,180	1,657,552	8,247,905	12,547,486	15,484,230*	7,752,071
China	759,895	890,765	7,984,003	9,791,156	15,349,290	6,955,022
Canada	806,618	1,261,845	4,602,644	7,100,642	11,441,510	5,042,652
Spain	350,254	852,784	4,391,220	8,039,331	10,541,845	4,835,087
United Arab Emirates	3,752	31,980	1,077,403	1,692,884	18,705,047	4,302,213
China, Hong Kong SAR	349,333	671,188	3,161,775	6,821,872	8,485,711	3,897,976
Korea, Republic of	87,280	438,935	3,303,414	6,459,074	8,297,395	3,717,220
Total	**24,500,085**	**40,486,441**	**172,130,462**	**253,746,166**	**290,825,418**	**156,337,714**
World total	34,748,770	56,630,704	255,355,968	353,147,624	447,497,428	229,476,099
% of world total	71	71	67	72	65	68

Exports

Countries	\	\	Years	\	\	Decadal average
	1961	1970	1980	1990	2000	
United States of America	5,187,350	7,507,566	42,921,186	45,210,987	56,479,900	31,461,398
France	1,246,491	2,962,836	18,519,111	33,432,321	33,390,182	17,910,188
Netherlands	1,267,473	3,149,676	16,091,315	30,927,503	27,884,332	15,864,060
Germany	388,354	1,362,708	11,021,979	20,374,986	24,147,297	11,459,065
United Kingdom	983,067	1,420,838	8,242,790	12,766,968	16,684,026	8,019,538
Australia	1,558,811	2,333,963	9,216,112	11,749,559	14,698,447	7,911,378
Canada	1,260,268	1,815,641	7,071,758	9,181,264	15,684,949	7,002,776
Italy	701,212	1,219,583	5,677,448	11,134,930	15,603,562	6,867,347
Brazil	1,169,525	1,946,375	9,320,492	8,763,781	12,761,338	6,792,302
China	380,869	1,147,785	4,554,142	10,207,810	13,076,473	5,873,416
Spain	375,823	767,164	3,566,320	7,825,934	13,999,088	5,306,866
Argentina	906,064	1,498,609	5,518,628	6,976,824	10,776,094	5,135,244
Denmark	826,872	1,191,745	5,222,539	8,290,189	8,788,582	4,863,985
Belgium-Luxembourg	341,240	1,095,694	6,369,385	11,787,599	17,619,979	3,918,784
Thailand	392,234	493,986	3,344,140	5,387,818	7,273,564	3,378,348
Total	**16,985,653**	**29,914,169**	**156,657,345**	**234,018,473**	**288,867,813**	**145,288,691**
World Total	32,217,186	52,075,640	234,255,267	326,243,879	410,548,587	211,068,112
% of world total	53	57	67	72	70	69

*Addition of data for Belgium and Luxembourg

SOURCE: Food and Agriculture Organization of the United Nations (FAOSTAT, on-line http://www.fao.org) May 2002.

Since the end of World War II, the global supply of cereals, the basic staples for most of humanity, has largely depended on the production and export capacity of some fifteen countries. In 1999, major cereal exporters held close to one-half of global cereal stocks (Food and Agriculture Organization of the United Nations, 2002; hereafter FAO). In the year 2000, the four largest cereal exporters, the United States, France, Canada, and Australia, produced over 495 million metric tons of cereals (wheat, maize, rice, sorghum, oats, and others), which amounted to 24 percent of the total world production, and exported 164.8 million metric tons of cereals, 61 percent of the total world exports of cereals for that year. However, in past decades this proportion had been much larger, reaching as much as 78 percent in 1980 (see Table 2).

In addition to trade, food transfers between main producers and main consumers include "food aid." Between 1970 and 2000, more than 336 million metric tons of cereals were shipped as food aid to countries in need.

TABLE 2

Main cereal exporters, 1961–2000 (Qty., Mt)

Countries	Years				
	1961	1970	1980	1990	2000
World Total	79,466,691	114,423,775	223,191,018	226,234,678	272,236,822
United States of America	31,796,032	40,406,383	112,905,797	92,615,939	87,358,248
France	4,180,590	10,283,517	19,637,116	30,897,774	32,746,384
Canada	12,112,152	14,896,455	21,866,888	23,092,252	22,885,090
Australia	6,205,202	8,357,127	19,466,766	15,013,192	21,819,313
Total 4	54,293,976	73,943,482	173,876,567	161,619,157	164,809,035
% of world total	68	65	78	71	61
Argentina	3,643,362	10,217,977	9,909,358	10,442,436	23,728,443
Germany	1,256,903	2,893,628	2,414,667	4,732,186	14,391,914
China	222,434	1,720,698	1,514,152	4,202,888	13,952,775
USSR	7,844,833	6,913,415	2,286,962	1,539,083	0
Thailand	2,140,932	2,517,588	5,158,421	5,280,948	6,206,293
United Kingdom	180,439	269,335	2,796,403	6,610,689	5,429,248
South Africa	1,181,180	1,299,770	3,780,404	2,229,861	632,776
Netherlands	304,489	1,479,634	1,659,856	4,225,808	1,214,274
Italy	284,749	1,385,875	1,845,074	2,435,261	2,179,490
Denmark	141,553	351,483	1,139,087	3,250,496	1,974,970
Belgium-Luxembourg	78,846	887,484	3,366,919	2,199,432	2,827,038*
Total 15	71,573,696	103,880,369	209,747,870	208,768,245	257,346,256
% of world total	90	91	94	92	87

*Addition of data for Belgium and Luxembourg

SOURCE: Food and Agriculture Organization of the United Nations (FAOSTAT, online http://www.fao.org), May 2002.

Over half of these shipments came from the United States alone. In 1990, the United States donated 7.2 million metric tons of cereals, 43.3 percent of which went to African countries, 21 percent to Latin American countries, and another 21 percent to countries in Asia. Despite its humanitarian character, food aid can also be used to the advantage of food donors through the conditions that may be attached to shipments and the adverse effects that these shipments may have on the domestic markets of the recipient countries (Mittal, 2002).

Food power has been used directly to pressure nations for a desired change of policy. In the second half of the twentieth century, food sanctions were applied against a handful of countries for a variety of purposes. For example, the United States embargoed a number of nations including Cuba, Iraq, Iran, Libya, and Sudan, impeding or severely restricting food trade between the United States and those countries.

Food Supply in the Twenty-First Century

In the twenty-first century, the food supply is conditioned by the rules of the global food market and global geopolitics, which affect decisions concerning the production and distribution of food at the national and local levels. The effective demand (purchasing power) of high-income buyers has precedence over the real demand of the nutritional needs of populations. For most people on earth, access to food depends on access to money and, for some,

on access to charity, and the expansion of agribusiness to the countries of the so-called Third World has seriously affected these countries' self-sufficiency in food. Food trade and food markets have become subject to rules over which the majority of farmers have no control, and this has serious implications for the livelihoods of entire populations.

In the large urban centers of the world, the regular supply of fresh produce concentrates in the expensive supermarkets of wealthy neighborhoods, while a large proportion of the population can go without enough to eat. Lack of access to food leads to undernourishment, a problem that affects more than 800 million people in the world, including many living in the rich, food-exporting countries.

Food supply has become subject to a complex set of interests that governments are finding increasingly more difficult to mediate. Cereal stocks at the global level seem to have begun a diminishing trend due to an overall decline in production and an overall increase in utilization. Estimates for the year 2000 indicated an expected 4 million tons, down from the opening levels (FAO, 2000).

Though the per capita supply of cereals has been growing steadily since 1961 in most regions of the world, food shortages afflict a large number of countries. In 2002, the FAO reported that a state of emergency existed in the food-supply systems of as many as thirty-four countries on four continents, including Europe (FAO/GIEWS, 2000). One of the factors that adversely affects real food supply per capita in many countries is the utilization of cereals as animal feed, which in 1999 amounted to 35.1 percent of total world cereal stocks (Faostat, World Food Balance Sheet, May 2002). Unless local small-scale production for self-consumption is protected and encouraged, continuous and adequate access to food cannot be guaranteed for the rural populations of the world. With rural-urban migration on the rise almost everywhere, the majority of populations in the world will soon be concentrated in cities, contributing to the expansion of already impoverished slums.

A series of fundamental changes in global trade and the international financial system is in order if food security for all is ever to be attained. In this regard, the efforts of civil organizations fighting for fair trade and a more egalitarian world society are crucial.

See also **Food Supply, Food Shortages; Political Economy.**

BIBLIOGRAPHY

Drèze, Jean, Amartya Kumar Sen, and Athar Hussain, eds. *The Political Economy of Hunger: Selected Essays.* Oxford: Clarendon, 1995.

Food and Agriculture Organization of the United Nations. "Current Agricultural Situation: Facts and Figures." In *The State of Food and Agriculture 2000.* Rome: Food and Agriculture Organization of the United Nations, 2000. Online document report available at http://www.fao.org/docrep/x4400e/, May 2002.

Food and Agriculture Organization of the United Nations and GIEWS [Global Information and Early Warning System on Food and Agriculture of the FAO]. "Countries Facing Exceptional Food Emergencies." Food Crops and Shortages 2, April 2002, p. 2. Food and Agriculture Organization of the United Nations. Online publication available at http://www.fao.org/WAICENT/faoinfo/economic/giews, May 2002.

Harris, Marvin. *Cannibals and Kings: The Origins of Cultures.* New York: Random House, 1977.

Korten, David. *When Corporations Rule the World.* West Hartford, Conn.: Kumarian, and San Francisco: Berrett-Koehler, 1995.

Mittal, Anuradha. "New Arms, New Wars: Food Security in the New World Order." In *Bangkok: Focus on the Global South.* Online document available at http://www.focusweb.org, May 2002.

Moore Lappé, Frances, Joseph Collins, and Peter Rosset, with Luis Esparza. *World Hunger: 12 Myths.* 2d ed., fully revised and updated. London: Earthscan, 1998.

Murphy, Sophia. "Managing the Invisible Hand: Markets, Farmers, and International Trade." Institute for Agriculture and Trade Policy. Online report available at http://www.wtowatch.org/library, 23 April 2002.

Sen, Amartya Kumar. *Hunger in the Contemporary World.* London: Development Economics Research Programme/Suntory and Toyota International Centres for Economics and Related Disciplines/London School of Economics, 1997.

Sen, Amartya Kumar. *Hunger and Entitlements: Research for Action.* Forssa, Finland: World Institute for Development Economics Research of the United Nations University, 1987.

Shiva, Vandana. *Stolen Harvest: The Hijacking of the Global Food Supply.* Cambridge, Mass.: South End Press, 2000.

Luis L. Esparza Serra

FOOD SUPPLY, FOOD SHORTAGES.

A nation's food supply is determined by composition and selection. The components of a food supply are limited by a number of factors, primarily climate and geography. The U.S. food supply is noticeably different from that of other nations as the twenty-first century begins. Americans are more likely to recognize food products than the specific ingredients in the seemingly endless array of products on supermarket shelves (some supermarkets stock over forty thousand different items). Fast-food outlets—a McDonald's, Taco Bell, or a Subway sandwich shop—are more recognizable than a steer, hog, chicken, or a bushel of wheat. Most such foods are slaughtered, processed, manufactured, and packaged; few are sold in bulk, as was common before World War II. Nearly all foods are shipped from distant places on pallets or in large containers, transported to huge warehouse storage facilities or to freezers close to cities, and trucked from there to be unpacked and displayed on supermarket shelves or served in fast-food outlets.

The United States enjoys a temperate climate especially hospitable to agriculture that supports the production of a wide variety of grains, fruits, and vegetables as well as milk, meat, poultry, and fish. Within the U.S. landmass, soil conditions and characteristics ensure an abundance of available farm acreage, which, in turn, assures a profuse supply of food—so much so, in fact, that the U.S. Congress authorizes programs that pay landowners to keep portions of their farmland lying fallow. Purchasing, storing, and maintaining food surpluses cost taxpayers more than paying farmers not to produce, making payments to idle farm acreage the cheaper alternative. Income also is a significant element in the composition of the food supply.

Composition of the U.S. Food Supply

Americans are among the wealthiest populations of the world, and their wealth enables most U.S. citizens to purchase from abroad any food not available from U.S. agriculture or fisheries. The United States is a magnet for the world's food supply, drawing an endless trade caravan of meats, pastas, spices and herbs, sauces, cheeses and other dairy products, wines and spirits, cakes and crackers, and fish as well as exotic and conventional fruits and vegetables, mostly fresh. While income is a means of expanding the selection of foods available in an indigenous food supply, income more often is a limiting factor in the availability of food in a population or in subgroups within a population.

Low-income families and individuals in the United States, for example, have a more limited food supply than do those with middle or higher incomes, although public policies today ease income barriers to a more adequate food supply by supplementing the purchasing power of low-income families and individuals. Still, even with the assistance provided by food stamps and other government programs, including school meals for children, low-income households can afford less for food than higher-income families, some $1,000 less annually per person, and, as a result, consume food measurably lower in nutritional value.

Populations in poor countries (euphemistically called "less developed countries" [LDCs]), in contrast, are limited by income to the food supply readily available where they live. Trade in either conventional or exotic foods is not an option, since many of the world's poor live outside a conventional marketing system. As a result, most citizens of LDCs grow or raise most of their food themselves, although imports are becoming increasingly important. In central Africa, for example, the food supply consists of locally produced staple foods such as maize, cassava, sweet potatoes, banana, millet, sorghum, and yams. Traditional vegetables, including the leaves of cassava and sweet potatoes, provide the vitamins and minerals otherwise largely lacking in these staple foods.

Food Supply: Sources

Cereals provide 69 percent of dry matter and 55 percent of the protein in the world's food supply by weight. Legumes—for example, beans—provide another 6 percent of dry matter and 13 percent of protein (Allard, 1999). Vegetables, fruit, meat and poultry, eggs, fish, nuts, sugar, and other sweeteners, in that descending order, provide the rest. People living in the United States and the countries in the European Union, as well as Canada, Japan, Australia, and New Zealand, consume a food supply with larger proportions of meat and poultry, dairy products, fruits and vegetables, fish, nuts, sugar, and oils and fat, a diet that delivers a substantially larger caloric load than that typically available in poor countries.

As personal incomes rise, the diet of individuals and nations shifts from basic food sources to those that provide a higher level of energy, or calories—animal products, more highly processed prepared foods, and oils and fat. Grains drop out of the human diet to become animal fodder as incomes rise, especially maize, oats, millet, and sorghum, which are then categorized as feed grains. Replacing grass and hay (traditional animal fodder), feed grains are fed to cattle, hogs, and chickens instead, reentering the food supply as beef, pork, poultry, milk, and other dairy products. Fish farming, or aquaculture, has emerged as a commercial source of freshwater fish and seafood in the last decade, and as a user of feed grain in rations fed to fish raised in underwater pens. Wheat is the major food grain in the United States, although rice consumption is increasing with the rising proportion of Americans of Asian and Latin American descent, for whom rice is the major food grain.

The food supply varies by nation and by geographic region, reflecting religious beliefs as well as cultural practices. Devout Muslims and Jews do not eat pork. Koreans, Chinese, Vietnamese, and other citizens of Southeast Asian nations consider both dogs and cats enjoyable sources of animal protein, and horsemeat, a staple in pet food in the United States, is a delicacy eagerly consumed by the French and other Europeans.

During the 1990s, the American people increased spending on food consumed outside the home by nearly 25 percent, a whopping increase compared to the 4 percent growth in consumption of food prepared and eaten at home during the same period.

By the end of the twentieth century, the U.S. was unable to visualize the source of its food supply from an agricultural perspective, that is, in terms of basic food groups, because a majority no longer live on farms. Instead, food had become an endless array of food products typically found on supermarket shelves, especially those that stock over forty thousand individual items. Most such foods are processed and packaged, and few are sold in bulk as was common sixty years ago. Nearly all were shipped from distant places, packaged in large containers, transported to huge warehouse storage facilities close to cities and metropolises, and trucked from there to be unpacked and displayed on supermarket shelves.

Transporting the food supply long distances requires that foods arrive in a "safe" condition, meaning that they will cause no harm when eaten. Processing and packaging are traditional methods essential to safely preserving food ingredients, either by drying fresh fruits and vegetables, fish, meat, and poultry, by freezing them, or by cooking and canning them before they are transported and distributed. Food processors and manufacturers strive to convince the public of the differences between brands through advertising and promotion, but the only differences are frequently superficial marketing "hooks" introduced to change consumers' perceptions of products in order to capture a larger share of their food dollars. Price competition keeps profit margins low. Basic ingredients do not change, but that fact can be hidden. For example, any breakfast cereal can be made to appear different and more appealing by producing it in different shapes or adding sugar, dried fruit, essential vitamins and minerals, or new flavoring or colors. Newly designed packaging, announced by a new advertising campaign, will successfully persuade consumers that the product itself is new and different.

A successful promotion is intended to achieve better differentiation of individual products, a product virtue that is more important than nutritional value. Processors do not ignore nutrition, however, especially if it has the virtue of enhancing product differentiation. Differentiation of a product is an essential marketing function that enables a food company to charge U.S. consumers more for, or to sell more of, a basic food grain than might otherwise be possible. The availability of forty different packages of a breakfast food containing corn cereal in the breakfast food section of the supermarket is not intended to provide variety for consumers. The goal is to divide the market into increasingly smaller segments within which more can be charged per ounce than can be extracted from consumers for simple cornflakes. The same segmentation game can be played in every category of processed food. Differentiation ensures that food companies do not compete on the basis of price, traditionally the distinguishing feature of an openly competitive, free market in capitalist systems. New food products quickly come and go, but the basic ingredients—flour, fat, sugar, flavoring, coloring, and preservatives—remain unchanged. An estimated twelve thousand new food products are introduced annually, and fewer than a hundred will remain on supermarket shelves after five years.

Food processors and supermarkets, squeezed by restaurants and fast-food companies into a smaller portion of the commercial food market, have defended their share of the food supply by developing products that contain the main entree of a meal or a full meal packaged in dried or frozen form. Breakfast cereals come in small packages containing a single portion. Different recipes are devised for wheat flour, fat, sugar, jams and jellies, and artificial flavoring in partially baked pastries that can be heated in the kitchen toaster as a breakfast food or as a snack, for example. Full meals are packaged frozen, to be heated in a microwave and served as a quick lunch or dinner.

As a food category, the entree items and full meal products can be differentiated from other food products, enabling food processors to charge a higher price for a product than its often meager ingredients would bring if sold individually. Within the packaged meal category, product differentiation tactics often promote convenience as well as health benefits, both strong personal objectives, especially among individuals in the upper-middle and higher income brackets, the primary targets of advertising and promotion campaigns. Supermarkets over the past decade have given more floor space to and hired more employees for deli counters that offer convenience foods as well as whole meals, or home-meal replacements.

Needless to say, advertising, promotion, product development, and packaging design are not free services. They are the cost of marketing the food supply in a postindustrial society and a service economy. While the proportion of the food dollar spent to eat out grew from 44 percent in 1990 to 47.5 percent by the end of the twentieth century, consumer spending for food increased by 37 percent, with marketing costs responsible for almost all of the increase. Marketing costs in the decade rose 45 percent, compared to a rise of 13 percent in the

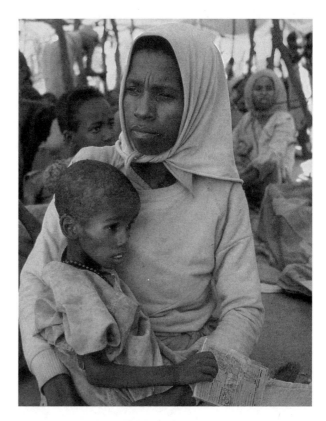

Mother with malnourished child in famine-stricken Somalia. COURTESY PHOTO RESEARCHERS, INC.

farm value of food purchases. Marketing consumed 80 percent of the trillion-dollar cost of the food supply system in the United States, leaving the actual value of the food supply at $200 billion, or 20 percent of the operational cost of the food system as the twenty-first century began. As some corn growers mournfully point out, the cost of the package containing cornflakes is more than the farmer is paid for the ingredients.

These shifts in how money is spent for food reflect seismic changes in the social tectonics of the U.S. economy at the end of the twentieth century. Among citizens of developed countries globally, Americans alone were working more hours each week as the century ended than when it began. Employment during the 1990s rose faster than in any decade since the end of World War II. The structure of the nation's workforce changed as well. The number of two-income households rose as more women entered the workforce, and wages grew faster, even as inflation declined.

The consequences of more real income and less leisure time drove changes in the food supply system. Consumers purchased more food overall, but more higher-cost processed and packaged in-home foods. The practice of spending to eat out at restaurants grew rapidly, especially at fast-food outlets. As the twenty-first century began, the money spent on fast food consumed nearly

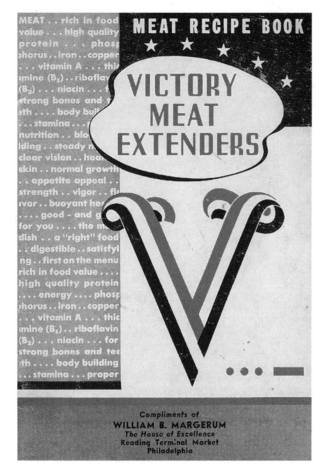

Due to wartime shortages, the National Live Stock and Meat Board in Chicago issued this 1944 booklet on tips for making the most of meat purchases during the national emergency. This included a pledge of the American homemaker: "I want to do my bit and more, to help America win the war." ROUGH-WOOD COLLECTION.

one of every four dollars spent to eat out. Only a decade earlier, in comparison, one dollar in ten was spent on restaurant meals. Wages and employment in the food supply system rose, all in response to the search for convenience.

Consumers were working more, earning more, and willing to pay more for convenience and for appliances like the microwave, which made convenience foods more convenient. By the end of the twentieth century, only one in three U.S. consumers said their food budget was a primary consideration in food purchases, while the other two said service and convenience topped their list. Oddly, as convenience became the hallmark of the U.S. food system in the twenty-first century, more space and attention was being given to kitchens in new home designs, especially as the size and amenities in homes increased. In addition, kitchen utensils with as much decorative appeal as utility were being featured in up-

scale department stores and shops catering to consumers aspiring to culinary sophistication.

The prosperity at the end of the twentieth century, combined with the largely benign condition of inflation, led to an effective overall reduction in the portion of disposable income spent on food in the United States. At the close of the 1990s, U.S. households were spending 10.4 percent of disposable personal income on food, down from 11.4 percent in 1990. Household spending in 1999 was greater in four expenditure categories—medical care, housing and home expenses, transportation, and services—than it was in the category of food, for one simple reason: with each additional dollar of income, the share of family income that must be spent on food is less than the share from the previous dollar. As real income rises, more family income is available for other needs. Wealthier families allocated far less by half than 10 percent of disposable income to food, while families at the lower end of the low-income category were spending up to 40 percent of their disposable income on food.

The Immutable Economics of Food

Regardless of the marketing ingenuity of food processors and supermarkets, or the culinary talent of restaurant chefs, the food system cannot escape the reality of the inflexible economics of food. The typical stomach can hold only a finite amount of food. After a certain point, the stomach becomes inelastic; the same is true of the economics of food. To put a finer point on the observation, an individual who has not eaten for twenty-four hours may be willing to pay twice the asking price for a tempting meal, but, once the meal has been eaten, few individuals will pay a dime more to consume the same meal immediately.

Food also obeys the law of inelasticity. The need for food is constant, and people who are starving will pay almost anything, do anything, to get enough to eat. Survival depends on a minimum intake of food, averaging between 1,800 to 2,400 calories per person daily, that will also ensure adequate levels, or stores, of essential oils, fats, vitamins, and minerals. Humans can, and do, survive on less, but at a physical and physiological price measured in stunted growth and susceptibility to chronic and infectious diseases. When food is scarce, food prices will increase; the more scarce food becomes, the more rapid the escalation in food prices.

When food is plentiful, in contrast, people will not pay more to obtain greater amounts of food than they need. Farmers who harvest more food than can be easily sold will be paid a substantially lower price for all the wheat, maize, rice, or hogs and cattle they sell in the market than they would receive without the excess production. When each farmer produces only slightly more one year than the last, the combined surplus can be so large as to devastate the income of all farmers, a condition that plagued U.S. agriculture for much of the twentieth century and now looms as a global condition. Farmers cannot withhold their individual surpluses since the amount is too small to make a difference, but each farmer suffers measurably when the overall surplus is so large that commodity prices fall and profits are destroyed. No individual, cooperative, or company has the resources to acquire and store the excess food.

Farmers, food processors, and consumers each cope differently with the inflexible fact of inelastic stomachs, all with varying degrees of government intervention. With a food supply in which the value of food accounts for only 20 percent of the cost of the system, food processors have the comparative advantage of size and few competitors. Consolidation among competitors occurred rapidly at all levels in the U.S. food supply system in the 1990s, thanks to the benign attitude of the federal government toward anticompetitive behavior, creating a marketplace with enormous advantages for the survivors. The massive size of food processors—four companies essentially control processing of beef and pork, three companies dominate the poultry industry, and even these seven firms are exploring further consolidation—allows processors to largely control what they will pay to producers.

Although commodity prices in the United States are low by all historic standards, the cost of food is not as significant a factor for company management as stability of supply and the ability to either stabilize (fix) the cost or negotiate the price of ingredients. Processors with few competitors need to fix the cost of ingredients over the life of the marketing plan for a food product. Those costs will be only one factor to consider in setting the level of product prices in the development of marketing strategies that will produce a profit. With price competition virtually eliminated for grocery food items, the price obtained through product differentiation is the dominant management concern.

From the consumer's perspective, food costs are actually declining as a portion of rising household income, and food price inflation is largely absent. Both conditions are substantially influenced by government fiscal and monetary policy. As long as these conditions prevail, consumers are less likely to be upset about the growing market power of food processors than they would be if food price inflation were escalating as much as it did in the 1970s. As odd as it sounds, inflation is not a food supply issue today because of the convenience factor. Food processors and supermarkets would inflate food prices if they could, but restaurant and fast-food outlets would take a bigger share of food spending if they did. As long as consumers choose to eat out more, the food industry is stymied by the competition over market share from restaurants and fast-food outlets. Processors and supermarkets have yet to develop an effective counterstrategy to the competition of convenience and are unable to raise prices as much as they would like. With the consumer food dollar almost evenly split between eating out and eating at home, the food processor is being forced to get

by with a smaller piece of the pie, so to speak. Consolidation in the processing industry is an inevitable response, dividing the consumer dollar among fewer participants.

An additional factor limiting the ability of the supermarket industry to raise food prices is a recent invasion of competitors, especially from "big box" discount retailers. Both Wal-Mart and Target are rapidly adding grocery merchandising sections to their existing stores and building new stores that emphasize groceries and food. As a result, supermarkets are being pressured not only by restaurants and fast-food outlets, but also by competition from discount stores. Supermarkets are taking the pragmatic approach, "if you can't beat them, join them," by marketing whole meals prepared in the store. While seven of every ten take-out meals sold in 2001 came from fast-food outlets, supermarkets accounted for almost two of ten, leaving the remaining one percent of the take-out market to restaurants. As long as consumers have the disposition and the disposable income to eat at restaurants or fast-food outlets, they also have the most effective strategy for playing suppliers in the food system against another.

Farmers cope with the changing trends in the food supply system with the one tool still available to them, aid from the federal government. In 1995, Congress enacted legislation to end government intervention in agriculture by phasing out income-support programs. However, when farm incomes fell in 1998 and in the following years, Congress quickly authorized emergency income payments and added another $30 billion over the next three years to already generous subsidies and government payments. In 2002, the first new farm legislation of the twenty-first century was adopted. The most generous in the sixty-year history of farm programs, the new legislation provided income support payments to farmers of over $19 billion a year for the following ten years. The scale of the subsidies allocated by Congress is unparalleled. Legislators in Washington have guaranteed that American farmers will receive nearly $200 billion in income payments over ten years, the equivalent of the farm share of annual consumer spending for food. Over 90 percent of farm output in the United States was harvested by some 200,000 farm operators who would receive most of the $19 billion in annual farm income payments. Globally, agriculture production is rising, a condition that experts predicted would drive down farm commodity prices further. If this pattern develops during the twenty-first century, even greater expenditures for farm support could be made by the federal government than had been projected under the existing farm legislation.

Immutable Law of Nutrition
If the food supply is governed by the economics of inelastic stomachs, it is also bound to the immutable law of nutritional consequences. People consume food because

MALNUTRITION

Malnutrition affects about 600 to 800 million people in the world, most of whom live in Africa and Asia, where food shortages occur more frequently and the food supply is tenuous and unpredictable. In Africa, the major cause is unstable governments combined with uncertain weather, a lethal social combination that undermines efforts to develop a more reliably productive agriculture capable of increasing domestic food production. Food assistance, mainly through the World Food Program, which distributes surplus food from developed countries, has been established worldwide to fill the calorie gap. However, food assistance treats the symptom, not the problem, and aggravates the search for long-term solutions by disrupting the agricultural economy when it is most vulnerable by displacing domestic markets.

of an instinct for survival, but life can be put in harm's way either by too little food or by eating too much food. People die of both starvation and gluttony. Nations are similarly at risk. If citizens, threatened by food shortages or famine, confront a food supply insufficient to fill shrunken stomachs, anarchy may ensue. A nation faces a no less compelling array of social, economic, and political problems when it confronts a food supply that is grossly greater than is needed. Surpluses can destroy the farming economy. If the nation dumps its surpluses on its neighbors, professing humanitarian impulses, the policy will destroy its neighbors' farming systems. If national leaders exhort people to eat their way out of the problem, or even if the surpluses are transformed into meat, poultry, and other forms of animal protein, then people will become overweight. In addition to surpluses, health costs will increase as well, and the national budget for health services will rise because obesity is a precursor to chronic diseases and overweight individuals are at risk of early death.

The U.S. public has come to accept that malnutrition is the consequence of too little food for too long a time. But malnutrition has two faces. It is a Janus-like condition of nutritional extremes, of either undernourishment or overnourishment, both of which may occur at the same time in a single population. In the United States and other developed countries, classic malnutrition, or undernourishment, most often occurs in predictable groups: women, children, the elderly, and the poor. The cause may vary, but malnutrition almost always accompanies poverty, which occurs more frequently

among these groups. Women are paid less than men for equal work, while four of every ten children live in poverty in the United States, where fewer than two of every ten families are poor. The proportion of the elderly who are poor continues to be greater than should be the case.

Malnutrition of the poor is not evident since undernourishment has few immediate, unique characteristics, although the condition will be visible eventually in the rising levels of infectious diseases, diarrhea, and tuberculosis. The overt signs of starvation, such as stunting, failure to thrive, kwashiorkor (extreme protein malnutrition, especially in children), or marasmus (chronic malnutrition, especially in children), are generally indicative of severe, widespread hunger throughout a population in which malnutrition already is extensive. Undernourishment in the United States, or in other highly developed nations, is not caused by food shortages but, instead, by barriers, almost always poverty, that block access to the food supply. There was no shortage of food in the world at the beginning of the twenty-first century, nor is there in the foreseeable future. Since the 1960s, the United States has established a series of federal nutrition programs to increase access to the food supply for groups of citizens at risk of hunger, including low-income families, children away from home, mothers and their infant children, and the elderly. The Food Stamp Program is intended to assist families and individuals, especially during rising unemployment and in seasonal periods when work is not available. The program also reaches families troubled by chronic unemployment and families in which the parents hold down two or more jobs but still earn only a poverty-level income. At peak unemployment in the early 1990s, nearly 25 million Americans were participating in the Food Stamp Program.

School meals, which include breakfast and lunch, are subsidized and served each day to more than 50 million schoolchildren, and schools receive additional subsidies to provide meals at nominal or no cost to over half of these children. Some 7 million mothers receive monthly certificates through the WIC (Women, Infants, and Children's) program to purchase infant formula and additional foods that provide nutrients needed especially by pregnant women and lactating mothers. The WIC Program also offers nutritional counseling and health information on pregnancy to expectant mothers. Over 2 million older Americans daily receive hot meals at nominal prices delivered to their homes or served in community centers through subsidies provided by the Older American Nutrition Program to community organizations. During the economic slowdown in 1991 and 1992, the federal government was spending over $40 billion a year on nutrition programs, including $27 billion on food stamps alone.

The unique characteristics of the U.S. food supply compared to other nations occur most notably in public policies. While the United States and the European

Union both subsidize their farm economies generously, other countries possess neither the wealth nor the political commitment to match this. At the beginning of the twenty-first century, the United States was projected to spend $200 billion over the next decade in farm income payments, and an estimated $350 to $400 billion for food assistance. No other nation allocates as much overall or as a percentage of its gross national product to ensure access to food for the poor as does the United States. The U.S. government has taken a benign view of economic concentration in the food system, permitting the accumulation of economic power among a few corporations in every sector of the industry, ranging from livestock slaughter to poultry processing, farm equipment and chemicals, as well as food manufacturing and retailing. The European Union, in comparison, is more vigilant regarding competition as an economic force in a free enterprise system.

See also **Agriculture since the Industrial Revolution; FAO (Food and Agriculture Organization); Fast Food; Food Banks; Food Pantries; Food Politics: United States; Food Security; Food Stamps; Food Supply and the Global Market; Food Trade Associations; Government Agencies; High-Technology Farming; Homelessness; Hunger Strikes; International Agencies; Political Economy; Poverty; School Meals; Take-out Food; WIC (Women, Infants, and Children's) Program.**

Rodney E. Leonard

FOOD TRADE ASSOCIATIONS. Since the time of the first Crusade (1095–1099), early food trade companies shipped raw specialty commodities (primarily spices) from exotic lands, first from Egypt and Syria, and later from China, India, and Indonesia, to market ports in the colonial world. The Italian trade families of Venice and Genoa were particularly active, most notably the Polo family, which brought goods from China between 1260 and 1294. Perhaps the most important of these shipments were seed stuffs, which were conveyed great distances, then planted on domestic soils and genetically groomed to flourish in their new habitats, to eventually become some of the staple commodity crops—such as maize and wheat—of human history. Bartering goods in both directions, the early trading companies contributed to the wealth of their risk-taking owners and sponsors who paid for their explorations.

The successful trade of even nonessentials developed dependencies on imported goods; tea and coffee, for instance, became so prized that their trade was eventually manipulated for political purposes. Frequently subsidized by royalty, food trade companies easily became players in the political arena. The East India Tea Company, which still exists today, was the beneficiary of tea taxes that Great Britain placed on its colonies in the early 1770s. When the practical Americans started drinking Dutch teas instead, the British placed tariffs on the Dutch teas, favoring their own trade association products at lower prices. That move was the impetus for the famed Boston Tea Party of 1773. After that, coffee rose quickly into American favor, having been introduced in 1600 to the West by Italian traders. So popular was the brew in the early 1960s that the coffee-producing and -consuming nations agreed to use export quotas to provide reasonable market prices and stabilize supplies. When that agreement was not renewed in 1989, the producers formed the Association of Coffee Producing Nations and developed the Coffee Retention Plan to balance supply and demand. Food trade associations had come of age and became a driving force in the global political arena.

Contemporary food trade associations may represent a commodity grower group, such as the National Cattlemen's Beef Association and National Corn Growers' Association in the United States; the Asociacion de Exportadores de Chile (Association of Chilean Exporters, or ASOEX, fruit exporters); or the Association of British Salted Fish Curers and Exporters, and the Pea Pickers and Pea Packers, in the United Kingdom. Or they can represent a group of commodities and products that share a trading platform or set of technologies, such as the Grocery Manufacturers Association (GMA), American Frozen Food Institute, Biotechnology Industry Organization, and the National Food Processors Association (NFPA) in the United States; or the Camara Nacional de Agricultura y Industria (National Chamber of Commerce for Agriculture and Industry) in Costa Rica.

These associations no longer physically trade food goods, but deal with a variety of issues that cannot be handled at the level of the food producers or processors individually, including coordination and collaboration in the marketplace on food safety, workers' rights, and agricultural health; public communication and education; distribution, pricing and marketing strategies; technical services; crisis management; and legal representation and lobbying in the international trade policy arena. Members (producers or processors), not owners or sponsors, reap the benefits of their efforts. Nowhere is this more apparent than in high-visibility marketing campaigns that have emerged for small-commodity products like raisins ("I heard it on the grapevine") and milk ("Got milk?").

Trade associations can be vitally important in legally defending an industry when it is involved in a trade dispute, for instance when it is charged with "dumping," as in the case of Chilean salmon defended in *Asociacion de Productores de Salmon y Trucha AG (Association of Salmon and Trout Producers)* v. *the United States International Trade Commission* (2 July 1999), where tariff penalties were greatly minimized. Mexico's Asociacion Agricola Local de Productores de Uva de Mesa (AALPUM) and Chile's ASOEX successfully cleared their table grape growers of dumping complaints by the Desert Grape Growers

League of California in the spring of 2001. Court and lobbying fees in international trade disputes can mount into the millions, far beyond the capacity of individual producers in developing countries where government support for the industry is nonexistent.

Trade associations can wield enough power to countermand multilateral international treaties. The World Trade Organization was established 1 January 1995 out of the General Agreement on Tariffs and Trade (GATT) of the Uruguay Round to adjudicate trade disputes according to a scientific risk-based assessment. Now, many food trade associations, like the science-based NFPA and the GMA, participate actively in that process, supplying regulatory and scientific experts to the WTO Codex Alimentarius Committees to prevent the formation of future technical barriers to trade.

See also **Civilization and Food**; **Codex Alimentarius**; **Commodity Price Supports**; **FAO (Food and Agriculture Organization)**; **Government Agencies**; **Government Agencies, U.S.**; **International Agencies**; **Maize.**

BIBLIOGRAPHY

Alden, John R. *A History of the American Revolution.* New York: Knopf, 1969. Reprint, New York: Da Capo, 1989.

Barty-King, Hugh. *Food for Man and Beast: The Story of the London Corn Trade Association, the London Cattle Food Trade Association and the Grain and Feed Trade Association, 1878–1978.* London: Hutchinson, 1978.

Grocery Manufacturers of America. Available at www.gma brands.com.

National Food Processors Association. Available at www.nfpa -food.org.

Robin Yeaton Woo

FOOD WASTE.   Food waste is the discarding of potentially usable food. Both edible and inedible foods may be considered garbage and therefore wasted. Edible foods are considered inedible when their quality deteriorates until they become unhealthy or noxious. Food deterioration occurs from microbial contamination or from rotting as a consequence of overproduction, storage problems, or improper preparation. Food waste also occurs through food use that returns little nutritional value, like overprocessing and overconsumption.

Edible foods are also wasted when cultural or individual preferences deem food undesirable. For example, some people dislike bread crusts, so they remove them and discard them. Societies with abundant food supplies often consider reusing leftover foods as inconvenient, while less food-rich societies regard food reuse as imperative. Specific parts of animals and plants considered edible in some cultures are considered inedible in others. Animal parts viewed as waste may include bones or shells, skins or scales, fat, blood, intestines, brains, eyes, and stomachs. Plant parts viewed as waste may include cores, seeds, stems, outer leaves, shells, rinds, husks, or peels.

Cultural Variations in Food Waste

Food systems in different cultures vary in the proportion of food waste that is discarded. Cultural variations exist in what is considered garbage, and understanding cultural food rules is crucial in examining food waste. For example, intestines and other internal organs are considered delicacies in China but are discarded as offal in many Western countries. Animal fats are consumed or used as fuel in societies like the Inuit, but in postindustrial nations fats are often trimmed and discarded to reduce caloric intake. Blood is an ingredient in dishes like black pudding in Britain but is discarded in many other societies.

Cultural differences in beliefs about what is edible versus inedible exist more often for animal foods than for plant foods. This may be because animals are similar to humans, so that edibility involves more symbolic meanings. Also, plant food wastes often constitute parts indigestible by humans that therefore have no nutritional value, such as vegetable rinds.

Moral values in most cultures admonish food waste. However, food protests and food riots may intentionally waste food to make ideological and ethical points. Many groups are proud of their efficient use of all parts of a slaughtered animal, such as Cajun claims to use "everything except the squeal" of hogs. Agricultural societies often feed plant food wastes to animals, while many industrial societies process by-products of animal slaughter into livestock feed. Such practices recycle undesired by-products into edible foods and minimize actual food waste. Some societies accept the waste of less-desirable portions of animals and plants as a sign that they have attained a state of affluence and can afford to consume only high-quality items.

Food Systems and Food Waste

Postindustrial societies waste food across all stages of the food system. Food production wastes preharvest food through natural disasters, diseases, or pests; harvested food by inefficient collection of edible crops or livestock; and postharvest food in storage or contamination losses. Food processing wastes food in spillage, spoilage, discarding substandard edible materials, or removing edible food parts in inefficient processing. Food distribution wastes food by offering more food than consumers will purchase and then discarding unsold products. Food acquisition wastes food when consumers purchase more food than they use. Food preparation wastes food by removing edible parts of foodstuffs, spilling or contaminating foods, and rendering foods inedible through improper handling and overcooking. Food consumption wastes food by taking larger portions than can be eaten or by spilling food. Digestion, transport, and metabolism of foods in the body waste nutrients through inefficient absorption, storage, or utilization, thereby failing to use all nutrients that were ingested.

Waste streams in the food system are the by-products of human production and consumption. Garbology, the study of human waste behaviors, identifies food waste as a significant portion of the total human waste stream. Food waste comprises about 10 percent of the total municipal solid waste streams in postindustrial nations and higher percentages in societies lacking mechanized refrigeration and durable packaging.

The four principal methods of disposing of food waste are dumping, burning, minimizing, and recycling. Dumping is the most common method of food waste disposal, but it may create sanitation and landfill problems. Burning food waste is convenient and minimizes the amount of solids needing to be disposed, but burning reduces air quality and is banned in many places. Minimizing food waste occurs through food trades, gifts, donations, and conservation during preparation and after consumption, such as reusing leftovers. Recycling often involves feeding food waste to livestock or composting food refuse. Compost can be used as fertilizer to grow more food, reducing the absolute food waste.

The Cost of Food Waste

Food waste significantly impacts environmental, economic, and community health. The accumulation of discarded food in landfills contributes to air and water pollution, and the burning of food refuse also affects air quality. Economic and nutritional losses are incurred from the calories lost in discarded food as well as from the energy and materials used to transport food waste to landfills. Wasted food means fewer nutrients are available for human consumption, which jeopardizes community food security.

There are also costs associated with the use of salvaged foodstuffs. For example, feeding animal slaughter by-products to livestock has caused outbreaks of bovine spongiform encephalopathy (BSE) and hoof and mouth disease in several European nations. Consumption of leftover foods that were not prepared or stored properly is implicated in many cases of foodborne illness.

Historical Changes in Food Waste

Historical transformations have changed the type and amount of food waste generated. Hunter-gatherer cultures often discarded bones as their primary food waste. The development of agriculture added more plant materials to the food waste stream. Industrialized agriculture increased organic waste by-products from large-scale food processing. Increased population growth and urbanization multiplied and concentrated the amount of food waste, which was increasingly dumped as the cities that generated waste became located farther from agricultural areas.

Historical shifts occurred in the conception of food waste. The term "garbage" originated in the French word for entrails and once referred exclusively to food waste. Later the word signified all refuse, since food waste embodies the most unacceptable characteristics of solid waste, putrefaction and attraction of vermin.

Material prosperity reduces the economic necessity for food conservation and reuse, and conspicuous consumption and disposal are demonstrations of social status. Food in postindustrial societies is inexpensive relative to total income, and wasting food is increasingly accepted. Technology that improves the durability of foods, such as plastic packaging, has reduced food waste from spoilage but has created a new waste problem as food packaging contributes more to the waste stream than food itself. Regardless of consumption and disposal practices, the growing world population has increased food waste.

See also **Consumption of Food; Meat.**

BIBLIOGRAPHY

Gallo, Anthony E. "Consumer Food Waste in the United States." *National Food Review* 3 (1980): 13–16.

Kantor, Linda S., Kathryn Lipton, Alden Manchester, and Victor Oliveria. "Estimating and Addressing America's Food Losses." *Food Review* 20 (1997): 2–12.

Rathje, William, and Cullen Murphy. *Rubbish! The Archaeology of Garbage.* New York: HarperCollins, 1992.

Strasser, Susan. *Waste and Want: A Social History of Trash.* New York: Metropolitan Books, 1999.

Jeffery Sobal
Mary Kay Nelson

FOODWAYS. The term "foodways" refers to the connection between food-related behavior and patterns of membership in cultural community, group, and society. In its most general usage, "foodways" refers to the systems of knowledge and expression related to food that vary with culture. For example, in modern America, foodways continue to represent cultural diversity within an increasingly interwoven society. In specific usage, "foodways" refers to those food-related behaviors that are believed to identify the primary cultural attributes of an individual or group of individuals; for example, it is in their foodways that Northern Italians are most easily distinguished from Southern Italians and Sicilians.

The first American usage of "foodways," without attribution of coinage, occurs in writings of the folklore initiative within the cultural New Deal—the program of civic reinvestment created by the administration of President Franklin D. Roosevelt in the early 1930s to combat the effects of the Great Depression. In a host of anthology publications, the publicly supported folklore work of the Federal Writers' Project celebrated American "stuff": traditional culture more easily identified by

The Makah Tribe prepares salmon for Makah Day Dinner, Neah Bay, Washington. COURTESY OF THE NATIONAL ARCHIVES AND RECORDS ADMINISTRATION.

its prevalence than its longevity. The director of the project's folklore activities, Benjamin Botkin, instructed fieldworkers to gather the evidence of tradition and creativity among America's living regional, ethnic, occupational, and spiritual communities—work songs, the calls of street vendors, festivals, tall tales, superstitions, and foodways.

In this context, foodways is a silent member within a category of expressive genres; like a festival, it is a "performed" tradition whose "texts" are activities that can be observed, and perhaps sampled, but are as emblematic of the people who produce those texts as the more conventionally recognized folk expressions that comprise collections and anthologies of published folklore. Botkin and his contemporaries also used the term "foodlore" on occasion to refer to foodways since, like folklore, it is a canon of shared beliefs or "lore" that is widely held but limited to a certain culture or situation.

Like its kindred terms "folkways" and "lifeways," "foodways" often echoes the popular anthropology of the 1950s—language carefully, if transparently, tailored to avoid infection by ethnocentrism and tuned to the broadest level of cultural comparison. Foodways is seen as a component of every culture, large or small, but one among several components artificially constructed at a level of analysis and comparison, just above the degree of particularity that might enable it to be easily understood. In its specification of the edible universe, foodways implies other categories containing elements equally innocuous yet laden with meaning: "shelterways," "clothesways," and perhaps "homeways," "workways," "schoolways," "healthways," "leisureways," or even "deathways." Each of these terms is logically sensible, but only "foodways" found its way, if by a slim thread, into contemporary usage.

The term "foodways" survived a period in folklore studies, roughly from the mid-1950s into the early 1970s, when what is now generally referred to as "material cul-

ture" in the United States did not rank as highly as the spoken word and the performed arts within the canon of folk expression. It is largely through the efforts of Don Yoder and Warren Roberts that the term was carried from one generation to another, from a period of relative low American academic interest into the current state of broad, heightened engagement.

In "material folk culture," the summary phrase of Henry Glassie's broad and renewing scholarship, foodways found revived utility in folklore studies. At the University of Pennsylvania and Indiana University, respectively, Yoder and Roberts prepared two generations of students to uphold broad applications of the term "tradition" (that is, inclusive of material folk culture) in their research. Since the late 1960s Yoder has documented the bearers of Pennsylvania's traditions, including those engaged in foodways, for the annual Pennsylvania Folklife Festival—an early example of collaboration between scholars and the general public that would arise later at the national level.

Since the 1970s, the percentage of American folklorists entering academe has been small in comparison to the number working in government-supported positions, located in arts-granting agencies, archives, and libraries as well as in foundations that are actively supporting the application of research to social issues. In both research and public programs, the early twenty-first-century generation of folklorists, more than half of whom were students of Yoder and Roberts, have found material expressions of tradition particularly useful in demonstrating the resilience of folk culture, the fundamental—and key—assertion of folklorists involved in public education.

In the 1980s, as the growing number of government-based programs continued to exercise their commitment to inclusion, many sought to engage recently emigrated peoples from Southeast Asia and Central America as nascent communities. With often limited resources, and language and translation challenges to contend with, a number of folklorists found in foodways a common ground for the presentation and comparison of contemporary tradition in action. In 1969, the Smithsonian Institution's annual Festival of American Folklife—whose advisory board over the years has included Yoder, Roberts, and Glassie—first presented foodways among festival programs that focused upon featured states or regions, ethnic communities, and occupational groups. Since its inception, the festival has included foodways as a way of focusing upon traditionally acquired skills and shared community values.

At the Smithsonian, the presentation of foodways in a festival setting became a model—a work-in-progress—that was emulated by state folklife program coordinators and festival directors. Built upon a foundation of field research that placed culinary traditions within the context of folklife genre, festival foodways presentations co-opted the "cooking show"—a presentation model made familiar by county fairs, food stores, and television. Here folklorists interviewed traditional cooks in the midst of preparing food and defined, in a way that few other public programs could, the concepts of observation and imitation, informal apprenticeship, and shared standards of appropriateness and taste.

In the early twenty-first century, foodways has generated little scholarship; however, many scholars have focused upon the cultural exchange within so-called food events, often attending to customs found in large-scale and socially significant occasions. Others, particularly those who work in both academic and public sectors of the discipline, have successfully identified matters of cultural consequences found in foodstuffs that are rapidly being depleted in their natural supply by commercial expansion into formerly wild areas. Folklorists Suzi Jones and Lynn Martin Graton, working in Alaska and Hawaii, respectively, have used the concept of foodways to describe and explain native and immigrant communities, natural resource management, and the viability of folk cultural processes.

There is both opportunity and need for more comprehensive foodways scholarship, the reappraisal of food-related traditions as a medium for creating cultural identity, and attention to the responsibilities of active tradition-bearers as teachers, conservators, and innovators. With improved standing in the American academy and the well-earned support of government agencies, foodways is poised to accommodate and frame the rapidly converging interests of scholarship and civic engagement.

See also **Folklore, Food in**; **Icon Foods**; **Religion and Food**; **United States: African American Foodways.**

BIBLIOGRAPHY

Freeman, Roland L. *The Arabbers of Baltimore*. Centreville, Md.: Tidewater, 1989.

Kirshenblatt-Gimblett, Barbara. *Destination Culture*. Berkeley: University of California Press, 1998.

Weaver, William Woys. *Sauerkraut Yankees*. Philadelphia: University of Pennsylvania Press, 1983.

Westmacott, Richard. *African-American Gardens and Yards in the Rural South*. Knoxville: University of Tennessee Press, 1992.

Charles Camp

FRANCE.

This entry includes six subentries:

FOOD AND CUISINE IN FRANCE

In 1826 a famous French gastronome, Brillat-Savarin, wrote among other things: "Animals feed, humans eat, but only those with refined taste dine," and "The creation of a new dish brings more happiness to humanity than the discovery of a new star." These two aphorisms are fundamental to an understanding of French attitudes toward food. On the one hand, food is not simply a source of nourishment, nor is it something everyone "naturally" appreciates. Only by cultivating discrimination (being attentive to tastes, colors, and textures) will food leave the realm of biological necessity and attain sensual heights. Secondly, creation is both essential and beneficial to society. It is the chef's duty to create, to advance the art of cookery and in so doing, provide pleasures that surpass those associated with more abstract achievements.

We will return to the importance of these two concepts later, since they are directly related to the prominent place French cuisine occupies in the world today. Before doing so, however, a look backward will help place French cuisine in a greater context and allow us to address several sensitive issues concerning its "birth" and evolution.

The Italian Controversy

An oft-repeated story maintains that French cuisine emerged from the "dark ages" of primitive eating only when Catherine de' Medici brought her Italian cooks to France in the mid-sixteenth century, for her marriage to Henry II in 1533. The French being more than apt students, the story goes, not only learned their lessons, but quickly surpassed their Italian masters in the art of fine cookery and . . . *Voilà!* French cuisine was born.

This legend has been repeated in popular histories of cooking for centuries, even in France. It was first evoked in 1739 in the preface to an innovative cookbook attributed to François Marin, *Les dons de comus*, where it is stated: "The Italians civilized all of Europe and it is they, without a doubt, who taught us how to eat. . . . For more than two centuries the French have enjoyed good cooking, but rest assured, dishes have never been as delicate, as expertly prepared, or better tasting, than they are today." A similar point of view is expressed by Le Chevalier de Jaucourt who authored the article on cuisine in Denis Diderot's famous *Encyclopédie* published in the 1750s:

> The Italians inherited the art of cookery from the Romans; it was they who introduced fine food to the French. . . . During the reign of Henry II, cooks from beyond the Alps came and settled in France, and we are eternally indebted to this motley band that served at Catherine de Medici's court. . . . The French, finely attuned to the flavors that should dominate in each dish, quickly surpassed their masters who were soon forgotten. From that moment on, as if they had successfully met the challenge of stressing what was important, they could pride themselves in the knowledge

that the taste of their cuisine had surpassed that of all others and reigned supreme in opulent kingdoms from North to South.

Thus, the simple cooking of ages past, having become more complex and refined from century to century, has today become a subject of study, a complex science about which numerous treatises constantly appear under titles such as *Le Cuisinier françois*, *Le Cuisinier royal*, *Le Cuisinier moderne*, *Les Dons de comus*, *L'école des officiers de bouche*, and many others, each one teaching a different method, which proves how futile it is to attempt to re-

duce to an established order what human beings, with their whims and changes of taste, search, invent, and imagine in the preparation of their food.

We will treat these points separately, starting with the reference to Catherine de' Medici and the Italian influence on French cuisine. Both of these eighteenth-century authors agree that the French have enjoyed good cooking "for more than two centuries," that is, since the sixteenth century. In fact, long before the young queen arrived in 1533, numerous sources bear witness to the sophistication of French cuisine.

Starting in the early fourteenth century, manuscript cookbooks were being written in France, one of which became extremely popular. This book, simply known as the *Viandier* (the term *viande* [meat] at that time referred to all eatables, hence a *viandier* was simply a cookbook) was said to be the work of one Taillevent, a chef in the royal kitchens of Charles V. The recipes we find in the *Viandier* are as rich and varied as those in contemporary Italian, English, Germany, or Spanish cookery manuscripts. This said, French cooks do not appear to have had a greater reputation than those in other European countries. They served dishes common to an "international repertoire" as well as some specific to France.

The situation seems to change in the sixteenth century but not it the way our two eighteenth-century authors suggest. Although a new generation of French cooks did rejuvenate cooking in France, the dishes they propose owe little or nothing to the Italian cuisine of the time, the style of which was radically different. Indeed, the earliest published cookbooks are German and French, not Italian, and barring an Italian dietetic work by Platina published in the 1470s that included some recipes from some fifty years earlier, not one Italian culinary treatise is translated into French. At a time when Catherine de' Medici was still a baby, travelers, including Italians visiting France, claim that French cooks are the best in Europe, and Rabelais, the most gourmand of writers, clearly prefers French dishes to those of any other nation since he frequently mentions those specific to the national repertoire in his gargantuan menus. In fact, there is no proof that Catherine de' Medici even brought her cooks with her to France!

No author living in the sixteenth century mentions the supposed superiority of Italian cookery, although Montaigne does marvel at the eloquence and precision of an Italian *maitre d'hôtel* describing the art of banqueting, and the expertise of Italian gardeners, confectioners, and carvers is not only recognized, but admired and copied. Nevertheless, notwithstanding the esteem in which Italians are held in the accessory arts of serving and confectionery, it is not until two centuries later that any hint of the so-called Italian influence on French cuisine per se appears in print. Be that as it may, French cooks do not achieve a clear dominance in the kitchens of Europe until the mid-seventeenth century.

The Beginnings of French Hegemony

Neither Marin nor Le Chevalier de Jaucourt gives a specific date for the rise of French cuisine. The latter does indicate that the French had "surpassed their masters" in the seventeenth century by including three seventeenth-century cookbooks (*Le Cuisinier françois*, *Le Cuisinier royal* and *L'école des officiers de bouche*) in his list of treatises devoted to the culinary arts. One of these books, *Le Cuisinier françois* of La Varenne, is the first to document the radical changes French cooking had undergone since the end of the Renaissance. Published for the first time in 1651,

La Varenne's book would be translated into several languages and remain in print for over one hundred years. In the preface to the English translation of 1653 we read, "Of all the cooks in the world, the French are esteemed the best," and from that time forward French predominance in the kitchen will continue its almost uninterrupted ascendancy.

A partial explanation for the influence of French cuisine lies in its vitality. The best professional chefs feel a duty to improve on the work of their predecessors in order to "advance" the art of cookery. Not only do they create new dishes, their cooking embodies new attitudes toward food, which often spread with the dissemination of the dishes they have invented. Over and over again, a new philosophy of cookery emerges, often in conflict with that of previous generations, always claiming to mark significant "progress" in the culinary art. In the eighteenth century, for instance, devotees compared the cooking of their *nouvelle cuisine* to alchemy, claiming to distill the essence of taste from the ingredients employed. A century later, a new generation of chefs led by Antonin Carême saw the cook more as an architect than a chemist. They encouraged the creation of monumental assemblages and developed a family of basic sauces, some of which are still in use today.

In turn, Auguste Escoffier in his *Guide culinaire* of 1903 rejected the elaborate cuisine developed by Carême, claiming that the "fast pace of modern life" no longer allowed chefs the leisure to prepare elaborated displays, and argued for a simplification of cuisine. It should be noted, in this context, that Escoffier was the first chef to obtain international recognition and to father a new school of cookery who did not work in a private home. Whereas previously the greatest French chefs all worked in aristocratic households or in royal kitchens, Escoffier built his reputation as a hotel chef at the Savoy Hotel in London and later at the newly created Ritz Hotel in Paris, before returning to London to the kitchens of the Carlton Hotel as an internationally acclaimed celebrity whose writings would form the basis of French cooking throughout the greater part of the twentieth century.

Gastronomy and Gastronomes

Food and cooking alone do not explain France's reputation in culinary matters. To recall Brillat-Savarin's words, "only people with refined taste know how to dine," and the French have not only cultivated the art of cookery but have long considered it an integral part of their culture: how one eats is as important as what one eats. Indeed, the French claim that they invented gastronomy and linguistically, this is certainly true. The term first appears in the title of an epic poem, *La Gastronomie* by Joseph Berchoux, published in 1803, its four cantos treating respectively the history of cuisine in antiquity, the first service, the second service, and the dessert of a banquet. The word rapidly came to designate the study of food and cookery as an art; those who excelled in this study, and for whom gastronomy was a central feature of their existence, were "gastronomes."

The gastronome was defined as a critical observer of the chef's work—not a chef. As professionals, gastronomes became food critics, the earliest of whom in the western world appear to be French. Among them, Grimod de la Reynière leads the list as the inventor of a new branch of literature with the publication of his *L'almanach des gourmands* from 1803 to 1812. In this yearly journal, he reviewed restaurants and published the results of tastings aimed at selecting the best artisans and products of his day, beginning a tradition of searching out quality that remains very much alive in the French mentality today.

L'exception française

One has only to contemplate the ferocious aversion of French consumers to hormone-fed beef and veal, to genetically modified food plants and the standardization of food in general, to understand that their relationship to food goes far beyond just eating—much to the bemusement and exasperation of France's trading partners. And where else but in France would the Education and Culture Ministries sponsor a national inventory of traditional food products, or classes teaching children how various foods are made and how to appreciate different tastes, smells, and textures?

The French approach to cookery, the institutions developed by its proponents and the gastronomic culture it glorifies have all contributed to the preeminence of French cuisine. Indeed, the very use of the term "cuisine," when applied to the food of another nation, implies that it has gone from simply being cooking to something more refined and complex—something closer to the French model. Naturally, the culinary superiority of France has been challenged in the past and continues to be challenged today, but no other cuisine has had such a sustained influence on the cooking practices of its neighbors, nor can any other claim to have exerted as universal an impact on professional cooks around the world, as that which developed and continues to evolve in France.

See also **Carême, Marie Antoine; Chef, The; Cookbooks; Cuisine, Evolution of; Escoffier, Georges-Auguste; La Varenne, Pierre François de'; Medici, Catherine de'; Middle Ages, European; Nouvelle Cuisine; Rabelais, François.**

BIBLIOGRAPHY

Flandrin, Jean-Louis, Philip Hyman, and Mary Hyman. "Introduction." In *Le Cuisinier françois* by La Varenne. Paris: Editions Montalba, 1983.

Hyman, Philip, and Mary Hyman. "La première nouvelle cuisine." In *L'honnête volupté: Art culinaire, art majeur,*" pp. 73–74. Paris: Editions Michel de Maule, 1989.

Mennell, Stephen. *All Manners of Food: Eating and Taste in England and France from the Middle Ages to the Present.* Oxford, Basil Blackwood, 1985.

Wheaton, Barbara Ketcham. *Savoring the Past: The French Kitchen and Table from 1300 to 1789.* Philadelphia: University of Pennsylvania Press, 1983.

Philip Hyman
Mary Hyman

NORTHERN FRENCH CUISINES

The Loire River has long served as a divide between northern and southern France. It runs from Nantes on the Atlantic coast to the south of Burgundy, where it veers south at Pouilly, though the French mentally continue the division line eastward to Geneva. Roughly half of France is north of the Nantes-Geneva line, including Brittany, the château country (Orléans to Tours), Normandy, Paris and the surrounding area known as Île-de-France, French Flanders, Alsace, Lorraine, Burgundy, and the Franche-Comté.

Farmers here are basically well-off. The wheat fields of the Beauce, just south of Paris, produce the finest wheat in France, Normandy is famous for its beef and cheese, and the lambs that graze near the sea in Brittany and in Picardy are among the most esteemed in France. Paris itself was once surrounded by vast gardens that supplied the capital's needs.

Beer, Gin, and Sugar Beets

Running along its most northerly perimeter and extending out to the tip of Brittany is France's longest coastline. From the English Channel to the Atlantic seaboard, fishing has always been a major industry. Herring was the dominant fish along the northeastern part of the Channel, and today salted and smoked herring are still a specialty there. French Flanders, however—like neighboring Belgium, with which it has strong cultural ties—does not spontaneously come to mind as a gastronomic haven. Coal mining was a major industry here, and those who survived the backbreaking work often sought relief in taverns and bars. Beer and hard liquor were consumed in great quantities, and a French version of gin (*genièvre*) wreaked havoc on the health of those who overindulged. It is therefore no surprise that this province holds the sad record of having the highest rate of cirrhosis of the liver in France.

One can nevertheless find something positive here: nowhere else in France is there as great a variety of traditional beers, of every conceivable taste and ranging in color from rich brown to amber, blond, and white. Not surprisingly, beer is the perfect accompaniment to the hearty local cuisine, whether one of the many forms of herring, a Flemish hotpot (*hochepot flamand*), or a pungent Maroilles, "the most delicate of strong cheeses." A by-product of beer production, brewer's yeast, also contributes to the character of the pastries, many of which use raised doughs, such as the light and airy Flemish-style waffles (*gaufres flamandes*) or briochelike cakes with names like *craquelin, cramique,* or *couquebottrom.*

Traditional ceramic terrine for *Alsatian Hasepfeffer* (*civet de lièvre*). Poterie artisanale Gérard Wehrling, Soufflenheim, Alsace (France), 1998. Rack of hare is baked in wine and gingerbread crumbs in this elaborate earthenware vessel, which also doubles as a serving dish. ROUGHWOOD COLLECTION. PHOTO CHEW & COMPANY.

The North is also the largest sugar-producing region of France. It has been ever since the British navy imposed the Continental blockade at the beginning of the nineteenth century, depriving France of cane sugar from its overseas colonies and prompting Napoleon to reward anyone who could apply a newly-discovered technique for producing sugar from beets on a commercial scale. The North quickly became a center of production of the precious commodity, and it is surely no coincidence that this is the only region where people use brown sugar (called *vergeoise* here), not only in desserts like the sumptuous sugar tart (*tarte au sucre*) with its light or dark brown-sugar filling, but in savory dishes prepared *à la flamande*, including the local blood sausage (*boudin*), sweet-sour red cabbage (*chou rouge*), and beef stewed in beer (*carbonade*).

Foie Gras and Sauerkraut

Like the ties between French Flanders and Belgium, Alsace, in the northeasternmost corner of France, shares many traits with Germany, its neighbor across the Rhine. Up until the treaty of Westphalia in the mid-seventeenth century, both Alsace and adjoining Lorraine were part of Germany. In the course of ensuing wars, they went back and forth between France and Germany until the end of World War II. As a result, trade with Germany has long been an important source of income for this region, as has tourism, which has increased in the course of time.

In this land of lager beers, *bretzels* (pretzels), and sausages—where white wines have names like Edelzwicker, Sylvaner, Riesling, and Gewürztraminer—Alsatian culture at first seems purely Germanic. Fat white Alsatian asparagus, which originated in Germany, is a springtime favorite served with slices of smoked ham and Alsatian Riesling. Even mustard is different here. Unlike the sharp Dijon-style mustard preferred elsewhere in France, the white mustard seeds used in Alsace result in a truly sweet mustard that reigns on virtually every table, as in Germany. The celebration of Saint Nicholas Day (6 December) is as important as Christmas in both places. In Alsace, it provides the occasion for making gingerbread effigies of the good bishop and *Mannala* (little man), a doll-shaped cookie associated exclusively with this day.

Not everything in Alsace has a German origin, however, and Alsatians proudly assert their differences with their imposing neighbor to the east. Not only are their wines and beers lighter, but a specific repertoire of dishes and a French penchant for fine gastronomy all distinguish them from their German cousins. A favorite Alsatian specialty that does not seem to have a German equivalent is *Bäckeoffe*, made by marinating beef, pork, and lamb in white wine and baking them slowly for several hours with sliced potatoes and onions in a special earthenware terrine. Even sauerkraut is prepared so differently here—braised in Alsatian white wine with smoked, salted, and fresh cuts of pork and served with additional Strasbourg sausages and liver dumplings—that Germans cross the river in droves to enjoy *choucroute à l'alsacienne* as a special treat.

The great cheese of Alsace is Muenster, a French-style soft, creamy cheese, albeit served with a decidedly un-French accompaniment of caraway seeds (called *cumin* here). Alsace is also the home of *foie gras*, a quintessentially French specialty that, curiously enough, appears to have been introduced by the large Jewish population that settled here. Over the centuries, the Jews perfected the art of force-feeding geese to increase the quantity of fat, to be used for cooking since pork fat was prohibited by their religion. The enlarged, buttery livers or *foie gras*, a by-product of this operation, had become a highly sought-after specialty by the eighteenth century. Unlike southwestern France (the site of Jewish immigration from Spain), where *foie gras* is most often baked simply in a terrine, the livers are traditionally baked in a pastry shell in Alsace.

Baba and Quiche

The Germanic influence is much less evident in neighboring Lorraine, where specialties more closely resemble those encountered elsewhere in France. One could name the *potée lorraine*, a poached salt pork and vegetable dinner very similar to the ubiquitous beef-based *pot-au-feu*, the *macarons* from Nancy, or the *madeleines* from Commercy. Another product specific to Lorraine, and the emblem of the region, is the *mirabelle*, a small yellow plum that is enjoyed eaten on its own, distilled to produce an aromatic brandy, made into preserves, or baked into a tart.

Lorraine is also the home of one the best known specialties in all of France—*quiche*. Mentioned as early as the sixteenth century and initially made with a simple filling of eggs and cream, it was prepared only in the region until the nineteenth century, then started to spread to the rest of country. Today the word, and the pastry, can be found around the world with a bacon-studded filling, an early-twentieth-century variant on the original, meatless filling rarely encountered today.

Like French Flanders and Alsace, Lorraine is beer-drinking country, where many pastries are made with egg- and yeast-rich doughs. The most famous of these is the *baba*, a light, raised cake with raisins. It is derived from a cake of the same name that was introduced in the eighteenth century by the exiled Polish king, Stanislas Leszczynsky, whose daughter, Marie, married King Louis XV of France. As Duke of Lorraine, Stanislas held court in Nancy, where local bakers adopted and perfected the baba. By the beginning of the nineteenth century, its fame had spread to Paris, where a pastry chef named Stohrer (whom many believe was from Lorraine) added the final touch of making individual babas and dousing them with rum.

Smoked Meats and Hefty Cheeses

Directly south of Lorraine is the mountainous region of Franche-Comté, sandwiched between Switzerland and Burgundy. It is a land of hilly, green pastures that produce some of the finest cheeses and meat products in all of France as well as some of the country's most unusual wines. The mountain cheeses, made from the milk of the local Montbéliard cow, range from the creamy *vacherin* of the Mont-d'or, encircled with a strip of spruce wood, to large, hard-pressed wheels of *comté*, the French version of gruyere. Every bit as fruity as its more familiar Swiss cousin, *comté* improves with age. Another cheese peculiar to the region is *cancoillotte*, made in the valleys. After skimming off all the cream to make butter, the milk is allowed to curdle naturally, the curds are dried, and the resulting *metton*, as it is called, is broken up and aged until it has become yellow and waxy. To make *cancoillotte*, a piece of *metton* is melted with butter and water and seasoned with garlic or caraway. Definitely an acquired taste, the creamy, pungent *cancoillotte* is a favorite local topping for baked or steamed potatoes, or scrambled eggs.

Unlike their treatment in most of France, meat products are traditionally smoked here, rather than simply salted and dried. This preference is related to the structure of the typical farmhouse of the area, built around a large central chimney called a *tuyé*. The ham from the Haut-Doubs, the sausages from the towns of Morteau and Montbéliard, and an unusual smoked beef tenderloin known as *bresi*—to name only these few—are among the finest *charcuterie* in France.

As for the wines, the most striking are the whites, made with a local grape variety, the *savagnin*. Their almost sherrylike taste is surprising at first but perfect with the *charcuterie*, cheeses, and cream-based dishes from the region, especially those garnished with morel and chanterelle mushrooms from the Jura mountains. The most astonishing is the "yellow wine" (*vin jaune*) produced near the village of Château Chalon. Always served at room temperature, it can be aged for up to a hundred years, and its particular fruit and walnut flavors are unique.

Snails, Wine, and Aperitifs

To the west of Franche-Comté lies Burgundy. The most famous dish associated with the region, *boeuf bourguignon*, combines wine and beef, two of Burgundy's most valued resources. Though wine comes immediately to mind when Burgundy is mentioned, there are few vineyards in the southern part of the region where equally famous white cattle are raised on small farms near the town of Charolles. A very large breed with tender, lean meat especially well suited to grilling and roasting, Charolais beef has few rivals in France, and the breed is now raised in some seventy countries worldwide.

Driving north on the road back toward Paris, one sees multicolored tiles covering rooftops in the valley that runs through some of France's most prestigious vineyards. There are virtually no imposing estates here, and the wines take their names from the towns, the most famous of which lie along the stretch of the N7 highway between Chalon-sur-Saône and Dijon: Chassagne-Montrachet, Meursault, Pommard, Aloxe-Corton, Vosne-Romanée, Vougeot. . . . Producers live in simple farmhouses and tend small plots of land, so one must know the names of the specific growers whose style one prefers. Production is small compared to Bordeaux and prices are, on the whole, higher.

For many, the food most associated with Burgundy is snails, once plentiful in the vineyards. Naturally, if they were not gathered, they feasted upon the precious grapes—a sort of eat-or-be-eaten situation. Burgundians long ago chose the first option, consuming them with such gusto that the local snail is now an endangered species that can be gathered for personal use, but not marketed. The large Burgundian snail (*Helix pomatia*) is harder to raise than its southern cousin the *petit gris* (*Helix aspersa*), so the majority of the *escargots de Bourgogne* sold in France are shipped alive to Burgundy from such faraway places as Turkey, where they are still plentiful in the wild and do not fit into the national diet.

In the upper end of the region, Dijon is famous for several specialties. *Moutarde de Dijon* has been renowned throughout France since the thirteenth century and is an indispensable item in French kitchens. The hot, tangy mustard enters into the *vinaigrette* salad dressing familiar to all, or into sauces of all kinds (particularly those for rabbit and pork), or is served alone to accompany a wide variety of dishes: grilled meats, the homey boiled-beef dinner or *pot-au-feu*, and even French fries, dipped into the mustard pot for an extra "zing."

Pain d'épice, a honey-rich gingerbread loaf, can be bought in shops throughout the city. Often eaten casually in the course of the day, Dijon's *pain d'épice* differs from others in that it is always made with wheat flour rather than rye, more popular in the rest of the country.

Crème de cassis, a lightly alcoholic, sweet blackcurrant liqueur produced in Dijon since at least the eighteenth century, can be sipped on its own, or added to a glass of dry white wine (traditionally from the aligoté grape). It was in this latter form that it became enormously popular starting in the 1950s, when the mayor of Dijon routinely served the mixture at public events. As a result, it is now known by his name—Kir—and served as an *aperitif* throughout France.

Pigs' trotters and . . . Champagne!
Given the celebrity of its wine, whose bubbles are synonymous with elegance, one might believe that Champagne, directly north of Burgundy, is a region with a highly sophisticated cuisine. Nothing could be much fur-

ther from the truth. Although the *pain d'épice* of Reims, the wine capital, has been famous for centuries and the pink ladyfingers made there (*biscuit de Reims*) are the ultimate in refinement, for the most part the cuisine of Champagne is hearty country fare. Particularly well-known is the *charcuterie* of Troyes, most notably the *andouillette*, a tripe sausage served either grilled with mustard or baked with a cream-shallot-mustard sauce. Other regional favorites include the boiled-vegetable and salt-pork *potée champeoise*, and *salade au lard*, a deceptively simple dandelion salad that has become the subject of such hot debate that a local historian wrote a 150-page book comparing the merits of different versions: Should the dandelion greens be cut or left whole? Should the bacon be fatty or lean, smoked or just salted? Should the potatoes be cooked in their skins or peeled? And so forth.

Another humble but delicious specialty from Champagne is grilled pigs' trotters *à la Sainte-Menehould*, delightfully creamy inside and crisp on the outside. Named for the town in which they have been served for over three hundred years, the trotters are simmered for up to fifty hours in an aromatic stock, then breaded, broiled, and eaten—bones and all.

Champagne also shares one very prestigious product with the Île-de-France, the region surrounding Paris immediately to the west. For hundreds of years, the northern half of Brie country belonged to the province of Champagne, with its capital at Meaux. The cheeses from the area have been famous since the fifteenth century, and when made with unpasteurized whole milk, *brie de Meaux* is still among the finest cheeses in France. After the French Revolution, however, Meaux was incorporated into the newly created *département* of the Seine-et-Marne, with its capital at Melun, which was (and still is) part of the Île-de-France. This, of course, did not stop farmers in the Marne *département*, to the east of the new administrative line, from continuing to make "Brie de Meaux" as they had for centuries. In 1980, when the coveted *appellation contrôlée* (Denomination of Protected Origin) status was awarded to the cheese, this fact was taken into account. To this day, a small proportion of the mammoth wheels of Brie that can be seen in Parisian cheese shops come from Champagne.

Feeding Paris
Along with cheeses from Brie, until very recently the Île-de-France could count on the farmland encircling Paris to come close to meeting the needs of the capital in fruits and vegetables. With the spread of suburbs since the 1960s, virtually all of the orchards and vegetable gardens have disappeared. The peaches from Montreuil and the succulent grapes from Thomery (trained against a labyrinth of sun-heated walls near Paris in order to ripen on all sides) are now a thing of the past, as are the mountains of fat white asparagus from Argenteuil that were once served at the finest tables. Nevertheless, although

the great majority of the once-famous fruits and vegetables developed in the Île-de-France are now produced outside of the region, their names remain, reminding us of the past glory of the cherries from Montmorency, the *champignons de Paris* (button mushrooms first cultivated in the limestone quarries that tunnel under Paris), or the delicate, pale-green dried beans *(flageolets)* from Chevrier.

All of this legendary produce, as well as the finest fish and meat from all around France, was sold for centuries at the equally legendary central wholesale market, les Halles, until 1969, when the demands of a constantly growing population and the paralyzing traffic jams it caused forced it outside of Paris, to Rungis. Nevertheless, the bistros that grew up around les Halles still thrive and continue to serve quintessentially Parisian dishes like steaming onion soup *(gratinée)*, calf's head *(tête de veau)* with a tangy vinaigrette or highly seasoned mayonnaise *(sauce gribiche)*, or the exquisitely simple but refined *boeuf à la ficelle*, beef tenderloin tied to a string, dipped for only minutes in an aromatic vegetable bouillon, served rare with the vegetables, and accompanied by coarse salt, mustard, and pickles or, for an even more refined presentation, by béarnaise sauce.

In the past, much of the produce that arrived in les Halles came from Picardy, directly north of the Île-de-France and sandwiched between Champagne on the east, Flanders on the north, and the English Channel and Normandy on the west. A rich agricultural province, Picardy's main city, Amiens, is only 137 kilometers (85 miles) from Nôtre-Dame. Parisian connoisseurs could order excellent lamb from Beauvais, duck pâtés *(pâté de canard)* from Amiens, eels baked in pastry *(pâté d'anguille)* from Abbeville in the north, and a wide variety of vegetables long before the existence of modern transportation. Artichokes from Laon, beans from Soissons, peas, and even potatoes were once important "exports," although today they can hardly compete with the same products shipped by train or truck from all over France. The small, moist macaroons from Amiens have been famous for well over a century, and few cakes can match the lightness of the Picard *gâteau battu*, a tall, fluted *brioche* shaped like a chef's hat.

Camembert and Calvados

To the west of Picardy, green pastures and half-timbered houses welcome you to Normandy. A land long famous for the quality of its butter and cream, Normandy is also a land of great cheeses, and the little town of Camembert can lay claim to producing what is arguably the most famous cheese in the entire country. Curiously, most people don't know that Camembert is a relatively recent invention, as cheeses go. Dating back to the eighteenth century, it is said to be a variant of Brie, and its popularity dates only from the nineteenth century, when railways made it possible to ship the cheese to distant markets. An authentic Camembert is made from unpasteurized whole milk and aged until its white crust is streaked with rust-colored stripes.

Those who associate Norman cooking with butter and cream are often surprised when they encounter another specialty—*tripes à la mode de Caen*. One of the gastronomic glories of the region, the tripe is simmered for hours with carrots, onions, and condiments before a dash of calvados is added as a finishing touch. Made by distilling apple cider (apples are another product indissociable from Normandy), calvados is a popular digestive brandy *(digestif)* both in and outside the region. It is as common as (and generally cheaper than) cognac, although the finest old calvados can equal its more famous rival in both taste and price.

Another unusual Norman specialty is duck—not just any duck, but a special breed developed in Rouen and slaughtered by suffocation so that blood remains inside. Only this duck should be used when preparing *canard à la Rouennaise*. Young and tender, it is cooked and served in a complex manner—which involves crushing the carcass in a specially designed silver press to recover the blood and juices for the making of a sumptuous sauce.

In addition, the Normandy seacoast is historically the site of intense fishing, and many ports are associated with specific fish. Fécamp, for example, was once an important center for the fish-curing industry. Inexpensive and nonperishable, salt cod and herring were in centuries past a staple throughout Europe, particularly sought-after during Lent when meat and poultry were banned. The curing industry has now vanished, but the fresh fish remain. Other ports are known for other specialties: particularly prized are the sole from Dieppe, the shrimp and lobsters from Cherbourg, and the oysters from Etretat and Granville.

Castles in France

As one travels south toward Orléans and the Loire valley, the culinary landscape changes. After the flat, wheat-growing plains of the Beauce around Chartres, game becomes plentiful, eel stewed in red wine is a popular dish, and white asparagus is abundant every spring. In Orléans, one can sample a delicious quince paste called *cotignac*, already famous in the sixteenth century, and the vinegar made in the city is considered the best in France. Some 37 kilometers (23 miles) south of Orléans lies Lamotte-Beuvron, the birthplace of one France's favorite desserts. It was here, in the modest Tatin hotel run by two sisters, that the famous *tarte tatin*, a rich and buttery caramelized apple tart baked upside down, is said to have been invented.

Nestled in the gentle hills along the Loire River from Orléans to Tours are the extraordinary châteaus built by the kings and high nobles of France. Rabelais was a native son of Chinon, and his love of good food is no wonder in this idyllic region of excellent lamb and poultry, fruity and delicate goat cheeses from Chavignol, Sainte-Maure, and Valençay, and wonderful pork products, among which the *rillettes de Tours*, a creamy, spreadable pâté, has no equal. Not to mention the local wines—light,

One of the oldest restaurants in Paris was the Boeuf à la Mode, which opened in 1792. Shown here is a detail from one of the restaurant's menus in 1919. The scene is intended to evoke an image of the restaurant in its heyday. ROUGHWOOD COLLECTION.

elegant reds from Chinon, Anjou, and Bourgueil, and lively whites from Vouvray, Pouilly, Quincy, and Sancerre—which are the perfect companion to these and other delicacies of the region.

A bit farther back from the river, caves hollowed out of the chalky hillsides are used for growing button mushrooms, and as one wends one's way westward, the lambs are joined by cattle; the Pays-de-la-Loire is the largest beef-producing region of France, providing 20 percent of the total production. Poultry is first-rate, especially in the *département* of the Sarthe, where the capon *(chapon)* from Le Mans has been famous since the sixteenth century.

Bagpipes and Butter Cakes

Proceeding west, one enters the Breton peninsula, which extends far out into the Atlantic, measuring about 150 kilometers (about 95 miles) from north to south at its widest point, but only half that at its tip. It is a province inhabited by one of France's most independent-minded peoples, who have long fought to preserve their traditional language and culture, descended as they are from

the Celts who fled here from Great Britain during the invasion of the Angles and Saxons starting in the fifth century. Not only are the Bretons trying to preserve their Celtic language, but they celebrate holidays and festive occasions to the sound of bagpipes, as do their Celtic cousins in the British Isles. A separatist movement would like to see this province secede from France, but most Bretons consider themselves thoroughly French and are proud to be so.

Contrary to most of France, virtually no cheese is produced here. The Bretons churn virtually all of their cream into butter which, unlike that made elsewhere in France, is preferred salted. The importance of butter is nowhere better appreciated than in the local pastries, whether in the form of cookies like the paper-thin *galettes* or the crumbly, shortbread-like *palets*, the *gâteau breton* (a sort of cake-sized *palet)*, or the inimitable *kouign-amann* (literally, "butter cake"), in which butter and sugar are rolled and folded together in a bread dough that is baked until caramelized. Although cider is the main beverage, this is also the only French province where buttermilk *(lait ribot)* is drunk, more often than not with savory buck-wheat pancakes *(galettes de blé noir)* or sweet wheaten *crêpes*, both spread out to an almost transparent thinness.

Given Brittany's extensive coastline, it is no surprise that the Bretons are a legendary seafaring people. From the sixteenth century onward, countless ships have set out from Nantes, Brest, and Saint-Malo, sailing thousands of miles to fish the great cod banks of Newfoundland. Sardines and mackerel are also plentiful, and, as in Normandy, the salt-cod trade once made towns like Saint-Malo the center of constant activity. Brittany is also a favorite vacation spot for those who wish to escape the crowded beaches in the south of France. Vacationers feast on seafood, particularly shellfish; most notable are lobsters, virtually absent from every other French coast and considered superior to the American variety that lives on the other side of the Atlantic.

Benefiting more than any other part of France from the Gulf Stream, the province has for centuries been renowned for the quality of its fruits and vegetables. In recent years, it has literally been transformed by industrious farmers growing cauliflower, strawberries, and even tomatoes. One vegetable that is especially associated with the region's agriculture is the globe artichoke. Despite competition in recent years from the purple artichoke grown in Spain and southern France, Breton artichokes are still highly sought-after, and plentiful, in markets throughout the country from June to October.

Northern Riches
Living in the most populated and by far the most industrial part of the country, few inhabitants of the northern half of France have suffered the hardships of those living in the most desolate parts of the south. Farmers in the north have benefited most from the presence of Paris in its center, since the French capital has always been a vast market for goods produced here. The extensive seacoast has been the source of a thriving fishing industry from the Middle Ages until today. Northern France is a patchwork of cultures where beer and cider can be more important than wine, not only on the table but in the dishes as well, although butter and cream are universally employed here. From the rugged, foggy coasts of Brittany to the green, low-lying mountains of the Franche-Comté, this gentle France is a far cry from the sun-baked fields, the olive trees, and the snowy heights of the Pyrenees and Alps only a few hundred miles to the south.

See also **Cheese**; **Germany, Austria, Switzerland**; **Italy**; **Mustard**; **Wine**.

BIBLIOGRAPHY
Conseil national des arts culinaires. *L'Inventaire du patrimoine culinaire de la France* [Inventory of the culinary patrimony of France]. Paris: Albin Michel: Nord Pas-de-Calais, 1994; Bourgogne, Franche-Comté, Pays de la Loire, Île-de-France, 1993; Bretagne, 1994; Lorraine, Alsace, 1998; Picardie, 1999; Champagne-Ardenne, 2000.

Hanicotte, Colette, Jean Froc, et al., eds. *La Cuisine des terroirs: 500 recettes* [Regional cuisine: 500 recipes]. Paris: Larousse, 2000.

Mary Hyman
Philip Hyman

SOUTHERN FRENCH CUISINES
Broadly speaking, southern France extends southward from the Loire River to the Mediterranean, and eastward from the Atlantic coast to the Alps along an imaginary line running from Nantes to Geneva. Numerous cultures and cuisines coexist in this vast area. Walnut oil and goose fat in the southwest give way to olive oil along the Mediterranean coast which, in turn, yields to butter in the foothills of the Alps.

Most of southern France is covered with grape vines but the wines they produce differ greatly from one another. South and east of the prestigious Bordeaux châteaus lie the vineyards that produce the earthy reds of Madiran and Cahors. Along the Mediterranean seacoast, the lighter reds and whites of Languedoc-Roussillon blend into the rosés of Provence. At their juncture, the Rhône Valley runs north, with full-bodied wines that range from the rich reds of Châteauneuf-du-Pape and Hermitage to the flowery white Condrieu, a far cry from the crisp white wines of Savoy, nestled in the Alps.

Although Bordeaux on the Atlantic seaboard, Toulouse in the southwest, Marseilles in the south, and Lyons in the northern Rhone Valley all function as regional capitals in southern France, none of them acts as a center for concentrating wealth and stimulating production as Paris does in the north. On the whole, the south is more varied from both a physical and culinary point of view.

Of Oysters and Mussels and Goat Cheese Cakes
Proceeding southward along the Atlantic coast from Nantes to Bordeaux by way of La Rochelle, one encounters two provinces rarely visited by the casual tourist: Poitou and Saintonge. Grouped together into the administrative region of Poitou-Charentes, this is a transition area that shares some aspects with the north of France and some with the south. One of the most famous butters in all of France, *beurre d'Echiré*, is produced here and butter-based dishes are common, though they in no way resemble those made in Brittany or Normandy. One of the most popular is *embeurré de choux*, literally "buttered cabbage," made by crushing boiled cabbage with a fork, then stirring in a healthy amount of fresh butter. Steamed new potatoes from the Île de Ré, served with butter and sprinkled with the sea salt (*fleur de sel*) also produced on this island off La Rochelle, are another treat far more sumptuous than the simplicity of the preparation would lead one to imagine. And the local goat cheese, called *cabichou*, although delicious on its own, is also turned into desserts, whether the tartlike *fromageau* or

the astonishing *tourteau fromagé*, with its jet black, rounded top and light, moist inside.

Curiously enough, the food most frequently associated with the Charentes is the snail, so much so that people here are called *les cagouilles* (snails). They like their snails—not the large Burgundian snail but the smaller, southwestern *petit gris*—grilled over an open fire or simmered in red wine. Mussels, too, are popular, particularly when transformed into *mouclade*, that is, opened over the heat with a little white wine, then finished with cream (and occasionally a pinch of curry powder!). Oysters from the Arcachon basin (*huîtres de Marennes*), both sought after and plentiful, are preferred raw on the half-shell here with an accompaniment of grilled sausages and a glass of white wine.

From Lamprey Eels to Foie Gras

South of the Charentes is Bordeaux. The wine capital of France, this city is also a major port with numerous links to the sea. Given its location on the estuary of the Gironde River, it is perhaps not surprising that the most emblematic fish of the region are estuary fish: shad, lamprey eel, and sturgeon. The first two swim in from the sea and up the Gironde in the spring and are highly prized by local gourmets who relish grilled shad with a sorrel sauce (*alose à l'oseille*) and prefer their lampreys in a red wine sauce thickened with the fish's own blood (*lamproie à la bordelaise*). In centuries past, however, the sturgeon was the king of fish, not only around Bordeaux but on aristocratic tables throughout France, where it reigned supreme until the end of the sixteenth century. By the end of the nineteenth century, however, the French had also discovered the joys of caviar, which so decimated the wild Atlantic sturgeon population that, since 1982, its fishing has been banned. In recent years, however, a slightly smaller species has been successfully farmed, permitting the curious to once again sample sturgeon and caviar from the Gironde.

South of Bordeaux a once treeless expanse known as the Landes stretches down the coast almost to Spain. Planted with pines over a century ago, it is still sparsely populated but attracts tourists in search of a pleasant beachfront with inexpensive holiday accommodations. In the Landes, and extending inland for many miles, geese and ducks have brought fortune and fame to farmers for centuries. Force-fed until their livers swell to enormous size, they are then sacrificed, producing *foie gras*, a luxury product highly sought after both in and outside the region.

Although *foie gras* is indisputably a French specialty today, it was probably introduced into the southwest by Spanish Jews fleeing religious persecution in the seventeenth century. They had perfected the art of force-feeding geese as a means of obtaining a ready supply of cooking fat (pork fat being prohibited by their religion), much as northern European Jews introduced *foie gras* into Alsace (see Northern French Cuisines). Today, goose *foie gras* is produced on a very small scale, but fattened duck

Legs of lamb rubbed with Provençal herbs (among them, French lavender) roast slowly beside a fire at the Bistro des Alpilles in St. Remy-de-Provence, France. © OWEN FRANKEN/ CORBIS.

livers are a major cottage industry. Easier to handle than geese and demanding a much shorter fattening period, the plump ducks also provide locals with two other highly prized specialties: duck steaks (*magret de canard*) and preserved duck (*confit de canard*). The thick steaks, made from the meaty breasts of the fattened ducks, started becoming popular in the 1970s when local restaurateurs began putting them on their menu. Previously they were salted, then simmered in a cauldron of fat until completely tender, like the rest of the bird, to make *confit*, which could be kept for several months packed in their cooking fat in large stoneware jars. Today, this ancient technique is carried one step further, and the *confit* is subject to a second preserving process by being sterilized and canned. Jars of *confit* can be kept on a kitchen shelf for many more months than the traditional preserve and are sold at roadside stands all year round.

The area northeast of the Landes, Périgord, produces perhaps the most expensive delicacy in all of France: black truffles. Specially trained dogs and pigs smell their location in the ground since, to this day, no one has found a way to successfully cultivate the elusive subterranean mushrooms, which explains their high price and scarcity even in France. Thinly sliced and barely warmed, truffles can be used to garnish many dishes. They are frequently served with *foie gras* or poultry although many people maintain that they are best with very simple foods—steamed potatoes with butter and salt, or creamy scrambled eggs, for example—or on their own, wrapped in waxed paper and buried in the embers until the truffle has been warmed through.

Although truffles are in season from December to March, they are in such high demand during the holiday season that patient gourmets wait to purchase them until after 15 January when prices drop to more "reasonable" levels. Like *foie gras*, canned truffles also form a lucrative part of the preserving industry, but neither of these exceptional foods survives the canning process unscathed. Though they are exported in this form around the world, they are in no way comparable to their fresh counterparts, which are rarely available outside of France.

Nations within a Nation: The Basque Country and French Catalonia

Although only 500 miles (800 kilometers) separate the Atlantic Ocean from the Mediterranean Sea, the culinary traditions that straddle the Pyrenees Mountains along these two seaboards are as different from each other as the people who created them. On the Atlantic coast is the Basque country that extends roughly from Bayonne to Bilbao. Much like the Bretons in the North, the fiercely nationalistic Basques have long demanded independence from both France and Spain and struggle to keep their native customs and unique language alive on both sides of the mountains. They are proud of their "differentness," which is reflected in their cuisine. Unlike almost any other in France, Basque cookery is marked by a preference for spicy tastes. A special variety of chili pepper grown near the town of Espelette is particularly sought after and used in preparing *piperade*, a spicy tomato stew, most often stirred into scrambled eggs and garnished with a slice of Bayonne ham, or served next to the ham with a fried egg on top. Inveterate fishermen, the Basques were among the first to exploit the great cod banks of Newfoundland in the sixteenth century, and their love of fish is expressed in dishes like *ttoro*, a fish stew, stuffed squid (*encornets farcis*), or sweet red *piquillo* peppers stuffed with a creamy codfish purée. Irouleguy wine is a perfect accompaniment to all these delicacies, unless one prefers to taste the local sparkling cider (*sagarnoa* in Basque), another specialty of this most remarkable corner of France. And to finish the meal in a typically unusual way, Basques like to serve their famous Ossau-Iraty sheep's cheese (*fromage de brebis des Pyrénées*), with orange marmalade or black cherry jam from the village of Itxassou and a glass of sweet Jurançon wine from the neighboring Béarn region just to the east.

Another product that arrived from the Americas four centuries ago and took hold in the traditional cuisines of the French southwest along with the chili pepper and its relatives is corn (maize). Originally a replacement for the once popular millet, ground cornmeal is used principally to make a bread (*pain de maïs* or *mesture*), and a thick porridge known variously as *cruchade*, *escauton*, or *millas*, eaten hot as a garnish with any number of stews or allowed to cool, cut into slices, pan fried in butter, and sprinkled with sugar for dessert. Cornmeal quickly became a staple in the peasant diet, and the grain had the added advantage of fattening both ducks and geese much more efficiently than native European cereals.

At the other end of the Pyrenees facing the Mediterranean is another community that takes great pains to preserve its proud traditions. Catalonia, a powerful nation during the Middle Ages, straddles the border between France and Spain, roughly from Perpignan to Tortosa, south of Barcelona on the Costa Brava. The Catalan language is still spoken on both sides of the Pyrenees, and Catalan nationalists have long argued that the two provinces should be united again to make an independent border state. Much of Catalonia hugs the Mediterranean and it comes as no surprise to find that the people excel in preparing seafood dishes of all kinds, among which are the *bullinada* (a fish soup similar to bouillabaisse), the *llagostada* made with spiny lobster (*langouste*), or the *pinyata* from Collioure, which includes everything from octopus, shellfish, and eels to red mullet cooked in a tomato sauce. Fresh anchovies, sardines, and tuna are also used to create many a Catalan dish but for centuries, the tiny village of Collioure, nestled near the Spanish border between the foot of the Pyrenees and the Mediterranean sea, has made a specialty of salting them. Used as condiments, or eaten alone, the salted anchovies (*anchois de Collioure*) are especially esteemed and used extensively in Catalan cooking. Unfortunately, they have become a rarity, and canned or salted anchovies from North Africa tend to take their place.

Fish are not the only strong point of Catalan cooking. It also boasts a wide range of pork products including an air-dried prosciutto-like ham called *gambajo*, and sausages (*embotits*) of all kinds that fall generally into two categories: *boutifarra*, or blood sausages, and *llonganissa*, long pork sausages that can be either fresh (*fresca*) or dried (*seca*). And no meal would be truly complete without *touron*, the multifaceted Catalan sweet that can be anything from white and creamy to crunchy and dark (with lots of almonds or pistachios), or a glass of one of the naturally sweet wines from Rivesaltes and Banyuls, either at the start of the meal or to accompany dessert.

Cassoulet, Clafoutis, and Cantal

North of the Pyrenees and east of the Landes is a vast expanse that continues the southwestern traditions of *foie gras* and *confit*, and where a third American "immigrant," the white kidney bean, has become the basis of yet another emblematic preparation, *cassoulet*, traditionally cooked and served in a large earthenware bowl known as a *cassole*—hence its name. As with most legendary dishes, the number of recipes is countless, but two towns claim to have invented it: Castelnaudary, where the beans are cooked only with pork products, and Toulouse, where lamb is added. Both include at least one kind of sausage and generally duck or goose *confit* as well. Although most people consider that the original *cassoulet* was that of Castelnaudary, each has its partisans who religiously defend their local version as the only "authentic" one.

Extending north of Toulouse, toward Limoges, are some of the finest orchards in France, producing the inimitable, plump prunes (*pruneaux*) of Agen, the sweet white grapes (*chasselas*) and greengage plums (*prunes Reine claude*) of Moissac, and the walnuts and melons of Quercy.

And although the Limousin has long been one of the most destitute regions in the entire country, it can nevertheless lay claim to producing not only some of the finest china in the world but beef, veal, lamb, and pork that are among the best in all of France. In centuries past, the impoverished peasants lived principally on a diet of chestnuts and a large variety of turnip called the *rave du Limousin*, one of the vegetables that is still a must in a true *potée limousine*, a one-pot boiled salt-pork and vegetable dinner. Another essential *potée* ingredient is the *mique* or *farcidure*, a dumpling (either plain or flavored with various leaf vegetables or herbs) originally made of millet flour, then corn flour, but more often today with wheat flour, which has become more widely available in the last half century or so. And no *potée limousine* would be complete without its accompaniment of *moutarde violette*, purple mustard from Brive-la-Gaillarde, which gets its color from the grape must with which it is still made.

By far the most famous of the specialties from this region is *clafoutis*, a Limousine cherry flan that has become a favorite all over France. But beware! In order to preserve the intense flavor of the black cherries and keep them from losing their juice, the people of the Limousin are adamant that the fruits must be baked with their pits!

To the east of the Limousin, in a vast, mountainous area called the Massif Central, lies the Auvergne, another very poor region where the peasants once survived on a diet of chestnuts, dairy products, and black rye bread baked into mammoth, round loaves. Nevertheless, it is a region that can be proud of its gastronomic heritage. Clermont-Ferrand has been famous for its fruit jellies (*pâtes de fruit*) since the sixteenth century, especially those made with apricots that were unequalled even in Paris, according to one early traveler. The sausages and hams made from chestnut-fed pigs and dried in the cool mountain air are sought after nationwide, as are the tiny green lentils from Le-Puy-en-Velay, considered to be distinctive enough to have been awarded the coveted AOC status (*Appellation d'origine contrôlée*) usually reserved for fine wines and cheeses. The *lentilles vertes du Puy* were so famous by the end of the eighteenth century that they were not only shipped all over southern France but as far as Italy, Spain, and Portugal.

Nevertheless, Auvergne's claim to fame, as well as that of the neighboring Rouergue, immediately to the south, is undoubtedly the quality of its cheeses. Most of them are made from cow's milk; among them are bleu d'Auvergne, tender Saint Nectaire, and Cantal, a large, thick cylindrical cheese whose taste ranges from buttery to pungent, depending on its age. When very young, it is used in cooking, often with potatoes in dishes like the crusty *truffade* or the creamy *aligot* that, when properly made, forms a rope when the spoon is lifted out of the pot and must be cut with scissors to be served!

Cantal is made over a large area, with famous variants from Salers in the Auvergne, made from the milk of mahogany-colored cows of the same name, and from

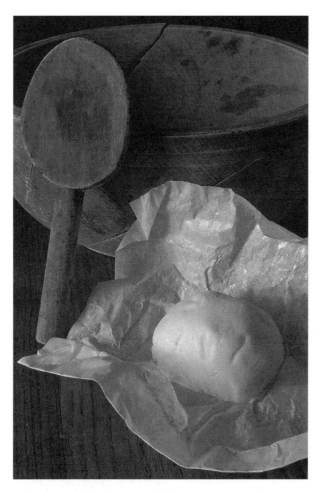

When asked why French cooking tastes the way it does, most chefs will reply "it's the butter." French butter is world renowned and the farmhouse butter from Brittany, shown here, is among the best. © MICHELLE GARRETT/CORBIS.

Laguiole (pronounced lye-ole), made from the milk of the Aubrac breed of cow in the area around Rodez in the Aveyron *département*. But the most celebrated cheese of this area is made from ewe's milk in and around the little town of Roquefort-sur-Soulzon near Millau, southeast of Rodez. In the course of fermentation, the cheese is strewn with crumbs of moldy rye bread, creating the greenish-blue pockets that give Roquefort cheese its distinctive look and taste.

Olives, Olive Oil, and Honey

Continuing south from Roquefort toward the Mediterranean coast, one passes through almond, apricot, and peach orchards, leaving the domain of lard, goose fat, and walnut oil and entering the realm where the olive reigns supreme. All along the crescent that forms the French Mediterranean coast, olive trees abound. Introduced by the Greeks, olives and olive oil have had a checkered history in Languedoc and Provence. Although the best oil

In an effort to reaffirm regional food identities, village fairs are cropping up all over France. This Renaissance fair at Salon-de-Provence features a rich variety of local pastries as well as reconstructions of Renaissance dishes. © GAIL MOONEY/CORBIS.

has always been a valuable export, in the not so distant past, inferior oil was burned in oil lamps. Even to this day, a green soap known as *Savon de Marseilles* is made from low-grade oils of the region.

Gastronomically speaking, the olives and olive oils of southern France are as varied as wines, as are their uses. At the western end, the inhabitants of Languedoc-Roussillon are partial to the slender, delicate green *picholine* and the darker green, crescent-shaped *lucque* with its almost lemony flavor; in the east, although the wrinkled brown olives from Nyons, in the southern Rhône Valley, have gained national renown, the people from Nice remain faithful to the tiny black olives produced in the hills rising up behind that city's famous pebble beaches. In between, the number of varieties and the ways of preparing them are countless, as are the flavors of black or green *tapenade*, an olive paste spread on toast as an appetizer.

Among the oils of southern France, those made in the Valley of Baux-de-Provence north of Arles, in Aix-en-Provence, in Nyons, and in Nice are the most sought after today. However, because oils can vary widely in taste depending on the variety of olive used and whether the fruits are pressed green or ripe, it is best to sample as many as possible since some go best with steamed vegetables, others with fish, and yet others are better adapted to making sauces, according to personal taste. In this part of the country, not only is olive oil ubiquitous in the preparation of savory dishes, it even enters into traditional pastries such as the *fougassette*, *pompe à l'huile*, or *gibassié*, an enriched hearth bread lightly flavored with orange-flower water that is the most substantial of the thirteen desserts served at a traditional Provençal Christmas banquet, or *gros souper de Noël* (the others being walnuts, hazelnuts, almonds, white nougat, black nougat, figs, raisins, dried apricots, peaches, apples or pears, fresh

mandarin oranges or clementines, a special melon called a *verdau*, and finally, either *calissons d'Aix* or fruit jellies from Apt).

Another southern product with extraordinary diversity is honey, which comes in as many flavors as there are aromatic flowers for the bees to gather pollen from: rosemary, thyme, and lavender from the plains, chestnut, heather, and any number of scrub plants from the hills. Of all these honeys, the most famous historically is that of Narbonne, a small town at the west end of the Mediterranean north of Perpignan, renowned for its incomparable rosemary honey (*miel de Narbonne*) since at least the twelfth century.

From Nîmes to Bastia

The image of Provençal cooking as based on olive oil, tomatoes, and garlic is a much abused stereotype. For centuries lard was the dominant fat in the southern French kitchen, olive oil being reserved for the many meatless days imposed by the Roman Catholic Church (which explains at least in part its lingering presence in festive pastries). Although garlic has been around since the Middle Ages, tomatoes, now the pride of the region, were not used on a wide scale until the end of the eighteenth century. Therefore, it comes as no surprise to find famous southern dishes that use no tomatoes. A particularly striking case in point is *brandade de morue*, a creamy purée of salt cod from Nîmes flavored with just a hint of garlic and into which warm olive oil and milk have been beaten. Another example is *daube de búuf*, an aromatic beef stew from Nice in which the bouquet garni always contains a piece of orange peel. Indeed, a great many of the traditional specialties sold in the street markets of Nice and other Provençal cities have not a hint of tomato: *socca*, a large, thin pancake made of chickpea flour; *pissaladière*, an onion-anchovy pizzalike tart with black olives; sardines, either grilled or stuffed with spinach. Among the desserts, one of the most astonishing is the *tourte de blettes* from Nice, a sweet tart filled with Swiss chard greens or spinach studded with pine nuts and raisins. And although vanilla, another newcomer from the Americas, is now a ubiquitous flavoring in pastries all over France, traditional cakes and cookies throughout the south—*fougassette*, *navette*, *gimblette d'Albi*, or the spectacular *gâteau à la broche* (baked on a spit), to name only those few—have remained faithful to lemon peel and orange-flower water, firmly entrenched here for centuries.

A rapid survey of French Mediterranean cooking would not be complete without a visit to Corsica, home of one of the most colorful figures in French history, Napoleon Bonaparte. Nicknamed *l'Île beauté* (the isle of beauty), Corsica became part of France only in 1768, after a forty-year struggle for independence from a thousand years of Italian domination. The local language and products are still heavily impregnated with their Italian heritage, yet maintain their differences. The Italian origin of pork products with names such as *coppa*, *prisuttu*, and *salamu* is clear, but the excellent quality of the semi-wild Corsican pigs, fattened on the chestnuts and acorns of the island's extensive forests (*le maquis*), sets them quite apart—to say nothing of the inimitable *ficatellu*, a pungent liver-based sausage, grilled when fresh, sliced like salami when dried. The Corsicans themselves subsisted for centuries on chestnuts, and chestnut flour is still used in many local specialties like *nicci* (thin crepes) or *castagnacciu* (chestnut cake). But perhaps the most emblematic products of the Isle of Beauty are *cabri*, baby goat, the high point of every festive occasion, and *brocciu*, the "national cheese of Corsica," made from the whey left over from the fabrication of other cheeses. Although it may be consumed as is, fresh or aged, *brocciu* often enters into desserts, whether fritters (*fritelle*), turnovers (*pastelle*), or the king of Corsican cheesecakes, *fiadone*.

The Northeast and Lyons

Just north of Nice the Alps begin, extending all the way to Geneva. The olive groves blend progressively into a land of pasture, cows, and butter. Cow's milk cheeses such as the orange-crusted Reblochon, the creamy Vacherin, or the gruyerelike Beaufort are the pride of the region. Rich potato dishes abound, the most famous being the *gratin dauphinois*, from around Grenoble, where thinly sliced potatoes are baked in cream until brown. To put cheese on top is considered heresy here (but typical of the Savoyard version of the dish made high in the Alps to the north). Another specialty associated all over France with Grenoble is walnuts. The large tender nuts, shipped in their shells throughout the country during the fall and winter seasons, are considered so specific to the area that they have been accorded their own prestigious AOC.

A small pocket of flat land lying roughly halfway between the Alps and the Rhone Valley prides itself on another unique AOC. Called Bresse, this area is familiar to all French gourmets as being the part of the country where the best chickens are raised. The white-feathered, blue-footed *poulet de Bresse* can sell for three to four times the price of other free-range birds. Served in the finest restaurants around the country, it is the only bird to have been awarded AOC status. Once a year the finest specimens are displayed to compete for blue ribbons in Bourg-en-Bresse. Capons and pullets are specially fattened, slaughtered, and wrapped tightly in linen to press the wings and legs into the fat, producing a smooth torpedo shape. The slightest flaw, a bruise or tear in the translucent skin, immediately eliminates the bird. The prize winners bring not only prestige but also considerable income to their owners since they are sold at a premium at the conclusion of the fair.

About forty miles (sixty kilometers) southwest of Bresse is Lyons, which prides itself on being "the gastronomic capital of France." Lyonnaise cuisine is very hearty, with a penchant for extremities, innards, sausages, and lots of onions. Small restaurants, called *bouchons*, perpetuate local traditions and serve such typically Lyon-

naise fare as sheep's trotters salad (*salade de pieds de mouton*), crunchy, pan-fried smooth tripe (*tablier de sapeur*), honeycomb tripe sauteed with onions (*gras-double à la lyonnaise*), pork sausage with potatoes (*saucisson lyonnais, pommes à l'huile*), as well as more refined dishes like pike dumplings with crayfish sauce (*quenelles de brochet, sauce nantua*), or a creamy cheese mixture laced with herbs and a little white wine called *cervelle des canuts*.

The French Paradox

Each part of France has its own culinary traditions. France's temperate climate, varied topography, different soils, and multiple coastlines combine to make it one of the richest agricultural countries in Europe. Nonetheless, like most industrial countries today, France's culinary landscape is changing. Although some foods like the wind-dried cod (stockfish) still favored in isolated communities in south-central France and in Nice rarely travel far from home, many that were once reserved for festive occasions are now consumed on a daily basis while others, once hardly eaten outside their place of origin, like *confit de canard*, are now readily available in shops and restaurants throughout the country.

The wide variety of French regional cuisines bears witness to the longevity of local cultural traditions—as well as of the country's inhabitants: France enjoys the lowest rate of cardiovascular disease in Europe (ahead of Portugal, Spain, and Italy) and, curiously enough, it is precisely in the southwest of French, the land of *foie gras* and *confit de canard*, that people enjoy the lowest rate of cardiovascular disease in the industrialized world outside of Japan. The famous French paradox. What is the secret? Nobody knows for sure, but goose and duck fat, garlic, and tannic red wines—the staples of the local diet along with a wide variety of fruits and vegetables—are all known to produce substances that protect the heart. Beyond that, the sheer beauty of a French open-air market with its multiplicity of fresh foodstuffs of every possible color and smell, and the enjoyment of savoring them at a leisurely meal with a glass of wine and good company, may provide part of the answer.

See also **Cheese; Fish; Iberian Peninsula; Wine.**

BIBLIOGRAPHY

Froc, J., Mary Hyman, and Philip Hyman, eds. *Inventaire du patrimoine culinaire de la France.* Paris: Michel Albin (Conseil national des arts culinaires). Volumes on Poitou-Charentes, 1994; Provence-Alpes-Côte d'Azur, Rhône-Alpes, 1995; Corse, Midi-Pyrénées, 1996; Aquitaine, 1997; Languedoc-Roussillon, Limousin, 1998.

Hanicotte, Colette, and Jean Froc, et al. *La cuisine des terroirs.* Paris: Larousse, 2000.

Stouff, Louis. *Ravitaillement et alimentation en Provence aux XIVe et XVe siècles.* Paris: Mouton and Co., 1970.

Mary Hyman
Philip Hyman

TRADITION AND CHANGE IN FRENCH CUISINE

France is a country with many cuisines. Some dishes are part of a national repertoire and generally referred to as "traditional family fare." Examples might be *pot-au-feu* (a boiled beef dinner), *gigot d'agneau* (roast leg of lamb), *vinaigrette* (oil and vinegar dressing), or *pâté de campagne* (country-style pâté). From North to South, these dishes can be found in most French homes. A second group of dishes is mainly, or only, encountered in specific regions. Typically based on ingredients native to the region, they include *choucroute* (sauerkraut) in Alsace, *galettes de sar-rasin* (thin buckwheat pancakes) in Brittany, *soupe de pois-sons* (fish soup) or the more elaborate *bouillabaisse* in Provence. Lastly, certain dishes are part of the *haute cui-sine* tradition, which includes dishes prepared by chefs both past and present. A vast group, this repertoire is constantly shifting as tastes evolve and culinary trends change. Such things as *Tournedos Rossini* (beef tenderloin topped with *foie gras*), *pêche Melba* (vanilla ice cream and peaches with fresh raspberry sauce), or the more recent *terrine de poissons* (fish pâté) or *salade folle* (a salad of foie gras and mixed greens) are all dishes that can be attrib-uted to specific periods of French culinary history, the first two evoking the *cuisine classique* of the early 1900s, the latter two the *nouvelle cuisine* of the 1970s.

Changing Fortunes

These various types of cuisine are not mutually exclusive. Béchamel sauce, said to have been created by Louis de Béchamel (1635–1688), was quickly adopted as part of the fashionable repertoire of the eighteenth century and went on to become a mainstay of nineteenth- and early-twentieth-century *cuisine classique*; today it is more likely to appear in private homes than on the menu of some trendy chef. *Boeuf bourguignon* has gone from being a "lo-cal" to a "traditional family" dish. Other regional fa-vorites, such as *magret de canard* (fattened-duck steaks), a specialty of the southwest, have been adopted by chefs committed to a more creative cuisine. This said, one is more likely to find elaborate French dishes than tradi-tional or regional ones in restaurants around the world. Only a handful of regional specialties (*cassoulet, bouill-abaisse, foie gras*) are known outside the country, and even then they are often misunderstood and misinterpreted. The vast majority of preparations identified with France and upon which the reputation of French cuisine stands are chefs' creations, some dated and old-fashioned (*sauce béarnaise, béchamel, crêpes Suzettes*), others more contem-porary (salmon with sorrel sauce, tropical fruit sorbets, flourless chocolate cakes).

La Nouvelle Cuisine

The exploits of fashionable chefs keep French cuisine alive beyond national boundaries and, to a large extent, influence eating habits within France itself. The most re-cent trend to remodel the way the world and the French think of food is *nouvelle cuisine* (literally, "new cooking").

Revolutionary in its beginnings, this movement is now thirty years old. Many of the dishes associated with it have lost their shock value and can now be found in mod-est households around the country. What was this culi-nary upheaval all about?

In 1972 two French food critics, Henri Gault and Christian Millau, noticed that several young chefs had started serving dishes with a noticeably different style from those of the past fifty years that had been based on Auguste Escoffier's early-twentieth-century reinterpre-tation of classic cuisine. As spokesmen for this new gener-ation of chefs, Gault and Millau became vocal exponents of the "new" cuisine, encouraging the rejection of what were now perceived as obsolete standards and the pur-suit of innovative dishes that reflected more personal tastes. They wrote and published a sort of manifesto, not too modestly called "the ten commandments of *nouvelle cuisine*," which not only gave *nouvelle cuisine* a base to grow on, but profoundly influenced the way many people thought about food and its preparation. The principles Gault and Millau propounded were the following:

1. *Reject unnecessarily complex preparations.* This basically meant abandoning many classic dishes that involved a multitude of sauces (each specific to an element in the final presentation), complicated garnishes, and elaborate preparations that sacrificed taste to ap-pearance. Chefs were invited to emphasize the in-herent nature of the foods they were preparing, such as by serving a roast partridge as it came from the oven with a light, simple sauce made from its pan juices and a little butter.

2. *Reduce cooking times.* It was better to undercook rather than overcook: green beans would be served "al dente" and fish would be cooked "slightly pink on the bone."

3. *Use seasonal produce.* Chefs were encouraged literally to shop daily and cook only what was found at the market that day.

4. *Shorten menus.* Greater attention was to be given to a small number of dishes rather than trying to im-press clients with a multitude of preparations that could not be given the attention they deserved. This said, *nouvelle cuisine* popularized "tasting menus" that allowed the curious to sample many dishes in very small quantities. These two ideas are not necessarily contradictory since tasting menus are generally served to entire tables only (not individuals), which means that there are fewer dishes to prepare than it might appear.

5. *Do not marinate meats or hang game.* This comple-mented the first "commandment" which called for respecting the natural tastes of foods. Gault and Mil-lau added that "marinating meat hides its taste . . . if game is hung at all it should only be for a very short time, otherwise its flavor is altered and an undesir-able fermentation begins." They did, however, ac-

cept the use of spices, particularly new and "exotic" ones, such as green peppercorns and fresh ginger, as a means of heightening flavors.

6. *Abandon heavy sauces.* This was a direct condemnation of such classics as *béchamel*, brown sauce, and other thick, flour-based sauces that produce an opaque coating. The idea was to use light sauces made by deglazing the pan juices with a liquid (wine, water, stock, etc.), and swirling in fresh butter.

7. *Promote regional cooking.* Traditional local dishes could be just as exciting as any others—if they had been "reinvented" according to *nouvelle cuisine* principles.

8. *Take an interest in new cooking methods and utensils.* Steamers, "dry-steam" ovens, and time-saving devices such as the food processor and blender should become standard equipment in the professional kitchen.

9. *Be health conscious.* Good eating is not incompatible with a healthy diet. The chef who best embodied this "commandment" was Michel Guérard, who created *cuisine minceur* (literally, slimness cooking) in the late 1970s. In keeping with this principle, chefs were encouraged to give greater importance to a wide variety of fresh vegetables than in the past.

10. *Be creative.* This speaks for itself.

Thanks to the enormous interest the media took in *nouvelle cuisine,* virtually all of the "commandments" had some effect on the way the French cooked and on their attitudes towards food. The principles would be adopted not only by chefs throughout the country but, in the course of time, by the general public, which was anxious to eat dishes more in tune with contemporary aesthetics and dietary concerns and welcomed the simplification of their preparation.

Beyond Cuisine

Movements such as *nouvelle cuisine* have not been the only force at work on the French diet. Another new term entered the French language at about the same time as *nouvelle cuisine*: *le fast-food.* Hamburgers and hot dogs were no strangers to France, but in the late 1970s American and British hamburger chains started to proliferate. Their success was at least partially due to the low prices they charged and their link with a foreign culture that was then in vogue. Immediately popular with the younger generation, their success was regarded with dismay by parents who lamented that their offspring had lost all interest in traditional cooking and that French cuisine was doomed to disappear. With the passage of time, however, these fears have proved to be unfounded. Despite the ongoing popularity of fast-food outlets among the young, as the youths of yesteryear mature and their incomes increase, they return to *cuisine* via the chefs' answer to the foreign invasion: the bistro.

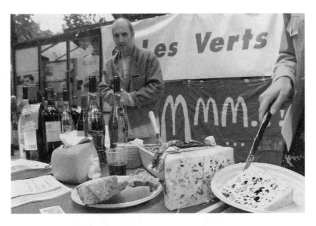

The "McDonaldization" of French cuisine is viewed in France as one of the most threatening influences on traditional cooking and eating habits. This protest was staged in July 2000 by the Green Party to protest the opening of the forty-sixth McDonald's in the French capital. French breads, pâtés, cheeses, and wines were distributed in front of McDonald's "golden arches." © REUTERS NEWMEDIA INC./CORBIS.

Bistros, old-fashioned, homey, reasonably priced places, are a French establishment dating from the end of the nineteenth century, but as the twentieth century drew to a close, the term came to be applied to any small establishment serving moderately-priced food—not necessarily "old-fashioned" or in the least "homey." Chef's bistros were adjoined to many famous and prestigious restaurants; in these bistros, one could sample toned-down versions of "the master's" cooking at bargain prices. Specialized bistros also began to appear, with those dedicated to fish cookery becoming particularly popular. Another spin-off of the fast-food challenge to the French palate was the wine bar, where a collection of regional hams, sausages, pâtés, and cheeses, or a small simple dish, could be enjoyed with a glass of wine.

In short, tradition and change constantly find new ways to coexist as each "lost generation" of French diners rediscovers the gastronomy it had so ardently rejected. Just as with *nouvelle cuisine,* the invasion of fast food has enriched and diversified the dining experience and provided yet another opportunity for France to show the world that its cuisine is alive and well—responding to new challenges and incorporating new ideas without losing sight of the foundations upon which it continues to build its reputation.

BIBLIOGRAPHY

Fischler, Claude. *L'Homnivore*. Paris: Éditions Odile Jacob, 1990.

Gault, Henri, and Christian Millau. *Gault et Millau se mettent à table.* Paris: Stock, 1976.

Hyman, Philip, and Mary Hyman. "Modèles culinaires et nouvelle cuisine française," *Culture Technique*, Juillet N°16 (1986): 347–349.

Hyman, Philip, and Mary Hyman. "La première nouvelle cuisine." In *L'Honnête volupté: art culinaire, art majeur*, edited by Paul Noirot et al., pp. 73–74. Paris: Éditions Michel de Maule, 1989.

Mary Hyman
Philip Hyman

WINE AND THE FRENCH MEAL

For the French, wine is not an alcohol but a beverage. Like most beverages, it is generally consumed at mealtimes and like bread, it is so much a part of most meals that many French people would not enjoy eating without drinking a little wine. Given its importance and the wide variety of French wines to choose from, they have devised a few simple rules for serving wine:

- White with fish, red with meat
- White before red
- Serve wines in ascending order (the best wine last)
- Drink wines of a region with foods from that region
- Drink reds at room temperature and whites chilled

Of course, the French being typically French, there are exceptions to every rule.

White with fish, red with meat

For the most part, this rule is respected, especially concerning beef and lamb. But there are important regional differences. In Alsace, for instance, white wine is served with both fish and meat. This is no doubt because the region produces very little red wine and because Alsatian whites go so well with pork and pork sausages that

The French meal invariably includes cheese. The French are among the world's highest consumers of cheese, but the cheese is generally eaten with wine. A waiter at Le Grand Vefour restaurant in Paris is shown here serving cheese from a cart. © OWEN FRANKEN/CORBIS.

the famous Alsatian *Choucroute* (sauerkraut with an assortment of salted and smoked pork products) is *never* served with red wine but with an Alsatian white wine (or beer). The full-bodied whites of Burgundy can also be served with poultry and go surprisingly well with *pâtés* of all kinds. In the Jura the distinctive sherry-flavored "yellow wine" (*vin jaune*) may be served with poultry or fish, especially when cooked with cream and morel mushrooms from the nearby mountains. In Bordeaux, oysters on the half shell are eaten with grilled link sausages, a delightful combination with which the wine of choice is a white Graves. Conversely, it is also in Bordeaux that one encounters the unusual practice of serving red wine with fish, most specifically lamprey eel, which is cooked in a red wine sauce.

White before red

This is true so long as the wine is dry, the case for most of the white wine produced in France. Sweet white wines or champagne, on the other hand, can be served at the end of the meal. Admittedly, this practice is dying out and, these days, one is more likely to be served a glass of sweet *sauternes* with a slice of *foie gras* as a starter than with dessert, and champagne is a favorite *apéritif* throughout the country.

Serve wines in ascending order (the best wine last)

Exponents of this idea argue that if the best wine is served first, all that follow will disappoint. Those who question this approach point out that cheese and dessert come in last place, hence the best wine would always be served with one of them. The problem is an obvious one: great wines are not always at their best with cheese (dessert wines are rarely served these days). Though certain wines can be exquisite with specific cheeses (Alsatian Riesling with Munster, red Burgundy with a pungent *époisses*) certain subtleties in very fine wines can be lost if the cheese they are served with is too pungent. One solution is to follow a complex, mature wine that was served with the main dish with a young, full-bodied wine carefully chosen to enhance the taste of the cheeses. The wine in question is so different from the preceding one that the two cannot really be compared, leaving the impression of progressing from a delicate, suave taste to a "stronger" one.

Drink wines of a region with foods from that region

Although this rule applies marvelously well to the foods and wines of the lesser-known regions, oddly enough the great wine-producing regions—Bordeaux, Burgundy, and Champagne—are not associated with a wide range of regional specialties. Though Burgundy is rich in natural resources, notably beef, too often *any* dish with a red wine sauce is (mistakenly) considered to be *bourguignon*. Few French people can name even one dish that is specifically associated with either Bordeaux or Champagne. This is not to say that they do not exist; they are simply unknown to the public outside the region. Bordeaux, for example, claims to produce some of the finest lamb in all of France (*agneau de Pauillac*) and every spring the *Bordelais* delight in grilling shad, fished in the Gironde estuary. Dishes one might encounter when traveling in Champagne often have no specific links to culinary traditions: add a splash of Champagne to virtually any dish and, *voilà!* you've made it *champenois*! The true specialties from that region are simple farmhouse food—poached salt pork and cabbage, tripe sausage, dandelion salad—hardly what one might accompany with a glass of vintage bubbly.

Reds at room temperature, whites chilled

This is perhaps one of the most misunderstood and frequently challenged practices in France. What exactly is "room temperature"? Essentially this means that wines should not appear to be cold when served. Too often, "room temperature" is interpreted to mean "warm," a terrible blunder. Though most of the best reds are still served "at room temperature" (60–63°F/16–17°C for Burgundies and 64–66°F/18°–19°C for Bordeaux) there is a growing tendency to serve young, fruity reds at "cellar temperature," cool but not cold (55°F/12°C). This is specifically the case of *Beaujolais* and the light reds from the Loire Valley.

Though white wines are generally brought to the table in an ice bucket, wine stewards in better restaurants often advise their clients to chill fine, full-bodied whites like those from Burgundy just long enough to bring them slightly below "cellar temperature" and feel cool to the tongue (about 48–50°F/9–10°C). Only young, very dry white wines, light rosés, or sparkling wines should be drunk truly cold.

One of the most dramatic exceptions to this rule concerns the famous "yellow wine" from the Jura. This is the only white wine made in France that is served at room temperature.

Wine and Pleasure

Ideally, a wine should enhance the food it is served with and vice versa. This is why wine is rarely served with salads unless they are made without vinegar because vinegar ruins the taste of wine. Most people are familiar with a few "perfect marriages" (oysters with *muscadet*, lamb with Bordeaux, Sauternes with *foie gras*) though several recent books have encouraged the exploration of more daring combinations like white wines with goat cheeses and pâtés, or light reds with certain fish like fresh grilled tuna or sardines. Nonetheless, the French have conservative tastes generally speaking, and are more likely to respect the rules given above then to break them (regional practices aside). Drinking wine is part of life, not an intellectual exercise, and what count most of all are the pleasures of the table—many French people could not imagine even a simple meal without a glass of wine.

Although wine, whatever its origin, is indispensable to a French meal, one should never conclude that the French are wine "experts." Most people are familiar with only a limited array of wines and do not anguish over making choices. On festive occasions, however, wine takes on central importance and much time might be spent selecting and orchestrating the serving of several wines. Foreign wines are still an oddity; indeed, those who live in wine-producing regions are often perfectly content to drink *only* wines from their area.

The French are more interested in enjoying their wines than in analyzing them. This is not to say that they do not pay attention when selecting wine, or that they are not attentive when wine is served. But they are more concerned with serving wines to enhance the pleasure of a meal than in anything else. This customarily implies personal discretion and moderation: getting drunk is considered antisocial and severely frowned upon.

See also **Dinner**; **Etiquette and Eating Habits**; **Meal**; **Table Talk**; **Wine**.

BIBLIOGRAPHY

Dumay, Raymond. *Guide du vin* [Guide to wine]. Paris: Le Livre de Poche, 1992.

Senderens, Alain. *Le vin et la table*. [Wine and the table]. Paris: Le Livre De Poche, 2000

Mary Hyman
Philip Hyman

FRENCH AND BRITISH COOKING COMPARED

England and France are two countries which, in world perspective, are actually rather similar. Their pattern of long-term development differs subtly in detail but in broad terms is equally similar, and their cultures and cuisines have been in reciprocal contact ever since the Middle Ages. Moreover, the alimentary raw materials available were broadly the same though not identical. How, then, did their strikingly different culinary cultures take shape?

Caricature is a serious danger in this field. What people eat is universally a potent ingredient of national and social stereotyping. That applies both to the formation of people's "we-images" of their own group and of their "they-images" of outsider groups. Food has long played a prominent part in the sense of national identity of both the English and the French, and it is very risky to accept their reciprocal stereotypes of each other's cuisine at face value. At the very least, one must not fall into the trap of comparing, say, the food of Paul Bocuse with that served at some British transport café, or French professional cuisine with English domestic cookery. Yet, the conclusion is that such common stereotypes as the rotund and rubicund John Bull sitting at a table of roast beef, or the lank and bony French cook smelling of garlic and spearing a frog leg with a fork really do have a kernel of truth in them, particularly in relation to underlying attitudes.

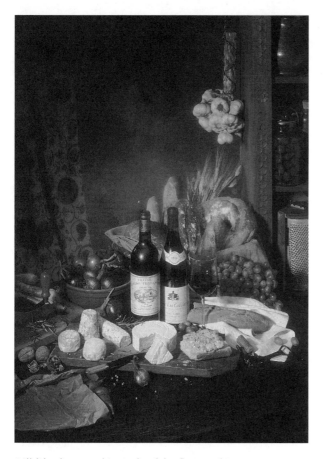

Still-life photographic study of the flavors of France. © MATTHIAS KULKA/CORBIS.

This investigation took as its baseline the late Middle Ages, reviewing the published documents and drawing upon the work of specialists, notably Stouff's outstanding monograph (1970) on late medieval Provence. The picture that emerges from such studies can be briefly summarized. First, the national differences in cuisine that we take for granted were as yet very little developed in medieval Europe. Members of the same estate of society ate in strikingly similar fashion throughout Western Europe. Before Columbus, many of the vegetables now seen as typically Mediterranean were unknown, so that, for example, the humble cabbage was as prominent an item in Provence as in Northumberland. Second, however, the differences between the estates were quite marked, though quantitative differences in consumption were possibly more striking than differences in quality (with an exception registered for a very small elite in really major courts). Stouff depicted graphically the increase in sheer quantity of food consumed as one progressed up the social ranks. Before the Black Death, this was especially marked in the case of meat, though subsequently meat was relatively abundant for the lower ranks, too. The famous gargantuan banquets thrown by kings and nobles to mark particular occasions were no-

table for their vast scale rather than the subtlety of the cooking; their motivation and social function resembled that of the potlatch among the Kwakiutl Indians. Only in the greatest princely courts, and even there probably only for the more special occasions, was the famous courtly cuisine with its elaborate mixtures and proliferation of spices to be found. The recipes found in the manuscripts, whether from France, Italy, or England, are strikingly similar.

Although the evidence from the Middle Ages is too sparse to be conclusive, the best guess from the similarity between surviving manuscripts from different places and periods is that the pace of change in matters culinary was then very slow in all strata of society. From the time of the Renaissance onward, however, the pace of change perceptibly quickens in these as in so many other aspects of everyday life (cf. Elias, 2000), at first among the secular upper classes and then very gradually among lower strata, too. We must be careful: the history of eating is a prime instance of what Elias has called "the polyphony of history." Marc Bloch contended that only in the nineteenth century was it possible to see "the beginning of a trend towards greater uniformity in food—speaking in very relative terms—from the top to the bottom of the social ladder (1970, p. 232)." Until then, the food and the cookery of the peasants in the countryside seem to have changed only extremely slowly over the centuries. It was something to be studied in the perspective of the *longue durée*. From the advent of the printed book, however, it is possible to trace a gradually accelerating pattern of change in the cookery of the upper and upper middle classes. If changes in technique and fashion never quite attain the pace of *histoire événementielle*—although the gastronomic myth-makers delight in representing the invention of new dishes as unique creations of great men on unique occasions (see Mennell, 1985, Chapter 10)— it could fairly be portrayed as *histoire des conjonctures*.

The first elaborate cuisine representing a definite change from the medieval traditions is to be found in the secular and religious courts of Renaissance Italy, but the leadership of Europe in culinary as in so many other facets of culture soon passed to France. Very detailed work by Jean-Louis Flandrin and his associates in Paris may be interpreted to show that French leadership goes back further, but from the appearance of La Varenne's famous book *Le Cuisinier François* in 1651, it does not require in-depth research to see that something recognizable to later eyes as a distinctively French style of cuisine has emerged. From then on, the cookery books are more numerous, and not only can advances in cookery techniques be seen, but it is quite clear that contemporaries were conscious of the rapid pace of change and of the importance of food as an aspect of fashion in courtly circles. By the 1740s, the first gastronomic controversies were being fought out in Paris between minor courtiers (Mennell, 1981). Although by then cookery books were being directed specifically at the bourgeoisie, and some

50

differentiation between courtly haute cuisine and domestic cookery was being codified, the models still clearly stemmed from courtly circles. One of the important consequences of this was that the spirit of thrift and economizing in the kitchen, which was very marked from an early date in England, was much less in evidence even in French cookery books, and something of the courtly functions of luxurious display heedless of the cost (cf. Elias, 1983) lived on until the present day in the French kitchen.

In England, the cookery books from the late sixteenth century onward depict a more rustic, "country housewife" style of cookery. They were still directed at readers among the nobility and gentry—this is not the food of the peasants—but they reflect their readers' greater continuing involvement in country life and pursuits than was the case among their French counterparts. There was for a time a line of English courtly cookery books too, but that tradition lost its vitality in England after the Civil Wars of the mid-seventeenth century, and from the early eighteenth century it is eclipsed by the resurgence of the "country housewife" style of book, written mainly by women, unlike those of the French and courtly traditions. The spirit of thrift and economy, often linked with an overt hostility to French extravagance, is strongly expressed.

This is a very compressed summary of only part of the evidence for differences in culinary culture between England and France. To counteract the necessary oversimplification, it must be emphasized that when speaking of "English cookery" and "French cookery," we are not dealing with two entirely separate things. French cookery had an early and continuing influence on English cookery, particularly through English cooks having worked in France and French cooks working for the very wealthiest English families. Yet there is a valid contrast. The food of the English gentry and prosperous farmers, depicted in the English cookery books, enjoyed a prestige of its own to which there was no equivalent at that date in France. From the technical point of view, there are also clear differences. The French developed a "cuisine of impregnation," replacing the antique "cuisine of mixtures." The use of cullis (the English translation of *coulis*) as a *fonds* and the proliferation of sauces—a process carried still further in France in the nineteenth century—was precisely not the foundation of English cookery. In England, continuities from the past were much more in evidence. The old pies and joints of meat remained the center of the English meal, whereas in France the focus of attention shifted to the ever-increasing variety of delicate little "made dishes."

What explanations can be offered for the rather different courses of development observed in the taste in food of the two countries?

One explanation has been so often repeated that it has the force of conventional wisdom. It is that meat (and

other raw materials) were so abundant and of such superior quality in England that it was not necessary to cook them with great skill, disguise their flavor, or eke them out in made dishes. This explanation is implausible. For one thing, the superiority and abundance of English raw materials is highly questionable. For another, this popular explanation rests on the implicit proposition that all human beings prefer the "natural" taste of foods, transformed as little as possible by the culinary arts, which are thus seen as little more than a forced adaptation to circumstance. There is no serious evidence for this proposition.

On the contrary, three more explicitly social strands of explanation bear closer examination. These are, first, the possible influence of Puritanism, or other religious differences between England and France; second, the role and influence of the court society, and, more generally, differences in the distribution of power and social stratification; and, third, the differing relationship between town and country on the two sides of the Channel.

The influence of religion on eating is certainly very strong and familiar in many of the world's cultures. But the contention, advanced by such popular writers as Philippa Pullar (1970), that Puritanism blighted the English kitchen needs to be treated with some skepticism. For one thing, it is not clear that the English Puritans of the mid-seventeenth century were at all the general killjoys of later stereotype; they certainly do not have much to say against enjoying one's food. Later, perhaps, as Dissenters, their outlook narrowed, but by then they were not in the prominent positions in society from which they might once have commanded taste-setting power. Moreover, it is often overlooked that, besides the sizeable Huguenot community, seventeenth-century France also saw an influential Jansenist current within Catholicism that has long been seen to have similarities to the Calvinist predestinarian kind of Protestantism. Yet no one has ever suggested that Jansenism permanently damaged French taste buds.

As for the royal and princely courts, their direct influence on the authors of French cookery books is plain to see. In the light particularly of Norbert Elias's account of the place of luxury and display in French court society (1978), it is highly likely that competition between courtiers would be acted out through their kitchens and their tables as in many other aspects of culture. An essential link in the argument is that the French nobility, having emerged on the losing side from a series of struggles with the king, became deracinated and defunctionalized—deprived of their roots in a rural way of life, deprived in particular of their relatively independent power bases and governmental functions in the provinces. This did not happen to the same extent in England. The power shifts that were the outcome of the Civil Wars, the Glorious Revolution of 1688, and the Hanoverian succession in 1714 nipped in the bud the growth of an absolutist monarchy and court society on the French model. The royal court in eighteenth-century England was more *primus inter pares;* noble houses and the gentry retained a relatively independent power and governmental function in the provinces; and the pressures toward competition through virtuosity in consumption were relatively less intense.

That connects with a third consideration. The relationship between town and country in England was rather different from that in France. It was not that England was a more rural country than France. Quite the contrary. London in the eighteenth century was absolutely bigger than Paris, and its population relatively still larger as a proportion of the nation as a whole. It is estimated that as many as one in six people in that period spent some part of their lives in London. Nevertheless, the prestige of the country way of life remained much higher in England than it did in France, and London and country society remained more closely interlocked than in France. A larger proportion of English noblemen and gentlemen spent a larger proportion of the year living on their country estates and largely eating the seasonal products of their lands than was the case in France. Rustication from court was dread punishment for a French courtier. Besides, it should not be forgotten that in a preindustrial economy the range of available foods was generally more limited in the country than in the markets of major cities. The very diversity of the products to be found in the principal markets of great cities is a prerequisite for the creation of a great diversity of made dishes. Haute cuisine is a characteristic of urban life.

Convergences: The Nineteenth and Twentieth Centuries

After the Napoleonic Wars, the divergence between English and French cuisines appeared to widen. What was actually happening was something rather more complicated. Certainly, French professional cuisine, founded in the aristocratic kitchens of the ancien régime, was raised to new heights through competition between the restaurants of nineteenth-century Paris. And there is a good deal of evidence that, especially in the latter half of the century, the rather fine English country cooking tradition declined and became coarsened. What appears to have happened was that French culinary hegemony in the higher circles of English society became far more firmly established than in the eighteenth century, when only a few of the greatest grandees had employed French chefs. French culinary colonialism now extended further down into the highest reaches of the middle class. Besides, the sheer number of families involved in London "Society" was growing very rapidly (Davidoff, 1973), and the intense competition created by this social inflation mimicked in some degree the competitive display found among French courtiers a century earlier.

It was not, however, likely that these conditions would favor the emergence of a separate and distinctive English haute cuisine. Something like the "dependency

theory" of "world-systems" theory applies to culinary colonialism as well as to colonialism proper. French cookery having already reached great heights, its techniques, recipes, rules, and vocabulary were there to be adopted by the colonized, just as about the same time the advanced state of many English sports led to the adoption of the games and their English vocabulary in many parts of the world.

The coarsening of the English "country housewife" tradition of cookery in the nineteenth century may have been due not just to the defection of the social model-setting circles to French cuisine but also, lower down the social scale, to the disruptive effects of very rapid urbanization and population growth on the transmission of traditional knowledge from mother to daughter. Urbanization took place in England far earlier and far more rapidly than in France. By the time the corresponding movement to the towns took place in France, largely during the twentieth century, the popular press and other mass media may to some extent have provided alternative channels for the maintenance of traditional knowledge.

That is to some extent speculative and requires deeper investigation. What becomes quite clear, however, is that by the 1960s, forces leading to convergence between the culinary cultures of France and England were dominant over the forces of divergence. That was to be seen quite clearly in the further diffusion of French influence down the English social scale through cookery columns in women's magazines and cookery programs on television. But far more important was the enormous growth of the food processing industry and its impact on the domestic kitchen in both countries and indeed throughout the developed world. That, and the growth of the fast-food industry, have become very powerful agents for the internationalization of food, and that has involved contrary yet interlinked trends both to standardization and to the greater diversity of styles in an increasingly cosmopolitan culinary culture. This applies not just to the actual dishes that come out of domestic and commercial kitchens, but also—in the richer countries—to social contrasts in eating. Both have been marked, in Elias's phrase, by "diminishing contrasts and increasing varieties."

In summary, France and England, two similar neighboring countries that had been in continuous contact with each other since the Middle Ages, nevertheless developed contrasting culinary cultures. The explanation for why that happened should not be sought not in any "innate" differences in the "taste" of English and French people, nor to any great extent in their natural endowments of alimentary raw materials, nor yet in religious differences. An answer lies rather in the divergence between their social structures from about the seventeenth century onward. In particular, competitive display and virtuoso consumption played a more compelling part in the absolutist monarchy that developed in France under Louis XIV and up to the Revolution than it did among the gentry and aristocracy in England after the defeat of the king in the Civil Wars in the mid-seventeenth century. Linked to these differences in stratification was a different relationship between the city and the country. French haute cuisine had its origins in courtly cookery, and courts are urban institutions. In contrast, the greater prestige of the country way of life in England is reflected in its cookery.

See also **British Isles: England.**

BIBLIOGRAPHY

Bloch, Marc. "Les aliments de l'ancienne France." In *Pour une Histoire de l'Alimentation,* edited by J. J. Hémardinquer, pp. 231–235. Paris: A. Colin, 1970.

Davidoff, Leonore. *The Best Circles: Society, Etiquette and the Season.* London: Croom Helm, 1973.

Elias, Norbert. *The Court Society.* Translated by Edmund Jephcott. Oxford: Blackwell, 1983.

Elias, Norbert. *The Civilizing Process: Sociogenetic and Psychogenetic Investigation.* Edited by Eric Dunning, Johan Goudslom, and Stephen Mennell. Translated by Edmund Jephcott. Oxford, U.K.: Blackwell, 2000.

Ferguson, Priscilla P. "A Cultural Field in the Making: Gastronomy in Nineteenth-Century France." *American Journal of Sociology* 104, 3 (1998): 597–641.

Flandrin, Jean-Louis, and Massimo Montanari, eds, *Food: A Culinary History from Antiquity to the Present.* English edition by Albert Sonnenfeld. Translated by Clarissa Botsford. New York: Columbia University Press, 1999.

Flandrin, Jean-Louis, Philip Hyman, and Mary Hyman. "La cuisine dans la littérature de colportage." Introduction to *La Varenne, Le Cuisinier François,* pp. 11–99. Paris: Montalba, 1983.

Goody, Jack. *Cooking, Cuisine and Class: A Study in Comparative Sociology.* Cambridge, U.K.: Cambridge University Press, 1982.

Mennell, Stephen. *All Manners of Food: Eating and Taste in England and France from the Middle Ages to the Present.* 2d ed. Champaign, Ill.: University of Illinois Press, 1996. First edition, 1985.

Mennell, Stephen, ed. *Lettre d'un pâtissier anglois et autres contributions à une polémique gastronomique du XVIIIe siècle.* Exeter: University of Exeter, 1981.

Pullar, Phillipa. *Consuming Passions: A History of English Food and Appetite.* London: Hamilton, 1970.

Stouff, Louis. *Ravitaillement et alimentation en Provence aux 14e et 15e siècles.* Paris: Mouton, 1970.

Wheaton, Barbara Ketcham. *Savouring the Past: The French Kitchen and Table from 1300 to 1789.* Philadelphia: University of Pennsylvania Press, 1983.

Stephen Mennell

FRENCH FRIES. In the United States, potatoes cut into long strips and fried in deep fat have been known as french fried potatoes, then french fries, and now just "fries."

French fried potatoes are a favorite food in countries around the world. What makes them so popular? Perhaps it is the flavor of the fat, or the salt—or both—that leads us to purchase the potatoes often. French fries do not require eating utensils in informal situations, which makes them easy to eat and to carry away from the point of purchase. The many restaurants selling french fires frequently combine servings of fries with another food, for example, fried fish or hamburgers. Also, these restaurants advertise widely, so we are tempted to buy french fried potatoes repeatedly.

Origin

There is disagreement as to the origin of this method of cooking potatoes. Because the term "French" is used in the name, many people give cooks in France credit for having first prepared french fries. A French writer of the nineteenth century who went by the name of Curnonsky (his real name was Maurice Edmond Sailland) said that if there were regional Parisian cooking, its greatest contribution to gastronomy would be *pommes frites* (French fried potatoes). Others have suggested that "French" refers to the way in which the potatoes are cut, into lengthwise strips, as with frenched green beans.

Legend has it that President Thomas Jefferson introduced the deep-fried potatoes at a state dinner in 1802 upon his return to the United States from a trip to France. There seems to be no record of them in the United States for about sixty years. Some restaurants were selling them by the 1860s, but this form of potatoes was not popular here until the 1920s when World War I veterans returned from Europe. Drive-in restaurants, opened in the 1930s and 1940s, sold french fries. Since they did not require a utensil, they were easy to eat while driving.

A British food history book states that "chipped" potatoes were introduced into Britain from France about 1870. The term "chips" is used to designate fries in Britain, while potato crisps is the British name for what are known as chips in North America. The British "chipped" potatoes were paired with fried fish and sold in shops instead of the sliced bread or baked potatoes that had accompanied fried fish since about 1850.

Preparation

In French cookbooks, one finds recipes for potatoes cut into many shapes before frying. For example: *pommes frites allumettes* (also called *julienne de pommes de terre*), which are matchstick-shaped; *pommes frites paille,* cut into thin straws; and *pommes gaufrettes,* which are waffle-shaped potatoes. It is not usual to find a recipe for plain *pommes frites. Pommes frites pont-neuf,* first sold in a Parisian restaurant on the Pont Neuf, may be the closest to our traditional shape for fries.

Recipes for souffléd potatoes are found often in French cookbooks. Souffléd potatoes were first made in 1837, when a dinner being prepared for King Louis Philippe and Queen Amelie was held up by the late arrival

The curse of nutritionists, the enemy of sustainable agriculture, the standby of the teenage diet, French fries are not only loaded with fat, but are also the subject of heated debate and a symbol of food globalization. © ROBERT YOUNG PELTON/CORBIS.

of the guests of honor. The chef took the potatoes off the heat before they were quite done, then put them back into hot fat just before serving. The potatoes puffed and were a great success at the dinner. French fries are said to be of best quality when they, too, are partially cooked at a lower temperature, then finished in fat that has been heated to a higher temperature; that has become the traditional way of preparing them. Some American cooks were doing this at home about 1950. American food writer Pam Anderson has developed what she calls a new way for home cooks to do fries, using less oil and raising the temperature of the oil toward the end of the cooking period, rather than removing the potatoes from the fat, then adding them back later. The method still depends on the two different temperatures for a good product.

In the United States, Russet Burbank potatoes are the variety used most for frozen fries. This variety does not grow well in other countries, so about half a million metric tons of frozen fries are exported annually. The greatest market for these is Asia, with the Japanese being the largest consumers. Other potato varieties, especially Bintje, are used fresh for fries in the Netherlands and France, and by some sellers on the East Coast of the United States.

One potato expert says that the best french fries are made in the Netherlands, where they are found on almost every street corner in Amsterdam. There, the fries are served with lots of ketchup, mayonnaise, and mustard on top. Others think the Belgians have the best fries, and

there are shops in New York City selling Belgian-style fries. The Belgians are known to eat *pommes frites* more often than the Americans. The correct term for potatoes is *pommes de terre*, "earth apples," but no one seems to be confused by *pommes frites*. Belgians might eat them every day, both with meals and as snacks. Along with coffee, *pommes frites* are known as Belgian staples. The potatoes are usually served with mayonnaise, tartar sauce, Russian dressing, or béarnaise sauce, and may be accompanied by pickles or pickled onions. In Paris, the best *pommes frites* are said to be made by Algerians, Turks, and Greeks, rather than by French cooks. In each of these countries fresh potatoes are used rather than frozen ones. Americans tend to like fries with tomato ketchup accompanying them, and, in the northernmost parts of the United

A Belgian writer says that *frites* shacks, small wooden shops selling fries along the sidewalks, have all but disappeared in Belgium. In the 1940s in the United States and Canada, there were trailers selling freshly cooked fries parked along the streets of small towns or at beaches.

States and in Canada, vinegar is the choice of topping, a practice probably adopted from the British.

The fat in which the potatoes are fried can make a big difference in flavor of the finished product. McDonald's fries used to be cooked in a mixture of vegetable oil and beef tallow, which gave them a unique flavor. This practice ceased when enough consumers complained about the saturated fat, and so all vegetable fat has been used, and no beef tallow, since 1990. The flavor was different, though, so natural beef flavor was added to the frozen fries, much to the outrage of vegetarians, who expected there to be no animal product in the potatoes. A Belgian recipe for *pommes frites* calls for beef kidney suet, which gives them a unique flavor.

A Dutch-Egyptian factory near Cairo uses palm oil for its fries. A *New York Times* food writer fries the potatoes in a mixture of peanut oil and duck fat with bacon added. Another suggestion is to use horse fat, which is difficult to obtain in the United States. Burger King coats the potatoes with a mixture of potato starch and rice flour, then uses liquid smoke for flavor, but does not tell consumers what kind of fat is used.

French Fries as an American Icon Food

In America, frozen french fries were sold at R. H. Macy in New York City in 1946. Maxon Food Systems of Long Island City introduced the fries, but the company failed. Idaho potato processor J. R. Simplot had chemists develop frozen french fries for his company in 1953. These did not catch on because the potatoes tasted best when reheated in hot fat and home cooks did not want to bother doing that for a convenience food. Simplot decided to aim at restaurant owners who would be interested in saving labor in preparing potatoes for frying.

In about 1966, McDonald's restaurants began selling Simplot's frozen french fries. The potato processor had a new factory built just to prepare the fries for McDonald's. Customers did not object to the frozen product, and the reduced labor cost meant that french fries became a very profitable menu item. By 1995, Simplot had produced two billion pounds of french fries and other frozen potato products in the northwestern United States and in China.

Residents of the Southeast United States eat more french fries than those of the rest of the country. The Midwest is next, with the West and the Northeast following in that order.

Monitoring the sugar content versus starch content of potatoes is important in getting top-quality fries. If there is too much sugar, the potatoes will brown too fast. Companies may add some sugar to the fries in the fall, and leach out sugar in the spring, in order to get uniform color and taste throughout the year. Storage temperatures will affect sugar content of the potatoes.

In 1960, Americans consumed eighty-one pounds of fresh potatoes per capita and approximately four pounds of frozen french fries. By 1971, the consumption of processed potatoes was greater than that of fresh potatoes. Frozen potatoes accounted for most of the processed potatoes. In 2001 the consumption was forty-nine pounds of fresh potatoes and over thirty-one pounds of frozen french fries. The thirty pounds is equal to about four servings of fries a week. About 67 percent of the fries are bought at fast-food restaurants, with other restaurants accounting for 13 percent of the market share. Americans aged sixty and above eat fewer fries than younger persons.

There are now two other American frozen potato processors larger than Simplot: Lamb Weston, part of ConAgra, and Ore-Ida, owned by Heinz Frozen Food. Both of these companies are located in the Northwest. Lamb Weston processes fries for McDonald's and makes more that 130 different types of fries, some of which are sold in school lunch programs. In 2002, Ore-Ida stimulated sales of frozen french fries by introducing Funky Kool Blue Fries (not made from blue varieties of potatoes, but artificially colored a brilliant blue), chocolate-flavored (and colored) fries, and cinnamon sugar fries.

Frozen french fries have been a profitable item for fast-food companies. In 2001, it was possible to buy the potatoes for about 30 cents a pound and sell french fries for around $6.00 a pound. Unfortunately, farmers get very little of the profits. Increasingly, big corporations own the farms, while the farmers who have been driven from the land are hired to manage the farms for the corporations.

See also **Fast Food**; **Fish and Chips**; **Hamburger**; **Icon Foods**; **Potato**; **Take-Out Food**.

BIBLIOGRAPHY

Fitzgibbons, Theodora. *The Food of the Western World. An Encyclopedia of Food from North America and Europe.* New York: Quadrangle/The New York Times, 1976.

Foods of the World. Recipes: A Quintet of Cuisines. New York: Time-Life Books, 1970

Hooker, Richard J. *Food and Drink in America.* New York: Bobbs-Merrill, 1981.

Joseph, Scott. "Americans Love, Love, Love Fries, for Better or Worse." *Orlando Sentinel*, 25 September 2001.

Lang, James. *Notes of a Potato Watcher.* College Station: Texas A&M University Press, 2001

Laudan, Rachel. "Fast Food, Slow Food, Home-Cooked Food." Presented at the International Association of Culinary Professionals 24th International Conference, San Diego, Calif. 20 April 2002.

Lin, Bling-Hwan, Gary Lucier, Jane Allshouse, and Linda Scott Kantor. "Fast Food Growth Boosts Frozen Potato Consumption." *Food Review* 24, no. 1 (January–April 2001): 38–45.

Schlosser, Eric. *Fast Food Nation. The Dark Side of the All-American Meal.* New York: HarperCollins, 2002.

Trager, James. *The Food Chronology. A Food Lover's Compendium of Events and Anecdotes, from Prehistory to the Present.* New York: Henry Holt, 1995

Walker, Reagan. "At Last, an End to Fast-food Monopoly on Fries." *FOODday. The Oregonian*, 4 June 2002.

Wells, Patricia. *The Paris Cookbook.* New York: HarperCollins, 2001.

Whitman, Joan, ed. *Craig Claiborne's New York Times Food Encyclopedia.* New York: The New York Times, 1985.

Wilson, C. Anne. *Food and Drink in Britain. From the Stone Age to Recent Times.* Chicago: Chicago Academy, 1991.

Mary Kelsey

FROZEN FOODS.   In the early twenty-first century, frozen foods are an important component of meals prepared and served in both homes and restaurants. They have expanded the kind and quality of meals served and continue to influence food preparations and consumption in this country. The variety of frozen foods in the market reflects the wide use of frozen foods in households. These include ethnic, vegetarian, fast foods, imported gourmet, dietary, and many others.

Early use of freezing occurred in parts of the world, such as Canada, where temperatures in winter drop below freezing for significant periods of time. When hunters brought game animals home in winter, it was possible to freeze the catch by using the outdoor environment as the freezer. It was also convenient on farms where butchering was done. These meats were frozen and used before temperatures moderated. Experiences like this demonstrated the advantages of freezing. Because the storage time was dependent on the weather, this procedure had limitations.

The advantages of freezing as a method of preservation prompted researchers to develop freezing technology. In 1842, a patent for freezing foods by immersion in a brine of ice and salt was issued to Henry Benjamin in Britain. Fish was first frozen in the United States in 1865, and in 1917, Clarence Birdseye began word on freezing foods for retail trade. The use of dif-

ferent refrigerants was one of the early needs examined. The possibility of freons as refrigerants was well received for industrial and consumer applications and led to their early incorporation into household freezers. These early models offered were large in size and were designed to be used for the game and butchering needs of farm families at that time. But soon after their introduction, it was obvious that they were extensively used to store fruits and vegetables, an attractive application for farm households who were growing their own produce. These early models were great successes, and they launched the freezing preservation of fruits and vegetables in this country.

The possibility of freezing preservation of fruits and vegetables became an important interest in the United States, catching the attention of many city apartment dwellers and suburban families who lived in small houses. Unable to accommodate the large-size freezers that appliance manufactures were selling to farm families, these householders teamed up with their neighbors to develop community freezers, where families could rent freezer space in a large freezer-locker rental operation. Although this solved the problem, it was less than convenient.

Questions were raised about the effect of freezing meats, fruits, and vegetables on the quality of the thawed

Photo of one of the original TV dinners, with its compartmentalized aluminum serving dish for turkey, mashed potatoes, and peas. COURTESY ARCHIVE PHOTOS, INC.

TV Dinner

In 1954 C. A. Swanson & Sons introduced TV dinners to consumers in the United States. Gerald Thomas, an executive at Swanson, conceived the idea after the company unexpectedly found itself with 520,000 pounds of unsold Thanksgiving Day turkeys (information available at any website on popular culture of the 1950s). The turkeys were being stored in refrigerated railroad cars moving coast to coast across the country because there was not enough storage space in the company's warehouses. Thomas also conceived of the idea of using aluminum trays with three separate compartments. Based on his experiences in World War II, when soldiers ate from a tray, commonly known as "mess gear," he wanted to solve the problem of different foods running together in their serving tray. He observed the lightweight metal trays then being utilized by the airline food industry to heat meals and adopted them for use with the TV dinner.

The TV dinner concept was not met with immediate approval or enthusiasm at Swanson, though, where two more traditional-thinking brothers owned and operated the company. It was not until the older brother, who opposed the idea, went on vacation that Thomas's idea became a reality. The first dinner contained turkey, corn bread stuffing, gravy, sweet potatoes, and buttered peas. Its packaging was designed to look like a TV. Because most consumers did not own freezers in 1954, the dinners were usually consumed on the day they were purchased.

The market for TV dinners, or "frozen food dinners or entrées" (as they have come to be described almost exclusively by the frozen food industry since the 1960s), has continued to expand over the past five decades, reflecting the values and concerns of a larger American society. The initial production order by Swanson was for five thousand dinners, at a cost of 98 cents to consumers. Within a year, Swanson sold more than ten million turkey TV dinners. To ensure successful sales of the TV dinner, Swanson created an ad campaign featuring Sue Swanson, who "re-assured housewives they needn't feel guilty about not cooking homemade meals for their families." During the 1960s the sale of frozen food entrées rose dramatically after it became well publicized that the first American astronauts to land on the moon ate prepared meals while in space. In the 1950s and 1960s these entrées featured mostly comfort foods, similar to the homemade dinners that "Mom" would make, such as meatloaf or fried chicken combined with mashed potatoes.

The microwave oven was then invented in the 1960s, and it became a standard feature in most American homes by the 1980s. This development further increased the convenience and attractiveness of TV dinners to consumers. The 1980s witnessed a rise in the production of ethnic, low-calorie, and budget entrées, whereas the 1990s saw an increase in the production of gourmet entréees, "kid cuisine," and "hearty portions." The new millennium has so far indicated increasing growth in the production of frozen food entrées that are either healthy or "wholesome."

The frozen dinner is currently the largest category within the frozen food market; it currently accounts for over $5 billion worth of supermarket sales annually. One of the ten most popular dinners served in American homes is now a TV dinner, and nearly half of all Americans purchase frozen entrées. Those individuals most likely to consume TV dinners are "blue-collar families, older couples, and retired singles," whereas those least likely to consume TV dinners are either more wealthy families living in the suburbs or poorer people living in the country (see *American Demographics* for further information). In addition, frozen dinners are being delivered increasingly across the country to individuals who are homebound because of poor health or functional impairment. Survey findings reported by the Frozen Food Institute in 2002 reveal that certain frozen foods are among the top three items that Americans would not want to live without.

Julie Locher

product, including its nutrient retention. The USDA and land grant universities responded to this concern with research studies to assess the impact of freezing on nutrients in fruits, vegetables, and meat, which are summarized by Karmas and Harris. The results of this work showed the nutritional advantages of frozen foods and gave recommendations for freezing methods aimed at retaining maximum quality and nutritional value.

During World War II, homemakers began to join the U.S. workforce in large numbers and appreciated the timesaving advantages of frozen food. The appliance and food industries noted the acceptance by consumers of both freezing preservation of foods and the small freezer sections in household refrigerators. Early models of refrigerators did not offer separate compressor units for the freezer section. As a result, these appliances provided only limited freezing capacity and ability to freeze. The development of appliances with freezing sections that had separate compressors that allowed the freezing section to successfully hold frozen foods in the frozen condition had a major impact on the consumer's ability to store food. The food industry has also responded to the abilities of the new refrigerator models to hold frozen food by introducing frozen foods such as entrees, vegetable, breads, fruits, desserts, juices, snack foods, and ice cream. The refrigerator and freezer combination appliance fits into small spaces and is especially appreciated by those living in apartments and small homes. In the early twenty-first century, few refrigerators do not include a freezer on a separate compressor.

In microwave heating, foods are placed in an electromagnetic field when they are positioned in the oven cavity and the microwave energy is turned on. Heat is generated by molecular friction among the free water molecules in the food load. Since a frozen food has a very small amount of unfrozen water that attracts the microwave energy first, the heat is generated in a small part of the food load and is rapidly absorbed by the frozen part. In frozen foods, a large part of the water is in the form of ice. While water readily absorbs microwaves, ice does not. Some of the water in frozen foods does not freeze; this may be due to the salt content. The unfrozen water absorbs microwaves quickly in the microwave appliance. As a consequence, the use of microwaves to thaw and cook food may result in "runaway heating," a situation in which the unfrozen water containing salts is boiling while next to it, areas of ice exist. To prevent this, a defrost program is recommended; this feature exposes the food load to microwave energy for a short time, then turns microwaves off for a slightly longer time, allowing the heat to be conducted to the ice. This cycle is repeated until thawing is completed and does not usually produce runaway heating.

See also **Birdseye, Clarence**; **Microwave**; **Preparation of Food**; **Preserving**.

BIBLIOGRAPHY

Burnett, Barbara. *Every Woman's Legal Guide*. Garden City, N.Y.: Doubleday, 1983.

Frozen Food Institute. Available at http://www.affi.com.

Jay, James M. *Modern Food Microbiology*. 6th ed. Gaithersburg, Md.: Aspen, 2000.

Keene, Linda. "Fame for the Inventor of the TV Dinner Is Frozen in Time." *Seattle Times*, 24 September 1999.

Institute of Food Technologists. "Effects of Food Processing on Nutritive Values: A Scientific Status Summary by the Institute of Food Technologists Expert Panel on Food Safety and Nutrition and the Committee on Public Information." *Food Technology* 40, 12 (1986): 109–116.

Karmas, Endel, and Harris, Robert S. *Nutritional Evaluation of Food Processing*. New York: Van Nostrand Reinhold, 1988.

"Penguin Power." *American Demographics* 21, issue 3 (March 1999): 21, 14–15.

"Swanson TV Dinners." Fifties Web Pop History—TV Dinner. Available at http://www.fiftiesweb.com/pop/tv-dinner.htm.

Gertrude Ambruster

FRUIT.

This entry includes three subentries:
Citrus Fruit
Temperate Fruit
Tropical and Subtropical Fruit

CITRUS FRUIT

Citrus fruits are native to southeastern Asia and are among the oldest fruit crops to be domesticated by humans. They are widely grown in all suitable subtropical and tropical climates and are consumed worldwide. The most important of the citrus fruits commonly eaten include sweet oranges, mandarins, lemons, limes, grapefruits, and pummelos. These are eaten fresh, juiced, and in processed products. Citrus fruits have well-documented nutritional and health benefits as well as industrial uses. Their beauty and utility were well described by Georges Gallesio in 1811:

> Of all the plants spread by nature upon the surface of the globe, there are none more beautiful than those we know under the names of citron, lemon, and orange trees which botanists have included under the technical and generic name *Citrus*. These charming trees are both useful and ornamental. No others equal them in beauty of leaf, delightful odor of flowers, or splendor and taste of fruit. No other plant supplies delicious confection, agreeable seasoning, perfume, essences, syrups, and the valuable aides so useful to colorers. In a word, these trees charm the eye, satisfy the smell, gratify the taste, serving both luxury and art and presenting to astonished man a union of all delights. These brilliant qualities have made the citrus a favorite in all countries.

Botany

Citrus fruits constitute several species of the genus *Citrus* of the subfamily Aurantiodeae of the plant family Rutaceae. The Aurantiodeae has a total of thirty-three mostly subtropical and tropical genera, a few of which have economic importance. Most genera originated in Southeast Asia: the Malaysian and Indonesian Archipelagos, the Indochinese Peninsula, India, and China. A few genera originated in Australia or Africa.

The citrus fruits proper are characterized by their distinctive fruit, the hesperidium, which is a berry with the internal fleshy parts divided into segments (typically 10 to 16) and surrounded by a separable skin. The name is derived from classical mythology, referring to the "golden apples" grown in the garden of the Hesperides (the daughters of Hesperus, the evening star), located in the far west, in Paradise. When grown naturally, citrus plants are generally small to large trees, with glossy alternate leaves having oil glands. The attractive and fragrant flowers have an annular disk and generally bloom in the early spring.

The genus *Citrus* is divided into two subgenera, *Citrus* and *Papeda*. The former contains "edible" citrus fruits (including some less than palatable varieties), while the latter consists of the papedas. These are a distinctive group, the fruits of which have high concentrations of droplets of acrid oil in the pulp vesicles, rendering them inedible due to the bitter, unpleasant flavor. The leaves are also distinctive as compared to those of the subgenus *Citrus*, having large, prominent petioles. The leaves of one species, *Citrus hystrix*, are used as a condiment in Southeast Asian cooking.

The taxonomy of *Citrus*, as a genus, is unclear. So, for that matter, is the taxonomy of the other thirty-two genera in the subfamily. Different authorities have recognized anywhere from 3 to 170 species of *Citrus*. Obviously, this large a difference is due to more than mere hair-splitting. The most commonly used systems, that of W. T. Swingle (see Reuther, Webber, and Batchelor, pp. 190–430) or its modifications, recognize about sixteen species.

Most of the difficulties in *Citrus* taxonomy arise due the free hybridization that can occur between different varieties and even between different species of *Citrus*. In fact, many of the other Aurantiodeae genera are capable of free hybridization with Citrus. The result is that many types of citrus arose from these hybridization events at some time in the past. A strict interpretation of the "species" concept would result in fewer types being awarded species rank, whereas a looser interpretation would result in a higher number of species. This problem is compounded by the numerous controlled hybridizations and selections made by humans with the goal of producing a more desirable fruit.

Currently, the generally accepted concept is that there are three primordial or fundamental Citrus species: *Citrus medica* (citrons), *Citrus maxima* (pummelos), and *Citrus reticulata* (mandarins). All other types of citrus currently existing arose from single or sequential hybridization events between these species or their offspring. This concept is supported by various types of studies: classical taxonomy, chemotaxonomy, and molecular analysis.

Edible citrus is generally divided into sweet oranges, sour oranges, mandarins, grapefruit, pummelos, lemons, limes, and citrons. Within each of these types there are various subtypes, as well as types that arose from free or controlled hybridization. Depending on the taxonomic system used, these subtypes and hybrids may or may not be accorded species status. Table 1 presents some basic information on these standard types of edible citrus. Some of this information is not strictly accurate in a scientific sense: Oroblanco is actually a hybrid of a pum-

melo and a grapefruit, but it is generally marketed as a grapefruit; Meyer is probably a low-acid natural hybrid of a lemon and a sweet orange, but it is usually marketed as a lemon; Mediterranean Sweet is probably more accurately referred to as a "limetta" rather than a sweet lemon. However, the idea is to present the reader with some general information on fruits that might be encountered and eaten. Some types (low-acid sweet oranges, sour oranges, citrons) are not of much importance commercially, while others (sweet lemons, sweet limes) are important in some regions of the world but not in others.

There are four types of sweet oranges. The navel oranges possess a small, secondary fruit in the stylar end of the main fruit. This is the navel. Since navel oranges were introduced to California from Brazil in 1873, they have assumed a primary importance throughout the world as a sweet orange for fresh consumption. Like the navel oranges, common sweet oranges mature during the winter. Because of the popularity of the navel as a fresh fruit, common oranges are generally grown mostly for processing, although they can be important locally as fresh fruits. Blood oranges have a pigment called anthocyanin in the rind and juice, producing a reddish blush that becomes more pronounced with cooler night temperatures in the fall. The blood oranges have a distinctive taste compared to other sweet oranges. Valencia oranges mature later than the other sweet oranges and are generally harvested in the late spring or summer. Low-acid oranges have about the same levels of sugars as regular sweet oranges, but much lower levels of acid, resulting in a rather bland flavor.

Mandarins are often referred to somewhat incorrectly as tangerines. The word "tangerine" was used in the nineteenth century to designate Mediterranean types of mandarins, and referred to the city of Tangier. This term later became associated with other types of mandarins. Mandarins are of ancient cultivation in China, their probable area of origin, and other parts of Asia. The common mandarins include such important varieties as Ponkan, which is widely grown in Asia under different names. The Satsumas are a distinctive, seedless, early maturing group apparently originating in Japan relatively recently as compared to the common mandarins. The Clementines are another distinctive group that apparently originated in Algeria as recently as the 1890s. There are now many different selections of Satsumas and Clementines. The hybrids of tangelo (crossed with pummelo or grapefruit) and tangor (crossed with sweet orange) are included here as types of mandarins since they are generally thought of by the public as being more like mandarins than the other parent.

Sour oranges are not often eaten as fresh fruit or used for processing. However, the fruit is used to produce marmalade, and the flowers of certain types are used in the production of perfume. The Bergamot, a sour orange hybrid, has a distinctively scented oil that is used in

TABLE 1

Edible citrus: A summary

Fruit type	Species	Known age (yrs)	Year named	Probable origin	Probable native habitat	Subtypes	Harvest period	Representative varieties
Sweet orange	C. sinensis	500	1757	hybrid	China	common sweet orange	winter	Pera Hamlin Pineapple Shamouti Itabora Westin
						navel orange	winter	Washington Newhall Bahianinha Atwood Navelina Lane's Late
						Valencia orange	summer	Olinda Valencia Late
						blood orange	winter	Moro Tarocco Ruby Sanguinelli
						acidless	winter	Succari Lima
Mandarin	C. reticulata	2000 (?)	1837	true species	China	common	fall–spring	Dancy Pixie Fairchild Ponkan Kinnow Imperial
						Satsuma	fall	Okitsu Wase Owari Aoshima Clausellina
						Clementine	fall–spring	Fina Oroval Nules Marisol
						tangor	winter–spring	Temple Murcott Ortanique King Iyo Ellendale
						tangelo	winter–spring	Orlando Minneola Seminole Hassaku
Sour orange	C. aurantium	900	1753	hybrid	China		winter	Seville
Grapefruit	C. paradisi	200	1930	hybrid	Barbados	white-fleshed	winter–spring	Marsh Duncan Oroblanco
						pink-fleshed	winter–spring	Marsh Pink Ruby Red Rio Red Star Ruby Flame
Pummelo	C. maxima	2000 (?)	1765	true species	China		winter–spring	Kao Panne Kao Phuang Thong Dee Banpeiyu Chandler Reinking

[continued]

TABLE 1 (CONTINUED)

Edible citrus: A summary

Fruit type	Species	Known age (yrs)	Year named	Probable origin	Probable native habitat	Subtypes	Harvest period	Representative varieties
Lemon	C. limon	800	1766	hybrid	India	acid	winter–spring	Fino Genoa Interdonato Monachello Villafranca Verna
						Eureka	variable	Taylor Allen Genoa
						Lisbon	winter–spring	Limoneira 8A Monroe Walker
						sweet	winter–spring	Dorshapo Mediterranean sweet Meyer
Lime	C. aurantifolia	700	1913	hybrid	Malaya	small acid	winter–spring	Mexican Galego Kagzi
						large acid	winter–spring	Persian Tahiti Bearss
						sweet	winter–spring	Palestine
Citron	C. medica	2300	1753	true species	India		winter–spring	Etrog Diamante Buddha's Hand

SOURCE: Compiled from various sources

---

teas as well as perfume. Sour oranges often make attractive ornamentals.

Pummelos are generally large fruit that originated in more tropical areas than most other types of citrus. They are commonly grown in southeastern Asia, where consumption is the highest. Pummelos are not eaten much outside of that area. The pummelos are a very diverse group, with large variations in size and shape, rind, flesh pigmentation, and acid level.

Grapefruit is another natural hybrid (probably pummelo crossed with sweet orange) arising relatively recently (in the eighteenth century). In the twentieth century, it became widely planted and was used for both fresh fruit and processing. White- and pink-fleshed varieties exist. The pink-fleshed varieties derive their color from the pigment lycopene and require high heat levels for good color development (in contrast to the blood oranges).

Lemons have not been identified as a wild species, and probably arose sometime in the remote past as a cross between a citron and a sour orange (itself probably a hybrid of pummelo and mandarin). Lemons are rather variable and it is sometimes difficult to distinguish between different varieties and types. Low-acid, sweet lemons also

exist. The limettas are similar to and more common than sweet lemons and are often referred to in this manner.

Limes are somewhat similar to lemons in appearance and ancestry, and the distinction between the two groups is not always clear. Like lemons, low-acid, sweet types exist. The acid lemons are generally divided into the large, fruited types (generally seedless) and the small-fruited, "Key" types.

Citrons were probably the oldest citrus fruit to be cultivated in the West, but today they are not widely grown. Citrons are a highly variable group including acid and sweet varieties, but to the general public they often resemble large lemons. Citrons are sometimes used in the production of a candied peel and in Jewish religious ritual. The citrons are aromatic and are occasionally grown as ornamentals.

The kumquats are not, strictly speaking, citrus fruits. They are, however, in the genus *Fortunella*, which is closely related to *Citrus* in the Aurantioideae. Kumquats are distinctive in that they have small fruits with a sweet, edible peel. The trees are small and attractive and they are generally grown as backyard trees rather than commercially. The most important varieties of kumquats are Nagami, Meiwa, and Marumi.

Natural History and Spread

As well stated in Reuther, Webber, and Batchelor, "The history of the spread of citrus reads like a romance. Even in very early times the beautiful appearance of both tree and fruit attracted the attention of travelers and received mention in their written narratives" (p. 1).

Citrus is native to and has its center of diversity in northeastern India, southern China, the Indochinese peninsula, and nearby archipelagos. A theoretical dividing line (the Tanaka line) runs southeastwardly from the northwest border of India, above Burma, through the Yunnan province of China, to south of the island of Hainan. Citron, lemon, lime, sweet and sour oranges, and pummelo originated south of this line, while mandarins and kumquats originated north of the line. The mandarins apparently developed along a line northeast of the Tanaka line, along the east China coast, through Formosa, and to Japan, while kumquats are found in a line crossing south-central China in an east-west direction.

The cultivation of citrus began in ancient times in these areas. In fact, citrus was one of the earliest crops to be exploited and domesticated by man. Probably cultivation of citrus began independently in several locations within the area of origin and spread throughout the Southeast Asian region, and eventually into the Middle East, Europe, and America.

The oldest mention of citrus fruits known is from China, in the Yu Kung, a book of tributes to the Emperor Ta Yu, who lived from about 2205 to 2197 B.C.E. This book mentions the use of various types of citrus as tributes to the emperor. Later writings describe other types of mandarins, sweet oranges, pummelos, and kumquats. The monograph on citriculture written in 1178 C.E. by Han Yen Chih mentions twenty-seven varieties of citrus. The earliest mention of citrus in Indian writings is from about 800 B.C.E. in a collection of devotional texts, the Vajasaneyi samhita. This text mentions citrons and lemons. Sweet oranges are not mentioned in Indian writing until about 100 C.E.

The sweet orange probably arose in southern China where both mandarins and pummelos were planted together. From there, it spread through Burma and Assam into India. Much the same route was probably followed by the mandarins. Mandarins also spread into Japan. This probably occurred in the middle of the first millennium C.E., but the first mention of mandarins in Japanese literature dates from the thirteenth century.

Conversely, the citron probably originated in northern India and spread northward into China later. The citron also spread from India westward to Medea (Persia) by the first millennium B.C.E., and then into Palestine and the Near East. It is supposed that it was brought to this area by Alexander the Great. The citron became established in Italy during Roman times. The sweet and sour oranges, lemons, and pummelos followed this route at a later date.

The Arabs were instrumental in introducing most of the citrus types to Europe and northern Africa. The invasion of southern Europe by the Moors introduced citrons, sour oranges, lemons, and pummelos to the Iberian Peninsula, which is still an important area of citriculture. However, the sweet orange was apparently not established in Europe until the fifteenth century C.E. This was probably due to an entirely different route by Portuguese trade with southern Asia. The mandarins were apparently not introduced to Europe until early in the nineteenth century, when they arrived directly from China. Kumquats were introduced from China in the middle of that same century.

Citrus can be, and is, grown in southern Europe. That citrus represented a new and appealing type of fruit and had more exacting climatic requirements created a sort of cult of citrus in the more northern areas of Europe that persists to this day. Since citrus cannot be grown outdoors in such areas as the British Isles, northern France, and Germany, special houses (later known as orangeries) were in use by the fourteenth century for growing oranges and citrons. Some of these structures, which can be considered precursors to modern greenhouses, are still standing. In some cases, the citrus overwintered in the orangeries and were brought outdoors to enjoy the brief and mild summers and to enchant the public.

Citrus was carried to America by the Spanish and Portuguese colonizers beginning in the sixteenth century with the second voyage of Columbus in 1493. From its initial establishment in the Caribbean islands, it spread to the mainland (Mexico) and from there into the southern United States and Latin America. Citrus was introduced into Florida earlier than into California. Citrus was introduced separately into Brazil by the Portuguese, who were also responsible for the introduction of citrus into West Africa. It had apparently been introduced to the African continent earlier by Arab or Indian traders. Citrus was introduced in Australia from Brazil in 1788 by the colonists of the First Fleet.

The World Citrus Industry

In the New World, as in the Old, wherever citrus was introduced it became a popular fruit. If climatic conditions were appropriate, citrus was planted for commercial and for personal use. It remains the most widely planted fruit, except for grapes, in the world today. Most grape production is for winemaking, so citrus is undoubtedly the most widely planted fruit for direct human consumption in the world.

Citrus is grown throughout the world in the "Citrus Belt" between approximately 40°N and 40°S latitude. Within this belt there are tropical, semitropical, and subtropical climates, and it is possible to grow citrus in all three. Although there is some influence of scion and rootstock in cold susceptibility, frost is the main climatic limitation to citrus production. At the northern and southern margins

The method for protecting lemon and orange trees during the winter along the Lake of Garda in northern Italy. At the beginning of cold weather, the orangerie was shuttered along the front and roofed over with moveable boards. From Johann Christoph Volkamer's *Nürnbergische Hesperides* (Nuremberg, 1708). ROUGHWOOD COLLECTION.

of production (Corsica, Japan, New Zealand), the mildness and shortness of the summers is a secondary constraint. In areas that have a Mediterranean climate, which has a long, dry summer, supplemental irrigation is necessary.

The majority of commercial production is in the subtropical regions between 20° and 40° northern and southern latitudes. In the tropics, flowering is often erratic, and fruit may mature throughout the year. Although fruit size is generally large in the tropics, fruit quality is usually lower. Fruit color is generally less intense and acids may be too low for good eating quality. Yellow-fleshed and high-acid types (lemons and limes) are not as affected by these factors and are widely grown in the tropics, as are pummelos. Although there is less large-scale commercial production in the tropics, citrus is important locally and when grown for personal consumption.

In the subtropical areas, the yearly cycle of flowering and fruit development, as well as vegetative growth, is more tightly regulated by climatic conditions. This results in a crop that matures at the same time and has higher fruit quality. Semitropical conditions are intermediate between tropical and subtropical conditions. These areas, which include such major production areas

as Brazil and Florida, produce high yields of citrus that is of acceptable quality. Fruit quality for fresh consumption is lower than in subtropical climates such as California and Spain, but most fruit produced in Brazil and Florida is grown for processing, which has slightly lower-quality standards.

Within these climatic types, there are some variations in types of citrus successfully produced. For example, varieties that are colored by lycopene, such as the pigmented grapefruits, do well in these semitropical climates, while those colored by anthocyanins (blood oranges) do better in areas with lower winter temperatures. In marginal areas such as Japan and New Zealand, early maturing varieties such as Satsumas are grown.

Brazil has been the largest producer of citrus for some time, followed by the United States. Other important producing countries include China, India, Spain, Morocco, Argentina, Italy, South Africa, Australia, Mexico, and Egypt. The relative ranking of these countries varies from year to year. Recently, there has been much interest in large-scale production in countries such as China and India, where the climate is suitable and labor and infrastructure inexpensive. There are many niches within the world citrus production. For instance, in the United States, Florida produces a large proportion of the sweet oranges, the majority of which are used in processing. California produces a higher quality sweet orange, with emphasis on navel varieties, which is eaten fresh and largely exported. Countries such as Spain and Morocco produce large quantities of mandarins for export to the United Kingdom and northern Europe. Some of the Southern Hemisphere countries export to major Northern Hemisphere producers during the off-season.

As with any industry, there have been changes over the years. In the last decades of the twentieth century, the trend has been toward increased global trade and yearlong availability in most major markets. Processed products have grown in importance. In fresh fruit, the trend has been toward easy-peeling, seedless mandarins and sweet oranges. In grapefruit, the pigmented varieties are becoming predominant.

Production

Citrus is produced in slightly different ways in different areas. Commercial production is more uniform throughout the world than is local or personal production, but there are some differences here as well. Many of the differences are in the nature of farming inputs rather than the production of trees. For instance, fertilization and irrigation are necessary in most areas. However, a more industrialized producer in an exporting country may utilize drip irrigation with inorganic fertilizers injected through the drip system, while a producer for the local market in a poor country or area may use manure and flood irrigation.

Citrus can be grown from seed; however, there are some disadvantages. In some cases, seedlings are not true-to-type with the mother tree; due to juvenility factors, seedling trees do not usually bear fruit until they are nearly a decade old; and they are vulnerable to unfavorable soil conditions, diseases, and so forth. For these reasons, most citrus produced throughout the world utilizes budded (grafted) trees.

A budded tree consists of two parts: the scion, which is the fruit variety, and the rootstock, which supports the scion in the soil environment. Rootstocks are chosen based on a number of factors, including compatibility with the scion, resistance to diseases or pests, adaptation to soil conditions, effect on fruit quality. Citrus rootstocks can be grown from seed, since the commonly used rootstocks are apomictic (and hence true-to-type), and there are no confirmed seed-transmitted systemic diseases of citrus. Production from seed is easier than from cuttings, the common method of production for rootstocks for most other tree crops.

The rootstock is usually of an appropriate size for budding about nine months to a year after germination, when it is about the diameter of a wood pencil. The scion variety is budded onto the rootstock by making an incision into the bark of the rootstock, inserting a bud removed from the scion variety, and wrapping it with tape. A callus should form between the rootstock and scion tissues in two to four weeks. With appropriate training, the young tree is ready for planting in the field in about another year.

Once planted, it is usually about two to three years before the tree begins to produce fruit. Full production is usually achieved at about ten years of age. Under appropriate conditions, citrus trees may live a long and productive life and achieve a fairly tall height. This was common in many older citrus-producing areas. Since about the 1970s, citrus production has become more cyclical, like that of other tree crops, and the life of an orchard may be no more than twenty to thirty years.

Citrus requires relatively little cultural manipulation compared to crops such as grapes and deciduous trees, which require pruning and extensive training. In some areas, however, such as the Mediterranean basin, mandarins and sweet orange may receive somewhat more manipulation than in areas such as California. Lemons grow vigorously upright and require more frequent topping. Irrigation and fertilization are necessary. Certain production problems or challenges in citrus have been successfully managed with the application of plant growth regulators. This is more established in citrus than in most other perennial crops.

In contrast to the relatively low cultural inputs for citrus, disease and pest management in this crop is more critical and challenging than for many others. Because citrus is grown in warm areas of the world, reproduction of insect pests is rapid and insect pressure can be great. The individual insect pests vary greatly with geographic area. Compared to other crops, citrus is also subject to a larger number of systemic, graft-transmissible diseases caused by virus and viruslike pathogens that can potentially devastate industries. The most important worldwide is the tristeza virus, which destroyed many thousands of hectares in California and South America starting in the 1930s. This has been managed in some areas by certification programs requiring the use of virus-tested propagative materials and in a few cases with eradication programs. Other diseases, such as greening and citrus variegated chlorosis, are equally deadly but less widespread throughout the world.

Citrus is harvested by hand. At this point, there have not been any widely accepted methods of mechanical harvest. The time of harvest is dictated by the market or in some cases by legal maturity standards. Citrus is more forgiving than some other crops in that harvesting can be delayed somewhat and fruit quality is not decreased too much by the extra time on the tree. This varies with variety. However, if fruit are left on the tree too long, quality deteriorates as acid levels decrease and the taste becomes insipid. Other fruit quality problems can also occur. After harvest, citrus can be stored at low (refrig-

Lemon vendors in Oaxaca, Mexico. Oil painting by Mexican artist Rocio Levito, 2002. PHOTO COURTESY OF THE ARTIST.

erated) temperatures for several months. This has had important implications in the development of the industry since the beginning of the twentieth century.

After harvest, commercial citrus is transported to a packinghouse. There, the fruit is washed, sorted and graded, treated with fungicides and waxes, and packed. In some cases, ethylene gas treatment is used for degreening. Citrus packing today is highly automated in some ways, with various sensors and other devices routing and sorting the fruit through a complexly routed pathway of conveyor belts, and bins. However, there is still a substantial amount of hand labor necessary for sorting, grading, and movement. After citrus is packed, it is transported away from the packinghouse and enters wholesale and retail market channels.

In addition to commercial production, citrus is widely grown for personal use in "door yards," roadsides, small subsistence plots. Growing citrus for this use is extremely variable. Trees are grown from seed, are grafted by the grower, are purchased from commercial sources, and so forth. Varietal selection is based on personal preference rather than economic factors. Citrus is also prized for its ornamental value and often serves a decorative purpose as well. There are some cultivars that are grown strictly as ornamentals, such as some variegated types and the Buddha's Hand citron.

Use of Citrus Fruits

Citrus is consumed fresh, juiced, and processed. The most nutritious ways of serving citrus are as fresh fruit or fresh-squeezed juice. Citrus fruits are well known for their vit-amin C content, but are also good sources of vitamin A, folic acid, and dietary fiber. Nutritional profiles of some citrus fruit and fresh juices are shown in Table 2.

Fresh citrus fruits can be stored for several days at room temperature or for several weeks in the refrigerator. Fresh-squeezed juice should be stored in the refrigerator and is stable at refrigerator temperatures for several weeks from a nutritional standpoint. However, there is often a loss of quality when fresh-squeezed juice is stored. This is especially true of navel orange juice.

Processing is an important part of the citrus market worldwide. Two of the major producers of citrus, Brazil and Florida, produce fruit predominantly for the processing trade. Low-grade and excess fruit from fresh market production may also be routed into processing. Where production is oriented toward producing citrus for processing, different varieties and to some extent different cultural practices are employed than when grown for fresh market. Criteria for harvest and quality standards are also different. Internal quality is paramount for processing citrus, whereas external appearance counts for more in fresh market fruit.

The most important use of citrus for processing is the production of frozen concentrated orange juice. The production of this is different from but equally as complex as packing fresh fruit. After fruit enter the plant, they are washed, juiced with a press or extractor, and strained to remove peel and rag. The juice then goes to the finisher, where excess pulp and essential oils are removed from the juice. It is then concentrated by an evaporator.

TABLE 2

Nutritive value of citrus fruits and raw juices

Fruit	Grapefruit	Grapefruit juice	Lemon	Lemon juice	Lime juice	Orange	Orange juice	Tangerine
Serving	1/2 grapefruit, raw, without peel, membrane, and seeds (3.75 in. diam., 1 lb. 1 oz., whole, with refuse)	Raw, 1 cup	1 lemon, raw, without peel and seeds (about 4 per lb. with peel and seeds)	Raw, 1 cup	Raw, 1 cup	1 orange, whole, raw, without peel and seeds (2.625 in. diam., about 2.5 per lb., with peel and seeds)	Raw, 1 cup	1 tangerine, raw, without peel and seeds (2.375 in. diam., about 4 per lb. with peel and seeds)
Grams	120	247	58	244	246	131	248	84
Water, %	91	90	89	91	90	87	88	88
Food energy, kcal	40	95	15	60	65	60	110	35
Carbohydrate, g	10	23	5	21	22	15	26	9
Protein, g	1	1	1	1	1	1	2	1
Fat, g	Tr	Tr	Tr	Tr	Tr	Tr	Tr	Tr
Fatty acids, saturated, g	Tr	Tr	Tr	Tr	Tr	Tr	0.1	Tr
Fatty acids, mono-unsaturated, g	Tr	Tr	Tr	Tr	Tr	Tr	0.1	Tr
Fatty acids, poly-unsaturated, g	Tr	0.1	0.1	Tr	0.1	Tr	0.1	Tr
Cholesterol, mg	0	0	0	0	0	0	0	0
Calcium, mg	14	22	15	17	22	52	27	12
Phosphorus, mg	10	37	9	15	17	18	42	8
Iron, mg	0.1	0.5	0.3	0.1	0.1	0.1	0.5	0.1
Potassium, mg	167	400	80	303	268	237	496	132
Sodium, mg	Tr	2	1	2	2	Tr	2	1
Vitamin A, IU	10	20	20	50	20	270	500	770
Thiamin, mg	0.04	0.10	0.02	0.07	0.05	0.11	0.22	0.09
Riboflavin, mg	0.02	0.05	0.01	0.02	0.02	0.05	0.07	0.02
Niacin, mg	0.3	0.5	0.1	0.2	0.2	0.4	1.0	0.1
Ascorbic acid, mg	41	94	31	112	72	70	124	26

SOURCE: Gebhardt and Matthews, pp. 20–26.

The bulk concentrate is stored in tank farms and transported in refrigerated trucks, train cars, or ships. The bulk concentrate is packaged into consumer- or industrial-sized containers. Frozen concentrate orange juice is sometimes reconstituted into "single strength orange juice." This is also produced directly without first being concentrated. Processing has little effect on the nutritional value of orange juice, but there is generally a loss of palatability. Grapefruit juice and to a lesser extent lemons, limes, and mandarins are processed similarly. These products are sometimes used to blend with other types of fruit juice or for the production of frozen confections. By-products of processing include essential oils and pulp. The latter is used for cattle feed. Other processed products of citrus include canned segments, segments in juice, pectin, jellies, and jams. Peel products are used for animal feed, marmalade, and shaved peel.

In addition to processing for juice and its associated by-products, there are minor industrial uses of citrus. Although essential oils are extracted as part of juice processing, in some instances trees are grown specifically for the production of these oils. The center of this industry is Calabria, Italy, and the main variety used is Bergamot, of which there are various selections. Citrus is also used to produce pesticides, cleaning products, and hair care products.

Health Benefits and Traditional Usage

In addition to the nutritional value and vitamin content of citrus, there are certain health benefits associated with some of the secondary products. For instance, various limonoid compounds, particularly D-limonene, have been shown to reduce tumorgenesis under experimental conditions. Carotenoids, such as lycopene, have been associated with decreased risks of heart attacks as well as general antioxidant activity. The high pectin content of some types of citrus contributes to soluble fiber consumption, which has been linked to increased cardiovascular health and reduced risk of certain types of cancer.

As might be expected with a crop utilized by humans for a number of millennia, these health benefits are reflected in the traditional use of citrus by indigenous people. Many of these uses are focused around the center of origin in China and India. However, health-related use of citrus has also been reported from traditional peoples in such areas as Fiji, Guatemala, and Chile. Citrus has been reported to be used for treatment of various illnesses, to reduce vomiting or diarrhea, and for regulating fertility. The sour orange has been reported to be used in voodoo ceremonies in Haiti.

Many of these uses are also associated with other plants in the subfamily Aurantiodeae. The kumquats have been mentioned already as being edible, but some other types of fruits are sometimes eaten by traditional peoples. Of particular note are the use of the leaves of *Murraya koenigii* as condiments and in the preparation of curry (the common name for this tree is curry leaf) and the use of Aegle marmelos ("Bael") for the preparation of teas. Other traditional uses reflect some of the properties suggested by the industrial use of citrus: insecticides and shampoos. As more insight into ethnopharmacology and secondary plant products is gained, it is possible that industrial use of citrus may increase, and probably some of these uses will reflect traditional uses of these plants.

See also **China**; **Dietary Guidelines**; **Ethnopharmacology**; **India**; **Scurvy**; **Southeast Asia**; **Vitamin C**.

BIBLIOGRAPHY

Davies, Frederick S., and L. Gene Albrigo. *Citrus*. Wallingford, Oxon, U.K.: CAB International, 1994.

Gallesio, Georges. *Traité du Citrus*. Paris: Fantin, 1811.

Gebhardt, Susan E., and Ruth H. Matthews. *Nutritive Value of Foods*. Home and Garden Bulletin No. 72, rev. ed. Washington, D.C.: United States Department of Agriculture, Human Nutrition Information Service, 1991.

Institute of Food Technologists Citrus Products Division. "Nutrition and Health Benefits of Citrus Fruit Products." *Food Technology* 48, no. 10 (November 1994): 103–139.

Kalt, Wilhelmina. "Health Functional Phytochemicals of Foods." *Horticultural Reviews* 27 (2001): 269–315.

Kimball, Dan A. *Citrus Processing: A Complete Guide*. 2d ed. Gaithersburg, Md.: Aspen Publications, 1999.

Reuther, Walter, Herbert John Webber, and Leon Dexter Batchelor, eds. *The Citrus Industry*. Vol. 1. *History, World Distribution, Botany, and Varieties*. Rev. ed. Berkeley: University of California, Division of Agricultural Sciences, 1967.

Rinzler, Carol A. *The New Complete Book of Food: A Nutritional, Medical, and Culinary Guide*. New York: Facts on File, 1999.

Saunt, James. *Citrus Varieties of the World*. 2d ed. Norwich, U.K.: Sinclair International, 2000.

Spiegel-Roy, Pinchas, and Eliezer E. Goldschmidt. *Biology of Citrus*. Cambridge and New York: Cambridge University Press, 1996.

Wardowski, Wilfred F., Steven Nagy, and William Grierson, eds. *Fresh Citrus Fruits*. Westport, Conn.: AVI, 1986.

Robert R. Krueger

TEMPERATE FRUIT

Many of the world's best-known and favorite fruits (such as apple, pear, peach, plum, grape, and strawberry) are adapted to climates in the middle latitudes and are known as temperate fruits. Temperate fruits have two climatic adaptations: they require some cold periods (dormancy) to complete their life cycle, which conditions their adaptation in tropical climates, and they have various degrees of winter hardiness, which conditions their adaptability in cold climates. Fruits that do not specifically require cold but have slight frost tolerance (citrus, fig, olive, persimmon, pomegranate) are known as subtropical fruits; they are not discussed here. In contrast, tropical fruits typically are very sensitive to cold and are often injured by low temperatures above freezing. Temperate fruits are usually classified by their growth habit as tree fruits (apple, pear, peach), vine fruits (grape, kiwifruit), or small fruits (strawberry, raspberry, currant, and blueberry). The term "small fruits" refers to the size of the plant and not necessarily the fruit. In the United Kingdom they are better known as bush fruits or soft fruits.

Tree Fruits

The best-known temperate tree fruits are members of the rose family (Rosaceae). These include the pome and stone fruits. Pome fruits (apple, pear, quince, and medlar) are fleshy fruits in which the outer portion is formed by expanded floral parts and receptacle. The stone fruits, all members of the genus *Prunus* (almond, apricot, cherry, peach, nectarine, and plum) are fleshy fruits that contain a stony pit (hence the name "stone fruits"), which encloses a solitary seed.

Apple (*Malus* × *domestica*) is the best known of the pome fruits. It has been known since antiquity and is grown in Siberia and northern China where winter temperatures can fall as low as –40°F and in high elevations in Colombia as well as Java, Indonesia, straddling the equator, where two crops can be produced in a single year provided leaves are stripped. While there are many species of *Malus*, the domesticated kinds seem to be derived from *M. siversii* indigenous to Kazakhstan and neighboring countries where forests of wild apple contain seedlings with all of the characteristics of the domesticated sorts. Apples are popular because they can be consumed in many ways: fresh, dried, or cooked and in liquid form as juice, alcoholic cider, or brandy (Calvados). Processed apples are appreciated as a filling for many bakery items and enjoyed as a sauce or concentrated as a butter. Some apples have a long storage life under refrigeration, in some cases as long as a year, especially under controlled atmospheres (low oxygen). In the United States the apple is the symbol of wholesomeness; "an apple a day keeps the doctor away" is a popular aphorism.

Pear (*Pyrus* species) can be divided into two types, the European pear (*P. communis*), which usually are consumed when they soften after harvest, and the Asian pear

Pears are a popular winter fruit because of their storing qualities. Shown here is the heirloom Seckel pear, which was discovered in the 1790s growing wild along the Delaware River by Philadelphia wine merchant Lorenz Seckel (1747–1823). The pear is believed to be a natural hybrid of older pear varieties brought to colonial America. FROM A NINETEENTH-CENTURY WOODCUT COURTESY OF THE ROUGHWOOD COLLECTION.

(*P. pyrifolia* and *P. ussuriensis*), which are consumed when crisp. The pear is as old a fruit crop as apple but is somewhat less popular in the West. This is probably because the postharvest ripening required makes it difficult to determine optimum quality, and some fruits contain grit (stone cells), which can be objectionable. Asian pears (known as *nashi* in Japan and as *li* in China) are probably more popular than apples in China, Japan, and Korea. Pears are closely related to apples and are consumed in similar ways.

The quince (*Cydonia oblonga*) is the third most important pome fruit. It is not very popular because most are too sour and astringent to be consumed raw, but it is excellent cooked, especially in preserves, jams, and jellies, to which sugar is added. Some types grown in warm climates soften and can be consumed raw. It is an important crop in Argentina. Some quinces are used as dwarfing rootstocks for pear. Quinces have a wonderful perfume and should be more widely grown but have passed into the realm of a neglected fruit. The Asian quinces (species of *Chaenomeles*) are often grown as or-

namentals, but there have been attempts to domesticate these species in the Balkans for juices and preserves.

Medlar (*Mespilus germanica*) is truly an almost forgotten fruit. It is mentioned and disparaged by Shakespeare, who notes that it must be almost rotten to be enjoyed. The medlar is inedible until an internal fermentation occurs, producing an aromatic taste that appeals to some. The medlar can still be found in Italian markets.

The peach, despite its scientific name (*Prunus persica*), which suggests a Persian origin, is native to China, where it has always been highly prized for the beauty of its flowers and fruit. The peach seems to have been introduced to Europe via Persia in the first century B.C.E. but may have been known to the Greek philosopher Theophrastus (372–287 B.C.E.), who writes of Persian fruit and Persian apple. The fruit was well known to the Romans, and pictures of peaches were found in Herculaneum, destroyed in the eruption of Vesuvius in 79 C.E. Peach germplasm was introduced to the United States by the Spanish in the sixteenth century and became naturalized, but quality was low. Introductions from China in the middle of the nineteenth century, particularly one called Chinese Cling, are the progenitors of modern American cultivars. Peach is now the most popular temperate summer fruit. There are a number of distinct types. The freestone types with melting flesh and white or yellow flesh are usually consumed fresh. The clingstone, rubbery-flesh types are used in processing. The nectarine, a peach with a nonfuzzy skin, resulted from a mutation. Peentao, a saucer-shaped, flat peach is another variant type. Breeding in the United States has created many cultivars of both peach and nectarine that are widely grown in Europe, and some have been reintroduced to China for greenhouse production.

Almond (*Prunus amygdalus*) is native to the hot arid regions of western Asia but was introduced to Greece and West Africa in prehistory. The flesh is leathery and inedible, although the very immature fruits are consumed in Arab countries. Unlike most stone fruits, which have a bitter seed due to hydrocyanic (prussic) acid, the seeds of almond are nonbitter and are the edible part of this fruit. This species is therefore discussed under nuts. The almond is the most extensively planted "fruit" in California and is widely grown in countries of the Mediterranean basin.

Cherries, one of the most popular early summer fruits, are a symbol of joy as expressed in a famous song line: "life is just a bowl of cherries." There are about thirty species of cherry. The edible types include sweet cherry (*Prunus avium*), a diploid with two sets of chromosomes ($2n = 16$), and tart (sour) cherry (*P. cerasus*), a tetraploid with four sets of chromosomes ($2n = 32$). Another tetraploid type called Duke cherry is derived from a hybrid between sweet and tart cherries. Cherries may be red, yellow, or bicolored and are consumed fresh, dried, or processed, including as a liquor called kirsch.

The Maraschino cherry is almost an artificial fruit in which cherries are brined, bleached, and then artificially colored and flavored with bitter almond oil. They are often used in a wonderful confection: chocolate-covered cherries. Cherries are now available over a long season in North American markets due to the efforts of American and Canadian breeders.

Apricot (*Prunus armeniaca*), an ancient fruit native to central Asia and China, was thought by the Greeks to have originated in Armenia, hence its scientific name. The beautiful, aromatic fruit with a velvety skin is consumed fresh, dried, and processed. Apricot liquor is well appreciated. The apricot blooms very early, is subject to spring frost, and is difficult to grow. This may explain why apricot has not become as important as peach, cherry, or plum. The beautifully flowered Chinese plum (*P. mume*) is more properly included with the apricots than the plums.

Plums are a diverse group of fruits, as exemplified by the many names by which they are known: bullaces, cherry plums, damsons, date plums, egg plums, greengages, mirabelles, plums, prunes, and sloes. Various species originated in Europe, Asia, and America. Two European species (*Prunus domestica* and *P. insititia*) are hexaploid, with six sets of chromosomes. The *domestica* plums include several groups of cultivars, such as greengage and prune types, while *P. insititia* includes bullaces, damsons, mirabelles, and St. Julien types. Among Asiatic species are *P. salicina* and *P. simonii*, the former of which includes both red- and green-fleshed Japanese plums. Many of these were introduced by Luther Burbank, with the red-fleshed Santa Rosa being the best known. *P. simonii* (apricot plum) is cultivated in China. There are a number of American plum species, but none are widely cultivated. At the start of the twenty-first century, the world plum industry is largely made up of *P. domestica* in Europe and *P. salicina* in Asia. Plums are consumed fresh or dried. Plums that dry without fermentation are called prune plums or simply prunes. They are dried down to very low moisture levels, in which state they can be stored for long periods of time. They are rehydrated when they are sold as packaged prunes, processed into jelly and jam (popular as a bakery filling), made into a diluted juice, or turned into brandy or cordials. The wrinkled dried fruit was widely consumed by senior citizens because of its laxative properties and thus became a source of comic derision. (It has been said that the turndown service at senior hostels includes a prune rather than a chocolate on the bed.) As a result, the industry has changed the name of prune to dried plum!

Vine Fruits

Grapes (species of *Vitis*, Vitaceae, or grape, family), one of the most important temperate fruit species, are usually grown on trellises. Total world production of this fruit is surpassed only by all citrus and species of *Musa* (banana and plantain). Grapes derived from the European species, *V. vinifera*, have been prized as the source of wine since antiquity. Although wine can be made from any sweet fruit, the grape is the preferred species because the combination of sugars, acids, and astringent substances such as tannins gives character to the product. The name of wines, such as cabernet sauvignon and pinot noir, refer to the grape cultivar. Because these wines have become a standard product there is great reluctance to change grape cultivars used for wine, but various clones have been selected throughout the many years they have been cultivated. Some grapes (known as table grapes) can also be enjoyed fresh; many of the new cultivars bred for this purpose are seedless. Nonalcoholic grape juice is enjoyed in the United States; this industry derives from Concord, a cultivar of the American species *V. labrusca*, the fox grape. American grapes are typically winter-hardy and have a slip skin and a unique flavor referred to as foxy. Concord juice in the United States is also used to make the sweet wine used traditionally in Jewish ceremonies, a product often derided by wine connoisseurs but still enjoyed by millions of ordinary folk. (When the astronaut Gene Cernan landed on the moon, he expressed his wonder at the sight with the famous expression "Man O Manischewitz," the name of a popular brand!) American grapes have long been grown in Japan, where their foxy flavor is appreciated. The large-fruited table grape Italia, widely appreciated in Europe, has a muscat flavor that is similar to the foxy flavor of *labrusca* grapes, many of which are sweet and pleasant but insipid. The strong-flavored muscadine (*V. rotundifolia*), native to the southern United States, has a small market in this area for fresh fruit, juice, and wine.

The kiwifruit (*Actinidia deliciosa*, Actinidiaceae) is an example of a fruit species that has been essentially domesticated in the twentieth century. It derives from a gathered Chinese fruit known as yangtao, which had long been appreciated in China but was collected rather than cultivated. Introduced to the United States and New Zealand early in the twentieth century by the plant explorer E. H. (Chinese) Wilson, it was referred to as Chinese gooseberries. Although it remained a curiosity in the United States, New Zealand growers and nurserymen succeeded in domesticating the crop by selecting suitable male and female clones (the plant is dioecious), as well as techniques for cultivation. One seedling selected by A. Hayward Wright and subsequently named Hayward became the mainstay of the world industry. The fruit was exported to the United States and promoted by Frieda Caplan, a marketer of new crops. In 1959 the relatively unattractive brown fruit received the new name kiwifruit after the kiwi, an endemic flightless bird often used as a nickname for New Zealanders. Kiwifruit has a pleasant but weak flavor with very high vitamin C content, but the nutritious quality of the fruit has not been promoted; rather, it was the beautiful and unique appearance of the sliced flesh, which is used as a garnish on bakery products or as a component of mixed fruit, that made this fruit popular worldwide. The long storage life of the fruit made it possible for New Zealand to export the fruit year-round. The popularity of the crop made millionaires of many New Zealand growers, but as kiwifruit began to be grown in such countries as the United States, Italy, and Chile, the boom crashed and New Zealand growers had to struggle to survive. Kiwifruit is consumed out of hand in New Zealand, usually scooped with a spoon, but this technique has not caught on, and further expansion is probably linked to development of a simple method for peeling. A yellow-fleshed kiwifruit marketed as Zespri Gold (*A. chinensis*) was introduced at the turn of the twenty-first century, and the New Zealand growers are attempting to control its distribution. It is too early to know if this will succeed. A small-fruited hardy American species (*A. arguta*), sometimes called tara fig, is now cultivated in gardens but this species has not been commercialized.

Small Fruits

Strawberry, the most widely grown small fruit, has an interesting history. Although a small-fruited species of strawberry (*Fragaria vesca*, a diploid species, $2n = 16$) is native to Europe, the modern strawberry is derived from hybrids between two octoploid ($2n = 56$) native American species, *F. virginiana*, indigenous to the East Coast of North America, and *F. chiloensis*, native to Chile. Hybrids between these two species were produced naturally in Brest, France, early in the eighteenth century when a pistillate clone of the large-fruited *F. chiloensis*, introduced by Amédée François Frezier, a French army officer, was interplanted with staminate plants of *F. virginiana*. The new hybrids (now known as *Fragaria* × *ananassa*, or pineapple-strawberry) initiated the modern strawberry industry. Breeding efforts through the years have resulted in tremendous advances as the plant was changed from a predominantly dioecious species with male and female plants to a hermaphroditic species, in which flowers contain both stamens and pistils. Fruit size has been greatly increased, and modern cultivars tend to be very firm-fleshed (too firm for some), with improved flavor and appearance. Although strawberries are grown in all temperate countries, the industry is now concentrated in some favored locations such as southern California in the United States, southern Spain, and various locations in Italy. Some strawberries now are grown in greenhouses.

The genus *Rubus* is very diverse. The cultivated *Rubus* species known as brambles includes red raspberry (*R. idaeus*), black raspberry (*R. occidentalis*), and blackberry (*Rubus species*), including various interspecific hybrids between raspberry and blackberry, such as loganberry, boysenberry, and tayberry. Brambles have delicious flavors but marketing has been a problem because of the soft texture of the fruit.

Cultivated species of *Vaccinium* and *Ericaceae* are berry crops domesticated in the twentieth century. Blueberry (various species) is native to the United States and grows in bushes of various heights. The blue fruits are easy to preserve by freezing and have become very popular in the United States because of their use as a fresh fruit and in muffins or pancakes. They are increasing in popularity in Europe and in New Zealand. The cranberry (*V. macrocarpon*) is an unusual berry crop because it is grown submerged in bogs. The fruits are too acid to be eaten raw and are consumed processed as jelly or as a sauce. In the United States cranberry is a favorite food for the feast of Thanksgiving. Sweetened dilute cranberry juice, consumed alone or mixed with other fruit juices, has become popular because of its therapeutic benefits in urinary tract problems of women. Lingonberry (*V. vitisidaea minus*) is native to northern regions of Europe, Asia, and North America. The bright red fruit has long been gathered from wild stands in Scandinavia, and a large commerce developed from this source. Attempts to domesticate the crop are based on the management of natural stands. There are a number of other native *Vacciniums*, such as bilberry (*V. myrtillus*) and bog bilberry (*V. uliginosum*), that have been considered as possible domesticates.

Cultivated *Ribes* species include a number of popular berries such as black currant (*Ribes nigrum*), red and white currant (*R. sativum* and *R. rubrum*), and gooseberries (*R. grossularia*). They are too acid to be consumed fresh and are essentially used for jams, jellies, and juice. Black currant was the source of ribena syrup, widely fed to British children during World War II as a source of vitamins. Black currant is not widely grown in North America because cultivation was discouraged and even made illegal because the plants were alternate hosts for white pine blister rust.

See also **Apple; Berries; Grapes and Grape Juice; Wine; Wine in the Modern World.**

BIBLIOGRAPHY

Galleta, Gene J., and David G. Himelrick, eds. *Small Fruit Management*. Englewood Cliffs, N.J.: Prentice Hall, 1990.

Jackson, David I., and Norman E. Looney. *Temperate and Subtropical Fruit Production*. 2d ed. Wallingford, Oxon., U.K.: CABI, 1999.

Melvin, Neil Westwood. *Temperate-Zone Pomology: Physiology and Culture*. 3d ed. Portland, Oreg.: Timber Press, 1993.

Roach, F. A. 1985. *Cultivated Fruits of Britain*. Oxford: Blackwell, 1985.

Ryugo, Kay. *Fruit Culture: Its Science and Art*. New York: Wiley, 1988.

Jules Janick

TROPICAL AND SUBTROPICAL

Tropical and subtropical fruits, in contrast with temperate fruits, can be broadly defined as those meeting all of the following criteria: crops that have their origin and commercial growing areas (when such exist) in the tropics or subtropics, plants that are evergreen and perennial, crops with a limited degree of frost resistance, and plants whose growth is practically nonexistent below 50°F (10°C) (with some exceptions according to species and individual age). A distinction between tropical and subtropical is possible if one considers that tropical species are not only sensitive to temperatures below 68°F (20°C) but indeed require a climate with average mean temperatures higher than 50°F (10°C) for the coldest month (Watson and Moncur, 1985, p. 3). Additionally most tropicals require humid environmental conditions. Examples of truly tropical crops are traditional fruits native to Southeast Asia, like mangosteen, durian, and rambutan. A good example of a typical subtropical fruit crop is the cherimoya, which when cultivated in cold subtropical areas may suffer some foliage loss during the winter with regrowth in spring. However, some fruit crops can be cultivated equally well in either the tropics or the subtropics, of which the banana and the avocado are the most outstanding examples.

Strictly speaking, the tropics extend between the Tropics of Cancer and Capricorn, at 23° north and south of the equator. But, agronomically speaking, these boundaries are too rigid. Not only do they contain areas, especially at higher altitudes, that do not conform to the climatic characteristics generally assigned to the tropics, but regions outside this belt have coastal areas or insular climates that may exhibit climatic conditions fitting properly in the tropics. This is the reason why some climatologists have extended the region to the thirtieth parallels (Nakasone and Paull, 1998, p.1). In any event the main feature associated with the tropics is not so much that of heat but rather steady warm temperatures throughout the year. J. A. Samson (1986, p. 1) gave a good working definition of the tropical climate: temperature averages around 80.6°F (27°C), with the warmest month being only a few degrees higher than the coldest and temperature differences between night and day, at any given time, being greater than those between winter and summer, and, finally, little variation in day length, with the longest day being less than thirteen hours long. In comparison, the subtropics have hotter summers and cooler winters. Humidity is also generally lower. Day length differences become greater with increased latitude. The limit for the subtropics is the isotherm of 50°F (10°C) average for the coldest month (Nakasone and Paull, 1998, p. 12).

Hundreds of tropical and subtropical fruits exist, but only some fifty are well known throughout most of the world (Martin et al., 1987, p.1). These are important production crops (see Box 1), although a considerable gap exists between world per capita consumption (54.9 kilograms per year) and estimated consumption saturation (about 100 to 120 kilograms per year) (Jansen and Subramanian, 2000). Production and trade figures allow the division of tropicals and subtropicals into three main categories (Galán Saúco, 1996) with some overlapping.

1. Major fruits, such as banana and plantain, citrus, coconut, mango, and pineapple.

2. Minor fruits, such as abiu, atemoya, avocado, breadfruit, carambola, cashew nut, cherimoya, durian, guava, jaboticaba, jackfruit, langsat, litchi, longan, macadamia, mangosteen, papaya, passion fruit, pulusan, rambutan, sapodilla, soursop, and white sapote.

3. Wild fruits belonging to diverse botanical families. These are not cultivated commercially in any country and are much in need of characterization, conservation (both in situ, including on farm, and ex situ), selection, and breeding.

Major-category fruits are cultivated in most tropical (and subtropical) countries and are well known in both local and export-import markets. Minor fruits are not so extensively cultivated, and consumption and trade tend to be more limited, both geographically and quantitatively. However, many are of considerable economic importance in their respective regional markets, as is the case with carambola, durian, and mangosteen, which are major fruits throughout Southeast Asia (Anang and Chan, 1999).

TABLE 1

Production of major tropical and subtropical fruits in 2000

Fruit	World production (x 1,000 t)	Important producing countries
Orange	66,055	Brazil, United States, India, Mexico, Spain, China, Italy, Egypt, Pakistan, Greece, South Africa
Banana	58,687	Burundi, Nigeria, Costa Rica, Mexico, Colombia, Ecuador, Brazil, India, Indonesia, Philippines, Papua New Guinea, Spain
Coconut	48,375	Indonesia, Philippines, India, Sri Lanka, Brazil, Thailand, Mexico, Vietnam, Malaysia, Papua New Guinea
Plantain	30,583	Colombia, Ecuador, Peru, Venezuela, Ivory Coast, Cameroon, Sri Lanka, Myanmar
Mango	24,975	India, Indonesia, Philippines, Thailand, Mexico, Haiti, Brazil, Nigeria
Papaya	8,426	Nigeria, Mexico, Brazil, China, India, Indonesia, Thailand, Sri Lanka
Avocado	2,331	Mexico, United States, Dominican Republic, Brazil, Colombia, Chile, South Africa, Indonesia, Israel, Spain
Pineapple	13,455	Philippines, India, Indonesia, China, Brazil, United States, Mexico, Nigeria, Vietnam

SOURCE: http://www.fao.org.

Botanical Aspects

Tropical and subtropical fruits include not only woody plants, such as the mango or the orange, but also herbaceous crops like the banana and vines like the passion fruit. Most botanical families can lay claim to at least one species of tropical or subtropical fruit. Franklin Martin and colleagues (1987) list some 137 families, and the best known are in Box 2.

From the botanical point of view, a fruit is the structure developed from flowers or inflorescences. In most cases the fruit consists only of the developed ovary, but it may include other parts of the flower, such as the pedicel, sepal, or receptacle, or even a portion of the seed stalk. As with temperate crops, many different fruit types appear among the tropicals and subtropicals, from single fruits, including berries, such as the avocado or orange; drupes, such as the mango; pomes, such as the loquat; capsules, such as the durian; nutlets, such as the litchi and the longan; to compound fruits, as in the typical syncarpium of the pineapple; or even a bunch of individual berries, as in the banana. To differentiate fruit crops from perennial vegetables whose fruits are also eaten, it is necessary to keep in mind that in a horticultural sense a fruit is something that is normally eaten fresh and out of hand. A number of exceptions exist, like the breadfruit and the plantain, considered fruits by all but only palatable when cooked, as if they were vegetables. Nuts, obviously not eaten out of hand, and some tree crops whose seeds are the only part eaten, are also included among tropicals and subtropicals in most horticultural books and as such are included in this entry.

TABLE 2

Best-known tropical and subtropical fruits and their botanical families

Family	Common names of species
Anacardiaceae	Mango, Cashew
Annonaceae	Cherimoya, Guanábana, Custard apple
Bombacaceae	Durian
Bromeliaceae	Pineapple
Cactaceae	Pitaya
Caricaceae	Papaya
Ebenaceae	Caki
Guttifferae	Mangosteen
Lauraceae	Avocado
Malphigiaceae	Acerola
Meliaceae	Langsat or Lanson
Moraceae	Breadfruit, Jackfruit
Musaceae	Banana, Plantain
Myrtaceae	Guava
Oxalidaceae	Carambola
Palmaceae	Coconut, Date
Passifloraceae	Passion fruit, Granadilla
Proteaceae	Macadamia
Rosaceae	Loquat
Rutaceae	Orange, Grapefruit, Mandarin
Sapindaceae	Litchi, Longan, Rambutan
Sapotaceae	Chicosapote, Lucuma
Solanaceae	Sweet pepino, Lulo, Tamarillo

Areas of Origin and Spread

Although most of the continents, including the islands throughout the Pacific, have contributed tropical and subtropical fruits (see Box 3), most of the best-known ones came from the tropical and subtropical regions of America (for example, papaya, avocado, pineapple, guava) and Asia (for example, orange and most citrus fruits, mango, banana, litchi). Only two commercially important fruits originated in Oceania, the macadamia in Australia (specifically Queensland) and the coconut in the Pacific, the latter to the extent that its origin is considered pantropical (Martin et al., 1987, p. 47). The only important fruit native to the African continent is the date. Europe, with no tropical and limited subtropical areas, has none.

Spread to the regions surrounding their areas of origin probably began early, as soon as humans realized their value in terms of nutrition and the variety they could add to the primitive diets of the time. The potential of some species to provide not only food but also shelter or clothing (some types of banana), wood, and medicine hastened distribution.

An outstanding example is the mango. Native to the Indo-Burman region, by the end of the fourth century C.E. it had spread to all the tropical countries of Southeast Asia (Galán Saúco, 1999, p. 36). The Arabs were apparently responsible for its spread to the east coast of Africa around 700 C.E. as an adjunct to their slaving ventures. Just as Malaysians introduced the banana to Madagascar some two centuries earlier, Islamic domination brought the orange to the Mediterranean and southern Europe. Crops from the Americas are not as well documented, but archaeological findings have shown connections between the cultures of Mexico and Peru dating as far back as 1000 B.C.E. (Purseglove, 1968, p.12), giving a solid opportunity for some tropical and subtropical fruits to spread around the warmer American lands.

Soon after the European discovery of America, the Old and New Worlds rapidly exchanged crops. The sixteenth-century monk Bartolomé de las Casas mentioned that orange seeds were carried from the island of La Gomera (Canary Islands, Spain) to Haiti on Christopher Columbus's second voyage in 1493 (Amador de los Ríos, 1851–1855, vol. 1, p. 3). It is similarly well documented that the banana was carried to Santo Domingo from the Canary Islands in 1516 (the Canaries were a routine last port of call for European ships facing an Atlantic crossing). After Columbus's voyages, a veritable avalanche of expeditions explored all corners of the world, and where the ships went, food went also, to say nothing of tasty fruits and easily propagated species. Between 1500 and 1650 Portuguese sailors connected Brazil and the Cape of Good Hope, touching Goa, Malacca, the Moluccas, Canton, and Macao, trading from there with Japan and Formosa. The Spanish Manila galleon route dominated shipping from 1565 to 1815, plying the seas between the Philippines and Mexico. Dutch, British, and French voyagers were also important in spreading tropical fruits around the world.

No hard and fast rule explains why some fruits spread quickly throughout the world while others remain limited in scope even in the twenty-first century. Several factors may be involved, among them crop adaptability, shelf life, ease of propagation (including the capacity to survive long voyages), size of the plant, multiplicity of uses (that is, other than as fresh fruit), and taste acceptance.

The excellent taste of the pineapple, the long-lasting viability of the plant's suckers as planting material, and the rapidity with which it produces fruit all account for its prompt appearance in Europe—albeit in glasshouses—and India as early as 1548 (Nagy and Shaw, 1980, p.16; Galán Saúco, 2001). Similar considerations apply to the banana and the papaya and even to woody perennial trees like the mango or the guava, which soon spread throughout the tropics and subtropics, even though their size precluded cultivation in greenhouses outside these areas. On the other hand true tropical trees are usually demanding in climate and in some cases are difficult to propagate. The mangosteen, rambutan, and durian (this last deemed by many people to have a peculiar taste) have remained confined almost exclusively to their area of origin in Southeast Asia. The mangosteen is notable among tropical fruits in that it has proven particularly intractable to most attempts to establish it outside of its area of origin via the usual method, which is selection or breeding of cultivars capable of adapting to environments different in climate or edaphic conditions. The species consists of a single genotype, which in essence means no genetic variation exists with which to breed or improve stock, and it is entirely possible that its evolution has ceased (Yaacob and Tindall, 1995, p. 25).

Nutritional and Medicinal Value

Despite the relatively low caloric values of tropical and subtropical fruits (banana and plantain and avocado are the notable exceptions), they play an important role in human diet mainly because of their high and diverse vitamin and mineral content. This has been of capital importance in the tropics, where people have been consuming them since ancient times, either by collecting fruit from the wild or by cultivating plants in kitchen gardens. They have become an important part of the diet of people in the developed countries of the world, especially among the health and fitness conscious. In a properly balanced diet, tropical and subtropical fruits may be an excellent component for the sports-oriented person. This is not to say that one can live by tropical fruits alone or that they can be considered staple fruits within the diet (again the banana and especially its relative the plantain are the exception in some tropical areas). But nutritionists have long recommended a minimum of one hundred grams of fruit per day and that it be as varied as possible. Toward the end of the twentieth century market campaigns commonly recommended consumption of five

A traditional Greek fig wheel, showing the manner in which figs were dried and shipped since ancient times. This photograph dates from 1910. ROUGHWOOD COLLECTION.

fruits per day, which, while it may have more to do with commerce than with science, does reinforce the value of fruit as a part of the human diet.

Tropical and subtropical fruits also have some medicinal properties. Many tropical fruits, notably the mango and the papaya, are a good source of carotene (provitamin A). An indication of the high content of this vitamin is the orange-yellow color of the flesh. Others, like all citrus fruits and the guava, are well known as good sources of ascorbic acid (vitamin C). In general they are not a good source of the B group of vitamins (thiamine, riboflavin, and niacin) except for nuts, which are also a good source of vitamin E, proteins, and fats (Martin et al., 1987, p. 7). Tropical and subtropical fruits are also rich in pectin, fiber, and cellulase, which promote intestinal motility. In common with other fruits, they are good sources of antioxidants, and some are also good sources of organic acids, which stimulate appetite and aid digestion.

Values for the chemical composition of tropical and subtropical fruits are widely available in many texts, some of which are included in the bibliography cited here, but the salient points related to general nutritional value follow. Banana is a good source of vitamins A, B, and C and riboflavin. Together with the tropical and subtropical nut fruits, the banana has the highest calorie content. It is low in protein and fat and rich in potassium. Easy to digest, it constitutes an excellent food for young and old alike and is recommended for athletes. Avocado has a good oil content (of the different avocado races, the West Indian types have the lowest) composed of highly digestible unsaturated fatty acids, and it is rich in folic acid. Some cultivars contain good quantities of proteins, vitamin A, riboflavin, and phosphorus.

All citrus fruits have fairly high amounts of vitamin C, as does the guava, which in turn contains fair amounts of niacin and iron. The papaya has high quantities of vitamins C and A as well as potassium and calcium, and it is low in carbohydrates. However, its outstanding feature, which distinguishes the papaya from all other fruits, is the fact that it contains papain, an enzyme that promotes digestion (although papain content does decrease as the fruit ripens). It is highly recommended for people with certain digestive disorders. The mango is rich in provitamin A and carbohydrates and is an acceptable source of vitamin C. The same is true of the passion fruit, which additionally has acceptable quantities of niacin. The pineapple is also rich in vitamin C and carbohydrates and is a good source of calcium, phosphorus, iron, potassium, and thiamine.

The litchi and the longan, most of the Annonaceae, and the durian are all good sources of carbohydrates and vitamin C. The durian also has fair amounts of iron and niacin. The mangosteen is considered by many to be one of the finest tasting fruits of all, according it the title of "queen of fruits" (Yaacob and Tindall, 1995, p. v). It is one of the lowest in nutritive value, but even so it can boast moderate quantities of calcium, phosphorus, ascorbic acid, and carbohydrates. The carambola is low in calories and rich in vitamin C, and it is an adequate source of vitamin A. It is prohibited for people with kidney problems (specifically stone formation) due to its high oxalic acid content, but new cultivars have been selected for lower oxalic content while maintaining sugar and vitamin levels (Galán Saúco et al., 1993, p. 5).

The macadamia nut is rich in protein, oil, iron, calcium, thiamine, riboflavin, and niacin. The subtropical date also has a high nutritive value. Rich in carbohydrates, it is a good source of vitamin A, potassium, and iron but is low in oils and sodium. The coconut is high in phosphorus, iron, proteins, and oils—in this case all saturated fatty acids, the consumption of which should be limited according to health recommendations. Coconut milk aids in balancing pH in the body due to its alkaline reaction.

The medicinal value of tropicals and subtropicals, both the fruits themselves and their actual plant parts (bark, roots, and even pollen), has long been acknowledged by the diverse peoples in and around their areas of origin. These regions are rich in recipes for preparing infusions, decoctions, syrups, pastes, jellies, juices, and so forth for myriad purposes. All the citrus fruits and several others rich in vitamin C are obviously useful to prevent colds and similar infections, while fruits rich in vitamin A

prevent dietary deficiencies, such as those leading to blindness. An excellent compilation of popular medicinal uses is in the book *Fruits of Warm Climates* (1987), written by Julia F. Morton, but a few examples follow.

The date has a high tannin content that is reportedly useful as an astringent in intestinal complaints and is good for sore throats, colds, and bronchial catarrh. Breadfruit is reported to reduce high blood pressure. Carambola fruit and pineapple juice are reportedly useful diuretics, while the flesh of the very young fruit of the pineapple is reputedly an abortifacient. The skin of the avocado and extracts of ripe and unripe fruits and seeds of the papaya reportedly have antibiotic properties. In traditional medicine a decoction of young mango leaves is recommended as a remedy for asthma, blenorraghia, and bronchitis. The roots, bark, leaves, and immature fruits of many tropical fruit crops are widely used in the tropics as astringents to stop gastroenteritis, diarrhea, and dysentery. A decoction of the boiled fruit of the sapodilla has also been reported useful in treating diarrhea. The flesh of the longan has been recommended for its febrifuge and vermifuge properties and as an antidote against some types of poisons. The infusion of passion fruit leaves, rich in the glycosid passiflorine, is reported to have sedative properties.

Consumption and Other Uses

The main method of consumption of most tropical and subtropical fruits is as fresh fruit. The breadfruit is the most important exception, as it is only eaten cooked. Nuts can be eaten directly or processed (roasted, candied, and so forth). Salads, both savory and sweet types, are prepared with many fruits. Indeed consumption is virtually as unlimited as the chef's imagination. Jams, jellies, juices (made with fresh fruits, concentrates, or frozen pulp), sauces, ice cream and sherbets, and other desserts and diverse confectionaries are typical of the uses to which tropical and subtropical fruits are put, both industrially and domestically. Infusions as social beverages, not as medicinal remedies, are made from many different fruits.

A specific product is baby food, especially made with "healthy" fruits like the banana or the papaya, based on different kinds of puree (industrially known as aseptic, chilled aseptic, or simply chilled purees). Flour is also made from the durian and the banana. Pickles and chutneys are made from many fruits, the most famous of which is mango chutney, a staple in Indian cuisine and highly esteemed by gourmets. Dips are also popular in many countries, of which perhaps the best known is avocado-based guacamole. Guava paste or spread is consumed, usually with bread and cheese, in many countries, particularly Cuba, Brazil, and the Canary Islands.

Besides their edible and pleasant fruits, the actual plants of several tropical and subtropical fruit crops are also put to good use. Descriptions of the many properties of parts other than fruits—wood, leaves, flowers, roots, seeds—are frequently dealt with in older texts (including, among others not yet mentioned, Popenoe, 1974 [1920]; Chandler, 1958; Singh, 1960; Purseglove, 1968; Ochse et al., 1972; Coronel, 1983), but a clear dearth of in-depth studies on many of these aspects is apparent. The potential of leaves or flower extracts as biological products for use against pests and diseases is in much the same situation and is an issue relevant to organic produce, of increasing importance to concerned consumers. Some outstanding examples of alternative uses follow.

Religious uses. Some orchards of date palms in the Mediterranean are maintained solely to supply young leaves used on Palm Sunday during the Christian Easter week.

Oils, perfumes, and the like. An essential oil is extracted from some citrus species, particularly from certain oranges and their flowers. Avocado oil, occasionally used for cooking, is a commercial product in some countries. Soaps, bath gels, and shampoos include extracts from different tropical and subtropical fruits. Loquat seed oil is used in soaps and paints.

Animal feed. Banana leaves, pseudostems, and fruits are fed to goats in several countries, particularly in the Canary Islands (Galán Saúco, 2001). Dried dates and their pits, breadfruit leaves, and mango seed kernels are used as feed in several countries. In India, Gandhi recommended using peanuts and mango seed kernels rather than expensive cereals and imported fodders (Galán Saúco, 1999, p. 44).

Textiles and paper. Fibers from pineapple and banana leaves are used in several places for papermaking and cloth, notably in the Philippines to make the typical loose-fitting shirts called guayaberas.

Handicrafts. Mature date palm leaves and avocado wood are excellent for decorative carvings.

Construction and furniture. The wood of breadfruit, citrus in general, guava, longan, mango, and mangosteen are regularly used for interior paneling or for furniture. The wood of the caki is highly prized. Banana and date palm leaves are a traditional roofing material in many regions.

Firewood. Orange wood is long lasting, while avocado wood is highly combustible. Mango wood is held in high esteem in Bangladesh, to the extent that the locals consider the best trees those that faithfully provide both wood and fruit (Galán Saúco, 1999, p. 44).

Other uses. For many years chewing gum (chicle) was made from sapodilla latex. Although the industry subsequently began to use artificial substances, the trend in favor of organic products may signify a return to traditional chicle. Garden brooms are made out of the stripped fruit clusters of the date palm. Fishermen in the Pacific have used the coconut as a fishing aid, chewing the coconut

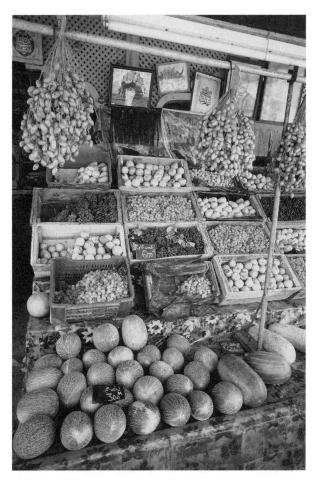

Dates, figs, jujubes, citrons, oranges, pomegranates, and a rich array of other fruits crowd this enticing stand in the market at Kairouan, Tunisia. © DAVE BARTRUFF/CORBIS.

meat and spitting the resulting mass onto the water to produce a glossy calm spot, smooth enough to allow a brief glimpse of the fish below the surface (Hawaii).

The potential for development of tropical fruits does not rely only on consumption. Planting tropical fruits for agroforestry and for urban horticulture are important endeavors. In fact tropical countries like Malaysia encourage and promote intercropping of suitable perennial fruits with compatible forest species (Anang and Chan, 1999). Many tropical fruit trees make beautiful ornamental plants not only capable of improving air quality but also capable of contributing to ecological stability. They are easy to handle in gardens or in industrial or community buildings and are adequate for planting along country roads. These considerations may involve new lines of research, particularly searching for cultivars that can be oriented toward wood (or flower) production. As indicated at the World Conference on Horticultural Research (WCHR) held in Rome in June 1998, international agencies and local authorities should work together with university and government scientists to promote the

DATES

The date palm (*Phoenix dactylifera*) has been cultivated in the Middle East since ancient times, where it has assumed a role as more than simply a source of food and become culturally associated with Islamic culture. In the words of the Prophet Muhammad, "There is among trees one tree which is blessed . . . it is the palm."

The date palm is adapted to areas with long, very hot summers with little rain, low humidity, and abundant underground water. This is expressed by the saying that the date palm "must have its feet in running water and its head in the fire of the sky." These conditions are found in oases and river valleys in the arid subtropical deserts of the Middle East, the area of origin of the date palm. This is the "Fertile Crescent," where agriculture in the Old World is thought to have arisen. The date palm has been cultivated in this area since about 7000 B.C.E., and was possibly one of the first crops domesticated. By 2000 B.C.E., date palm culture had spread to Palestine, Arabia, Egypt, North Africa, and western India.

Date palms or their wild progenitors were undoubtedly used by man even before actual cultivation began. A date palm oasis must have been a welcome sight to those crossing the desert. Here were water, shade, and fresh and dried fruits high in carbohydrates. The dried fruits were easily stored and transported after leaving the oasis. The date palm also supplied building material, fiber, fuel, animal feed, honey (syrup), and wine.

The date palm had great spiritual and cultural significance to peoples of the region. It is depicted on many ancient tablets, bas-reliefs, and so forth. The date palm is mentioned a number of times in Jewish and Christian writings, but achieved its greatest esteem in Islamic culture. The date palm was consecrated by Muhammad in both his public and private life, and is prominently mentioned in the Koran and in other Islamic writings. Date consumption spread from Arabia along with Islam, and dates are now eaten by Muslims in areas unsuitable for their production, such as Indonesia and Thailand. Date culture eventually spread to non-Islamic countries with suitable growing conditions, but its culture and consumption in these areas is minor compared to that in the Islamic world.

In the early twenty-first century, the Middle East is still the center of date production and consumption. The largest producers of dates are Egypt, Iran, Iraq, and Saudi Arabia. Most dates are consumed locally, but there is some export, mostly to other Islamic countries that do not have suitable growing conditions. Production of dates is highly specialized and labor-intensive. There are great variations in date growing practices: from traditional oasis culture to modern industrial plantings. The United States has led the way in mechanization of date production, but this practice is spreading to other countries as they modernize.

There are thousands of local varieties of dates grown in the Middle East. Other countries have a more limited number of varieties derived from a few importations. Recently, *barhee* and *medjool* have become increasingly prominent due to their use as foundation materials for tissue-cultured plants. The use of tissue-cultured plants has become common in some countries as the increase in land area devoted to date culture has expanded beyond that which can be planted with offshoots, the traditional method of propagation.

Dates are consumed fresh or in processed form. Fresh market dates are divided into dry, semidry, and soft varieties. In Middle Eastern countries, they are also eaten in the early *khalal* stage. Dates are nutritious, being high in carbohydrate and fiber. In most varieties, the sugar content is mostly invert sugar (glucose and fructose), with only low levels of sucrose. Processed products are more common in the Middle East, where large amounts of dates are produced, than they are elsewhere. Processed products include sugars, pastes, flours, preserves, syrups, and fermentation products.

Robert R. Krueger

utilization of horticultural plants in large metropolitan areas (Gosselin et al., 1999).

Commercialization and Trade

In addition to citrus and the banana, four other tropical and subtropical fruits, pineapple, mango, avocado, and papaya, dominate the fresh fruit export trade (see Box 4). Pineapple clearly leads the ranking in processed fruits with a wide range of products, although juice and rings in syrup are the best known.

Many other tropical and subtropical fruits are no longer exotic products in world markets, having become firmly established with guaranteed supply and reasonable prices. Carambola, guava, litchi, mangosteen, passion fruit, and rambutan have experienced notable development. The main importers of most of these tropical and subtropical fruits are the European Union, the United States, Japan, Canada, and China.

Exports of fresh fruits are mainly by ship or surface transport. Postharvest techniques for extending the shelf life of most tropical and subtropical fruits have been mastered, and refrigerated boats (some even providing controlled atmosphere installations) move these commodities from production countries to their ultimate markets with ease. A small proportion of the major fruits, particularly pineapple, mango, and papaya, are transported by air, either destined specially for gourmet or niche markets or for celebrations at certain times of the year, such as Christmas and New Year's, when they command higher prices. Some of the minor crops, still considered exotics, like the mangosteen and the rambutan, have a more difficult postharvest life and therefore are exported by air.

Many countries from virtually all the continents have designated specific areas for production of fruits destined purely for export. Those countries include India, Malaysia, Thailand, and China in Asia; the Philippines and Australia in Oceania; South Africa and Ivory Coast in Africa; Mexico, Brazil, the United States, Peru, Costa Rica, and Chile in North and South America; Spain in Europe; and Israel.

While banana, pineapple, and citrus have a long history of international trade, the avocado trade burst upon the scene in the 1970s. The mango did not become a well-known fruit (from a consumption point of view) until the 1990s, with Mexico as the leading exporter. The papaya and the litchi may still revolutionize trade.

Of particular relevance for the development of tropical and subtropical fruit trade is the World Trade Organization (WTO) agreement in Marrakech on 15 April 1994 following the conclusion of the Uruguayan round of General Agreement on Tariffs and Trade (GATT) talks. Basically these agreements established the principle of free trade not exposed to arbitrary market entrance taxes, and obligate signatory countries (in practice most of the world) to use only sanitary and phytosanitary quarantine measures based on solid scientific information, thus effectively halting the use of these measures as a loophole to arbitrarily restrict imports.

As in other commodities, an interesting market is developing for organically produced tropical and subtropical fruits, and organic pineapples and bananas are available in Western markets.

International Forum on Tropical and Subtropical Fruits

Many organizations and horticultural societies at national and international levels are dedicated to particular tropical or subtropical fruits (or a closely related group). Their members include amateurs, growers, researchers and academics, handlers, traders, and consumers. By reason of both magnitude and global concern, some of these merit special mention.

The International Society of Horticultural Science (ISHS), headquartered in Louvain, Belgium, has established a Commission of Tropical and Subtropical Horti-

culture with working groups in specific tropical and subtropical fruits. The ISHS meets regularly in different countries to discuss aspects of production, research, and trade of these fruits, and it holds an international congress every four years, which congregates a minimum of four thousand people.

The Interamerican Society of Tropical Horticulture was formerly known as the Tropical Region of the American Society of Horticultural Science. It holds annual meetings in different American countries with tropical crops to discuss the same issues mentioned above but including vegetables and ornamental plants.

The Intergovernmental Group on Bananas and on Tropical Fruits, under the auspices of the Food and Agriculture Organization of the United Nations (FAO), meets every two years to discuss issues related to marketing and trade.

See also **Banana and Plantain**; **Durian**; **Nuts**; **Vegetables**.

BIBLIOGRAPHY

Amador de Los Ríos, José. *Historia General y Natural de las Indias, Islas y Tierra-Firme del Mar Océano, por el Capitán Gonzalo Fernández de Oviedo y Valdés* (General and natural history of the Indies, islands, and Terra Firme of the Ocean Sea). Critical edition. 4 vols. Madrid: Impr. de Real Academia de la Historia, 1851–1855.

Anang, S., and Y. K. Chan. "Recent Developments of the Fruit Industry in Malaysia." Paper presented at the FAO–IGG on Bananas and on Tropical Fruits. Gold Coast, Australia, 4–8 May 1999.

Chandler, William Henry. *Evergreen Orchards.* Philadelphia: Lea and Febiger, 1958.

Coronel, Robert E. *Promising Fruits of the Philippines.* College, Laguna, Philippines: College of Agriculture, University of the Philippines at Los Baòos, 1983.

Galán Saúco, Víctor. 1999. *El Cultivo del Mango* (The cultivation of the mango). Madrid: Ediciones Mundi-Prensa, 1999.

Galán Saúco, Víctor. "Current Situation, Trends, and Future of Agronomic Research on Tropical Fruits." In *Proceedings of the International Conference on Tropical Fruits, Kuala Lumpur, Malaysia, 23–26 July 1996.*

Galán Saúco, Víctor. "Greenhouse Cultivation of Tropical Fruits." International Symposium on Tropical and Subtropical Fruits. Cairns, Australia, 26 November–1 December 2001; *Acta Horticulturae* 575 (2002): 727–735.

Galán Saúco, Victor, Umberto G. Menini, and H. Don Tindall. *Carambola Cultivation.* FAO Plant Production and Protection Paper 108. Rome: Food and Agriculture Organization of the United Nations, 1993.

Gosselin, A., S. Yelle, and B. Dansereau. 1999. "Policy Issues in University Horticultural Research." *Acta Horticulturae* 495 (1999): 511–515.

Hawaii. "Canoe Plants of Ancient Hawaii." Available at http://hawaii-nation.org.

Jansen, M. J. J., and B. Subramaniam. "Long-term Perspectives of Fruit and Other Tree Crops in the New Century." *Acta Horticulturae* 531 (2000): 23–27.

Martin, Franklin W., Carl W. Campbell, and Ruth M. Ruberté. *Perennial Edible Fruits of the Tropics: An Inventory.* Washington, D.C.: U.S. Department of Agriculture, Agricultural Research Service, 1987.

Morton, Julia F. *Fruits of Warm Climates.* Miami, Fla.: Morton, 1987.

Munier, Pierre. *Le Palmier-Dattier* [The Date palm]. Paris: Maisonneuve and Larose, 1973.

Nagy, Steven, and Philip E. Shaw. *Tropical and Subtropical Fruits: Composition, Properties, and Uses.* Westport, Conn.: Avi, 1980.

Nakasone, Henry Y., and Robert E. Paull. *Tropical Fruits.* New York: Cab International, 1998.

Ochse, J. J., M. J. Soule, M. J. Dickman, and C. Wehlburg. *Cultivo y Mejoramiento de Plantas Tropicales y Subtropicales* [Cultivation and improvement of tropical and subtropical plants]. 2 vols. México: Limusa-Wiley, 1972.

Popenoe, Paul B. *Date Growing in the Old and New Worlds.* Altadena, Calif.: West India Gardens, 1913.

Popenoe, Wilson. *Manual of Tropical and Subtropical Fruits.* New York: Hafner Press, 1974. Facsimile of the original 1920 edition.

Purseglove, J. W. *Tropical Crops: Dicotyledons.* 2 vols. New York: Wiley, 1968.

Samson, J. A. *Tropical Fruits.* 2d ed. New York: Longman, 1986.

Singh, Lal Behari. *The Mango: Botany, Cultivation, and Utilization.* New York: Interscience Publishers, 1960.

Watson, B. J., and M. Moncur. *Criteria for Determining Survival: Commercial and Best Minimum July Temperatures for Various Tropical Fruits in Australia (S. Hemisphere).* Queensland, Australia: Wet Tropical Regional Publication, 1985.

Yaacob, Othman, and H. D. Tindall. *Mangosteen Cultivation.* FAO Plant Production and Protection Paper 129. Rome: Food and Agriculture Organization of the United Nations, 1995.

Zaid, Abdelouahhab. *Date Palm Cultivation.* Rome: Food and Agriculture Organization of the United Nations, 1999.

Víctor Galán Saúco

FRYING. Fried foods, though widely considered indelicate, are also among the most ephemeral. Regarding fried foods, a Chinese proverb states: It is better that your guests wait for their meal, than that the meal wait for the guests. Fried dishes cannot wait, and if allowed to stand, rising interior steam causes them to lose their crisp exterior and, thereby, their character.

Frying is a means of heat transfer that works by both conduction (direct contact) and convection (the natural movement of molecules in a fluid). Like broiling, boiling, and baking, frying is a method of cooking, but unlike water-based cooking (boiling, braising, or steaming), frying uses dry heat. Oil wicks moisture away from food surfaces. Because oil heats to a higher temperature than water, frying is faster than boiling, and fried surfaces, rather than becoming soft as they do when boiled,

broiled, or steamed, coagulate. The resulting fried food is incomparably tasty, crisp, and beautiful. Frying comprises not only deep-frying and pan-frying, but also the cooking method used to prepare common foods such as pancakes and fried eggs as well as less-known foods such as the Indian dish *dalia uppma*, an herbed bulgur with fried vegetables. Most, but not all, of the world's cultures have practiced frying.

Some fried foods are so popular that they can be identified as cultural stereotypes. American french fries and Middle Eastern falafel (chickpea or fava bean fritters) are examples. Native Americans of the Southwest are known for fry bread, and corn dogs are associated with New York's Coney Island. The American South has southern fried chicken, while in Asia, sweet potatoes are fried and served from vendors' carts. In Mexico, on the *zócalo* (the central square), vendors working from carts sell *churros*, a deep-fried pastry.

Advantages and Disadvantages

Through the ages, frying has remained popular because it adds an outside layer of flavor and crunch to soft foods, such as eggplant and okra. In addition, frying cooks and browns beautifully. It adds texture and yields the smooth and taste-imparting feel that comes only from various oils and fats.

On the negative side, the process of deep-fat frying is dangerous and requires special equipment and controlled environments. To avoid the overflow of hot oil from the pan, large temperature-controlled deep fryers are used, and these pans are filled only about one-third of their depth with oil. In addition, to maintain the desired high temperature, deep fryers are not filled with food, but rather, food is fried in small batches. Moist foods are not placed in hot oil because they cause boiling and popping, which can be dangerous. To avoid burns and fires protective gloves and clothing, long-handled utensils, as well as fire extinguishers and baking soda, are used. Unlike water, oil can catch on fire, and oil fires spread quickly. If a pan of oil catches fire, the pan is covered with a lid, doused with salt, or sprayed with a fire extinguisher. A stream of water is not effective in dousing an oil fire.

The use of oils and fats has also become a health concern. Those who support frying claim that with fast, clean frying, only a small amount of oil remains on the food, and certain oils and fats are healthier than others. Olive oil and canola oil, monounsaturated vegetable oils, are recommended for human consumption, while saturated oils, such as palm and coconut oil, or saturated fats, such as butter or lard, are not recommended. Canola oil is considered good for one's health because of its ratio of linoleic acid (an omega-6 fatty acid) to linolenic acid (an omega-3). A balance of omega-6s and omega-3s is an asset to health, with other oils often lacking the omega-3s. Canola oil offers the best balance for omega-3 and omega-6 fatty acids.

Methods of Frying and Equipment

Frying methods include sautéing, stir-frying, pan-frying, and deep-fat frying. These styles of frying form a continuum based on the amount of oil used, with sautéing using the least oil and deep-fat frying using the most.

Each of the principal frying methods is associated with a particular pan. Pan-frying is practiced in stainless steel, aluminum, and heavy cast-iron skillets, all with sloping sides. To sauté, there exists a French sauterne or sauté pan, which is wide like a skillet, but has low and straight sides. Deep-frying occurs in the deep fryer or wok, with either a fry basket insert, the long-handled slotted skimmer, or, as in China, the spider (small basket) attached to a long bamboo handle. Deep-frying thermometers are used to help the cook maintain a constant temperature. Finally, when fried foods, such as bacon or potato chips, are removed from the oil, they are placed on drip racks or paper towels. Deep-fat fryers are available in many sizes, from large multigallon commercial vats to small personal fryers that hold two or three cups of oil.

Other frying pans, too, are associated with specific foods. In crêpe pans, thin pancakes are cooked in a style associated with classical French cooking. Round or oval omelet pans are used to fry omelets. Heavy cast-iron chicken fryers are deep pans that include nippled lids that allow moisture to drip back onto the frying chicken. Restaurant kitchens often fry eggs, pancakes, sausages, and sandwiches on large steel frying surfaces called griddles, but home cooks can purchase small, hand-held griddle pans for the same purpose.

With a wok, many foods are stir-fried in the style of several Asian traditions. Woks are available as self-contained electric units or as wide, deeply sloped circular pans that fit over a gas flame. They are often sold with lids so that foods can be steamed for part of the cooking time. Before vegetables, seafood, poultry, or meats are added to the stir-fry pan, a small amount of oil is heated to a high temperature. In China, where stir-frying is an ancient tradition as well as a modern art form, small pieces of food are placed in a large pan over intense heat, and they are stirred quickly as they cook.

Oils and Fats

Frying fats may be solid or liquid. In selecting an oil or fat, the oil should be fresh and clean. Its flavor should not overpower the food being cooked, and monounsaturated vegetable oils have been recommended for presumed health reasons. Solid vegetable shortenings contain emulsifiers, which make them good for use in cakes, but poor for frying. The emulsifiers lower smoke points to about 370°F. Margarine and butter spreads are also not recommended for frying as they contain a variety of fats and even water.

Butter is a special case, as it adds much-valued flavor to many foods. Butter, however, until it is clarified, contains milk solids and burns at about 250°F. When the solids are removed by clarification, butter is an improved medium for frying, and its smoke point rises to 375°F. In India, both solids and water are removed from butter, and the resulting ghee or *usli* ghee is used for pan- and deep-frying. Lard as well as chicken, duck, and goose fats are also used successfully for frying. They impart excellent flavor but prompt health concerns among some researchers.

The purest flavor and safest frying are achieved when oil and fats are used one time. If frying is continuous for long periods, the oil requires changing, as it begins to darken or deteriorate. If frying oil is too hot, it will burn or break down, and if too cold, or less than about 300°F, the food being fried will absorb too much oil and become greasy.

Smoke Points

Frying is faster than boiling or steaming because oils get hotter than do water or steam. Smoke points, however, limit maximum possible frying temperatures. Oil is too hot when it reaches the smoke point, the temperature at which the oil starts to smoke, deteriorate, and burn. Too much heat causes gaseous fumes and chemically active, free fatty acids to negatively impact flavor. Maintaining the optimum temperature can be challenging, as each time oil is used, it picks up food particles, breaks down, and loses its ability to absorb heat. In addition, over-used or rancid oil smells and tastes bad.

Oils deteriorate by oxidation or contact with the air, and heat speeds this process. Thus, in storage and cooking, contact with air should be minimized. For deep-frying, a deep and narrow pan is better than a shallow, wide one because it allows for less air contact.

Suitable frying oils have high smoke points; the higher the smoke point, the faster the cooking. Depending on the oil, smoke points range from a low 250°F to a high 520°F. For example, while water boils at 212°F, the favored frying oils such as olive, peanut, and canola have smoke points ranging from 410°F to 437°F and are best heated to 365°F. This temperature cooks food quickly yet does not burn these oils.

Cultural Differences

During the British colonial period, frying spread from Europe to the Americas and Africa. American colonists adapted frying with great frenzy, and in a *Harper's* magazine story of 1866, Americans were said to be eating, "Fried ham, fried eggs, fried liver, fried steak, fried fish, fried oysters, fried potatoes, and last, but not least, fried hash." These preparations, as well as doughnuts, pancakes, and fritters, were served "morning, noon, and night," according to the magazine contributor, who thought that Americans consumed too much fried food.

Due to a lack of either resources or technology, frying was absent from some ancient cultures. Early European scholars writing about the food among the original inhabitants of the New World could not believe that these cultures did not have oil and did not fry. Because these cultures did not have use of rotary motion, they could not reduce their quantities of peanuts or other seeds to oil. While European cultures used round wheels, Native Americans ground maize and other grains with a to-and-fro motion. After Europeans arrived, some Native Americans found the unfamiliar cooking oils and fats repulsive. In modern Latin America, with some exceptions, such as street fair food, fried tortillas, and *pescado frito* (fried fish), frying is not among the significant methods of cooking.

Foods, especially meats, were fried during the first century C.E. in many cultures around the Mediterranean. In Rome the term "frying," or *frigere*, had two meanings, first, the toasting of grains in a dry skillet, and second, cooking in oil. From the eighth to the fifteenth century, fats and frying played an essential role in Arab cooking. Sheep tail fat was a frying delicacy; books from this region and period tell how to extract, clarify, perfume, color, and store this fat, which was used to finish-fry boiled meats. During the same period, Andalusia, Maghreb, and Syria were known for their olive oil, which was exported to Iraq and Egypt. The modern practice of browning, or lightly searing, meats through frying before stewing is described in Arab literature, also from this period. The result of this practice is that outer surfaces are slightly burned, and this enhances the flavor of stews.

Sautéing and Pan-frying

The first step in preparing an Indian curry is to heat a small amount of oil and then quickly sauté a variety of herbs and spices. Similarly, Chinese cooks pre-heat oil, often with garlic, before stir-frying. High heat releases flavor and aroma. Stew meats, for example, are often pan-fried to seal juices and develop surface flavor. In French and American kitchens, sautéing is used to quickly fry vegetables and other foods with little oil.

Pan-frying is the use of a shallow, slope-sided frying pan or skillet to cook in oil. Like deep-frying, it depends on conduction and convection. In pan-frying, a layer of oil has four functions: it lubricates the surface; increases contact between the food and the pan; reduces cooking time; and increases flavor and color.

When frying battered fish or chicken, the oil covers the pan but not the food, but when frying pancakes, the oil is but a thin film to keep the batter from sticking. Asian cooks fry rice with all kinds of meats, seafood, vegetables, and nuts. Chinese fried rice is pan-fried in a skillet with very little oil, perhaps one tablespoon per cup of rice. The challenge of pan-frying thick items such as chicken parts is to cook to the center without burning the surface. The Chinese have effectively solved this problem by slicing foods thin enough so the surface and interior cook in the same time.

Deep-Fat Frying

With deep-fat frying, foods are submerged in hot oil. Because of the expense of the oil or because of the difficulty of this method, deep-frying is associated with celebra-

tions, festivals, and street carnivals. American street fair vendors commonly serve deep-fried corn dogs, elephant ears, and funnel cakes. Deep-fat frying, also called deep-frying, is popular for breads, like southern cornmeal hush puppies, as well as for battered food, such as seafood or vegetables. Some food categories such as tempura, croquettes, and fritters are always deep-fried.

In India, *poori* breads are deep-fried, while *paratha* breads of whole wheat, potato, pea, chickpea, and corn are both griddle- and shallow-fried. *Poori* bread is a puffed up whole-wheat bread, much like *chapati*, another Indian bread that rather than being deep-fried is fried or "baked" on a griddle.

While European and Western cooks deep-fry with a single frying, the Chinese deep-fry in stages. After being marinated, foods are then deep-fried at a low temperature, maybe 290°F, and later finish-fried at a high temperature, 365°F to 385°F. This staged cooking increases crispness and color.

Batters reduce surface moisture, and a dryer surface reduces initial boiling. In addition, batters add color, flavor, and texture to many deep-fat fried foods, with green tomatoes, eggplant, okra, and even ice cream being examples of foods that are battered before they are fried. A meunière is a thin, light breading, or flour dusting, often used on fish and popular in traditional French kitchens. But batters can also be thick, as in the case of double, triple, or breaded coatings used for fried fish and chicken.

In summary, frying is quite expensive, somewhat controversial, almost universal, and very pleasing. The quick removal of moisture from food surfaces through the wicking effect of hot oil is a cooking method that will remain popular in homes and restaurants and at public events.

See also **Baking; Boiling; Broiling; Butter; Fats; Oil; Roasting; Stew; United States: The South; Utensils, Cooking.**

BIBLIOGRAPHY

Corriher, Shirley O. *Cookwise: The Hows and Whys of Successful Cooking.* New York: Morrow, 1997.

Devi, Yamuna. *The Art of Indian Vegetarian Cooking: Lord Krishna's Cuisine.* New York: Bala Books, 1987.

Kirschmann, Gayla J. *Nutrition Almanac.* 4th ed. New York: McGraw-Hill, 1996.

Miller, Gloria Bley. *The Thousand Recipe Chinese Cookbook.* New York: Grosset and Dunlap, 1970.

Rodgers, Rick. *Fried and True: Crispy and Delicious Dishes for Appetizers to Desserts.* San Francisco: Chronicle Books, 1999.

Sohn, Mark F. *Mountain Country Cooking: A Gathering of the Best Recipes from the Smokies to the Blue Ridge.* New York: St. Martin's Press, 1996.

Sonnenfeld, Albert, English ed. *Food: A Culinary History from Antiquity to the Present,* edited by Jean-Louis Flandrin and Massimo Montanari. New York: Columbia University Press, 1999.

Mark F. Sohn

FUNCTIONAL FOODS. The term "functional foods" refers to foods and their components that may provide a health benefit beyond basic nutrition. Functional foods do more than meet minimum daily nutrient requirements—they also can play a role in reducing the risk of disease and promoting good health. Biologically active components in functional foods impart health benefits or desirable physiological effects.

All foods have a function when consumed in proper balance as part of an overall healthy diet. Functional foods may include whole foods, such as fruits and vegetables, which represent the simplest example. Those foods that have been fortified, enriched, or enhanced with nutrients, phytochemicals, or botanicals, as well as dietary supplements, also fall within the realm of functional foods.

The functional attributes of many traditional foods are only now being discovered. Examples include phytoestrogens in soy foods and a variety of antioxidants in fruits and vegetables, such as lycopene in tomatoes. Still, new food products are being developed with beneficial components, with a focus on wellness and the reduced risk of chronic disease (i.e., foods and beverages containing pre- and probiotics to maintain gastrointestinal health, calcium-fortified beverages to maintain bone health, and dressings and spreads containing plant stanol and sterol esters, which may decrease the risk of heart disease).

History

Over two thousand years ago Hippocrates said, "Let food be thy medicine." Although the concept of functional foods is not entirely new, it has evolved considerably over the years. In the early 1900s food manufacturers in the United States began adding iodine to salt in an effort to prevent goiter, representing one of the first attempts at creating a functional food through fortification.

Other twentieth-century examples include vitamin A and D fortification of milk and niacin and folic acid fortification of grains. These early fortification examples, however, focused on reducing the risk of diseases of deficiency. In the latter part of the twentieth century, consumers began to focus on wellness and the reduction of chronic disease. Research now focuses frequently on the promotion of health through many lifestyle factors, including the consumption of an optimal diet. As of 2002, researchers have identified hundreds of food components with functional qualities, and they continue to make new discoveries surrounding the complex benefits of phytochemicals in foods.

Demand

Consumer interest in the relationship between diet and health has increased the demand for information on functional foods. Rapid advances in science and technology, increasing health-care costs, changes in food laws affecting label and product claims, an aging population, and a rising interest in attaining wellness through diet are

WHAT IS THE RELATIONSHIP BETWEEN FOOD BIOTECHNOLOGY AND FUNCTIONAL FOODS?

Although many of the nutritional compounds in functional foods are either naturally present or added during processing, some may be the result of agricultural breeding techniques, including conventional crossbreeding and, in the future, food biotechnology.

Crossbreeding to produce a plant for a specific genetic trait, such as higher sulforaphane-containing broccoli, can take as long as a decade or more. Modern biotechnology, however, makes it possible to select a specific genetic trait from any plant and move it into the genetic code of another plant in a much shorter time span, and with more precision than crossbreeding allows.

Researchers are working with farmers around the world to develop dozens of functional foods through the use of this promising technology. For example, a high-oleic acid soybean oil has been developed through biotechnology to have the health benefits of soybeans (possible protection against heart disease) without the saturated fat content of other cooking oils. Other research holds promise for boosting levels of beneficial components such as carotenoids in fruits and vegetables.

among the factors fueling U.S. interest in functional foods. Credible scientific research indicates many potential health benefits from food components. These benefits could expand the health claims now permitted by the U.S. Food and Drug Administration (FDA).

Consumer Attitudes

The International Food Information Council (IFIC) has been researching awareness of, and attitudes about, functional foods, through both qualitative and quantitative research. In 2002 telephone surveys with U.S. consumers were conducted, building on quantitative data collected in 1998 and 2000.

As in 1998 and 2000, the vast majority of consumers believe that they have a "great amount" of control over their own health. Also, in comparing the effects of nutrition, exercise, and family health history on health, consumers believe that nutrition plays the greatest role (71 percent versus 63 percent and 41 percent, respectively). Therefore, it is no surprise that 93 percent of Americans believe that some foods have health benefits that go beyond basic nutrition and that 85 percent are interested

TABLE 1

Examples of functional components*

Class/Components	Source*	Potential benefit
Carotenoids		
Alpha-carotene	carrots	Neutralizes free radicals that may cause damage to cells
Beta-carotene	various fruits, vegetables	Neutralizes free radicals
Lutein	green vegetables	Contributes to maintenance of vision
Lycopene	tomatoes and tomato products (ketchup, sauces, etc.)	May reduce risk of prostate cancer
Zeaxanthin	eggs, citrus, corn	Contributes to maintenance of vision
Collagen Hydrolysate		
Collagen Hydrolysate	gelatin	May help alleviate some symptoms associated with osteoarthritis
Dietary Fiber		
Insoluble fiber	wheat bran	May reduce risk of breast and/or colon cancer
Beta glucan**	oats	Reduces risk of cardiovascular disease (CVD)
Soluble fiber**	psyllium	Reduces risk of CVD
Whole grains**	cereal grains	Reduce risk of CVD
Fatty Acids		
Omega-3 fatty acids, DHA/EPA	tuna; fish and marine oils	May reduce risk of CVD and improve mental, visual functions
Conjugated linoleic acid (CLA)	cheese, meat products	May improve body composition, may decrease risk of certain cancers
Flavonoids		
Anthocyanidins	fruits	Neutralize free radicals, may reduce risk of cancer
Catechins	tea	Neutralize free radicals, may reduce risk of cancer
Flavanones	citrus	Neutralize free radicals, may reduce risk of cancer
Flavones	fruits/vegetables	Neutralize free radicals, may reduce risk of cancer
Glucosinolates, Indoles, Isothiocyanates		
Sulphoraphane	cruciferous vegetables (broccoli, kale), horseradish	Neutralizes free radicals, may reduce risk of cancer
Phenols		
Caffeic acid		
ferulic acid	fruits, vegetables, citrus	Antioxidantlike activities, may reduce risk of degenerative diseases like heart disease and eye disease
Plant Stanols/Sterols		
Stanol/stanol ester**	corn, soy, wheat, wood oils	May reduce the risk of coronary hear disease (CHD) by lowering blood cholesterol levels
Prebiotic/Probiotics		
Fructo-oligosaccharides (FOS)	Jerusalem artichokes, shallots, onion powder	May improve gastrointestinal health
Lactobacillus	yogurt, other dairy	May improve gastrointestinal health
Saponins		
Saponins	soybeans, soy foods, soy protein-containing foods	May lower LDL cholesterol, contains anticancer enzymes
Soy Protein		
Soy Protein**	soybeans and soy-based foods	1 ounce per day may reduce risk of heat disease
Phytoestrogens		
Isoflavones, daidzein, genistein	soybeans and soy-based foods	May reduce symptoms of menopause, such as hot flashes
Lignans	flax, rye, vegetables	May protect against heart disease and some cancers; lowers LDL cholesterol, total cholesterol, and triglycerides
Sulfides/Thiols		
Diallyl sulfide	onions, garlic, olives, leeks, scallions	Lowers LDL cholesterol, maintains healthy immune system
Allyl methyl trisulfide, dithiolthiones	cruciferous vegetables	Lowers LDL cholesterol, maintains healthy immune system
Tannins		
Proanthocyanidins	cranberries, cranberry products, cocoa, chocolate	May improve urinary tract health and reduce risk of CVD

*Examples are not an all-inclusive list.
** FDA-approved health claim established for component.

in learning more about such foods. These levels of interest have been consistently strong since 1998.

The top ten foods that consumers identify as having a health benefit beyond basic nutrition include broccoli (9 percent), fish or fish oil (9 percent), green, leafy vegetables (9 percent), oranges or orange juice (9 percent), carrots (8 percent), garlic (7 percent), fiber (6 percent), milk (6 percent), calcium (5 percent), oats/oat bran/oatmeal (6 percent), and tomatoes (6 percent). The top five foods have remained consistent for the past three surveys; they are associated with America's top health concerns. Cardiovascular disease factors, including heart disease/attack, high blood pressure, stroke, and high cholesterol, remain the primary collective concern of American consumers. Cancer continues to concern almost a third (30 percent) of all consumers. Other areas of worry include weight (17 percent), diabetes (17 percent), and nutrition/diet (12 percent).

Almost two-thirds (63 percent) of Americans say they are eating at least one food in order to receive a functional health benefit. Although not significantly different from the 2000 results (59 percent), this does represent a significant increase since 1998 (53 percent).

Finally, the terms "functional foods" and "nutraceuticals" are often used to describe foods that may have health benefits beyond basic nutrition. "Functional foods" is preferred over "nutraceuticals" two to one (62 percent versus 31 percent). In reality, all foods have some function even if it is mostly taste and enjoyment. In addition, health benefits can be reaped from an apple, yogurt, or a filet of salmon as much as from calcium-fortified fruit juice or a supplement.

Scientific Criteria

Many academic, scientific, and regulatory organizations are considering ways to establish the scientific basis to support claims for functional components or the foods containing them. FDA regulates food products according to their intended use and the nature of claims made on the package. Three types of claims are allowed on food and dietary supplement labels: (1) structure and function claims describing effects on the normal function of the body; (2) disease risk-reduction (health) claims implying relationships between components in the diet and diseases or health conditions, as approved by FDA and supported by significant scientific agreement; and (3) content claims.

Whereas science can confirm broad connections between some foods or eating patterns and health benefits, it is still not known how all individual food components work and whether there are synergistic effects among compounds. For example, numerous studies suggest that the consumption of a diet rich in whole grains, fruits, and vegetables is associated with a decreased risk of prostate, bladder, esophageal, stomach, and other cancers. However, the interactions among various components in these

HOW CAN MORE FUNCTIONAL FOODS BE ADDED TO THE DIET?

The most effective way to reap the health benefits from foods is to eat a balanced and varied diet, including whole grains, lean meats, low-fat dairy products, legumes, fruits and vegetables, as well as foods with added beneficial components. Watch labels and read articles for information about foods and health. Before deciding to make any major dietary changes, however, take the time to evaluate your personal health and speak to your health-care provider on ways to help reduce the risk of certain diseases. It is also important to remember that there is no magic bullet that can cure or prevent health concerns, even when eaten in abundance. The best advice is to choose foods wisely from each level of the food guide pyramid in order to incorporate many potentially beneficial components into the diet.

foods continue to be elucidated. The roles of vitamins, minerals, fiber, antioxidants, and other phytonutrients do not stand alone.

A large body of credible scientific research is needed to confirm the benefits of any particular food or component. Although scientific studies point to many functional components in foods that provide added health benefits, more research is needed to determine which components are responsible for the beneficial effects as well as how individual components interact. The scientific community is still in the early stages of understanding the potential for functional foods. For functional foods to deliver their potential public-health benefits, consumers must have a clear understanding of and a strong confidence level in the scientific criteria that are used to document health effects and claims.

Functional foods are an important part of wellness, which includes a balanced diet and physical activity. The good news with functional foods is that what one does eat may be more important for health than what one does not eat. Individuals should consume a wide variety of foods, including the examples listed in Table 1. These examples are not "magic bullets." The best advice is to include a variety of foods from each of the food groups, which would incorporate many potentially beneficial components.

See also **Biotechnology; Food Safety; Fruit; Health and Disease; Hippocrates; Nutraceuticals; Vegetables.**

Wendy Reinhardt

FUNGI. Fungi—sing. fungus; from the Greek *sphongis* (sponge)—are nonphotosynthetic and thus must absorb nutrients from organic matter formed by other organisms. The great majority of fungi obtain their food from dead organic matter and hence are known as saprophytes; a relatively small percentage derive their food from other living organisms and are known as parasites. Fungi may be unicellular (yeasts) or multicellular (mushrooms) and their cell walls usually contain chitin or cellulose and b-glucan. They may produce sexually or asexually by means of spores that are roughly comparable with the seeds of higher plants.

The fungal kingdom offers enormous biodiversity with over seventy thousand known species and an estimated 1.5 million species. According to molecular evidence (16S-like ribosome RNA sequences), the fungi may have originated from protozoan ancestors before the kingdoms Animalia and Plantae split; there is strong evidence that Fungi are closer to Animalia than Plantae

(Hawksworth et al.). Fungi are associated with some of the earliest remains of land plants. Some scientists believe that lichens (a stable self-supporting association of a fungus and an alga) might be transmigrants, the earliest colonizers of land.

Fungi have contributed to the shaping of humankind's welfare since the beginning of civilization. Fungi are recognized as both beneficial and harmful in their relationship to humans although this role is predominantly beneficial. They are responsible for a major portion of food deterioration in developing countries; however, the preservative effects of fermentation of foods and beverages with fungi are well-known benefits, including organic acids, alcohol, antibiotics, pigments, vitamins, growth regulators, immunomodulating agents, and enzymes. Finally, various types of edible mushrooms are consumed as an important part of human diets in many countries.

Fungi and Food Processing

Fungi used in food processing have been an integral part of the human diet since the beginning of civilization. In such foods, fungi are the agents responsible for imparting special flavors, textures, odors, or consistencies to food products. Fungi such as *Aspergillus* spp., *Rhizopus* spp., *Penicillium* spp., *Neurospora* spp., *Cladosporium* spp., and *Mucor* spp., as well as yeasts and many others have long been used to process a number of food products from soybeans to peanuts, rice, gram, maize, cassava, taro, and cacao beans.

Fungal enzymes. Food formulation using enzymes derived from fungi has undergone a rebirth in recent years. Enzyme suppliers have improved their ability to supply single-activity enzymes that do not have undesirable side activities (see Table 1 for a list of commercial fungal enzymes and their uses). Enzyme products have found increasing application for improving product clarity and yield and in replacing costly physical processes such as heating.

Cheese manufacture. Two general types of cheese are made with fungi as the ripening agents. Roquefort cheese is an example of cheese that is ripened primarily by growth of fungi (*Penicillium roquefortii*) throughout the cheese mass. Brie cheese is an example of one type of soft cheese that is ripened by the growth of fungi (*Penicillium camemberti*) on the outside of the cheese mass. In both types of cheeses, the fungi grow and release protein and fat-degrading enzymes that soften and ripen the cheese. Roquefort cheese requires about two months to ripen while Brie cheese requires only about one month to ripen.

Baker's yeast. Leavening, a process whereby batter or dough is caused to rise via the production of gas, especially carbon dioxide, was first discovered in Egypt. Today, most of the bread, cakes, cookies, and the like consumed by the public are prepared from leavened bat-

TABLE 1

List, source, and uses of enzymes derived from fungi for food manufacture

Enzyme	Source	Use
α-Amylase, amyloglucosidase	*Aspergillus niger* *A. oryzae* *Rhizopus* spp.	Hydrolysis of starch in production of beer, bread; manufacture of high-fructose syrups
α-Galactosidase	*Mortierella vinacea*	Hydrolysis of raffinose to sucrose and galactose during sugar refining
Catalase	*Aspergillus niger* *Penicillium vitale*	Remove excess hydrogen peroxide formed during cake baking or that may be added during pasteurization of milk and cheese
Cellulase	*Aspergillus niger* *Trichoderma viride*	Improve palatability of low-quality vegetables, accelerate drying of vegetables, alter texture of foods, increase flavor of commercial mushrooms
Hemicellulase	*Aspergillus niger* *Trichoderma viride*	Manufacture of instant coffee
Invertase	Yeasts *Aspergillus* spp.	Increases sweetness in confections; yields soft center in chocolate-covered candies
Lactase	*Aspergillus niger* *A. oryzae*	Hydrolysis of lactose in milk products, enabling their use by lactose-intolerant individuals; production of syrups for use as sweetening agents
Lipase	*Candida* spp. *Aspergillus* spp. *Mucor* spp. *Rhizopus* spp.	Used for flavor development in cheese, chocolate crumb, apple wine, and cooking fats; improved whipping properties of egg whites; fish processing
Naringinase	*Aspergillus niger*	Reduce bitter flavonone glycoside derivative found in some citrus products
Nuclease	*Penicillium* spp.	Flavor enhancers
Pectic Enzymes	*Aspergillus niger* *Penicillium notatum* *Botrytis cinerea*	Remove turbidity from fresh fruit juices; removal of pectins before concentrating juice; clarifying agent in wine
Protease	*Aspergillus* spp. *Mucor pusillus*	Meat tenderizer; remove bitter flavors, replace rennin in cheese manufacture, chill-proofing of beer; reduce elasticity of glutin proteins in bread
Rennet	*Mucor* spp.	Milk coagulation in cheese manufacture
Tannase	*Aspergillus niger*	Treat insoluable material that forms during manufacture of instant tea

SOURCE: Adapted from: Beuchat (1987) and Moore-Landecker (1995)

ter or dough. Most cakes and cookies are leavened chemically (by using baking powder) while most bread is leavened by yeasts (such as *Saccharomyces cerevisiae*). Yeasts develop and reproduce by producing buds on mother cells that subsequently enlarge and produce more buds. During growth, carbohydrates in the dough are metabolized to carbon dioxide that is trapped in the dough in the form of bubbles. During the leavening process, alcohol may accumulate in the dough to as high as 0.5 percent. The alcohol is driven off during baking and helps give the bread a pleasant aroma.

Edible Mushrooms

Mushrooms have a long history of human consumption. Traces of puffball fungi have been found in Stone Age settlements. Over 4,500 years ago in ancient Egypt only pharaohs were permitted to eat mushrooms, which they believed were "sons of the gods" sent down to earth on lightning bolts announced by claps of thunder. The legend that mushrooms may have originated from thunder and lightning also existed among people of other ethnic groups. In Roman folklore, some fungi were believed to spring from the ground in places struck by a thunderbolt. In the Hindu tradition, there was a god named Soma that manifested himself to the priests in the form of hallucinogenic fluids. Some scientists believe that Soma was the fly mushroom, *Amanita muscaria*. A similar legend

may have existed among the inhabitants of the highlands of Guatemala and Mexico, where even today the people refer to *A. muscaria* by a common name meaning thunderbolt (Lowy).

Cultivated species. The cultivation of edible mushrooms worldwide reached 6.16 million metric tons in 1997, up from 1.26 million tons in 1981 (Table 2; Chang). This represents a 12 percent annual increase. Six mushroom genera accounted for 87 percent of the total mushroom supply (Table 2). These were *Agaricus* (31.8%), *Lentinula* (25.4%), *Pleurotus* (14.2%), *Auricularia* (7.9%), *Flammulina* (4.6%), and *Volvariella* (3%). China produced 3.92 million tons of mushrooms in 1997, or 63.6 percent of the total world output. The major mushroom of commerce in China is *L. edodes*, which accounts for 35 percent of the total output for that country. China currently produces 88 percent of the total world production of *L. edodes*.

Agaricus bisporus (button mushroom). The cultivation of the button mushroom originated in the Paris region in France. Melon growers in this region discovered how mushrooms could be grown and started cultivating them in 1650. By the mid 1700s it was discovered that *A. bisporus* could grow without light, and that very favorable conditions for growing mushrooms prevailed in subterranean tunnels and caves. As a result of this discovery,

TABLE 2

World production of cultivated edible mushrooms in 1981, 1990, and 1997

Species	1981 Fresh Wt (x 1,000 t)	%	1990 Fresh Wt (x 1,000 t)	%	1997 Fresh Wt (x 1,000 t)	%
Agaricus bisporus	900.0	71.6	1,424.0	37.8	1,955.9	31.8
Lentinula edodes	180.0	14.3	393.0	10.4	1,564.4	25.4
Pleurotus spp.	35.0	2.8	900.0	23.9	875.6	14.2
Auricularia spp.	10.0	0.8	400.0	10.6	485.3	7.9
Volvariella volvacea	54.0	4.3	207.0	5.5	180.8	3.0
Flammulina velutipes	60.0	4.8	143.0	3.8	284.7	3.0
Tremella spp.	-	-	105.0	2.8	130.5	2.1
Hypsizygus spp.	-	-	22.6	0.6	74.2	1.2
Pholiota spp.	17.0	1.3	22.0	0.6	55.5	0.9
Grifola frondosa	-	-	7.0	0.2	33.1	0.5
Others	1.2	0.1	139.4	3.7	518.4	8.4
Total	**1,257.2**	**100.0**	**3,763.0**	**100.0**	**6,158.4**	**100.0**

SOURCE: Chang, 1999

successful culture was undertaken inside the numerous caves that were excavated for building stones and for gypsum. The caves presented, from a climatic point of view, several advantages over the previous growing conditions in open air. Factors such as temperature and relative humidity were much more constant in caves compared with aboveground conditions.

From France, mushroom cultivation spread to other parts of the world. The business grew and soon spread to England and other countries. By 1825, the first mushroom crops were being produced in caves in Holland. In 1865, mushroom culture entered the United States via England and the first mushrooms were grown on a small scale on Long Island, New York; by 1870 the industry had begun to develop.

Detail view of cepes (*Boletus edulis*), one of the most highly prized of all culinary mushrooms. PHOTO ANDRÉ BARANOWSKI.

The button mushroom is produced commercially on a selective substrate prepared by composting mixtures of wheat straw, hay, corncobs, horse manure, or combinations thereof. The finished compost should have a nitrogen (N) content of 2–2.5 percent, and to reach such a level, nitrogen-rich supplements must be added. Inorganic nitrogen supplements can be added but only to provide part of the necessary amount. Organic sources of nitrogren include oilseed meal, brewers' grain, malt sprouts, and poultry manure.

Once the compost has been prepared, it is seeded with mushroom spawn that is prepared from a mother culture maintained by a spawn laboratory. Spawn is prepared by inoculating a pure culture of the mushroom onto steam-sterilized grain, usually rye or millet. Approximately one liter (500 g) of spawn is used to seed 0.5 m² of production surface that is contained in trays or beds inside environment-controlled production houses. Spawn run (vegetative growth of the mycelium) lasts ten to fourteen days, then a layer of neutralized peat moss (casing) is placed on top of the colonized compost to stimulate production of mushrooms. Approximately ten to fourteen days after casing, mushrooms are ready for harvest.

Lentinula edodes (shiitake). Production of shiitake worldwide increased more than sevenfold in the fourteen-year period from 1983 (207,000 t) to 1997 (1,573,000 t; Chang). Most of this increase occurred in China, where more than ten million part- and full-time farmers cultivate shiitake. Shiitake is widely consumed in China, yet one-third of production is exported. In 1997, China produced approximately 88 percent of the total world output (Chang). In the United States, production of shiitake is a relatively new enterprise, having begun only in the late 1970s. In 1990, the United States produced 1,123 tons of shiitake and by 1999 production reached 3,941 tons, a 3.5-fold increase (USDA). This increase in production was due, in part, to increased production efficiency and to increasing consumer demand. Farmers have learned to provide the specialized management this crop requires, thereby reducing production costs. The amount of controlled-environment production surface devoted to growing shiitake on synthetic logs has increased 2.9 fold from 1990 to 1999 (74,200 m² to 212,400 m², respectively).

Sawdust is the most popular basal ingredient used in synthetic formulations of substrate for producing shiitake in the United States, but other basal ingredients may include straw, corncobs, or both. Starch-based supplements (20–60 percent dry weight) such as wheat bran, rice bran, millet, rye, and maize may be added to the mix. These supplements serve as nutrients to provide a more optimal growth medium (Royse).

Pleurotus* spp. *(oyster mushroom). Oyster mushroom production increased at a rapid rate worldwide during the 1980s and then decreased slightly during the 1990s (Table 2). From 1986 to 1997, oyster mushroom production increased from 169,000 tons to 917,000 tons (a 5.4-fold increase). China was responsible for most of the production increase. In the United States, production of oyster mushrooms was 1,647 tons in 2001, up 2 percent from the previous year (USDA).

In the United States, the primary ingredients used for *Pleurotus* spp. production are chopped wheat straw or cottonseed hulls or mixtures thereof. After completion of pasteurization (140°F [60°C] for one to two hours) the substrate is cooled and spawned with the desired strain. There are several species of oyster mushrooms cultivated, with various colors of fruiting body. In Japan, bottle production of oyster mushrooms is most common. Substrate is filled into bottles, sterilized, and inoculated with *Pleurotus* spawn. Upon completion of the spawn run, bottle lids are removed and mushrooms emerge from the surface of the substrate. After the mushrooms are harvested they are weighed and packaged for shipment to market.

Auricularia* spp. *(wood ear mushroom). Total production of *Auricularia* spp. in 1997 exceeded 485,000 metric tons (fresh weight; Table 2). This value is an increase of 366,000 tons or fourfold over 1986 levels (Chang). *Auricularia* spp. production now represents about 8 percent of the total cultivated mushroom supply worldwide.

Auricularia auricula and *A. polytricha* commonly are produced on a synthetic medium consisting of sawdust, cottonseed hulls, bran, and other cereal grains or on natural logs of broadleaf trees. For synthetic medium production of Auricularias, the substrate may be composted for up to five days or used directly after mixing. The medium is filled into heat-resistant polypropylene bags and sterilized (substrate temperature 240°F [121°C]) for sixty minutes. After the substrate has cooled, it is inocu-

While the white truffles of Italy are best eaten raw, France's black truffles (*Tuber melanosporum*) are most flavorful when cooked. This French society of truffle devotees meets annually to herald the beginning of the truffle season. PHOTO ANDRÉ BARANOWSKI.

lated with either grain or sawdust spawn. Light intensity of more than 500 lux during the spawn run may result in premature formation of primordia. Temperature, light intensity, and relative humidity all interact to influence the nature and quality of the mushrooms.

Flammulina velutipes* *(enokitake). Worldwide production of *F. velutipes* has increased from about 100,000 metric tons in 1986 to about 285,000 tons in 1997. Japan is the main producer of enokitake. In the United States, enokitake production has increased at an estimated rate of 25 percent or more per year for the last four years. However, only about 60 tons of enokitake were produced in the United States in 2001.

Production of most enokitake in Japan is based on synthetic substrate contained in polypropylene bottles. Substrates (primarily sawdust and rice bran; 4:1 ratio) are mechanically mixed and filled into heat-resistant bottles with a capacity of 800 to 1,000 ml. Sawdust primarily from *Cryptomeria japonica*, *Chamaecyparis obtusa*, or aged (nine to twelve months) *Pinus* spp. appears to offer the best yields. In the United States, a sterilized, bran-supplemented medium, consisting primarily of corncobs, serves as the primary medium. When the substrate is fully colonized, the original inoculum is removed mechanically from the surface of the substrate and the bottles may be placed upside down for a few days.

To further improve quality during fruiting, temperatures are lowered to 37° to 46°F (3 to 8°C) until harvest. As the mushrooms begin to elongate above the lip of the bottle, a plastic collar is placed around the neck and secured with a Velcro® strip. This collar serves to hold the mushrooms in place so that they are long and straight. When the mushrooms are thirteen to fourteen cm long, the collars are removed and the mushrooms are pulled as a bunch from the substrate. The mushrooms then are vacuum packed and placed into boxes for shipment to market.

Grifola frondosa (maitake). Japan is the major producer and consumer of maitake. Commercial production of maitake in Japan began in 1981 (325 t) and by 1997 reached 32,000 tons (a 98-fold increase). Maitake is produced primarily in the Japanese provinces of Niigata, Nagano, Gunnma, and Shizuoka. Other countries, such as the United States, began maitake production in the early 1990s. Maitake production in the United States in 2001 was estimated at about 84 tons.

Most maitake is marketed as food. However, maitake has been shown to have both antitumor and antiviral properties. Powdered fruit bodies are used in the production of many health foods such as maitake tea, whole powder, granules, drinks, and tablets. Maitake also is believed to lower blood pressure, reduce cholesterol, and reduce the symptoms of chronic fatigue syndrome.

Commercial production of most *G. frondosa* is on synthetic substrate contained in polypropylene bottles or bags. A common substrate used for production is hardwood sawdust supplemented with rice bran or wheat bran in a 5:1 ratio, respectively. Other formulas include hardwood sawdust (70 percent based on oven dry weight basis) supplemented with white millet (20 percent) and wheat bran (10 percent). Some growers may add soil to the mix to stimulate fruit body formation. For production in bags, the moistened substrate is filled into microfiltered polypropylene bags and sterilized to kill unwanted competitive microorganisms. After cooling (sixteen to twenty hours), the substrate is inoculated and the bags are heat-sealed and shaken to uniformly distribute the spawn throughout the substrate. Spawn run lasts about thirty to fifty days depending on strain and substrate formulation.

Volvariella volvacea (straw mushroom). Cultivation of *V. volvaceae* is believed to have begun in China as early as 1822. In the 1930s, straw mushroom cultivation began in the Philippines, Malaysia, and other Southeast Asian countries. Production of the straw mushroom increased from 54,000 tons in 1981 to about 181,000 tons in 1997 (about 3 percent of the total mushroom supply).

Many agricultural by-products and waste materials have been used to produce the straw mushroom. These include paddy straw, water hyacinth, oil palm bunch, oil palm pericarp waste, banana leaves and sawdust, cotton waste, and sugarcane waste. *Volvariella* is well suited for cultivation in the tropics because of its requirement for higher production temperatures. In addition, the mushroom can be grown on nonpasteurized substrate, which is more desirable for low-input agricultural practices.

In recent years, cotton wastes (discarded after sorting in textile mills) have become popular as substrates for straw mushroom production. Cotton waste gives higher and more stable biological efficiencies (30 to 45 percent), earlier fructification (four days after spawning) and harvesting (first nine days after spawning) than that obtained using straw as a substratum. Semi-industrialization of paddy straw cultivation on cotton wastes has occurred in Hong Kong, Taiwan, and Indonesia as a result of the introduction of this method.

Wild mushrooms. In many developing countries, the collection and sale of wild edible mushrooms has become an important source of income for many people in remote forested regions. Despite a relatively short growing season, wild mushrooms provide many families with 50 to 100 percent of their income. World trade in wild, edible mushrooms is estimated at more than $7 billion annually (Arora). The global trade in matsutake (*Tricholoma matsutake*), the most expensive wild mushrooms after truffles, is estimated at $3 to $5 billion. Matsutake may sell for as much as $200 apiece in Tokyo markets. The King Bolete (*Boletus edulis*; also known as porcini, cepe, borovik, etc.) is the most popular wild mushroom of Europe. These may be served fresh in some upscale restaurants. Dried boletes are famous for their concentrated flavor and choice aroma and are available year round from almost anywhere in the world. Other wild mushrooms available on world markets include chanterelles (*Cantharellus cibarius*), morels (*Morchella* spp.), hedgehog mushrooms (*Hydnum repandum*), lobster mushrooms (*Hypomyces lactifluorum*), candy caps (*Lactarius fragilis*), and cauliflower mushrooms (*Sparassis crispa*).

WARNING: Collecting and ingesting wild mushrooms without the presence of an expert to correctly identify specimens can be very dangerous and should be discouraged since there are several deadly mushrooms that look like edible wild ones.

Mycotoxins

Mycotoxins are chemical compounds produced by fungi growing on organic substances such as corn, cottonseed, or peanuts that, when ingested, have some undesirable effect on humans or on an animal consuming them. Adverse effects can range from vomiting to weight loss, various types of tumors, and in some cases, death. Over one hundred toxic compounds produced by fungi have been identified, and about forty-five of these occur in grain crops. Some mycotoxins are rare in occurrence while others such as aflatoxin are common in some years. The seriousness of the mycotoxin problem varies with the year, the crop being grown, and the intended use of the crop product. Most mycotoxins affect the blood, kidneys, skin, or central nervous system, and some may cause cancer.

MUSHROOM COLLECTORS

The consumption of wild mushrooms has a lengthy history, dating back well over two millennia and extending throughout the world. For over two hundred years, mushrooms have been a cultivated crop as well. Despite somewhat negative images of mushrooms in the popular imagination and despite the possibility of real danger in their consumption, they have long been valued for their culinary and psychedelic properties. In 300 B.C. Theophrastus recorded that mushrooms were valued as food and for trade. Pliny, Juvenal, Martial, and Cicero all considered mushrooms to be great delicacies, and the Roman emperor Claudius was allegedly poisoned by a plate of mushrooms. Mushrooms are also mentioned in the Hindu Rig Veda and were eaten on the Indian subcontinent. Mushrooms were probably consumed for food and for their psychedelic properties in Mesoamerica, Siberia, and Scandinavia. Some suggest that the biblical "manna from heaven" was a fungus. By the eighteenth-century reign of Louis XIV, mushrooms were cultivated in caves near Paris. During the nineteenth century mushrooming became a popular leisure pursuit in Europe and America, and by the end of the century mushroom societies were formed.

One estimate placed the number of mushroomers in the United States at thirty million in the early 1980s. A survey conducted at the same time found that 22 percent of Americans collect wild mushrooms, and 15 percent consume mushrooms they find. In the nations of eastern, central, and southern Europe with stronger mushroom cultures, these figures would likely be higher. Mushroom societies are found in every region of the United States, as well as Canada and Europe. In the United States, mushroom societies were founded in Boston and Minneapolis in the late nineteenth century. The North American Mycological Association, covering the United States and Canada, has approximately 2,000 members. These clubs organize talks, dinners, sharing of advice, and forays to mushroom collecting sites.

Novices worry about the toxic qualities of wild mushrooms. Despite this, the number of mushroom fatalities, at least in the United States, is very low. In some years, there are no fatalities although illnesses or hospitalizations might occur as a result of the misidentification of mushrooms, the contamination of otherwise edible specimens, or allergic reactions. Among the edible wild mushrooms that are most widely collected in the United States and Europe are morels, chanterelles, puffballs, boletes, and coral mushrooms. While the collection of wild mushrooms has increased in the past decades, the hobby is limited, and the greatest growth in "wild mushrooms" is likely to occur when these foods become cultivated and therefore perceived as safe to consume.

Gary Alan Fine

The genera of fungi of greatest importance to humans with respect to natural poisoning outbreaks are *Aspergillus*, *Penicillium*, and *Fusarium*. The *Aspergillus flavus* group produces aflatoxins (at least eighteen types known) that are considered the most important from the viewpoint of a direct hazard to human health. *Aspergillus flavus* is a common fungus that is found in soil, air, and decaying plant residues. Infection by *A. flavus* and subsequent aflatoxin production can occur in the field, in transit, or in storage. Most reports indicate that infection occurs in the field, while aflatoxin production can occur whenever the product is exposed to favorable conditions, either in the field or in storage.

Control of aflatoxin includes prevention of fungal growth, removal of toxins, and inactivation of toxin. Most control efforts have been directed toward control of aflatoxins in peanuts and corn. Hand picking, electronic sorting, and air classification accomplish control of aflatoxin in processed peanut products. Removal of shriveled, rancid, or discolored kernels has proven the most practical way of limiting aflatoxin contamination in peanuts.

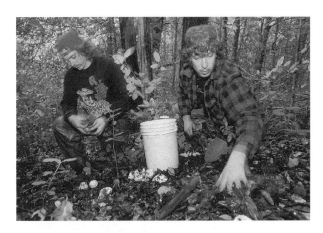

In areas of the country with cool weather and heavy rainfall, mushroom collecting is a full-time occupation. These brothers make a living collecting a variety of mushrooms in Oregon's coastal forests. © DAN LAMONT/CORBIS.

BIBLIOGRAPHY

Arora, D. "The Global Mushroom Trade." *California Wild* 52, no. 4 (fall 1999):16–17.

Beuchat, Larry R. *Food and Beverage Mycology.* 2d ed. New York: Van Nostrand Reinhold, 1987.

Chang, S. T. "World Production of Cultivated Edible and Medicinal Mushrooms in 1997 with Emphasis on *Lentinus edodes* (Berk.) Sing. in China." *International Journal of Medicinal Mushrooms* 1 (1999):273–282.

Findlay, W. P. K. *Fungi: Folklore, Fiction, and Fact.* Eureka, Calif.: Mad River Press, 1982.

Fine, Gary Alan. *Morel Tales: The Culture of Mushrooming.* Cambridge: Harvard University Press, 1998.

Friedman, Sara Ann. *Celebrating the Wild Mushroom.* New York: Dodd, Mead, 1986.

Hawksworth, D. L., P. M. Kirk, B. C. Sutton, and D. N. Pegler. *Ainsworth and Bisby's Dictionary of the Fungi.* Wallingford, U.K.: CAB International, 1995.

Lowy, B. "*Amanita muscaria* and the Thunderbolt Legend in Guatemala and Mexico." *Mycologia* 66 (1974): 188–190.

Moore-Landecker, Elizabeth M. *Fundamentals of the Fungi.* 4th ed. Upper Saddle River, N.J.: Simon & Schuster, 1996.

Royse, Daniel J. "Specialty Mushrooms and Their Cultivation." *Horticultural Reviews* 19 (1997): 59–97.

United States Department of Agriculture. *Mushrooms.* Washington, D.C.: National Agricultural Statistics Service, Agricultural Statistics Board, 2001.

Wasson, R. Gordon. *Soma: Divine Mushroom of Immortality.* New York: Harcourt Brace Jovanovich, 1968.

Daniel J. Royse

FUSION CUISINE. Fusion cuisine is the deliberate combination of elements from two or more spatially or temporally distinct cuisines. Transcending conventional geographical and historical boundaries, it is a unique form of cuisine particular to today's postmodern world. The precise origin of the term "fusion cuisine" is uncertain although "culinary globalization," "new world cuisine," "new American cuisine," and "new Australian cuisine," all other names for fusion cuisine, have their roots in the 1970s in the emergence in France of nouvelle cuisine, which combined elements of French and, primarily, Japanese cooking (Sokolov, 1992). As nouvelle cuisine spread to other nations, it combined with elements of the foods of the host country. As Adam Gopnik has observed, while the Enlightenment of new cooking took place in France, the Revolution occurred elsewhere. Indeed, fusion cuisine has emanated primarily from the United States and Australia, but has spread to other parts of the world as well. Fusion cuisine may have taken off in the United States and Australia, because of those countries' short history relative to the rest of the world, their unique immigration histories, their lack of a cuisine that is clearly recognized by other parts of the world, and, most importantly, their lack of a culinary tradition.

As fusion cuisine evolves, many more ethnic and regional cuisines beyond French are being combined to form new hybrids. Exemplars of fusion cuisine include Pacific Rim cooking predominant in Australia and New Zealand, and Norman Van Aken's New World Cuisine (combining Latin, Caribbean, Asian, and American elements) found in the United States. An example of a specific fusion dish that combines classic Chinese recipes with French techniques and Mexican ingredients is Susanna Foo's pan-seared sweetbreads with veal dumplings made with ancho chili and served with Sichuan pickled relish and crispy shallots.

Fusion cuisine is distinct from historical combinations of cuisines, such as those that occurred in the sixteenth century when foodstuffs from the New and Old worlds mixed. It is also different from Creole cooking, which combines elements of French, African, Acadian, and Native American cooking. Geographers have described the long history of foodstuffs crossing geographical borders and the ways in which food is socially constructed through various processes (Cook and Crang, 1996; Bell and Valentine, 1997). Earlier forms of cuisine that combined elements from different regions or ethnic groups were reactive, rather than proactive, as is today's fusion cuisine. These cuisines emerged slowly from the everyday cooking practices that occurred within individual households and local communities. In contrast, fusion cuisine has developed rapidly and has found its way into everyday kitchens and restaurants as a direct consequence of the concerted and conscious activities of cultural intermediaries in the form of professional cooks, celebrity chefs, and cookbook authors. Fusion cuisine is an innovative and experimental process that demands from its practitioners the constant creation or re-creation of elements into novel food forms.

The social and cultural conditions that have contributed to the development of fusion cuisine, as well as most forms of contemporary cuisines, include increasing processes of globalization, increasing cultural flows through media and travel, the rise of a consumer culture, the modern food system, the expansion of the cookbook industry, the increased prominence of chefs throughout the world, the growth of the food and restaurant industry, and a greater concern with healthy lifestyles. Images constantly bombard the world, increase consumer knowledge, and escalate demand. Further, advances in technology have made foodstuffs from around the world available to all at any time. Boundaries are eliminated through the Internet, television, and the convenience and affordability of travel. Further, as consumers become increasingly concerned with living healthier lifestyles, the idea of mixing the healthiest elements from a variety of cuisines becomes appealing. For example, steaming and grilling may replace frying as a method of cooking, while herbs and spices are used in place of butter. The combination of these cultural and economic elements increases the likelihood that many culinary forms and combinations will exist.

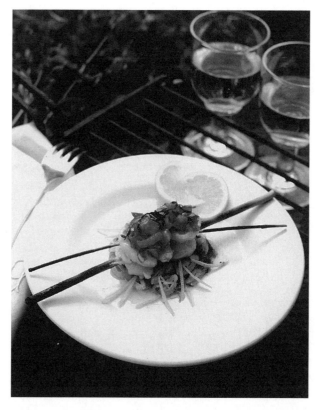

Described as a blend of flavors and ingredients from different cultures, of different presentation styles, even of different cooking techniques, fusion cuisine has become a popular modern metaphor for hotel cookery around the world. Whether East has met West (or vice versa) successfully has been an ongoing discussion among food critics. PHOTO BY ANDRÉ BARANOWSKI.

Fusion cuisine, like fusion music and religion, appeals to multiculturalism, diversity, and novelty; it is also quite easy to market. It is an expression of the contemporary world of images and actively promotes a blending and diversity of cultures. It is a global cuisine in the sense that its elements are representative of cultures from around the world. One of the most interesting developments associated with fusion cuisine is that no single culture, with the exception of the French, dominates. Fusion cuisine combines elements of what are traditionally referred to as ethnic or regional cuisines, and may provide an opportunity to mainstream various ethnic and regional cuisines as well as provide opportunities for immigrant and minority chefs. Additionally, because of the hegemony of French cooking that persists in the culinary world, combining elements of French cooking may elevate the status of various ethnic and regional cuisines in a way that might not be accomplished otherwise.

Fusion cuisine has been met with mixed reactions because it is characterized by its lack of rules, or perhaps more accurately, by the precept that the rules ought to change constantly. Fischler claimed that contemporary gastronomy might be better thought of as "gastro-anomy" increasingly characterized by its lack of normative structure. Critics argue that practitioners of fusion cuisine deconstruct French and other cuisines (which do have codified culinary traditions and are clearly understood as unique culinary languages), and reassemble them into "new culinary sentences" that are not grammatically correct. Another related and frequently echoed criticism of fusion cuisine is that it is a haphazard mixing of cultures that lacks a respect for tradition. Further, particular cuisines become more or less popular as part of the hybrid, depending upon what is "hot" at the moment and not necessarily upon what tastes good. Because of increasing processes of globalization and consumerism, it is unlikely that fusion cuisine is going away any time soon. There are limitless possible combinations yet to be created.

See also **France: Tradition and Change in French Cuisine**; **Nouvelle Cuisine**; **United States: Ethnic Cuisines**.

BIBLIOGRAPHY

Bell, David, and Gill Valentine. *Consuming Geographies: We Are Where We Eat.* London: Routledge, 1997.

Cook, Ian, and Philip Crang. "The World on a Plate: Culinary Culture, Displacement, and Geographical Knowledge." *Journal of Material Culture* 1 (1996): 131–153.

Cwiertka, Katarzyna. "Culinary Globalization and Japan." *Japan Echo* 26 (June 1999): 52–58.

Fischler, Claude. "Food Habits, Social Change, and the Nature/Culture Dilemma." *Social Science Information* 19 (1980): 937–953.

Gopnik, Adam. "The Politics of Food: Is There a Crisis in French Cooking?" *The New Yorker* (28 April and 5 May 1997): 150–161.

Heffernan, Greg. "Pacific Rim Fusion Cooking." Proceedings of the World Association of Cooks Societies, 28th World Congress, New Zealand Chefs Association Inc., Melbourne, Australia, 1998. Available at www.chef.co.nz/chefs/html/pacific_rim_cooking.html.

Rice, William. "Together at Last: Americans Embrace Fusion Dishes." *Chicago Tribune*, 14 January 1998. Available at www.freep.com/fun/food/qfuse14ew.htm.

Sokolov, Raymond. *Why We Eat What We Eat: How the Encounter between the New World and the Old Changed the Way Everyone on the Planet Eats.* New York: Summit, 1991.

Symons, Michael. "Eating into Thinking: Explorations in the Sociology of Cuisine." Ph.D. diss., Flinders University of South Australia, 1991.

Julie L. Locher

G

GADGETS, KITCHEN. *See* **Kitchen Gadgets.**

GAME.   The importance of nondomesticated animals, or game, in the human diet is unclear. Some anthropologists have argued that the advent of hunting game with tools was the critical development in the evolution of humans, resulting in such cultural characteristics as male aggression, sophisticated tools, and the sexual division of labor. The role of game in the human diet can more clearly be understood in light of ecological, nutritional, evolutionary, and cross-cultural information.

Except in the high latitudes occupied by peoples such as the Inuit, plants are generally the most abundant food source. Game is rarer than plants due to the second law of thermodynamics: As one moves up the food chain from plants, to herbivores, to carnivores, one finds that there is less to eat at the higher levels because energy is lost at each step in the chain. Not only is game rarer than plant foods, it may also be more difficult to obtain. Plants may protect themselves with thorns or toxins, but they do not hide or run away as animals do. These two points suggest that people might always choose plants over game as food sources. However, due to a process called biological magnification, game provides more concentrated packages of nutrients than do plants. In addition, some plant foods are difficult to digest without processing. Hence, some anthropologists classify game as "high-quality" foods and plants as "low-quality" foods.

Human nutritional requirements and digestive physiology suggest that at least some game is required in the diet. With the exception of vitamin B_{12}, humans can obtain all the nutrients they require from plant foods. Vitamin B_{12} can only be found in animal products. Humans require only 2.4 micrograms of vitamin B_{12} per day and can generally store sufficient amounts for up to twenty years, but a chronic lack of vitamin B_{12} in the diet may cause pernicious anemia, fatigue, and damage to the nervous system, and in children compromise growth. The need for protein is often the basis of arguments that humans require meat in their diet. While for humans game is a good source of protein, the required amino acids may be obtained from a mix of plant foods. In some regions, such as the Arctic, there is relatively little plant life; thus,

humans there generally require game to meet their protein requirements. Although humans are clearly capable of digesting game, their gut has a long digestion time similar to that of apes, which are primarily folivorous (Milton, 2000). In addition, it is possible that too much game may compromise human health. Game is generally leaner than meat from domesticated animals, and too much lean meat increases a person's metabolic rate such that ingested energy is used entirely to digest the food eaten. Consequently, lean meat must be eaten with energy-rich foods such as fat or carbohydrates. Furthermore, high-protein consumption may exceed the liver's ability to metabolize amino acids.

Human nutritional requirements and digestive kinetics are a function of the evolutionary history of the species. Therefore, an understanding of game in the human diet requires a consideration of the diets of human ancestors. It should be borne in mind that the role of game in the diets of human ancestors may be overemphasized, because plant food remains are less likely to be preserved in the fossil record than animal food remains. In addition, any plant food remains that do exist may have been overlooked by early researchers working with the perception that hunting was paramount in the subsistence strategies of human ancestors.

Hominids in Africa 4 to 2.5 million years ago did not leave archaeological traces such as "kitchen middens" and stone tools. Consequently, little is known of their diets. In lieu of archaeological data, dietary inferences have been made on the basis of paleoecological reconstructions, craniodental morphology, dental wear, chimpanzee behavior, and stable isotope analyses of their remains. Paleoecological reconstructions, craniodental morphology, and dental wear suggest that these first hominids subsisted primarily on fleshy fruits and leaves. Using chimpanzees as models for the behaviors of the first hominids also leads to the conclusion that they had a diet that was primarily vegetarian with an occasional animal product. This agrees with a stable isotope analysis of the bones of a three-million-year-old *Australopithecus africanus* from South Africa that indicates this hominid ate fruits, leaves, large quantities of grasses and sedges or animals that ate these plants, or both (Sponheimer and Lee-Thorp, 1999). Interestingly, the researchers suggest that these hominids may have been capable of procuring game prior to the development of stone tools.

The evidence of 2.5 million years ago in Tanzania's Olduvai Gorge points to both tool makers and the consumption of game. Animal bones with cut marks indicative of butchering found in association with these tools indicate that the hominids who lived there ate game. How these bones were obtained is a subject of debate, because cut marks on the bones are sometimes found overlying tooth marks of carnivores, suggesting scavenging by the hominids. Some researchers argue for hunting or for confrontational scavenging in which groups of people drove carnivores off still-fleshy animals. Others argue that these people practiced passive scavenging from carcasses that had already been largely consumed. While evidence that might resolve this debate is sparse, the simplicity of the Oldowan tools may favor more passive scavenging (Klein, 2000).

Around 1.8 million years ago *Homo erectus* appears in the fossil record with a greatly expanded brain and more refined tools. The expansion of the brain dramatically increased the energy requirements, as the brain uses energy as much as ten times faster than average body tissue. Hence, it has been argued that increased access to high-quality, readily digestible flesh and marrow may have been essential for brain enlargement. However, corms, tubers, and other subterranean plant foods might have provided equal or greater nutrition for effort, and most historically recorded African hunter-gatherers exploited them heavily (Klein, 2000). Moreover, while there are many animal bones associated with *H. erectus* sites, there are few cut marks on the bones and a lot of carnivore teeth marks, suggesting that the fossil assemblage may not be due to human activity but to people inhabiting the same waterside sites as those favored by other animals.

The use of fire renders game a more viable food, as heating makes the tissue more digestible. So archaeological evidence of fire might help determine the consumption of game. The earliest possible site for fire is Locality 1 in Zhoukoudien, China (600,000–400,000 years ago), but this has been disputed due to the lack of mineral ash in deposits. To date, the earliest undisputed sites are deposits from 200,000 years ago in African, West Asian, and European caves.

The origin of Neanderthals around 130,000 years ago brings clear evidence of hunting of game. This conclusion is reached on the basis of faunal remains associated with Neanderthal living sites, wear patterns on their tools, and the analysis of stable isotopes and trace elements in their skeletal remains. Stable isotope analysis has been used in particular to compare the diets of Neanderthals with subsequent *Homo sapiens*. Such an analysis of nine *H. sapiens* and five Neanderthals from the European mid–Upper Paleolithic (about 20,000–28,000 years ago) indicates that the Neanderthals had diets composed primarily of large terrestrial herbivores, whereas *H. sapiens* had a broader diet with a heavy reliance on freshwater resources (Richards et al., 2001). M. P. Richards and colleagues conclude that this transition was made possible by refined technology that made it easier to capture freshwater game. Stable isotope analysis of *H. sapiens* skeletons from sites in Israel dating from 70,000 to 10,000 years before the present reveals an increase in plant foods in the diet 20,000 years ago (Schoeninger, 1982). The change, it is argued, was due to refined technology for processing plant foods.

Hunter-Gatherers

While anatomically near-modern people were present in Africa by 130,000 years ago, not until around 10,000 years ago were plants and animals domesticated. This means that for at least 77 percent of the time the species has been in existence, humans have obtained food by hunting and gathering. Hence, many of behavioral propensities, dietary requirements, and biocultural responses to food likely evolved prior to the advent of agriculture (Bogin, 2001). Given this, ethnographic and archaeological data concerning the diets of hunter-gatherers help explain the role of game in human diets.

As with the paleoanthropological data, studies of hunter-gatherer diets are biased by the perception among early researchers that hunting was the most important subsistence strategy. An additional problem in describing the natural or ideal diet of hunter-gatherers is the tremendous variation documented for such diets (Jenike, 2001). Despite the cultural and geographic diversity of hunter-gatherers, spanning from the rainforests of central Africa to the Arctic tundra of Baffin Island, similarities exist across these groups (Bogin, 2001). First, foragers consume a diverse array of food items; 105 species of plants and 144 species of animals among the !Kung San of southern Africa's Kalahari Desert, 90 species of plants and animals among the Ache of Paraguay's tropical forest (Hill and Hurtado, 1989), and 10 species of plants and 33 species of animals among the Dogrib of subarctic Canada (Hayden, 1981). Second, gathered rather than hunted foods are the primary source of dietary energy for most foragers. Richard B. Lee (1968) reported that, among 58 foraging societies, the primary subsistence base was gathering for 29, fishing for 18, and hunting for 11. Of those who relied on fishing or hunting, almost all were north or south of the fortieth parallel, a region researchers believed was not occupied by Paleolithic foragers. A review of the data in 2000 for 229 hunter-gatherer groups concluded that animal protein and fat provided up to 45 to 65 percent of the energy consumed and that 73 percent of these groups acquired as much as 56 to 65 percent of the energy they consume from animal foods (Cordain et al., 2000). When greater than 35 percent of the energy is from animal foods, the extra is from aquatic game.

The importance of game in the diets of many hunter-gatherer groups is apparent in paleoecological reconstructions as well. Tim Flannery (2001), for example, writes that 13,000 years ago in North America, a sparse human population drove much of the megafauna to extinction by hunting.

Nonhuman Primates

Given humans' close evolutionary relationship with apes and monkeys, a final line of evidence to consider is the importance of game in the diets of nonhuman primates. In general, most nonhuman primates appear to eat little animal matter because of the difficulty of obtaining it and a gut poorly suited to the digestion of animal matter (Milton, 2000).

This is not to say that game does not form an important part of the diet of some nonhuman primates. For example, observations of chimpanzees in different African sites reveals that they hunt often (Mitwani et al., 2002). The vast majority of the game hunted and eaten is red colobus monkeys, hunted primarily by males four to ten times per month with a success rate greater than 50 percent. The hunts entail a high cost in both energy expended and risks taken. Once caught, the meat is selectively shared with members of the troop. Interestingly, the chimpanzees do not appear to hunt to meet a nutritional need, as they hunt primarily during the seasons when fruit is abundant. Rather, among chimpanzees, game may be a political tool used to increase one's genetic contribution to subsequent generations (Mitwani et al., 2002). By sharing the meat, the hunter builds alliances within the troop. These alliances enable a chimpanzee to establish and maintain a high rank that appears to confer mating and reproductive advantages.

Ecological factors suggest that if humans were to choose their diet on the basis of availability alone, they would choose one composed primarily of plant foods. But, given the concentration of nutrients found in game and the difficulty of digesting some plant foods, they would likely wish to complement the plant foods with game. Nutritional considerations indicate that at least some game is required in the diet.

Conclusion

Paleoanthropological data reveal that human ancestors of 4 to 2.5 million years ago ate primarily plant foods and possibly some game. Only at 2.5 million years ago does definitive evidence of the consumption of animals, obtained via scavenging or possibly hunting, appear. The expansion of the brains of human ancestors 1.8 million years ago does not necessarily mean they increased their consumption of animal foods. Rather, they may have increased their energy intake via the consumption of energy-rich plants. The Neanderthals of 130,000 years ago were the first hominids for whom game was a staple of the diet. *H. sapiens* also consumed game, albeit a greater variety and less focused on megafauna. Data from hunter-gatherers indicate they consumed a wide variety of plants and animals and that, by and large, plant rather than an-

The fallow deer as depicted in Edward Topsell's *Historie of Fourefooted Beasts* (London, 1658). The fallow deer was one of the most prized game animals of the medieval hunt. ROUGHWOOD COLLECTION.

imal products provided the bulk of the calories consumed. Studies of nonhuman primates document that game is regularly consumed among some species. Although the nutritional implications of this behavior are not clear, it does appear to have cultural implications among chimpanzees, where meat is shared by males to enhance their reproductive potential. Each line of evidence considered here suggests that, beginning 2.5 million years ago, game formed part of the diet of human ancestors, and that plant foods have provided the bulk of human calories. In short, game was a part of the diets of early hominids and hunter-gatherers, but plants predominated in the diet. The evidence is insufficient to clearly evaluate the impact of this subsistence strategy on human behavior.

See also **Agriculture, Origins of; Evolution; Hunting and Gathering; Mammals; Prehistoric Societies.**

BIBLIOGRAPHY

Bogin, Barry. *The Growth of Humanity.* New York: Wiley-Liss, 2001.

Cordain, Loren, Janette Brand Miller, S. Boyd Eaton, Neil Mann, Susanne H. A. Holt, and John D. Speth. "Plant-Animal Subsistence Ratios and Macronutrient Energy

Estimations in Worldwide Hunter-Gatherer Diets." *American Journal of Clinical Nutrition* 71 (2000): 682–692.

Flannery, Tim. *The Eternal Frontier: An Ecological History of North America and Its Peoples.* New York: Atlantic Monthly Press, 2001.

Hayden, B. "Subsistence and Ecological Adaptations of Modern Hunter/Gatherers." In *Omnivorous Primates*, edited by Robert S. O. Harding and Geza Teleki. New York: Columbia University Press, 1981.

Hill, Kim, and A. Magdalena Hurtado. "Hunter-Gatherers of the New World." *American Scientist* 77 (1989): 436–443.

Jenike, Mark R. "Nutritional Ecology: Diet, Physical Activity, and Body Size." In *Hunter-Gatherers: An Interdisciplinary Perspective*, edited by Catherine Panter-Brick, Robert H. Layton, and Peter Rowley-Conwy. Cambridge: Cambridge University Press, 2001.

Klein, Richard G. "Archaeology and the Evolution of Human Behavior." *Evolutionary Anthropology* 9 (2000): 17–36.

Lee, Richard B. *The Dobe !Kung.* New York: Holt, Rinehart and Winston, 1984.

Lee, Richard B. "What Hunters Do for a Living; or, How to Make Out on Scarce Resources." In *Man the Hunter*, edited by Richard B. Lee and Irven DeVore. Chicago: Aldine Publishing, 1968.

Milton, Katherine. "Hunter-Gatherer Diets: A Different Perspective." *American Journal of Clinical Nutrition* 71 (2000): 665–667.

Mitwani, John C., David P. Watts, and Martin N. Muller. "Recent Developments in the Study of Wild Chimpanzee Behavior." *Evolutionary Anthropology* 11 (January 2002): 9–25.

Richards, Michael P., Paul B. Pettitt, Mary C. Stiner, and Erik Trinkaus. "Stable Isotope Evidence for Increasing Dietary Breadth in the European Mid-Upper Paleolithic." *Proceedings of the National Academy of Sciences* 98 (2001): 6528–6532.

Schoeninger, Margaret J. "Diet and the Evolution of Modern Human Form in the Middle East." *American Journal of Physical Anthropology* 58 (1982): 383–403.

Sponheimer, Matt, and Julia A. Lee-Thorp. "Isotopic Evidence for the Diet of an Early Hominid *Australopithecus africanus.*" *Science* 283 (1999): 368–370.

Warren M. Wilson

GAMERITH, ANNI. Anni Gamerith (1906–1990) was one of the most famous European food ethnologists, known for her fieldwork and her theoretical insights. Born in Austria and a teacher by profession, Gamerith received her doctorate late in life at the University of Graz. The same university later gave her an honorary professorship for her scientific achievements. Her theory about the structure of traditional cookery was put forward for the first time at the First International Symposion of Ethnological Food Research held at Lund, Sweden, in 1970. This immediately won her international recognition. She proposed that there was an interdependence between food, cooking utensils, and cooking processes on the one hand and the fireplace on the other.

In essence, the type of food produced by a culture was dependent on one of two basic technologies. In former times, before the so-called *Sparherd* (literally "fuel-frugal" kitchen range) was invented, kitchen fireplaces were designed either for an open fire (hearth) or for a cooking oven. The hearth with its open fire could be close to the floor (where the cook had to bend down) or as high as a table (where the cook could stand upright while cooking). The food was boiled in the hot water of an iron kettle (hanging over the fire) or fried in the hot fat of an iron three-legged pan (standing over the fire). The food prepared in this way included both meat, which was often boiled, and various kinds of pancakes, with the dough fried in different ways. During the whole process of preparing the food on the hearth, the cook could intervene at any time.

Preparing the food in the cooking oven was another matter. Here, the food was cooked in the superheated air of the oven. Once the food was placed in the oven, the oven door was shut, and the door stayed shut to avoid having the oven cool down. The pots and pans used in this case were ceramic and were placed in the oven through the small hole in front by special devices called "pot forks" (*Ofengabel*) or "pot forks with wheels" (*Ofenwagen*). The food systems connected with the hearth and the cooking oven as the two main places of food preparation were structurally different and, according to Gamerith, could be referred to as "hearth food" (*Herdkost*) and "cooking oven food" (*Ofenkost*). In former times a region was characterized by one category or the other.

Woodcut from the *Neu-vermehrtes künstliches Koch-Büchlein* [New, Improved Artful Manual of Cookery] published anonymously about 1650. While the cook turns a roast on a spit, sausages are being smoked above the fire. Leaning against the wall is a pot fork for moving hot cookpots on the hearth. COURTESY HANS WEISS. ROUGHWOOD COLLECTION.

This 1840s Austrian woodcut shows a newly installed cast-iron cooking range with a bake oven in the back. The iron pots on the stove have undergone a radical redesign to account for the new technology. COURTESY HANS WIESS. ROUGHWOOD COLLECTION.

The *Sparherd* or kitchen range changed the situation completely. The incentive for its invention was the necessity of saving wood (hence the name, German *sparen* meaning 'to save'). The kitchen range combined the two formerly separate principles of preparing food: the hot surface of this stove is equivalent to the open fire (allowing boiling or frying), while the baking oven corresponds to the cooking oven (where one could bake or braise). With this innovation, the two previously separate food systems could be combined, and the former differences between areas where one method or the other was dominant disappeared.

Gamerith had encountered these exclusive systems in her fieldwork and was finally successful in finding the theoretical explanation. She also found a classification for the many different kinds of gruel and concerned herself very early with old methods of processing cereals from the aspect of nutrition. She was involved to a great extent in the organization of the museum at Feldbach, Austria, with its special attention to rural material culture in general, including many objects that were relevant for ethnological food research. In the museum at Stainz, Austria—again due to Anni Gamerith—food plays an important role.

See also **Germany, Austria, Switzerland; Hearth Cookery; Preparation of Food.**

BIBLIOGRAPHY

Gamerith, Anni. "Feuerstättenbedingte Kochtechniken und Speisen." *Ethnologia Scandinavica* 1 (1971): 78–85.

Gamerith, Anni. *Speise und Trank im südoststeirischen Bauernland.* Grazer Beiträge zur Europäischen Ethnologie Bd. 1. Graz: Akademische Druck- u. Verlagsanstalt, 1988.

For further publications see "Rund um das bäuerliche Essen." *Festschrift zum 80. Geburtstag von Anni Gamerith.* Feldbach 1986. Also contains a curriculum vitae written by herself.

Edith Hörandner

GARDENING AND KITCHEN GARDENS.

The purpose of the kitchen garden is to supply the household to which it belongs with culinary herbs, fruit, and vegetables. There are, however, different types of households, and likewise different kinds of kitchen gardens. This entry deals mostly with the walled kitchen gardens that were created in northern Europe, and in particular in Great Britain, during the eighteenth, nineteenth, and early twentieth centuries.

Types of Kitchen Garden
The earliest garden of any kind was surely one that supplied its owner with edible and, to a certain extent, medicinal or useful household plants. People created

An organic kitchen garden at the Centre for Alternative Technology, Machnylleth, Wales. © JULIE MEECH; ECOSCENE/CORBIS.

such gardens in prehistoric times and they are still made today, albeit on a small scale and with fewer medicinal or household plants.

A productive garden requires certain essential elements that are common to all: They are usually situated close to the homestead; they need fertile soil, a supply of water, shelter from the worst of the weather, and protection from thieving birds, beasts, and people. Kitchen gardens with these basic requirements can be found in rocky, compost-filled craters on tropical islands; on cold, windswept seaside beaches; on rooftops in the center of huge towns; on narrow strips of land beneath ancient city walls; on river islets; and on terraced mountainsides. Security is provided by low stone or mud walls, hedges of thorns or spiky cacti, wooden or reed palings, ditches or moats, old bedsteads, and wire netting. Water comes from nearby springs, streams, rivers, or pools. In spite of the ingenuity required to make them productive, the produce of these gardens is likely to be erratic, as they are dependent on the seasons both for clement weather and rain; for this reason, and also because they usually have no supporting structures such as glasshouses, work sheds, or storage rooms, these gardens must be termed "primitive."

The country dweller's cottage kitchen garden forms another category. Lying somewhere between the basic, or primitive, kitchen garden and the much larger, walled kitchen garden, the typical cottager's garden forms the very surroundings of the cottage itself with flower beds, fruit trees, narrow paths, and small lawns as well as an open, cultivated vegetable patch. It might include a little

orchard, bee hives, a pigsty, and a poultry house. The whole would be surrounded by a stout hedge, fence, or low wall. Before the arrival of modern piped water on tap, water would have been supplied by a well or a pump. The amount of produce grown on the vegetable patch might be sufficient to provide the family with a surplus of staples for storing over the winter, but the area would not necessarily be big enough to grow vegetables in succession, and the owners might not be able to afford a glasshouse, heated or unheated, for out-of-season luxuries. It could though, be laid out in a decorative manner, with a mixture of flowers and vegetables, trained fruit trees, and topiaried hedges.

The decorative kitchen garden, one designed as much for beauty as utility, is a constantly recurring theme in kitchen gardening. In the early twentieth century, when the fashion for this kind of kitchen garden had a little revival, it was referred to by English-speaking gardeners as the *potager*, an affectation that simply means "kitchen garden" in French.

Although well suited to it, the *potager* style of gardening is not confined to the cottage garden; it can be carried out on a vast scale as, for example, in the gardens of the Château of Villandry on the Loire in France, and it was often seen in walled kitchen gardens, too. In spirit the *potager* is poetic, inspired by classical Roman works such as Virgil's *Georgics* (see especially *Georgic* 4) and *Hortulus*, a poem on gardening written about 840 by the monk Walafrid Strabo. Renaissance gardens, too, with their vine- and jasmine-covered arbors, statues, urns, and fountains; clean sandy walks lined with clipped box, pinks, or herbs; little pavilions or gazebos at each corner overlooking the countryside beyond; and juxtapositions of fruit, flowers, and vegetables within were as pleasant to look at, contemplate, and walk in as they were useful. The theme continues into the seventeenth and eighteenth centuries, with the gradual removal of the kitchen garden from close proximity to the house and the separation of the garden as a whole into various compartments. The essayist Sir William Temple in his *Epicurus* of 1685 describes this arrangement: "so as to be like one of the Rooms out of which you step into another." By the end of the eighteenth century, kitchen gardens in many of the larger estates had been removed to a considerable distance from the house. George Carter in his catalogue for the exhibition of the work of the landscape designer Humphry Repton notes that Repton wished the walk toward the kitchen garden to be as ornamental as the kitchen garden itself (pp. 67–68). Once there, the visitor would find features similar to those described in sixteenth- and seventeenth-century manuals on gardening: gazebos, fruit trees trained over hoops to provide shady walks, and beds lined by flowers with the more ornamental kinds of vegetable on show, the commoner kinds concealed. In winter, the visitor could seek the warmth and beauty of the glasshouses.

The garden at Villandry is a Renaissance pastiche; it was created on a sixteenth-century site in the twentieth century, and is based on contemporary designs for *parterres* by Androuet de Cerceau—not that there is any evidence that de Cerceau used vegetables in this way. In practice, in many a modern *jardin potager*, the *parterre*-like layout of the beds, and the heights and colors of the plants therein are of more importance than the supply of food to the household. When the cropping of one cabbage can jeopardize the beauty of a whole row, this type of kitchen garden begins to look like a plaything.

For town-dwellers, fruit and vegetables have always been available from shops, itinerant tradesmen, and markets. These outlets were supplied with produce grown in outlying commercial market gardens, many of which specialized in only one or two kinds of fruit or vegetable (asparagus, strawberries, mushrooms, or grapes, for example). From the late nineteenth century onward, produce markets depended increasingly on stuff imported from abroad, and it is this factor—plus the relative cheapness of bought food compared to the cost of growing one's own—that has contributed to the demise of the great walled kitchen gardens. On the other hand, with the creation of the allotment system in the early nineteenth century, town-dwellers (ranging from wealthy tradesmen to artisans of the working class) were, and still are, enabled to raise a few fruits, flowers, and vegetables of their own on communal, rented plots provided either by philanthropists, speculators, or the municipality on the outskirts of towns. The original purpose of the allotment system was to offer a healthy pastime for heads of households who might otherwise squander their time and money in public houses and other dens of vice. Ten such gardens would occupy one acre and in 1835, according to William Howitt, in *Rural Life in England*, there were, on the outskirts of the English manufacturing town of Nottingham alone, "upwards of 5000 gardens, the bulk of which are occupied by the working class" (pp. 550–553).

Allotment gardens, traditionally equipped with little huts or summer houses, are still in use throughout Great Britain and Europe, providing their tenants, as they did in the past, with welcome retreats from the noise and dust of the city, as well as a healthy occupation and a supply of wholesome fresh food. Market gardens, with their vast glasshouses and forcing beds are not, for the purposes of this article, strictly kitchen gardens, although they supply similar produce, but the allotment garden is definitely in the kitchen garden category, being private and noncommercial.

Walled kitchen gardens invariably formed part of the gardens attached to any substantial country house. Unlike the other domestic kitchen gardens described above, these gardens were huge, occupying anything from one to twenty acres, commensurate in size with households often consisting of more servants than family, and capable of providing enough produce for feasts, balls, banquets, and numerous staying guests as well.

By the beginning of the twentieth century, kitchen gardens had reached the peak of perfection: the rarest and best of fruits, flowers, and vegetables were to be found here, raised by teams of highly skilled gardeners who used the latest in horticultural technology. This is not to say that the wealthier classes were alone in their love of luxury—plus a degree of natural curiosity and competitiveness—but peaches, melons, muscats, and pineapples cannot be raised in one's own garden without considerable financial means.

These gardens supplied their masters with a succession of fruits and vegetables all year round, both delicacies and staples, and with ornamental plants and flowers for the house and for personal adornment. Indeed, the demise of these great gardens, which began after World War I, and was virtually complete by the end of World War II, is largely due to such fruits and vegetables being cheaply available to everyone in a supermarket. The modern shopper might be surprised to learn that from the late eighteenth century onward, glasshouses in these walled gardens were providing heat and shelter for tropical fruits and orchids as well as more temperate plants. Forcing beds ensured that there would be new potatoes, asparagus, and strawberries for Christmas and in early spring; mushrooms were grown in dark, heated sheds, to be available at all times; insulated and ventilated storage rooms kept grapes, apples, and pears in perfect condition over winter and into springtime. Common roots and vegetables such as onions, cabbages, and pumpkins were likewise stored in specially constructed cellars and attics. Garden produce was even frozen, and kept in ice-houses. The kitchens made surpluses into pickles and preserves, and if the family was staying in town, fresh fruit, flowers, and vegetables—washed, trimmed, and packed in hampers—were sent up as required by the gardeners.

Design

In layout, walled kitchen gardens show a marked similarity to one another; this is due to their being essentially working gardens, the design of which is led by function and has evolved through practice. Ideally they are rectangular, with the longest walls facing the sun; lean-to hothouses are ranged against the sunny side of the northernmost wall; sheds behind them (known as "back sheds") house boilers or furnaces to heat the glasshouses, workrooms, storage rooms, and tool rooms, the men's mess room, the head gardener's office, his seed room, the mushroom house, and sometimes a *bothy* or hut for the unmarried gardeners. The head gardener is given a house for himself and his family, often built onto the walls themselves, and always as close as possible to the hothouses, so that he can keep a close watch on them and their contents. Forcing pits, frames, and hot beds occupy a separate yard beside or behind the back sheds, as does an enclosure for packing materials, poles and posts, fuel, composts, and manures. The "slip garden" (the area outside the main walls) was also cultivated, usually with the more robust vegetables or with soft fruits. The slip in front of the southernmost wall was sometimes used as an ornamental flower garden, especially if it was the garden through which visitors from the house might pass on their way to view the kitchen garden.

With the exception of glasshouses, which were not seen in kitchen gardens until the early eighteenth century, and then only rarely, the monastic, royal, and aristocratic gardens of medieval Europe were very similar; they were modeled on treatises written by classical authorities such as Pliny, Cato, Varro, and Columella. Situated conveniently close to the back kitchens and the stables or home farm (which provided dung), stoutly defended by walls of mud, brick, or stone (depending on the locality), they were laid out if possible on land sloping toward the sun, on a four-square grid, with long, narrow raised beds.

The layout of the beds and paths was dictated by a watering system in which the paths between the beds acted as channels, the water coming either from central ponds, reservoirs beyond the garden, or wells, tanks, and cisterns within it. It was distributed in water carts, or by pumps and water wheels. The invention of the hydraulic ram in the mid-nineteenth century allowed gardens to be made on higher ground than would have been possible before. The invention of the horse-drawn seed drill in the late seventeenth century, whereby seed was sown in rows on flat ground, was taken up at first by farmers and then by market gardeners, effectively doing away with

raised beds in the larger gardens of the more northern parts of Europe.

Diversity of Plants

The variety of plants grown in the earliest kitchen gardens was dependent on locality; those known to thrive in the wild were taken in and "improved" by selective breeding, fertile soil, shelter, and abundant watering. Travelers, merchants, nurserymen, and itinerant seedsmen introduced novelties from further afield. With the voyages of discovery made by Europeans from the fifteenth century onward, plants from across the world were brought into Spain, Portugal, France, Italy, the Netherlands, and Britain. They were taken to the gardens of botanists and apothecaries, as well as the kitchen and flower gardens of enthusiasts, to be assessed as much for their economic or medicinal values as for their edibility or beauty.

These introductions were challenging to the gardener. Many of them needed protection over winter and heat in order to survive. The hot bed, a flat-topped mound of warm, fermenting horse dung covered by a bed of rich, sifted soil and surmounted by a protective frame, was introduced to Moorish Spain by the Arabs in the eleventh century, but was not used in the rest of Europe until four centuries later, when it was used for raising the seedlings of exotics, melons, cucumbers and out-of-season salads. Orangeries (also known as conservatories or greenhouses) were used for conserving citrus fruits and other exotic greens. Originally a dark, well-insulated overwintering shed, the orangery gradually evolved into a high-windowed ornamental building, with heat provided by small smoky stoves. Dutch gardeners led the way in seventeenth-century stove and glasshouse development. They made their orangeries lighter by giving them sloping glass fronts; they improved ventilation and perfected a system of underfloor heating by means of hot-air flues heated by small furnaces at the back of the house. With the discovery toward the end of the seventeenth century of how to raise pineapples, they introduced the use of hot beds heated by fermenting tan bark, in place of horse dung.

By the 1720s, British gardeners had overtaken the Dutch in horticultural invention. Gripped by a mania for growing pineapples, they developed glazed, heated pits and glasshouses expressly for that fruit, eventually adapting the system to suit vines, peaches, and tropical plants. With the industrial revolution, which began in Britain, came the invention of the steam boiler and later the hot water boiler, as well as the glassworks and foundries for the manufacture of iron-framed glasshouses in which to raise these plants, and a new, industrial wealthy middle class to enjoy them.

Even before the sixteenth century, Flemish and French gardeners were masters in the cultivation of fruit. They raised innumerable varieties of hardy fruits such as plums, apples, pears, and cherries, as well as figs, grapes, and the more tender, early-flowering apricots, almonds, peaches, and nectarines. They were experts in grafting and in training trees to grow as fans, espaliers, cordons, and free-standing dwarfs. With the arrival in Britain of the Dutch King William III, in 1688, this style of fruit growing became fashionable in British gardens where, until then, fruit growing had been concentrated mostly on hardy orchard fruits. As on the Continent, dwarf fruit trees, pruned to form decorative balls, goblets, spindles or pyramids, were used ornamentally in beds lining the kitchen garden paths, or were even given a *jardin clos*, an enclosed fruit garden of their own. Fruit trees with branches trained as horizontal bars (espaliers), as single, double, or treble stems, either upright, oblique, or horizontal (cordons), or as branches trained into a flat palm or fan shape (fans) needed the support of free-standing trellises or high walls. Walls were especially needed too, to accommodate the more tender wall-fruits.

An Industrial Quality

Thus the walls surrounding the kitchen gardens of northern Europe and Great Britain increased both in height and extent. Gardens of more than four acres were divided and subdivided by yet more walls, some of which were heated by horizontal, serpentine flues running from small fireplaces situated at the back.

High garden walls were beneficial to wall-fruits, created a benign, sheltering microclimate within the garden, provided support for taller, more extensive glasshouses and back sheds, and hid the whole process of growing kitchen produce from sight, giving the place a secretive air. It should be noted, though, that this complex was the headquarters of the gardens as a whole; it was where the entire workforce assembled and received orders, where the garden boys were educated by the head gardener, where equipment was kept, and all the choicest plants raised and nurtured.

It was also becoming increasingly industrial. For a visitor to an early-nineteenth-century kitchen garden, as described by Jane Austen in *Northanger Abbey*: "The walls seemed countless in number, endless in length; a village of hot-houses seemed to arise among them, and a whole parish to be at work within the inclosure." She does not mention the numerous smoking chimneys perched above hot walls and glass houses—or how, on a windy day, strawy dung from frames, pits, and hot beds would be blowing about and there would be a noticeable smell of rotting cabbage leaves, celery, onions, and leeks. These aspects, and even the very sight of "a whole parish" going to and fro with their barrows and carts, were less pleasing to eighteenth- and nineteenth-century gentlefolk.

The Landscape Movement

Apart from the sensibilities of its owners, the landscape movement was to some extent responsible for the removal of the kitchen garden with its high walls to some distance from the house. If it could still be seen, it was screened by beds of tall, ornamental shrubs or, if the screen was to act as a shelter belt as well, by tall forest trees. "If from your best room windows any objects should intercept your sight," wrote landscape designer J. Trusler in his *Elements of Modern Gardening* (1784), "go to the top of the house and from thence select the best distance and background, preserving in the piece such of the buildings and plantations as will suit the composition. . . ." Not everyone agreed; the political reformer William Cobbett, in his *English Gardener* thought it "the most miserable taste to seek to poke away the kitchen garden, in order to get it out of sight" (p. 8).

At the beginning of the twenty-first century, these arguments seem trivial, for the gardens are in ruins, with little but the walls to be seen. But there is some hope for their revival. Local communities see them as sources of fresh, organic produce; others will use them as living museums in which to teach old horticultural skills, and display long-forgotten fruits and vegetables.

See also **British Isles: England; Fruit; Food Production, History of; Horticulture; Organic Farming and Gardening; Vegetables**.

BIBLIOGRAPHY

Bradley, Richard. *New Improvements of Planting and Gardening*. 3d ed. London: Mears, 1719 and 1720.

Campbell, Susan. *Charleston Kedding: A History of Kitchen Gardening*. London: Ebury, 1996.

Campbell, Susan. *Cottesbrooke: An English Kitchen Garden*. London: Century, 1987.

Campbell, Susan. *Walled Kitchen Gardens*. Princes Risborough: Shire, 1998.

Carter, George, Patrick Goode, and Kedrun Laurie, eds. *In the Catalogue for the Exhibition: Humphry Repton Landscape Gardener, 1752–1818*. Norwich: Sainsbury Centre for Visual Arts, 1982.

Cobbett, William. *The English Gardener*. Oxford: Oxford University Press, 1980. Original edition published in 1833.

Davies, Jennifer. *The Victorian Kitchen Garden*. London: BBC Books, 1987.

Evelyn, John. *The Compleat Gard'ner*. Translated from the French *Instructions pour les jardins frutiers et potagers* by Jean-Baptiste de la Quintinye, 1690. London: Gillyflower, 1693.

Howitt, William. *Rural Life of England*. 3rd ed. London: Longmans, Brown, Green, and Longmans, 1844.

Loudon, John Claudius. *Encyclopaedia of Gardening*. 5th ed. London: Longman, Rees, Orme, Brown, and Green, 1835.

M'Intosh, Charles. *The Book of the Garden*. 2 vols. Edinburgh, 1853–1855.

Morgan, Joan, and Alison Richards. *A Paradise Out of a Common Field*. London: Century, 1990.

Mountain, Dydymus (alias Thomas Hill). *The Gardener's Labyrinth*. New York. London: Garland, 1982. Facsimile of 1577.

Svieking, Alber Forbes, ed. *Sir William Temple upon the Gardens of Epicurus with Other Seventeenth-Century Essays*. Gollancz, 1902.

Thomson, Robert. *The Gardener's Assistant, Practical and Scientific.* 1st ed. 6 vols. Glasgow, 1859.

Trusler, Dr. John (attributed). *Elements of Modern Gardening: or, the Art of Laying Out of Pleasure Grounds, Ornamenting Farms, and Embellishing Views Round about Our Houses.* London: Logographic Press, 1784.

Wilson, C. Anne, ed. *The Country House Kitchen Garden, 1600–1950.* London: Sutton Publishing with the National Trust, 1998.

Susan Campbell

GARLIC. *See* **Onions and Other Allium Plants.**

GASTRONOMY. Most dictionaries define gastronomy as "the art and science of good eating," or "the art and science of fine eating." The etymology of the word is generally attributed to the title of a poem by French attorney Joseph Berchoux, "Gastronomie" (1801). Early descriptive writings often assume gluttony. One versed in gastronomy is said to be a gastronome, while a gastronomist is one who unites theory with practice and thus becomes a gourmand (gourmet).

The original suffix root of gastronomy derives from the Greek word *nomos*, meaning 'laws that govern', which led to the notion that gastronomes are those who only dwell upon classic and haute cuisine. Implied too is that "the art and science of good eating" is confined to expensive, lavish, and complex meals requiring equally expensive silver and china. Fortunately, as is the case with so many rules and regulations, such rigidity of form can become uncomfortable. One so-called early proponent of gastronomy asserted that a true gastronomist should shun diversity—a rather narrow footnote by today's understanding.

Gastronomy has evolved from its original dictionary meaning to the point that it really would be best studied broken down into subsets by culture.

A further denotation of *nomos*, 'the sum of knowledge of a specific subject', gives gastronomy a meaning that includes a person's command of the totality of knowledge regarding the art and science of good food and eating. Rather than just beautifying the ritual of consumption, gastronomy now entails an appreciation and understanding of the many avenues of cooking and food production. For example, today's gastronomist would do well to have some knowledge regarding food chemistry and physics, food history, foodways, and culinary anthropology, including a link to the many cultures of the world via computer technology.

One should seek a better understanding of agriculture, aquaculture, and the technology of newer cooking

Copper engraving called "Au Gourmand," used as a letterhead on an 1816 bill of Paris *traiteur* Corcellet at the Palais Royal. This bill was charged to Anthony Morris of Philadelphia, who was visiting Paris at the time. ROUGHWOOD COLLECTION.

methods and equipment, as well as information on the impact of eating and diet upon health, including food-borne disease and worldwide ecology. Gastronomy should promote lessons on how to taste, savor, and fully sensualize the dining experience, whether it is a family meal at home or a special dining-out event.

Simpler repasts should be enraptured alongside the grandest banquets. Standing at a seaside fish market and savoring a freshly shucked oyster just harvested and chilled from the sea can be savored as much as the expensive three-hour feast served in a banquet hall.

There is a tendency to judge food and cooking solely by what it looks like. When dining out, taste and aroma are demoted in favor of stylistic architecture. People, especially Americans, are losing the ability and sensibility of how to taste. Americans no longer savor or appreciate the joy and satisfaction of eating. Entertaining and pleasant conversations over dinner seem to have disappeared; food fads come and go before ever having had a chance to even establish an identity. It is time to relearn or reemphasize how the senses can be used to fully appreciate and relish the hedonistic pleasures of life. People are equipped with the necessary anatomy and physiology to elevate a boring biological function to one of life's greatest pleasures.

See also **Appetite; Brillat-Savarin, Anthelme; Catherine de' Medici; Eating: Anatomy and Physiology of Eating; Icon Foods; Larousse Gastronomique; La Varenne, Pierre François de; Pleasure and Food; Sensation and the Senses; Slow Food.**

BIBLIOGRAPHY

Montagné, Prosper. *Larousse gastronomique: The Encyclopedia of Food, Wine, and Cookery.* Edited by Charlotte Turgeon and Nina Froud. New York: Crown, 1961. First English edition.

Montagné, Prosper. *Larousse gastronomique: The New American Edition of the World's Greatest Culinary Encyclopedia.* Edited by Jennifer Harvey Lang. New York: Crown, 1988. Second English edition.

Montagné, Prosper. *Larousse gastronomique: The World's Greatest Culinary Encyclopedia.* Edited by Jennifer Harvey Lang. New York: Clarkson Potter, 2001. Third English edition.

Simon, André Louis. *A Concise Encyclopaedia of Gastronomy.* Complete and unabridged. New York: Harcourt, Brace, 1952.

Szathmáry, Louis. *American Gastronomy: An Illustrated Portfolio of Recipes and Culinary History.* Chicago: Regnery, 1974.

Fritz Blank

GELATIN. Gelatin (also gelatine, jelly in Britain, jelly powder in Canada, and *gelée* in France) is a flavorless, transparent thickener derived from animal collagen that dissolves when heated and congeals when cooled, allowing foods to set. This versatile ingredient provides unique textural and sensory properties to both savory and sweet foodstuffs such as mousses, gummy bears, Turkish Delight, nougat, jellied soups, Bavarian cream, aspic, and Jell-O.

Gelatin is composed of protein molecules, made up of chains of amino acids. When placed in liquid, the molecules swell and then dissolve, and the chains separate. After cooling, they re-form as tightly as before. In the warmth of the mouth, they melt, providing excellent flavor release. This property and gelatin's easy digestability and absorption by the body makes gelled desserts appropriate for children, invalids, and the elderly.

Nutritional value of gelatin was recognized as early as the Napoleonic Wars (1800–1815) when the French used it as a source of protein during the English blockade. Commercial gelatin contains no fat or cholesterol and few calories, making it popular with people who have diet and heart concerns. Commercial manufacturers claim that gelatin promotes nail and hair growth, as well as flexible joints and healthy bones. However, the protein in gelatin is missing an amino acid and thus is not absorbed as a complete protein by the body.

Making Gelatin

The discovery of gelatin was probably serendipitous: When animal bones and hides are boiled in water, the broth that results will set upon cooling. From the Middle Ages through the eighteenth century, making gelatin was a daylong, laborious process in which cattle hooves were boiled for six hours. The stock was clarified as it dripped through a jelly bag, boiled again, and then allowed to sit. Not surprisingly, production was limited to wealthy households with many servants. Another early

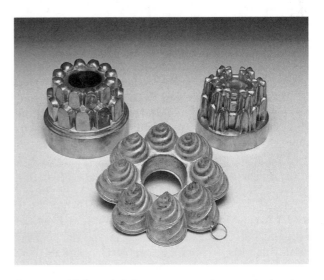

Copper molds for gelatin became extremely ornate in the nineteenth century. Different colors of gelatin, as well as different flavors, were often layered together in molds to create elaborate patterns for the table. Copper molds from England, circa 1870. ROUGHWOOD COLLECTION. PHOTO BY CHEW & COMPANY.

Part of the early success of Jell-O was its strong marketing appeal to children. This 1908 Jell-O brochure shows two disappointed children who have just been served baked apples instead of the Jell-O they expected. ROUGHWOOD COLLECTION.

JELL-O

Jell-O has become a cultural icon in the United States. Invented by Pearle Bixby Wait in 1897, (the name Jell-O was coined by his wife, May), this flavored gelatin's longevity is credited to its convenience for dessert, its popularity, especially with children, and its ability to inspire smiles, jokes, and playfulness. Beginning with strawberry, raspberry, orange, and lemon, Jell-O in the early twenty-first century comes in twenty-three flavors, including white sparkling grape, watermelon, and passion fruit. Strawberry is the best seller. Over a million boxes are sold every day; Salt Lake City, Utah, is the number-one consumer city.

Aside from thousands of inventive serving ideas (including one from 1930 for forcing set Jell-O through a potato ricer), Jell-O has spawned collectors (of original boxes, early advertising, recipe booklets, molds, glasses); Jell-O shots (alcoholic treats made by mixing in liquor); Jell-O wrestling (sometimes in the nude in large vats); the Jell-O Museum in Le Roy, N.Y.; an attempt to measure the brain waves of Jell-O; and countless websites.

Not everyone thinks Jell-O is benign. During the 1950s, when femininity was defined as docility, complicated molded constructions with fruits precisely placed according to pattern were popular, raising questions about a foodstuff that controls and keeps things in their place. One researcher claims that the marketing of Jell-O depicts women as inept homemakers. It is hard not to wonder about the larger social message of "perfection salad," a prescribed concoction of cabbage, celery, and red peppers in tomato Jell-O, popular at the turn of the twentieth century. Such prescription becomes a symbol of conformity and stifles creativity.

source of gelatin in the Middle Ages was hartshorn (antlers of the hart deer).

Today, the substance is manufactured commercially all over the world. In the United States most gelatin is derived from pig skin. Strictly speaking, this is not a kosher practice (although interpretations vary), and it is not permissible under Islamic dietary law. An alternative, isinglass (made from the air bladders of sturgeon), is acceptable to the religious and vegetarians. Another alternative is agar, made from a variety of red seaweed, commonly used in Japan where it is known as *kanten* and used in the manufacture of ice cream. Cattle form the basis of gelatin in France and Britain, raising safety concerns about transmission of mad cow disease even in the United States where some gelatin is imported from Europe.

Commercially manufactured gelatin is packaged in ¼-ounce envelopes of desiccated granules; paper-thin sheets, known as leaves (used in jelled Central and Eastern European desserts and aspics); and meltable blocks (Great Britain). In Latin America, gelatin is often mixed with milk or cream instead of water for the popular creamy desserts. In Russia, gelatin encases pigs' feet and other meats.

Aside from home and restaurant cooking, gelatin has wide application in the food industry where its functional properties are used to gel, thicken, stabilize, emulsify, bind, film, foam and whip prepared foods. Among other items, gelatin is incorporated into marshmallows, cake mixes, frostings, bakery glazes, meringues, ice cream, coffee, and powdered milk.

Medieval Beginnings

Elaborate molded jellies began to grace aristocratic British banquet tables in the fourteenth century. In the Late Medieval period (the 1400s) through the 1500s, cooks made savory and sweet jellied dishes using meat, chopped fine, mixed with cream or almond milk that was flavored with spices, rosewater, or sugar to fashion creations known as cullis, gellys, or brawn. In 1754, the first English patent for the manufacture of gelatin was granted. During the Victorian era, copper, and later aluminum, molds were introduced, which made possible the presentation of tall, shimmering creations. Unflavored dried gelatin became available in 1842 from the J and G Company of Edinburgh, Scotland.

Gelatin had an esteemed role in classic French cuisine. Escoffier's legendary *Guide Culinaire* (1903) includes a chapter on aspic jellies (savory gels) in which the great chef named two kinds: one flavored with champagne; the other with sherry, Marsala, or Madeira. Surprisingly, he mused that aspics might be even more important than stock, the bastion of Gallic cooking, because a cold meat, poultry, or fish entree (known as *chaud-froid*) is nothing without its glimmering coating of aspic. He warned that the value of the aspic decreased in direct proportion to its increasing firmness. The ideal was a softer consistency so aspic could even be served in a sauceboat. Gelatin also figured in many classic French desserts like blanc-mange, charlottes, mousses, and Bavarian creams.

Gelatin in the United States

In America, in 1845, Peter Cooper, inventor of the steam locomotive, secured a patent for a gelatin dessert powder called Portable Gelatin, requiring only the addition of hot water. The same year, the J and G Company began exporting its Cox Gelatin to the United States. The new formulas never gained much popularity, however, and as late as 1879 when the classic *Housekeeping in Old Virginia* was published, editor Marion Cabell Tyrer, while admitting that jelly made of calves and hogs was "more troublesome," claimed it was more nutritious than Cox's or Nelson's desiccated formulas. Plymouth Rock Gelatin Company of Boston patented its Phosphated Gelatin in 1889. In 1894, Charles Knox introduced granulated gelatin, making the brand something of a household word. This opened the way for a plethora of American recipes that gained popularity, particularly during the 1950s when chiffon pie and tomato aspic (made of gelatin and tomato juice) became staples.

Although Jell-O is considered déclassé in upscale restaurants, gelatin was resurrected and frenchfied by American chefs in the late 1990s, who reverted to calling the sweets "gelées." These creative formulas have been limited only by imagination since virtually any liquid can be used—coffee, champagne, grape and beet juice, rosé wine, sangria, and fruit poaching liquids. What began in the Middle Ages as an elite food has come full circle and returned to gourmet status.

See also **Escoffier, Georges-Auguste**; **Medieval Banquet**; **Proteins and Amino Acids**; **Icon Foods**; **Women and Food**.

BIBLIOGRAPHY

Wyman, Carolyn. *JELL-O: A Biography, The History and Mystery of "America's Most Famous Dessert."* San Diego, Calif., New York and London: Harcourt, 2001. Contains material on gelatin as well.

Shapiro, Laura. *Perfection Salad: Women and Cooking at the Turn of the Century.* New York: Farrar, Straus and Giroux, 1986.

Belluscio, Lynne. *The JELL-O Reader.* Le Roy, N.Y.: Le Roy Pennysaver, 1998. A collection of forty articles by the director of the Le Roy Historical Society. Also contains material on gelatin.

Berzok, Linda Murray. "My Mother's Recipes: The Diary of a Swedish American Daughter and Mother." *In Pilaf, Pozole, and Pad Thai: American Women and Ethnic Food*, edited by Sherrie A. Inness. Amherst, Mass.: University of Massachusetts Press, 2001. The social meaning, for women, of Jell-O molded salads.

Linda Murray Berzok

GENDER AND FOOD.

Across many cultures and epochs, people have constituted, expressed, and bridged gender differences through foodways—the beliefs and behaviors surrounding the production, distribution, and consumption of food. Through the division of labor, alimentary exchanges, access to food, and the meanings surrounding eating, men and women have enacted their identity, roles, and power.

Gender and Food Production

In many cultures, men and women define their economic relationships in food-centered productive roles. In hunting-gathering and pre-industrial farming cultures, men and women share in food production but have distinct roles. Among the !Kung of the Kalahari Desert, for example, women gather vegetable foods and men hunt animals. Although women produce the great majority of the food, men produce highly desired meat, and thus the contributions of both sexes are relatively equally valued, which contributes to the gender egalitarianism that is a hallmark of the !Kung. In Wamira, Papua New Guinea, men and women contribute to growing taro at different stages in the agricultural cycle: men prepare the soil and plant the tubers; women weed the gardens and tend the growing plants; men harvest the mature tubers (Kahn, 1986). They promote gender interdependence and mutual respect by symbolically linking their complementary roles in the production of taro to those in the reproduction of children. Among share-cropping peasants in Tuscany in the first half of the twentieth century, men focused on producing grain, grapes, and olives, while women took care of the family vegetable garden and the courtyard animals. Women also helped harvest the major crops, gathered wild foods, and preserved and prepared key comestibles. Because women's productive work was associated closely with their taken-for-granted reproductive roles in the home, it was less highly valued than men's contributions to food production.

Around the globe, women predominate in the lowest status, lowest paying, and most servile roles in agribusiness and the food industry as fieldworkers, waitresses, fast-food servers, and cannery and meatpacking workers. In rural Iowa, for example, women were almost completely excluded from the pork-packing industry when jobs were unionized and pay was good. They entered the industry in increasing numbers in the 1980s,

The tension between male and female views of food and cookery is satirized in this picture of the helpless husband and the amused wife. © H. ARMSTRONG ROBERTS/CORBIS.

when wages were falling, and at the end of the twentieth century they were still almost always relegated to the poorest paying packing and cleaning jobs in the plant rather than the better-paying cut and kill jobs (Fink, 1998).

Women are almost universally in charge of cooking and feeding, starting with breast-feeding the newborn. Through breast-feeding, women forge deep bonds with children and give them the best possible food, yet across the globe, breast-feeding has declined under the flood of commercial formulas. While formula has been beneficial to some women who cannot or do not want to breast-feed, it lacks the many benefits of breast milk and has contributed to the disempowerment of mothers who have lost confidence in their bodies and control of their children's food (Blum, 1999; Van Esterik, 1989; Whitaker, 2000).

Women's labor to produce, preserve, prepare, serve, and clean up food sometimes brings recognition and value, as among Ecuadorian peasants. But often women's food roles are devalued, especially under conditions of capitalist economic development, as in late-twentieth-century central Italy, where women's food roles became isolated in the home and separated from valued, public production. Florentine women struggle to balance their

desire to work outside the home with traditional expectations that they prepare elaborate meals for both lunch and supper. They suffer conflicts that men, free from culinary expectations, do not face. As in Italy, in England and the United States women's food roles in the home are sometimes problematic because they are "naturally" assigned to women and the labor involved is both underestimated and undervalued. Women are obligated by custom and culture to cook and please their husbands while subordinating their own desires (Charles and Kerr, 1988; DeVault, 1991). In lesbian and gay households, feeding work is undervalued and confers low status, so many couples tend to minimize its significance and the implicit subordination of the partner who does it (Carrington, 1999).

Gender and Food Consumption

Food consumption signifies gender and sexuality in diverse cultures. Eating often stands for intercourse, foods for sexual parts. Among the Wamira, taro represents male virility, and the size and fullness of the tubers stand for the potency of their producer. Male and female identities are expressed through association with foods and rules about consumption. The Hua of Papua New Guinea classify foods into two main categories: *koroko*, or female foods, are wet, cold, fertile, soft, and fast growing; *baker'a*, or male foods, are dry, hot, infertile, hard, and slow growing. Hua men and women believe they can gain some of each other's powers and attenuate gender differences by eating each other's foods (Meigs, 1984). In other cultures, however, rules about food consumption promote hierarchical conceptions of gender. In nineteenth-century American bourgeois homes, women were discouraged from eating meat, which was believed to stimulate excessive sexual appetite. Late-twentieth-century U.S. college students still believed that men should eat lots of meat and women should eat lighter foods, such as salads. They valued hearty appetite and big bodies in men, but preferred dainty eating and small bodies in women, thereby forcing women to deny their appetites and reduce themselves (Brumberg, 1988).

In Western cultures for at least seven centuries, women have much more commonly than men practiced extreme fasting and compulsive eating to communicate unspoken longings for autonomy, control, and power. A significant number of medieval women used food refusal and miraculous emissions of breast milk as expressions of piety and spiritual power. Middle-class nineteenth-century American girls refused food to demand attention and speak their needs for full personhood. Many U.S. girls at the turn of the twenty-first century struggle for control by pursuing excessive thinness through extreme fasting or bingeing and purging, while others eat compulsively to numb the pain of abuse. Yet women from many cultures have forged positive relationships with their bodies that allow different and more ample forms of body beauty. In cultures as disparate as Fiji and Flo-

MALE COOKS IN THE MID-TWENTIETH CENTURY

Insights into the gender-based division of labor in American culture are beautifully illustrated by cookbooks that were written by men for other men in the first half of the twentieth century. Among other things, they illustrate that, just like women, men had to deal with the consequences of being fettered by other people's notions of what was a permissible interest or occupation. Men were expected to do important, well-paying work, and if they happened to be interested in cooking, they were expected to be executive chefs. Men who wrote cookbooks could write without embarrassment about the pursuit and preparation of wild game, perhaps, or the perils of outdoor barbecuing, but everyday home cooking was understood to be women's work.

Nevertheless, men interested in writing recipes for home cooks managed to do so without losing their self-respect, but in order to pull it off they had to set themselves apart from women. Authors had to prove that male cooks were more creative and inspired than women, who were understood to be more concerned with the mundane task of getting three meals a day on the table. Male cooks had to convince themselves and others that, unlike women, their approach to food was spirited and adventurous, not weighted down by frets over level measurements or undue concerns about nutrition. The concern of the male cook, of course, was to appear masculine enough not to be mistaken for a sissy or the least bit effeminate; he would prove his legitimacy by establishing his superiority over women.

Certain American foods have been linked either to men or to women, creating stereotypes that designate light, sweet foods such as jams, jellies, and cupcakes as female, while male food is heavy and spicy, with the only acceptable vegetable being potatoes.

Male gourmets were happy to see the prohibition of alcohol lifted in 1933 so that they could occupy themselves with matching good food to good wines. Seeking like-minded companions, they formed societies to share their interest in fine food. J. George Frederick, founder and first president of the New York Gourmet Society, established his leadership by creating "A Gourmet's Code of Modern Dining," published in his book, *Cooking as Men Like It* (1939).

Frederick has clear ideas about differences between men and women in their approaches to food. While he credits women with having made some striking advances in their cooking, he finds them too occupied with cleanliness, purity, and nutrition, rather than what is "savory and tasteful" or "varied and succulent," the priorities of men.

While old ways of thinking tend to persist, new styles of eating would suggest that at the start of the twenty-first century, men who like to cook and bake can do so without feeling their manhood challenged, and women who have no interest in domesticity will perhaps no longer be considered unnatural.

See also **Cookbooks; Division of Labor; Time; United States: African American Foodways.**

Barbara Haber

---

rence, people decry thinness as evidence of social neglect and celebrate women's plumpness as a reflection of well-being and fertility.

Gender and Food Distribution

In food exchanges, men and women create meaningful relationships and demonstrate wealth and power. In many agricultural and hunting-gathering societies, men give away food to acquire and demonstrate political leadership. In Wamira, Papua New Guinea, men gain allies and shame enemies through massive food feasts. Women in many cultures exercise influence over family members by giving or withholding food, and they contribute to establishing hierarchy in the family by allocation of delicacies. When serving the soup, Ecuadorian Indian peasant women show favor by distribution of the prized chunks of meat, and they express ire at husbands by failing to prepare dinner, a grave insult and social transgression

(Weismantel, 1988). In many cultures, women and men initiate relationships by eating together—whether as a date among Western college students or as a marriage proclamation by sharing yams among the Trobriand Islanders. Feasts celebrate community and gender cooperation across all cultures. For example, in Tresnuraghes, Sardinia, for the feast of Saint Mark, shepherds donate sheep, which their wives cook and distribute—solidifying community, demonstrating wealth, and sharing food widely.

In many cultures, gender hierarchy is expressed through access to food. Often women have less access to food than men, a practice supported by their economic dependence, by beliefs that they need less, and by pregnancy food taboos. The Mbum Kpau, for example, prohibit women from eating chicken or goat lest they die in childbirth or suffer sterility, a major tragedy because of the importance of childbearing to these women. While in practice the prohibitions have little effect on daily consumption, they reinforce men's power by emphasizing their right to meat and other preferred foods (O'Laughlin, 1974). Under conditions of food deficiency, women are particularly vulnerable to hunger, along with children and the elderly, because they generally have less power over food and other resources than men. In Malawi, under normal conditions, women controlled grain stores and lived close to their relatives in matrilineal and matrilocal households. But in the 1949 famine, crops failed and women had no grain to control. Wage labor, exclusively practiced by men, was the only way to gain access to food, but many men left their wives' households to search for food in the villages where they were born, so women lost access to men's labor and wages while still being responsible for feeding children, the elderly, and themselves (Vaughn, 1987). Under conditions of food insecurity, male power over food is particularly salient, but even under conditions of food security, gender relations play an important role in food production, distribution, and consumption across cultures and time periods.

See also **Anorexia, Bulimia; Anthropology and Food; Division of Labor; Lactation; Milk, Human; Sex and Food; Symbol, Food as; Taboos; Time; Women and Food**.

BIBLIOGRAPHY

Becker, Anne. *Body, Self, and Society: The View from Fiji*. Philadelphia: University of Pennsylvania Press, 1995.

Blum, Linda. *At the Breast: Ideologies of Breastfeeding and Motherhood in the Contemporary United States*. Boston: Beacon Press, 1999.

Brumberg, Joan Jacobs. *Fasting Girls: The Emergence of Anorexia Nervosa as a Modern Disease*. Cambridge: Harvard University Press, 1988.

Bynum, Caroline Walker. *Holy Feast and Holy Fast: The Religious Significance of Food to Medieval Women*. Berkeley: University of California Press, 1987.

Carrington, Christopher. *No Place Like Home: Relationships and Family Life among Lesbians and Gay Men*. Chicago: University of Chicago Press, 1999.

Charles, Nickie, and Marion Kerr. *Women, Food and Families*. Manchester, U.K., and New York: Manchester University Press, 1988.

Chernin, Kim. *The Hungry Self: Women, Eating and Identity*. New York: Times Books, 1985.

Counihan, Carole. *The Anthropology of Food and Body: Gender, Meaning and Power*. New York: Routledge, 1999.

De Grazia, Victoria, ed. *The Sex of Things: Gender and Consumption in Historical Perspective*. Berkeley: University of California Press, 1996.

DeVault, Marjorie L. *Feeding the Family: The Social Organization of Caring as Gendered Work*. Chicago: University of Chicago Press, 1991.

Fink, Deborah. *Cutting into the Meatpacking Line: Workers and Change in the Rural Midwest*. Chapel Hill: University of North Carolina Press, 1998.

Inness, Sherrie A., ed. *Kitchen Culture in America: Popular Representations of Food, Gender, and Race*. Philadelphia: University of Pennsylvania, 2001.

Kahn, Miriam. *Always Hungry, Never Greedy: Food and the Expression of Gender in a Melanesian Society*. Cambridge, U.K., and New York: Cambridge University Press, 1986.

Meigs, Anna S. *Food, Sex, and Pollution: A New Guinea Religion*. New Brunswick, N.J.: Rutgers University Press, 1984.

O'Laughlin, Bridget. "Mediation of Contradiction: Why Mbum Women Do Not Eat Chicken." In *Woman, Culture, and Society*, edited by Michelle Zimbalist Rosaldo and Louise Lamphere, pp. 301–318. Stanford: Stanford University Press, 1974.

Paules, Greta Foff. *Dishing It Out: Power and Resistance among Waitresses in a New Jersey Restaurant*. Philadelphia: Temple University Press, 1991.

Shapiro, Laura. *Perfection Salad: Women and Cooking at the Turn of the Century*. New York: Farrar, Straus, and Giroux, 1986.

Thompson, Becky W. *A Hunger So Wide and So Deep: American Women Speak Out on Eating Problems*. Minneapolis: University of Minnesota Press, 1994.

Van Esterik, Penny. *Beyond the Breast-Bottle Controversy*. New Brunswick, N.J.: Rutgers University Press, 1989.

Vaughan, Megan. *The Story of an African Famine: Gender and Famine in Twentieth-Century Malawi*. Cambridge, U.K., and New York: Cambridge University Press, 1987.

Weismantel, Mary J. *Food, Gender, and Poverty in the Ecuadorian Andes*. Philadelphia: University of Pennsylvania Press, 1988.

Whitaker, Elizabeth Dixon. *Measuring Mamma's Milk: Fascism and the Medicalization of Maternity in Italy*. Ann Arbor: University of Michigan Press, 2000.

Carole M. Counihan

GENE EXPRESSION, NUTRIENT REGULATION OF.

The human genome (or genetic material) is comprised of deoxyribonucleic acid (DNA) that encodes information required for all life processes, including growth, development, reproduction, and even cell death. The functional units within the genome are called genes. Genes are hereditary regions of DNA that encode functional molecules, either proteins or ribonucleic acid (RNA) species. The human genome encodes approximately 100,000 genes on 23 chromosomes. DNA resides in a specific compartment within the cell, known as the nucleus. Each nucleated human cell within an individual, regardless of its origin, contains identical DNA. However, the genetic code is expressed or read differently in each cell type. Gene expression refers to the processes in which the genetic code is deciphered to produce a functional macromolecule, either protein or RNA. While some genes are expressed in all cells, others are expressed exclusively in certain tissues or organs. This selective reading of the code imparts very different chemical, functional, and morphological properties to each cell type and ultimately defines the function of a tissue or organ. Genes can also display temporal specific expression. For example, some genes are expressed only in the fetus, while other genes are not expressed until puberty or adulthood. Therefore, human DNA not only contains all of the genes required to assemble a human organism, but also encodes information that directs where, when, and how much an individual gene will be expressed.

Mechanisms of Gene Expression

Genes encode proteins. Proteins are polymers of amino acid building blocks that serve a variety of biological functions. Proteins can function as intracellular scaffolds that maintain cell integrity; others are transporters that permit specific nutrients and other small molecules to enter the cell. Proteins also can be enzymes that catalyze the many chemical reactions required for cell survival. While DNA is present in the nucleus, protein synthesis occurs in the cytoplasm, a separate compartment within the cell. Therefore, an intermediate molecule is needed to transfer the genetic information from the nuclear compartment that contains the code to the cytoplasmic compartment where the code is read. This intermediate molecule is termed "messenger RNA," and it is a short-lived functional copy of the genetic code. The process by which the genetic code, DNA, is copied to make a messenger RNA molecule occurs in the nucleus and is termed "transcription." The process of reading the genetic code from a messenger RNA molecule occurs in the cytoplasm and is termed "translation." The end product of translation is a protein molecule.

The expression of some genes is predetermined and cannot be altered. However, the expression of other genes, particularly those involved in nutrient storage, processing, and metabolism, is dynamic, and can be influenced by the cell's environment. Therefore, in some instances, gene expression can be an adaptive process. It is now well established that the expression of many genes is, in part, constrained by the nutrient environment—giving credence to the old adage, "you are what you eat." There are more than forty nutrients that are essential for mammals, and deficiencies in any of these nutrients have direct impacts on health. The cellular demand for these nutrients can vary as a function of growth, development, age, reproductive status, and immunity. However, for many organisms, the availability of nutrients can vary daily, weekly, and, in some cases, seasonally without notable changes in health. This is because organisms adapt to nutrient supply by altering gene expression. This alteration, in turn, enables cells to increase their storage capacity for certain nutrients, alter the absorption or excretion of certain nutrients, use alternative metabolic pathways, or reprogram metabolic pathways.

Nutrients as Informational Molecules

If organisms have evolved the ability to reprogram themselves for optimal utilization of the available nutrient resources, then the implication is that a nutrient is not merely

FAMILIAL HYPERCHOLESTEROLEMIA

Familial hypercholesterolemia is a disease that results from genetic mutations in the low-density lipoprotein (LDL) receptor. It is one of the most common inborn errors of metabolism. Individuals with one mutated copy of the gene (referred to as heterozygotes for this mutation) number about one in five hundred, whereas one in a million individuals carry two mutated copies of this gene (referred to as homozygotes for a mutation). LDL receptors are necessary for transporting LDL into cells from serum. LDL is a major cholesterol transport lipoprotein in human plasma, and individuals with LDL receptor mutations accumulate LDL in serum because LDL transport into cells is impaired. Plasma cholesterol levels from affected heterozygotes range from 350 to 550 mg/dl, and these values can exceed 1000 mg/dl for affected homozygotes. Individuals with elevated serum cholesterol have a high risk for developing heart disease at very young ages.

Cholesterol is an important component of cell membranes, and it serves to decrease their fluidity. Mammals can synthesize cholesterol in the absence of sufficient dietary cholesterol, but the endogenous biosynthesis is tightly regulated and inhibited by dietary cholesterol supply. A transcription factor known as SREBP (Sterol Response Element Binding Protein) regulates the expression of a gene that encodes a key enzyme that is necessary for cholesterol biosynthesis. When dietary intake of cholesterol is adequate, this transcription factor is sequestered in the membranes of the Golgi compartment of the cell and is inactive. When cellular cholesterol levels fall, however, the membranes in the Golgi become more fluid. This results in the liberation of SREBP from the membrane and enables it to travel to the nucleus, where it can activate the expression of genes that are necessary for cholesterol biosynthesis. Through this regulation, cholesterol biosynthesis occurs only when dietary sources are limited. However, this mechanism of gene regulation fails in familial hypercholesterolemia. Because LDL cholesterol is not effectively transported into cells, the cells cannot sense extracellular cholesterol levels, and therefore cellular SREBP activity and cholesterol biosynthesis is constantly activated. Activated cholesterol biosynthesis serves to further increase serum LDL concentrations in affected individuals.

a chemical component required for a particular metabolic function, but also that it plays an informational or signaling role in the cell. As with any system that transmits

TABLE 1

Nuclear receptors and their associated ligands

Ligands	Nuclear receptors
Hormone Activating Ligands	
3,5,3'-L-triiodothyronine	TR
testosterone	AR
progesterone	PR
aldosterone	MR
cortisol	GR
17β-estradiol	ER
androstanol	CARβ
pregnenolone-16-carbonitrile	PXR
25-hydroxycholesterol	SF1
Vitamin Activating Ligands	
dihydrovitamin D3	VDR
all-trans retinoic acid	RAR
9-*cis* retinoic acid	RXR
Metabolite Activating Ligands	
leukotriene B4	PPARα
8(S)-HETE	PPARα
15-deoxy-12,14-prostaglandin J2	PPARγ
22(R)-hydroxycholesterol	LXR
CDCA (bile acids)	FXR
palmitoyl-CoA	HNF-4

information, the signal must have a sensor or receiver that can accept, decode, and relay the information that has been transmitted. Cellular proteins that receive and transmit this information are termed "receptors." The receptors then must relay this information via a transducing mechanism to the part of the cell that is capable of reprogramming the cell to adapt to the new environmental conditions. This reprogramming can occur in the cell nucleus or cytoplasm. It can involve changes in the expression of genes (transcription and translation), the stability of messenger RNA and protein, or the activity of proteins. The key principle behind nutrient control of gene expression is specificity. Each receptor must have the capability of binding a nutrient-signaling molecule with specificity and should initiate an adaptive change.

Nutrient Control of RNA Synthesis
The best-understood signaling molecules are hormones such as estrogen and testosterone. A hormone is produced by a particular tissue and causes a specific biological change in the same tissue or a different tissue located elsewhere in the body. In some cases, these molecules can enter a cell and bind to a particular protein molecule, termed a "nuclear receptor." The receptor-hormone complex then travels to the nucleus, binds very specific regions of the DNA, and turns on the expression of genes not normally expressed in the absence of the hormone. This change in gene expression imparts new functional roles to individual cells, which can impact the entire organism greatly. In this manner, diverse biological processes can be initiated, including puberty or menstruation. Certain nutrients can also influence gene expression in a similar manner. Nutrients, including

vitamin A, vitamin D, and certain fatty acids, bind nuclear receptors and influence the expression of genes. These nutrient receptors enable cells to sense their nutrient environment and adjust cellular metabolism accordingly by altering the expression of genes.

Nutrient Control of Protein Synthesis
Nuclear receptors are effective in reprogramming DNA transcription to adapt to nutrient environments. Other mechanisms exist to alter gene expression without changing rates of DNA transcription. In fact, alteration of translation is a common mechanism that permits cells to adapt rapidly to changing nutrient environments. Iron is the paradigm for nutrient regulation of gene expression at the level of translation. Iron is a critical component of many metabolic proteins and enzymes involved in oxygen transport, energy metabolism, and DNA synthesis. Iron deficiency results in several disease states, including anemia. Therefore, the body must retain sufficient iron stores to stave off such pathologies. However, iron is also a potent oxidant and, if not bound by proteins in the cell, it can destroy DNA and proteins, and catalyze events that initiate cancer. Therefore, the body must store iron, but in such a manner that prevents the iron from destroying the integrity of its cells. Cells are protected from the deleterious effects of iron by sequestering it in a protein shell called ferritin. Cellular iron is stored in ferritin until required. Ferritin synthesis is rapidly induced when cells are exposed to iron and this increased synthesis is directly regulated by iron. Cells contain an iron-sensing protein called the iron regulatory protein (IRP). This protein binds either iron or ferritin messenger RNA but cannot bind both molecules simultaneously. When iron is not available to the cell, the intracellular concentration of nonprotein-bound iron is very low and IRP does not contain bound iron. This results in IRP being available to bind ferritin messenger RNA, which stops new ferritin synthesis. However, when cells are exposed to iron, IRP contains a bound iron molecule and cannot bind ferritin messenger RNA, and ferritin synthesis occurs. In this manner, the iron storage protein ferritin is only synthesized when it is required to store new iron.

Permanent Adaptation to Nutrient Supply
There is accumulating evidence that prenatal and postnatal nutrition can permanently alter cellular metabolism by altering gene expression throughout adulthood, a phenomenon termed "metabolic imprinting." Low birth weight, which occurred in infants born to survivors of the Dutch Famine of 1944–1945, has been linked to an increased risk of chronic disease later in life, including adult obesity, insulin resistance, hypertension, and cardiovascular disease. The susceptibility to these disease states is influenced both by dietary habits as well as one's genetic predisposition or heritage. Although the biological basis for metabolic imprinting is not yet proven, the suggestion that gene expression can be programmed by fetal and postnatal nutrient environment has far-reaching im-

plications. For many adult chronic disease states, dietary management is an important component of the therapy. If metabolic imprinting occurs, dietary management early in life may also be advantageous in preventing numerous chronic disease states that do not surface until adulthood.

Nutritional Modulation of Gene Expression in Health and Disease

The relationships between nutrient availability and adaptive changes in gene expression are critical to understanding the role of nutrition in health and disease. For many nutrients, either dietary insufficiency or excess can result in or contribute to disease onset. Nutrient modulation of gene expression serves to protect the cell from the deleterious effects of both under-nutrition and over-nutrition. Hereditary hyperferritinemia-cataract syndrome is a human disorder associated with altered regulation of iron homeostasis. Affected individuals have mutations in a ferritin gene that result in the synthesis of a ferritin messenger RNA that encodes a normal functional ferritin protein, but the mutation does not permit IRP to bind to the messenger RNA and stop translation. Therefore, these individuals can no longer regulate ferritin levels in response to changes in iron intake. As a result of this mutation, these individuals contract early-onset bilateral cataract associated with a progressive decrease in visual acuity. Ongoing research is identifying many other nutrient-related disease states that result from disregulation of nutrient control of gene expression.

See also **Cholesterol; Combination of Proteins; Genetic Engineering; Genetics; Malnutrition: Protein-Energy Malnutrition; Nutrients; Proteins and Amino Acids**.

BIBLIOGRAPHY

Alberts, Bruce, et al. *Molecular Biology of the Cell.* 3d ed. New York: Garland, 2002.

Allerson, Charles R., M. Cazzola, and Tracey A. Rouault. "Clinical Severity and Thermodynamic Effects of Iron-Responsive Element Mutations in Hereditary Hyperferritinemia-Cataract Syndrome." *Journal of Biological Chemistry* 274 (1999): 26439–26447.

Berdanier, Carolyn D., and James L. Hargrove. "Nutrient Receptors and Gene Expression." In *Nutrition and Gene Expression*, edited by Carolyn D. Berdanier and James L. Hargrove. Boca Raton, Fla.: CRC Press, 1993.

Mikulits, Wolfgang, Matthias Schranzhofer, Hartmut Beug, and Ernst W. Müllner. "Post-Transcriptional Control via Iron-Responsive Elements: The Impact of Aberrations in Hereditary Disease." *Mutation Research* 437 (1999): 219–230.

Repa, Joyce J., and David J. Mangelsdorf. "The Role of Orphan Nuclear Receptors in the Regulation of Cholesterol Homeostasis." *Annual Review of Cellular and Developmental Biology* 16 (2000): 459–481.

Waterland, Robert A., and Cutberto Garza. "Potential Mechanisms of Metabolic Imprinting that Lead to Chronic Disease." *American Journal of Clinical Nutrition* 69 (1999): 179–197.

Patrick J. Stover

GENETIC ENGINEERING. Genetic engineering involves the directed alteration of an organism's DNA (deoxyribonucleic acid)—that is, its genetic material. This technology has been applied to microbes, plants, and animals, and consequently used to modify foods, animal feedstuffs, and food-processing reagents.

Domestication and improvement of plants and animals for agriculture initially relied on identification of individuals with desirable characteristics from among natural populations. Applying knowledge of genetics to the breeding of plants and animals resulted in more rapid progress and remains vitally important to agricultural development. Traditional breeding, however, is constrained by the boundaries of sexual compatibility, which limits the choice of parents that can be used as sources of genes and traits to improve a specific crop or animal to those that can produce progeny through sexual reproduction. Genetic engineering expands the source of genes that can be used to modify the characteristics of plants and animals.

Technology of Genetic Engineering

Genetic engineering requires three fundamental technologies: the ability to isolate and modify the DNA of specific individual genes; an understanding of the mechanisms that regulate how genes function and how these can be manipulated; and the capacity to transfer genes into an organism. These have all been developed following the discovery of the structure of DNA in 1953. Genetic engineering of microbes was first reported in 1973, followed in the next decade by similar achievements in plants and animals. Because DNA is the genetic material in all organisms, genes for genetic engineering can be taken from any source, or even synthesized. Modification of genes may be necessary, particularly in regions that control how they operate, in order for the genes to function effectively in the recipient organism. *Agrobacterium tumefaciens*, a bacterium that transfers DNA into plant cells as part of its normal life cycle, is used commonly to transfer genes into plants, although other methods such as the "gene gun" also have been developed. Genetically engineered plants are technically "transgenic organisms," as they contain transferred genes. However, they are frequently referred to as "genetically modified organisms," or GMOs, and the products derived from them are described as "genetically modified," or GM foods. These terms can be confusing, as essentially all cultivated plants have been genetically modified through breeding and selection—for example, the many varieties of cultivated onions possess numerous qualities that distinguish them from each other and especially from the wild onions from which they originated.

Application of Genetic Engineering in Agriculture

The first genetically engineered crops were planted on a large scale in 1996. By 2001 more than fifty million hectares were planted worldwide with transgenic crops. The first generation of these crops has been altered in ways that improve the efficiency of crop production by modifying the tolerance of plants to herbicides and insect pests. Broad-spectrum herbicides are able to kill almost all plants. A prerequisite for using chemicals to control weeds in a crop is that the crop itself must be resistant to the herbicide. Genetic engineering has been used to develop plants (specifically soybean, canola, corn, and cotton) with resistance to two broad-spectrum herbicides, glyphosate and glufosinate, which are sold under the trademarks Roundup and Liberty, respectively. Glyphosate-tolerant soybeans have been adopted rapidly in some countries, notably the United States and Argentina, and accounted for approximately 46 percent of the soybean acreage worldwide in 2001. Herbicide use has not declined in these crops but the specific herbicides that are used have changed.

Insect pests can damage crops during the growing season and also after harvest. A variety of methods, including cultural practices and insecticides, are used to control insect damage. Genetic engineering has provided novel approaches to this problem. The bacterium *Bacillus thuringiensis* (*Bt*) produces proteins that are toxic to some types of insects, and *Bt* spores have been used as insecticides for decades. Genes encoding *Bt* toxin proteins have been isolated, modified so they function in plants, and transferred into crop plants including corn, potato, and cotton. These engineered *Bt* crops are more resistant to such insects as the European corn borer, Colorado potato beetle, and cotton bollworm than are their nonengineered counterparts. The introduction of *Bt* cotton has resulted in reduced use of insecticides on this crop in some regions of the United States. Growers of *Bt* crops are required to plant a portion of their acreage with varieties that do not carry the *Bt* gene, in an effort to delay the development of insect populations with resistance to *Bt* toxins.

The Flavr Savr tomato, developed in the 1980s by Calgene, a biotechnology company in California, was the first food produced from a genetically engineered plant. These tomatoes ripened more slowly and had an extended shelf life. However, for a number of reasons—including production problems and consumer skepticism—this product was not a commercial success and was withdrawn in 1996, after less than three years on the market. Melons and raspberries have also been engineered to have delayed ripening but have not been produced commercially. Transgenic papayas with resistance to ring spot virus also have been developed. These were grown successfully in Hawaii, where the papaya industry was devastated by this debilitating disease. A similar approach was used to produce virus-resistant summer squash and against other viruses affecting a wide variety of foodstuffs.

The first generation of transgenic crops for the most part were designed to improve the efficiency of crop production, an ongoing objective for genetic engineers. Additionally, the techniques of genetic engineering can be used to alter the nutritional composition of foods. The transfer into rice of three genes that function to produce beta-carotene in the seed resulted in "golden rice." Once consumed, beta-carotene can be converted to vitamin A, the degree of this conversion being dependent upon a number of factors that relate to the source of the beta-carotene, the diet, and the individual consumer. In less-developed countries, vitamin A deficiency is widespread among those with a restricted diet, and is responsible for increased mortality and blindness in children. Although the efficacy of transgenic rice in reducing disease has not been established, it demonstrates the potential use of genetic engineering for nutritional enhancement in many crops. Other applications of genetic engineering of animal and human foods include removing allergens from foods such as peanuts, increasing the level of essential vitamins and nutrients in foods, and producing foods possessed of vaccines and other beneficial compounds.

Genetically engineered microbes also are used to produce proteins for food processing. Chymosin (or rennin), an enzyme used in cheese production, traditionally is obtained from the stomach of veal calves. However, the gene encoding this enzyme was transferred into microbes, and the enzyme now can be produced in bulk by purifying it from large microbe cultures. Chymosin prepared from transgenic microbes has more predictable properties than the animal product and is used to produce more than fifty percent of hard cheeses in the United States. Other enzymes used in food processing are produced by similar methods. For example, bovine growth hormone (BGH) is produced in large quantities from transgenic microbes and is given to cows to increase milk production.

Regulation of Genetic Engineering

In the United States, three federal agencies—Food and Drug Administration (FDA), Environmental Protection Agency (EPA), and Department of Agriculture (USDA)—are involved in regulating transgenic crops. Similar systems are in place in other countries as well. Companies that have developed this technology generally are supportive of the current regulatory framework. Nevertheless, the development of transgenic crops and the introduction of foods that contain products from these plants in the 1990s generated tremendous controversy, notably in Europe. Proponents of genetic engineering have argued that the addition of one or two well-characterized genes into crop plants that have a history of safe use is unlikely to affect materially the properties of these plants. Opponents suggest that this technology has not been tested adequately and the public should not be exposed to unknown and unnecessary food-based risks.

Safety concerns include the possibility that this technology will reduce the nutritional content of foods and introduce novel allergens or other toxins into foods. Opponents have sought more extensive testing and mandatory labeling of products that contain genetically engineered foods so that consumers can choose whether or not to eat such items. The impact of transgenic crops on the environment also has been questioned. Pests are likely to develop resistance to toxins produced by transgenic plants, raising doubts about the sustainability of this approach. However, transgenic technology also has the potential to reduce the use of chemical pesticides for crop production, which most regard as a positive development. Transfer of genes from engineered crops to other plants might also occur—for example, making weeds resistant to a specific herbicide or expanding the range of a plant so that it can grow in new locations.

This new technology also brings forth social, economic, and ethical issues, many of which are reflected by a wide political debate. One subject of concern is that most of the technology enabling genetic engineering of crop plants is controlled by a small number of companies. Much of this control is achieved through ownership of intellectual property, such as patents on genes, methods to produce transgenic plants, and the plant material that is the basis for crop improvement. Companies that manage agricultural inputs, such as seeds, pesticides, and fertilizers, as well as food processing and retail operations, function increasingly on a global scale. Opponents of globalization have criticized genetic engineering as one factor that is contributing to this trend and have expressed concern that both farmers and consumers will have limited choice in who supplies their needs. Opposition to genetic engineering also has come from religious groups who believe that tampering with genes in this way is unnatural—that is, inconsistent with the divine domain of nature—and should not be allowed.

Development of methods to genetically modify plants that extend beyond the limits of normal sexual reproduction has the potential to change many aspects of food production. Some of the first generations of products of this technology were adopted readily by most farmers but, as with other new technologies, there are many opponents. If this technology eventually receives widespread acceptance, it is likely that genetically engineered products will be found in almost everything that humans and domesticated animals eat.

See also **Additives**; **Agronomy**; **Biotechnology**; **High-Technology Farming**; **History of Food Production**.

BIBLIOGRAPHY

Charles, Daniel. *Lords of the Harvest: Biotech, Big Money, and the Future of Food.* Cambridge, Mass.: Perseus Publishing, 2001. A history of the development of agricultural biotechnology and genetically engineered foods.

Colorado State University. *Transgenic Crops: An Introduction and Resource Guide.* Available at http://www.colostate.edu/programs/lifesciences/TransgenicCrops/

Ervin, David, Sandra Batie, Rick Welsh, Chantal Carpentier, Jacqueline Fern, Nessa Richman, and Mary Schulz. *Transgenic Crops: An Environmental Assessment.* Morrilton, Ark.: Winrock International, 2000. Available at http://www.winrock.org/Transgenic.pdf

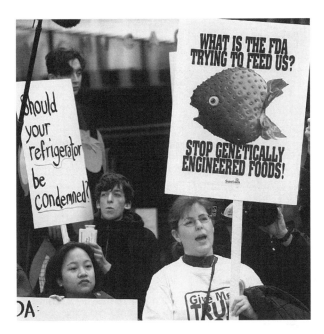

Genetically engineered foods have caused widespread concern, even open protest, as in the case of this demonstration against the Federal Food and Drug Administration in Chicago. Much of the concern is not centered on the science itself, but on the social and ethical ramifications, the economic implications, and the lack of accountability for "genetic pollution." PHOTO COURTESY OF AP/WIDE WORLD PHOTOS.

Nuffield Council on Bioethics. *Genetically Modified Crops: The Ethical and Social Issues.* London: Nuffield Council on Bioethics, 1999. A report from the United Kingdom that addresses consumer issues.

Pew Initiative on Food and Biotechnology. *Harvest on the Horizon: Future Uses of Agricultural Biotechnology.* Washington D.C.: Pew Initiative, 2001. Available at http://pewagbiotech.org/research/harvest/

Watson, James, Michael Gilman, Jan Witkowski, and Mark Zoller. *Recombinant DNA.* 2nd ed. New York: W. H. Freeman, 1992. A detailed description of the science behind genetic engineering.

Peter Goldsbrough

GENETICS. Since the first efforts were made to cultivate plants, humans have employed genetics to breed crops with improved taste, hardiness, or yield. The long history of genetics and nutrition can be felt even today, and permeates many aspects of our daily life. Home gardeners can purchase seeds that will grow in particular soils, produce fruit at various times of the year, or grow in sunshine or shade. Local supermarkets sell supersweet varieties of corn and fruits such as the tangelo, made from crossing grapefruits with tangerines. The "Green Revolution," which began with the identification of a high-yield strain of wheat, has resulted in dramatic increases in food production around the world. With the advent

FIGURE 1

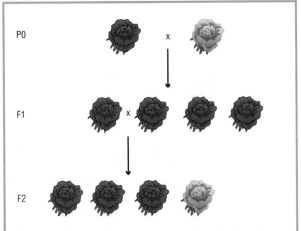

Phenotype of Mendel's plants. Mendel crossed "pure-breeding" purple-flowered plants with pure-breeding white-flowered plants. These parental plants (P0 generation) were derived from plant stock that always gave rise to purple- or white-flowered plants. When crossed to one another, however, they only produced purple-flowered plants in the F1 generation. When two F1 plants were crossed, Mendel was able to recover white-flowered plants. Mendel repeated his results for other traits as well, including plant height, pea shape, pea color, pod color, leaf position, and pod shape.

of genetic engineering, new, disease resistant crops have been developed, with the promise of reducing requirements for pesticide use.

Plants are not the only organism to be subjected to genetic breeding programs by humans. Yeast strains for baking bread or producing alcoholic beverages have been cultured for centuries. Meatier turkeys and cows that give more milk are the product of animal breeding efforts. Some have argued that the genetic manipulation of foodstuffs has gone too far, emphasizing crops that can withstand long storage times, transportation to markets, and handling by the consumer over any selection for flavor. Others worry that genetic engineering gives us unprecedented, and perhaps dangerous, opportunities to mix and match desired traits. It is nevertheless apparent that genetics has had an enormous impact upon society.

What is genetics? Simply put, genetics is the study of hereditary variation. This variation, in essence, is the diversity of life as it exists in all its forms on earth. For example, there are perhaps some 300,000 different species of flowering plants. What makes each of these plants different from one another? Perhaps even more amazing than this variation between species, there are astounding levels of variation that can be found even within a species. There are, for example, some 6,000 different varieties of apples alone. Genetics aims to understand how this variation occurs between species as well as within species. The term "phenotype" is used to describe any differences that can be observed or measured. For example, the possession of yellow kernels is a phenotype of a particular strain of corn, which distinguishes it from strains that possess white kernels. The two may have phe-

notypes in common (e.g., they both have white flowers or are supersweet) in addition to the differing phenotype of yellow and white kernels. Genetics examines the ground rules regarding how these phenotypes are passed on, or inherited, from one generation to the next.

Gregor Mendel, the Father of Genetics

While genetic breeding has been practiced for many hundreds of years, the true science of genetics began with Gregor Mendel, an Austrian monk who published his seminal work in the mid-1800s. At the time, genes had not been identified; indeed, the term itself would not be coined until 1909. How traits could be inherited from one generation to another was entirely unclear. Charles Darwin himself proposed the pangenesis theory, in which traits from the parents are passed to their children in a process that "blends" them together. In this theory, children represent a melding of the two parental sets of traits. They in turn would pass their traits on to their children, further blending together the traits of their respective parents. This model of how genetics operates can be contrasted with the particulate theory, in which traits are retained on small particles passed from one generation to the next. While Darwin's model would seem to be consistent with what we can observe in our own children, Mendel's carefully performed and insightful experiments clearly supported the particulate theory, and laid down the basic principles of the inheritance of phenotypes.

Mendel discovered his principles working with pea plants, which were raised not only for their experimental value but also as a food source for the monastery. Mendel's seminal idea was to identify clearly defined and distinct traits among these plants, and determine how these phenotypes were passed from one generation to the next. For example, Mendel identified plants that possessed either white flowers or purple flowers, but not both. He then crossed these two different variants with one another (the "parental," or P0 generation), and examined the flower color of the resulting progeny plants in the filial, or F1, generation. If the blending theory were correct, one might expect pink flowers to be produced in the F1 plants. Instead, Mendel obtained only purple flowered plants. If these F1 purple-flowered plants were then interbred with one another, producing an F2 generation of plants, Mendel saw once again pea plants with white flowers. Thus, even though this particular trait (white flowers) had not been seen at all in the F1 generation, it had been retained, and could be recovered in the F2 generation. These results clearly supported the particulate theory.

To obtain his results, Mendel studied the transmission of seven distinct phenotypes among some 28,000 pea plants, and synthesized them into a mathematical model of genetic inheritance. In doing so, he did what had never been done before; he quantified his results. From an analysis of his data, he was able to infer several key principles. He argued that there must exist determinants that specify particular phenotypes, a feature we now recognize as genes. He also argued that these determinants are located on particles, one of which is donated by the father, and one by the mother. These particles, now known to be chromosomes, produce a progeny plant that has one determinant for flower color donated by the mother, and one determinant for flower color donated by the father. The phenotype of the progeny plant will depend upon the particular combination of determinants it receives from its parents. Mendel deduced that the determinant for the production of purple flowers (represented as "P") is dominant over the determinant to produce white flowers (represented as "p"). Conversely, the white flower determinant is recessive in the presence of the purple-flower determinant. Two copies of the purple-determinant (P/P) in a plant, one maternal and one paternal, results in purple flowers. One purple and one white flower determinant (P/p) still produces purple flowers. Only if a plant receives two white flower determinants (p/p) will it possess white flowers.

Mendel's results were not widely known at the time. Some thirty-five years later, his work was "rediscovered" by geneticists who had repeated his results in other organisms. The implications of Mendel's work were revolutionary. For the first time, it was possible to observe the patterns of inherited phenotypes of a plant, animal, insect, or bacterium, and deduce, with mathematical precision, the expected genotypes of these organisms. It is a tribute to the work of Mendel and others of his time that their results were obtained despite not knowing that genes were encoded by DNA or how genes act to produce the observed phenotype.

Single Gene Effects

Part of Mendel's success was due to his implicit recognition that there are two primary types of variation: discontinuous and continuous. In discontinuous variation, a particular phenotype can be found in a population in at least two distinct forms. For example, Mendel's peas possessed purple or white flowers, and not both. On the other hand, in continuous variation, a range of similar phenotypes can be observed in the population. An example of this among humans might be the observation that noses come in all shapes and sizes. In most instances, genetics has focused predominantly upon discontinuous variants, as the associated phenotypes can be clearly recognized and categorized. As it turns out, many of the phenotypes that fall into this group can be associated with alterations in the function of a single gene. In our purple versus white flower example, the gene that is normally responsible for giving the plant its purple color has been mutated, such that it no longer functions. In the absence of this gene, white, or uncolored, flowers are produced. The different forms of this same gene (P, indicating normal or wild-type function, and p, indicating altered or mutant function) are called alleles. If an allele is widely represented in the population, as is the case

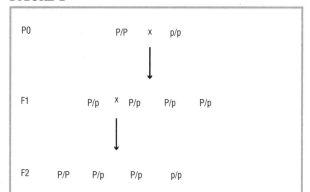

Genotype of Mendel's plants, as shown in Figure 1. As the parental plants are pure-breeding, they must each carry two identical determinants—either two copies of the "P," or purple flower determinant, or two copies of "p," the white flower determinant. Their progeny in the F1 will receive one determinant from each parent, so that all plants will carry a P and a p determinant. In the F2, plants can receive either a P or a p from either parent. Those receiving two p determinants will have white flowers.

among white or purple flowers in pea plants, they are termed polymorphisms.

Polymorphisms can be identified in other organisms as well. However, in humans, there are also additional issues of ethnicity and race. A common polymorphism among Asians, for example, is a particular allele of the alcohol dehydrogenase 2 (Adh2) gene. This allele negatively affects the enzyme's ability to metabolize alcohol, and is possessed by more than 90 percent of the Japanese population. In the European population, on the other hand, less than 10 percent have this allele. Similarly, lactose intolerance is due to allelic variation in the lactase gene. An allele that leads to low activity of lactase following early childhood is common in Africans and Asians (>80 percent), and rarer in Caucasians (17–50 percent). These relatively common polymorphisms are just a few of the many thousands of alleles known to exist in humans.

Why these polymorphisms exist is not clear, although it can be hypothesized that they either do no harm to individuals who harbor these particular alleles, or, if they are in fact somewhat harmful, are nonetheless still of some benefit. This can be described as the fitness of the allele. For example, as many as 10–20 percent of the European population bears a polymorphism in the gene encoding methylenetetrahydrofolate reductase (MTHFR). These individuals have a greater risk of neural tube defects, such as spina bifida, due to the fact that this allele affects folate metabolism. Why then, is such a polymorphism maintained in such a high percentage of the population? The answer may lie in the observation that individuals with this polymorphism have an increased efficiency of blood clotting. As mortality resulting from bleeding after childbirth was a common occurrence, this would be beneficial to individuals bearing this polymorphism. While it is often dangerous to speculate why a polymorphism exists, if this reduction in risk is substantiated, it would

FIGURE 3

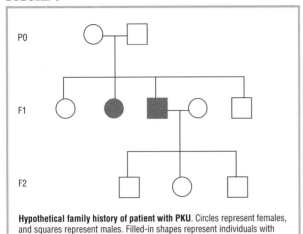

Hypothetical family history of patient with PKU. Circles represent females, and squares represent males. Filled-in shapes represent individuals with PKU. Note that the parental generation and F2 generation do not exhibit disease.

obviously be of benefit both to the individual and the population as a whole.

While we have centered this discussion around polymorphisms, on occasion, an allele will arise that affects only a small percentage of the population. Although these rare variants are uncommon (<1 percent of the population), they make up a large proportion of the patients that are hospitalized for medically related conditions. One such example would be phenylketonuria, which occurs in one out of every 10,000 births. This medical condition is due to a mutation in the phenylalanine hydroxylase gene, and leads to a failure to metabolize phenylalanine containing compounds, such as aspartame. If unrecognized, infants with PKU invariably develop mental retardation. This can be avoided by monitoring dietary intake to eliminate phenylalanine-containing compounds. How is PKU inherited from one generation to another? The fields of medical genetics and genetic counseling encompass the analysis of family histories, so as to better treat individuals who are at risk from these illnesses. If we examine the family history of a typical patient that has PKU, we might observe the following:

In this case, neither parent in the P0 generation suffers from the disease, but some of their children do. Applying principles learned from Mendel's work, we can infer the genotype of the family members from this phenotypic analysis:

From the study of this family history, it is clear that PKU is inherited in a recessive manner. Adults who are heterozygous for mutations in the phenylalanine hydroxylase gene (K/k; possessing one wild-type or normal allele and one mutant allele) do not have PKU. Only those with two mutant copies (k/k) display the condition. Thus, Mendel's laws apply equally well to humans as they do to peas. Interestingly, however, while the phenotype of PKU patients indicates a recessive inheritance of this

condition, an analysis of the genotype of these patients and the population in general reveals the existence of more than 400 alleles of the phenylalanine hydroxylase gene. This astounding degree of allelic heterogeneity indicates that most PKU patients indeed possess two mutant alleles of the hydroxylase gene, but that these two alleles are likely to be completely different. The phenotypic effect is the same; elimination or severe alteration of the normal function of the gene leads to PKU. The molecular basis of this defect, however, is dependent upon the specific alleles that are involved. It is plain to see that the field of molecular genetics, which examines the actual genes responsible for these defects, is an important complement to more traditional genetic phenotypic observations.

While the examples we have looked at so far have comprised diseases or phenotypic traits that are inherited in a recessive fashion, many diseases are inherited in a dominant manner. In these instances, a single copy of the mutant allele is sufficient to confer, at least partially, a medically associated condition. An example of this might be familial hypercholesterolemia, which is associated with an inability to properly metabolize cholesterol. A family history of patients with this affliction might appear thus:

Compare the rate of occurrence of this condition with that of PKU. Only a single copy of the mutant allele is required to produce at least some phenotype in cases of familial cholesterolemia. In many of these dominantly inherited diseases, individuals that possess two mutant alleles are much more strongly affected than individuals with one mutant and one wild-type allele. In familial hypercholesterolemia, homozygous patients (those with two mutant alleles; H/H) rarely live past the age of 30. These individuals are rare, however, occurring in perhaps one in one million. Heterozygous individuals (those with one mutant and one wild-type allele; H/h), on the other hand, are extremely common, and are present in perhaps one in 500. These individuals have a higher propensity for premature heart disease due to the buildup of atherosclerotic plaques, but without the severity of phenotype exhibited by homozygous individuals.

These examples illustrate just a few of the more than 1400 single-gene disorders that have been identified. It has been estimated that in any one individual, perhaps 20 percent of all genetic loci are heterozygous. This suggests that a striking degree of individuality exists at the genetic level. This allelic variation may explain, for example, the differential response of individuals to environmental, dietary, or pharmacological effects.

Multiple Gene Interactions

So far, we have discussed examples of phenotypes that can be traced to alterations of a single gene. While great strides have been made in identifying genes that are associated with a particular phenotype, it is clear that we are far from understanding how genes interact with one another as a whole. For example, many genetic disorders are thought to result from the interplay of multiple genes with epigenetic, or environmental, influences, such as diet. One means of trying to understand these multifactorial disorders and how genes and the environment interact is to examine at a molecular level how genes function. While Mendel derived his results from observing the phenotype of his plants, a molecular geneticist might ask, what is the actual gene that is responsible for production of purple pigment? What is its sequence? How does it function in the plant cell to produce color? With what other genes does it interact?

DNA has often been called the "blueprint of life," and indeed, DNA is the thread that ties almost all life on earth together. Rules that govern the replication of DNA and its transmission to daughter cells (e.g., during cell division) are the same in nearly all organisms. But if DNA is DNA whether or not it is found within a fly or a human, how is it possible to obtain such diverse organisms? The answer, of course, is that the genes that exist within DNA are different from flies to humans. One might suspect that these two diverse organisms would possess radically different sets of genes, separated as they are by over 600 million years of evolution. With the advent of the Human Genome Project, it has become possible to directly test this hypothesis. Once the entire sequence of human DNA was known, it was compared to the sequence of *Drosophila melanogaster*, a fruitfly that has been used for over one hundred years as a genetic model. This comparison revealed an astonishing 40 percent of all genes in the human have similar counterparts in the fruit fly. While this figure is still tentative, and gene number is hardly an adequate means of comparing differences among species, it underscores yet again that genetic principles learned in model organisms, such as the fruit fly, can have important theoretical and practical applications in understanding human genetics.

If variation between species is accomplished, at least in part, by genes that are unique to flies or humans, how does variation occur within a species? All cells in the human body, with the exception of those involved in the production of sperm or ovum, contain identical DNA sequences, and therefore identical sets of genes. How is it then, that a skin cell will develop differently from a hair cell, if both contain the same DNA? The answer is that each cell may contain the same genes, but not all the genes will be expressed in each cell. Current estimates suggest that there are approximately 50,000 genes in the human genome. Any given cell type, however, is thought to express some 15,000 of these genes. Thus, a hair cell will express 15,000 genes, but these genes will be somewhat different from the 15,000 that are expressed by a skin cell. It is this differential gene expression that leads to the differences in observed phenotype between the two cell types. In a similar vein, two noses located on the faces of two different individuals may well be specified by the same 15,000 genes, but slight differences in their expression from one individual to the next may well explain

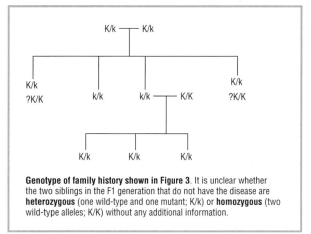

FIGURE 4

Genotype of family history shown in Figure 3. It is unclear whether the two siblings in the F1 generation that do not have the disease are **heterozygous** (one wild-type and one mutant; K/k) or **homozygous** (two wild-type alleles; K/K) without any additional information.

the somewhat petite nose on one and the rather large proboscis on the other. The growing field of genomics aims to study, at a global level, the interactions of all of the genes that contribute toward a particular phenotype.

If it does indeed require 15,000 genes to produce any given cell in the body, then mutant alleles that arise in any one of these genes may, or may not, strongly affect the development of that cell. Alleles of certain genes may alter the color of the cell, or perhaps its ability to metabolize phenylalanine-containing products. Or it is possible that an alteration in just one gene among 15,000 may have no discernable effect at all. How these thousands of genes interact with one another to produce a given trait is perhaps the biggest challenge that faces the molecular geneticist studying genomics today. Moreover, these genetic interactions are often complicated by epigenetic influences as well. Nutrition, in particular, has very strong effects on gene expression. Many multifactorial diseases, such as diabetes, are thought to be associated with both genetic and environmental risk factors. A given family history may, to the medical geneticist, indicate a predisposition towards diabetes, but other factors, such as diet and exercise, are also thought to influence the development of this disease.

One particularly fascinating example of the link between nutrition and genetics is the effect of diet upon aging. Unusual longevity in humans has often been attributed by these self-same individuals as directly associated with the manner in which they have lived their life. Whether it is a glass of wine each day, eliminating red meat, or ingesting large quantities of vitamin C, these individuals claim to have identified the reason behind their advanced years. How much can truly be attributed to these epigenetic influences, and how much is based upon the individual's particular genetic makeup? Research in model organisms such as the fruit fly has identified a handful of genes that seem to strongly affect the lifespan of the fly. Mutations in the methuselah gene, for example, allows flies to survive more than 35 percent longer

FIGURE 5

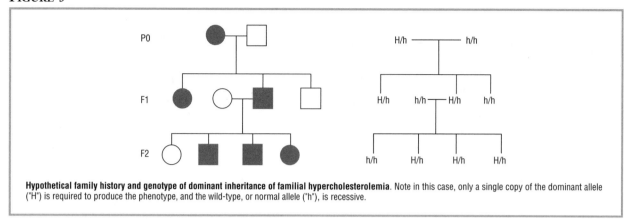

Hypothetical family history and genotype of dominant inheritance of familial hypercholesterolemia. Note in this case, only a single copy of the dominant allele ("H") is required to produce the phenotype, and the wild-type, or normal allele ("h"), is recessive.

than their normal lifespan. This astonishing result suggests that aging may actually be strongly influenced by a limited number of genes, many of which are involved in metabolism. On the other hand, it has long been known that reducing the calorie intake of rodents by 40 percent can also markedly increase their lifespan. The new field of genomics has begun trying to identify the molecular basis for this increase in longevity, by comparing how many genes are differentially expressed between calorie-restricted rodents and their non-restricted counterparts. It was found that hundreds of genes had been affected, including a large number known to be involved in metabolic processes. Thus, the effects of nutrition on aging can be profound. How much of this is due to our genes? How much can attributed to single genes? How much is due to our caloric intake? The answer to this "age-old" question remains to be determined.

A similarly tantalizing example demonstrating the link between nutrition and genetics lies in the area of control of bodyweight. Mice that are homozygous mutant for a particular allele of the obese gene (ob/ob) are grossly overweight. The excitement that surrounded this result centered around the possibility that weight gain might be strongly influenced by individual genes, and that no amount of dietary control or exercise can alleviate its effects. This, of course, has been shown to be a gross oversimplification, and it is clear that many genes are involved in the regulation of body weight. Nevertheless, it is apparent that the field of genetics is gradually beginning to unravel some of the major problems in nutrition and biology today.

Conclusions

The practice of genetics is as old as the human race, and yet as a science, it is still in its infancy. The study of genetics stretches across all of biology, and has grown to include many sub-specialties within the field. Cytogenetics, for example, is the study of chromosomal defects, such as trisomy 21. Molecular genetics is the analysis of individual genes, such as Adh2, and their function within the cell. Population genetics studies the frequency with which polymorphisms of Adh2 occur within large subsets of individual organisms. Medical genetics searches to identify patterns of inheritance of diseases within patients, and the effect of epigenetic influences such as diet and exercise. And finally, genomics tries to understand how genes behave as a whole to specify particular cell types or phenotypes. Together, these diverse but interrelated fields aim to understand how variation is established and maintained within biology.

See also **Agriculture since the Industrial Revolution; Crop Improvement; Gene Expression, Nutrient Regulation of; Genetic Engineering.**

BIBLIOGRAPHY

Brown, P. O., D. Botstein. "Exploring the New World of the Genome with DNA Microarrays." *Nature Genetics* 21 (1 Suppl) (1999): 33–37.

Griffiths, Anthony J. F., J. H. Miller, David T. Suzuki, Richard C.Lewontin, and William M. Gelbart. *An Introduction to Genetic Analysis.* 7th ed. New York: Freeman, 2000.

Jorde, Lynn B., John C. Carey, Michael J. Bamshad, and Raymond L. White. *Medical Genetics.* 2d. ed. St. Louis: Mosby, 1999.

Lee, C. K., Weindruch Klopp, T. A. Prolla. "Gene Expression Profile of Aging and its Retardation by Caloric Restriction." *Science* 285 (1999): 1390–1393.

David Ming Lin

GEOGRAPHY. Food is grown in a one place, distributed to another place, and eaten in yet another place. Food is affected by culture, by economics, and by politics. Food affects our bodies, our relationships with other people, and our relationship with the land. This is the "food system," a system that encapsulates where and how food is produced, how it reaches our mouths, and why we eat what we do.

Anthropologists, nutritionists, historians, sociologists, and philosophers have long been concerned with different aspects of the food system. So too—and increasingly—are geographers.

Geography has a lot to say about food. A subject often misconceived as being concerned solely with maps and mapping, it is actually a philosophically and topically pluralistic discipline that is concerned with spatial processes in the human and physical environment. With a focus on both the spatial aspects of human existence and natural features, geographers are uniquely qualified to study a system that is, as Atkins and Bowler say in *Food in Society* (p. 13), "squeezed into a fault line between environment and society." Geographers seek to conceptualize the food system as a spatial construct that is driven in part by processes that operate from one physically definable and socially constructed space to another. Scale-dependent concepts such as regional, local, and global, location, place, and space, are the basis of questions geographers ask of the food system: Where is food grown and why? What are the processes controlling the movement of food from place to place? Why do we eat what we do? Why do we buy food where we do? How is food consumption related to production? Why is food consumption high in some parts of the world and low in others? Geographers think spatially. They also think systematically, theorizing about the relative roles of the environment and human beings as participants in the system under study and how they interact.

In the academy there are many different types of geographers, all of whom have a potential interest in food. Physical, economic, social, urban, rural, cultural, medical, and agricultural geographers all have their respective emphases on the analysis of the food system. All told, they study the production, consumption, provision, and distribution of food, from the local to the global, from feast to famine. And, as a tool, geographers can use relatively new computer-aided mapping techniques, especially geographical information systems (GIS) to map and analyze spatial data as it pertains to food systems.

Food production and how and why it varies over space is studied in physical and human geography. Physical geographers seek to explain the spatial arrangement of food crops throughout the world by analyzing the environmental factors that limit or promote food production, such as climate, soil, and topography. Human geographers look to the explanatory power of history, economics, and politics and place a greater emphasis on the role of agricultural (food production) systems in affecting how much food is produced and where. They seek to describe the systems—whether as subsistent, intensive, extensive, or industrial—and ask how social, organizational, and technological changes within the system are affected by spatial processes and how they in turn affect spatial outcomes. Geographers have helped pioneer the understanding of food production as an "industrialized" system, a system bound up with processes of economic development that subsequently affects where and how much food is produced.

Food production also has an impact on the environment. One of the first disciplines to recognize the human

The influence of food production on geography is clearly evident in this aerial view of Kansas farmlands. Circular fields designed to accommodate irrigation systems cluster around a free-flowing river while open grasslands occupy the intervening space. COURTESY OF AP/WIDE WORLD PHOTOS.

impact on the environment, geography has long identified the environmental impact of modern agriculture. Hydrologists and soil scientists measure the impact of fertilizers, pesticides, and irrigation on water and soil quality. Desertification and deforestation are environmental issues identified by geographers as outcomes, in part, of food production. In turn, rural and developmental geographers take up the challenge of assessing the impact of environmental changes on local people and national economies.

In terms of food consumption, geographers argue that "place matters" in what people eat. Traditionally, geography has looked at regional patterns of diet, but over the past three decades focus has shifted to the symbolic meaning and cultural identity of food—to the way, in other words, that human beings use food to construct a place-related identity, either real or imaginary. Cuisines create a sense of identity; restaurant locations indicate spatially spreading food trends; the perception of what is "ethnic" and "local" food reveals the way we see ourselves fitting into society socially and geographically.

Food provision and retailing are another aspect of consumption studies within geography. Geographers seek to explain the spatial patterning of food retailers: Why, in many cases, do certain neighborhoods have very few food stores while others are supersaturated? Using the notion of "competitive spaces," geographers in the United Kingdom have been able to identify supermarket locating decisions as a response not only to state-imposed locational regulations, but to the market advantage of locating in a "competitive space."

Geography also asks how spaces of food consumption are linked with spaces of food production. An inherently geographical phenomenon, food is distributed in a variety of ways: national transportation systems, global trade, or local exchanges. Geographers have extended the study of these food distribution networks by seeking to uncover the relations between the site of raw food production and the site of consumption. Using the conceptual approach of "commodity chains," geographers trace food items from the point of consumption back through the chain of retail, wholesale, processing, and agricultural production, taking into account transportation, labor processes, technology, and politics. And in the related "food network" concept, institutional intermediaries such as state regulation and international agreements are added into the chain. Developments in this field have been spurred by increasing worldwide interest in the trend toward the replacement of national by international institutions, global sourcing of products, and the centralization of strategic assets, trends often conceptualized by the term "globalization." Geographers have highlighted, in particular, the local, regional, and national response to globalization, often finding that globalization in some way strengthens the local nature of food production.

Linking food production and consumption in terms of supply and demand is also very much part of the geographical tradition. Geographers ask why it is that in some regions and communities of the world people do not have enough to eat, whereas in others there is overnutrition. Some geographers analyze the spaces of hunger in terms of economics and social relations, others in terms of population growth and environmental limits on food production. Again, geographers are uniquely poised to ask questions about society and the environment. Space, it seems, unites them both.

See also **Distribution of Food**; **Environment**; **Food Production, History of**; **Population and Demographics**.

BIBLIOGRAPHY

Atkins, Peter, and Ian Bowler. *Food in Society: Economy, Culture, Geography*. London: Arnold, 2001.

Bell, David, and Gill Valentine. *Consuming Geographies: We Are Where We Eat*. London: Routledge, 1997.

Goodman, David, and Michael J. Watts, eds. *Globalising Food: Agrarian Questions and Global Restructuring*. London: Routledge, 1997.

Goudie, Andrew. *The Human Impact on the Natural Environment*. Cambridge, Mass.: MIT Press, 2000.

Grigg, David. *An Introduction to Agricultural Geography*. London: Routledge, 1995.

Marsden, Terry, Andrew Flynn, and Michelle Harrison. *Consuming Interests: The Social Provision of Foods*. London: UCL Press, 2000.

Shortridge, Barbara G., and James R. Shortridge, eds. *The Taste of American Place*. Lanham, Md.: Rowman & Littlefield, 1998.

Smil, Vaclav. *Feeding the World: A Challenge for the Twenty-first Century*. Cambridge, Mass.: MIT Press, 2000.

Tansey, Geoff, and Tony Worsley. *The Food System: A Guide*. London: Earthscan, 1995.

Wrigley, Neil, and Michelle Lowe, eds. *Retailing, Consumption and Capital: Towards the New Retail Geography*. Harlow, Essex, U.K.: Longman, 1996.

Corinna Hawkes

GEOPHAGY. Geophagy, the consumption of earth, is widespread in various animal taxa, including birds, reptiles, and mammals. Among the latter it is reported in rats, ungulates, and primates, and in many human populations. The most frequently consumed soils are generally rich in clay, and the qualities of clay appear to be the stimulus for geophagy. The prevalence of this practice suggests that it is not aberrant behavior, but rather that it may have some functional significance related to diet and ecology. Several overlapping hypotheses have been proposed to explain the existence of geophagy, and clay consumption in particular: (1) clay provides supplemental minerals that may be lacking in the routine diet; (2) clay has the capacity to adsorb toxic secondary compounds widely distributed in plant foods; (3) clay protects the gastrointestinal tract from chemical and biological insult, and thus counters gastrointestinal disease. Support exists for all of these hypotheses depending on ecological context and taxon and indicates that geophagy is likely to be associated with positive biological effects.

The unique chemical structure of clays allows them to have these biological functions. Clays are associated with a variety of soil types, and are formed by routine weathering forces. All clays have similar properties: a large surface area, which derives from the organization of silicon-oxygen tetrahedrons in hexagonal networks, and an ability to bind and exchange minerals because of the dense localization of hydroxyl ions and oxygen in the tetrahedron structures. Clays are commonly composed of aluminum, magnesium, iron, and calcium, which can engage in mineral exchanges. Clays also have colloidal properties that make them adsorbent of water and other organic compounds. Commonly consumed clay types include: kaolin, smectite, montmorillonite, halloysite, and allophane.

Geophagy is well-described among ungulates, which seem to derive significant mineral nutrition (especially sodium, calcium, and magnesium) from eating earth, and among rats, who appear to use clay to detoxify a highly omnivorous and opportunistic diet. Gilardi and others found that parrots in Peru consumed large amounts of clay-rich soils, which served to detoxify a seed-based diet that was high in secondary compounds and to protect the cells that line the gastrointestinal tract from these toxic chemicals. Within the primate order, apes and monkeys consume soils that contain valuable minerals along with the clay metahalloysite, which counteracts diarrhea.

Among humans, the consumption of clay takes a variety of forms. In some cultural contexts, clay is an integral part of cuisine. Timothy Johns has documented the use of clay sauces with potatoes among highland Andean populations. Consumed in this way, clay adsorbs the toxic glycoalkaloid (solanine) in the potato cultigens that are the staple foods of this region. Clay is also used in the production of acorn bread by both Native Americans and Sicilians (Johns and Duquette, 1991). In this example, baking with clay reduces the toxicity of tannins in acorns, and improves the overall nutrient composition of this food. Clay is also used for specific medicinal purposes, most often to counteract gastrointestinal illness such as nausea, heartburn, or diarrhea (Vermeer and Ferrell Jr., 1985). Consumed in tablet or liquid suspension (as in Kaopectate®), clay has these effects by slowing gastrointestinal motility, binding toxins or pathogenic microorganisms, and buffering acids of the upper gastrointestinal tract. It is important to note that since clay can adsorb a variety of chemical compounds, it can also interfere with the absorption of pharmaceuticals such as antimalarial drugs (chloroquine).

Beyond the routine use of clay in cuisine, clay consumption is often correlated with pregnancy in humans (Lagercrantz, 1958). The practice is reported most frequently among Africans and African Americans, although it is found in many other populations. Women report that clay eases the nausea and vomiting that often occur during the first trimester. This is likely due to the ability of clay to buffer the gastrointestinal tract and adsorb toxins, to which the embryo is especially vulnerable during early development. Clay consumption often continues throughout pregnancy, and clay may provide supplemental calcium, the demand for which increases during pregnancy to form the fetal skeleton. Support for this analysis comes from Andrea S. Wiley and Solomon H. Katz's study (1998) of geophagy in African populations, which demonstrated that clay consumption was significantly more common in populations that did not consume milk and that relied heavily on toxin-rich plant foods. Hence clay may serve as a detoxicant as well as a source of calcium; both are particularly important for nondairying, agricultural populations. Many sub-Saharan African clays (especially those derived from termite mounds) have been found to be rich in calcium (Hunter, 1993). Importantly, clays are frequently baked before consumption, thus reducing the potential for microbial contamination. When clay is not readily available, laun-

ACORN BREAD

Processing of acorns for consumption is laborious and time-consuming, but the large quantity of tannins in acorns makes them inedible unless some mechanism for their removal is employed. In traditional Native American cuisine, acorns were first hulled (sometimes after boiling, to make it easier to extract the nutmeats) and pounded into a coarse flour with a stone mortar and pestle. Then, a variety of leaching techniques could be employed, including putting the flour in a basket or woven bag or digging a hole in a sandy bank along a river and allowing water to flow through the flour for up to several days. Or the flour could be put in a hole in the ground that was lined with leaves or pine boughs; water was then poured over it numerous times. The leaching removed the bitter tannins, thereby making the acorn flour both more palatable and more digestible. The flour was then placed into a tightly woven basket with water and very hot rocks to make a boiled acorn mush. It could also be molded into patties and fried, or the flour could be dried and then made into a stiff dough and slowly baked in a smoldering fire to produce bread. In contexts where leaching was not practiced or was insufficient to reduce the bitterness of acorns, acorn meal was mixed with clay and water and baked in an earth oven for several hours to produce acorn bread.

dry starch is sometimes consumed by pregnant women, although this is not likely to be associated with the same health benefits as clay.

BIBLIOGRAPHY

Hunter, John M. "Macroterme Geophagy and Pregnancy Clays in Southern Africa." *Journal of Cultural Geography* 14, no. 1 (1993): 69–92.

Johns, Timothy, and Martin Duquette. "Detoxification and Mineral Supplementation as Functions of Geophagy." *American Journal of Clinical Nutrition* 53 (1991): 448–456.

Lagercrantz, Sture. "Geophagical Customs in Africa and among the Negroes in America." *Studia Ethnographica Upsaliensia* 17 (1958): 24–81.

Vermeer, Donald E., and Ray E. Ferrell Jr. "Nigerian Geophagical Clay: A Traditional Antidiarrheal Pharmaceutical." *Science* 227 (1985): 634–636.

Wiley, Andrea S., and Solomon H. Katz. "Geophagy in Pregnancy: A Test of a Hypothesis." *Current Anthropology* 39, no. 4 (1998): 532–545.

Andrea S. Wiley

GERMANY, AUSTRIA, SWITZERLAND. These three nations represent the heartland of German-speaking Europe, although their present borders by no means demarcate the farthest geographical extent of German culture and its historical influence. Modern Germany came into existence in 1871 out of an amalgam of petty dukedoms and small kingdoms that traced their origins to the Holy Roman Empire of the Middle Ages. Modern Austria was created in 1918 out of the German-speaking provinces of the former Austro-Hungarian Empire. Its borders have been stable since then. Switzerland's political independence began in 1291 with an uprising led by William Tell, but the long struggle was not complete until 1412, when peace was made with the House of Habsburg. The Habsburgs, who later created the Austrian empire, were originally Swiss, and the ruin of their castle can still be seen in Canton Aargau. While the political evolution of German-speaking Europe is complex, the culinary divisions are far more distinctly defined.

The largest division is based on religion. Northern and eastern Germany are mostly Protestant (Lutheran), while the South is Roman Catholic. Austria is predominantly Roman Catholic. Switzerland is Roman Catholic and Protestant Reformed (Calvinist). These religious differences have had a great influence on foodways and eating habits. In the Protestant areas of Germany, many older religious festivals were discarded. One of the most important changes, however, was the abolishment of fasting except during Lent. The Protestants also gave up the big Carnival processions and the feasting that accompanied them. The German Pietists in particular abjured drinking, gluttony, and carousing with dance. Thus, northern Germany's food habits became markedly different from those of the South. Differences in religion also affected the movement and acceptance of various new customs such as the Christmas tree, which slowly moved south into Bavaria and Austria during the nineteenth century.

While religion has created an overlying framework for the culinary culture of German-speaking Europe, geography has played a fundamental historical role. The Rhine River Valley, which begins at Lake Constance in Switzerland, has been a major cradle of culture for thousands of years. It was the homeland of the ancient Gauls, whose preference for pork and beer is still deeply embedded in German culture. The Rhine Valley became the most important military region of the Roman Empire, and for a short period of time, Trier, Germany, was the capital of the Empire. The vestiges of Roman culture, such as viticulture, sausage making, pretzels, gingerbread, even half-timbered architecture, have all come to represent core features of traditional culture in these three countries. The most significant geographic feature, however, is the Alps, rugged mountains that form a physical barrier between German-speaking Europe and the Mediterranean. The high mountain regions of Bavaria, Switzerland, and western Austria have evolved a cuisine that is quite distinct from that of the rest of German-speaking Europe. Its focal point is dairying, with milk products and cheese forming the major components.

While the geographic barriers are significant, it is also important to keep in mind that German-speaking Europe is not one monolithic culture. It is composed of many regional cultures and dialects. Alemannic-speaking southwest Germany, Alsace, and Switzerland are home to a very distinct food culture—and the richest agricultural regions—while the Plattdeutsch area of northern Germany, centered on the swampy lowlands bordering the North Sea and the Baltic, offers yet another culinary identity: tea drinking, fish cookery, beer, foods using oats or buckwheat, and very dark rye breads.

Since the 1970s, there has been a revival of interest in dialects and regional cookery and an impressive outpouring of cookbooks exploring local cuisines and food products. This has been a revival in the most literal sense because scholars in all three countries began studying regional foods and foodways in the 1840s; thus the accumulated food literature is extensive and a full century ahead of what has been undertaken in the United States. The *Wörter und Sachen* (Terms and Objects) movement of the early 1900s was particularly active in recording traditional foods and terminologies. Unfortunately, the National Socialist Party, which came to power in Germany in 1933, employed this research toward political ends. Since 1945, the words *ethnisch* ('ethnic') and *Volk* ('folk') in German have carried such a pejorative association with Nazi propaganda that their use is now generally avoided in serious scholarly writings about food.

There is also a sharp dichotomy between the culinary writings of scholarship and the culinary writing of popular cookbooks. Mass-market cookbooks have created the idea of a national German or Austrian cuisine, whereas food scholars have decried this as artificial and misleading, since there are only regional or highly localized cooking traditions, which do not represent the political boundaries of the country. These local traditions often overflow the borders into adjoining countries such as France, Slovakia, Slovenia, and even northern Italy.

Germany

The present Federal Republic of Germany came into being in 1945 out of the ashes of the Third Reich. It was assembled from the western German states then under Allied occupation, specifically the forces of the United States, Britain, and France. The eastern German states were occupied by the Soviet Union and became the German Democratic Republic. In 1989, with the fall of Communism, the eastern and western states were reunified. The former German states of Silesia, Pomerania, East and West Prussia, and the city state of Danzig (modern Gdansk) are now permanently incorporated into Poland. Since the ethnic Germans living in those areas were evicted in 1945, the culinary cultures of the German regions incorporated into Poland are a matter of history,

although considerable ethnographic material has been preserved from the pre-1945 era. Many traditional recipes from this region, such as *Königsberger Klopse* (Königsberg dumplings) still appear in many German cookbooks. Refugees from these regions have tried to keep their dialects and cooking styles alive through cooking clubs and similar organizations.

There are now thirteen states comprising modern Germany. They include, from north to south: Schleswig-Holstein, Mecklenburg-Vorpommern, Niedersachsen, Brandenburg, Sachsen-Anhalt, Sachsen, Thüringen, Hessen, Nordrhein-Westfalen, Rheinland-Pfalz, Saarland, Baden-Württemberg, and Bayern (Bavaria). Each of these states is further subdivided into smaller regions,

The German Renaissance kitchen as depicted in Balthasar Staindl's *Ein künstlich vnd nützlichs Kochbuch* [An Artful and Useful Cookbook], first printed at Augsburg in 1544. COURTESY OF HANS WEISS. ROUGHWOOD COLLECTION.

some with very distinct local cuisines. For example, the wines and foods of Franconia in northern Bavaria are quite different from the rest of the state; the Pfalz, the southernmost area of Rheinland-Pfalz, is world famous for its wines, and locally well-known for its figs and chestnuts and its onion pies.

It is important to know these German states because popular cookbooks tend to treat regional cookery on a statewide basis—thus, there are Bavarian cookbooks, Saxon cookbooks, and so on. The most detailed cookbooks in terms of local cuisine, however, are the ones that focus on a particular valley or county (*Kreis*), such as Annelene von der Haar's *Das Kochbuch aus Ostfriesland* (The East Frisian cookbook), which deals with an area bordering on the Netherlands. The Frisians are the brunt of many German jokes about gluttony and thickheaded farmers, so this cookbook carries far more symbolism for the German reader than it would for outsiders. A unifying theme in most of the regional cookbooks written today is nostalgia for rural life in the village and a closer tie to nature, even to wild foods. In reality, preindustrial

Germany was a harsh place for peasants, and recurring famine was commonplace.

Dietary patterns of preindustrial Germany. Until the beginning of the nineteenth century, mass poverty and famine were integral parts of daily life in most of German-speaking Europe. The majority of the population subsisted on grains that were either eaten in the form of thick gruel cooked in milk or water or converted into flat cakes, coarse breads, a variety of small rolls, dumplings, noodles, and thick soups. (Baker's goods, such as *Lebkuchen, Gugelhupf, Strudel,* and Austrian *Nockerln,* were rarely made in the home and were eaten only on special occasions.) The grains were rich in carbohydrates and, when consumed in quantity, covered daily energy requirements. Fava beans, lentils, and peas helped to offset the shortage of protein in the grain-based diet. Analysis of the diet in poorhouses and hospices for which records survive has underscored anecdotal evidence of a widespread lack of many vital vitamins and minerals. Thus, various degrees of malnutrition were common in the countryside.

124

Meat, fish, and butter, as well as eggs, were reserved for special occasions. In general, it was much more common for peasants to sell these food products at market than to eat them themselves. As a result, urban dwellers consumed much more meat, fish, butter, and eggs than their rural cousins. Meat was held in such high esteem that it was viewed as a prerogative of only the well-off and persons of high social rank. It was also abundant only for short periods of time (such as in the fall) and remained expensive well into the nineteenth century. The high status of meat consumption became so ingrained in German culture that today, now that Germans have a high standard of living, meat in some form is usually consumed with every meal. This is nowhere more evident than in the flesh-rich pages of the late Hannelore Kohl's *Culinary Voyage through Germany* (1997), which is a fair representation of what middle-class Germans like to eat.

Most German historians today agree that, by 1800, many of the rural poor and a large portion of the urban working class expended 70 to 80 percent of their income on food, normally in the form of barter. This imbalance was exacerbated by the low consumption of fresh fruits and vegetables until the 1860s. The full value of these foods was not recognized by popular cookbook writers until the 1920s, when there was a large surge of interest in raw foods, fruitarian diets, vegetarianism, and spa cuisine. The German cinema shifted concepts of physical beauty by featuring women who were obviously thin, whereas in the past, a Rubenesque figure had been considered the desired norm. Many books like Sophie Sukup's 1927 *Iss Dich Schlank*! (Eat yourself thin!) proclaimed a new dietary regime based on raw and garden-fresh foods.

Until that time, most fruits and vegetables had been consumed in preserved form, which lowered the vitamin content. Cane sugar was well known to confectioners, and the rich used it in ample quantities, but it never played a role in the German working-class diet. Sugar did not enter that diet in a large way until the introduction of beet sugar. Most German sugar-based products today employ beet rather than cane sugar. Gram for gram, beet sugar is now so much cheaper than meat that it has replaced meat in the form of junk and snack foods.

Until the end of the nineteenth century, a large majority of the rural population in German-speaking Europe was self-sufficient in terms of supplying daily food needs. Most households oriented their menus according to what could be obtained in the nearest market, and these menus did not vary greatly through the course of the year. Regional customs and the season determined the rhythm of consumption, but by today's standards, this cooking would be considered monotonous, nutrient-deficient, hard to digest, even at times disgusting because of the heavy-handed use of lard and other animal fats. It is ironic that with the prosperity which Germany has enjoyed since World War II, culinary writers have painted a picture of the past that is much rosier than what actually occurred—a truism for most European peasant cookeries. Rich dishes that were only eaten on rare occasions are now treated like daily fare, and restaurants specializing in traditional cookery, especially establishments catering to tourists, provide menus that resemble old-time wedding banquets rather than typical meals. This is not to say that German Europe has not created a cuisine with many noteworthy dishes, yet it is true that these dishes have lost much of their original cultural context.

Germany's food revolution. German Europe's gradual transition to a modern diet began in piecemeal fashion. In parts of Prussia, in some of the more enlightened dukedoms and principalities, cottage and small-scale industries were encouraged during the late 1700s. This created a cash economy that allowed the workers more freedom to purchase luxury items like tea, coffee, and chocolate. Northern Germany's dynastic ties to the British crown opened northern ports to English colonial goods. It is not surprising then that port cities like Hamburg and Lübeck now fall within the German "tea belt," while southern cities like Munich are solidly within the confines of the *Kaffeeklatch*.

Tea drinking in the north also brought with it a new preference for white bread and butter as a side dish, and this culinary troika soon displaced the traditional gruels served at breakfast and during main meals. In the south, coffee drinking moved northward out of Austria, accompanied by a preference for sweet pastries eaten with the coffee. This trend also pushed aside traditional gruels, substituting in their stead such innovations as coffee soup (*Kaffeesuppe*), where bits of bread or cake were crumbled into the coffee so that it could be eaten with a dainty spoon.

The rise in white-bread consumption tied to coffee and tea revolutionized German milling practices and changed German agriculture. The growing bread demand caused a shift away from traditional grains like millet, buckwheat, barley, and oats in favor of rye and wheat. Oats underwent the largest decline in consumption even though they were often the grain of choice in many German-speaking regions for hundreds of years. They have continued as a crop largely for cattle fodder, although they are beginning to return as a health food. In spite of the large shift to bread, there were pockets in rural areas where the older gruel-based eating patterns persisted into the early twentieth century.

The second factor in the German food revolution was the coming of the potato. Potatoes had been known in Germany since the 1500s and were grown as curiosities in many botanical collections. Some of the earliest European depictions of the potato appeared in German herbals, yet the plant was largely despised even as cattle feed. Only after the devastating famines of 1770–1771 and 1816–1817 did the potato achieve widespread acceptance. This occurred in concert with efforts by several German

Alpine butter mold from the Tyrol, circa 1890. These molds, which depict mountain deer, edelweiss, and other symbols of alpine culture, were made as mementos for Victorian-era tourists. ROUGHWOOD COLLECTION. PHOTO CHEW & COMPANY.

monarchs to encourage the peasantry to rely on potatoes rather than grains and bread as a mainstay of the diet. This promotional effort was in part self-serving since the governments at that time realized that potatoes were cheaper than bread, easy to store, and more reliable than grain, especially in Germany's climate. In terms of yield, potatoes also fed more people per acre than grain. Thus, for a combination of reasons, the potato became one of the "pillars" of modern German cookery, especially in the north. In the south, where flour-based dumplings were a dietary mainstay, the potato never quite achieved the same central dietary role. To this day, the potato is still only a side-dish food in southern Germany, Austria, and Switzerland. It is also converted into dumplings in those regional cuisines.

The third factor that played a decisive role in the German food revolution was the increase in alcohol consumption, especially in the form of spirits or hard liquor. Grain and fruit alcohol was distilled by many peasants in the seventeenth century, but this was mostly to make good use of the residues from wine pressing or from cider. Furthermore, the distilled beverages were treated more as medicine than as social drinks. Around 1800, German chemists discovered that spirits could be distilled from potatoes, and this opened the door to what is known in Germany as the "Brandy Plague" (*Branntweinseuche*). The plague spread in step with the rising popularity of potato production, especially among the large land holders in northeastern Germany. The benefits were obvious: potato *Schnaps* provided yet another source of income for the landowner. Furthermore, the potato scraps left over from distilling could be used to fodder pigs (yet another

sideline business). But cheap *Schnaps* weaned peasant drinkers away from beer to such an extent that production ceased in many areas of Germany, with the result that beer brewing became concentrated in the hands of large urban breweries. The unspoken side effect of the Brandy Plague was the concomitant rise in alcoholism. However, in traditional wine-growing regions, old drinking habits prevailed. The Brandy Plague never touched the Mosel Valley, the Pfalz, or the vineyard villages of Swabia.

After its establishment in 1871, the Second German Reich experienced rapid industrialization and a tremendous population explosion. The growth in the population of cities was accelerated by migration of labor from the countryside. Due to technological improvements in agriculture, the food supply throughout German Europe increased dramatically, and meat consumption rose with it. Fear of food shortages and famine very quickly disappeared almost within a generation. Only after World War I and during World War II did Germany suffer again from widespread food shortages. Today there are roughly 230,000 registered food products available in German stores on a daily basis.

All of these sociological and economic changes in German diet did not go unnoticed by cookbook writers. German-speaking Europe, like England, has a long tradition of middle-class cookbooks that may be studied as barometers of culinary change. The first of these is doubtless the *Kuchenmeistery*, a pamphlet cookbook first printed in Nürnberg about 1485. It was not until the latter part of the eighteenth century, after the appearance of a number of general reflections on the culture of eating, that a true "bourgeois cuisine" began to take shape in German culinary literature. This is referred to in German as *bürgerliche Kochkunst*, a concept which has no precise analogy in English.

The underlying themes of this literature were economy, rational meal preparation, taste improvements over traditional recipes, and new meal regimes under the rubric of *Hausmannskost* (fare for the working husband). This new literature for "plain kitchens" as opposed to aristocratic kitchens appealed to urban housewives. The great German classic of this genre was the *Kochbuch für die gewöhnliche und feinere Küche* (Cookbook for plain and elegant cookery) written in 1845 by Henriette Davidis, the daughter of a Westphalian minister. This book passed through new editions almost every year until 1900—long after the author's death in 1876. Davidis also wrote the first cookbook on the preparation of horsemeat in 1848, and a collection of her recipes was published for German-American immigrants in Milwaukee during the 1870s. She was in every respect reigning queen of the kitchen of imperial Germany.

Towards the end of the nineteenth century, there was a growing recognition in Germany, Austria, and Switzerland that cookbooks had become a mirror of the whole culinary culture. This led to a realization that the peculiarities of regional cookeries promoted feelings of regional identity and even a sense of nationalism. Cooking literature turned abruptly away from French cuisine in favor of regionalisms, even regional dialect food terms. In some cases, this genre has evolved even further, as in the case of Swabian cookbooks printed entirely in Swabian dialect.

It is possible today to dip into these regional cookbooks to extract a few examples of some of Germany's best-known traditional dishes: *gefüllter Saumagen* (stuffed pig's stomach) of the Pfalz; *Specktorte* (bacon tart) of Saarbrücken; *Panhas* (scrapple) and *Rievkooche* or *Reibekuchen* (shredded potato patties) of Nordrhein-Westfalen; *Schleizer Bambser* (sugary potato dumplings) of Thüringen; Christmas *Stollen* (fruit cake) of Saxony; Nürnberg *Lebkuchen* (gingerbread), *Schmalznudeln* (deep-fried yeast dough), and Franconian *Blaue Zipfel* (sausage stew) of Bavaria; *Käsespätzle* (cheese spaetzle) and *Schupfnudeln* (finger dumplings) of Baden-Württemburg; *Pommischer Mandelkringel* (ring-shaped almond cake) of Mecklenburg-Vorpommern, and *Rote Grütze* (pudding of mashed tart fruit with oatmeal and cream) of Hamburg and Schleswig-Holstein. Not the least of course are *Sauerbraten* and the German pretzel. German pretzel bakeries have even gone so far as to underwrite the continued growing of spelt wheat (*Triticum dicoccum*, var. *spelta*), the ancient grain associated with pretzel making since the early Middle Ages. Spelt, under the label of *Grünkern* (dried unripe whole grains) has also become a symbol of the latest wave in German cookery: green cuisine or ecological fare.

***Green cuisine* (Ökokost).** This concept came into being through the German Ecological Movement (called the "Greens"), which promoted a total reassessment of the food chain and its connection to the environment. The movement had its roots in German health-reform movements of the late nineteenth century but adjusted those concepts in more modern terms. Essentially, green cuisine is a cookery in which all agrarian products must be free of artificial ingredients, additives, and chemical taints; only food in its most natural form is acceptable. In general, this type of food is grown by farmers who follow organic growing methods and is very closely connected with the mainstreaming of vegetarianism. Although the Green Party has many followers in Germany and wields considerable influence in several regional parliaments, the overall market for such food was small until 1999. The outbreak of hoof-and-mouth disease and mad cow disease caused a large drop in meat consumption and sent many German consumers in the direction of *Ökokost*. The market sector for this type of food has now trebled, but it is still not the choice of a majority of Germans.

German cookery today. Prior to World War II, Berlin was Germany's cultural and culinary capital, although Munich was arguably the "Berlin of the South." With the

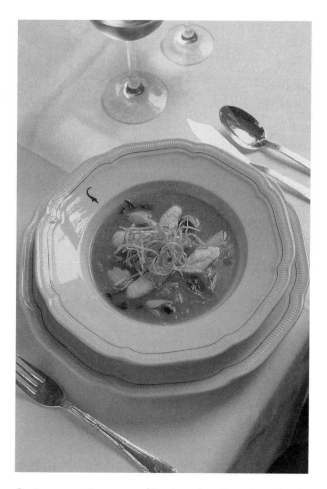

Contemporary German cooking is undergoing reinvention in the hands of chefs influenced by French nouvelle cuisine. This study in tomato soup as food and art was prepared at Die Ente Restaurant in the Hotel Schwarzbauch, Wiesbaden, Germany. © BOB KRIST/CORBIS.

massive destruction of Berlin's downtown area during the war and the movement of the capital to Bonn, the center of gravity shifted decisively to Munich. Munich remains today the country's most energized culinary center and has attracted many new and creative chefs. It is also home to the *Oktoberfest*, which is known throughout the world for its beer and sausages. The *Oktoberfest* began in the early nineteenth century as an agricultural fair showcasing the products of Bavaria. It was intended to encourage Bavarian agriculture and a sense of national pride (at the time, Bavaria was an independent kingdom). Today, the event has become a tourist mecca and the conduit for a type of tourist cuisine called "Bavarian cooking" that has been replicated in mini-*Oktoberfests* all over the world.

The best German cookery is found in small restaurants and inns, often in the countryside and not far from vineyards. There has been an attempt by many chefs to lighten up the traditional cuisine, to explore unusual local produce, and to reinterpret recipes according to new dietary demands, such as less fat and smaller portions of meat. Whether this trend will lead to yet another German food revolution, only time will tell.

Austria

The Republic of Austria was created in 1918 out of the German-speaking provinces of the former Austro-Hungarian Empire. Modern Austria consists of eight provinces plus the capital city of Vienna, which for elective purposes is treated as a province. From east to west, the provinces include Burgenland, Niederösterreich, Oberösterreich, Steiermark, Kärnten, Tyrol, Salzburg, and Vorarlberg. Each of these regions is remarkably different from the other in spite of the small size of the country. Much of the western part of the country straddles extremely high mountains, and this alpine environment has played an important role in the development of regional foods and foodways.

The economic development and general trends experienced by Germany during the nineteenth century also occurred in much of the Austro-Hungarian Empire, with famine and poverty widespread in the countryside. Much of the wealth was concentrated in large cities, especially Vienna, Budapest, and Prague, where the landed aristocracy congregated. When Vienna was cut off from its Slavic and Hungarian provinces in 1918, much of the former industrial development lay outside the borders of the new country. The great imperial city found itself at the hub of a wheel with only a few remaining spokes. Due to the rugged terrain of the western provinces, that region continued to be largely agricultural and pastoral and remains so even today, although tourism and skiing are important sources of local income.

Any discussion of the food culture of Austria must first take into account the enormous historical influence that Vienna has had on the foods and eating habits of the country. But Vienna's role in this culinary evolution is relatively recent. The city was not a capital during the Middle Ages, and during the eighteenth century, when it was home to the Habsburg monarchy, it was still a small town by European standards. It was not until the Congress of Vienna in 1815 that the city established itself as a major center of culinary activity. Vast sums of money were spent during that period and gave rise to the light-hearted party life for which the city became famous. This reputation continued to grow rapidly as Vienna's wealth attracted culinary talent from all over Europe, yet the city did not take on the grand imperial appearance it has today until after the medieval city walls were demolished in 1857. However, several cultural themes came together in a unique way that gave rise to a distinctively Viennese way of life.

The first of these was coffee. There is a degree of murkiness about the origins of coffee drinking in Vienna, yet there is solid archival evidence that it was being drunk in private homes as early as 1665. The first public coffeehouse opened in 1683 and after that, coffee (along with chocolate and tea) became a common beverage in Viennese establishments frequented by men. It is fairly clear that the coffee habit came to the Viennese via the Turks living in areas then occupied by the Ottoman Empire, but the reasons for coffee's eventually preempting other exotic beverages cannot be ascertained from the historical record. Perhaps it was the association with Turkish luxury, or the fact that coffee could be consumed with very sweet foods to offset the bitterness. Whatever the reason, coffee found a natural marriage with sweet pastries in Vienna, and this union of bitter-and-sweet became the keystone of the Viennese coffeehouses of the nineteenth century. Furthermore, Vienna became the gateway for coffee drinking throughout the Upper Danube Basin. The coffee habit also moved west into southern Germany and Switzerland—accompanied by the silver trays of rich pastries.

Viennese pastries were not invented in Vienna, although they were undoubtedly refined and perfected there. Most of the pastries trace their cultural origins to Bohemia or Hungary or to some other far-flung part of the old Austrian Empire. It was the coming together of these various festive foods that made the Viennese dessert table so distinctive. It was, in fact, a cornucopia of the best Central Europe had to offer. The idea that Vienna had acquired a cuisine of its own began in cookbook literature intended for women who lived in more provincial parts of the empire but who wanted to be thoroughly up-to-date. Anna Dorn's *Neuestes Universal-oder Grosses Wiener-Kochbuch* (Newest universal, or large Viennese cookbook), issued in 1827, is one example of this genre. It lies halfway between the older aristocratic cookbooks composed by royal cooks or anonymous noblewomen and the later *bürgerliche Kochkunst* of Germany. Like the first Polish cookbook, Austria's first cookbook was written by an aristocrat, although the author is as yet unidentified. The cookbook was called *Ein Koch- und Artzeney-Buch* (A book of cookery and household medicine). It was published at Graz in Steiermark in 1686.

Another theme in Vienna's culinary evolution was the creation of a furniture and decorative style now called Biedermeier. It took shape during the 1830s and drew upon neoclassical themes for its inspiration. Vienna produced some of the most extraordinary furniture during this period, combining blond Hungarian oak with dark woods from the hinterlands, and then furnishing coffeehouses and restaurants with the most voluptuous combinations of color and classical ornament. This style of design found its counterpart in foods, and many surviving cookbooks, especially the hand-illustrated ones for professional bakers and chefs, offer an amazing array of richly ornamented dishes so refined in appearance that they must have startled the country bumpkins accustomed to seeing only dumplings and tarts on special occasions. Viennese cooking continued to evolve throughout the nineteenth century, but it never escaped its core identification with Biedermeier style. If this essence of Viennese cuisine could be expressed in a few words, then it has been captured succinctly in Joseph Wechsberg's essay "Tafelspitz for the Hofrat," which describes in minute detail the art of preparing a very special Viennese, and only Viennese, cut of beef.

The third theme in the evolution of Viennese cookery is the *Heurigen*. These are extremely informal family-owned snack-houses whose primary function is to sell light foods to accompany year-old local wines. Authentic *Heurigen* are owned by small-scale vintners who sell their own wines and no other. When the houses are open, the owners hang a pine branch or a wreath of evergreens over the door. Menus consist of cold cuts, bread, sausage, walnuts, perhaps even some home-cooked food, but the meals are not considered dinner. After the close of the business day, Viennese flee to the countryside to spend a relaxed evening in their favorite *Heurigen*. This social institution is very firmly established, but there are also *faux Heurigen* whose primary clientele is tourists seeking out "the *Heurigen* experience." These houses are easy to spot because they are surrounded by buses and cars with foreign license plates.

There are over 140,000 acres of vineyards throughout Austria, mostly planted in the native *Grüner Veltliner* (for white wine). This has given rise to *Heurigen* far beyond the Viennese countryside. While this development is doubtless good business for small places in out-of-the-way locations and is especially beneficial to large commercial wineries, the two institutions are not the same. For Viennese, the *Heurigen* experience represents a momentary return to the countryside, a reality check against the oversophistication of city life and an opportunity to taste "real" Austrian food of the sort grandmother used to make. This interest in culinary roots is something that took shape after World War I, after the country shrank to its present size, and especially after the coming of the automobile, which made evening trips to the country possible.

It is significant that Katharina Prato's great Austrian classic *Süddeutsche Küche* (South German cookery), which first appeared at Graz in 1858 and passed through more than seventy editions, made no mention of Austrian cuisine. Prato was from an aristocratic family, and her world view, like that of other Austrians of her day, encompassed the empire and its most refined culinary riches, not the food of the peasants. By degrees, the *Heurigen* have taken this view in the opposite direction, and this has moved hand-in-hand with Austrian scholarship on the country's most interesting traditional foods and customs.

The list of individuals who have contributed to the formation of a new Austrian culinary identity is indeed long, but two names do stand head and shoulders above the rest. They are Ernst Burgstaller and Anni Gamerith. Both were scholars with an ethnographic approach to their subject, although Gamerith was also intensely interested in traditional horticulture and actively helped to preserve endangered heirloom food plants. Burgstaller's *Österreichisches Festtagsgebäck* (Austrian festive breads and pastries) is a model of what can be learned about a country by studying its foods on a village-by-village basis. Burgstaller's maps outlining regional customs and foods have formed the basis for many regional food studies that have followed, such as Brigitte and Siegfried W. de Rachewiltz's *Tiroler Brot* (Tyrolean bread). On the other hand, Gamerith's literary output was huge, and many of her studies take a holistic approach to food. *Lebendiges Ganzkorn* (Living grain) followed the entire story of whole-food grains in Steiermark, their agricultural history, the old horticultural knowledge surrounding their planting and harvest, the old methods of milling and storage, and finally, their conversion into food and bread, including recipes.

Food in Austria today. Gamerith's approach may have been influenced to some extent by the writings of Rudolf Steiner, whose theories on biodynamic agriculture not only originated in Austria, but are still widely practiced there to one degree or another. Because of the lack of large open agricultural lands, Austrian farmers have concentrated on intensive agriculture on small plots of land. Organic farming is extremely popular, and the country supplies a large amount of its own food. Interest in heirloom fruits and vegetables is high and is well-coordinated under the grass-roots organization *Arche Noah* (Noah's Ark), which is headquartered at Schloss Schiltern. The most recent trend in Vienna's leading restaurants has been a turn away from the old imperial cuisine so popular with tourists, and the placement of new emphasis on seasonal local produce and traditional cooking methods. Thus the cuisine of the countryside is now finding new status on high-end menus in the creative hands of numerous young chefs.

Tourism still plays an important role in Austrian cookery, but the differences between native Austrian fare and what tourists consume are growing ever wider. Travel writers and food journalists created a Viennese experience that the tourist still seeks out, such as a requisite slice of *Sachertorte*, a dish of *Kaiserschmarrn*, coffee at Demels, and the ever-present tins of *Mozartkugeln* (chocolate balls). This is culture for outsiders, a caricature of Austria as highly packaged and as devoid of "authenticity" as the blaring echoes of *The Sound of Music* that roll through the cobblestone streets of Salzburg every summer day.

Switzerland

Modern Switzerland began in 1291 with the confederation of the three original cantons: Uri, Schwyz, and Unterwalden. After that the confederation grew piecemeal fashion with the addition of several new cantons after the Swiss declared independence from foreign domination in 1648. The last cantons to join the confederation were Neuchâtel, Valais, and Genève in 1815. This created the modern borders of the country. Today there are twenty-three cantons, the largest being Graubünden, Ticino, Valais, Berne, and Vaud. While the country has four official languages (French, German, Italian, and Romansh), German is the dominant language, especially since it is the language of business and banking. However, it is not the oldest language of the country.

Romansh or Rhaeto-Romance is a relic language surviving from Roman times. A mixture of Latin and Celtic, it was at one time spoken over a much larger part of Switzerland than the present Engadin region in Graubünden where it is now centered. The Romansh Badrutt family brought this cultural milieu to world attention when it established luxury hotels at St. Moritz. However, sister dialects of Romansh were spoken in Austria and, during the early Middle Ages, over much of what is now Bavaria and Baden-Württemberg. In culinary terms, it is the Romansh culture of Switzerland that provides a direct link to the cookery of ancient Helvetia. When the Swiss think of the roots of their culture, and about symbols of cultural identity, it is Romansh and the ancient Helvetians that come to mind. This is their idea of Swissness and is the reason the country's currency bears the name of the Helvetic Confederation.

In spite of the fact that the Swiss gained political independence in 1648, the country never evolved a national food identity. Today, most outsiders probably think of fondue or Emmenthaler cheese when they think of Switzerland, but the Swiss are fiercely loyal to their cantonal identities; thus it is much more reasonable to discuss the cookery of Bern, or of Vaud, or of Zürich, than to lump everything together into one pot. While it may be overly simplistic to break the food story down into the major Swiss language groups, it is true that the cookery of the German-speaking cantons is different from the cookery of the French and Italian cantons—yet with a great deal of overlapping.

The peculiarities of Swiss cuisine have been studied in minute detail by the Swiss themselves, and there are innumerable books tackling the subject. For example, Werner Meyer's *Hirsebrei und Hellebarde* (Millet mush and halberds) traces the shifts in Swiss diet that occurred during the late Middle Ages and the 1500s. From a cantonal standpoint, the best studies thus far are those by the Swiss food historian Albert Hauser, who launched a series of cantonal food histories with the publication of *Vom Essen und Trinken im Alten Zürich* (Eating and drinking in old-time Zurich) in 1961. This was followed by similar studies of Bern and other cantons.

Since the Renaissance came early to Switzerland, and since Basel became a great center for the study of humanism, Swiss books dealing with culinary topics have appeared steadily since the 1500s. Yet a peculiarly Swiss identity did not begin to appear until the eighteenth century. Mostly it took the form of cookbooks written for the wives of rich burgers, as in the case of the anonymous *Bernisches Koch-Büchlein* (Little Bernese cookbook), which is known from its second edition of 1749 (and recently reprinted in facsimile). It first appeared about 1720, although no copies have survived of that edition. The contents of the cookbook, while Swiss in the use of the Bernese dialect of German, make no effort to cover Bernese culinary specialties. It is more of a guide to what was then fashionable, with many adaptations of French recipes.

The same could be said of other cantonal cookbooks, such as Crescentia Bohrer's *Freiburger Kochbuch* (Freiburg cookbook), published in 1836. It was not until later in the nineteenth century that the word "Swiss" begins to appear in cookbook titles, no doubt the result of a rising sense of nationalism. One of these books was Jenny Lina Ebert's *Die Schweizerische Köchin* (The Swiss cook), which was published in 1870 and 1871. Like Bohrer's, Ebert's cookbook embraced *bürgerliche Kochkunst*, and the fact that she used the feminine *Köchin* is significant. This was a book intended for housewives.

The overwhelming body of Swiss culinary literature has been written by men for professional cooks. This phenomenon is due to one very important contribution the Swiss have made to the food world: the development of the hotel industry and hotel cookery. The English discovered Switzerland's Alps during excursions to Italy. The romantic landscapes, the quaint chalets, yodeling peasants, hillsides covered with goats, windswept meadows, glaciers—it was a universe far removed from the apple orchards of Kent. It began with the English renting rooms in farmhouses, but the astute Swiss were quick to observe that more rent-paying Englishmen and their families could be packed into country inns with expanded sleeping and dining arrangements, and thus the hotel industry was born. The construction of the Swiss railroad system made it possible for middle-class tourists to reach most parts of the country. By the 1860s, Switzerland was dotted with hotels situated in scenic locations, and considerable advertising copy was devoted to the fact that the fresh mountain air, the crystal-clear glacial waters, and the fresh cheese and butter were far healthier for the constitution than the thick coal smogs of London. In order to run these hotels profitably and efficiently, the Swiss also established training schools in management and in hotel cooking. They are still masters of this industry, and hotel chefs the world over are quick to mention their Swiss diplomas.

In concert with the movement of tourists into the country there was a movement of Swiss talent abroad. Overcrowding of farmland, food shortages, and economic downturns convinced a number of Swiss to emigrate and to apply their talents elsewhere. Dolf Kaiser has traced this migration in his book *Fast ein Volk von Zuckerbäckern?* (Almost a nation of confectioners?), which outlines in great detail how Swiss from Graubünden came to manage the great hotels, confection shops, and cafés of Europe. This emigration included the Delmonico family, which established a well-known restaurant in New York, as well as many, many other famous names in the world of food: Café Josty in Berlin, the restaurant Köhl in

The *Stube* or stove room was the center of family life in the old German farmhouse. The *Eckbank* (corner bench) along the wall served as seating for the one-pot meals eaten from a common bowl. This photograph from about 1900 shows the interior of a south German farmhouse *Stube*. ROUGH-WOOD COLLECTION.

Odessa (Russia), the Café Chinoise in St. Petersburg, Café Tosio in Warsaw, Klainguti & Company in Genoa, and the Café Gilli in Florence, to name a few. If there were one cookbook that served as a text for this expatriate Swiss food network, it was Giacomo Perini's richly illustrated *Der Schweizerzuckerbäcker* (The Swiss confectioner), which was published at Weimar, Germany, in 1852. Because it was written for a small circle of confectioners and thumbed to shreds, very few copies now survive, and it is today one of the rarest of all Swiss cookery books. Furthermore, the term "Swiss" in this context does not refer to a national style of cooking, but to an established reputation among Swiss confectioners for a high level of professionalism.

Swiss confectioners were especially renowned for their chocolates. In 1876 the Swiss confectioner Daniel Peter created milk chocolate by combining milk powder with the chocolate formula. His powdered milk had been manufactured by Henri Nestlé as a product for babies, but it became obvious from this discovery that greater money could be made with this new kind of chocolate. Nestlé's name has been associated with milk chocolate and instant chocolate ever since. Nestlé is now a large international corporation headquartered in Vevey, Switzerland. Another Swiss contribution came from Rodolphe Lindt, who in 1880 developed the technique for conching chocolate, a process that permitted much firmer and more highly ornamental candies, as well as the ability to insert fillings.

Swiss cooking today. Tourism has to some extent "decantonalized" modern Swiss cooking. In order to meet the expectations of foreign visitors, Swiss hoteliers and restaurateurs are quick to supply a roster of well-known menu items like fondue, raclette, *rösti* (grated potato pancakes), Basler *Leckerli* (Basel-style gingerbread), Zürich Hotpot (*Gumbis*), and a long list of recipes based on lake fish. In Swiss home cooking and in the cooking of the small inns frequented by the Swiss themselves, especially places where there is a fixed *Stammtisch* (reserved tables for regular local customers), the food is decidedly different and at times far superior to hotel fare. There is also a strong movement to capture traditional dishes in cookbooks with a highly localized focus. Fritz Gfeller's *Rezepte aus dem Emmental* (Recipes from the Emmental) represents an attempt by the chef of a popular country inn to take the farmhouse cookery of his famous valley and put it into a cultural context with stories about each recipe and the rather remarkable local characters connected with them. Dialect recipe titles like *Zueguet-Schnitzu* (Schnitzel in the style of a Zueguet farm) tell us that this is a cookbook intended mostly for Swiss eyes.

Likewise, *Aargauer Rezepte* (Aargau recipes) by Dora Schärer, Betty Pircher, and Yvonne Fauser is also a collection of local recipes, but one assembled by three instructors in schools of home economics. They have taken rustic traditional foods and revamped them according to modern cooking techniques and food presentation. This is an important strand in domestic Swiss cooking because it is an attempt to insulate the nation's cuisine from the homogenization of the European Union, to which Switzerland does not belong.

Finally, it goes without saying that some of the most famous French restaurants in the world are not inside France. The Swiss penchant for high professionalism and artistic creativity in food are perhaps strongest in *Suisse romande*, in the French-speaking cantons facing Lake Geneva. One of the recent culinary heroes of that region is Fredy Girardet, a native of Canton Vaud, whose restaurant in the village of Crissier has been recognized as one of the world's great culinary meccas.

See also **Balkan Countries; Central Europe; Chocolate; Christmas; Cookbooks; France; Gamerith, Anni; Gingerbread; Italy; Low Countries; Middle Ages, European; Pastry; Potato; Sausage; Shrove Tuesday; United States,** *subentries on* **Ethnic Cuisines** *and* **Pennsylvania Dutch Food.**

BIBLIOGRAPHY

Benker, Gertrud. *In alten Küchen* [In old-time kitchens]. Munich: Callwey, 1987.

Bernisches Koch-Büchlein [The little Bernese cookbook]. Bern: Gottschall & Companie, 1749.

Böhmer, Günter. *Die Welt des Biedermeier* [The Biedermeier world]. Munich: Kurt Desch, 1968.

Burgstaller, Ernst. *Österreichisches Festtagsgebäck* [Austrian festive breads and pastries]. Linz: Rudolf Trauner, 1983.

Burnett, John, and Derek J. Oddy, eds. *The Origins and Development of Food Policies in Europe*. London: Leicester University Press, 1994.

Davidis, Henriette. *Praktisches Kochbuch für die gewöhnliche und feinere Küche* [Practical cookbook for plain and elegant cookery]. Bielefeld: Velhagen und Klasing, 1845.

Davis, Belinda. *Home Fires Burning: Food, Politics, and Everyday Life in World War I Berlin*. Chapel Hill: University of North Carolina Press, 2000.

Dorn, Anna. *Neuestes Universal- oder Grosses Wiener-Kochbuch* [Newest universal, or large Viennese cookbook]. Vienna: Tendler & von Manstein, 1827.

Ebert, Jenny Lina. *Die Schweizer Köchin* [The Swiss cook]. Bern: Rudolf Jenni, 1870 & 1871. Issued in two parts.

Gamerith, Anni. *Lebendiges Ganzkorn* [Living grain]. Bad Goisern (Austria): "Neues Leben," 1956.

Gfeller, Fritz. *Rezepte aus dem Emmental* [Recipes from the Emmental]. Bern: Hallwag, 1996.

Girardet, Fredy. *The Cuisine of Fredy Girardet*. Translated and annotated by Michael and Judith Hill. New York: William Morrow, 1985.

Haar, Annelene von der. *Das Kochbuch aus Ostfriesland* [The East Frisian cookbook]. Münster: W. Hölker, 1975.

Hartog, Adel den, ed. *Food Technology, Science and Marketing: The European Diet in the Twentieth Century*. Phantassie (Scotland): Tuckwell Press, 1995.

Hauser, Albert. *Vom Essen unde Trinken im Alten Zürich* [Eating and drinking in old-time Zurich]. Zurich: Verlag Berichthaus, 1961.

Heise, Ulla. *Kaffee und Kaffee-Haus* [Coffee and the coffee house]. Hildesheim: Olms Presse, 1987.

Horn, Erna. *Bayern Tafelt* [Bavaria at the table]. Munich: Prestel-Verlag, 1980.

Kaiser, Dolf. *Fast ein Volk von Zuckerbäckern?* [Almost a nation of confectioners?]. Zurich: Verlag Neue Zürcher Zeitung, 1985.

Ein Koch- und Artzney-Buch [A Book of cookery and household medicine]. Graz: Widmannstetterschen Erben, 1686.

Kohl, Hannelore, editor. *A Culinary Voyage through Germany*. New York: Abbeville Press, 1997.

Loewen, Nancy. *Food in Germany (International Food Library)*. Vero Beach, Fla.: Rourke Book Company, 1991.

Meyer, Werner. *Hirsebrei und Hellebarde* [Millet mush and halberds]. Olten/Freiburg-im-Breisgau: Walter-Verlag, 1985.

Neunteufl, Herta. *Kochkunst im Barock* [Cookery in the baroque age]. Graz/Vienna: Leykam-Verlag, 1976.

Perini, Giacomo. *Der Schweizerzuckerbäcker* [The Swiss confectioner]. Weimar: B. Fr. Voigt, 1852.

Rachewiltz, Brigitte, and Siegfried W. De. *Tiroler Brot* [Tyrolean bread]. Innsbruck: Tyrolia-Verlag, 1984.

Sandgruber, Roman. "Nutrition in Austria in the Industrial Age." *European Food History: A Research Review*, edited by Hans J. Teuteberg, pp. 146–147. Leicester: Leicester University Press, 1992).

Schärer, Dora, Betty Pircher, and Yvonne Fauser. *Aargauer Rezepte* [Aargau recipes]. Aarau: AT Verlag, 1984.

Scharfenberg, Horst. *Die deutsche Küche* [The German kitchen]. Bern: Hallwag, 1980.

Sukup, Sophie. *Iss dich schlank!* [Eat Yourself Thin!]. Stuttgart: Franckh'sche Verlagshandlung, 1927.

Teuteberg, Hans J. "The Diet as the Object of Historical Analysis in Germany." In *European Food History: A Research Review*, edited by Hans J. Teuteberg, pp. 109–128. Leicester: Leicester University Press, 1992.

Wechsberg, Joseph. "Tafelspitz for the Hofrat." In *Blue Trout and Black Truffles: Peregrinations of an Epicure*, edited by Joseph Wechsberg, pp. 70–82. New York: Knopf, 1953.

Wiegelmann, Günther. *Alltags-und Festspeisen* [Daily fare and festive foods]. Marburg: N. G. Elwert, 1967.

Wiswe, Hans. *Kulturgeschichte der Kochkunst* [Cultural history of cookery]. Munich: Heinz Moos, 1970.

William Woys Weaver
with material on Germany from Hans-Jürgen Teuteberg

GINGERBREAD. The word "gingerbread" has evolved in English over the past five hundred years to include a highly diversified range of ginger-flavored foods. In its original medieval meaning, gingerbread was characterized as a "bread stuff," which meant something edible, a dry finger food consumed as an adjunct to the meal, although in this case unusual in taste and texture, and commonly eaten as a medicine due to its effect on the bodily humors. The earliest references to gingerbread in medieval English cookery books are quite clear on this point, since they refer to brittle gingerbread preparations made mostly of ginger and sugar. In short, medieval English gingerbread was a medical candy, but parallel to this was a large family of honey-based cakes or cookies known in German as *Lebkuchen*. *Lebkuchen* are the central subject of this discussion. In English they were known as honey cakes.

Honey cakes trace their ancestry to ancient Rome. Among food historians the general consensus is to define the *Lebkuchen* as a highly spiced honey cake baked in a *clebanus* or portable oven. The literal meaning of *Lebkuchen* is thought to be 'clebanus cake', something baked originally in the ancient Roman dining room and served directly to the guests. The Romans often baked honey cakes in the shape of a heart, and for this reason their honey cakes were associated with weddings and, by extension, were edible love tokens on a par with the modern box of luxury chocolates. Gingerbread has branched out into several types of cakes or cookies, not all of them sweetened with honey.

By the 1500s English gingerbreads had evolved into highly spiced crisp cookies, like the German *Lebkuchen* ornamented with stamped designs or cut into innumerable shapes and patterns. These cookies were popular during the winter months and were usually dipped in wine or cider when eaten. This is the so-called crisp ginger cake of colonial North America, which survives in the commercial ginger snap cookies. Gingerbread cookies were also popular as Christmas tree ornaments. With the introduction of inexpensive tin cookie cutters during the late nineteenth century and the ease with which cookies could be baked in cast-iron stoves, ornamental gingerbread cookies became a fixed feature of domestic cookery.

The introduction of saleratus and other chemical leavenings during this same period also changed American gingerbread, and soft gingerbread or gingerbread cake developed. In the United States the term "gingerbread" is more commonly associated with a chemically leavened spice cake than with the crisp cookies of the eighteenth and nineteenth centuries.

Prior to becoming a branch of domestic cookery, gingerbread baking of all kinds was generally the preserve of the professional baker. In many European countries gingerbread bakers were a distinct subunit of the bakers' guild. Since no guilds existed in America, this pattern was not continued there, yet in the German-speaking communities of Pennsylvania and Maryland individuals continued this specialized tradition until the beginning of the twentieth century.

One of the important adjuncts of professional gingerbread baking was the carving of the molds used to stamp the cookies with patterns. Both the carving of molds and the baking of the gingerbreads were male tasks, although the baker's wife and daughters often worked as decorators. The most elaborate gingerbreads were also

Iced gingerbread from a 1680s mold showing how these cookies looked when fully ornamented. Cookie and icing by William Woys Weaver.

iced, so the ornamental images were not only raised on the surface of the cookies but were also visually colorful. Bakers called this "applying makeup." Cookies were also gilded with gold leaf, the origin of the idiom "to take the gilt off the gingerbread." The decorated gingerbreads were often kept rather than eaten, used as wall decorations or put on display in a glass cabinet. Many bakeries made show cookies of giant sizes for their shop windows as part of Christmas advertising. The gingerbread bakers of Belgium and Holland were well known for such large cookies, and considerable literature describes the various schools of mold carving that once existed in those countries.

A discussion of gingerbread and its history invariably turns to a discussion of the molds because the finest ones represent a branch of popular art that has been recognized and studied by numerous European museums. Some of the best-known centers of mold carving were Lyon (France), Nürnberg (Germany), Ulm (Germany), Toruń; (Poland), Pesth (Hungary), and Prague (Czech

Gingerbread mold depicting Willem III (1650–1702) of the Netherlands. Early-nineteenth-century copy of an older design. The stadtholder was a popular theme with Dutch gingerbread bakers. This mold yields cookies about 36 inches tall, and was only used by professional bakers who had ovens large enough to accommodate cookies of this size. ROUGHWOOD COLLECTION. PHOTO CHEW & COMPANY.

Republic). The Bread Museum in Ulm, Germany, and the Ethnographic Museum in Toruń, Poland, possess two of the largest mold collections in Europe.

Molds were an important means for mass producing a design. But to make honey cakes, bakers had also to process honey by removing it from the combs. Thus in the workshops where honey and beeswax were processed, two different types of molds were used, one for gingerbreads and one for wax figures. For the production of gingerbreads, the molds were carved into wooden blocks. The wood had to be hard, for example, oak or boxwood, since a single mold had to serve for the production of thousands of gingerbreads.

Carved molds were made either by special carvers or by the gingerbread bakers themselves. The bakers had to learn how to carve molds during their apprenticeships and as journeymen. Of course not everyone had great talent for carving, but at least every baker could produce molds as they were needed, for instance, when a mold was too worn out for further use and had to be replaced, when a new motif was in demand, or when a special design had to be made to order.

The characteristic ingredients for the gingerbread dough were honey, flour, and potash. The dough was normally made in the fall and allowed to undergo an enzyme reaction over a period of two or three months. The dough became soft and rubbery, but it was also rather dry in texture and required considerable strength to be handled. It was pressed into the mold and then "beaten out," that is, the baker slapped and punched the backside of the mold until the gingerbread relief fell out. One journeyman or the master baker produced hundreds of cookies a day. In the oven the cookies with their raised patterns were dried at a low temperature rather than baked in order to preserve the image and keep it from warping.

The range of motifs was wide, and even a simple workshop in the country had a number of different motifs in stock. Foremost among them were hearts, babies, and riders, which can be called classical motifs. Next are the motifs referring to the great feasts of the Christian calendar, such as Christmas and Easter, and the great events in human life, especially the wedding, which was the climax in the life cycle for the individual as well as for the community. When noble families combined forces by marrying their children, usually a so-called "allied coat of arms" was created and carved. Stamped gingerbreads showing this motif were handed out among the wedding guests. Producing offspring was a main aim of marriage, therefore the bride could be presented with gingerbreads showing babies, tokens of well wishing and wishful thinking at the same time.

As far as the Christian calendar feasts were concerned, Christmas motifs took the lead. Among them, the Nativity and the Adoration of the Three Kings were most frequent, but other aspects, such as the feast day of Adam and Eve on 24 December, were represented also. The depiction, especially of these Christmas motifs, was often in the Baroque style because the designs reached their most elaborate forms during the 1600s. However, when such molds had to be replaced, the new carvings were often copies of the worn-out pieces, even including the dates of the originals. Thus a gingerbread mold made as late as the middle or even the second half of the nineteenth century can show all the stylistic criteria of two hundred years earlier.

In Catholic areas the range of religious motifs also included various saints and places of pilgrimage. The religious gingerbread reliefs were bought for the respective occasions. The big Christmas and Easter gingerbreads were shared by the family. The name day (saint's day) was more important than the birthday (the name day was interpreted as the day of the heavenly birth); consequently a gingerbread relief of the patron saint was often presented to a person as a present on his or her name day. Going on a pilgrimage was a common and regular event. A gingerbread depicting the miraculous image of the place of pilgrimage was carried home. (The custom survives, with paper replacing the gingerbread memento.)

A considerable number of gingerbread motifs were dedicated to news, and gingerbreads served as a kind of history book or newspaper. The "portraits" of emperors and kings or empresses and queens (for example, of Empress Maria Theresa of Austria-Hungary or of Emperor Charles the Great) were presented to the public in gingerbread images as well as in copperplate engravings. There were pictures of the giraffe the Egyptian ruler Mehemed Ali gave to the Austrian emperor in 1828 and of the first steamship on the Danube, the *Maria Anna*, as well as a portrayal of the 1817 European famine that was actually a sociocritical parody of the exorbitant prices of grain. These images represented the big news of the day.

The gingerbreads were sold in the workshops and on the markets. The producers went to the seasonal markets during the year but also set up their stalls on the place before the church on Sundays. The churchgoers were regular customers attending Mass and market together. Gingerbread reliefs were presented to children and grown-ups alike. For children they were sweets and toys (especially babies, riders, soldiers, swords, pistols, trumpets, animals, and at the beginning of the school year, alphabets and school scenes).

Gingerbread molds are no longer produced or in use commercially. Plain gingerbreads, that is, without reliefs, are common. Saint Nicholas, visiting the children on the evening of 5 December, always has gingerbreads among his gifts, and gingerbread hearts with written axioms ("With Love!" "For Friendship!") can be bought at fairs. Gingerbread molds have become collector's items and often are quite expensive since few have survived.

See also **Baking**; **Bread**; **Cake and Pancake**; **Candy and Confections**; **Christianity**; **Christmas**; **Easter**; **Feasts, Festivals, and Fasts.**

Reverse side of the mold above depicting Willem III's wife. ROUGHWOOD COLLECTION. PHOTO CHEW & COMPANY.

BIBLIOGRAPHY

Germanisches Nationalmuseum Nürnberg. *Festliches Backwerk* [Festive cookies]. Edited by Klaus Pechstein and Ursulla Elwart. Nürnberg, Germany: Nationalmuseum, 1981.

Hipp, Hans. *Lebzelten, Wachsstöcke, Votivgaben: Handwerk und Brauch* [Gingerbreads, wax sticks, and religious votives: Craft and custom]. Pfaffenhofen, Germany: W. Ludwig, 1983.

Hörandner, Edith. *Model: Geschnitzte Formen für Lebkuchen, Spekulatius und Springerle.* [Molds: Carved forms for gingerbread, speculatius, and springerle]. Munich: Callwey, 1982.

Kruszelnicka, Janina. *Pierniki Torunskie* [Toruń gingerbreads]. Toruń, Poland: Ministertswo Kultury i Stucki, 1956.

Mai, Paul, ed. *"Das Werk der Fleissigen Bienen": Geformtes Wachs aus einer Alten Lebzelterei* [The work of the busy bee: Molded wax from an old gingerbread shop]. Munich and Zurich, Switzerland: Schnell and Steiner, 1984.

Vienna Museum für Volkskunde. *Lebzeltenmodel aus Österreich* [Gingerbread molds from Austria]. Edited by Leopold Schmidt. Vienna: Österreichisches Museums für Volkskunde, 1972.

Weiner, Piroska. *Carved Honeycake Moulds.* Budapest, Hungary: Corvina Press, 1964.

Edith Hörandner

GOAT. Goats are one of the earliest domesticated animals, providing humankind with milk, meat, hides, and fiber. They include several species of small, cloven-hoofed ruminants constituting the genus *Capra*. Similar to other ruminants, including cows and sheep, goats process plant roughage through a fermentation process within their compartmentalized stomachs, and they chew regurgitated, partially digested food known as cud.

THE LAND OF MILK AND HONEY

The Talmud explains that the biblical description of a land "flowing with milk and honey" actually refers to goats foraging in fig trees. The figs were so ripe that sweet juice (called fruit honey) dripped everywhere, and the goats were so well-nourished their udders overflowed with milk. The milk and honey literally spilled across the land.

—Ketubot *111b*, Megilla *6a and* Ramban, Shmot *3:8*.

*

The Old French word for slaughtering and cutting up meat is *boucheron,* from the term for a he-goat, *bouc*. It is also the root of the English words "butcher," "buck" (a male goat), and, perhaps, the slang term "butch."

Unlike other ruminants, goats are agile browsers, preferring to reach upwards for foods such as the leaves, fruit, and bark of small trees rather than grazing on grasses. When the desired foods are unavailable, however, goats will consume any plant material accessible. It is this foraging ability and flexibility of diet that has secured the importance of goats as a food source in the world's subsistence economies.

Domestication

Wild ancestors of modern goats, known as Persian or Bezoar goats (*Capra aegagrus*) once roamed from South Asia to Crete. It is believed human goatherding began 10,000 years ago in the Zagros highlands of western Iran, as evidenced through selective slaughter of young males. DNA studies support that domestication began at that time due to the rapid growth of the goat population. Domesticated goats (*Capra hircus*) demonstrate remarkable genetic uniformity worldwide. Genetic analysis suggests that goats were a commonly traded in ancient times, which dispersed the population to Europe, Africa, and Asia. Later, they provided a convenient source of milk and meat aboard the ships of European explorers, who introduced goats to the New World.

Breeds

Selective breeding of goats has resulted in animals smaller than their ancestors, and with greater diversity of coat length, texture, and color. Noses are straight or convex; ears vary from negligible external organs to pendulous and droopy. Both males (bucks) and females

(does) are horned. Hornless (polled) animals have been bred, though the recessive polled trait is associated with infertility. (Goat horns are frequently removed after they bud to prevent accidents.) One characteristic that has not changed with domestication is goat intelligence, judged superior to that of dogs. Numerous breeds have been developed for meat, milk, and fiber (including angora for mohair, and cashmere), in addition to being bred for hardiness and suitability to specific geographic regions.

Distribution

The Food and Agriculture Organization of the United Nations estimates that in 2001 close to 693 million goats were kept worldwide, with 95 percent of all stock found in developing countries. This compares to 1.3 billion cattle and 1 billion sheep. Regionally, South Asia has the most goats, with 205 million head, followed by East and Southeast Asia, due largely to the 157 million in China. Other nations with significant goat populations (in descending order) are India, Pakistan, Bangladesh, Iran, Nigeria, Ethiopia, Burkina Faso, Brazil, Indonesia, Kenya, Mali, Mexico, Mongolia, and Somalia.

Official statistics on goat meat and milk greatly underestimate production since many goats are raised for personal family use. Primarily nations with large numbers of animals accounted for the most meat: over one-third of the global supply in 2001 came from China. Other significant producers include India, Pakistan, Bangladesh, Nigeria, Sudan, and Iran. Commercial milk production did not correlate so closely with number of head, however, reflecting cultural differences in dairy food use. In 2001, major producers were India, Bangladesh, and Sudan, followed by Pakistan, Somalia, Spain, Russia, France, and Greece.

Goat Products

Meat. Goat meat has a taste similar to mutton, with a slightly gamy flavor. It is lower in fat than either beef or mutton (due to a fat layer exterior to the muscle rather than marbled through it), and can be drier. The United States Department of Agriculture describes quality goat meat as firm and finely grained. The color can vary between females and males, from light pink to bright red. Kids, defined as under one year old, are often slaughtered at three to five months of age. Their meat is less flavorful and juicy, but more tender than the meat of older goats.

Goat meat is an important protein source in South Asia, the Middle East, and Africa. It is consumed regularly in some parts of Latin America, such as the Caribbean, Mexico, and Brazil, and is regionally popular in China, Korea, Indonesia, the Philippines, Greece, Italy, Portugal, and Spain. The entire goat is usually consumed. An eviscerated carcass is typically cut, flesh and bone, into cubes for stewing, used in dishes such as curried goat and garlic-flavored *caldereta*, a Spanish specialty found also in Latin America and the Philippines. Roasted goat is popular worldwide, often considered a special-occasion food. In Saudi Arabia, the cavity is stuffed with rice, fruits, and nuts. Jerked goat leg, heavily seasoned before cooking over allspice wood, is a Jamaican specialty.

Organ meats are eaten, too. Goat's head soup is prepared in most regions where the meat is consumed. The dish is known as *isiewu* in Nigeria; the eyes are considered a delicacy. In Morocco, kidneys, liver, heart, lung, and pancreas are added to the meat to make goat *tagine*. In Kyrgyzstan, the testicles are roasted separately over the fire for consumption by men, and washed down with vodka. In the Philippines, *paklay* is an Ilocano specialty that combines goat intestines with sour fruits, such as unripe pineapple.

There are few taboos regarding goat meat, and it is accepted by all major religions that permit eating meat. Jewish consumption is often dependent on kosher processing, and for Muslims it must be slaughtered according to *halal* rules. In some regions goats, especially kids, are associated with certain religious holidays, particularly Passover, Easter, and Ramadan. Goat meat is usually classified as a hot or *yang* food in the Chinese philosophical system of yin/yang, and preferentially consumed during the winter months.

Goat meat is not well-accepted by a majority of Americans due to negative associations with garbage-eating and the unpleasant odor of the buck during rut. Exceptions are found among ethnic populations and in the Southwest, where Spanish-Mexican influences have popularized barbequed or pit-roasted *cabrito* (suckling kid). Enterprising goat ranchers in the United States market goat jerky and sausages as *cabrito*, or as the more French-sounding *chevon*.

Dairy Foods. Goat's milk is traditionally consumed fresh, fermented as yogurt, and processed into butter and cheese. While goat's milk is a significant protein food in areas where grazing land is limited, goats lactate seasonally and produce lower quantities of milk than do cows, reducing availability. Fresh milk is a common beverage in South Asia, parts of the Middle East, and Greece and is an occasional dietary addition in other goat-raising nations (with the exception of China and Korea). In Europe, evaporated, canned, and powdered goat's milk products are popular. Cow's milk desserts are occasionally made from goat's milk as well, such as ice cream or the Latin American caramelized milk sweet known as *dulce de leche* or *cajeta*.

Goat's milk cheeses are favored in the Middle East, and in parts of Europe and Latin America. They are processed and classified similarly to cheeses prepared from other milks. Soft and semisoft unripened (unaged) cheeses predominate, often home-made. Most are delicate, spreadable, snowy white in color, with a light, tart flavor. Many are marketed under the generic term

Milking a goat herd in Palestine, circa 1915. While men or boys may have tended the goat herds, it was the traditional role of the women to milk the goats and to make goat cheese. ROUGHWOOD COLLECTION.

Chèvre (French for goat's cheese) and may be named for their shape, such as buttons or pyramids. Fewer firm and ripened (aged) goat's cheeses are produced; examples are *Crottin* and *Sancerre*. Some cheeses traditionally made with goat's, cow's, or sheep's milk blends include Feta, *Fromage Frais*, *Gjetost*, *Kaseri*, and *Queso Fresco*.

Health Value

Meat. Goat meat is nutritionally notable for combining the advantages of red meat with those of white meat or poultry. Goat meat provides similar amounts of protein when compared to the composite nutritional value for beef, but is 80 percent lower in total fat, most of which is unsaturated. Goat meat is also lower in fat than pork, lamb, and skinless chicken breasts. Iron content in goat meat is 70 percent higher than in beef and 200 percent higher than chicken. Cholesterol levels are similar to beef, pork, and lamb, however.

Milk. Goat's milk is a vitamin- and mineral-rich protein food (see Table 1), shown to be a suitable substitute

Goats metabolize and process the yellow- and orange-colored carotenes found in plants much more efficiently than do cows, which is the reason the milk is white, not cream-colored, and the fat is colorless (a drawback for butter).

*

Xanadu cheese, which blends a mixture of cow's and goat's cheeses, was popular in the American South during the nineteenth century. It was a staple food for the Union Army while in the South, and was so disliked it was banned from consumption after the South was defeated.

for cow's milk in feeding malnourished children. Yet, it is the differences in the fat, protein, and carbohydrate composition of goat's milk that account for its reputation as a healthy food. The fat contains a high proportion of small- and medium-chain fatty acids, which increases absorbability and contributes to the tangy flavor. It is lower in casein proteins than is cow's milk, resulting in much smaller curd (protein clump) formation in the stomach, another factor in digestibility. Goat's milk is naturally homogenized because it also lacks the protein agglutinin, so the fat stays dispersed in the milk and does not form cream at the top. Lactose, a sugar found in all milks, is slightly lower in goat's than in cow's milk, so individuals with lactose intolerance (the inability to digest lactose, resulting in intestinal discomfort) may tolerate goat's milk better.

Goat's milk is often touted as an alternative for individuals with allergies to cow's milk. Goat's milk may be better tolerated, yet it can cause adverse reactions in individuals who are extremely sensitive to caseins or other proteins, such as lactoglobulins. Conversely, individuals who tolerate cow's milk may show sensitivity to goat's milk. Some parents of infants and toddlers prefer goat's milk to cow's milk or formula due to its superior digestibility, but nutritional adequacy is dependent on fortification, particularly folate. Use of unpasteurized (raw) goat's milk or dairy foods has serious health risks, including brucellosis, listeriosis, staphylococcus infection, salmonella poisoning, and toxoplasmosis.

See also **Cheese**; **Dairy Products**; **Meat**.

BIBLIOGRAPHY

Addrizzo, John R. "Use of Goat Milk and Goat Meat as Therapeutic Aids in Cardiovascular Diseases." In *Meat Goat Production and Marketing Handbook*, edited by Frank Pinkerton and B. W. Pinkerton. Raleigh, N.C.: Rural Economic Development Center, 1994.

Food and Agriculture Organization of the United Nations. FAOSTAT: Agriculture Data. Available at http://apps.fao.org/page/collections?subset=agriculture. 2001.

Harwell, Lynn, and Frank Pinkerton. "Consumer Demand for Goat Meat." In *Meat Goat Production and Marketing Handbook*, edited by Frank Pinkerton and B. W. Pinkerton. Raleigh, N.C.: Rural Economic Development Center, 1994.

Luikart, Gordon, et al. "Multiple Maternal Origins and Weak Phylogeographic Structure in Domestic Goats." *Proceedings of the National Academy of Sciences* 98 (8 May 2001): 5927.

Razafindrakoto, Odile, et al. "Goat's Milk as a Substitute for Cow's Milk in Undernourished Children: a Randomized Double-Blind Clinical Trial," *Pediatrics* 94 (1994): 65.

United States Department of Agriculture Food Safety and Inspection Service. *Food Safety of Goat and Horse.* Washington D.C., 1997.

United States Department of Agriculture, Agricultural Research Service. *USDA Nutrient Database for Standard Reference*, Release 14. Nutrient Data Laboratory Home Page, Available at http://www.nal.usda.gov/fnic/foodcomp. 2001.

Zeder, Melinda A., and Brian Hesse. "The Initial Domestication of Goats (*Capra hircus*) in the Zagros Mountains 10,000 Years Ago," *Science* 287 (24 March 2000): 2254.

Pamela Goyan Kittler

TABLE 1

Selected nutrients in milk

(1 cup/244 grams)

	Calories	Protein (g)	Fat (g)	Carbohydrate (g)	Calcium (mg)	Potassium (mg)	Vitamin A (IU)	Vitamin D (IU)	Folate (mcg)	Vitamin B-12 (mcg)
Goat	168	8.9	10.1	10.8	326.9	487.7	451.4	29.3	2.4	0.2
Cow	149	8.0	8.1	11.4	290.4	370.9	307.4	97.6	12.2	0.9

GOITER. *See* **Iodine.**

GOODFELLOW, ELIZABETH. Elizabeth Goodfellow (1768–1851) was an American pastry cook, confectioner, and cooking school instructor. Her full married
name was Elizabeth Baker Pierson Coane Goodfellow.
Through her daughter Sarah Pierson, the wife of the
French Quaker Michel Bouvier, Goodfellow was an ancestor of Jacqueline Bouvier Kennedy Onassis. Illustrious
connections aside, Goodfellow's antecedents remain obscure, though she was probably born in Maryland, and the
source of her extraordinary culinary training is unknown.
Yet as an advocate of native ingredients and of an American style of cooking, she was one of the most creative
forces in American cookery during the early nineteenth
century. She was a teacher, friend, and mentor to Eliza
Leslie, who expounded Goodfellow's culinary philosophies in all of her highly successful cookbooks.

By the time of her third marriage, to the Philadelphia clockmaker William Goodfellow in 1808, Elizabeth
Goodfellow had established herself as one of the leading
pastry cooks and confectioners in the city and had become well known throughout the country for her cooking school, which she operated in association with several

Carte de visite with the photo portrait of Elizabeth Goodfellow.
Copied from a daguerreotype about 1851 and probably given
out as a memento to guests at her funeral. This rare portrait
was discovered by genealogist Francis James Dallet and acquired by the Roughwood Collection in 1997. COURTESY ROUGH-
WOOD COLLECTION.

**"MRS. GOODFELLOW'S
INDIAN MEAL POUND CAKE"**

The structure of this recipe is pure Goodfellow. Even
though the ingredients are not listed in the order in
which they are used, a certain logic emerges, since the
weights of the dry ingredients depends on the eggs.
The Indian meal referred to was a coarse, starchy flour
made from Menomonee white flour corn that resembled *masa harina*.

Eight eggs
The weight of eight eggs in powdered sugar
The weight of six eggs in Indian meal, sifted
Half a pound of butter
One nutmeg, grated, or a teaspoonful of cinna-
mon

Stir the butter and sugar to a cream. Beat the eggs
very light. Stir the meal and eggs, alternately, into the
butter and sugar. Grate in the nutmeg. Stir well. Butter a tin pan, put in the mixture, and bake it in a moderate oven. (Leslie, 1828, p. 61)

---

boarding schools for young girls. In her cooking school
Goodfellow prepared budding debutantes for marriage
by teaching them recipes for rich sideboard dishes, like
beef à la mode, and innumerable pastries and cakes for
formal teas, including her own inventions Spanish buns,
Indian meal pound cake, rose jumbles, and perhaps her
most famous dish, lemon pudding, the prototype for the
American lemon meringue pie.

The core of Goodfellow's lectures survives in Leslie's
Seventy-five Receipts for Pastry, Cakes, and Sweetmeats
(1828) and in numerous manuscript cookery books compiled by other Goodfellow students. Unlike her contemporary and business competitor Hannah Hungary
Widdifield, Goodfellow never published a book. One of
her former students from the South issued a cookbook
in 1853 called *Cookery as It Should Be* and claimed that it

embodied all the best of the Goodfellow school of cookery. It did not, as Leslie curtly pointed out in a contemporary review, since Goodfellow would have been "horrified" by the use of chemical leavens and other glaring culinary flaws.

Leslie's work preserves Goodfellow's maxims, such as the one relating to pound cakes: "Up-weight of flour, and down-weight of everything else" (p. 520). One of Goodfellow's most important contributions was to insist that, in recipe writing, all ingredients be listed first. On this point alone she was many years ahead of her times.

See also **Cookbooks; Education About Food; Leslie, Eliza; Recipe; United States.**

BIBLIOGRAPHY

For genealogical data see the Goodfellow papers at the Genealogical Society of Pennsylvania, courtesy of Frances James Dallett. For original cooking school recipes see Hannah Marshall Haines, "Receipt Book" (Philadelphia, 1811–1824), available at the Wyck Association in Philadelphia. Also see Mrs. Frederick Sidney Giger, *Colonial Receipt Book* (Philadelphia: Winston, 1907); and Eliza Leslie, *Seventy-five Receipts for Pastry, Cakes, and Sweetmeats* (Boston: Munroe and Francis, 1828), as well as Eliza Leslie, *Miss Leslie's Cook Book* (Philadelphia: T. B. Peterson, 1881).

William Woys Weaver

GOURDS. *See* **Squash and Gourds.**

GOUT. *See* **Health and Disease.**

GOVERNMENT AGENCIES. National governments often play a major role in the production, distribution, trade, and safety of food. Nowhere is the government food system as elaborate and extensive as in the United States. Bureaucracy in every type of political system has been built up around food regulations and laws; inspection, quarantine, laboratory analysis and certification; epidemiology and surveillance of food-borne disease; and systems management. Which agency performs which function varies among governments.

In any country, there is a fundamental need to sustain as much production as possible in order to feed the population. Government-controlled price-support systems are often put in place to guarantee a certain amount of commodity production. These systems stabilize income for farmers, who supply essential crops, and they allow for competition in domestic and global marketplaces. A Ministry of Agriculture usually performs farm-aid services, in which plant and animal production are combined, or such tasks may be undertaken by a more comprehensive Ministry of Agriculture, Fisheries, and Forests, which also oversees fishing and wood production. The function of such agencies may include introducing new technologies to enhance production, as well as educating consumers about new products, such as those derived from agricultural biotechnology. Agricultural agencies may also dispense government-subsidized seed stocks, license plant hybrids, and manage national grain reserves to protect the country against famine. Agency experts or advisory committees made up of outside experts may compile government manuals of good agricultural practices. Regulatory officials in such agencies are responsible for defining regulations that assure food safety and high-quality products for trade. Such officials may also represent national trade interests and work to harmonize international regulations with officials from other countries in arenas like the World Trade Organization or Codex Alimentarius.

It is often said that hunger and food-supply problems in many countries in the developing world are not the result of a lack of food but of a lack of infrastructure for the equitable dissemination of food. Effective governmental management of distribution systems (roads, railroads, etc.) through a Ministry of Transportation can be of vital importance in feeding a population efficiently. A Ministry of Commerce may also assist both in domestic distribution, through oversight of the marketplace, and in international distribution, through a system of import and export regulations, tariffs, permits, and certification, which may also be the tasks of a Ministry of Trade.

A Ministry of Public Health may be involved in issues of food safety and nutrition. This agency is usually responsible for licensing or running analytical laboratories and may be involved in tracking food-borne disease outbreaks. International trade standards enforce low tolerances for agricultural chemicals and pesticides, filth, toxins, and contaminants. Thus, foods that enter into international trade may be of higher quality than those that are relegated to the domestic marketplace, thereby creating a double standard for food production. As a result, domestic consumers in developing nations may receive inferior-quality food, in addition to insufficient amounts of food. A Ministry of the Environment may be a governmental player in the food production arena as well, since pesticides and chemicals used in food production may exert a negative impact on the environment.

Traditionally, this multi-agency situation in governments has set one agency against another, vying for political support and the finances to run programs, especially when resources are extremely limited. A government that encourages interaction among various agencies is often more successful. Due to the heavy emphasis that has been placed on food safety in most nations, there has been a trend toward the establishment of single national food-safety agencies. The trendsetter in this regard was Canada, which is serviced by the Canadian Food Inspection Agency (CFIA). The CFIA combined into one agency the authorities of four traditional departments involved in food-safety regulation and quality control of food production and processing; export certification; and import permits and quarantine. The French Food Safety Agency (AFSSA) and the new Belize Animal Health Authority (BAHA) are two other examples of consolidated agencies.

The effective performance of all functions involving the food-supply chain is vital to sustaining leadership in government. Without an adequate or safe food supply or a viable economy resulting from ample agricultural production, a hungry public may challenge or overthrow that leadership. The appointed officials who lead these governmental agencies face intense political pressures. Thus the tenure of such an official may be quite brief, with Ministers of Agriculture staying in office an average of fourteen months in Latin America in 2000. First in Great Britain and then in several other European countries, the leadership and structure of agencies responsible for food safety were completely changed in the wake of "mad cow" disease scandals. Public confidence in the government's ability to protect public health plunged to new depths, and whole parties in power were overthrown. In a world where information flows quite freely, governmental agencies are expected to function transparently and keep the public well informed of issues involving the safety of their food supply.

A relatively new tool for regulatory decision making in regard to food production and processes is risk assessment. To appease a wary public and facilitate operations, some governments are adding new agencies to provide such scientific analysis and make recommendations for risk management and communication. The European Union (EU) is setting up an umbrella food-safety agency, the European Food Safety Authority (EFSA), which will provide risk assessment and scientific advice to the European Commission, its Parliament, and member states, as well as to the public. Japan is also setting up an independent scientific risk-assessment authority to reestablish public confidence in that government.

The extent of a government's food-agency infrastructure depends on the importance of agriculture to a national economy and, of course, the size of that economy. Thus, in the developing world, agencies that exist may be extremely important but may have limited capacity and resources. Food agencies in such countries may rely heavily on private sector partnerships where some functions, particularly those involving trade, may be performed by cooperatives of producers working in their own best interests. An example is the Association of Exporters of Chile (ASOEX), which devised a quality production system for Chilean fruits and financed legal costs

associated with allegations of grape dumping in the United States.

See also **Codex Alimentarius; Commodity Price Supports; FAO (Food and Agriculture Organization); Food Security; Food Supply and the Global Food Market; International Agencies; National Cuisines, Idea of; Political Economy.**

WORLD HEALTH ORGANIZATION

The World Health Organization (WHO), an agency of the United Nations, addresses food safety and foodborne illness, among many other issues. It focuses largely on providing national governments with expert and technical advice on food regulation and the improvement of food safety programs. Along with the Food and Agriculture Organization (FAO), the WHO created the Codex Alimentarius Commission, which publishes guidelines for production, processing, and manufacturing of foods to facilitate international commerce. The WHO also develops and publishes information for food handlers and consumers in an effort to prevent foodborne illness. It collects data on foodborne illness to help guide national and international policies and interventions.

The WHO examines new technologies, such as food irradiation to kill pathogenic organisms, by investigating and publishing reports on the benefits and drawbacks of the technologies. In conjunction with overseeing Codex activities, the WHO seeks to reduce barriers to the world food trade caused by unnecessary or unscientific regulations.

The WHO provides advice to travelers on the consumption of food and water, including the dictums "Make sure your food has been thoroughly cooked and is still hot when served" and "Cook it, peel it, or leave it" for fruits and vegetables. In addition the organization provides information regarding what to do if the precautions fail and the traveler develops diarrhea. The WHO has published "Essential Safety Requirements for Street-Vended Food" to address a common but largely unregulated worldwide food distribution system. It also publishes "Guidelines for Drinking-Water Quality" and technical reports on food additives, drug and pesticide residues in food, and the development of dietary guidelines, among other topics.

Richard L. Lobb

BIBLIOGRAPHY

Doering, Ronald L. "Reforming Canada's Food Inspection System: The Case of the Canadian Food Inspection Agency (CFIA)." *Journal of the Association of Food and Drug Officials* 62, no. 3 (1998): 1–15.

European Food Safety Authority website. Available at http://www.europa.eu.int/comm/food.

The World Health Organization's web site is available at www.who.int.

Robin Yeaton Woo

GOVERNMENT AGENCIES, U.S. Several departments and agencies of the United States government have responsibility for various aspects of food production, marketing, regulation, safety, and consumer protection. Government agencies serve a multiplicity of purposes, but the net effect of U.S. government policy is to provide an abundance of food at relatively low cost.

The United States Department of Agriculture (USDA) has prime responsibility for encouraging agriculture and food production, which it does through a host of programs aimed at the farm community. It administers a program of price supports for major commodities, such as corn, wheat, rice and soybeans, which makes payments to farmers if the market prices fall below target levels. The program is viewed as a "safety net" for farmers and as a boon to consumers since it calls forth abundant supplies of basic commodities. It has the potential of costing the government billions of dollars per year, the actual amount depending on market prices. The existence of such enormous subsidies is often an issue with the United States's international trading partners, despite the fact that many of them also subsidize their farmers.

Prices of other goods, such as milk, are supported through federally enforced marketing orders that set minimum prices paid to farmers. Programs for specific crops of fruits, vegetables, and nuts are intended to stabilize supplies and market prices. Some crops, from almonds to avocados, and some animal products, such as beef, pork, and milk, have programs supported by producers and enforced by the government to raise money for advertising and marketing.

Food safety is a major concern of several agencies, including the USDA's Food Safety and Inspection Service (FSIS), the Food and Drug Administration (FDA), and the Environmental Protection Agency (EPA). FSIS provides mandatory, carcass-by-carcass inspection of slaughtered livestock and poultry to ensure that meat and poultry products are wholesome and not adulterated. At the turn of the twenty-first century, more than seven thousand FSIS inspectors work in meat and poultry plants across the country; some states have equivalent, federally recognized programs in which the inspectors are employed by the state. FSIS also monitors processing plants for cleanliness and the avoidance of known hazards (such

as foreign matter in meat and poultry). The agency also oversees labeling; no statements or claims can be made on meat and poultry packaging that are not first approved by FSIS.

The Agricultural Marketing Service offers a voluntary but widely used grading program for meat and poultry, fruits and vegetables (both fresh and processed), milk and dairy products, and eggs. Only products with the top grade in each category are normally sold at retail. Producers pay for the grading inspections.

Food products other than meat and poultry are generally the responsibility of the FDA's Center for Food Safety and Applied Nutrition (CFSAN), which sets standards for products other than meat and poultry. Because, as of 2001, CFSAN employs fewer than eight hundred inspectors to monitor more than fifty thousand processing plants, it relies mainly on sampling and oversight of quality assurance systems to ensure product safety.

The federal agency with primary responsibility for seafood is the National Marine Fisheries Service (NMFS) of the National Oceanographic and Atmospheric Administration (NOAA) in the Department of Commerce. NMFS offers a voluntary seafood inspection program to the industry that allows products to carry the mark "Processed Under Federal Inspection" and/or a seal "U.S. Grade A." NMFS estimates that about 17 percent of the seafood consumed in the United States is certified under the auspices of the seafood inspection program.

FDA also regulates the labeling of food packages according to the name of the product, its ingredients, and nutritional value, among other information. It regulates the meaning of label terms such as "light" or "low-fat." Data developed or reviewed by the FDA and USDA provide the basis for the Nutrition Facts labels required on packaged food.

The Environmental Protection Agency sets tolerances for pesticide residues in or on food products or in animal feeds. These tolerance levels, which are set at very low levels, are enforced by CFSAN and FSIS through random sampling of food products and feed.

As a major player in the world food trade, the United States participates in Codex Alimentarius, the international body that fosters trade by creating widely recognized standards. The U.S. office of Codex is housed at the USDA's Food Safety and Inspection Service, and officials from FSIS, FDA, and EPA coordinate Codex activities for the U.S. government.

USDA's Food and Nutrition Service administers food assistance, programs intended to help the economically disadvantaged get more to eat and to understand better the importance of proper nutrition. The food stamp program is one of the nation's largest welfare programs, providing benefits to needy people to increase their food purchasing power. The Special Supplemental Nutrition Program for Women, Infants, and Children, known as WIC, provides nutritious food supplements and

142

nutrition counseling to pregnant women and to the mothers of infants and children up to five years of age. Low-income schoolchildren are provided with free or low-cost breakfast and lunch, and the milk program provides milk to children in schools and child-care institutions that do not have federally supported meal programs.

USDA's Center for Nutrition Policy and Promotion works with the Department of Health and Human Services to promote the Dietary Guidelines for Americans and the Food Guide Pyramid, which provides general advice on how much people should eat from the various food groups to achieve nutritional balance.

The Federal Trade Commission has the power to take action against false and misleading advertising of food as well as other products through an administrative action or by seeking a court injunction. It can also investigate mislabeled products not covered by other federal laws, such as milk jugs not filled as stated on the label.

Foods contaminated with pathogenic microorganisms or toxins pose a significant risk of illness and death in the United States. The Centers for Disease Control and Prevention (CDC) of the Department of Health and Human Services (HHS) investigates major outbreaks of food-borne illness and collects data on outbreaks from local and state health departments.

Foods imported into the United States are legally required to meet the same standards as those produced in the United States. As with domestic products, imports other than meat and poultry are regulated by the Food and Drug Administration, which can conduct product sampling to ensure that the foods meet health, safety, and labeling standards. Meat and poultry is regulated by the FSIS, which inspects processing plants in other countries to determine if they meet U.S. requirements. FSIS also determines whether the foreign country's inspection system is equivalent to that of the United States. Countries meeting those requirements can export food products to the United States, subject to quotas, tariffs, and other restrictions, and subject to inspection by U.S. officials upon arrival in the country.

Agents of the Department of Agriculture and the U.S. Customs Service enforce regulations on food items carried by travelers to the United States. Travelers are prohibited from bringing in fresh, dried, and canned meats and meat products from most foreign countries. Some fruits, vegetables, and plants may be brought into the United States without advance permission, but they must be declared, inspected, and found free of pests.

The United States is a major donor to international relief efforts. The U.S. Agency for International Development (USAID) operates the Food for Peace (FFP) program under Public Law 480. The agency donates commodities such as wheat, corn, rice, and soybean meal to private voluntary organizations, cooperatives, and international organizations, such as the United Nations World Food Program.

The Special Trade Representative (USTR) negotiates food trade agreements (along with non-food agreements) with foreign countries and, in so doing, relies on the expertise and information of the USDA's Foreign Agriculture Service (FAS). FAS also provides information on trade opportunities to U.S. exporters.

The U.S. government regulates food at virtually every stage of production, processing, and marketing. Federal programs in place since the 1930s encourage the production of food and fiber. Consumer issues, food safety most prominent among them, have been an important topic of federal regulation since the passage of the Pure Food and Drug Act in 1906 and have become even more important in recent years with the rise of consumer consciousness.

See also **Codex Alimentarius; Commodity Price Supports; FAO (Food and Agriculture Organization); Food Safety; Food Stamps; Food Trade Associations; Government Agencies; Inspections; International Agencies; Labeling, Food; Toxins, Unnatural, and Food Safety; WIC (Women, Infants, and Children's) Program.**

BIBLIOGRAPHY

Institute of Medicine and National Research Council. *Ensuring Safe Food: From Production to Consumption.* Washington, D.C.: National Academy Press, 1998.

The United States Government Manual. Washington, D.C.: Government Printing Office, 2000.

Richard L. Lobb

GRAIN RESERVES.

GRAIN RESERVES. Grain is the foundation of the world's diet. Since the beginning of agriculture, farmers have recognized the need to manage stocks of grain to prevent starvation in times of scarcity. In the Hebrew Bible, the Egyptians were directed to stockpile seven years of harvests in preparation for seven years of famine. In North America, early Indians overwintered grain reserves in woven baskets within pits dug into soil. Now, most grain is stored in metal bins or warehouses on or near the farms that produce the grain. Good sanitation is important, since significant grain losses may occur due to spoilage, rodents, and insects. The primary purpose of grain reserves is to help cope with food emergencies, but grain reserves are also used to stabilize grain prices and as a loan commodity.

Food Security

Food security in the fullest sense would mean that all people at all times have access to adequate quantities of safe and nutritious food. To ensure food security, many countries stockpile strategic grain reserves (SGRs). Grains are an easy-to-store and nutritious way to provide the basic needs of a population facing a food emergency until alternative food supplies can be arranged. Countries with abundant supplies of grain will frequently sell or loan their stores of grain to countries without an adequate supply. SGRs are costly to establish and maintain. The United Nations Food and Agriculture Organization (FAO) and the World Bank recommend a grain reserve sufficient to cover three or four months' consumption, plus a cash reserve to import food. In the United States an SGR of up to 4 million metric tons of wheat, corn, sorghum, and rice is reserved for international humanitarian purposes.

Some countries—for example, India—are able to reserve large quantities of grain but lack the distribution system necessary to supply all areas of the country. In contrast, sometimes too much grain is reserved. In 1999 and 2000, China accumulated large stocks of low-quality grain at a time when consumers were demanding higher-quality grain. In response, China discarded its low-quality, low-value grain reserves.

Food emergencies can result from natural causes, such as pest outbreaks sparked by drought, floods, storms, earthquakes, or crop failures, as well as from war and terrorism. Due to advances in agricultural science, between 1950 and 1980 grainland productivity (yields per unit acre) and world cultivated acreage increased significantly, resulting in an abundance of world food. However, since 1980 the rate of food production increase has slowed, while population growth has continued to rise. Many countries are facing both population increases and shortages of resources that are important to agriculture—such as oil, topsoil, water, and undeveloped farmland.

Stabilizing Grain Prices

In the United States, grain reserves have been used to protect farmers from wheat and feed grain production shortfalls and to provide a buffer against unusually sharp price movements. For example, under a farm commodity program administered by the USDA Consolidated Farm Service Agency (CFSA) in 2002, farmers place their grain in government-managed storage and receive an extended loan or advance deficiency payment against a target grain price.

Ceres

Since 1930, atop the Chicago Board of Trade building, a 6-ton cast aluminum statue of Ceres has held a bag of corn in her right hand and a sheaf of wheat in her left. Ceres was created by sculptor John Storrs and is a symbol of the close association between the Chicago Board of Trade and agriculture. According to Roman mythology, Ceres (Demeter in Greek mythology) is the goddess of food grains and patroness of corn trade. She is associated with the ground from which crops spring, the bread produced from grain, and the work necessary to raise crops. Ceres presided over the distribution of grain to the urban poor. The word "cereals" is derived from her name.

See also **Agronomy; Cereal Grains and Pseudo-Cereals; Commodity Price Supports; Wheat.**

BIBLIOGRAPHY

Chicago Board of Trade. *Profile Ceres.* Available at http://www .cbot.com/150/e3/dep/ceres-body.html.

Committee for the National Institute for the Environment. *Agriculture: A Glossary of Terms, Programs, and Laws.* Congressional Research Service Report for Congress.

Gale, Fred, Hsin-Hui Hsu, Bryan Lohmar, and Francis Tuan. "China's Grain Policy at a Crossroads." Economic Research Service/USDA. *Agricultural Outlook* (September 2001): 14–17.

Lynton-Evans, John. *Strategic Grain Reserves: Guidelines for Their Establishment, Management, and Operation.* Rome: Food and Agriculture Organization of the United Nations, 1997

Morford, Mark P., and Robert J. Lenardon. *Classical Mythology.* 6th ed. New York: Longman, 1985.

Sayagues, Mercedes. "SADC Cereal Goal: More Trade, Smaller Reserves." *Africa Recovery* 11, no. 2 (October 1997): 17.

USDA Consolidated Farm Service Agency. Available at usda .gov/factbook/007a.pdf.

Patricia S. Michalak

GRAINS. *See* **Barley; Cereal Grains and Pseudo-Cereals; Wheat.**

GRAPES AND GRAPE JUICE.

There is culinary potential in nearly every part of a grapevine: the skins (food coloring), the pulp and juice (jams, vinegars, wines, and brandies), the seeds (oil), the leaves (dolmas), and even the wood, which makes aromatic fuel for grilling and smoking.

In size, shape, color, flavor, texture, sweetness, acidity, astringency, and relative seed presence, the grape is almost infinitely variable. French ampelographer (vine expert) Pierre Galet counts more than 9,600 varieties among the nearly twenty million acres of grapes grown on all continents except Antarctica (Galet, 2000). And, although many older varieties have disappeared from commercial production, new varieties are constantly being created and tested by breeders.

Approximately 50 percent of all commercial vineyards are in Europe. Over half of all grapes are used for wine production. The rest are consumed fresh; canned; as raisins, jams, or juice; or distilled (Monette, 1988).

Grapes are unique in their ability to achieve Epicurean heights in an astonishing range of conditions: fresh, dry, unripe (sparkling wines like champagne), over-ripe (dessert wines like port), frozen (the vinous nectar *Eiswein*), evaporated and acidified (balsamic vinegar), slimed over with yeast (sherry), and even rotten with mold (another vinous nectar, sauternes).

No other fruit has reached so broadly or deeply into human culture as the grape. Art, history, psychology, medicine, politics, world trade, and religion are all infused with the imagery and substance of vineyards (John-

TABLE 1

Grapevine "family tree."		
Genus and Species	**Selected Varieties**	**Comments**
(American) *Vitis* or *Muscadinia rotundifolia*	Scuppernong, Magnolia	The fruit and flavor of muscadines is virtually unknown outside the southeastern United States. Relatively low sugar, low acid, very thick skin, few large berries per bunch that ripens very unevenly. Fruity dessert wines are traditional, although some newly developed varieties have more neutral flavors and can be made into table wine.
(American) *Vitis aestivalis*	Norton, Lenoir	This is the American species most suited to dry table wine. The fruit is late-ripening but has high sugar, high acid, low pH, thick skin, unstable color, vinous flavor, and is always seeded. There are relatively few small berries per bunch
(American) *Vitis labrusca*	Catawba, Concord, Isabella, Niagara, Steuben. Note: these varieties may not be pure species	This species has relatively low sugar, low acid, low pH, soft pulp with thick skin, few moderate-size berries per bunch. Best suited for consumption fresh or as juice and jelly. Not suited for dry table wine, but can make pleasant sparkling, aperitif, and sweet fruity wines. Fruit flavors described as foxy or like passion fruit.
(American) *Vitis berlandieri, riparia,* and *rupestris*	Riparia Gloire, Rupestris du Lot, SO4, 5 BB, 3309C, 110 R	These species are used mostly as phylloxera-resistant rootstocks to replace the tender roots of *V. vinifera*, but they are also in the parentage of European-American hybrids. *Riparia* berries are small, mostly black, contain high acid, and being early ripening can achieve fairly high sugar and herbaceous flavor.
(Eurasian) *Vitis vinifera*	Chasselas, Flame Seedless, Muscat blanc, Sangiovese, Sauvignon blanc, Syrah, Riesling	High sugar content, sometimes seedless, colors of many hues. Bunch and berry size is highly variable, but mostly better-filled bunches than American types. Table grapes that ship well, all types of wine grapes from mundane to sublime, and the best raisins.

son, 1989). Before the advent of modern medicine in the nineteenth century, unhealthy water was often rendered harmless and limbs saved from amputation by the antiseptic properties of wine. All forms and transformations of the grape enliven basic foods and are not only healthy but therapeutic.

Grapes and Their Origins

Wild vines are common around the globe. In the family Vitaceae, there are more than a thousand species divided among sixteen living and two fossil genera, including *Ampelopsis, Parthenocissus* (both used for ornamental purposes), and *Vitis*, the "grapevine" genus. The French botanist J. P. de Tournefort first defined the genus *Vitis* in 1700, and it was one of the first plant genera studied by the great botanist Linnaeus (Galet, 1979). The word *vitis* means 'vine' or 'centurion's staff' in Latin. It derives from the verb *viere*, meaning 'to braid or weave together', and is descriptive of climbing vines entwined with tree branches.

There are approximately sixty-five named *Vitis* species native to the temperate zones of Asia, Central America, and North America. A majority of the approximately two dozen North American species are found east of the Rocky Mountains. Unlike *Vitis vinifera*, which has a long (more than seven-thousand-year) history of cultivation, native American species remained largely in a wild

state until European colonists began to select among them for their fruit quality and disease resistance.

Grape seeds carry the embryo of genetic material from two parents, thus every seedling is genetically unique. Purposeful and natural crosses have led to improved varieties over time (Morton, 1985). As food, grape seeds are high in fatty acids yet low in their effect on blood cholesterol levels. With a high smoking point, grapeseed oil is the secret to truly French "French fries."

As the source of food and drink, the grape is generally divided into two camps—the Eurasian (*Vitis vinifera*) and the North American (see Table 1).

Sine Qua Non: American Roots for European Grapes

It was only after the phylloxera (plant louse) crisis in 1860s Europe that the roots of American vines became far more precious than their fruit, and hybridization became as important to the creation of new rootstocks as it had been to the creation of interesting new grape varieties. Technically speaking, a hybrid is the offspring of two individuals that differ by at least one gene and can be the progeny of crosses between varieties of the same or different species—and rarely of different genera, as is the case with *Vitis* × *Muscadinia* crosses. Hybrids between American and European types—for example, Foch,

The Temperance Movement raised the popularity of table grapes and especially of grape juice. It was even used by some churches for Communion wine. This circa 1904 brochure promotes grape juice from the Finger Lakes Region of New York, where viticulture was already well established. ROUGHWOOD COLLECTION.

Chambourcin, Seyval, and Vidal Blanc—can be good choices for vineyards where cold temperatures or fungal disease pressures make growing vinifera varieties difficult or uneconomical.

Grape Juice

Raw grape juice, with help from passing yeasts, naturally ferments into wine first, then turns into vinegar. In fact, only timely and deliberate action prevents this from occurring. Pasteurization is the most common method for keeping grape juice from infusing itself with alcohol or acetic acid. American varieties make strongly flavored and deeply colored single-strength juice. By comparison, vinifera grapes would be quite insipid and cloying because of their high sugar content. This can be corrected by acidifying the grape juice with lemon juice, ascorbic acid, or tartaric acid. Most grape juices benefit from dilution with water or seltzer. Adding ginger ale to Concord grape juice creates the approved designated-driver libation "purple passion." One would think that muscat varieties would make charming grape juice, but their special aromas and flavor do not survive the pasteurization process. (Cirami, 1996).

Grape juice is adept at transmutation. The juice of very unripe grapes, known as verjuice or green juice, is an acidic substitute for citrus called for occasionally for sauces or deglazing. Slightly unripe grape juice can be used for sparkling wine.

Highly acid but ripe grapes are the main ingredients for a potable grape foam produced in the French appellation of Crépy, just over the border with Switzerland. Fresh Chasselas must is put into a small stainless steel keg along with a few family-secret ingredients. By New Year's, when the tap is opened, white foam will blast out into waiting flutes. Consumption begins immediately, as it is considered bad luck to allow the foam to settle into a liquid of young wine.

Food writer Harry Nickles (1969) describes another use for grape juice—a sweetmeat made in a village near Sparta from fresh unfermented grape syrup (*epsima*) and flour. The process involves boiling the juice to reduce the volume and increase the sweetness, then adding the ashes of burned vine canes to clarify the juice as it settles. After decanting the sediment and straining, the liquid is further reduced by boiling. Finally, flour is added and the mixture is poured into a shallow pan where it cools into a chewy confection known as *grouta*.

In France fresh juice is boiled down into a syrup and simmered with other fruits to create a jam without sugar called *raisiné*.

Dried Grapes

Dried grapes are known as sultanas or raisins (both seedless and seeded), and even as currants. They are found in recipes for many types of food—from meat stuffing to vegetarian couscous, from teetotaler baked goods to sauces and fruitcakes soaked in rum, port, or brandy.

Whereas it is generally fermented or distilled in Europe, grape sugar is particularly important in the cuisine of the Middle East. Sun-dried raisins are one form of portable grapes. Drying causes grapes to lose their water, but they retain their minerals, vitamins, fiber and about 324 calories per 100 grams. Another method of concentrating grapes for transporting is to repeatedly dip a string into grape juice and allow it to dry. Eventually many layers of dried grape juice will create sort of grape sugar candle.

Black Corinth or Zante (from the Ionian island of Zákinthos) currant grapes are a classic product of Greece. Without treatment with growth regulators such as gibberellin, the vines produce tiny, mostly seedless grapes, which make soft, tart little raisins that lend themselves to baked goods and stuffings.

Currants often join pine nuts and rice in a cocoon of grape leaves or dolmas. These leaves can be harvested any time in the growing season and briefly blanched before using. Or they can be found preserved in a saline and acid solution in glass jars at specialty shops. Generally speaking, the leaves of vinifera table grapes are ideal for this purpose, whereas the leathery and hairy-backed leaves of native American vines are not.

Vines Beyond the Grape

Grapevines can provide welcome shade to patios. To avoid bees at the barbecue, however, one should consider planting male-rootstock varieties—such as Riparia Gloire or SO4—with large leaves (also good for dolmas) and no fruit. After the leaves have fallen, the canes from these patio vines can be woven into durable and functional wreaths and baskets for the kitchen. Chopped sections of grape canes can be stored in small paper bags for later addition to the smoker along with hickory or fruitwoods. The smoke has a strong flavor, so a little goes a long way.

See also **Beer; Fermented Beverages other than Wine or Beer; Fruit: Temperate Fruit; Wine.**

BIBLIOGRAPHY

Cirami, Richard. *Tablegrapes for the Home Garden: A Practical Guide to Growing Tablegrapes in Your Garden*. Australia: Winetitles, 1996.

Galet, Pierre. *A Practical Ampelography: Grapevine Identification*. Translated and adapted by Lucie Morton. New York and London: Cornell University Press, 1979.

Galet, Pierre. *Dictionnaire Encyclopédique de Cépages*. Paris: Hachette Livre, 2000.

Johnson, Hugh. *Vintage: The Story of Wine*. New York: Simon and Schuster. 1989.

Lang, Jenifer Harvey, ed. *Larousse Gastronomique: The New American Edition of the World's Greatest Culinary Encyclopedia*. New York: Crown, 1990.

Monette, P. L. "Grapevine (*Vitis vinifera* L.)." In *Biotechnology in Agriculture and Forestry*, Vol. 6. Crops II ed. Y. P. S. Bajaj, pp. 3–37. Berlin and New York: Springer-Verlag, 1988.

Morton, Lucie. *Winegrowing in Eastern America*. Ithaca, N.Y.: Cornell University Press, 1985.

Munson, Thomas V. *Foundations of American Grape Culture*. 1909. Reprinted by the Denison Public Library, Denison, Tex., 1975.

Nickles, Harry G. and the Editors of Time-Life Books. *Middle Eastern Cooking*. New York: Time-Life Books, 1969.

Lucie Morton

GRAVY. The term "gravy" first appears in Middle English as *gravé* and is presumed to derive from French, since the word may be found in numerous medieval French cookbooks. The original medieval meaning was precise: the *gravé* consisted of the natural cooking juices that flowed from roasting meat. By implication, this meat was spit-roasted, and therefore two important implements were required to make and collect the gravy: a flesh fork for piercing the meat in order to increase the flow of drippings, and a dripping pan beneath the roast, designed to collect the gravy for use at table. Normally the gravy was skimmed of fat, salted, and then sent up as a sauce, although presalting was not necessary, since this could be accomplished to taste at table. The term in this sense has been replaced today by *jus*, as in beefsteak *au jus*.

The medieval roasted meat with *gravé* was generally served rare and not likely to have a counterpart in contemporary Byzantine cookery, since the Eastern Church forbade the consumption of blood or bloody food. Among Byzantine Christians, the gravy of pork, mutton, goat, and the mouflon of Cyprus (a species of wild goat prepared like venison) was often reduced over high heat and mixed with *garum* (fish sauce) or wine, as reported by several medieval travelers. The preparation was then served as a dipping sauce, since the meat was cut up into small pieces and eaten with a fork. The idea of treating gravy as a sauce base is extremely old and may in fact trace back to antiquity. The debate among purists as to whether gravy with additional ingredients constitutes a sauce has not been settled, and probably never will be.

With the revival of sauce cookery in seventeenth-century France, gravy underwent numerous sophistications with the addition of herbs, wine, and other highly flavored ingredients. The English custom of boiling mint or calendula blossoms with clear mutton gravy dates from this same period and was brought to colonial America. The most common addition to gravy, however, was drawn butter, which remained popular into the nineteenth century.

In his *Cooks and Confectioners Dictionary* (London, 1726), John Nott used the term "gravy" in several senses, including the meat stock or bouillon known as a "restaurant," or restorative. His recipe for Gravy Broth (served as a soup course) is typical of the period in its blurring of the distinctions between gravy, soup, and sauce:

> Take a fleshy Piece of Beef, not fat, spit it and roast it; and, when it begins to roast, slash it with a Knife to make the Gravy run out, and keep it continually basting with what comes from it, mix'd with Claret; cut it often, and baste it 'till all the Gravy be come out, put this Gravy into a Sauce-pan over a few Coals; put some Salt, whole Spice, and Lemon-peel, and let it simmer: Put some Sippets in a Dish, pour in your Gravy, garnish your Dish with Oranges and Lemons, and serve it up.

Sippets were small triangular pieces of toasted bread, and the orange and lemon slices were placed around the

Dripping pan (Russian iron), stand (wrought iron), and basting spoon (wrought iron), some of the traditional implements for making gravy. All of the utensils are American and date from the 1790s. The pan was placed under a joint of meat turning on a spit so that the drippings could be collected and used as gravy. ROUGHWOOD COLLECTION. PHOTO CHEW & COMPANY.

rim of the dish. The whole spices and lemon peel were strained out before the gravy broth was poured over the bread. The use of spices, vegetables, and other ingredients to heighten the flavor of gravy became common in English household cookery by the Victorian period. For example, in Eliza Acton's *Modern Cookery* (Philadelphia, 1848) adapted for the American market, there are fifteen recipes for gravy, most of them somewhat complex and more typical of what might be found in an urban rather than rural household.

In rural cookery of this period, it became common practice both in England and America to add flour or roux (cooked flour and fat) to gravy in order to thicken it. This was especially common for dishes served at breakfast or supper. Some period writers considered this an adulteration, while others treated it as an economical and practical way to extend the pan drippings. The Gravy for Chops, which appeared in *Cookery as It Should Be* (Philadelphia, 1855) is typical and resembles the type of gravy most Americans associate with the Victorian era:

Take out your chops when cooked; keep a large spoonful of fat in which they were cooked, in the pan;

dredge in as much flour as will make it a paste; rub this well together over the fire, until a light brown; then pour in as much boiling water as will reduce it to the thickness of cream, and add a tablespoonful of mushroom catsup and a little salt; let this simmer five minutes, and pour it through a sieve over the steak.

This type of quickly made gravy became popular in the United States as a fast food, especially after the Civil War, once iron cookstoves became a standard kitchen fixture. Milk was also commonly added to create a genre of white gravies as opposed to the common brown ones of the past. Chicken gravy over waffles, hashed beef gravy over fried potatoes, red bean gravy on ham, fried tomato gravy—the list of preparations is long with many, many regional variations. Easy to make, they became popular adjuncts to camp cookery and dishes prepared by men in hunting lodges, boat outings, and other outdoor activities.

The demand for convenience soon led to the development of commercial products imitating the homemade preparations. Thus we find prethickened gravies sold in cans, jars, and even in powder form to be reconstituted with boiling water. In America, the term has came to sig-

TOMATO SOP

Slice firm, ripe tomatoes; roll in flour and fry in equal parts of lard and butter until brown on both sides. Remove several slices to a platter, stir those remaining with flour and small lumps of butter: then thicken with milk and season to taste. Sop with bread or toast.

FROM: C. Mac Sheridan, *The Stag Cook Book: Written for Men by Men* (New York: George H. Doran Co., 1922), 95.

nify any kind of homemade sauce, from the giblet gravy served with turkey at Thanksgiving, to tomato sauce made by Italian Americans for pasta. In this sense, the word "gravy" has been employed in advertising to imply that the commercial product tastes homemade. But one feature has never changed. Real homemade gravies always contain the essential juices of the thing being cooked, whether pan drippings from a pork chop or the juice that runs out of a tomato.

See also **Restaurants; Sauces; Soup.**

BIBLIOGRAPHY

Davidson, Alan. *The Oxford Companion to Food*. Oxford: Oxford University Press, 1999.

Flandrin, J. L. "Brouets, potages, et bouillons." *Médiévales* 5 (November 1983): 5–14.

Weaver, William Woys. *America Eats: Forms of Edible Folk Art*. New York: Museum of American Folk Art: Perennial Library, 1989.

Weaver, William Woys. "White Gravies in American Popular Diet." In *Food in Change: Eating Habits from the Middle Ages to the Present Day*, edited by Alexander Fenton and Eszter Kisbán. Edinburgh: J. Donald Publishers, 1986: 41–52.

William Woys Weaver

GREECE, ANCIENT. The appreciation of food in ancient Greece—by those who had the time and money—marks the beginning of what is known today as gastronomy. Greek literary texts (especially comic plays) of around 350 B.C.E. present detailed discussions of which foods were consumed, how much they cost, and how they would be prepared. From the same period one can trace the beginnings of the idea that each city would have its own local food specialities and its own distinctive wine. Adherents of the medical tradition begun by Hippocrates were developing dietary theories and compiling handbooks that dealt with the contribution made by individual foodstuffs to human health.

An interest in food and wine is evident in the oldest Greek literature. Alcman, lyric poet of Sparta, in a surviving verse fragment, lists five fine wines of the southern Peloponnese; in another, hot bean soup is jokingly demanded as payment for poetry. Hesiod's *Works and Days*, a poem of farming and practical lore, tells of the hot June days when "goats are fattest and wine best and women lustiest and men weakest. . . . Then we need rocky shade and Bibline wine and creamy barley mash and the last milk of the goats, and the meat of a foraging cow that has not calved . . . and from an ever-flowing unpolluted spring to pour three of water and to make the fourth be wine" (*Works and Days*, lines 587–596). Many of the focal events in the two great Homeric epics, the *Iliad* and the *Odyssey*, take place around shared meals of roast meat and red wine. Odysseus's description of the palace of Phaeacia is a reminder that fruit was prized and seasonal varieties had been developed: "Outside the yard is a big orchard on both sides of the gates . . . where tall trees spread their leaves, pears and pomegranates and shiny-fruited apples and sweet figs and leafy olives; their fruit never fails or falls short, winter or summer, all the year, but the West Wind, blowing, fertilises some and ripens others" (*Odyssey*, Book 7, lines 112–119). These texts were written before 600 B.C.E., and they set the scene for later gastronomy. Most notably, they also highlight olives (for olive oil) and wine. Archaeology shows that these two products already had been important in Greece for well over a thousand years: they remained essential components of the Greek diet throughout ancient times and are still so today. From prehistoric sites, including the Minoan palace at Knossos in Crete, there are vats and plentiful storage jars for oil and wine. From Classical times there are many fine paintings on cups and wine jars showing the olive and grape harvests, the marketing of oil, and the joys of wine. The god Dionysus, with his train of drunken male satyrs and ecstatic female maenads, features in many such paintings, as if to remind the viewer that wine and its pleasures are a divine gift.

In Greek terms any proper meal had three components, *sitos* (the staple: wheat bread or barley mash or one of the pulses), *opson* (the relish: fish, meat, vegetable, cheese, or just olive oil) and *oinos* (wine, the universal drink). The trouble with ancient Greek gourmets was that they were largely *opsophagoi*, "relish-eaters": they put too much emphasis on fine fish and other relishes, and not enough on simple, wholesome bread. Even worse were the frequent meat-eaters, like the greedy god Heracles and the north Aegean peoples (Macedonians, Thracians, and Greeks of Thessaly), or excessive wine-drinkers—a "barbaric" habit reputed by many Greeks to have killed Alexander of Macedon in 323 B.C.E.

Barley grew well in Greece, but it did not make good bread; nor did emmer, the wheat species that grew best locally. Broths, porridges, and mashes were made with these. Athens and some other cities imported bread wheat from Sicily, North Africa, and the northern Black Sea

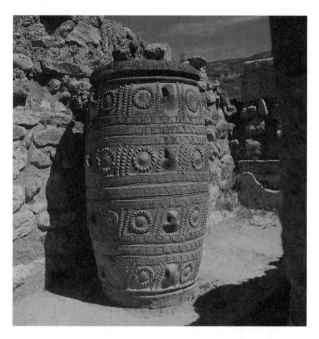

A *pithos* in the palace of Minos at Knossos, Crete. These pottery jars, often five feet tall, were designed to store grain, oil, and wine. Ropes were run through the lug handles on the sides so that a team of workers could move it to another location in the royal cellars. © ROGER WOOD/CORBIS.

coasts, and the Athenian market became famous for its fine industrially baked bread.

In Athens and many other Greek cities, fish was available at the market—expensive, as fine fish still is in Greece, but very fresh. Europe's first gourmet writer, Archestratus (c.350 B.C.E.), wrote extensively on the types of fish that should be sought in specific cities, during which season, at what price, and the manner in which it should be cooked. "The bonito, in autumn when the Pleiades set, you can prepare in any way you please. . . . But here is the very best way for you to deal with this fish. You need fig leaves and oregano (not very much), no cheese, no nonsense. Just wrap it up nicely in fig leaves fastened with string, then hide it under hot ashes and keep a watch on the time: don't overcook it. Get it from Byzantium, if you want it to be good. . . ." Some later readers knew Archestratus's poem under the title *Gastronomia* (Rules for the stomach), the origin of our modern word "gastronomy." A stone inscription dating to the third century found in the small city of Acraephia, not far north of Athens, sets out an official market price for over twenty kinds of fish, a sign of the close interest that governments took in this trade.

Meat was a different matter—expensive, like fish, but in short supply. Livestock was not, and will never be, abundant in much of Greece, owing to the mountainous topography and the consequent shortage of good pasture land. In addition, animals could not simply be killed but

needed to be sacrificed to a god. Meat was thus a relatively small part of the diet, a rarity enjoyed at city festivals (free to citizens), celebrations, family events (when participants spent as much as they could afford), and other special occasions. The sacrificial butcher-priest, the *mageiros*, who was always male, served also as cook on these occasions; the art of cookery was named for this profession, *mageirike techne* (sacrificer's art).

Imported flavorings included *garos* (fish sauce), from the Black Sea coasts; *rous* (sumach, from Syria); and *silphion*, a now-extinct spice from North Africa, similar to asafetida. Coriander, cumin, and many other native aromatics were in use. Mastic, native to the island of Chios, was used to aromatize bread and spiced wine, and also as a natural chewing gum to freshen the breath. A rich source of information on classical Greek food is *The Deipnosophists* (Professors at dinner), written by the scholar Athenaeus around 200 C.E.

In the Classical period, the fifth and fourth centuries B.C.E., Greeks ate two meals a day: a lighter *ariston* (breakfast) late in the morning and a fuller *deipnon* (dinner) in the evening. Breakfast called for bread and olive oil, perhaps with fresh or dried fruit, and red wine. Dinner was a more serious matter, and might well be followed by a *symposion* (symposium, drinking party). Typically dinner consisted of two courses. The first was a selection of tasty small dishes, some of them resembling modern Greek *mezedes* (appetizers): shellfish, such as oysters, mussels, and clams, other seafood, salads and cooked vegetables, and fresh fruit. The main course might have included fine fresh fish dishes, delicacies such as sliced salted tuna, and perhaps meat. No wine was taken with dinner. A libation of neat (or undiluted) wine (offered to the gods and tasted by humans) marked the beginning of the symposium, with dried fruits and nuts, cakes perhaps flavored with sesame and saffron and drenched in honey, and plenty more wine, always diluted with water: how much water was a matter for endless discussion.

At both dinner and symposium the proper custom was to recline, a fashion that Greeks had learned from the Near East. At all meals at which guests might be present, men and women ate separately. At sacrifices and open-air meals they formed separate circles (but some religious ceremonies were for women only or for men only). At home only male diners used the *andron* (dining room), which literally means "men's room."

Conversation languished while the business of eating went forward. The symposium was the occasion for talk, both serious and lighthearted; it was also a time for composing and reciting poetry, and for music and dance performed by the participants or by hired artists (usually slaves), including the ubiquitous *auletrides* (flute-girls). These performers, along with other entertainers and *hetairai* (courtesans), breached the rule of separation of the sexes. Symposia might continue all night, drunkenness supervening slowly but surely, since one could not prop-

Greek *calyx krater* from the sixth century B.C.E. These vessels served as mixing bowls for wine and water and held about six to seven gallons. They were the focal point of the ancient Greek symposia, or drinking parties. COLLECTION OF THE METROPOLITAN MUSEUM OF ART. © BETTMANN/CORBIS.

erly refuse to drink; inhibitions disappeared. While some symposia turned into orgies, others formed the backdrop for some of the greatest intellectual achievements of Greece. A symposium just like those described here is the setting for the philosophical discussion of love that is recorded in Plato's *Symposium*.

Were symposia only enjoyed by an elite? This question is controversial, and the meager evidence can be read in more than one way. Certainly there were great differences in access to food between the rich, who could spend time on eating and entertainment and could have as much meat and fine fish as they wanted, and the very poor, who subsisted largely on pulses (chickpeas, fava beans, and others less nourishing), green vegetables, and roots and fruits (and maybe snails) gathered from the wild. In famine years, many citizens were reduced to such a diet.

See also **Ancient Kitchen, The; Gastronomy; Mediterranean Diet; Rome and the Roman Empire; Table Talk; Wheat: Wheat as a Food; Wine in the Ancient World**.

BIBLIOGRAPHY

Athenaeus. *The Deipnosophists*. Edited and translated by C. B. Gulick. 7 vols. Cambridge, Mass.: Harvard University Press, 1927–1941.

Dalby, Andrew. *Siren Feasts: A History of Food and Gastronomy in Greece*. London and New York: Routledge, 1996.

Dalby, Andrew, and Sally Grainger. *The Classical Cookbook*. London and Los Angeles: British Museum Press/John Paul Getty Museum Press, 1996.

Davidson, James. *Courtesans and Fishcakes: The Consuming Passions of Classical Athens*. London: Harper Collins, 1997.

Garnsey, Peter. *Food and Society in Classical Antiquity*. Cambridge, U.K.: Cambridge University Press, 1999. Valuable study guide, important on food shortages and food of the poor.

Murray, Oswyn, ed. *Sympotica: A Symposium on the Symposion*. Oxford.: Oxford University Press, 1990.

Olson, S. Douglas, and Alexander Sens. *Archestratos of Gela; Greek Culture and Cuisine in the Fourth Century B.C.E.*: Text, Translation and Commentary. Oxford: Oxford University Press, 2000.

Slater, William J., ed. *Dining in a Classical Context*. Ann Arbor: University of Michigan Press, 1991.

Wilkins, John, et al., eds. *Food in Antiquity*. Exeter, U.K.: Exeter University Press, 1995.

Andrew Dalby

GREECE AND CRETE. Greeks, until recently, have been mainly vegetarian not by choice but by necessity. In the mountainous Greek countryside it was not possible to pasture large herds and provide meat for everybody. In ancient times and even recently, meat was

a rare, festive dish, consumed on Sundays, at Easter and Christmas, and for important family feasts. The traditional Greek diet and the similar diet of the people of Crete—Greece's largest island—are mainly based on regional and seasonal agricultural produce: vegetables, leafy greens (*horta*), various kinds of dandelion and chicory, mustard greens, both sweet and bitter, and amaranth shoots in the summer. The greens are either foraged from the hills and fields or cultivated. Grains, mainly in the form of homemade bread, were the basic staple, complemented with fruity olive oil, olives, beans and other legumes, local cheeses, yogurt, occasionally fresh or cured fish, and sometimes meat.

Typical dishes are vegetable stews—green beans, zucchini, artichokes, or leafy greens cooked in olive oil with onions or garlic and fresh or canned tomato or lemon juice during the winter. Tomatoes, zucchini, and eggplants are also stuffed with rice, sometimes with the addition of ground meat. Beans, chickpeas, and lentils are made into soups, while all seasonal vegetables and greens are also used to make the stuffing for pies wrapped in homemade or commercial phyllo pastry. *Hortopita* (greens pie), also called *spanakopita* (spinach pie), is probably the most common example. Lots of flat leaf parsley and the intensely fragrant dried wild oregano are the most common herbs used in Greek cooking. Celery, dill, and wild fennel are also used fresh, while mint is added to some dishes, fresh but also dried. Bay leaves flavor meat stews, and cinnamon is used in most tomato sauces and

meat stews, sometimes together with cloves. *Stifado* (rabbit, hare, or veal stew with pearl onions in red wine sauce) is scented with bay leaves, cinnamon, and cloves.

Only after the mid-1960s, as the country became more affluent, did meat gradually begin to play a significant role in people's everyday diet. Around that time, the Greek demographic structure changed. At least four out of ten middle-aged Greeks who, in the early twenty-first century, lived in the big cities—Athens and Thessaloniki—came originally from agricultural areas. They moved with their families to the cities during the last forty years of the twentieth century, bringing with them the cooking and culinary habits practiced in the villages by their mothers and grandmothers.

Most people have kept their ancestors' village homes and visit them on long weekends, summer holidays, and at Christmas and Easter. Many have also kept much of their land, so it is common for Greek families to produce the olive oil they consume—about forty pounds per person each year. And when they don't produce it themselves, they buy it from friends who have a surplus. This reflects Greek society's largely agricultural past. Olive oil is not just the primary fat used in Greek cooking, but is also basic to Greek people's identity. It is tied to every ritual, both folk and religious, that marks the crucial events in the cycle of life. Priests anoint infants with olive oil when they are christened, and the bodies of the deceased are embalmed with olive oil and wine prior to burial.

The roasting of lambs at Easter is a community-wide festivity. The women of a village near Corinth are shown here preparing the huge outdoor barbecue in 1994. © DAVID G. HOUSER/CORBIS.

Bread was the basic staple food up until the mid-1960s, as it used to be in ancient and Byzantine times. Although now they can afford a great variety of foods, Greeks still consume enormous quantities of bread. Traditional breads are often made with a combination of wheat, barley, and sometimes corn flour, using sour old-dough starter as leavening. Barley, easily growing in the dry and difficult climate of southern Greece and on the islands, was for many centuries the staple food of the ancients. It was ground and eaten as porridge or made into flat breads. Today in Crete and on the other islands, *paximadia* (rusks)—slices of twice baked and completely dry barley bread, which need to be briefly soaked in water to soften them—are still very popular. *Paximadia* keep well for many months and were the ideal food for sailors. They were only baked every two or three months, so they made good use of the oven heat, as wood was always in short supply in most arid Greek islands.

Lunch, eaten around 2 P.M., and dinner, eaten after 8:30 P.M. and often at 10:00 at night or even later, are the two principal meals of the day. Breakfast is usually just a cup of coffee, occasionally accompanied by a cookie or biscuit. Meals include a salad of fresh raw or blanched seasonal vegetables or greens, and end with seasonal fruits. Wine accompanies most meals. Greece has many old indigenous varieties of grapes that produce wonderful wines that have now started to be exported and appreciated by connoisseurs. Some of the best-known Greek grape varieties are *Xinomavro*, which produces the deep red wine of Macedonia; *Aigiorgitiko*, which produces

the red from Nemea in the Peloponnese; *Asyrtiko*, which produces a fruity white from the island of Santorini; and *Moschofilero*, which produces the fragrant fruity white from Mantineia in the central Peloponnese.

Sweets were originally part of the festive table, which almost always involves meat, usually lamb on most occasions. Now, of course, sweets tend to be eaten at all times of the day.

With its many islands, Greece probably has more boats per capita than cars. Nevertheless, fish and seafood have never been plentiful enough to become a staple for the people who live near the sea. The fish and seafood of the Aegean are exceptionally delicious but scarce, and the best fish that islanders manage to catch is sold to the big cities for much-needed cash. Red mullet, sea bream, grouper, mackerel, bonito, swordfish, smooth hound, sardines and anchovies, spiny lobster, octopus, calamari, cattlefish, and cockles are the most common of the many kinds of fish one can find in the market, especially in the winter.

The Venetians and Genoans, who ruled most of the country during the Middle Ages, and later the Ottoman Turks, who made Greece part of their empire and remained the rulers of northern Greece and Crete until the early 1900s, have all left their marks on Greek cooking. (The use of yogurt in cooking and baking, more prominent in Crete, is the result of the Ottoman influence.) But the rules of the Greek Orthodox Church are by far the most important element in shaping people's eating habits. Even nonreligious Greeks often abstain from

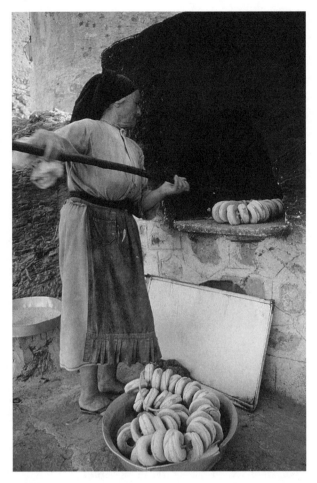

Woman baking rusks at Karpathos, Dodecanese, Greece. These rings of hard-baked rye dough are kept for use the year around for dunking in coffee or wine. © FRANZ-MARC-FREI/CORBIS.

Many dishes are still closely related to religious holidays, although pizza and hamburgers, as well as *gyro* and the ubiquitous "Greek Salad" tend to banalize modern Greek food. *Magiritsa*, a delicious soup made from chopped lamb's innards, scallions, and dill, with a tart egg-and-lemon sauce, is only eaten after the midnight Resurrection Mass on Good Saturday. Pork is associated with the Christmas and New Year tables. Christmas has become a major holiday only during the past forty years. Pigs are raised by most families, especially on the islands, and are slaughtered in December to make sausages and other smoked or salted meats that are used as flavorings in vegetable or legume dishes throughout the year. At the festive table, one finds head cheese and stewed pork with winter vegetables such as celeriac and greens, often cooked with *avgolemono* (egg and lemon sauce). Ground pork is the stuffing for *lahanodolmades* (cabbage leaves), the Christmas dish in Macedonia. Fish, a symbol of Christianity, is consumed on Annunciation Day (25 March), and always at the solemn meals that follow funerals.

Greek food follows the seasons. In the homes cooks do not make stuffed tomatoes or *melitzanosalata* (eggplant dip, made by mixing chopped grilled eggplant with garlic, olive oil, lemon, and parsley) in the winter, although these vegetables are now available all year round. The frugal Greek cooks ingeniously combine seasonal ingredients to create dishes that modern dieticians now use as

foods deriving from animals—meat, dairy products, and eggs—during the fast days that precede Easter, Christmas, and other religious occasions. It is notable that even the McDonald's restaurants in Greece serve special menus during those days. This is the reason that many traditional dishes, such as stuffed vegetables and phyllo-wrapped pies, come in two versions: one with meat (sometimes called the "festive") or with cheese, and one without, for the fast days.

The numerous religious holidays are scattered throughout the year. These holidays have often evolved from ancient celebrations. Easter, Greece's most important feast, seems to have its roots in the pagan agricultural spring festivals of antiquity. Celebrated in the open country, amid fragrant herbs and multicolored flowers, the Easter table features tiny, succulent locally raised and fed spit-roasted lamb or kid and salads of wild greens, tender raw artichokes, and fresh fava beans. The traditional Easter sweets are made with *myzithra*, a generic name for the various regional creamy fresh sheep's milk cheeses of the season.

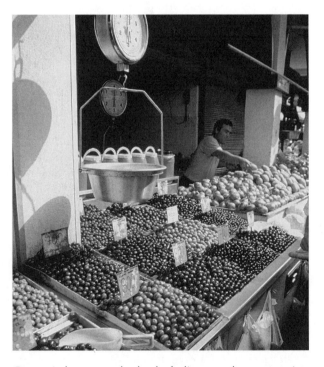

Greece is known as the land of olives, as the great variety found in any market will easily attest. Thirteen different types of olives are available at this stand in the Central Market in Thessaloniki in northern Greece. © JOHN HESELTINE/CORBIS.

models for the famed healthy Mediterranean Diet. This highly recommended diet was the result of a study by an American, Dr. Ancel Keys, and his associates, who compared the daily food intake and the overall health condition of the inhabitants of seven countries in the early 1960s. They found that the Greeks, and more specifically the inhabitants of Crete, fared best of all.

See also **Christianity: Eastern Orthodox; Mediterranean Diet.**

BIBLIOGRAPHY

Athenaeus. *The Deipnosophists* (7 volumes). Loeb Classical Library. Cambridge, Mass.: Harvard University Press, 1971.

Bober, Phyllis Pray. *Art, Culture, and Cuisine: Ancient and Medieval Gastronomy.* Chicago: The University of Chicago Press, 1999.

Dalby, Andrew. *Siren Feasts: A History of Food and Gastronomy in Greece.* London and New York: Routledge, 1997.

Keys, Ancel. *Seven Countries: A Multivariate Analysis of Death and Coronary Heart Disease.* Cambridge, Mass.: Harvard University Press, 1980.

Kremezi, Aglaia. *The Foods of Greece.* New York: Stewart, Tabori, and Chang, 1993.

Kremezi, Aglaia. *The Foods of the Greek Islands.* Boston and New York: Houghton Mifflin, 2000.

Aglaia Kremezi

GREEN REVOLUTION. The Green Revolution was the notable increase in cereal-grains production in Mexico, India, Pakistan, the Philippines, and other developing countries in the 1960s and 1970s. This trend resulted from the introduction of hybrid strains of wheat, rice, and corn (maize) and the adoption of modern agricultural technologies, including irrigation and heavy doses of chemical fertilizer. The Green Revolution was launched by research establishments in Mexico and the Philippines that were funded by the governments of those nations, international donor organizations, and the U.S. government. Similar work is still being carried out by a network of institutes around the world.

The Green Revolution was based on years of painstaking scientific research, but when it was deployed in the field, it yielded dramatic results, nearly doubling wheat production in a few years. The extra food produced by the Green Revolution is generally considered to have averted famine in India and Pakistan; it also allowed many developing countries to keep up with the population growth that many observers had expected would outstrip food production. The leader of a Mexican research term, U.S. agronomist Norman Borlaug, was instrumental in introducing the new wheat to India and Pakistan and was awarded the Nobel Peace Prize in 1970.

Borlaug (b. 1914) was hired in 1944 to run a wheat-research program established by the Rockefeller

Foundation and the government of Mexico in an effort to make that country self-sufficient in the production and distribution of cereal grains. Borlaug's team developed varieties of wheat that grew well in various climatic conditions and benefited from heavy doses of chemical fertilizer, more so than the traditional plant varieties. Wheat yield per acre rose fourfold from 1944 to 1970. Mexico, which had previously had to import wheat, became a self-sufficient cereal-grain producer by 1956.

The key breakthrough in Mexico was the breeding of short-stemmed wheat that grew to lesser heights than other varieties. Whereas tall plants tend both to shade their neighbors from sunlight and topple over before harvesting, uniformly short stalks grow more evenly and are easier to harvest. The Mexican dwarf wheat was first released to farmers in 1961 and resulted in a doubling of the average yield. Borlaug described the twenty years from 1944 to 1964 as the "silent revolution" that set the stage for the more dramatic Green Revolution to follow.

In the 1960s, many observers felt that widespread famine was inevitable in the developing world and that the population would surpass the means of food production, with disastrous results in countries such as India. The United Nations Food and Agriculture Organization calculated that 56 percent of the human race lived in countries with an average per-capita food supply of 2,200 calories per day or less, which is barely at subsistence level (cited by Mann, p. 1038). Biologist Paul Ehrlich predicted in his 1968 bestseller *The Population Bomb* that "hundreds of millions" would starve to death in the 1970s and 1980s "in spite of any crash programs embarked upon" at the time he wrote his book (Ehrlich, p. xi).

In 1963, just such a devastating famine had threatened India and Pakistan. Borlaug went to the subcontinent to try to persuade governments to import the new varieties of wheat. Not until 1965 was Borlaug able to overcome resistance to the relatively unfamiliar crop and its foreign seeds and bring in hundreds of tons of seed to jump-start production. The new plants caught on rapidly. By the 1969–1970 crop season—about the time Ehrlich was dismissing "crash programs"—55 percent of the 35 million acres of wheat in Pakistan and 35 percent of India's 35 million acres of wheat were sown with the Mexican dwarf varieties or varieties derived from them. New production technologies were also introduced, such as a greater reliance on chemical fertilizer and pesticides and the drilling of thousands of wells for controlled irrigation. Government policies that encouraged these new styles of production provided loans that helped farmers adopt it.

Wheat production in Pakistan nearly doubled in five years, going from 4.6 million tons in 1965 (a record at the time) to 8.4 million tons in 1970. India went from 12.3 million tons of wheat in 1965 to 20 million tons in

Norman Borlaug, the acknowledged "father" of the Green Revolution. © AP/WIDE WORLD PHOTOS.

1970. Both nations were self-sufficient in cereal production by 1974.

As important as the wheat program was, however, rice remains the world's most important food crop, providing 35–80 percent of the calories consumed by people in Asia. The International Rice Research Institute in the Philippines was founded in 1960 and was funded by the Ford and Rockefeller Foundations, the government of the Philippines, and the U.S. Agency for International Development. This organization was to do for rice what the Mexican program had done for wheat. Scientists addressed the problem of intermittent flooding of rice paddies by developing strains of rice that would thrive even when submerged in three feet of water. The new varieties produced five times as much rice as the traditional deepwater varieties and opened flood-prone land to rice cultivation. Other varieties were dwarf (for the same reasons as the wheat), or more disease-resistant, or more suited to tropical climates. Scientists crossed thirty-eight different breeds of rice to create IR8, which doubled yields and became known as "miracle rice." IR8 served as the catalyst for what became known as the Green Revolution. By the end of the twentieth century, more than 60 percent of the world's rice fields were

planted with varieties developed by research institutes and related developers. A pest-resistant variety known as IR36 was planted on nearly 28 million acres, a record amount for a single food-plant variety.

In addition to Mexico, Pakistan, India, and the Philippines, countries benefiting from the Green Revolution included Afghanistan, Sri Lanka, China, Indonesia, Iran, Kenya, Malaya, Morocco, Thailand, Tunisia, and Turkey. The Green Revolution contributed to the overall economic growth of these nations by increasing the incomes of farmers (who were then able to afford tractors and other modern equipment), the use of electrical energy, and consumer goods, thus increasing the pace and volume of trade and commerce.

As successful as the Green Revolution was, the wholesale transfer of technology to the developing world had its critics. Some objected to the use of chemical fertilizer, which augmented or replaced animal manure or mineral fertilizer. Others objected to the use of pesticides, some of which are believed to be persistent in the environment. The use of irrigation was also criticized, as it often required drilling wells and tapping underground water sources, as was the encouragement of farming in areas formerly considered marginal, such as flood-prone regions in Bangladesh. The very fact that the new crop varieties were developed with foreign support caused some critics to label the entire program imperialistic. Critics also argued that the Green Revolution primarily benefited large farm operations that could more easily obtain fertilizer, pesticides, and modern equipment, and that it helped displace poorer farmers from the land, driving them into urban slums. Critics also pointed out that the heavy use of fertilizer and irrigation causes long-term degradation of the soil.

Proponents of the Green Revolution argued that it contributed to environmental preservation because it improved the productivity of land already in agricultural production and thus saved millions of acres that would otherwise have been put into agricultural use. It is estimated that if cropland productivity had not tripled in the second half of the twentieth century, it would have been necessary to clear half of the world's remaining forestland for conversion to agriculture (Brown, *Eco-Economy*).

However, the rates at which production increased in the early years of the program could not continue indefinitely, which caused some to question the "sustainability" of the new style. For example, rice yields per acre in South Korea grew nearly 60 percent from 1961 to 1977, but only 1 percent from 1977 to 2000 (Brown et al., *State of the World 2001*, p. 51). Rice production in Asia as a whole grew an average of 3.2 percent per year from 1967 to 1984 but only 1.5 percent per year from 1984 to 1996 (Dawe, p. 948). Some of the leveling-off of yields stemmed from natural limits on plant growth, but economics also played a role. For example, as rice harvests increased, prices fell, thus discouraging more aggressive production. Also, population growth in Asia slowed, thus reducing the rate of growth of the demand for rice. In addition, incomes rose, which prompted people to eat less rice and more of other types of food.

The success of the Green Revolution also depended on the fact that many of the host countries—such as Mexico, India, Pakistan, the Philippines, and China—had relatively stable governments and fairly well-developed infrastructures. These factors permitted these countries to diffuse both the new seeds and technology and to bring the products to market in an effective manner. The challenges were far more difficult in places such as Africa, where governments were unstable and roads and water resources were less developed. For example, in mid-1990s Mozambique, improved corn grew well in the northern part of the country, but civil unrest and an inadequate transportation system left much of the harvest to rot (Mann, p. 1038). According to the report by David Gately, with the exception of a few countries such as Kenya, where corn yields quadrupled in the 1970s, Africa benefited far less from the Green Revolution than Asian countries and is still threatened periodically with famine.

The Green Revolution could not have been launched without the scientific work done at the research institutes in Mexico and the Philippines. The two original institutes have given rise to an international network of research establishments dedicated to agricultural improvement, technology transfer, and the development of agricultural resources, including trained personnel, in the developing countries. A total of sixteen autonomous centers form the Consultative Group on International Agricultural Research (CGIAR), which operates under the direction of the World Bank. These centers address issues concerning tropical agriculture, dry-area farming, corn, potatoes, wheat, rice, livestock, forestry, and aquatic resources, among others.

Future advances in agricultural productivity depend on the development of new varieties of plants such as sorghum and millet, which are mainstays in African countries and other less-developed areas, and on the introduction of appropriate agricultural technology. This will probably include biotechnology—the genetic alteration of food plants to give them desirable characteristics. For example, farmers in Africa are plagued by hardy, invasive weeds that can quickly overrun a cultivated plot and compel the farmer to abandon it and move on to virgin land. If the plot were planted with corn, soybeans, or other crops that are genetically altered to resist herbicide, then the farmer could more easily control the weeds and harvest a successful crop. Scientists are also developing a genetically modified strain of rice fortified with vitamin A that is intended to help ward off blindness in children, which will be especially useful in developing countries. While people have expressed concern about the environmental impact of genetically modified food plants, such plants are well established in the United States and some other countries and are likely to catch on in the developing world as well.

See also **Agriculture since the Industrial Revolution; Biotechnology; Crop Improvement; Ecology and Food; FAO (Food and Agriculture Organization); Food Safety; Food Supply and the Global Food Market; Food Trade Associations; Government Agencies; High-Technology Farming; Horticulture; Hunger, Physiology of; Inspection; International Agencies; Political Economy**.

BIBLIOGRAPHY

Borlaug, Norman. "The Green Revolution, Peace, and Humanity." Nobel Lecture. Delivered 11 December 1970. Available at http://www.nobel.se.

Brown, Lester R. *Eco-Economy: Building an Economy for the Earth.* New York: Norton, 2001.

Brown, Lester R., et al., eds. *State of the World 2001: A Worldwatch Institute Report on Progress Toward a Sustainable Society.* New York: Norton, 2001.

Dawe, David. "Re-Energizing the Green Revolution in Rice." *American Journal of Agricultural Economics* 80 (1998): 948–953.

Easterbrook, Gregg. "Forgotten Benefactor of Humanity." *The Atlantic Monthly* 279, no. 1 (January 1997): 75–82.

Ehrlich, Paul R. *The Population Bomb.* Revised and expanded. New York: Sierra Club / Ballantine, 1971. A reprint of the 1968 edition.

Gately, David. "Backgrounder: The Past 25 Years: Successes, Failures, and Lessons Learned in Feeding the World." International Food Policy Research Institute, Washington, D.C., 2001. Available at http://www.ifpri.cgiar.org/2020/backgrnd/25years.htm.

Lappé, Frances Moore, Joseph Collins, and Peter Rosset. *World Hunger: 12 Myths.* New York: Grove Press, 1998.

Mann, Charles. "Reseeding the Green Revolution." *Science* 277 (1997): 1038–1043.

Walsh, John. "The Greening of the Green Revolution." *Science* 242 (1991): 26.

Richard L. Lobb

GREENHOUSE HORTICULTURE.

Plant cultivation is influenced by various factors, such as soil quality, water availability, and climatic conditions. Techniques have been developed either to adapt food crops to their environment (as by breeding and selecting plants more resistant to drought or with shorter production cycles), or to adjust the environment (for example, temperature, nutrient supply) to meet plant needs. Practical means of modifying the environment surrounding the plants have involved methods such as the use of windbreaks, mulches, plant or row covers, and cold frames. These methods of protecting plants may be described as passive methods since they only raise barriers between the plants and their environment, and do not control the environment. Some types of garden frames (hotbeds, heated frames) may be heated by artificial means, but do not actually provide for any control of the environment.

The only method of food crop production that makes use of control of the environment is greenhouse production. Modern greenhouse production is also referred to as controlled environment agriculture (CEA). With the use of a greenhouse, it is possible to cultivate food-producing plants in locations and at times when climatic conditions would adversely affect them or even prevent them from growing. Also, when climatic conditions allow outdoor plant cultivation, greenhouses can be used to protect crops against weather phenomena (such as wind, excessive rain, or hail) that would negatively affect them. For the purpose of this article, the term "greenhouse" is defined as a structure covered with a transparent or translucid material, in which environmental conditions can be modified or controlled, for the cultivation of plants. Tunnels are also used to modify environmental conditions for plant production, but are not usually considered greenhouses. Since the distinction between greenhouses and tunnels is not always clear in the literature, both structures, when high enough for people to move and work freely in them, will be considered together.

Food Produced in Greenhouses

Although greenhouses have been in existence since 1800 (or earlier), and greenhouse food production started to develop as an industry in the second half of the nineteenth century, the largest growth and expansion of the greenhouse industry occurred throughout the world following World War II. Today, food production in greenhouses can be found in all continents. Most popular food crops grown in greenhouses are tomato (beefsteak, cluster, Italian, cherry), cucumber, and sweet pepper. Other greenhouse grown vegetables include watermelon, muskmelon, summer squash, zucchini, lettuce, eggplant, snap beans, celery, cabbage, radish, Welsh onion, and asparagus. Fruits such as grapes, strawberry, banana, pineapple, papaya, orange, mandarin, cherry, and fig, as well as culinary and medicinal herbs, are also grown in greenhouses.

Today's Greenhouses

Covering materials. The main greenhouse covering materials are glass and polyethylene (PE). Glass has been used since the early days of greenhouses. The introduction of PE film after World War II was the main reason for the expansion of greenhouse production around the world, and it is now the most widely used covering material in the world. Glass-covered greenhouses are concentrated mainly in northern Europe and North America. The low cost of the PE greenhouse is the main reason for its high popularity, especially in developing countries. In recent years, the use of PE-greenhouses has even spread to northern regions. Research has shown that, under Canadian climatic conditions, heating costs of a double-layer PE-greenhouse are 20 to 30 percent lower than for a glass-covered greenhouse. Most of the greenhouses built now in Canada are covered with PE. Standard PE film blocks the ultraviolet, but not the infrared radiation, and has a short durability. However, improved PE films retain the infrared, but allow the ultraviolet, radiation (necessary for the bees, used for pollination of plants, to orient themselves)in the greenhouse, and are more durable. Polyvinyl chloride (PVC), another plastic film used to cover greenhouses, is used mostly in Japan. Other covering materials for greenhouses include rigid plastic acrylic, fiberglass, polycarbonate, and PVC panels, but their use is generally limited because of their high cost, compared to PE. Beside glass and PE, polycarbonate is often used on the sidewalls of polyethylene greenhouses in northern regions because of its good insulation, durability, and reasonable cost.

Technology in the greenhouse. Greenhouses come in many styles and sizes, from the original houses with minimal climate control (furnace and vents) to the modern 10-ha (25-acre) or more, multispan greenhouses with high-tech climate controls (sophisticated and powerful heating system, CO_2 enrichment, evaporative cooling pads, exhaust fans, roof vents, thermal/shade curtain, computer controls, light sensors). Most sophisticated greenhouses are generally found in the developed, northern countries. Phytotrons are highly sophisticated structures that allow for accurate control of environmental conditions including light, and are generally used for scientific research in universities and research institutes. However, phytotrons cannot be considered greenhouses since they are not covered with a transparent material.

The degree of environment control needed depends on various factors. The first factor is the location of the greenhouse (local climatic conditions). Northern regions are characterized by cold winters and warm summers. If the objective is to grow plants all year long, then such large differences in climatic conditions between winter and summer require a high-tech greenhouse. In regions such as the Mediterranean (Spain, Italy, Morocco, Greece), the mild winter climate does not require the use of powerful heating systems, and low-tech greenhouses are sufficient for winter production. However, these regions have very hot summers, and the use of a low-tech greenhouse may not provide satisfactory temperature control to grow plants during summertime.

The production schedule also affects the level of environment control and thus the level of technology. A greenhouse in northern regions may require a high level of climate control if the objective is to grow crops all year long (or long-season crops). If the objective is only to extend the production season (e.g., one early crop in spring), then a less sophisticated greenhouse could be satisfactory.

Optimal growing conditions differ from one species to another. For example, lettuce prefers cooler temperatures than cucumber. Thus, the crop grown in the greenhouse may influence the level of environment control needed or desired. A low-tech greenhouse may provide

TABLE 1

Estimated greenhouse area (ha) and important food crops grown in greenhouses worldwide

Country	Total area	Food crops area	Hydroponic	Important food crops		
China	360 000	(-)ᶻ	140ʸ	Cucumber (-)ˣ	Tomato (-)ˣ	Sweet pepper (-)ˣ
Spain	55 000	> 50 000	4 000 (10)	Melons (-)	Tomato (-)	Sweet pepper (-)
Japan	52 571	43 950 (84)	655 (1.5)	Tomato (15)	Cantaloupe (13)	Strawberry (13)
Italy	26 000	21 000 (81)	400 (1.9)	Tomato (-)	Zucchini (-)	Sweet pepper (-)
Korea	21 061	(-)	(-)	Cucumber (-)	Chinese cabbage (-)	Tomato (-)
Western North Africaʷ	11 400	> 7 900	(-)	Tomato (47)	Sweet pepper (25)	Cucumber (8)
Turkey	10 800	9 000 (83)	(-)	Tomato (-)	Cucumber (-)	Melon (-)
The Netherlands	10 800	4 335 (40)	2 895 (72)	Tomato (30)	Sweet pepper (23)	Cucumber (16)
France	9 100	6 500	(-)	Tomato (-)	Cucumber (-)	Strawberry (-)
United States	5 000	300 (6)	300 (100)	Tomato (-)	Cucumber (-)	Lettuce (-)
Greece	4 620	3 790 (82)	60 (1.6)	Tomato (-)	Cucumber (-)	Eggplant (-)
Middle Eastʷ	4 300	3700 (86)	(-)	Tomato (65)	Cucumber (21)	Sweet pepper (10)
Germany	3 300	(-)	(-)	Tomato (-)	Cucumber (-)	Lettuce (-)
Belgium	2 250	1 600 (71)	850 (53)	Tomato (38)	Lettuce & herbs (19)	Cucumber (5)
United-Kingdom	1 600	(-)	(-)	Tomato (-)	Cucumber (-)	Lettuce (-)
Canada	1 470	756 (51)	600 (80)	Tomato (56)	Cucumber (24)	Sweet pepper (16)
Arabic peninsulaʷ	(-)	1930	(-)	Cucumber (53)	Tomato (28)	(-)
Eastern North Africaʷ	(-)	1700	(-)	Cucumber (38)	Sweet pepper (34)	Tomato (20)
Mexico	(-)	350	17.5 (5)	Tomato (-)	(-)	(-)
Brazil	(-)	(-)	50	Lettuce (-)	Arugula (-)	Watercress (-)

ᶻ Value in parenthesis: percentage of greenhouse area used for food crops in each country, calculated over total greenhouse area; (-) = unavailable data.
ʸ Value in parenthesis: percentage of greenhouse area with hydroponic systems in each country, calculated over greenhouse area for food crops; (-) = unavailable data.
ˣ Value in parenthesis: percentage of greenhouse area for major crops in each country, calculated over greenhouse area for food crops; (-) = unavailable data.
ʷ These regions include the following countries (in order of importance of their greenhouse industry): Western North Africa: Morocco, Algeria, Tunisia; Eastern North Africa: Lybia, Egypt; Middle East: Jordan, Lebanon, Syria; Arabic peninsula: Saudi Arabia, Kuwait, United Arab Emirates, Iraq, Bahrain, Qatar.

sufficient climate control for lettuce but not for cucumber, depending on the location of the greenhouse and the production schedule.

Economic development also plays a role in the level of technology used in the greenhouse. In developing countries, growers may not be able to afford the most sophisticated equipment, and may lack technical expertise and technical support.

Greenhouses in desert regions. Although greenhouses were developed in northern regions as a means of protecting crops against cold temperatures, and are therefore generally associated with cold climates, they are also used in arid regions such as Saudi Arabia. In such regions, the objective of the greenhouse is to protect plants from the excessive solar radiation and temperature, and to prevent excessive water loss by plants (especially since water resources are generally limited in those regions). Therefore, technology in greenhouses in these regions is directed toward cooling.

Artificial lighting. In northern countries, high-tech greenhouses can provide optimal growing conditions (temperature, humidity, carbon dioxide) for vegetable crops even during the coldest winter months. However, even with excellent climate control, yield and quality of crops grown during these months are low due to the low light level available. Research has shown that it is possible to produce good yield of high-quality produce during the winter months by using artificial light to supplement the natural radiation. The most common artificial lighting is the high-pressure sodium lamp. The high cost of electric energy in many regions is the most important factor preventing an increased use of artificial light.

Production Systems

Growing in soil. Since the early days of greenhouses, plants have been grown in soil or in soil-filled containers. The first technique for fertilizing plants, which is still in use today in organic production, was the use of manure. Today, fertilization of plants can also be accomplished by incorporating chemical fertilizers in the soil, or by distributing fertilizers dissolved in water (so-called fertigation) to plants with a drip (trickle) irrigation system. Intensive and repetitive cultivation of crops on the same soil generally results in a degradation of soil properties and fertility. Salt accumulation may be another problem in soil cultivation. Incorporation of manure, compost, and other organic materials into soil can be used to improve its structure and replenish its fertility. However, ensuring perfect fertilization of plants grown in soil is still a difficult task. Furthermore, intensive and repetitive cultivation of crops on the same soil can also result in insect or disease infestation. Soil replacement and soil fumigation are two solutions, but the first technique is expensive and the second is not always successful. Greenhouse production in soil is still used widely.

TABLE 2

Estimated area (ha) of protected crops per region and type of structure

	Greenhouses + Tunnels		
	Plastic	Glass	Total
Asia	440 000	3 000	443 000
Mediterranean	97 000	8 000	105 000
Americas	15 600	4 000	19 600
Europe*	16 700	25 800	42 500
Africa + Middle East*	17 000	-	17 000
Total	586 300	40 800	627 100

*Excludes European countries on the Mediterranean Sea.

Growing without Soil

In order to better control fertilization for optimizing plant growth and yield, and also to avoid the problems occurring in soil, growing systems that do not use soil (soilless) were developed for the cultivation of greenhouse crops. These soilless systems can be classified in two groups: liquid (water) and solid (artificial substrates that are either inorganic or organic). Systems using water as a growing medium are the nutrient film technique (NFT), deep flow technique (DFT), and aeroponics. Common inorganic media are rockwool, vermiculite, perlite, and clay pellets. Organic substrates are peat, coconut coir, sawdust, and straw. Inorganic and organic substrates are usually contained in bags, and plants are irrigated with a complete nutrient solution distributed by a drip irrigation system. The excess of nutrient solution can either be allowed to leak into the ground or is recuperated and recirculated (after treatment) to plants. In liquid systems, plant roots are continuously exposed to nutrient solution, which is not leaked into the ground.

Growing methods using artificial substrates or water are known as soilless culture or hydroponics. Hydroponics is literally defined as the growing of plants in water, but the plants are actually grown in a complete nutrient solution. Ideally, the term *hydroponics* should be reserved for water culture, and the term *soilless culture* for plant cultivation on artificial substrates. In practice, the terms *hydroponics* and *soilless culture* are used indiscriminately to describe water and substrate-based systems.

Although official statistics are unavailable, hydroponic systems are known to be used extensively for food production in greenhouses. The most popular soilless medium for hydroponic vegetable production is rockwool. The nutrient film technique is also often used, but to a much lesser extend than rockwool. In some regions, the availability of low-cost materials may provide alternative substrates. For example, in British Columbia, sawdust, a residue of the large forestry industry, is commonly used as a substrate. Both aeroponics and DFT remain in little use today.

Insect and Disease Control in Greenhouses

One objective of hydroponics is to avoid insects and diseases that may occur in soil. In a soilless culture system, such as rockwool, it is easy to remove infected plants. However, spread of diseases can occur very quickly in systems where nutrient solution is recirculated. Methods such as filtration of the nutrient solution, and disinfection with ozone or ultraviolet light, have been developed to eliminate pathogens that may be present in the nutrient solution. However, these methods are often expensive and not completely effective.

Greenhouses are used to create and maintain an environment ideal for plants. However, this environment is often favorable for insects and pathogens too. In the past, the control of insects and diseases in greenhouses was accomplished with the use of pesticides, but over time both insects and diseases have developed resistance to such pesticides, while consumers have begun to demand pesticide-free produce. Biological agents are now used to control whitefly, thrips, aphids, and two-spotted spider mite in greenhouses; few reliable biological agents are currently available for the control of diseases.

Research on Greenhouse Food Crops

In countries or regions where greenhouse production is an important industry, government and universities are generally involved in research on greenhouse production. The general objective of the research is to improve yield and quality of produce and profitability of production, by investigating all aspects of greenhouse production: greenhouse design and covering materials, growing methods, environment controls, substrates, plant nutrition, plant pathology, and insect control. Grower associations may also be involved in the development of research priorities, and may contribute financially to the expenses of research.

Due to the presence of a large and technologically advanced greenhouse industry in the Netherlands, the most notable research institutions are found there. The Research Station for Floriculture and Glasshouse Vegetables (under the Ministry of Agriculture, Nature Conservancy and Fisheries) has five sites. The other important Dutch institution is the University of Wageningen.

In the United Kingdom, Horticulture Research International (HRI), the largest horticultural research establishment in the world, maintains an active research program on greenhouse crops and provides its services (from fundamental research to technology transfer) to research councils, government departments, growers, and commercial industries, in the European Community (EC) and other countries.

In the Americas, the Greenhouse and Processing Crops Research Centre (GPCRC; Agriculture and Agri-Food Canada) is the largest research facility specializing in greenhouse vegetables. The GPCRC is a leading mem-

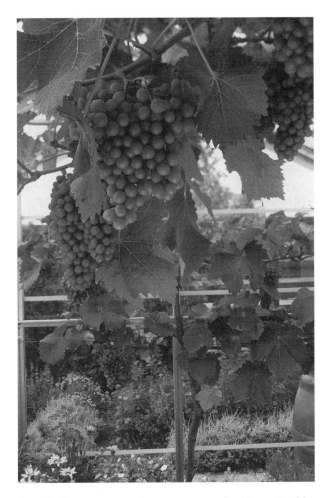

Organically grown greenhouse grapes at the Henry Double-day Research Association's headquarters in Ryton, England, near Coventry. During the Roman period, England's climate was considerably warmer, and grapes could be cultivated into the Midlands. Today, grapes can be grown only in Kent, in southeastern England; otherwise, table and wine grapes must be raised under glass. © MICHAEL BOYS/CORBIS.

ber of the Canadian Network for Greenhouse Vegetable Research.

Japan, Spain, and Israel are some of the other countries with important research programs in horticulture, including greenhouse food production.

The International Society for Horticultural Science (ISHS) is an international organization of horticultural scientists, which aims at promoting research in all branches of horticulture, including greenhouse food production. Within the ISHS, there are various commissions and working groups related to greenhouse production.

Future of Greenhouse Food Production

As the world population continues to increase, and more agricultural land is lost to urban development, intensive food production in greenhouses may play a more impor-

tant role in food production. Furthermore, improving economic conditions in developing countries and an increasing preoccupation with health and nutrition will increase demand for high-quality food products. Through controlled climate and reduced pesticide use, greenhouses can meet this consumer demand. Foods with improved health characteristics or containing nutraceuticals (substances with pharmaceutical or health-beneficial properties that can be extracted or purified from plants) can be grown pesticide-free in greenhouses.

See also **Chili Peppers**; **Crop Improvement**; **Cucumbers, Melons, and Other Cucurbits**; **High-Technology Farming**; **Horticulture**; **Tomato**.

BIBLIOGRAPHY

Bakker, J. C., G. P. A. Bot, H. Challa, and N. J. Van de Braak, eds. *Greenhouse Climate Control: An Integrated Approach.* Wageningen, The Netherlands: Wageningen Pers, 1995.

Dalrymple, Dana G. *Controlled Environment Agriculture: A Global Review of Greenhouse Food Production.* U.S. Department of Agriculture, Economic Research Service, Foreign Agricultural Economic Report no. 89. Washington, D.C.: USDA, 1973.

Dorais, Martine, ed., *Proceedings of the 4th International ISHS Symposium on Artificial Lighting.* Leuven, Belgium: International Society for Horticultural Science.

Baudoin, W. O. "Protected Cultivation in the Mediterranean Region." *Acta Horticulturae* 486, (1999): 23–30.

Centre de Recherche en Horticulture, Université Laval, Québec, Qué. Canada (Horticultural Research Centre, Laval University, Quebec City, Que., Canada). Available at http://www.crh.ulaval.ca

Costa, J. Miguel, and Ep Heuvelink, eds. *Greenhouse Horticulture in Almería (Spain): Report on a Study Tour 24–29 January 2000.* Wageningen, The Netherlands: Horticultural Production Chains Group, Wageningen University, 2000.

Graves, Chris J. "The Nutrient Film Technique." *Horticultural Reviews* 5 (1983): 1–44.

Greenhouse and Processing Crops Research Centre, Agriculture and Agri-Food Canada, Harrow, Ont., Canada. Available at http://res2.agr.ca/harrow

Giacomelli, Gene A., and William J. Roberts. "Greenhouse Covering Systems." *HortTechnology* 3, no.1 (1993): 50–58.

Hanan, J. J. *Greenhouses: Advanced Technology for Protected Horticulture.* Boca Raton, Fla.: CRC Press, 1998.

Hashimoto, Y., G. P. S. Bot, W. Day, H.-J. Tantau, and H. Nonami, eds. *The Computerized Greenhouse: Automatic Control Application in Plant Production.* San Diego, Calif.: Academic Press, 1993.

Hix, John. *The Glasshouse.* 2d ed. London: Phaidon, 1996.

International Working Group on Soilless Culture. *Proceedings of the International Congress on Soilless Culture.* Wageningen, Netherlands: Secretariat of IWOCS, 1973-

Jensen, Merle H., and Alan J. Malter. *Protected Agriculture: A Global Review.* World Bank Technical Paper no. 253. Washington, D.C.: World Bank, 1995.

Jensen, Merle H., and W. L. Collins. "Hydroponic Vegetable Production." *Horticultural Reviews* 7 (1985): 483–558.

Martin, Inigo. *The Horticultural Industry in Spain.* 3d ed. Asturias, Spain: Inigo Martin, Cabru, 2001.

Nisen, A., M. Grafiadellis, R. Jimenez, G. La Malfa, P. F. Martinez-Garcia, A. Monteiro, H. Verlodt, O. de Villele, C. H. von Zabeltitz, I. Denis, and W. O. Baudoin, eds. *Protected Cultivation in the Mediterranean Climate.* Food and Agriculture Organization, Plant Production Protection Paper no. 90. Rome, 1990.

Papadopoulos, Athanasios P., ed. *Acta Horticulturae no. 481, vol. 1 and 2. Proceedings of the International Symposium on Growing Media and Hydroponics.* Leuven, Belgium: International Society for Horticultural Science, 1999.

Savage, A. J., ed. *Hydroponics Worldwide: State of the Art in Soilless Crop Production.* Honolulu, Hawaii: International Center for Special Studies, 1985.

Statistics Canada. *Greenhouse, Sod and Nursery Industries.* Catalog no. 22-202-XIB, 1999.

Wittwer, Sylvan H., "World-wide Use of Plastics in Horticultural Production." *HortTechnology* 3, no.1 (1993): 6–19.

Wittwer, Sylvan H., and Nicolas Castilla. "Protected Cultivation of Horticultural Crops Worldwide." *HortTechnology* 5, no. 1 (1995): 6–23.

Zhang, Zhibin. "Update Development of Protected Cultivation in Mainland China." *Chronica Horticulturae* 39, no. 2 (1999): 11–15.

Athanasios P. Papadopoulos
Dominique-André Demers

GREENS. *See* **Leaf Vegetables; Lettuce; Salad; Vegetables.**

GRILLING. Grilling is a fast, dry method of cooking tender cuts of meat and vegetables with radiant heat directed from below or from above. Its chief benefit is that it provides for the maximum amount of browning. In addition, a well-seasoned grill imparts a distinct flavor of its own to food cooked on it.

Virtually every American man either feels himself to be a master of outdoor grilling or experiences a twinge of guilt at falling short. The backyard barbecue has become for many the epitome of the suburban good life.

Grilling owes part of its appeal to its apparent simplicity: humans, fire, and meat. But many people are deceived by what looks like a simple process, and a lot of good food ends up ruined unnecessarily. Worse yet, some of the most delicious uses of the outdoor grill are ignored.

It is important to understand that grilling is not the same as barbecuing, even though both can be done on the same covered grill wheeled out of the garage on Sunday afternoons. Barbecue is an indirect slow-cooking process that uses long periods of exposure to low heat to tenderize tough cuts like brisket and chuck steak. It is generally agreed that the correct barbecue temperatures are from 180°F to 300°F. During the hours of cooking, extra flavor can be imparted from the smoky character of the grill, from the fuel used, and from sauces that are applied regularly. It is possible to get and satisfy a sudden impulse to grill. Barbecue, on the other hand, is a matter that requires planning, careful thought, and the provision of some form of amusement for the chef.

Methods of Grilling
Grilling can be divided into three major cooking styles, depending on how the heat source is configured. But all agree that the heat used must be above 500°F. The under-heat technique and grill roasting have the advantage of flavor enhancement from the grill itself; other methods only simulate some of the attributes of grilling.

In traditional or under-heat grilling, food is placed on a rack or grill bars over a gas or charcoal grill. Because of the fast nature of the cooking process, it is necessary to preheat the grill and the racks.

In top-heat grilling or broiling, used mostly in restaurants, the food is placed under a salamander, a professional overhead cooking oven. Again the grill (broiler) must be preheated, for quick searing. The process does produce a fine grill quality, but falls short in two areas. It does not leave the distinct grill marks so prized by many chefs and grill fanatics alike, and it also does not impart a smoke flavor.

Pan grilling, the third main method, is suitable for the most tender cuts. The food is cooked directly on a heavy cast-iron pan or ridged griddle pan. The cooking surface should be lightly seasoned to avoid sticking. One advantage of this method is that the food can be seared on a ridged pan, then finished in the preheated oven. This professional method is practical when preparing banquet menus, because the chef can be sure of consistently cooking to the same degree of doneness.

Other techniques. Grill roasting or indirect grilling is a hybrid technique. The procedure uses a conventional grill in a nontraditional way: fire is ignited under part of the grill, the food is placed over the unheated or coolest part of the grill, and the grill lid is closed. Some of the flavor of the grill is imparted to the food, which is usually browned over the heated part. Grill roasting is best for foods that are already tender but have a larger mass; birds and fish are good candidates.

Grill smoking is another variation on indirect grilling. Before you start to grill, place a metal dish or foil package containing moistened wood chips or herbs below the grill and over the fire. The heat will make lots of smoke that will fill the closed grill and flavor the food. This is a particularly good technique to use with brined foods.

Grilling Basics
In terms of grilling tips, simple common sense is the rule. Always trim excessive fat off meat; this will help stop flare-

Grilling is a popular method of cooking for outdoor meals, especially during the summer. Entire menus can be created from grilled vegetables, meats, and fish. There is also a shift in the gender of the cooks, since grilling is commonly perceived as a male task. PHOTO BY ANDRÉ BARANOWSKI.

up, which adds a combustion taste to grilled foods. Always remove silver skin and connective tissue; silver skin does not dissolve when cooking, and connective tissue can cause meat to warp on the grill as the elastin shrinks.

As is true with all high-heat cooking, the best results come from food of uniform thickness. Trim the tapered ends from chicken breasts and vegetables and cook separately or reserve for another use. If grilling a vegetable—asparagus, for instance—try to select pieces that are of uniform thickness. Cutting other vegetables on a mandoline—a compact, hand-operated wood- or stainless steel-frame slicing and cutting machine with various adjustable blades—makes uniform thickness easy to obtain.

Dry ingredients that are exposed to high heat brown, their protein transformed by a series of changes called the Maillard reactions. Browned meats are much more flavorful, and when people say that they love the smell of cooked meat, they are in fact admiring the aromas that accompany browning. Maillard reactions take place only at temperatures well above the boiling point of water, so it is essential to pat meat that is wet or marinated dry before grilling. Meat and vegetables can also be brushed with oil or rubbed with infused oil. This actually facili-

tates browning while it adds flavor and prevents items from sticking to grids.

Season at the last minute. Never (except when braising) let meat sit in a coat of salt. Instead, add salt or salt-and-spice mixtures immediately before cooking. If salt is left on the surface it draws out the juices and toughens the meat. Be careful not to burn spices. With dry herb-and-spice rubs used to impart flavor, brush off excess before grilling; an option is to brush over the surface with oil before cooking, to prevent burning dry-rub ingredients.

When using natural fuel (charcoal) make sure coals are the correct temperature, and burnt down. A two-second hand count (meaning you can't hold your hand over the grill for more than two seconds) is the rule for a grill between 450°F and 500°F. Nothing imparts a bad resin flavor like charcoal that is not fully ignited and a cool grill.

The Science of Grilling

Some understanding of cooking chemistry helps in grilling. Chefs are reexamining the use of brining or salting to produce juicy items today, and it is only a matter of time before the consumer catches on to this technique.

Brining—soaking lean cuts in salted water—preserves moisture. For fish, pork, chicken, or shrimp, prepare a brine with one cup of kosher salt per gallon of water (some brines also call for a small amount of sugar). Soak chicken in brine for two to twenty-four hours, other foods for as little as an hour. Rinse well, pat dry, and use the indirect method described above. The science behind the brine is simple; meat proteins are made up of amino acids, some of which are highly charged. They interact with the salt ions in the brine to open their structure and to dramatically increase their water-holding capacity. The salt actually moves into the meat, and extra water is also absorbed; on the grill, the salt in the meat holds on to the moisture, and so does the protein. The result is a juicier product, even from the high heat of the grill or the medium-high heat of grill roasting. Another way to impart flavor is by use of marinades and basting. Before cooking, meat proteins and vegetables may be marinated in mixtures of oil with vinegar, wine or citrus juice, herbs and spices, and other ingredients to help tenderize and add flavor. Marinades should always be blotted dry before grilling.

The process of grilling must also be defined in terms of the fuel used. There are several different types of grills, but gas and charcoal are by far the most common. They are also the source of the great grill debate: efficiency versus flavor. Today, gas grills represent about 60 percent of sales to household consumers. It is clear that they have their advantages, the most touted being ease of use, not having to add more fuel during long cookouts, and a juicy end product. Grilling purists, however, argue that hardwood charcoal gives a better flavor, and a smoky, drier character. The fuel source for charcoal grills has been recognized for at least five thousand years. No one is certain who discovered charcoal, but evidence of early use has been found all over the world. What most consumers may not know is that charcoal is actually wood; it is created by heating wood to high temperatures. Charcoal does provide a distinctive flavor that is not easily reproduced. And with the use of hardwoods like hickory, cherry, and mesquite, the flavor profile of the final product may have infinite variety. It is a tough decision for many people: the convenience of a gas grill against the flavor of charcoal.

See also **Barbecue; Broiling; Hearth Cookery; Marinating and Marinades; Meat; Roasting.**

BIBLIOGRAPHY

Cooks Illustrated Editors. *How to Barbecue and Roast on the Grill.* Cooks Illustrated Library. Boston: Boston Common Press, 1999.

Fuller, Kristi M., ed. *The New Grilling Book.* Des Moines, Iowa: Better Homes and Gardens, 2000.

McGee, Harold. *On Food and Cooking: The Science and Lore of the Kitchen.* New York: Scribners, 1984.

Francis McFadden

GRIMOD DE LA REYNIÈRE. Named Alexandre-Balthazar-Laurent by an aristocratic mother and a farmer father, Grimod de la Reynière (1758–1837) was a rich eccentric with extravagant ways. He began a career as a theater critic but became one of the first to develop French gastronomic literature through the eight volumes of his *L'Almanach des gourmands,* which he published from 1803 to 1812. He originated the double genre of food critic and restaurant guide, providing practical information as well as critical standards. These were formulated by his jury of tasters, twelve friends who met weekly at the five-hour dinners he staged in his Paris home.

In 1808 his *Manuel des amphitryons,* a condensation of the material of the almanac, established the idea that the consuming public wanted guidance from an authoritative judge. The application of judge and jury to table matters was appropriate to the chaos of post-Revolutionary Paris and to the beginning of public restaurants during the transition from "ancient" to modern French cuisine. Such autocratic judgment created enemies and, forced to leave Paris in 1812, La Reynière sent out a public notice of his death and staged a funeral banquet in order to predict, accurately as it turned out, how very few friends would attend. He spent the rest of his life in retirement in the countryside, married to the actress who had been his mistress.

La Reynière's influence in creating a critical guide for bourgeois consumers and gastronomes in the newly de-

Grimod's fondness for the flesh of game and that of actresses is evident in this fanciful recipe:

"Stuff an olive with capers and anchovies and put it in a garden warbler. Put the garden warbler in an ortolan, the ortolan in a lark, the lark in a thrush, the thrush in a quail, the quail in a larded lapwing, the lapwing in a plover, the plover in a red-legged partridge, the partridge in a woodcock—as tender as Mlle Volnais, the woodcock in a teal, the teal in a guinea fowl, the guinea fowl in a duck, the duck in a fattened pullet—as white as Mlle Belmont, as fleshy as Mlle Vienne, and as fat as Mlle Contat, the pullet in a pheasant, the pheasant in a duck, the duck in a turkey—white and fat like Mlle Arsène, and finally, the turkey in a bustard."

—*Larousse Gastronomique, p. 532*

"The local wine, a dinner at your friends' house, and music performed by amateurs are three things to be equally dreaded."

—*Larousse Gastronomique, p. 531*

mocratized theaters of the table, in houses and in restaurants, extends to this day. While the prose and outlook of his contemporary gastronome, Brillat-Savarin, were more humane, Grimod's delight in staging dining scenes that were theatrically absurd and macabre, a sort of *cuisine noire* (black-comedy cuisine), is peculiarly modern.

See also **Brillat-Savarin**; **Chef**; **France**.

BIBLIOGRAPHY

Béarn, Pierre. *Grimod de la Reynière*. Paris: Gallimard, 1930.

Desnoiresterres, Gustave. *Grimod de La Reynière et Son Groupe; D'après des Documents Entièrements Inédits* [Grimod de La Reynière and his group; from unedited documents]. Paris: Didier et cie, 1877.

Grimod de La Reynière, A. B. L. *Grimod de La Reynière: Écrits Gastronomiques* [Gastronomic writings]. Paris: Union Générale d'Éditions, 1978.

Mennell, Stephen. *All Manners of Food: Eating and Taste in England and France from the Middle Ages to the Present*. Oxford and New York: Blackwell, 1985.

Rival, Ned. *Grimod de La Reynière: Le Gourmand Gentilhomme*. Paris: Le Pré aux clercs, 1983.

Betty Fussell

GROCERY STORES. *See* **Retailing of Food.**

H

HALLOWEEN. Halloween (also Hallowe'en) is thought to have derived from a pre-Christian festival known as Samhain (pronounced "Sah-wen") celebrated among the Celtic peoples. The various peoples whom we now refer to as "Celts" once lived across Europe, but in time came to inhabit the areas known today as Ireland, Scotland, Wales, Brittany, and Cornwall. Modern Irish, Welsh, and Scots peoples are the descendants of these peoples, as are their Gaelic languages.

History

Samhain was the principal feast day of the year; it was the New Year's Day of a year that began on 1 November. Traditionally, bonfires were lit as part of the celebration. It was believed that the spirits of those who had died during the previous twelve months were granted access into the otherworld during Samhain. Thus, spirits were said to be traveling on that evening, as the Celtic day was counted from sundown to sundown.

Scholars know little about the actual practices and beliefs associated with Samhain. Most accounts were not written down until centuries after the conversion of Ireland to Christianity (c. 300 C.E.), and then by Christian monks recording ancient sagas. From the evidence, we know that Samhain was a focal point of the yearly cycle, and that traditions of leaving out offerings of food and drink to comfort the wandering spirits had joined the bonfire custom. Also, the tradition of mumming—dressing in disguise and performing from home to home in exchange for food or drink, as well as pranking, perhaps in imitation of the wandering spirits, or simply as a customary activity found throughout Europe—had become part of the occasion. With the acceptance of Christianity, the dates of the pre-Christian festivals were used as occasions for church feast and holy days. The first day of November became, in the sixth century, the Feast of All Saints, or All Hallows. Many of the folk traditions surrounding this occasion continued, and the Eve of All Hallows, Hallow Evening, has become conflated into the word "Hallowe'en." In the ninth century, 2 November was assigned the Feast of All Souls, a day set aside for prayers for all the faithful departed who had died during the previous year.

Halloween was brought to North America with Irish and British colonists, although it was not widely observed until the large influx of European immigrants in the nineteenth century, especially the Irish fleeing the potato famine in the 1840s and thereafter. In the United States, Hallowe'en, celebrated on 31 October, was a time for parties and pranking. As a festival of autumn, the fruits, vegetables, and foods associated with it are those of the harvest. Games were and are still played with apples, and the primary symbol of Halloween is the jack-o'-lantern, the great, carved pumpkin. Likewise, both apple pie and pumpkin pie are commonly served.

Samhain in Ireland

In Ireland, however, Halloween is much more a harvest festival than it is in the United States, where Thanksgiving has become the official day of thanks for abundance. As Samhain, November Eve was one of the four great quarter days of the year, each one marking the beginning of a new season. Samhain also marked the start of a new year. Halloween commands a place of honor in Ireland today greater than in the United States. And in fact it functions much like Thanksgiving does here. Family meals and a gathering of relatives are common. There is pranking throughout the season, and Halloween rhyming, in which young people go from door to door for weeks in advance of 31 October, present a rhyme or perform a song of some sort, in return for nuts, apples, or money. The money is spent on fireworks. Also well in advance of the actual day, lanterns are carved out of large turnips, called swedes, or rutabegas in the United States. These are given a face and a handle, and are carried about or set on walls to create a spooky atmosphere. When the old tradition of the turnip lantern was brought to the new world, settlers found the already hollow pumpkin to be preferable to the hard turnip, and so the pumpkin replaced the turnip in the United States. But the pumpkin is a fruit introduced to Europeans by Native Americans and is not native to Ireland, Great Britain, or the rest of Europe.

By carving a face on a turnip or a pumpkin, one transforms the organic item into a cultural one. The jack-o'-lantern is the wandering spirit of a man who was refused entry into either heaven or hell in the afterlife. He is condemned to wander this earth, carrying a lantern to guide his way. He is a trickster; he will lead hapless souls who follow his light to no good. The turnip lantern is said to represent the spirits of the dead—ghosts. The organic

Apple dunking was a popular Halloween activity in nineteenth-century America, as shown here in an 1879 engraving. ROUGH-WOOD COLLECTION.

items are made to reference the supernatural. Also, they are turned into another kind of cultural item: food. Pumpkin pies and mashed turnips are foods of the season, and represent domestic aspects of Halloween. The wild, unpredictable outside and the safe, nuturing inside are two poles of this festival. Halloween combines danger and safety, as when trick-or-treaters in the United States are invited in for cider and doughnuts. In Ireland, the inversive elements usually precede the day itself, which is given over to parties, special meals, and traditional games. These games are often played with the seasonal foods, such as dunking for apples, but they are also used in a playful way as divination games. For instance, Halloween in Ireland is also known as Nut Crack Night, because a common game is to place two nuts together near the hearth, name them for an adolescent or courting couple, then see what the effect of the heat is on the nuts. If they explode and pop away from each other, their relationship is doomed.

Divination and Halloween food come together in the apple tarts (pies) and the cakes known as barm brack. Barm brack means speckled bread. It is a corn loaf, and it is baked with tokens inside, usually a ring, but also a thimble, or a button. To get the ring means you will be married; the button suggests bachelorhood for a man, and

a thimble, spinsterhood for a woman. There may be other tokens as well. The apple tart is also baked with charms, usually a coin (preferably silver). This means good luck for the recipient. These food customs are widespread in Ireland—one sees the bakeshops advertising their apple tarts and barm bracks "with rings and mottoes." Likewise, in the supermarkets, quantities of apples, hazelnuts, peanuts in the shell (called monkeynuts), and even coconuts are displayed alongside soft drinks and false faces.

Many are the divination games and rites of Halloween. It is said, for instance, that one should peel an apple continuously, so that the peel is in one long piece, and then toss it over one's left shoulder. The peel will land and form the initial of one's future love. Typically, these games are played by girls, to whom the indoor, domestic, nurturing realm is given, while the adolescent boys collect bonfire materials and engage in games of macho daring with firecrackers. Halloween is in these ways very gendered.

According to some accounts, the Halloween supper has featured a roast fowl or even meat, but as the day before a Holy Day of Obligation in the Catholic Church, Halloween has traditionally been a day of abstinence from meat. The dishes most associated with Halloween in Ireland—colcannon, champ, and boxty—are all made from root vegetables and earthy harvests such as potatoes and cabbage. Champ is mashed potatoes, frequently with leeks, and served with a pool of melted butter in the top. Colcannon is potatoes and cabbage. Boxty is mashed potatoes mixed with grated raw potatoes, onion, and cabbage, which are then boiled, cut into portions and fried.

These traditional foods are emblematic of Halloween for many in Ireland. Sometimes, portions were left out for the fairies. In an article published in 1958, K. M. Harris quotes a man who recalls his mother putting salt on the head of each child to prevent them from being taken away by the "wee people" on Halloween. He also recounts her placing a thimble-full of salt on each plate. If the salt fell down that person would die in the next twelve months. These beliefs indicate the continued association of food with the supernatural, and perhaps echo the "old" new year's day of Samhain in the idea that what happens on this night affects the next twelve months.

Periods of transition and seasonal change frequently are felt to be times when the barriers between the natural and the supernatural—between our world and the otherworld—are opened. During such times, spirits and otherworldly creatures such as fairies are especially active. They are dangerous and must be appeased; thus the offerings of food. But they are also tricksters, and can be imitated, thus lending an air of inversion to Halloween.

Halloween in the United States
In the United States, 31 October has become a major celebration that appeals to adults as well as children, as shown by the elaborate homemade and store-bought dec-

orations people use to decorate their homes, and also by the adult street festivals, masquerades, and parties found all over the United States. Commercially, Halloween has become second only to Christmas in the amount of revenue it generates.

Ironically, by the mid-twentieth century, Halloween in the United States had become almost exclusively a children's event. The custom of trick-or-treating (the American version of Halloween rhyming) seems to have been introduced in the 1930s as an alternative to the children's pranking activities—sometimes dangerous, such as logs in the road; always a nuisance (Tuleja, 1994). Trick-or-treating became a widespread activity after World War II. While treats could include apples and homemade sweets, the favored treat was commercially produced candy. In the United States, then, Halloween has always reflected the commercial culture of capitalism. Apocryphal stories known as "urban legends" have circulated about poisoned treats and apples with razor blades hidden in them. While there has been no substantial verification of the stories, the belief is widespread. The result is that homemade treats and natural fruits are looked at suspiciously—many communities offer Halloween treat X-raying services. Now so more than ever, the commercially produced sweet is preferred (Ellis, 1994).

By the late twentieth century, as the generation that had enjoyed Halloween as children became adults, the holiday returned to being one in which different age groups engaged. College students hosted large costume parties. Cities such as New York, Boston, Washington, D.C., and San Francisco had major street festivals. As a day of public costuming and inversion, a time when people confronted images of the taboo—representations of death, evil, and chaos, Halloween had long been used by the gay population as a "safe" time to parade in drag, to publicly display an identity that they must keep hidden the rest of the year. By the end of the twentieth century, the rest of the population joined them to create a kind of national Mardi Gras. Unlike the actual Fat Tuesday, however, this carnival is in the autumn, and it combines seasonal images of the harvest with images of human death (ghosts and skeletons) as well as other unspeakables. Halloween is a time when it is safe to play with our fears, to allow our demons to come out from under the bed and take center stage once a year.

See also **British Isles,** *subentries on* **England** *and* **Ireland; Christianity; Day of the Dead; Feasts, Festivals, and Fasts; Holidays; Shrove Tuesday.**

BIBLIOGRAPHY

Ellis, Bill. "'Safe' Spooks: New Hallowe'en Traditions in Response to Sadism Legends." In *Hallowe'en and Other Festivals of Death and Life,* edited by Jack Jack Santino, pp. 24–44. Knoxville: University of Tennessee Press, 1994.

Harris, K. M. "Extracts from the Committee's Collection." *Ulster Folklife* 4 (1958): 37–49.

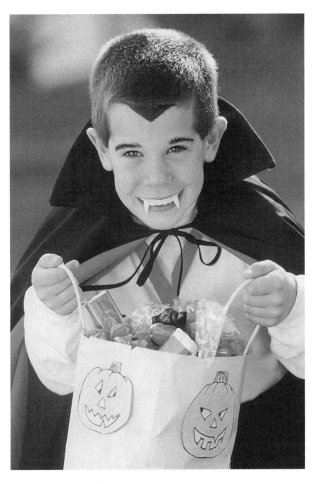

The most recent development in the evolution of the American Halloween is the costumed trick-or-treater. It began in the 1920s and has become a national custom, especially for children. © ED BOCK/CORBIS.

Santino, Jack. *All Around the Year: Holidays and Celebrations in American Life.* Champaign-Urbana: University of Illinois Press, 1994.

Santino, Jack, ed. *Hallowe'en and Other Festivals of Death and Life.* Knoxville: University of Tennessee Press, 1994.

Santino, Jack. *The Hallowed Eve: Dimensions of Culture in a Calendar Festival in Northern Ireland.* Lexington: The University Press of Kentucky, 1998.

Tuleja, Tad. "Trick or Treat: Pre-texts and Contexts." In *Hallowe'en and Other Festivals of Death and Life,* edited by Jack Santino, pp. 82–102. Knoxville: University of Tennessee Press, 1994.

Jack Santino

HAMBURGER. Humans have consumed beef in scraped, chopped, hashed, and minced forms since the domestication of the cow. Its main advantage was that it was an efficient way of using many smaller parts of the cow, including fat, organs, brains, and so on. To this

FIRST LOCATED HAMBURG(ER) RECIPE?

To make Hamburgh Sausages
    Take a pound of Beef, mince it very small, with half a Pound of the best Suet; then mix three Quarters of a Pound of Suet cut in large Pieces; then season it with Pepper, Cloves, Nutmeg, a great Quantity of Garlic cut small, some white Wine Vinegar, some Bay Salt, a Glass of red Wine, and one of Rum; mix all these very well together, then take the largest Gut you can find, stuff it very tight; then hang it up a Chimney, and smoke it with Saw-dust for a Week or ten Days; hang them in the Air, till they are dry, and they will keep a Year. They are very good boiled in Peas Porridge, and roasted with toasted Bread under it, or in an Amlet.

SOURCE: Hannah Glasse. *Art of Cookery Made Plain and Easy.* 6th ed. London, 1758, p. 370.

mixture could be added parts of other animals, plants, spices, flavorings, and adulterations. The resulting product can be easily shaped into different forms and prepared in a variety of ways—raw in steak tartare, molded into flat cakes or croquets, baked in a loaf, boiled and served in soups, barbecued or roasted and served on a bun, fried into meat balls, or stuffed into sausages with spices and herbs for later consumption.

Origin of Hamburger
The invention of the twentieth-century hamburger sandwich is the result of long developmental processes. Beginning in the fifteenth century, minced beef was a valued delicacy throughout Europe. In northern Germany, lightly fried chopped meat was called *Frikadelle*. Similar words are found in other European languages, and the root may be "farce," deriving from Latin *farcere* (to stuff). In English the term "forcemeat" was defined by Randle Holme in "The Academy of Armory" (Chester, 1688) as "meat with a stuffing of herbs, or other things made to that purpose."

    Hashed beef was made into sausage in several different regions of Europe. In places such as Bologna, Russia, and Hamburg, beef was often combined with other meats and other ingredients. The German city of Hamburg was known for its beef sausage, which migrated to England by the mid-eighteenth century. One recipe, titled "Hamburgh Sausage," appeared in Hannah Glasse's 1758 *The Art of Cookery Made Plain and Easy*. It consisted of chopped beef, suet, and spices. Although the author recommended that this sausage be served with toasted

bread, no evidence suggests that the sausage was served as a sandwich.

    Hannah Glasse's cookbook was also among the most common in Colonial America, although it was not published in the United States until 1805. This American edition did contain the "Hamburgh Sausage" recipe with slight revisions.

    The frequently cited "Hamburg Steak" on the Delmonico's restaurant menu dated 1834 was neither served as a sandwich nor composed of ground beef. With the popularization of the meat grinder in America about 1850, ground beef became a possibility. Recipes for it appeared in cookbooks from other countries, such as in Henriette Davidis's *Praktisches Kochbuch für die Deutschen in Amerika*. In American cookbooks, these recipes were frequently called "Beefsteak à la Hamburg." This recipe was so associated with the United States that the 1899 edition of Blüher's *Rechtschreibung der Speisen und Getränke* reported without explanation that chopped beefsteak was called "Hamburg steak" in America. Ground beef was also called "Salisbury steak," which was named in honor of the American physician James H. Salisbury (1823–1905), who wrote *The Relation of Alimentation and Disease* (New York, 1888). Salisbury believed that scraped lean beef, flattened into cakes and broiled, was among the best foods for those who were ailing. As scraping beef was a difficult task, common recipes for it just recommended grinding the beef, a process not recommended by Salisbury. Scraped or ground, Salisbury steak could be served with toast, but it was not served as a sandwich.

The Sandwich
The sandwich—a filling between two slices of bread that can be consumed by hand—is said to have been popularized by the Fourth Earl of Sandwich (1718–1792). This mode of eating became so popular in England that it was mentioned in several diaries and in Samuel Johnson's 1755 *Dictionary of the English Language*. Shortly thereafter, cooks and hosts began experimenting with various fillings other than sliced beef.

    Sandwiches migrated to the United States before the Civil War. In the mid-nineteenth century, sandwiches consisted of a filling composed of lean slices of cold meat between two thin pieces of bread flavored with mustard and ketchup. They were served in bars and saloons, where patrons could easily consume them without the need of knives, forks, or plates. During the late nineteenth century, interest in the sandwich rapidly expanded to include boned fish, sardines, cheese, boiled eggs, stewed fruit, chopped nuts, mushrooms, chicken, watercress, sardines, and jelly and jam. Many salads, such as chicken and lobster, were converted into sandwiches. By 1900, hundreds of different fillings were consumed in sandwiches.

Hamburger Sandwiches
Several legends have grown up concerning who first served hamburger sandwiches in America. A hamburger

sandwich is defined as a hot ground-beef patty between two slices of bread. It is not likely that any of the early claims put forth are accurate: sandwiches were composed of thin bread requiring thin fillings. Thin bread would also not have been able to contain the juices exuded from hot ground hamburger.

The first known published reference to a "hamburger sandwich" appeared in an article in the *New York Tribune*, which noted that this "new innovation" was served at the 1904 St. Louis Exposition. While it is possible that hamburger sandwiches were constructed well before this date at small stands and diners, the fair gave them national exposure and national diffusion resulted.

Hamburgers served in stands and diners in many regions of the United States attracted the working class. In a diner in Wichita, Kansas, a short-order cook named J. Walter Anderson flattened the meat balls and placed them in a bun; he developed the first commercial bun for hamburgers. In 1916 Anderson opened his own hamburger stand and sold them at five cents apiece to attract customers. To sell sandwiches at this price, Anderson streamlined his operation. To make certain that his clients were aware of what was contained in his hamburger, he ground his own beef and let his customers watch him doing it. His business was so successful that he opened three additional stands within four years. His success brought competitors, and the streets of Wichita had many hamburger stands. In 1921 he went into business with Edgar Waldo "Billy" Ingram. Ingram repackaged Anderson's hamburger stands architecturally into castles, and gave the operation the name "White Castle." Ingram insisted on standardization of all the stands, and he required employees to maintain strict standards of cleanliness, eventually requiring uniforms. This was extremely successful, and White Castle began expanding beyond Wichita. By 1924 the company had expanded to Omaha, then to Kansas City, then St. Louis, and the expansion continued. Ingram declared White Castle to be a national operation with forty-four outlets by 1930. He standardized the operation by opening meat-processing and bun-baking operations.

White Castle imitators, including some with the word "white" in their name, such as White Tower, spread across the United States. Ed Gold launched another hamburger chain, Wimpy Grills, in 1934. This featured the ten-cent "Wimpy" burger named after the cartoon character J. Wellington Wimpy, who immortalized the phrase: "I would gladly pay you tomorrow for a hamburger today" in a Popeye cartoon released in 1929. Wimpy Grills was the first fast-food corporation to expand abroad. Another competitor was Bob Wian, who founded Bob's Big Boy chain in southern California in 1936. He featured an upscale double-patty burger and franchised his operation, which quickly spread from coast to coast.

Within a few decades of the launch of White Castle, the hamburger had become America's national sand-

The American hamburger has become a food culture of its own. This humorous sign for the Bun Boy Restaurant was photographed in southern Indiana. © PHILIP GOULD/CORBIS.

wich. Through small hamburger stands and national franchise chains, hamburgers were sold through hundreds of outlets throughout America.

McDonald's

The prewar enlargement paled by comparison with the expansion of hamburger establishments after World War II. Returning from the war, many military personnel married, had children, bought cars, and moved to the suburbs. Focusing on those suburbanites with growing families and stretched incomes, Richard and Maurice McDonald designed a hamburger restaurant incorporating assembly-line efficiency into a commercial kitchen. This efficiency helped them to reduce their expenses and therefore permitted them to sell hamburgers at a low price. They hoped that the lower price would increase the number of customers, generating a greater volume with higher profits. To test their ideas, they opened an octagonal-shaped hamburger stand in San Bernardino, California, in 1948. Their operation did not include indoor tables, and it required that customers line up to place their orders and then eat in their cars: this eliminated the need for waitresses, which further reduced their expenses. The McDonalds sped up the process of making hamburgers through a series of innovations. They also decided to concentrate on selling just a few items: hamburgers, cheeseburgers, French fries, sodas, and shakes. These efforts to streamline and mass-produce hamburgers paid off. In 1951, they grossed $275,000.

As efficient as their internal operation was, the McDonald brothers concluded that they needed a new architectural design for the outside of their restaurant. Richard came up with the idea of constructing "golden arches" right through the roof which sloped upward toward the front, thus creating one of the most well-known architectural symbols in the world.

With the success of their newly designed operation, the McDonald brothers made another important decision: they franchised their operation. Franchising permitted others to build McDonald's drive-ins throughout the nation that were based on the design developed in San Bernardino. Those receiving franchises paid the McDonald brothers a fee and a percentage of their sales. In 1953 newly-designed McDonald's franchises opened in Phoenix, Arizona, and Downey, California.

At this time, McDonald's was just one of several new fast-food hamburger chains. In Los Angeles, Carl Karcher started selling hamburgers in 1946. In San Diego, Jack in the Box had been launched in 1951 and sported the first drive-through service. Three years later in Miami, James McLamore and David Edgerton founded Insta-Burger King, which later evolved into the Burger King chain.

To make the shakes quickly, the McDonald brothers purchased Multimixers—machines that mixed six shakes simultaneously. Ray Kroc, a Multimixer salesman, visited the McDonald brothers' operation in 1954 and was so impressed with their efficient operation that he arranged with the McDonald brothers to sell franchises. In 1955, Kroc opened his own McDonald's restaurant in Des Plaines, Illinois, and streamlined the operation even further. By the end of 1957, there were thirty-seven McDonald's. Two years later, the total exceeded one hundred establishments, and this doubled the following year. In 1961 Kroc bought out the McDonald brothers for $2.7 million and opened Hamburger University in Elk Grove, Illinois. McDonald's operations throughout America rapidly expanded.

McDonald's success encouraged competition, and many other fast-food chains adopted methods developed by the McDonald brothers and Kroc. Dave Thomas opened his first Wendy's restaurant in 1962 in Columbus, Ohio. Fast-food establishments underwent tremendous growth beginning in the mid-1960s. By 2000 there were more than 11,800 McDonald's, 6,298 Burger Kings, and 3,721 Wendy's fast-food establishments in the United States. Since there are an estimated 160,000 fast-food restaurants, it is estimated that the first job of one out of ten Americans is in a fast-food establishment.

Problems

Despite the rapid success of fast-food and soft-drink enterprises throughout the world, hamburgers and fast food have been condemned almost from the beginning. Until the arrival of White Castle, many potential customers avoided hamburger stands because of the lack of cleanliness of some establishments. Also, as low cost was an important factor in the hamburger business, many sellers adulterated the ground beef with other ingredients, leading many Americans to consider the hamburger an unhealthy food. In *100,000,000 Guinea Pigs* (1933), Arthur Kallet and F. J. Schlink claimed that hamburgers contained preservatives, which restored the color of the ground beef and destroyed the odor of spoilage.

Another concern has focused on fast-food advertising targeted at youth. McDonald's, for instance, developed cartoon characters such as Ronald McDonald. The "Happy Meal" with toys was launched in 1979. McDonald's has subsequently added children's play areas to many establishments and, like Burger King, has developed numerous tie-ins with major children's motion pictures.

Fast-food chains have been sensitive to a variety of health and environmental issues. For instance, McDonald's has reduced the fat content of its hamburgers, encourages recycling in some restaurants, refuses to buy beef from Brazil, and changed the wrappings of Big Macs and Quarter Pounders to make them more biodegradable.

Eric Schlosser's *Fast Food Nation: The Dark Side of the All-American Meal* maintains that the enormous growth of the fast-food industry has caused conditions in the big slaughterhouses to pose serious health concerns. Schlosser and others also blame fast food for a rise in obesity, which is among America's most serious health problems.

There has been heated criticism of the effects of fast food on local cultures and businesses. Serious nutritional, environmental, and cultural questions about fast food remain. As the homogenization of food choices continues worldwide, some consider the rapid expansion of fast-food chains as examples of an insidious American imperialism that is destroying local cultures and values. McDonald's success abroad has cause deep resentment by others who see the company as a symbol for the United States, and who believe that McDonald's expansion threatens local culinary traditions. In France, a sheep farmer named José Bové demolished a McDonald's restaurant that was nearing completion. Similar actions have occurred in other European countries.

Globalization

Despite condemnation throughout the world, the hamburger sandwich is one of the most successful foods in the world. The attraction of the hamburger is that it is inexpensive, convenient, and filling. Hamburgers are also versatile. At the minimum, hamburger sandwiches consist of just cooked ground beef in a bun. To this can be added hundreds of sliced and diced vegetables, condiments and spices, the most common of which are tomatoes, onions, mayonnaise, ketchup, mustard, pickle relish, salt, and pepper. Hamburger sandwiches with special seasonings and ingredients have proliferated. In 1984, Gyula Décsy's *Hamburger for America and the World* catalogued more than eight hundred hamburgers in the United States alone. These were a small fraction of the variety of hamburgers available today.

Hamburger establishments also caught on quickly in Canada and the United Kingdom. McDonald's opened its first Canadian restaurant in 1967 and created its International Division in 1969. By 1988 McDonald's had

2,600 locations abroad. Six years later, that number exceeded 4,500 restaurants in 73 other countries. In 2002 there were more than 28,000 restaurants in about 120 countries. McDonald's has over 1,000 restaurants in Japan alone. Measured by volume of customers, the most popular restaurant in Japan is McDonald's. France has 538 McDonald's restaurants; Australia, 615; Germany (the home of the original "hamburger"), 743; United Kingdom, 693; and Canada almost 900. The world's largest McDonald's is located near Red Square in Moscow, where a Big Mac lunch costs the equivalent of a week's paycheck. When McDonald's opened its first restaurant in Minsk, over 4,000 Belorussians showed up, forcing the operators to call in the police for crowd control. McDonald's boasts 127 restaurants in China—one of which overlooks Tiananmen Square in Beijing. Today, McDonald's international sales are $15 billion out of a total of almost $32 billion. Of its total revenue, 59 percent of its corporate profits are generated by restaurants in countries other than the United States.

There are many reasons for the success of fast-food chains in other countries. Most chains have adapted to foreign cultures, including revising the ingredients in hamburgers. In addition to efficient service and cultural sensitivity, other factors contributing to this success abroad are cleanliness of fast food establishments, family atmospheres, clean bathrooms, and air-conditioning. At the beginning of the twenty-first century, there were few countries that did not sport a fast-food establishment selling hamburgers. Foreign hamburger establishments are expanding at a faster pace than are hamburger establishments in the United States. With this rapid expansion, hamburgers are now a global food.

See also **Cattle; Delmonico Family; Fast Food; French Fries; Meat; Restaurants; Sandwich; Take-out Food.**

BIBLIOGRAPHY

Boas, Max, and Steve Chain. *Big Mac: The Unauthorized Story of McDonald's.* New York: Dutton, 1976.

Décsy, Gyula. *Hamburger for America and the World: A Handbook of the Transworld Hamburger Culture.* Transworld Identity Series, vol. 3. Bloomington, Ind.: Eurora European Research Association, 1984.

De Gouy, Louis P. *The Burger Book: Tasty Ways to Serve Ground Meat.* New York: Greenberg, 1951.

Halberstam, David. *The Fifties.* New York: Villard Books, 1993. (Chapter 11 [pp. 155–172] discusses Richard and Maurice McDonald, Ray Kroc, and the origins of the McDonald's empire.)

Hogan, David Gerard. *Selling 'em by the Sack: White Castle and the Creation of American Food.* New York: New York University Press, 1997.

Kallet, Arthur, and F. J. Schlink. *100,000,000 Guinea Pigs: Dangers in Everyday Foods, Drugs, and Cosmetics.* New York: Vanguard, 1933.

Kroc, Ray, with Robert Anderson. *Grinding It Out: The Making of McDonald's.* Chicago: Henry Regnery, 1977.

Love, John F. *McDonald's behind the Arches.* Rev. ed. New York: Bantam, 1995.

Ritzer, George. *The McDonaldization of Society: An Investigation into the Changing Character of Contemporary Social Life.* Rev. ed. Thousand Oaks, Calif.: Pine Forge Press, 1996.

Schlosser, Eric. *Fast Food Nation: The Dark Side of the All-American Meal.* Boston and New York: Houghton Mifflin, 2001.

Tennyson, Jeffrey. *Hamburger Heaven: The Illustrated History of the Hamburger.* New York: Hyperion, 1993.

Vidal, John. *McLibel: Burger Culture on Trial.* New York: New Press, 1997.

Watson, James L., ed. *Golden Arches East: McDonald's in East Asia.* Stanford, Calif.: Stanford University Press, 1997.

Andrew F. Smith

HARVESTING. Harvesting is the act of removing a crop from where it was growing and moving it to a more secure location for processing, consumption, or storage. Some root crops and tree fruit can be left in the field or orchard and harvested as needed, but most crops reach a period of maximum quality—that is, they ripen or mature—and will deteriorate if left exposed to the elements. While the major factor determining the time of harvest is the maturity of the crop, other factors such as weather, availability of harvest equipment, pickers, packing and storage facilities, and transport are important considerations.

Economic and marketing issues are often even more important than considerations of maturity in deciding when to harvest a commodity. Before the crop can be harvested, the grower must be sure that there is a demand for the crop and that the price is sufficient to make harvesting the crop profitable. If the price is less than adequate to cover the costs of production, harvesting, and marketing, growers are faced with the difficult decision whether to harvest and store the crop, to wait for a better market, or to cut their losses and leave the crop in the field.

The Process of Harvesting

Harvesting can be separated into three steps. The plant part of interest must be identified, detached from the rest of the plant, and then collected in a container suitable for transport from the field. The harvesting of all the major agronomic crops (grains of cereals and legumes) has been mechanized. The resistance of dried cereal and legume seeds (for example, corn, rice, wheat, and soybeans) to physical damage allows the first and second steps to be combined in a threshing machine or combine that separates the seeds from the rest of the harvested plant. The grain (seeds) is then loaded in bulk containers and transported to silos for additional cleaning, grading, fumigation, and temporary storage.

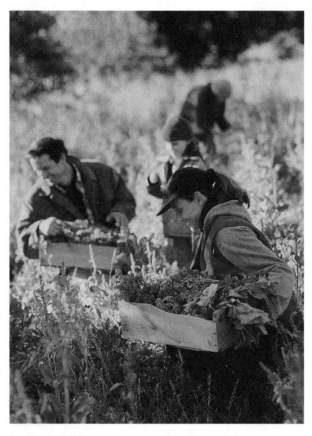

Community Supported Agriculture (CSA) started in Japan in 1965 and has since spread to many parts of the world. Families buy shares of a season's crop and are delivered food on a weekly basis. Some farms allow shareholders to harvest the food themselves. This family is gathering broccoli. © DAVID MARTINEZ/CORBIS.

In contrast to the dry grains and legumes, most horticultural crops (fleshy fruits such as apples and tomatoes, ornamentals, and vegetables) are hand harvested for the fresh market. Some mechanical harvesting is done, but the damage incurred is usually so severe that the fruits and vegetables are only fit for processing. Some fruits (for example, apple, pear, and tomato) evolved to ensure seed distribution by enticing animals to eat the attractive (in appearance, aroma, and flavor) fruit. Therefore, they are almost always attached to the plant by a specialized structure that contains an "abscission zone" which permits the ripe fruit to be easily separated from the tree. Other fruit, such as bananas, citrus, peppers, and all vegetables (for example, cabbage, broccoli, carrots, lettuce, and squash) do not develop an abscission zone and must be cut from the plant.

Only human beings have the unique combination of eyes, brain, and hands that permits the rapid identification and harvest of delicate and perishable materials with minimal loss and bruising. Some mechanical aids such as cherry pickers, ladders, picking bags or baskets, stem clip-

pers, and wheelbarrows are used by harvesters to make their work easier, faster, and safer. Harvesters can be trained to select only those fruits or vegetables that are of the correct maturity, size, or shape, thus greatly reducing the amount of material that must be removed on the sorting and grading line in the packing shed. In fact, many vegetables and berries are harvested directly into retail containers without further sizing or grading. Most other horticultural crops are harvested into field bins that are taken to packing sheds where the commodities are cleaned, sorted, graded, inspected, packed, cooled, and stored before being transported to regional markets.

The Social Importance of the Harvest

The time of harvest is one of the most important phases of the agricultural calendar since it marks a point in time when the crops have survived natural disasters and are ready to be gathered in. The period in late summer just before the harvest could be a time of famine because of poor harvests the preceding season or an inability to store food from the last harvest. It is not surprising then that the fall harvest festivals were such joyous times, for they heralded the end of this all too frequent seasonal famine and ushered in a time of plenty. There have been harvest celebrations for as long as people have gathered seasonally abundant food for storage and later consumption. Cultures as diverse as the Chinese, Egyptian, Greek, Hindu, Mayan, and Roman developed elaborate harvest customs that included songs, rituals, prayers, and special dishes.

Thanksgiving Day is perhaps the most universally observed harvest ritual in the United States and Canada, although these days are not communal in the sense of traditional village feasting. In the United States, Thanksgiving Day celebrates the first harvest of Dutch and English settlers who arrived in America almost four hundred years ago aboard the *Mayflower*. About fifty years before these Pilgrims, the observation of another Thanksgiving Day was started in what is now Newfoundland. Centuries later they were recognized as official holidays in their respective countries. However, for thousands of years before the European invasion, Native Americans had developed many traditional harvest celebrations. The Wampanoag Indians who inhabited the site occupied by the Pilgrims had three thanksgiving harvest festivals during the year: one for the maple tree and its syrup, one for picking berries, and one for the food they had grown and gathered that year.

County and regional fairs were often scheduled after the harvest so local farmers could sell some of their harvest to merchants, exchange experiences about the previous season, learn new farming techniques, exhibit their finest crops, compete for awards, and generally engage in a communal celebration. Other harvest-related events included parades, special religious services, and a large feast with traditional native dishes. In North America these include cranberry sauce, pumpkin pie, succotash, sweet corn, pecan pie, turkey, and wild rice stuffing. Succotash is a native North American dish that can be prepared today by combining whole-kernel sweet corn with Lima or broad beans in a sauce made from cream and flour. The cream (1 cup) and flour (¼ cup) are boiled for a few minutes with constant stirring, and then the sweet corn (one cup) and beans (2 cups) are added and the mixture heated for another 8 minutes. Addition of meat stock, bits of meat, green peppers, squash, and seasoning transforms this basic recipe into the many regional variations consumed throughout Eastern North America.

The Harvest Home celebrations of earlier times are dying out as the number of people engaged in farming declines because of mechanization, and as urban populations become disconnected from the actual growing of crops. In the past, the whole rural community worked together to harvest crops before the storms of late autumn arrived. The first or last fruits of the harvest were often accorded special religious significance and either offered to the gods, or kept safe as a talisman to be used to protect the planting of the crop next season. Cutting of the last sheaf and carrying it in procession to shelter symbolized the bringing of the harvest home, and was greeted with great rejoicing accompanied by music, dancing, and elaborate feasting. One of the traditional Harvest Home dishes was frumenty, a wheat pudding made with boiled milk, almond extract, honey, egg yolk, and raisins. The milk (1¾ cup), almond extract (½ teaspoon), and honey (2 tablespoon) are brought to a boil, the heat reduced, and the cracked wheat (1 cup) added with stirring until all the liquid is absorbed (about 15 min.). The yolk of one egg is then stirred in and ¼ cup of raisins is added. The pudding is served either hot or cold.

See also **Feasts, Festivals, and Fasts**; **Horticulture**; **Thanksgiving**.

BIBLIOGRAPHY

Jackson, Ellen B. *The Autumn Equinox: Celebrating the Harvest.* Highland Park, N.J.: Millbrook Press, 2000.

Kader, A.Adel, ed. *Postharvest Technology of Horticultural Crops.* 3rd ed. San Diego: University of California Agricultural and Natural Resources Publication, 2002.

Kavasch, E. Barrie. *Enduring Harvest: Native American Foods and Festivals for Every Season.* Old Saybrook, Conn.: Globe Pequot Press, 1995.

Penner, Lucille R. *The Thanksgiving Book.* New York: Hastings House, 1986.

Mikal E. Saltveit

HEALTH AND DISEASE. The relationships among food, health, and disease are myriad and complex. We consume food every day, and it provides the resources we need to carry out life-sustaining functions. Hence it comes as no surprise that one's diet can affect profoundly one's daily and long-term physiological health and well-being. Qualities of a diet and the foods that comprise it have the potential to make one sick, but they also can act to reduce one's risk of acute or chronic diseases.

All of the formal medical traditions of the world recognize a close connection between diet and an individual's health. One theme common to Mediterranean, Middle Eastern, and South and East Asian traditional medical systems is the ascription of humoral qualities to foods (for example, foods that are "heating" or "cooling" to the body). In these traditional systems, an individual's diet is manipulated to include or exclude foods with specific properties in order to correct putative humoral imbalances or disease states. In contemporary biomedicine, the link between food and disease most often is articulated with regard to the compositional qualities of foods and the ways that diets high or low in specific foods (and hence nutrients and other plant constituents) have harmful or beneficial effects on the body.

Benefits of Nutrient Diversity
There are numerous ways in which diets comprised of specific foods containing or lacking a given nutrient contribute to health or disease. For example, a diet that includes few or no animal products may result in anemia due to a deficiency in iron and/or vitamin B_{12}. On the other hand, a diet high in animal products but low in fruits and vegetables may contribute to specific vitamin deficiencies. Scurvy (a disease caused by vitamin C deficiency) was recognized first among sailors on long-distance sea voyages, as they had no source of fresh fruits or vegetables. An unprocessed corn-based diet is known to result in the disease pellagra, caused by a deficiency of niacin, one of the B vitamins. Up through the early twentieth century, there was a well-defined "pellagra belt" through the southern United States, where corn was consumed widely.

A diet comprised of diverse foods generally is considered to be the best way to prevent nutrient-deficiency diseases. Early humans lived by hunting and gathering, and they ate a broad array of plant and animal foods, although this varied by season and geography. Modern hunter-gatherers of the Kalahari Desert in southern Africa are known to exploit more than eighty species of plant foods, and no specific nutrient deficiencies have been reported among these groups. However, with the transition to agriculture, which happened in many parts of the world around 10,000 years ago, dietary diversity declined notably as populations began to cultivate a narrow array of staple crops (such as wheat, rice, potatoes, and millet). Iron deficiencies and severe growth deficits due to undernutrition become apparent in the skeletons of early farmers.

Effects of Food Processing
Some of these nutritional problems were resolved as populations evolved different means of processing staple

foods that enhanced dietary nutrient profiles. Indeed, in the postagricultural period, food-processing techniques became crucial for reducing the negative health impacts of reliance on a few foods. Native populations of the Americas that had a long tradition of reliance on maize (corn) prepared it in such a way as to avoid the problem of niacin deficiency. Corn was boiled in a solution containing lime (calcium carbonate, ash, etc.); this process resulted in the liberation of niacin from an undigestible complex, and also improved the food's amino-acid balances. When corn was introduced to Europe during the Columbian period, the lack of a tradition for its processing led to outbreaks of pellagra. A similar example is the leavening of wheat to make bread, or fermentation to make beer. Both of these processes increase the bioavailability of the minerals calcium, iron, and zinc. When soybeans are processed into bean curd, as is common in East Asia, they lose their protease inhibitors, which interfere with protein digestion.

On the other hand, it is also the case that some food-processing techniques—such as heating, boiling, or drying—can destroy vitamins in foods. Vitamin C degrades in the presence of heat and aridity; folic acid and thiamine likewise are sensitive to heat. Some of the other B vitamins break down in the presence of alkaline or acidic conditions. Others, such as vitamins B_6 and B_{12}, are quite stable under most cooking conditions. Milling and polishing rice into smooth white grains, which are valued highly in East Asian cuisine, reduce the protein and thiamine content of rice, and contribute to the risk of the disease beriberi (thiamine deficiency). Industrial processing of foods often reduces their nutrient profile, but many foods, especially those that are consumed widely such as cereals, are enriched to replace lost nutrients. In addition, grilling or broiling meats until they are well-charred has been associated with the production of the chemical compound Benzo(a)pyrene, which has been linked to gastrointestinal cancers.

Nonnutritive Food Components
When diets are derived largely from plant foods, particular combinations of food are known to improve the overall dietary quality, particularly with respect to the balance of essential amino acids. Corn, for example, is low in the amino acids lysine and tryptophan, but in native American cuisine, corn is often combined with legumes that are rich in those amino acids. Likewise, the combination of rice and legumes can provide the full array of essential amino acids. A peanut butter sandwich, a staple in the diet of many American children, contains complementary amino acids from the wheat and peanuts.

However, it is not only the nutrient composition of foods that is relevant to disease. Other qualities of foods —especially plant foods—recently have been found to contain other chemicals that reduce the risk of certain diseases. Phytochemicals derived from plant foods may reduce the risk of some cancers, while others may protect against heart disease and/or diabetes. Some potentially important phytochemicals include polyphenols (in red wine and green tea) and carotenoids (in orange, yellow, and green vegetables). Many of these have been found to have antioxidant effects and may prevent cell damage from oxygen-free radicals. Widespread consumption of red wine has been credited by some with the "French Paradox," the observation that, although the French tend to eat foods high in fat, their consumption of red wine may offset some of the risk of cardiovascular disease usually associated with such diets. Phytoestrogens, a form of isoflavones found in legumes such as soybeans, may reduce the risk of many cancers, especially breast cancer, by binding to estrogen receptors, and these also may reduce bone loss associated with osteoporosis. Proteins in soybeans also may reduce cholesterol levels and thus reduce the risk of heart disease. The organosulfur constituents of garlic may inhibit platelet aggregation and reduce blood lipids, thereby reducing the risk of coronary heart disease. Tannins (found in tea, coffee, cocoa, red wine, and some legumes and grains) and phytates are hypoglycemic, and may contribute to reduced risk of diabetes.

Other plant compounds have links to infectious disease, such as the protozoan disease malaria, which is a common disease (and often life-threatening) in tropical and semitropical areas. Manioc (*Manihot esculenta*; also called cassava or yuca), a widely cultivated root crop in the tropics, contains cyanogens, which appear to inhibit the growth of the malaria parasite in red blood cells. Likewise, fava beans contain vicine, a potent oxidant that disrupts malarial reproduction in red blood cells. However, individuals who are deficient in the enzyme G-6PD (a deficiency most common in Mediterranean populations) are susceptible to the potentially fatal anemia, favism, because their red blood cells are extremely vulnerable to destruction by potent oxidants such as vicine.

Many secondary compounds in plants do not have such salutary effects, or their benefits are tempered by potential negative effects on health. The cyanogens in manioc, lima beans, and other foods can interfere with thyroid function, glucose metabolism, growth and development, and other important physiological functions. Cruciferous vegetables such as cabbage contain thiocyanate compounds that act as goitrogens, and thereby contribute to thyroid disease. Tannins, which are distributed widely among plant foods, inhibit protein digestion and interfere with iron absorption. The ingestion of solanine, a glycoalkaloid found in commercial strains of potatoes that have been exposed to light, or in many wild varieties, can lead to serious gastrointestinal and neurological symptoms. Interestingly, traditional modes of consuming potatoes among Andean populations appear to reduce the risk of solanine exposure; their potatoes are consumed often with a clay-based slurry, which effectively detoxifies them.

176

Food-Consumption Concerns Linked to Population Profiles

There are cases in which the health effects associated with the consumption of particular foods vary in significant ways among diverse populations. For example, the ability to produce the enzyme lactase (which breaks down the milk sugar lactose) in adulthood is rare among human populations. This ability persists in highest frequencies through adulthood among northern Europeans and pastoral populations in Africa and other areas. Fresh milk consumption played an important role in maintaining health in the history of these populations, and they evolved lactase persistence as a dietary adaptation. When adults with low levels of small-intestinal lactase activity consume fresh milk (the food highest in lactose), they often experience cramps, bloating, diarrhea, and other forms of gastrointestinal distress. This is less of a problem when milk is consumed after processing into yogurt or cheese, as lactose is either fermented or removed during their production.

In populations that only recently have begun relying on wheat production there is a high frequency of celiac disease, an allergic response to wheat protein (gluten). There is some suggestion that African Americans may be more sensitive to salt than are other sectors of the population, and that, consequently, salt consumption by African Americans increases blood pressure and contributes to an incidence of hypertension greater than in other groups.

In the most general sense, both underconsumption and overconsumption of foods can lead to chronic disease. Not surprisingly, these two ends of the consumption spectrum tend to occur in poor and wealthy populations, respectively. It is estimated that more than 1.2 billion people suffer from deficiencies of calories and protein. A similar number suffer from problems related to the overconsumption of calories. Both are associated with deficiencies of micronutrients. It has been suggested that more than half of the world's disease burden derives from nutrition-related sources.

Overconsumption of calorie-rich foods became the norm in wealthy countries during the late twentieth century. Such foods became mass produced, more readily available, and relatively inexpensive. Today supermarket shelves are lined with potato chips, candy, cookies, crackers, soda, and all kinds of other calorie-dense foods. Fast-food restaurants specialize in ever-larger servings of high-calorie foods that are quickly prepared and consumed. Most of these are highly processed, and although they are rich in calories, they are often low in vitamins, minerals, and phytochemicals. It is widely accepted that, when combined with a sedentary lifestyle, diets high in such foods contribute to a broad array of chronic health conditions, most significantly cardiovascular disease (CVD), diabetes, cancer, and hypertension. It is now estimated that more than half of Americans are overweight, and almost one-quarter are obese, which is itself a risk

factor for these diseases. In addition, an increasing number of children are now obese, and "adult-onset" (Type 2) diabetes is appearing with alarming frequency in adolescents. More than 75 percent of all mortality in the United States is due to CVD and cancer, but death rates from stroke and heart attacks have declined since the 1970s. This has been attributed, in part, to reduced consumption of saturated fat from red meat, whole milk, butter, and lard. There are several studies indicating that a low-fat diet based largely on vegetables, fruits, whole grains, legumes, with relatively small amounts of animal protein (especially from fish) is associated with increased longevity and reduced risk of chronic disease.

Problems related to the overconsumption of high-calorie foods are not unique to the industrialized world. As countries are integrated into the global economy and populations increasingly become urbanized, there has been a global shift in dietary patterns and health conditions that appear to accompany those new consumption habits. Interestingly, such changes are remarkably consistent across countries, and may reflect a panhuman preference for foods rich in calories, which historically have been quite limited in the diet. Generally the consumption of fats and sweets has increased, and the use of traditional whole-grain foods and traditional modes of processing has declined. Fast-food outlets such as Kentucky Fried Chicken and McDonalds have become ubiquitous in urban centers throughout the world. Active lifestyles are being replaced with sedentism, as people move away from subsistence agriculture into clerical and factory jobs. As a result, the chronic diseases that heretofore had predominated in wealthy industrialized countries are becoming globalized. For example, the global diabetes rates seen in 2000 are expected to double by 2025, with the majority of that growth occurring in developing countries.

On the other hand, undernutrition, also referred to as protein-energy malnutrition (PEM), often occurs under conditions of food scarcity and is associated with a wide range of negative health effects. More than 10 percent of the world's population suffers from chronic hunger, and undernutrition may be responsible for as many as twenty million deaths per year. It is important to realize that hunger is not the result of too little food being produced for too many people in the world; it is essentially a problem with the way that food is distributed unevenly among the world's populations. Children are especially vulnerable to PEM, as they have higher protein and energy needs per unit of body weight than do adults. When calories and protein are chronically scarce in childhood, permanent stunting and retarded development occur. In its acute form, PEM results in wasting (dramatically reduced weight relative to height) and it is potentially fatal. More routinely, PEM increases vulnerability to infectious disease, since energy, protein, and certain vitamins and minerals play crucial roles in immune function. In environmental contexts in which infectious disease (especially diarrheal disease) is common, the combination of PEM and infection can provoke a rapid deterioration of health that can lead to death. A common stage for this progression to manifest itself is weaning, the period when children make the transition away from breast milk (which contains nutrients and disease-suppressing maternal immunoglobulins) to an adult-type diet. It is not uncommon for children to become more vulnerable to infection when they are weaned prematurely and are unable to consume sufficient nutrient-dense foods to maintain growth.

In the 1800s, baby bottles were developed and cow's milk was developed into infant formula as an alternative to breast milk. The practice of formula-feeding peaked in the United States in the years following World War II; breast-feeding is now on the rise again in most parts of the world, although it remains uncommon past the early months in most industrialized countries. Most research amply demonstrates the health benefits of breast-feeding: substitution of formula for breast milk is associated with increased risks of numerous health problems including SIDS (sudden infant death syndrome), ear infections, diabetes, breast cancer, and allergies.

Controversy erupted in the early 1970s over the promotion of formula by multinational corporations in the developing world. Formula was marketed heavily and inappropriately, and health personnel began to encourage mothers to feed their children formula rather than nurse them. Formula, which was costly, often was prepared in dilute form with contaminated water. Its use in this way increased infant morbidity and mortality and generated much attention among the media and international health organizations, ultimately resulting in a ban on formula promotion by multinational corporations.

As the links between diet and disease have become more widely known, there has been a trend toward more healthful eating habits in industrialized societies. However, this trend is not uniform within such populations. Numerous studies have shown that obesity, the eating habits that contribute to it, and the diseases associated with it, especially diabetes, have increased among lower socioeconomic groups. The reasons behind this trend are complex, but as noted above, foods high in starches, fats, and sugars are now cheap and readily available. Those high in protein (meat, dairy products) and fresh fruits and vegetables are relatively less accessible and more expensive, and are consumed less commonly by the poor. Moreover, in the United States, fast-food outlets are locating preferentially in areas serving poorer communities. This has led to the curious, yet commonplace, phenomenon in wealthy countries whereby weight is correlated inversely with wealth. Historically, of course, the reverse would have been the case, as is still evident in many developing countries.

See also **Anthropology and Food; Baby Food; Disease: Metabolic Diseases; Fast Food; Food Politics: United** States; Lactation; Malnutrition; Medicine; Milk, Human; Niacin Deficiency (Pellagra); Nutrients; Nutrition; Obesity; Paleonutrition, Methods of; Political Economy; Population and Demographics; Salt; Sodium; Vitamins.

BIBLIOGRAPHY

Cohen, Mark Nathan. *Health and the Rise of Civilization.* New Haven, Conn.: Yale University Press, 1991.

Diamond, Jared. "The Saltshaker's Curse." *Natural History* (October 1991): 22–26.

Gardner, Gary, and Brian Halweil. *Underfed and Overfed: The Global Epidemic of Malnutrition,* edited by Jane A. Peterson. Worldwatch Paper 150. Washington, D.C.: Worldwatch Institute, 2000.

Jackson, Fatimah Linda Collier. "Secondary Compounds in Plants (Allelochemicals) as Promoters of Human Biological Variability." *Annual Review of Anthropology* 202 (1991): 505–546.

Johns, Timothy. "The Chemical Ecology of Human Ingestive Behaviors." *Annual Review of Anthropology* 28 (1999): 27–50.

Katz, Solomon H. "Food and Biocultural Evolution: A Model for the Investigation of Modern Nutritional Problems." In *Nutritional Anthropology,* edited by F. E. Johnston. New York: Alan R. Liss, 1987.

Lappé, Frances Moore, Joseph Collins, and Peter Rosset. *World Hunger: Twelve Myths.* New York: Grove Press, 1998.

Lee, Richard B. "What Hunters Do for a Living, or, How to Make Out on Scarce Resources." In *Man the Hunter,* edited by Richard B. Lee and Irven DeVore. Chicago: Aldine, 1969.

Liebman, Bonnie, and David Schardt. "Diet and Health: Ten Megatrends." *Nutrition Action* 28, no. 1 (January/February 2001): 3–12.

Martorell, Reynaldo. "Interrelationship between Diet, Infectious Disease, and Nutritional Status." In *Social and Biological Predictors of Nutritional Status, Physical Growth, and Neurological Development,* edited by Lawrence S. Greene and Francis S. Johnston. New York: Academic Press, 1980.

McGee, Harold. *On Food and Cooking: The Science and Lore of the Kitchen.* New York: Simon and Schuster, 1984.

Stuart-Macadam, Patricia, and Katherine A. Dettwyler, eds. *Breastfeeding: Biocultural Perspectives.* New York: Aldine de Gruyter, 1995.

Van Esterik, Penny. *Beyond the Breast-Bottle Controversy.* New Brunswick, N.J.: Rutgers University Press, 1989.

Wardlaw, Gordon M., and Paul M. Insel. *Perspectives in Nutrition.* New York: Mosby, 1996.

Andrea S. Wiley

HEALTH FOODS. The concept of "health food" is attributed to the 1830s Popular Health movement whose founders included Sylvester Graham, father of graham crackers. Reacting against professional medicine, the movement emphasized temperate living, lay knowledge and health care, and health foods as part of the broader

178

feminist and class struggle. A simple vegetarian diet, including whole wheat, and exercise were promoted for physiological and spiritual reform to a more natural, uncomplicated life. Meat, white flour, and alcohol were among the stimulating sinful foods.

John H. Kellogg and his brother Will were the first to become millionaires from "food faddism" (Herbert and Barrett, 1981, p. 87). The Seventh-Day Adventists founded a religious colony and sanitarium at Battle Creek, Michigan, where Kellogg's clients "detoxified" via enemas and high-fiber diets, including cornflakes. By 1899, the Kellogg cereal company's cornflakes competed with Post Grape-Nuts, the latter a supposed cure for appendicitis, malaria, consumption, and loose teeth. Charles W. Post was a former Kellogg patient. Kellogg and the Post Division of General Foods remain giant cereal manufacturers.

While scientists quantified protein, carbohydrate, fat, and later the vitamin and mineral composition of food in the late 1800s and early 1900s, agriculture and industry augmented production. Public health sanitation and vaccinations minimized infections, and the increased stable food supply fed a growing population more fit to work the factories, farms, and military. As home economists taught the nutritional food groups recommended by the U.S. Department of Agriculture (USDA), profiteers promoted grander elixirs via speeches, newspapers, books, magazines, and doctors, dentists, and chiropractors with dubious degrees.

Beginning in 1906, the Food and Drug Administration (FDA) restricted health claims on food and drug packaging, but marketers could nevertheless exercise free speech by offering information in books, magazines, and brochures. *Prevention* and *Let's Live* magazines began publication in 1950 and 1933, respectively; the latter was initially called *California Health News*. They promoted vitamins, food preparation, and exercise and warned of pollution dangers. In the era of World War II victory gardens, Rodale Press began publication of *Organic Gardening and Farming* in 1942; this later became *Organic Gardening* and then simply *OG*. In 1980, Rodale Press grossed $80 million with 2.4 million *Prevention* and one million *Organic Gardening and Farming* subscribers (Herbert and Barrett, 1981, p. 99). Amway, Shaklee, and Neo-Life used door-to-door sales to distribute high-priced vitamins with brochures and books; in 1980 these three companies grossed about $700 million from food supplements (Herbert and Barrett, 1981, p. 22).

Health Food and the Counterculture

The 1960s and 1970s counterculture youth questioned the political and economic values of capitalism and experimented with alternative lifestyles. University students created community gardens, cooperative grocery stores, health-food restaurants, buying clubs, and organic farms. Ecology and health food became "cool." Notions of balance were sought from formerly less acknowledged eco-

logical studies and from Eastern or Native American philosophies. In the early 1900s, USDA staff had explored sustainable Far Eastern agricultural practices, but these foods and methods received little attention until organic farming became popular in the 1960s and 1970s. Brown rice, wheat germ, honey, nuts, sprouts, and Eastern foods like yogurt, hummus, falafel, tofu, and stir-fried vegetables were considered healthy, and environmentally sound if they were produced locally and organically. Vegetarian diets, of the non-red meat, lacto-ovo, macrobiotic, and vegan varieties, were adopted to eat low on the food chain or to avoid killing animals. Sugar, white bread, and red meat were considered unhealthy.

The health-food business recognized a market in the counterculture. Adelle Davis, with books like *Let's Eat Right to Keep Fit*, promoted vitamins and natural foods to prevent psychological metabolic disorders as well as cancer. The Atkins Diet promised thinness through consumption of protein foods, fruits, and vegetables, but few carbohydrates. While exploring non-Western religions and cultures, youth tried ethnic foods, spices, herbs, and recreational drugs. While ethnic variety entered American cuisine, doctors bemoaned the fact that people were not seeking medical treatment but were using useless or harmful herbs and concoctions. Laypeople sought self-reliance over "the establishment" with traditional natural products to achieve holistic mental and physical health.

The professional certification of Registered Dietitian became required by many states in the 1970s and 1980s. In 1973, the FDA required enriched or fortified foods to be labeled with ingredients and Recommended Daily Allowance values for protein and seven essential vitamins and minerals.

Small-Scale to Global Mass Marketing

By the 1990s, as the counterculture matured, health-food issues saw compromise such as more integration of nutrition and preventative medicine in medical practice, or scientific evaluation of physiological properties in food beyond macro- and micronutrients. International conservation-development projects found wide use of herbal medicines to the extent that the World Health Organization promoted traditional medicine to cut health-care costs. The U.S. National Institutes of Health researched herbal medicine claims. A recent *Physicians' Desk Reference* describes herbal uses and contraindications. FDA food label regulations gradually permitted scientifically tested nutrient content claims (for example, "low-fat," "high fiber"), structure/function claims (for example, calcium aids in the growth and maintenance of bones), and a few health claims (for example, calcium reduces the risk of osteoporosis). In December 2000, the USDA defined national organic food standards to regulate health-food claims and to facilitate national and international trade. U.S. organic food sales increased from $178 million in 1980 to $1 billion in 1990 and $7.8 billion in 2000 (Mergentine, 1994, p. 164; Myers and Rorie, 2000).

Natural product sales (including whole foods, organics, supplements, and household products) grew from $1.9 billion in 1980, to $4.2 billion in 1990, and to $32 billion in 2000 (Spencer, 2001). Small cooperative health-food stores persisted, but large "one-stop" natural grocery stores opened in the 1980s and 1990s. Convenience attracted the "hippie" become "yuppie" professionals who retained health and environmental concerns but had little time to produce, obtain, or cook food. Mergers and acquisitions occurred as conventional food conglomerates bought out natural food product lines or whole companies. Regular chain grocery stores carried more organic foods besides conventional foods. The Internet provided both health-food magazine and retailer advertising as well as access to university and medical school websites. The Internet health-food market was initially profitable, but plateaued with delivery limited to nonperishables. Scientifically verified "functional foods" became popular, whether in regular meals, sports foods, or weight reduction. Consequently, antioxidants, fatty acids, phytoestrogens, flavinoids, pro- and prebiotics, are now promoted in a Functional Food Pyramid, mirroring the conventional USDA food pyramid adopted in 1992. Both nutrition education models acknowledge growing scientific evidence that fruits, vegetables, and grains are important to health, with lower emphasis on animal-derived food, compared to the Four Food Groups model used since 1958.

"Functional food," "designer food," and "nutraceutical" are used interchangeably. This is problematic in global trade regulation since food and drugs are compartmentalized differently in international regulatory agencies. Functional food is conventional food, but demonstrates physiological benefits and/or reduces the risk of chronic disease beyond basic nutritional functions. A nutraceutical is a product produced from foods but sold in pill, powder, and other medicinal forms not generally associated with food and demonstrated to have physiological benefit or provide protection against chronic disease (Stephen, 1998, p. 404). The American Dietetic Association classifies all food as functional at some physiological level, but suggests that "functional food" includes unmodified food as well as modified food. While some sports enthusiasts or dieters favor modified processed foods with higher nutrient content, many Americans and Europeans buy organic foods because they worry about allergic reactions and environmental hazards caused by genetic modification.

See also **Functional Foods; Kellogg, John Harvey; Natural Foods; Nutraceuticals; Organic Foods; Vegetarianism.**

BIBLIOGRAPHY

American Dietetic Association. "Functional Foods—Position of ADA." *Journal of the American Dietetic Association* 99 (1999): 1278–1285.

Belasco, Warren J. *Appetite for Change: How the Counterculture Took on the Food Industry, 1966–1988*. New York: Pantheon, 1989.

Davis, Adelle. *Let's Eat Right to Keep Fit*. Newly Revised and Updated. New York: Harcourt, Brace, and Jovanovich, 1970.

Dubisch, Jill. "You Are What You Eat: Religious Aspects of the Health Food Movement." In *Nutritional Anthropology: Biocultural Perspectives on Food and Nutrition*, edited by Alan H. Goodman, Darna L. Dufour, and Gretel H. Pelto. Mountain View, Calif.: Mayfield, 2000.

Functional Foods for Health. Functional Food Guide Pyramid. Southern Illinois University/CFAR/University of Illinois Functional Foods for Health Program, 2000. http://www.ag.uiuc.edu/ffh/health/bw_pyramid.html.

Herbert, Victor, and Stephen Barrett. *Vitamins and "Health" Foods: The Great American Hustle*. Philadelphia: George F. Stickley, 1981.

Mergentine, Ken. "The USA Perspective." In *Handbook of Organic Food Processing and Production*, edited by Simon Wright. London: Blackie Academic and Professional, 1994.

Myers, Steve, and Somlynn Rorie. "Facts and Stats: The Year in Review." *Organic & Natural News* 12 (2000): http://www.organicandnaturalnews.com/articles/0c1feat1.html. Virgo Publishing, 2001.

Spencer, Marty Traynor. "Natural Product Sales Top $32 B." *Natural Foods Merchandiser* (June 2001). Available at http://www.healthwellexchange.com/nfm-online/nfm_backs/Jun_01/sales.cfm.

Stephen, A. M. "Regulatory Aspects of Functional Foods." In *Functional Foods: Biochemical & Processing Aspects*, edited by G. Mazza. Lancaster, Pa.: Technomic, 1998.

Whorton, J. C. "Historical Development of Vegetarianism." *American Journal of Clinical Nutrition* 59 (1994): 1103S–1009S.

Sabrina H. B. Hardenbergh
Hea-Ran L. Ashraf

HEARTH COOKERY. The field of hearth cookery, in its most general sense, is immensely broad, encompassing standard kitchen practice from ancient human settlements to present-day cultures throughout the world. The twentieth century has seen the growth of this new study as historians and social and physical scientists worldwide have found it a source of illumination in traditional areas of research. Among them, one thinks of gender and work, family structure, economics and status, technology, ethnicity and acculturation, and health. Growing numbers of interdisciplinary publications attest to its value, as does its use in living history museums throughout the world. The traditional foods of the hearth have become fashionable in barbecue pits and smokehouses of both professionals and aficionados, in the recreated foods of brick-oven pizzas and artisanal bakeries, and in the restaurants of imaginative chefs using their dining-room fireplaces to simultaneously cook for their patrons and entertain them.

Reflector oven for open hearth cooking. Philadelphia, ca. 1855. Tin and cast iron. Joints of meat were roasted on the spit, which was turned by hand. In England, these implements were referred to as Dutch ovens. ROUGHWOOD COLLECTION. PHOTO CHEW & COMPANY.

Despite vast differences between ethnic cuisines, this far-flung cookery practice may be described as a relatively simple array of basic cooking utensils used at a hearth, or fire-site. The hearth was usually situated at floor level and held the burning fuel (chiefly but not exclusively local wood); the flames, embers, and radiating heat did the work. More the exception than the rule, a few cultures developed convenient raised hearths, often built eighteen inches or so above floor level; despite this variation, the utensils and cookery principles remained the same. Where fuel was abundant, home brick or clay ovens were used as well. Until relatively recent innovations in fuels and technologies, hearth cooking was the predominant way (indeed, often the only way) of cooking.

The American Hearth

American hearths have existed since the Stone Age in various degrees of modernization. Pre-Columbian Native American cookery sites were usually simple, their utensils often fashioned artfully from natural substances—wood, clay, stone, bone, shell, and hide. The family cooking site was generally out of doors and typically consisted of a flat stone-lined shallow pit, sometimes hold-

ing a small tripod of stones to support rounded clay pots or stone griddles. This was commonly augmented by deeper cooking pits in which food was buried for steaming, and with smoking and roasting racks of wood. Indoor cookery, appropriate for inclement seasons or for security, was a simplified version in which smoke escaped through the roof.

The earliest Europeans in the New World brought a working concept of the hearth that was in many ways similar and had in common frequent use of clay pots, tripods or legged trivets, large rounded forms, and flat griddles. Major differences were largely a consequence of the Old World metallurgy hitherto unknown in the Americas, and they added clear advantages of strength, transportability, durability, and more subtle heat transmission.

Seventeenth-century American colonists, following European architectural innovation, improved on their earlier floor fires and roof smoke holes by installing fireplaces with extended stone or brick hearths and chimneys. This new workspace was safer, more flexible, efficient, and comfortable, but hardly simple. As temperatures directly over the flames often exceed 600°F

THE DUTCH OVEN

The history of certain pot forms is informed by early recipes. The following cooking directions seem to suggest an early Dutch oven, and what was also known as "bake kettle" technique.

"To bake an apple [egg] fritter" . . .
    place a little fire on the lid and let it bake this way."

—*De Verstandige Kok (*The Intelligent Cook*), Amsterdam, 1683*

One hundred fifty years later, Mary Randolph described the use of a Dutch oven as a *bain marie* in her recipe:

"To Make Custards
    Fill the custard cups, put on the covers, and set them in a Dutch oven with water, but not enough to risk its boiling into the cups, Do not put on the top of the oven."

—Mary Randolph, *The Virginia Housewife*, 1824, p. 180

(315°C), control of cooking temperatures was a technological challenge. Small three-legged clay, bronze, or iron pots were perched over small subsidiary fires or piles of glowing embers shoveled from the main fire onto the hearth. In addition, horizontal lug poles were installed high in the chimney; and from these hung iron trammels of several designs, their adjustable hooks capable of suspending pots at variable levels. The cook "turned" the temperature up or down by moving pots toward or away from the heat. In the early eighteenth century, innovative swinging cranes added the possibility of adjusting hanging pots and their contents without the work of lifting them.

Fire and Heat Management

Hearth cooking was characterized not so much by the recipes, which varied widely according to time and place, as by general knowledge of fuels and heat regulation and the maintenance of steady heat in the face of ever-changing temperatures. Fires waxed and waned as fuels ignited, blazing up into flames, and then subsided into glowing coals or embers. Good cooks used this varying heat to advantage, shifting pots according to the state of the fire and the needs of the dish. For example, when boiling water, one hung the kettle close to the hottest flames, but when warming milk (which burns easily), one set the pot on the hearth away from the scorching tem-

peratures and, along with stirring, may have rotated it 180 degrees periodically for even cooking.

The experienced cook judged cooking temperatures with sensory clues—visual, auditory, olfactory, and tactile. Heat was estimated repeatedly through the cooking processes by holding one's hand between the fire and the pot, by the sounds of frying or boiling, and by the appearance of the coals.

Fuels

Fire temperatures were regulated by the choice of fuel. Most pine burns cool; osage orange and sassafras are very hot. Hard woods (for example, hard maples, oak, fruit, or nut), aged and split, were most desirable, but not without cost. In the American colonies, where wood was often abundant, firewood production demanded long hours invested in felling trees and then cutting, hauling, splitting, and stacking. Yet even with this apparently unending richness, there were places where people were forced to cook over peat (by the mid-eighteenth century, Long Island had depleted its forests) or buffalo chips (the prairies). These situations paralleled those of Ireland, India, China, and nomadic Asia, where similar substitutions were necessary. Consequently, the roaring kitchen fire, a necessity for producing beds of coals, was desirable but not always standard. Wood for cooking fires was sometimes conserved by fine splitting, which had added advantages of efficiency, faster ignition, and more responsive heat replenishment. In combination with flames and embers, assorted sizes of wood enabled the cook to prepare a number of dishes at one time, each pot at its most appropriate temperature.

In maintaining desired warmth, a variety of techniques involved adding, removing, and resituating fuel. For example, a log set into the flames creates a temporary barrier and a cool spot above it; but as it catches fire, it creates a hot spot. Similarly, enlarging the air channels inside the fire increases its rate of burning, while consolidating the fuel and cutting off air supply slows it down.

The Pots

The pots and their technologies were also players in temperature maintenance. Colonists imported or manufactured the designs from home that traditionally worked well with fire, and incorporated special features that added to their effectiveness. Some pots had their own legs for straddling the coals, or used high cooking trivets for that purpose. Larger kettles also incorporated swinging bale handles that hung them from a trammel and crane S-hooks. Many had rounded or bulbous bottoms that transmitted the heat evenly, without the angular corners in which food could burn. Their long handles allowed the cook to avoid the blasting heat of the central fire, as did a variety of long-handled forged hand utensils (spoons, ladles, skimmers, turners, forks, etc.). Like European antecedents, they were made of iron, brass, bell-metal, copper, tin, and ceramics. One New World adaptation, the cast-iron "American Dutch oven," boasted a heavy deep-rimmed lid to hold coals above and three stilt legs to straddle coals below.

Basic *batteries de cuisine* included assorted cast-iron kettles, water kettles, spiders (frying pans), posnets (saucepans), and griddles, as well as open kettles and pans of cast brass or bell-metal. These heavy pots worked well with wet cooking techniques. However, for dry-heat cookery and high-temperature processes such as frying and broiling, hand-forged metals, being better conductors, were formed into spiders (frying pans) and gridirons (broilers). Tin reflecting ovens made superlative roasters. An array of these pots was common in middling or average kitchens. One's economic status was reflected in the range of utensils: where less fortunate families were perhaps limited to a cooking kettle, water kettle, and frying pan, privileged families owned larger assortments and varied sizes of the basics, supplemented with specialized equipment such as wafer irons, chafing dishes, mounted clock jacks to turn roasts on heavy spits, decorative copper or ceramic molds, or hand-forged geared grinders.

The Cuisine

Cooking with fire has always had the potential for both simple and complex cuisines. The simple hearths of remote and rural areas or those of people of modest means have produced the one-pot dishes (simmered soups, porridges, or stews), roasted meats, and simple baking that have been the mainstay of daily cooking everywhere. At the other extreme are the culinary heights of the Roman and Ottoman empires, Persia, India, China, Mexico, France, and Italy, in which simple equipment and fuel have been no obstacle to fine sauces and elaborate confections. The early introduction of bronze and iron utensils in wealthier and more cosmopolitan urban civilizations enlarged the range of their hearths, enabling such possibilities as the high-temperature deep-fried *kunafa*, a crisp medieval Arabic bread. To this day, the hearth remains the center of food preparation in both primitive and modernized homes throughout the world and figures in such basic preparations as lightly crisped, griddle-baked Mexican tortillas or Moroccan flatbreads.

The average colonial American cook of moderate means had the skills and resources to turn out complex family meals, undaunted by fire-tending, stooping to floor or crane levels, and relatively primitive equipment. Her success actually had little to do with hearth limitations, depending more on the time of year and seasonal homegrown food availability, on access to imported ingredients (in particular, sugars, spices, and other flavorings), and on the amount of time and help she had for preparations. Seventeenth- and eighteenth-century European cookbooks used in the colonies show a wide array of recipes and varied techniques, among them boiling, simmering, roasting, frying, sautéing, fine baking, preserving, and candying.

FIRESIDE COOKERY

The following is a selection of wonderful recipes from the original eighteenth- and nineteenth-century sources:

Batter Cakes

"Boil two cups of small hominy very soft and add an equal quantity of corn meal with a little salt, and a large spoonful of butter; make it into a thin batter with three eggs, and a sufficient quantity of milk, beat all together some time, and bake them on a griddle or in waffle irons . . ."

—Mary Randolph, *The Virginia Housewife*, 1824, p. 171

Wafers

"Make a very thin batter with eggs, milk, butter, and powdered loaf sugar, to your taste; pour it into wafer-irons, bake them very quick, without browning; roll them as you take them from the irons."

—Mary Randolph, *The Virginia Housewife*, 1824, p. 173

Not all fireside cookery was that simple. This somewhat more complex dish was offered by Hannah Glasses's *Art of Cookery*, 1747.

A Jugged Hare

"Cut it in little Pieces, lard them here and there with little Slips of Bacon, feafon them with a very little Pepper and Salt, put them into an earthen Jugg, with a Blade or two of Mace, an Onion ftuck with Cloves, and a Bundle of Sweet Herbs; cover the Jugg or Jar you do it in, fo clofe, that nothing can get in, then fet it in a Pot of boiling Water, keep the Water boiling, and three Hours will do it, then turn it out into the Difh, and take out the Onion and Sweet Herbs, and fend it to the Table hot."

—Hannah Glasse, *The Art of Cookery*, 1747, p. 50

By all historical accounts, among them Karen and John Hess's *The Taste of America*, and the experiences of such food historians as Sandra L. Oliver in recreating these recipes today, the food of accomplished early cooks met the highest standards of the modern palate. For example, roasting even unseasoned fowl and red meat in an open tin reflecting oven set against the fire produced a product far superior to that of its modern gas or electric counterpart. The technique produced a juicy and tender texture, good crust or skin, and slight smokiness, and generally enhanced natural flavor. Likewise, one's daily cornbread, prepared in a heavy Dutch oven, boasted

KITCHEN EQUIPMENT

The nineteenth-century overlap of hearth and cookstove technologies is most apparent in early trade catalogs. For example, *Catalogue of Savery & Co.'s Castings* (Philadelphia: circa 1855) offered assorted stovetop griddles and kettles (flat bottoms, no legs), and various three-legged hearth pots such as skillets, griddles, kettles, Dutch ovens, and spiders (pp. 4–25).

delicate moistness and a wonderful crust unequaled in modern ovens.

American Hearth-to-Cookstove Transitions

In the 1790s, when over 90 percent of Americans were farming, hearth cooking was the sole means of meal preparation in both countryside and city. With the growth of cities in the nineteenth century and the gradual introduction of cookstoves, it survived in closest association with rural life. The new cookstove, developed and popularized in growing cities by 1850, presented a major force in women's changing social roles and the cuisine, but for many years kitchens reflected an overlap in the use of these technologies. Well into the twentieth century there were still communities, notably in remote areas of Appalachia, where hearth cookery sustained life.

The earliest kitchen hearths were associated with relatively small homes in which they were the focus of the house, and the center of much work and socializing. They offered not only cooking heat, but also a warm wintertime house. In time, and with the trend to enlarging American homes, they were distanced from expanded specialized dining and living rooms. At times they were relegated to a separate building (especially in the South and on wealthy farms or plantations), as families sought to remove themselves from the sounds, smells, and dangers of the work. The passing of the hearth in favor of the cookstove was not always lauded; some average families mourned the loss of the congenial kitchen fireside, fearful that both the cuisine and the family were doomed.

Social Implications

The experience of contemporary hearth cooks has added to the correction of past assumptions and misconceptions; for example, the experienced home cook could indeed produce delicious complex meals on a daily basis. There was no inherent danger in long clothing—to the contrary, the natural fibers did not flame (only smolder), while skirts and sleeves provided comfort, insulating the body from the heat. There was more threat from tipped kettles and scalding.

In addition, the activity has reinforced the concept of a strong family unit: despite gender work divisions, there were clear advantages to social cooperation—the quality and quantity of family food depended on it. The large body of economically viable skills and knowledge that were specifically women's, the oral tradition of recipe and cookery transmission, the time and strength required, the daily distinctions between drudgery and creativity, and the need to juggle hearth tasks with other necessary chores are only some of the areas informing the current interpretation of social history.

If nothing else, in pinpointing individual and family behavior, it supports a strong case for individualization that surviving cooking manuscripts do not convey.

See also **Iron Cookstove, The**.

BIBLIOGRAPHY

Note: Relatively little has been written on hearth cookery processes. Some information may be gleaned from a close reading of eighteenth-century cookbooks. Modern interpretations are sometimes included in the introductory chapters of facsimile editions and reprints of early works. Books on antiques or trade catalogs are helpful.

Feild, Rachel. *Irons in the Fire: A History of Cooking Equipment.* U.K.: Crowood Press, 1984. Study of English equipment and hearth processes that were the basis of cookery in most American colonies. Careful research, good illustrations.

Franklin, Linda Campbell. *Three Hundred Years of Kitchen Collectibles.*, 4th edition. Iola, Wisc.: Krause Publications, 1997. Exhaustive illustrated compendium of the equipment, well-documented.

Glasse, Hannah. *The Art of Cookery Made Plain and Easy.* London: 1747; facsimile edition London: Prospect Books, 1983. Reprinted throughout the eighteenth century and used widely in the American colonies, with an American edition in 1805. Good source of recipes used by English-Americans.

Harrison, Molly. *The Kitchen in History.* New York: Scribners, 1972. Broad sweep of kitchen evolution, with some detail on equipment and processes.

Hess, John L., and Karen Hess. *The Taste of America.* New York: Grossman Press, 1977. Evaluation of cuisines then and now.

Lecoq, Raymond. *Les Objets de la Vie Domestique: Utensiles en Fer de la Cuisine et du Foyer des Origines au XIXe Siecle.* Paris: Berger-Levrault, 1979.

Martha Washington's Booke of Cookery and Booke of Sweetmeats. Transcribed by Karen Hess. New York: Columbia University Press, 1995. Heavily researched and annotated sixteenth-century English cooking manuscript; intermittent discussion of early implements.

Oliver, Sandra L. "Introduction" and "The Buckinghams: Saltwater Farming." In *Saltwater Foodways: New Englanders and Their Food at Sea and Ashore, in the Nineteenth Century.* Mystic, Conn.: Mystic Seaport Museum, Inc., 1995. Equipment and processes.

Randolph, Mary. *The Virginia Housewife: or, Methodical Cook.* Washington, D.C.: Davis and Force, 1824; facsimile edition with Historical Notes and Commentaries by Karen Hess. Columbia, S.C.: University of South Carolina Press, 1984. First Southern American cookbook. Fine recipes for the hearth.

Sloat, Caroline. "Hearth Cookery." In *Old Sturbridge Village Cookbook*, edited by Caroline Sloat. Chester, Conn.: The Globe Pequot Press, 1984. Equipment and processes for the modern historian at the hearth.

Alice Ross

HÉDIARD, FERDINAND. Born in Loupe, a village near Chartres, Hédiard (1832–1898) became interested in the world of imported foods at a young age when he discovered at the port of Le Havre all kinds of cargo from Martinique, Haiti, Guadeloupe, and the Lesser Antilles, all part of the colonial French empire at the time. Fired with the mission of introducing the French to the food wonders he had experienced as a young boy, he opened his first store at the age of twenty-three, in 1850. In 1854, he opened a larger store, which he called "Comptoir d'épices et des Colonies," (trading post selling the products of the colonies), in effect, the first French grocery store. He imported island commodities such as rum, cacao, coffee, bananas, and other tropical fruits and made them all available to a public—including the painter Eugène Delacroix, who lived in the neighborhood—that had never experienced such a taste of the exotic.

As the French empire expanded, Hédiard's business grew. He made a big splash exhibiting the pride of his importations at the 1867 Paris World's Fair, and in 1880 he opened another store in Paris, much more fully realized than the first, at 21 place de la Madeleine, where the flagship store still stands. In 1889, he penned a book of recipes (still in print) to show off the best use of his exotic products. Over its long history, the store has drawn the notice of the rich and famous, such as the writers Alexandre Dumas, Colette, and Jean Cocteau; performing artists such as Jean Gabin, Marlene Dietrich, and Charlie Chaplin; and a loyal following of princes, maharajas, and politicians.

Upon his death, he left the business to his daughter Marie-Blanche and her husband, Max Kusel, who operated it for a time, after which a series of owners have continued the operation in expanded but somewhat changed form.

In 1920, the store's pastry chefs developed a special line of marzipan candies. In 1935, what became the store's signature gold-foil-wrapped packages were developed. The store was modernized in 1950. In 1969, to handle the growing demand worldwide for the Hédiard line, a facility near Nîmes in the Gard Valley opened for the artisanal production of jams, conserves, fruit pastes, glacéed fruits, and other products. Expansion to five additional city locations throughout Paris and three locations in the

suburbs followed in the 1970s. To commemorate the 150-year anniversary, a restaurant was opened at the place de la Madeleine location. Since 2001, an Hédiard website is bringing the world to Hédiard—not bad for a company founded by a man who never left French soil.

See also **Candy and Confections**; **Chef**; **France**; **Retailing of Food**.

BIBLIOGRAPHY

Kusel-Hédiard, Benita. *Le Carnet de Recettes de Ferdinand Hédiard* [Notebook of Ferdinand Hédiard's recipes]. Paris: Le Cherche Midi Editeur, 1998.

Hédiard website: www.hediard.fr.

Robert Wemischner

HERBICIDES. Weeds have been deemed undesirable during much of human history for their negative influence on crop production, their unsightly appearance in the landscape, and in some cases their toxic properties and negative effects on human and animal health. Consequently, weed control is as old as the discovery of agriculture, eight to ten thousand years ago. Techniques for weed control have progressed from the employment of intensive human labor to complex systems involving mechanical, chemical, and biological methods. The earliest methods to eliminate weeds involved physical removal by grubbing or hoeing, followed by cultivation practices using first draft animals and then tractors. Since 1945, the use of chemical herbicides has become the predominant weed control technique in many parts of the world.

Chemicals have been suggested for weed control since antiquity. Theophrastus (372–287 B.C.E.) mentions killing trees by pouring olive oil over their roots. Cato (234–149 B.C.E.) advocated the use of amurca (the watery residue left after the oil is drained from crushed olives) for weed control. Other chemicals include sodium chloride, sulfuric acid, sodium arsenite, copper sulfate, iron sulfate, carbon bisulfate, arsenic trichloride, and petroleum oils. The first synthetic herbicide, 2-methyl-4,6-dinitrophenol (dinitro) was developed in France in 1932 for selective weed control in beans. In 1940 ammonium sulfamate was introduced for control of woody plants.

The chemical herbicide age began in 1941 when R. Pokorny first synthesized 2,4-dichlorophenoxy acetic acid (2,4-D) and reported that it had growth-regulating effects on plants. E. J. Krause of the University of Chicago later suggested that 2,4-D might be used to kill weeds, which stimulated research to test this and other newly synthesized chemicals for weed control in the field. These herbicides proved effective, and in 1945 the American Chemical Paint Company was awarded a patent for 2,4-D as a weed killer. The great potential of synthetic herbicides to control weeds and reduce human labor stimulated the birth of the herbicide chemical industry, resulting in the development of over 180 herbicides for weed control by the end of the twentieth century.

Herbicides are now primarily developed in the private sector. Chemists typically synthesize a variety of compounds, which are screened for their ability to control weeds and then modified and formulated for efficient use. Present herbicides tend to have very low mammalian toxicity because they inhibit biochemical pathways that are unique to plants.

There are a number of chemical classes of herbicides and various mechanisms by which herbicides kill plants. Herbicides generally act by inhibiting specific cellular functions, including photosynthesis, plant-specific amino acid biosynthesis, pigment formation, shoot and root growth, cell membranes, cellulose biosynthesis, lipid biosynthesis, and growth hormone activity.

Herbicides may be applied in many ways. Some herbicides are applied to the soil and absorbed by the plant root and/or shoot and move to their site of inhibition within the plant. Others are primarily applied to emerged foliage and either have an immediate contact effect on the foliage by burning or desiccation, or are translocated throughout the plant, leading to total plant death (systemics). Most soil-applied herbicides kill weed seedlings as they emerge from the soil, while foliage-applied herbicides control emerged weeds and can kill quite large plants.

Herbicide selectivity, the ability to kill weeds but not crops, can be accomplished either by directed application or through biochemical mechanisms. Placement of the herbicide to avoid contact with the crop is widely used. For example, tree crops with deep roots often do not absorb soil-applied herbicides. While it is an effective herbicide for killing most broadleaf plants (dicots), 2,4-D is ineffective on most grassy weeds (monocots). This makes it useful in monocot crops, such as grains and turf. Others selectively kill monocot grasses but not dicots, making them effective in crops such as soybean. Some crops metabolize an applied herbicide to an inactive form while the weeds cannot, so the weed is killed, but the crop is not harmed. For example, atrazine is metabolized to an inactive form by maize while weeds are killed.

In many weed and crop situations there are no good selectivity mechanisms for herbicides. With the advent of recombinant DNA technology (genetic engineering) certain crop plants, such as soybean, corn, and cotton, have been made resistant to nonselective herbicides such as glyphosate by adding genes that make the crop immune to the herbicide. This technology is expected to increase, though its rate of acceptance has been slowed by the reluctance of the food industry to utilize transgenic crops because of concerns expressed by certain consumer advocacy groups.

Modern agriculture in the United States is almost inconceivable without the use of herbicides. Herbicides reduce labor inputs for weed control and make it possible to control weeds where cultivation is infeasible. They reduce the need for mechanical cultivation that can injure crop plants and lead to soil degradation via structure loss and compaction. Herbicides allow the use of no-till crop production, which reduces the need for plowing, now considered a destructive practice. Efficient weed control improves crop growth by reducing weed competition for nutrients and water, and results in improved harvesting and crop quality.

A Source of Controversy

Despite the obvious advantages of herbicides, their use has raised concerns relating to human health and the environment. Since herbicides are toxic to plants, critics have questioned their toxicity to other organisms exposed directly or indirectly. The persistence of some herbicides in the environment has led to concerns relating to their carryover in the soil and effects on subsequent crops as well as their influences, due to drift or volatilization, on non-target plants. Furthermore, through repeated exposure to herbicides, many weeds have become resistant, which reduces the efficacy of previously effective herbicides.

Other concerns involve herbicide costs, the requirement for additional equipment for precision application, and questions relating to proper disposal of unused herbicides.

The advantages and disadvantages of herbicide use are thoroughly evaluated by the U.S. Environmental Protection Agency (EPA) prior to registration and labeling of any new compound. All new pesticides must be granted a registration, permitting their distribution, sale, and use. The EPA assesses a wide variety of potential human health and environmental effects associated with use of the product, including the particular site or crop on which it is to be used; the amount, frequency and timing of its use; and recommended storage and container disposal practices.

In evaluating a pesticide registration application, the registrant must provide data from tests done according to specific EPA guidelines conducted under recognized "Good Laboratory Practice." Results of these tests determine whether a pesticide has the potential to cause adverse effects on humans, wildlife, fish, or plants, including endangered species and non-target organisms, as well as possible contamination of surface water or groundwater from leaching, runoff, and spray drift. The potential human risks evaluated include short-term toxicity and long-term effects, such as cancer and reproductive system disorders. A pesticide will only be registered if it is determined that it can be used to perform its intended function without unreasonably adverse effects on applicators, consumers, or the environment. The EPA also must approve the specific language that appears on each pesticide label; the product can only be legally used according to label directions. The EPA continually evaluates herbicides as to their safety, and any compound that is found to cause any adverse effect is immediately removed from the market.

At the present time herbicides provide consistent, broad-spectrum, and effective weed management in an economical manner. In the future, herbicides will be required to pass even more stringent tests related to their safety. While new-generation herbicides will likely be applied at even lower doses with less environmental persistence and exceedingly low toxicity to non-target organisms, herbicides are now recognized as only one factor in efficient weed control. Weed management is an ever-evolving system that will continue to use an integrated approach, combining cultural, mechanical, chemical, and biological techniques. In this process, however, herbicides will remain an essential component for weed control to help insure a sustainable food production system that reduces unacceptable risks to the environment while producing an abundant and safe food supply.

See also **Agricultural Research**; **Contaminants, Chemical**; **Ecology and Food**; **Government Agencies**; **Pesticides**; **Safety, Food**; **Toxins, Unnatural, and Food Safety**.

BIBLIOGRAPHY

Monaco, Thomas J., Stephen C. Weller, and Floyd M. Ashton. *Weed Science: Principles and Practices.* 4th ed. New York: Wiley, 2002.

Zimdahl, Robert L. *Fundamentals of Weed Science.* 2d ed. San Diego, Calif.: Academic Press, 1999.

Stephen C. Weller

HERBS AND SPICES. The terms "herb" and "spice" describe plants or parts of plants used for medicine, cooking, and pleasure all over the world. These plants number in the thousands and come from almost every plant family known. This makes it almost impossible to generalize about their uses and properties. However, a treatment of this length could not be written without generalizations, so it is important to keep in mind that for every statement made one or more exceptions exist.

Definitions

Herbs are the green, leafy parts of plants. They are most efficacious and flavorsome when used fresh, and they are mostly grown in temperate to hot regions. Spices are derived from any part of a plant that is not a leaf: for example, cloves are flower buds, cinnamon is bark, ginger is a root, peppercorns are berries, nigella is seed, cumin is a fruit, saffron is stigmas, cardamom is pods and seeds, and asafetida is a gum. Spices are usually used in small amounts, are best used dry (the drying process often enhances the flavor), and most grow in subtropical or tropical climates. One single plant can be both an herb and a spice. Aromatic seeds like dill are a spice, while dill leaves are an herb. However, coriander and hamburg parsley roots, garlic and fennel bulbs are all regarded as herbs rather than spices.

What Do They Look Like?

Herbs and spices cover the complete range of growth habits and sizes of plants, and they can be annuals, biennials, perennials, trees, shrubs, climbers, and grasses. They grow in a wide range of conditions and habitats from the tropics to polar regions. They can be found at sea level, some even grow in the sea or in fresh water, and others grow near the tops of the highest mountains. Despite this diversity it is true that many of the better-known herbs and spices fall into distinct groups. One group contains those plants found in the Lamiaceae (mint family). They are characterized by young stems that are four-angled, simple opposite leaves, and flowers with five more or less fused petals. Glands on these plants usually contain volatile fragrant oils. Most originate in the Mediterranean or Central Asia and are used as potherbs, to make perfumes, and in the manufacture of pharmaceutical products. Well-known herbs such as basil, bergamot, calamint, hyssop, lavender, lemon balm, mint, rosemary, sage, savory, and thyme are in this family.

In the Apiaceae (carrot family) are important herbs and spices such as angelica, anise, caraway, chervil, coriander, cumin, dill, fennel, gotu kola, lovage, and parsley. These plants mostly originate from temperate regions all over the world. They are characterized by being aromatic and having hollow stems and dissected leaves arranged in spirals, often attached by a base that sheathes the stem. The usually small, five-petaled flowers appear in umbels and are followed by strongly scented fruits (often called seeds). The leaves of many of these plants are important herbs, while the fruits are widely used spices.

French tarragon is in the Asteraceae (daisy family), members of which grow mostly in temperate regions all over the world. Plants in this group usually have simple or dissected leaves arranged in spirals. Flowers are usually tiny discs grouped together in compact heads and surrounded by a ring of ray flowers with straplike petals. Other herbs in this family include burdock, chamomile, chicory, dandelion, marigolds, pyrethrum, safflower, wormwood, and yarrow. Some are important culinary herbs, while others are important medicinal herbs. The group also includes herbs used to kill and repel insects and to produce dyes.

The Lauraceae (laurel family) consists mostly of aromatic, evergreen shrubs and trees originating from warm and tropical regions of Southeast Asia and northern South America. The herbs and spices in this family include sweet bay, camphor, cassia, cinnamon, and sassafras.

Allspice, cloves, cajuput oil, eucalyptus, and myrtle are all in the Myrtaceae (myrtle family). These are trees and shrubs that grow in tropical and warm areas of the world. They bear scented leaves containing important essential oils, and many also bear edible fruit.

Some important root spices are in the Zingiberaceae (ginger family). These plants mostly grow from thickened

The formal herb garden at the Henry Doubleday Research Association's garden center, Ryton, near Coventry, England. Featured here are golden feverfew, lady's mantle, and tansy. The Ryton gardens are open to the public and offer programs on growing herbs organically. © MICHAEL BOYS/CORBIS.

aromatic rhizomes with large, upright, alternate leaves. They are mostly found in tropical and subtropical regions of the world. In this family are cardamom, Chinese keys, galangal, gingers, torch ginger, turmeric, and zedoary.

History

Archaeological evidence shows that the use of spices and herbs dates back to long before recorded history, when human ancestors first added sharp-flavored leaves to early cooking pots. Roaming hunter-gatherer groups experimented with leaves, roots, flowers, and seeds, so over time they built up a precious compendium of knowledge that was passed from one generation to the next. As civilization progressed and nomadic tribes settled in one place, herbs and spices were not just collected from the wild but were deliberately sown near dwelling places. By the beginning of the agricultural period plants were collected from the wild and grown near dwellings for food, flavor, medicine, fuel, decoration, dyes, poison, and weapons and to alter early humans' sense of reality.

The earliest written records come from ancient Egyptian, Chinese, and Indian cultures. The Ebers Papyrus that dates from 1550 B.C.E. describes some eight hundred different medicinal remedies and numerous medicinal procedures. Early Egyptians used spices and herbs in medicine, as cosmetics and perfumes, for embalming, in cooking, and to kill and repel pests.

Trade

The ancient trade in some spices was highly lucrative. Black pepper was the most lucrative of all, although cassia and cinnamon were essential ingredients in Egyptian embalmment. Taprobane (Sri Lanka) was well known to the Greeks and Romans, and trade with it is described in

the Byzantine topography of Cosmas Indicopleustes. The earliest known Chinese records of the uses of plants date from 2700 B.C.E., from the herbal compiled by Emperor Chin Nong. In India the Vedic literature of about 1500–1200 B.C.E. describes many different plants used in religious ceremonies. When the Queen of Sheba visited King Solomon in the tenth century B.C.E., she offered gifts of rare and sought-after spices and herbs, probably with the hope of increasing and expanding the existing trade in these commodities.

Evidence of trading and use of herbs and spices is in the writings, among others, of the Greek physician Dioscorides and the Roman civil servant Pliny the Elder in the first century C.E. The spread of the Roman Empire also spread herbs such as rosemary, savory, garlic, and thyme into northern Europe and Britain. Romans took with them precious supplies of spices like pepper and ginger. The fall of the Roman Empire accompanied a dramatic decrease in trade until the eighth century and the spread of the Muslim Empire, when once again spices and herbs were on the move and were widely used in medicine and cooking. After the Norman conquest of Britain, spices such as ginger, cloves, mace, and pepper were once again found on the tables of wealthy Britons.

Later the ongoing search for and trade in other valuable spices, which at different times have been worth as much as gold, led to some of the great voyages of discovery. Ginger, pepper, cloves, cinnamon, galangal, mace, and nutmeg were the reasons for battles fought, fortunes made and lost, and new worlds discovered. These spices launched Europe and Britain, attempting to satiate their desires for these exotic ingredients, into the age of exploration. Christopher Columbus discovered America while searching for a new sea route to the Spice Islands. In 1498 Vasco da Gama, the Portuguese navigator, rounded the Cape of Good Hope and established a new spice route to India and beyond. Magellan eventually found the western route to the Spice Islands in the 1520s. In the following centuries the Portuguese, Dutch, and British fought wars for control of these routes and the islands where many of the spices grew.

Modern methods of preservation led to a decrease in the use of spices in many Western countries, and at the same time, with modern methods of transportation, spices became ubiquitous and relatively cheap.

Growing Herbs and Spices

In the past herbs and spices were grown in gardens and harvested for use in the home, or they were collected from the wild, in what was known as wild crafting. As the demand for herbs and spices increased, they were also grown on a small scale as agricultural crops. The growth, harvest, and processing of herbs and spices was and in many cases has remained a labor-intensive enterprise. Consequently these crops often were grown in countries where labor was cheap. In the early twenty-first century Egypt grew and exported large quantities of anise, basil,

TABLE 1

Common culinary herbs

Name*	Description	Climate, place of origin	Part used	Uses
Basil *Ocimum* species Lamiaceae	Annual, small shrub	Tropical to warm temperate, Asia and Africa	Fresh leaves, young stems	Tomato dishes, salad, stuffings, sauces, soups
Bay leaves *Laurus nobilis* Lauraceae	Perennial, medium tree	Temperate, Mediterranean	Fresh or dried leaves	Soups, stews, stir-fries, sauces, meats, desserts
Bergamot *Monarda didyma* Lamiaceae	Herbaceous perennial, medium	Temperate, North America	Fresh or dried leaves and flowers	Salads, pork, chicken, seafood, eggs, drinks, teas
Chervil *Anthriscus cerefolium* Apiaceae	Annual, small shrub	Temperate, Europe and Western Asia	Fresh leaves	Salads, stir-fries, sauces, cheese, garnishes
Chives *Allium shoeoprasum* Alliaceae	Herbaceous perennial, small clumps	Cold temperate, Yugoslavia, Siberia, Asia Minor	Fresh and dried leaves and flowers	Salads, stir-fries, sauces, cheese, breads, garnishes
Cilantro *Coriandrum sativum* Apiaceae	Annual, small shrub	Temperate, Europe	Fresh leaves, flowers, roots, dried seeds	Salads, stir-fries, soups, chicken, fish, eggs, garnishes
Curry leaf *Murraya koenigii* Rutaceae	Perennial, small tree	Tropical and subtropical, Asia	Fresh and dried leaves	Curries, pickles, chutneys, fish, vegetables, rice
Dill *Anethum graveolens* Apiaceae	Annual, tall shrub	Temperate, Southwest Asia	Fresh and dried leaves, dried seeds	Salads, stir-fries, chicken, seafood, sauces, garnishes
Fennel *Foeniculum vulgare* Apiaceae	Herbaceous perennial, tall shrub	Temperate, Mediterranean seeds	Fresh and dried leaves, fresh stem base, dried seeds	Salads, stir-fries, eggs, seafood, sauces, soups, vegetables
Garlic chives *Allum tuberosum* Alliaceae	Herbaceous perennial, small clump	Temperate, Southeast Asia	Fresh leaves flowers, buds, flower stems	Salads, stir-fries, sauces, soups, cheese, garnishes
Gotu kola *Centella asiatica* Apiaceae	Perennial, low spreading groundcover	Tropical to warm temperate, Asia and Australasia	Fresh leaves	Salads, soups, rice, garnishes
Lemongrass *Cymbopogon citratus* Poaceae	Perennial, clumping grass	Tropical to warm temperate, India and Ceylon	Fresh and dried leaves and stems	Soups, stir-fries, beef, chicken, seafood, sauces, teas
Marjoram and oregano *Origanum* species Lamiaceae	Herbaceous perennial, spreading clumps	Temperate Mediterranean to East Asia	Fresh and dried leaves	Soups, stews, sauces, cheese, breads, eggs, vegetables
Mint *Mentha* species Lamiaceae	Herbaceous perennial, spreading clumps	Temperate, Europe, Asia, Africa	Fresh and dried leaves	Salads, sauces, lamb, chicken, seafood, garnishes, drinks, teas
Parsley *Petroselinum crispum* Apiaceae	Biennial, low-growing clump	Temperate, Europe	Fresh and dried leaves	Salads, sauces, cheese, garnishes on most foods
Rosemary *Rosmarinus officinalis* Lamiaceae	Woody perennial, medium bush	Temperate, Mediterranean	Fresh and dried leaves	Stews, sauces, soups, stuffings, breads, eggs, teas
Sage *Salvia officinalis* Lamiaceae	Woody perennial, medium bush	Temperate, Mediterranean and North Africa	Fresh and dried leaves	Stews, sauces, soups, stuffings, breads, eggs, teas
Tarragon *Artemisia dracunculus* Asteraceae	Herbaceous perennial, spreading clump	Temperate, Central and Eastern Europe, Southern Russia	Fresh and dried leaves	Salads, soups, stews, chicken, seafood, eggs, vegetables
Thyme *Thymus* species Lamiaceae	Perennial, low bush or spreading clump	Temperate, Europe and Asia	Fresh and dried leaves	Stews, sauces, soups, stuffings, breads, eggs, teas
Watercress *Nasturtium officinale* Brassicaceae	Perennial, spreading clump	Temperate, Europe and Southwest Asia	Fresh leaves	Salads, soups, sauces, eggs, garnishes

*Garlic is not included here as it is discussed in the text.

Fresh nutmegs are red. The shell covering is dried and called mace. © Bob Krist/CORBIS.

caraway, dill, and fennel; China produced fennel, garlic, ginger, and cumin; India grew celery seed, fennel, and turmeric; and Croatia produced sage, savory, and rosemary, to name a few. At that time the herb and spice industry could be divided into three main categories, essential oils, medicinal crops, and culinary herbs and spices (fresh and dried).

Essential Oils

Essential oils are usually found in specialized oil cells or ducts in plants. Oils from aromatic plants are generally volatile, so they are extracted by water or steam distillation. Some volatile and most nonvolatile essential oils are obtained by solvent extraction. The aromatic, resinous product obtained from nonvolatile oils is known as an oleoresin. Oleoresins are concentrated and are widely used in the food industry. For example, pepper oleoresins are used in processed food, while turmeric oleoresin is a common natural coloring agent in food and pharmaceuticals. Essential oils are produced and processed all over the world, and France, Brazil, China, Spain, and Mexico are among the largest producers. These oils are often the by-products of another industry, and citrus oils, extracted from the skins of oranges, lemons, and limes, account for a large proportion of the essential oil industry. Pine and cedarwood oils are by-products of the timber industry. Of the herbs and spices planted specifically for oil production, anise, bergamot, citronella, lemongrass, lavender, mints, and rosemary are probably the most widely grown. Mints represent the largest essential-oil crop in the United States. Dill is also an important oil crop, used mostly in the manufacture of pickles.

Medicinal Herbs and Spices

It is particularly important that medicinal herbs and spices are grown in ideal rather than marginal conditions so the proportion of medicinal constituents is maximized.

Usually the constituents of medicinal value to humans are secondary metabolites produced by plants for purposes other than growth. Advocates for organic gardening insist that conditions most closely approximating wild conditions are best for growing herbs, especially medicinal herbs, because the use of pesticides and herbicides can alter the plants' constituents, thereby altering their flavors and medicinal attributes.

Wild Herbs and Spices

Wild crafting of herbs and spices occurs all over the world. Some herbs, such as echinacea and goldenseal, have become rare in the wild because of overharvesting. Although all herbs can be cultivated, one school of thought says the best medicinal herbs are taken from the wild, so pressure on wild herb populations in all parts of the world continues. Conversely, some cultivated herbs have escaped into the wild, where they have become problem weeds. Harvesting these from the wild helps keep them under control while providing plenty of raw material for processing.

Culinary Herbs

In the past culinary herbs and spices were collected from the wild or grown in gardens among vegetables and flowers. By the twenty-first century, although the traditions of collecting flavorings from the wild and growing a few herbs in gardens continued, more people in Western countries demanded interesting and exotic flavors with their foods. This trend produced a proliferation of fresh, processed, frozen, and dried herbs and spices on supermarket shelves and a burgeoning industry to support these demands. In these Western countries the processed herb market is mostly supplied by companies that dry, process, package, and transport the produce to market. These companies are usually supplied by contract growers, often from other countries. Many herbs are dried for use as herb teas as well as for flavorings. A smaller but increasing market exists for biodynamically and organically grown herbs, both dried and fresh.

Culinary Spices

Most commercially grown herbs are produced in temperate regions, as are the seed spices, such as coriander, dill, cumin, caraway, and fennel. Most spices, however, are indigenous to and are grown commercially in subtropical and tropical regions. Each spice is usually grown in just a handful of countries and then exported all over the world. For example, the best cinnamon still comes from its native Sri Lanka; cassia come from China, Indonesia, and Vietnam; cloves come from the Moluccas, Zanzibar, and Madagascar; pepper comes from India, Indonesia, and Malaysia; and ginger comes from Jamaica, Nigeria, and India. The spice saffron is native to more temperate regions, and most of it is grown in and exported from Spain, Kashmir, Greece, and Iran.

Drying Spices

Spices are usually dried straight after harvest, either in the sun or in drying rooms. The drying ensures that essential oils and oleoresins are largely preserved intact. As some spices dry, enzymes and chemicals in the spice react to create a different flavor. For example, when peppercorns are dried in the sun, the volatile oil piperine is formed, thus giving dried peppercorns their unique flavor. Vanilla beans also only develop their flavor after months of careful, slow drying. Once dry, spices are best stored in airtight containers to preserve their volatile oils. These oils are released by the application of heat (frying, roasting, boiling) and are absorbed by the food, which takes on a new flavor. Many spices are ground after drying. But once they are ground they lose their flavor much more quickly, so it is best to use freshly ground spices when possible. Whole spices can be stored away from direct light for up to three years, ground spices only for about one year.

Fresh Herbs

The fresh herb market in Western countries saw enormous growth in the last decade of the twentieth century with an increase in the variety of herbs available for purchase. As the size of this market increased, some herbs moved from a niche product to one fully integrated with fresh market vegetables, so they are grown, harvested, packaged, transported, and marketed in the same way as vegetables. Even so, fresh herbs tend to be grown on smaller farms and are often sold in smaller specialty grocers, farmers' markets, and roadside stalls. In the supermarkets fresh herbs, often hydroponically grown in greenhouses, are sold in bunches or increasingly in pots. At the beginning of the twenty-first century the fresh herbs available for sale at the Los Angeles wholesale fruit and vegetable market included anise, arugula (rocket), basil, chives, cilantro, dill, epasote, lemongrass, marjoram, mint, oregano, parsley, rosemary, sage, sorrel, tarragon, thyme, and watercress. The variety of herbs available is increasing with demands from immigrants for herbs from their native countries and a general wish for a greater variety in herb flavors.

Everyday Ingredients

Most people eat or use herbs and spices in some form every day, in vanilla ice cream, chili and Worcestershire sauces, alcoholic drinks such as gin, in cinnamon buns and in seed breads. Herbs flavor toothpaste and cough medicines, and they are drunk as teas and added to vinegars, oils, and sauces. The scents and flavors of herbs and spices originate from the essential oils in the plant material. These oils are a complex combination of organic compounds such as alcohols, esters, and aldehydes. So the growth, harvest, and drying of herbs and spices aims to maximize the preservation of these oils and thereby the scents and flavors. This is also true of the preparation and cooking of herbs and spices. For maximum flavor herbs should be harvested at the last possible moment

CLASSIC HERB COMBINATIONS

Bouquet Garni
This name is given to any small bunch of fresh herbs tied together and added to sauces, stock, soups, stews, and casseroles. The herbs are removed before serving. The basic combination is one bay leaf, a sprig of parsley, and a sprig of thyme. Other herbs used in bouquet garni are lemon balm, tarragon, fennel, rosemary, sage, and oregano.

Fines Herbes
A classic French combination of equal amounts of finely chopped chervil, chives, parsley, and tarragon. This mixture is used with soups, sauces, eggs, grilled meats, and fish. Lovage and fennel are sometimes added.

Herbes de Provence
A mixture of herbs that thrive in southern France during the summer: marjoram, oregano, rosemary, savory, and thyme. Use fresh or dried on any Mediterranean-style dish, pizza, stew, kebabs, and tomato dishes.

and chopped just before use. If this is not possible, purchased herbs should look as fresh as possible (no wilting or bruised or brown leaves) and should be stored in plastic bags in the refrigerator until needed, preferably not more than a few days. Again they should be chopped just before use.

Dried Herbs

Dried herbs should be green (not brown) and should retain a lot of flavor when crushed. They should be purchased in small amounts and used before the use-by date. Drying an herb or spice reduces the water content, and if done properly it concentrates the flavor. For this reason using only a quarter to a third of what one would use if the herb were fresh will produce the same flavor. Some herbs retain more flavor than others when dried. Basil, chives, parsley, chervil, and coriander leaves all lose some flavor components when dried, while rosemary, sage, and oregano stay much the same, just more concentrated.

Using Herbs

Many fresh herbs should only be added near the end of cooking, otherwise their flavors are lost. Herbs such as cilantro, parsley, chervil, dill, and basil should all be added in the last few minutes of cooking or should be sprinkled over a dish just before serving. Dried herbs and some of the more strongly flavored fresh herbs like rosemary, sage, and bay can be cooked for much longer. In parts of the Mediterranean and in some Asian countries, it is usual to serve a bowl of assorted fresh herbs or a salad made predominantly of herbs with the meal. This serves the twofold purpose of stimulating and revitalizing the palate and aiding digestion.

Green sauces are also popular in many cultures and can be used to add piquancy to an otherwise bland meal. These sauces are made by pounding fresh green herbs with a pestle in a mortar or a food processor. They can be as simple as a single abundant herb, a clove of garlic, and drizzle of olive oil all pounded together. They can be as complex as Italian pesto (pine nuts and basil), North African *chermoula* (coriander, mint, and parsley leaves), French sauce *verte* (parsley, tarragon, chervil, and chives leaves), and Yemeni *zhoug* (coriander and parsley leaves), all of which also require a range of spices and other ingredients. These sauces are spread on bread, spooned into pasta or rice, added to soup, used as a marinade, spread over cooked meat, or used as a dip.

Much Southeast Asian cooking, especially in Vietnam and Thailand, demands fresh rather than dried herbs to obtain their distinctive flavors. Cilantro leaves and roots, lemongrass, garlic, ginger, turmeric, and chili are used fresh in traditional dishes from these countries. In contrast, Middle Eastern dishes use mainly dried and ground ginger and turmeric.

Using Spices

Spices are an essential component of cuisines from all over the world. Spicy food is not necessarily hot. The heat in spicy food usually comes from pepper or chili. If these are not added to a spice mix, the dish will not have any heat. Nearly all spices are dried before use. They are best purchased whole and ground just before needed. If this is not possible, then one can buy ground individual spices or mixtures a little at a time and use them within twelve months. Many spices, whether used whole or ground, need to be lightly cooked before use. This enhances and in some cases changes the flavor of the spice. Whole spices can be spread over a tray and dry roasted for a few minutes in a hot oven. They can then be ground or left whole and added straight to a dish. Ground spices are best gently fried, without oil, in a frying pan for up to sixty seconds.

Mixtures

Spice mixtures, which vary from country to country, are judicious combinations of spices that give a balance of flavors, often with surprising highlights. The various tastes of spices are usually categorized into five taste groups, sweet, pungent, tangy, hot, and amalgamating. Curry, for example, is a spice mixture that involves the selective use of pungent and aromatic spices. Some of these spices, like coriander, are added to almost every mixture; others, like star anise, are only rarely added to achieve a specific flavor.

Seed spices are an important component of many different breads, where they complement the carbohydrates and contain oils that aid digestion. Poppy and sesame seeds are used on bread rolls, nigella and black sesame seeds on Turkish breads, and caraway and dill seeds in and on many European breads. This use dates from antiquity, when different seed spices were used in cakes, biscuits, and breads to improve flavor and to help digestion.

Traditional Uses

Hundreds of herbs and spices have been used in cultures all over the world for thousands of years. During this time countless traditions, myths, and rituals have evolved. The following gives just a taste of some of these.

In times past foul or nasty odors were often associated with evil, while sweet, fragrant scents indicated goodness and purity. Herbs and spices with strong or unpleasant scents were avoided, while the sweetly scented ones masked bad odors and protected against evil. Spices in particular were in demand to improve preservation and to disguise the flavor of rotten or foul-tasting food. The Romans used ginger to counteract rancidity. Ginger is also associated with the rites and passages of life. It is given to new mothers all over Asia to restore strength and vigor, while the Chinese see ginger as a warming (yang) and stimulating food, believing it calms and purifies. Closely related turmeric is used in Indian ceremonies to anoint brides, while in Thailand it is used to anoint novice monks before ordination.

Dill is an herb and a seed spice with a long history. Romans fed it to their gladiators to confer vitality, and in medieval times it was added to love potions. Some Americans know it as "meeting house seed" because at one time dill seeds were chewed to dull the pangs of hunger during long religious services. Parsley grew wild on remote Grecian hillsides, but the ancient Greeks did not usually eat it. They used it in funerals and as a symbol of death; to be "in need of parsley" meant that one was seriously ill. In early medieval England the slow and patchy germination of parsley was explained by the suggestion that, once sown, parsley went nine times to the devil and back before sprouting. Those with worries about hair loss were advised to sprinkle their heads with parsley seeds three times a year. Rosemary is another herb with connections to funerary rights. In France rosemary was customarily placed in the hands of the deceased before burial, and in England sprigs of rosemary were thrown into the open grave. Rosemary was also believed to aid memory. Greek students twined rosemary in their hair, believing the scent would stimulate memory. Tradition has it that where rosemary flourishes the women are in charge, while according to an Arabic proverb a person whose sage grows well will live forever.

The statuesque herb angelica has been used in pagan and Christian festivals for centuries. It is indigenous to cold northern Europe, and its name is derived from a legend in which an angel appears to a monk in a dream

CLASSIC SPICE COMBINATIONS

Panch Phora
1 tsp. brown mustard
1 tsp. cumin
1 tsp. fennel
1 tsp. fenugreek
1 tsp. nigella

Whole seed mixture; fry or roast to release full flavor. Add to vegetables, seafood, breads, and pulses.

Pickling Spices
3 tsp. black pepper
3 tsp. yellow mustard seed
4 dried bird's eye chilis
3 tsp. allspice berries
3 tsp. dill seed
1 tsp. mace blades
1 crumbled cinnamon stick
2 crumbled bay leaves
2 tsp. cloves
4 tsp. ground ginger

Whole seed mixture, used to make pickles, chutneys, and spiced vinegar. Can be wrapped in muslin and removed before bottling.

Garam Masala
2 tsp. black peppercorns
1 cinnamon stick
1 tsp. cloves
2 tsp. cardamom seeds
2 tsp. cumin seeds

Grind the spices. Many different forms of this recipe exist, but they generally revolve around the same spices. Optional extras include bay leaves, coriander seeds, mace, and nutmeg. Use with fish, poultry, other meats, most vegetables, rice, pulses, and eggs.

Mixed Spices
1 cinnamon stick
1 tsp. allspice berries
1 tsp. whole cloves
2 tsp. grated nutmeg
2 tsp. ground ginger

Grind the whole spices. A traditional English mixture. Use in desserts, pies, cakes, and biscuits.

Basic Curry
10 tsp. coriander seed
5 tsp. cumin seed
1 tsp. brown mustard seed
5 whole bird's-eye chili
1 tsp. fenugreek seed
1 tsp. whole peppercorns
2 tsp. ground turmeric

Roast the whole spices, grind and mix all the spices together. Hundreds of different curries exist with varying combinations of the above spices. Other spices that can be used in curry mixes are fennel, cinnamon, cloves, cardamom, ginger, and curry leaves.

Mexican Chili Powder
5 tsp. chili powder
3 tsp. ground cumin seed
2 tsp. sweet paprika

Use to flavor chili con carne and other bean and minced beef recipes.

Quatre Épices
5 tsp. ground black pepper
2 tsp. ground cloves
2 tsp. ground ginger
2 tsp. ground nutmeg

A French spice mixture. Use in preserved meats like salami, with game meats, and with slow-cooked beef and chicken dishes.

Chinese Five-Spice Powder
1 tsp. black peppercorns
1 tsp. ground cassia
1 tsp. cloves
3 tsp. fennel seed
5 whole star anise

Grind the whole spices. Use with stir-fried vegetables and as a marinade for seafood, chicken, pork, and duck.

---

and tells him this plant can cure the plague. It was also believed that angelica protected a person carrying it against witches and their spells. Other sweet herbs such as lavender and rosemary sweetened washing water to scent clothes and, strewed around rooms, repelled insects and masked unpleasant smells.

Herbs and Spices in the Twenty-first Century
Modern medicine led to a decrease in the use of herbal medicines in Western countries in the twentieth century. Nevertheless herbal remedies remain widely used in many poorer parts of the world, and herbal remedies have begun to regain popularity in the West. Many old uses

TABLE 2

20 common culinary spices

Name*	Description	Place of origin, climate	Part used	Quality and taste	Uses
Allspice *Pimenta dioica* Myrtaceae	Perennial, tall evergreen tree	Tropical, America and West Indies whole and ground	Dried and cured unripe berries	Pungent, clovelike	Sweets and cakes, pickles, preserved meats, curries
Caraway *Carum carvi* Apiaceae	Biennial, medium clump	Temperate, Europe and West Asia	Dried seeds, fresh leaves and roots mixes	Pungent, earthy with anise and orange	Breads, cheeses, pork, sausages, apples, cabbage, pastes, spice
Cardamom *Elettaria cardamomum* Zingiberaceae	Perennial, medium clump	Tropical, India	Dried pods and seeds, fresh leaves	Pungent, warm, camphorous	Fruits, cakes, biscuits, custards, curries, rice
Cassia *Cinnamomum aromaticum* Lauraceae	Perennial, tall evergreen tree	Tropical, Burma	Dried bark, whole and ground	Sweet, strong, slightly bitter	Pastries, cakes, biscuits, curries, spice blends
Chili *Capsicum* species Solanaceae	Short-lived perennial, perennial, small bushes to small trees	Tropical, America	Fresh and dried fruits and seeds	Hot, fruity	Spice blends, curries, pastes, sauces, sambals, pickles, dips
Cinnamon *Cinnamomum zeylanicum* Lauraceae	Perennial, medium evergreen tree	Tropical, Southern India and Sri Lanka	Dried bark, whole and ground	Sweet, mild, warm, woody	Stewed fruits, rice, curries, spice blends, sweet dishes, cakes, breads
Cloves *Syzygium aromaticum* Myrtaceae	Perennial, medium evergreen tree	Tropical, Moluccas	Dried flower buds	Pungent, camphorous, spicy, slightly peppery	Curries, spice blends, spiced wines, stewed fruits, custards, pickles, meats
Coriander *Coriandrum sativum* Apiaceae	Annual, small shrub	Temperate, Europe	Dried seeds, whole and ground	Amalgamating, citrus and sage	Cakes, pies, biscuits, fruits, curries, spice blends, pickles, sauces
Cumin *Cuminum cyminum* Apiaceae	Annual, small shrub	Temperate, Mediterranean	Dried seeds, whole and ground	Pungent, earthy sweet flavor	Curries, spice blends, rice, fish, lamb, breads, pickles, vegetables
Fennel *Foeniculum vulgare* Apiaceae	Herbaceous perennial, tall shrub	Temperate, Mediterranean	Dried seeds, whole and ground	Amalgamating, sweet anise	Salads, soups, spice blends, pastas, breads, sausages
Fenugreek *Trigonella foenum-graecum* Fabaceae	Annual, small, slender	Temperate, Southern Europe and Asia	Dried seeds, whole or dried leaves from seeds	Pungent, spicy and bitter	Vegetable and fish curries, spice blends, sprouts grown
Ginger *Zingiber officinale* Zingiberaceae	Perennial, spreading clump	Tropical, Asia	Fresh and dried, whole and ground roots	Pungent, spicy, sweet, warm to hot	Biscuits, cakes, fish, meats, vegetables, curries
Juniper *Juniperus communis* Cupressaceae	Perennial, shrubs to medium trees	Temperate, Europe and Asia	Dried berries	Pungent, savory, spicy, pine	Game meats, duck, pork, chicken, soups, stews
Nigella *Nigella sativa* Ranunculaceae	Annual, medium, erect	Temperate, Southwest Asia	Seeds	Pungent, black, bitter, slightly metallic tasting	Breads, spice blends, potatoes, curries
Nutmeg and Mace *Myristica fragrans* Myristicaceae	Perennial, evergreen medium tree	Tropical, Indonesia	Nutmeg-seeds, Mace-placental seed coverings, dried, whole or ground	Nutmeg-sweet, warm, aromatic Mace-pungent, spicy, sweet	Nutmeg-root vegetables, custards, cakes, biscuits Mace-seafood, meat sauces
Pepper *Piper nigrum* Piperaceae	Perennial, climber	Tropical, Southern India and Sri Lanka	Dried or pickled fruits	Hot, pungent, fragrant	Most savory foods
Saffron *Crocus sativus* Iridaceae	Perennial, small, bulbous	Temperate, probably Greece	Dried stigmas woody, fragrant	Pungent, earthy,	Rice, seafood, chicken, cakes
Star anise *Illicium verum* Illiaceae	Perennial, evergreen, small tree	Warm temperate to tropical, China and Vietnam	Dried fruits woody, aniseed	Pungent, spicy,	Vegetables, fruits, strong seafood, cured meats, sweet dishes
Turmeric *Curcuma longa* Zingiberaceae	Perennial, leafy clump	Tropical, India	Fresh and dried, whole and ground roots	Amalgamating, spicy, bitter	Spice blends, curries, fish, stir-fries, rice
Vanilla *Vanilla planifolia* Orchidaceae	Perennial, climbing orchid	Tropical, Florida, West Indies, Central and South America	Cured seed capsules	Sweet, fragrant	Desserts, cakes, biscuits, ice creams, sugar, chicken

*Mustard is not included here as it is discussed in the text.

of herbs have been confirmed by scientists, while new uses are being found. For example, Taxol is extracted from yew trees to treat some cancers.

See also **Ethnobotany**; **Myth and Legend, Food in**; **Sensation and the Senses**.

BIBLIOGRAPHY

Boxer, Arabella, Jocasta Innes, Charlotte Parry-Crooke, and Lewis Esson. *The Encyclopedia of Herbs, Spices, and Flavourings.* London: Octopus Books, 1984.

Chapman, Pat. *Pat Chapman's Curry Bible.* London: Hodder and Stoughton, 1997.

Garland, Sarah. *The Herb and Spice Book.* Lane Cove, New South Wales, Australia: Hodder and Stoughton, 1979.

Hemphill, Ian. *Spice Notes: A Cook's Compendium of Herbs and Spices.* Sydney: Pan Macmillan Australia, 2000.

Huxley, Anthony, ed. *The New Royal Horticultural Society Dictionary of Gardening.* London: Macmillan Reference, 1999.

Manfield, Christine. *Spice.* Ringwood, Victoria: Penguin Books Australia, 1999.

Ortiz, Elisabeth Lambert, ed. *The Encyclopedia of Herbs, Spices, and Flavorings.* New York: Dorling Kindersley, 1992.

Simon, James E. "Essential Oils and Culinary Herbs." In *Advances in New Crops,* edited by Jules Janick and James E. Simon. Portland, Ore.: Timber Press, 1990.

Woodward, Penny. *Penny Woodward's Australian Herbal.* South Melbourne: Hyland House, 1996.

Penny Woodward

HERDING. Domestication of animals for food began about 10,000 years ago in the Near East, in the western part of the Fertile Crescent. This coincided with a period of climatic warming following the last retreat of the Pleistocene glaciation in Europe and Asia. Livestock provided a more regular supply of food that tended to mitigate, but not entirely eliminate, the seasonal patterns of resource availability that faced the hunter and gatherer. The Neolithic pattern of keeping animals for food followed shortly after the earliest domestication of plants in the same area of the Near East. Since that time other grazing and browsing animals were domesticated and their origins have been found at different sites around the globe. Table 1 lists major domestic species with earliest dates and places of domestication. All of these species can provide food in the form of meat, organs, marrow, blood, milk, or fat, although some function as draught, pack, or riding animals, and provide wool, hides, skins, hooves, and dung. When the earliest animals were domesticated, they were reserved for slaughter and their meat was used for food. Today, the livestock species listed in Table 1 constitute more than 3,000 breeds or domestic subspecies and provide a variety of foods and materials.

About 6,000 to 7,000 years ago, domestic animals began to be used for milking, wool production, and other purposes in addition to meat in what Andrew Sherratt (1981) has called the "secondary products revolution." Milk production or dairying may have been practiced more than 7,000 years ago in the Near East since there is evidence for milking cattle and ovicaprids (sheep/goats) in Neolithic Europe that dates back to 6,000 years ago. A significant problem in the cultural development of dairying was the biological evolution of tolerance to milk sugar—lactose—through production of the digestive enzyme—lactase—beyond infancy by children and adults. Almost certainly the ability to utilize lactose by breaking down this disaccharide sugar into its digestible monosaccharides occurred by natural selection. The picture of adult lactose tolerance is a complex one of relationships among genetics, digestive physiology, and digestive enzyme adaptation. However, this is one of the best examples that we have of culture change (pastoralism to dairying) actually producing biological change (in genetics of populations) through natural selection.

Animal domestication and herding spread from centers in Eurasia to Europe, South and East Asia, and Africa. The pig was dispersed from Southeast Asia to New Guinea by least 3,000 years ago, and then later to the Pacific Islands. Much later, following Columbus's discovery, European domesticated animals were transported to the New World. In the indigenous New World, the Andean llama and alpaca were the only animals herded throughout North and South America.

Traditions of agro-pastoralism arose in moist areas or areas capable of irrigation: in marginal, semiarid, or arid lands, transhumant (seasonal migrations) and nomadic herding predominated. David Harris (1996) noted

TABLE 1

Earliest Domestication of Major Livestock Species

Dates are in approximate years before the present

Common Name	Species	Date	Place	Reference
Goats	*Capra* sp.	10,000	Near East (SW Asia)	1
Sheep	*Ovis* sp.	9,000	Near East	1
Pigs	*Sus* sp.	9,000	Near East, China	2
Cattle	*Bos* sp.	8,000	Near East, India	3
Horses	*Equus caballus*	6,000	Eurasian steppes	4
Water Buffalo	*Babalus babalis*	6,000	China	5
Camelids	*Llama* sp.	6,000	Central Andes	6
Donkeys	*Equus asinus*	5,000	NE Africa	4
Camels	*Camelus* sp.	5,000	Arabia (dromedary) Central Asia (bactrian)	7
Yak	*Bos grunniens*	>2,000	Tibetan Plateau	8
Reindeer	*Rangifer tarandus*	<2,000	Northern Eurasia	9

References: [1]Legge (1996), [2]Clutton-Brock (1979), [3]Clutton-Brock (1989), [4]Clutton-Brock (1992), [5]Olsen (1993), [6]Novoa and Wheeler (1984), [7]Köhler-Rollefson (1996), [8]Olsen (1990), [9]Aikio (1989).

Herding yaks in the Do Tarap Valley of Nepal. © CRAIG LOVELL/CORBIS.

that the early Near East Neolithic (about 8,000 years ago) a "package" of foods that included cereals, pulses, goats, and sheep was particularly effective in providing a diet that contributed to population growth and expansion, and the spread of new subsistence practices.

Today, non-Western herding practices range from nomadic pastoralism in Africa, the Near East, and Asia to agro-pastoralism in the Mediterranean, Near East, Africa, and Asia. Diets are highly variable: some populations consume large amounts of animal products, whereas others trade animal products for cereals and sugar, and still others use animal products only to supplement a largely vegetarian diet. Since the earliest period of domestication, livestock have always contributed foods that are high in energy, balanced in nutrients, and both high and balanced in amino acids and the quality of protein. The cultural selection for a balanced diet became crucial to human health when the predominance of cereal and root crops in intensive agriculture contributed to dramatic population increases.

Several examples of pastoral diets can be drawn from Africa. There is considerable variation in food intake, where animal products constituted between 80 percent (Turkana) and 21 percent (Fulani and Baggara) of dietary intakes as a proportion of caloric intake. Moreover, in all these dairying populations milk is said to be a staple food. Other sources of human dietary variation are: (1) animal productivity, (2) seasonal changes, (3) the mix of animal species, breeds, and herd composition, (4) the patterns of animal use, and (5) trade practices. Animal productivity depends on the breeds of livestock, the forage productivity of the environment, and the patterns of herd management—such as ranching, sedentary, transhumant, or nomadic (Little et al. 1999). Well-fed stock will be larger and have more muscle mass and greater body fat deposits. Seasonal changes in semiarid ecosystems lead to loss of body fat and muscle mass in livestock, reduced milk pro-

duction in lactating females, and lower fat content of milk (Galvin and Little 1999). Different livestock species, breeds, and age/sex groups show variable food productivity; for example, dairy herds will have high proportions of females and high reproductive rates (population increase). Patterns of livestock use vary from largely food production (meat, milk, blood), to use of animals for traction, packing, or riding. In the case of Andean camelids, llamas are principally pack animals, while alpacas provide wool and meat. Trade of animal products for cultivated foods can substantially enrich diets. The concept of "verticality" in highland pastoral peoples entails exchanging of animal products for cultivated food from lowland populations. This is practiced by Indian Bakkarwal sheep and goat herders and by Peruvian Quechua llama and alpaca herders. Pastoralists depending principally on livestock products for food often will have very high protein intakes but low energy (calorie) intakes. Conversely, pastoralists who trade some of their animal products for cereal foods are likely to have adequate protein and higher energy intakes.

Herding of livestock is practiced today on all continents from tropical grasslands to Arctic tundra. More than 75 percent of world meat production in grassland-based ecosystems is from North America, South Amer-

PRIONS AND MAD COW DISEASE

Prion diseases are produced by infectious agents that are proteins. These prion proteins resist inactivation by normal procedures because they do not have a normal nucleic acid genetic makeup. Prion diseases are often referred to as transmissible spongiform encephalopathies (TSE) because of the damage caused to the brain. The two livestock prion diseases that are known today are scrapie in sheep and bovine spongiform encephalopathy (mad cow disease) in cattle. Mad cow disease is transmissible to humans, and another human prion disease, kuru, was probably originally transmitted to humans through a modified form of scrapie via another prion disease called Creutzfeldt-Jacob disease. Mad cow disease is an example of a domestic zoonosis, that is, a disease that is transmitted from a domestic animal to humans. Two other domestic zoonoses that can be transmitted from livestock to humans are brucellosis or ungulent fever (present in goats, sheep, cattle, and pigs) and anthrax (present largely in cattle).

DEFORESTATION AND LIVESTOCK GRAZING

Deforestation dates back in antiquity to the first rise of cities in the Near East about 5,000 years ago. Yet 2,000 years ago, in Roman times, 90 percent of Europe was still forested. Today, there are many causes of deforestation—living space for an increasing human population, agriculture, charcoal production, use of wood for fuel, commercial logging, and others. However, deforestation for herding of livestock, especially cattle, is one of the least productive uses for land. Increasing demands for beef and increasing numbers of fast-food chains internationally have contributed to the growth of cattle ranches in North and South America. It is estimated that more than 10 million hectares (24.7 million acres) of tropical forest are lost each year, and of these losses, about 10 percent or one million hectares are lost to grazing lands.

ica, Western Europe, Japan, Australia, and New Zealand. Residents of these major Western livestock producing nations (especially the United States, Argentina, and Australia) consume substantial amounts of animal protein and fat calories. Such dietary practices, when combined with sedentary physical activities, have contributed to high rates of cardiovascular disease in many of these Western nations. Another liability resulting from the close contact of humans and livestock are "zoonoses," that is, diseases that originate in animal populations but are transmitted to humans. Examples are bacterial cattle diseases such as anthrax and brucellosis that are widespread around the world. Scrapie in sheep and mad cow disease are neurological degenerative diseases produced by pathogens called prions. When contracted by humans, they are almost always fatal.

Livestock productivity as food is low when compared to agricultural productivity, and requires either vast grazing lands or substantial importation and use of feed (Jordan 1993). Increasing demand for animal protein has certainly contributed to deforestation through cutting and burning of forests to maintain grasslands. And livestock manure is one of the major pollutants of bodies of water in the United States (Cincotta and Engelman, 2000). An estimate of the global livestock body mass in 1950 was about 340 million metric tons (3.4×10^{11} kg). This biomass of livestock nearly doubled to an estimated 600 million metric tons (6.0×10^{11} kg) in the year 2000 (Cincotta and Engelman, 2000). In contrast, non-Western livestock production in marginal lands that are unsuitable for agriculture (transhumant or nomadic herding) is an efficient system of animal food production that

is not environmentally degrading. However, this system of keeping herds represents an exceedingly small proportion of worldwide livestock productivity.

See also **Goat**; **Mammals**; **Meat**; **Sheep**.

BIBLIOGRAPHY

Aikio, P. "The Changing Role of the Reindeer in the Life of the Sámi." In *The Walking Larder: Patterns of Domestication, Pastoralism, and Predation*, edited by Juliet Clutton-Brock, pp.169-184. London: Unwin Hyman, 1989.

Cincotta, Richard P., and Robert Engelman. *Nature's Place: Human Population and the Future of Biological Diversity*. Washington, D.C.: Population Action International, 2000.

Clutton-Brock, Juliet. "The Mammalian Remains from the Jericho Tell." *Proceedings of the Prehistoric Society* 45 (1979): 135–158.

Clutton-Brock, Juliet. "Cattle in Ancient North Africa." In *The Walking Larder: Patterns of Domestication, Pastoralism, and Predation*, edited by Juliet Clutton-Brock, pp. 200–206. London: Unwin Hyman, 1989.

Clutton-Brock, Juliet. *Horse Power: A History of the Horse and the Donkey in Human Societies*. Cambridge, Mass.: Harvard University Press, 1992.

Galvin, Kathleen A. "Nutritional Ecology of Pastoralists in Dry Tropical Africa." *American Journal of Human Biology* 4 (1992): 209–221.

Harris, David R. "The Origins and Spread of Agriculture and Pastoralism in Eurasia: An Overview." In *The Origins and Spread of Agriculture and Pastoralism in Eurasia*, edited by David R. Harris, pp. 552–573. Washington, D.C.: Smithsonian Institution Press, 1996.

Köhler-Rollefson, Ilse. "The One-Humped Camel in Asia: Origin, Utilization and Mechanisms of Dispersal." In *The Origins and Spread of Agriculture and Pastoralism in Eurasia*, edited by David R. Harris, pp. 282–294. Washington, D.C.: Smithsonian Institution Press, 1996.

Legge, Tony. "The Beginning of Caprine Domestication in Southwest Asia." In *The Origins and Spread of Agriculture and Pastoralism in Eurasia*, edited by David R. Harris, pp. 238–262. Washington, D.C.: Smithsonian Institution Press, 1996.

Little, Michael A., Rada Dyson-Hudson, and J. Terrence McCabe. "Ecology of South Turkana." In *Turkana Herders of the Dry Savanna: Ecology and Biobehavioral Response of Nomads to an Uncertain Environment*, edited by Michael A. Little and Paul W. Leslie, pp. 43–65. Oxford: Oxford University Press, 1999.

Novoa, C., and Jane C. Wheeler. "Llama and Alpaca." In *Evolution of Domesticated Animals*, edited by Ian Mason, pp. 116–128. London: Longman, 1984.

Olsen, S. J. "Fossil Ancestry of the Yak: Its Cultural Significance and Domestication in Tibet." *Proceedings of the Philadelphia Academy of Natural Sciences* 142 (1990): 73–100.

Olsen, S. J. "Evidence of Early Domestication of the Water Buffalo in China." In *Skeletons in Her Cupboard: Festschrift for Juliet Clutton-Brock*, edited by A. Clason, S. Payne, and H-P. Uerpmann, pp. 151–156. Oxford: Oxbow Monograph 34, 1993.

Sherratt, Andrew. "Plough and Pastoralism: Aspects of the Secondary Products Revolution." In *Pattern of the Past: Studies in Honor of David Clarke*, edited by Ian Hodder, Glynn Isaac, and Norman Hammond, pp. 261–305. Cambridge, U.K.: Cambridge University Press, 1981.

Michael A. Little

HERODOTUS. Known as the "Father of History," Herodotus (c. 484–424 B.C.E.) was born on the southwest coast of Asia Minor in Halicarnassus, which was at that time a Greek-speaking city ruled by Artemisia, queen of Caria, under the overlordship of the Persian Empire. Herodotus traveled widely in that empire and in Greece. Eventually, exiled from Halicarnassus, and having spent some years in Athens (where he gave regular readings of his work), he joined the new colony of Thurii in southern Italy, where he died.

Herodotus is the author of the earliest surviving work of history and one of the masterpieces of Greek literature. It is owing to him that the word "history" came to mean what it does: he introduces his book as "the inquiries (*historiai*) of Herodotus of Halicarnassus." The usual title in English translations is *The Histories*. His purpose was to explore the interaction, peaceful and warlike, between Europe (particularly Greece) and Asia (particularly the Persian Empire). Some of his best stories are of kings, but he takes just as much interest in the adventures of differently privileged people—physicians, athletes, merchants, priests, and cooks.

Book 2 of Herodotus's *Histories* focuses on Egypt (then subject to Persia) and North Africa. Books 1 and 3 include much information on Babylonia, Lydia, and other Persian provinces. Book 4 includes a survey of the peoples of Scythia (the Russian steppes).

One of the means by which Herodotus characterizes peoples is through their food behavior. His descriptions of the Egyptians, Persians, and other highly civilized peoples among whom he had lived are far more nuanced than those of "barbarian" peoples, most of whom he knew only by hearsay. The underlying message to his audience is different in the two cases. He was rightly impressed by the long history of civilization in Egypt and Babylonia and by the efficiency of the Persians: he seems to encourage the reflection that the lifestyle of these peoples is logical in its own terms, sometimes more logical than that of the Greeks, and may have been instrumental in their successes. Barbarian tribes, by contrast, are shown as making stranger and stranger food choices as they recede farther and farther towards the edge of the world, from agriculturalists to pastoral nomads to cannibals.

A structural anthropologist before the term was invented, Herodotus is not one to waste a promising structure. He asserts, and it is likely enough, that if the Persians took a decision while drunk, they made a rule to reconsider it when sober. Few authors between Herodotus and Lévi-Strauss would have dared to add, as Herodotus does, that if the Persians took a decision while sober, they made a rule to reconsider it when they were drunk (*Histories*, book 1, section 133).

Herodotus is preeminent as a historian of the conflict of cultures. Throughout his work, food behavior is often the focus for sensitive and striking portrayals of culture clash. When Persian ambassadors visited the king of Macedonia, their stupidity in demanding the company of women at dinner, in conflict with local custom, was justly rewarded: the "women" who entered the dining hall were young men in disguise, armed with daggers, and the ambassadors were never heard of again (*Histories*, book 5, sections 18–20).

See also **Africa: North Africa**; **Greece, Ancient**.

BIBLIOGRAPHY

Hartog, François. *The Mirror of Herodotus: The Representation of the Other in the Writing of History*. Berkeley: University of California Press, 1988.

Herodotus. *The Histories*. Translated by Aubrey de Selincourt. Baltimore and Harmondsworth: Penguin, 1954.

Thomas, Rosalind. *Herodotus in Context: Ethnography, Science, and the Art of Persuasion*. Cambridge, U.K.: Cambridge University Press, 2000.

Andrew Dalby

HIGH-TECHNOLOGY FARMING. During the twentieth century, farming changed more than at any time since it began. Crop and animal production in the United States went from a labor intensive to a capital-intensive operation. What caused these changes?

Crop Production

The revolutions in crop production started with the mechanical revolution that began with the plow, the planter, and the reaper, and the shift from horsepower to tractor power. The mechanical revolution started after the turn of the twentieth century with the replacement of the horse with modern tractors, combines, and cotton pickers. Since that time, machinery design has kept pace with the increased tractor power.

The second revolution in crop production began with the introduction of hybrid corn in the 1930s. Since then, average U.S. corn yields have increased from 25 bushels in 1930 to more than 140 bushels per acre today. Corn hybrids, along with other practices, greatly enhanced growing conditions so the genetic potential of the hybrid is expressed during most years. The plant breeding revolution has had similar impact on yield of other crops like rice, wheat, and soybean.

The third revolution in crop production came with the increased availability of fertilizers, particularly nitrogen fertilizer. The fertility revolution gained momentum

Hydroponic farming is demonstrated with cultures of lettuce at Disney's Epcot Center, Orlando, Florida. © JOSEPH SOHM; CHROMOSOHM, INC./CORBIS.

when munitions plants built during World War II were converted into factories for making nitrogen fertilizer. The ready availability of nitrogen fertilizer, along with better understanding of fertility through soil testing, improved fertilizer application and crop growth. Other nutrients like limestone, phosphorus, and potassium helped achieve the genetic potential of the crop. Fertilizer applications are still improving through variable rate applications as part of precision agriculture. Virtually every American farmer uses fertilizer to increase crop yields.

The fourth revolution is in the use of herbicides, insecticides, and fungicides to control weeds, insects and diseases that reduce crop growth. This revolution began in the 1950s. Modern weed control practices enable farmers to plant crops much earlier. Now corn and other crops grow during more favorable moisture and temperature conditions without competition from weeds for light, water, and nutrients.

The fifth revolution in crop production is the biotechnology revolution. It did not influence crop production until about 1995. Present benefits include better quality seed such as canola, insect resistant seed such as bollworm resistant cotton and corn borer resistant corn, seed with herbicide resistance such as soybeans, cotton, and corn. Many other changes are imminent. Use of seeds with herbicide, insect and disease resistance impact favorably on the environment because they replace less environmentally friendly chemicals. The revolution in biotechnology promises to increase quantity and quality of the foods we eat.

The sixth revolution in crop production is the new availability of computers, software, and satellites. This technology enables what is often referred to as precision agriculture (PA). Precision agriculture technology enables advances from a data-poor to a data-rich environment. Previously, yields were measured by fields; now it is possible to measure yield continuously. The Internet affects farmers' business practices just as it does other types of business.

Livestock Production

The farm livestock sector has changed dramatically in the past fifty years. Farms have gone from mixed crop and livestock operations to specialized livestock enterprises. Economic factors—the comparative cost of land, labor, capital, and environmental regulations—have brought about these changes. The cost of labor and land per animal fell dramatically while capital investment and environmental costs increased. Farms with small herds and flocks yielded to large specialized farms with large animal concentrations.

Before 1950, farms had many different crops, including hay and pasture, as well as various types of animals: cattle, hogs, and chickens. In the twenty-first century, there are large specialized farms: dairies, beef feedlots, hog operations, and chicken and turkey houses.

Such operations use small land areas or are housed entirely inside buildings. Many animal units can be managed with small amounts of labor. The result is animal farms where all the best health controls are available and applied to keep herds and flocks healthy.

Computer technology has increased the amount and way data is collected. Dairies know the daily and annual milk output for every cow in the herd; hog farmers know the weight gain and feed conversion efficiency of every sire used in their breeding operation; cattle feedlot managers know the weight gain and the carcass quality of every animal; and poultry producers know the feed-to-meat ratio of their broilers and the egg production of each laying hen.

The ease of obtaining data by computer and the ready availability of well designed equipment and buildings has decreased labor and enabled increases in size of animal operations. Increases in the economic efficiency of producing meat and eggs have reduced the cost of products at the grocery store. While many small animal operations exist, most production is from larger operations. Biotechnology's promise for animal agriculture is comparable for crop production and will lead to many new products.

Animals such as cattle, sheep, and goats still graze land too rolling, too dry, or otherwise not suited for crop production. Such cow-calf and sheep operations harvest the biomass that would otherwise be uneconomical to harvest and supply feedlots with animals. Land well suited for crop production—flat, with adequate rainfall or available irrigation—has reduced animal grazing during the past twenty to fifty years.

Summary

Crop and animal agriculture has changed more in the past century than it has since farming began many millennia ago. Modern-day crop production practices, often called precision agriculture (PA), benefited from all earlier revolutions in crop production. Precision agriculture technology developed because of ubiquitous and inexpensive computational power, software (GIS), and satellite location systems (GPS). Precision agriculture equipment enables variable-rate fertilizer, herbicide, plant population, and yield assessment. Wide adoption of PA equipment will occur as it becomes economical. Technology has moved crop production from a high labor and low capital intensive to a low labor and high capital intensive industry. Typical Midwest Corn Belt farms have gone from less than 160 acres to more than 500 acres. The labor necessary to produce a bushel of corn decreased from more than thirty minutes in 1930 to a fraction of a minute in 2002. Availability of high powered well designed equipment; well-adapted hybrids and varieties; precise weed, insect, and disease control; improved plant and animal genetics; and improved animal health have all contributed to the revolution in plant production we have discussed. Biotechnology and computer

revolutions enable us to manage large operations and design crops and animals that will be more nutritious in the future. Consumers are the major beneficiary of these developments since food purchases now requires less than 10 percent of average income.

See also **Agriculture, Origins of; Agriculture since the Industrial Revolution; Agronomy; Crop Improvement; Food Production, History of; Food Supply and the Global Food Market; Food Supply, Food Shortages; Green Revolution; Herbicides; Horticulture; Livestock Production; Pesticides.**

BIBLIOGRAPHY

Conway, Gordon. *The Doubly Green Revolution: Food for All in the Twenty-first Century*. Ithaca, N.Y.: Comstock Publishing, 1997.

Lal, Rattan. "Viewpoint: A Modest Proposal for the Year 2001: We Can Control Greenhouse Gases and Feed the World . . .with Proper Soil Management." *Journal of Soil and Water Conservation* 55, no. 4 (2000): 429–433.

Manning, Richard. *Food's Frontier: The Next Green Revolution*. New York: North Point Press, 2000.

Runge, E. C. A., and Frank M. Hons. "Precision Agriculture: Development of a Hierarchy of Variables Influencing Crop Yields." In *Proceedings of the Fourth International Conference on Precision Agriculture*, edited by P. C. Robert, R. H. Rust, and W. E. Larson, part A, pp. 143–158. St. Paul, Minn., July, 1998.

E. C. A. Runge

HINDU FESTIVALS.

HINDU FESTIVALS. India is a land of bewildering diversity, a unique and colorful mosaic of people of various faiths. There is a festival for every reason and for every season. Many festivals celebrate various harvests, commemorate great historical figures and events, or express devotion to the deities. Every celebration centers around the rituals of prayer and seeking of blessings, and involves the decoration of homes, wearing of new clothes, music, dancing, and feasting. Festivals are an expression of the spirit of celebration. They are observed with enthusiasm and gaiety and are occasions when the greater family and friends come together. They also present women with an opportunity to socialize. Many of these festivals are associated with special foods.

Among the most important Hindu festivals are Makar Sankranti, Shivratri, Holi, Onam, Ganesh Chaturthi, Dussehra, and Diwali. They are celebrated throughout the country in various forms.

Makar Sankranti

Also referred to as Lohri in the North and as Pongal in parts of the South, Makar Sankranti is a celebration of the "ascent" of the sun to the North. The festival marks the coldest day of the winter (14 January), after which the biting cold begins to taper off. In the North, the festival is marked by the lighting of bonfires, into which sweets, rice, and popcorn are thrown as offerings. In the South, prayers are offered to the sun god, because without the sun, there would be no harvest. During the festival, the most commonly eaten foods are sesame seeds and jaggery sweets, rice cooked with milk, jaggery (called *pongal*), and sugar drops. Jaggery is a dark crude sugar made from palms.

Shivratri

Shivrati literally means the night of Shiva. It is celebrated in February and March. Devotees of Shiva abstain from eating food throughout the day and only break their fast the following morning after a night of worship. The offerings of food to the deity comprise "cooling" foods, because Shiva was said to be hot-tempered. These include milk, water, honey, and the leaves of the wood apple tree (*aegle marmelos*), which are said to be cooling. Another food popular at this festival is *thandai*, a drink made with milk, almonds, and hemp seed. Hemp seed is said to have been dear to Shiva and is thus imbibed as part of the festivities.

Holi

Celebrated essentially in northern India, this boisterous festival heralds the onset of spring (in mid-March). It is a festival of color, and people smear each other with colored powder and spray each other with colored water. Singing and dancing add to the gaiety of the occasion. It is variously associated with Krishna (as is evident in the particularly extensive celebrations at Vrindavan and Mathura, the two places associated with Krishna) and Shiva. Legend has it that the celebration of Holi is actually a recreation of the marriage procession of Shiva. The delicacies eaten during this festival include *malpua* (fresh bread soaked in a sugar syrup), *puranpoli* (unleavened wheat bread stuffed with lentils and jaggery and baked on a griddle), and *gujjiyas* (flour patties stuffed with milk solids, sugar, almonds, and raisins and then deep-fried).

Onam

Onam, the harvest festival, is traditionally celebrated in Kerala (in August–September). The harvest has been reaped and the granaries are full; therefore it is time to rejoice.

Ganesh Chaturthi

Celebrated essentially in Maharashtra, this festival celebrates the birthday of Ganesha, the elephant-headed god who is the son of Shiva and Parvati. Ganesha is the remover of all obstacles and difficulties; he is the one who will grant success in all human endeavors. Therefore, no new venture is started without first praying to Ganesha. His image is installed in individual homes for a period of hours or days leading up to the festival, at which point those same images are displayed in a procession with much singing and dancing, and then immersed in running water. Ganesha's favorite food *modak* (a wheat flour pastry stuffed with coconut and jaggery and baked on a

Women worshipping the sun god during the Chhat Puja Festival held on the banks of the Hooghly River in Calcutta. Devotees arrive at sunset and spend the night in prayer. The women shown here are sending offerings into the river. © REUTERS NEW MEDIA INC./CORBIS.

griddle) is offered to the deity and served throughout the festival's duration.

Dussehra

Celebrated in October, Dussehra commemorates the victory of good over evil, and culminates in the burning in effigy of Ravana and the triumph of Rama. It is celebrated in various ways throughout the country, often with much music and dancing, and lasts for ten days. During this time, there are public performances of the Ramlila (the story of the Hindu epic, the Ramayana). On the day of Dussehra, new accounts are opened, and new ventures started.

Diwali

Celebrated twenty-one days after Dussehra, this festival commemorates Rama's return to his hometown, Ayodhya, after having been in exile for fourteen years. While Dussehra celebrates Rama's victory over Ravana, Diwali celebrates his return. Thousands of oil lamps are lit to welcome him home, making it a night of enchantment. Homes are decorated, and sweets are exchanged between family and friends. Fireworks and festivities are part of the celebrations. On this day, the goddess of wealth, Lakshmi, is worshipped.

See also **Fasting and Abstinence: Hinduism and Buddhism; Feasts, Festivals, and Fasts; Festivals of Food; Hinduism; India; Religion and Food; Weddings.**

BIBLIOGRAPHY

Freed, Stanley A., and Ruth S. Freed. *Hindu Festivals in a North Indian Village.* Anthropological Papers of the American Museum of Natural History. New York: American Museum of Natural History, 1998.

Gupta, Shakti M. *Festivals, Fairs, and Fasts of India.* New Delhi: Clarion Books, 1991.

Ministry of Information and Broadcasting. *Festivals of India*. New Delhi: Ministry of Information and Broadcasting, Publications Division, 1977. Originally published 1956.

Welbon, Guy R., and Glenn E. Yocum, eds. *Religious Festivals in South India and Sri Lanka*. New Delhi: Manohar, 1982

Thangam Philip

HINDUISM. Hinduism is a religion, a philosophy, and a way of life. It guides people along paths that will ultimately lead to the individual soul (Atman) becoming one with the Universal Consciousness.

The religion recognizes that everyone is different and has a unique intellectual and spiritual outlook. Therefore, it allows people to develop and grow at their own pace by making different spiritual paths available to them. It allows various schools of thought under its broad principles. It also allows for freedom of worship so that individuals may be guided by their own spiritual experiences. This freedom of worship permits individuals to worship in any place, be it a church, mosque, or *gurudwara*. The tolerance shown by this religion to other faiths is unmatched. Hinduism has never been imposed on anyone, whether on a subjugated people through wars, or by offering spiritual or economic benefits to the poor.

The strength of Hinduism lies in its adaptability to the infinite diversity of human nature. It has a highly spiritual and abstract side suited to the philosopher, a practical and concrete side suited to the worldly individual, an aesthetic and ceremonial side suited to the person of poetic feeling and imagination, and a quiescent and contemplative side suited to the lover of peace and seclusion.

Hinduism is also unique in that it has adapted itself to include numerous ideals and precepts of other religions, such as those of Jainism and Buddhism. For instance, among many communities, offerings of rice and ghee (or clarified butter) took the place of animal sacrifice—a compromise with Vedic ritualism. Many of the early Aryans had been meat eaters, but under the influence of Buddhist and Jain ideas, numerous groups of Brahmins and non-Brahmins became vegetarian.

Another feature unique to Hinduism is its belief that liberation or deliverance (*moksha*) can be achieved in this life itself: one does not have to wait for a heaven after death.

Hindu Beliefs as Reflected in Food

Rebirth or reincarnation. The Hindus believe that one must go through several births and rebirths before attaining liberation. The hardships of the current world are a result of the actions of a previous life that have to be atoned for in the present life.

Karma. The law of karma (or action) also supports the above theory. It suggests that every action has a similar or related reaction. Although it is not possible to change one's past life, it is possible for one to shape the future and to pave the way for a better life in rebirth through the actions of the present.

Dharma. Dharma refers to duties that have to be performed at different stages of one's life. These must be completed without a thought of possible rewards or benefits and should also be accomplished to the best of one's ability. They are responsible for the prevailing social order in the world. There are four stages of Dharma:

- Student or Brahmachari—This first phase involves living and studying with a guru.
- Householder or Grihastha—This next phase starts with marriage.
- Retirees or Vanaprastha—The third phase occurs when the duties of child rearing and work are over.
- Sanyasi—This is the final phase when all worldly desires are renounced and the individual spends all of his or her time in meditation.

Hindu Scriptures

Hinduism is based on the Eternal Truth as it has been explicitly defined in the scriptures:

1. The Srutis come from the Vedas, of divine origin and unchangeable. They encapsulate the greatest truths.

2. The Smritis, referred to as the Dharma Shashtras, are of human composition. They govern the daily conduct of people, including the actions of the individual, the community, and the nation, and may change over time.

3. The epics are those stories or fables in which the philosophy of the Vedas is told. The most important epics are the Ramayana and the Mahabharata.

4. The Puranas are the Hindu scriptures that convey the truths of the Vedas and the Dharma Shashtras in the form of tales. These stories form the basis of religious education for the common man.

5. The Agamas record the doctrine for the worship of different deities, including Shiva, Vishnu, and Shakti.

6. The Darshanas encompass the six schools of Hindu philosophy; they guide scholars.

Hindu Gods and Goddesses

Hinduism has many gods and goddesses, some of whom were worshipped by early peoples who later came into contact with this faith. The aim of Hinduism is not the worship of any one of these deities, but rather the means with which the individual soul or Atman will become one with the Brahman, or the Universal Soul. Among the most commonly worshipped gods are:

- Nirguna Brahman—The Universal Soul who transcends time and space and is formless.

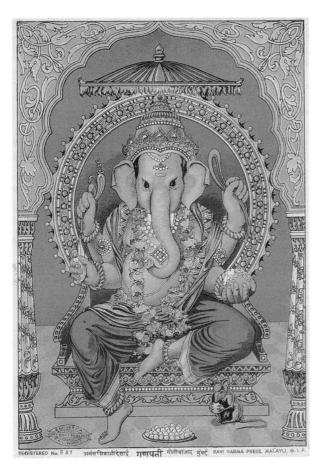

Popular print of Ganesa, the Hindu god of wisdom and prudence. He is usually depicted as a man with an elephant's head. The print dates from circa 1930. ROUGHWOOD COLLECTION.

- Saguna Brahman—The concept of Ichwara, the Great God, with a form upon which the individual mind may fixate during prayer and meditation.

- The Trinity—As personified by the three attributes of Ichwara, including their feminine dimensions: creation (Brahman), preservation (Vishnu), and destruction (Shiva).

Attaining *Moksha*

There are essentially three paths to attain oneness with the Universal Consciousness:

1. Bhakti yoga (the path of devotion)—The vast majority of people choose this path of single-minded devotion to a favorite god.

2. Karma yoga (the path of action)—Those who choose this path believe in the dictum "work is worship." No job is too menial or too low for this devotée, as all work is a means of realizing God.

3. Jnana yoga (the path of knowledge)—This is perhaps the most difficult of the three paths and therefore

chosen by very few, usually scholars. Knowledge of the Vedas, Upanishads, and Bhagavad Gita is essential.

See also **Buddhism**; **Fasting and Abstinence: Hinduism and Buddhism**; **Festivals of Food**; **Hindu Festivals**; **India**; **Religion and Food**; **Weddings**.

BIBLIOGRAPHY

Khare, R. S., ed. *The Eternal Food: Gastronomic Ideas and Experiences of Hindus and Buddhists.* SUNY Series in Hinduism. Albany: State University of New York Press, 1992.

Morgan, Kenneth William. *Asian Religions: An Introduction to the Study of Hinduism, Buddhism, Islam, Confucianism, and Taoism.* New York: Macmillan, 1964.

Ross, Nancy Wilson. *Hinduism, Buddhism, Zen: An Introduction to Their Meaning and Their Arts.* London: Faber & Faber, 1968.

Toomey, Paul M. *Food from the Mouth of Krishna: Feasts and Festivities in a North Indian Pilgrimage Centre.* Delhi, India: Hindustan, 1994.

Thangam Philip

HIPPOCRATES. Hippocrates (460–377 B.C.E.), a disciple of Democritus, was a Greek physician who is now considered the father of Western medicine. Born on the Greek island of Cos, he was associated with the cult of Asclepius, the Greek god of healing whose staff entwined with a serpent became the symbol of medicine. In the seventh century B.C.E, Asclepius, aided by his two daughters, Hygeia and Panacea, superseded Apollo as the greatest of the healing gods, and temples in his name were built to heal the sick. According to legend, the centaur Chiron taught Asclepius pharmaceutical knowledge about drug plants.

Hippocrates, considered the originator of a Greek school of healing, was the first to clearly expound the concept that diseases had natural rather than supernatural causes. Various works attributed to him and to his school are contained in the Hippocratic Collection, which includes The Hippocratic Oath, Aphorisms, and various medical works. He was an expert in diagnosis, predicting the course of disease. Based on the color and pallor of the ill person, disease was considered to be an imbalance of the four "humors"—blood, phlegm, yellow bile, and black bile—a concept that was to affect medicine for the next two thousand years. This concept persists in the following terms that describe distinctive temperaments: sanguine (warm and ardent), phlegmatic (sluggish, apathetic), and bilious (ill humored). Healing emphasis was placed on purges, attempts to purify the body from the illness produced by excesses or imbalance of humors. Hippocrates particularly noted the influence of food and diet on health, recommending moderation.

In the work *On Ancient Medicine*, Hippocrates notes differences in individual responses to food. He comments on the fact that some can eat cheese to satiety while others do not bear it well, a diagnosis of what we would now call lactose intolerance. The use of drugs was also an area of study: between two hundred and four hundred herbs were mentioned by the school of Hippocrates.

See also **Greece, Ancient; Health and Disease; Medicine; Pythagoras.**

BIBLIOGRAPHY

Hippocrates. *Hippocratic Collection*, in eight volumes. Loeb Classical Library. Cambridge, Mass.: Harvard University Press, 1923–1988.

Hippocrates. *Ancient Medicine. Airs, Waters, Places. Epidemics 1 & 3. The Oath. Precepts. Nutriment.* Vol. I in the eight-volume *Hippocratic Collection.* Loeb Classical Library. Cambridge, Mass.: Harvard University Press, 1923.

Jouanna, Jacques. *Hippocrates.* Translated by M. B. DeBevoise. Baltimore, Md.: Johns Hopkins University Press, 1999. Original edition: *Hippocrate.* Paris: Fayard, 1992.

Jules Janick

HOLIDAYS.

Holidays are "holy days," when people interrupt the profane, mundane round of production and celebrate with the preparation and eating of special foods and meals. The two basic forms of holidays are a festival (from Latin *festum* for 'feast'), when people break their normal weekly, monthly, or annual routine to celebrate together, and a vacation (in the sense of leaving their homes and workplaces empty), when an often longer disruption may be accompanied by dislocation, as people change residences or travel.

Festivals

Traditionally, festivals have enjoyed an explicitly religious interpretation, so that the Sabbath of Jews, Christians, and Muslims is a God-ordained day of rest. Many holidays have been associated with seasonal change, and the New Year is celebrated in many calendars, notably the Chinese, with brilliant feasts. Other festivals have been national, ordered by governments to honor founding events and heroes, such as Bastille Day (14 July) in France. Further holidays might commemorate children, an emperor's birthday, the achievements of war veterans or the working class. Australians take legislated days off for horse races.

Festival foods often feature in cookery books, such as the multivolume *Foods and the World* series of Time-Life (1968–1971). Conversely, festival foods are often described in surveys of holidays around the world, such as *Holidays and Festivals* (1999). Traditionally, women have worked together for several days on elaborate preparations, such as finely decorated confectionery and pastries, which have been keenly anticipated each year and have long remained poignant reminders of local, ethnic, and religious affiliations.

Eating and drinking might become especially abundant at harvest festivals and the breaking of a fast, as when Carnival concludes the Christian Lent and at the end of Ramadan, the ninth month of the Muslim year. Particular foods might be featured, such as the lamb and unleavened bread of the Jewish Passover. The Hindu festival of lights, Divali, celebrates the longest night of the year (which falls in October or November in the Western calendar) with gifts of sweets, which vary immensely across the subcontinent. The Scottish *haggis*, which is a boiled sheep's stomach stuffed with mutton offal and oats, is a triumph of symbolic grandeur if not culinary, typical of midwinter and so featuring at *hogmanay* (New Year's Eve) and again on Burns Night (25 January), which commemorates the birthday of poet Robert Burns, who praised the *haggis* as the "great chieftain o' the puddin'-race."

Thanksgiving (the last Thursday in November) is a national American feast on which families dine on turkey and traditional accompaniments. The warmer weather of Independence Day (4 July) encourages parades and more casual, outdoor eating, especially barbecued chicken and perhaps an apple pie or red, white, and blue cake. Particular foods tend not to be associated with newer holidays, and yet the community mindedness of Martin Luther King's Day (the third Monday in January) might be reflected in sharing minority cuisines and decorating paper bags for food deliveries to the needy.

Vacations

Monarchs frequently took their court on an extended voyage through the countryside from palace to palace. Other leisured classes have long avoided either extreme of temperature by "summering" or "wintering" at an alternate house or resort. With the expansion of rail and road networks and the democratization of the annual break, more people took vacations. They could grow up knowing life on the farm from childhood holidays spent with cousins, could visit distant relatives when several national holidays coincide (such as Christmas–New Year's and the Japanese "Golden Week"), and could experience the products of hotel, restaurant, and other kitchens, sometimes in foreign countries, where everything might be closed for an unexpected holiday of pageantry and feasting.

The Effect of Globalization on Holidays

Whether in premodern China, ancient Rome, medieval Europe, or modern industrial societies, the proportion of holidays has remained remarkably constant—approximately one day in three. However, with globalization, and more continuous production and consumption, fewer collective breaks are observed. The seasonal emphasis is giving way to consumer weekends, a few national days, plus individual annual leave. Religious feasts are losing out to sport and entertainment, gift-giving breaks such as Christmas are commercially exploited, and vacations are serviced by organized leisure and tourism industries.

The innocent "holiday mood," which has been relished not just by the holidaymakers but novelists and screenwriters, is in danger of being lost. Holidays provide scenic locations, laid-back atmospheres, and breaks in everyday routines for the unexpected to happen. A gem of the French cinema, Jean Renoir's *Une partie de campagne* (often translated as A Day in the Country, 1936/46), centers around a Parisian family picnic at a country inn, during which two men invite the mother and betrothed daughter to go boating. In *Le Rayon vert* (The Green Ray or Summer, 1986), director Eric Rohmer shifts his listless heroine to various French holiday destinations, and she memorably justifies her vegetarianism over an outdoor lunch. Hollywood has often taken teenagers on summer holidays for lessons in growing up, their chosen meal typically milkshakes and hamburgers.

The association between holidays and foods may be lessening, yet it persists in many ways, and understanding the genesis of holidays assists in continuing to reinvent them.

Explaining Holidays

The Russian author Mikhail Bakhtin in *Rabelais and His World* (1968) analyzed the carnivalesque, the inversions when aristocrats and servants change places, when scatological humor temporarily undermines the dominant ideology, and when eating reappears as a "grotesque" reality. More conventionally, such boisterous breaks as Mardi Gras are often said to "release" pent-up energy that might otherwise be destructive.

Other social scientists have viewed holy days as "sacred" moments that give shape to otherwise "profane" time. Developing this approach from Émile Durkheim, anthropologist Edmund Leach asks in "Two Essays concerning the Symbolic Representation of Time" (1961) why people dress up in "false noses" or, more precisely, adopt three types of behavior: increased formality (such as an English Sunday), masquerade (New Year's Eve revelry), and role reversal (Mardi Gras). He then argues that such activities generate and reinforce sacred time (so that "transgressive" and "sacred" accounts are not so different). Such holidays contribute to social cohesion, not only reinforcing a common interpretation of the world, but also facilitating a rhythmic pattern of activities and so the "ordering of time."

Food is then usually regarded as "symbolic" of sacred time. Yet the inverse often makes better sense because holidays are grounded in cycles of food production. The interruption in "profane" routine by joy, revelry, or contemplation generates the holy. A harvest festival is an obvious case, when an intense burst of consumption follows a busy period of gathering and preserving, and when people are no doubt so profoundly thankful that they bring these crops before the gods.

Likewise, lamb might "represent" Easter, but while offering first fruits might come to "symbolize" spring,

before that, the rejoicing at their arrival generates the concept of spring. The word "Easter" comes from the old English *easter* or *eastre*, a festival of spring, and its lambs, eggs, and rabbits are more than mere "symbols" of spring; they are spring. The Jewish festival of Passover derives from the Hebrew's nomadic origins, when the new growth would have supported extended gatherings, celebrated by sacrificing some of the newly increased flock. Since Jesus had been put to death around the time of Passover, Christians adopted the symbolism of Jesus as a sacrificial lamb.

The trappings of Christmas belong to the phalanx of "pagan" midwinter festivals; the merrymaking and exchange of presents join the ancient Roman festival of Saturnalia and other cheering anticipations of cornucopia. With no certain tradition as to the date of Jesus' birth, Emperor Constantine chose the winter solstice, possibly to "compete" with the other festival, as often stated, but more likely to place Jesus' birthday appropriately at the beginning of the year.

Not only the seasonal festivals but also the weekly are based on the food supply. In different cultures, weeks have comprised three, four, five, six, seven, ten, or other number of days. With few exceptions, these have been organized around the market cycle. A strict periodicity must be maintained for both the circuit of sellers and the attendance of buyers. The Christian world took the seven-day week from the Jews, who had adopted it from the Babylonians.

Marking out the market week and seasonal year, festivals dramatize the cycles of food production and consumption upon which our survival depends. The feasts become time-keeping devices, proto-calendars. For, in another inversion of a common assumption, holy days were not the products of formal calendars, but their antecedents. Festivals originally had ecological dates, because they related closely to winter scarcity, bud-burst, arrival of flocks of birds or schools of fish, the weakening of the monsoon, and other natural cues. With precise astronomical observations, central authorities then created rational calendars and so, eventually, more "exact" festivals.

Upholding Holidays

Commercialism has boosted Christmas, Mother's Day, Father's Day, and others. Among ancient holidays that have gained new life, Valentine's Day encourages couples to dine out, and Japanese women to give chocolates. The food and drink industries have introduced a range of festivals, not the least the return of weekend farmers' markets, and annual food and wine fairs replete with tastings and grand banquets.

The mobility of global populations might have made many holidays anachronistic in that traditional meals are out of season; for example, Christmas turkey and plum pudding are absurd in the middle of the hottest days, as happens in the Southern Hemisphere. Yet people adapt, and many Australians enjoy the heavy fare during their winter, on 25 June or 25 July (for some reason, seven months out seems to be preferred). People invent their own rituals to surround a global television event, such as the annual telecast of the Academy Awards.

The individualization of holidays encourages new approaches. The registration of precise dates of birth has helped make this an important anniversary; many people ask for their birthday off from work, and even attach an appropriately seasonal food or meal. Married couples, probably having conducted much of their courtship over dinner, having founded their new household at a wedding breakfast, and then having gone on a honeymoon, celebrate wedding anniversaries at a romantic dinner at a restaurant or weekend retreat. Perhaps they celebrate other milestones, such as the departure of children from the "nest." People take other rites of passage seriously, such as reaching adulthood at the age of eighteen or twenty-one.

Influential American and British cookery writers discovered the joys of traditional European cuisines on sojourns after World War II. Many others now make an annual gastronomic tour, steered by the "stars" in restaurant guidebooks. Food and wine-producing areas have become tourist attractions. Enthusiasts take cooking lessons in Tuscan villas.

More modestly, a holiday is a chance to catch up with household chores, for a city worker to spend time in the kitchen, or for everyone to go on a picnic. People shift to a beach or mountain house to get away from the clamor of newspapers, television, and junk mail, and go fishing or hunting. Stressed workers still need time to read, to chat over coffee, to walk along the beach, to linger over meals, to philosophize into the night. Even more fundamentally, human beings need to keep in touch with the seasons. Given the range of the world's climates, clinging to the best local products is a force for difference.

See also **Buddhism; Christianity; Christmas; Day of the Dead; Easter; Epiphany; Fasting and Abstinence; Feasts, Festivals, and Fasts; Hindu Festivals; Hinduism; Islam; Judaism; Passover; Shrove Tuesday; Thanksgiving; Wedding Cake; Weddings.**

BIBLIOGRAPHY

Bakhtin, Mikhail. *Rabelais and His World*. Translated by Hélène Iswolsky. Bloomington: University of Indiana Press, 1984.

Editors of Time-Life Books. *Foods of the World*. 27 volumes. New York: Time-Life Books, 1968–1971.

Holidays and Festivals. New York: Macmillan Library Reference, 1999.

Leach, Edmund. "Two Essays Concerning the Symbolic Representation of Time: (1) Cronus and Chronos (2) Time and False Noses." In *Rethinking Anthropology*, pp. 124–136. London: Athlone Press, University of London Press, 1961.

Tun, Li-ch'ên. *Annual Customs and Festivals in Peking*. Translated by Derk Bodde. Hong Kong: Hong Kong University Press, 1965.

Zerubavel, Eviatar. *Hidden Rhythms: Schedules and Calendars in Social Life*. Chicago: University of Chicago Press, 1981.

Michael Symons

HOLLAND. *See* **Low Countries.**

HOME ECONOMICS. From its beginnings, the profession of home economics, also called family and consumer sciences, closely paralleled the general development of education for women. Home economics developed out of political, economic, and technical conditions in the last half of the nineteenth century. Before then, formal training for women was virtually nonexistent. What did exist was the realization that obligations of the home extended beyond its walls. The discipline was begun by men and women, including Ellen H. Richards, Wilbur O. Atwater, Edward L. Youmans, and Isabel Bevier, who aimed to develop a profession that understood the obligations of and opportunities for women. They wanted to use scientific principles and processes to enhance management of households, and they wanted to make home and family effective parts of the world's social fabric.

Family and consumer sciences or home economics, as taught and practiced in the United States and abroad, has a broad and comprehensive focus. A plethora of names, including domestic science, living science, home science, home science education, human ecology, human sciences, practical life studies, household technology, science of living, family and household education, family and nutritional studies, and nutrition and consumer studies, also have been used to describe the discipline, whose purpose is to meet specific and general needs of individuals and families. Although the names were numerous, a single widely accepted definition was adopted at the 1902 Lake Placid Conference on Home Economics, one of ten such conferences held annually from 1899 to 1908 devoted to the study of laws, conditions, principles, and ideas concerned with a person's immediate physical environment, his or her nature as a social being, and the interrelationships therein.

Founding Home Economics

Publications, such as Catharine Beecher's *A Treatise on Domestic Economy* (1841), and legislation, including the Morrill Act (1862), probably provided the impetus for the Lake Placid conferences. The Morrill Act devoted federal lands to support the development of colleges of agriculture and mechanical arts. This helped shape the field of home economics because women subsequently were admitted to these land-grant colleges, as they were called, and to some private institutions, such as Oberlin College in Ohio.

The first home economics class in an institution of higher learning was offered at Iowa State College in 1871 and was called "domestic economy." Kansas Agricultural College began its domestic economy curriculum two years later, and Illinois Industrial University followed a year after that. These and the others that followed helped women apply theories in arts and sciences to everyday living. As they studied domestic economy along with some classical curricula and as theirs became an academic discipline, educational opportunities for women expanded.

Concurrently the interest in adult education courses expanded. Prior to the last quarter of the nineteenth century, women's work was mostly needlecraft, sewing, and cooking; the work was done at home; and women received little formal educational training for these tasks. Some classes in cookery existed, such as those at the Boston Cooking School begun by Maria Parloa, and Mothers Clubs and Reading Circles developed. In time, all of these organizations had major impacts on communities. Mothers Clubs and Reading Circles became Parent Teacher Associations, and the Society of the Study of Child Nature became the Child Study Association.

Ellen Richards influenced the field of home economics and all of women's work. Considered the founder of the profession of home economics, she became in 1873 the first woman to earn a bachelor of science degree at the Massachusetts Institute of Technology (after earning an A.B. from Vassar in 1870). She published *The Chemistry of Cooking and Cleaning* and a manual for housekeepers, both in 1881. Some years later she worked on an exhibit in Chicago for the World's Columbian Exhibition (1890) based on her nutrition experiments. This exhibit was influential in establishing the first school lunch program in 1894.

Academic and adult education courses as well as increased immigration, industrialization, and urbanization added impetus for the development of this discipline, initiated at the first Lake Placid Conference on Home Economics in 1899. Three years later the conference founded a national organization, the American Association of Home Economics (AHEA), which actually began its work in 1909. The goals of AHEA were to improve living conditions in homes, institutional households, and communities. Conference participants selected subject matter that stressed family applications and developed academic requirements in cultural, technical, and vocational venues. These originally included the areas of food, clothing, shelter, and institutional management and shortly thereafter expanded to include child development, personal and family relationships, consumer education, home management, and housing.

Participants at the Lake Placid conferences designed the discipline's educational requirements in natural and social sciences and the arts and humanities for elementary and secondary schools and institutions of higher education. They also developed ways to access funding to implement these goals, including advocating passage of the Smith-Lever Act of 1914 and the Smith-Hughes Act of 1917. These two acts established, respectively, the Cooperative Extension Bureau and education in home economics at precollege and college levels. These efforts developed ties between institutions of higher education and teacher preparation.

World War I created demands for professionals trained in institutional management and dietetics, natural situations for home economists. After the war, additional demands arose in public health, community feeding, school lunch supervision, consumer protection, and related areas. These demands expanded the discipline's activities well beyond cooking and sewing. During the depression of the 1930s, home economists were further called upon for advice in managing family needs. These newer roles required that institutions of higher education develop and emphasize research and divide their educational offerings into narrower specialties.

These circumstances, along with a 1930 AHEA report, changed training for professionals. The training kept physiological, psychological, economic, social, and political perspectives; increased emphasis on sociology, economics, and philosophy; and decreased required courses in education, science, and home economics. This shifted the emphasis from home-related skills to those needed in away-from-home situations. Additional changes during and after World War II expanded preparation and broadened professionals' areas of service.

The AHEA suggested ways to strengthen family life, expanding offerings and reducing skills courses for the five largest areas of the profession, that is, home economics education; child development and family relations; textiles, clothing, and fashion merchandising; general home economics; and food, nutrition, and dietetics. Building on the basic disciplines, the AHEA promoted more research relating to nutrition, child development, consumer economics, and home management to increase the discipline's impact on families, homes, consumers, legislation, and technology, and on all types of households and related institutions.

Late Twentieth-Century Developments

No other discipline integrates so many applied and theoretical areas of education or reaches out as far as home economics. Many conferences, committees, and research efforts have kept the AHEA and its constituents current. In the 1960s efforts were expended toward accreditation of all undergraduate programs, achieved in 1967. The eleventh Lake Placid Conference met in 1973 to revitalize values and to develop future directions to broaden home and family life into an ecosystem conceptualization, emphasizing interdependence of people in rapidly changing environments. In the 1980s the organization focused on certification of professionals, which began in 1986.

Reaching out to meet the demands on professionals, AHEA was instrumental in organizing a professional summit to build consensus among five related organizations, including the AHEA, the home economics division of the American Vocational Association, the Association of Administrators of Home Economics, the National Association of Extension Home Economists, and the National Council of Administrators of Home Economics. At a conference in Scottsdale, Arizona, in 1993 these organizations opted to change the discipline's name from home economics to family and consumer sciences (FCS), for which the memberships favorably voted the following year. In 1997 national standards for middle and high schools were developed and adopted for FCS education, focusing on content, process, and competencies.

Positioning itself for the twenty-first century, the profession developed additional ways to empower individuals and families to take charge of their lives, to maximize their potential, and to function independently and interdependently. To further these means of empowerment, FCS and related professionals work together to create opportunities and options for their diverse constituencies, and they have made strides to increase minority membership and leadership. In addition, they have set standards for integration and application of knowledge among all peoples and constituencies. FCS professionals, with the help of others who share the same goals, have moved women's work toward the center of higher education. They have impacted society and continue to work so all professionals can see efforts in the home and the community increased and gender marginalization reduced.

The national organization, renamed the American Association of Family and Consumer Sciences (AAFCS; renaming effective 1994), promotes improvements in individual and family life. Its efforts effect changes in areas such as food, nutrition, textiles, clothing, family relationships, child development, family resource management, design, housing, and consumer studies. Using its unique, integrated approach, it strengthens and empowers individuals, families, and communities, enhancing the quality of life. The profession strives for positive change in the multifaceted environments and ecosystems in which people live, work, and otherwise partake of life.

See also **Extension Services; Nutritionists; Professionalization; School Meals; Women and Food.**

BIBLIOGRAPHY

American Association of Family and Consumer Sciences. *Themes in Family and Consumer Sciences: A Book of Readings.* Volume 2. Alexandria, Va.: American Association of Family and Consumer Sciences, 2001, p. 563.

American Home Economics Association. *The Context for Professional in Human, Family and Consumer Sciences.* Volume 1. Washington, D.C.: American Home Economics Association, 1996.

American Home Economics Association. *Scottsdale Meeting: Positioning the Profession for the 21st Century.* Washington, D.C.: American Home Economics Association, 1993.

Brown, Marjorie, and, Beatrice Paolucci. *Home Economics: A Definition.* Washington, D.C.: American Home Economics Association, 1993.

Hunt, Caroline L. *The Life of Ellen Richards.* 8th ed. Washington, D.C.: American Home Economics Association, 1980.

Pundt, Helen. *AHEA: A History of Excellence.* Washington, D.C.: American Home Economics Association, 1980.

Stage, Sarah, and Virginia B. Vincenti. *Rethinking Home Economics: Women and the History of a Profession.* Alexandria, Va.: American Association of Family and Consumer Sciences, 2000.

Jacqueline M. Newman

HOMELESSNESS. No nation is without its homeless. In the United States alone, between 280,000 and 600,000 men, women, and children are homeless each night, according to differing estimates. They are without permanent lodging because of poverty, lack of affordable housing, low wages, substance abuse, mental illness, or domestic violence. In many other countries, however, civil unrest, war, and famines bring about homelessness. At the beginning of the twenty-first century, there were more than eleven million homeless worldwide.

Paramount among the problems facing the homeless are poor nutrition and hunger. They can be life-threatening, especially among refugees. Protein-energy malnutrition is a major contributory cause of death among newly displaced refugees. International relief organizations and the United Nations set up refugee camps and make the distribution of nutritionally adequate food rations a high priority. The homeless in the United States often do not experience such extreme food deprivations. However, many are often chronically undernourished. Compared to other groups at risk for hunger, the homeless are at greatest risk, being ten times more likely to go without food for a day compared to the poor. Few are able to obtain three meals a day, and many go at least one day a month without any food. Scant research indicates that many have caloric intakes far below recommended levels and may have inadequate intakes of calcium, folacin, iron, magnesium, or zinc. Their low-calorie diets, which tend to be high in fat, cholesterol, and sodium and inadequate in essential nutrients, may further compromise the already poor health status of the homeless.

While many rely on homeless shelters, especially in winter months, a large number find refuge in cars, abandoned buildings, on grates, in parks, or, other outdoor places. Most have been without a fixed and regular night-time residence for more than one year. Lacking a stable home environment and cooking and storage facilities exacerbates their inability to obtain an adequate, varied, and healthy diet. While it is not uncommon to see a home-less person panhandling or scavenging for food through trash cans, most depend on soup kitchens and shelters for the major portion of their daily nourishment. Soup kitchens and shelters typically serve one meal a day on-site, although some shelters permit their residents to pre-pare and cook their own meals. Those who are substance abusers or have mental health problems are more likely to resort to obtaining food from trash cans or begging, compared to those without these health conditions.

Participation in the Food Stamp Program, the gov-ernment's largest antihunger program, is unusually low among the homeless. While homeless advocates specu-late that most of the homeless are eligible, they argue that barriers such as documentation of identity or ad-ministrative burdens prevent many from participating. The difficulty of making effective use of food stamp ben-efits without adequate cooking and storage facilities is also a barrier. While the Food Stamp Program does per-mit states to contract with restaurants to serve meals at concessional prices to the homeless, such authorizations are uncommon among states.

See also **Body Composition; Caloric Intake; Class, Social; Food Banks; Food Pantries; Food Politics: United States; Food Stamps; Food Supply, Food Shortages; Hunger, Physiology of; Poverty; Soup Kitchens.**

BIBLIOGRAPHY

Burt, M. R., et al.. *Homelessness: Programs and the People They Serve.* Washington, D.C.: U.S. Department of Housing and Urban Development, Office of Policy Development and Research, 1999.

Lindsey, A. T. *Food and Nutrition Resource Guide for Homeless Shelters, Soup Kitchens and Food Banks.* Washington, D.C.: United States Department of Agriculture, 1998.

Patricia McGrath Morris

HORS D'OEUVRES. *See* **Dinner; Meal.**

HORSE.
For the last five thousand years, the horse has of been of greater human interest for its strength than as a source of meat. The domestication of the horse is considered to have taken place in the present-day Ukraine in the fourth millennium B.C.E., and the practice spread from there. Prior to that, wild horses had been caught for food and seem to have been eaten by most peoples that adopted them during the first three thousand years of their domestication, though other, work-oriented kinds of use were more important.

The people of ancient Greece and Rome despised horse eating, although it was still practiced among the Germanic peoples and Asian nomads at that time. The Asian nomads also made a common use of mare's milk and "koumiss"; in fact, fermented mare's milk has been

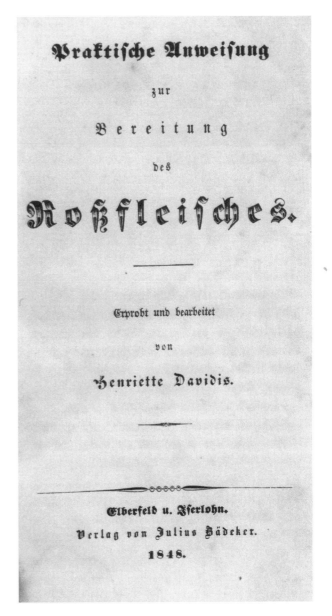

Title page of the first cookbook to deal with the preparation and cooking of horse meat. It was written by Henriette Da-vidis, one of the most popular cookbook authors of nineteenth-century Germany. The book was issued during a period of widespread famine and political upheaval. COURTESY OF HANS WEISS. ROUGHWOOD COLLECTION.

an important foodstuff in the steppes of Central Asia and is still a common drink there, and is also known in Scan-dinavia and the former Soviet Republics. Boeuf tartar is believed to originate from Asian Nomads, who preferred horsemeat to beef and therefore many think that this dish was originally made from horsemeat. Horsemeat is still an important food in Mongolia and Japan. The Japanese like to use it in their famous teriyaki. Horses are bred for food in many places in Asia, as in Mongolia, Central Asia, and Japan.

The dietary restrictions of Jews, Muslims, and most Hindus do not allow horsemeat in the diet. The practice of sacrificing horses and in some cases consuming their meat has been widespread in Europe and South Asia from the beginning of their domestication. It was part of pagan Germanic ceremonies and its importance in pagan religion is probably the reason why it was despised by Christians. Horsemeat is the only foodstuff that Christianity has abolished from the diet for religious reasons. Canon law forbade the eating of horses, and most of the Christian societies in Europe adopted that ban. This ban was for the most part abolished in first half of the nineteenth century in the Christian countries of Europe. Now horsemeat is eaten in most of the European countries, and in France, Belgium, Italy, Switzerland, and Iceland horses are bred for food production, although horse has not yet become a considerable part of the diet in any of these countries. The French and Flemish consume the most horsemeat in Europe, but the highest rate of consumption has amounted to only about five percent of that of beef. In the last decades of twentieth century the consumption of horsemeat dropped. One reason was that meat was cheaper when it was a byproduct of raising horses for uses that machines have mostly taken over now. Another reason is the increased opposition to eating horsemeat by animal rights activists. Activists in the United Kingdom have fought against eating horsemeat for decades, and in America the campaign against horse slaughtering for food is also prominent. Some American Indians are traditionally horse eaters, but the average consumption in the United States is low, although horsemeat is readily available. French immigrants make up a considerable part of the horse eaters. In many places in the Americas, as in the United States (the leading producer of horsemeat), Argentina, and Canada, horses are bred for their meat but it is mostly exported.

Horsemeat is darker red than beef and venison. Raw horsemeat is also more fibrous, and if kept for a while, it becomes rapidly black in color. It is more than 50 percent lower in fat and energy than beef, but of comparable nutritional value. After slaughter, foals and horses up to about two years old are usually chopped and prepared in ways similar to cattle and served as various kinds of steaks and goulashes, although special recipes for horsemeat are rare in the cookbooks of the Western world. The meat is easy to digest and the taste generally falls somewhere between beef and venison but a bit sweeter than either. Meat of older horses is commonly salted, smoked, or made into sausages. It can be very difficult to distinguish foal meat and beef, if it is spiced the right way. Hence in many places measures have been taken to prevent selling of horsemeat as beef. Older horses tend to be fatter, and horsefat is yellowish in color and not considered good in taste. The horsefat gets quickly rancid if not properly conserved, and horsemeat deteriorates more rapidly than beef. The fat, when melted, becomes oillike, and has been used for bread baking in northern Europe.

See also **Asia, Central**; **Cattle**; **China**; **Dairy Products**; **Goat**; **Japan**; **Mammals**; **Meat**; **Pig**; **Taboos**.

BIBLIOGRAPHY

Buell, Paul D., and Eugene Anderson, eds. *A Soup for the Quan: Chinese Dietary Medicine of the Mongol Era as Seen in Hu Szu-Hus Yishan cheng-yao: Introduction, Translation, Commentary and Chinese Text*. London: Kegan Paul International, 2000.

Kiple, Kenneth F., and Kriemhild Coneè Ornelas, eds. *The Cambridge World History of Food. Volume I*. Cambridge, U.K.: Cambridge Unversity Press, 2000.

Milk and Milk Products from Medieval to Modern Times. Proceedings of the Ninth International Conference on Ethnological Food Research. Ireland, 1992; edited by Patricia Lysaght. Edinburgh: Canongate in association with the Department of Irish Folklore, University College Dublin, 1994.

Rögnvaldardóttir, Nanna. *Matarást* [An Icelandic encyclopedia on food and cooking]. Reykjavík, 1998.

Schwabe, Calvin W. *Unmentionable Cuisine*. Charlottesville: University Press of Virginia, 1979.

Hallgerður Gísladóttir

HORTICULTURE.

Horticulture, literally garden culture, is a part of crop agriculture that also includes agronomy and forestry. By tradition, horticulture deals with garden crops such as fruits, nuts, vegetables, culinary herbs and spices, beverage crops, and medicinals, as well as ornamental plants. Agronomy is involved with grains, pasture grasses and forages, oilseeds, fiber crops, and industrial crops such as sugarcane, while forestry is involved with trees grown for timber and fiber as well as the incidental wildlife. The edible horticultural crops are used entirely as human food and are often utilized in the living state and thus highly perishable. In contrast, edible agronomic crops are often utilized in the nonliving state, are highly processed, are often used for animal feed, and usually contain a high percentage of dry matter. The precise distinction between horticultural and agronomic crops is traditional. In general, horticultural crops are intensively cultivated and warrant a large input of capital, labor, and technology per unit area of land, but in modern agriculture, horticultural crops may be extensively grown while many agronomic crops are now intensively cultivated. Many crops are claimed by more than one discipline. Horticulture is practiced in large agricultural operations, in small farm enterprises, and in home gardens.

Horticultural Arts

Horticulture is associated with a number of intensive practices that collectively make up the horticultural arts. These include various propagation techniques incorporating special plant structures such as bulbs, corms, or runners; the use of layers or cuttings; budding and grafting; and micropropagation involving tissue culture. Cultural practices include soil preparation, direct planting or transplanting; fertilization; weed, disease, and pest control; training and pruning; the use of controlled environments such as greenhouses or plastic tunnels; applications of chemical growth regulators; various harvest and handling methods; and various postharvest treatments to extend shelf life. Other practices associated with horticulture are breeding and genetic techniques for crop improvement, marketing methods, and food processing. Ornamental horticulture, not considered here, includes added practices associated with landscape architecture and the floral arts. While horticulture is an ancient art with many of its practices empirically derived, present-day horticultural arts are intimately associated with science, so that modern horticultural science is one of the most advanced parts of agriculture. Recently some horticultural growers have attempted to reduce or even eliminate reliance on inorganic fertilizers and pesticides through the incorporation of ecologically based practices (integrated crop management).

Horticultural Food Crops

Horticultural food crops include an enormous array of species that are grouped in various ways.

Fruits. Fruits of woody perennial plants have long been prized for sources of refreshment, for their delightful flavors and aromas, and as nourishing foods. Fruit crops can be defined as temperate, subtropical, and tropical depending on their temperature requirements. Temperate fruits are deciduous (drop their leaves in the cold period) and undergo dormancy requiring a certain amount of low temperatures (chilling period) before growth is resumed in the spring. Subtropical fruits require a very short chilling period. Tropical fruits are usually evergreen and are extremely cold-sensitive. Within these groupings fruit crops are usually grouped by taxonomic affinity. The temperate fruits include the pome fruits (apple, pear, quince, medlar), stone fruits (apricot, cherry, peach and its smooth-skin variant the nectarine, and plum), vine fruits (grape and kiwifruit), and small or bush fruits (strawberry; blueberry, cranberry, and lingonberry; brambles such as blackberry, raspberry, and various hybrids; currants and gooseberries). The subtropical fruits include citrus (citron, grapefruit, the tropical pomelo, sweet orange, lemon, lime, mandarins, and various hybrids such as the tangor or tangelo); and fruits associated with Mediterranean climates (avocado, cactus pear, carob, fig, loquat, persimmon, pomegranate). There are hundreds of tropical fruits, of which the most important are banana and plantain, mango, papaya, and pineapple, but there are hundreds of others with regional interest, including acerola, akee, carambola, cherimoya, durian, guava, litchi, mangosteen, passion fruit, rambutan, sapodilla, and soursop.

Nuts. The important tree nuts that enter into international trade include almonds, Brazil nuts, cashews, chest-

CROP PROPAGATION

Horticultural crops are multiplied sexually (seed propagation) or asexually (clonal or vegetative propagation). Many vegetables and herbaceous (soft-stemmed) ornamentals are seed-propagated (beans, tomato, petunia). However, some seed is produced by nonsexual means (apomixis—bluegrass, many citrus, mango), and plants produced by this type of seed are considered vegetatively or clonally propagated. Clonal propagation occurs naturally in many horticultural crops through special vegetative structures such as the tubers of potato, the runners of strawberry, the cloves (corms) of garlic, or the bulbs of tulip. Clonal propagation can be achieved by cuttings, where pieces of the plant regenerate missing parts. Thus, shoot cuttings regenerate roots (grape), root cuttings regenerate shoots (sweet potato), and leaf cuttings regenerate shoots and roots (African violet). Most fruit crops are propagated using grafting techniques where plants are physically joined together, in which the combination of parts achieves physical union through tissue regeneration to grow as a single plant. The part of the combination that provides the root is called the stock; the added piece is called the scion. When the scion consists of a single bud only, the process is referred to as budding. A modern form of vegetatative propagation is called micropropagation and involves tissue culture—the aseptic growth of cells, tissues, or organs in artificial media.

This technique permits very rapid propagation and is widely used for many foliage plants. It is commonly used to produce disease-free stock of strawberry, which are later propagated in the field by runners.

nuts, hazelnuts, macadamias, pistachios, pecans and hickories, and walnuts.

Beverage crops. Beverage crops include the subtropical crops—coffee, tea, and maté—and the tropical cacao used for cocoa and the confection chocolate.

Vegetables. Vegetables are typically herbaceous (soft-stemmed) plants in which various parts are used as food, including roots, tubers, leaves, fruit, or seed. There are various groupings based on the part consumed and taxonomic affinity. Vegetables include the root crops (beet, carrot, cassava, celeriac, dasheen, horseradish, parsnip, potato, salsify, turnip, radish, rutabaga, and sweet potato, as well as some little-known Andean tubers such as oca, mashua or anu, and ulluco, and root crops such as arracacha, maca, and yacon); bulb or corm crops including the pungent alliums (chive, garlic, leek, onion, shallots,

PLANT DOMESTICATION

The greatest advances in horticulture, the selection and domestication of our useful crops, were made in prehistory by farmers unknown and unsung. The basic techniques of horticulture were well established by ancient cultures in antiquity (5000 to 1500 years ago). In fact, a complete record of horticulture practices is illustrated in the tomb artwork of ancient Egypt. The horticultural technology of antiquity includes basic propagation techniques (seed handling, grafting, use of cuttings); planting and cultivation (plowing, seed bed preparation, weeding), irrigation technology involving water storage, lifting, and channeling; storage technology such as granaries; fertilization and crop rotation; plant selection; basic food technology (fermentation technology in bread- and winemaking, drying, and pickling), and even the beginning of protected culture (the Romans had a primitive greenhouse using mica for cucumber forcing).

and chive); salad or leafy crops (arugula or rocket, celery, chicory, cress, endive, lettuce, parsley); cole crops or crucifers (cabbage, cauliflower, broccoli, brussels sprouts, kohlrabi, Chinese cabbage, and various Asian types such as bok choy); potherbs or greens (chard, collards, dandelion, celeriac, kale, mustard, orach, spinach, New Zealand spinach); solanaceous fruits (eggplant, sweet and hot peppers, tomato and husk tomato), cucurbits, also known as melon or vine crops (chayote, cucumber, muskmelon, pumpkin, squash, watermelon); legumes or pulse crops in which the seed is consumed (adzuki bean, broad bean, chickpea, common bean, cowpea, lima bean, mung bean, rice beans, tepary bean, urdbean, garden pea, and pigeon pea). Some vegetables are perennial (artichoke, asparagus, Jerusalem artichoke, rhubarb, sea kale). Some agronomic crops are consumed as a vegetable in various stages, and these types are included as horticultural crops. Examples include sweet corn (the immature ears of a sweet type of maize), immature vegetable soybean or edamame, and the young leaves of amaranth.

Culinary herbs and spices. Aromatic plants used for culinary purposes are called herbs when they are temperate species and spices when they are tropical. Examples include allspice, anise, basil, capsicums, caraway, cardamom, cinnamon, chervil, clove, coriander, cumin, dill, fennel, funugreek, garlic, ginger, laurel, marjoram, mint, mustard, nutmeg and mace, onion, organum, parsley, pepper, poppy seed, rosemary, saffron, sage, savory, sesame, star anise, tarragon, thyme, and turmeric.

Horticultural Societies
The field of horticulture has a great many organizations and societies devoted to all phases of horticulture, including amateurs and fanciers, growers and handlers, researchers, and academics. There are plant societies devoted to individual or groups of crops, trade organizations devoted to the production and marketing of individual horticultural crops, and scientific societies devoted to scientific research. In the United States, the principal society devoted to the science of horticulture is the American Society for Horticultural Science (founded 1903) with offices in Alexandria, Virginia. The society publishes three scholarly journals as well as books, and conducts annual meetings. Examples of other scientific societies in the United States include the American Pomological Society, devoted to fruits and nuts, and the American Potato Society. Growers of horticultural crops are also organized in state societies. Many countries have a national scientific society devoted to horticulture. The International Society for Horticultural Science located in Leuven, Belgium, sponsors international horticultural congresses every four years.

Horticultural Education
Horticulture is a recognized part of the curricula in agriculture worldwide. In the United States many land grant universities have horticulture departments devoted to undergraduate education leading to the B.S. degree. Most of these departments provide advanced training leading to the M.S. and Ph.D. degree. However, since the 1990s

THE MORRILL ACTS

The land-grant universities trace their origins to the Morrill Act signed by Abraham Lincoln in 1862, a famous piece of legislation sponsored by Justin Smith Morrill of Massachusetts. Monies from the sale of public lands (30,000 acres for each of its Senate and House members) were to be used as a trust fund to endow a college where practical education in agriculture and engineering would be emphasized. The Agricultural Experiment Stations associated with the land-grant colleges trace to legislation (Hatch Act of 1887) sponsored by William H. Hatch of Missouri. In 1890, the Second Morrill Act was passed and provided direct annual appropriations and forbade racial discrimination in admission to colleges receiving the funds. States were allowed to escape this provision if separate institutions were maintained and a number of the "1890 colleges" in various states open to African Americans became known as "black colleges."

The bounties of horticulture are celebrated in this still-life painting by French artist Hippolyte Chaignet. Collection of the Musée des Beaux-Arts. © ARCHIVO ICONOGRAFICO, S. A./CORBIS.

there has been a trend for horticulture and agronomy departments to combine into either a Crop Science or Plant Science department. A number of schools give two-year programs leading to associate degrees.

See also **Agriculture since the Industrial Revolution; Agriculture, Origins of; Aquaculture; Climate and Food; Extension Services; Farmers' Markets; Gardening and Kitchen Gardens; Genetic Engineering; Greenhouse Horticulture; High-Technology Farming; Organic Agriculture; Organic Farming and Gardening; Organic Food; Prehistoric Societies: Food Producers; Sustainable Agriculture.**

BIBLIOGRAPHY

Bailey, L. H. 1914. *The Standard Cyclopedia of Horticulture.* New York: Macmillan, 1914.

Bailey, L. H., Ethel Zoe Bailey, and the Staff of the Liberty Hyde Bailey Hortorium. *Hortus Third: A Concise Dictionary of Plants Cultivated in the United States and Canada.* New York: Macmillan, 1976.

Brewster, James L. *Onions and Other Vegetable Alliums.* New York: CABI, 1994.

Brickell, Christopher, and David Joyce. *The American Horticultural Society Pruning and Training.* New York: DK Publishing, 1996.

Davidson, Harold, Roy Mecklenburg, and Curtis Peterson. *Nursery Management: Administration and Culture.* 4th ed. Upper Saddle River, N.J.: Prentice-Hall, 2000.

Davies, Frederick S., and L. Gene Albrigo. *Citrus.* New York: CABI, 1994.

Decoteau, Dennis R. *Vegetable Crops.* Upper Saddle River, N.J.: Prentice-Hall, 2000.

Dole, John M., and Harold F. Wilkins. *Floriculture: Principles and Species.* Upper Saddle River, N.J.: Prentice-Hall, 1999.

Everett, Thomas H., ed. *The New York Botanical Garden Illustrated Encyclopedia of Horticulture.* New York: Garland, 1981.

Galleta, Gene J., David Glenn Himelrick, and Lynda E. Chandler. *Small Fruit Crop Management.* Englewood Cliffs, N.J.: Prentice-Hall, 1990.

Harris, Richard Wilson, James R. Clark, and Nelda P. Matheny. *Arboriculture: Integrated Management of Landscape Trees, Shrubs, and Vines.* Upper Saddle River, N.J.: Prentice-Hall, 1999.

Hartmann, Hudson T., et al. *Plant Propagation: Principles and Practices.* 6th ed. Upper Saddle, River, N.J.: Prentice-Hall, 1997.

Huxley, Anthony, ed. *The New Royal Horticultural Society Dictionary of Gardening.* New York: Grove's Dictionaries, 1999.

Janick, Jules. *Horticultural Reviews*. New York: Wiley, 1983 to present.

Janick, Jules. *Horticultural Science*. 4th ed. New York: Freeman, 1986.

Janick, Jules, et al. *Plant Science: An Introduction to World Crops*. 3d ed. San Francisco: Freeman, 1981.

Morton, Julia Frances. *Fruits of Warm Climates*. Edited by Curtis F. Dowling. Miami, Fla., and Winterville, N.C.: Morton, 1987.

Nakasone, Henry Y., and Robert E. Paull. *Tropical Fruits*. New York: CABI, 1998.

Parry, John W. *Spices: Morphology, Histology, Chemistry*. 2nd ed. 2 vols. New York: Chemical Publishing, 1969.

Robinson, Richard W. *Cucurbits*. New York: CABI, 1997.

Vaughan, J. G., and Catherine A. Geissler. *The New Oxford Book of Food Plants*. Oxford: Oxford University Press, 1997.

Westwood, Melvin N. *Temperate-Zone Pomology: Physiology and Culture*. 3d ed. Portland, Ore.: Timber Press, 1993.

K. C. Willson. *Coffee, Cocoa and Tea*. New York: CABI, 1999.

Jules Janick

HOUSEHOLD. Definitions of what constitutes a household have always been dynamic and dependent on political, historical, and cultural factors. Prior to the nineteenth century, typical households were large and agriculturally self-sustaining, with most family members contributing to homestead productivity. The industrial revolution in Europe and the United States brought about changes in household and family structure that influenced fertility patterns and household size, including changes in gender roles and definitions of modernity.

The contemporary American household continues to change in composition and size. Married couples comprised 78 percent of households in 1950, but this percentage dropped dramatically over the next forty years to a low of 53 percent in 1998. The average size of the American household has also decreased in recent years. Over half of American households (57 percent) now consist of only one or two people, compared to an average of 3.1 persons in 1970 (USDS, 2001).

Other nations have also experienced rapid shifts in household size and composition. In their 2000/2001 General Household Survey, the National Statistics Office of Britain reported a doubling and tripling, respectively, of one-person and two-person households between 1971 and 2000. The percentage of married-couple households with dependent children dropped from 31 percent of all households in 1979 to 21 percent in 2000 (Walker et al., 2001).

The basic definition of "household" given by the U.S. Census is "all the persons who occupy a housing unit." The only qualification is that there can be no more than eight persons not related to the head of the household; the unit then becomes "group quarters" (USCB,

1999). Another governmental definition of household, determined by the Food and Nutrition Service (FNS) division of the U.S. Department of Agriculture, is "individuals who live in a residential unit and purchase and prepare food together." This definition plays an important role in the Food Stamp Program, as the household is the basic unit on which benefits are granted. According to Food Stamp Program policy, people who share a housing unit but do not prepare and purchase food together are not considered a household. Thus, food is a crucial component of the Food Stamp Program's definition, even if not of that of the U.S. Census.

Food also plays a role in how other countries define a household. In the view of the Swiss Household Panel, one criterion that defines a household is whether household members share a meal at least once every week. Anthropologists and others often define a household in terms of food preparation and consumption: all individuals who consume food from one hearth belong to a household. Central to this is the idea of "commensality," or food sharing, and anthropologists have often documented the key role of food in the formation and maintenance of social relations both within the household and beyond. Nutritionists and economists have often used the household as a primary unit of analysis. While the household appears to be a "natural unit" for studies of food consumption and nutrition, this conceptualization poses a problem in many parts of Africa and Asia where households are polygamous or where "extended family" households are common.

Anthropologists are increasingly engaged in the examination of household dynamics, focusing on social interactions, marital-sexual power relations, and work or food allocation. Recent research has shown that household composition and size can play a considerable role in dietary intake and distribution. In some settings or cultures, particularly where food resources are insecure, gender or age discrimination may result in unequal food distribution among some household members.

Many cultures also assign significantly different positions and/or status levels to males and females. The types of high-social-value foods vary between cultures, but depending on the kind of food, its restriction could have significant nutritional implications for one gender or the other. Some cultural groups, such as the Chagga of Tanzania, have distinct food prescriptions and proscriptions for men and women. Males are proscribed against eating green vegetables, so females in households are ultimately the only members consuming these foods. Other societies may prohibit women from receiving foods considered to be of high social value, such as meat or animal products, particularly during pregnancy or lactation. However, these cultural norms of proscription or prohibition do not always reflect behavioral adherence. Women denied meat may be at higher risk for protein and iron deficiencies. In rural Nepal, unequal food distribution and cultural beliefs were shown to influence inadequate micronutrient intakes by women, and plate-sharing within households was protective among children for mild xerophthalmia, a clinical deficiency of vitamin A. Cultural beliefs, then, can influence both positive and negative nutrition and health outcomes.

To investigate nutrition and health status within and across households, it is important to understand the complex interrelationships of the overall environment. This is the strength of a biocultural approach that situates individuals and households within specific cultural and social settings.

See also **Anthropology and Food; Division of Labor; Food Stamps; Gender and Food; Malnutrition; Nutritional Anthropology; Places of Consumption; Population and Demographics; Time.**

BIBILIOGRAPHY

Bentley, Margaret E., and Pelto, Gretel H. "The Household Production of Nutrition." *Social Science and Medicine* 33, no. 10 (1991): 1101–1102.

Castner, Laura, and Randy Rosso. *Characteristics of Food Stamp Households Fiscal Year 1998*. Alexandria, Va.: U.S. Department of Agriculture, Food and Nutrition Service, 2000.

Messer, Ellen. "Intra-Household Allocation of Food and Health Care: Current Findings and Understandings." *Social Science and Medicine* 44, no. 11 (1997): 1675–1684.

Pelto, Gretel H. "Intrahousehold Food Distribution Patterns." In *Malnutrition: Determinants and Consequences*, edited by Philip L. White and Nancy Selvey. New York: Liss, 1984.

Pelto, Gretel, and Pertti Pelto. "Anthropological Methodologies for Assessing Household Organization and Structure." In *Methods for the Evaluation of the Impact of Food and Nutrition Programmes*, edited by David Sahn, Richard Lockwood, and Nevin S. Scrimshaw. Tokyo: United Nations University, 1984.

Ruether, Rosemary Radford. *Christianity and the Making of the Modern Family*. Boston: Beacon Press, 2000.

Walker, Alison, et al. *Living in Britain: Results from the 2000/01 General Household Survey*. London: Office for National Statistics, 2001.

United States Census Bureau. *State Household and Housing Unit Estimation Methodology: 1990–1998*. Washington, D.C.: U.S. Census Bureau, 1999.

United States Department of State. "The American Family, by the Numbers." *U.S. Society and Values* 6 (2001): 8–10.

Margaret E. Bentley
Erin Fields

HUMOR, FOOD IN.
Humor and laughter are unique to humans and separate them from other animals. While all social and cultural aspects of human existence are subject to humor, food and sex are the most widespread topics because they are the fundamental biological bases of human existence. Food habits and sexual practices show considerable cross-cultural variations.

Food is a handy weapon for humor on the stage. Actor Bert Lahr is seen here cooking (with a pinch of Old Dutch Cleanser) on stage during a performance of *George White's Scandals* at the New Amsterdam Theatre in New York. © JOHN SPRINGER COLLECTION/CORBIS.

People in different cultures have definite views not only of the foods they eat but also of what constitutes a potential food. Ethnocentrism reigns supreme in matters of food and food habits.

Humor in individual societies targets food and eating habits while humor at the universal level focuses on cross-cultural differences in food habits, food values, and ideologies. No single comprehensive, cross-cultural treatment of food-related humor exists, although there is an extensive literature on the foods and food habits of people in specific societies. This essay discusses the humor of food, primarily in the United States.

Forms, Techniques, and Topics of Food-Related Humor
Verbal and nonverbal humor is primarily based on incongruity and takes various forms: jokes, puns, riddles, funny stories, parodies, ludicrous definitions, malapropisms, one-liners, caricatures, cartoons, pranks, and practical jokes. Cartoons and caricature generally use visual humor while pranks and practical jokes exploit social situations. However, almost all types of humor depend on language. The techniques used in humor are exaggeration, ludicrous imitation, reversal and contrariness, and

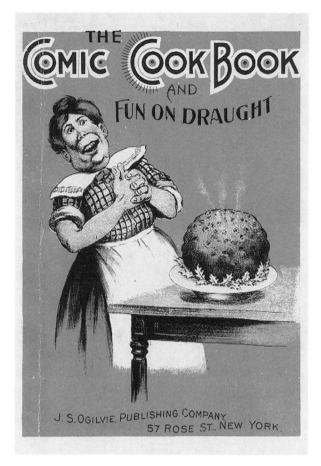

Food has always been an easy target for humor. This spoof on cookery and dining manners was sold at New York newsstands as a Christmas joke book in 1890. It contains several chapters on various branches of cookery, including recipes. ROUGHWOOD COLLECTION.

trivializing everyday life events. Topics include genuine and fictional recipes; fast-food and other restaurants; chefs and fast-food cooks; butchers, housewives, waiters, and customers; cooking processes; eating habits of various ethnic groups; food ingredients; and eating utensils.

Jokes

Jokes are the most popular type of food humor. Jokes take many forms and include other types of humor. They include riddles, one-liners, word play, ethnic jokes, and so on. A major characteristic of jokes is the surprise punch line. Over the last fifty years, many collections of all types of jokes have been published. The introduction of the Internet has helped disseminate thousands of jokes all over the world. There exist Internet "The A-Z Jokes Collections" and new jokes are added daily.

Jokes either exaggerate or overturn common cultural practices, and target cultural roles and professions related to cooking and eating, making them incongruous. Jokes focus on the contradictions between cultural perceptions of ideal recipes, appropriate food habits, and roles, on the one hand, and social reality on the other. Among jokes relating to food professions, those relating to waiters are especially popular, and the question-answer format is most common. Generally, waiters provide the punch line by their culturally inappropriate and incongruous answers to customers' complaints.

Pranks and Practical Jokes

Pranks and practical jokes are an important aspect of all informal and formal social interactions. Generally, individuals, but occasionally groups, are the butt of these jokes, especially at parties, weddings, and other similar social gatherings. The aim is to surprise and embarrass the chosen target, and this is accomplished through unexpected actions such as a pie in the face, removal of some clothing thereby revealing "private" body parts, pouring water or liquor on a person or a group of people, or throwing smelly foods at the victim(s). Some pranks are so well established in the United States that the victims expect them, thereby canceling the element of surprise. A popular ritual in the United States is a "roast," a banquet in honor of a celebrity who is subjected to humorous tongue-in-cheek jibes and insults by friends. The target is figuratively roasted until he or she is totally embarrassed, to the amusement of the participants.

Cartoons

Cartoons are a very widespread and popular form of humor. In the United States, daily newspapers are full of cartoon strips, many of which focus on food. The two best known are "Blondie" and "Beetle Bailey." Blondie's husband Dagwood is famous for his appetite and huge sandwiches. The waiter and the cook at the diner where Dagwood eats his lunch are also humorous characters. The catering business started by Blondie has led to several hilarious episodes. While "Sarge" in the Beetle Bailey cartoon strip is known for his gluttony, the army cook is notorious for his awful cooking, and his food is disliked and made fun of by the soldiers. The "Far Side" cartoon series by Gary Larson has had several food-related cartoons, especially episodes which depict anthropologists being boiled in the cauldron by wild tribes. Jack Ziegler's cartoon collection "Hamburger Madness" demonstrates the zany aspects of fast food. The cartoons on the front and back covers portray the ubiquity of hamburger in the world.

Caricatures and Parodies

Caricature and parody involve creatively ludicrous imitations of aspects of food, emphasizing the contrast between its serious and trivial aspects. Humorous cookbooks (to be discussed below) caricature diners, chefs, utensils, gadgets, and cooking itself. While caricature emphasizes the visual attributes of its subject, parody focuses on language and style. It is the incongruity between the

HOT DOGS AND NEGATIVE STEREOTYPES

Americans have always had a strong negative reaction to members of some Asian societies who eat dog meat. This has much to do with the American cultural belief that one does not eat pet animals. Yet one of the most popular fast foods in the United States is named the "hot dog." How did this come about? Why do Americans call the food in question by this name when they intensely dislike the idea of eating dogs? And why is this name readily accepted? One could say, after all, "what's in a name?" But we all believe that names are important. People have a general belief in the magical ability of words. Even many Americans who do not believe in the power of words want to know when they visit a physician what they are suffering from, and they are satisfied only when the physician actually names their illness. Hence the puzzle and the irony of the name "hot dog." It is true that hot dogs do not contain dog meat. But it is interesting to contemplate how the name originated and how it became widespread. Hot dogs are also known as frankfurters and wieners. They are a type of sausage. J. J. Schnebel (at "hot dog" in "Who Cooked that up?" http://members.cox.net/ starview/) provides a brief history of this food from the time of the ancient Greeks through the Middle Ages to modern America. The names "frankfurter" and "wiener" are derived from the names of the two European cities, in which sausages were manufactured and were a popular food item: Frankfurt in Germany and Vienna (Wien) in Austria. This food was also called "dachshund sausage" because of the similarity of its shape to the German dog used in hunting badgers; thus the word is a combination of two German words, *hund* meaning hound and *dachs* meaning badger. The name continued to be used by German immigrants who began to sell these sausages in New York City in the 1860s. These sausages gradually became popular as fast foods to be served at picnics, and to be consumed for a quick lunch on the street, in restaurants, and at baseball games.

Schnebel credits the sports cartoonist Thomas Dorgan of the *New York Journal* for inventing the name "hot dog." Dorgan wanted draw a cartoon of a "barking" sausage steaming in its roll—which was until then known as dachshund sausage—being eaten at baseball games in New York. He did not know the spelling of the word "dachshund" so instead he used "hot dog" and the name caught on.

The joke below titled "Americans Eating Dogs" illustrates how ethnic stereotypes are mutual, with an added twist emphasizing the similarity of a hot dog to the male organ of procreation in humans and many other animals.

Two foreign nuns have just arrived in the United States by boat and one says to the other, "I hear that the people of this country actually eat dogs."

"Odd," her companion replies, "but if we shall live in America, we might as well do as the Americans do."

Nodding emphatically, the Mother Superior points to a hot dog vendor and they both walk toward the cart.

"Two dogs, please," says one.

The vendor is only too pleased to oblige and wraps both hot dogs in foil and hands them over the counter. Excited, the nuns hurry over to a bench and begin to unwrap their "dogs."

The Mother Superior is first to open hers. She begins to blush and then, staring at it for a moment, leans over to the other nun and whispers cautiously, "What part did you get?"

---

serious and trivial that is amusing. Asian cultures that emphasize food rituals are often subjected to such parodies. Television has occasionally emphasized caricature in regularly featured cooking shows. In the United States there is now a twenty-four-hour channel devoted to cooking shows, some of which tend to lean toward caricature.

Sitcoms have their share of the humor of cooking, involving episodes where inept men and woman take a stab at cooking and end up in total chaos. Fun is also made of exaggerated rituals connected with selling and buying ready-made food. The episodes of the "Soup Nazi" in the popular sitcom *Seinfeld* are worth noting here. Customers have to stand in line, politely ask for the kind of soup they want, pay the right change, and move to the side in a drill-like fashion. The cook and proprietor named the "Soup Nazi" by the main four characters in the show can, and does, refuse his soup to anyone who does not obey this ritualistic etiquette or displeases him in any way. Yet, people line up outside his joint to taste his soup. The *Seinfeld* episodes devoted to this theme and involving the four major characters are hilarious.

Well-known food dishes and their names are subject to parody that works both ways. Known foods and recipes, and other food-related events, actions, states, and so forth are manipulated to sound like famous book or movie titles and these, in turn, are altered to remind the readers of famous recipes, as illustrated in *To Grill a Mockingbird And Other Tasty Titles*, concocted and illustrated by Ruth Young and Mitchell Rose. A few examples from it are "The World According to Carp," which is described

WAITER JOKES

Among all food jokes, the most popular seem to be those making fun of waiters. Such jokes portray waiters as rude and not interested in the orders and complaints of the customer; in other words, waiters are not seen as true professionals. However, these jokes also focus on the presumed ability of waiters to answer any customer complaints with witty and unexpected one-upmanship, thereby creating an incongruous situation. The preferred format of waiter jokes is question and answer. The following are a few examples.

1. Customer: Waiter, there is a dead spider in my soup!
   Waiter: Yes, Sir, they can't stand the boiling water!
2. Customer: Waiter, waiter, there is a fly in my soup!
   Waiter: Not so loud, Sir, everyone will want one!
3. Customer: There is a small slug in my salad !
   Waiter: Sorry, Sir, I'll get you a bigger one!
4. Question: Why do waiters prefer elephants to flies?
   Answer: Have you ever heard anyone complaining of an elephant in their soup?
5. Customer: Waiter, waiter, there is a spider in my soup!
   Send for the manager!
   Waiter: It's no good, Sir, he's frightened of them too.

as "Smash nationwide bestseller by a writer's writer! Meet T. S. (Terribly Salable) Carp, porpoiseful young novelist, and discover the best love story New England has produced since "Ethan Fromage"; "Lady Chatterley's Liver"; "Moby Duck"; and "The Soufflé Also Rises." The illustrations accompanying each tasty title are exaggerated and amusing.

Imaginary food recipes focusing on the personality traits of famous people are favorite areas of food humor. This kind of humor is difficult to categorize, although it probably comes under the heading of parody. *Freud's Own Cookbook* by James Hillman and Charles Boer (1984) and *Jean-Paul Sartre's Cooking Diary* (author unknown) are two such examples. The first describes such dishes as "Slips of the Tongue in Madeira Sauce" (p. 48)," "Erogenous Scones" (p. 75), and "Incredible Oedipal Pie" (p. 76), that are reminiscent of concepts developed by Freud and his friends and colleagues. The Sartre book consists of philosophical musing about cooking and recipes.

One-Liners, Puns, Riddles, and Word Play

These closely related and occasionally overlapping genres of humor are devoted to comments about common-sense rules of eating, dieting, low-calorie foods, overeating, obesity, food fads, and favorite, and addictive, foods of individuals and groups. Incongruity is the result of such techniques as reversal, exaggeration, and double meaning. Note the following: "Eating should never make you sad, unless it is a mourning meal"; "Visibly upset from the whole ordeal, the grape juice started to whine"; "I used to work at the sugar packaging factory. Then my position was dissolved"; "The upper crust of society is composed of a lot of crumbs held together by dough"; "If you eat something, but no one else sees you eat it, it has no calories."

Consumption humor is contrary to the common-sense constraints concerning what to eat and how much. Everyone has particular food addictions and many believe in the dictum of living to eat rather than eating to live! Humor focuses on such shortcomings. Note these one-liners: "If we are what we eat, then I am easy, fast, and cheap"; "A balanced diet is a cookie in each hand"; "No one thinks of any 'rules' associated with the when, where, and how chocolate should be eaten." We have the riddle: "Q.: Why is there no such organization as Choca-holics Anonymous? A: Because no one wants to quit eating chocolate."

Humor associating food with various aspects of human anatomy and sexual activities is widespread and popular. For example: "Q: What did one strawberry say to the other strawberry? A: If we hadn't been found in the same bed together we wouldn't be in this jam!" Note "The Life Story of An Egg": "So you think your life is bad, then just think how bad the life of an egg is. . . . You only get laid once. You only get eaten once. It takes four minutes to get hard and two minutes to get soft. You have to share a box with eleven other guys. And the only chick that ever sat on your face was your mother!"

Dictionaries of food items and related terms with creatively outrageous or absurd meanings are another type of humor, as illustrated by *A Cook's Dictionary* by Henry Beard and Roy McKie. They "bring new meaning to matters of taste." The very definition of the word "cooking" on the cover page is given as "1.n. the art of using appliances and utensils to convert ingredients and seasonings into excuses and apologies." A "chef" is defined as "any cook who swears in French," while "health food" is defined as "any food whose flavor is indistinguishable from that of the package in which it is sold." This dictionary also includes cartoon-style humorous sketches of food-related activities.

See also: **Feasts, Festivals, and Fasts; Folklore, Food in; Sex and Food; Table Talk.**

BIBLIOGRAPHY

Apte, Mahadev L. *Humor and Laughter: An Anthropological Approach*. Ithaca, N.Y.: Cornell University Press, 1985.

Fieldhouse, Paul. *Food and Nutrition: Customs and Culture*, 2d ed. London: Chapman & Hall, 1995.

Barr, Ann, and Paul Levy. *The Official F*O*O*D*I*E Handbook*. London: Ebury Press, National Magazine House, 1984.

Beard, Henry, and Roy McKie. *A Cook's Dictionary*. New York: Workman Publishing, 1985.

Hillman, James, and Charles Boer. eds. *Freud's Own Cookbook*. New York: Harper & Row, 1985.

Young, Ruth, and Mitchell Rose. *To Grill a Mockingbird and Other Tasty Titles*. New York: Penguin Books, 1985.

Ziegler, Jack. *Hamburger Madness: Cartoons by Jack Ziegler*. New York: Harcourt Brace Jovanovich, 1980.

Mahadev Apte

HUNGARY. *See* **Central Europe.**

HUNGER, PHYSIOLOGY OF. Hunger is the set of internal experiences that lead a human or animal to seek food. Appetite describes the preferences that surround the selection of food that is found. For many people, hunger is a set of feelings often focused on the stomach. It may be associated with contractions of the stomach or intestine, and described as "emptiness." Indeed, many of the early ideas about hunger and its opposite, satiety, were described in terms of stomach contractions or stomach distension. Increased physiological understanding has yielded the information that the stomach and intestine are only one part of the system experienced as hunger.

A drive to eat food can be produced by damage to selected parts of the brain, usually located in the hypothalamus near the pituitary. When this area is damaged, animals and humans become voracious eaters and become obese. This indicates that there are sections of the brain that can inhibit food intake that, when destroyed, fail to do this. Alternatively, there are other regions of the brain (lateral hypothalamus) where damage in either humans or animals produces reduced food intake and wasting.

The connections between what happens in the body and how the brain recognizes it have advanced by leaps and bounds since the 1970s. One of the first discoveries was that many of the same messages or signals that are found in the stomach and intestine are also found in the brain. These so-called gut-brain messages can serve to stimulate or inhibit feeding. As a general rule, the ones produced and released in the body tend to inhibit feeding. Thus cholecystokinin, a hormone that causes the gallbladder to contract, also inhibits food intake. This peptide works both in the body and when put into the brain. Another gut-brain hormone is ghrelin. In contrast to cholecystokinin, ghrelin stimulates food intake whether injected into the body or into the brain. The fat cells are another source of important signals for hunger. The most important of these sources is a hormone called leptin. When this hormone is absent in either humans or animals, massive obesity results. When this hormone is given back, hunger immediately subsides, indicating the important role that this hormone plays in the control of hunger. The amount of leptin released from fat cells increases as the total body fat increases. It thus serves as a circulating marker for the level of fatness. Once in the circulation, leptin acts on the brain. Through a lock-and-key mechanism, leptin changes the formation of four other hormones in the brain that regulate eating. When leptin is high, the release of two peptides (neuropeptide Y and agouti-related peptide) in the brain is reduced and two other hormones (cocaine-amphetamine regulated transcript and proopiomelanocortin) are released. Acting in concert, this combination of hormones reduces feeding and relieves the sensations of hunger. Conversely, when leptin is low, the opposite situation occurs, and hunger develops along with the search for food.

Insulin is a second major hormone in the body that signals hunger. In diabetic patients who take insulin and tightly control their blood sugars, mild degrees of obesity frequently develop. Similarly, some of the drugs for treating obesity (sulfonylureas and peroxisome proferator-activated receptor-γ agonists) produce weight gains. One likely way this happens is through reducing blood glucose that in turn signals the need for food.

The role of circulating glucose in the initiation of hunger has been advanced considerably. Beginning with studies in animals, it was found that a small drop of about 10 percent in glucose preceded the onset of many but not all meals. When this drop in glucose was prevented, the animal did not eat at the expected time. That is, hunger had been prevented by manipulating glucose. The glucose-stimulated hunger can be provoked by giving a drug that mimics the key nerve (vagus) that supplies the pancreas to release insulin. Studies in human beings also found that a small drop in glucose preceded many meals. It has been long known that there were lock-and-key systems in the brain responding to glucose or its deficiency. The experiments described above suggest that the brain signals a small release of insulin that leads to a transient decrease in glucose, which in the "primed" animal produces an internal feeling of hunger.

These many signals for feeding can increase the intake of all available foods, or they can signal intake of certain foods. We know that when we have eaten our fill of turkey at Thanksgiving, there is still room for pumpkin pie or ice cream. The loss of hunger for one food after it is eaten is known as sensory specific satiety, that is, the overall drive to eat can be regulated in parts. This is consistent with the finding that some of the signals described earlier stimulate one type of food intake or another, but not necessarily all. Thus, some signals are known that will specifically reduce the intake of fat and others, carbohydrate.

Obesity results from changes in leptin or damage to the brain. From studies on the control of feeding, it is known that at least two monamine neurotransmitters (norepinephrine and serotonin) in the brain play a particularly important role. These neurotransmitters have been the subject of considerable interest, since most of the medications used to treat obesity influence hunger through changing levels of one or both of these neurotransmitters. As more is learned about the control of hunger, a steady source of new targets is available that can be used to develop future medications for the treatment of obesity.

See also **Acceptance and Rejection; Anorexia, Bulimia; Appetite; Eating: Anatomy and Physiology of Eating; Obesity; Sensation and the Senses.**

BIBLIOGRAPHY

Bessesen, D. H., and R. Kushner. *Evaluation and Management of Obesity.* Center for Obesity Research and Education. Philadelphia: Hanley & Belfus, 2002.

Bray, George A., and F. L. Greenway. "Current and Potential Drugs for Treatment for Obesity." *Endocrinology Review* 99, no. 20: 805–875.

Bray, George A. *Contemporary Diagnosis and Management of Obesity.* Newtown, Pa.: Handbooks in Health Care, 1998.

National Heart, Lung, and Blood Institute (NHLBI). Obesity Education Initiative. Expert Panel on the Identification, Evaluation, and Treatment of Overweight and Obesity in Adults. *Clinical Guidelines on the Identification, Evaluation, and Treatment of Overweight and Obesity in Adults—The Evidence Report. Obesity Research* 6 (1998) (Suppl 2): 51S–209S. Review.

Yanovski, J., and S. Z. Yanovski. "Obesity." *New England Journal of Medicine* 346, no. 8 (2002): 591–602.

George A. Bray

HUNGER STRIKES. The hunger strike is a type of political resistance notable for deploying deliberate self-starvation to protest alleged injustice and abuses of power. Food plays a central and paradoxical role in these acts by virtue of its conspicuous literal absence, yet compelling figurative presence. Hereby, the substantive rejection of material food comprises the main tactical strategy of hunger strikes, while the evocative symbolisms of food and food denial inscribe the moral messages conveyed by proactive martyrdom for a cause.

History and Political Agendas

Although the origins of hunger striking are obscure and its venerable history sketchy, it is known from diverse cultures and varying historical epochs dating back to antiquity. Hunger strikes were described in the lore of ancient India, and were well-established practices in medieval Celtic societies. In the early decades of the twentieth century, British suffragettes deployed hunger strikes to gain women's right to vote; and in the closing decades, hunger-striking Chinese students in Tiananmen Square petitioned for democratic reforms, and Tibetan monks

staged public fasts outside the United Nations to spotlight their struggles for self-determination. The hunger strikes of Mahatma Gandhi in British-occupied India, Andrei Sakharov in the Soviet Union, Nelson Mandela in apartheid South Africa, and Bobby Sands of the Irish Republican Army, made these individuals renowned in their respective days. In modern times starvation rebellions have been geographically widespread and have championed numerous political causes, ranging from wholesale indictments of totalitarian power to more localized claims for citizens' entitlements within late capitalist democracies.

Instances from the 1980s and 1990s include Chinese women seeking asylum in the United States on the grounds that the one-child policy (and consequent forced abortions) are a form of political persecution, Iranian refugees resisting deportation from France, Kurdish fasters in Turkish jails petitioning to be accorded political-prisoner status, Israeli physicians on hunger strike for better wages, and American activists lobbying to abolish homelessness. Hunger strikes have been directed against nuclear proliferation, unjust imprisonment, immigration policies, and military actions; and they have been undertaken to champion political sovereignty, environmental protection, education reform, animal welfare, and the rights of workers, farmers, and minorities.

Common Characteristics

As their mode of operation, all hunger strikes share in common the principles of nonviolence, a claim to martyrdom for a cause, and an appeal to a universalized ethics that aims to indict by shaming the opponent. Modern applications are further framed by their appropriation of democratic and human rights discourses, and by their potential to capitalize on the vast and rapid circulation of sensational spectacles in a global media network.

In general the issues that incite hunger strikes have either been failed by, or fall outside the purview of, official legislation. By necessity, then, these strategies are designed to circumvent conventional systems of jurisprudence. Nonetheless, in dramatizing an interrogation via a tacit appeal to a public "jury," the hunger strike is structurally analogous to courtroom trials, such that it can be said to function as a kind of "meta-juridical trial." This trial is launched when the hunger-striking protagonist declares self-starvation, and thereby extends his quest for justice in the vulnerability of existence. Such deliberate martyrdom puts the body in an escalating "state of emergency" that graphically tests the resolve of the activist while simultaneously attesting to the depth of commitment. Taking oneself hostage to endorse a political agenda in effect constitutes the initial accusation, or "prosecutorial gesture," whereby the characteristically private act of not eating paradoxically transforms into a public indictment of an (allegedly) unjust system and its overseers. Under conventional trials, language—in the form of law codes and legal arguments—is the established tool of power and order. Yet, in the meta-juridical trials set in motion by hunger strikes, the authority of language is symbolically displaced, to be superseded by food as an alternative medium of communication. In other words, food provides a symbolic vocabulary in the political resistance movement that makes starvation (nonfood) a weapon of social reform.

Food as Symbol

The meaning-making enterprise of hunger strikes strategically exploits the complex and contradictory significance of food, which has been ambivalently endowed with both positive and negative associations in numerous cultures throughout history. Complementary to its role as vital nourishment, food characteristically betokens hospitality and charity, commands an exalted status at major life events, and is a special marker of ideology and identity. Food's beneficence is encoded in language: for example, "com-pan-ionship" in English means "the sharing of bread," thereby etymologically connecting friendship to a fundamental staple of Western cuisine. In its constructive essence, then, food is a preeminent material catalyst of human sociality and a signifier of shared community. Given its multifaceted centrality in human relations, the repudiation of food by hunger strikers can be read as an analogical rejection of community. In the manner that putrid food is inedible and can provide no nutritional sustenance, an unjust society is deemed uninhabitable and can offer no political-moral integrity. This leads to the self-exile of the faster, voluntarily removed from the (allegedly) corrupt circle of sociality.

The refusal of food engenders moralistic messages. For, despite its widely celebrated virtues, it is the intentional abstinence from food that has long been considered a ritual of purification in many religious traditions. Moreover, such self-disciplining still sends ethical (as well as aesthetic) messages in contemporary popular culture. According to Judeo-Christian teachings, the transgression of eating the forbidden fruit launched humankind's original fall from paradise; and gluttony was considered foremost among the seven deadly medieval sins. Abstinence from food provided one escape from these beastly temptations of the flesh, and accorded a path to greater spirituality that placed fasters outside the inherently violent food chain of consumption. It is upon this pious path of nonconsumption that hunger strikers embark, seeking some claim to moral righteousness by virtue of their excess asceticism. The faster's refusal to incorporate food asserts the individual body as sacrosanct and autonomous, and (through the symbolic substitution of food for community) safeguards the boundaries of the self against infiltration by a demoralized system. Importantly, in the striker's brief moment in the public limelight, self-starvation functions as an emphatic character sketch that stages a contest of willpower and suffering in order to prove dedication. By association, these performances strive to pair the political faster with the moral connotations that underlie willingness to sacrifice oneself for one's beliefs.

By ransoming the body as the battleground of resistance, the hunger strike seeks to redefine political issues as existential matters, and replace abstract rules with an impending crisis of life or death. Whether its diplomacy is better characterized as "nonviolent penetration of the heart" (to quote Gandhi) or as "political blackmail" (to cite his opponent, Viceroy Linlithgow), the act is one of keen, if nonetheless desperate, negotiation. Hereby, the violence fasters inflict on their own bodies (which are literally consumed by starvation) symbolically parallels the violence they contend power has inflicted on them (which "consumes" their moral integrity). The striker's purposeful hunger for food thus makes concrete an unfulfilled hunger for justice that can only be satisfied by a reformation of the political-moral order.

Communal Bond

In the iconoclastic logic of the goal-oriented fast, such reformation begins with the private suffering of the martyr put forth as a call to collective action. Just as trespasses of justice are deemed to be public concerns, the individual in need (and in pain) is deemed to be a matter of collective accountability. The individual's need for food invokes a primary interrelationship, based on food sharing as an archetype of caretaking. Insofar as premeditated self-starvation delves into the corporeal conditions of existence, it attempts to forge the commonality of hunger (an experience, to some degree, familiar to all) into an elementary, alimentary bond between striker and spectator. This bond is offered as the foundation for a code of ethics that seeks to mobilize righteousness from mutual responsibility for one another's physical and moral well-being. To ignore a cry for justice (and/or food) is tantamount to a shameful rejection of human mutual dependency.

Hence, in mirroring the violence of power and challenging its humanity, political martyrs endeavor to shame the (proclaimed) perpetrators of injustice. Reliant on its audience, the hunger performance summons civil witnesses to participate in this shaming and speak out against abuses of power. Through this unconventional diplomacy, hunger strikers appoint themselves scapegoats who map the ethical trespasses of an errant society onto their sacrificial bodies (a move which provocatively advertises sociopolitical inequities as undeniably bodily concerns). Here, food symbolism—with its mercurial nature—reemerges. For the messages underlying these political rituals of transformation are consonant with the healing and nurturing significance of food, which, when blessed and shared (witness consumption of the scapegoat, the totem, the transubstantiated bread of communion) can be sustaining, as can society, when purged of corruption. An end to the political fast, and the striker's consequent return to the community of food sharing, symbolizes redemption of the collective moral good.

See also **Consumer Protests; Food as a Weapon of War; Symbol, Food as**.

BIBLIOGRAPHY

Bell, Rudolph M., and William N. Davis. *Holy Anorexia*. Chicago: University of Chicago Press, 1987.

Beresford, David. *Ten Men Dead: The Story of the 1981 Irish Hunger Strike*. New York: Atlantic Monthly Press, 1987.

Collins, T. *The Irish Hunger Strike*. Dublin and Belfast: White Island Book Company, 1986.

Ellman, Maude. *The Hunger Artists: Starving, Writing, and Imprisonment*. Cambridge, Mass.: Harvard University Press, 1993.

Green, Barbara. *Spectacular Confessions: Autobiography, Performative Activism and the Sites of Suffrage 1905-1938*. London: MacMillan, 1997.

Harbury, Jennifer K. *Searching for Everardo: A Story of Love, War and the CIA in Guatemala*. New York: Warner, 2000.

Harpham, Geoffrey Galt. *The Ascetic Imperative in Culture and Criticism*. Chicago: The University of Chicago Press, 1987.

Landzelius, Kyra. "Hunger Strikes: The Dramaturgy of Starvation Politics," in *Einstein Meets Magritte: Science, Nature, Human Action and Society, Volume VIII: Man and Nature - A World in Transition*, edited by Diederik Aerts, pp. 83–90. Dordrecht: Kluwer Academic Publishers, 1999.

Landzelius, Kyra. "Back to the Garden: The Primordial Hunger Strike." *Proceedings of the Semiotic Society of America*, 1997, pp. 161–168.

Kyra Landzelius

HUNTING AND GATHERING.

Hunting and gathering, or more generally stated as foraging, can be defined as a mode of subsistence in which all food is obtained from wild resources without any reliance on domesticated plants or animals. This has been the dominant means of subsistence for 99.5 percent of the 2.5 million years of human existence. It was only in the last ten thousand years or so that people began to domesticate and produce food in some areas, while in other areas hunting and gathering continued up until the nineteenth and twentieth centuries. Within this time period and throughout the many different geographical regions that people inhabited, there has been tremendous variation in food consumption. We will examine some of the major geographical, cultural, and temporal trends within this great diversity, as well as some common misconceptions.

Among the most prevalent misconceptions are the following:

1. People relying on wild foods had to work constantly in order to obtain enough to eat, and thus had no time to develop the arts of civilized life. In reality, quantification of time use among contemporary hunter-gatherers living in comparatively harsh environments has demonstrated that even these foragers spend only two to five hours a day in obtaining food, leaving far more time for leisure than "civilized" people have.

2. Hunter-gatherers are frequently on the brink of starvation and are generally malnourished. In contrast to this view, recent studies have shown that most hunter-gatherers experience infrequent famines and are generally better nourished than neighboring or comparable agriculturalists due in part to the wider variety of foods that hunter-gatherers usually obtain and the lack of reliance on the narrow range of starch-rich plants that tend to typify agricultural and horticultural societies.

3. Hunting was the predominant source of food for hunter-gatherers. In fact, except for Arctic and Subarctic areas, plant foods were the most abundant and reliable foods and provided most of the daily fares (see Lee and DeVore 1986, Hayden, 1981). Surprisingly, hunters in most hunter-gatherer societies only manage to kill a few large game animals (over 10 kg) per year (Hawkes et al., p. 687).

4. Meat has a higher caloric value than vegetable foods. In fact, they are often of equal value (Eaton et al., p. 80).

5. Meat was always hunted. However, large proportions of the meat obtained even among contemporary hunter-gatherers is scavenged from kills of other animals.

6. Meat was the major goal of hunting. In reality, fat is much more important (Hayden, 1981; Speth and Spielmann).

One example is seen among the Australian Aborigines, who, after bringing down a kangaroo, cut open the abdominal cavity of the animal in order to determine the fat content. If there is insufficient fat on the animal, it is not eaten but left in the bush. Similar behavior is recorded in James Woodburn's film *The Hadza* (1966). There are also a number of accounts of hunter-gatherers who were starving despite the fact that they were eating large amounts of very lean meat. This is sometimes referred to as "rabbit starvation" in North America since it historically involved the reliance on lean rabbits by hunter-gatherers. Fat was critically important among hunter-gatherers for proper metabolism, for obtaining essential fatty acids, and for adequate calories to maintain body temperatures during cold periods.

While animals may not have been the major staple of most hunter-gatherer diets, ethnographically they were universally highly valued far above other types of foods. Successful hunting of animals conferred great status on individuals (Hawkes et al.), and hunting was almost universally carried out by men, while women and children gathered plants and small animals such as lizards, mice, or frogs.

Evolutionary Trends

The origin of hunting is hotly debated. Wooden spears have been recovered from deposits over 400,000 years old, and reasonable arguments have been advanced for hunting going back to the Lower Paleolithic, some two million years or more ago. Other scholars argue that there was a prolonged period encompassing the Lower Paleolithic and perhaps the Middle Paleolithic, when people (proto-people) relied primarily on scavenged rather than hunted meat. There is little evidence for the use of plant foods from these early periods, but they undoubtedly played important roles in the overall subsistence diet.

Up until twenty thousand years ago or so, we must assume that all food was either eaten raw or was roasted on open fires (the initial use of fire is also disputed, but seems definitely to be in place by 400,000 years ago). Until the end of the Paleolithic, there is no evidence of boiling containers or the heating of rocks to boil liquids. Ethnographically, there appears to have been no hunter-gatherers that made any alcoholic beverages either.

It is only around twenty thousand years ago that fire-cracked rocks begin to appear and were probably used in boiling foods such as vegetables and the first bone soups (for extracting the bone fats). Some five to ten thousand years later, the first evidence for the systematic exploitation of a wide range of new food types appears. This includes the first evidence for grass seed use (grinders), systematic fishing (net sinkers, fishhooks, leisters, and fish remains), and semi-toxic nuts like acorns. The expansion of food resources used together with the new technological inventions that made this possible is sometimes referred to as the "Mesolithic" technology or exploitation pattern. It is this pattern that persisted in most areas of the world where hunter-gatherers survived until contemporary times.

Choice of Foods

The choice of which plant, fish, insect, bird, and animal species were to be used for food was initially constrained by the regional environments that groups lived in and by the relative abundances at different trophic levels. In the Arctic, there are simply not many plant foods available for most of the year; in deserts, there are no fish; in each environment, the nature of the plants and animals will differ somewhat, but there will always be fewer (and more dangerous) carnivores than herbivores and more plants than herbivores. It is not possible or meaningful to catalog all such variations; however, it is possible to understand hunter-gatherer choices of foods in other ways using general trends or categories.

Although there is some variation between cultures in terms of what is considered to taste good, taste is frequently an important factor in determining which species are preferred to eat. Very strong-tasting flesh tends to be avoided (e.g., crows, mutton birds, mountain sheep [at least in the Northwest of North America]). Very fibrous

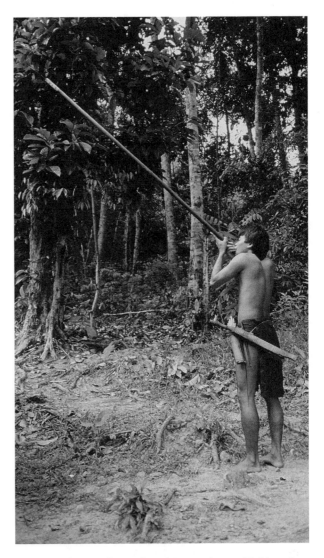

The nomadic Dayak peoples of Borneo hunt with blowpipes and preserve many features of a primitive lifestyle based on hunting and gathering. © CHARLES AND JOSETTE LENARS/CORBIS.

or woody plants are less desirable than those with more fleshy tubers or fruits. There are also many plants that are mildly toxic or produce undesirable effects when eaten in varying amounts.

Transcending these considerations, it has often been observed that species that are rich in fats, oils, starches, or sugars are avidly sought by hunter-gatherers. This appears to be due to the fact that high caloric foods are relatively rare in the wild. Wild animals are very lean during most of the year, averaging only about 4 percent fat versus the 29 percent fat content that is typical for domesticated animals (Eaton et al., p. 80). Bears are often favorite foods because they store large amounts of fat for winter hibernation; beavers are favored for the same reason. In southeastern Australia, streams were modified and canals constructed in order to capture large numbers of migrating, oil-rich eels. Elsewhere, in eastern Australia, large gatherings of people occurred in order to harvest bushel loads of oil-rich moths in their mountain mating locations. In central Australia, witchity grubs were relished for the same reason, although only a few could be obtained at a time. Honey is another insect product greatly sought after by hunter-gatherers. Starch-rich tubers, nuts, and grains were also eagerly sought. In contrast to the more vegetarian agriculturalists of later times, salt does not appear to have been a major concern for most foragers, probably because of the natural salt content in the meat that they consumed.

There were also foods sought for more special dietary purposes. While berries might not provide many calories, they were often rich in vitamins necessary for good health. Keene has shown that the need for hides, vitamin C, and calcium were major nutritional bottlenecks among some groups of hunter-gatherers and that these considerations determined which animals and how many were hunted.

Some animals and plants were also avoided due to totemic or other cultural taboos. These might vary from individual to individual and from group to group. Some groups ate their domesticated dogs, others did not; the Tasmanians ate fish in their early prehistory, but avoided fish completely in their later prehistory. It is often difficult to discern any logic or pattern to these kinds of food prohibitions.

Finally, some scholars have tried to use optimal foraging theory to model hunter-gatherers' food choices. Winterhalder and Smith explain this theory, which postulates that resources that provide the best returns for the time and effort invested in their procurement and processing should be the most intensively used, and that all resources can be ranked relative to each other in these terms. The initial applications of this theory used caloric returns as the measure of theoretical desirability. Researchers attempted to calculate travel time, harvesting time, processing time, and caloric returns. The results did not fit the model expectations very well, but perhaps given all of the other factors that influence food choices (listed above), this may not be too surprising. In addition, risk factors probably play important roles. Food species that can be reliably obtained on a day-to-day basis may be preferred over foods that can only be obtained more sporadically, even if the reliable foods require more time and energy to obtain on average. Thus, plant foods, shellfish, and abundant small animals like lizards are sometimes the mainstays of hunter-gatherer diets while scarcer, more mobile types of food such as large game animals are eaten more episodically.

Of all the lower ranked food types requiring more effort, grass seeds constitute something of a special case. O'Connell and Hawkes observe that grass seeds are particularly inefficient sources of food in Australia, although many groups used them. It is therefore difficult to un-

derstand why they were used, and especially to understand why they only began to be used in the last fifteen thousand years or so of hunter-gatherer evolution. There are no seed grinding tools in the world archaeological record up to that time. Certainly, grass seeds contain starches, oils, and protein in desirable proportions. It is primarily the collection and processing costs that seem to have made this type of food unattractive, although some wild stands of wheat in the Near East can be harvested at the rate of one kg per hour as shown by experiments using Mesolithic type technology. One might expect the use of seeds for food to occur first in these more productive types of environments; however, it is curious that the Tasmanians never used grass seeds despite the occurrence of large seeded species similar to those in the Near East, whereas a number of Australian groups used several smaller seeded species. Various researchers have suggested that grass seeds may have begun to be used due to population pressures, or due to advances in processing and collecting technologies, or due to the emergence of prestige feasts, a topic to be pursued below.

The Effect of Food on Culture

The nature of food resources used by hunter-gatherers has many ramifications for understanding their cultures. For most simple hunter-gatherers, or "foragers," wild food resources are scarce, fluctuating, and susceptible to overexploitation. Thus, population densities are very low (usually only supporting one person for every ten to one hundred square kilometers); group sizes are small (twenty to fifty people); the groups are nomadic (moving every few weeks to new resource areas); little if any food is stored; sharing food with others in the group is the normal (often obligatory) practice; intergroup alliances are formed to access refuges in times of famine; feasting is limited to sharing meat and fat from large desirable game animals; private ownership of resources and most other items is absent or rudimentary; borrowing is rampant; societies are comparatively egalitarian; and competitive or aggrandizing behavior is not tolerated (Hayden, 1993). This was probably the nature of most hunter-gather groups during most of the Paleolithic. In contemporary terms, the Hadza of East Africa and the Central Australian hunter-gatherers exemplify this type of adaptation.

Toward the end of the Paleolithic, and increasingly during the Mesolithic, there is evidence of dramatic changes in some of the richer environments of the world, especially along the richer riparian habitats and migration routes (whether terrestrial or marine). In the richest habitats, "complex" hunter-gatherers emerged. Population densities rose dramatically, groups became semi-sedentary or fully sedentary, storage of foods became important, new technologies appeared for obtaining and processing new species in massive quantities (especially fish, nuts, and seeds), large plant roasting pits occur for the first time (up to eight meters in diameter in the Northwest), prestige objects appear and testify to private ownership of wealth as well as important socioeconomic differences, sharing is more limited, and debt-structured or competitive feasting emerged for the first time in human history. Northwest Coast cultures are perhaps the best examples of complex hunter-gatherers with their massive harvesting and storage of salmon, eulachon, halibut, or other fish species; their heavy use of shellfish; and their use of sea mammal blubber for feasting.

Feasting and Domestication

Above all, as documented in Dietler and Hayden, it is the use of feasting to create debts, to obtain desirable goods and services, to craft political power, to establish close social relationships, and to transform surplus food production that is perhaps the most important turning point in the history of the use of food and in the evolution of human culture. Up until the development of surplus-based feasting, which provided sociopolitical and economic benefits, all animal species, including human beings, could only use as much food as they, or their co-residents, could eat themselves. This placed an absolute ecological limit on the utility of food. However, with the advent of feasting forms that conferred major advantages on hosts (such as better alliances, more [or more desirable] spouses, and more socioeconomic/political power), a new ecological paradigm was created without parallel in the natural world up until the emergence of complex hunter-gatherers. For the first time, as much surplus foods could be used (and transformed into other desirable items or relationships) as could be produced. This created an open-ended, positive-feedback relationship between resource production and practical benefits. The more that could be produced, the greater the sociopolitical and economic advantages that could be obtained; and the greater the sociopolitical or economic advantages, the more food could be produced; and so on. It is, above all, the establishment of this kind of positive feedback relationship through feasting that has most likely created the geometrically increasing rate of population, technological complexity, and political complexity that has characterized the past fifteen thousand years.

The establishment of feasts based on surplus production, and the host's desire to impress guests or make them beholden to him, may well have been among the factors responsible for the development of food production and the domestication of plants and animals some ten to twelve thousand years ago. Katz and Voigt have suggested, for instance, that cereal grains may have been domesticated primarily as a means of producing alcoholic beverages such as beer. In fact, there are no alcoholic beverages recorded for simple foragers, but it is possible that alcohol first began to be produced in the context of complex hunter-gatherer prestige feasting as among the Gunditjmara hunter-gatherers of southeastern Australia. On the Northwest (Pacific) Coast, there were certainly potlatches that featured starches (clover roots) and intoxicants (tobacco) as central parts of the feasts.

There are many other theories that purport to account for the development of domesticated animals and plants, such as climatic changes and population pressures. In support of the feasting and surplus model of domestication, it can be noted that among complex hunter-gatherers such as the Ainu of Japan, bear cubs were captured in the wild and raised for a year by wealthy families specifically for consumption at special prestige feasts. Moreover, domestic animals in traditional societies appear to be eaten exclusively in the context of feasts. Similarly, starchy clover roots and cinquefoil roots were tended and grown in Northwest Coast societies for use in feasting. In all these feasting contexts, the most prestigeous foods are those with high lipid, starch, or sugar contents (fish oil, blubber, bear meat, deer fat, seeds, clover roots). These are the foods that were given to the most prestigeous guests. These are the foods for which extra efforts were expended in order to produce. Rather than being forced by population pressures and famine to use foods that required great effort to produce, it may have been the importance of impressing guests at feasts that accounts for the extra efforts used to procure and prepare such low ranked but highly desirable foods as grass seeds, clover roots, and bear meat. This is especially true in complex hunter-gatherer societies where other more highly ranked foods are plentiful (e.g., in the Mesolithic/Epipaleolithic archaeological cultures of the Near East, and in the ethnographic Japanese and Northwest Coast cultures). The highly desirable foods used to impress important guests in complex hunter-gatherer feasts exhibit the same characteristics as those that were eventually domesticated and that we find in supermarkets today. The fruits are the largest, most succulent available; the vegetables are the least fibrous and highest in starches or oils; the meats have the highest fat contents. There is a world of difference between the use of foods by simple foragers and complex hunter-gatherers, and we are far more similar in our use of foods to complex hunter-gatherers than we are to the use of foods by simple foragers, even though the vast majority (99 percent) of our physical, mental, and emotional evolution occurred in the context of simple foraging.

See also **Agriculture, Origins of; Anthropology and Food; Evolution; Game; Mammals; Prehistoric Societies: Food Foragers**.

BIBLIOGRAPHY

Dietler, Michael, and Brian Hayden, eds. Feasts: *Archaeological and Ethnographic Perspectives on Food, Politics, and Power.* Washington, D.C.: Smithsonian Institution Press, 2001.

Eaton, S. Boyd, Marjorie Shostack, and Melvin Konner. *The Paleolithic Prescription.* New York: Harper and Row, 1988.

Hawkes, Kristen, James O'Connell, and Nichoas Blurton Jones. "Hunting and Nuclear Families." *Current Anthropology* 42 (2001): 681–709.

Hayden, Brian. "The Cultural Capacities of Neandertals: A Review and Re-evaluation." *Journal of Human Evolution* 24(1993): 113–146.

Hayden, Brian. "Subsistence and Ecological Adaptations of Modern Hunter-Gatherers." In *Omnivorous Primates.* Edited by Robert Harding and Geza Teleki. New York: Columbia University Press, 1981.

Katz, Solomon, and Mary Voigt. "Bread and Beer: The Early Use of Cereals in Human Diet." *Expedition* 28, no. 2 (1986): 23–34.

Kelly, Robert. *The Foraging Spectrum.* Washington, D.C.: Smithsonian Institution Press, 1995.

Keene, Arthur. "Optimal Foraging in a Nonmarginal Environment: A Model of Prehistoric Subsistence Strategies in Michigan." In *Hunter-gatherer Foraging Strategies.* Edited by Bruce Winterhalder and Eric Smith. Chicago: University of Chicago Press, 1981.

Lee, Richard, and Irven DeVore, eds. *Man the Hunter.* Chicago: Aldine, 1968.

O'Connell, James, and Kristen Hawkes. "Alyawara Plant Use and Optimal Foraging Theory." In *Hunter-Gatherer Foraging Straegies.* Edited by Bruce Winterhalder and Eric Smith. Chicago: University of Chicago Press, 1981.

Speth, John, and Kathrine Spielmann. "Energy Source, Protein Metabolism, and Hunter-gatherer Subsistence Strategies." *Journal of Anthropological Archaeology* 2 (1983): 1–31.

Winterhalder, Bruce, and Eric Smith, eds. *Hunter-Gatherer Foraging Stratgegies.* Chicago: University of Chicago Press, 1981.

Brian Hayden

HYPERTENSION. *See* **Health and Disease; Salt; Sodium.**

IBERIAN PENINSULA.

This entry comprises three subentries:
Overview
Portugal
Spain

OVERVIEW

The Iberian Peninsula, in southwestern Europe, is occupied by Spain and Portugal. It is separated from the main continent by the Pyrenees and surrounded by the Atlantic Ocean to the northwest and west and the Mediterranean to the south and east.

The characteristics and features of Iberian cuisine cannot be understood without reference to the culinary influence of the Romans, Arabs, Jews, and Christians, and the dietary exchange that followed the conquest of America and colonialism in Africa and the Far East. However, Rome did not conquer the Basque country, and the Arabic heritage never reached the northwestern fringe of the Peninsula.

When former Muslim areas came under Christian rule, Muslims were forced to adopt Christianity. The expulsion of these so-called Moriscos from the Peninsula in the seventeenth century was the end of Moorish culinary system in Iberian lands. However, some Moorish elements are still discernible in Peninsular cuisine, particularly in regions where Moors or Moriscos remained for a longer time. These regions are Alentejo, Algarve, Andalusia, Aragón, Extremadura, Murcia, and Valencia.

Contact between Moors and Christians
Moorish foodways influenced the cuisine of Christian upper classes during the Umayyad caliphate and Taifas' periods (tenth to twelfth centuries), during which Al-Andalus (the Iberian Muslim kingdoms) served as a cultural model. Secondly, there was a certain amount of cultural contact between Moors and Christians during long peaceful periods of time in frontier lands. Moorish culinary influence was also the product of years of interaction between Moorish and Christian communities in cities in which, after the Christian conquest, Muslims were confined to ghettos. Another point of contact between Muslim and Christian culture was through the kingdom of Granada, the last Muslim territory in the Peninsula, conquered in 1492.

The Morisco rebellion in the kingdom of Granada (1568–1570), the relocation of the Granadan Moriscos around the kingdom of Castile, and their resistance to integration into Christian society despite the pressures of the Inquisition produced in Christians an aversion toward Moorish foodways. This aversion did not stop the culinary exchange, and, in fact, the influence of Christian culture and foodways on Moorish cuisine led to the disappearance of certain Moorish culinary practices. Often there was a substitution, addition, or different combination of ingredients and dietary practices. The outcome was a cuisine that contained some Moorish components but had different flavors, smells, colors, and textures.

Moorish Culinary Contributions
Expiración García in *La Alimentación* (Food), Lucie Bolens in *La cuisine andalouse* (Andalusian cuisine), and Manuela Marín in *Cuisine d'Orient* (Eastern cuisine) have described Al-Andalus cuisine. However, contemporary Iberian cuisine has only a few elements of this Al-Andalus cuisine. In the Iberian Peninsula, these culinary features are marked by the prevalence or use of certain ingredients, dishes, methods of cooking, or ways of eating that were once typical of Al Andalus but devoid of any religious meaning. These features having a Moorish heritage are the following:

Communal sharing from the same dish. Examples of such shared dishes are paella, *migas* (fried breadcrumbs or semolina), and *gachas* and *papas* (porridges). This practice of sharing is no longer as prevalent as it once was.

Predominance of yellow, green, and white colors. Yellow is common in most rice dishes, in fish stews with rice or noodles, and in some chickpea stews. White is typical of some sweet rice puddings (*arroz con leche* and *arroz dolce*), some porridges, and some soups such as *ajo blanco* (a white garlic soup), the original gazpacho, *gazpachuelo* (a fish and egg soup), and various almond soups. Green is the dominant color of some Portuguese dishes prepared with coriander, although the *sopa verde* (green soup) cannot be included in this category.

Use of saffron, cumin, and coriander. Coriander is rarely found in traditional Spanish cuisine but is very popular in Portugal, especially in dishes from Alentejo; some food

writers relate this use to African influences. Saffron is used both to color and to flavor rice dishes, legume stews, and meat casseroles. Cumin seasons some legume stews, sausages, and dishes of meat or fish.

Spiced stews made from chickpeas, lentils, and fresh or dried broad beans. Examples of such legume and bean stews include *potaje de garbanzos, potaje de lentejas, fava rica,* and *favas con coentro.* The consumption of broad beans, however, has diminished during the last sixty years. Bulgur, or cracked wheat, is still included in some dishes from the Alpujarras region in Andalusia.

Savory or sweet porridges, made from different grain flours. These porridges, such as *gachas* and *papas,* were also the basis of Roman cuisine.

Dishes made with breadcrumbs or slices of bread. Breadcrumbs or torn-up slices of bread are used for thicken-

ing and giving texture to many varieties of gazpacho and other kinds of soups (*açorda, sopa de ajo, ensopados,* and *sopas secas*). Breadcrumbs are also the main ingredient in *migas,* a traditional and popular dish. There are some factors that relate the recipe for *migas,* in its Andalusian version, to the recipe for couscous. The first element is the way in which *migas* are cooked. A sort of steam cooking is produced through the sauteeing and continuous stirring of the semolina or the crumbs (these are previously soaked and drained) and gives a golden and granulated appearance to the dish. *Migas,* similarly to couscous, serve as the base for a wide range of other ingredients such as fresh fruit, fried vegetables, fried or roasted fish or sausages, and even sweets. Finally, *migas,* like couscous, are eaten from the pan in which they were prepared; the pan is placed on the table, and the whole family eats from it.

A LINK BETWEEN *MIGAS* AND COUSCOUS

Southern Spain's *Migas,* a dish of sautéed breadcrumbs or semolina, are a derivative of couscous, a staple dish of steamed semolina. The following is an excerpt from *A Recipe from an Anonymous Andalusian Cookbook of the Thirteenth Century,* translated by Charles Perry:

> I have seen a couscous made with crumbs of the finest white bread—for this one you take crumbs and rub with the palm on the platter, as one rubs the soup, and let the bread be neither cold nor very hot; put it in a pierced pot and when its steam has left, throw it on the platter and rub with fat or moisten with the broth of the meat prepared for it.

Spiced fritters and desserts. Various doughnutlike fritters (*buñuelos, boladinhos, roscos, filhós, pestiños*) and desserts (*alcorza, alfeñique, alajú,* nougat, and marzipan) are made by combining honey or sugar, egg yolks, cinnamon, and sometimes ground almonds.

Other popular foods and dishes. Flatbreads, either baked (*pão estentido*) or fried (*pão de sertã, torta*), stuffed eggs, stuffed eggplants, vermicelli stew, spiced meatballs, shish kebabs (*pinchos morunos, espetada*), and quince paste are current Iberian foods also mentioned in Arab cookbooks.

See also **Africa: North Africa; Couscous; France; Islam; Italy**.

BIBLIOGRAPHY

Bolens, Lucie. *La cuisine andalouse, un art de vivre: Xie–XIIIe siècle.* [Andalusian cuisine, an art of living: 11th–13th centuries]. Paris: Albin Michel, 1990.

García, Expiración. "La alimentación en la Andalucía Islámica: Estudio histórico y bromatológico" [Food in Islamic Andalusia: An historical and dietetic study]. *Andalucía Islámica,* 2–3 (1981–1982): 139–177 and 4–5 (1983–1986): 237–278.

Marín, Manuela. "Cuisine d'Orient, cuisine d'Occident." [Eastern cuisine, Western cuisine]. *Médiévales* 33 (1997): 9–21.

Teresa de Castro

PORTUGAL

Although smaller than the state of Indiana, Portugal was the seat of a great European empire, and its trading network has marked its culture and cuisine. Even before nationhood, Portugal was successively invaded by Celts, Phoenicians, Greeks, Romans, Visigoths, Swabians, and Moors, and was influenced by these cultures. The birth of the Portuguese nation dates back to 1139, when Afonso Henriques took the title king of Portugal, after a major victory against the Moors, although the south remained under Moorish rule until 1250. Spain and Portugal signed the 1494 Treaty of Tordesillas, under papal auspices, dividing the New Worlds between them. The Spanish claimed the Americas, while the Portuguese acquired Brazil and the Spice Route, from Africa to Timor. Portugal's last trading colony, Macao, established in 1557, peacefully reverted to Chinese control at the end of 1999. Portuguese traders brought back to Europe a treasure of spices such as cardamom, pepper, ginger, curry, saffron, and paprika, as well as other exotic foods, such as rice and tea from Asia, coffee and long pepper from Africa, peppers, tomatoes, potatoes, tropical fruits, and peanuts from Brazil. All ingredients form part of Portuguese cuisine today. As Jean Anderson notes in *The Food of Portugal,* the ingenious combination of Old and New World foods differentiates Portuguese cooking from Spanish (p. 10).

Regions

Portugal faces the Atlantic, whereas Spain, except for Galicia, identifies itself as Mediterranean. In the north, Minho province is a green garden of small plots and vineyards. Inland, Trás-os-Montes is a land of stark mountain ranges and hills with a severe climate. The Douro River, rising in Spain, flows to Oporto, through steep-terraced vineyards. The three Beira provinces form the Portuguese heartland, with the highest mountains. The center of the empire, Lisbon's Estremadura province received much wealth from the colonies, as is evident in its varied cuisine. The gentle plains of Ribatejo along the banks of the Tagus provide pastureland. Alentejo, meaning "beyond the Tagus," is a vast expanse of cork oak, olive trees, and wheat fields along the Spanish border. The Moorish occupiers remained longest in southernmost Algarve, leaving their influences on the architecture, customs, and food. Portugal's only remaining overseas territories are the Atlantic archipelagos: Madeira and the Azores.

Portuguese Eating Habits

Although young people tend to favor international fast foods, the rest of the Portuguese still prefer slow cuisine and fresh fish and vegetables. Portuguese families are increasingly dependent on hypermarkets—giant supermarkets that function like compact department stores—springing up everywhere, but the weekly farmers' markets are still very popular. Portuguese households begin the day with a continental breakfast of coffee and milk with bread and butter, honey, or jam. The main meal takes place at lunch, with an appetizer (*acepipes*) like fresh cheese or codfish balls, one course—generally meat and vegetables—and dessert. Country loaves, more refined rolls, or cornbread appear with every meal. A lighter supper can start with soup, one course of perhaps fish, and fruit. There is usually a midmorning break for coffee and a roll, and children take a midafternoon snack of sandwiches and milk. Most elegant teahouses, where ladies of

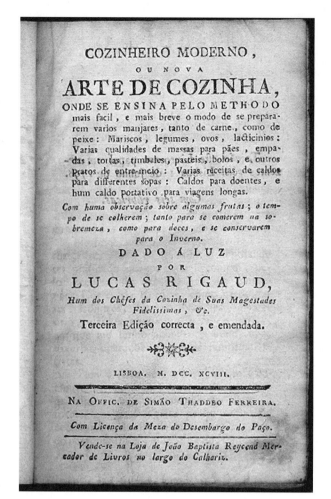

COZINHEIRO MODERNO,
ou nova
ARTE DE COZINHA,
ONDE SE ENSINA PELO METHODO
mais facil, e mais breve o modo de se prepara-
rem varios manjares, tanto de carne, como de
peixe: Mariscos, legumes, ovos, lacticinios:
Varias qualidades de massas para pães, empa-
das, tortas, timbales, pasteis, bolos, e, outros
pratos de entre-meio: Varias receitas de caldos
para differentes sopas: Caldos para doentes, e
hum caldo portativo para viagens longas.

Com huma observação sobre algumas frutas; o tem-
po de se colherem; tanto para se comerem na so-
bremeza, como para doces, e se conservarem
para o Inverno.

DADO Á LUZ
POR
LUCAS RIGAUD,
Hum dos Chéfes da Cozinha de Suas Magestades
Fidelissimas, &c.

Terceira Edição correcta, e emendada.

LISBOA. M. DCC. XCVIII.

NA OFFIC. DE SIMÃO THADDEO FERREIRA.

Com Licença da Meza do Desembargo do Paço.

Vende-se na Loja de João Baptista Reycend Mer-
cador de Livros no largo do Calhariz.

Title page of the 1798 Portuguese edition of *The Modern Cook or New Art of Cookery*, written by Lucas Rigaud. This cookbook was popular in Spain and Portugal during the eighteenth century. ROUGHWOOD COLLECTION.

leisure used to indulge in rich egg and sugar cakes, have closed with changing work habits, but pastry shops serve the seventeenth-century convent sweets.

Meal times. Typically, Portuguese meal hours are closer to those of the French than the Spanish: They do not share their Iberian neighbors' midafternoon repasts and siestas or midnight suppers, except on Christmas and New Year's Eve. Lunchtime is 1:00 P.M., and many work-places still close from 1:00 to 3:00 P.M. The traditional dinner hour is 8:00 P.M.

Weekly cycle. Traditional dishes like *caldeirada* (fish or shellfish stew) and *cozido á portugesa* (boiled meat and vegetables) are served in homes on weekends to allow for more time for food preparation. Portuguese families also like to eat out on weekends. Many popular restaurants offer generous half-portions, but even so, prices have soared faster than wages, and the average family is going out less.

Seasonal Cycle

With its temperate Gulf Stream climate, coastal Portugal does not suffer the extreme temperatures of inland Iberia. It rarely freezes, and fresh fruits and vegetables are available year round, although they vary with the seasons. Even sardines come in seasons, fatter and juicier from June through October. At year's end there is the *matança* or the killing of the pig, and the smoking of lean meat and stuffing sausages to last through the winter. Basically the Portuguese eat the same substantial meals all year. Inland, however, where summer temperatures can hover over 100°F (37°C), lighter wines are served and occasionally *gaspacho*, a cold tomato and cucumber soup, similar to its Spanish cousin *gazpacho*. There are also *escabeches*, cold marinated meats, for scalding summer days.

Feasts and special occasions. Religious feasts, with special foods, are still important in this Roman Catholic country. Christmas Eve supper usually features the national favorite *bacalhau cozido* or boiled dried codfish, with cabbage, potatoes, and hard-boiled eggs, smothered in garlic and olive oil. (Portuguese fishermen have been sailing to Newfoundland for cod since the fifteenth century, salting and drying it at sea. But in response to European fishing restrictions imposed in the 1990s, Portugal imports cod from Norway, which is more expensive.) On Christmas Day, the main course features roast turkey, and for dessert there is *rabanadas*, slices of bread dipped in eggs, honey, red wine, sugar, and cinnamon, and fried.

At Easter, lamb or young goat is marinated overnight in white wine, roasted, and served with baked potatoes. Lamb soup uses the lamb's heart, liver, lungs, tripe, blood, and plenty of stale bread. A popular Easter dessert is cottage cheese tarts.

Every region has a saint's festival with special foods. Lisboners pay homage to Saint Anthony with a costume parade, block parties, grilled sardines, and red wine. Oporto celebrates St. John with fireworks, street dancing, cabbage soup, and red wine. The Templar city of Tomar honors the Holy Spirit, with the Festival of Crowns, a cortege of girls, wearing tall crowns of fresh loaves of bread and paper flowers, accompanied by merrymaking and a panoply of sweets like almond cheese cakes and pumpkin tarts.

Other festive occasions include birthdays, weddings, baptisms, and first communions. These used to call for elaborate banquets, but in the early twenty-first century the menu is simpler: traditional dishes like tripe, hake filets, roast lamb, baked rice, and egg and sugar tarts.

Regional Foods and Wines

As communications have improved in this compact country, more regional dishes have acquired national status. *Cozido á portugesa*, the hearty Portuguese boiled dinner, with chicken, spareribs, sausages, and vegetables originates from Estremadura but is found everywhere. Other national favorites include green soup with shredded cab-

PORT WINE

Originally port was a dry red table wine and came from the Upper Douro Valley some 2,000 years ago. Then in 1820, exceptionally warm weather produced unusually sweet grapes and the full, rich dessert wine that the English adored. To satisfy eager English customers, port wine producers added brandy, which stopped the fermentation early and preserved the high sugar level of the grapes, raising the alcohol level to about 20 percent. The process of producing port is now mechanized. The new wine is no longer transported in *rabelos,* flat-bottomed sailboats, but trucked to the port wine lodges, at Gaia across from Oporto. There it is blended and stored to mature.

The French now consume more port than the British, Pasquale Iocca of the Portuguese Trade Commission emphasizes in the *Food of Portugal* (Anderson, 2001). He points out that the British still favor vintage port ten to fifty years old, whereas the French prefer tawny port aged three to five years in casks.

bage and potatoes from the Minho, fish or shellfish stew found all along the coast, baked dried codfish (the fish is first soaked in liquid before cooking) with onions and potatoes originally from Oporto, and *açordas,* or creamy dry bread soups from Alentejo. The national sauce of crushed tomatoes, green peppers, and onions is the universal condiment. The "national" dessert is *arroz-doce*—rice pudding.

While Port and Madeira dessert wines have gained worldwide recognition, Portuguese table wines are beginning to attract more attention. There are some fifty officially demarcated wine-growing regions. The best reds come from the Alentejo, although those from Beira are better known. Increasingly popular is the effervescent white *vinho verde* or new wine, from the Minho. Excellent natural and carbonated mineral waters come from Beira and Trás-os-Montes.

Between the Minho and Douro food culture. Minho province, blessed by rivers, fertile farmland, trellised vineyards, and a fruitful sea, is home to an exceptionally varied cuisine. From the Minho and Lima Rivers come salmon trout and lamprey. Atlantic specialties include sardines grilled on pine needles, octopus stew, and shad vinaigrette. Pork is the dominant meat, with delicacies like pork cubes marinated in *vinho verde.*

Oporto's unlikely favorite food is tripe. In fact, the native people are known as *tripeiros* or tripe-eaters because in the fourteenth century they donated all their

meat to feed the navy in its defense of Lisbon against Juan I of Castile. The *Portuenses* were left with the innards, which they learned to use in many innovative ways.

Estremadura food culture. Naturally the richest, most cosmopolitan cuisine is found in the capital, reflecting the diverse population, who settled here from all over Portugal. Lisbon's specialties range from stuffed crab and lobster *açorda* to rice and turnip greens or codfish hash. Then there is café beefsteak, with cream sauce and french fries, which made its debut in popular cafés and is now a regular in many homes. Over the past decade, immigrants from the former colonies of Angola, Goa, and Macao

MADEIRA

It was the visionary Prince Henry who first brought Malvasia grapes from Crete in the fifteenth century to Madeira as the basis for the island's important wine industry. The special intense quality of Madeira wines comes mainly from the basaltic soil and mild climate. Like port, Madeira is fortified with brandy to ensure its quality during shipping, but it acquired its distinctive, slightly scorched flavor by chance. Sometime in the seventeenth century, a case of Madeira was forgotten in the hold of a ship when it reached its destination in the New World. The wine returned to Madeira considerably enriched after its lengthy sea voyage twice through the steamy tropics. Subsequently, Madeira merchants began to send their wines on long tours to enhance the sweetness and aging. Then they found they could get the same results by a process of steaming the wine at home.

Queen Catherine of Bragança, the Portuguese wife of King Charles II of England, was indirectly responsible for the popularity of Madeira wines in colonial America, according to Pasquale Iocca of the Portuguese Trade Commission. In the *Food of Portugal* he points out that because of Queen Catherine's influence, Madeiras were the only European wines exempted from the 1665 export ban and shipped duty-free to the English colonies. The signing of the Declaration of Independence was celebrated with glasses of Madeira, and George and Martha Washington used to drink a pint of Madeira every evening with dinner.

Madeira exports virtually halted after the island's vineyards were devastated by disease in 1852. Several English companies that were involved in producing and shipping Madeira helped to reconstitute the vineyards. By 1900, Madeiras were back better than ever, but Americans had meanwhile switched to sherry.

231

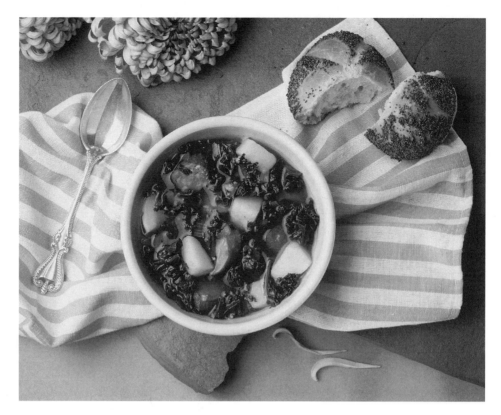

Couve tronchuda is a variety of Portuguese open-headed cabbage dating from ancient times. It is still a traditional ingredient in Portuguese cookery and serves as the main ingredient in this cabbage and sausage soup. © BECKY LUIGART-STAYNER/CORBIS.

have established new ethnic restaurants in Lisbon, which are certain to influence future eating habits.

Alentejo food culture. Portugal's least developed region, the Alentejo has produced the most imaginative dishes. Frugal housewives have ingeniously used the staple ingredients bread, olive oil, and garlic to produce outstanding dishes. *Açorda á alentejana* is a creamy bread puree with coriander and poached eggs. Another dry soup is *migas*, crumbled bread and olive oil, cooked with cubes of beef, pork, and bacon. The most astonishing combination is pork and clams, with pork loin marinated in chili sauce—the flavors meld together beautifully.

Food culture of Madeira and the Azores. In 1425, Portuguese navigators discovered uninhabited, forested islands, some 350 miles off the Moroccan coast, which they called Madeira (wood in Portuguese). Realizing the islands' importance as a stopover for transatlantic shipping, Prince Henry, in the fifteenth century, sent over settlers, mostly from the Minho, to plant sugar cane and vineyards. Despite the distance, Madeira's cuisine is very Portuguese, enhanced with other influences. Fresh tuna steaks and scabbard fish are marinated in garlic and olive oil and fried, but served with fried cornmeal and even corn-on-the-cob. The local *cozido* includes the usual pork and vegetables, but also sweet potatoes, green pumpkin,

and couscous. Madeira's fruit salad, however, is strictly local and includes papaya and passion fruit.

The nine Azores have the closest ties to the United States. In the old days, whaling crews from the Azores sailed to New England and California, many settling there with their families, who still visit the islands in summertime. Commercial whaling has stopped, but many Açoreanos live by fishing, and fish is an important part of the diet. Fish soup Azores style includes the local catch: haddock, porgy, grouper, mackerel, swordfish, eel, and squid or octopus. Dairy farming and cheese making are also important activities, and the fragrant, moist cheese from São Jorge Island is a bestseller on the mainland.

Food culture of other regions. In the wild, hilly Trás-os-Montes, the pig is "king" and fed with table scraps. In the past, the prevalence of pork caused problems for the many Jewish converts. Maria de Lourdes Modesto recounts in *Traditional Portuguese Cooking* how the "new Christians" invented *alheiras*, a delicious, porkless sausage based on partridge, to escape detection by the Inquisition's spies (p. 47). *Alheiras* are still popular, but sometimes include pork.

Mountain folk of Upper Beira are masters with leftovers. After roasting a baby goat that is basted with white wine, the head is boiled for broth, the backbone and the

FURNAS

One of the most traditional dishes of the Azores is *cozido de lagoa das furnas* (boiled dinner from Furnas Lake). This lake on São Miguel Island is a volcanic crater, and the beach contains numerous *caldeiras* or small caverns spewing sulfur. Chunks of beef, pork, and chicken, sausages, bacon, turnips, carrots, potatoes, and red peppers, covered with cabbage leaves, are put into an aluminum pan, with the lid tightly shut. The pan is placed in a cloth bag, with a long string, and let down into a *caldeira,* then covered with a wood board and volcanic sand. The *cozido* takes about five hours to cook in the steaming ground—the ultimate in Slow Food.

heart, liver, and lungs stewed, and the cutlets are fried and always served with boiled potatoes. Beira also produces Portugal's creamiest cheese, made from long-horned sheep that feed on wild herbs in a demarcated zone of the Estrela Mountains.

The Ribatejo, with its alluvial plains, is famous for its dark full-bodied red wines and substantive dishes like stone soup made from pig's ear, *chouriço* (a spicy sausage), ham, and red kidney beans.

Algarve's clean beaches, sun, mild sea, and air temperatures have made it Portugal's primary tourist resort, and this situation has threatened it with a loss of identity. By avoiding international establishments, it is still possible to find original Algarve seafood dishes, like octopus with rice, tuna steaks in onion sauce, or squid stuffed with ham and *chouriço.*

See also **Cheese**; **Crustaceans and Shellfish**; **Feasts, Festivals, and Fasts**; **Fish**; **Meat, Salted**; **Mollusks**; **Sausage**; **Slow Food**; **Vegetables**; **Wine**.

BIBLIOGRAPHY

Anderson, Jean. *The Food of Portugal.* Revised edition. New York: Morrow, 2001.

Modesto, Maria de Lourdes. *Traditional Portuguese Cooking.* Translated by Fernanda Naylor. Lisbon and São Paulo, 1989.

Modesto, Maria de Lourdes, and Afonso Praça. *Festas e Comeres do Povo Português.* 2 vols. Lisbon and São Paulo: Editorial Verbo, 1999.

Pedrosa, Ines, ed. "Comidas Restaurantes Pratos Tradicionais." In *Guia O Melhor de Portugal* [Guide to the best in Portugal], vol. 5. Lisbon: Expresso, 1998.

Saramago, Alfredo, ed. "Sabores Vinhos Enchidos Queijos Doces." In *Guia O Melhor de Portugal* [Guide to the best in Portugal], vol. 6. Lisbon: Expresso, 1998.

Marvine Howe

SPAIN

Spain, situated on the westernmost peninsula of Europe and opening to the Atlantic Ocean on the northwest, historically has been oriented toward the Mediterranean both in its climate and in the temperament of its people. First settled by Celts, then invaded by Phoenicians, Greeks, and finally the Romans, who consolidated the peninsula into one province, ancient Spain became one of the most important agricultural regions of the Roman Empire. Following the Romans came the Goths, then Nordic invaders, and finally the Arabs, so that during the Middle Ages the country fragmented into many small kingdoms. Those former kingdoms roughly correspond to the provinces and regional cultures comprising modern Spain. Each of the invading peoples added its own identity to the rich mixture known as Spanish cuisine.

The Main Cultural Regions

Galicia, which has Celtic roots, is in the far northwest of Spain, and to the east are Asturias and the Basque country, whose culture and language predate Roman Spain. To the east of Asturias are Navarre and Catalonia, two important kingdoms during the Middle Ages that established Spain as a major maritime power in the Mediterranean. Along the western border with Portugal is Extremadura, and in the Spanish heartland to the east are Old and New Castile. Along the Mediterranean coast in the South, opposite Africa, are Andalusia and the Comunidades of Valencia and Murcia, all with distinctive regional cookeries and internationally known wines. The Arabic influence was strong in these regions and lingered in many aspects of the culture, perhaps best typified by the great Moorish palace of the Alhambra in Granada. Of course many islands are part of Spain, among them the Balearic Islands of Minorca, Majorca, and Ibiza and the Canary Islands off the Atlantic coast of Africa. No matter how Spanish culture is studied, it is obvious that this huge diversity rather than any one element of it defines the cuisine of modern Spain.

Added to this diversity is the climate. In the northern coastal area the weather is generally cool, even rainy, whereas in the central and southern parts of the country the climate is hot and dry like other parts of the Mediterranean. Thus even in its kitchen gardens and agriculture, the country exhibits a great diversity. In addition several gastronomic riches of the New World, including the tomato, the potato, the capsicum pepper, cacao, and vanilla, reached Europe via the Spanish Empire.

The Characteristics of Spanish Eating Habits

Not until the late twentieth century did a "national" Spanish characteristic for the times and places of food

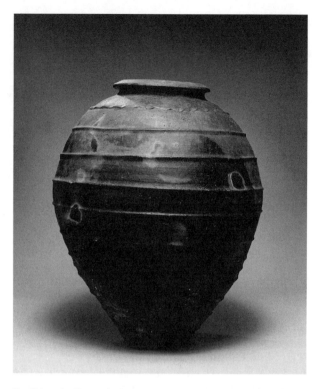

Traditional olive oil storage jar. Spain, seventeenth century. Gray earthenware. The design is based on the ancient Roman *dolium*. The exterior of the jar was sealed with pitch (still extant), then sunken into the floor of the cellar. ROUGHWOOD COLLECTION. PHOTO CHEW & COMPANY.

consumption emerge. Previously the family determined such patterns locally, but new family structures and work customs shifted the patterns dramatically. The typical pattern became two main meals (midday dinner and supper), a light breakfast, and two optional meals (tapas and *merienda*). Breakfast, the first meal, generally corresponds to the European continental breakfast, consisting of a quickly eaten, fortifying menu based on pastries, small breads, coffee, milk, butter, and marmalade, and it is essentially of French origin. Alternatively something totally Spanish, such as *churros* and *porras* (fritters) can be substituted.

Main meals. The most typical feature of the meal schedule is the tendency for Spaniards to delay the timing as much as possible. When midday dinner is adjusted to the work schedule, it usually takes place at around 2:00 P.M. On the other hand, when festivities or vacations allow more flexibility, Spaniards tend to postpone it until 4:00 in the afternoon for relaxation or friendly reunions or because of the earlier consumption of tapas. The most significant feature of the Spanish midday dinner is to prolong it as late into the day as possible with the help of desserts, liqueurs, and coffee. Its only rival activity is the siesta or midday nap. This dinner involves a major consumption of food. After the Spanish Civil War (1936–

1939) families began to eat at the table three main dishes plus appetizers, cheeses, and dessert. Subsequently this pattern devolved into two main dishes and dessert.

The traditional Spanish supper usually takes place around 10:00 P.M., also in the home. It is characterized by its pretension of being light, although it consists again of two main dishes and dessert. Vegetables and fish are often preferred to assure that it is less heavy than the midday meal.

Meals between meals. Spaniards, being of a relaxed, Mediterranean temperament, have created a minimeal between breakfast and midday dinner. This meal, called an appetizer elsewhere in the world, is referred to in Spain by the verb *tapeo* (to eat tapas). Drinks and food are of equal importance to eating tapas. It is also popular among Spaniards to not eat the tapas in one establishment but rather to stroll through various eateries throughout the course of the morning.

A classical tapa can be eaten with a toothpick, in small pots or bowls with a fork, or on top of a piece of bread. All of these variations have their own descriptive nomenclatures based on appearance: *pinchos, cazuelitas,* and *montados.* Drinks of low alcoholic content, such as beer and wine, are always drunk with the tapas. In the South wines such as Jerez, Fino, and Mazanilla are served. Usually the higher the alcoholic content of the beverage served, the smaller the quantity of food consumed until, at the far extreme, tapas simply become dried fruits and olives.

Merienda. *Merienda* is the meal between the midday meal and supper. Generally it is a meal for socializing during afternoon visits or during a game of cards, or for children and the elderly who require extra nourishment between fixed meals. The drink most representative of the Spanish merienda is chocolate. Spanish-style chocolate is characterized by its thickness, although it is traditional to drink it in small cups called jícaras accompanied by absorbent cookies that can be dipped into the chocolate.

Another *merienda*, easy to eat during journeys, is the *bocadillo*. This is the equivalent of the sandwich, but it is prepared with a whole loaf of Spanish bread. During times of food shortages, *bocadillos* have been filled with sliced quince or a little grated chocolate. The more classical *bocadillos* are made of *serrano* ham and *manchego* cheese.

The *bocadillo* has undergone a gradual evolution. It is used as a quick meal suitable for any hour of the day since all of the basic types of nutrients can be put into the loaf, such as chorizo (a spicy pork sausage), *calamares a la romana* (squid fried in butter), sardines, or *tortilla a la española* (Spanish omelet). For excursions to the countryside something special is created, *bocadillo* filled with breaded filet of beef.

The weekly meal cycle. The Spanish housewife generally makes a clear distinction between the everyday meal and the festive meal, especially on Sundays. Traditionally it was possible for working husbands and schoolchildren to eat in their own homes every day, and only manual laborers were obliged to eat at work. Housewives created a varied menu by distributing dishes representative of each day of the week—for example, Monday macaroni, Tuesday lentils, Wednesday stew, Thursday broiled fish, Friday porridge, Saturday salads, and Sunday paella. Depending on the economic means of the family, beef could be a choice, especially for Sundays. This custom continues in the "dish of the day" on restaurant menus.

The Seasonal Cycle
In spite of the geographical diversity of Spain, a shared seasonal climatic variation is common to all parts of the country. Thus, except for the colder regions, summer tends to be hot throughout Spain, which defines the character of summer meals. The foods of the warm season favor easy preparation and light, refreshing ingredients, such as salads and gazpachos. The basic ingredients of a typical salad are lettuce and tomatoes, and the simple salad dressing—olive oil, wine vinegar, and salt—is prepared at the beginning of the meal by the guests themselves. This custom has continued in public restaurants. When the server places the cruet stand on the table, it is a sign that one of the dishes will include lettuce.

The "king" of all the first course dishes is gazpacho, one of the great contributions of Spanish cooking to hot weather cuisine. It is similar to a cold tomato soup, but in gazpacho all the ingredients, ripe tomatoes, cucumbers, green sweet peppers, garlic, olive oil, salt, and vinegar, are raw and are liquefied. Cold water is added to thin the soup. At restaurants it is served with garnishes, consisting of the same ingredients cut into small pieces, and small bits of bread.

In Spain the cold season is associated with the consumption of legumes. Lentils are part of a tasty repertoire of everyday meals, but when Spaniards want to feel satisfied, they think of garbanzo stew. When they want to feel extremely full, they think of the *fabada asturiana*. The *fabada* is a thick stew of white beans and pork products from the region of Asturias on the coast of northern Spain.

The Festive Cycle
The celebrations that have influenced Spanish gastronomy the most are the religious feasts, notably Christmas, a time when major excess prevails. The traditional feast days are Christmas Eve dinner on 24 December, Christmas Day dinner on 25 December, New Year's supper on 1 January, Three Kings supper (Epiphany Eve) on 5 January, Epiphany breakfast on 6 January, and Epiphany dinner on 6 January.

During the Middle Ages, Christmas Eve dinner followed a vigil, and from this period a light dish called *sopa de almendras* (almond soup) survived as a nostalgic relic. Only after midnight mass, or *misa de gallo*, could the great gastronomic excesses begin. Eventually this became the preeminent family dinner. The traditional dishes have continued, although they have evolved over time. Earlier the meal consisted of savoy or red cabbage and fish, usually red porgy, but grilled leg of lamb has become the porgy's competitor.

Certain Spanish confections, such as *turrones*, *marzapán*, and *polvorones*, convey a nostalgic dimension to Christmas, since they are only consumed at this time. The Christmas meal is family oriented, and turkey is the main dish. New Year's festivities tend to lose their family orientation, since New Year's Eve is a supper prelude to a party outside the home. Consequently it is light and easy to prepare, generally a cold meal of various seafoods, especially prawns. The cheapest and most common prawns are baptized with plenty of Catalan Cava (Spanish champagne).

Three Kings' supper on Epiphany Eve is a magical night for children, since they wait for gifts from the Three Kings of the East. The breakfast on Epiphany morning would not be of major importance were it not for the fact that the Magi have brought a *roscón*, a large, round, braided bread flavored with orange-flower water and decorated with crystal sugar, chopped almonds, and dried fruits. Spaniards give each other *roscones de Reyes* until every house has a great accumulation of them.

Lent is a period of recovery, forty days of penitence preceding the celebrations of the death and resurrection of Jesus. The traditional vigils and fasts during these forty days have developed many variations over time, yet the vigil dishes and the dishes of nourishment for days of fasting are a form of nostalgia or remembrance. The representative dish of a vigil is a *potaje* consisting mainly of garbanzos, dried codfish, spinach or cabbage, hard-boiled eggs, and a touch of cumin. During Lenten fasting one characteristic sweet, called *torrija*, is consumed. It is made with sliced bread soaked in milk and sugar, dipped in an egg batter, fried in olive oil, and drowned in wine, orange juice, or honey.

In addition to these great religious observances, each region of Spain has its own patron saint, who is celebrated with some characteristic meal. The confections made in the saint's honor add a special note to the extraordinary fare of the celebration and have given rise to numerous types of *rosquillas*, *panecillos*, and *bollos* ornamented with saintly symbols. Remarkably bakers invent new recipes for modern festivities, so many traditional observances are revitalized on a daily basis.

The Regional Cookeries of Spain
Because Spain has varied regional identities and diverse agricultural districts, regional cooking has acquired a special meaning. Besides the different languages and dialects, regionalism is thoroughly manifested in highly varied

gastronomic traditions. In spite of this localization, many dishes have become popular over the entire country.

Local inns and taverns have a commercial interest in exposing consumers to dishes representative of the region. These can be identified by their last names, such as *a la gallega, a la asturiana, a la riojana, a la catalana, a la valenciana, a la murciana, a la andaluza,* just to mention a few specialties. Obviously these dishes are not always accurately prepared outside their regional settings, but they do allude to distinct culinary styles. Each regional capital has centers, called Casas Regionales, representing the cultures of other regions. These centers normally include restaurants that serve food typical of the regions they represent. All of Spain's regional cookeries are accompanied by an enormous diversity of wines that gradually have become certified by their nominations of origin, including sparkling Catalans, red Riojanos with a *ribera del Duero* body, and full-flavored Andalusians, plus a series of local liqueurs, the outstanding one being Anis.

Basque cookery. The importance of Basque cookery rests on the great Basque love for gastronomy and on the high quality of the natural products from that region, of which fish is the most important. In Basque country the clubs called Sociedad Gastronomica are exclusively for men. Whatever food they prepare themselves, they must also eat. The purpose of this society is to conserve traditional Basque cookery, but the members also are mindful of creative new cooking techniques. Out of this region great chefs, including those from the Basque part of France, given its close proximity, have emerged with innovative talents. In any city of Spain a restaurant run by a Basque chef will be well known for the high quality of its cookery.

Of the fish caught along the Basque coasts, the most notable is hake, which is also one of the most expensive. However, its closest relative, weakfish, is generally less expensive and equally tasteful. The best dark-fleshed fish also come from these waters, such as bonito and tuna. Basque sardines and anchovies have earned international popularity, and an industry has developed around preserving sardines and salted anchovies in oil.

Among the dishes most representative of Basque cookery, hake in green sauce stands out, as does *marmitako,* a stew composed of chopped bonito and potatoes with olive oil. The Basque secret of preparing codfish *al pil-pil* is the peculiar pan-shaking movement that must occur at the correct moment of cooking to emulsify the sauce. The typical wine from this region is *txacolí,* a young wine of low alcoholic content.

Castilian cookery. The central part of Spain is an extensive region known historically as the two Castiles. It is an area characterized by plateaus and a continental climate, cold winters and hot, dry summers. The area is rich in cereal products and herds of wool-producing animals, both sheep and goats. During the cold season residents consume legumes, most commonly garbanzos and lentils. Castilian-style garbanzos have given their name to the famous dish *el cocido madrileño.* Grain products hold an important place among the region's numerous shepherds, who make a light meal—by frying flour or pieces of bread in olive oil, garlic, ground red pepper, and bacon—called *migas de pastor.*

From Castile comes the best quality Spanish lamb, which when grilled attains a level of specialty by virtue of its utter simplicity. This area of Spain is also famous for its traditional method of grilling lamb and suckling pig. The cold, dry winters are traditionally the time for pork butchering, resulting in the famous chorizo sausage. This region also produces the famous *manchego* sheep's milk cheese, which gets its aromatic flavor from the wild herbs growing in the pastures where the sheep graze.

The cookery of Valencia. This style of Spanish cookery is famous for its clever use of rice. It has been said that the region's cooks are capable of producing 365 rice recipes, one for each day of the year. The two most famous rice recipes from this region are *paella valenciana* and *paella alicantina.*

Spanish rice is cooked with a precise proportion of grain to water so, at the end of the cooking process, the grains are perfectly fluffy, with no stickiness from excess water. The *bomba* variety of rice is ideal for paella, since it absorbs the stock surrounding it, producing the best texture.

The classic *paella valenciana* is composed of elements from the kitchen garden, chicken, rabbit, vegetables, and snails. *Paella alicantina* is essentially composed of seafood. It is visually attractive, presented at the table with shellfish, lobsters, shrimp, and prawns arranged radiating from the center. In both types of *paella,* saffron is essential to give the rice a yellow color and a distinctive flavor.

Andalusian cookery. Andalusia is one of the world's major producers of olive oil, and it has a bountiful seacoast and hot Mediterranean weather. These characteristics have given the regional cuisine its primary features, the refreshing gazpachos, the fried fish, and a style of cookery generally easy to prepare and accompanied by richly flavored wines. Andalusian fish fries are especially famous, and the best cured ham comes from this region.

The high quality of the region's ham is due to the fact that the *cerdo ibérico* (Iberian pig) breed is raised mostly in this region. The pigs' special diet in the pasture and a unique curing process contribute to the fine flavor of these hams, which are classified as *serrano* (plain cured) and *bellota* (acorn ham). *Bellota* comes from Iberian pigs fed on acorns, which achieves a flavor somewhat on the sweet side. This ham is of such prestige that it has been called Spanish "caviar."

Other regions. In addition to the culinary regions already mentioned, Galicia includes the best seafood, Ri-

PAELLA VALENCIANA

The paella is the pan used to cook this legendary dish, and valenciana refers to Valencia, the region of Spain on the shores of the Mediterranean where it originated. It is typically cooked outdoors in the countryside on a dry wood fire. The paella must be set at a suitable height to be surrounded by the flames during the first part of the cooking, and the fire must be kept burning at the correct strength.

Generally a good paella depends not so much on the quality of the ingredients as on combining all the components in the correct proportions. The five basic elements—oil, water, rice, heat, and cooking receptacle—need to be balanced with an almost mathematical precision. The experience and personal touch of whoever is in charge of the cooking are also of utmost importance.

The preparation of a paella in the countryside is a ritualistic festive occasion, which can sometimes turn into a gastronomic debate! The relaxed, lighthearted atmosphere is punctuated with jokes and comments on the progress of the food.

The experience culminates when the paella is deemed ready, removed from the fire, and carried to the table.

Ingredients:

6½ oz. (200 gr) fresh or dried large lima (butter) beans, or *fava* (broad) beans, soaked overnight
4½ cups (2 qt. / 2 l) water
²/₃ cup (5 fl. oz. / 155 ml) olive oil
1½ lb. (750 gr) chicken, in chunks
1 lb. (500 gr) rabbit or lean pork, in chunks
8 oz. (250 gr) green beans, trimmed and halved
1 tomato (3½ oz. / 100 gr) peeled and finely chopped
1 teaspoon paprika
salt
12 small land snails or 1 sprig rosemary
2 pinches saffron
2½ cups (13 oz. / 410 gr) medium grain rice.

Put the lima beans on to boil in 2 cups (16 fl oz. / 500 ml) of water.

Heat the oil in an 18-in. (45-cm) paella (shallow metal pan) and fry the chicken and rabbit chunks, turning to ensure even cooking. Add the green beans and fry gently. Keeping the heat low, add the tomato, then the paprika, immediately followed by the rest of the water.

Add the lima beans with the cooking water. Add salt and bring quickly to a boil, then turn down the heat and continue cooking until the meat is cooked (45–60 minutes).

Add the snails or rosemary. Check the seasoning and add the saffron. Turn up the heat and add the rice, spreading it out as evenly as possible. Cook quickly for the first 10 minutes then turn down the heat gradually for another 8–10 minutes.

Taste the rice to check if it is done. The grains should be soft but still quite firm inside. Remove from the heat and allow to rest 5 minutes before serving. Serves 4.

Lourdes March

oja produces the highest quality Spanish wines, Catalan cookery is notable, and many subregions are incorporated within the larger provinces. The cookery of Galicia in particular benefits from the rugged coastline, ideal for nurturing quality seafood. Furthermore, its inland prairies produce beef and veal famous throughout the country. The delicious empanadas of medieval origin are made with the products of both land and sea.

The cookeries of Navarre and of the Rioja region enjoy the benefit of being in areas with special microclimates, and they are privileged with many bays and river valleys, where rich soils produce appealing vegetables. These vegetables are the ingredients in excellent stews that have encouraged mammoth feasts.

Catalan cooks, in their desires to rescue local traditions and to blend them with an innovative curiosity, compete with the Basques for first place in the Spanish kitchen. Their emphasis on grills and wood-burning fires is most likely of Roman heritage. As in Roman times clay tiles are used in cooking mushrooms, vegetables, fish, and meats. Catalan sauces or *picadas* are made by pounding mixtures of aromatic ingredients, such as garlic, dried fruits, tomatoes, herbs, olive oil, salt, and even cookies to give them a surprisingly sweet flavor. The weight of tradition is also reflected in Catalonia's varied ornamental confectionery.

Other regional foods, of no less importance, include the Murcian, with its fish chowders and the cookery of the Balearic archipelago, probably the most ancient style of cooking in Spain. Extremadura on the Portuguese border and the Canary Islands possess culinary riches inherited from Spain's age of discovery. From their cities came the curious voyagers who inaugurated Spain's expansion into a world empire, the true beginning of globalization.

BIBLIOGRAPHY

Balzola, Asun, and Alicia Ríos. *Cuentos Rellenos*. Madrid, Spain: Editorial Gaviota, 1999. (19 cuentos relativos a la tradición oral gastronómica española).

Ríos, Alicia, and Lourdes March, *The Heritage of Spanish Cooking*. New York: Random House, 1991.

Alicia Ríos

*Translated from the Spanish by
Enrique Balladares-Castellón*

ICE CREAM. Ice cream, or iced cream as it was originally called, was once narrowly defined as a luxury dessert made of cream, sugar, and sometimes fruit congealed over ice. The techniques for making water ices and sorbets probably led to experimentation with cream and milk in Italy during the Renaissance although no recipes survive. On the other hand, there is clear literary evidence that this experimentation underwent considerable refinement in France during the seventeenth century, and that it was the French court of Louis XIV that first served ice creams at banquets. The use of snow and ice to cool wines was known to the Romans, and sorbets were well known to the Persians and Byzantine Greeks. It does not take a large leap in technology to go from sorbets to frozen creams, yet it was the use of sweet cream from cow's milk that originally made true ice cream possible. In fact, it is the rich milk from certain breeds of cattle that further defines the texture and flavor of this product.

Early Techniques

The original technique for making ice cream was relatively simple, although it was predicated on a good supply of ice or well-packed snow. A large pewter basin was filled with coarsely broken ice, over which the confectioner scattered salt. Salt lowers the melting temperature of the ice and thus induces evaporation. Another smaller pewter basin was set into the salted ice. This basin contained the cream, sugar (usually in the form of syrup), and flavoring—lemon being by far the most popular ice cream flavor until the 1850s. The small basin was then turned by hand and the cream mixture stirred gently until it congealed due to the cooling action of evaporation. Otherwise, it was still-frozen, then beaten once firm. This method is found in numerous recipes surviving from the latter half of the sixteenth century, as well as in quite a few eighteenth-century printed cookbooks, including the *Receipts of Mary Eales* and Hannah Glasse's *Compleat Confectioner*.

The cookbook of Mary Eales, which appeared in 1718, is considered the first to feature an ice cream recipe printed in English, and it varies in technique from the basin method just described. Eales placed her cream in pails in an ice chest and still-froze them, a method developed by professional French confectioners and similar in shape to the crank-turned freezers of the nineteenth century. The appearance of ice cream in domestic cookbooks of the period may be taken as evidence that ice cream had moved from strictly palace fare of earlier times to the tables of the literate well-to-do. This is confirmed in America by a 1744 reference to ice cream on the dessert table of Governor Blandon of Maryland—a thing to be marveled at and noted diligently in a dinner guest's diary. The governor's ice cream was served with fresh strawberries, a foreshadowing of the ubiquitous strawberry and ice cream festivals that today have become such an integral part of the American cultural scene. As for Governor Blandon, it goes without saying that many wealthy colonial Americans owned icehouses, which made such luxuries possible.

Implicit in the operation of making ice cream was the use of metal that transfers the cold temperature of the ice as quickly as possible to the cream. Pewter was the preferred metal of most ice cream makers down to the end of the nineteenth century, when it was replaced by other alloys. The reasons for replacing pewter were several: it pitted easily and it was soft. Complex molds made of pewter would eventually warp or bend, especially around the area of the hinges, which would lead to leaks and imperfectly shaped molded ices. Most important, pewter reacted chemically with acids in ice creams, thus forming toxic lead salts. This realization did not occur to confectioners until the chemistry of food became better understood; thus, it is highly probable that toxins in ice cream contributed to some of the maladies suffered by consumers in the past. This was certainly the case prior to pasteurization because freezing cream or milk does not kill microbes or prevent enzyme breakdown. However, none of these modern concerns affected the historical popularity of ice cream in Europe or America. It would probably be more accurate to say that ice cream became such a rage that its negative effects on the body were rarely mentioned even in medical literature. The loudest critics of ice cream bemoaned the costliness, for ice cream was indeed an expensive indulgence until the invention of the commercial ice cream maker in the late 1840s.

If French confectioners brought ice cream to the attention of the world by serving it at the French court, these same confectioners also codified the art of making ice cream so that, by the middle of the eighteenth century, numerous books could be consulted on ice cream making from A to Z. While the basin method was generally a technique employed in household confectionery, professionals made ice creams in ice chests and experimented with various substances to enhance freezing, including alum and saltpeter. The French also coined the term *fromage glacé* for true iced cream and introduced such unusual flavorings as cinnamon, chocolate, bergamot, and orange flower petals. The French in addition developed the concept of serving ice cream in tiny glasses, normally arranged on glass salvers. These standing displays, sometimes stacked very high, are depicted in quite a few confectionery books and necessitated the invention of tiny pointed spoons for eating the creams.

As ice creams became more fashionable, the formulas for making them also became more and more complex. This was especially true for ice creams that were molded because they required a firmer body than the old hand-whipped sorts. Cutting cream with milk and the addition of eggs, all of which was gently cooked until thick, became one of the signature methods used by French confectioners. Modern American ice cream producers generally call such cooked egg-thickened ice creams "French," as in French vanilla ice cream, although in the nineteenth century Sarah Rorer in Philadelphia and Agnes Marshall in London categorized them emphatically as Neapolitan. In fact, cooking the milk or cream was practiced by more than just French confectioners, and in America at least it was associated primarily with Italians. Neapolitan ice cream was also a specific flavor combination: three distinct layers, one green (pistachio), one white (vanilla), and one orange (orange flavor) in imitation when sliced of the Italian national flag.

The Popularity of Ice Cream

The French Revolution did much to spread the popularity of ice cream, especially in England and America, where refugee confectioners set up business. Some of the most active French confectioners settled in New York and Philadelphia, and their advertisements for ice creams are common in American newspapers from the 1790s into the 1820s. It was also during this period that ice cream gardens developed. They featured a confectionery shop where a variety of sweet foods were prepared, where wines and lemonades were served, and even elaborately planted flower gardens and, on occasion, musical entertainment. Since the best cream was seasonal—May and June being the optimal months—the ice cream gardens also offered cooked food to such an extent that many of them resembled outdoor restaurants. The cookery, however, was light, and for the most part appealed to women and children, since they could not enter oyster houses or taverns unless accompanied by a male. Ice cream gardens became safe havens where even teenage girls could socialize (or flirt) with budding admirers. Furthermore, ice cream gardens were off-limits to African Americans; thus in cities like Philadelphia, a number of black cooks established their own counterparts. Once commercial ice cream became less expensive, the ice cream garden was replicated by churches as a fundraising event under the name of an ice cream social.

The most famous ice cream in nineteenth-century America came from Philadelphia owing to the proximity of fine dairies, rich pasturage on which to feed the cows, and no small amount of local ingenuity. While several French confectioners established a penchant for rich ice creams during the 1790s, especially the demand for finely molded *fromages glacés* at supper parties and balls, it was the Parkinson family who put Philadelphia ice cream on the map.

George Parkinson and his wife Eleanor created a confectionery business that made Philadelphia vanilla ice

Puss-in-boots ice cream mold. New York, circa 1881. Pewter alloy (cleaned). Like period gingerbread molds, themes for ice cream molds were derived from popular culture. In this case, the mold design is based on an 1881 Christmas trade card (next page). ROUGHWOOD COLLECTION. PHOTO CHEW & COMPANY.

cream a synonym for the city's haute cuisine. Their son James opened a restaurant in the early 1840s with an ice cream garden in the back—situated in the center of an elaborately pruned collection of roses. Parkinson's sales bills, advertisements, and surviving menus offer a rich selection of ice creams and ice cream sculptures. When Swedish singer Jenny Lind visited Philadelphia in 1850, Parkinson sent to her hotel room an ice cream harp complete with an ice cream nightingale perched on top (the singer was nicknamed the "Swedish Nightingale," hence the allusion). The ice cream was served on a huge silver platter together with a Bohemian glass ice cream service, molded jellies, and "iris-colored" cakes. Parkinson's showmanship did not go unrewarded. The story of the ice cream and Lind's response made national headlines. Parkinson's ice cream flamboyances and another important local development in the history of ice cream probably worked together to establish this food as a national dish. Ice cream is certainly viewed today as an American food, but its transformation would never have happened without Eber C. Seaman.

The Impact of the Crank-Turned Ice Cream Machine

Seaman was a New Jersey Quaker who invented a crank-turned ice cream machine, which he patented in 1848. His invention was first tested in the ice cream saloon of Mrs. E. A. Harbach, a Philadelphia confectioner also famous for her candies. Until the invention of Seaman's device, ice cream had to be made in small batches by

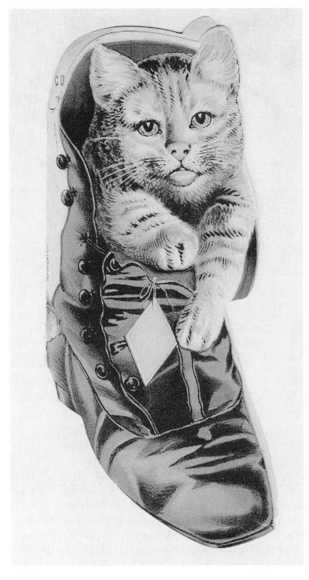

Chromolithograph folding trade card issued for Christmas 1881 by the Philadelphia dry goods store Sharpless & Sons. ROUGHWOOD COLLECTION.

hand. Seaman's crank-turned machine allowed one person to turn out many large batches of ice cream in a matter of hours. This brought down the unit cost of ice cream so that, within a short period of time, it became little more than a street commodity. Seaman's invention is what allowed the American love affair with ice cream to blossom. His large commercial machine was soon miniaturized so that anyone with a supply of ice could make their own ice cream by the quart or gallon. Thus, the hand-turned ice cream machine became a common household utensil by the 1880s, and numerous pamphlet-sized cookbooks were sold to go with them, all including detailed directions for ice cream recipes. One of the most popular brands of ice cream machine was the White

Mountain, which gained many testimonials from leading cooks of the day.

Sarah Tyson Rorer of Philadelphia was a champion of such ice cream pamphleteering, primarily in her role of product endorsement. Rorer's New England counterpart was Mary J. Lincoln of the Boston Cooking School, whose magazines are today a gold mine of period ice cream recipes and illustrations, especially of the odd ways in which the creams were styled for presentation. One wonders whether her ice cream in the shape of a beef tongue realistically colored would have appealed to all sensibilities. On the other side of the Atlantic, Agnes B. Marshall of London not only offered her own patented ice cream freezer, a rich selection of elaborate ice cream molds, but also Marshall's patent ice cave for transporting ice creams to picnics, and two technical books on the subject: *The Book of Ices* (1894) and *Fancy Ices* (1922). Her domination of the late Victorian world of ice cream outshines the likes of either Rorer or Lincoln, and her cookery books are now considered classics of their genre. While Marshall is now part of history, her popularization of iced soufflés and especially of iced puddings has been long-lasting, especially in British cookery.

The future of ice cream, however, was not prophesized in the books of Marshall, but by Rorer. She broke down ice creams into these pragmatic categories: Philadelphia ice cream (using cream only), Neapolitan ice creams (frozen custards employing eggs), and ice creams from condensed milk or a product called evaporated cream. She also included in her 1913 cookbook a recipe for an "Alaska Bake" that was ice cream baked under a thick coating of meringue. In the last two examples, she was somewhat forward-looking in that baked Alaska became popular by the 1920s, and the shift away from natural ingredients to all sorts of artificial additives was already beginning to overtake commercial ice cream production in the early 1900s.

The first step in this evolution was the introduction of condensed milk by Gail Borden in 1856. Commercial thickeners appeared during the 1870s in the form of powders, such as powdered egg yolks, then various gelatin products, both animal- and plant-based. Finally, in 1899 the French introduced homogenizers that largely served as cream substitutes. This led to ice cream powders.

Espoused Health Benefits

Home ice cream making was always fraught with uncertainties, especially the achievement of good texture. Ice cream powder was introduced as a fail-safe remedy with health benefits thrown in for good measure. As one 1908 Jell-O cookbook claimed, "the healthfulness of good ice cream is beyond question. In many cases of illness the patients crave ice cream, and doctors and nurses tell us that it is usually good for them." This reasoning harks back to the Italian sorbets of the eighteenth century, which were often administered to patients suffering from high temperature. But those ices were primarily water

Advertisement from circa 1935 showing the "Happy Cone," which later became known as the Skyscraper. Its tall, phallic shape was made possible by a specially patented scoop. COURTESY OF JUNE V. ISALY AND BRIAN BUTKO.

and sweetened fruit juice, which the body metabolizes differently from dairy-based products.

The health slant was doubtless an attempt to adjust to the Pure Foods Act of 1906 because this same point is echoed across the board in most confectionery advertising of the period. After the United States acquired Cuba, the per capita consumption of sugar soared. Sugar began to permeate all aspects of the American diet, and this trend has not stopped. Yet, as an antidote to demon rum, the fountains of sugar at the ice cream parlor ("parlor" denotes respectability) or local drugstore became the morally correct culinary altar for Methodists, Baptists, and other dry denominations. It was in that blue law milieu that the ice cream sundae was born at Two Rivers, Michigan, in 1881. The sundae transformed plain ice cream into a rapture of chocolate syrup, chopped nuts, and candy tidbits known as nonpareils.

Ice Cream as a Part of Street Culture

Meanwhile, in cities where large communities of Italians settled, the hokey-pokey man became a fixture of popular street culture. He was an ice cream vendor and moving sandwich stand par excellence, with a small pushcart and a variety of Neapolitan flavors—Naples being the presumed origin of all the ice creamers in that line of work. The hokey-pokey man sold ice creams in paper cups and in paper cones so that customers could walk and eat at the same time. They also sold ice cream called penny licks. These were little glasses that contained a penny's worth of ice cream, a marketing gimmick aimed primarily at children. When the ice cream was eaten, the glass was given back to the vendor, who then washed it and refilled it for the next customer. The hokey-pokey man gave rise to a flavor of ice cream in cities like New York and London. In Philadelphia, his name attached itself to a hokey sandwich made with an antipasto salad of cold meats and lettuce now known as the hoagie.

The Ice-Cream Cone

The inventor of the ice-cream cone is not known, although claims abound. There is ample evidence that the concept existed in several forms long before the debut of the cone at the St. Louis World's Fair in 1904. The benefit of the cone was that the ice cream container could be eaten, yet if one is to accept the research of Brian Butko (2001), there was considerable resistance to the idea when it first attracted public attention. Hygiene was one reason, sticky fingers another. The public perception of ice cream was that it should be clean, like milk itself, a food that was both basic and culturally defining. The ice cream parlor and the drugstore soda fountain probably did more to help the ice cream cone gain acceptability in the long run, but it was the carefully wrapped ice cream snacks of the 1920s that eventually captured the market.

That ice cream should assume its hallowed place beside the drug counter during Prohibition may seem at first glance the most remarkable of fates, but it was the original idea that ice cream was both safe and healthy that allowed it to invade the domain of the local apothecary. Temperance instilled Americans with a love of drugs as a substitute for luxury: patent medicines were mostly alcohol, and the tempering qualities of ice cream were not known to cause a Fourth of July picnic to degenerate into debauchery. Perhaps this is one reason why American ice cream evolved into yet another branch of frozen snacks during the 1920s. Perhaps it was also due to a shift in lifestyles and altruistic spin-offs geared toward Hollywood and a need to provide movie theaters with frozen finger foods. Whatever the reason, one of the most important additions to the ice cream story arrived in the form of ice cream "novelties," to use a term then current.

Ice Cream Novelties

This included such portable snack foods as the ice-cream sandwich, the popsicle, and the Klondike, which is today the most popular of all ice cream products of this type. Most of these foods were born about the same time. Eskimo Pies were first marketed in 1921. Good Humor's ice cream "suckers" initially appeared in Youngstown, Ohio, in 1922. And in response to the success of Eskimo Pies, Isaly's of Pittsburgh created the Klondike, its polar bear logo curiously similar to the polar bear used by Mar-

shall in her famous book of ices. Isaly's went on to become a household name in the Midwest, and their popular skyscraper cones left no doubt that even ice cream could assume phallic meanings.

Ice Cream in the Twenty-First Century

Ice cream has now come full circle. Most of it is extremely cheap and for this reason it has lost its sexiness. Low-fat dieticians have decried it as the frozen grease that clogs our veins. Ice cream has become for many the moral opposite of granola or a raw carrot. However, people gorge on ice cream that they feel is safer, which has not only lost its cream, but instead is made entirely of nondairy products, euphemisms for ingredients that never passed through a cow. It might be far more healthful to eat real ice cream in moderation and enjoy a long walk afterwards. This seems to be the rallying cry of the Slow Food Movement and other present-day culinary groups dedicated to revitalizing ice cream, and to restoring its flavor and cultural significance.

See also **Additives; Dairy Products; Icon Foods; Sherbet and Sorbet; Slow Food; Snacks.**

BIBLIOGRAPHY

Butko, Brian. *Klondikes, Chipped Ham, and Skyscraper Cones.* Mechanicsburg, Penn.: Stackpole, 2001.

Ciocca, Giuseppe. *Gelati. Dolci freddi, rinfreschi, bebite refrigeranti.* Milan: 1926.

Cox, J. Stevens. *Ice-Creams of Queen Victoria's Reign.* St. Peter Port (Guernsey): Toucan Press, 1970.

Eales, Mary. *Mrs. Eales' Receipts.* London: Meere, 1718.

Emy. *L'art de bien faire les glaces d'office.* Paris: Le Clerc, 1768.

David, Elizabeth. "Hunt the Ice Cream." *Petits propos culinaires* 1 (1979): 8–13.

David, Elizabeth. "*Fromages glacés* and Iced Creams." *Petits propos culinaires* 2 (1979): 23–35.

Harris, Henry G., and S. P. Borella. *All about Ices, Jellies, Creams, and Conserves.* London: Maclaren and Sons, 1926.

Hyde, K. A., and J. Rothwell. *Ice Cream.* Edinburgh, Scotland: Churchill Livingstone, 1973.

Marshall, Agnes B. *The Book of Ices.* London: Marshall's School of Cookery, 1894.

Marshall, Agnes B. *Fancy Ices.* London: Marshall's School of Cookery, 1922.

Nutt, Frederick. *The Complete Confectioner.* New York: Richard Scott, 1807.

Parkinson, Eleanor. *The Complete Confectioner, Pastry-Cook, and Baker.* Philadelphia: Lea and Blanchard, 1844.

Rorer, Sarah Tyson. *Mrs. Rorer's Ice Creams, Water Ices, Frozen Puddings.* Philadelphia: Arnold and Company, 1913.

Senn, Charles Herman. *Ices and How to Make Them.* London: Universal Cookery and Food Association, 1900.

Stallings, W. S. *Ice Creams and Water Ices in 17th and 18th Century England.* London: Prospect Books, 1979. Issued as a supplement to *Petits propos culinaires* 3.

Williams, Mrs. H. Llewellyn. *The Ice Book. Iced Beverages, Ice Creams, and Ices.* New York: Wehman, 1891.

William Woys Weaver

ICON FOODS. The term "icon" was first used during the Middle Ages as a religious word suggesting images, figures, signs, or objects representing sacred elements. They were fabricated items meant to recreate or suggest something or someone consecrated or divine. Icons themselves are pictures, signs, or resemblances of seemingly more significant things or people. They are slightly different from symbols or indexes in that they have meanings of their own; however, they develop elaborate meanings when used in reference to something more significant. Icons, tangible signs of something larger, are displayed as pictures, objects, and even food, whereas indexes and symbols have meaning only in relationship to another object. It is through the icon that people gain access and learn about the object. Icons are signs that stand for or define something else (Parmentier, 1994; Peirce, 1931).

In the twenty-first century the term "icon" often implies an object representing something else, but even this definition has evolved. Within popular culture, icons are not necessarily just representative of something else but also may be something that receives an extraordinary amount of attention, praise, and idolization. "Iconic" can also mean formulaic or repetitive, as is seen in logos and other illustrative representations. And icons themselves change meanings over time.

The word "icon" today has largely lost its religious and spiritual attachment. Rather, icons are used in secular settings. Examples of icons are found throughout popular culture in movies, books, stories, clothing, music, celebrities, and food. Specific icon foods, when consumed or even just imagined, immediately suggest links to specific places, culturally bound groups, or communities.

Icon foods are always fair game for parody, and, conversely, many icons are also themes for food. The Eiffel Tower, Leaning Tower of Pisa, and the Statue of Liberty have often been reproduced in ice cream or candy. Here we have the Liberty Bell (1876 copper mold complete with faux crack) sold under the guise of walnut ice cream at the U. S. Centennial. To the right is a George Washington cast iron cookie print (for Washington's Birthday), which reappears as a patriotic motif on the preserve jar in "Preserves" (Volume 3, page 153), and a "Liberty" cookie mold for a New England Fourth of July picnic. ROUGHWOOD COLLECTION. PHOTO CHEW & COMPANY.

They are used within a cultural context, exploring how specific foods mirror express groups of people, as opposed to the original religious meanings and connotations of the term "icon." Icon foods and their images also have different meanings for different groups of people, whether grouped by nationality, ethnicity, religious affiliation, or ideological beliefs.

Personal Identity, Group Identity, National Identity

Icon foods help define individual, group, and national identity. The difficulty here is determining whether inside members of a group deem the food iconic or outsiders consider it representative of the group.

Specific foods or food practices may serve as icons for individual people's beliefs or values, as seen in the example of vegetarianism. Corporate identity may also be defined by food icons, as in crediting producers on restaurant menus or the use of fast-food logos. Ethnic groups are often defined by specific foods, considered quintessential to their cultures. National, regional, racial, religious, and ethnic identities are often dictated by specific icon foods. Sometimes these foods are selected by the group itself, as with the state-created Israeli cuisine; southern American grits; Louisiana "crawfish"; Maryland blue crab; Maine lobster; Florida orange juice; Massachusetts cranberries; Vermont maple syrup; Texas chili; New York bagels; Alsatian *choucroute garnie*; French croissants, cassoulet, and ratatouille; Japanese sushi, Scottish haggis; German wursts; Austrian Sacher torte; and Antiguan pepper pot. Sometimes outsiders choose foods they judge iconic for groups they are not members of, often with negative references.

Iconic Food Logos and People

Throughout the world, but predominantly in the United States, food logos for famous food companies represent the whole of American culture and the values of capitalism and enterprise. Around the world America is synonymous with McDonald's. The commonly recognized McDonald's "golden arches" are a representation of modern corporate worship. Other large-scale food company logos are known worldwide also. It is not the foods themselves that suggest the country but in these cases the food businesses that symbolize entire nations. For example, Heineken, Fosters Lager, and Guinness Stout are all brands of beer, but each conjures up specific images of its home country and people, Holland, Australia, and Ireland, respectively. Similarly food clip art emphasizes the visual aspects of food over its taste. It is not the actual food but the image of the food or of the food company and what that image represents. For example, Ronald McDonald is an icon, but he is not a food, a restaurant, or even a person.

The famous Andy Warhol Campbell's soup artwork is an example of a pedestrian food product elevated to iconic proportions. The labels and branding of many other established and popular packaged food products, including Heinz ketchup, Tabasco sauce, Yoo-Hoo chocolate drink, and Oreo cookies, are iconic. In these examples, iconic seems to mean "has been that way for a long time." It is recognizable. People may also serve as food or culinary icons, symbolizing the highest levels of culinary prowess (Julia Child, George-Auguste Escoffier, and Marie Antoine Carême) or representing food values (Alice Waters) or food commercialism (Emeril Lagasse).

See also **Metaphor, Food as**; **Religion and Food**; **United States**.

BIBLIOGRAPHY

Belasco, Warren, and Philip Scranton, eds. *Food Nations: Selling Taste in Consumer Societies.* New York: Routledge, 2002.

Parmentier, Richard J. *Signs in Society: Studies in Semiotic Anthropology.* Advances in Semiotics series. Bloomington: Indiana University Press, 1994.

Peirce, Charles S. *Collected Papers of Charles Sanders Peirce.* Edited by Charles Hartshorne and Paul Weiss. Cambridge, Mass.: Harvard University Press, 1931.

Shortridge, Barbara G., and James R. Shortridge, eds. *The Taste of American Place: A Reader on Regional and Ethnic Foods.* Lanham, Md.: Rowman and Littlefield, 1998.

Jennifer Berg

IMMUNE SYSTEM REGULATION AND NUTRIENTS. Chicken soup, herbal tea, and vitamin C pills take on special meaning in cold and flu season. But beyond their possible role in treatment and comfort, nutrients are essential and fundamental parts of immune system function. To understand nutrient-immune interactions, it is helpful to understand how the body's immune system functions in general.

The human immune system has evolved to the state where it cannot only maintain continual vigilance against new challenges, but can "learn" from past challenges and "remember" more efficient means of resolving those challenges if they are ever encountered again. The numerous cooperative mechanisms by which the immune system addresses (but does not "remember") novel challenges are collectively termed "innate immunity." These mechanisms include proteins that can bind to or neutralize a wide variety of foreign particles, and cells that can phagocitize foreign particles to remove them from the body. In the process of neutralizing and removing foreign particles, other cells within the immune system (mainly dendritic cells) transport samples of the foreign particles (antigens) to specialized tissues and organs (spleen, lymph nodes, Peyer's patches) where naive cells (T cells and B cells) not previously exposed to foreign particles can adapt their surface molecules (through gene recombination) in order to increase the efficiency with which later encounters with the foreign particle can be resolved. These adapted cells and associated specialized proteins (immunoglobulins—proteins that function as antibodies) provide immunological memory of past encounters and form what is termed "acquired immunity."

The body's ability to resolve infections can be likened to the running of a race. The infectious agent must elude detection by the immune system until it can proliferate and establish itself within the body. The earlier the body can detect this infection (by maintaining a critical concentration of innate immune system cells and proteins throughout the body) and the faster the body can produce new protective cells and proteins, the better the chance of winning the race. The key steps in this process—efficient communication and rapid biosynthesis—are constrained by the availability of raw material, and in the body, raw material means nutrients. In this light, well-established nutritional principles can also be regarded as immunological paradigms.

Biosynthesis: Building New Cells and Proteins

The immune system is continually producing a remarkable number of new cells and proteins to provide a broad repertoire of potential immune responses and maintain functional concentrations in the periphery. An average adult has nearly six pounds of bone marrow, which produces about one trillion white blood cells per day, accounting for 8 percent or more of the total protein synthesis in the body. About 60 percent of bone-marrow biosynthesis is devoted to producing neutrophils (innate immune system phagocytes), amounting to about 100 billion cells a day, which then survive only one to two days in circulation. Studies in laboratory rats indicate that in the acquired immune system, cell turnover is ten times higher in the thymus than in the liver. Of the millions of naive T cells and B cells produced in the thymus and bone marrow every day, only about 3 to 5 percent of T cells and 10 to 20 percent of B cells pass positive and negative selection steps to reach the periphery and enter the "race" that was described.

As for proteins, more than two-thirds of the IgA (an acquired immune system protein useful in protecting mucosal surfaces—eyes, mouth, etc.) produced by the body every day (more than three grams per day for a 155-pound person) is secreted onto the body's mucosal surfaces for short-term disposal. Immunoglobulins also account for a significant fraction of total blood protein (second only to albumin) and must be replenished continually at a rate of about six grams of immunoglobulins per day for a 155-pound person. Clearly, maintaining the immune system is a demanding process for the human body.

On the cellular level, upon activation, a lymphocyte doubles the amount of intracellular energy (ATP—that is, adenosine triphosphate) committed to protein synthesis (up to 20 percent of total cell energy use), while nucleotide synthesis begins consuming about 10 percent of the cell's energy. This ATP is ultimately derived from dietary macronutrients (protein, carbohydrate, or fat) through metabolic steps that require thiamin, riboflavin, biotin, pantothenic acid, and niacin. When ATP supply is limited, protein and nucleotide syntheses are the first cellular processes to suffer. The building of proteins and nucleotides from amino acids also requires folate, vitamin B_6, and vitamin B_{12} as the essential cofactors. Enzymes that build immunologically active proteins and cells also rely on diet-derived transitional metal atoms (iron, zinc, copper, etc.) for stability and to serve as functional centers. For example, ribonucleotide reductase is a rate-limiting enzyme in nucleotide synthesis, but the only way to maintain the loosely bound iron atom in its functional center is with adequate dietary iron intake. When deprived of multiple nutrients during malnutrition, these immunological processes are clearly compromised as exemplified by reduced thymus mass, lower IgA secretion, and poor proliferation of immune cells in vitro.

Signaling and Gene Regulation

The ability to expand or direct an immune response depends on communication between and within cells. In the innate immune system, various cells can produce signaling molecules (eicosanoids, chemokines, etc.) that attract phagocytes to the site of a challenge (inflammation) while alerting the rest of the immune system. In the acquired immune system, the adaptation of immune cells can be directed toward more efficacious products by signals between cells (cytokines, receptor interaction, etc.) and inside of cells (intracellular signaling molecules, nuclear binding factors, etc.).

Perhaps the clearest relationship between essential nutrients and immune system signaling is the transformation of dietary essential fatty acids into eicosanoids. Certain kinds of fat, which synthesize polyunsaturated fatty acids, are essential to life. These fatty acids are classified as omega-3 or omega-6 fatty acids based on their chemical structure. These fatty acids are used by the body to manufacture eicosanoids (prostaglandins, thromboxanes, and leukotrienes) that regulate inflammation and other body functions. At a molecular level, the distinction between dietary intake of omega-3 versus omega-6 fats is functionally important since eicosanoids derived from omega-3 fats do not produce as much inflammation as omega-6 fats.

An area of immunological research that has rapidly expanded in recent years is the discovery and characterization of proteins that carry signals between the cell surface and nucleus as well as where these proteins bind within various genes. Both vitamin A and vitamin D regulate gene expression by binding to specific gene sequences including, for example, the genes that regulate production of the antiviral protein interferon-gamma. A deficiency of either of these vitamins can impair immune function. Pharmacological doses of vitamin D have been investigated for their therapeutic potential in autoimmune disorders.

Immune system cells also initiate intracellular signals in response to oxidation. Oxidative stress induces expression of intracellular proteins (AP-1 and NF-kB), which leads to increased production of pro-inflammatory signaling molecules (such as cytokines and chemokines) and their receptors. Vitamin E, vitamin C, and other antioxidants can reduce NF-kB expression, which may contribute to their wide variety of effects on the immune system. Intracellular oxidation state also may alter acquired immune responses, but further research is needed to determine if dietary antioxidants can modify oxidation-sensitive genes and proteins.

Life-Cycle Stages

Different stages of the life cycle have unique nutritional demands and are characterized by unique immunological functionality. Both young children and the elderly have clear age-related immune function deficiencies. In addition, many children in the United States do not meet their daily requirements for several immunologically relevant nutrients, including vitamin E, iron, zinc, and vitamin B_6. The elderly may also have difficulty meeting their requirements for vitamin B_{12}, zinc, vitamin E, iron, vitamin D, and vitamin B_6 as a result of physiological changes due to aging or to inadequate dietary intakes. Pregnant and lactating women are remarkable because they produce acquired immune system products for the sole apparent purpose of export to the infant. Likewise, pregnant and lactating women frequently do not meet their nutritional demands for folate, vitamin B_6, iron, and zinc. Few studies have examined the interaction between nutrients and life-cycle–dependent immune outcomes in otherwise healthy people, but the available data indicate that these interactions have immunological impact—for example, vitamin E among the elderly and iron among postpartum women. Given the susceptibility of these populations to infectious disease, a better understanding of nutrient-immune life-cycle interactions is needed to promote optimal immune status through adequate nutrition.

Nonnutritive Food Components and the Immune Response

For immunologists, developing more efficacious vaccines and certain anticancer agents is a process of improving immune system performance. As nutritional paradigms have shifted from preventing deficiency to promoting optimal health, nutrition scientists have also sought to improve immune system performance. Many in vivo studies have examined more or less purified food components like phytochemicals (polyphenols), herbs, and carotenoids. Such studies frequently use classic immunological tests—cell proliferation, blood lymphocyte counts, skin hypersensitivity responses, etc.—but the results of these tests should be interpreted with caution. For example, a food component that increases cell proliferation may be

beneficial if it is the protective cells that proliferate more readily. Conversely, increased cell proliferation would be harmful if autoreactive T-cell or B-cell clones were expanded or inflammatory responses were boosted inappropriately. Although these measures are useful for preliminary identification of nutrient-immune interactions, additional studies using efficacy-related immune measures (infectious disease risk, vaccine titers, etc.) are needed before such phenomena can be termed beneficial.

Summary

To maintain immunological competence, the immune system must quickly alert the body to foreign challenges and rapidly manufacture the cells and proteins needed to stop exponentially dividing infectious organisms. It is apparent that some essential nutrients are signaling molecules. Others can be rate-limiting factors in cell division and protein synthesis. The brevity of this review has prohibited the exploration of many other important nutritional immunology topics: nutrient interactions with infectious agents, treatment of autoimmune disorders, cancer biology, and metabolic functions of nutrients unrelated to biosynthesis or signal transduction. Clearly, the most venerable nutritional paradigms of growth and development are important for shaping the magnitude and character of immune responses.

See also **Fats; Gene Expression, Nutrient Regulation of; Iron; Nutrients; Vitamins: Overview; Vitamins: Water-Soluble and Fat-Soluble Vitamins**.

BIBLIOGRAPHY

Buttgereit, F., G.-R. Burmester, and M. D. Brand. "Bioenergetics of Immune Functions: Fundamental and Therapeutic Aspects." *Immunology Today* 21 (2000): 192–199.

Delves P. J., and I. M. Roitt. "The Immune System: First of Two Parts." *New England Journal of Medicine* 343 (2000): 37–49.

Delves P. J., and I. M. Roitt. "The Immune System: Second of Two Parts." *New England Journal of Medicine* 343 (2000): 108–117.

Inserra, P. F, S. K. Ardestani, and R. R. Watson. "Antioxidants and Immune Function." In *Antioxidants and Disease Prevention*, edited by H. S. Garewal, pp. 19–29. New York: CRC Press, 1997.

James, M. J., R. A. Gibson, and L. G. Cleland. "Dietary Polyunsaturated Fatty Acids and Inflammatory Mediator Production." *American Journal of Clinical Nutrition* 71 (2000): 343S–348S.

Prentice, A. M. "The Thymus: A Barometer of Malnutrition." *British Journal of Nutrition* 81 (1999): 345–347.

Ross, A. C, and U. G. Hammerling. "Retinoids and the Immune System." In *The Retinoids: Biology, Chemistry and Medicine*, edited by M. B. Sporn, A. B. Roberts, and D. S. Goodman, 2nd ed., pp. 521–543. New York: Raven Press, 1994.

J. Paul Zimmer

INCA EMPIRE. The imperial Inca state was built upon thousands of years of cultural history and diverse elaborate statecraft of the Andean region of western South America, beginning in the thirteenth century C.E. Though the empire was short-lived (it was conquered by Spain in the sixteenth century), the Inca of the Cuzco valley brought together hundreds of groups, including speakers of many mutually exclusive languages from the dry western South American coasts to the verdant Amazonian foothills, from warm and moist valleys of modern Columbia to the dry Atacama Desert of Chile and the dry mountains of northwestern Argentina. They conquered this territory in less than sixty years. Among their many tools for statecraft were food production, storage, and feasting. When they conquered they divided the lands for the state, for the sun (the focus of their religion), and for local use. In this way the conquered people had to work all of the land, though most of the produce was for the Inca rulers; produce was taken to and stored in highly regularized storage buildings called *qolqa* placed at administrative centers (*tambo*) throughout the empire. Food had great cultural value and carried the histories of the consumers in every meal. The recipe and type of plant variety used identified a person's background, much as clothing did. The Inca encouraged these differences, to keep account of the groups that they codified in a hierarchical record-keeping organization, with the local leaders reporting to Inca administrators.

All social events were marked with food and gift exchanges. These feasting activities occurred at the conquest of new peoples, but also at the renewal of group allegiances and all religious ceremonies. John Rowe notes that the value of crops was so great that at the start of planting season, between September and November, when the rains began, the Sapa Inca (king) himself would join the religious assembly to make the first hole in the ground for maize (corn) planting in a sacred field of the religious authorities. While men had to make the holes in the ground, women had to place the seed in the earth. Singing accompanied this activity, recounting major military victories. After this planting was begun, beer was provided to all workers. The crops were tended throughout the rainy season, to keep animals from eating them, until harvest, which began around May when the rains tapered off. In the highlands, harvest was accompanied by large cooked meals, primarily of potatoes, in the fields, to repay helpers.

When the Inca arrived on the borders of a group they wanted to conquer, they would send emissaries ahead to ask if the group wanted to join the Inca state or would rather fight. If the group chose to join and not fight, a date would be set for a ceremony. On that date, the Inca military leaders would arrive in the territory bearing gifts of fine clothing, elaborate imperial ceramics, and jewelry, for the new local leaders to take on the emblems of the Inca state. If the local leaders accepted these gifts and their takeover, there would be a feast of

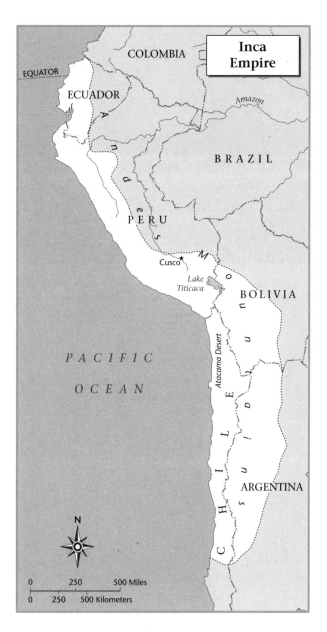

beer and meat. These events focused on specific dishes, ceramics, and cuisine. Tamara Bray reports that there were three highly standardized receptacles to present food at these state occasions; a jar or *arybaloid*, a plate, and a cup or *keru*. The jar was to serve liquid, always a fermented beer called *chicha* in Quechua, the Inca language. This vessel shape is the oldest ceramic shape in the Andes. This beverage could be made out of many plant items, the strongest being the fruit from a leguminous tree of the warm valleys and coasts, *Schinus molle*, called *molle*. *Chicha* could also be made from quinoa (*Chenopodium quinoa*), an annual grain that grows in the high mountains, but the most common and of highest value was *chicha* from maize (*Zea mays*). (In fact, it is clear that the Inca made maize the state crop and focused much of their conquests on the warmer intermontane valleys

Ancient terraced fields at Mora, Peru. By terracing fields into the sides of steep mountains, the Inca were able to increase their food production many times over. © CHRIS RAINIER/CORBIS.

See also **Beer: From Late Egyptian Times to the Nineteenth Century; Central America; Maize; Mexico; Mexico and Central America, Pre-Columbian; South America.**

BIBLIOGRAPHY

Bray, Tamara. "To Dine Splendidly." Paper presented at "The Culinary Equipment of Early States: The Political Dimensions of State Pottery Symposium" at the 65th Annual Meeting of the Society for American Archaeology, Philadelphia, 2000.

Rowe, John Howland. "Inca Culture at the Time of the Spanish Conquest." In *Handbook of the South American Indians*, edited by Julian H. Steward. Washington, D.C.: Government Printing Office, 1946–1959.

Christine A. Hastorf

INDIA.

This entry contains three subentries:
Moghul India
Northern India
Southern India

MOGHUL INDIA

Indian cuisine reached its zenith in the royal kitchens of the kings, nawabs, and maharajas —the one-time rulers of India's princely states who patronized art and culture, and enjoyed a lavish lifestyle. Among the varied cuisines that were native to India or borrowed from other world cultures and amalgamated within the Indian milieu, the one that stands at the forefront is "Moghlai cuisine," named for the era of the Grand Moghuls during which time it developed and became immensely popular. So rich and grand was this cuisine that it left a lasting impact on and influenced other equally grand cuisines—the Awadhi cuisine of Lucknow and of the Rampur royal family in North India and the Hyderabadi cuisine within the state of Nizam in the Deccan region.

In spite of multiple invasions—by the Aryans in 200 B.C.E., the Greeks led by Alexander the Great in 326 B.C.E., the Moghuls in the sixteenth century, the British in the eighteenth and nineteenth centuries, and the more limited incursions of the Mongols, Huns, Arabs, Turks, Afghans, Portuguese, and Dutch in between—India still managed to establish and maintain its own unique cuisine, with that of the Moghuls being a major influence.

Muslim incursions into India began as early as 712 C.E. However, their presence only began to be felt around 1000 C.E., starting with the raids of Mahmud Ghaznavi. The first Muslim kingdom was declared in India in the twelfth century with the establishment of the "Delhi sultanate," although it was not until 1526 that Babur the Mughal, a descendant of Tamerlane and Genghis Khan, successfully invaded the Punjab and proclaimed himself emperor of India. Humayun, Akbar, Je-

and coasts.) This beer would be consumed in highly decorated tumbler-shaped cups made of ceramic or wood. This vessel probably became an important item used in ritual consumption in the earlier Middle Horizon states. The plate was an innovation for dry food presentation in the Andes. This would be how the dried camelid meat (*charqui*), boiled potatoes (*papa*), or toasted corn kernels (*kamcha*) would have been presented. Outside of the imperial Inca feasts such dried foods would have been presented on nicely woven cloth, as is still done in the countryside in the early twenty-first century. The Inca controlled hunting of large game, primarily two kinds of deer (*loyco* and *taroka*) and guanaco, for their pleasure, making these species a less common foodstuff than in earlier times.

Most of the populace typically ate something quite different. There were two main meals a day. The first was a thick soup eaten out of bowls in the midmorning after early tending of herds. It was made of potatoes, quinoa, or maize in the highlands, depending on the elevation of the farmer, and of lima beans or maize on the coast. The highland evening meal at dusk was consumed after a day in the fields and usually was solid food consisting of beans or boiled potatoes with a spicy sauce of chili peppers and wild herbs, eaten out of a common cooking jar with wooden spoons or on woven cloth. Meat was sometimes included, but it was usually only reserved for feast days. This would often be llamas or alpacas (camelids) in the higher areas, or guinea pigs (*cuyes*), and less often wild ducks, rabbits, and other small animals caught in the fields. Along the coast, fish, shellfish, and also seaweed would have been a common soup base as well as an addition to the evening meal, again spiced with chili peppers and wild herbs.

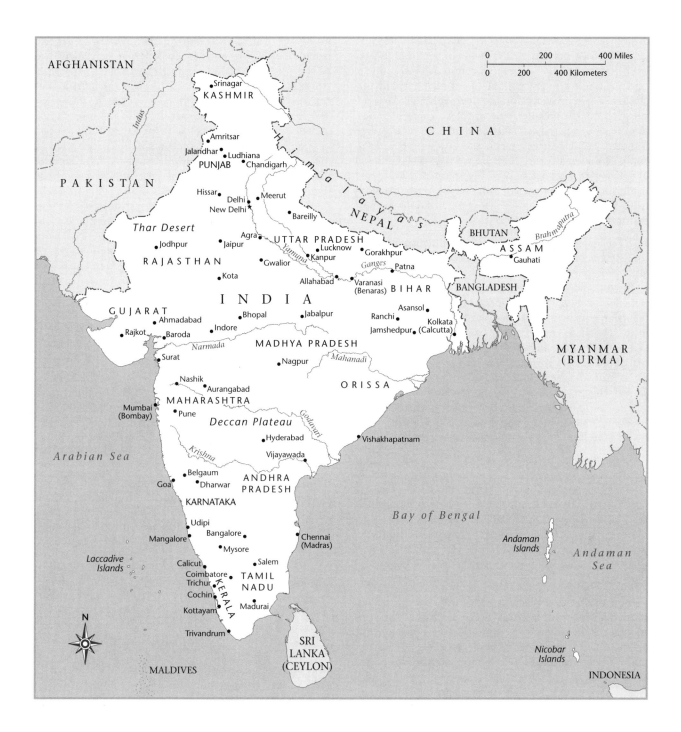

hangir, Shah Jehan, and Aurangzeb, with whose death in 1707 C.E. the empire effectively came to a close, followed Babur as emperor.

During Babur's rule, a Moghul era with unparelleled power flourished. Architectural projects involving the construction of great cities, palaces, mosques, and monuments were executed in North India. This time period also marked the genesis of a "cuisine" later designated as Moghuls' cuisine in India. While cherishing their cuisine, Babur and his successors, soon titled Grand Moghuls, inadvertently enhanced many facets of Indian life. They in-

troduced a unique grandeur and style to an otherwise austere Indian hospitality.

Moghul cuisine is classified as the richest and most lavish cuisine of North India. It revolves around lamb preparations for which it is famous. Prepared with cream, luscious fruits, and almonds, and served with rich *pulaos* (preparations of rice), the gamut of lamb preparations can be described in one sentence: "A really superb North Indian cook can produce a different lamb dish for every day of the year." History, tradition, and religion have encouraged North Indian cooks to experiment with lamb dishes. Because of their Muslim backgrounds, Moghul kitchens could not use pork. The use of beef was also actively discouraged in a predominantly Hindu country. And, neither geography nor habit permitted the ready inclusion of fish or seafood in the diet. Although Moghlai cuisine came to include some excellent chicken dishes, they never compared in quality or scope with the supreme Moghlai culinary achievement, the inspired cooking of lamb. It was mandatory that the animal be slaughtered by cutting the jugular vein with a sharpened knife and while uttering the name of Allah. The meat produced from this type of slaughter, that is, by bleeding the animal to death, was called *halal* meat.

To the somewhat austere Hindu dining ambience, the Muslims brought a refined and courtly etiquette of both group and individual dining, and of sharing food and fellowship. Food items indigenous to India were enriched with nuts, raisins, spices, and ghee (clarified butter). These included meat and rice dishes (*pulaos*), dressed meats (kebabs), stuffed items (*samosas*), desserts (*halwa* and stewed fruit), and sweetened drinks (*falooda* and sherbet). New dishes enriched the cuisine of the land, like those made of wheat finely ground with meat (*halim* and *harisa*), the frozen *kulfi*, a rich ice cream of milk solids, or the *jalebi* (a sweet made from gram flour, which is deep-fried and sweetened in sugar syrup). The Muslims influenced both the style and substance of Indian food.

Moghlai cuisine consists generally of *sharbat i labgir* (a very sweet sherbet), *naan e tanuk* (light bread), *naan e tanuri* (chapatis cooked in tandoors), *samosas* (whole wheat pastry stuffed with meat, onion, etc.), mutton, the flesh of birds such as quail and sparrow, *halwa*, and *sabuni sakar* (a mixture of almonds, honey, and sesame oil). Wine was also customarily served. After the meal, it was customary to serve betel leaf to refresh the palate and to aid digestion.

Vast table settings and spreads were commonplace. However, most eating was done by hand, although spoons and knives were used for serving and carving. The hospitality of the elite Moghuls was legendary. It was often the case that a nobleman's entire staff would be fed their main midday meal at his home. This would comprise *naan* (bread baked in a tandoor), goat meat, chicken *biryani*, a cup of wine, sherbet, and betel leaf. Frequently, the nobles ate their meals together and the unconsumed food would be distributed to beggars.

During the reign of Akbar, there were three classes of cooked dishes. The first, called *safiyana*, was consumed on Akbar's days of abstinence. No meat was eaten on these days, and the dishes were either rice- or wheat-based. The rice-based dishes included *zard birinj* (saffron rice), *khuska* (boiled rice), *khichri* (a dry preparation of rice and lentils cooked together), and *sheer birinj* (rice cooked with milk and sweetened). The wheat-based dishes included *chichi* (essentially the gluten of wheat isolated by washing and then seasoned). Also included in the

meal were lentils, *palak saag* (spinach), *halwa* (a generic name for a dessert made by cooking one ingredient like carrots with milk solids and clarified butter, and then sweetening it with sugar), and sherbets. Both meat and rice cooked together, or meat and wheat prepared together, constituted the next set of dishes. Those with rice included *pulaos*, *biryanis*, *shulla* (a spicy mix of rice, lentils, and meat), and *shurba* (a thick soup). Those with wheat included *halim* and *harisa* (both are made by pounding wheat and meat together with spices), and *kashk* and *qutab* (both prepared with meat and wheat with different spices). The third class of cooked dishes were those in which meat was cooked with *ghee* (clarified butter), spices, curd, eggs, and so forth, to yield dishes such as *yakhni* (a mutton preparation), kebabs, *dopiyaza* (literally, "twice onions," once at the start of cooking in ground form and then later sliced and fried), *mussaman* (a mélange of minced meat, onions, herbs, and spices used as a stuffing), *dumpukh* (meat or vegetable dry-cooked in a heavy-bottomed, tightly sealed pan on a slow fire), *qaliya* (a meat dish cooked with a vegetable, in which the gravy is thick and saucelike), and *malghuba* (a spicy meat dish).

Variations of bread served were either thick, made from wheat flour and baked in an oven, or thin, made from unleavened dough and baked on iron plates using a dough of either wheat or *khushka* (boiled rice). The Persian Muslims preferred leavened bread baked in an underground oven. The *paratha* (whole wheat bread, layered with fat and baked on a griddle) was an adaptation of the deep-fried *pooris* (whole wheat dough, rolled out and deep-fried). The more affluent Muslims ate *baqar khani* (leavened bread enriched with clarified butter), whereas *shirmal* (a sweet baked bun-type bread) was even more upscale than *baqar khani*.

Raw materials came from various places: rice from Bharaij, Gwalior, Rajori, and Nimlah; *ghee* from Hissar; ducks, water fowl, and certain vegetables from Kashmir; and fruits from across the northwestern borders as well as from all over the country. Babur's personal fascination with Indian fruits was evident in his description of them, his names for the fruits sometimes making a technical comment on their variety: the citrus phylum-orange, lime, citron, *santhra* and *galgal* (both are species of orange), *jambiri lime* (rough lemon), *amritphal* (perhaps the mandarin orange), and *amal bid* (a citrus fruit).

A favorite breakfast for common Muslims was *naan* accompanied by *kheema* (minced meat) or kebabs. Rice and onions, and rice-based desserts, such as *phirni* (rice flour cooked with milk and sweetened), *sheer birinj* (rice and milk cooked together and then sweetened) blended with milk and sugar, *halwas*, and dried fruits were other delicacies. The Muslims also adopted the Hindu habit of chewing betel leaves stuffed with areca nuts and spices after a meal.

Eminent citizens who lived in grandeur relished serving opulent preparations, which could number as many as fifty types at a time. Most of the preparations served were those inspired by the Persians and Iranians, and included such dishes as *khormas* (meat, chicken, or fish with a sauce of creamy consistency), kebabs, *rotis* (unleavened bread), and *pulaos*. The marriage of the Persian Princess Noor Jehan to Indian Prince Jehangir also contributed to the import of many delicacies to India and this had its own profound effect on Moghul cuisine.

The art of retaining the rudimentary character of a food preparation while incorporating multiple seasonings was mastered by Indian chefs. A classic illustration is the preparation of Moghlai *biryani*. This dish is also a model for the fusion characteristic of cooking from a bygone era. Two odd or incompatible ingredients—rice and lamb—were not only marinated, but also married with spices, curds, saffron, an aromatic mixture of spices, and garnished with *varq* (silver leaves).

Although there is room for modification or different styles in *biryani*, its basic formula is as steadfast as that of another speciality, kebabs. Through the multiple processing of lamb, which was minced, steamed, skewered, broiled, cubed, or sliced, Moghul chefs demonstrated great dexterity in the preparation of this dish. The two most popular dishes in the kebab family were *shammi* kebab (a combination of minced lamb, nuts, and chickpeas, stuffed with chopped onions and green chilies) and *nargisi* kebab (a hard-boiled egg covered with a preparation of minced lamb, onions, spices, and herbs, and then deep-fried).

Chefs were trained to present their food as impressively as possible. Some even went as far as preparing *khichri* (a rice and lentil preparation) with almonds and pistachio nuts, which were cut to resemble grains of rice and lentils. This was all done for visual effect. Colors also played a major role in food presentation. Various permutations and combinations were used to make the appearance of the dish as attractive as the taste.

The Moghuls introduced rich, milk-based sweets in India. Tiny bits of bread coated with sugar and ghee were prepared for the ceremonies of *Fatiha* (prayers offered to one's ancestors) and *Niyaz* (prayers offered to the Prophet). *Malida* (a sweet made with broken bread, sugar, and ghee, although the bread is often replaced with semolina) was another sweet dish. Gradually, milk, which had been thickened by boiling it down, replaced flour in the preparation of sweets. The Moghuls were also fond of candies and conserves. During their reign, *murabbas* (sweetened preserves) and *achars* (pickles) were developed and commonly used. *Halwa*, a sweet item, would be made with a variety of ingredients, from which it would take its name. For instance, if made from carrots, it would be called "carrot" *halwa*, if made from lentils, it would be called "lentil" *halwa*, and so on. *Halwa* is said to be of Arab origin. The most popular *halwa*s with the Muslims were *sohan* (a sticky wheat confection), *papri* (a crispy sweet confection made with wheat and sugar), *habshi*

(made with wheat, reduced milk, and sugar), and *dudhia* (made with bottle gourd, reduced milk, and sugar). *Barfi* (a dry, white, soft sweet like a milk cake) originated in Persia (*baraf* means snow in the Persian language). *Balu shahi* (a sweet, glazed wheat patty), *khurme* (a date-shaped sweet), *nuktiyan* (a sweet dish made of wheat and sugar shaped as small beads), *gulab jamun* (croquettes made of milk solids, deep-fried until golden brown, and then soaked in sugar syrup), and *dar behisht* (a sweet dish of rice flour and thickened milk) were all developed during this era. *Jalebis* originated in Arabia, where they are called *zalabia* (a gram flour batter, piped out in circles in hot oil, deep-fried until crisp, and then soaked in sugar syrup).

Food that was served at feasts at home or transported to another setting was called *tora*. This comprised a *pulao* (a rice-based dish); *muzafar* (a sweet, rich rice dish flavored with saffron); *mutanjan* (meat, sugar, and rice with spices); *shirmal* (a sweet baked bun-type bread); *safaida* (a simple sweet rice dish); fried aubergine; *shir birinj* (a rich sweet rice dish boiled in milk); *qaurma* (a meat curry); *arvi* (a fried vegetable with meat); *shammi kababs* (croquettes of meat and lentils); and *murabba* (sweetened preserves), *achar*, pickles, and chutney.

Regional environments influenced dietary rituals in India. Meat or any type of flesh is forbidden after a funeral. No food is cooked in the house of mourning for forty days after the death. Women who are seven months pregnant receive vegetables, dried fruit, and cake on their laps. After an engagement ceremony, dates and sugar are distributed to the family of the groom-to-be. At the wedding, the bride and her kinswomen eat from the same plate, a practice that would be unthinkable in the Hindu world. Islamic festivals such as *Bakrid*, *Id*, and *Moharram* are celebrated all over India. The foods consumed by the community have a strong Islamic influence. *Maleeda* (broken bread, sugar, and ghee) is a common ritual offering.

The Moghul emperors relished the practice of eating *paan* (betel leaf). Two betel leaves formed one *bira*: One leaf was stuffed with *supari* (betel nut) and *kattha* (*Acacia catechu*, heartwood extract), and the other leaf would have *chuna* (lime). Sometimes, the betel leaves contained *kapur* (camphor) and musk. When chewed, this sweetened the breath and reddened the lips. *Paan*s were bestowed as a mark of royal favor on courtiers. By the end of the seventeenth century, a *paandaan* (a container for betel leaves and other ingredients) was given as a royal present to ambassadors and nobles.

The Moghul emperors favored water from the Ganges River. People with the highest integrity oversaw the transportation and distribution of water, from the source to its points of consumption. The water was tasted before consumption as a precautionary measure against poisoning. The use of wine was neither prescribed nor forbidden in the Mughal fraternity.

Devout Muslims celebrate three main festivals, each of which is replete with its own food requirements:

- *Ramadan* is observed as a time of fasting and austerity. During this period, Muslims fast from sunrise to sunset, breaking their fast only with the setting sun. The month culminates in the festival of *'Id al-fitr*, where alms are distributed. Traditionally, *sheer qurma* (a sweet dish of milk, vermicelli, nuts, and dried fruits) is made on this day and offered to family and guests. *Haleem* and *harees*a are other dishes that are commonly eaten at this celebration as they are very nutritious.

- *Id uz zuha*, or *Bakrid*, commemorates the sacrifice of Ishak by prophet Ibrahim in the name of God. However, God instructs Ibrahim to sacrifice a ram instead. On this day, Muslims sacrifice lambs, goats, rams, and cows and feast on ritual *pulaos, biryanis*, curries, and roasts. These are then sent to family and friends not in attendance.

- *Muharram* is observed in honor of the saint Hussain, who fell in battle against Yazid, the tyrant ruler of Arabia. Meat is strictly avoided on this day. *Khubooli* (a simple austere dish of rice and chickpea lentils), yogurt and rice, and *zarda* (a sweet dish made with rice) are prepared and offered in prayers.

See also **Asia, Central; Hindu Festivals; Hinduism; Islam; Middle East; Ramadan; Religion and Food; Zoroastrianism**.

BIBLIOGRAPHY

Acharya, K. T. *Indian Food: A Historical Companion*. 1994.

Acharya, K. T. *A Historical Dictionary of Indian Food*. 1998.

Ansari, Muhammad Azhar. *Social Life of the Mughal Emperors, 1526–1707*. New Delhi, 1974.

Rao, Shavaji, and Shalini Devi Holkar. *Cooking of the Maharajas*. New York: Viking, 1975.

Rau, Shanta Rama. *The Cooking of India*. New York: Time Life Books, 1975.

Sharar, Abdul Halim. *Lucknow: The Last Phase of the Oriental Culture*. London: Paul Elek, 1975.

Thangam Philip

NORTHERN INDIA

India is a vast country. Its geography and climate vary tremendously, from the landlocked mountains and the fertile Indo Gangetic plains in the North, to the arid Deccan plateau and the coastal regions of the South. It is these differences that have given India a rich and varied tradition of food.

India is made up of people from several faiths, and the gulfs between them are substantial, including dietary customs and prohibitions. Thus, the Hindus and Sikhs will not eat beef; the orthodox Hindus and Jains avoid onion and garlic, considered "passion-inducing"; the Parsis, who came to India in the seventh century from Persia, gave up eating beef as a gesture of thanks to the Hindu ruler who gave them asylum; and the Muslims and Jews abstain from pork but relish beef, the meat of sheep, and chicken.

Although India is associated strongly with the concept of vegetarianism, which came into being with the advent of the faiths of Buddhism and Jainism in the sixth century B.C.E., the majority of people in India are, however, nonvegetarian. In Punjab, chicken, lamb, and goat meat are relished, and in Kashmir, the Kashmiri pundits are known for their love of meat and famous *wazwan*s (feasts), where up to thirty nonvegetarian courses may be served. Nonetheless, in most Indian families where meat is consumed, this occurs no more than one day a week, usually on a Sunday afternoon. For many other families, meat is consumed only three or four times a year, usually at weddings. In many middle-class families in the North, it is common to find women who do not partake of meat, fish, or eggs, while the men in the family do. The consumption of meat in these areas is sometimes associated with masculinity.

Outside Influences

India is a melting pot of people of all religions and races, its diversity resulting from countless invasions and migrations, including those of Alexander the Great (356–323 B.C.E.). Invaders came in search of wealth and soon discovered India's spices.

The food of North India was greatly influenced by the Persians, who entered India in the eleventh century. From the thirteenth to sixteenth centuries, Mongolian conquerors brought with them Afghan and Persian cuisine, the rich and fragrant foods of their regions. This marked the start of luxurious eating. Pilafs and *biryanis* (meat-based pilafs), garnishes of *varak* (sheets of pounded silver), spicy *kormas* (braised meat in creamy sauces), *koftas* (grilled, spicy meatballs), and *kababs* graced the tables of the emperors and intermingled Hindu and Muslim cuisines: the meat dishes of the Middle East combined with the spicy gravies that were indigenous to India. And, Muslim *naans* (bread cooked in a tandoor) and *chapatis* (bread cooked on a griddle) were consumed side by side with the more traditional *pooris* (bread made from whole wheat flour and fried in oil) and *bhathuras* (bread made from white flour and yeast and then deep-fried in oil). The idea of ending a meal with a confection also originated in the Middle East. Most of these were made of almonds, rice, wheat flour, or coconut, sweetened with sugar, and scented with rose water.

More recently, Indian cuisine has been influenced by the British, particularly in certain sections of society, such as the army and among educated, urban professionals. They institutionalized the use of white bread, as well as sandwiches, toast, and tea drinking.

SUSHRUTA SAMHITA

The *Sushruta Samhita* is an ancient Ayurvedic text, dating back to 600 B.C.E. This traditional healing practice originated almost five thousand years ago, and its theory influenced Greek and Chinese medicine. According to Ayurvedic theory, the human body is made up of five elements: air *(vayu)*, water *(jala)*, fire *(agni)*, earth *(prithvi)*, and space *(akash)*. These combine to form the constitution of the body. Any imbalance in this constitution produces disease, and Ayurveda aims to correct such imbalances by the use of suitable counter-substances.

Food plays an important role in countering the imbalances. There are six basic tastes, which are made up of two elements each: sweet (earth and water), sour (fire and earth), salty (fire and water), bitter (space and air), and astringent (earth and air).

As these elements also form the constitution of the body, the choice of food should be such that it reduces the predominant elements within the body, so that a balance exists between them. When the elements are in equilibrium, one will enjoy good health. However, what may be beneficial for one person might not suit another. Diets therefore vary from person to person, depending on age, sex, climate, and other variables.

The *Sushruta Samhita* suggests that foods be varied in taste according to the season: spring (pungent), summer (sweet and cold), monsoons (salty and sour), autumn (sweet), and winter (pungent and oily). The use of correct foods in different seasons will presumably prevent the onset of disease.

Seasonality of Cuisines

The well-defined seasons of India bring with them a series of particular fruits and vegetables. Thus, menus and diets vary considerably year round—from lush berries in the early days of summer to ripe watermelons available during the later hot weeks of the same season. Certain seasons are associated with specific foods, according to the *Sushruta Samhita*, an ancient medical text, written around 600 B.C.E. It recommends pungent foods in spring, sweet and cold in summer, salty and sour during the rains, sweet in autumn, and greasy and hot in winter.

In Kashmir, where the winters are cold, the staple diet of meat, fish, and rice is supplemented with vegetables that have been sun-dried during the summer months. Seasonality also extends to herbs and spices. During the cold months of winter, "heat-generating" spices like cinnamon, cardamom, cloves, black pepper, and chilies are used in cooking to keep the body warm. Mace is consid-

ered taboo in summer, whereas poppy seeds are regarded as cooling during the summer months.

Foods of the Northern Region: Kashmir, Punjab, Uttar Pradeshi, and Rajasthan

Traditionally, Indian food is served as a complete meal in one course. It is composed of several vegetables, a *dal* (a purée of lentils), and a central starch, which is the main source of calories. Yogurt, relishes, and chutneys are served on the side. In the North, the starch is unleavened bread, such as *chapati* (a flat griddle bread). People in the North tend to eat more wheat and maize, which are easily available and made into bread.

Pulses high in protein, carbohydrates, and fiber have always played an important part in the diet of Indians. For vegetarians, pulses provide essential proteins.

The most commonly eaten meats are chicken, mutton, and fish. A rice-based sweet usually signifies the end of a meal. Savory and sweet snacks are very popular, but do not correspond to specific meals or dishes. Northern India has a great tradition of "snacking."

Alcohol is not consumed along with food, but iced water or *lassi* (a yogurt-based drink) usually accompanies the meal. Aperitifs like *kanji* (made from fermented carrots and mustard seeds), *aam panna* (raw mango juice), *jaljeera* (made from tamarind juice and cumin seeds), and *nimbupani* (fresh lime juice) are the favored drinks in the North.

North Indians place great emphasis on the use of milk and milk products in their cuisine. This is particularly true of the Punjabis, who use a great deal of ghee

SNACKING IN INDIA

Indians love to snack and have a penchant for light, spicy foods. This has given rise to a whole new cuisine called *chaats,* a generic name for several salty snacks that originated in Delhi. They leave a spicy, lingering taste in the mouth and are usually eaten during mid-morning or at teatime.

Chaats come in a wide variety of savory tidbits, spiced mainly with *ajwain* (bishop's weed). They are consumed with two chutneys: the fresh and tangy mint chutney and a tamarind-based chutney called *sonth.* Most chutney preparations are vegetarian and have potatoes and/or lentils as the base. Almost all have some fried components. *Chaat* tends to be bought rather than made at home, and is eaten at roadside stalls, where it is served in bowls made out of leaves.

THE TANDOOR AND TANDOORI CUISINE

Tandoors are clay ovens that are air-dried, embedded in sand or earth, and fired with either wood or charcoal at the bottom. The heat generated is distributed up the sides of the oven. The average temperature within a tandoor ranges between 1,112 to 1,472°F (600 to 800°C). Some tandoors can withstand extreme heat, up to 2,552°F (1,400°C).

Tandoors are most commonly used in Punjab. It is a versatile piece of equipment and can be used to cook meats, kebabs, breads, and *dal* (lentil purée) with equal ease. Over recent years, there have been variations in the types of tandoors available: from gas-operated models to electric ones. However, in the final analysis, the flavor from the original charcoal-fired tandoor is unsurpassable. Tradition holds that a tandoor in regular use improves the flavor of anything cooked in it, because the heated clay releases a mellow fragrance that permeates the food. In the case of meats, the final taste is a result of the smoke that emanates from the marinade which has dripped on the hot charcoal.

Tandoors are used to cook a variety of meats and breads. The prerequisite for cooking meats in the tandoor is that they must be marinated. The popularity enjoyed by Indian cuisine around the world can be attributed, in large measure, to the tandoor, because it uses very little oil or fat for cooking and the foods thus cooked are moderately spiced.

Prior to use, the tandoor has to be seasoned. This is done by rubbing the inside walls of the tandoor with a paste of spinach or any other green, leafy vegetable. After this has dried, a mixture of mustard oil, buttermilk, jaggery, and salt is applied over the paste. The tandoor is then heated by lighting a small fire at the base, so that the temperature rises gradually. If the temperature rises too fast, the internal walls will crack and it will not be possible to control the temperature. Once heated, the mixture will peel off, and it has to be reapplied three or four times to properly season the tandoor. Finally, the inside walls need to be sprinkled with brine and allowed to dry.

(clarified butter), white butter, *paneer* (homemade cottage cheese), and cream in their cooking. For those who cannot afford or tolerate ghee, the preferred oils are mustard and peanut.

Tandoori cuisine has its origins in the northwest frontier province, now in Pakistan. The cuisine gets its name from the tandoor (the oven in which the food is prepared) and has contributed to the growing popularization of Punjabi cuisine throughout the world. In many cases, tandoori cuisine is synonymous with Indian cuisine.

Northern Indian Cuisine by State

Kashmir. Kashmiri cuisine is a unique blend of Indian, Iranian, and Afghani cuisines. It is essentially meat-based and centered on a main course of rice. Unlike the Brahmins in other parts of the country, the Kashmiri Brahmins are nonvegetarian.

The abundance of dried fruit and nuts (walnuts, dates, and apricots) in the region has inspired their use in desserts, curries, and snacks. Sauces for curries are made from dairy-rich products.

A local spinachlike green called *haak* is popular in the summer months, as are lotus roots, which are used as a meat substitute. Fresh vegetables are abundant in the summer, including a prized variety of mushrooms called *guhchi*, used only for special occasions. Fresh fish is favored in the summer, while smoked meat, dried fish, and sun-dried vegetables are used in the winter.

Kashmir is also known for a very special green tea called *kahwa*, flavored with saffron, cardamom, and almonds and served from a samovar, a large metal kettle, which originated in the Russian steppes.

Punjab. Punjabi cuisine is simple, substantial, and robust, reflecting the extremes in climate and the industrious nature of its people. It forms a distinctive part of the culture. Everyday meals are centered on bread; there are a great variety of flat breads. *Parathas* (breads that are plain or stuffed with shredded, seasonal vegetables, seasoned with herbs and spices, and baked on a hot griddle) are favored for breakfast, served with a dollop of homemade butter.

Main meals throughout the year would comprise one *dal*, at least one seasonal vegetable, *chapatis* or *parathas*, and yogurt. *Lassi* (a yogurt shake) accompanies the midday meal, and pickles are served on the side. Some of the more popular dishes include a variety of locally grown legumes and *dals*, cooked whole or split, *saag* (spinach), *mutter paneer* (homemade cottage cheese cooked with peas), and *baingan bhartha* (smoked eggplant cooked with tomato). Punjabis are fond of nonvegetarian food like tandoori chicken, chicken curry, and meat *koftas* (meatballs in gravy). Sweets are welcomed; carrot *halva* (grated carrots cooked with milk solids and clarified butter and garnished with almonds) served hot is a favorite in winter, while chilled *kheer* (rice pudding) is popular during the summer. *Makki ki roti* (corn bread) and *sarson ka saag* (mustard greens) served with white butter is another well-liked winter dish. Rice, which is prepared only for special occasions, is rarely served plain. It is made with cumin or fried onions or, in winter, jaggery. Punjabis prefer aromatic basmati rice, especially at banquets and large social gatherings.

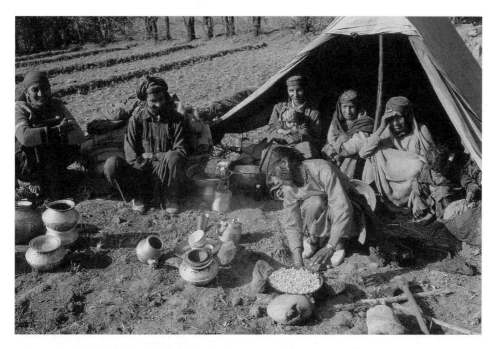

Bakarwal gypsy family preparing chapatis over a camp fire at Sonamarg, India. The Bakarwal gypsies are a nomadic group who travel between the Jammu lowlands of India and the mountains of Afghanistan. © LINDSAY HEBBERD/CORBIS.

Dhabbas are roadside eateries, commonly found on the highways in North India, particularly in Punjab. They were formerly frequented by truck drivers, criss-crossing the vast subcontinent in search of a hot, home-cooked meal. Today, *dhabbas* have sprung up not only on the highways, but also in urban areas as well, and are frequented by a cross section of society. They typically have a limited menu of one *dal*, one vegetable, and one meat dish served with a variety of breads. The menu varies daily and the food cooked is always fresh because refrigeration is lacking.

Uttar Pradesh. This state is best categorized by the cities of Benaras (Varanasi), which is traditionally Hindu in character, and Lucknow, which is traditionally Muslim in character.

Varanasi is one of India's holiest cities, bisected by the Ganges River, the waters of which are said to wash away a lifetime of sins. Many Hindus use the water from the Ganges for cooking and for sacred ceremonies. Breakfast in Varanasi consists of *pooris* (whole wheat bread that puffs up when deep-fried) or *kachoris* (whole wheat bread stuffed with split peas or fenugreek greens and deep-fried), eaten with *aloo bhaji* (potatoes spiced with ginger, cumin, and dried mango powder) or *aloo koda* (a combination of potatoes and pumpkin). Meals tend to be vegetarian and stick to the following formula: one *dal*, one or two seasonal vegetables, *chapatis* or some other form of traditional bread, yogurt, with side dishes of pickles and relish. People in this region are very fond of sweets, and a variety are available year round. These in-

clude *malai gujiyas* (sheets of reduced milk, folded over mounds of sweetened nuts), *lal peras* (deep red, caramelized sweetmeats), and *malpuas* (sweetened pancakes).

In Lucknow, a typical breakfast consists of *parathas* (whole wheat bread plain or stuffed with shredded vegetables and baked on a griddle) or *kulcha* (flat sour dough bread), eaten with spicy fried liver and *andey ki bhujia* (scrambled eggs cooked with chopped onions, tomatoes, green coriander, and green chilies).

The average middle-class family will eat a *salaan* (meat gravy with a seasonal vegetable), a vegetable *bhujia* (a dry preparation of vegetables), boiled rice, and *dal* for dinner. The upper-middle-class family will supplement this with a kebab or another meat dish and *kheer* (a creamy, chilled rice pudding). Occasionally, a *korma* (meat curry) replaces the *salaan*, and a *biryani* or *pulao* replaces the more ordinary boiled rice. For those with a sweet tooth, the typical summer sweet is a *guramba* (unripe mangoes cooked with sugar and semolina), and during the winter, *rasawal* (rice cooked with sugarcane juice). Family dinners tend to be very elaborate. Lucknow is also well known for its kebabs, particularly the *kakori kebab*, which is made by pounding meat and fat until it becomes a paste. To this poppy seeds, cloves, and other ground spices are added, and the pounding continues until the meat turns almost gluey. This mixture is then wrapped around skewers and grilled over live charcoal.

Rajasthan. Rajasthani cuisine has been influenced by the availability of food resources in the desert state and by the warlike lifestyle of the Maharajas. The food had to be cooked in such a way that it would last for several days when the men went off to war. The scarcity of water gave rise to a cuisine that is cooked with very little or no water. This is especially true of the desert belt, where milk, buttermilk, or ghee is often substituted for water.

The princely families of Rajasthan were obsessed with *shikar* (hunting) and enjoyed game. Their meat delicacies are incomparable. During the hunts, meats, including poultry, game, and fish, are marinated, skewered, and grilled over live fires to make *soola kebabs*. Within the ancient palaces, the recipes were a closely guarded secret. Game is cooked in several ways. Rabbit, deer, and boar are prized, and what is not consumed is pickled for later use.

At the other end of the spectrum are the Marwaris, who are strict vegetarians and will not even use garlic and onion in their cuisine. Dried lentils and beans from indigenous plants are the staples of a Rajasthani diet, as wheat and rice do not grow in the desert. *Bajra* (millet) and *makki* (maize) are used for making various kinds of bread. The Marwaris use a lot of pulses and gram flour in their cuisine as vegetables are scarce in the desert climate. *Moong dal khilni* (a dry preparation of lentils, tossed in a mixture of spices), *moong godi ki subzi* (grape-sized dumplings of green gram, which has been ground to a paste and sun-dried), and *gatte ki subzi* (rolls of gram flour, steamed and cooked in buttermilk sauce) are delicacies in this region. Other innovations include the use of mango powder as a substitute for tomatoes, and asafoetida, to enhance taste in the absence of garlic and onions. Sweets are also very popular.

Feasting and Fasting

A proverb in North India says "after a fast, a feasting; and after a feasting, a fast." Festivals in India always revolve around food: either through feasting, fasting, or feeding someone. They are numerous, and celebrate harvests and the prevalence of good over evil in stories related to gods and goddesses. Food is an important part of any celebratory event. No festival or celebration is complete without sweets, which are said to ward off evil spirits. In North India, some of the popular festivals are Lohri, Holi, Janmashtami, and Diwali.

Lohri (the winter solstice) is a festival connected to the solar year. It is also celebrated as a harvest festival in many parts of the country. *Til laddus* (a sweet made from sesame seeds) is distributed among family and friends and eaten throughout North India. *Til* is considered auspicious and "heating," an important attribute given the cold weather prevalent at that time of year. Another traditional preparation on this day is *khichari* (a preparation of rice and lentils cooked together).

Holi is the festival of color that celebrates the end of winter and the coming of warm weather. The crops have been cut, threshed, stored, or sold. People of all ages celebrate by throwing color on each other. The festival is also celebrated with special sweets. In the North, families and friends share *gujiyas* made with *khoya* and nut stuffing (wheat pastry with a stuffing of milk solids and nuts) and sugar *batashas* (sugar flakes). *Thandai*, a chilled, milk-based drink flavored with almonds, cardamom, rose petals, and whole pepper, is synonymous with Holi and is routinely served to all celebrants or guests.

Janmashtami is associated with Krishna. The food prepared on this day is prepared from milk and curds, much beloved by him. A part of the festivities includes filling a large earthen pot with milk, curds, butter, honey, and fruit and suspending this pot from a height of between twenty and forty feet. Sporting young men and boys form human pyramids to bring the pot down and to claim its prized contents. Many families fast on this day, but one meal is allowed. This meal includes fruit, sweets, nuts, and curds.

Diwali, the festival of lights, commemorates the victory of good over evil. It is also the day when Lakshmi, the consort of Vishnu and the goddess of prosperity, is worshiped. Lakshmi and Vishnu are said to dwell in the celestial *Kheer Sagar* (the ocean of milk). This is the origin of the word *kheer*, a popular confection of milk and rice that is prepared on almost all festive occasions as an auspicious offering to placate the gods, after which it is served to the priests and guests. The preparation of *kheer* is a must on Diwali.

Diwali signifies the onset of winter. The harvest is over, and it is time for a change in diet that is more appropriate to the winter season. On this auspicious day, unleavened bread, which is traditionally baked, is fried, perhaps to symbolically display prosperity with the extravagant use of fat. This may also be because during the winter months, the body requires more calories to combat the cold, and richer foods become easier to digest. The affluent eat dried fruits, nuts, and sweetmeats, while others gorge themselves on *kheel khilone* (puffed rice and candied sugar figurines). There is a great emphasis on sweets, with gifts of sweets exchanged between family, friends, and business associates.

The most elaborate festival has to be Wazwan, a Kashmiri feast, that was introduced to India about five hundred years ago from Central Asia. It is a blend of the culinary styles of the Mughals and Persians who were Muslim on the one hand, and the Kashmiri pundits who are Hindu Brahmins on the other hand. As many as forty courses may be served during Wazwan, with at least twelve and up to thirty courses being nonvegetarian.

There are numerous fasts in India. Each day of the week is dedicated to one of the many Hindu deities. Those with particularly strong religious sentiments fast on the day dedicated to their favorite deity. For example, those who believe in Hanuman will fast on a Tuesday. These fasts require that only one meal, without cereal and salt, be eaten throughout the day, although fruit, nuts, sweets, curds, and liquids are allowed. Muslims in

KASHMIRI WAZWAN

A Wazwan is a Kashmiri feast held to celebrate any occasion. It is a formal affair, and the number of people invited to attend could exceed one thousand, depending on the occasion and the social status of the host.

The Wazwan is a blend of cuisines of the Kashmiri Pundits, Mughals, and Persians. The concept of the Wazwan is more than five hundred years old and has its roots in Central Asia. The central starch for the meal is rice and there are several meat preparations. The Wazwan often includes up to forty courses, of which at least twelve and as many as thirty may be meat-based.

Traditional cooks called Wazas prepare the elaborate meal. Being a Waza is hereditary; it is passed from father to son. Four senior Wazas are required along with twelve assistants to prepare the feast for one thousand guests. If the Wazwan is a dinner, they start cooking at sunrise and continue preparing food until sunset. For a lunch, the Wazas arrive the previous evening and cook through the night.

The planning of the feast can take days and the cooking many hours. It begins early in the morning and continues throughout the day, with a whole retinue of people including butchers and assistants working to prepare the meal. There are no shortcuts in the preparation of food. The sheep are slaughtered using the *halal* method (bleeding the animal) on the day of the feast. Different cuts of meat are used for different preparations: ribs for *tubbak maz* (ribs simmered with black cardamom, turmeric, and salt, and fried in clarified butter); marrow bones, neck, and rump as well as the breast for *rogan josh* (meat curry simmered in yogurt with red kashmiri chilies and saffron); various cuts of meat for *seekh kebabs* (minced meat ground with spices and grilled on skewers); and meat from the backbone and tail for *aab ghosht* (meat cooked in a milky sauce). All the fat trimmed from the meat is saved for the preparation of *gushtaba* and *rishta kebabs*. These are prepared by pounding the meat and fat separately to a paste. To every kilogram of meat, 250 grams of fat are added, and the pounding continues with the addition of black cardamom and other spices. These are then formed into smooth round kebabs (a quarter pound for each *gushtaba* and half that size for each *rishta kebab*) and simmered in huge cauldrons with yogurt, whole spices, and salt.

The vessels used for cooking are like the large, flat copper platters used to serve the food; many of them have a traditional *chinar* (maple) leaf design on them. The guests sit on the floor around the plates: four guests to each plate. The Wazas serve the food: In addition to all the meat preparations, there is also *haak* (a green, leafy vegetablelike spinach), tomato *paneer* (cream cheese cooked with tomatoes), various chutneys like green chili and walnut, as well as plain yogurt. *Gushtaba* marks the end of the meal. The sweets generally served include *sooji ka halwa* (a semolina sweet cooked with clarified butter) and *phirni* (a rice flour and milk dessert). Finally, hot cups of *kahwa* (green kashmiri tea flavored with saffron and cardamom and garnished with sliced almonds) are poured from samovars to aid in the digestion of the feast.

India observe Ramadan and fast for the entire month, rising at 4 A.M. to eat a small meal and breaking their fast at sundown with a full meal, including meat. This fast does not permit the consumption of food or drink throughout the daylight hours.

Another rigorous Hindu fast is *karwa chauth*. Punjabi women observe this fast for the welfare of their husbands. They wake up before sunrise and eat *sargi* (food that has been given to them by their mothers-in-law). This includes one pasta item, fruit, sweets, and *matthis* (fried savory made from flour). Throughout the day, they are not permitted to eat or drink anything until moonrise. Then, after prayers, a full meal is allowed.

Religious Significance of Food

Rice. Rice has an important place in Hindu religious ceremonies. During weddings, it is thrown into the fire because it is the symbol of fertility. When the Hindu bride leaves her maternal home for the last time, she throws fistfuls of rice over her head, signifying the riches of her childhood home. Similarly, when she enters the home of her husband for the first time, she knocks over pots of rice that line the entrance to the house. The extent to which the grains spill across the floor denotes the prosperity the bride will bring to her new family.

Rice is also a traditional dish in the daily menu offerings at the temple. Legend has it that an ancient king dreamed Lord Jagannath had asked him to introduce boiled rice in the menu at the temple. The monks, unwilling to partake of the plain food, even when the king told them of his dream, decided to feed it to a dumb monk first to see if he regained his powers of speech before accepting the rice as temple food. According to legend, not only did the monk retrieve his powers of speech, he also recited all the verses from the Vedas.

Mango. Mango leaves and fruit also have religious connotations. It is said that mango is the favored fruit of Ganesha, the deity who can remove any obstacles. All those who wish to have their desires fulfilled string a garland of mango leaves on their front doors.

Ghee. Because it is considered pure, ghee has great religious significance. It is used in all Hindu ceremonies, burned in every temple lamp, and used during cremation.

Kara Prasad. Associated with the Sikh community of Punjab, an offering (or *prasad*) of wheat flour, clarified butter, and sugar in equal amounts is made to the gods symbolizing universal brotherhood. During its preparation, hymns are sung in the food's praise. The *prasad* is made and served by devotees at the *Gurudwara* (a Sikh place of worship); it seeks to break down barriers of caste.

See also **Asia, Central; Buddhism; Civilization and Food; Hindu Festivals; Hinduism; Islam; Religion and Food; Rice; Weddings**.

BIBLIOGRAPHY

"About Ayurveda: The Traditional Medicine of India." Available at http://www.Mothernature.com.

Acharya, K. T. "A Slice of India, Food as a Part of Health." Available at http://www.Britannica.co.in.

"Ayurveda, Basics," "Ayurveda, History," and "Ayurveda, Diet and Fasting." Available at http:www.medybiz.com.

Bagla, Pallava, and Subhadra Menon. "The Story of Rice." *The India Magazine* 9 (February 1989): 60–70.

Chandra, Sarat. "Food for the Gods." *The India Magazine* 9 (February 1989): 28–36.

Cole, Owen W., and Piara Singh Sambhi. *The Sikhs: Their Religious Beliefs and Practices*. Brighton: Sussex Academic Press, 1995.

Hiremath, Laxmi. "Delicacies of India," "Feast of Kashmir, Delicacies of India," and "Punjabi Standard, Delicacies of India." Available at http://www.indolink.com/Recipe/laxmi.

Holkar, Shalini. "Seasoning through the Seasons." *The India Magazine* 4, no. 1 (December 1983): 46–55.

Holkar, Shalini. "Wazwan, A Kashmiri Feast." *The India Magazine* 7 (April 1987): 33–39.

"Indian Cuisine, Festival and Recipes." Available at http://www.shubhyatra.com/htm/cuisine. See especially sections on the Holi, Janmashtami, and Makar Sankranti.

Jaffrey, Madhur. *A Taste of India*. London: Pavilion, 1989.

Kiritsinghe, Buddhadasa P. "The Mango, Spiritually and Culturally Indian but Universally a Gourmet's Delight." *The India Magazine* 4, no. 6 (May 1984): 38–41.

Maleta, Andreas. "The Holy Cow." *The India Magazine* 7 (January 1987): 16–27.

"Punjabi Cuisine" and "Rajasthani Cuisine." Available at http://www.indianvisit.com/ivnew/thecountry/culture.

Rau, Santha Rama. *The Cooking of India, Foods of the World*. New York: Time Life Books, 1970.

Sunny, Sashi. "High Life, Partying in Kashmir ... Wazwan Style." *Savvy Cookbook* (July–August 1998): 109–111.

Taneja, Meera. *Indian Regional Cookery*. London: Mills and Boon Ltd., 1980.

Taneja, Meera. *New Indian Cookery*. London: Fontana, 1983.

"Vegetarianism in India." Available at http://www.sscnet.ucla.edu/southasia/culture/cuisine/vegetar.html.

Thangam Philip

SOUTHERN INDIA

Southern India has been exposed to a variety of enriching influences through the years, including a number from Southeast Asia and Africa. Coconut and banana derive from Southeast Asia, betel leaf, areca nut, sago palm, and certain yams from Africa. Although the six tastes enjoined by Vedic practice are still more or less observed during a meal in most parts of India, the actual order in which the items are eaten differs from region to region. Broadly speaking, the South has a common order, and the arrangement of food items on a banana leaf used for eating is similar in Andhra Pradesh, Karnataka, Tamil Nadu, and Kerala.

Andhra Pradesh

The food from Andhra Pradesh is renowned for its sharp and pungent flavor. As in most southern states, the *dosa* (fermented rice flour and lentil pancake) is common everywhere. However, the favorite remains *pesarattu*, a rice pancake with a filling of semolina and onions, cooked together. This is served with *sambar* (a spicy lentil preparation) and a variety of chutneys. Rice is a staple food in the region. No meal in Andhra is complete without the famous Andhra pickles that come in several varieties. *Rasam*, a spicy lentil soup, is common to the entire southern region, but interestingly, mulligatawny soup derives its name from the Telugu *mulligatanni* or black pepper water.

Hyderabadi food is distinct, having been influenced by renowned Moghlai cuisine. The kitchens of the Nizams combined the Muslim influence of the Moghlai court with a predominantly Hindu subculture to create a cuisine that is the ultimate in fine dining.

Hyderabadi cuisine includes *biriyani* (rice layered with mutton and cooked), *haleem* (wheat pounded with mutton), *baghare baigan* (roasted eggplant), and tomato *kut* (a tomato chutney). The repertoire is rich and vast, both in vegetarian and nonvegetarian fare. What also distinguishes Hyderabadi food is its sourness, clearly a Telugu influence. Souring enhances the taste of the food and is considered good for the heart and for digestion. The various souring agents used in Indian foods primarily reduce spoilage by microorganisms and also counteract the pungency resulting from the use of red or green chilies. The favorite souring agents are lemon and tamarind, although dishes like the *khormas* (meat curries with a creamy consistency) are soured with yogurt, and some dishes of Western origin, such as lamb chops, are soured with vinegar. Green mango when in season is a favorite souring agent for meat dishes and dals. Another favorite is *narangi*, a sour citrus fruit, which is used to flavor various dishes. The tomato too is often used to sour a dish rather than as a vegetable. In Southern and Western India, *ambada* (roselle leaves), a kind of spinach with a distinct sour taste, is another great favorite. Fresh or dried prawns, chicken, or meat cooked with *ambada* can be quite delicious, as is common dal soured with *ambada*. Sour berries called *karonda* (*Carissa caranda*) and sour fruits such as *kamrak* (star fruit or carambola) are also used to sour meat dishes.

Hyderabadi food can, in addition, be hot and spicy, another Telugu influence. Specialties include several dishes that are picklelike in flavor: *chatni gosht* (chutney meat), *achar gosht* (pickle-meat curry), *achar ke aloo* (pickle-potato dish), and *mirchi ka salan* (picklelike dish of green peppers and special herbs).

Chili peppers are used in Hyderabadi cooking in several ways—they can be chopped, ground into paste, slit, and deseeded, or an entire chili can be inserted in the dish. Certain red chili powders, especially those that come from the coastal Andhra region, have a flaming red color and a hot taste.

The procedure of seasoning, or *baghar*, is used in Hyderabad to great effect in order to infuse a dramatic nuance of taste into a dish. In *baghar*, food is seasoned by a process of dropping chilies, herbs, and spices into hot oil and then pouring that concoction over a dish while it is still sizzling. There are also exotic methods of seasoning that are quite unique to Hyderabad. In a lentil curry called *thikri ki dal*, a piece of freshly fired earthen pot is broken, heated until red hot, and added to the dish so that the rich aromatic flavor of the earth is captured. Similarly, in a dish called *kabab kheema* (minced kebab), a piece of red-hot coal is deposited in the center of the cooking pan and covered immediately so that the kebab absorbs the smoke and flavor of the burning coal.

Certain spices that are hardly used in North Indian cuisines are rather commonly used in Hyderabad, quite obviously due to Muslim-Moghlai influence. These are *shah jeera* (black cumin), *khus khus* (poppy seeds), *magaz* (seeds of muskmelon and watermelon), and *kabab chini* (cassia buds). Another spice used very often in Hyderabad, a South Indian legacy, is *til* (sesame seeds), which is scarcely used in the North.

A magical mix of various herbs and spices called *bhojwar masala* is indeed a Hyderabad offering to Indian cuisine. It is used in dishes like *baghara baigan* (seasoned eggplant), *mirchi ka salan* (green chili curry), and *mahi gosht* (a meat dish), and contains a mixture of coriander seeds, sesame seeds, cumin seeds, bay leaf, groundnut, dried coconut, and a lichen with an exotic aroma curiously called *pathar ka phool* (stoneflower). Another mix of herbs and spices from Hyderabad and much more exotic is *potli ka masala*, thus named because herbs and spices are tied in a *potli*, a sack of muslin cloth, and placed in

Sugar is an important agricultural product from southern India, where it has been grown for several thousand years. This shows workers processing sugar in the open air. © ENZO & PAOLO RAGAZZINI/CORBIS.

the cooking dish. *Potli ka masala* is used mostly in *nehari*, a broth of pig's feet and goat's tongue, and *chakna*, a tavern dish of meat and organs. This mixture of spices is very different in taste and is literally an orchestra of fragrances. It includes sandalwood powder, dried vetiver roots, dried rose petals, bay leaves, coriander seeds, black cardamom, cassia buds, *pathar ka phool*, *gehunwala* (a kind of grain), *pan ki jadi* or *kulanjan* (a lesser variety of galingale), and *kapur kachri* (*Hedylium spicatum*).

Hyderabadi cuisine is more nonvegetarian than vegetarian, but the repertoire of Hyderabadi vegetarian fare is also complex and indicative of a high level of cooking skill. Hyderabadi prefer rice to bread, although *phulka* and *paratha* are also eaten. An earthy Maharashtrian bread made from an Indian millet called *jawari ki roti* is very popular. Nonetheless, rice is overwhelmingly preferred. It is said that nearly forty varieties of *biryani* are made in Hyderabad, including *pulao*. In Hyderabad a delicious mixed-vegetable *biryani* called *tahiri* is often served. It is said that throwing a handful of it on the ground in a spray will test the quality of a cooked *biryani*. If each grain of rice falls separately from the other and the grains do not stick together, then the *biryani* has made the grade.

Hyderabad is also a curry paradise. Broadly speaking, Hyderabadi curries come in five to six forms. One is *shorva* (or *shorba*), a thin, soupy curry with dumplings of meat and a vegetable, which could be potato, okra, some of the gourds, or colocasia, and soured with tamarind and

MIRCH KA SAALAN
(WHOLE GREEN CHILIES IN A MASALA GRAVY)

Mirch ka saalan is among the better-known Hyderabadi dishes. Since it keeps well for several days, the Hyderabadi often carry it with them on long road or rail journeys.

Preparation time   40 minutes
Cooking time   25 minutes
Serves   6–8 persons

Ingredients

Green chilies, large	8–9 ounces, slit on one side
Onions	4, cut into 4–6 pieces each
Ginger	1-inch piece
Garlic	½ pod, with the skin removed
Coriander seeds	1 tablespoon
Cumin seeds	1 teaspoon
Sesame seeds	3 tablespoons
Peanuts	½ cup
Poppy seeds	1½ teaspoon
Dried coconut (*copra*)	about 1 ounce
Fenugreek seeds	¼ teaspoon
Turmeric powder	¼ teaspoon
Red chili powder	1 teaspoon
Jaggery or sugar	1 teaspoon
Tamarind	2½ ounces
Curry leaves	a few
Cooking oil	1 cup
Salt	To taste

Method

Soak tamarind in about 1 cup of warm water. Mash and sieve to obtain tamarind water. Discard seeds and other residues. Set aside

Roast the onions on a griddle until they soften and turn a pale golden brown. Then dry-roast together over medium heat the coriander seeds, sesame seeds, peanuts, cumin seeds, poppy seeds, dried coconut (*copra*), and fenugreek seeds until their shade darkens very slightly and they start emitting an aroma.

Grind together the onions, roasted spices, ginger, garlic, salt, turmeric, red chili powder, and jaggery or sugar into a fine paste. Mix with the tamarind water.

Heat oil. Add the green chilies. As soon as they acquire a few golden brown spots, remove from the pan and set aside. Add curry leaves to the oil and, after a few seconds, the ground spices. Cook for about 5–10 minutes. Then add the green chilies. Cook over medium heat, stirring occasionally. Add a little water while cooking, if desired. Cook for another few minutes until the oil rises to the surface. The dish should have a fairly thick consistency.

a bit of yogurt. It is flaming red in color and can also be quite hot in taste as it is blended with red chili powder. Then there is *khorma*, which is a meat, chicken, or fish dish with a creamy consistency as it is flavored and soured with yogurt and spiced with red chili powder. All *khormas* are yogurt-based dishes. Then there are the thicker curries called *khalias*, which again are meat dishes with a vegetable in which the gravy is thick and saucelike. There are also the *bhuna* dishes, which are not exactly dry, as the name suggests, but have very little sauce, in which the mixture of spices coats the meat. Another group of curries without a specific name are those flavored with *baghar* or seasoning. In addition, there are some other curries outside these categories, but with a texture and flavor all their own.

Indians rarely bake their foods, except perhaps in the celebrated clay oven called the tandoor. Hyderabad, however, boasts of a few unique baked dishes, not surprisingly all made of minced meat. Most of these are actually *kabab*-like or are baked *kababs*, except perhaps the savory called *tootak*, made of semolina and minced meat. Some of the baked foods are obviously imports, from Arabian countries and Iran.

The gourmets of Hyderabad have incorporated other Arab dishes into their culinary repertoire, and the most spectacular of these is perhaps *muzbi*, in which an entire goat is stuffed with *pulao*, chicken, boiled eggs, and nuts and raisins, and then cooked. There is also *marag*, a rich broth of mutton and marrow, and the famous *nehari*, another fine broth of tongue and pig's feet. The Turks introduced Hyderabadi to *shawarma*, slices of goat's meat upon a special skewer. All these dishes have been subjected to Hyderabadi interpretation, and abundant use of unique Indian spices has imparted to them their own local flavor.

Another nonvegetarian category in which Hyderabadi food offers tremendous variety and culinary excitement is minced meat. *Kheema* or minced meat has a certain versatility that allows it to be cooked in several ways. A mince dish is not supposed to be watery and therefore has very little gravy. However, it goes very well with rice or bread. Several *kababs* are made with mince, as are baked dishes and savories. Mince also lends itself well to stuffing. In a group of dishes called *dulmay*, like the Greek and Armenian *dolma*, mince is stuffed in onion, potato, capsicum (sweet and hot peppers), and even fruits like apple and guava.

As in the West, there is a certain order in the manner in which food is taken in Hyderabad. Food is eaten in courses, but not served in courses. Everything is placed on the table at the same time, but eaten in a set order. A dry dish, generically called *gazak* (or appetizer), is first consumed. It could be a *kabab*, a savory, or even fried fish. The *gazak* is followed by *khalia*, a semidry mutton curry, which is eaten with *phulka* (a thin dry chapati). Then comes the *shorva* or *khorma*, which generally contains a vegetable. Alternatively, a *biryani* might be served in place of the *shorva*. Similar order prevails in the presented food at weddings and parties, only the fare is more sumptuous and has greater variety. At parties and celebrations, at least two varieties of *gazak* and two types of *biryani* are served. A chicken dish and mutton curry are also offered to guests, along with bread. For dessert, favorites include *double ka meetha* (a bread pudding), called *shahi turka* in the North, and *khubbani ka meetha*, an apricot dessert served with fresh cream.

No introduction to Hyderbadi cuisine would be complete without a word on its pickles. Since the Indian passion is for foods sour and pungent, one predilection is pickles made of green mango, lemon, tamarind, green chili, and even sour fruits like the *kamrak* (star fruit). The pickles are all seasoned and flavored with vinegar.

The Hyderabadi *paan* (betel leaf) is well known. Making a good *paan* is a delicate process and is often an exercise in *nazakat* (elegance). The Hyderabadi prefer the South Indian leaf. It is soft and does not have the coarseness or pungency of some other leaves. Each leaf is fastidiously cleaned of all its veins in order to soften it further. Both the *katha* and *chuna* (slaked lime) are processed at home. The *katha* is also treated with rose water. At the end of a meal, a silver *paandaan* (a container for the betel leaf preparation) is brought out and the lady of the house makes the *paan* with her own hands. The *paan* is rarely given by hand. It is placed in a miniature silver tray and offered with the right hand. (Food in Indian homes is always served and eaten with the right hand. The left hand is not used for either purpose, for traditionally the practice in Hindu homes is that the right hand is used to receive and/or give.) At parties, *paans* are decorated with *chandi ka varq* (silver leaf) before being served.

Andhra cuisine is largely vegetarian, except for the coastal areas, which show a preference for seafood. Fish and prawns are curried in sesame and coconut oils, flavored with freshly ground black pepper, and then eaten with rice. For vegetarians, rice is served with *sambar* (a spicy lentil preparation) and vegetables. *Pakodas* (potatoes or onions dipped in gram flour batter and deep-fried), *vadas* (fried dumplings made from split black gram) in steaming hot sambar, or *idlis* (steamed rice dumplings) are served as snacks. The Portuguese word for grain, *grão*, was first applied in India to the Bengal gram or chickpea, and later applied generally to all pulses; thus arose the terms red gram, green gram, black gram, horsegram, etc. Gram's use is unknown outside India.

A wide variety of fruit grows in Andhra Pradesh. These include custard apples (*Anomas*), grapes, apricots, and mangoes.

Karnataka

Writings on food in Kannada date back approximately a thousand years. Rice was the premier food after the tenth century C.E. in Karnataka. Four varieties of a cooked rice-

A traditional Thali tray in Madras, India. Each bowl contains a small portion of a vegetarian dish. © LINDSAY HEBBERD/CORBIS.

ghee combination dish flavored with garlic and salt, called *kattogara*, were prevalent. Crushed *papads* was added to yield one variation, crisp-fried *sandiges*, made of the ash gourd made for another, and various cooked greens gave rise to yet other variations. By mixing in lime, *huli* (a spicy lentil preparation), turmeric, tamarind, or the powders of roasted rice and split chickpeas, flavors could be easily changed. Cooking the rice in water in which, as a preliminary step, the leaves of *tulasi* (holy basil) were boiled resulted in "curd rice" (a traditional preparation) that would keep for several days.

An exceptionally large number of wheat preparations also continue to be consumed. Karnataka consumes roughly equal amounts of rice, wheat, and *ragi* (millet). The wheat foods may be roasted, baked, steamed, or fried. Roasting can take several forms. *Mucchal roti* is baked between plates, with live coal above and below, and *kivichu roti* on a *kavali* or *tava* (flat griddle plate) with a little ghee (clarified butter). Several *tava*-roasted rotis may be mounted one over the other with a pierced stick and flavored with ghee, sugar, edible camphor, and *thale* (Palmyra) flower to yield *chucchuroti*. A stack of ghee-smeared circles mounted one over the other, *savaduroti*, is baked on a griddle under cover of a cup. A cup cover above, live coals below, and a ball of dough within yield *uduru roti*, from which the blackened crust is peeled off before consumption. *Mandige* or *mandage* is a delicate baked product: when baked on a heated tile, it is called *white mandige*, and when overheated but still very soft, it is called *ushnavarta mandige*. The stuffing may be varied. Sugar and ghee yield *khanda mandige*; multilayered fillings of cooked *chana*, coconut shreds, dates, and raisins result in a *mandige* variation called *perane hurige*. Today the *mandige* of Belgaum is a very large and fine *paratha* stuffed with finely ground sugar containing cardamom powder, baked on an upturned clay pot, and folded into a moderately stiff rectangle.

True baking within a seal of wheat dough, called *kanika* in Kannada, is used to make the *bhojanadhika roti*, in which *mandige* broken up into small pieces is mixed with milk, cream, coconut milk, mango juice, and sugar, and then pressed into a ball. This is placed within a covering of wheat dough and baked under seal on a hot tile with frequent turning of the vessel. When done, the upper crust is sliced off, and ghee and sugar are poured on the *roti* before it is consumed.

Wheat dough made with sweetened milk or even cream, rolled out into circles and then deep-fried, yields *yeriappa* and *babara*. Balls of dough made with wheat flour, curds, and sweetened cream are deep-fried to produce *pavuda*. A less viscous wheat batter prepared with sweetened milk is forced through a hole made at the base of a coconut shell cup (the usual extrusion device) directly into hot ghee for ropelike *chilumuri*.

Some preparations have been frequently mentioned throughout the centuries. *Melogara* is a dish of pulses and greens, with coconut gratings, but many variations are prevalent. To make it, *mung dal* (split green gram), *avarai* (flat beans), *urad dal* (split black gram), fresh *chana* (split chickpeas), or *tuvar dal* (split red gram) are first cooked with sesame seeds, then cooked again with greens, drumsticks, grapefruit, salt, and coconut gratings, and finally mixed with ghee and tempered with asafetida (gum resin) and thick milk. Even wheat dough pieces rolled into thin strands and fried may be added to *melogara*. Vegetables used for *melogara* are pretreated. Certain leaves are first washed in lime water before cooking, other greens are washed in turmeric water, and yet others with common salt or alkaline ashes. The *surana* root is first boiled with betel leaves, or soaked in rice water and then cooked with tamarind leaves. A *melogara* of dal and beans may be sweet, sour, or spicy.

There are many kinds of relish in this cuisine. *Balaka* is now made by soaking large chilies in salt water, drying them, and then frying the chilies in oil when needed as a crisp and spicy accompaniment to food. Historically, some twenty kinds of *balaka* have been prepared using various vegetables and their peels. Deep-fried items eaten as crisp and crunchy accompaniments to a meal include *chakkali* (called *murukku* in Tamil Nadu), a circular mass of continually widening rings extruded from a thick rice-*urad* (split black gram) batter, and numerous *sandige*, irregular lumps of spiced rice-*urad* batter, sesame powder, onion, or even vegetable skins like those of the ashgourd, sun-dried first, and then deep-fried until crisp in very hot oil. Curd-based relishes with greens and raw vegetables are called by various names, such as *pacchadi*, *kacchadi*, *krasara kacchadi* (this contains milk with curds), *palidya* (one variety is called *kajja*), *thambuli* (with greens and coconut gratings), and *raita* (a commonly used condiment today). *Kosamris* are uncooked relishes made from *chana* or mungbean sprouts (green gram), which are soaked in water until they soften and swell, and then garnished with salt, mustard seeds, and fresh coriander.

In the cuisine of Karnataka, there has been a vast variety of sweet items, and they have altered little over a millennium. Sweet boiled rice, rice *payasam* (rice cooked in milk and then sweetened), rice-derived *vermicelli payasam* (vermicelli pasta cooked in milk and sweetened), mixed *rice-wheat payasam* (a mixture of rice and wheat cooked in milk and sweetened), *rice kadabu* with a sweet filling, and deep-fried delicacies of rice flour and jaggery (now called *athirasa*) are all based on rice. Wheat, especially in the form of semolina, is suitable for the preparation of sweets; from it, *kesari bhath* (sweetened rice flavored with saffron), *ghrtapura* (a fried ball), *payasam* (*kajjaya*), and *ladduge* are made. Wheat vermicelli is extruded to a fine consistency from hard wheat dough (it is then known as *pheni*) and usually eaten with sugared milk. Sweet wheat rotis stuffed with a mash of boiled *chana*, jaggery (brown palm sap sugar), and coconut constitute *purige*, *hurige*, or the later *holige*; a thinner drier form is *obattu*, and there is also the rolled-up cylindrical form called *surali holige*. Rolled-out pieces of dough are fried in various forms and then dusted with castor sugar to make *phenis* and *chirotti*; *madhunala* is a small tube of dough (of wheat, rice, and *chana* with added mashed banana) filled with sugar, sealed at both ends, and then deep-fried. *Karaji kayi* is a half-moon puff with a sweet stuffing; if only sugar constitutes the stuffing, the result is *sakkare burunde*. Pulse flours of *chana* and black gram are also used to make sweetmeats. *Boondi* grains made from them are sweetened with sugar syrup and shaped into *ladduge*, *pinda*, *moti chur*, and *manohara unde*. *Jilabi*, tasty as nectar, are made of *chana* flour. Milk is the major ingredient for sweet *payasa*, as well as *hal unde* (balls of sweetened milk solids) and *halaugu*. *Shikharini* consists of curd solids lightly spiced and sweetened.

A typical breakfast in the region includes *idli* (made by fermenting a mixture of ground rice and split black gram) and *vada* (made from split black gram), accompanied by *sambar* (a spicy lentil preparation) and a coconut chutney, lemon rice, *upitu* (a savory dish made from semolina), or *kesari bhath* (a sweet made from semolina and flavored with saffron).

Vermicelli upma (a savory dish made with vermicelli pasta) is used as a snack in-between meals. The main meals are usually rice-based. Rice is eaten with clarified butter. This is followed by rice with *rasam* (a thin lentil soup), rice with *sambar*, and rice with curds for the final course. Usually, two vegetables called *palyas* accompany the meal. These are dry-cooked vegetables with green chilies, cumin, and grated coconut. A salad called *kosamri* is also eaten with the meal.

The Kodavas, Mangaloreans, and Udipis are distinct communities within the state; each has its own specialities.

Perched on the highlands of southern Karnataka in the Kodagu district are a warlike and distinctive people with a unique cuisine. Rice is eaten boiled or as a distinctive ghee-coated product (*nai kulu*), or as a *pulao* with firm meat chunks and every grain coated evenly with a mixture of spices. Rice is also transformed in numerous ways, and each has a distinct nonvegetarian accompaniment. The *akkiroti* based on a rice dough rolled out on a wet cloth is roasted and eaten with a spicy sesame chutney, a red pumpkin (*kumbla*) curry, or with a dry and salty dish of bamboo shoot chiplets (these shoots are also pickled).

With the *pulao* goes a tasty relish of ripe wild mangoes in a curd base called *mangay pajji*. A paper-thin, soft rice pancake, *neer dosai*, is accompanied by a chicken curry, into which a lot of fresh coconut is added. The *nu puttu* of Kodagu is the strandlike *idi appam* of South India, once eaten with jaggery water, but now with any liquid curry. Steamed balls of cooked and mashed rice constitute *kadambuttu*, which is paired with a pork dish with a very thick mixture of spices, of which an essential ingredient is the sun-drawn extract of the kokum fruit, locally called *kachampuli* (*kerala kudampuli garcunia cambogia*). Its acidity serves to keep the fat on meat firm and springy. A breakfast dish, *paputtu*, is prepared from rice grits mixed with grated coconut and milk, and then steamed in metal pans. This is often eaten with either pork curry or ghee and the honey so plentifully found in Kodagu. Another breakfast dish is *thaliya puttu*, made from a batter of ground rice, fenugreek seeds, and soda bicarbonate, fermented overnight and steamed. Two fish are commonly used in this cuisine. One is the sardine, *matthi meen*, and the other the tiny whitebait (*koyle meen*), cooked and eaten bones and all. There are also two popular desserts and both are based on the banana. Well-ripened fruits are mashed with the powder of roasted rice, to which a little fenugreek is added, to make uncooked *thambuttu*, which is eaten with ghee, fresh coconut gratings, and whole-roasted sesame seeds. To make *koale puttu*, mashed banana and small wedges of mature coconut are steamed in a banana leaf packet, which is opened to give a brown slab; the mixture is then eaten either hot or cold with fresh butter. The name is derived from *koovale puttu*, originally made with the soft, weepy variety of jackfruit called *koovale*.

Tamil Nadu

Located in the South of India on its Eastern coast, Tamil Nadu has a large Hindu population. The large community of Brahmins are vegetarian, hence, the state is primarily vegetarian by nature. The main cooking method in the South is steaming. As a result of this, every single home is equipped with a variety of small and large steaming pots. The word "curry" originated in Tamil Nadu. Contrary to popular belief that a curry is a dish with a gravy, curries in Tamil Nadu are dry, spiced dishes without gravy.

Most of the south, and particularly Tamil Nadu, has a hot climate, and this has been used to prepare some of the most delicious and nutritious dishes that require fermentation. For this process, no yeast is used, as the

THE UDIPIS

The Udipi region is on the coastal stretch of Karnataka, sandwiched between Goa and Kerala. The Krishna temple in the area is famous for training young boys (from the age of ten years) to work in the kitchen. All boys start as apprentices and gradually learn the trade. Thereafter, they are free to seek employment elsewhere. This has given rise to a whole chain of "Udipi restaurants" throughout Maharashtra and Karnataka. The food served at any of these places is completely standardized, with each item having the same weight, volume, and appearance. Long before the concept of chain restaurants came about in the West, along with the accompanying standardization of foods, the ubiquitous Udipi restaurant was already making its presence felt in India!

THE MANGALOREANS

The Christian community of Mangaloreans are an integral part of Karnataka. However, their food is quite different from Hindu cuisine, being as nonvegetarian as the Hindus are vegetarian. In fact, it has several similarities with the coastal cuisine of Kerala: both make use of coconut milk and similar spices. Seafood, being readily available, is also consumed in large quantities, as is heavily spiced pork.

average temperature of 25°C does the work quite effortlessly. To counteract the heat, cooling ingredients such as tamarind are employed to great effect.

Idlis, small, savory rice cakes, made slightly sour by overnight fermentation and steamed the following morning, are served as breakfast to millions in the South. The process relies almost entirely on the weather to change a batter of ground rice and split peas into a light froth, which then only requires a quick steaming to become a deliciously light, highly nutritious, and very digestible breakfast.

South Indians are serious coffee drinkers. They make strong filter coffee, but do not drink it strong, preferring to mix it with lots of hot milk. The proportions vary from house to house. Sometimes, as little as 20 percent coffee is in an individual serving, and at other times it is a neat balance of half and half. Before the coffee is poured into separate glasses or cups, there is one more ritual to be performed: that of pouring the mixture from one vessel to another at some height in order to raise a head of froth.

ACHAR KE ALOO
(POTATOES IN A PICKLE SAUCE)

Preparation time	15 minutes
Cooking time	45 minutes
Serves	6–8 persons

Ingredients

Potatoes	1½–2 pounds
Onions	5, ground to a paste
Ginger paste	1½ teaspoon
Garlic paste	1½ teaspoon
Red chili powder	1½ teaspoon
Turmeric powder	1½ teaspoon
Vinegar	1/3 cup
Sugar	2 teaspoons
Salt	To taste

For tempering

Nigella seeds	1 teaspoon
Mustard seeds	½ teaspoon
Cumin seeds	1 teaspoon
Whole red chilies	8

Method

Boil the potatoes. Peel and cut into 1-inch-sized pieces

Heat oil. Fry the potatoes until they are golden. Set aside. Leave about 2/3 cup of oil and remove the rest. Next fry the onions until they are golden brown. Add the ginger and garlic paste and fry a little. Next add salt, turmeric, and chili powder, and then the fried potatoes. Add about half a cup of water and cook over low heat for approximately 5 minutes until the spices are well blended and a small amount of gravy remains. Turn off the heat. Mix sugar in vinegar and add to the dish. Transfer all to the serving dish.

Heat 2 tablespoons of oil. Add the dry whole red chilies, mustard seeds, cumin seeds, and finally the nigella seeds. When the mustard seeds begin to crackle and the red chilies darken, pour the tempering over the dish.

A *dosa* is more satisfying than a simple pancake, as it is golden red and crisp on one side, smooth and white on the other. Made from almost the same batter, both *idlis* and *dosas* are the traditional breads of the South, as nourishing and digestible (due to the fermentation process) as they are delicious. They may be eaten with butter and honey or with chutneys, or they may be stuffed with a spicy blend of potatoes and onions. All these breads are unleavened and prepared in two stages. First, each round is cooked briefly on a preheated griddle; then, the par-tially cooked bread is held over an open flame for a few seconds. The direct heat causes moisture in the dough to turn quickly to steam, puffing the bread while the cooking is completed. For a crisper effect, unleavened dough may be cooked completely on the griddle until well browned on both sides.

The main staple in Tamil Nadu is rice. Simple vegetarian lunches consist of three courses, each eaten with rice. A typical lunch menu would be rice and *rasam* (a highly spiced lentil soup) and a preparation made from vegetables. This is followed by more rice for the second course, with *sambar* (a preparation of lentils) and *papadams*. The last course comprises rice, yogurt, and pickles. Southern meals tend to end this way: hot, fiery courses followed by bland, soothing ones.

Vegetarian meals using the same basic theme of rice, *rasam*, *sambar*, and yogurt may in skillful hands become much more elegant and elaborate. Examples include *rasavangi*, a kind of heady *sambar* with the tiniest of eggplants (aubergines) bobbing about in it; *vendakai curry*, delightfully crisp fritters made by dipping sections of okra into a spicy chickpea flour batter and frying them; *keerai poricha kootu*, a kind of thick soupy stew of lentils, spinach, and fresh coconut; and the popular *rasavade*, made with savory *urad dal* (split black gram) doughnuts, immersed in *rasam* just long enough to soften and soak up all the liquid's tart and fiery flavor.

Chettinad

Traders, merchants, and money-lenders by profession, the Chettiyars of Chettinad have traveled the seas freely since ancient times. Their wealth is enormous, and the Chettiyars are very comfortable with and open about this. They are known to begin collecting dowries for their daughters at birth. The Chettinad region of southern India that comprises Madurai, Virudhunagar, and adjoining regions is dry and arid. The cuisine of the region reflects this and also the fact that the early Chettiyars were traders in spices. Therefore, their cuisine is spicy (fiery hot) and rich in its variety of spices, the most prominent being peppercorn and red chilies.

In Chettinad a meal is traditionally eaten off a banana leaf. Some popular preparations are *meen varuval*, fried fish; *varuval kola*, fried meatballs made with a very creamy paste of meat, cashews, poppy seeds, coconut, fennel, and fenugreek seeds; *koli kolambu*, chicken cooked in spicy tamarind water; *kari kolambu*, meat cooked with roasted coriander seed and tomatoes. There are also dishes made from mixed vegetables cooked with the second water used for washing rice (*mandi*) or *idi appams*, freshly made rice vermicelli, seasoned with mustard seeds and *urad dal* (split black gram), as well as dishes made from banana flowers, banana stems, dried mango, and assorted pickles and sweets. Fennel and roasted and powdered fenugreek are the predominant spices in Chettinad chicken, fish, and vegetable preparations.

Koli uppu varuval, a kind of peppered fried chicken, is a dish that has gained immense popularity outside the Chettinad region.

Kerala

Kerala is a bit of heaven on earth. Located as it is on the West coast of India, with a long coastline, the food of the state has been influenced greatly by its climate and geographic location. There is a wealth of seafood, and the swaying coconut palms all along the coastline have resulted in the extensive use of coconut and coconut oil in the local cuisine. Other foods locally produced and consumed include many types of bananas and jackfruit. Kerala is well known for its spices. In fact, the Greeks, Romans, Arabs, and Chinese all came to Kerala to trade. Later, Portuguese, Dutch, French, and English explorers arrived to profit from the lucrative spice trade.

Black pepper is the main spice grown in Kerala. It was used in the past as currency, to pay tributes and ransoms. Other spices that grow in the area include nutmeg, cinnamon, cardamom, cloves, ginger, and turmeric. Tamarind trees and the curry leaf tree (*Murraya koenigii*) are visible everywhere; the aromatic curry leaf has greatly influenced the cuisine of the Keralites as a result. Kerala also produces large amounts of coffee and tea, and manicured tea gardens can be seen on the hills of the region. There are three major communities residing in Kerala. Hindus, Muslims, and Syrian Christians make up the bulk of the population of the state, although there are other minority communities, including Jews.

Each community has its own distinctive cuisine. Unlike the royal families of other states such as Hyderabad and Mysore, those of both Travancore and the state of Cochin are extremely austere and spartan in their food habits and lifestyle, although they are great scholars and lovers of art. Other states were known for their opulence, both in lifestyle and cuisine, but this is lacking among the royal families of Kerala. However, during the Onam festival, all Keralites enjoy a festive meal. Nonetheless, there is no special cuisine that can be attributed to them.

The Syrian Christians. Breakfast for all Keralites, whatever their religion, is the popular *appam* (also called hoppers), a pancake, or *palappam*. These are rice flour pancakes, which have soft, thick spongy centers and lace-like, thin, crisp edges. The Syrian Christians eat *palappam* with a meat stew, whereas the Hindu community comprising the Nampoothiris and Nairs eat it with a mix of vegetables (*aviyal*).

There are two other breakfast items common to all Keralites. The first is *idiappam* (cooked rice noodles or string hoppers), eaten with sweetened coconut milk or with a meat or chicken curry. The second is *puttu* (made of coarsely ground rice flour and coconut shreds, which are alternately layered in a bamboo tube, and steamed by affixing the bamboo tube to the mouth of a vessel containing boiling water). Being rather dry, *puttu* is commonly eaten with bananas or with a spicy dry chickpea curry.

Kuzhal appam is a fried crisp curled up like a tube; it is typically Syrian Christian. There are two other *appams* popular with this group, and both are sweet. *Acchappam* is a deep-fried rose cookie made of rice, the name derived from the frame (*acchu*) needed to make it. *Naiappam*, called *athirasam* in Tamil Nadu, is a deep-fried, chewy, dark doughnut fashioned from toddy (fresh or fermented palm sap), fermented rice, and jaggery.

Another rice-coconut combination uses fried rice and is called *avilose*, a Syrian Christian speciality. It can be molded into an *unda* (ball) with coconut palm treacle. *Churuttu* (which literally means cigar) is also rice-based; it has a crisp, translucent outer case, filled with *avilose* and coconut palm treacle. *Khumbilappam*, eaten by all Keralites, consists of a mash of ripe jackfruit, roasted rice flour, and jaggery, folded in the form of a triangle in a cassia leaf and steamed. During jackfruit season, a preserve called *chakka varattiyathu* is made with jackfruit, jaggery, and cardamom. This preserve is served continuously throughout jackfruit season.

Syrian Christians in Kerala eat beef, and *eracchi olarthiyuthu* (fried meat) is a daily food item, which is also served during weddings. It is a dry dish of cubed beef boiled with spices and pieces of coconut and then sautéed in oil. *Kappa kari*, pieces of tapioca cooked with ground coconut and tempered with oil, is another favorite dish among this community. Most curries, including meat, always have a lot of coconut milk.

In Kottayam and Trichur, both sea and river fish distinguish local fare. In Kottayam, the fish is cooked using a sour fruit rind (*Garcinia cambogia*), locally called *kudampuli*. *Meen vevichathu*, fish in a fiery red chili sauce, has a characteristic sour and smoky flavor, resulting from the *kudampuli*.

In Trichur, tender mango is the souring agent used along with coconut milk. *Meen pattichadhu* includes very small fishlike oil sardines, or even prawns with coconut gratings. A hot favorite with the laity and priests alike is *mappas*, a mildly spiced chicken curry with a thin coconut gravy.

A special sweet traditionally served at weddings is *thayirum pazham pani*, coconut palm treacle, which is poured on ripe bananas, mashed together, and then eaten with curd and rice.

The Muslims. The Muslims of Kerala are called *moplahs*; they are direct decendants of Arab traders who married local Kerala women. Although the Kerala freely use rice, coconut, and jaggery, an Arab influence may be clearly observed in their *biriyanis* and a ground wheat-and-meat porridge, called *aleesa*, elsewhere referred to as *harisa*.

The Muslim kind of roti is the distinctive *podi patthiri*, a flat thin rice chapati made from a boiled mash of rice, baked on a *tava* (flat griddle plate), and dipped in coconut milk. *Aripatthiri* is a thicker version of this made from parboiled rice and flattened out on a cloth or banana leaf to prevent it from sticking. *Naipatthiri* is a deep-fried *puri* of raw rice powder with some coconut, fried to a golden brown. All these *patthiris* are eaten at breakfast with a mutton curry. Steamed *puttus*, eaten with small bananas, are also commonly consumed as the morning repast. A wedding-eve feast may include *nai choru*, rice fried lightly in ghee with onions, cloves, cinnamon, and cardamom to taste, and finally boiled to a finish. A wedding dinner generally includes a *biriyani* of mutton, chicken, fish, or prawns that is finished by arranging the separately prepared flesh and the cooked rice in layers and then baking them with live coals above and below. Several flavored soups are made from both rice and wheat, with added coconut or coconut milk, and spices. A whole-wheat porridge with minced mutton cooked in coconut milk is called *kiskiya*. A distinctive and unusual sweet is *mutta mala* (egg garlands), chainlike strings of egg yolk cooked in sugar syrup but later removed from it. *Mutta mala* is frequently served with a snowlike pudding called *pinnanthappam* made from the separated egg whites that have been whisked up with the remaining sugar syrup, steamed, and then cut into diamond shapes. This dish is indicative of the Portuguese influence in the area.

The Hindus. There are three main communities within the Hindu group, each with its own distinct cuisine: the Thiyas, Nairs, and Nampoorthiris.

The Thiyas are a community that formerly tapped palm sap, but have now entered many other professions. *Appam* and stew are typical breakfast fare, the stew being varied: fish in coconut sauce with tiny pieces of mango, mutton in coconut milk, or simply a sugared thick coconut milk. A specialty bread is *naipatthal*, in the shape of a starfish. The curd of favor is *pacchadi* (a dish made of beaten curd with cooked vegetable marrow and coconut ground with mustard seeds, and then tempered again with mustard seeds and oil). A popular dessert is *prathaman*, split green gram boiled in coconut milk and flavored with palm jaggery, cardamom, and ginger powder, and laced with fried cashews, raisins, and coconut chips.

The *Nairs* were the original warrior class of Kerala, whose cooking skills later led to their employment as professional chefs to nonvegetarian families all over the South. Breakfast typically consists of *palappam* or bamboo-steamed *puttu*, eaten with sweetened milk and tiny bananas. Certain vegetable specialities, although eaten by all Keralites, have special Nair associations. *Aviyal* is a mixture of green bananas, drumsticks, various beans, and green cashews (distinct to Nair cuisine), cooked with ground coconut and a little sour curd, and then topped with some coconut oil. *Kalan* is similar, but uses green bananas alone, with a gravy of yogurt, ground coconut, cumin, and green chilies. *Olan* is a dish of white pumpkin and dried beans cooked in coconut milk; fresh coconut oil is poured on top of it after the cooking pot is removed from the fire. A Nair wedding feast will generally include several types of *pacchadis*, pickles, chips, and *payasams* based on milk, coconut milk, rice, dal, and fried vermicelli. No meat is served at a wedding, although it is part of the typical diet. Such domestic meat and chicken dishes, although spiced, use a great deal of fresh coconut and coconut milk for tempering. A yogurt dish containing small pieces of ash gourd or raw mango cooked with coconut, curds, and chili paste is called *pulisseri*. A sweet mango chutneylike dish called *puli inju* (fried sliced ginger in a tamarind chili jaggery sauce) is served daily.

The *Nampoothiris* are the Brahmins of Kerala who probably first arrived there around the third century B.C.E. They are strict vegetarians who favor the *idli*, *dosai*, and *puttu* for breakfast with a coconut or curd accompaniment, and eat their rice with *kootu* (a preparation of mixed vegetables), *kalan*, and *olan*. The use of garlic in cooking is avoided. Other vegetable preparations consumed include *thoran*, which is usually made from runner beans, sliced fine and then steamed and tossed with grated coconut, ground turmeric, cumin, and green chilies and tempered with oil. Other bean varieties such as field beans, sword beans, green bananas, amaranthus, cabbage, and peas can all be made into *thoran* and eaten with rice. *Aviyal* and *erusseri*, a pumpkin curry, are also included in the Nampoothiri menu.

All Keralites eat yellow banana chips fried in coconut oil and lightly salted. The *payasam* of Kerala is made with rice and milk, but *prathamans* use milk, dried fruit, and dal or paper-thin shreds of a rice roll, which are then precooked and added to the sweetened milk to yield *palada prathaman*. Memorial services held once a year for ancestors routinely include *chatha pulisseri* in their menu. This is a sour buttermilk preparation with pepper, salt, and coconut paste that is thickened through boiling.

See also **Curry; Hinduism; Islam; Rice.**

BIBLIOGRAPHY

Achaya, K. T. *A Historical Dictionary of Indian Food.* New Delhi, India: Oxford University Press, 1994.

Achaya, K. T. *Indian Food—A Historical Companion.* New Delhi, India: Oxford University Press, 1994.

Jaffery, M. *A Taste of India.* London: Pavilion, 1985.

Karan, P. *Hyderabadi Cuisine.* India: HarperCollins, 1998.

Philip, Thangam E. *Modern Cookery for Teaching and the Trade.* Vol. 1. Singapore: Longman, 1965.

OTHER RESOURCES

Additional information on specific cuisines available at http://www.diwalimela.com

http://www.bawarchi.com

http://www.indiacultureonline.com

http://www.rediff.com

http://www.indiaexpress.com

Thangam Philip

INDONESIA. *See* **Southeast Asia.**

INDUSTRIALIZATION. *See* **Agriculture since the Industrial Revolution; Packaging and Canning.**

INDUS VALLEY. The food on which the diverse peoples of ancient India lived is a subject that has received some attention since archaeologists can recover bones, teeth, and carbonized seeds from their excavations. The period covered in this entry has come to be called the Indus Age (Possehl, 1999), that period in Pakistan and northwestern India which stretches from the beginnings of farming and herding around 7000 B.C.E. through the Early Iron Age to about 500 B.C.E. This period encompasses the Indus Civilization (2500–1900 B.C.E.), the Indian subcontinent's first period of urbanization (Fig. 1).

It was centered on the Indus Valley and the Punjab, but there were important settlements in southern Baluchistan, Gujarat, northern Rajasthan, Haryana, and western Uttar Pradesh (Fig. 2).

From the point of view of soil, water, and climate, these are regions suitable for the growing of wheat and barley and the raising of cattle, sheep, and goats on a significant scale. This is the constellation of plants and animals on which the earliest farmers and herders thrived, from the Mediterranean Sea to the lands of the Indus civilization.

A glimpse at an early period of farming and herding in this region is available from the site of Mehrgarh, on the Kachi plain of the Indus Valley. Around 7000 B.C.E., the inhabitants of this village lived mostly on domesticated, naked six-row barley, along with two other varieties of domesticated barley. Einkorn, emmer, and hard wheat were present in smaller amounts. The noncereals include the Indian jujube, a cherry-sized fruit; grapes; and dates. Sugar would have come from honey.

The use of domesticated rice by the peoples of the Indus civilization is not fully documented. However, by the second millennium B.C.E., it was the staple food grain at the site of Pirak, near Mehrgarh on the Kachi plain.

The animal economy of early Mehrgarh was dominated by twelve species of what can be termed "wild big game": gazelle, swamp deer, nilgai, blackbuck, onager,

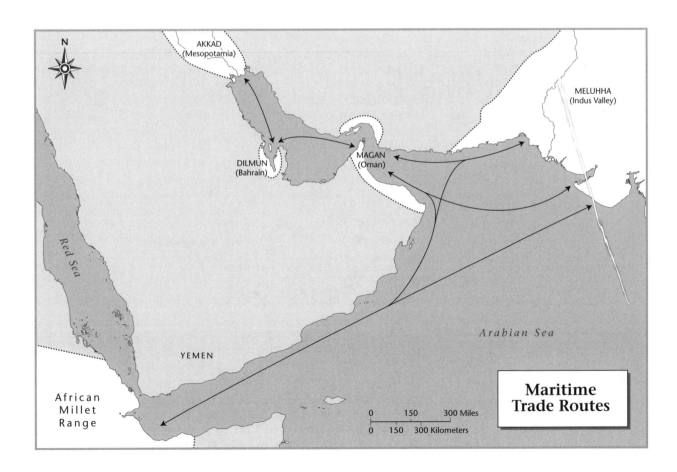

Maritime Trade Routes

FIGURE 1

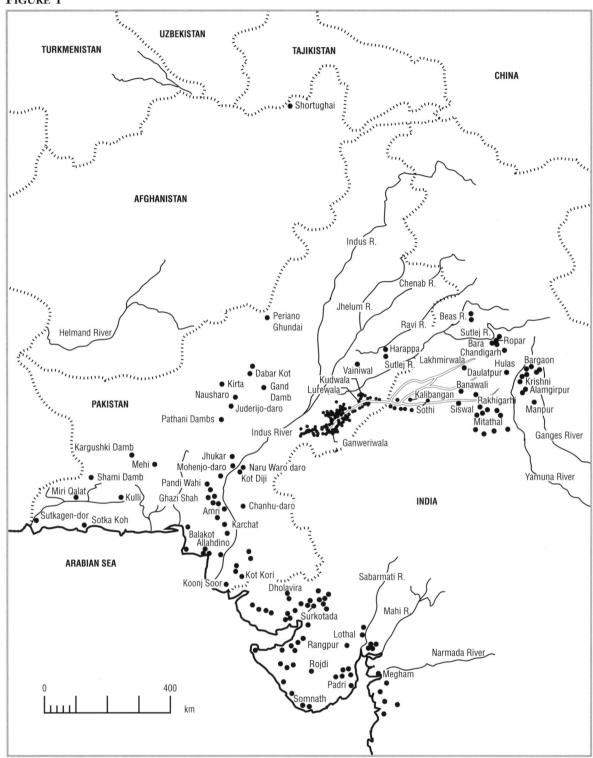

spotted deer, water buffalo, sheep, goat, cattle, pig, and elephant. These are animals that would have lived on the Kachi plain itself and the hills that surround it. The virtual absence of fish and bird remains suggests that the swampy environments near Mehrgarh were little exploited, but no screening was undertaken at the Mehrgarh site, and the recovery of fish and bird bone was therefore somewhat compromised.

268

FIGURE 2

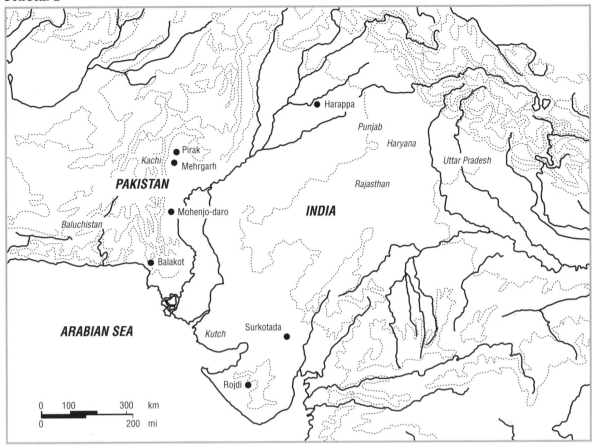

Meadow has noted the following concerning the subsistence economy of early Mehrgarh:

1. Goats were kept from the time of the first occupation of the site.

2. Cattle and sheep are likely to have been domesticated from local wild stock during Periods I and II (c. 7000–5000 B.C.E.).

3. Size diminution in goats was largely complete by late Period I, in cattle by Period II, and in sheep perhaps not until Period III.

4. The development of animal keeping by the ancient inhabitants of Mehrgarh took place in the context of cereal crop cultivation, the building of substantial mud brick structures, and the existence of social differentiation and long distance trade networks as attested by the presence of marine shells, lapis lazuli, and turquoise in even the earliest graves (p. 311).

From this evidence one can see that the development of food production and the domestication of the plants and animals appears to have been a local phenomenon, not one that came to the subcontinent by diffusion from the west.

Crops and Herds: Hunters, Gatherers, and Fishermen

From about 5000 B.C.E. the peoples of the Indus Valley and surrounding regions lived on a variety of food resources, both domesticated and wild. The base of the diet would have been the two cereals: barley first, and wheat second. They also cultivated various peas, beans and other pulses and exploited dates. Cotton seeds may have been present in Period II at Mehrgarh. One generally thinks of cotton as a fiber crop, but cotton oil is an important and nutritious commodity. Sesame was also domesticated in the Indus region, almost certainly for its oil. Most of these crops are grown in the winter season. For many millennia winter was the principal agricultural growing season in the subcontinent.

Extensive archaeology and archaeobotanical work in Gujarat, the southeastern "domain" of the Indus civilization, has produced evidence for the breadth of food resources used by the Indus peoples. A pot filled with seeds was recovered from the site of Surkotada. A number of seeds belonged to cultigens like Italian foxtail millet, green foxtail, and finger millet. The foxtail millet and finger millet were also found at the Sorath Harappan site of Rojdi (Weber, p. 119).

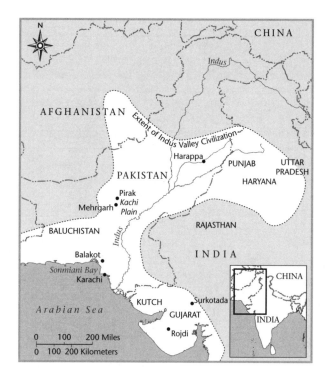

The chicken seems to have been first domesticated in China, but a case can be made that this was separately accomplished in the Indus region, where it is descended from the Indian Red Jungle Fowl, a beautifully colored bird. The male is a glossy deep orange-red, with long, yellowish neck feathers. The tail is shiny metallic black with long, arching sickle-shaped feathers. The underparts of the wild bird are blackish brown. This magnificent creature shares little in common with the almost pathetic white broiler stock now raised around the world. The wild chickens were eaten, and the eggs were probably a part of the diet.

Sedentary, village-based agriculture was complemented by herding, hunting and the gathering of additional plants. This served to expand and broaden the food base. We know from extensive analysis of animal remains that the peoples of the Indus civilization were cattle keepers on a grand scale. They also kept domesticated sheep and goats, as well as water buffalo. These animals were the source of a host of products from food to traction and of valuable materials such as fiber, leather, sinew, bone, and horn. Milk and milk products would have been very important to the Indus peoples. It is interesting to note that the subcontinent has never been a place where cheeses were prepared, but butter, *ghee* (clarified butter), and various forms of yogurt are widely known and may have their beginnings in the period being discussed here. The pig seems to have stayed wild, but it was hunted along with the animals listed above as "big game" that were not domesticated. Pigs and elephants were the source of ivory for the Indus peoples.

The aforementioned pot from Surkotada also produced large numbers of seeds from wild grass and sedges and other wild plants. This, and parallel evidence from Rojdi, informs us that gathering of wild plant material was an important part of the subsistence strategy, at least in some places. The Indian jujube was then, and is today, another food product gathered from wild trees.

Evidence for the use of fish and shellfish is spotty and not robust in the Indus region prior to the Indus civilization. After about 2500 B.C.E., however, the use of these maritime and riverine resources increased markedly. It is clear, for example, that fish contributed significantly to the diet of the Harappan inhabitants of Balakot, just to the west of Karachi near Sonmiani Bay on the coast of the Arabian Sea. They were eating a grunt, a fish that inhabits lagoons and sea areas with sandy bottoms and is taken today by fishermen who use gill nets in Sonmiani Bay. The peoples of the Indus civilization were great fish lovers. The Indus River teems with various species that were caught and eaten. The Harappans made very nice copper or bronze fishhooks, with an eye to take the line (Fig. 3).

Large fish vertebrae have been found at some Kutch Harappan sites. Salted and/or dried fish were traded over large distances during the Mature Harappan, as documented by the presence of a marine species at the Indus civilization city of Harappa.

The peoples of the Indus civilization ate considerable quantities of shellfish and turned the shells into beautiful artifacts: bangles, beads, ladles, figurines, rings, and inlay. The gastropods included five "shank" type shells and three bivalves, or clamlike animals. At Balakot one species of "shank" and the grunt seem to have dominated the diet of the Harappans.

We do know that these protohistoric peoples ate plenty of meat, including beef. Whether any of them were vegetarians has not been determined. Some of them could have been, but the widespread modern Indian tradition of vegetarianism, and the special respect that Hindus have for cattle, came later. Modern Indian vegetarianism has many bases, but key to it historically is the philosophical concept of *ahimsa* (noninjury), which is a part of the In-

FIGURE 3

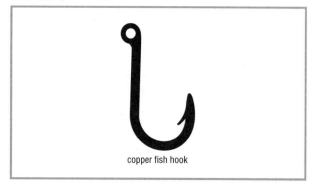

copper fish hook

dian intellectual achievement of the second half of the first millennium B.C.E.

Dietary Innovation with African Millets

The food grains of the early Indus Age were winter grasses, barley, and wheat. These do well in the northwestern region of the subcontinent where there is enough winter rain and snow to sustain them. But the main period of rainfall for the subcontinent as a whole is the summer monsoon, which lasts from June to November. This is the hot season, and the winter grasses, as well as the other winter crops that the peoples of the Indus Age used, were not well adapted to it. It turns out that the subcontinent does not have any large-seeded summer-season cereals that could be domesticated, so there was something of an environmental bind for the expansion of agriculture outside the northwestern region with its winter rainfall.

This environmental bind was broken to a large extent when three millets from Africa became available to the farmers of ancient India. These plants were sorghum, pearl millet, and finger millet, all of which evolved in a belt across Africa just below the southern margin of the Sahara desert. Evidence for maritime trade between the Indus civilization and Mesopotamia comes to us from cuneiform texts and artifacts recovered from archaeological excavations. The texts speak of Mesopotamian venture capitalists who mounted maritime trading expeditions to three lands: Dilmun, Magan, and Meluhha, identified in order as Bahrain Island, Oman, and the Indus civilization (Possehl 1997: 133–137). They brought large quantities of copper back to Mesopotamia. Sailors of the Indus civilization reached Oman and the Arabian Gulf, since quantities of common Indus pottery have been found there along with other Indus artifacts.

The presence of the African millets in archaeological sites dating from 2400 to 2000 B.C.E. in Yemen, Oman, and the subcontinent implies that one leg of this maritime trade extended to the mouth of the Red Sea, where Indus sailors, probably short on food supplies, acquired local grains (the millets) for the trip home. These are the large-seeded summer cereals on which an entire subsistence system can be based. They begin to appear in the archaeological record of the Indus civilization about 2400 B.C.E.—first finger millet, then pearl millet, and finally sorghum at the end of the third millennium.

The resulting modification to the subcontinent's subsistence pattern was slow and complex. The process was certainly not linear, with millets replacing other crops, and the massive acceptance of farming by hunter-gatherers. But over time these three African millets have made a massive contribution to the Indian economy because they were so well adapted to the summer monsoon wet season. Some measure of this success can be seen in modern statistics on cereal production in India. The three African millets are all in the list of the six most productive cereals, as seen in Table 1.

TABLE 1

Production of the top six cereals in India

Grain	Amount in thousands of tons
Rice	70,667
Wheat	53,995
Sorghum	10,518
Corn	8,332
Pearl Millet	7,787
Finger Millet	2,379
All cereals	156,550

SOURCE: Government of India. *Indian Agriculture in Brief.* 23rd ed. Delhi: Ministry of Agriculture, 1990.

Ceramics and Food

Archaeologists have identified a few pottery shapes that can be associated with food and cooking in specific enough ways that they are interesting to talk about. There is a cooking pot, today called a *handi* in most north Indian languages (Fig. 4).

FIGURE 4

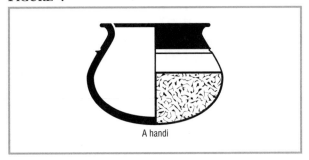

A handi

Shards from the bottoms of these pots are often fire-blackened, and they were sometimes protected against thermal shock with a coating of clay placed on the bottom after the pot was fired. The dish- or bowl-on-stand (Fig. 5). looks like a raised plate, just the sort of thing

FIGURE 5

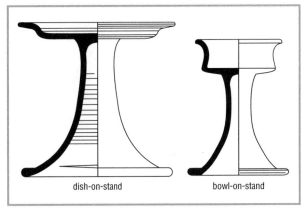

dish-on-stand   bowl-on-stand

that a person who ate sitting on the floor would use to raise his or her dinner closer to the mouth. There are lots of globular pots, often with surface treatments that significantly increase the surface area of the pot. One of these ceramic types is called "wet ware" (Fig. 6), which

FIGURE 6

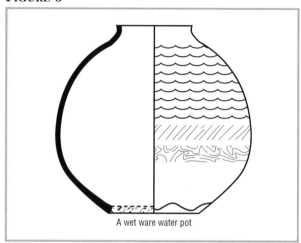

A wet ware water pot

was made by applying a viscous slurry of very fine clay over the body of a formed pot. The resulting pattern is both a decoration and functional since the many ridges increase the surface area of the pot, allowing for maximum evaporation, which kept the water in them cool. There are also small teacups (Fig. 7) with perforated han-

FIGURE 7

tea cup

dles, which look much like their modern counterparts, and probably functioned in much the same way, as well as copper-bronze frying pans (Fig. 8).

FIGURE 8

copper-bronze frying pan

Food and Eating in Ancient India

Based on what is known one can imagine an eating scene in a home during the Indus civilization. People seem to have eaten while sitting on the floor, which was probably covered with a rug or a mat. They were served their food in a dish or bowl on a stand. The meal could have included flat, unleavened bread of barely or wheat flour, ground at home between stones. This would have been accompanied by meat: chicken, goat, sheep, water buffalo, or even beef. At times the flesh of wild ungulates would have been available. Fish and shellfish would have broadened this portion of the diet. Various peas and pulses would have added a vegetable component to the meals; and chicken eggs may have been included. A fruit component to the meal, possibly a dessert, would have come from honey, dates, grapes and the jujube. Milk from cows, buffalo, sheep and goats would have been available, and could have added great diversity of taste to the ancient diet. Cool liquids would have come from spherical pots, like those in wet ware, and been consumed in ceramic tableware, possibly even the little tea cups. Although butter was probably prepared, since it goes rancid so quickly in hot climates, the more stable clarified form, known as *ghee* in contemporary India, was also prepared. Other oils, for cooking and consumption, would have come from sesame and cotton seeds.

Cooking would have included roasting, boiling, and baking, as suggested by the *handi*-shaped pots, and frying, as documented by the copper-bronze frying pans. By 1500 B.C.E. the *tandoor*, a clay oven, is documented. This implies that this distinctive cuisine of modern India and Pakistan has a 3,500-year history.

There would have been almost no refrigeration, so many foods would have been eaten fresh, and seasonal availability would have had an important impact on the diet. But some forms of preservation were probably known. Food grains can be stored for years if kept dry. Clarified butter keeps for months. Dried and/or salted meat and fish are implied by the presence of maritime fish at Harappa, five hundred miles from the sea.

There is much to be learned on this topic of food in protohistoric times in South Asia. But there is an outline, and that will surely be filled out over time.

See also **Butter; Cereal Grains; India.**

BIBLIOGRAPHY

Meadow, Richard H. "Animal Domestication in the Middle East: A Revised View from the Eastern Margin." In *Harappan Civilization: A Recent Perspective*. 2d ed. Edited by Gregory L. Possehl. Delhi: Oxford & IBH and the American Institute of Indian Studies, 1993.

Possehl, Gregory L. "Seafaring Merchants of Meluhha." In *South Asian Archaeology 1995*. Edited by Bridget Allchin. Delhi: Oxford & IBH, 1997.

Possehl, Gregory L. *Indus Age: The Beginnings*. Philadelphia: University of Pennsylvania Press, 1999.

19191919191919191919191919191919191919Weber, Steven A. *Plants and Harappan Subsistence: An Example of Stability and Change from Rojdi*. Delhi: Oxford & IBH and the American Institute of Indian Studies, 1991.

Gregory L. Possehl

INFANT FORMULA. *See* **Baby Food; Lactation; Milk, Human.**

INSPECTION. Among the many systems that assure food safety, inspection is one of the most critical and difficult. As the global trade of food increased over time, veterinary experts of the Organization International des Epizooties (OIE) addressed the scientific challenge of confining animal diseases, which are the origin of most food-borne pathogens. In 1951 the spread of plant pests through trade became the concern of the International Plant Protection Committee (IPPC) of the Food and Agriculture Organization (FAO). As a result, the World Health Organization (WHO) and FAO organized a set of international standards, the Codex Alimentarius, which describes preferred methods of food production to minimize contaminants and toxicants to keep them below acceptable tolerance levels, with recommendations from the OIE and IPPC. In the early twenty-first century, the Sanitary and Phytosanitary Agreement (SPS) was the system that governed how inspection standards may be used in the fair trade of foods. This agreement was established by members of the 1994 Uruguay Round of the General Agreement on Tariffs and Trade (GATT). Together, Codex and SPS work to improve the quality of traded foods, limit the movement of crop pests and animal diseases, and mediate fair trade.

In the United States, inspection is performed by several different agencies, such as the Department of Agriculture, the Food and Drug Administration, the National Oceanographic and Aeronautic Administration, and the U.S. Customs Service. The following laws empower these agencies to perform inspections: the Federal Meat Inspection Act (1906), the Seafood Inspection Act (1934), and the Federal Food, Drug, and Cosmetic Act (1938) (Table 1). While the U.S. Department of Agriculture (USDA) cannot demand that a plant be closed, and while product recalls are voluntary, the withdrawal of all inspectors effectively means a plant can no longer ship its products since inspection is mandatory. The Food and Drug Administration (FDA) has authority to inspect food production facilities overseas, reject foods from entry into the United States, and even pull defective products off of store shelves.

U.S. Customs authorities assist in processing food imports at 150 ports of entry. In 2000, the FDA's limited resources allowed direct physical inspection of only 1 percent of imports. Still the system manages to catch problems (logging in over eight million lines of import

TABLE 1

U.S. food inspection system

Food	Agency/office	Target
Meat, poultry, and processed egg products	USDA Food Safety and Inspection Service (FSIS)	Pathogens, filth, drug residues
Imported plants and pests, live animals	USDA Animal and Plant Health Inspection Service (APHIS)	Crop diseases
Fresh plant foods and eggs, processed foods, seafood, and dairy	FDA Office of Regulatory Affairs (ORA)	Pathogens, toxins, filth, pesticides, additives

detentions annually). In one season the reasons given for rejection of imports included: filth (32 percent); microbial pathogens and molds (17 percent); low-acid canned foods (12.5 percent); defective or misleading labeling (10 percent); pesticides and heavy metals (11.5 percent); decomposition (7.5 percent); and food additives (6.5 percent).

If an inspector suspects that products are unsafe, items can be detained automatically (especially if a number of previous shipments have been defective). An agency usually has a month to test the product and make a decision on its admissibility, but the importer may apply for early release after five days if the product is perishable. Permanently detained food must be remanufactured to acceptable standards, destroyed, or removed from the country within a certain period of time (three months in the United States).

In other countries inspection of imports may be a local, national, or regional endeavor. The Canadian Food Inspection Agency (CFIA) is the inspection authority in that country. In Central America, the Organismo Internacional Regional de Sanidad Agropecuaria, or International Regional Organization for Plant and Animal Sanitation (OIRSA), is the agency responsible for testing imports and assuring their safety.

Issues that arise from inspection are of two main types: political and scientific. First, if the reason for detention of an inspected food item is not transparent and scientifically valid, the importing country may be accused of erecting a trade barrier. Second, adequate sampling and testing are technically difficult. Traditionally, meat and poultry were inspected through organoleptic or sensory evaluation (smell, sight, touch), which worked for detection of gross filth, decomposition, and molds, but not for detection of microbial pathogens. Agents have begun to perform microbiological tests on meat and poultry, but such tests must be rapid, accurate, and relatively inexpensive to be useful. Perishable foods that are detained too long may not be fit for consumption by the time test results are available. Tests for many pathogens

are still in development; agents often test for common pathogens like salmonella and *E. coli*, which serve as biomarkers for the existence of other pathogens in a food sample.

Even when an excellent testing procedure is available, sampling poses a problem, especially in the case of solid or semi-solid foods. Contamination may be isolated in one part of a carcass, a head of lettuce, or a production run of some other food. Sampling the entire product would eliminate the worry that a pathogen was missed, but there would be no product left to eat. Thus an elaborate science of statistical testing has evolved to ascertain with reasonable probability whether a product is contaminated based on a certain number of samples of a certain size. Still, there is no guarantee that the product is safe or that subsequent abuse will not render it unsafe.

To streamline the inspection process, many countries require government-validated export certificates to verify whether a product contains what the label says it does and that it has been approved for safety and offered for consumption in the country that produces it. Making certification an internationally harmonious process is the focus of the Codex Committee for Food Import and Export Inspection and Certification Systems.

See also **Codex Alimentarius; FAO (Food and Agriculture Organization); Food Safety; Food Trade Associations; Government Agencies; International Agencies**.

BIBLIOGRAPHY

Codex Alimentarius website with links to WTO, OIE, IPPC. Available at http://www.codexalimentarius.net.

Food and Drug Administration website. Available at http://www.fda.gov. See the Office of Regulatory Affairs information on import inspections.

World Trade Organization website. Available at http://www.wto.org. Contains Sanitary and Phytosanitary Agreement information. See the agreement on the Application of Sanitary and Phytosanitary Measures.

USDA websites. Available at http://www.fsis.usda.gov and http://www.aphis.usda.gov.

Robin Yeaton Woo

INTAKE. Intake is an umbrella term that refers to the act of taking something in. The term "intake" is often used in relation to food and drink, to describe how and how much is ingested. It also relates to behavior, since mental processing is involved in the action of eating and drinking. That is, physical and social stimuli are involved in feeding and drinking behaviors in terms of controlling the movements of gathering and ingesting materials; internal stimuli such as metabolism and circulating substrates also play a role. Intake of food and drink interests natural and social sciences as it is a vital behavior to sustain life that is also shaped by culture and society.

Behavioral Organization of Intake

The behavioral organization of intake involves perception of the sensory characteristics of food and drink. Physical and chemical properties of food and drink that can be sensed by the eater provide information about their nature. Orosensory attributes (that is, those relating to both taste and the other senses) can be detected by sight and sound, smell, irritance, taste, and touch. Food and drink can be appealing based on their orosensory properties. And the first mouthfuls of food can send substrates around the body within minutes.

Intake can be adjusted according to nutritional needs when orosensory characteristics are associated with the postingestive (metabolic) effects of food and drink. Orosensory characteristics can thus become cues that predict postingestional effects specific to foods and drinks. These cues can be unlearned (innate, sweet taste) or learned (acquired, bitter taste). While sweet stimuli mean energy, perhaps from carbohydrate, bitter stimuli are a cue to alkaloid toxins. From an evolutionary standpoint, it has been hypothesized that the liking for sweetness ensured animals' survival. In animals and humans, learning plays an important role in food intake. The acquisition of a taste for nutrients and an aversion for toxic substance are also vital. Behavioral and physiological analysis of the learning of pre- and postingestive control of intake was developed by French physiologist Jacques Le Magnen. His original contributions include findings on conditioned sensory aversions, carbohydrate-conditioned sensory preferences, and control of meal size.

Social and Cultural Organization of Intake

Intake is also organized according to food availability. In terms of the latter, we see the great contrast between industrialized countries where food is available in abundance and Third World countries where hunger afflicts poor people due to food scarcity. Our ancestors' intake was mainly dependent on plant food gathering, hunting, and fishing. Later on, domestication of food and animals and the development of food preservation enabled human societies to improve food availability. However, in parts of the world not well suited for cultivation, pastoralists still acquire their food from their herds of domesticated animals. Herding allows them to transform nonedible plant matter into animal products.

Intake is also determined by the culture of human groups. Learned cultural knowledge affects food choices. Socially transmitted knowledge about food includes norms, religious, or cult values, as well as myths, superstitions, taboos, and fads. The intake of certain kinds of plant and animal foods can be culturally prohibited. For example, cattle are killed for meat in many parts of the world, while traditional Hindus forbid killing cattle for meat because of their use in agriculture. Dogs serve as pets and companions in American culture while serving as food in other cultures, illustrating how intake is motivated by symbolic values of the food rather than its survival value. However, sociocultural influences do not act alone and interact with the individual's biology to determine intake.

Control of Intake

Investigations concerned with the control of intake have used various peripheral and central approaches. This has led to theories of the mechanisms controlling intake, such as the glucostatic (transient change of blood glucose), the lipostatic (fat metabolism and body fat stores), the thermostatic (thermic effect of food), and the aminostatic (essential amino acid) hypotheses. Although intake was shown to be facilitated or inhibited by a variety of substrates, the behavioral mechanisms remain to be identified. Neural bases of food intake have evolved from the those prevalent in the 1950s, focusing on appetite and satiety brain centers located in the hypothalamus, to the current hypothesis that macronutrient intake is controlled by precise synaptic pathways. Food intake might indeed be guided by macronutrient selection. However, experiments that involve presenting laboratory animals with two or more diets differing in their nutrient content in an attempt to understand brain mechanisms that control intake involves the inclusion of confounding factors. Indeed, many drugs that affect central nervous system neurotransmitters and peptides also act on sensory pathways. Therefore, unless the confounding sensory attributes of food have been excluded, one cannot conclude that the subsequent food intake is controlled by the macronutrients. This principle was applied by examining studies using sensorily contrasting forms of various macronutrients, and only brain serotonin was found to affect carbohydrate intake while the effects of catecholamines and opiates on macronutrients were not substantiated.

Intake is also motivated by factors external to the food or the drink itself. Age, sex, physiological state, nutritional state, emotions, stress, number of people present, peer groups, food trends, social pressures (body image), as well as beliefs related to food safety (for example, food beliefs related to mad cow disease, genetically modified foods, pesticide-free or organic food) are known to influence intake. Other external factors that affect intake include food availability, food cost, as well as environmental factors (season, temperature, and so forth). In addition, animal and human studies have revealed that food and macronutrient intake is related to circadian rhythms, and that food intake is concentrated during the period of main activity (for example, during the day) and is related to predictable rhythms of macronutrient selection.

Expressing Intake

Intake of food and drink is often estimated by dietary measurement of daily intake of energy (kilocalorie [kcal], kilojoules [kJ]) and nutrients (carbohydrate, protein, lipid, vitamins, and minerals). Units such as the gram (g),

milligram (mg), microgram (μg), International Unit (IU), and so forth are used, as well as established human nutrition methodologies such as food diary, food recalls, food frequency questionnaires, and so on. Intakes are then qualified as adequate or inadequate based on nutritional recommendations. Nutritional research methods need to be improved by assessing cognitive perception and control of eating.

Facilitated intake and its inhibition are expressed in various ways. Among terms used to describe facilitated intake or events surrounding it are appetite, hunger, palatability, motivation to eat, and (sensory) preference. If intake is inhibited, terms such as satiety, satiation, appetite inhibition, or even satiety disinhibition are used. These terms are often used to interpret sets of quantitative data such as amount eaten during the day, meal size, ingestion rate, or numbers calculated from scales rating the hunger state. Although these measurements do not assess cognitive processes controlling intake, their direction is translated into words describing behaviors. The experimental design is therefore crucial to identify causal processes involved in intake; for example, unchanged quantitative intake while rate of intake is reduced could be interpreted as decreased pleasure while sensory preference remains unaffected.

Implications

Insufficient intake results in chronic malnutrition and periodic massive starvation. Related health problems are numerous, and include the impact of the permanent effect of energy–protein deficiency on brain development (in early childhood), parasitic diseases, and high rates of infant mortality. Controlling population growth and a better allocation of resources were proposed as solutions to world hunger. The problem of hunger could also be alleviated by technology transfer in which new technologies and crop variety could improve food production.

Disordered intake can lead to health problems such as obesity, cardiovascular disease, diabetes, alcoholism, as well as disordered eating in athletes and the eating disorders of restrictive eaters, anorexics, and bulimics. Interestingly, these health problems often arise in countries where food is abundant. Intake of specific macronutrients has been linked to diseases, for example, intake of carbohydrates has been linked to diabetes, and fat intake has been linked to heart disease, as well as to some cancers. Therefore, a better understanding of how intake is controlled could provide precious tools enabling one to intervene effectively or even prevent the development of nutrition-related pathologies.

See also **Acceptance and Rejection; Appetite; Assessment of Nutritional Status; Eating: Anatomy and Physiology of Eating; Health and Disease; Malnutrition; Metabolic Imprinting and Programming; Sensation and the Senses.**

BIBLIOGRAPHY

Berthoud, Hans-Rudolf, and Randy J. Seeley. *Neural and Metabolic Control of Macronutrient Intake*. Boca Raton, Fla.: CRC, 2000.

Booth, David A. *Psychology of Nutrition*. London: Taylor & Francis, 1994.

Peoples, James, and Garrick Bailey. *Humanity: An Introduction to Cultural Anthropology*. Belmont, Calif.: West/Wadsworth, 1997.

Stricker, Edward M. *Handbook of Behavioral Neurobiology*, vol. 10, *Neurobiology of Food and Fluid Intake*. New York: Plenum, 1990.

Thibault, Louise, and David A. Booth. "Macronutrient-Specific Dietary Selection in Rodents and Its Neural Bases." *Neuroscience and Biobehavioral Reviews* 23 (1999): 457–528.

Thibault, Louise, and David A. Booth, eds. "The Role of Orosensory and Postingestive Effects of Food in the Control of Intake. Jacques Le Magnen, 1955–1963." *Appetite* 33 (1999): 1–59.

Louise Thibault

INTERNATIONAL AGENCIES.

The second half of the twentieth century witnessed the growth of a type of social institution that plays an important role in food and nutrition policies and programs throughout the world. These institutions, which are commonly referred to as "international agencies," are usually constituted as suborganizations within larger sociopolitical organizational structures. One set of such institutions are the "multilaterals," which include many governments, particularly the agencies of the United Nations (UN), or those of the European Union. A second set of agencies, often referred to as "bilaterals," are the aid organizations established by national governments in the industrialized world, including those of the European states, the United States, and Canada, as well as Australia and Japan. A third type, with activities that closely parallel those of the UN and governmental agencies, includes nongovernmental organizations (NGOs) or private voluntary organizations (PVOs). These may be religious or "faith-based" agencies that are administratively connected to religious organizations or are closely affiliated with such organizations, or they may be independent groups, such as the Helen Keller Foundation or Save the Children. Many of these NGOs receive funds from bilateral and multilateral agencies.

Agencies of the United Nations

The establishment of the various agencies in the UN system began with the founding of the UN in 1945. During the following half-century, new agencies were added as needs were redefined and expanded. The current body of UN agencies whose work involves food and/or nutrition are the Asian Development Bank (ADB), Food and Agriculture Organization (FAO), International Atomic Energy Agency (IAEA), International Fund for Agricul-

tural Development (IFAD), International Labor Organization (ILO), Joint United Nations Programme on HIV/AIDS (UNAIDS), United Nations Development Programme (UNDP), United Nations Educational, Scientific, and Cultural Organization (UNESCO), United Nations Population Fund (UNFPA), United Nations High Commissioner for Refugees (UNHCR), United Nations Children's Fund (UNICEF), United Nations Research Institute for Social Development (UNRISD), World Food Programme (WFP), World Health Organization (WHO), and the World Bank.

Agency Goals and Functions

One of the principal motivations underlying the establishment and operation of international agencies was to provide vehicles for directing resources—economic, technical, and technological—from resource-rich countries to resource-poor countries. Other political, economic, and social interests also shape the motivations and activities of agencies. Moreover, the fact that international agencies are generally not freestanding institutions, but part of larger sociopolitical units, is one of several characteristics that affect their mission, administrative organization, philosophy, policy, and activities.

The purposes of both UN and non-UN agencies whose work relates to food and nutrition can be summarized by one or more of the following goals: establishing technical norms, providing funding, providing technical assistance, or delivering services. Within the UN system, the various agencies were established with distinct, yet complementary, mandates and were given different, but often overlapping, sectors of action. Thus, WHO and FAO were set up as technical agencies with responsibilities for technical norms and technical assistance, whereas UNICEF was designed to support and deliver services through funding and technical support, and the World Bank was designed to provide funds.

Obstacles, Challenges, and Persistence

In their efforts to further the health and welfare of populations with respect to food and nutrition, international agencies face multiple challenges. An examination of these challenges helps to explain the gaps between stated goals and realities of agency activities that make them frequent subjects of controversy and criticism. Some of these challenges relate to the structure of international collaboration and conflict regardless of the focus of action, while others are specific to characteristics of social action related to food and nutrition.

A primary challenge for establishing complementary activities at country and community levels is that agencies' activities are based on widely differing philosophies of how to promote and sustain development. Bilateral agencies represent countries with different economic and political agendas. These differ not only between nations, but also within nations, as is evident from the policy changes that accompany shifts in government when different political parties are in power. Within the UN system itself, there are also different philosophies and constituencies, which are evident not only between agencies, but also within them. The NGOs and PVOs represent still other sets of values and theories about what needs to be done and how to do it.

International agencies face serious challenges in reconciling definitions of needs as perceived on one hand by technical advisers, high-level political representatives, and international advocacy groups, and on the other with the needs articulated by recipient groups, from national-level politicians and civil administrators to regional and community-level spokesmen. These conflicting interpretations arise from multiple sources and cover a range of issues, including ethical concerns and competing values about fairness, justice and "whose reality counts," priorities for action in the face of limited resources, and differing perspectives on the causes and consequences of food and nutrition problems. A related factor that affects many aspects of food and nutrition policies and programs is that most agencies, especially the bilaterals, have to answer to the political constituencies who control the resources they require to carry out their work. Indeed the basic organization of development activities into the categories of "donors" and "recipients" create structural barriers that pose significant challenges to meeting population needs.

Another common problem, which relates to the demands from "donor constituencies," is that the time frame for research, program development, and evaluation is typically much too short. As a consequence, agencies are forced to take shortcuts that jeopardize the achievement of goals. As a result, the potential to learn from experience is reduced, and there are inadequate opportunities to make adjustments to improve programs.

Special challenges for food and nutrition activities stem from the fact that throughout the world they relate to multiple and very different social sectors. Food is the provenance of agriculture and various economic sectors of producers and marketing concerns. It is also the source of nutrients, which are the provenance of nutrition and health sectors. Both national governments and international agencies tend to divide food and nutrition responsibilities among multiple organizational units, which often results in conflicting goals and serious fragmentation of efforts. Even within a particular sector, such as health agencies, differing orientations may result in conflicting approaches to nutrition and health education in communities.

In 1977 the UN established the Subcommittee on Nutrition (SCN), under the aegis of the Administrative Committee on Coordination (ACC), as a mechanism for communication among the various UN agencies with responsibilities in food and nutrition. The ACC/SCN, which meets yearly and compiles and disseminates technical reports through its office in Geneva, Switzerland, also seeks the participation of bilaterals and NGOs. This

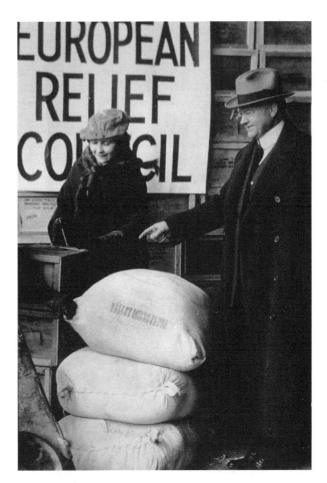

Commerce Secretary (later President) Herbert Hoover inspects food shipments for the European Relief Council in the early 1920s. Food was sent to help Europe recover from the devastation of World War I and its aftermath. COURTESY OF ARCHIVE PHOTOS, INC.

small organization has no mandated authority to resolve differences but provides a forum for exchange and debate. Its existence is threatened by hostility from some of its constituent agencies who fear that SCN activities may reveal weaknesses in their own operations, and at least one of SCN's components, the Advisory Group on Nutrition (AGN), which was composed of senior experts from outside the UN system, has been dismantled.

The example of the tribulations of the SCN provides a glimpse of the shortcomings in motivations, organization, and action that are typical of international agencies. There are, however, two critical questions to answer before recommending curtailing or abolishing these agencies. The first is, "Would the poor and hungry be better off without these agencies?" Historical comparisons of situations where the agencies have and have not been active reveal that the presence of the agencies has been favorable. Without them, the only major interests affecting food and nutrition are commercial and political—neither of which care much about the poor.

The second question is, "Can the system or its constituents be improved?" Greater intellectual attention is required to address such important issues as updating the mandates of international agencies to modern realities, instituting better accountability for all international agencies (including bilaterals and NGOs), and increasing resources to improve diet and nutrition worldwide. At the level of agencies, a high priority is developing better methods for more effective cooperation between agencies and populations. While there are many difficult barriers to improving agency functioning, dedicated people who work in and with international agencies find many opportunities to make improvements.

See also **Codex Alimentarius; Food and Agriculture Organization (FAO); Food Supply and the Global Food Market; Food Trade Organizations; Government Agencies; Political Economy.**

Gretel Pelto
Jean-Pierre Habicht

INTESTINAL FLORA. "The entire world is covered with a layer of feces. Granted it is thicker in some places than in others, but a solid layer, nevertheless. . . ." This is how a wizened professor used to begin his clinical parasitology course for microbiology graduate students. Naturally all the students laughed, only to learn during the ensuing months that the statement is profoundly true. The lesson also bears truth in that fecal microorganisms arise from within the bowels of the digestive tract. The human intestine is home to an invisible and remarkable biosphere of living organisms dedicated to preserving its own existence. Humans serve as host to these billions and trillions of organisms that function in effect as a single living entity.

In fair exchange, during our lifespan, our gut flora provides us with health, protects us from disease, and serves as the major labor force to digest almost everything we eat—from artichokes to zebu.

The population of microbes that inhabit our intestines is made up of hundreds of different species of bacteria and other organisms. By far the vast majority of these are anaerobic, which means they do not multiply in the presence of oxygen. Since few if any anaerobes are defined as classic pathogens, by and large these anaerobes are only of interest to culinarians because they function to metabolize and break down what we eat and make it available to be absorbed and used as fuel and energy for our own body. Other species that require air (oxygen) to live are more commonly known by the general public, and a few have even achieved stardom, mainly because of their predilection to cause disease. Thus, certain bacteria such as *staphylococcus, E. coli, salmonella, shigella, enterobacter,* and others have become well recognized, if not feared—almost to the point of being a phobia—by some people, especially in the United States. Most people seem to be confused by too many overstated, highly publicized warnings, along with too many recommendations from too many different sources.

A list of the scientific names of all the different microorganisms that inhabit the human gut, sometimes described as autochthonous flora, would be very lengthy. Some understanding of science is required, however, in order to appreciate the very complex relationship we have with the microbial world living inside and on our bodies, which in turn help maintain the delicate balance between health and disease. Most important is the fact that each living human being has a rather steadfast and distinct microbial profile. This profile is almost as identifiable as a fingerprint.

When foreign bacteria are introduced to our profile, the ecosystem reacts rather quickly to disallow these species to proliferate. Accordingly, disease is not a normal finding; rather, we, for most of our existence, maintain ourselves in a general state of good health.

Some remarkable studies have demonstrated that even when our intestinal microbiologic profile is disrupted to the point of causing disease, for instance, in the case of traveler's diarrhea, the body mounts a tremendous effort to return itself to its normal healthful state, and in doing so somehow the original microbial profile returns. What we eat and how old we are does play a major role in the overall state of our live-in microbial population, and on occasion shifts of our profile do occur. For example, this happens when the microbes adjust to accommodate the various types of food we ingest. So, if we eat a diet of all starches, those species of organisms which thrive on starches will increase their relative numbers in relation to the frequency and amount of starch which we consume. When one considers diseases that are due to intestinal microbiota, it is also important to know what "pathologic bolus" means. Simply put, this phrase refers to the minimal number of pathogenic organisms needed to be ingested in order to cause a specific disease. It is usually expressed as numbers in powers of ten per gram or milliliter of menstruum. This number ranges from very large to very small, depending on the specific organism and disease. So, while certain diseases require huge numbers of bacteria in order to initiate illness, others require very few bacteria.

For example, not all *salmonella* species are pathogenic, and those that are generally require that a large pathologic bolus be ingested to produce illness. On the other hand, most species of *shigella* are intrinsically "pathogenic," and it takes only a small number to cause symptoms. It has been found, in this example, that *salmonellae* generally are susceptible to destruction by acidity of the stomach, and few survive to enter the intestines where the actual infection takes place. Shigellae, on the other hand, are able to withstand the acidity of our gastric juices and arrive in the intestine viable and ready to set up (unwanted) residence and cause disease.

Other major factors also play heavily in defining health and disease. Paramount to this struggle are the status of our overall nutritional habits and secondly the maintenance of the immune system and understanding how it functions to protect us from invading organisms.

In general, well-fed people are less likely to catch infectious diseases of any sort, and with some exceptions, the incidence and severity of dysenterylike diseases are also lessened if we follow a well-balanced diet. The amazing increase in the average height of individuals after the introduction of better food and balanced diets in certain Third World populations, which occurred in one single generation, is testimony to the tremendous impact diet plays in this regard. Individuals who suffer from underlying diseases and conditions that compromise the normal function of our immune system are much more vulnerable to life-threatening diseases caused by bacteria, viruses, and other organisms than are average citizens. Likewise, those who have lost protection due to impairment or destruction of the skin are much more likely to become ill. The causative agents in these cases are produced not only by recognized pathogens, but also come from normally benign species of so-called normal (or commensal) flora. Almost 90 percent of mortalities in burn patients are due to infection and sepsis. Furthermore, most of these deadly infections are produced by the patient's own intrinsic internal microorganisms. Notable for this discussion is that most foodborne diseases are indeed usually attributed to microbial species of the enteric type—"enteric" meaning those normally found in the digestive tract. When they are allowed to proliferate in nutrient-rich unrefrigerated foods such as potato salad, bacterial and viral "food poisoning" is likely, and outbreaks continue to afflict even the most civilized nations.

The most common cause of both direct and cross-contamination of foods, which ultimately can lead to such outbreaks, is unofficially labeled in medical vernacular the "fecal/hand/mouth" route—not a polite description, but accurate. Furthermore, although refrigeration and proper storage—and to a lesser degree chemical disinfection—are important, human hands remain the most villainous of vectors of food-borne disease. More important, frequent handwashing with regular soap and hot water remains the absolute best means of prevention.

See also **Digestion; Eating: Anatomy and Physiology of Eating; Health and Disease**.

BIBLIOGRAPHY

Blank, Fritz. "Food on the Move: Travelers' Diarrhea: The Science of 'Montezuma's Revenge.'" Proceedings of the Oxford Symposium on Food and Cookery. Oxford, U.K., 1996.

Schaedler, Russell W., and René Dubos. "The Ecology of the Digestive Tract." Proceedings of the Cholera Research Symposium. Washington, D.C.: U.S. Department of Health, Education and Welfare, 1965.

Dubos, René, and Russell W. Schaedler. "Some Biological Effects of the Digestive Flora." American Journal of the Medical Sciences 244, no. 3 (September 1962).

Fritz Blank

INTRAVENOUS FEEDING. *See* **Enteral and Parenteral Nutrition.**

INUIT. The northern indigenous peoples known as Eskimo or Inuit (not including the Russian Inuit and Yupiget) numbered approximately 143,582 in 2002. In the United States, Alaskan Eskimos (Inuit, Yupiit, Yupiget, and others) numbered 55,674 according to the 1990 census (U.S. Bureau of the Census, personal communication, May 2002). In Canada, Inuit numbered 41,800 in the 1996 census, while the nation of Greenland, formerly a Danish territory, had an Inuit population of 46,108 in 2001. Alaskan Eskimos live in rural coastal villages, along northern rivers, in isolated island or northern interior valleys and, increasingly, in regional population centers such as Anchorage, Barrow, Fairbanks, Kotzebue, and Nome. In Canada, despite rising migration rates to the south, most Inuit live in fifty-five rural communities located in Nunavut, the Northwest Territories, Quebec province, Newfoundland, and Labrador. In Greenland, too, Inuit live in coastal villages, although those who live in population centers such as Nuuk are increasing.

In Alaska, Canada, and Greenland, names such as Inuit, Yupiit, and Yupiget identify Eskimos as "the people" or "the real people." Regardless of location or name, food is a critical feature of identity for all. (The term "Eskimo" is used here because it includes all groups.) Identity is often expressed as a longing for locally harvested and prepared foods by those who find themselves separated from traditional homeland communities. Local foods are referred to as "our" food, "real" food, or, in Alaska, simply "Eskimo" food. In Canada, such foods are called "country" food. Among the Alaskan Yupiget of St. Lawrence Island, for instance, the term *neqepik* means "real" food, while imported foods are called *laluramka* or "white people's" food (Jolles, 2002).

Across the north, dietary habits and cultural meanings attached to food are similar, due partly to adaptation to a common arctic ecosystem and partly to similar socioeconomic conditions, which keep unemployment rates as high as 50 to 80 percent. Under such conditions, subsistence-oriented hunting, fishing, and gathering activities, vital to community survival, are performed year-round. In Nunavut, Canada, alone, replacing subsistence foods with equivalent amounts of beef, chicken, and pork would cost an estimated $30 to $35 million annually.

Types of harvested foods depend on local environments and overall resource availability. In 2002, in In-

Whale and walrus meat drying in the open air at Hoopers Bay, Alaska. FROM AN ANTIQUE PHOTOGRAPH, COURTESY OF THE LIBRARY OF CONGRESS.

galiq, Little Diomede Island, Alaska, for example, severe weather plus political and physical isolation at the Russian-American border one mile distant necessitated a substantial dependence on local foods. Diomede subsistence resources include bearded seals, ringed seals, spotted seals, walrus, and polar bears. In summer, the community harvests migrating water fowl such as auklets, puffins, and murres, along with their eggs. In late summer, wild greens and berries are harvested and stored. In winter (December through mid-May), the community takes Alaska blue king crabs through the sea ice and trades a portion of the harvest with mainland Alaskan Eskimo communities for unavailable foods such as caribou. Altogether, Ingaliq subsistence foods include more than forty marine mammal, plant, avian, fish, and shellfish resources. Local harvests in Diomede and elsewhere in the North are supplemented with expensive, imported, commercially available goods from Native cooperative stores, Hudson Bay Company franchises, and other small multipurpose stores found throughout the north.

In Alaska, meat and fish are the centerpieces of Eskimo diets and constitute 90 percent of locally harvested foods. In addition, communities take several types of whales: bowhead, gray, minke, and beluga, or white. Reindeer (introduced in the late 1890s by the U.S. government and managed by local villages), moose, caribou, and a newly reintroduced resource, musk oxen (available to hunters in 1995) are also taken. Numerous migratory seabirds are hunted during late spring and early fall, as is the ptarmigan, a permanent resident. Fish are prominent in southwestern coastal diets, especially salmon. Herring, tomcod, Arctic char, grayling, flounder, sculpin, and halibut also contribute to the diet. Clams are taken from walrus stomachs. Ground squirrels, once commonly harvested for their furs and their meat, are seldom taken any more. While meat is the mainstay, wild greens and berries are much sought. At least thirty species of plants are collected for food purposes from the land and from the beaches (Jones, 1983; Schofield, 1989, 1993).

For Canadian Inuit, diet in the early twenty-first century also consisted of two major classes of food, Inuit food or "country" food, and *Qallunaat*, or "white people's" food. "Country" foods include caribou, Arctic hare, ptarmigan, ringed seal, bearded seal, walrus, polar bear, beluga whale, migrating fish (Arctic char, Atlantic salmon, and Pacific salmon), and migratory birds (Canada goose, common eider, king eider, and black guillemots). "White people's" food includes items shipped from southern Canada and purchased at local stores, including fresh fruits and vegetables, canned goods, processed foods, and dry goods.

In Alaska, especially in the most northern communities, it was once common to consume uncooked meats. This has become less common with the introduction of such modern conveniences as microwaves, refrigerators, propane-fueled stoves, and the like. However, in Canada, the preference for uncooked meats is still a significant cultural feature. This practice became a powerful marker of Inuit identity in the post–World War II era as Canadian Inuit experienced more sustained contact with Europeans and Canadians of European descent such as missionaries, teachers, and administrators. Consumption of raw or frozen foods, a practice typically disdained by non-Inuit, intensified boundaries separating Inuit and non-Inuit (Brody, 1975), and fostered increased social unity and political activism among Inuit who sought to protect and promote their hunting and fishing rights and to achieve local resource management in Inuit homelands.

Greenland Inuit obtain their food from two major sources: local land, seas, and lakes (called "country" food) and through local store purchases and via mail order. The main subsistence foods are ringed seal, beluga whale, caribou, bearded seal, and polar bear as well as a wide variety of fish, including cod, capelin, Atlantic salmon, Arctic char, and Greenland halibut. One feature that distinguishes the Inuit of Greenland from Canadian and Alaskan Eskimos is the abundance of small-scale fisheries, which include fish plants that provide a number of settlements with seasonal employment (Dahl, 2000). In addition to subsistence production, many Greenlandic Inuit are also involved in large-scale commercial fishing operations, and fishing products, including shrimp, Greenlandic halibut and crabs are Greenland's major exports. Many of the companies are owned and maintained by Inuit. Finally, there are approximately sixty sheep farms in southwest Greenland that produce lamb and other products for both domestic and international markets.

Food management in Eskimo communities combines traditional practices with modern convenience. Subsistence meats are often "half-dried" on outdoor meat racks, cooked (boiled), and stored in containers of seal oil or, alternatively, stored in home freezers, either "half-dried" or fresh. Greens, roots, and berries are more often stored in freezers, although some residents also use seal oil. Traditional underground or semiunderground food caches are gradually becoming a part of the past, while home freezer storage and consumption of fresh frozen foods has become increasingly common. In the late twentieth century and early twenty-first, in spite of significant changes in food storage methods, locally harvested foods from the land and the sea remained a major component of Eskimo food consumption. However, while "country" food or "real" food still defines ethnic and cultural boundaries in the North, "white people's" food is increasingly popular among young people, whether in Alaska (Jolles, 2002), Canada, or Greenland (Searles, 2002). The presence of contaminants in locally harvested foods is a major concern in the Arctic, for example, PCP, and is under discussion in all of the affected regions. It is unclear how this information, along with changing lifeways, will modify Eskimo diets.

See also **Arctic; Canada: Native Peoples.**

BIBLIOGRAPHY

Anderson, Douglas, Ray Bane, Richard K. Nelson, Wanni W. Anderson, and Nita Sheldon. *Kuuvanmiit Subsistence: Traditional Eskimo Life in the Latter Twentieth Century.* Washington, D.C.: National Park Service, U.S. Department of the Interior, 1977.

Brody, Hugh. *The People's Land: Eskimos and Whites in the Eastern Arctic.* Harmondsworth, England: Penguin, 1975.

Dahl, Jens. *Saqqaq: An Inuit Hunting Community in the Modern World.* Toronto, Canada: University of Toronto Press, 2000.

Jolles, Carol Zane, with Elinor Mikaghaq Oozeva, elder advisor. *Faith, Food, and Family in a Yupik Whaling Community.* Seattle, Wash.: University of Washington Press, 2002.

Jones, Anore. *Nauriat Niginaqtuat: The Plants That We Eat.* Kotzebue, Alaska: Maniilaq Association, 1983.

Searles, Edmund. "Food and the Making of Modern Inuit Identities." *Food and Foodways* 10 (2002): 55–78.

Carol Zane Jolles
Edmund Searles

IODINE. Iodine is an essential dietary element necessary for normal development and function of all vertebrates. Its sole physiological function is as a constituent of the thyroid hormones, thyroxine and triiodothyronine. It is removed from the blood by the thyroid gland for storage in organic form where it is found as iodinated amino acids in peptide linkage in thyroglobulin, a high-molecular weight protein.

Iodine is widely but usually sparsely distributed in nature, so that in vast areas of the world the supply in customary diets is marginal or insufficient. It has been estimated that over two billion persons are at risk of disorders attributable to iodine deficiency. Among these disorders are goiter, impaired intellectual function, growth retardation, reduced fecundity, lowered work capacity, increased rates of fetal loss and infant mortality, deafness, and in extreme instances a well-defined but somewhat

varied constellation of physical findings collectively known as cretinism. Cretins are recognized by severe mental deficiency, disturbances in gait, impaired or absent hearing, and other neurological defects, but the signs and symptoms in these individuals may be subtle. These features merge with those of the less impaired members of the same community or nearby countryside where they may appear in lesser severity.

The iodine content of edible plants is largely dependent on the iodine content of the soil on which they are grown. The iodine content of foods of animal origin depends on the iodine in their food. Iodine is concentrated in milk, and is found in relatively high concentration in sea fish, who are at the upper levels of the food chain that contains algae. Some sea fish concentrate iodine from sea water. The only structure among the vertebrates that contains a significant amount of iodine is the thyroid gland.

Role of Iodine in Disease

For centuries the disorders arising from iodine deficiency have been recognized in well-defined regions. These have been called "goiter belts." Switzerland was included in the goiter belt until the iodine deficiency in that country was corrected in the first half of the twentieth century. Until recent years iodine deficiency was a recognized disorder in the United States, especially the Midwest and West, where goiter was commonplace. Iodine deficiency has been a major public health problem in the Andean region and eastward, in large areas of central and north Africa, in the Middle Eastern countries, in India, and in eastern and central Europe, and even today in localized regions of western Europe. Fortunately, remarkable headway has been made in elimination of iodine deficiency through various methods of supplementing diets.

Goiter is only one of the many consequences of iodine deficiency, and is relatively trivial when compared with the damaging effects of iodine deficiency on the nervous system. From the human point of view, it is more correct to speak of "endemic mental deficiency" than "endemic goiter."

Endemic thyroid disease has traditionally been considered a feature of iodine deficiency in the mountainous regions of the world. Endemic thyroid disease is found in regions of high elevation, but has also been common where glacial run-offs occur and in floodplains where there has been chronic leaching of the soil. Such geographic regions include the Gangetic plain and much of India and southeastern Asia, the Himalayan region, and central Africa, where the iodine deficiency disorders are frequent and severe; the coastal regions of western Europe are marginally iodine deficient. Endemic iodine deficiency can be detected almost anywhere with currently available sensitive techniques. In the United States until recently the mean intake of iodine was excessive, but recently has been rapidly falling into a normal range. The recent precipitous fall in iodine consumption in the United States has led to concern that iodine deficiency may again become a problem if the present rate of decline continues. The need for monitoring iodine intake is apparent. This is customarily done by measuring the iodine content of urine from a fair sample of the population under observation.

The optimal daily adult iodine intake is about 150 μ g/day, about half that for children and infants. This figure rises to about 200 μ g during pregnancy, but under normal circumstances there is wide latitude in intake because of the ability of the normal thyroid system to compensate for varying levels of supply. The thyroid and pituitary through a feedback relationship provide a highly efficient regulatory system. If iodine intake falls below about 50 μ g/day the pituitary gland becomes stimulated to increase its iodine uptake and hormone production, and, if the iodine supply exceeds needs, the pituitary shuts down appropriately.

Iodine is readily absorbed by the stomach and upper gastrointestinal tract. Iodine in chemical combination is released in the gut and absorbed; it may be rapidly taken up by the thyroid gland or excreted in the urine. Only a small fraction appears in the stool. Exceptions occur when iodine is in chemical combination with such drugs used as radio-contrast agents and amiodarone, the widely used cardiac medication.

Iodine Deficiency and Disease

Certain chemical agents found in some foods interfere with the uptake or utilization of iodine by the thyroid. Among these are the cyanoglycosides found in cassava (manioc), a component of millet, and a variety of chemical agents and some unidentified substances found in the effluent water from rock formations and in factory discharges. It must be stressed that the inhibitory effect of these substances may be bypassed if there is an ample supply of iodine in the diet, but their effect may be critical if the iodine intake is marginal or lower.

When marginal or low iodine intake is identified in a geographic regions such as a district or country, an effort should be made to correct the deficiency. A variety of techniques have been employed. These include distribution of iodine solution to school attendees, candies containing potassium iodide, addition of iodine to drinking water, and the use of canisters containing iodine that is slowly released into sources of drinking water. None of these methods has proved to be widely accepted. In addition, it should be stressed that the primary target for the prevention of neurological damage due to iodine deficiency is the pregnant and nursing mother.

Prevention of Iodine Deficiency

The most effective and widely employed method for correcting iodine deficiency is salt iodization. The technique is simple, inexpensive, and effective. Potassium iodate rather than iodide salts is used because it is more stable when mixed with salt. Nevertheless certain problems must be corrected. Unscrupulous traders may sharply increase the cost of iodized salt to the consumer. If improperly stored the iodine may sublime and be lost from the salt. If addition of iodine by the manufacturer is not done carefully the salt may be overiodinated. In certain cases, especially those in which people have nodular goiters resulting from prolonged iodine deficiency, thyrotoxicosis may result, which may be subtle in onset and chronic, with unwanted or disastrous results. Careful and continued monitoring of dietary supplementation by iodized salt must be done, as with all food additives.

Promotion of salt iodization, especially in areas of particular need in the developing world, has been a health priority of many public and private agencies, including the World Health Organization, UNICEF, the International Council for Prevention of the Iodine Deficiency Disorders, and others. One of the principal problems with programs of salt iodization is that governments tend to lose interest, and the programs lapse, leading to recurrence of the iodine deficiency disorders. Again, constant monitoring is the key to continued success.

Injections of heavily iodinated poppyseed and other oils have been tried in mass campaigns, first in New Guinea; these methods have since been widely employed elsewhere. These are the same oils that have been widely used as radio-contrast agents. The results have been impressive. The iodine is slowly released from the oil and may be effective for two or more years. The oral route has also been used to administer the oils, but effectiveness is less prolonged. The disadvantages of programs using iodinated oil are principally cost and the requirement for sterile needles and trained personnel, which may be difficult to obtain in remote regions. Iodine-induced thyrotoxicosis may occur after administration of iodinated oil.

A unique and successful method of iodine distribution has recently been introduced. This method can be used in regions where iodine can be drip-added to irrigation water. It has been used in the desert regions of western China with salutary human benefit, and with a highly satisfactory effect on livestock production. The problems with this method are the need for skilled personnel to add the iodine to the irrigation system at the right time and rate, and the fact that it is only feasible when it is possible to add iodine to irrigation water. A somewhat similar technique that has proved beneficial is adding iodine to a municipal water supply. As with other methods of iodine supplementation, skilled maintenance of the program is essential, and the subsequent appearance of thyrotoxicosis is unknown.

Summary

Iodine is thinly distributed in the earth's crust, and much of the human population lives in regions that have marginal or insufficient iodine. Mountainous regions, floodplains, and regions where there has been extensive leaching of iodine from the soil may not provide suffi-

Fish Fish in the Giannino Restaurant, Milan, Italy, 1949. Such enticing displays of high-quality ingredients are far more common in European restaurants than in those in the United States. The photograph itself is a study in period food styling. Roughwood Collection.

Top: **Fish** This hand-tinted engraving called *Philadelphia Taste Displayed* shows the interior of an 1830s American oyster cellar with its private booths, its black owner James Prosser, and the complete absence of women. City ordinances in early America forbade women and children from entering these establishments, which specialized in turtle soup, pepperpot, and seafood. Roughwood Collection.

Bottom: **Fish/Sea Fish** Food styling in the Victorian period relied heavily on an abundance of garnishes, as in the case of this poached salmon from Alphonse Gouffeé's *Royal Cookery Book* (London, 1868). Roughwood Collection.

Top: **Flowers** Nasturtiums were introduced from Peru in the 1500s. Both the leaves and the flowers were used in cooking and are still popular today as salad garnishes. Photo by William Woys Weaver.

Below: **France/Southern French Cuisines** Fried fish at Chez Fonfon, Marseille, France. © Owen Franken/CORBIS.

Herbs and Spices The Egyptian Market in modern Istanbul evokes the culinary riches of the former Ottoman and Byzantine empires. Ground herbs and spices are arranged in neat hills. © Paul Hardy/CORBIS.

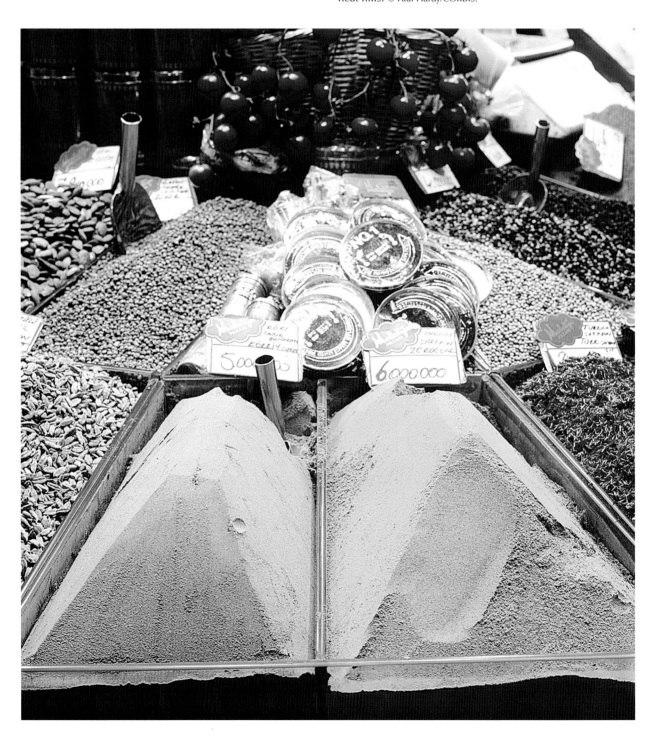

Bottom, left: **Gelatin** One of the keys to the early success of Jell-O was its pitch to children and the use of children in its advertising campaigns. The "Jell-O girl" is featured on the cover of this 1924 booklet containing recipes and pictures of her on every page. Roughwood Collection.

Top, right: **Ice Cream** Victorian ice creams achieved elaborate designs and flavor combinations. This chromolithograph plate from Garrett's *Encyclopedia of Practical Cookery* (London, circa 1880) proves that Victorian confectioners also possessed a sense of playful whimsy. Roughwood Collection.

Bottom, right: **Ice Cream** The hokey-pokey man was once a familiar figure in American cities with large Italian populations. He was a street vendor who sold ice creams, water ices, and a variety of light foods. This circa 1890 chromolithograph "scrap" picture was meant to be pasted to a gingerbread cookie and thus serve as a Christmas tree ornament. Roughwood Collection.

Luxury Nineteenth-century opulence is depicted in this contemporary painting of the banquet hall in Yildiz Palace, Istanbul. Courtesy of The Museum of Fine Arts, Istanbul. © Archivo Iconografico, S.A./CORBIS.

Inset: **Luxury** Oriental opulence was also a popular theme in Victorian table design, as in the case of this Persian pattern silver by Tiffany & Company of New York. © Peter Hartholdt/CORBIS.

Top: **Markets** Cherry vendor in the old Philadelphia market shambles. Produce was formerly sold loose, which necessitated both an array of baskets and an assistant to carry them. From *The Useful and the Beautiful* (Philadelphia, 1850). Roughwood Collection.

Below: **Markets** Fresh vegetable and fruit stand in Quebec City, Canada. © Philip Gould/CORBIS.

TOUJOURS FRAIS
ALWAYS FRESH

Left: **Mexico** Tortilla vendor in Yucatán, Mexico. © Liba Taylor/CORBIS.

Top right: **Mexico** Peppers and a tomato worm from Maria Sibylla Merian's *Metamorphosis Insectorum Surinamensium* (The Hague, 1705). Merian's primary interest was insects, but she used plant and vegetable props in all of her renderings. Unlike Raphaelle Peale, whose paintings are botanically correct, Merian's pepper plant is actually a collage of different species and varieties all growing from the same branch. (See Peale's still life with tomato in volume 3, color insert page 5.) Roughwood Collection.

Bottom right: **Mexico** Cactus pears *(Opuntia ficus-indica)* are generally harvested in the summer. Fruits with red pulp are prized in the United States and Europe, whereas Mexicans generally prefer fruit with green pulp. Photo courtesy of Park S. Noble.

cient iodine for human needs. The result is the appearance of iodine deficiency disorders, which include neurological damage, goiter, increased fetal and infant mortality, deafness, and diminished human energy and resulting economic underproductivity. Iodine deficiency is a major public health problem for a large fraction of the world's population.

Wherever marginal or insufficient iodine exists, implementation of iodine supplementation is required. This may be done by supplementing table salt with iodine, administration of iodinated oil by injection or orally, or addition of iodine to the drinking water. It is essential that a monitoring system be in place to ensure that the population is receiving an adequate iodine intake. Care must be exercised to avoid an excess of iodine, which might induce thyrotoxicosis.

See also **Body Composition; Fluoride; International Agencies; Malnutrition; Nutrition; Nutrition Transition: Worldwide Diet Change; Salt; Sodium; Trace Elements.**

BIBLIOGRAPHY

Braverman, L. E., and R. D. Utiger, eds. *Thyroid: A Fundamental and Clinical Text.* 7th ed. Philadelphia: Lippincott, Williams, & Wilkins, 2000.

De Long, G. R., J. Robbins, and P. G. Condliffe, eds. *Iodine and the Brain.* New York: Plenum. 1989

De Long, et al. "Effect on infant mortality of iodination of irrigation water in a severely iodine-deficient area of China." *Lancet* 360 (1997).

Fernandez, R. L. *A Simple Matter of Salt.* Berkeley: University of California Press, 1990.

Gaitan, F., ed. *Environmental Goitrogenesis.* Boca Raton, Fla.: CRC Press, 1989.

Hetzel, B. S. *The Story of Iodine Deficiency.* New York: Oxford University Press, 1989.

Hetzel, B. S., and C. S. Pandav. *S.O.S. for a Billion.* Bombay: Oxford University Press, 1996.

Stanbury, John B., and John T. Dunn. "Iodine and the Iodine Deficiency Disorders." In *Present Knowledge in Nutrition,* 8th ed., edited by B. A. Bowman and R. M. Russell, p. 344. Washington, D.C.: ILSI Press, 2000.

Stanbury, J. B., et al. "Iodine-Induced Hyperthyroidism: Occurrence and Epidemiology." *Thyroid* 8 (1998).

World Health Organization. *Assessment of Iodine Deficiency Disorders and Monitoring their Elimination.* 2nd ed. World Health Organization, 2001.

John Stanbury
John T. Dunn

IRAN. The art of sophisticated cookery in Iran can be traced to antiquity. It has, according to existing literature, preserved its basic mode of preparation for more than a thousand years, enhanced by refinement of dishes and new recipes created in the kitchens of royalty and or-

Detail of a seventeenth-century miniature showing an outdoor banquet of Abbas I of Persia. The carafes on the small carpet contain red wine. © ARCHIVO ICONOGRAFICO, S.A./CORBIS.

dinary folk. Iranian food is prepared with such delicate subtlety that every ingredient used can be tasted and every aromatic spice added can be appreciated.

Food of Ancient Persia

History. The Persian Achaemenid empire, founded by Cyrus the Great in 549 B.C.E., dominated the ancient world for almost two centuries. At the height of its power it extended from the Indus in the east to Asia Minor and Egypt in the west, uniting Medes, Persians, and Parthians, as well as many other tribes and peoples, in fealty to the dynasty. Presumably the people living in that vast expanse with its varied climates each formed their own culinary culture according to indigenous food products, naturally available, grown, or reared. Yet all cultures converged at the Achaemenid court and were elaborately manifested at the table of the king of kings.

There are no known recipes left of that period. The references to food in the Avesta and Elamite tablets from Persepolis dated 509–494 B.C.E. indicate that the Achaemenid diet consisted of dairy products from cows, sheep, goats, and mares; meat from oxen, rams, goats, and wild or reared fowls; grains for making bread; ales; wines; dried fruit; and nuts and seeds also used for pressing oil.

Each season, the nomad kings and the court moved from capital to capital. Winter was spent in Babylon or Susa, where the wine was fermented from dates and grapes; spring in Ecbatana, where meat, dairy products, and herbs were ample; and autumn in Persepolis, where fruit, wild vegetables, and seeds were in abundance.

Narratives by Greek authors of the period reveal the sumptuous preparation and the abundance of food in that fertile realm. Ctesias (405–397 B.C.E.) and Dinon indicate that 15,000 men ate daily in the court of the Achaemenid king of kings. The Greek writer Polyaenus (second century C.E.) recounts that the food brought to the court for distribution as well as for the preparation of three meals a day was formulated by Cyrus and engraved on a bronze column. It included great quantities of different grades of wheat, barley, and rye, floured or treated; grains of corn and parsley; salt; male livestock; gazelles; poultry; geese; pigeons; small wild birds; dairy; watercress; onions and garlic; pickled radishes and beetroots; cured capers; juice of sweet apples; conserve of sour pomegranates; honey; oils of almond, terebinth, sesame seed, and acanthus; raisins dark and light; nuts; sweetened seeds; vinegar; mustard, anise, cumin, celery, and safflower seeds; saffron; cardamom; and dill flower. Xenophon (430–355 B.C.E.) notes that what was served at the king's table was prepared in exquisite taste by expert cooks and bakers who were engaged in a constant search for new recipes and would invent a variety of pastries and cakes.

Herodotus (fifth century B.C.E.) relates that the Persians ate varied desserts and sweets. Birthdays were celebrated by giving great feasts. Side dishes, served at regular intervals, punctuated the introduction of the principal dishes. Large animals, including big fowl like ostrich, were stuffed and roasted whole; birds were stuffed and seasoned with capers. Meat cured in sophisticated fashion was served.

The Greek historian Diodorus Siculus (first century B.C.E.) reflects on the variety of delicacies brought from Persia to Babylon, in particular fish from the Persian Gulf. Polyaenus remarks on the exquisite mixture of cardamom and other spices, vinegar, and pepper, and upon the use of aromatic herbs from which oil was also extracted for medicinal purposes.

It is said that soldiers normally received meat and bread, but on long journeys and campaigns were sustained by onion soup and bread. To this day *eshkaneh*, basically made with onions, flour, and turmeric, is cooked in different parts of Iran. Seasonal or dried herbs and fruit—dried or fresh—are added, and, combined with one or two eggs, the dish can serve a big family. It remains the food of the populace, while the stuffed beast or fowl, *boghlameh*, is served mainly at tribal feasts by those who can afford the luxury. Pierre Briant, quoting Polyaenus, remarks in *Histoire de l'Empire Perse* (p. 300) that when Alexander the Great defeated Darius III and seized Persepolis (331 B.C.E.), ordering the bronze pillars to be destroyed, he said with laughter that such a diet weakens the body and the mind and was the cause of the defeat of the Persians.

Following Alexander's demise, his successors, the Seleucid Greek rulers (323–64 B.C.E.), were overthrown by the Parthians of western Iran. The Parthians (250 B.C.E.–224 C.E.) revived the national spirit that came to full flowering under their successors, the Sassanians (224–652 C.E.). The culinary culture of the aristocracy and preparation of food in this period are revealed in a rare Pahlavi manuscript, "King Husrav and His Boy" (translated: J. Unvala, Paris), a reliable source that withstood the destruction of libraries by the Islamic army in 636 or 637. In the text Khosrow II and a companion discuss, among the pleasures of life, the variety of Epicurean cuisine. Some dishes are in certain ways similar to what is eaten in the early twenty-first century in certain parts of Iran. For example, the boy recommends that the meat of a two-month-old kid fed on mother's milk and cow's milk marinated with herbs be cooked and served with whey (*kashk*). In Yazd (central Iran), Kerman, and Azerbaijan, *bōzghōrmēh* is still a popular dish. It features chunks of goat's meat or mutton as a dominant substitute, fried with chopped onions, seasoned with turmeric and cinnamon, sprinkled with tarragon and mint or saffron, and topped by thick yogurt or *kashk*. As for sweets, almond, walnut, and pistachio are used in making delicate cookies, as they were many years ago. A jelly made with quince juice is now called *mōjassaméh-ye beh*. In jams and preserves the peel of *baalang*, a large citrus fruit, is still popular in Fars and Gilan provinces. Quince jam continues to be made in most parts. Cucumber and walnut jams and pickles are remembered recipes in Qazvin.

Other later sources, too, elaborate the sophisticated Sassanid cuisine. An eleventh-century scholar, Tha'alebi of Neishapur, describes in his "History" a variety of dishes including wild birds and other game, fish, lamb, and veal marinated in vinegar, mustard, stock, garlic, dill, and green and black cumin, or in yogurt, flavored with spices, and stewed, broiled, or roasted according to different recipes; barbecued chicken flavored with cane sugar, skewered and grilled; stuffed vine leaves; puddings made of rice, milk, honey, butter, eggs, and rosewater; and delicacies and sweets using countless aromatics. He mentions that peasants marinated their meat in brine and pomegranate juice.

Festivals. Festivals were frequent in ancient Persia. For the ancient Persian herdsmen and farmers, the revival of nature in the spring was a terrestrial renewal of life, so people equated the New Year with the spring equinox. Before the equinox, reverence for the seven *Ēmshāspands* (archangels) in the Zoroastrian religion was symbolized in seven cereals and pulses grown in clay pots to predict the quality of the next harvest. In the five leap days (the year being 360 days) preceding *Nōwrūz* (New Year's festival), festivities would begin. Food, including milk and honey, sweetmeats, nuts, and dried fruits, was prepared and bonfires were lit on rooftops to attract the *Farvahars*, or guardian angels of the ancestors, who would descend for the annual reception in which wining and dining continued for five days following *Nōwrūz*.

Yaldā is still celebrated, marking the birth of Mithra on the longest night of the year. Throughout the long night of *Yaldā*, fresh fruit specially preserved for the oc-

casion, seven kinds of nuts, and a range of dried fruit were consumed in a joyous vigil held to drive out the darkness in anticipation of the sun's rebirth. Apart from *Mehrgān* or *Sadēh* little is known of other such festivals.

After the Arab invasion in the seventh century, a great number of Zoroastrians migrated to India, taking with them their culinary culture. However, the art of Persian cookery and the etiquette of eating (*ādāb-é sōfrēh*) at a spread (*sōfrēh*) laden with a colorful array of food survived. These, in later years, highly influenced the Arab, the Ottoman, and the Indian culinary cultures.

In the eighth century, Iranians who helped the Abbasid caliphs gain power passed on the refined Sassanid recipes to Baghdad. This is apparent in a range of cookery books written in Arabic in subsequent centuries.

In the fifteenth century, the haute cuisine that evolved at the Ottoman court was in the style of the Teimurid court of Persia. From the sixteenth century, when a descendant of the Teimurid dynasty in Iran established the Moghul empire in Delhi, the first cookery books, written in Persian and Urdu by Iranian scholars of the imperial court, appeared. In parallel, cookery books were written in Iran by master chefs in the Safavid court and in the nineteenth century in the Qājār court of Nā ser od-Dīn Shāh, showing further refinement in the art of cooking, of rice, in particular.

Modern Iranian Cuisine

Rice. Rice in Iran is steamed to a unique perfection, bringing out its full flavor and fragrance, turning the grains into light, fluffy *chēlōw* (plain rice) that may be eaten with *khōrēsh* (stew) or grilled meat (*chēlōw kabāb*). Rice can be steamed with meat, herbs, vegetables, sour cherries, or pulses in many varieties, colors, and mixtures (*pōlōw*) as a crisp crust (*tah-dig*) is formed at the bottom of the cooking vessel. It can be garnished with saffron, barberries, and slivers of orange peel, pistachio, and almond. Rice with beaten eggs, yogurt, and saffron, steamed with layers of cooked meat, eggplant (aubergine), or spinach turns into yet another sumptuous dish known as *tahchin*.

The best rice is grown in the Caspian provinces of Gīlān and Māzandarān; it is also cultivated in limited quantity in the Lenjān district of Ēsfahān and along the Qēzēl Ōzan River near Zanjān. The major grades of quality long-grain rice, with their elongated form and characteristic fragrance, Sadri Dōmsīah and Tārōm, are the best known for perfume and taste.

Stews. Iranian cuisine in general is the art of cooking the available nutrients in a way that pleases the eye and the palate and balances the functions of the body. Recipes consider food's properties and elements to formulate an equation in which the ingredients blend harmoniously, each counterbalancing the excess effect of the other on the digestive system.

Khōrēsh, derived from the Persian verb *khōrdan* (to eat), is a kind of stew prepared to these rules. The base for every *khōrēsh* is fried onions (garlic is added in the northern and southern regions), meat or poultry, the appropriate spices and seasoning. These are left to simmer in water to a desired consistency, then lightly fried vegetables, herbs, or fruit are added. Depending on vegetables and herbs in season, countless varieties are made all over Iran. For example, chopped mint and parsley would make *khōrēsh-é na'najafari* with celery, or, in the spring, rhubarb, greengages, acanthus, or young green almonds with verjuice (sour grape juice) as seasoning. The famous *khōrēsh-é fēsēnjān*, which turns into a thick light or dark brown sauce, is made of ground walnuts seasoned with pomegranate juice or paste and has a sweet and sour taste. The cooling effect of pomegranate juice balances the warm and rich property of walnuts. This is an autumn and winter *khōrēsh* customarily made with duck, or with chicken or meatballs as substitutes. In late autumn it can be made with ripe walnuts and pomegranate juice. In winter chunks of eggplant or pumpkin, dried prunes, and apricots may be added. It is then called *mōtanjan*. A further derivation is *anar-āvīj* (pomegranate paste or juice and herbs), prepared in the Caspian region. Another speciality is *khōrēsh-é ghōrmēh-sabzi* made with mixed herbs and red kidney beans (in the south, black-eyed beans) with whole dried limes used for fragrance, freshness, and seasoning. Also common is *khōrēsh-e gheimeh* (diced meat) with split peas, served plain or with fried potato sticks and dried lime as seasoning or eggplant, zucchini (courgettes), or celery with sour grapes as seasoning, quinces, or apples with sweetened vinegar as seasoning, etc. A luxury, known from the imperial court of the Qājārs (nineteenth century), is *gheimēh-mōrassa'* (jeweled diced meat), which in place of split peas uses skinned whole pistachios with ample saffron for aroma and color.

Khōrāk and side dishes.

Khōrāk, also derived from the verb *khōrdan* ('to eat') cooked with or without meat, cover an extensive range and reflect the significant contributions of Gīlān and Azerbaijan provinces. Among these dishes are *kabāb*, a variation of charcoal-grilled meat, fowl, or fish; *shāmi*—meat cooked with split peas pounded and kneaded with eggs, ground cumin, and saffron, shaped in a round patty and deep-fried; *kūkū*, a form of thick puffed omelette or soufflé of different vegetables or herbs; *dōlmēh*—stuffed vegetables or vine or cabbage leaves; *tās-kabāb*, meticulously arranged layers of onion, meat, tomatoes, carrots, eggplant, potatoes, and quinces or apples (depending on the season), sprinkled with cardamom and cinnamon, chopped dried lime, and prunes steam-cooked in its own juice on low heat; *kashk-bādēm-jān*—fried eggplant topped with *kashk* (whey) and tastefully garnished; *mīrzāghāsēmi*, grilled eggplant cooked with garlic, tomatoes, and eggs. Side dishes are prepared with various vegetables cooked or raw and mixed with yogurt seasoned with aromatic herbs.

Fish.

Fish is cooked in a variety of ways in the Caspian Sea provinces and alongside the Persian Gulf and the Arabian Sea. In the Khuzistan region well-spiced baked fish seasoned with tamarind is among the specialities whereas in the Caspian area it is barbecued or stuffed with herbs, including dried pomegranate seeds, baked and served with bitter oranges. The Caspian caviar is an important item for export, and the large grey and the rare golden of the Iranian coast are famous among connoisseurs.

Bread.

Bread or *nān* is revered as a gift from God. Except in the rice-growing areas along the Caspian coast, it is the staple food of Iranians. *Khōrēshs* and *khōrāks* are eaten with *nān* as well as rice. Made in a flat form, the most common varieties of bread are *sangak* (baked on pebbles), *tāftūn*, thin *lavāsh*, thick *barbari*, *nān-é shīrmāl* (dough mixed with milk), and crispy *nān-é rōghani* (dough mixed with butter).

Soups.

Āsh is the general name for a thick soup made with herbs, rice, or pulses with or without meat, served plain or variably seasoned. It is another prominent and universal feature of Iranian cuisine. The recipe for *āsh-e sac* (spinach soup) has been passed down from the Sassanid era. *Āsh* cooked using barley, wheat, or noodles and *kashk* is a convenient dish in tribal life. *Ābgūsht* (literally meat juice) is made with mutton, onions, turmeric, chickpeas, pinto beans, tomatoes, potatoes, and dried lime; the stock is separated and the rest is pounded into a paste. It is the sustaining food of all classes. Other variations of *ābgūsht* are derived from this basic form. Another soup is known as *kallēh-pācheh* (sheep's head and pig's feet in a bouillon); when homemade, tripe is often added. *Halīm* is a homogeneous porridgelike soup made with wheat and pounded meat of lamb, turkey, or goose, garnished with melted butter and powdered cinnamon. *Kūftēh* refers to tiny to very large meatballs in onion-based soup. The *kūftēh tabrīyi* of Azerbaijan is so large that it can hold a chicken, an egg, prunes, barberries, orange peel, and almonds in its center.

There are cold soups for summer. *Ābdūgh*, a soup made from cucumber, raisins, and herbs in diluted yogurt is everybody's meal. *Ēshkanēh*, made with fresh fruit such as sour cherries, is both refreshing and filling.

Confections and preserves.

A common confection is *hālva*, prepared from flour, butter, diluted sugar, saffron, and rosewater. *Tar hālva*, a sophisticated version of *hālva*, is prepared with ground rice instead of flour and with crushed orange peel or yellow rose petals. Other well-known desserts are *shōllēhzard*, made with rice, water, butter, sugar, saffron, and almond slivers and garnished with cinnamon and crushed pistachio; *masqati*, made with starch, water, sugar, butter, cardamom, and almond slivers; and *yakhdarbēhēsht*, prepared with starch, milk, and sugar. All are perfumed with rosewater or orange-blossom water.

Jams, preserves, *torshis* (pickles), and sherbets (soft and refreshing cold drinks) such as *sērkangēbin*, made of sugar water, vinegar, and mint, and others prepared with the juice of rhubarb or various fruits, are prominent features of Iranian culinary culture. The techniques of long conservation of herbs, vegetables, meat, fish, and dairy have been passed on from one generation to another and have been developed in homes mainly by women, the keepers of the household.

Cookies and pastries. Cookies and pastries in Iran are generally delicate in form with a subtle aroma, prepared with variation on basic recipes in different regions. *Bāghlava*, made with phyllo pastry, finely ground almonds or pistachio, sugar and light syrup, flavored with cardamom and rosewater, finely cut into small diamond-shaped pieces, is a popular confection. Now commercially produced, it was conventionally a homemade product except in Yazd, where confectioners, as a cherished tradition, have specialized in its production. Similarly, numerous *petit fours*, made with finely ground rice or chickpeas or coconut or almond, are produced. Apart from Yazd, as examples, Esfahān specializes in the production of *gaz* (nugat); Qum in *sōhān* (a kind of fudge made of germinated wheat, garnished with crushed pistachio); Kērmānshāh and Qazvīn in *nān-é bērēnji* (rice cookies) and *kāk* or *nān-é yōkhēh* (a fine phyllo made of flour, butter, eggs, and milk, rolled and cut into small pieces, baked and sprayed with powdered sugar); the specialty of Shīrāz is *nōghl* (sugared slivered almond or pistachio, or muskwillow seed). In rural and tribal areas, *kōlūcheh*, a kind of shortbread, is popularly produced, mainly for festivities.

Street food. Hot steaming beetroots, grilled pumpkins, baked potatoes, boiled broad beans, and cooked lentils served with powdered Persian marjoram seed sold by peddlers in winter, and liver *kabābs* rolled in flatbread with or without fresh herbs and chopped onions sold all year round are characteristic features of the popular culture. As further examples, a number of puddings and sweetmeats as well as dried barberry or prunella soaked in water for the juice can be added to the list.

Persian food has not reached the international market. Until the early decades of the twentieth century, people holding high functions or the aristocracy saw to their business in the outer quarters of their home. They were fed together with their employees, assistants, and guests by the *kārkhānēh* (workshop), as the kitchen was known in a big household. It was in such kitchens that great chefs trained cooks who specialized in certain branches of cooking and accepted apprentices to ensure the continuity of the tradition.

Commercial sale of food was limited to *qahvēhkhē-neh* (coffee or, in fact, tea houses), where basic dishes are prepared; *chēlōw-kabābīs*, where only rice and kabobs are served; and certain shops that function only very early in the morning or late in the evening, selling one item like rice pudding, *halīm*, or tripe. Restaurants are a post–World War I phenomenon mainly introduced by Ar-

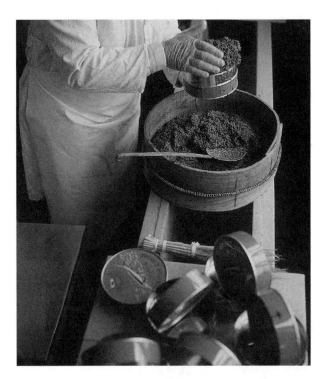

Modern Iran is famous for its high-quality caviar. This scene is from a caviar cannery in Bandar Pahlavi. © ROGER WOOD/CORBIS.

menian, Caucasian, and Russian émigrés from the former Soviet Union. They introduced their own cookery rather than commercializing the Persian cuisine.

Feasts and rituals. Cookies, dried fruit, nuts, and sweets are prepared for *Nōwrūz* (the New Year festival). The traditional dish for New Year's Eve is *sabzi-pōlōw* (rice with herbs) with fried or smoked fish. On New Year's Day *rēshtēh-pōlōw* (noodles with rice), spiced and artfully garnished, is served. Festivities end with a picnic on the thirteenth day, at which *āsh-é rēshtēh* (noodle soup made with herbs, pulses, and *kashk*) and *bāghēla-pōlōw* (rice steamed with broad beans and dill) are the main features.

Observation of religious mourning is customary during the first ten days of the first month of the lunar Islamic calendar to commemorate the martyrdom of Hossein, the grandson of the prophet Muhammad. The occasion includes offerings in the form of food and puddings to the poor. Rice and *khōrēshs* are served in the evenings. On the tenth day, the well-to-do offer puddings such as *shōllēhzard* or *hālva* to ensure good health for the loved ones. In the month of Ramadan a whole range of sophisticated condiments of fine quality are made available for those fasting and feasting during daylight hours.

See also **Bread; Feasts, Festivals, and Fasts; Herbs and Spices; Herodotus; Islam; Mesopotamia, Ancient; Rice; Soup; Stew; Zoroastrianism.**

BIBLIOGRAPHY

Abu Eshaq Shirazi, Mowlana. *Divan-e At'ameh*, edited and published by Mirza Habib Esfahani. Istanbul, a.h. 1302/ 1884–1885. Gives recipes in satirical poetry. The edition includes a glossary by the editor.

Afshar, Iraj, ed., *Ashpazi-ye Dōwrēh-ye Safavi: Matn-e Dōw Rāsē lēh az ān Dōwrēh*. Tehran: Entesharat-e Seda va Sima, a.h. 1360/1981. Includes two major works on cookery from the Safavid period, *Kārnēmeh: dar Bāb-e Tabbākhi va San'at-e Ān of Hāji Mohammad Ali Bāvarchi Baghdādi*, a.h. 927/1521 a.d, pp. 33–184; and *Māddat al-Hayāt of Nurallāh*, a.h. 1003/1594–1595 a.d., pp. 185–256. This also includes a valuable list of references to a number of Arabic and Persian manuscripts and rare nineteenth-century prints.

Āshpazbāshi, Mīrza Ali Akbar Khān. *Sōfrēh-yé At'ameh*. Tehran: Bōnyād-é Farhang-é Iran, a.h. 1352/1974. Written by the chef at the Court of Nāser od-Dīn Shāh in 1883–1884 at the request of Dr. Desire Tholozan.

Batmangelij, Najmieh K. *A Taste of Persia: An Introduction to Persian Cooking*. London and New York: I. B. Tauris, 1999.

Briant, Pierre. *Histoire de l'Empire Perse: de Cyrus à Alexandre*. Paris: Fayard, 1996.

Daryabandari, Najaf. *Kētāb-é Mōstatāb-e Āshpazi: Az Sīr tā Piyāz*, in co-operation with Fahimeh Rastkar, 2 vols. Tehran: Nashr-e Kārnāmēh, a.h. 1379/2000.

Ghanoonparvar, Mohammad R. *Persian Cuisine, Book Two: Regional and Modern Foods*. Lexington, Ky.: Mazdâ, 1982–1984. In English and Persian.

Mōntazami, Rosa. *Hōnar-e Āshpazi*. 9th ed. Tehran: Shērkat Offset, a.h. 1361/1982, 1st edition printed in a.h. 1347/1968.

Richard, Josephine (Nēshāt-ed-Dōlēh). *Tabbakhi-ye Nēshāt*. Tehran, n.d.

Richard Khan, Yūsēf (Mō'addab-al-Mōlk). *Rēsālēh-yé Tabbākhi*. Tehran, 1903.

Roden, Claudia. *The New Book of Middle Eastern Food*. Rev. ed. New York: Knopf, 2000.

Sancisi-Weerdenberg, Heleen. "Persian Food: Stereotypes and Political Identity." In *Food in Antiquity*, edited by John Wilkins, David Harvey, and Mike Dobson, pp. 286–302. Exeter: University of Exeter Press, 1995.

Shaida, Margaret. *The Legendary Cuisine of Persia*. Henley-on-Thames, U.K.: Lieuse, 1992.

Simmons, Shirin. *A Treasury of Persian Cuisine*. East Sussex, England: Book Guild, 2002.

Wilkins, John, David Harvey, and Mike Dobson, eds. *Food in Antiquity*. Exeter: University of Exeter Press, 1995.

Yarshater, Ehsan, ed. *Encyclopaedia Iranica*. (Articles on cookbooks, cooking, *berenj*, and cookies.) London; Boston: Routledge & Kegan Paul, 1983–1989; Costa Mesa, Calif.: Mazdâ Pulishers, 1990–.

Zubaida, Sami, and Richard Tapper, eds. *Culinary Cultures of the Middle East*. London and New York: I. B. Tauris, 1994.

Maryam Matine-Daftary

IRELAND. *See* **British Isles.**

IRON. Iron is the second most abundant mineral on earth and is an essential nutrient for nearly all organisms. Iron is necessary for many varied functions in mammals, including the synthesis of DNA, the generation of energy from macronutrients by aerobic respiration, and the transport and metabolism of oxygen. Iron is highly reactive and is potentially toxic at high levels of intake; therefore, its utilization and storage present a major challenge for biological systems. Cellular iron exists primarily in its reduced ferrous (Fe^{+2}) and oxidized ferric (Fe^{+3}) states, and conversion of the mineral between these states serves to catalyze many reactions. One example is Fenton's reaction, whereby hydrogen peroxide is converted to highly reactive hydroxyl radicals ($^{\cdot}OH$).

$$Fe_2^+ + H_2O_2 \rightarrow Fe_3^+ + OH^- \ {}^{\cdot}OH \quad \text{(Fenton's reaction)}$$

Both ferric iron and the hydroxyl radicals generated by free iron in this reaction directly damage tissues by randomly inducing DNA strand breaks and by oxidizing and thereby damaging cellular proteins, lipids, metabolic cofactors, and nucleic acids. Therefore, it is not surprising that most iron in the cell is bound or sequestered by proteins, so that the concentration of free iron is very low (usually less than $1 \times 10{-}18$ moles per liter). Many iron-binding proteins are enzymes that harness and bring specificity to the reactive properties of iron, whereas other proteins store or transport iron (Table 1). Protein-bound iron can accept electrons during enzyme-catalyzed reactions, enable proteins to recognize and bind substrates, and assist in the formation of defined protein structures.

Dietary Forms and Factors Affecting Iron Requirements

The Recommended Daily Allowance (RDA) for iron is 8 milligrams per day for men and postmenopausal women and 18 milligrams per day for premenopausal women. Adult males contain about 4 grams of total body iron (50 milligrams per kilogram of body weight), whereas menstruating women contain 40 milligrams per kilogram of body weight. Full-term infants are born with sufficient

TABLE 1

Representative proteins that bind iron

Protein	Function
Transport and Storage Proteins	
DMT1	Intestinal iron uptake
FP1	Intestinal iron export
Ferritin	Iron storage
Enzymes	
Ribonucleotide reductase	Synthesis of DNA precursors
Cysteine dioxygenase	Amino acid metabolism
Oxygen carriers	
Hemoglobin	
Myoglobin	

iron stores to meet metabolic demands for the first 4 months of life. Breast milk contains 0.2 mg iron/liter; breast-feeding infants receive about 0.27 milligrams per day.

There are two natural dietary forms of iron: (1) inorganic salts of ferric iron, and (2) iron bound to a cyclic carbon ring called heme in the form of hemoglobin and myoglobin in meat products. Inorganic iron is readily liberated from food in the acidic lumen of the stomach but is not absorbed well in the small intestine because of its poor solubility at physiological pH and because it is sequestered by many dietary components that hinder absorption, including phytates, polyphenols, calcium, and fiber. Therefore, only a small percentage of injected iron salts are actually absorbed into the body, thereby indicating that iron salts have a low bioavailability, or ability to be effectively absorbed. However, other low-molecular-weight dietary components bind inorganic iron and facilitate its absorption. These compounds, which include vitamin C and lactic acids, are commonly found in citrus and deciduous fruits and are known as metal chelators. In addition, an unidentified "meat factor" present in animal tissue also enhances the absorption of iron salts. Finally, heme iron has a much greater bioavailability than iron salts because fewer factors interfere with its absorption and it displays greater solubility in water. Hence, heme iron can account for up to 35 percent of absorbed iron in diets when accounting for only 10 percent of total dietary iron intake. In the United States, artificially fortified foods in the form of fortified grain products are a major source of dietary iron and account for nearly 50 percent of all iron consumed.

Iron absorption and transport from the intestinal lumen to the circulatory system is tightly regulated and complex. Enterocyte cells, which are responsible for the uptake and transport of nutrients from the intestinal mucosa, mediate the uptake and transport of iron to the plasma. These cells, once mature, function for only 48 to 72 hours before they are shed and excreted. The capacity of the mature enterocyte to transport inorganic iron is determined very early in its development and is inversely proportional to plasma iron status. The enterocyte iron transport protein, DMT1 (divalent metal transporter), facilitates iron uptake from the intestinal lumen into the enterocyte. DMT1 concentrations at the cell surface are increased when whole-body iron stores are depleted, which increases the rate of cellular iron accumulation into the enterocyte once it is matured. The induction of DMT1 protein synthesis results from increased DMT1 messenger RNA levels. During iron deficiency, the iron regulatory protein (IRP) binds to the 3' untranslated region of the DMT1 messenger RNA and increases its stability. Heme iron is transported into the enterocyte from the intestinal lumen by an unidentified heme iron receptor, and cellular enzymes in the enterocyte release iron from the heme ring. Iron is exported from the basolateral surface of the enterocyte to plasma by the iron transport protein ferroportin1 (Fp1). Fp1 is believed to assist in the direct transfer of iron to a soluble plasma iron transport protein called transferrin. Transferrin facilitates the delivery of two molecules of iron among the sites of absorption and storage and to all tissues and organs. The transferrin-iron complex enters the cell by binding to a specific protein, the transferrin receptor, which is present on the plasma membrane of all cells. Once transferrin binds to its receptor, the receptor-transferrin complex is engulfed by the cell, forming an internal vesicle called an endosome. Once in the cell, iron is released from transferrin by the acidification of the endosome, and the transferrin receptor is recycled to the cell surface where it can bind additional transferrin molecules.

Iron Physiology

Intestinal absorption is the primary mechanism that regulates whole body iron concentrations. There are no specific mechanisms to remove excess iron from mammals. Inorganic iron excretion is limited because of its low solubility in aqueous environments and therefore daily iron loss is minimal in the absence of blood loss. Fecal (from shed enterocytes and biliary heme products), urogenital, and integumental losses account for 4 mg/day of iron loss. Menstruation, blood donation, and pregnancy also can cause significant iron loss. Variations in iron status and requirements are influenced by individual genetic makeup as well as by differences in menstrual losses. The latter averages 0.6 mg/day but can greatly exceed that value in the individual, resulting in a need to absorb an additional 3 to 4 mg/day to maintain adequate iron status. An additional 4 to 5 mg/day of iron must be absorbed during pregnancy. States of rapid growth during childhood through adolescence also increase iron requirements.

Most absorbed iron is used by the bone marrow to make hemoglobin, an abundant protein that binds and distributes oxygen throughout the body. The remaining iron is distributed to other tissues where it is incorporated into iron-requiring proteins or stored. Nearly 70 percent of total body iron is present in red blood cells bound to hemoglobin. Another 15 percent is bound to metabolic enzymes and numerous other proteins, including muscle myoglobin, which transports oxygen to the mitochondria, and cytochromes, which act as electron carriers during respiration. The remaining iron is stored in the liver, spleen, and macrophages and can be distributed to other cells during states of dietary iron deficiency. The primary iron storage protein is ferritin, which is a hollow sphere comprised of 24 protein subunits. One ferritin molecule can store about 3,000 ferric iron molecules that can be mobilized readily when required. There are two types of ferritin subunits, heavy-chain and light-chain ferritin. Heavy-chain ferritin sequesters Fe^{+2} and oxidizes it to Fe^{+3}; light-chain ferritin aids in the formation of the mineral iron core within the protein. Tissue, gender, hormones, and iron status can influence the ratio of heavy-chain and light-chain sub-units that comprise a ferritin molecule, but the physiological significance of this ratio is not well understood.

Consequences of Altered Iron Status

Iron deficiency is the most common of all micronutrient deficiencies in the world, and the anemia that results affects an estimated 2 billion people. Dietary iron deficiency results in reduced iron stores in the liver, bone marrow, and spleen, followed by diminished erythropoiesis, which is the production of red blood cells, and anemia, and ultimately results in decreased activity of iron-dependent enzymes. Iron uptake in the intestine is responsive to total body stores such that iron-deficient individuals display increased iron absorption as described above. Clinical manifestations of iron deficiency include impaired endurance exercise due to an inability to deliver oxygen to tissues, microcytic anemia, glossitis, and blue scerra. Maternal iron deficiency during pregnancy is associated with several adverse outcomes for the newborn infant, including premature delivery, low birth weight, permanent cognitive deficits, developmental delay, and a wide range of behavioral disturbances. The onset of anemia and depletion of tissue iron concentrations occur concurrently, whereas the other negative consequences of iron deficiency occur after hemoglobin concentrations fall.

The tolerable upper level intake for iron for adults is 45 mg/day; intakes that exceed this level result in gastrointestinal distress. Dietary overload can occur, although it is uncommon, except in individuals with primary hereditary hemochromatosis, an iron-storage disease, which can result in up to fifty-fold increases in storage iron deposits. Hemochromatosis most commonly results from a common genetic mutation or genetic polymorphism in the HFE gene that is prevalent in populations of European descent but can also result from mutations in other iron-related proteins including a transferrin receptor. The HFE protein is involved in intestinal regulation of iron accumulation, but its precise biochemical function is unknown. This genetic disorder, if untreated by regular phlebotomy, results in liver cirrhosis, cadiomyopathy, arthritis, and cancer.

See also **Gene Expression, Nutrient Regulation of; Nutrients; Nutrient Bioavailability**.

BIBLIOGRAPHY

Standing Committee on the Scientific Evaluation of Dietary Reference Intakes, Food and Nutrition Board, Institute of Medicine. Washington, D.C.: National Academy Press, 2001. Dietary Reference Intakes for vitamin A, vitamin K, arsenic, boron, chromium, iodine, iron, manganese, molybdenum, nickel, silicon, vanadium, and zinc.

Griffiths, William, and Timothy Cox. "Haemochromatosis: Novel Gene Discovery and the Molecular Pathophysiology of Iron Metabolism." *Human Molecular Genetics* 9 (2000): 2377–2382.

Patrick J. Stover

IRON COOKSTOVE, THE.

The cast-iron cookstove, a constructed range that totally encases the fire, is a relatively recent development in the history of cookery, and an outgrowth of earlier cooking devices made of stone, brick, clay, and tile. The English term "stove" has a history of its own, and has been used for centuries to designate a variety of early cooking devices in which the fire was not enclosed. For example, one precursor to the cookstove involved a raised hearth which, like the later ranges, was waist high, but supported open fires. These, along with structures for partially enclosed fires and portable braziers called stoves, are helpful in tracing the origins of what was to become the nineteenth-century cast-iron cookstove.

Early History

For thousands of years before the advent of cookstoves, people cooked over open flames. Depending on materials and technologies at hand, various cultures have worked out a cooking surface heated by a fire below. These are exemplified by the Russian domed clay stove and the Japanese *kamado*. Some had holes in the cooking surface to bring cooking pots into direct contact with the flames. Their open fires were easily tended but smoky and somewhat inefficient. More advanced early cultures, among them the Chinese Han Dynasty, used the ceramic *tsao*, a very early range in which the fire was enclosed. The late medieval period and the Renaissance brought many changes because of the greater use of iron. With the growth of cities and consolidation of power, there was a trend toward elaborate cuisines and larger kitchens. Commercial establishments and wealthy or aristocratic households, having more means and more need, were the first to explore various types of "stoves."

The stew stove, one of these cookstove progenitors, was a bank or row of open-top or grill-like "burners," each over its own fire. Its role in the kitchen was as an adjunct to the large roasting fireplaces. For example, the stew stoves of sixteenth-century Italian chef Scappi were made of brick and clay; those of his contemporaries were often made of tile or stone. In such stoves, the fire was not totally enclosed, but they offered individually regulated temperatures and a waist-high surface. In later centuries, this form was sometimes adapted to quantity cookery, using permanently installed large cast-iron or copper kettles, each over their own fireboxes, and used for the preparation of substantial stews and soups. The German architect and engineer Georg Andreas Böckler designed a brick range that followed this principle (Frankfurt, 1666); subsequently others devised cast-iron frames and fireboxes. Like Scappi's stoves, they were usually limited to professional kitchens.

Renaissance ironworkers built on smelting and casting innovations of the medieval period, and developed cast-iron stoves. Böckler's *Furnologia, or: The Art of Domestic Stoves* described such a stove, one that produced coals to be used in a fireplace and another with a horizontal surface for household cooking. Subsequently, the English industrial revolution improved blast furnaces, increased production, and popularized iron stoves in both professional and industrial cookery, and in privileged households. For example, Denis Diderot recorded their use by French candy makers in his *Encyclopédie*, 1758.

Northern Europeans (especially Germans and Scandinavians) had stoves early, possibly as a response to their cold winters. In England they were sometimes installed alongside the grate system, used as free-standing ranges, and sometimes employed steam, ultimately developing into the English institution, the AGA stove.

The American Cookstove
Cookstoves were not new to the colonies: Mary Randolph suggested a brick version (probably a stew stove) in 1824.

By the end of the 1700s early American scientists such as Benjamin Franklin and Count Rumford had worked out further ideas leading to the development of home cookstoves. In the early 1800s New Yorker Jordan Mott manufactured the first American stoves, supplementary adjuncts to the traditional hearth. At first quite small in size, they were placed free-standing in front of the fireplace, their stovepipes carrying the smoke to the fireplace chimney. As they became larger and more complex, they usurped the hearth entirely and were installed directly within the fireplace.

The antebellum period brought many cookstove innovations, among them expanded surface area, multiple lids, dual ovens, warming ovens or shelves, additional storage space, and water boiler shelves. By 1850, most urban middle-class hearths had given way to stoves. The changeover was uneven, slower to reach the lower economic levels and more remote areas.

The cookstove itself demanded new designs for pots and pans. Age-old legs and rounded bottoms, so workable on the hearth, were no longer effective, and were replaced by flat bottoms that could absorb heat by direct contact with the heated surface. A few boiling kettles retained the rounded bottom and short legs (to prevent tipping), and were set into an open lid hole, the hottest setting possible; others were further redesigned with bottom insets that fit down inside the open lid "eye." Trade catalogs of the mid- to late nineteenth century continued to reflect a period of hearth-stove overlap, and supplied cooking utensils for both. With increasing specialization, stovetop equipment expanded to include such adaptations as saucepans, boilers, kettles, skillets, pancake and waffle irons, coffee roasters, toasters, and short-handled utensils.

How They Worked
The workings and maintenance of cookstoves were demanding. Between the firebox and the chimney, a series of manual dampers and levers controlled the air and smoke flow, the rate of burning, and consequently the cooking temperatures. The fire was lit with all dampers open, after which adjustments redirected the heat and smoke to a passageway surrounding the oven to heat it. As the ovens were without self-regulating thermostats, overheating was prevented by opening oven doors temporarily, cutting down on the fire's air flow. To maintain temperature, the cook checked the relatively small firebox, testing for heat by hand, and stoked it frequently. Such instructions on cookstove management were included in nineteenth-century cookbooks.

Cooking temperatures were also controlled by the position of the pot on the stovetop. The area nearest the firebox was by far the hottest; the farthest corners were the coolest. As the oven was hottest near the wall between the firebox and the oven, one used the farthest side of the oven and turned the pans regularly (rather than positioning the shelves). Cookstoves were notoriously eccentric. A good cook learned their vagaries and adapted.

There was now more choice in fuel. Hardwoods were preferred over soft, as always, as they created more heat and lasted longer. Coal was preferable to wood in that it produced more heat for a longer period of time and was easier to procure and handle in urban kitchens, but it triggered debates over possible danger from its fumes.

General Assessment

Cast-iron cookstoves brought about a major revolution in many aspects of cookery, notably the technology of the kitchen, the character of cuisine, and the role of home cooks.

The new "ranges" influenced cooking technology throughout the Western world. In cultures that had little iron, the designs of cast-iron stoves were applied to newer versions of their earlier traditional stoves. For example, the Russian domed stove evolved into a clay-covered brick bank stove, at first used by the upper classes, and eventually adopted into peasant homes. The Alsatian brick cookstove and the Bavarian stone and tile stove followed a similar pattern.

The attraction of new stoves overcame their shortcomings. Cooks benefited from waist-high, flexible cooking, less bending and lifting, less smoke, and no ash in the food. Their ovens achieved and maintained desired temperatures in far less time, enabling daily baking, and permitted more flexible menus. They heated the house

THE COAL STOVE

Stoves for coal should be carefully put up, as if the pipe gapes, the coal gas may occasion death.

Catharine Beecher, *Treatise on Domestic Economy*, 1841

Anthracite coal is one of the most difficult fuels for the beginner to manage; but once having learned its requirements, it will be found one of the most satisfactory and constant of friends.

Maria Parloa, *Home Economics*, 1898

You may take the poetry of an open wood fire of the present day, but to me in those early days it was only dismal prose, and I am grateful to have lived in the time of anthracite coal.

Diary of Mary Bennett, 1868

more efficiently in winter, and were easily taken apart and reassembled in summer kitchens. However, in comparison with hearth cooking, they did not roast or bake well, were notoriously drafty and finicky, and required arduous cleaning. Some decried the loss of the hearth, declaring that the center of family life was threatened and with it the family itself.

The cookstove had far-reaching effects on cookery and the domestic life of nineteenth-century men and women. Well suited to city life and the growing cash economy, it eliminated the task of producing one's own fuel. Women, now changing their role from farm producer to city consumer, enjoyed the convenience, and

Cooking with gas is not as new as many people think. This 1884 gas stove advertisement depicts an iron cookstove with all units working at full capacity. ROUGHWOOD COLLECTION.

THOREAU ON STOVES

I used a small cooking-stove for economy . . . but it did not keep fire so well as the open fireplace. Cooking was then, for the most part, no longer a poetic, but merely a chemic process. . . . The stove not only took up room and scented the house, but it concealed the fire, and I felt as if I had lost a companion. You can always see a face in the fire.

Henry David Thoreau, *Walden*, 1846

used their growing discretionary time for philanthropic community welfare. Growing interest in fashionable dining likewise stimulated a far wider range of daily cooking and baking. Simultaneously, a drop in the cost of sugar, flour, and spices led to elaborate home baking, candy making, preserving and canning, and the consumption of snack foods. The gradual development of chemical leaveners, well adapted to the quickly fired cookstove, replaced much yeast baking and encouraged new and revised recipes—especially for quick breads and iced layer cakes.

See also **Hearth Cookery.**

BIBLIOGRAPHY

Brewer, Priscilla J. *From Fireplace to Cookstove: Technology and the Domestic Ideal in America.* Syracuse, N.Y.: Syracuse University Press, 2000.

Cowan, Ruth Schwartz. *More Work for Mother: The Ironies of Household Technology from the Open Hearth to the Microwave.* New York: Basic Books, 1983.

da Messisbugo, Cristoforo. *Banchetti.* 1549. Facsimile edition. Venice: Neri Pozza, 1976?

Diderot. *Recuell De Planches.* Paris: 1758. Compact edition. New York: Redex Microprint, 1969.

Feild, Rachel. *Irons in the Fire: A History of Cooking Equipment.* Marlborough, U.K.: Crowood, 1984.

Franklin, Linda Campbell. *Three Hundred Years of Kitchen Collectibles,* 4th ed. Iola, Wisc.: Krause, 1997.

Hardyment, Christina. *Behind the Scenes: Domestic Arrangements in Historic Houses.* London: National Trust Enterprises, 1992.

Hess, John L., and Karen Hess. *The Taste of America.* New York: Grossman Press, 1977.

Lecoq, Raymond. *Les Objets de la Vie Domestique: Utensiles en Fer de la Cuisine et du Foyer des Origines au XIXe Siècle.* Paris: Berger-Levrault, 1979.

Leviner, Betty Crowe. "The Stew Stove at the Governor's Palace, Williamsburg." Unpublished report. Williamsburg, Va.: Colonial Williamsburg Foundation, April 1994.

Mohs, K. *Die Entwicklung des Backofens vom Back-Stein zum selbstaetigen Backofen. Eine kulturgeschichtliche Studie* [The development of the bakeoven from the bakestone to the self-starting oven]. Stuttgart: Werner & Phleiderer, 1926.

Oliver, Sandra L. "Introduction" and "The Buckinghams: Saltwater Farming." In *Saltwater Foodways: New Englanders and Their Food at Sea and Ashore, in the Nineteenth Century.* Mystic, Conn.: Mystic Seaport Museum, Inc., 1995.

Alice Ross

ISLAM.

This entry includes three subentries:
Shi'ite Islam
Sunni Islam
Sufism

SHI'ITE ISLAM

Shi'a comprise 10 to 15 percent of the world Muslim population, and are concentrated in the Middle East, particularly in Iran, where Shi'ism is the state religion. Shi'a differ from the majority Sunni Muslims in matters of religious authority and leadership arising from disputes over the legitimate succession to Muhammad, with Shi'a supporting the claim of 'Ali, grandson of the Prophet, and his family and descendants. The teachings of the Qur'an are strictly interpreted and followed. However, the basic pattern of observances, including food-related behavior, is similar for Shi'a and Sunnis.

Role of Food in Religious Tradition

Islamic food practices are derived first from the Qur'an and secondly from the hadith—the sayings and deeds of Muhammad. Pre-Islamic Arabs had few food prohibitions, and these were more a matter of local custom, specific to particular tribes. The food laws of the Qur'an provided one way of uniting the tribes in common observances, at the same time differentiating the Muslims from the Jews. The use of food to create and maintain boundaries and common identities is common among the world's religions.

Islamic law influences diet by prohibiting or restricting certain foods, based on Jewish dietary laws as mentioned in the Qur'an, and by requiring fasting and feasting at specific times of year. It also enjoins moderation and reasonableness in all things and commends hospitality. Food was strongly linked to hospitality in Arabic cultures and the sharing of food was encouraged by Muhammad as a means of creating common bonds and sharing in common blessings.

Shi'a follow general Qur'anic food regulations. In the Qur'an food is mentioned frequently as a fundamental beneficence, a Divine blessing. Believers are exhorted to eat of the good things with which God has supplied them and are given only minimal dietary restrictions. Forbidden, or *halal*, is that which dies naturally, blood, swine's flesh, and that over which any name other than God's has been invoked. Also prohibited are meat of the ass, of carnivorous animals such as the tiger, fox, dog, and leopard, which kill prey by using their paws, and of birds of prey. Alcohol is forbidden, along with any other substance that is debilitating to the faculties. The meat of permitted animals is only *halal* if slaughtered in accordance with Islamic law, by cutting the throat while pronouncing the words "Bismillah. Allah Akbar" ("I begin with God's name: God is great").

Further food regulations are contained in the hadith and have been elaborated over time by various schools of Islamic jurisprudence. Foods are allocated to one of the five categories of action in Islamic law: obligatory, recommended, neutral, disapproved, or prohibited. Each school of jurisprudence categorizes foods differently, though the differences between Shi'a and Sunnis is, on the whole, of little practical everyday significance. Foods or parts of animals forbidden based on exclusively Shi'ite hadiths include hare and porcupine, fish without scales, sea creatures with shells (except shrimp is allowed), rabbits, and certain body parts such as the gallbladder and spleen.

Qur'anic food laws are seen as a sign of God's will, but there is no sin in eating prohibited foods in small quantities if essential to sustain life. Sunnis generally permit the consumption of meat slaughtered by Jews or Christians, while Shi'a do so only if necessity dictates. As in all religions, the strictness with which dietary laws and guidelines are observed differs with social status and circumstances, depending on the commitment to practice.

Fasting

There are different categories of fasting in Islam: those that are obligatory; those that are recommended but which may be broken without penalty; those that are blameworthy and discouraged; and those that are forbidden. Obligatory fasts include the month of Ramadan, expiatory fasts performed as *kaffarah* (atonement) for breaking the Ramadan fast, and those performed in fulfillment of a vow. The chief obligatory fast is Ramadan. Shi'a generally break the fast a few minutes after the sun has set and commence the fast a few minutes before dawn. In both instances the intent is to ensure that the full fasting period is observed. The exemption categories for the fast are similar for Shi'a and Sunnis, though with some variations in interpretation. For Shi'a fasting is not valid if it would cause or aggravate illness or intensify pain or delay recovery; to do so is to cause harm, which is prohibited. Pregnant women in the final trimester and nursing mothers ought to break their fast if there is danger of harm. To continue fasting in such circumstances is not valid. In both instances breaking the fast is optional for Sunnis. Acute hunger, unless life-threatening, is not a sufficient reason for Shi'a to break the fast, but is acceptable to Sunnis. There are other differences relating to travelers, to what precisely breaks the fast, and to what is required in the way of restitution for infractions. The most serious infraction, sexual intercourse with a spouse, is punished with extended fasting and fines in both Shi'ite and Sunni law; such fines include freeing a slave, feeding sixty poor, or fasting for two consecutive months.

Muhurram, the first month of the Muslim year, is a time of major public affirmations of Shi'a beliefs. The one-day fast of Ashura, which falls on the 10th of Muhurram, was, according to Sunni tradition, instituted by Muhammad in imitation of the Jewish practice of marking the deliverance of the children of Israel from the Pharoah. Although the fast was soon abrogated in favor of Ramadan, it remained as a voluntary observance. For Sunni Muslims Ashura is a joyous festival, commemorated precisely because it is Sunnah—the Way of the Prophet. But for Shi'a it is a time of mourning, the anniversary of the murder of Husayn, son of 'Ali and grand-son of Muhammad, by the Caliph Yazid at the battle of Kerbala. Husayn opposed caliphate rule and was killed in an attempt to restore the imamate. Shi'a mark this occasion with large public parades, at which loud lamentations are accompanied by beating of drums and penitents who scourge themselves with whips or knives. In some places dancers enact scenes from Kerbala and decorated replicas of the martyrs' tombs are carried through the streets. A specific Shi'a practice during Muhurram is the provision of food and drink to the community. In Shi'a neighborhoods children distribute ladles of water to passersby, while tables of food may be set up for the poor. This allows believers to symbolically compensate for the fact that Husayn was allowed to die hungry and thirsty while, at the same time, alleviating the thirst and hunger of the oppressed.

Supererogatory fasts are meritorious for all Muslims on any day when fasting is not specifically forbidden. The first and last Thursdays and the 13th, 14th, and 15th of each month are particularly auspicious, as are a number of other days during the year. It is reprehensible to single out Fridays or Saturdays for fasting, or to fast on Naw Rouz (New Year) or on the day preceding Ramadan. Fasting is forbidden on the first days of 'Id al-fitr and 'Id al-adha. For Shi'a fasting is also forbidden on the 9th of Muhurram, as on this day the enemies of Husayn fasted in preparation for the battle of Kerbala.

Holidays and Festivals

Shi'a observe the major Islamic festivals of 'Id al-fitr and 'Id al-adha, as well as commemorating many events in the lives of the Imams. 'Id al-fitr is a three-day festival following the Ramadan fast and is celebrated to give thanks to God for providing the strength to complete the fast. It is marked with visiting, gift-giving and preparation, and exchange of favorite foods. Specially prepared sweet dishes are characteristic of the festival, giving it the popular name of Sweet Id. 'Id al-Adha, the feast of sacrifice, is a four-day public holiday occurring at the end of the pilgrimage to Mecca. It celebrates Abraham's complete obedience to God in being willing to sacrifice his son Ishmael, and God's dispensation in allowing Abraham to substitute a sacrificial ram. At public ceremonies the imam sacrifices a sheep for the community. Every Muslim who can afford it should sacrifice at home a goat, lamb, cow, or camel and share the meat with family and friends and with the poor.

'Id al-Ghadir, held on the eighteenth day of the month of pilgrimage, is a Shi'ite feast instituted in 962 C.E. to commemorate the events of Ghadir Khumm, when Shi'a believe that the Prophet designated 'Ali as his successor. This is not observed by Sunnis.

See also **Fasting and Abstinence: Islam; Ramadan.**

BIBLIOGRAPHY

Abbas, Ali, ed. *A Shi'ite Encyclopedia.* Available on the Internet at http:/www.al-Islam.org/encyclopedia/chapter7/3.html.

This section of the on-line encyclopedia provides minute detail on the variations in Ramadan fasting requirements among schools of Islamic jurisprudence.

Glasse, C. *A Concise Encyclopedia of Islam.* San Francisco: Harper and Row, 1989.

Tabataba'i, Muhammad. *Shi'ite Islam.* Translated by Seyyid Hossain Nasr. New York: Albany State University Press, 1975.

Paul Fieldhouse

SUNNI ISLAM

"Islam" comes from the Arabic word meaning 'peace' and 'submission'. For Muslims around the world it is a way of life requiring absolute submission to the will of God. Islam dates from 622 C.E. and is based on the prophetic revelations of Muhammad. From its Middle Eastern roots Islam has spread around the world and, with over a billion followers, is the second largest of the world's religions, after Christianity. About 15 percent of Muslims live in the Arab world and another 25 percent in Africa. Substantial parts of Asia are predominantly Muslim, with Indonesia having the largest Muslim community. There are also significant Muslim populations in Europe and the Americas. The three main Islamic sects are the Sunni, who comprise about 90 percent of all Muslims, Shi'ites, and Sufis. In addition, there are numerous small sects and subsects, such as Ahmaddis, 'Alawites, and Wahhabis, that differ in degrees of orthodoxy and practice.

Although they accept the divine status of the Jewish and Christian revelations, Muslims believe that Muhammad was the "Seal of the Prophets," the last of God's messengers. The word of God as revealed to Muhammad is recorded in the Holy Qur'an, the infallible guide to Muslim conduct. Further guidance is provided by the *sunna*, the authoritative example of the Prophet, whose words and deeds are recorded in the *hadith* (literally 'tiding' or 'information'; more broadly 'every word, deed, and approval attributed to Muhammad'). "Sunni," derived from "sunna," describes allegiance to the ways of the Prophet. Within the Sunni tradition there are four schools of jurisprudence (Hanifis, Malikis, Shafis, Hanbalis) that differ in their interpretations and applications of religious law, including some minor issues related to food.

Role of Food in Religious Tradition

Prior to the advent of Muhammad, food practices among the Arab peoples of the Middle East were diverse. The establishment of common Islamic food laws united these diverse groups, at the same time differentiating the new religion from Judaism. In several places in the Qur'an, Muhammad refers to the restrictive food laws of the Jews as a burden imposed on them for sins, noting that there were few food restrictions prior to the revelation of the Torah (4:160; 6:146). While he retained certain elements of Jewish food law, such as the prohibition on pork,

Muhammad proclaimed food as a general beneficence, a gift from God to be enjoyed by His people without undue burden. "O ye who believe! Eat of the good things that We have provided you, and be grateful to Allah if it is Him ye worship" (2:172).

Islamic laws regarding food are found particularly in three Qur'anic *suras* (chapters), The Cow (2), The Table (5), and Cattle (6), respectively. In addition, the sayings and actions of Muhammad, as recorded in the *hadith*, provide detailed guidance to acceptable food practices. Food is classified as lawful (*halal*) or unlawful (*haram*). Between these is the category of doubtful or suspect (*mashbooh*). *Halal* signifies food that is acceptable in the sight of God; it includes all food that is not classified as *haram* or *mashbooh*: milk from cows, sheep, camels, and goats, honey, fish, vegetables, fruit, legumes, nuts, and grains. Most animals are *halal*: "Lawful unto you (for food) are all four-footed animals, with the exceptions named" (5:1). However, to be *halal*, meat must come from animals slaughtered ritually in a way (similar to Jewish practice) intended to spare them unnecessary suffering. The words "Bismillah. Allah Akbar" ("I begin with God's name: God is great") are pronounced over the animal as its throat is slit, allowing the blood to drain. In fact, kosher food is generally acceptable to Sunni Muslims: "The food of the People of the Book is lawful for you, and yours is lawful unto them" (5.5). Also, similar to kosher practice, in the marketplace meats and other products are certified *halal* by authoritative Islamic agencies and are stamped with a *halal* seal.

The opposite of *halal* is *haram* food—that which is unacceptable. Pork is the preeminent example of a *haram* food, the only meat specifically forbidden in the Qur'an. Blood, and that which dies naturally (carrion), as well as food over which any other name than God's has been invoked, are *haram* (5.3). Also prohibited in the *hadith* are flesh of the ass, carnivorous animals, such as the tiger, fox, dog, and leopard, which kill prey by using their paws, and birds of prey. Fish must be alive when taken from the sea or river, and only fish that have fins and scales are allowed, which excludes shellfish and eels. Shrimp are generally considered *halal*; however there is some disagreement over this within the Hanafi school of jurisprudence. Land animals without ears, such as frogs and snakes, are prohibited. Foods contaminated by *haram* substances themselves become *haram*. Alcohol is *haram*, along with other mind-altering substances. However, there are several references to wine in the Qur'an that illustrate changing attitudes toward alcohol: wine is acknowledged to have some benefit, but which is outweighed by harm (2:219); believers are exhorted not to pray while under the influence of intoxicants (4:43); and it is expressly prohibited as "an abomination of Satan's handiwork" (5:90). The latter, together with guidance found in the *hadith*, forms the basis for most modern interpretations, which view alcohol as both morally and socially unacceptable. Other intoxicants that cloud the mind are also forbidden, though this is a gray area. For example, the chewing of *qat* ("khat," *Catha edulis*), a plant whose leaves contain a mild stimulant, is common in Yemen. Coffee consumption has also been controversial at times, though sixteenth-century attempts to ban it proved impossible to enforce. While coffee is a symbol of hospitality in some Arab countries, it may be avoided by devout Muslims. It is worth noting though that some Muslims, notably Sufis, interpret the Qur'anic verses in other ways and do not prohibit wine. Wine drinking is also acceptable to 'Alawites, especially in a sacramental context.

If a person is uncertain whether a food is *halal* or *haram*, then it is *mashbooh*—doubtful or suspect—and should be avoided. Ingredients such as emulsifiers, gelatin, and enzymes used in processed foods fall into this category as the animal origin of the constituents may be unknown. Some food manufacturers and Islamic authorities produce lists of foods and ingredients classified as *halal* or *haram* as a guide to food choice.

There are regional, social, familial, and individual variations in the strictness with which food laws are adhered to. Some Chinese Muslims, for example, openly consume pork. Concern for one's health or obligations stemming from hospitality are reasons for transgressing normative food behaviors. "But if one is forced by necessity [to eat forbidden foods], without wilful disobedience, nor transgressing due limits—then is he guiltless. For Allah is Oft-forgiving Most Merciful" (2:173).

Fasting and Feasting

Fasting (*sawm*) is one of the Five Pillars of Islam and, as such, is an important religious duty. Muslim fasts require complete abstention from food and drink between the hours of sunrise and sunset. Fasting at different times of year may be obligatory (*wajib*), recommended (*mustahab*), discouraged (*makruh*), or forbidden (*muharam*). The main obligatory fast of the Muslim calendar is that of Ramadan, which lasts for the entire month. Also obligatory is fasting for kaffarah—atonement for infractions of the Ramadan fast—and fasts made in fulfillment of vows. Fasting is considered *mustahab* on all days of the year on which it has not been prohibited. It is specifically stressed for the thirteenth, fourteenth, and fifteenth of each month in imitation of the Prophet, and on Mondays and Thursdays. *Ashura* is a one-day fast held on the tenth day of Muhurram, instituted by Muhammad in imitation of the Jewish holiday Pesach (Passover), which marks the delivery of the children of Israel from the Pharoah. Although *Ashura* was replaced in the second year of Muhammad's dispensation by Ramadan, it remains as an optional fast.

It is *makruh* to single out Fridays and Saturdays (the Muslim and Jewish Sabbaths) for fasting or to fast on the day preceding Ramadan or on *Naw Rouz*. Fasting is *muharam* on the days of the 'Id al-Fitr and 'Id al-Adha festivals. To be valid, fasting must be undertaken with correct spiritual intent (*niyyah*), which should be renewed each day. Fasting is incumbent on all sane adult Muslims, with exemptions made for pregnant, nursing, and menstruating women, for travelers, and for those in ill health. The exceptions are seen as evidence of the statement that Allah does not want to place an undue burden on His people (2:185). Deliberate infractions of the Ramadan fast are subject to either *kaffarah* (atonement) or *qada* (restitution), though unintentional lapses are not punished. Some differences exist between schools of jurisprudence as to the detailed practices and penalties associated with fasting. For example, Sunnis may break the fast if they suffer acute hunger; Shi'ites may not unless there is risk of illness.

Certain foods have a particular symbolic value because they recall the practices of Muhammad. Thus, fasts are traditionally broken with dates and water, followed by lentil soup and often a salad before the main course, which is more a matter of local custom.

Holidays and Festivals

During the Ramadan fast Muslims may consume more food than at other times of the year, for Ramadan is an essentially joyous occasion, a time for giving thanks to God. Feasting in the evening is common, and special foods are commonly prepared at family and community meals. Ramadan food specialities vary across Islamic cultures, for example, Syrian *shakreeyeh* (lamb in minty yogurt sauce), Turkish *kaahk Ramazan* (sourdough crescent rolls), and Moroccan *harira* (lamb and lentil stew).

At the close of Ramadan comes the three-day festival of 'Id al-Fitr, commonly known as "Sweet Id." The celebration is a way of thanking Allah for providing Muslims with the strength to have fasted successfully, and it is marked with feasting and gift-giving. It is characterized by the serving of sweet dishes, such as *sawaiyan*, a fine vermicelli boiled with milk and sugar. In Malaysia, *ketupat*, rice cooked in coconut leaves, and *rendang*, a spicy beef dish, are prepared especially for this occasion. 'Id al-Adha, the feast of sacrifice, occurs at the end of the pilgrimage to Mecca. It was previously a four-day festival, now much diminished, in which all adult male Muslims sacrificed a lamb, goat, or cow. Islamic prescriptions require that the sacrificial meat be divided into three equal portions: one for the family, one for friends, relatives, and neighbors, and one for charity. This is in remembrance of God's mercy in allowing Abraham to sacrifice a ram instead of his son, Ishmael. *Ashura* is a joyous occasion for Sunnis, though it is a solemn historical remembrance for Shi'ites.

See also **Africa: North Africa; Asia, Central; Christianity; Fasting and Abstinence; Feasts, Festivals, and Fasts; Holidays; Iberian Peninsula; Iran; Judaism; Middle East; Religion and Food.**

BIBLIOGRAPHY

All citations from the Qur'an are taken from:

'Ali, 'Abdullah Yusuf. *The Meaning of the Holy* Qur'an. 9th ed. Beltsville, Md.: Amana, 1998.

Abbas, Ali, ed. *A Shi'ite Encyclopedia*. Available on-line at: http://www.al-Islam.org/encyclopedia/chapter7/3.html

Hussaini, Mohammed M. *Islamic Dietary Concepts and Practice*. Chicago: Islamic Food and Nutrition Council of America, 1993.

Welch, Andrew T. "Islam." In *A New Handbook of Living Religions*, edited by John R. Hinnells, pp. 162–235. Cambridge, Mass.: Blackwell, 1997.

Paul Fieldhouse

SUFISM

Sufis are members of a small Islamic sect that arose as a protest against the growing worldliness of Muslims after the time of the Prophet. Sufis strive to imitate the words and deeds of Muhammad, and traditionally adopt a life of poverty and abstinence. Although Sufism is firmly anchored in orthodox Islamic doctrine, it emphasizes the inner pursuit of love, obedience, and devotion to God over concern with the outward law or *shari'a*, and is often associated with mysticism and esotericism. There are hundreds of Sufi orders that have developed within different cultural contexts so that there is no one Sufi way.

Role of Food in the Sufi Tradition

Sufis are guided by the *adab*, written treatises that prescribe manners or norms of conduct modeled on the life of Muhammad, which includes the food sayings and practices of the Prophet in minute detail. Muhammad praises the virtues of hospitality, generosity, and moderation, and food was and is clearly seen as a means of encouraging these virtues. As an integral part of the daily spiritual life of Sufis, food provides a way of sharing in the greatest of Divine blessings, of creating unity among people and of linking to all creation. Hospitality and eating together were highly commended by Muhammad and, since early times, Sufis have been associated with the serving of food to others. Communal kitchens and guest lodges for feeding the poor and travelers were features of early Sufi settlements, a tradition that continues in Sahas, or Sufi centers where massive concrete tables may serve up to one hundred diners at a sitting. At *moulid* festivals, feeding stations are set up to offer food and drink to passers-by.

Food Symbolism and Rituals

There is extensive use of food imagery and metaphor in Sufi writings. Sugar and other sweet foods represent the sweetness of piety and community with God, while salt symbolizes purity and incorruptibility. Bread is regarded as sacred in Islam and is treated reverentially. Through the pronouncement of *Bismallah* during the bread-making process, the bread is imbued with spiritual power or *baraka*, which is shared by those who eat the bread. The transformation of the raw wheat to finished bread is used as an analogy for Sufi spiritual development.

Sufi ritual observances (*dhikr*) are concerned with remembrance of God through exaltation and praise. Singing, dancing, and drumming are commonly part of such rituals, as is sharing of food. For example, *ashura* is a dish that takes its name from the festival celebrated by all followers of Islam. During preparation of the *ashura*, Mevlevi Sufis stir the pot in a special way while pronouncing the name of God. Sharing the *ashura* then becomes a way of spreading remembrance of God in the form of bodily nourishment.

Holidays and Festivals

Sufis observe general Muslim holidays and festivals. *Ashura* has particular significance for Sufis and Shi'a. In addition, they celebrate numerous saints' days, or *moulids*. Major *moulid* festivals attract hundreds of thousands of people and can last for two to three weeks. Sufi orders set up hospitality stations (*khidamet*) in public buildings, in tents, or simply on cloths spread on the ground. Drink and (usually) food are offered to passers-by, and must be accepted as the food contains the *baraka* of the saint being honored and therefore confers spiritual blessing on the recipient. For the poor, these stations provide an additional opportunity for physical as well as spiritual nourishment.

Fasting and Feasting

Fasting is an essential feature of Sufism, especially during the forty-day retreat undertaken by initiates in many orders. Early Sufis placed great emphasis on asceticism in the pursuit of self-control and suppression of worldly desires. Eating was seen to be an important source of potential harm to the new initiate, and there are many Sufi stories of extreme restraint. Later, excessive fasting came to be viewed as unfavorably as excessive eating, for the message of the *adab* was one of moderation. Indeed, Muhammad even enjoined His followers to break a fast if invited to eat, for to refuse an invitation to share in God's blessing was wrong.

Food and Social Circumstance: Prescriptions and Proscription

While the asceticism of early Sufism has largely disappeared, gluttony is frowned upon and moderation is enjoined. Sufis follow Qur'anic injunctions regarding food and are usually fastidious about observing the prohibition on pork consumption. While many Muslims do eat meat other than pork, Sufi teachings recommend that such meat be consumed only in small quantities. Some orders, both ancient and modern, have praised vegetarianism as a more compassionate practice, and have viewed animal consumption as conducive to animalistic behavior.

See also **Fasting and Abstinence: Islam; Iran; Islam: Shi'ite Islam; Islam: Sunni Islam; Middle East; Religion and Food.**

BIBLIOGRAPHY

Hoffman, Valerie. "Eating and Fasting for God in the Sufi Tradition." *Journal of the American Academy of Religion* 62, no. 3 (1995): 465–484.

Reynolds, Gabriel Said. "The Sufi Approach to Food: A Case Study of Adab." *The Muslim World* 90 (2000): 198–217.

Seidel, Kathleen. *Serving the Guest: A Sufi Cookbook and Art Gallery 2000*. Site posted August 2001. Available on the Internet at http://www.superluminal.com/cookbook/.

Paul Fieldhouse

ISRAEL. *See* Judaism; Middle East.

ITALY.

> *This entry includes four subentries:*
> Northern Italy
> Southern Italy
> The Italian Meal
> Tradition in Italian Cuisine

NORTHERN ITALY

Northern Italy occupies an area that stretches from the southern Alps south to the Po valley and from the northernmost coast of the Tyrrhenian Sea in Liguria west to the coast of the Adriatic Sea on the northeastern side of Italy. Northern Italian cuisine is distinguished from those of Central, Southern Peninsular, and Insular Italian by the predominant use of butter, cream, cheeses, rice, potatoes, baccalá (dried salted codfish), polenta (corn mush), wines used for cooking, hams, sausages, beef, chicken, and venison, and the occasional use of a much lighter olive oil—produced in limited quantities in the regions of Emilia-Romagna, Veneto, Trentino, and Lombardy—than that of the south.

It is the culinary expression of eight regions where dumplings of all sizes and shapes have been prepared since at least the twelfth century B.C.E. Processed regional foods also include regional meat and fish specialties, such as *Bresaola* (Valle d'Aosta air-dried beef), *Mocetta* (Valle D'Aosta's air-dried mountain goat ham), *Mosciame* (Ligurian dried filet of tuna and dolphin), *Missoltitt* (Lake Como's sun-dried smelts), *Gianchetti* (blanched baby anchovies), *Ciccioli* (lard-rendered pork scraps), *Speck* (Alto Adige's air-cured bacon), *Mortadella* (baloney from Bologna), and several varieties of *Prosciutto* (air-dried ham).

Northern Italian cuisine favors mild-tasting, creamy, meat-rich, and nutritious dishes inspired by a territory that is an extended vineyard. It has also produced many dishes and specialties that originated with ancient Roman Catholic religious traditions. Besides creating Christmas and Easter specialties such as *Panettone* (Christmas fruitcake), *Colomba* Pasquale (a dove-shaped cake prepared

BOILED MEAT

Boiled meat was less desirable than roasted meat in many societies. A story told by Marcel Rouff (Hazan, 1980, p. 273) illustrates how one cook overcame this prejudice. Dodin-Bouffant served it to the Prince of Eurasia, who was offended at first to be served such a low-status food, but he soon changed his mind about boiled beef. When Dodin-Bouffant's formidable boiled beef finally arrived—reviled, despised, and an insult to the Prince and all of gastronomy—it was monstrously imposing, borne on a huge platter, and held so high and at arm's length by the head chef that at first the anxious guests were unable to catch a glimpse of it. However, when it was lowered onto the table with straining caution, there were several minutes of stunned silence. Each guest recovered his composure in a characteristic way. Rabaz and Magot inwardly berated themselves for having doubted the Master; Trifouille was seized with panic before such genius; Beaubois trembled with emotion. As for the Prince of Eurasia, his reaction wavered among the worthy desire to make a duke of Dodin-Bouffant, as Napoleon had wished to make a duke of Corneille (a seventeenth-century French dramatist); a wild longing to offer the gastronome half of his fortune and his throne if only he would agree to oversee his banquets; annoyance at being taught such an obvious lesson; and impatience to taste the heady enchantments of the culinary marvel set before him.

Judit Katona-Apte

during Easter), *Uovo di Pasqua* (chocolate Easter egg), Northern Italian cuisine also includes dishes that follow Catholic Church mandates regarding food including "no-meat-on-Friday" or "fat and meat during Carnival prior to Lent" with specialties such as *Crostoli* (fried, and sometimes twisted, ribbons of dough), also called *Sfrappole, Fritole, Chiacchere, Lattughe, Nastri, Grostul,* or *Zeppole,* depending on the regional dialect.

Favorite ingredients of this cuisine are wild foods such as frogs, snails, truffles, mushrooms, and nuts. Typical first-course dishes of Northern Italy include stuffed ring- or square-shaped pasta—tortelli, tortellini, tortelloni, ravioli, agnoli, agnolotti, pansotti, capelletti, and capellacci—served either in clear broth or topped with sauces. Northern Italy is also home to gnocchi (finger-sized potato dumplings), lasagna, world-famous cheeses —Gorgonzola, Fontina, Taleggio, Mascarpone, Parmigiano Reggiano, and Grana Padano—and innumerable

varieties of risotto (creamed rice): risotto with truffles (*Risotto con Tartufi*), buds of hops (*Risotto ai Bruscanzoli*), red-and-white chicory (*Risotto al Radicchio*), dandelion (*Risotto coi Brusaoci*), frogs (*Risotto con le Rane*), snails (*Risotto e Lumache*), baby pig tails (*Risotto con Codine di Maiale*), chicken livers (*Risotto con Fegatini di Pollo*), filets of lake perch (*Risotto con Filetti di Pesce Persico*), sausage meat (*Risotto con Luganege*), peas (*Risi e Bisi*), asparagus (*Risotto e Sparaghi*), artichokes (*Risotto coi Carciofi*), porcini mushrooms (*Risotto ai Funghi*), and squid with its black ink (*Risotto Nero alle Seppie*).

Northern Italian desserts are creamy and rich rather than sweet: *Zuccotto* (Lombardy's cupola-shaped whipped

Polenta maker. From a woodcut printed in Milan about 1860. ROUGHWOOD COLLECTION.

Northern Italy is comprised of several small geographically defined areas distinguished by specialty dishes that feature locally grown and foraged foods.

The Alpine Range Area
The Alpine Range Area contains portions of northern Piedmont and northern Friuli-Venezia Giulia and the regions of Trentino-Alto Adige and Aosta. In the south, the Alpine Range gradually opens onto a wide valley of well-tended fruit orchards and vineyards and an expanse of farmlands and plains.

Trentino-Alto Adige. Three cultural traditions (German, Italian, and Ladin [northern Italian and Swiss]), which at times have clashed politically, have produced a cuisine that offers an array of specialties made with potatoes, cabbage, barley, and rye or other foods procured by hunting or forest foraging. Specialties in Trentino-Alto Adige use snails, chestnuts, wild nuts, wild mushrooms, and meats from domesticated animals. The region's cuisine reflects the taste for wines and *Grappa* (brandy made from distilled grape skins; also regionally called "schnaps"), preserved and air-cured or smoked sausages and meats, slow-cooking stews and soups with barley, freshwater fish from volcanic lakes and glacial streams, lots of sauerkraut, dumplings of all sizes and shapes, dry and long-lasting rye breads, and simple fruit-rich desserts such as Strudel.

Specialty dishes of this region reflect the influences of German and Swiss cuisines and include *Risotto al Teroldego* (rice with red Teroldego wine), *Spezzatino alla Pusterese* (paprika-flavored beef stew), *Tortel di Patate* (potato pancakes), *Torta di Mele* (apple cake), *Carre di Maiale con Crauti* (pork shoulder with sauerkraut), *Pollo al Cren* (stewed chicken in horseradish gravy), and *Camoscio alla Tirolese* (stewed mountain goat Tirolean-style).

Veneto and Friuli Venezia Giulia. Both of these northeastern areas of Italy share a border with Austria, and lie near Slovenia and the former Yugoslavia. Both Veneto and Friuli Venezia Giulia are renowned for their vegetables such as radicchio (a red winter lettuce similar to chicory), fennel, and asparagus. Both regions are also famous for their sausages and hams, for example, a prosciutto from San Daniele, as well as a fruity sparkling white wine (*Prosecco di Conegliano*). Venice and Trieste, port cities on the Adriatic Sea, boast a thriving fishing industry.

Specialty dishes of this area reflect both the cultural influences of German and Slavic cuisines and the foods available from the land and sea. Some of the most notable dishes include *Lasagna al Papavero* (lasagna with a poppy seed stuffing), *Suf* (a watery corn mush), *Cialzons* (stuffed pasta pockets), *Verze Impinide* (stuffed cabbage leaves), *Capriolo in Salmi* (stewed deer), *Us in Fonghet* (eggs with porcini mushrooms), *Risotto al Tagio* (rice with eel and shrimp), *Polenta e Osei* (corn mush and roasted birds), *Sardele in Soar* (marinated and fried anchovies),

cream and chocolate trifle), *Profiterol* (Lombardy's chocolate-glazed and cream-filled pastry puffs), *Tiramisu* (Venetia and Lombardy's layered zabaglione trifle), *Monte Bianco* (Piedmont's liqueur-flavored chestnut and whipped cream dessert), *Strudel* (Alto Adige's fruit-filled strudel), and *Sbrisolona* (Emilia-Romagna's dry pound cake).

Food portions for Northern Italian meals are small or moderate. What is considered most important is the variety of courses and the type of dishes, not the amount of food. Classic meals are served either with wine or mineral water, which can be sparkling or natural. Over time, multicultural influences from abroad, especially of German, central European, or U.S. origin, have introduced the serving of beer (*birra*) or coke (*coca*) with certain specialties such as *Wuerstel con Crauti* (German sausages with sauerkraut) or pizza. Sweet beverages, sodas, or milk shakes may be graciously tolerated by Italians if they are served by foreigners with classic Northern Italian meals, but they are not recommended according to classic serving standards.

pork caul), *Minestra di Riso, Latte, e Castagne* (chestnut chowder with rice), *Tajarin* (very fine ribbon pasta similar to angel hair), *Lumache al Barbera* (snails stewed in red Barbera wine), *Leper alla Vignarola* (hare stewed in wine and grapes), *Rane Ripiene* (stuffed frogs), and *Zabajone* (egg custard with Marsala wine).

Lombardy

The wealthy, industrialized region of Lombardy is located within the Piedmont and Lombardy Plains Region and shares its eastern border with Switzerland. The cuisine of this region includes lots of rice, plenty of meat, some olive oil, brightly colored, expensive ingredients such as saffron and candied fruit, famous soft cheeses named for the town or area where they originate—Gorgonzola, Taleggio, and Certosa—lake or river fish, and pasta pockets. Lombardy is also famous for its ice cream factories.

Lombardy's specialty recipes feature hearty, one-dish meals: *Buseca* (stewed tripe), *Caseula* (sausages, spare ribs, and ham hocks with stewed cabbage), *Polenta Vuncia* (corn mush with butter, cheese, and sage leaves), *Luc-*

PANETTONE

Panettone appeared in northern Italy around the fifteenth century. Professional bakers probably developed panettone since the process involved is highly complex and requires facilities and equipment that the home kitchen of the past lacked. As the bread's popularity grew, people began to speculate about its origin. The most popular legend concerns a young Milanese nobleman who fell in love with the daughter of a baker, named Toni. To impress the girl's father, the young man disguised himself as a baker's boy and invented a sweet, wonderful bread of rare delicacy and unusual size with a top shaped like a church dome. This new, fruitcakelike bread enjoyed enormous success, with people coming to the bakery in droves at all hours to purchase the magnificent *Pan de Toni* (Tony's Bread).

Judit Katona-Apte

---

and *Insalata di Radicchio alla Vicentina* (Vicenza-style radicchio salad with bacon dressing).

Valle d'Aosta and Piemonte (Piedmont). These regions both fall within the Alpine Range Area and the Piedmont and Lombardy Plain Area, and share borders with France and Switzerland. This geographical proximity is reflected in similar methods of food production and culinary traditions influenced by French and Swiss cuisines. The cooks of Valle d'Aosta and Piemonte, like those of Trentino-Alto Adige, use mushrooms, truffles, berries, and nuts foraged on the southern mountain slopes.

Valle d'Aosta's recipes use *Jambon de Bosses* (cured ham), *Bresaola* (cured beef), *Mocetta* (mountain goat ham), chunky soups topped with mountain cheeses, stews made with game, for example, mountain goat, deer, hare, and pheasant, *lard d'Arnad* (bacon lard), frogs, snails, white and black truffles, fleshy and thorny cardons (or cardoons, relatives of the artichoke), rare ovuli mushrooms (egg-shaped *amanita avoidea*), celery, cabbage, asparagus, potatoes, carrots, and cold-climate grains—rye, buckwheat, barley, and lots of corn mush (polenta). Piemonte is home to the world-renowned sparkling white wine, Asti Spumante, *Savoiardi* (ladyfinger cookies from the province of Savoia), *Gianduiotti* (chocolates made in Turin), and Fontina cheese.

Typical dishes of these regions include *Grissini* (thin bread sticks), *Bagna Cauda* (mixed vegetables with anchovy oil dip), *Griva* (meat loaf wrapped and baked in

---

PORCHETTA

Although eating meat was regarded as disgusting by the upper classes in imperial Rome, pork, along with bread, was distributed among the poor in the streets to maintain order.

Porchetta, roast suckling pig, is probably of Etruscan origin, and remains popular in areas that once comprised Etruria. A young pig is deboned, stuffed with a mixture of herbs, salt, and pepper, and roasted whole in a wood-burning oven. There are regional differences in the stuffing: stalks and leaves of wild fennel and garlic in Umbria, wild herbs in the Marches, and rosemary and garlic in Rome. In Sardinia, the dish is called *porceddu* and is flavored with myrtle leaves. While the herbs vary, pepper is its most distinctive spice.

At one time, *porchetta* may have been a mountain food, favored in the winter and prepared primarily for feasts. *Porchetta* has become a regular item at fairs and weekly markets such as *porta portese* (the Sunday morning market) in Rome, where it is sold from the back of trucks or wagons. The slices of *porchetta* are served between the halves of a roll without accompaniments.

Judit Katona-Apte

Truffle harvesting near Norcia, Umbria, Italy. © OWEN FRANKEN/ CORBIS.

resources of its geography. Nevertheless, this region has given the world several popular dishes, for example, focaccia (olive oil bread) and pesto (a pasta sauce made of basil, pine nut, and garlic). Seafood common in Ligurian recipes includes breams (*paraghi* and *saraghi*), red mullets (*triglie*), herring (*nasello*), swordfish (*pesce spada*), mussels (*muscoli*), blanched baby anchovies or sardines (*gianchetti*, also called *bianchetti*), and air-dried filets of delfin or tuna (*mosciame*).

Typical Ligurian dishes include *Trofie al pesto* (twisted pasta dumplings with pesto sauce), *Pansoti alla Salsa di Noci* (pasta pockets filled with an herb stuffing and topped with walnut sauce), *Moscardini alla Genovese* (Genoa-style stuffed squid), *Torta di Bietole* (swiss chard quiche), *Stoccafisso in Umido* (dried codfish soaked and then stewed), *Mitili alla Spezzina* (La Spezia-style stuffed mussels), *Castagnaccio* (chestnut-flour cake moistened with olive oil), and several stuffed vegetable dishes, for example, stuffed artichokes or zucchini flowers.

Emilia-Romagna

Emilia-Romagna, with its eastern coast along the Adriatic Sea, is probably the culinary divide between Northern and Central Italian cuisines. It is centrally located and touches the regions of Piemonte, Lombardy, Veneto, Liguria, Tuscany, and the Marches. In addition to its plentiful seafood resources, which include sole, hake, herring, mullet, turbot, monkfish, grouper, clams, mussels, cuttlefish, and mantis shrimp, Emilia-Romagna is famous for its lasagna, ragu (a meat sauce), meat-filled tortellini, and Parmesan cheese (Parmigiano Reggiano). The city of Modena is well known for its prosciutto, balsamic vinegar, and several sausage specialties, which include *Coppa* (pork sausage), *Pancetta* (pork belly sausage), *Cotechino* (pork meat and rind sausage), *Mortadella*, and *Zampone*, pork leg stuffed with meat and rind. Parma is also famous for its prosciutto.

Typical dishes that incorporate Emilia-Romagna's specialties include *Brodetto* (fish and seafood chowder), *Canocchie Al'olio e Prezzemolo* (shrimp snappers in olive oil and parsley dressing), *Anolini in Brood* (ring-shaped pasta pockets in broth), *Polpettone alla Bolognese* (Bologna-style meat loaf), *Erbazzone all'Emiliana* (Emilia-style quiche of onions and greens), *Cotechino in Galera* (cotechino sausage encased in meat loaf and cooked in red wine), *Asparagi alla Parmigiana* (Parma-style asparagus with Parmesan cheese), *Fagioli e Cotiche* (beans cooked with boiled pork rinds), *Bollito Misto* (mixed boiled meats), and *Lumache alla Piacentina* (Parma-style stewed snails). *Piadina*, a thin, parched, unleavened bread wheel, is also a specialty of this region.

Parmigiano Reggiano and Grana Padano

No discussion of Northern Italian cuisine can ignore two of its fine cheeses, Parmigiano Reggiano and Grana Padano. Both must be matured very slowly.

cio in Stufato (wine-moistened stewed pike), *Laciaditt* (apple fritters), *Cotoletta alla Milanese* (Milan-style breaded veal cutlet), *Frittata di Rane* (a frittata with frog), and *Zuppa alla Pavese* (Pavia-style bread soup with cheese and raw eggs).

Liguria

Liguria, located in the southern portion of Northern Italy, borders France and touches the Piedmont and Emilia-Romagna areas as well as Tuscany, a region of central Italy. It is a coastal region and its port cities—Genoa, La Spezia, and Imperia—provide its cooks with fish and other varieties of seafood. The copious use of locally produced olive oil is undoubtedly the most notable ingredient in Ligurian cuisine, an element that distinguishes it from the other regional cuisines of Northern Italy. It is used in raw, cooked, and fried dishes, for making pasta sauces with nuts and herbs, for moistening bread, and in desserts.

Ligurian cooking reflects its proximity to the food resources of the Ligurian Sea and the limited agricultural

Parmigiano Reggiano, usually called Parmesan cheese, has been made regionally since the early thirteenth century and has become a symbol of classic Italian cuisine. It is a semi-fat, hard, flaky cheese made of raw cow's milk, recognizable by its large, wheel-shaped forms, covered by a yellow wax rind, and marked with the dotted brand name, Parmigiano Reggiano. Commonly used as a grated cheese, it has a delicate, fragrant, and unique flavor that it imparts to foods. Under Italian law, Parmigiano Reggiano has a prescribed ripening period, usually about two years. It is produced according to traditional Parmigiano Reggiano methods in plants located in specific areas of Emilia-Romagna, which include Parma and Reggio-Emilia. Other Northern Italian locales that produce Parmigiano Reggiano are Bologna, Mantova, and Modena.

Grana Padano is cooked, cylindrical, semi-fat, hard, grainy cheese. First made at the beginning of the millennium by Cistercian monks in Lombardy, near Chiaravalle, it became known as *grana* (literally, 'grain') due to its grainy consistency. It is commonly used as a table cheese, but, like Parmigiano Reggiano, it is also used as a grated cheese. It is produced in the Po Valley and Delta region in Bologna, Mantova, Asti, Cuneo, Brescia, Como, Cremona, Milan, Trento, Treviso, Venezia, Verona, Ferrara, Piacenza, Ravenna, and other cities throughout the area.

BIBLIOGRAPHY

Alberini, Massimo. *Storia della cucina Italiana*. Casale Montferrato, AL: Piemme, 1992.

Barilla. *The Four Seasons of Pasta: The Recipe Book*. Westport, Conn.: Barilla.

Biagi, Enzo. *La Geografia di Enzo Biagi: Italia*. Milan: Rizzoli, 1975.

Carnacina and Veronelli. *La Cucina Rustica: Italia Settentrionale*. Milan: Rizzoli, 1966.

Gosetti della Salda, Anna. *Le Ricette Regionali*. Milan: Casa Editrice Solares, 1967.

Hazan, Marcella. *The Classic Italian Cookbook*. London: McMillan, 1980.

McKnight, Kent, and Vera McKnight. *Mushrooms: A Field Guide to Mushrooms*. Boston: Houghton Mifflin, 1987.

Maier-Bruck, Franz. *Das Grosse Sacher-Kochbuch*. Munich: Schuler, 1975.

Mariani, John. *The Dictionary of Italian Food and Drink*. New York: Broadway, 1998.

Morricone-Pedicino. *Dizionario dietetico degli alimenti*. Milan: Garzanti, 1986.

Ogrizek, Doré, ed. *Italy*. New York: McGraw-Hill, n.d.

Palombi, Arturo, and Mario Santarelli. *Gli Animali Commestibili dei Mari d'Italia*. Milan: Ulrico Hoepli, 1986.

Parisi, Livio. *Il Garda in Pentola*. Verona: Settore Tutela Faunistico Ambientale, 1996.

Paoletti, Pier Maria. *I Ristoranti di Panorama: 252 Itinerari Gastronomici alla Scoperta della Buona Tavola Italiana*. Milan: Mondadori, 1975.

Piccinardi, Antonio. *Dizionario di Gastronomia*. Milan: Rizzoli, 1993.

Plachutta and Wagner. *Die Gute Küche: Das Oesterreichische Jahrhundert Kochbuch*. Vienna: Donauland Kremayr and Scheriau, 1993.

Root, Waverly. *The Food of Italy*. New York: Vintage, 1997.

Testi, Antonio. *Il Libro dei Funghi d'Italia*. Verona: Demetra, 1995.

Zanoni, Mario. *A Tavola con Maria Luigi: Il Servizio di Bocca della Duchessa di Parma dal 1815 al 1847*. Parma: Artegrafica Silva, 1991.

Elisabeth Giacon Castleman

SOUTHERN ITALY

For the purpose of this entry, southern Italy is defined as Rome and all areas south of Rome (see map). Many ethnic groups, such as the Greeks, Spaniards, and Arabs, have passed through southern Italy over the millennia and influenced its cuisines. Traditionally, southern Italians have been much poorer than their northern counterparts. The poverty of the south has resulted in unique regional cuisines that bear little resemblance to the dairy-based cuisines of the north. Rome, traditionally part of middle Italy, today has a cuisine more southern than northern in temperament.

Interestingly, the ancestors of most Italian Americans are from the South; the dire poverty of southern Italy led to large-scale emigration from regions like Campania, Calabria, and Sicily to the United States. It follows logically that Italian-American cuisine is mainly derived from the cuisines of southern Italy. Pizza, pastas with tomato sauce, organ meats, and eggplant-based dishes are all common components of both southern Italian and Italian-American cuisine. Southern Italy is a historically poor region, and so the population used what they had available—inexpensive ingredients like capers and olives, hot peppers, garlic, and anchovies—to create flavorful and unique dishes. Unlike the northern pastas from regions such as Emilia-Romagna, southern pastas are made without eggs and from harder flour and are often shaped rather than rolled, resulting in a chewier pasta like *orecchiette* ("little ears") from Apulia (Puglia) or *conchiglie* (shells) from Campania. These less-rich pastas need heavier sauces.

In the South there are few cows, so beef, butter, and cream are not part of the diet. The favored cheese is *mozzarella di bufala*, which is made here wholly or largely from buffalo milk (that is, the milk of the water buffalo, not that of the American bison), which has a distinctive taste. There are also goats and sheep—yielding meat and cheeses—and pigs and chickens. Lamb dominates mountain cooking. In the past, young spring lamb was reserved for important occasions such as Easter or weddings and baptisms, but today it is more common and often available year-round. Near the coasts, saltwater fish such as *spigola* (sea bass), *orata* (bream), and *dentice* (dentex, a fish related to the porgy), as well as a variety of shellfish and cuttlefish, are available.

Olive oil is produced around the Apennines and in southern Apulia, and is used all over the South. Suitable soil and temperature contribute to an abundance of vegetables and fruits, and many types of herbs are also produced. Eggplant is a major food item, as it grows better in the South than in the North and can be prepared in many different ways; *melanzana*, the Italian word for eggplant, derives from *mela insana* ("noxious apple").

Rome, Naples, and Sicily are places that non-Italians are familiar with; however, there are other regions in Southern Italy, and some of their food culture is also described here.

Rome

Rome is truly the Eternal City. Its rich and fascinating history includes the elaborate public and private feasts held by ancient Roman emperors. That said, modern Roman cuisine is actually quite simple and much influenced by other regions. Dishes are prepared simply with a few inexpensive ingredients. Antipasti are not elaborate, pasta sauces are quick to prepare, and there is a large variety of vegetables (especially leafy greens).

Historically, Rome was the place where cattle were butchered, and so Romans are famous for their use of the *quinto quarto*, or fifth quarter, the organ meats and parts of the cattle that were left over after butchering. Two famous Roman dishes, *coda alla vaccinara*, a stew of oxtail braised for a long time with celery, carrots, onions, tomatoes, herbs, and spices in white wine, and *rigatoni alla pajata* or *pagliata*, short, tubular pasta with beef or veal intestines in a tomato sauce, were born around the communal slaughterhouse in Testaccio.

A popular meat is lamb, which is usually roasted in the oven (*abbacchio al forno*) and served with potatoes. Examples of other meat dishes considered very Roman are *pollo alla Romana*, chicken with red and yellow peppers; *saltimbocca alla Romana* (literally, jump into the mouth) made of thin slices of veal, prosciutto, and sage; and *trippa alla Romana*, which is tripe in a tomato and mint sauce.

Bucatini all'amatriciana (tubular pasta with bacon and tomato sauce) originated from country kitchens, where bacon, olive oil, and fresh tomatoes were plentiful. Fettuccine Alfredo is just *pasta al burro* (pasta with butter) from Alfredo's restaurant in Rome. Some other popular pasta sauces are *cacio e pepe* (pecorino cheese and pepper), *carbonara* (bacon, eggs, and pecorino and Parmesan cheeses) and *arrabbiata* (hot pepper and tomatoes). *Gnocchi alla Romana* are dumplings made of semolina, eggs, milk, and cheese. *Spaghetti alla puttanesca* (literally, spaghetti whorestyle) is made with olives, anchovies, and capers.

There are also soups, all with some version of pasta in them, such as *stracciatelle* (literally, "little rags"), so named from the thin batter of egg, flour, and Parmesan that is poured into the chicken or beef broth used. Others feature herbs, such as lentil soup flavored with *nepitella* (wild mint) and bean soup flavored with rosemary. There are also *minestra de ceci e pasta* (soup with chickpeas and pasta) and *zuppa di arzilla* (fish soup).

Romans say it takes four people to make a proper salad: a spendthrift for the oil, a miser for the vinegar, a wise man for seasoning, and a madman for mixing. *Panzanella* is bread salad with tomatoes, cucumbers, onion, basil, and dressing. A classic Roman winter salad is *puntarelle*, shoots of a particular variety of chicory with a bitter undertone, tossed with a dressing made with olive oil, anchovies, garlic, and lemon juice. Some salads are a mix of greens sometimes called *misticanza*, preferably with the addition of *rughetta* (also called *rucola*, *rocola*, and, as it is in English, *arugula*). More recently tomatoes, shredded carrots, and even canned maize (corn) may be added to salads.

Artichokes are also seasonal and popular as in *carciofi alla Romana* (Roman style), which are stood upright in a pan as they cook with garlic, mint, parsley, and an abundant drizzle of olive oil. Another famous preparation is made from *romanesco* artichokes, which are round and lack a spiny choke. These reach gastronomic heights when prepared *alla giudia* (Jewish style), in which the artichokes are flattened and deep-fried to look like golden sunflowers and their leaves have a delicious nutty crunchiness. This dish has contributed to the fame of the restaurants in the Roman ghetto.

Also popular in Rome are such stuffed vegetables as tomatoes stuffed with rice and mozzarella, or zucchini stuffed with chopped meat. Then there are vegetables, mainly greens, that are prepared *all'agro* (with a lemon-juice dressing) or *in padella* (stir-fried).

Rome is partial to frying: *fritto misto* (mixed fry) can contain shrimp and *calamari* (squid); or artichoke and brain; or different cheeses; or a mixture of vegetables; or *supplì al telefono*, a croquette of rice with mozzarella cheese in the middle—when one bites into it the mozzarella flows out in long threads, as in a telephone cord. The famous *fiori di zucca* (zucchini flowers) are stuffed with mozzarella and anchovy and dipped in batter before frying. Cod is also batter-dipped and fried (*baccalà filetti*).

Pecorino romano and ricotta are the most favored cheeses. Ricotta, a soft sheep's milk cheese, is prepared inside wicker baskets.

Rosette (hollow, very crisp rolls) are very characteristic of Rome, as is *casareccio*, a chewy, peasant-style bread.

Favorite desserts in Rome are fresh fruits, especially strawberries from Nemi (a town on the outskirts of Rome), or *macedonia* (fruit salad). Many other popular desserts have originated elsewhere, such as *tiramisu* (literally, "pick me up"), made of mascarpone (a very creamy, soft cheese, typically made from cow's milk), ladyfingers, coffee, and other ingredients specific to the home or restaurant; *torta de la nonna* (cake with custard and pine nuts); *panna cotta* (boiled cream), served with a variety of toppings, such as berries, chocolate, and caramel; *profiteroles* (mounds of little cream puffs drizzled with chocolate); and *gelato* (ice cream) in flavors such as lemon, coconut, orange, and pineapple, frozen and served in a container made of the skin or shell of its source.

Examples of foods reserved for specific festive occasions in Rome are lentils with *cotechino* and *zampone* (varieties of pork sausage), served on New Year's Eve; *porchetta* (roast stuffed pork), traditional at the festival of Noantri in Trastevere; *pan giallo*, a fruit-and-nut cake served at Christmas; *bigne di Giuseppe* (fried doughnuts), filled with cream or chocolate eaten for Father's Day; and *maritozzi* (raisin buns), traditional for Lent.

Campania and Naples

Naples has long guided the gastronomy of the region and its cooking has had the most influence on the way non-Italians regard Italian food. It is said that the true Neapolitan is poor, but likes to eat well and is proud of the invention of three of the tastiest food items: pizza, tomato sauce, and macaroni. Poor immigrants exported Neapolitan cuisine, rich in tomato sauce, garlic, olive oil, and black olives, to the United States and elsewhere. As meat and seafood were out of reach for the poor at home, the transported cuisine used more meat but fewer vegetables; the classic Italian-American dish, spaghetti with meatballs, for example, is not common in Italy. Immigrants also used more garlic and oregano.

But Naples was a kingdom that in the households of the nobility also had a refined cuisine that required extensive effort; a simple *ragù* (sauce), for example, took many hours to prepare. The master of the kitchen of the noble palaces was the *monzu* (a term derived from the French *monsieur*), a combination of cook and artist, revered and respected by all. He was responsible for the preparation of elaborate and rich court cuisine with dishes like *braciolla* (stuffed beef roll), mozzarella *in carozza* (fried mozzarella sandwich), and *timballi* of pasta or rice with eggplant, cheese, and tomato. Desserts like *baba* (a cake made of yeast dough with syrup) and *sfogliatelle* (literally, "little sheets"—flaky pastry wrapped around sweet items) were lavish and unusual. *Spumone*, an ice-cream confection in strips of colors, is also native to Naples.

The cuisine of Campania and of Naples is rich in vegetables and pasta, often layered in casserole dishes. But the Neapolitans also prepare refined seafood dishes such as *zuppa di vongole* (clam soup), or spaghetti *con le vongole in salsa bianca* (with clams in white sauce), or *cozze in culla* (tomatoes stuffed with mussels and a mixture of capers, chopped parsley, oregano, and bread crumbs). A Neapolitan dish still eaten at home is *minestra marinata*, made with pork fat and boiled greens. The richness of the soup depends on the economic conditions of the family; this was the basic daily meal until the arrival of pasta.

The people of Naples were the first to accept the tomato from the New World, at a time when other Europeans believed it to be poisonous.

Arguably, Naples's biggest contribution to world cuisine is pizza. Royalty played an important role in the development of pizza: For example, *pizza Margherita* reflects the three colors in the Italian flag (basil for green, cheese for white, and tomato for red) and was created specifically for King Umberto I's consort, Queen Margherita. Queen Maria Carolina, the moody and autocratic wife of King Ferdinando I of Naples, offered pizza to her entire court.

In the towns of Campania, including Naples, life takes place in the streets. In the working-class districts of Naples, the streets seem to consist of one long outdoor food shop. This tradition has roots in the past when people spent most of their days outdoors. Housing was cramped and uncomfortable, but the weather was warm, very conducive to outdoor living. Even today, one can observe that people spend much time in bars or in piazzas or just sitting on chairs in front of their doors. Until 1800, all kinds of food were eaten outdoors, including macaroni, pizza, and seafood. There was the macaroni vendor, for instance, who scooped out pasta from huge cauldrons and for a few pennies more offered it with tomato sauce or with boiled *polpi* (octopuses) served in a cup with their steaming fragrant broth.

Sicily

Sicily, the Mediterranean island in the sun, close to North Africa, enjoys strong Greek and Arab influences. Its cuisine, specifically its cooking style, has influenced the food culture of Italy and of other parts of the world. On the eastern side of the island, the cuisine is sober and mild, avoids sweet and sour tastes, and is less generous with sugar in sauces; whereas in the western part of Sicily, the influence is Saracen, with strong contrasts and flavors. It is thus not surprising that one of the specialties of Trapani, a seaport in northwestern Sicily, is *cuscusu* (couscous).

The dish more people associate with the island than any other is caponata, a cooked eggplant delight consumed cold and made with a number of ingredients such as celery, capers, anchovies, chilies, olives, tomatoes, and vinegar. It comes in many varieties; some are purely vegetarian, whereas the Palermo version can also contain fish.

Eggplant dishes are definitely favored in Sicily, as are tomatoes and pasta. Pasta varieties are abundant and are often baked into *timballi* (timbales); the most famous of these is *timballo di anellini*, made with ring-shaped dried pasta, *balsamello* (béchamel sauce), ground beef, chicken, peas, and vegetables, all wrapped in lettuce leaves and baked in a mold. A local specialty is spaghetti *con sarde* (with sardines), often prepared with raisins and nuts as well. Sicilian pizza is usually thicker than other varieties, and has anchovies. The fish of the Adriatic Sea are different from those of the Tyrrhenian Sea, and in Sicily there are swordfish from the warm water.

Sicilian cuisine has its own terminology: *arancini* (literally, little oranges) are fried balls of rice, meat, and grated cheese; *quaglie* (quails) are eggplants sliced open and fried in oil; and *falsemagre* (false thins) are meatballs made with salami, hard-boiled eggs, parsley, and other ingredients. Eggplant dishes are often given the appellation *Norma*, as in spaghetti *alla Norma*.

The cheese-making tradition in Sicily is very important. Cheese is a nourishing food that can be processed at the household level and is easily transported and preserved. That is the reason for the heavy reliance on cheese by poor people. Some of the favorites are *pecorino Siciliano*, a cheese with a hard consistency that is made from the ewe's milk and is aged and salted; *Ragusano*, a pear-shaped cheese made from cow's milk, which received its name from the practice of suspending the cheese from a beam with a cord; *caciocavallo Palermitano*, similar to Ragusano but having a pungent odor and a piquant flavor due to the type of grass eaten by the cows; *tuma*, pecorino before it has been salted; and *primosale*, salted only once (*provola* is a smoked version).

Ricotta is made from fresh ewe's milk and is extensively used in Sicilian cooking. Salted and baked ricotta cheeses have been developed in response to the need to preserve them. *Canestrato* owes its name to the pattern created by the wicker baskets in which it is pressed. It is made from ewe's or cow's milk and probably originated from attempts to make pecorino, for which it can be substituted in cooking.

Sicily exceeds all the other regions of Italy in its abundance of sweets, fruits, and ice creams. Candied fruits, sweets made with almond paste, and ice cream are available everywhere. *Cassata* (brick-shaped sponge cake filled with ricotta, candied fruit, and marzipan) may be the most famous of Sicilian desserts. Many of the recipes for Sicilian sweets come from monasteries, and until the turn of the twentieth century their entire production went to the clergy and to Sicily's aristocrats. Some recipes remain a mystery: the nuns of Santo Spirito, for example, refuse to reveal their secrets for making the sweet dessert they sell at their convent in Agrigento, or at the orphanage in Erice. Fortunately, these traditional sweets live on during the religious festivals such as Easter, when desserts made from almond paste in the form of fruits, sheep, and patron saints are sold.

Apulia

Apulia is a region in southeasternmost Italy producing wheat and a variety of vegetables—tomatoes, artichokes, lettuce, fennel, peppers, and onions—citrus fruits, olives, almonds, figs (some dried with almond flavoring), and grapes. Add to this a sea full of fish, as well as fields for grazing, and the result is a variety of ingredients that can easily be combined into a sumptuous cuisine.

Homemade pasta is found in unusual shapes like the *orecchiette* traditionally paired with broccoli rabe, or *cavatelli* (literally, little plugs). For Sunday dinner a favorite is *maccheroni al forno* (baked macaroni), a pie filled with little meatballs, sliced hard-boiled eggs, pieces of artichoke, salami, and cheese. *Ciceri e tria* is composed of fried pasta strips with chickpeas.

Since the sea surrounds three-quarters of the area of Apulia, seafood products are abundant and popular. Sea turtle, oysters, mussels, cuttlefish, and octopus are cooked in simple ways, sometimes even eaten raw in the markets. The dominant meat is lamb, roasted, stewed, or even fried. *Gniumerieddi* are lamb innards cooked with pecorino cheese. Beef is used for either meat sauce or small meatballs, possibly because in poorer times the only cattle to be slaughtered were old and produced tough steaks.

Due to the popularity of lamb and the enormous flocks, cheese made from sheep's milk is very popular, including fresh ricotta and pecorino. A typical snack of this region is the *calzone* (literally, big sock), pizza dough spread with onions, black olives, capers, tomatoes, pecorino cheese, anchovies, and parsley; closed and pinched around the edges; and baked in the oven.

Homegrown yellow and white melons, sweet watermelons and grapes, and *cotognata*, a quince concentrate, are considered appropriate choices for ending a meal.

Abruzzi e Molise

Most of the great cooks of Italy come from the region of Abruzzi, where the fame of the local cooks, who were often highly sought-after by nobles living in other parts of the kingdom, began in the sixteenth century. This geographical area is known for strong flavors: *peperoncino* (hot red pepper) is used to flavor many dishes, and a favorite sauce for pasta is *aglio, olio e peperoncino* (garlic, olive oil, and hot red pepper), which can be heavy going for those not accustomed to spicy food. *Alla chitarra* (guitar-style) is a well-known pasta named after the utensil used for cutting it.

Ideally, the cuisine of Abruzzi is divided between that of the sea and that of the mountains. The first has the classic *brodetto* (fish stew of many different fish) as a principal dish. Other dishes include fried fish and fish in sauces served with pasta, as well as freshwater fish, such as mountain trout and river shrimp. Lamb is the popular meat: *agnello all'arrabbiata* (literally, angry lamb) is a favored spicy entrée. Pizza *sette occhi* is a dessert in which the pastry strips resemble seven eyes.

Among the unique dishes of Molise is *p'lenta d'iragn*, a white polenta made with potatoes and wheat, and served with tomato sauce. *Scamorza* (a cheese similar to mozzarella) is a popular item from the region and is usually served grilled.

Basilicata and Calabria

Basilicata is known for spicy cuisine: as its inhabitants were poor, they made their fare more interesting with the use of spices, such as ginger. Sausages in some parts of northern Italy are still called by an old name for Basilicata (*lucania* or *licanica* or *luganega*), and so are some pasta dishes, such as *cavatelli alla lucana* with mushroom and sausage, or *cavateglie e patate*, pasta and potatoes with a ragù of rabbit and pork. Pasta dishes are often named after towns, such as *orecchiette alla Materana* (a town in Basilicata), which has a sauce made of vegetables and arugula. Other pasta dishes are frequently served *all'arrabbiata*.

In Calabria, pizza is called *pitta* (flat) and is served without tomatoes; *ciambotta* (big mixture) is a vegetable stew of eggplant, potatoes, tomatoes, and onions; *morseddu* (little morsel) is a traditional breakfast dish of pork-tripe stew with liver and herbs served in a pitta; *licurdia* is onion-and-potato soup; and *millecosedde* (thousand things) is a soup of dried beans and vegetables with pasta.

See also **Pasta; Pizza.**

BIBLIOGRAPHY

Bugialli, Giuliano. *Traditional Recipes from the Regions of Italy.* New York: Morrow, 1998.

Johns, Pamela Sheldon. *Italian Food Artisans: Traditions and Recipes.* San Francisco: Chronicle Books, 2000.

Mariani, John. *The Dictionary of Italian Food and Drink.* New York: Broadway Books, 1998.

Root, Waverley. *The Food of Italy.* New York: Vintage Books, 1977.

Scully, Terence, ed. and trans. *The Neapolitan Recipe Collection: Cuoco Napolitano.* (New York, Pierpont Library, MS Buhler 19). Critical Edition and English Translation. Ann Arbor: University of Michigan Press, 2000.

Judit Katona-Apte

THE ITALIAN MEAL

Meals are a central part of Italian family life. Italians are passionate about food and eating, and much of their socializing is done around the sharing of meals. As with most cultures, there are specific dishes associated with specific Italian holidays. Unlike many Western societies, however, Italians have not embraced a multitude of foreign and ethnic ingredients. Although Italian cities have many more foreign and fast-food restaurants than they did ten years ago, most Italian restaurants—and indeed most homes as well—take a more traditional and conservative approach to meals. "Fusion" and "nouvelle cuisine" are not terms commonly associated with Italian meals.

Fast food is popular with the young. Eating fast food is more a social than a culinary experience, and signifies conformity to a peer group, an identity independent of one's household, modernity versus tradition, and being in the company of, and behaving according to the rules of, chosen friends as opposed to family.

Due to Italian attention to tradition, there are reactions. Movements such as *il ricupero* (the retrieval) and *la riscoperta* (the rediscovery) are founded to maintain tradition in the modern world. The best-known such initiative is the "slow-food movement" that began in Italy in 1986 to challenge "fast food," which was believed to harm health, destroy the environment, and wipe out traditional cuisine. By 1999, thirty Italian towns had designated themselves "Slow Cities," where regional tradition in food, parks, and similar values are emphasized over traffic, neon signs, noise, and fast-food chains.

Shopping and Meal Preparation

The traditional Italian housewife shopped daily. Her morning visit to the open-air market was a form of ritual. In separate stalls she would purchase fruits and vegetables, fish or meat, eggs, cheese, and *salumi* (cold cuts), depending upon what was in season and what she needed. If she needed something more in the afternoon, she could pop out to the *latteria* for fresh milk, the *alimentari* (grocery store) for bread, cold cuts, cheese, and packaged foods, the *macelleria* for meat, or the *frutteria* for fruits and vegetables. These small family-owned stores populated every neighborhood. Today, however, things are changing. Supermarkets, especially the megastores, are rapidly replacing small neighborhood shops.

The designation of housewife (though she is likely to be a working woman) above is deliberate, for in traditional Italian society gender roles are closely associated with food preparation. In the home, women are responsible for meals. Men may cook occasionally or prepare a specific dish, but the responsibility for daily cooking rests with women.

Eating Out

Average Italians do not socialize in their homes with friends and acquaintances; meals at home are usually shared with family members. Eating in restaurants with family, friends, and business associates is quite common. On weekends it is not unusual to see extended families of four generations eating at a large table. There are many different types of eating places, as described below.

A *ristorante* is traditionally a proper restaurant. *Ristoranti* have attractive table settings, starched tablecloths and napkins, and numerous choices for every course. To be a waiter is a career opportunity, and many stay with the same restaurant for a lifetime. Female waiters are still infrequent but are increasing in number.

A *trattoria* is a small eatery with a limited menu. An *osteria* is a less sophisticated eating place frequented by neighborhood people, with a few characteristic dishes. Both are simple, family-run operations, in which people often sit at common tables, large sheets of butcher paper under their plates. A pizzeria is an eating establishment specializing in pizza. Some serve only pizza, salads, and antipasti (appetizers), while others also serve pasta dishes and a limited choice of meat dishes.

An *enoteca* is distinguished by its large selection of wine; a limited selection of dishes is served there, usually comprising cold salads and other appetizers. Recently, many have started serving a limited menu of hot foods. A *tavola calda* (snack bar serving hot food, often cafeteria-style) is not considered a restaurant and is used for quick snacks, usually at lunchtime. A *rosticceria* (rotisserie or grill) sells ready-to-eat foods such as grilled chicken, pizza by the slice, roasted potatoes, cooked vegetables, and some baked-pasta dishes to take home. Some of these distinctions are disappearing in the modern world; it is chic today to call a restaurant a *trattoria* or *osteria*, and *enoteche* have become popular eating places.

Coffee Bars. Bars serving mainly coffee during the day are a very important part of Italian social life. The number of ways Italians drink coffee seems to be endless: *espresso* (small but strong), *cappuccino* (espresso with steamed milk), *lungo* (with extra steam), *ristretto* (very strong), *caffè latte* (with much hot milk), *macchiato* (spotted with milk), *corretto* (with a shot of brandy or grappa), *doppio* (double), and *caffè Haag* (decaffeinated), to mention just a few. Romans claim that the quality of the coffee is determined by the three Ms: *Mano, Macchina*, and *Miscela* (hand, machine, and mixture). Italians drink their espresso quickly, unlike other Europeans, who sip it for a long time. Bars also serve fruit juices (*spremuta* or *sugo*), as well as *gelato* (ice cream), *granita* (flavored ices), and, recently, iced tea during the hot season.

People gather in bars to have a drink and a snack. They stand at the counter and read the newspaper. As Italians are avid soccer aficionados, they are likely to be loudly discussing last night's game. Bars that have tables, especially outside, charge extra for sitting at them.

Food Events

Historically, Italians had their major meal, or *pasto*, in the middle of the day, and then rested. Workers would go home to eat and return to the workplace in the afternoon. Today, distances are greater and more people work away from home, and so in many households, *pranzo*, the main meal, is now eaten in the evening. The exception is the Sunday midday meal, considered by many to be the most important meal of the week. On Sunday afternoons (often post-Mass), extended families will gather for large, lengthy multicourse meals.

Breakfast, *piccola colazione* or *prima colazione*, is not a major meal for most Italians. It is usually taken at a bar and includes coffee (often cappuccino) with a pastry such as a *cornetto*, the Italian equivalent of a croissant. There are many types of *cornetti*: plain, or filled with chocolate, cream of rice, jam (called *marmellata*), or custard. Other popular pastries are the brioche and the doughnut.

Structure of a Meal

Most people, when they think of an Italian meal, think of pasta. And while an Italian meal is much more than that, it is indeed the pasta (or at any rate the pasta course) that sets the Italian meal apart. The common American or European practice of serving stews and braises over noodles, rice, or dumplings is not found in Italy. Instead, these starches are served on their own, as a separate course. (The exception is potatoes, which are considered a vegetable, not a starch, and are often served with grilled meats.) Normally, the starch course will be prepared with its own separate sauce, though in the home the starch may be served with the sauce from a stewed or braised dish, followed by the meat from the same dish as a second course.

At first glance, a meal in Italy appears strictly structured. The traditional meal contains at least four courses: the antipasto; the *primo* (first course) of pasta, rice, polenta, or soup; the *secondo* (second course) of meat or fish; and the *dolce* (dessert). However, these multicourse meals are no longer daily occurrences for most Italians. At home, they may have just one or two courses for dinner, and the order of these limited courses contains some flexibility. While the *primo* would never follow the *secondo* (as is obvious from the names), Italians will eat meals of antipasto followed by *primo*; or *primo* followed by antipasto; or, less commonly, antipasto followed by *secondo*, or *secondo* served with selected antipasti on the side. They will not, however, eat two dishes that are considered *primo* together, such as soup followed by pasta, a sequence common in central European meals but shunned by Italians.

Despite eating fewer courses at home, Italians tend to regard eating out as an occasion for a more traditional three- or four-course meal. Bread, wine, and water accompany all meals (except, of course, breakfast), no matter how many courses are served.

Antipasti

Formal meals start with antipasti. There is tremendous range and regional variation, and in many situations an antipasto could be considered an elaborate meal by itself.

There are several bread-based preparations that may be included with an antipasto. Most typical are *bruschetta* (known in Tuscany as *fett'unta*)—toasted or grilled bread rubbed with garlic and drizzled with fruity olive oil (chopped tomatoes or other toppings can also be added); and *crostini*, thin slices of toast covered with an assortment of pastes made from chicken livers, mushrooms, truffles, artichokes, olives, bone marrow, and so forth.

One may find any or all of the following on an antipasto table: marinated cold vegetables such as eggplant, zucchini, whole small onions, and peppers; boiled greens such as spinach, *cicoria* (chicory), and broccoli rabe; anchovies, seafood salad, and mushrooms marinated in olive oil; frittatas (unfolded filled omelettes); *affettato* (cold cuts) of cured meats such as salami, prosciutto, mortadella, smoked tongue, and sausage.

There are also cheeses, especially mozzarella, Parmesan, and pecorino. The favored cheese is *mozzarella di bufala*, which is made at least partly from buffalo milk (that is, the milk of the water buffalo, not that of the American bison) and has a distinctive taste. Some popular cold antipasti are not on the buffet but can be ordered from the menu. Perhaps the most famous example of this is prosciutto and melon (or in season, figs). Other popular ordered antipasti are carpaccio (very thin slices of raw beef or fish), and *bresaola* (cured air-dried beef) drizzled with olive oil.

Antipasti can also be fried and served warm. *Crocchette* (croquettes) are popular; one type is *suppli* (rice balls filled with cheese or ground meat, dredged in breadcrumbs, and fried). There are olive *ascolane* (fried stuffed olives), *baccalà filetti* (dried salt cod, fileted and fried), and vegetables dipped in batter and fried. The famous *fiori di zucca* (zucchini flowers) are stuffed with mozzarella and anchovies before being dipped in batter for frying.

Primo

Primi piatti or just *primi* are felt to constitute the first course of an Italian meal, though they follow the antipasti. This course includes either pasta, rice, gnocchi, or polenta with sauce, or soups containing pasta, rice, or *farro* (spelt—an ancient variety of wheat).

Pasta et al. The variety of pasta shapes and sauces is seemingly infinite. Regions and even villages often have their own specific creations. A few examples are offered here.

It is important for Italians to match the shape of the pasta with the sauce, though they allow much flexibility. Certain pastas are always mentioned within the context of a sauce, such as *bucatini all'amatriciana* (tubular pasta with a tomato and bacon sauce), or *fettuccine all'Alfredo* (fresh egg noodles with butter, cream, and Parmesan), or *spaghetti alla carbonara* (spaghetti with bacon, eggs, cheese, and pepper); but substitutions can be made. At restaurants, waiters recite what is available by the shape of pasta—penne, spaghetti, fettuccine—and expect the customer to state what sauce should go on it. While almost any combination is possible, there are "rules." One general rule is that smooth sauces are appropriate on long pasta, and sauces with chunks of vegetables or meats are better on small pasta shapes, which trap the chunks. Another is that fresh egg pastas work better with butter-based sauces than olive oil–based ones. In the dairy-rich north of Italy, fresh egg pastas are very popular, whereas in the olive oil–dominated south, dried or eggless pastas predominate. An important "rule" is that all pastas are consumed without a spoon (that is, with just a fork), even spaghetti.

Fresh egg pastas include noodles such as fettuccine, *tagliarini*, and *pappardelle* (all ribbon-shaped in various widths), and filled pastas such as ravioli, tortellini (small, hand-pinched, ring-shaped), and *agnolotti* (small, half-moon-shaped). Popular dried pastas include spaghetti, penne (short, thick, tubular, cut diagonally), and *farfalle*

POLENTA AND SHRIMP

1 cup polenta or quick-cooking cornmeal
1 tsp. salt
5 cups of water or milk (or part water, part milk)
2 tbsp. butter
2 pounds shrimp, shelled and deveined
1 lb sausage (kielbasa or chorizo), cut into slices
1 onion, sliced
3 slices of bacon (optional)
1/4 cup vegetable oil (less if bacon is used)
2 cloves of garlic
Seasoning: salt, pepper, and cayenne to taste

Make polenta: bring 5 cups of water or milk (or part water, part milk) to a boil in a heavy pot (best to use nonsticking surface). Lower the heat to simmer, add salt and slowly add the polenta (best sprinkled by hand) and stir with a wire whisk or wooden spoon until it forms a mush. This should take from about 7 to 15 minutes. If the cornmeal is less processed it may take a little longer. Add butter and mix it in.

Make shrimp: cut bacon into 1-inch pieces and render in large frying pan. When most of the fat has separated, add the onion and garlic and stir fry for 3–5 minutes. Add the shrimp and seasoning, and cook until it turns pink, then add the sausage and stir until sausage is warmed through.

Pour polenta into serving platter, and pour shrimp mixture on top. Serve at once.

(bowties). Some pasta types are quite specifically associated with a certain region, as is the case with *orecchiette* (little ears), a traditional pasta from Apulia *(Puglia)*.

Risotto is a uniquely Italian way of cooking rice, resulting in a dish with a creamy consistency. Risotto is best made with special types of rice such as *arborio, canaroli,* or *vialone nano*. Popular renderings include *Milanese* (that is, with saffron—*risotto Milanese*, unlike other risottos, is traditionally served with osso buco, a meat dish, as a *secondo), con funghi* (with mushrooms), *con frutti di mare* (with seafood), and *nero* (with squid ink).

Polenta (thick cornmeal mush) is typically a northern dish. It can be soft and creamy with a sauce on top (often tomato with sausage and pork ribs), or it can be cut into shapes and baked, fried, or grilled. It is traditionally a cool-weather dish served on a wooden plate.

Gnocchi (dumplings) are either *di farina* (made from wheat flour) or *di patate* (made from potato). There are also *gnocchi alla romana*, made of semolina flour and traditionally served on Thursdays in Rome. *Crespelle* (crepes) may also be a first course and can be filled with meat or with cheese and spinach.

Sauces. Most pasta sauces are either butter- or olive oil–based. Tomatoes are probably the next most frequent ingredient, particularly in the south. An important component of baked pastas from Emilia-Romagna is *balsamella* (béchamel sauce). Whatever the sauce (called *sugo* or *salsa*), the most important thing is just to moisten the pasta with it; Italian pasta is served with much less sauce than its American counterpart.

The best-known sauces are probably *ragù alla bolognese*, made of vegetables, tomatoes, cream, and beef and simmered for a long time, and *pesto alla genovese*, a mixture of fresh basil, garlic, pine nuts, pecorino cheese, and olive oil that is traditionally served over a mixture of *trenette* (thin strips of pasta), potatoes, and green beans.

Other popular pasta sauces are *quattro formaggi* (four cheeses); *boscaiolo* (woodsman-style), containing mushrooms, peas, ham, tomatoes, cream, or whatever the chef wants to add "from the forest"; *arrabbiata* (literally, angry), a tomato sauce with hot peppers; as well as many for seafood (which are served without cheese).

Secondo

The *primo* is followed by a usually more austere second course of meat or fish and *contorno*, a vegetable or salad side dish.

Meats and fish. Meat and fish can be prepared in a variety of ways: grilled, roasted, or baked; braised with vegetables; fried, as in *fritto misto* (mixed fry); or boiled (*bollito*) and served with *salsa verde* (a piquant green sauce made with parsley) or *mostarda* (a sweet-and-sour condiment). Regional specialties include *fiorentina*, a Tuscan T-bone steak usually served rare, and osso buco, veal shanks in butter, garlic, anchovies, grated lemon peel, and herbs from Lombardy. *Trippa alla bolognese* is tripe with bacon, onion, garlic, and parsley, while *trippa alla romana* is tripe with tomatoes and mint. *Fegato* (liver, usually calf's liver) can be prepared *alla veneziana*, (with onions), or with sage, or grilled, or Milan-style (dipped in egg and bread crumbs and fried). Large porcini mushrooms are often treated like meat: grilled and drizzled with olive oil, garlic, and parsley as a *secondo*.

While lamb is more popular roasted or grilled, veal is prepared in many different ways. *Saltimbocca* (literally, leap into the mouth) is a dish of veal, prosciutto, and sage associated with Rome, while *scallopine alla bolognese* is veal layered with prosciutto and boiled potatoes. Thin slices of veal are often prepared in light sauces flavored with Marsala or lemon juice.

Chicken and turkey are also favored. *Pollo alla diaviola* is a spicy chicken: in Abruzzi it is sautéed with hot red pepper, in Tuscany with black pepper, and in Florence with ginger. Chicken Marengo is named after a battle won by Napoleon and contains chicken, brandy, tomatoes, olives, crayfish, and poached eggs on toast. Stuffed turkey is popular in Lombardy.

Pork is extremely popular, either as chops, roasted with fennel and rosemary as in porchetta, or made into sausages like *zampone* and *cotechino*, the former stuffed into pigs' feet.

Game, especially *cinghiale* (wild boar), *lepre* (hare), *piccioncino* (squab), venison, and pheasant, is available in season.

There is an abundance of both freshwater and saltwater fish, such as *spigola* (sea bass), *rombo* (turbot), *orata* (bream), *dentice* (dentex, a marine fish related to the porgy), and *sogliola* (sole), as well as tuna, swordfish, and *anguilla* (eel). These fish are often served grilled. *Frittura di paranza* is a dish of small fish fried in oil. Fish baked with potatoes is also a favored preparation.

Seppie (cuttlefish), *calamari* (squid), *polpi*, *polpettini*, and *moscardini* (types of octopus), and a variety of shellfish are also consumed. There are more shellfish in Italy than there are popular terms in English for them; for example, *scampi*, *gamberi*, *gamberetti*, *gamberoni*, *mazzancole*, and *canocchia* may be types of shrimp, prawn, or crayfish. *Cozze* and *muscoli* are mussels, and *vongole* (clams), *poveraccia* (poor or small clams), and *vongole veraci* (true or large clams) are all popular. There are many varieties of shellfish used mainly for antipasti such as *dattero* (date mussel—so called because its shell resembles the fruit), and various others called *cuore di mare* ("heart of the sea"), *tartufo di mare* (truffle of the sea), and so on.

Contorno. Vegetables are frequently just boiled and served at room temperature, to be drizzled with olive oil and lemon. Sometimes they are marinated in olive oil. More creative ways of cooking them include *sformato*, a creamed pudding of vegetables such as spinach or zucchini; *agrodolce*, a sweet-and-sour preparation; *in padella* (stir-fried, often with hot peppers and/or garlic); and *trifolato*, sautéed with garlic and parsley in olive oil.

Carciofi (artichokes) are seasonal and very popular. They can be prepared in a variety of ways; two favorites are *alla romana* (Roman style—made with garlic parsley, mint, and olive oil), and *alla giudia* (Jewish style—deep-fried whole, or cut into wedges and fried, or stuffed). Other popular stuffed vegetables are tomatoes stuffed with rice and mozzarella, zucchini stuffed with chopped meat, and eggplant stuffed with cheese or bread crumbs.

Fresh salads are usually dressed with olive oil and vinegar. *Panzanella* is bread salad made with stale bread, tomatoes, cucumbers, onion, and basil. *Caprese*, a dish of sliced tomatoes and mozzarella drizzled with olive oil and chopped basil, is available in Italian restaurants all over the world.

A classic seasonal Roman salad is *puntarelle*, shoots of a particular variety of chicory, picked while still young and tender and tossed with a dressing made with anchovies, garlic, and lemon juice. Some salads are a mix of greens and may include *rughetta* (also called *rucola*, *rocola*, and, as it is in English, *arugula*).

Dolce

The next course in the Italian meal is dolce (dessert). Due to geography and climate, there are abundant varieties of fruit available most of the year, though the more interesting ones are seasonal. Many berries, figs, grapes, *nespole* (medlars—round orange-colored fruit of a tree in the rose family, which, like the persimmon, is inedible until overripe), watermelon, and Sicilian blood oranges are still seasonal. Fruits are either served in bowls of water, or cut into large chunks on a platter (watermelon), or as fruit salads; if a mixed salad, it is called *macedonia*, but salads of specific fruits, such as berries, are also possible.

The best-known Italian dessert today is *tiramisu* (literally, "pick me up"), composed of mascarpone (a very creamy, soft cheese, typically made from cow's milk), ladyfingers, coffee, and other ingredients specific to the home or restaurant. Then there are zabaglione, a light fluffy whip of egg yolks and Marsala; *torta della nonna* (grandmother's cake), made with custard and pine nuts; *panna cotta* (boiled cream), served with a variety of toppings, such as berries, chocolate, and caramel; *profiteroles* (mounds of little cream puffs filled with ice cream and drizzled with chocolate); *crem caramel*; *zuppa inglese* (literally, "English soup"), a triflelike concoction; and many different types and flavors of *gelato*. Other desserts are based on ricotta (for instance, cannoli, crisp pastry shells filled with sweetened ricotta), almonds, sponge cake (for example, *cassata*, often flavored with an alcoholic beverage such as maraschino—a wild-cherry liqueur), and chestnuts. *Monte bianco* (Mont Blanc) is a seasonal dessert of chestnut puree, brittle meringue, and whipped cream. *Crostate* are open-faced tarts filled with ricotta or jam.

Though it is technically the last course, the Italian meal does not quite end with dessert. Italians always drink their espressos after, not with, their dessert. And with or after the coffee, there are always *digestivi*—alcoholic beverages so named because they are believed to help digestion. They are made with herbs or fruit. *Amaro* (for example, *averna* and *montenegro*), *sambucca*, and *limoncello* are popular examples. The meal may also finish with almond biscotti, called *cantucci* in Tuscany, which are dipped in Vin Santo (literally, holy wine), Moscato, or Marsala—sweet dessert wines.

See also **Crustaceans and Shellfish**; **Pasta**; **Slow Food**.

BIBLIOGRAPHY

Bugialli, Giuliano. *Giuliano Bugialli's Foods of Italy.* New York: Stewart, Tabori, and Chang, 1984.

Carluccio, Antonio, and Priscilla Carluccio. *Carluccio's Complete Italian Food.* New York: Rizzoli, 1997.

Fant, Maureen B., and Howard M. Isaacs. *Dictionary of Italian Cuisine.* New York: HarperCollins, 1998.

Hazan, Marcella. *Essentials of Classic Italian Cooking.* New York: Knopf, 1992.

Mariani, John. *The Dictionary of Italian Food and Drink.* New York: Broadway Books, 1998.

Paolini, Davide, and Michela Vuga. *From Rice to Risotto.* London: Kea & Cartago, 2000.

Root, Waverley. *The Food of Italy.* New York: Vintage Books, 1977.

Judit Katona-Apte

TRADITION IN ITALIAN CUISINE

The reason so many people fall in love with Italy has much to do with its cuisine. Italian cooking has been influenced by diverse groups of people and places, historically and in modern times. The Americas, for instance, had a huge influence on Italian cuisine. Tomato sauce, polenta, and anything *piccante* (hot) would not exist in Italian cuisine without the introduction of tomatoes, maize (corn), and peppers—all plants native to the Americas.

The world has adopted parts of Italy's cuisine, but not the structure of its meals. In Italy a meal is a leisurely sequence of events served in courses on separate plates, each appearing in the appropriate sequence. Americans often find it frustrating for a meal to be so lengthy, but, for Italians, dinner is often the main event and the focus of celebrations.

The cooking style is usually quite simple. There are no really elaborate sauces, and what sauces do exist are used only in small amounts, just enough to moisten pasta or delicately anoint meat or fish. Italian chefs claim, with some justification, that the secret to Italian cooking is *sapori e saperi* (flavors and skills), which implies doing little to excellent fresh ingredients.

Similarities and Differences

While there are many differences between regions, and between households within a region, the concept of Italian food would not exist unless there were many similarities as well. There is a tendency for food experts to stress the differences instead of the similarities within the Italian food tradition. But there is much that links it as a single cuisine. Some examples are the structure of the meal, the pasta course, and potatoes used as a vegetable rather than as a staple source of carbohydrates. There is also the ubiquitous antipasto of sausages and cheeses. The types of sausage and cheese may be local—in *Remembrance of Tastes Past*, Davide Paolini estimates over sixteen hundred types—but nonetheless they are all cold cuts and cheese served on a plate before the pasta course. There are also rules common to almost all Italian cooking, such as not pairing cheese with seafood, or lemon with tomato sauce.

Having said all that, there *are* regional cuisines, and restaurants tend to be specific to a region. A restaurant serving dishes from too many regions would not be popular with Italians. There are also many foods associated with specific localities. Among the best-known examples

Many traditional Italian dishes can be traced to the Renaissance or Middle Ages. This simple preparation of prawns and clams with parsley reflects the continuity of this rich culinary tradition. Prepared at San Fruttuoso, Italy, in 2000. © OWEN FRANKEN/CORBIS.

are pizza with Naples, saffron risotto with Milan, Austrian-type dumplings with Trentino, balsamic vinegar with Modena, *fiorentina* steak with Tuscany, polenta with Venice, prosciutto and Parmesan cheese with Parma, *ragù* with Bologna, pesto with Genoa, truffles with Umbria, sheep's-milk cheese with Sardinia, and chocolate with Perugia.

Festivals

Every Italian region has a tradition of its own with regard to Carnival, Easter, Christmas, and other holidays. Most foods prepared for them are sweet, but there are some savory dishes as well.

The best-known New Year's dish is lentils with *cotechino* or *zampone* (both pork sausages, the former stuffed into a pig's foot). The lentils represent coins and thus richness. *Croccanti* are brittle caramel and almond candies, which, molded into various shapes, decorate the center of the table at New Year's dinner. *Torta della Befana* is a fruit tart with a bean hidden inside (whoever finds the bean is crowned king or queen for the day) and is traditional for the Feast of the Magi.

For San Giuseppe Day on 19 March, *sfince* (called *zeppole* in Naples), fried dough seasoned with honey of Saracen origin, is popular in Sicily. For the feast of San Giovanni on June 24th, *tortelli* filled with greens and ricotta are traditional in Parma. *Amatriciana*, a pasta sauce of bacon and tomato, is traditionally served on the Sunday following *Ferragosto* (Assumption Day). *Bigne di*

Giuseppe (fried doughnuts) filled with cream or chocolate are eaten for Father's Day in Rome.

Carnival is a holiday full of food symbolism. Mardi Gras is literally Fat Tuesday, and the term *Carnevale* derives from Old Italian *carnelevare* (removal of meat). Both of these are major celebrations to initiate Lent, a period when people deprive themselves of some favorite food or other pleasure. *Quaresimali*, for example, are hard almond cookies prepared especially for Lent. *Pizza del giovedì grasso*, two circles of pizza with a filling of pork, cheese, eggs, and lemon, is served on the last Thursday before Lent. *Maritozzi* (raisin buns) are traditional for Lent in Rome.

On the Amalfi Coast and throughout much of the South, there is *migliaccio di polenta*, a casserole of polenta, sausage, and cheese. In Abruzzi, a Carnival dish of crepes in broth with Parmesan is consumed. Carnival is also an occasion for simple fritters: *chiacchiere* in Lombardy, *cenci* in Tuscany, and *frappe* in Rome may sound quite different, but they look and taste very similar—fried crunchy pastry strips sprinkled with powdered sugar. *Sanguinaccio* (literally, "blood pudding") is a chocolate dessert served at Carnival time around Naples.

A large variety of foods are made to celebrate Easter, from soups to main dishes to sweets, with egg as the dominant ingredient. *Pancotto*, for example, is bread soup containing butter, oil, salt, cheese, and egg, and is a traditional Easter dish in Lombardy. *Brodetto* is an egg-and-lemon soup made at Easter in Florence. An Easter *torta* (cake) can be sweet or savory. *Torta Pasqualine*, for example, is an Easter dish from Liguria traditionally made with thirty-three sheets of very thin pastry, to symbolize each year of Christ's life. The sheets are filled with greens, artichokes, ricotta, and hard-boiled eggs.

Pizza can also be savory or sweet. *Pizza di Pasqua ternata* is a sweet Easter pizza topped with preserved fruits and nuts from the Umbrian town of Terni. *Ciambella* or *brazedela* is a ring-shaped, traditional Easter breakfast bun in Emilia-Romagna. In Naples, Easter is celebrated with *pastiera*, a type of ricotta pie. *Colomba Pasquale* (Easter dove) is a popular bird-shaped Easter cake.

Every Italian region has its own tradition with regard to Christmas sweets. Instead of fruitcake, there are a variety of fruit breads. In Liguria there is *pandolce*, made with candied fruits, nuts, and flavorings. In Tuscany there is *panforte*, also called *panforte di Siena*, a hard, flat concoction popular since the thirteenth century. This characteristic sweet, made of toasted nuts stirred into hot honey caramel, has many virtues, including the fact that it can be stored for long periods of time.

Since the 1950s, *panettone* (literally, "Tony's bread") has become popular all over Italy at Christmas time. The custom of consuming *panettone*, especially during the year-end holiday season, spread from Milan throughout Italy. There are variations, however. *Pampepato* is a Christmas cake from Ferrara made with pepper, chocolate, spices, and almonds. In Rome the Christmas cake is *pan giallo*, a fruit-and-nut cake, originally made with saffron, thus its name, which literally means yellow bread.

In Naples women prepare for the arrival of Christmas with delicacies made of *pasta di mandorla* (marzipan) and with *struffoli*, tiny pieces of soft pastry formed into balls, fried, coated with honey, and sprinkled with bright and colorful candied sugar and pieces of candied fruit peel. Sicily has *cuccidatu* or *bruccellato*, a ring-shaped cake stuffed with dried figs, raisins, and nuts, and spiced with cloves and cinnamon.

Christmas also provides its share of savory specialties. In many homes, fish is the preferred main course for Christmas Eve dinner. In Lombardy, stuffed turkey and *tortelli* (similar to ravioli) filled with squash and crushed amaretto cookies are traditional for Christmas, while in Bologna tortellini (small, hand-pinched, filled ring-shaped pasta) is traditional for Christmas Day.

Papassine is a traditional Sardinian sweet for all occasions—Easter, Christmas, and All Saints' Day, for example—made with dried fruit, lard, orange, and eggs.

BIBLIOGRAPHY

Bianchi, Anne. *Italian Festival Food: Recipes and Traditions from Italy's Regional Country Food Fairs*. New York: Macmillan, 1999.

Bonino, Maddalena. *The Festive Food of Italy*. London: Kyle Cathie, 1991.

Mariani, John. *The Dictionary of Italian Food and Drink*. New York: Broadway Books, 1998.

Root, Waverley. *The Food of Italy*. New York: Vintage Books, 1977.

Judit Katona-Apte

J-K

JAMS, JELLIES, AND PRESERVES. An atmosphere evoking both enchantment and delight surrounds the consumption of jams, jellies, and preserves. Children and adults alike enjoy sweet quince paste from Spain, orange marmalade from Scotland, candied fruit from France, or ginger in heavy syrup, an English specialty. No doubt they would be surprised if told that there is not the least gastronomical ambition to be found in the origin of these delicacies—only the need to preserve fruit and other plants. They would be even more surprised to find out that the earliest confectioners were apothecaries, and the first preserves nothing but medicines. Sick people were very lucky in those days: they were permitted to eat sweetmeats to their hearts' content.

Preserving Food

Since prehistoric times, people have been very concerned about starvation, so they have protected themselves against hard times by storing the products of their crops and harvests. Various preserving methods were elaborated over the course of centuries; the earliest ones consisted in storing fruits far away from air and light, desiccating them, or preserving them in an antiseptic bath.

In the first century C.E., the Roman agronomist Columella described these techniques in his work *De re rustica*. According to Columella, the ideal means to preserve pears or peaches consisted of putting them in small wooden boxes, which were to be carefully closed so that air could not get in. As for figs and grapes, they were to be dried in the sunshine. Finally, Columella suggested the use of a preservative to retard decomposition, called *conditio* (from Latin *condire*, 'to condite, or preserve'. This use of *conditiones* to preserve food was called *conditus* (or *conditum*). There are various types of *conditiones*—salt, vinegar, sweeteners—that have preservative properties and do not exclude each other; in other words, their effects are cumulative.

Fruit pickled in vinegar and salt. Apicius, a Roman gastronome who lived in the time of Columella, preserved peaches in a mixture of salt, brine, and vinegar. Pickled fruit and vegetables are the modern version. But by its very nature, fruit needs sweet *conditiones*, which emphasize its flavor and heighten its fragrance. Since they did not know of the existence of sugar (see below), the ancients suggested several alternatives.

Fruit preserved in sweet wine. One alternative was *passum*, a high-alcohol, very mild wine made of raisins and used by Columella for pears and plums. The fruit was picked a short time before becoming ripe and was placed in a terracotta receptacle coated with pitch. It was then covered with *passum* so as to be soaked in liquor. A plaster-coated lid was placed on top. These *conditi in passum* can be seen as the forerunners of today's fruit in liquor.

Fruit preserved in wine syrup. Also used was *sapa* or *defrutum*, grape must that has been cooked and reduced by two-thirds or one-third, respectively. Columella used it for apples, pears, and sorbs. To make sure they were submerged in the syrup, a handful of dried fennel was placed on top. The lid was carefully coated with plaster and pitch so that air could not get in. This fruit bath of thick sugary grape juice is the forerunner of fruit preserved in syrup, which is now sterilized in order to protect it against decomposition.

Fruit preserved in sweet-sour pickle. Columella also concocted a sweet-sour *conditio* with vinegar and either *sapa* or *defrutum* for sorbs, plums, sloes, pears, and apples picked before they were fully ripe. They were then dried for one day in the shade. A mixture consisting of equal parts vinegar and *sapa* or *defrutum* was poured on the fruit. Columella recommended adding a bit of salt to prevent infestation by small worms or other animals. Finally, he made it clear that the fruit could be preserved even longer by adding two-thirds of *sapa* and one-third of vinegar. Our cherries in vinegar, which are served with stews and pâtés, are based on the same principle: they are covered with a bath consisting of a sweet element (two-fifths of sugar) and vinegar (three-fifths). We should not be surprised at the use of salt in the Roman recipe. It is a flavor enhancer, provided it is used in small quantities.

Apicius suggested another sweet-sour *conditio* based on *sapa* and blackberry juice. It was poured on blackberries placed in a glass vessel. The author specified that they could be preserved for a long time in this manner.

Melomeli and Marmalade. And—last but not least—there is honey. Its preserving properties have been recognized for a very long time. The corpse of Alexander the Great is said to have been kept in honey. Columella therefore claimed that honey stopped putrefaction and protected a corpse from decomposition for several years. Columella was, however, reluctant to use it for his fruit *conditi*, as he believed that fruit preserved in honey lost its flavor. J. André, in *L'alimentation et la cuisine à Rome*, suggests that his reluctance might be due to the fact that the production of honey was rather limited in those days.

Nevertheless, Apicius used honey as a *conditio* for figs, apples, plums, pears, and cherries: "Gather them carefully with their stalks and put them in honey so that they do not touch each other." Apicius paid particular attention to quinces, which he preserved in a mixture of honey and *defrutum*: "Choose faultless quinces with their twigs and leaves, and put them in a receptacle, and pour over honey and *defrutum*; you will keep them for a long time." In fact, Columella also made an exception for quinces, and he likewise recommended preserving them in honey. According to Columella, quinces should be picked when the sky is clear and the moon on the wane; they should be wiped and put into a new receptacle filled up to the rim with excellent very liquid honey, so that each fruit is covered. Not only does this method preserve fruit, but it also yields a drink called *melomeli* (from Greek *melon*, 'quince' and *meli*, 'honey'), administered to sick people when they run a fever.

The Greek physician Dioscorides, who was Columella's contemporary, gave a slightly different recipe in his herbarium entitled *De materia medica*. *Melomeli*, which he called *cydonomeli* (from Cydonia in Crete, where the best quinces were produced), appears in the chapter about wines: "First of all, quinces should be deseeded, then entirely covered with honey, which becomes good after one year and tastes like *oenomeli* (honeyed wine)." So, according to Dioscorides, quinces are to be deseeded first—in other words, opened and not left whole—unlike Columella's recipe.

Additionally, Dioscorides gave two recipes for *cydonites oenos*, "quince wine." In the first one, quinces are to be cut in pieces like turnips and then deseeded. For twelve pounds of fruit, forty liters of must are needed to cover them. The mixture should macerate for thirty days until the wine gets clearer. In the second recipe, quinces are crushed and the juice is squeezed out. The proportion is five liters of juice to one pint of honey, and the whole is then mixed up.

Melomeli and *cydonites oenos* have the same therapeutic properties: they are astringent, facilitate digestion, relieve dysentery, and are good for people with liver, kidney, or urinary ailments—a real cure-all, if you add the antipyretic qualities ascribed by Columella to his *melomeli*.

According to modern-day experimentation with these ancient recipes, both *melomeli* and *cydonites oenos* are slightly fermented drinks tasting like mead, with a very fruity and particularly original flavor. Dioscorides was actually right when he compared them to honeyed wine.

It is rather surprising to note that *melomeli* (also spelled *malomellus* in the seventh century), which is not a jam, is the origin of the word "marmalade," derived from it via Spanish *membrillo* and Portuguese *marmelo*, both meaning 'a quince'. Indeed, before it became, from the seventeenth century onward, "a jellied conserve of Sevilla oranges (with such alternatives as lime, grapefruit, lemon, or ginger), marmalade was a preserve confected from quinces boiled with honey or sugar" (Wilson, 1985, p. 15). The ancients did not know marmalades made of citrus fruit (they were introduced by the Arabs in the Middle Ages—see below), but they created jelly, jam, and quince paste.

Quince Paste

In the second century C.E., the Greek physician Galen wrote that the Romans were importing quince paste (*meloplacounta*, derived from *melon*, 'a quince', and *plakounta*, 'a tablet') from the Iberian Peninsula: "It is firm and hard, and has been brought to Rome in very large quantities. It consists of honey and crushed quinces cooked in honey." It is not only a delicacy, but also a medicine aimed at strengthening a debilitated stomach, as the distinguished physician put it.

So, according to Galen, quince paste originated in Spain. It has remained up to now a specialty of the Iberian Peninsula (*pasta de membrillo* in Spain and *marmelada* in Portugal). Unfortunately, Galen does not give the recipe for this confection. It is, however, to be found in a late text of Byzantine origin attributed to the last representative of Greek medicine, Paul of Aegina (seventh century): "Six pounds of quinces are cooked in wine until they have softened up. Then they are crushed. Eight pounds of honey are added and the whole is cooked slowly until the mass doesn't leave the slightest trace on the hand. Various drugs are added to the paste, which is eventually divided into half-ounce tablets."

Quince Jelly

Galen also gives the recipe for a drug based on quince juice that he claims to have invented and is particularly appropriate for stomach ailments. This drug survived for centuries under the name of *diamelon* or *cydonitum*. Its preparation involves mixing two parts quince juice, two parts honey, and one part vinegar. Ginger and pepper are optional. The mixture is cooked until it has thickened to the consistency of honey (*melistos pachos*). Modern-day experimentation with this ancient recipe has yielded a beautiful translucent red jelly with a pleasing peppery flavor.

Quince Jam

In the fourth century C.E., the Roman agronomist Palladius revived Galen's quince jelly, which he called *cydonitum*. He added a second formula: "You first peel ripe quinces, you cut them into small pieces, excluding the hard parts you may find inside. You then boil them in honey, until the mixture has been reduced by half, and you sprinkle it with fine pepper while they are cooking."

If the ancients did indeed know about pectic fermentation (pectin makes the process of jelling possible), they did not make the most of it. In fact, they only applied it to quinces, which are actually rich in pectin; when they are cooked with an acid (like vinegar in *diamelon*), jelling takes place almost automatically. C. Anne Wilson, in *The Book of Marmalade*, explains that the ancients preferred fruit "in their fresh, uncooked state to fruit preserved in wine, syrup, vinegar, or honey." Quinces were an exception, because, if not totally ripe, they remained hard even in honey. It was to avoid that risk that quinces were precooked. This led to the discovery of pectic fermentation. "The high pectic content of some other sharp fruits may never have been discovered because there was no incentive to precook them in honey. So quinces remained unchallenged in the field of the pectin-jellied conserve."

Another Fruit Jam

There is another jam in Greco-Roman medieval literature: *diaoporon* or *medicamentum ex pomis*, which is at the same time an antidiarrheic and good for digestion. Various fruits (apples, pears, pomegranates, and especially quinces) are cooked in honey, *sapa*, and must (the pulp and skins of grapes)—"*donec omnia quae indita sunt liquata in unitatem quadam coeant*"—until all ingredients have been reduced to a uniform mass, according to Celsius, a Roman physician of the first century C.E. As for Columella, he indicated that *diaoporon* must be cooked—"*donec crassamen in modum fecis existat*"—until it has reached the consistency of feces. This is in fact what it looks like when it has been cooked in that manner. Its flavor, however, is not unpleasant, as Celsius experienced ("*id gustu non insuave est*"). This is a rather surprising comment for Celsius, since he wrote at the beginning of his treatise, *De Medicina*, that "all *condita* are unserviceable for two reasons, because more is taken owing to their sweetness, and even what is moderate is still digested with some difficulty."

Fruit and Honey Syrups

The ancients also knew of other fruit and honey preserves. Criton, a Greek physician who lived at the beginning of the first century C.E., created *diaroion*, the forerunner of grenadine. It is made of pomegranate juice, cooked until it has reached the consistency of lime (*gloiou pachos*), honey, and, optionally, drugs such as myrrh. *Diaroion* is particularly appropriate in the treatment of mouth ailments.

Then, there is the blackberry-based *diamoron*, a famous remedy created by Heras (a contemporary of Criton), which is still mentioned in modern pharmacopoeias. It is prepared in the same way as *diaroion* and has the same therapeutic effects. It has also been found to be effective in treating gum inflammation.

Nougat and Marzipan

The ancients paved the way for honey and dried-fruit preserves with almonds as the main ingredient. This mixture eventually gave birth to marzipan and nougat, and the Arabs (see below) developed the manufacturing technique.

At the end of the fifth century B.C.E., the *Hippocratic Corpus*—in fact, just a few parts were written by Hippocrates himself—gives an interesting formula to cure pleurisy. The ingredients are honey (with an emollient effect on the throat), scilla (a bulbous herb useful as an expectorant), and almonds (with well-known cough-suppressing properties). The recipe is as follows: "Cut scilla bulbs into slices and cook them in water; when they have boiled, tip the water; pour water again and cook the scilla again until it looks mushy and well cooked); crush it in equal pieces, add roasted cumin, white sesame, fresh almonds; crush all these substances in honey." This may be the forerunner of marzipan.

As for Galen, he suggested a cough mixture made of sweet almonds and honey with other dried fruit such as pine kernels (which also have cough-suppressing properties), grilled flaxseeds, flag, and tragacanth gum (which have the same therapeutic effects). A modern version is to cook the mixture and let it cool down under a weight. The result is a delicious candy tasting like the famous black nougat from Provence served at Christmastime.

The Arab Contribution

It was not until Arab times (in the times of the Caliphate of Baghdad, more particularly the Abbasid dynasty) that there was some progress in the sciences. It should be noted, however, that much of the confectionery technology attributed to the Arabs was in fact developed in Sassanian Persia and known to the Byzantine Greeks. Further, sugar was not much used in the Near East until a system of irrigation could be developed and a source of wood could be found for processing it.

First, the Arabs introduced sugar in medicines and in cooking. Sugar diluted in water yielded a new confection called *sharab* in Arab and *syrupus* in Latin. Sugar syrup was used to manufacture various preserves and sweetmeats, more particularly *sharab al-fawaki* (*syrupus de fructibus*), an updated version of *diaroion* and *diamoron* in which Arabs replaced honey with sugar and used various comfits and sweetmeats such as fudge, tatty, and marshmallow.

Moreover, the Arabs went deeper into the subject of pectic fermentation. They created the first marmalades of citrus fruit; most of them, however, were candied in honey, not in sugar: an example is the lemon marmalade of Avicenna (980–1037). (Islamic traditions often use honey over any other form of sugar although they were one of the first to have sugar.)

In Spain, the Arabs developed the traditional fruit pastes (see above) by creating new varieties with roses, violets, orange peels, kernels, and green walnuts (well known in Byzantine Armenia). They were also made with honey. As for the traditional quince paste, it was sugar-candied from the thirteenth century onward.

Finally, the Arabs developed dried-fruit pastas and created various kinds of marzipan and nougat—sometimes with honey, sometimes with sugar.

Pseudo-Mesue: the father of European confectionery. Pseudo-Mesue, a twelfth-century physician probably of Italian origin, was the person who introduced Arab confections into Christian countries. He also invented new ones. He wrote jam recipes (apple, plum, peach) that were revolutionary for his time because they were made with sugar, not with honey.

It was not until the late Middle Ages that confectionery developed into what it is now. New recipe books evidencing this evolution were published. *The Libre de totes manieres de confits*, drawn up in the fifteenth century and written in Catalan, had many imitators during the Renaissance. They include: *De secreti* by Alexis of Piedmont (Venice, 1555), the preserves-maker of the French physician and astrologer Nostradamus (Lyons, 1555), and *The Treasurie of Commodious Conceits and Hidden Secrets* by John Partridge (1573).

See also **Apicius; Candy and Confections; Compote; Condiments; Fruit; Greece, Ancient; Hippocrates; Islam; Middle East; Rome and the Roman Empire; Sugar and Sweeteners; Sugar Crops and Natural Sweeteners; Syrup.**

BIBLIOGRAPHY.

André, J. *L'alimentation et la Cuisine à Rome*. Paris: 1981.

Arberry, A. J. "A Baghdad Cookery Book." *Islamic Culture* 13, (1939).

Hippocrates. Hippocratic Collection, in eight volumes. Loeb Classical Library. Cambridge, Mass.: Harvard University Press, 1923–1988.

Hippocrates. *Ancient Medicine. Airs, Waters, Places. Epidemics 1 & 3. The Oath. Precepts. Nutriment.* Volume 1 in the eight-volume Hippocratic Collection. Loeb Classical Library. Cambridge, Mass.: Harvard University Press, 1923.

McKibben J., and N. J. Engeseth. "Honey as a Protective Agent against Lipid Oxidation in Ground Turkey." *Journal of Agricultural and Food Chemistry* 50, no. 3 (2002): pp. 592–595.

Miranda, A. H. *Traduccion espanola de un manuscrito anonimo de siglo XIII sobre la cocina hispano-magribi*. Madrid: 1966.

Plouvier, Liliane. "La confiserie européenne au Moyen-Age." *Medium Aevum Quotidianum* 13 (1988).

Shephard, Sue. *Pickled, Potted, and Canned: The Story of Food Preserving*. London: Headline, 2000.

Wilson, C. Anne. *The Book of Marmalade*. London: Constable, 1985.

Liliane Plouvier

Translated from the French by Christian Labarre

JAPAN.

This entry includes two subentries:
Traditional Japanese Cuisine
Contemporary Issues in Japanese Cuisine

TRADITIONAL JAPANESE CUISINE

The Japanese eat three meals a day, and afternoon and late-night snacking is normal. This popular expectation of three meals a day dates to the middle of the Edo period (1600–1868) (Tsuji and Ishige, 1983, p. 306). One traditional definition of a meal in Japan is that it includes rice, soup, pickles, and at least one side dish. In normal home cooking these components are usually served together rather than as separate courses. In specialty restaurants, the main course is sometimes served first accompanied by sake (rice wine), followed by rice, soup, and pickles to mark the end of the meal.

Rice

Rice has been cultivated in Japan in wet paddies for about two thousand years. Introduced from southern China, the preference in Japan has always been for a glutinous, short-grained variety. Traditionally rice is boiled or steamed, and in modern kitchens it is usually prepared in automatic rice cookers.

The words for cooked rice in modern Japanese, *meshi* and *gohan*, are also used to mean a "meal." The degree to which rice has been the central staple of Japanese food is debated (Ohnuki-Tierney, 1993, pp. 30–43), and historically rice has been supplemented by other carbohydrates, such as millet and sweet potatoes. Nonetheless rice is idealized as the core of any Japanese meal. If noodles constitute the main starch of a meal, rice is not served, but such a meal is also considered more of a snack than a proper meal. Gretchen Mittwer points out that the midday noodle snack became popular in early historic periods, when only two meals per day were eaten (Mittwer, 1989, p. 23).

Rice, sake, and the pounded-rice paste called *mochi* are powerful symbols in Japan. Rice and its products symbolize the relation of Japanese people to their deities, the nature of community in Japan, and Japan's history and aesthetics, and in the end rice is a symbol of the Japanese self (Ohnuki-Tierney, 1993, pp. 8–11, 127–131).

Soups

Three major ingredients, which may be used together or separately, create the basic stock of a Japanese soup (dashi). The first is *katsuo-bushi*, or dried bonito. The bonito is dried and processed to create hard, woodlike pieces that are easily stored. A planelike tool is used to take shavings from it that are dropped into hot water, then strained out. Instant powders are often substituted. The second major ingredient is kelp (*konbu*), which is also available as an instant powder. *Konbu* and *katsuo-bushi* often are used together to create a stock. The third ingredient, shiitake mushrooms, are boiled with or without kelp to create a vegetarian soup stock used, for example, in *shoojin-ryoori*, the vegetarian cuisine of Buddhist temples (Ishige, 2000, p. 1178).

Two main types of soups are based on these stocks. Clear soups *(suimono)* are considered light and elegant and are served in lacquered bowls with lids. A bit of salt and soy sauce is added to the broth along with two or three small bits of solid food, perhaps a piece of fish, a sliver of vegetable, and an aromatic garnish. When the lid is lifted, the delicate fragrance escapes, and the aesthetic arrangement of the solid foods within the bowl is an added enjoyment (Tsuji, 1980, p. 151).

Miso soups comprise the second major class of soups. Miso is a paste made from soybeans and barley inoculated with a fungal culture and allowed to cure for a year or more. A great variety of misos exist, some smooth, others chunky. They range in color from light beige (called "white") to medium red or brown to nearly black. Some are sweet, while others are quite salty. Because this is a bean-based ingredient, miso soups are a rich source of protein.

To make a miso soup, a variety of miso is selected and dissolved in hot stock. The cook adds seasonal vegetables, such as parboiled fiddlehead ferns or eggplant, and perhaps a few cubes of tofu (white, mild-tasting curds made from soy milk). Miso soup is more common than the clear soups, and more filling as well.

Pickles

Japanese pickles *(tsukemono)* are primarily pickled vegetables. They exist in great variety and add texture and diversity to even a simple menu. Originally pickling preserved vegetables for use through the winter, but pickles have come to occupy a place in the menu year-round.

Daikon radishes, Chinese cabbages, cucumbers, eggplants, and turnips are often pickled. Rubbing the vegetable in salt, then placing a weight on top to force out liquids is a common method, as is packing the vegetables in miso, sake, sake lees, or rice bran. The use of vinegar is a relatively less-important pickling method in Japan (Yoneda, 1982, pp. 89–92).

Green, unripened Japanese plums *(ume)* are the only fruit regularly pickled, and they are prepared with salt and red perilla leaves *(shiso)*. The resulting pickle, called *umeboshi*, is salty, sour, and red. It is considered an appetite stimulant, consequently it is often served with breakfast (Richie, 1985, p. 85). *Umeboshi* is commonly used to flavor *onigiri*, a favorite picnic food, which is a ball of rice with something inside.

Traditionally pickles were made at home, and many regional specialties developed. However, most consumers buy pickles in supermarkets or department stores. There open vats of decoratively arranged pickles are displayed, and the attractively pungent smells are obvious immedi-

ately upon entering the store. Pickles are also frequently sold as regional souvenirs.

Side Dishes

Side dishes, *okazu*, add savor to the rice that is traditionally understood as the central portion of the meal. Non-Japanese people are tempted to call some of these the entrée of the meal, as the side dishes might include grilled fish or deep-fried pork *(tonkatsu)*, but this is at odds with the traditional understanding. Side dishes could also include sweet vinegared cucumbers, steamed enoki mushrooms, or *hijiki* seaweed stewed with carrots. A simple meal might have only one side dish, but elaborate meals would have many. Some major *okazu* include salads, tofu, seafood, and meat.

Salads. Traditional salads are served cold and can be divided into two basic categories, vinegared salads *(sunomono)* and salads with heavier dressings *(aemono)*. The vinegar-based dressings usually include a basic soup stock (dashi) and soy sauce and might also include some fruit juice, ginger, or grated daikon radish as well. Heavier dressings are often made with pureed tofu, ground sesame seeds, or miso.

Like the soups, which call for seasonally available fillings, salads highlight seasonal materials, including fruits, vegetables, and fish or shellfish. Depending on the materials, some might be steamed, parboiled, or grilled in preparation, but they are always cooled and dried before the salad is assembled. Typical salads might include crab with thinly sliced cucumbers in a vinegar and ginger

Seaweed has been an ingredient in traditional Japanese cookery for many centuries. It is a rich source of iodine and trace elements. Shown here is kelp. COURTESY OF FIELD MARK PUBLICATIONS.

dressing or parboiled spinach dressed with ground sesame seeds, soy sauce, dashi, and a bit of sugar (Tsuji, 1980, pp. 241–242, 247, 253).

Tofu. Mentioned above as a common ingredient for miso soup and as a base for thick dressings, tofu has attained worldwide recognition. It was originally brought to Japan from China, perhaps in the 900s by the delegations of Buddhist priests who studied there. As priests were allowed to eat neither meat nor fish, this high protein food was doubtless appreciated. By the 1100s tofu was widely used in Japan.

To make tofu, soybeans are cooked, then strained. The resulting liquid is soy milk. A coagulating agent is added to the soy milk, and the resulting curds are shaped into blocks. Tofu is an inexpensive ingredient that lends itself to many styles of preparation. In the 1780s two best-selling books each promised one hundred tofu recipes (Richie, 1985, pp. 34–41).

Two simple ways of serving tofu are popular. *Hiyayakko* is chilled tofu cut into bite-sized pieces and served with a dipping sauce of soy sauce and grated ginger or chopped scallions. *Yudoofu* is tofu cut into cubes and heated in hot water seasoned with kelp. Once warm, the cubes are lifted out and dipped in a heated sauce flavored with grated daikon radish.

Iridoofu is made by stirring tofu over heat with bits of carrots, shiitake mushrooms, and snow peas. *Dengaku* is tofu roasted on bamboo skewers, then spread with flavored miso and roasted again.

Tofu can be deep-fried. Cut into thick slices and dredged in potato starch, it is fried to make *agedashi-doofu* and is served with a sweetened soy sauce dip. Cut into thin slices and double-fried, *usuage* is often sliced in thin strips and used in boiled dishes because it holds together well, or it is used as a small edible pouch for sweet vinegared rice to make *inari-zushi*.

In addition to the raw and fried versions, tofu is freeze-dried. This product is easily stored, and when reconstituted with water, it has a distinctive spongelike texture. It is often simmered with vegetables or put into soups. Known commonly as *koori-doofu* and *shimi-doofu*, this tofu is also called *kooya-doofu* or Kooya tofu. It is said that monks on cold Mount Kooya discovered their tofu was frozen. When in their thriftiness they used it anyway, they were pleasantly surprised.

Seafood. Japan is surrounded by the sea. Both cold and warm currents lap the islands, creating a variety of ecological niches. This in turn supplies Japan with a variety of fish, shellfish, and marine vegetables. The general attitude in Japan is that the freshest fish are best enjoyed raw. Fish that are not as fresh should be grilled with salt, and fish of even lesser freshness should be stewed with soy sauce or miso (Ishige, 2000, p. 1177).

Since the Edo period raw fish has been served as sashimi, sliced into bite-sized pieces and garnished. Grated daikon radish or wasabi, a Japanese root product related to horseradish that adds pungent flavor, is provided along with a small side bowl of dipping sauce. The radish or wasabi condiment is added to the dipping sauce to taste, then the fish slices are dipped and eaten. In casual home cooking this dipping sauce might simply be soy sauce, but in restaurants it is often soy sauce reduced with sake (Tsuji, 1980, pp. 159–160). Before the Edo period raw fish was usually served as *namasu*, in which it is sliced and marinated in flavored rice vinegar, but with the advent of commercial-scale soy sauce production, the shift was to sashimi (Ishige, 2000, p. 1177).

Also in the Edo period sushi arose, originally a means of preserving fish. The fish was salted, then packed in cooked rice. With lactic acid fermentation, the rice developed a vinegarlike taste and preserved the fish, but the rice was discarded when the fish was served. By the 1400s people began to eat the rice as well, and in the Edo period slices of fresh fish were served atop small mounds of vinegared rice, often with a dab of wasabi added to the top of the rice (Ishige, 2000, p. 1177). This came to be known internationally as sushi, but more properly this style that developed in Edo (now Tokyo) in the early 1800s is *nigiri-zushi*. The older tradition of western Japan, particularly of Osaka, was to pack vinegared rice into a mold, cover the rice with marinated fish, remove the contents from the mold, then slice the resulting loaf into bite-sized pieces (Richie, 1985, p. 15; Tsuji, 1980, p. 288).

A great many vegetables are harvested from the seas. Kelp was mentioned above for its importance in making soup stock. *Wakame* is often used as a solid ingredient in soup and might be mixed with a variety of seaweeds in vinegared salads. Agar-agar *(kanten)* is important in traditional confections. Nori is well known as the nearly black paperlike sheets that wrap certain types of sushi (Tsuji, 1980, pp. 54–55, 72–73, 79–80, 97).

Meat. Eating meat was long a taboo in Japan. An imperial decree against eating several kinds of meats was issued in 675 C.E. In the Heian period (ninth to twelfth centuries), with the increased importance of Buddhism, meat eating largely disappeared in cities, though professional hunters were still active in remote areas. Nevertheless animals were not raised for slaughter. Cattle existed only for pulling carts and plows, and even their milk was not used. Buddhist priests were further enjoined from eating fish also, but the general populace ignored this stricture (Ishige, 2000, p. 1176).

Following Ishige's assertion that "traditional cuisine" is that of the Edo period, beef, popularized in the Meiji period (1868–1912), might be outside the focus of this article (Ishige, 2000, p. 1181). The innovations of the Meiji period succeeded, however, because they adapted to the norms of traditional cuisine (Cwiertka, 1999, p. 54), and the smooth shift eventually came to be seen as continuity.

With the opening of Japan to the West in the 1850s, the country quickly began to incorporate aspects of Western life, often with a catch-up mentality. In the 1860s the first slaughterhouse for cattle was built, and by the early 1870s beef eating was a fad. In 1873 the emperor endorsed the new custom. This gave rise to the dish called sukiyaki, in which beef is simmered in a traditional broth of sweetened soy sauce and sake along with other traditional items, such as grilled tofu, shiitake mushrooms, and chrysanthemum greens *(shungiku)* (Richie, 1985, pp. 21–25). The popularization of pork seems to have followed in the 1930s in the form of *tonkatsu*, a deep-fried, breaded pork cutlet (Richie, 1985, pp. 49–51).

This popular acceptance of distinctly foreign foods is paralleled in Japanese history by tempura, the crisply coated, deep-fried fish and vegetables known around the world. The Portuguese were a presence in Japan in the second half of the sixteenth century, and they apparently batter-fried their fish. The method spread, and by the mid-1700s tempura was popular, sold mainly from street carts (Ishige, 2000, p. 1177).

Beverages

The two most representative beverages of Japan are tea and sake. Tea was first imported into Japan in the 800s from China. The tea was formed into bricks, then allowed to cure by fermentation. These blocks of tea were powdered and boiled. After some popularity among the aristocracy, tea drinking in Japan died out. It was reintroduced in the 1200s, this time as powdered green tea. This is the tea of the famed tea ceremony of Japan, but its popularity was limited, perhaps due to the complex rituals associated with the drink. Sometime in the 1600s tea was reintroduced to Japan, this time as an infusion made with the green leaf. This style of tea has become dominant in Japan and is served in homes, offices, and restaurants. In the Meiji period black, Western-style tea was introduced, and by the 1920s it was widely popular (Ishige, 2000, pp. 1180, 1182; Kumakura, 1999, p. 40).

Sake, like rice and *mochi*, carries symbolic importance. It is offered to Shinto deities both at home altars and at large public shrines, and it is the drink that seals the marriage in any Shinto wedding ceremony. Although sake has a long history, modern sake is clear and has a higher alcohol content (15 to 17 percent) than before the twentieth century. Steamed white rice is inoculated with a mold called *kofi (Aspergillum oryzae)*, which starts the fermentation. About two days later, sake yeast *(Saccharomyces cerevisiae)* is added. Including refining, sake is produced in forty-five to sixty days. Sake does not improve with age; it should be consumed soon after production. Special cups and serving bottles are used for sake, and a fairly elaborate serving etiquette accompanies pouring drinks. While beer and whiskey are more popular than sake, the serving etiquette of these two drinks is based on that of sake (Tsuji, 1980, pp. 336–340).

Seasonality

The Japanese often pride themselves on the seasonality of their traditional food. In the mass market many foods are available without regard to season, but most traditional Japanese meals include seasonal aspects. As noted above, the solid ingredients in soups and the selection of materials for salads both announce the season in everyday meals.

Certain foods are only harvested and sold seasonally. The puffer or blowfish (fugu), which can quickly kill the eater if the poisonous liver is not properly removed, is available only in cold months, when the poison is said to be less potent (Richie, 1985, pp. 47–48). A fragrant and expensive mushroom, *matsutake*, is only found in the fall. The *ayu*, a fresh-water fish rather like a trout, is a food for early summer.

Some special days are marked by serving particular dishes. On 7 January it is traditional to eat a rice porridge made with seven springtime herbs *(nanakusa-gayu)*. In August, on the day of the ox as calculated by a traditional ephemeris, people eat grilled eel (or more innovatively some form of beef) to strengthen themselves to withstand the remaining days of summer. On the first day of winter many homes serve *tooji kabocha*, pumpkin cooked with sweet *azuki* beans.

Other foods are served differently in different seasons. Some prefer *soba* noodles served cold with a small cup of cold dipping sauce on the side, but the same noodles are more often served in a bowl of hot broth in the winter. Early in the Edo period sake was warmed only in fall and winter (Ishige, 2000, p. 1180). Since then it has often been served warm throughout the year, but after the 1990s cold sake experienced a resurgence, especially in the summer. Miso soup as served in the cuisine of the tea ceremony is a blend of red miso with white. In the depths of winter the mixture is almost completely red

BENTO BOX

Japanese *bento*, or *obento*, is a meal compartmentalized in a lidded box, usually made of lacquered wood. Often square or rectangular in shape, there are also round and oval types in which cut bamboo leaves are used to separate each food item. A *bento* box typically contains rice, pickles, braised vegetables, and a protein such as fish, poultry, or meat, each placed in individual sections. The new, internationally popular *bento* box lunch, served in a humble wooden or plastic box and usually offered by Japanese restaurants, is directly related to the *makunouchi* (meaning "between curtains") *bento* developed during the Edo period (1600–1868). This type of box lunch was intended as a conventional meal to be eaten during intermission at kabuki plays. During the same period, a more stylish type of *bento* box, called *shokado bento*, evolved in Osaka. In this type, each food item is placed in a small individual porcelain or lacquered wood dish, and then in a larger lacquered square or rectangular box. *Shokado bento* are not meant to be used as portable lunch boxes. Displaying colorful food rather artfully (much like traditional *kaiseki*, the elegant multi-course meals served prior to formal tea ceremonies), the *shokado bento* can be ordered in restaurants and other formal settings.

During the Meiji (1868–1912) and Taisho (1912–1926) periods, and with the arrival of railway stations, the *eki-ben* (meaning "station meal") box evolved. These boxes, although made of plastic or other light-weight material, are still available, often offering regional foods related to the station where people board the train. *Eki-ben* is, perhaps, also related to the original lunch-on-the-go given to the soldiers of the Heian period (794–1192). Once called *tonjiki* (meaning "soldier's meal"), *onigiri* is a handful of rice with salty fish or pickles set in the center and wrapped triangularly with *nori* (dried laver sheet), a common red algae.

Consistent with the Japanese appreciation for specificity, there are various types of *bento* box meals related to the particular individual or event. For example, a mother might prepare *tsugaku bento* for her child's school lunch or *aisai* (meaning "beloved wife") *bento* for her husband to take to work. *Koraku bento* are prepared for outdoor activities (for example, hiking), *domu bento* are sold at baseball stadiums, and *hokaben bento* are take-out meals.

BIBLIOGRAPHY

Ashkenazi, Michael, and Jeanne Jacob. *The Essence of Japanese Cuisine: An Essay on Food and Culture.* Surrey, England: Curzon, 2000.

Kamekura, Junichi, Mamaru Watanabe, and Gideon Bosker. *Ekiben: The Art of the Japanese Box Lunch.* San Francisco: Chronicle, 1989.

Mitsukuni, Yoshida, and Sesoko Tsune, eds. *Naorai: Communion of the Table.* Hiroshima: Mazda Motor Corp., 1989.

Corinne Trang

miso, which is considered hearty and warming. Into spring more white miso is blended in, and by summer it is almost completely white miso, which is considered a much lighter dish.

The dishes and plates on which food is served are also seasonally appropriate. The deep, warm-looking bowls of winter gradually give way to the flatter, more airy and open-looking bowls of summer. Glass, because it reminds one of ice, is used to give a cool look to a set of summer dishes. Dishes might also have painted decorations appropriate to the seasons, such as cherry blossoms for spring or colored leaves for fall.

Seasonal sweets. Seasonality is also marked in Japan by serving sweets associated with particular seasons or holidays. The doll festival is a minor holiday on 3 March. Families with girls display elaborate sets of decorative dolls that represent the imperial court of the Heian period. Girls might have parties at their homes and serve two traditional foods, *hishi-mochi*, diamond-shaped multicolored sweets made with puffed rice, and *amazake*, an unclarified, milky-white sake sweetened and flavored with ginger. *Arare* and *amazake* are sold in department stores and local convenience stores ahead of the festival date and are often shared as snacks (*o-sanji* or *o-yatsu*) for afternoon breaks in offices and other workplaces. While people with daughters to celebrate on this day have an obvious reason to buy and serve these sweets, many others do so as well. These two dishes are recognized as seasonal foods and are available once a year.

Other minor holidays are associated with particular sweets, such as the vernal and autumnal equinoxes, boys' day (5 May), and the celebration of the full moon of fall. The cherry blossom season also has its own associated sweets.

The New Year. Of all the holidays in Japan, New Year's is by far the most elaborate. It is celebrated on 1 Janu-

Contemporary variation on a traditional bento box as served at a Japanese restaurant in New York City, 2002. PHOTO CORINNE TRANG.

the rice between each stroke. The resulting dough was cut into small balls or rolled into a large sheet and later cut into squares. Today, most people buy processed *mochi.*

It is traditional that no (substantial) cooking takes place for the first three days of the new year, so elaborate side dishes are prepared at the end of the year and beautifully arranged in decorative lacquered boxes for the New Year feast. While many housewives preserve this tradition, others order these traditional dishes ahead of time from caterers.

On the last night of the year, it is traditional to eat buckwheat noodles, *soba,* called *toshi-koshi soba* (crossing-the-years *soba*). The noodles are served in a hot broth, typically garnished with scallions, fish sausage *(kamaboko),* or perhaps a piece of batter-fried shrimp (tempura). These long and thin noodles are eaten in the hope that life may be long and thin (virtuously upright).

On the morning of 1 January the family eats the most ritually elaborate meal of the year together. The foods prepared for this meal are called *o-sechi ryoori.* Many are good luck foods because of some pun or metaphorical connection with desired traits. The meal typically begins with a drink of *otoso,* a sweet, spiced sake. A sweet life is further ensured by eating such foods as small candied fish or chestnuts in a sweet potato comfit. Red snapper *(tai)* is eaten because its name recalls the word *omedetai* (auspicious). Sweetened black beans *(mame)* are eaten to become hard working *(mame)* in the new year. A kind of seaweed, *kombu,* is eaten because it sounds like the word for being happy *(yorokobu).* Special chopsticks made of willow are often used at this meal so in the new year the family members will be as flexible in body and mind as a willow tree.

The single most important dish of this meal, however, is the soup, called *ozooni.* Many regional variations of this soup exist. In eastern and northern Japan (including Tokyo) it is typically a clear soup with a few vegetables, while in the west (including Kyoto and Osaka) the soup is made with white miso. Regardless, if it is soup for New Year's morning that has *mochi* in it, it is called *ozooni.* This pounded rice paste, *mochi,* is considered the very essence of rice (Ishige, 2000, p. 1176). Since for centuries rice was a food for the elite and a traditional offering to the Shinto deities, to eat rice essence helps begin the new year right. Traditionally *mochi* is eaten instead of rice for the first three days of the year. Besides being eaten in soup, it is also boiled and dipped in a mixture of sugar and powdered soybeans *(kinako)* or grilled, wrapped in small strips of nori seaweed, and dipped in sweetened soy sauce.

BIBLIOGRAPHY

Ashkenazi, Michael, and Jeanne Jacob. *The Essence of Japanese Cuisine: An Essay on Food and Culture.* Philadelphia: University of Pennsylvania Press, 2000. Outstanding and

ary of the Western calendar, and most stores and offices are closed until 3 January. Special trains run all night shuttling people to major Shinto shrines, where they pray for a good year. Children receive envelopes containing money from their parents, relatives, and family friends, and large bundles of postcards with New Year's greetings are delivered on New Year's Day.

Through December many workplaces and university clubs hold year-end parties. These are often elaborate feasts of traditional Japanese food washed down with copious amounts of beer, whiskey, and sake. These parties are called *boonen-kai,* literally a gathering for "forgetting the year," specifically burying grudges of the past. Some groups host more abstemious Christmas parties instead, at which the food is usually Western and the drinks include sparkling wine.

In the last few days of the year, a New Year's delicacy called *mochi* was made traditionally. Glutinous rice was steamed, then put in a large mortar standing about two and a half feet tall and two to three feet in diameter. One person would swing a large mallet, pounding the mass of rice, while a second person reached in and turned accessible contextualization of Japanese food from a social science perspective.

Brennan, Jennifer. "Japan." In *The Oxford Companion to Food*, edited by Alan Davidson, pp. 413–415. Oxford: Oxford University Press, 1999.

Cwiertka, Katarzyna. "How Cooking Became a Hobby." In *The Culture of Japan as Seen through Its Leisure*, edited by Sepp Linhart and Sabine Frühstück, pp. 41–58. Albany: State University of New York Press, 1998.

Ekuan, Kenji. *The Aesthetics of the Japanese Lunchbox*. Edited by David B. Stewart. Cambridge, Mass.: MIT Press, 1998. Using Japanese food arrangement as a paradigm, the author expands to a general theory of Japanese design.

Frost, Griffith, and John Gaunter. *Saké: Pure and Simple*. Berkeley, Calif.: Stone Bridge Press, 1999.

Hosking, Richard. *A Dictionary of Japanese Food: Ingredients and Culture*. Boston: Tuttle Publishing, 1972. Names of Japanese ingredients with good English descriptions.

Ishige, Naomichi. "Japan." In *The Cambridge World History of Food*, edited by Kenneth F. Kiple and Kriemhild Coneè Ornelas, vol. 2, pp. 1175–1183. Cambridge, U.K.: Cambridge University Press, 2000.

Kondo, Hiroshi. *Sake: A Drinker's Guide*. Tokyo: Kodansha International, 1984.

Kumakura, Isao. "Tea and Japan's Culinary Revolution." *Japan Echo* 26, no. 2 (April 1999): 39–43.

Mittwer, Gretchen. "Tea Sweets: A Historical Study." *Chanoyu Quarterly* 57 (1989): 18–34.

Nakano, Makiko. *Makiko's Diary: A Merchant Wife in 1910 Kyoto*. Translated and annotated by Kazuko Smith. Stanford, Calif.: Stanford University Press, 1995.

Ohnuki-Tierney, Emiko. *Rice as Self: Japanese Identities through Time*. Princeton, N.J.: Princeton University Press, 1993.

Richie, Donald. *A Taste of Japan*. Tokyo: Kodansha International, 1985. Essays on various Japanese foods by a major interpreter of Japan to the West. Well illustrated.

Rodríguez del Alisal, María-Dolores. "Japanese Lunch Boxes: From Convenient Snack to the Convenience Store." In *Consumption and Material Culture in Contemporary Japan*, edited by Michael Ashkenazi and John Clammer, pp. 40–80. London: Kegan Paul, 2000.

Tsuchiya, Yoshio. *A Feast for the Eyes: The Japanese Art of Food Arrangement*. Tokyo: Kodansha International, 1985.

Tsuji, Shizuo. "Cooking, Japanese." In *Kodansha Encyclopedia of Japan*, vol. 2, pp. 20–25. Tokyo: Kodansha International, 1983.

Tsuji, Shizuo. *Japanese Cooking: A Simple Art*. Tokyo: Kodansha International, 1980.

Tsuji, Shizuo, and Naomichi Ishige. "Food and Eating." In *Kodansha Encyclopedia of Japan*, vol. 2, pp. 304–307. Tokyo: Kodansha International, 1983.

Yoneda, Soei, Koei Hoshino, and Kim Schuefftan. *Good Food from a Japanese Temple*. Tokyo: Kodansha International, 1982. Subsequently republished as *The Heart of Japanese Cuisine* (Tokyo: Kodansha, 1987). A practical and nuanced introduction to Japanese cooking.

James-Henry Holland

CONTEMPORARY ISSUES IN JAPANESE CUISINE

The twentieth century, and a few decades preceding it, was for Japanese cuisine a time of diminishing contrasts and increasing variety. During this period the food habits of the Japanese people advanced in two opposite directions. On the one hand, the dietary practices thus far restricted to the urban population spread to all areas of the country. On the other hand, it was a time of revolutionary change in the range of available foodstuffs and in applied cooking techniques. Never before had foreign food infiltrated Japanese cuisine to such an extent as it did during the twentieth century.

The Making of a National Cuisine

By the 1950s, the abundant regional variety and sharp class distinctions in diet that had been characteristic of premodern Japan gave way to a relatively homogeneous cuisine. The discrepancy between the sophisticated meals of the elite, the simple fare of the townsfolk, and the meager nourishment of peasants gradually faded away. Although the trade in local specialties flourished under the rise of capitalism, regional flavor had become by the late twentieth century the exception rather than the rule in the dietary culture of the Japanese people (Noguchi, 1994, pp. 323–326).

Urbanization has been largely responsible for the blending of regional food habits in modern Japan. The migration of great numbers of Japanese to Korea, Manchuria, and other colonies, and their repatriation after 1945, contributed to it as well. Modern food preservation technologies, such as canning and freezing, along with the popularization of foreign food, also played an important role in making the Japanese diet uniform. The increasing impact of mass media and home-economics education, as well as rising living standards, were other crucial factors in this process.

First of all, the rice-centered meal pattern consisting of a serving of rice, a bowl of soup, pickles (*tsukemono*), and side dishes had by the mid-twentieth century become a national standard. This pattern developed around the thirteenth century in the kitchens of wealthy warriors and monks, spread to less affluent samurai and townspeople during the following centuries, but only became the norm in peasant households in the wake of World War II. The daily diet of the rural population of Japan had thus far been composed of hearty soups; various types of millet, buckwheat, and barley, rather than rice, were their staples. Although rice has, since ancient times, been the most important crop in Japan, forming the center of its economy, a rice-based diet has for centuries been unattainable for the majority of the population (Ohnuki-Tierney, 1993, pp. 30–43).

The same holds true for soy sauce—nowadays regarded as the prevalent Japanese flavoring, the essence of Japanese cuisine. It should be mentioned that before the modernization of the country began in the late nineteenth century, peasants constituted more than 80 percent of the population. It is only since the beginning of the twentieth century that soy sauce has become affordable for every Japanese family. Before this shift took place, soybean paste (*miso*) had been the principal flavoring in farm households. Along with the factors mentioned earlier, the increased efficiency in production and retailing of soy sauce in the twentieth century helped it assume the position of Japan's national condiment.

Multicultural Eating

World War II is generally regarded as the watershed between the traditional and modern culinary culture in Japan. The food shortage of the 1940s diminished dietary prejudices, the American Occupation (1945–1952) instigated a powerful Westernizing influence, and the 1960s economic boom provided the means for the majority of the population to re-create affluent meals of the past and to mimic foreign food fashions (White, 2002, pp. 64–73).

Indeed, the economic affluence of the 1970s and 1980s supported extensive Westernization of Japanese food habits. A clear decrease in rice, soybean, and fish consumption, and a concomitant rise in red meat, dairy, and wheat consumption is just one of many indicators of this shift.

The year 1971 serves as a symbolic point marking the beginning of Japan catching up with the rest of the world in culinary culture. In that year the first McDonald's outlet was opened in Tokyo, soon followed by other American fast-food chains, ice-cream parlors, and steakhouses. The late 1980s and early 1990s witnessed the rise of the so-called ethnic food (*esunikku ryori*) boom. The ethnic-food category encompassed a variety of South and Southeast Asian cuisines as well as other culinary rarities such as Caribbean and Ethiopian cooking. This interchange of trends has turned Japanese cities into multicultural melting pots, hardly different in this respect from their counterparts elsewhere in the world. French, Italian, Chinese, Korean, and Indian are ubiquitous geographical headings on restaurant billboards in contemporary Japan.

Not only the restaurant culture underwent extensive transformation during the last decades of the twentieth century. Japanese home menus are less adventurous, yet by no means do they lack foreign influence. Most foreign dishes are incorporated as side dishes into the rice-centered meal pattern with soup and pickles. Dishes such as curried rice, spaghetti, and Chinese-style fried noodles are exceptions to this rule as they already constitute a meal.

The school lunch system, introduced in 1947 by the Allied Occupation authorities as a means of improving the nutrition of Japanese children, had a profound impact on the Westernization of Japanese home cooking. School lunches differed markedly from the typical Japanese meal in their strong emphasis on bread and milk, often combined with Western-style dishes such as curry

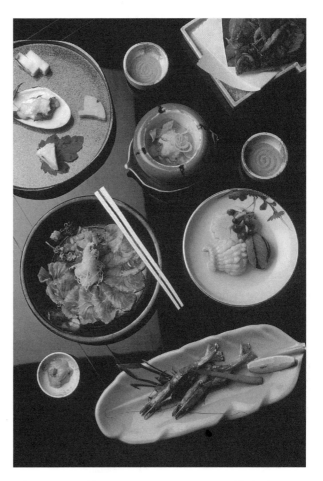

When Japan's older generation eats out, more likely than not, the meal of choice will be found in a quiet country inn, as in this dinner served at Miyabo Roykan in Kanazawa, Japan. © BOB KRIST/CORBIS.

stew, hamburger steak, spaghetti with meat sauce, and salad (Ehara, 1999). The kinds and combinations of foods served at school not only influenced children's tastes, but also indirectly affected the meals served in their homes. The postwar generations of children raised on such school lunches have grown into adults with tastes distinctly different from those of their parents and grandparents. The mass media and home-economics education provided Japanese women with the skills and expertise to satisfy the new food tastes of their families.

Accommodating Foreign Food

Although internationalization of Japanese cuisine has been proceeding rapidly from the 1960s onward, it was not entirely a product of post–World War II decades. The first signs of Western influence could already be seen in the late nineteenth century, soon after the opening of Japanese ports to foreign trade and the launch of a series of social and economic reforms.

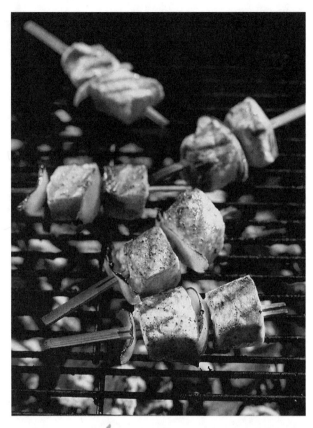

Young Japanese prefer to drink beer and eat *yakomono* (grilled foods) rather than more traditional dishes. Grilled chicken and fish (shown here) are among the most popular. PHOTO BY ANDRÉ BARANOWSKI.

The first Western-style restaurants in Japan opened in the 1860s in port towns that were designated to receive foreign ships and accommodate Western settlements. These restaurants were at first targeted exclusively at Western clientele. With the growing popularity of Western-style dining among the Japanese upper classes, however, Western-style restaurants began to cater to the Japanese customer as well. By the late 1880s, each provincial city in Japan had at least one Western-style restaurant, and within the next few decades a great many Western-style diners (*yoshokuya*) mushroomed throughout the country. They provided less affluent Japanese citizens with domesticated versions of Western-style dishes, such as fried fish, beefsteak, veal cutlet, croquettes, omelets, and stew. These dishes were not served as components of set menus consisting of several courses, as was the general practice at more expensive establishments, but were to be ordered à la carte and usually served accompanied by a plate of Japanese-style boiled rice. For the working classes, these Western-style diners were their only opportunity to try food that was different from what they usually had at home. Western-style cookery was not to enter Japanese folk kitchens until several decades later.

The early twentieth century did witness, however, the rise of a hybrid style of Japanese-Western home cooking among the nouveau-riche class of white-collar urban professionals. Middle-class housewives looking for diversion in their domestic chores ardently embraced this new eclectic cuisine (Cwiertka, 1998, pp. 49–54). Next to Western-style dishes, Chinese-style recipes began to be prominently featured in household literature from the 1920s onward—a decade after cheap eateries run by Chinese immigrants became popular in Japanese cities. Western and Chinese cooking techniques such as panfrying, stewing, and deep-frying of breaded meat and fish enlarged the variety of Japanese cookery. By the 1930s, the Japanese-Western-Chinese culinary triptych was firmly established as the foundation of modern Japanese foodways. The incorporation of Western-style and Chinese-style dishes into the diet of the Japanese armed forces contributed greatly to the popularization of this new food among all segments of society (Cwiertka, 2002, pp. 7–15).

Food Safety

From the 1970s onward, when rice-centered cuisine had reached the entire population and was about to be challenged by the encroachment of foreign food, a concern about sufficient food supply gradually shifted toward food safety (Jussaume, Hisano, and Taniguchi, 2000). Consumer awareness about the risks of food contamination and the connection between environmental pollution and food production grew steadily. In 1973, the National Association of Consumer Cooperatives (now known as the Japan Consumer Cooperatives Union) began to emphasize food safety in its marketing strategies. Various consumer groups advocating organic farming and reduction of food imports became active all over Japan. The issue attracted wide public attention in the late 1980s and early 1990s, when pressure from the United States and some European countries to open Japan's rice market met with violent opposition in Japan. A current example of the mainstreaming of the food-safety movement is the fact that the Japanese public strongly opposes genetically modified foods despite assurances from the Japanese government about their safety.

With the first Japanese case of bovine spongiform encephalopathy reported in 2001, and an increase in the incidence of child obesity and coronary diseases, it seems that Japanese consumers have not only added Western foods to their menus, but now have some of the same worries about food as Europeans and Americans.

See also **China**; **Korea**; **Southeast Asia**; **Tea**.

BIBLIOGRAPHY

Cwiertka, Katarzyna. "How Cooking Became a Hobby: Changes in Attitude Towards Cooking in Early Twentieth Century Japan." In *The Culture of Japan as Seen Through Its Leisure*, edited by Sabine Frühstück and Sepp Linhart, pp. 41–58. New York: State University of New York Press, 1998.

Cwiertka, Katarzyna. "Munching on Modernity: Popularizing Military Diet in Wartime and Postwar Japan." *Asian Anthropology* 1, no. 1 (2002), 1–30.

Ehara, Ayako. "School Meals and Japan's Changing Diet." *Japan Echo* 26, no. 4 (August 1999): 56–60.

Jussaume, Raymond A., Jr., Shuji Hisano, and Yoshimitsu Taniguchi. " Food Safety in Japan." In *Japanstudien* 12, edited by Nicola Liscutin and René Haak, pp. 211–228. Munich: Iudicium, 2000.

Noguchi, Paul. "Savor Slowly: *Ekiben*—The Fast Food of High-Speed Japan." *Ethnology* 33, no. 4 (Fall 1994): 317–330.

Ohnuki-Tierney, Emiko. *Rice as Self*. Princeton, N.J.: Princeton University Press, 1993.

White, Merry I. "Ladies Who Lunch: Young Women and the Domestic Fallacy in Japan." In *Asian Food: The Global and the Local*, edited by Katarzyna Cwiertka with Boudewijn Walraven, pp. 63–75. Honolulu: University of Hawaii Press, 2002.

Katarzyna J. Cwiertka

Ceramic bucket for kugel and steamed pudding. Saarland, Germany, circa 1890–1915. Used in cooking classes of the *Verein für Fraueninteressen* (Women's Topical Club) in Landau, Germany, until about 1918. The club membership was largely Jewish. ROUGHWOOD COLLECTION. PHOTO CHEW & COMPANY.

JUDAISM.

Jewish food is primarily defined by the dietary laws of Judaism. The Judaic religion is prescriptive in the selection, cooking preparation, and consumption of specific food items. Daily practice is meticulously structured to comply with Jewish law, the Halakhah, and the community of Jews is organized as a community of religiously complying eaters. Specific dishes, food combinations, and cooking preparations are prescribed for religious festivals. Throughout their history of multiple migrations and diaspora (dispersion), the Jews have been in contact with different cultures, languages, and cuisines. This has generated a diversified Jewish cuisine.

Dietary Laws

Under the classifying terminology of kosher versus nonkosher, the system of dietary prescriptions and prohibitions in Judaism primarily involves the consumption of animal flesh, and is codified in the Pentateuch, in Leviticus (chapter 11). Typical edible animals are domestic, have a vegetarian diet, and are physiologically "plain," that is, not affected by any disease or anatomical or physiological defect. In fact, as Mary Douglas has pointed out in *Purity and Danger*, the dietary prohibitions of Leviticus include a biblical narrative logic. They are organized along the mythological lines that structure the cosmological section of Genesis. Thus the animal kingdom is classified into three categories: those living on the earth, those living in the water, and those living in the air. In the first category, only mammal quadruped ruminants with split hooves are allowed on the Jewish table. Striking exceptions to this rule are emphatically mentioned in the text. Among the animals living on the earth, the swine, the camel, the hare, and the rock-badger are specifically excluded from the Jewish table because they satisfy only one condition for edibility; that is, either they are a ruminant, or they have a split hoof, instead of both

conditions required. The category of animals living in the air also functions as an exclusive system, when it provides a list of animals strictly prohibited on the table. Most of these animals are carnivorous birds, while the bat is eliminated for being a flying mammal, an utmost abomination by the Leviticus standards. Finally, animals living in the water should have fins and scales to be considered "pure" and edible, while those crawling on the earth or living underground are also considered "impure."

In addition to these dietary prohibitions concerning the selection of animals based on anatomical and physiological criteria, biblical law forbids the consumption of blood (Deuteronomy 12:23) and the mixture, in the kitchen and at the table, of dairy foods and meat dishes (Exodus 23:19). The former rule thus requires the strict observance of slaughtering techniques designed to evacuate the largest amount of blood from meat cuts before they are distributed to the marketplace. Some secular scholars have interpreted the regulation of Jewish food practices by religious law and sacred scriptures as evidence that the idea of God is at the core of the Jewish table. This spirit, although viewed by some as being motivated by hygienic concerns, has generated a complex system of community institutional organization that involves the technical training of rabbinical slaughterers (*shohatim*), their appointment in slaughtering houses, and the establishment of a system of verification of the

Vollständiges
praktisches Kochbuch
für die jüdische Küche

The 1910 edition of Josephine Gumprich's *Complete Practical Cookbook for the Jewish Kitchen*, which first appeared at Trier, Germany, in 1888. This book was popular with Jews in Europe and ran through several editions. ROUGHWOOD COLLECTION.

good omen. Most holiday menus are linked to the religious festivals and have a narrative function. Examples include the fried pastries served during Hanukkah. The holiday of Hanukkah is a ritual celebration of the biblical section narrating the Maccabees' victory over the Seleucid Greeks in the second century B.C.E. and the following miracle that kept the ritual oil lit for eight days in the Second Jerusalem Temple after it had been devastated by the Greek armies. Thus, in the Jewish communities of central and eastern European origin, the tradition requires that latkes, fried potato pancakes, be served. The equivalent in the Jewish traditions of the Mediterranean and the Middle East is usually fried buns served with honey. Purim celebrations include the baking of multiple pastries, a playful reminder of the defeat of Haman. Thus, Ashkenazic families serve *hamantashen* or "Haman's hats," poppy seed–filled triangular pastries.

The Jewish festival of Passover, a ritual narration of the Jewish slaves' exodus from Pharaoh's Egypt, includes special food prescriptions. During the eight days of the holiday, the only bread allowed for consumption is unleavened bread, to commemorate the bread that the slaves took in their hasty overnight flight from slavery. This unleavened bread, called matzo in Hebrew, is industrially baked today as a thin square flat cracker according to the Ashkenazic (eastern and central European) tradition. In Sephardic (Mediterranean and Middle Eastern) traditions, matzo has a round shape. The Passover food restrictions also require that no leavened substance be included either in the kitchen and menus or in the household at all. Some North African Jewish communities exclude rice from their Passover diet. Some also exclude chicken for fear of finding grain in the gizzard. Thus most Passover pastries and carbohydrate dishes are prepared with matzo flour or cracked matzo. Ashkenazic Jews traditionally serve matzo balls boiled in chicken soup, matzo brei (a fried, egg-coated matzo pancake), while North African Jews often enjoy the flavors of a couscous made out of cracked matzo.

Shavuot, or festival of the Torah, is marked by the consumption of honey and dairy foods, with which the Torah is allegorically identified. *Blintzes*, cheese pancakes, are displayed on Ashkenazic tables, while Sephardic traditions include yogurt or *baklava*. The favorite dishes served for Rosh Hashanah (Jewish new year) include heavily sweetened dishes such as the Ashkenazic *tzimmes* (a sweet carrot and raisin stew) and honey cake, all of which are designed to welcome a good and sweet new year. The fall festival of Sukkoth (also Sukkot) includes *borsht*, a beet and cabbage-based soup, served in households of Polish origin.

enforcement of dietary laws. The latter requirement is often handled by secular agencies, in collaboration with local rabbinical authorities. In New York, for example, the presence of the largest urban Jewish population in the world has generated a system in which the state government is in charge of the enforcement of kosher laws in the local food stores, especially those selling meat displayed as being kosher (Fried, 2000).

Jewish Festival Foods

At the core of all Jewish festival tables is the sanctified bread, or challah. Oven-baked and usually excluding dairy ingredients, the loaves are braided, though other shapes can be found in various Jewish traditions. Another typical festive dish is the Ashkenazic gefilte fish (Yiddish, "stuffed fish"), opening sabbath or holiday meals as a

Sabbath Foods

The Jews' food history is characterized by their many migrations and their status as a minority group. From this viewpoint, it is as diverse as Jewish cultures, languages, and community experiences have been, as Jews have related to the multiple cultures and populations they have been in contact with throughout the world. Jewish food has operated, both practically and symbolically, and not unlike Jewish languages, as Jewish versions of local nutritional habits. An illustration can be found in most dishes served for the most important holiday of the Jewish ritual calendar, the Sabbath. The *tshulent* is the Ashkenazic version of this sabbatical dish. The Yiddish name of this dish includes two French words, *chaud* ('warm') and *lent* ('slow'), a linguistic combination testifying not only to the many influences on Jewish culture and languages, but also to the specifically Jewish character of this dish's cooking technique. It is in effect cooked slowly for about twelve hours between the beginning of Sabbath (Friday night) and the Saturday lunch. This long and slow cooking is the result of the sabbatical prohibition on lighting fire during the twenty-four hours between Friday night and Saturday night. This implies that once the Sabbath candle is lit on Friday evening, any food starting to cook then will end up being overcooked when it is consumed on Saturday. In North Africa and the Middle East, this dish is called by either of the Arabic terms *dfina* or *tfina* ('buried'), *skhina* or *hammin* ('warm'). The first set of terms refers to the burying of the pot underneath blankets or even in an underground oven designed to keep warmth in. The second set of terms refers to the permanent warmth of the dish. All Sabbath dishes are composed of heavy and varied ingredients found in the local marketplace: beef, grain, potatoes, vegetables, peas or beans. In eastern North Africa, the tradition was to use green vegetables such as spinach or Swiss chard, fresh fava beans, or cardoons. This ingredient use is probably a custom borrowed from local Muslim neighbors. Muslims of these regions serve very green dishes for major holiday dinners, in the belief that green was the Prophet's favorite color. Thus local Jews have integrated this color symbol into their own major holidays.

The many migrations that have affected the Jews of eastern Europe, North Africa, and the Middle East throughout the twentieth century have resulted, in the early twenty-first century, in the massive secularization of the Jewish migrants in the hosting countries. Traditional Jewish food has thus become a marker of ethnic identity rather than a part of religious observance. On the other side, these traditional dishes, because they are the last ritual items to be given up in the process of Jewish secularization, constitute practical and social frameworks allowing religious observance to be maintained, even in its minimal scope.

See also **Bagel**; **Bread, Symbolism of**; **Christianity**; **Diaspora**; **Fasting and Abstinence: Judaism**; **Feasts, Festivals, and Fasts**; **Islam**; **Passover**; **Religion and Food**; **Taboos**; **United States: Ethnic Cuisines**.

BIBLIOGRAPHY

Bahloul, Joëlle. *Le culte de la table dressée: Rites et traditions de la table juive algérienne*. Paris: A.-M. Métailié, 1983.

Cernea, Ruth Fredman. *The Passover Seder: Afikoman in Exile.* Philadelphia: University of Pennsylvania Press, 1981.

Douglas, Mary. *Purity and Danger; An Analysis of Concepts of Pollution and Taboo.* New York: Praeger, 1966.

Fried, Joseph P. "Court Ruling Highlights Divergences on 'Kosher.'" *New York Times*, 5 August 2000, B3(L).

Milgrom, Jacob. "The Biblical Diet Laws As an Ethical System." *Interpretation* 17 (1963 [Union Theological Seminary, Richmond,Virginia]): 288–301.

Nathan, Joan. *The Jewish Holiday Kitchen.* New York: Schocken Books. 1988.

Roden, Claudia. *The Book of Jewish Food: An Odyssey from Samarkand to New York.* New York: Knopf, 1996.

Soler, Jean. "The Semiotics of Food in the Bible." In *Food and Drink in History*, edited by Robert Forster and Orest Ranum. Baltimore: Johns Hopkins University Press, 1979.

Joëlle Bahloul

JUICE. *See* **Fruit; Grapes and Grape Juice.**

KASHRUT, LAWS OF. *See* **Judaism; Passover.**

KELLOGG, JOHN HARVEY. John Harvey Kellogg (1852–1943) was born in Tyrone, Michigan. When he was four years old, his family moved to Battle Creek, Michigan, where his father was one of the founders of the Western Reform Institute, a Seventh-Day Adventist health clinic specializing in hydrotherapy ("the water cure") and vegetarianism. The Seventh-Day Adventists were the largest American religious denomination to endorse vegetarianism. Kellogg enrolled at Bellevue Hospital College in New York after completing his undergraduate work, where he studied medicine. In 1876, upon completion of his studies, Kellogg took over administration of the Western Reform Institute. He subsequently changed its name to the Sanitarium and enforced a strict vegetarian culinary regimen. Under his guidance, the Sanitarium was visited by America's rich and famous people and Kellogg's beliefs became widely disseminated.

Assisted by his younger brother Will K. Kellogg (1860–1951), John H. Kellogg experimented with rolling, flattening, and baking whole grains. The resulting flakes were a culinary success at the Sanitarium, and the Kelloggs decided to mass-produce and sell them through mail order. Imitators soon sprang up and churned out numerous similar products, including Grape Nuts and Post Toasties developed by C. W. Post, who had been a patient at the Sanitarium. Kellogg's creation had launched the commercial cold cereal industry.

John Harvey Kellogg also rolled other products, such as nuts, thus creating nut butters, which he believed were a substitute for cow's butter. While nut butters were made from all available nuts, peanuts were the least ex-

Photo portrait of John Harvey Kellogg. COURTESY AP/WIDE WORLD PHOTOS.

pensive nut. The Kelloggs created the Sanitas Nut Food Company, and again Will was placed in charge. Due in large part to the efforts of the Kellogg brothers, peanut butter quickly became an American favorite.

To develop further the commercial possibilities, the Kelloggs incorporated the Toasted Corn Flake Company in 1906. John H. Kellogg was the majority stockholder, but he distributed part of this stock among the Sanitarium doctors. Will Kellogg bought up the stock until he personally owned the majority of shares. Will promptly put his signature on the box and renamed the company that was ultimately to become Kellogg Co. To enhance sales, Will added sugar and other additives to the recipe and increased sales through advertising not as a health food for the ill, but as an enjoyable and convenient breakfast food for everyone. The two brothers went through years of legal battles over the name, but in the end Will won. For years the brothers never spoke to each other.

Later, John Harvey Kellogg confronted a variety of other problems. About 1906 the Seventh-Day Adventists excommunicated Dr. Kellogg and eventually severed ties with the Sanitarium. However, he survived until the Depression hit, and the Sanitarium began to lose money. It continued in operation until 1942, when it was sold. Kellogg died the following year.

Will Kellogg remained as president of the Kellogg Company until 1929, but remained as chairman of the Board until his death in 1951. In 1930 he established the W. K. Kellogg Foundation in Battle Creek, one of America's foremost philanthropic institutions.

See also **Breakfast; Cereal Grains and Pseudo-Cereals; Cereals, Cold; Peanut Butter; Wheat.**

BIBLIOGRAPHY

Carson, Gerald. *Cornflake Crusade.* New York: Rinehart & Company, 1957.

Kellogg, John H. *Household Manual.* Battle Creek, Mich.: The Office of the Health Reformer, 1877.

Powell, Horace B. *The Original Has This Signature—W. K. Kellogg.* Englewood Cliffs, N.J.: Prentice-Hall, 1956.

Andrew F. Smith

KETCHUP. *See* **Condiments.**

KITCHEN GADGETS. One of the earliest recorded uses of the term "gadget" was in 1886 as a nautical term referring to a small, somewhat specialized contrivance. It is unclear when the term first entered kitchen parlance, but the *Oxford English Dictionary* records the earliest use of the expression "kitchen gadget" as 1951 in the *Good Housekeeping Home Encyclopedia*, which remarked that kitchen gadgets are often discarded because it takes too much time to clean them.

A popular contemporary taxonomy of kitchen technology must account for the essential ambiguity of the term. Terms like "gadget," "utensil," "accoutrement," "tool," and "appliance" overlap. A kitchen gadget may be a specialized artifact used for the preparation of a single kind of dish or for performing one specific function across a variety of dishes. As such, it can be distinguished if only in a general sense from the broader term "kitchen utensil," which would include multipurpose and essential kitchen equipment, such as chefs' knives and large appliances like ovens and refrigerators. In modern usage the term "kitchen gadget" also may be pejorative. It is often used to refer to novelty items, gimmicky and cheap kitchen equipment that purports to ease the burdens of homemakers. As the usage in the *Good Housekeeping Home Encyclopedia* indicated, gadgets may be the kinds of products that accumulate in the back of kitchen drawers until they are discarded. Another aspect of the gadget is its symbolic character. Gadgets may be displayed as items that represent taste, newness, or status.

Although the term "gadget" originated in the late Victorian era, it is often used retroactively to refer to pre-Victorian forms of specialized kitchen equipment. Providing an account of early kitchen tools is difficult as such items rarely made their way onto household inventories. It is well established that, apart from the kitchens of the aristocracy, pre-Victorian cookery, at least in the British Isles, was almost entirely a matter of boiling in a pot, cauldron, or kettle; baking in an oven or on a bake stone; and roasting on a spit. A number of devices were designed to assist the pre-Victorian cook with each of these kitchen tasks.

Victorian Gadgets

The jack was one of the most useful Victorian aids. Roasting spits, also known as "broches," "peakes," or "flesh pikes," were mounted in the fireplace. A jack is a device that rotates the roasting spit without the constant attention of the cook. A great variety of techniques for spit rotation were designed over the years. The earliest jacks relied on a system of weights akin to those in a weight-driven clock for their slow and steady movement. Another early form of jack was the smokejack, first imported into England from Germany in the second half of the sixteenth century. The force of air and smoke rising in the fireplace chimney powered this kind of jack. Perhaps the most unusual were the animal-powered jacks, which relied on animals, such as dogs or geese. Geese were considered a better source of power, as dogs quickly became bored with the work and were far craftier than geese at shirking their duties. The most popular kind of jack was the windup or spring jack, which the Swedish botanist and noted traveler Pehr Kalm observed in almost every English home he visited in 1748.

Another kitchen implement from this era was the tin roaster. In its earliest form, a piece of wood lined with reflective tin was placed next to the meat to reflect the heat back and increase cooking efficiency. This arrangement evolved into a small and elegant device that only occupied the width of the fire bars. The tin roaster consisted of a tin enclosure to reflect heat back onto the meat, a dripping pan, and a door on the front through which the cook could baste and otherwise attend to the meat. Tin roasters often incorporated that other essential roasting gadget, a windup or bottle jack.

Another common kind of hearth-front gadget was the toaster. Hearthstones, a variety of toasting forks, and hinged devices mounted on the side of the hearth were all used to toast bread. One of the more common devices was the hearth toaster, a long-handled piece of cast iron that held the bread between small arches that could be swiveled to toast both sides of the bread.

Boiling and simmering called for some arrangement to regulate temperature by shifting pots closer to or farther away from the fire. The most basic technique used a series of pothooks or hangers of varying lengths. Another technique used a chain wrapped around a rod so it could be rotated. The chimney crane was perhaps the most elegant of these devices. The rod and hook techniques could only be used to move a pot up and down, whereas the chimney crane could move a pot through three dimensions. This afforded much more precise heat regulation than the hook or rod techniques and allowed the cook to move the pot out of the fireplace without directly picking it up. The chimney crane saw wide use, especially in southeastern England from the sixteenth century through the eighteenth century.

Within the great houses, an altogether more sophisticated battery of kitchen equipment existed. For example, inventories of the British estate Ham House from the 1670s and 1680s list sixty-two kinds of items. This list includes such specialized equipment as a tin apple roaster, colanders, a tin grater, a three-chain jack, a fish kettle and a carp pan with false bottoms, numerous larding pins, several mortars and pestles, pastry peels, a "rowling" (rolling) pin, skimmers, lark spits, iron toasting tongs, a wooden whisk, and a sieve (made of hair) along with the sundry common items like knives, pots, pans, and skillets.

The list of items at Ham House includes a number of "basons" (basins) of undesignated use. It is a safe assumption that they may be freezing basins. Hannah Glasse published several editions of *The Art of Cookery Made Plain and Easy* from 1747 on. Each edition included instructions for making ice cream using two pewter basins, one with a tightly fitted lid enclosed within the larger basin. She suggested two kinds of basins. One, manufactured in France, was tall and cylindrical; the other was three-cornered and wedge-shaped. The wedge basin was used with three other identically shaped basins so the cook could make a multihued circle of ice cream.

During the Victorian era, the use of the hand-cranked ice cream machine became widespread. The English inventor William Fuller sold a pamphlet titled *A Manual Containing Numerous Original Recipes for Preparing Neapolitan Ices* along with a hand-cranked machine patented in 1853. The machines of Fuller and his competitors were popular with professional confectioners and the wealthier and innovative set. They were not in common use at the household level. The first hand-cranked machine was patented in the United States in 1848, and domestic versions were available in the 1860s. By the 1880s numerous hand-cranked machines were designed for the domestic market, and many were still available in the early twenty-first century. The basic ice cream machine is a coopered wooden bucket into which an enclosed rotating chamber is inserted. A hand crank rotates the chamber. The chamber is surrounded by ice and salt, which reduces the chamber's temperature low enough to congeal its contents.

Some of the characteristic beliefs of modernity are that everything can be known and that all nature can be mastered if one applies sufficient time, expertise, and specialized technology to the task. This positivism was the prevalent mindset of the Victorian era. It should come as no surprise that the term "gadget" originated in the 1880s as the Victorian era saw an immense explosion in the

TABLE 1

Gadgets and their requisites

Gadget	Requisite
Jack: weighted	Hearth
Jack: smoke	Hearth and flue
Jack: windup or bottle	Hearth
Jack: animal-powered	Hearth and obedient dog or goose
Tin roaster	Hearth
Toaster	Hearth or for modern forms electricity
Pothooks and hangers	Hearth
Chimney crane	Hearth
Tin apple roaster	Hearth
Ice-cream maker: manual	Ice, salt, and muscle power
Ice-cream maker: electric	Electricity and either ice and salt or a refrigerator with a freezer compartment
Eggbeater	Muscle power
Stand mixer	Electricity and a variety of attachments, such as a whisk, flat paddle, or dough hook. Numerous other gadgets can be powered by a stand mixer, such as can openers, slicers and shredders, food grinders, fruit and vegetable strainers, grain mills, citrus juicers, pasta makers, and sausage stuffers.
Cafetiere	Ground, roasted coffee and hot water
Espresso maker	Hot water or electricity and finely ground, roasted coffee beans
Goblin	Electricity and tea
Coffee grinder	Electricity and roasted coffee beans
Coffee roaster	Electricity and raw coffee beans
Percolator	Electricity or alcohol for heat and roasted coffee beans
Drip coffee machine	Electricity, filter, and roasted coffee beans

development of small and highly specialized tools. This proliferation of specialized technology existed across all spheres of human activity, including the domestic, where kitchen gadgets flourished. The number of kitchen gadgets invented or in widespread use for the first time during the Victorian era was immense.

A book like Isabella Beeton's *The Book of Household Management* (1861) was representative of this Victorian positivism. Beeton set out in 1,112 pages to inform the homemaker how to micromanage every aspect of domestic economy. Her list of thirty-seven essential kitchen utensils, including a bread grater, was far more involved than the kitchen inventories of most British households in the preceding century.

This era saw the invention of many new kitchen gadgets, including the apple peeler, other specialized peelers, the mechanical eggbeater, the mechanical dough mixer, bread toasters, potato mashers, coffee grinders, food choppers, and waffle irons. The African American inventor John Thomas White was issued a patent for a lemon squeezer in 1896. It consisted of two pieces of wood connected by a hinge. The bottom piece included a slotted opening so the juice of the lemon could pass through when the two pieces were squeezed together.

Modern Gadgets

Many modern kitchen gadgets are simply updated and electrified forms of kitchen gadgets developed in the Victorian era. The aforementioned home ice-cream makers are representative of this trend. In the 1950s electric models of the ice-cream maker were introduced. The earliest models simply replaced the hand crank with an electric motor. Models from the late 1960s were designed to fit into a refrigerator freezer. In the 1960s the two most prevalent kinds of contemporary ice-cream makers were developed. The relatively inexpensive prefreeze models featured an insert filled with refrigerant that was prefrozen in the refrigerator freezer. The second kind of ice-cream maker used a small, built-in freezer to congeal the ice cream or sorbet.

The toaster is another updated item. The first electric toasters were built in the early twentieth century immediately after the invention of a nickel and chromium alloy, trademarked as NiChrome, was used to make the first high-temperature electric heating elements. The first commercially viable electric toaster was the General Electric D-12, an open affair mounted on a ceramic base. Electrical toasters underwent a number of innovations, including metal and plastic enclosures and various slot sizes to accommodate changing tastes in bread. Toasters designed specifically for bagels have become common. The combination toaster and oven was popular in the 1980s, but its acceptance has steadily declined due to its general ineffectiveness at both toasting and performing the duties of a small oven.

The toaster oven is one of the more widespread representatives of the multiple-function gadget. The numerous representatives of these devices range from the ill-fated combination nutmeg grater and corkscrew patented by George Blanchard in 1856 to the kitchen equipment advertised on late-night television that can do "all this and so much more." Perhaps the most successful multipurpose kitchen gadgets are the appliances manufactured by companies like Bosch, KitchenAid, and Sunbeam derived from the 1884 eggbeater design of the African American inventor Willie Johnson. His eggbeater was powered by a driving wheel in conjunction with a system of gears and pulleys that rotated a set of beaters, blades, or stirrers.

The eggbeater was an updated and mechanized version of the kitchen whisk that further evolved into a wide variety of gadgets. One of the most significant was the electric mixer. The first American patent for an electric mixer was filed in 1885 by Rufus W. Eastman. The earliest electric mixers were large, clunky machines that in the twenty-first century would look more at home in a wood shop than in the kitchen. By the 1930s at least a dozen manufacturers made electric mixers, including the nearly ubiquitous Hobart (KitchenAid) and the Hamilton Sunbeam. The Sunbeam Mixmaster model M4A, which was first manufactured in 1930, was relatively streamlined in comparison to its competitors. Its name "Mixmaster" eventually became the generic term for a stand mixer.

The new stand mixers were not really gadgets so much as constellations of gadgets. The Sunbeam Mixmaster was advertised as capable, given the right attachments, of mixing, mashing, whipping, creaming, stirring, beating, extracting fruit juice, chopping, grinding, and blending. A twenty-first century advertisement for the KitchenAid Stand Mixer lists attachable accessories that include a can opener, a rotor slicer and shredder, a food grinder, a fruit and vegetable strainer, a food tray, a grain mill, a citrus juicer, a pouring shield, a pasta maker, a sausage stuffer, a flat beater, a dough hook, and a whisk.

Coffee and tea have inspired quite a few gadgets over the years, including kettles, cafetieres, espresso makers, goblins, grinders, roasters, percolators, and drip machines. The tea goblin or the teasmade is one of the more unusual kitchen inventions. This was a British invention of the 1930s that made tea on a timer. Goblins often featured alarm clocks, lamps, heating elements, and devices for placing the tea into the hot water. Coffee was traditionally prepared by the Turkish method of boiling the coffee until the development in 1806 in Germany of the percolator by the American Count Rumford, who saw coffee drinking as an alternative to the hard-drinking lifestyle of German workers. The drip coffee maker soon followed. Early models were heated by burning alcohol, replaced by electrical elements in the early twentieth century. Other inventions included the steam espresso maker, which forces steam through the ground coffee until it is condensed on the other side, and the cafetiere, of which the most popular model worldwide is the Danish Bodum. Americans have preferred drip and percolator models, and Italians have preferred espresso makers that rely on various mechanisms, from pressurized cylinders to straight steam pressure, to force steam through the coffee grounds.

Coffee and espresso makers have accumulated attachments to much the same extent as the stand mixer. The difference lies in the purpose of these attachments. Coffee and espresso appurtenances are components of the machine designed to complement a cup of coffee rather than to perform a wide range of kitchen tasks. These appurtenances include devices for scalding and frothing milk and grinding coffee built directly into the machine. Some coffee makers emulate the tea goblin. On a timer, they grind the coffee beans, insert the grounds into the filter, and then make the coffee.

Kitchen equipment is tied to representations of status, and coffee-making equipment is an ideal example. The first electric percolators were designed as elegant table centerpieces, and most coffee was preground and sold in vacuum-sealed tins. By the 1980s percolators were no longer considered the height of sophistication. An elegant North American coffee drinker used a drip coffee maker and ground his or her own beans. By the twenty-first century, a European method was preferred. An Alessi-designed cafetiere or an Italian espresso maker, such as one of the pressurized La Pavoni machines, or even a stovetop steam-pressured espresso maker signified good taste.

See also **Beeton, Isabella; Coffee; Preparation of Food; Utensils, Cooking.**

BIBLIOGRAPHY

David, Elizabeth. *Harvest of the Cold Months: The Social History of Ice and Ices.* New York: Viking, 1985.

David, Elizabeth. "Hunt the Ice Cream." *Petit Propos Culinaires* 1 (1979): 8–13.

Davidson, Caroline. "Historic Kitchen Restoration: The Example of Ham House." *Petit Propos Culinaires* 12 (November 1982): 46–55.

Davidson, Caroline. *A Woman's Work Is Never Done.* London: Chatto and Windus, 1986.

Fearn, Jacqueline. *Domestic Bygones.* Shire Album 20. Aylesbury, U.K.: Shire Publications, 1977.

"Inventors." Available at http://inventors.about.com/library/weekly/aa122000a.htm.

Petroski, Henry. *The Evolution of Useful Things.* New York: Vintage Books, 1994.

"Sunbeam Mixmaster: The Mixer Americans Grew Up With." Available at http://www.angelfire.com/home/flexibleshaft/Sunbeam2.html.

Webb, Pauline, and Mark Suggitt. *Gadgets and Necessities: An Encyclopedia of Household Innovations.* Santa Barbara, Calif.: ABC–CLIO, 2000.

Weber, Max. "Science as a Vocation." In *Max Weber: Selections from His Works.* New York: Crowell, 1963.

Wesley Dean

KITCHENS, RESTAURANT.

With the debut of executive chef Gray Kunz's $1 million kitchen at the restaurant Lespinasse in New York City's St. Regis Hotel in 1994, the restaurant kitchen became a showplace and status marker for American chefs. Cast-iron ranges from France, cool-to-the-touch induction stoves from Japan, fast-churning ice-cream machines from Italy have become de rigueur for any cook worth his *fleur de sel*. But despite the push for state-of-the-art technology in kitchen design, the organization of the staff and the layout of the workspace have not changed much since Georges-Auguste Escoffier's day.

Kitchen Organization

In addition to codifying and modernizing the culinary repertoire, Escoffier is credited with streamlining the organization of the kitchen. "I myself have often been forced to make profound changes in my restaurant service to meet the need of the ultra rapid pace of modern life," he wrote in his memoirs at the turn of the twentieth century (p. 119). His solution was a kitchen organization based on principles of efficiency and division of labor that grew out of the Industrial Revolution. The tasks involved in assembling the meal are divided among different "stations" (*parties* in French), each with its team of cooks. The various elements of any finished dish may come from as many as five or six stations. Together, the team of chefs in the kitchen is known as the *brigade*. In English, the chefs who prepare the places during service are known collectively as the line. It is interesting to note that in many kitchens, no matter their ethnicity, French kitchen terms are usually mixed up with whatever language is spoken.

At the top of the kitchen hierarchy is the executive chef. In a hotel, the executive chef oversees all food preparation in the property's various food service outlets; the role is largely administrative. In a restaurant, the executive chef's duties are usually more hands-on. Now that so many restaurant chefs have multiple restaurants under their command, however, their role has also become more administrative in scope. Below the executive chef is the *chef de cuisine*. This is the person directly in charge of managing the kitchen. The cooks all report to the *chef de cuisine*, who in turn reports to the executive chef. To help oversee the smooth management of the kitchen, the *chef de cuisine* usually has one or two *sous-chefs* (literally "under chefs"). The responsibilities of the *sous-chefs* are often divided by meal period—for instance there will be a lunch *sous-chef* and a dinner *sous-chef*. The breakdown of the *chefs de partie*—"station chefs" or "line cooks" in English—is determined by the breadth and scope of the menu (not to mention the space available in the kitchen) and their tasks at hand. Thus, the *saucier* is responsible for making the sauces and stocks. Because of the emphasis Escoffier placed on sauces in his culinary repertoire, the saucier traditionally holds an exalted status in the kitchen. The *rôtisseur* is responsible for meats and roasts, the *poissonier*, fish. A *grillardin* does the grilling, a *potager* makes the soups (*potages*, in French). Vegetables and other side dishes are the charge of the *entremetier*. The *friturier* mans the fryer. The *garde-manger* is in charge of the cold pantry, from which issues forth hors d'oeuvres, salads, garnishes, and other cold preparations. During the eighteenth and nineteenth centuries, when large presentation pieces and ornate garnishes were an important element in traditional French service, the role of the *garde-manger* was elevated in status. The *pâtissier* is in charge of the pastries and other baking. A *chocolatier* would be responsible for chocolate items. Further divisions and subdivisions are also possible.

Depending on the demands placed on the staff, within the different stations there may be multiple cooks and assistants. Young apprentices known as *commis* or *sta-*

giaires are plentiful in large kitchens, for they are generally strong, eager, and willing to work for little pay. A *tournant* is an experienced chef who can fill in at any station should the cooks become backed-up during service (referred to colloquially in English as "being in the weeds"), or should someone not show up to work.

The expediter (*aboyeur*, in French, or "barker") is the person to whom the orders from the dining room are given by the waitstaff or, more likely these days, by the computerized ordering system. This is the role the executive chef often takes during service (often to the dismay of the staff; most executive chefs make poor expediters). The expediter is responsible for timing the preparation of a table's order so that all of the various components from the different stations are completed at exactly the same moment. This ensures that the food is served at its prime and contributes to the smooth operation of the restaurant and the maximum satisfaction of each guest is an important task.

Variations among Kitchens

The breakdown of the *brigade* differs from restaurant to restaurant. In reality, only the largest, most expensive restaurants follow Escoffier's organization to the letter, but a surprising number are based on his model. Most kitchens are organized around a compressed version of the traditional hierarchy. With modern technology and convenience foods (of which, based on his memoirs, Escoffier would likely have been a champion), it is possible for as few as three line cooks to turn out hundreds of meals, albeit of questionable quality.

Perhaps the most important factor in determining the organization of the kitchen is the menu, which itself is an outgrowth of the overall concept of the restaurant. The array of dishes, the variety of cooking techniques, and the intricacy of garnishes all have a direct impact on the way the kitchen functions. In planning the menu it is imperative that the chef consider the impact new items will have on each station of the kitchen. The second most important factor in the design of the kitchen and the division of labor is the physical layout of the space. No matter how heavy the demands placed by the menu on a particular station, if there is not enough space for the cooks to work comfortably, efficiency will suffer. Kitchens also reflect the personality and management style of the chef in charge. Some chefs prefer to divide stations based on the natural divisions of the menu. Thus, you will sometimes hear stations referred to by the terms "hot apps" (hot appetizers) or "salads."

Different styles of cuisine require different divisions of labor. In Italian restaurants, the pasta station becomes supremely important. In seafood restaurants, naturally, multiple fish cooks are required. Some types of cooking require a different organization altogether. Chinese restaurants are able to offer a vast number of dishes because of the way the kitchen is set up. Each chef has a workspace with at least one wok (usually several) and a

The classic restaurant kitchen drew for its inspiration upon the structure and labor organization of the royal kitchens of Europe. Depicted here is the well-organized kitchen of the Hofburg (royal palace) in Berlin in 1861. Note that all the cooks are wearing uniforms that define their station or pecking order in the hierarchy of the kitchen command. ROUGHWOOD COLLECTION.

huge array of ingredients at the ready. One dish at a time is prepared and sent out to the table as it is finished. This accounts for (or results from) a style of eating that is totally different from the Western model. In Japanese restaurants, the cooking is sometimes done right in front of the guests by the principal chef and his assistants. Although in the West we are familiar with this set-up in sushi and *teppanyaki* restaurants, in Japan other types of restaurants are molded into this configuration. Exemplary Mexican, French, and Italian restaurants in Tokyo are set up according to this sushi-bar model.

Although the "open kitchen" concept became popular in restaurant design in California in the 1980s and has since spread throughout the country, these kitchens, which afford diners a peek into the inner workings of the restaurant, are usually organized according to the traditional French model, not the Japanese. Similarly, the rise in popularity in the 1990s of "chef tables"—dining tables actually located in the thick of the kitchen commotion—offer an up-close view of the fine-dining kitchen.

Some American chefs make a point of shunning the traditional hierarchical organization of the kitchen alto-

gether. The two most renowned are probably Alice Waters at Chez Panisse in Berkeley, California, and Barry Wine at the former Quilted Giraffe in New York City. Both chefs pride themselves on the democratic ideology that governed their kitchens, giving each cook a more or less equal say in the decision-making process. Although the reasons behind the adaptation of this democratic model were very different—Waters came out of the Berkeley hippie movement of the 1960s and 1970s; Wine aspired to have the most innovative and creative restaurant in the high-flying 1980s—both succeeded in producing world-class restaurants that attracted international acclaim.

Social Interaction
Because of the high-pressure environment of most restaurant kitchens, they act as crucibles of social interaction. Despite formidable attempts to organize the kitchen into a smooth running "assembly line," systems and chains of command often break down. George Orwell's *Down and Out in Paris and London* (1933) offered a vivid glimpse of life in a large Parisian kitchen at the

beginning of the last century. Some seventy-five years later, the grit of kitchen life has again captured the popular imagination, with tell-all books such as Anthony Bourdain's *Kitchen Confidential* (2000) topping bestseller charts. In *Kitchens* (1996), sociologist Gary Fine offers a more scholarly portrait of kitchen life. Fine produced an ethnographic sociological study of work and human interaction in the restaurant kitchen environment. Fine spent several months in the kitchens of four restaurants that covered the spectrum of dining establishments from chain to fine dining. His study examines kitchen life through the filters of economic, class, and aesthetic considerations. He notes:

> [Cooks] face enormous challenges, toiling in an environment less pastoral than infernal. Cooks must ready the kitchen several hours before customers arrive, not knowing precisely how many to expect. Preparation must permit flexibility, depending on the walk-in trade and last-minute reservations. They must then be ready to cook numerous dishes, simultaneously and without warning, with sufficient speed that those with whom they must deal—servers and ultimately diners—do not become frustrated. Cooks have several masters. Restaurants are both service and production units, and, so, cooks work simultaneously for customers and management (p. 19).

Fine's findings emphasize the importance of the organization of the kitchen on the overall success of the restaurant and on the satisfaction derived from those who work in the restaurant kitchen environment.

See also **Chef; Escoffier, Georges-Auguste; Kitchen Gadgets; Kitchen Pantry and Larder; Places of Consumption; Preparation of Food; Restaurants; Serving of Food; Workers, Food.**

BIBLIOGRAPHY

Bourdain, Anthony. *Kitchen Confidential: Adventures in the Culinary Underbelly.* New York: Bloomsbury, 2000.

Escoffier, Auguste. *Memories of My Life.* Translated by Laurence Escoffier. New York: Van Nostrand Reinhold, 1997.

Fine, Gary Alan. *Kitchens: The Culture of Restaurant Work.* Berkeley, Calif.: University of California Press, 1996.

Orwell, George. *Down and Out in Paris and London.* New York: Harcourt, Brace, 1950. Original edition published in 1933.

Mitchell Davis

KOREA. Owing to the popularity of Korean barbecue (*kalbi* and *pulgogi*) outside Korea, Korean cuisine is often thought of as meat-based when compared with other Asian cuisines. However, in essence it has for centuries depended largely on vegetables and, to a lesser degree, on seafood. In fact, the consumption of animal products (beef, pork, chicken, eggs, milk, and dairy products) in Korea increased more than twenty times in the last three decades of the twentieth century, mainly due to economic affluence.

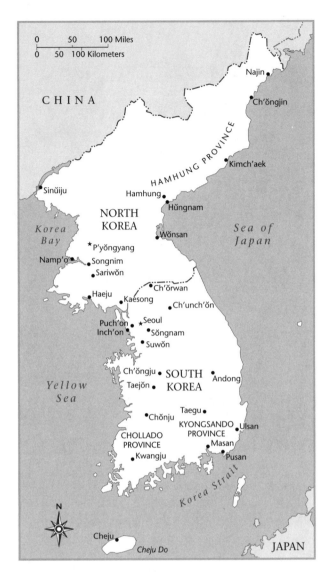

Chinese, Japanese, and Western (particularly American and Italian) influences are becoming increasingly visible, especially outside the home. Yogurt and Western-style sweets have become the staples of Korean children, and American fast-food chains (McDonalds, KFC, and Pizza Hut), particularly popular among the youth, are successively enlarging their share of the Korean restaurant market. Koreans of older generations prefer Chinese restaurants, which have been popular for several decades, to the more recent Japanese and Italian establishments. Chinese food is often cooked at home as well.

Yet, despite all these foreign influences, the daily fare of most Koreans, outside or inside the home, still consists of rice, soup, and side dishes—a meal structure that has barely changed for centuries.

The Korean Meal
There are few differences among the food Koreans consume at each meal. Supper is usually more elaborate than

breakfast and lunch, but generally speaking, every meal is centered on plain boiled rice (*pap*), soup (bouillon-like *kuk* or a more hearty *t'ang*), and pickled vegetables (*kimchi*). Side dishes (*panch'an*) extend this core, and their number depends on the occasion. Three to five side dishes are the norm in contemporary households.

Stews (*tchigae, tchim, chŏn'gol*) and soused or sautéed greens (*namul, pokkŭm*) constitute the majority of side dishes, complemented by grilled dishes (*kui* or *sanjŏk*) made of seafood, beef, pork, or chicken. Stews tend to acquire the position of a semi-main dish, as does *pulgogi*, turning into a center of the meal accompanied by a bowl of rice, smaller *panch'an*, and dipping sauces. Big-bowl dishes such as fried rice (*pokkŭmbap*), beef soup with rice (*sŏlŏngt'ang*), and mixed rice (*pibimbap*) are served in a similar fashion, with small portions of greens and pickles on the side.

Rice boiled or steamed with beans, other grains, or vegetables may be served instead of plain boiled rice. A variety of wheat and buckwheat noodles (*kuksu*) also frequently appear on the Korean table. Noodles are usually served in soupy liquids, while stuffed dumplings (*mandu*) can be either steamed, panfried, or simmered in soups (*manduguk*). Noodles and dumplings are popular lunch dishes. Flavored rice porridges (*chuk*) are less commonplace than rice, noodles, and dumplings, but still retain a notable place in Korean cuisine.

Chili pepper, sesame (seed and oil), garlic, and spring onions, along with soy sauce (*kanjang*), soybean paste (*toenjang*), and red bean paste (*koch'ujang*) constitute what might be called a Korean "flavoring principle." The combination of all or a selection of these ingredients gives Korean dishes their characteristic taste. Ginger, semi-sweet rice wine (*ch'ŏngju*), and honey or sugar are the other crucial components of the Korean flavor.

Kimchi

Pickled vegetables, generally referred to by the name of *kimchi*, are the most basic, indispensable element of every Korean meal. Neither a feast nor a most meager fare would be complete without it. For centuries *kimchi* was the sole side dish to accompany the staple of Korea's poor, whether it was barley, millet, or, for the fortunate few, rice. It was also a fundamental meal component in affluent households. Three kinds of *kimchi* were always served, regardless of how many side dishes were to appear on the table. To a contemporary Korean, rice and *kimchi* are the defining elements of a minimal acceptable meal. Yet, it is *kimchi*, not rice, that is regarded as the symbol of Korean culture.

There are hundreds of varieties of *kimchi*. Every region, village, and even family used to cherish its own special recipe, applying slightly different preparation methods and using slightly different ingredients. Napa cabbage (*Brassica chinensis* or *Brassica pekinensis*) made into *paech'u kimchi* is the most common type, followed by radishes (*Raphanus sativus*) made into *kkaktugi kimchi*. Basically, vegetables are placed for several hours in brine, washed with fresh water, and drained. Then, flavorings such as ginger, chili pepper, spring onions, garlic, and raw or fermented seafood are added, and the mixture is packed into pickling crocks and allowed to age.

Since the 1960s, when factory-made *kimchi* appeared on the market for the first time, the number of urban families who continue to make their own *kimchi* has gradually diminished. With the rising consumption of meat and seafood, and the popularization of Western-style food, the quantity of *kimchi* consumed by Koreans has declined as well. An average Korean consumes approximately forty pounds of *kimchi* on a yearly basis.

Yet, *kimchi* is still considered to be the most important element of the Korean meal and quintessentially Korean by Koreans and foreigners alike. Despite this cultural symbolism, *kimchi* has evolved relatively recently to the form we know today. The so-called "white *kimchi*" (*paek kimchi*), which is still popular in the early twenty-first century, resembles most closely the original version.

The addition of chili pepper came about in the mid-eighteenth century and gave *kimchi* its characteristic red color and pungent taste. Fermented seafood (*chŏtkal*), which has been included in the pickling from the late nineteenth century onward, not only enriched the taste of *kimchi*, but also increased its regional diversity. While at the end of the seventeenth century only eleven types of *kimchi* were classified, the regional variety of *chŏtkal* (some regions use shellfish, others anchovies or other kinds of fish) contributed to the development of several hundred varieties of *kimchi*. The type of vegetables that are pickled also changed. Gourd melon, cucumber, and eggplant have been used since ancient times; today napa cabbage and radish are the most common varieties.

The Table Setting

With a few exceptions, all components of the meal are on the table at one time. A set of a spoon and metal chopsticks is used while eating. Rice, soup, and other liquids are eaten with the former, side dishes with the latter. Soup and rice are served in individual bowls, but side dishes are often shared by more than one diner. Nowadays, bowls are usually made of stoneware, steel, or plastic, but for special occasions white porcelain tableware is used. In the past, the upper classes dined from brass bowls in the winter and porcelain ones during the hot summer months. A silver set of chopsticks and a spoon was considered most elegant. Less affluent sections of the population generally dined from earthenware, using wooden chopsticks and spoons. According to Korean etiquette, it is considered inelegant to lift bowls from the table. They stay on the table during the entire meal, unlike in the rest of East Asia, where it is customary to lift bowls up to the mouth while eating.

The majority of restaurants in Korea have two dining areas: one with Western-style tables and chairs, and one with an elevated floor where customers seated on cushions dine at low tables. Similarly, most Korean households use Western-style tables with chairs on a daily basis (the table is usually placed in the kitchen), but share meals at a low table with short legs, seated on cushions laid on the floor, when guests are entertained.

The most traditional dining setting is a small table designed for one or two persons. In upper-class households, there was no common dining room and such tables were laid in the kitchen and carried out to different parts of the house, where family members dined, divided according to age, gender, and position. Such dining arrangements reflected the hierarchical ideology of premodern Korea. The shared dining table with short legs became popular in the early decades of the twentieth century and by the 1960s spread all over the country, widely replacing the ubiquitous individual table. This transition was followed by the diffusion of Western-style table and chairs in the 1980s. Yet, even today, traditional tables designed for one are still used in some restaurants, student apartments, and average Korean households.

Food and Drink for Special Occasions

From the fifteenth century onward, Confucianism began to replace Buddhism as the strongest cultural influence in Korea. Various festivals and their celebration in Korea are closely related either to Buddhism or to Confucianism. These events are always marked by special food, with noodles, red beans, and many kinds of rice cakes playing a prominent role in festive meals and snacks. Because Korean meals traditionally did not include desserts, festivals were among the few occasions when sweet snacks were served, except in upper-class families, where sweet afternoon snacks were regularly prepared.

Throughout the ages, each festival food has acquired a symbolic meaning or a function that justifies its use at a specific occasion. Noodles, for example, are appropriate for birthdays because they symbolize long life. Red-bean porridge (*p'atchuk*) with sweet rice balls (*kyŏngdan*) eaten on the day of the winter solstice is said to prevent colds and drive away ghosts. Colorful rice cake (*mujigae ttŏk*) is prepared for a child's first birthday in the hope that the child will enjoy a wide range of accomplishments.

Certain occasions are inseparable from the food that is served during their celebration. The Harvest Moon Festival (*Ch'usŏk*), for example, is unimaginable without pine needle–scented rice cakes (*songp'yŏn*), and lunar New Year's Day celebrations (*Sŏllal*) would not be complete without rice cake soup (*ttŏkkuk*). "How many bowls of rice cake soup have you eaten?" is a polite way of asking about someone's age, as if failing to eat a bowl of rice cake soup would deprive a person from a complete New Year's experience.

Garnishing (*komyŏng*) is taken very seriously in traditional Korean cooking and becomes especially pronounced in festival food. Three-color garnish is made with egg yolk (yellow), egg white (white), and Korean watercress (green). Five-color garnish includes these with the addition of chili pepper threads (red) and stone-ear mushrooms (black).

Drinks are another medium used to celebrate special occasions. *Porich'a*, scorched-rice tea made by boiling water over the rice that sticks to the bottom of the cooking pot, used to be the most important daily beverage in Korea. Today, along with water, it remains an important drink to accompany meals. For celebrations, most Koreans drink either *soju* or beer. *Soju* is a kind of distilled liquor made of grain or sweet potatoes, with an alcohol content of up to 45 percent. Although it is often claimed to have been introduced to Korea in the thirteenth century through trade with the Mongols and Chinese, it is not clear whether the contemporary version has any connection with its ancestor apart from the name. Beer was introduced by the Japanese in the late nineteenth century and began to be produced on a large scale in the early 1930s.

A large variety of homemade wines (which are strictly speaking ales) flavored with ginseng, pine needles, chrysanthemum, cherry, plum, or apricot blossoms, herbs, and fruits were popular before the turn of the twentieth century. The ban on homemade wines during the Japanese colonial period (1910–1945) had a devastating effect on this part of the Korean tradition. The use of rice for wine making continued to be prohibited after the liberation, due to the shortage of rice. The ban on rice wine was lifted in 1971, and various efforts have been undertaken since to revive local wine making in Korea. In 1985, for example, the government designated many traditional wines as cultural assets. *Makkŏlli*, a milky rice wine with an alcohol content of 6 to 8 percent, also known under the name "farmer's wine" (*nongju*), is one of the most popular alcoholic drinks in contemporary Korea.

Alcohol is never drunk in Korea without elaborate snacking. Practically all side dishes can be served for this purpose and are called *anju* at such occasions. *Anju* can be small like French hors d'oeuvres or Spanish tapas but are not always small. Stews and large savory pancakes (*chŏn*), including vegetables, meat, and seafood, are typical snacks to accompany drinking.

The Historical Overview

The foundation of Korean cuisine was formed between the seventh and thirteenth centuries, with important modifications taking place in the eighteen and nineteenth centuries. As was the case with other aspects of Korean culture, Korean cuisine developed under the strong influence of its powerful neighbor—China. As in adjoining regions of East Asia, rice and fermented soybean products (soy sauce, soybean paste, and soybean curd) occupy a prominent place in the diet of the Korean people. The "rice–soup–side dishes" structure of the meal and the use of chopsticks to consume it are other indicators of the

Korean men celebrating the traditional Confucian New Year, which includes both prayers and food. Photographed 1 January 1988 in Seoul, Korea. © NATHAN BENN/CORBIS.

impact that Chinese civilization exerted on Korean foodways. The emphasis on five elements in Korean cuisine, for example, five flavors (salty, sweet, sour, hot, and bitter) and five colors of garnish, has Chinese origins as well. It should be emphasized, however, that despite this heritage, Korean cuisine has developed into a distinctive entity of its own, with more differences from Chinese cuisine than similarities to it.

The technology of rice cultivation was brought to the northern parts of the Korean peninsula from China, probably late in the second millennium B.C.E., but rice became a staple of the Korean diet only in the Silla period (668–935 C.E.). In fact, before the second half of the twentieth century, rice was not a staple for everyone, but was rather a symbol of wealth. The old phrase "white rice with meat soup," for example, connotes the good life, while tacitly acknowledging that not everyone could afford either rice or meat. Millet, barley, and buckwheat accompanied by *kimchi* and vegetable soup were the daily fare of the majority of the Korean population.

Vegetarian Buddhist influences in Korea did not, apart from the clergy, have much impact on food habits. Beef, pork, lamb, chicken, and various types of game were regularly consumed by the Korean upper classes. Still, before the economic growth of the 1970s, the eating of meat was a luxury for the common people in Korea. Farmers, who formed the majority of the Korean population, rarely ate meat except for three days in summer when dog stew was served and a special day in winter when sparrow, wild boar, or wild rabbit was prepared. In

both cases, the eating of meat was intended to strengthen physical resistance to extreme weather conditions (Walraven, 2002).

The techniques for making wine and *chang* (a semiliquid predecessor of soy sauce and soybean paste) were also introduced from China, and by the seventh century were already highly advanced. This was also the time when fermented seafood (*chŏtkal*) developed, along with vegetables preserved in salt. The latter eventually evolved into *kimchi* pickles.

Chili pepper was brought to Korea at the end of the sixteenth century, most probably via Japan. It became widely cultivated a century later and by the twentieth century was an integral part of Korean cuisine. As well as being an indispensable component in *kimchi* making, chili pepper contributes to the flavoring of the majority of Korean dishes through chili pepper powder (*koch'u karu*) and red bean paste (*koch'ujang*). Both are not only used extensively in the kitchen but often appear on the table as a relish.

It should be mentioned that the extensive use of chili pepper, and consequently the pungent taste of Korean cooking, was not originally characteristic of all Korea, but rather a feature of the Kyŏngsang province occupying the southeastern part of the peninsula. The diet of the southwestern provinces and the territory covering contemporary North Korea used to feature less spicy dishes than was the case in Kyŏngsang. Urbanization and the development of modern transport and communication networks led to the gradual decline of regional differences

Street vendors in Kyoonggi-do, South Korea, peel and chop vegetables to prepare kimchi, a spicy cabbage relish served with most Korean meals. © MICHAEL FREEMAN/CORBIS.

in the Korean diet. These differences, however, have by no means completely disappeared. Ch'ŏrwŏn, for example, is famous for *makkŏlli* wine, Ch'unch'ŏn for its chicken barbecue (*talkkalbi*), and Hamhung province for its cold noodles (*naengmyŏn*). The cooking of the southwestern provinces tends to be generally less spicy than the rest of the country. Chŏlla province, in particular, tenaciously retains its culinary distinctiveness.

Along with a gradual decline in regional differences and the democratization of the Korean foodways, the twentieth century marked the time of the modernization of production, processing, distribution, and consumption of food in Korea. This started during the Japanese occupation and continued in South Korea after the Korean War (1950–1953).

The Japanese introduced modern farming techniques and Western-style food processing. The railway system and the highway network erected by the colonizer led to the centralization of markets and modernization of retailing. Japanese and Korean physicians created the foundation of Korean dietetics, and affluent Korean women got acquainted with the Western science of nutrition through Western-inspired Japanese home economics education.

After the Korean War, South Korea continued to modernize under the strong influence of the United States. American dietary influences have become particularly visible since the 1980s but have not been widely welcome. While foreign products are desirable for the status and novelty they impart, the Korean people generally disapprove of the country's growing reliance on food imports (Pemberton, 2002; Bak, 1997). The increasing consumption of meat, for example, led to a rise in the number of livestock in Korea, making this mountainous country with almost no pasture largely dependent on imported feedstuffs. This and similar issues play an important role in the dietary consciousness of the Korean population today.

See also **China; Condiments; Fermented Beverages Other than Wine or Beer; Places of Consumption; Rice; Soup; Southeast Asia; Soy; Wine, Nongrape**.

BIBLIOGRAPHY

Bak, Sangmee. "McDonald's in Seoul: Food Choices, Identity, and Nationalism." In *Golden Arches East: McDonald's in East Asia*, edited by James L. Watson. Stanford, Calif.: Stanford University Press, 1997.

340

Chu, Young-ha. "Origin and Change in Kimch'i Culture." *Korea Journal* (Summer 1995): 18–29.

Kim, Joungwon, ed. *Korean Cultural Heritage.* Vol. 4, *Traditional Lifestyles.* Seoul: Korea Foundation, 1994.

Kim, Kwang-ok. "Contested Terrain of Imagination: Chinese Food in Korea." In *Changing Chinese Foodways in Asia,* edited by David Y. H. Wu and Tan Chee-beng. Hong Kong: The Chinese University Press, 2001.

Pemberton, Robert W. "Wild-gathered Foods as Countercurrents to Dietary Globalisation in South Korea." In *Asian Food: The Global and the Local,* edited by Katarzyna Cwiertka with Boudewijn Walraven. Honolulu: University of Hawaii Press, 2001.

Walraven, Boudewijn C. A. "Bardot Soup and Confucians' Meat: Food and Korean Identity in Global Context." In *Asian Food: The Global and the Local,* edited by Katarzyna Cwiertka with Boudewijn Walraven. Honolulu: University of Hawaii Press, 2001.

Katarzyna J. Cwiertka

KOSHER LAWS. *See* **Judaism; Passover.**

KWANZAA. Unlike December holidays steeped in centuries-old traditions, Kwanzaa, the African American year-end feast, was not established until 1966 by Maulana Karenga, a cultural nationalist. The celebration, which occurs annually from 26 December to 1 January, is based on a compilation of several harvest festivals and celebrations from around the African continent. During the holiday week most Kwanzaa celebrants use a menu of traditional African American dishes, foods from the "mother continent," and foods from the African diaspora. The word "Kwanzaa" comes from the Swahili expression "matunda ya kwanza," meaning 'first fruits of the harvest,' but the American Kwanzaa is distinguished from the African one by the addition of a second "a" in the second syllable.

The holiday was originally celebrated by cultural nationalists who wished to express pan-African solidarity. In the intervening years, however, it has become a rapidly growing tradition with over 18 million people of all political leanings and in all walks of life celebrating the week following 26 December as a time of feasting, fasting, and self-examination.

The holiday is not designed as a replacement for or alternative to any of the other year-end festivities like the Christian Christmas, the Jewish Hanukkah, or the Hindu Divali (Festival of Lights, celebrating Laksmi, the goddess of wealth; also called "Diwali" or "Dewali"). Rather, it is a time for reflection and self-examination that can replace or be celebrated jointly with any or all of the year-end holidays.

The celebration of Kwanzaa is guided by the Nguzo Saba, the seven principles of self-awareness, so each day

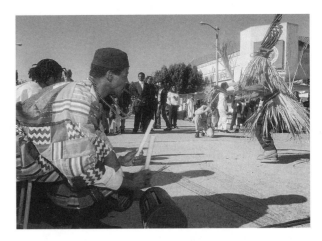

Dancer dressed as Chi Wara, the antelope who represents New Year at a Kwanzaa festival in Leimert Park, Los Angeles. COURTESY AP/WIDE WORLD PHOTOS.

of the week-long festival is devoted to the celebration of one of the building blocks of self-awareness.

Umoja—Unity
Kujichagulia—Self-Determination
Ujima—Collective Work and Responsibility
Ujamaa—Cooperative Economics
Nia—Purpose
Kuumba—Creativity (The feast of karamu is held on this day and is a public celebration at which the community gathers to celebrate the holiday.)
Imani—Faith

The number seven is at the core of the celebration. There are seven days, seven principles, and seven symbols of the holiday. The *mazao* are the fruits of the harvest that are a part of the celebration table, and the *mkeka* is the mat on which they are arranged. The *kinara*, the seven-branched candlestick, holds the *mishumaa saba*, the seven candles (three red, three green, and one black) that are lit every evening: first the black candle, symbolizing the people, and then, alternating, the red and green candles, symbolizing the principle that without struggle, there is no attainment.

Each Kwanzaa table has a centerpiece. On each centerpiece there are *muhindi* (also *vibunzi*), ears of corn, one for each child in the family who is still at home. If there are no children in the family, there is a single ear to remind the celebrants that, in the words of the proverb, "it takes a village to raise a child." The *kikombe cha umoja*, the chalice of unity, is the cup that is passed around or from which the ceremonial libation is poured. Finally, there are the *zawadi*, gifts, which should be educational and emphasize growth and self-knowledge.

BIBLIOGRAPHY

Copage, Eric V. *Kwanzaa: An African-American Celebration of Culture and Cooking.* New York: Morrow, 1991.

Harris, Jessica B. *A Kwanzaa Keepsake: Celebrating the Holiday with New Traditions and Feasts.* New York: Simon & Schuster, 1995.

Karenga, Maulana. *Kwanzaa: Origin, Concepts, Practice.* Inglewood, Calif.: Kawaida, 1977.

Karenga, Maulana. *The African-American Holiday of Kwanzaa: A Celebration of Family, Community, and Culture.* Los Angeles: University of Sankore Press, 1988.

Jessica B. Harris

L

LABELING, FOOD. Food products offered for sale in the United States are subject to a number of legal requirements regarding what information must, may, and may not appear on the package label. Food labels serve many purposes. The label identifies what the product is and how much of it there is, alerts individuals to the presence of allergenic ingredients, and provides nutritional information to enable consumers to make healthy dietary choices. Many of the regulations governing food labeling are extremely detailed, often specifying the placement and minimum type size of required information.

The term "label" refers to any written, printed, or graphic matter on the food's immediate container. "Labeling" includes the label and any other written, printed, or graphic matter accompanying the product in commerce (e.g., point-of-sale pamphlets). Most label information is required to appear on either the "principal display panel" (PDP) or the "information panel." The PDP is the part of the label most likely to be displayed to, and examined by, consumers under customary conditions of retail sale. The information panel is generally the panel contiguous to, and to the right of, the PDP. If that panel is unusable or too small, the next panel to the right of it may serve as the information panel. If the top of the container is the PDP, the information panel may be any panel adjacent to the PDP.

Government Agencies and Governing Laws

The U.S. Food and Drug Administration (FDA) is the federal government agency that administers and enforces labeling requirements for all foods (except meat and poultry) under the Federal Food, Drug, and Cosmetic Act (FD&C Act) and the Fair Packaging and Labeling Act. The U.S. Department of Agriculture (USDA) administers and enforces labeling rules applicable to meat and poultry products under the Federal Meat Inspection Act and the Poultry Products Inspection Act. While the FDA does not require, or offer, prior approval of food labels, the USDA requires government approval of most meat and poultry product labels prior to their use in U.S. commerce.

Other federal agencies play a role in regulating food labeling as well. The U.S. Customs Service requires country-of-origin marking on the labels of imported food products. The U.S. Treasury Department's Bureau of Alcohol, Tobacco, and Firearms (BATF) regulates the labeling of alcoholic beverages. The Federal Trade Commission (FTC) regulates the advertising of food products.

Federal law preempts inconsistent state laws in most areas of food labeling, but there are some aspects of labeling where states may and do impose their own requirements. For example, some states have promulgated their own labeling requirements regarding safety warnings, use-by or sell-by dating, and religious dietary laws.

General prohibition against misbranding. Federal law provides that a food product may be deemed "misbranded" if any part of its labeling is false or misleading. This general provision establishes misbranding even where no specific regulatory requirement has been violated. A food also may be deemed misbranded if any required information is not presented prominently enough—that is, likely to be read and understood by the ordinary consumer under usual conditions of purchase and use.

Mandatory Label Information

Statement of identity. The statement of identity (i.e., the name of the product) must be presented on the PDP. Both the FDA and the USDA have regulations establishing "standards of identity" for certain foods. These regulations prescribe the composition of a food and specify the name of the food to be used in labeling. For example, a food composed of tomato concentrate, vinegar, and spices must be identified as "catsup," "ketchup," or "catchup." However, not all statements of identity are dictated with such specificity. For any given product, the statement of identity is one of the following:

1. The name of the food as specified in any applicable federal law or regulation, such as a standard of identity (e.g., "ketchup") or a federal common or usual name regulation (e.g, "peanut spread")

2. The common or usual name of the food, established by common usage (e.g., "French toast")

3. An appropriately descriptive term (e.g., "hard candy")

4. A fanciful name commonly used by the public when the nature of the food is obvious (e.g., "candy corn").

Label (circa 1910) for a can of fancy lima beans showing the food product on one side and the company trademark on the other. While these old labels are attractive graphically, food labeling has evolved considerably since that time, with a full listing of ingredients, nutritional analysis, bar codes for scanning the price, and even country of origin. ROUGHWOOD COLLECTION.

Net quantity of contents. The net quantity of contents must be presented on the PDP of the food label in measures both English avoirdupois (i.e., ounces, pounds, etc.) and metric (i.e., liters, grams, etc.). For meat and poultry products, the net contents declaration is required to appear only in avoirdupois measure.

Nutrition facts. The amounts of certain nutrients present in one serving of the food product must be presented in the "nutrition facts" panel. Similar products have the same serving size so that consumers can easily compare nutrient levels. Nutrition facts must state the serving size (i.e., the size of one serving) and, unless the product contains only a single serving, the number of servings in the package. Generally, the following nutrients must be declared: calories, calories from fat, total fat, saturated fat, cholesterol, sodium, total carbohydrate, dietary fiber, sugars, protein, vitamin A, vitamin C, calcium, and iron. If other vitamins or minerals are added to the food, they also must be declared.

The graphic requirements for nutrition facts are highly detailed. Nutrition facts generally must appear on the PDP or the information panel. They must appear on the same panel as the ingredients list and the signature line, unless there are space constraints.

Raw fruits and vegetables and raw seafood, which frequently are sold in unpackaged form, are exempt from mandatory nutrition labeling. Instead, the twenty most frequently consumed varieties of fruits, vegetables, and seafood are subject to voluntary nutrition labeling guidelines that apply to retailers of these products. Single-ingredient raw meat and poultry products are likewise subject to a voluntary, retail-level nutrition-labeling program. It should also be noted that restaurant and food-service foods are exempt from nutrition-labeling requirements.

Ingredients list. Each ingredient present in a food product must be listed by its common or usual name in descending order of predominance by weight. While most ingredients must be identified by their specific name, use of generic names is permitted for certain ingredients (e.g., "spices," "natural flavor"). Special rules apply to the listing of certain types of ingredients. For example, chemical preservatives must be listed by their name, followed by a description of their function—such as "BHT (a preservative)." Certified color additives must be identified by their specific name (e.g., "Yellow 5" or "FD&C Blue 1 Lake"), but color additives not subject to certification may be listed using a generic term (e.g., "artificial color") or a specific name followed by a description of its function (e.g., "caramel color").

An ingredient that itself contains two or more ingredients must be listed in one of two ways:

1. By declaring the common or usual name of the ingredient followed by a parenthetical listing all of its components—for example, "milk chocolate (sugar, cocoa butter, milk, chocolate liquor, soy lecithin, vanilla)," or

2. By listing each component of the multicomponent ingredient without declaring the multicomponent ingredient itself—for example, "sugar, cocoa butter, milk, chocolate liquor, soy lecithin, vanilla."

The ingredients list may appear on either the PDP or the information panel, but it usually appears on the information panel. It must appear on the same panel as the nutrition facts and the signature line unless space constraints prevent such placement.

Signature line. The name and place of business of the manufacturer, packer, or distributor is typically called the "signature line" and must be presented on the same panel as the ingredients list and nutrition facts (usually the information panel), unless space constraints preclude such placement. If the name is not that of the manufacturer, it must be preceded by a qualifying phrase stating the firm's relation to the product (e.g., "manufactured for" or "distributed by"). The signature line must include a city or town, state (or country, if outside the United States), and ZIP code (or mailing code if outside the United States). A street address must be provided unless the firm is listed in a current city or telephone directory.

Label Information Required in Specific Cases

In specific circumstances—particularly when additional information could protect or otherwise benefit the consumer—specialized labeling may be required.

Warning and information statements. Certain products are required to present warning or information statements on their labels. For example, foods containing the artificial sweetener aspartame must bear the following statement in capital letters: "phenylketonurics: contains phenylalanine." Other food products required to bear warning or information statements on their labels include the following:

1. Foods that contain the fat replacer olestra

2. Foods that contain the artificial sweetener sorbitol (daily ingestion of 50 grams or more)

3. Foods that contain the artificial sweetener mannitol (daily ingestion of 20 grams or more)

4. Foods that contain dry psyllium husk and that bear a health claim linking consumption of soluble fiber from psyllium husk with reduced risk of coronary heart disease

5. Irradiated foods

6. Fresh eggs (in consumer packages)

7. Foods packaged in self-pressurized containers and intended to be expelled from the package under pressure

8. Foods that contain, or are manufactured with, chlorofluorocarbon or other ozone-depleting substances

9. Juices or juice-containing beverages that have not been processed so as to produce a minimum five-log (i.e., 100,000-fold) reduction in the most resistant pathogen of public health significance (e.g., *E. coli*) likely to occur in that product

10. Meat and poultry products that require special handling to maintain wholesomeness

11. Foods that contain any meat or poultry that is not ready-to-eat.

Juices. Certain categories of food products are subject to special labeling requirements. Among the most commonly consumed of such products are the numerous varieties of juices available on the market. Any beverage containing fruit or vegetable juice is required to present a percent juice declaration (e.g., "100 percent juice" or "contains 50 percent orange juice"). This declaration must appear near the top of the information panel and is usually placed directly above the nutrition facts. If a beverage contains less than 100 percent juice and its state-

ment of identity includes the word "juice," it must also include a qualifying term such as "drink," "beverage," or "cocktail." If one or more of the juices in the product is made from concentrate, the statement of identity must be qualified with the words "from concentrate" or "reconstituted."

Country-of-origin marking. Imported foods are required to bear country-of-origin marking (e.g., "product of Italy"). Country-of-origin marking must appear in a conspicuous place and as legibly, indelibly, and permanently as possible. Placing country-of-origin marking immediately beneath the signature line is often ideal. If the signature line states a U.S. address, it should be followed by country-of-origin marking to avoid misleading consumers about the product's geographic origin.

Flavor designation. If the label (other than in the ingredients list), labeling, or advertising for a food makes a representation (such as by words or pictures) about the food's primary recognizable flavor, that flavor is considered its "characterizing flavor" and must accompany the statement of identity on the PDP.

Nutrient content claims. If a food product's label includes a relative nutrient content claim (e.g., "reduced fat," "light," or "added calcium"), the nutrient content claim must be accompanied by information identifying the reference food and explaining how much the nutrient in question has been reduced or added. In addition, use of certain nutrient content claims triggers the need to include additional nutrient declarations in the nutrition facts. For instance, a claim about potassium content triggers the requirement to declare the actual potassium content in the nutrition facts.

Optional Label Information

Nutrient content claims. A nutrient content claim is any representation that characterizes the level of a nutrient in a food product (e.g., "low fat," or "sugar free"). A nutrient content claim must comply with the specific criteria for that particular claim. For instance, to make a "low fat" claim, a food must contain three grams or less total fat per reference amount customarily consumed (RACC). (The RACC, as established by the FDA, is the amount of food normally consumed per eating occasion by persons four years of age or older.)

A label statement about the actual amount or percentage of a nutrient in a food ("5 grams of fat per serving") is permitted, provided it is truthful and not misleading and does not characterize the level of the nutrient in the food. If the statement implicitly characterizes the level of the nutrient ("just 5 grams of fat per serving"), it is an implied nutrient content claim and must either meet the requirements for the implied nutrient content claim ("low fat"), or bear a disclaimer that the food does not meet those requirements ("just 5 grams of fat per serving, not a low-fat food"). Statements such as "contains the same amount of potassium as a banana" or "as much calcium as milk" are permitted, provided the reference food qualifies as a "good source" of the nutrient and the labeled product has at least an equivalent level of the nutrient per serving.

Health claims. A health claim is any representation that characterizes the relationship between any substance and a disease (such as coronary heart disease) or health-related condition (such as hypertension). A "substance" is a specific food or component of a food. A health claim must either be authorized by FDA regulation, or be an accurate representation of a current "authoritative statement" of a scientific body of the U.S. government with official responsibility for public health research related to human nutrition (e.g., the National Institutes of Health). Health claims based on an authoritative statement require premarket notification to FDA—an example is the FDA-approved health claim regarding the substance potassium and the conditions hypertension and stroke. Since 2001 the FDA has authorized the following health claims by regulation:

TABLE 1

Health claims authorized by FDA	
Substance	**Disease or Health-Related Condition**
calcium	osteoporosis
sodium	hypertension
dietary fat	cancer
saturated fat and cholesterol	coronary heart disease
dietary fiber in grains, fruits, and vegetables	cancer and coronary heart disease
soluble fiber from specific food sources (e.g., oat bran, oatmeal, psyllium husk)	coronary heart disease
fruits and vegetables	cancer
folic acid	neural tube defects
sugar alcohols	dental caries
soy protein	coronary heart disease
plant sterol and stanol esters	coronary heart disease

USDA regulations currently prohibit meat and poultry products from bearing health claims.

Like nutrient content claims, health claims must comply with both general requirements applicable to all health claims and specific criteria for the particular health claim being made. For example, to be eligible to bear a claim about soy protein and risk of coronary heart disease, a food must contain at least 6.25 grams of soy protein per RACC, must qualify as a low-cholesterol and low-saturated-fat food, and must qualify as a low-fat food.

To bear a health claim, a food may not contain disqualifying levels of certain nutrients—total fat (13 grams), saturated fat (4 grams), cholesterol (60 milligrams), or sodium (480 milligrams)—per RACC or per labeled serv-

ing. Under what is known as the "jelly bean rule," a food making a health claim must contain per RACC, prior to any nutrient addition, a minimum level of at least one of the following nutrients: vitamin A (500 international units or more), vitamin C (6 milligrams or more), calcium (100 milligrams or more), iron (1.8 milligrams or more), protein (5 grams or more), or dietary fiber (2.5 grams or more). The purpose of the so-called jelly bean rule is to prevent a food of little nutritional value from bearing a health claim simply because the food has been fortified. Reasonably, the health claim that links sugar alcohols to dental caries is exempt from the jelly bean rule.

The wording and placement of health claims are highly regulated.

Structure and function claims. A truthful statement that a food or any ingredient helps maintain a structure or any function of the body may be made in labeling (e.g., "cranberry juice may help maintain a healthy urinary tract"). The manufacturer or distributor making the claim must have scientific evidence supporting the claim.

Other claims. A number of other claims that may be made on food labels are also regulated. The FDA has requirements for claims that a food is "fresh" or "healthy." The USDA has regulations defining "organic." The FTC limits the use of the claim "new" to a period of six months after a product is introduced into the market. Provided the information given is truthful and not misleading, a food may bear a claim about the presence of an ingredient perceived to add value ("made with real fruit") or about the absence of a nonnutritive ingredient ("no preservatives").

Symbols on food labels. Food labels may bear a variety of symbols or logos. Some of these are required. For example, irradiated whole foods are required to carry the radura symbol (i.e., the international symbol of food irradiation, which resembles a flower in a circle), and all meat and poultry products are required to bear the USDA official inspection mark. Other symbols are optional. These include the Uniform Product Code (UPC; the most familiar bar code) and symbols indicating that a food product is kosher.

Recipes and miscellaneous information. Food labels may carry a wide variety of other optional items, including such things as recipes, promotions, and "romance copy" (e.g., information extolling the virtues of a product or describing its history). Such information is permitted, provided it is truthful and not misleading.

Prohibited Label Information

Any information that is false or misleading in any particular will render a product misbranded. In determining whether a food label is false or misleading, both affirmative representations and omissions of material facts may be considered. Certain information is clearly prohibited from the labeling of food products. This includes unauthorized nutrient content claims (for instance, claiming "high in omega-3 fatty acids"), health claims not authorized by FDA or supported by an authoritative statement, and disease claims (for instance, claiming "helps lower blood pressure" would subject a product to regulation as a drug).

Language Specifications

All mandatory label information in the United States must appear in English. If labeling includes foreign language words of a type that are likely to bring the product to the attention of consumers who do not understand English, then all mandatory information must appear in both English and the foreign language. Certain foreign language words will not trigger dual-language labeling—for example, an accepted name for which there is no English equivalent (such as "antipasto"), a foreign name used in a standard of identity (such as "spaghetti"), and the use of one or more foreign language words in a brand name, motto, or trademarked design.

In Puerto Rico and other U.S. territories where the predominant language is other than English, the predominant language may be substituted for English, except in the case of the USDA inspection mark on meat and poultry products, which must appear in English.

See also **Additives; Food Politics: United States; Government Agencies, U.S.; Health and Disease; Inspection; Marketing of Food; Nutrition.**

BIBLIOGRAPHY

Olsson, Philip C., Richard L. Frank, David F. Weeda, et al. *U.S. Food Labeling Guide*. Washington, D.C.: Food Institute.

U.S. Department of Agriculture, Food Safety and Inspection Service, Office of Policy, Program Development, and Evaluation. *Labeling and Consumer Protection Staff: Ten Most Commonly Asked Questions*. Available at 2002.http://www.fsis.usda.gov/OPPDE/larc/TenQuestions.htm.

U.S. Food and Drug Administration, Center for Food Safety and Applied Nutrition. *A Food Labeling Guide*. Available at http://www.cfsan.fda.gov/dms/flg-toc.html.

U.S. Food and Drug Administration, Center for Food Safety and Applied Nutrition. *Food Labeling Questions and Answers*. 1993. Available at http://vm.cfsan.fda.gov/lrd/qa2.html.

U.S. Food and Drug Administration, Center for Food Safety and Applied Nutrition. *Food Labeling Questions and Answers, Volume 2: A Guide for Restaurants and Other Retail Establishments*. 1996. Available at http://www.cfsan.fda.gov/frf/qaintro.html.

U.S. Food and Drug Administration, Office of Regulatory Affairs. *Compliance Policy Guides Manual*. 2002. Available at www.fda.gov/ora/compliance_ref/cpg.

Richard L. Frank
Robert A. Hahn

LACTATION. Lactation refers to the ability of mammals, warm-blooded, backboned animals, to nourish their young with milk produced by the mammary glands. Many other distinguishing features separate mammals into families that include over four thousand species. The milk of each species is specifically engineered for the growth and developmental needs of that species. In fact studies of the characteristics of the milk can predict the growth rate of both body and brain and the developmental maturity of the offspring at birth. It is also possible to predict the feeding patterns that vary from the whale, which feeds its young every three to four days and has extremely high-fat milk (50 percent), to the human, who initially feeds the infant every two to three hours and has low-protein, low-fat milk (3.4 percent). Some of the world's finest scientists have turned their attention to human lactation and have not only deciphered the micronutrients of human milk but have studied the nutrient needs of the human infant, especially as they pertain to brain development and physical growth. Research also has explained the physiology of human lactation.

Historically, in times of wealth and prosperity, women of higher socioeconomic levels have sought substitute feedings for their infants to "free" themselves of the burden of breast-feeding. Dogma and ritual have developed in different cultures of the world around nursing. It is significant that the Qur'an states that women should nurse their infants for two years. In the Old Testament, the Book of Psalms refers to the value of mother's milk. Pope John Paul II stated that the women of the world should provide their milk for their infants.

When bottle-feeding became more available for the average mother due to the discovery of sterilization, followed by the availability of prepared formulas, the trend toward bottle-feeding increased from 1930 to 1950. Well-educated women led the march to the bottle because they wanted to raise their infants by the book, with scientific information. In the second half of the twentieth century, these same educated women sought a different mode of childbirth in which the mother was prepared and in control. Concomitant with this, well-educated women began looking at breast-feeding as the most appropriate course for their infants.

In 1978 a bipartisan congressional committee charged with the responsibility of designing a health plan for the United States established the year 1990 as the target date for accomplishing several health goals. In addition to statements regarding decreasing hypertension, obesity, and smoking, the committee stated that 75 percent of women should leave the hospital breast-feeding and at least 35 percent should still be breast-feeding at six months. Many of the goals were not accomplished, and in 1990 they were rewritten with a target date of 2000. In 2000 they were rewritten for 2010, aiming at 75 percent of mothers initiating breast-feeding, 50 percent continuing for six months, and 25 percent continuing for a full year. The World Health Organization Code for Infant Feeding was developed in 1981, and the most industrialized countries of the world endorsed this policy, which supported breast-feeding and rejected the promotion of artificial feedings and advertisement of these feedings to the public. The United States did not sign until 1994. The Institute of Medicine, through the Subcommittee on Nutrition during Lactation, confirmed the position that all women, under ordinary circumstances, should breast-feed their infants and further stated that breast-feeding was ideal, even if the mother's diet was not perfect. The American Academy of Pediatrics, joined by the American College of Obstetrics and Gynecology, stated in 1997 that infants should be exclusively breast-fed for five to six months. They further stated that breast-feeding should continue as weaning foods are added through the first year of life and then for as long thereafter as the mother and the infant choose

Significance of Breast-Feeding to Health

Why have all of these important groups spoken out so strongly in favor of breast-feeding? The knowledge that human milk is for the human infant has been accepted for centuries. In the late twentieth century, however, considerable scientific investigation established unequivocally that breast-feeding is associated with a reduced incidence of infection in the infant, including reduced incidences of gastrointestinal, upper and lower respiratory, ear, and urinary tract infections. Immunologic data have shown reduced incidences of childhood-onset cancers, especially lymphoma and acute lymphocytic leukemia. Crohn's disease, celiac disease, and childhood-onset diabetes also are reduced when infants are breast-fed for at least four months. Probably the most dramatic information published in multiple articles is the relationship between breast-feeding and infant development. A study by Niles Newton compared the developmental progress of breast-fed and bottle-fed three-year-olds. Alan Lucas, Ruth Morley, T. J. Cole, and others reported a multisite study that compared premature babies given their mother's milk by feeding tube with infants given premature-infant formula. The group studied them at eighteen months and followed them until seven and a half to eight years of age. The study showed an 8.5-point difference when the data were adjusted for socioeconomic status and education of the mother. The eighteen-year study by L. John Horwood and David M. Fergusson in New Zealand showed a measurable difference at eighteen years of age in school outcomes and behaviors related to whether or not the children were breast-fed in infancy. Although these studies have been criticized for design flaws, many scientists accept their findings. These results are in addition to the compelling psychologic benefit to the mother and the infant in their relationship during breast-feeding.

Facilitating the Decision to Breast-Feed

A mother needs an opportunity to make an informed decision about how to feed her infant. If a mother comes to pregnancy without any information on this process, it is the health care provider's responsibility to see that she is well informed about the benefits of breast-feeding for her baby, for herself, and for society so she can make a decision that will be optimal.

The economic benefit of breast-feeding. A simple calculation of the cost of buying formula does not reflect completely the monetary benefits of breast-feeding. It costs between $60 and $80 a month to purchase infant formula, $700 to $1,000 for the first year of life. Careful studies in controlled populations, such as in health maintenance organizations, have demonstrated in multiple reports that infants who are not breast-fed have an increased number of illnesses, visits to the doctor, prescription medications, and hospitalizations compared with their breast-fed counterparts. The estimate per infant of the health care costs not to breast-feed is between $600 and $1,000 per year. This estimate does not include the reduction in the onset of chronic illnesses that may last a lifetime, such as diabetes, Crohn's disease, and allergies.

Benefits to the mother. The benefits of breast-feeding to the mother are often ignored. Women who breast-feed return to their prepregnant, physiologic states more rapidly. The uterus involutes, the postpartum blood loss is reduced, and the woman returns to her physiologic weight as well. Among other possible benefits are reduced incidences of long-term obesity, breast cancer, ovarian cancer, and most remarkably long-term osteoporosis. Although breast-feeding is not a contraceptive, it significantly affects the fertility in the childbearing years by suppressing ovulation.

Establishing lactation. Critical information about the mother's potential for a good milk supply is obtained during pregnancy. When the obstetrician does the early examination of the breasts in the first trimester, the breasts should be evaluated with respect to their potential for producing milk. Unusually small, unusually large, asymmetric, or tubular-shaped breasts may pose a problem. Prior surgery of the breast should be discussed. Lumpectomies and augmentation mammoplasty are not contraindications. Reduction mammoplasty, however, may pose a problem if the integrity of the ducts was interrupted. The obstetrician should also evaluate the breasts' responses to the hormones of pregnancy, the degree of increase in size of the breasts, and changes in the areola and nipple. The obstetrician should discuss with the mother her intentions to breast-feed and address any questions she may have. The mother should be encouraged to attend breast-feeding preparation classes, which are commonly available at hospitals with maternity services and at local mothers' groups.

The breast prepares for lactation during pregnancy by enhancing the ductal system and developing lacteal cells that will produce the milk. From about sixteen weeks in gestation on, the breast is capable of making milk if the fetus is delivered. During pregnancy the placenta produces a prolactin-inhibiting hormone (PIH) that blocks the breast from responding to the abundant prolactin of pregnancy. Once the placenta is delivered, the PIH drops, and the breast responds to the hormones oxytocin and prolactin.

The key response of the breast following delivery is called the ejection or letdown reflex, prompted by two major hormones, oxytocin and prolactin. Oxytocin causes myoepithelial cells to contract. Thus when the baby stimulates the breast by suckling, a message is sent via the peripheral nervous system to the mother's brain and pituitary to release oxytocin, which in turn causes the myoepithelial cells that surround the alveoli and the ductal system to contract, ejecting the milk from the ducts. Suckling at the breast also stimulates the release of prolactin, the hormone that stimulates the lacteal cells to produce milk. Prolactin is not released unless the breast is stimulated. Oxytocin, however, may be released when the mother sees her baby or hears her baby cry or as a result of other stimulating sensory pathways.

It is recommended that the infant be put to breast as soon after delivery as is possible. The infant has been sucking and swallowing in utero, consuming considerable amniotic fluid, from about fourteen weeks gestation on, so he or she is ready to begin breast-feeding.

To put the infant to breast, the infant is held with his or her abdomen against the mother's and the infant looking directly at the breast. The mother supports the breast with her hand, keeping her fingers behind the areola and gently compressing it. The mother strokes the center of the infant's lower lip with the nipple. This stimulates the infant to open his or her mouth, extend his or her tongue, and draw the nipple and the areola into his or her mouth. The baby's tongue compresses the elongated nipple and areola against his or her hard palate. The peristaltic motion of the tongue stimulates the letdown reflex, and milk is released and swallowed. Infants should be fed when hungry, which is eight to twelve times a day initially. No other food or drink is necessary during exclusive breast-feeding for up to six months.

See also **Baby Food; Dairy Products; Milk, Human.**

BIBLIOGRAPHY

American Academy of Pediatrics Work Group on Breastfeeding. "Breastfeeding and the Use of Human Milk." *Pediatrics* 100 (1997): 1035.

Ball, Thomas M., and Anne L. Wright. "Health Care Costs of Formula-Feeding in the First Year of Life." *Pediatrics* 103 (1999): 870.

Biancuzzo, Marie. *Breastfeeding the Newborn: Clinical Strategies for Nurses.* St. Louis, Mo.: Mosby, 1999.

Horwood, L. John, and David M. Fergusson. "Breastfeeding and Later Cognitive and Academic Outcomes." *Pediatrics* 101 (1998): 39.

Huggins, Kathleen. *The Nursing Mother's Companion.* 4th ed. Boston: Harvard Common Press, 1999.

Institute of Medicine, Subcommittee on Nutrition during Lactation. *Nutrition during Lactation.* Washington, D.C.: National Academy Press, 1991.

Lawrence, Ruth A., and Robert M. Lawrence. *Breastfeeding: A Guide for the Medical Profession.* 5th ed. St. Louis, Mo.: Mosby, 1999.

Lucas, Alan, Ruth Morley, T. J. Cole, et al. "Breast Milk and Subsequent Intelligence Quotient in Children Born Preterm." *Lancet* 339 (1992): 261.

Newton, Niles. "Psychological Differences between Breast and Bottle Feeding." *American Journal of Clinical Nutrition* 24 (1971): 993.

United States Department of Health and Human Services. *Healthy People 2010.* Conference ed. in 2 vols. Washington, D.C.: U.S. Department of Health and Human Services, 2000.

Ruth A. Lawrence

LAMB. *See* **Mammals; Meat; Sheep.**

LAMB STEW. Lamb stew is a preparation in which tough cuts of lamb (by definition, taken from a sheep younger than one year of age in Europe or younger than two years of age in the United States, at the time of slaughter) or mutton (lamb's counterpart on the older side of the dividing line) are cut into small pieces, seared in hot fat, and simmered slowly in a flavored liquid until moist and tender; in the process, its liquid medium becomes a glossy sauce rich with the flavors of the meat. The tender, high-status rack portion of the lamb comprises only four percent of its live weight. Most other parts of the meat—leg, shank, shoulder, breast, neck, arm, and trim—increase in both flavor and toughness with the age and activity level of the sheep. Such cuts are best prepared with a method that can at once tenderize the meat, preserve its moistness, and mellow its flavor. Stewing fits these needs particularly well.

Stewing is most effective on older, tougher cuts of meat rich with collagen—a stiff protein found in connective tissue. With ample exposure to sufficiently high temperatures for a length of time relative to the muscle's toughness, slow stewing converts collagen to gelatin, yielding tender bits of meat perfumed with the cooking liquid, and a sauce rich with sheen and body. A simmer just below the boiling point is ideal, as such a temperature is sufficiently hot to make the gelatin soluble over time, yet gentle enough to keep the muscle moist and tender, rather than causing constriction and exudation of most of its juices, as would occur under a rolling boil. Such processes constitute the physical and chemical basis of stewing lamb. The cooks and the influence of the prevailing culture determine whether the stew is made with breast, shoulder, or neck; cooked in a clay, cast iron, or copper-bottom pot; or flavored with rosemary and red wine, dill and lemon, or cardamom and ginger.

A testament to the effectiveness of the stewing method for lamb and mutton (here used somewhat interchangeably, owing to the varied legal definitions) is the plethora of national, regional, and individual variations found in a diverse array of cultures. (See the Table for some of these variations.) Throughout Europe and the Mediterranean, lamb stews are typically flavored with ingredients like wine, garlic, rosemary, thyme, parsley and other herbs, and bacon, onion, carrot, celery, cabbage, tomato, or potato. From northern to southern Africa, lamb stews vary from the Moroccan *tangine* (or *tagine*) to Ethiopian versions with butter and *berbere*, a chili and spice paste, to South African European-style

TABLE 1

A sample of national and regional variations of lamb stew

Region/Country, Name(s)	Key Flavoring Ingredients
Europe	
Spain, *estufado de cordero*	Chorizo sausage and blood sausage, garlic, wine.
France, *navarin d'agneau; printanier*	Turnips, root vegetables, wine; spring vegetables.
Norway, *lammestuing*	Cabbage and peppercorns.
Ireland, Irish stew	Potatoes and onions.
Basque region	Garlic, onions, carrots, potatoes, wine.
Africa	
South Africa, *lensieskos*	Lentils, ginger, tomatoes, chili, garlic.
Ethiopia, *sega wat*	Butter, onion, *berbere* chili and spice paste.
Morocco, lamb *tangine*	Carrot, chickpeas, spices, garlic, *harissa* chili paste.
Eastern Asia	
India, *kashmiri gosht; badami gosht*	Nuts, yogurt, onions, spices including cardamom, cloves, turmeric, coriander, chilies, saffron.
China, hot pot	Soy sauce, chili paste, garlic, ginger, scallion, rice wine.
Americas	
Native Andean, *huatia*	Uncultivated herbs, chilies.
Cuba, *chilindron de carnero*	Bacon, lime, onion, bell pepper, tomato, garlic, cumin, oregano.
Middle East and Arab World	
khoresche esfanaj	Lemon, dill, and green vegetables.
keshkeg herriseh	Porridge of lamb and wheat with onion, bay leaf.
Syria, *yukhnee*	Tomatoes, garlic, onion, spices.
Persia, *khoresh qormeh sabzi*	Red beans, onion, turmeric, lemon, fresh herbs.
Persia, Armenia, Morocco, and elsewhere	Apricots, garlic, onion, lemon, spices including turmeric, coriander, ginger, cayenne, cumin.
Turkey, *pirpirim asi*	Assorted pulses, uncultivated greens.
Sephardim, *msouki*	Onion, garlic, fava beans, fresh peas, *harissa* chili paste, nutmeg.
Egypt, *fatta*	Pilaf-style rice and bread with stewed mutton.

stews of lamb and legumes. In China, lamb stews are flavored with fermented sauces; in India, they are thickly flavored with spices, nuts, and yogurt, as they are in many other parts of Asia. Throughout much of Oceania and in parts of the United States, where lamb is big business, the stews incorporate flavors from throughout Europe, Africa, and Asia. Even in traditional cuisines of North America, where lamb is a relative newcomer, it is often substituted for indigenous meats, as an example, for alpaca meat in the Andean stew *huatia*.

But it is in the Middle East and the Arab World, more than anywhere else, where lamb stew has the broadest variety of manifestations—from a lamb-and-wheat porridge, to a stew with fresh dill and lemon, to some with red beans or fava beans, or with other legumes, many with apricots and spices, and even more containing tomatoes.

While there is likely no definitive answer as to why lamb stew is so important in the Middle East, there are some strong clues, both material and intangible, that can help to explain its centrality. The most evident reason is that Mesopotamia is the home of the domesticated lamb, with a tradition of raising sheep for wool and meat that goes back more than ten thousand years. Nearly as ancient is lamb's religious significance: roasted sheep ranked high in status among the early Semitic sacrifices, both prebiblical and biblical; and the paschal lamb of both Passover and Easter underlie references to Christ as the "Lamb of God." Even today, Christians in the Middle East and Mediterranean traditionally serve roast lamb for Easter; Sephardim serve stewed lamb for Passover; and Arabs serve roast or stewed lamb for nearly every feast—births, marriages, and death anniversaries, in addition to those of strictly religious celebrations.

Moreover, elements of lamb stew indicate some of the shared values of Middle Eastern culture. Societies of the Middle East as well as others consider it good etiquette to serve food in tender bite-size morsels as a display of time, effort, and hospitality on the part of the host, who would not have guests struggle to consume their food. Whole roast lamb is often presented and served off the bone, in contrast to the European tradition of displaying a formidable roasted joint or whole animal. A rich stew of lamb also highlights the accompanying rice, couscous, bread, or grain, accompaniments of simple integrity that complement the richness of the lamb. Many Middle Eastern people also place additional value on the local origins of the sheep, which is considered far superior to imported lamb, beef, or poultry, and is certainly preferred to pork, forbidden among observant Muslims and Jews.

Lamb stew has a deep history and tradition, a common base with seemingly infinite variations, a strong, complex, and pervasive flavor, and firm entrenchment in the surrounding culture. It is often seen as symbolic of the people and region of the Middle East.

BIBLIOGRAPHY

Cox, Beverly. "*Huatia*, an Andean Winter Stew." *Native Peoples* 13, no. 2 (February/March 2000): 42–43.

McGee, Harold. *On Food and Cooking*. New York: Collier Books, 1984.

Romans, John R., William J. Costello, C. Wendell Carlson, Marion L. Greaser, and Kevin W. Jones. *The Meat We Eat*. Danville, Ill.: Interstate Publishers, 2001.

Ward, Susie, Claire Clifton, and Jenny Stacey. *The Gourmet Atlas*. New York: Macmillan, 1997.

Wolfert, Paula. *Paula Wolfert's World of Food*. New York: Harper Collins, 1994.

Zubaida, Sami, and Richard Tapper, eds. *Culinary Cultures of the Middle East*. London: I. B. Tauris Publishers, 1994.

Jonathan Deutsch

LANGUAGE ABOUT FOOD. Foods can be named according to different levels of generality. The basic level terms (Rosch, "Principles of Categorization") are the most consistent across languages in that translation equivalents can be readily found. Examples of basic level terms are "apple," "potato," "rice," "coffee," "turkey," "salmon," and "snails." This level often corresponds to scientific taxonomies. More specifically, varietal or breed terms tend to be compounds consisting of a modifier plus a basic term, as in "Jonathan apple," "jasmine rice," "sockeye salmon," or "green-lipped mussel."

Higher level categories are more variable across languages than are basic level terms and often result in different, incompatible classifications. Whether a tomato is a fruit or a vegetable depends on the purpose of the classification. For scientific purposes, it is a fruit (as are squash and bell peppers), since it contains the seed for reproduction. However, for culinary purposes, a tomato is a vegetable in Europe and North America. In Taiwan, where tomatoes are eaten for dessert, along with sweet fruits, it would be a fruit. English-speakers classify potatoes as vegetables, but German-speakers are not likely to consider the *Kartoffel* (potato) to be included in the German word *Gemüse*, translated as "vegetable" but not coextensive with the English category.

There are many named categories based on cultural, dietary, and religious practices. According to Jewish dietary laws, the term *kosher* designates foods acceptable for Jews to eat, and *tref* (a Yiddish word) designates pork, shellfish, and other foods forbidden to eat. Another distinction is between *milchig*, describing dairy products, and *fleishig*, describing meat products, which include poultry but not fish. Items from these two categories are not to be eaten at the same meal. *Pareve* products are made without milk or meat, and can be eaten at dairy or meat meals.

Foods can be classified by their primary biochemical composition into carbohydrates, proteins, and fat for health and other dietary purposes. Vegetarians distinguish between "vegans," who eat no animal products, and "ovo-lacto-vegetarians," who eat eggs and milk products.

There are many informal and slang words for food in general: "chow," "grub," "mess," and "eats" are a few examples.

Words for Meals
English has various names for the customary times of day when people eat. "Meal" is a general term that includes breakfast, lunch, and supper (or dinner). "Dinner" is the largest meal, which can be midday or evening, depending on the region and culture. "Supper" is an evening meal, but for many people in the United States, "supper" and "dinner" are synonyms. The *Longman Lexicon of Contemporary English* (p. 217) contrasts meal terms for the British middle class and working class, and for Scotland in general. British middle-class words are similar to American usage, with the addition of "(afternoon) tea." In Scotland and among the British working class, "dinner" is served at noon, tea is served around 4 P.M., "(high) tea" is a light cooked meal served between 5 and 6 P.M., while "supper" is a small meal between 9 and 10 P.M.

In contrast to "meal," the term "snack" refers to food eaten between meals. Fancy or elaborate meals, especially those served on special occasions, are termed "feasts" or "banquets."

For meals with several courses, the courses are generally named according to the order in which they are served. In English the first course is the "appetizer" (or "starter" or "hors d'oeuvre"), followed by the main course or "entrée," and finally the "dessert." Although many English culinary terms are taken from French, usually with the French meaning, the sense of "entrée" has undergone a slight semantic shift. Traditional formal French dinners typically consisted of five courses: the *hors d'oeuvre* (literally "out of the work," often a soup or pâté), then the *entrée*, usually fish, followed by the *plat principal* (or *plat de résistance*, *pièce de résistance*), then *fromage* (cheese), and finally *dessert*.

Cooking Vocabulary
Preparing food by cooking is a universal practice in human societies, and every language has words to differentiate cooking methods. In English, "cook" is a general term with more specific words: "boil" (cook in water), "bake" (cook with dry heat in an enclosed space), "grill" or "broil" (cook over/under an open flame), "roast" (originally, cook on a spit over an open flame, but now partly synonymous with "bake"), and "fry" (cook in fat). English has highly specific words, including "steam," "poach" (cook gently in water), "deep-fry" or "French-fry" (submerge in hot oil), "sauté" or "pan-fry" (fry quickly in fat), or "stew" (cook slowly for a long time), "simmer" (gently boil), "braise" (sauté then simmer), and "barbecue." A relatively recent addition is "microwave."

Although German is closely related to English, the same concepts are expressed with somewhat fewer words. *Kochen* can mean "cook in general" or "boil" as a specific cooking method. *Braten* covers pan-frying, grilling, and broiling, while *backen* is the general word for "bake." Other words are *sieden* (boil, simmer), *rösten* (roast), and *grillen*, a specific term for grilling. *Dünsten*, *schmoren*, and *dämpfen* (braise, stew) are more specific.

Polish, like German, uses one word, *gotawać*, for cooking in general and for boiling. Other words are *smażyć* (fry), *duscić* (stew), and *piec* (bake, roast).

In Japanese the general term for cooking is *nitaki* or *ryoori-suru* (prepare food). *Niru* is a general term for boiling, with two subterms: *yuderu* for boiling solid food and *taku* for boiling or steaming rice. *Musu* means 'steam'. *Yaku* covers baking, roasting, broiling and frying, but there are specific words as well: *ageru* (deep-fry), *itameru* (stir-fry), *aburu* (grill or broil).

The general term for 'cook' in Mandarin Chinese is *shāo*. Its basic meaning is 'burn', and in context it can also be interpreted as 'bake', 'roast', or 'boil'. Other cooking words are *zhǔ* (boil), *zhēng* (steam), *chǎo* (stir fry) and *jiān* (fry in a little oil), *zhà* (deep-fry), and *káo*, a general word which covers baking, roasting, and broiling. More specific words include *dùn* (stew in broth or sauce) and *mēn* (cook slowly in a covered pot).

Amharic, a Semitic language spoken in Ethiopia, uses the term *bessela* (cook), with specific words for cooking methods and type of food cooked: *fella* for boiling liquids, *k'ek'k'elle* for boiling solid food, *gagger* for baking bread, *t'ebbese* for frying or roasting meat, and *k'olla* for parching grain.

In general, languages have a variety of different words for cooking methods based largely on whether water, oil, dry heat, or an open flame is used. There is almost always a specific word for "boil," and often this is also the general word for "cook." Grilling (broiling), baking, roasting, and frying can be denoted by different words, but frequently these are combined into one or two general words.

Eating and Drinking Vocabulary

All languages have words for eating and drinking. In English, the distinction is whether solids or liquids are consumed. German, in addition to *trinken* (drink), contrasts *essen* (eating by humans) and *fressen* (eating by animals). Navajo has a general word for "eat," and several specific ones whose use depends on the amount, shape, and consistency of the food eaten. (Corresponding distinctions occur in Navajo verbs for handling food, but not in verbs for cooking, which depend on the cooking method.)

English has two sets of specific verbs for eating. The first set comprises intransitive verbs for eating meals or amounts of food: these include "dine," "lunch," "snack," and "nosh." The second set comprises transitive verbs that describe the manner of eating or drinking: these include "gobble," "munch," "nibble," "lick," "guzzle," "sip," "wolf down," and "slurp" (Fellbaum and Kegl, 1989).

Words for Wine

Although we can perceive only four basic tastes—sweet, sour, bitter, and salty—we can perceive thousands of odors. These odors fall into a few basic categories: floral, ethereal, musky, resinous, foul, and acrid (Ackerman, p. 11). The sense of smell is extremely sensitive and selective. "Our olfactory threshold is about 6,000 to 10,000 times as sensitive as that for taste" (Amerine et al., 1959, p. 483). What we perceive as taste is really a combination of taste and smell.

A very large, creative vocabulary has been developed to describe the taste and smell of wines, and new words are continuously invented. The vocabulary includes scientific-technical terms mostly used by experts (for example, "malo-lactic fermentation," "botrytis nose"), and widely used varietal names, like "Chardonnay" and "Pinot Noir." Some words are descriptive: for example, wines can be "sweet" and "dry." However, a large part of the vocabulary consists of words that have both a descriptive and evaluative component. A wine with a high acid content can be "tart," if it is judged desirable, or "sour," if undesirable. A wine's "body," a function of dissolved solids (tannin, acids, and fruit extracts) and alcohol, can be either "heavy" or "light," words that are evaluatively neutral. "Rich" and "big" are positive terms for "heavy," while "coarse" is negative. "Thin" and "watery" are negative terms for the neutral term "light."

The purely descriptive and descriptive-evaluative words are usually divided into the following three categories: "Taste"—sweet or dry (residual sugar or no sugar), sour (acidic), and bitter (tannic); "bouquet and aroma"—the smell of the wine; and "texture"—the feel of the wine in the mouth. This last category of texture includes body, and also includes sensations such as prickliness from certain acids and astringency from tannin. Positive texture words include "smooth" and its synonyms "soft," "silky," "velvety." Negative descriptors include "rough," "hard," and "harsh."

The numerous descriptors for specific tastes and smells are based on a similarity to some fruits, vegetables, or other objects. Wines can be "fruity," "vegetal," or more specifically, have the taste or smell of any fruit (cherry, apple, melon), vegetable (green bean, asparagus, bell pepper), spice (cinnamon, nutmeg), or herb (thyme, peppermint). Wines can also be "meaty," "yeasty," "perfumed," "flowery," or "smoky." These specific descriptors are nouns or adjectives derived from nouns.

Perhaps the most interesting, most discussed, and most ridiculed aspect of wine description is based on metaphor. "Body," the weight of the wine, gives rise to an open set of semantic extensions. Since heavy things are usually big, various size words are used as synonyms: "huge," "massive," "mammoth." Other metaphors based on the human body include "muscular," "brawny," "fat," "fleshy," "stout," "beefy," "big-boned," and "chunky" for heavy wines, and "lean," "sleek," "sinewy," "svelte," and "thin" for light wines.

352

LAPPS

The "structure" of a wine is its solid components—"the combined effect of elements such as acidity, tannin, glycerin, alcohol and sugar as they related to a wine's texture" (Steiman, p. 231). The concept of structure has generated terms like "backbone," "frame," and "framework."

Especially interesting and creative are metaphors based on personality and character. Wines, whose properties are immediately apparent, can be "generous," "approachable," "assertive," "bold," "brash," "loud," "sassy," "flamboyant," or "in-your-face." Wines with subtler properties are "shy," "sly," "reserved," "reticent," or "subtle." Many terms based on human personality are mainly evaluative: "agile," "charming," "classy," "diplomatic," "friendly," "graceful," "polished," "refined," and "elegant" are positive, while "aggressive," "stingy," and "mean" are negative.

Some wine descriptors are based on age and the life cycle. "Young" and "old" are a function not only of when a wine was made but also of its stage of development from grape juice to drinkable wine to vinegar. Wines that are too young can be "immature," "green," "closed," "dumb" (mute), "tight," (tightly closed, tightly wound), or "locked in." Wines at the peak of drinkability are "open," "mature," "ripe," "developed," "evolved," or "mellow." Wines that are too old can be described as "withered," "dying," "decrepit," "over-the-hill," or "senile."

"Balance" is the way in which the various wine components interact. Positive descriptors include "balanced," "harmonious," "integrated," "focused," "formed," "coordinated," and "well-defined." Negative words are "unbalanced," "unharmonious," "diffuse," "disjointed," "uncoordinated," and "muddled."

In the vocabulary of wine description, synonyms can be added for existing concepts. "Big" is a conventional word for full-bodied wines, and general mechanisms of semantic extension allow speakers to generate descriptors like "gigantic," "towering," or "elephantine" to express the same idea with greater rhetorical effect.

French, German, Italian, Spanish, and other languages spoken in wine-growing countries also have extensive wine vocabularies that cover scientific-technical, common descriptive, and evaluative meanings. Vocabularies for beer, coffee, and tea have many parallels, and even share many of the same words (for example, "rich," "light," "deep").

BIBLIOGRAPHY

Ackerman, Diane. *A Natural History of the Senses.* New York: Vintage, 1991.

Amerine, M. A., E. B. Roessler, and F. Filipello. "Modern Sensory Methods of Evaluating Wine." *Hilgardia: A Journal of Agricultural Science Published by the California Agricultural Experiment Station* 28, 18 (June 1959): 177–567.

Cook's and Diner's Dictionary: A Lexicon of Food, Wine, and Culinary Terms. New York: Funk & Wagnalls, 1968.

Fellbaum, Christiane, and Judy Kegl. "Taxonomic Structure and Object Deletion in the English Verbal System." In *Proceedings of the Sixth Eastern States Conference on Linguistics,* edited by K. deJong and Y. No, pp. 94-103. Columbus: Ohio State University, 1989.

Lehrer, Adrienne. *Semantic Fields and Lexical Structure.* Amsterdam: North Holland, 1974.

Lehrer, Adrienne. *Wine and Conversation.* Bloomington: Indiana University Press, 1983.

Longman Lexicon of Contemporary English. Burnt Mill, Harlow, Essex, U.K.: Longman, 1981.

Rosch, Eleanor. "Principles of Categorization." In *Cognition and Categorization,* edited by E. Rosch and L. Lloyd. Hillsdale, N.J.: Lawrence Erlbaum Associates, 1978.

Steiman, Harvey. *Essentials of Wine.* Philadelphia: Wine Spectator Press, 2000.

Adrienne Lehrer

LAPPS. The Sami (Lapps) are a native minority of northern Norway, Sweden, Finland, and the Kola Peninsula in Russia. Their territory was once much larger than it is today, especially in Finland. The Sami land is not homogeneous, but is divided into different ecological zones ranging from the coast of the Arctic Sea via the high mountains of Scandinavia to the northern forests. From a historical perspective, this territory supports various types of economies, with a focus on reindeer breeding, reindeer hunting, hunting combined with fishing in the sea and in lakes (in some regions combined with small farms), or pursuit of sea mammals. It is also important to connect the economy to different types of consumption with the emphasis on reindeer meat or milk, game and fish, and seal. Vegetables, berries such as cloudberries, bilberries, and lingonberries, and (infrequently) bread can also be seen as complements. Mercantile goods like flour, coffee, liquor, and horse meat, complete the picture.

The transition from hunters and fishers to reindeer herders began at different times in different parts of the widespread Sami territory. For example, the Sami practice of reindeer hunting combined with a nomadic lifestyle has existed in Sweden ever since the end of the Middle Ages.

The reindeer has long been the comprehensive symbol of Sami food culture, and today reindeer meat is exploited by restaurant culture of the Nordic countries, outside of the Sami territory. There one can find it on menus as roast reindeer (for example, under the name of *suovas*) or as small pieces of meat in a sauce with mashed potatoes and lingonberry (*renskav*).

Formerly the Sami used almost every part of the reindeer as food, including viscera, minced and cooked udder, hooves, and the brain (as an ingredient in bread). Reindeer cheese was once considered a delicacy, even as a commercial product, as were the tongue and heart. Reindeer milk could also be mixed with angelica and sorrel.

353

A Lapp herding reindeer on the tundra near Arrisovarre, Norway. © FARRELL GREHAN/CORBIS.

Samis traditionally boiled meat and fish. Dried fish (salmon and pike) were a replacement for bread and were also a trade commodity. In the nomadic society there was no oven in the Sami tent—the infrequently consumed bread was made of purchased barley (and later, wheat) on the hot hearth.

Breakfast was not a traditional Sami meal. In the nineteenth century it became a coffee meal or snack. Boiling meat and fish at noon and in the evening was the most common kind of traditional cooking. The principal meal was served in the evening. Traditionally, cooking in Sami culture was a male duty.

After the slaughtering of reindeer, a symbolic meal was traditionally served. This *renkok* (formerly and especially in gastronomic literature referred to as *lappkok*) consisted of marrowbone, liver, tongue, or heart boiled in a fat gravy. One can find such a meal at restaurants, especially in Lapland. Also, until the twentieth century, the Sami served a feast with boiled meat and a fat gravy after a successful bear hunt.

The money market has brought Western foodstuffs to the Sami food culture—at first as status food but gradually more and more as basic food—but at the same time, reindeer meat has retained its strong symbolic value for Sami identity.

See also **Canada: Native Peoples; Inuit; Mammals, Sea; Nordic Countries; Russia; Siberia.**

BIBLIOGRAPHY

Bosi, Roberto. *The Lapps.* Westport, Conn.: Greenwood Press, 1976.

Fjellström, Phebe. *Samernas samhälle i tradition och nutid* [Lappish society in tradition and the present day]. Stockholm: P. A. Norstedt & Söners Bokförlag, 1985.

Ruong, Israel. "Sami Usage and Customs." *The Sami National Minority in Sweden,* edited by Birgitta Jahreskog. Stockholm: Almqvist & Wiksell International in collaboration with Humanities Press, Atlantic Highlands, N.J., 1982.

Vorren, Ørnuly, and Ernst Manker. *Lapp Life and Customs: A Survey.* Translated from the Norwegian by Kathleen McFarlane. New York: Oxford University Press, 1962.

Kurt Genrup

LAROUSSE GASTRONOMIQUE. The chef Prosper Montagné's *Larousse gastronomique* was first published in France in 1938. Alongside Georges-Auguste Escoffier's *Le guide culinaire* and Louis Saulnier's *Le répertoire de la cuisine,* the *Larousse gastronomique* became one of the key reference works on French national and regional cuisine for the professional chef. The *Larousse gastronomique* is a reference text that codifies a history of the French culinary arts from the distant past to the present day in encyclopedic form. Entries cover such items as culinary terminology, foods, kitchen equipment, techniques, national cuisines, regional French cuisines, and historically significant chefs and restaurants.

Montagné's work signaled a break with the preceding era of French cookery as exemplified by the architectural creations of Marie Antoine Carême. Montagné emphasized dishes that were simple by Carême's standards, and the shortened menus were delivered in the Russian style service—meals were served in courses on individual plates. This philosophy inspired the name of his culinary encyclopedia. Montagné covered the range from the relatively new haute cuisine to French provincial and home cooking with some attention to classic dishes of other nations.

Three editions of the *Larousse gastronomique* have been published in English. The first edition, published in 1961, was an Anglo-American venture edited by Charlotte Turgeon and Nina Froud. A fairly direct translation of the Montagné text, this edition included updated food science entries and English and American measurements. One translator is the noted British food writer Patience Gray and it concludes with an additional reading list compiled by Elizabeth David.

Jennifer Harvey Lang edited the English second edition, published in 1988, from the 1984 French edition compiled and directed by Robert J. Courtine. Courtine's introduction describes the first edition as a monumental work, albeit one in need of some refurbishment. These new editions take into account technical innovations, advancements in food science, and a new culture of dining characterized by simpler meals and a dietary palette expanded through travel and global commerce. Yet the core achievements of Montagné, including his recipes and technical advice on classical and regional French dishes, are preserved.

For the third English edition, published in 2001, Jennifer Harvey Lang worked from a new French edition edited by Joël Robuchon, the president of the Gastronomy committee of the Librairie Larousse. This edition claims to have retained the classic dishes and techniques of the original edition with a newfound sensitivity to global influences in technique, presentation, ingredients, and recipes. It is 1,350 pages, over 150 pages longer than the preceding English edition and it includes two hundred new recipes and four hundred new entries.

The *Larousse gastronomique* no longer sits alone—if it ever did—on the shelves of professional chefs. Although considered a classic reference text on classical French dishes, ingredients, and techniques, the contemporary chef has access to numerous books that cover the same ground. Furthermore, the third edition addresses some elements of a growing interest in fusion cuisine and the cuisines of other nations, but it cannot provide the detail of more specialized cookbooks. Nevertheless, it covers an immense breadth of culinary material, justifying its continued importance.

See also **Carême, Marie Antoine; Chef, the; Cookbooks; Escoffier, Georges-Auguste; France; Gastronomy.**

BIBLIOGRAPHY

Montagné, Prosper. *Larousse gastronomique: The Encyclopedia of Food, Wine, and Cookery.* Edited by Charlotte Turgeon and Nina Froud. New York: Crown, 1961. First English edition.

Montagné, Prosper. *Larousse gastronomique: The New American Edition of the World's Greatest Culinary Encyclopedia.* Edited by Jennifer Harvey Lang. New York: Crown, 1988. Second English edition.

Montagné, Prosper. *Larousse gastronomique: The World's Greatest Culinary Encyclopedia.* Edited by Jennifer Harvey Lang. New York: Clarkson Potter, 2001. Third English edition.

Wesley R. Dean

LAST SUPPER, THE. The final meal of Jesus with his followers in Jerusalem the evening before his crucifixion on the orders of Pilate in or around 30 C.E. is called the Last Supper. During the meal Jesus is said to have expressed a desire to be remembered by breaking bread and sharing a cup of wine, inspiring the central ritual of Christianity variously called the Eucharist, Mass, Lord's Supper, or Holy Communion. Leonardo da Vinci's fresco, executed in Milan in the 1490s, is probably the best-known pictorial representation of the Last Supper.

The participants left no firsthand reports of the Last Supper. Instead, varying accounts were handed down and recorded two or more decades afterward in books eventually collected into the New Testament (Matt. 26:17–30, Mark 14:12–25, Luke 22:7–38, John 13–17, and 1 Cor. 11:23–29). These and noncanonical sources, notably *Didache* 10 and 9 (in presumed chronological order), are the origin of a variety of liturgies, including washing one another's feet (John 13:14), so the details are open to conjecture.

Throughout his mission Jesus shared meals so enthusiastically that he was accused of being a glutton and a drunkard (Luke 7:33–34; Matt. 11:18–19). Thus it is plausible that he would have told companions to seek out an upper room in a house, where he organized supper before being seized by Roman authorities.

In the eastern Mediterranean the standard beverage, staple, and accompaniment were wine or water, bread, and a range of relishes, including fish. These all featured in both Jesus' reported sharing (such as the mass distribution of loaves and fishes) and early versions of the subsequent Christian agapes (love feasts) and Eucharists (thanksgivings).

Any familiar religious shape to the last meal would have been Jewish, since Jesus did not seem to have intended to inaugurate another religion. In that context the presence of women might have been quickly ignored in favor of twelve male disciples representing the twelve

The Last Supper is a recurring image in Christian art. This scene is a detail from the tympanum of the late-thirteenth-century cathedral at Strasbourg, France.

tribes of Israel. Some sources associate the Last Supper with Passover, the Jewish holiday of unleavened bread and spring lamb, which presumably would have taken the group to Jerusalem and which subsequently provided the timing of Easter, along with the symbol of Jesus' own sacrifice.

His followers soon believed that Jesus used distinctive words of institution over the bread and cup. These might have emerged from Passover procedures, as argued by Joachim Jeremias in *The Eucharistic Words of Jesus* (1966), and Jesus would surely have employed some form of Jewish thanksgiving or *berakah* standardly used as a grace before food. Yet Dennis E. Smith and Hal Taussig, in *Many Tables* (1990), argue for a Greco-Roman setting for the meal or more plausibly for early interpretations, so the bread and cup derive from the formal *deipnon* or dinner and subsequent *symposion* or talking over a shared drinking cup.

In Paul's influential version, probably written in 53–54 C.E., the key points are that Jesus took a loaf of bread, gave thanks, broke it, and said: "This is my body which is given for you. Do this in remembrance of me." After supper Jesus said: "This cup is the new covenant in my blood. Do this, as often you drink it, in remembrance of me" (1 Cor. 11:23–25). Accredited priests then trans-

formed the bread and cup into Jesus' actual flesh and blood, and this transubstantiation was added to the matters for rancor and division. Some Protestants even retreated so far as to commemorate a self-proclaimed eater, drinker, and server entirely without bread or wine.

See also **Christianity: Eastern Orthodox Christianity;**
Christianity: Western Christianity; Judaism.

BIBLIOGRAPHY

Jeremias, Joachim. *The Eucharistic Words of Jesus.* Translated by Norman Perrin. London: S. C. M. Press, 1966.

Smith, Dennis E., and Hal Taussig. *Many Tables: The Eucharist in the New Testament and Liturgy Today.* Philadelphia: Trinity Press International, 1990.

Symons, Michael. "From Agape to Eucharist: Jesus' Meals and the Early Church." *Food and Foodways* 8, no. 1 (1999): 33–54.

Michael Symons

LA VARENNE. Little is known about the life of François Pierre (1618–1678), who signed with the name La Varenne. One account states that he was born in the Burgundian town of Chalon-sur-Saône and died in Dijon in 1678, and we know that from approximately 1640 to 1650 he worked in the kitchens of the Marquis d'Uxelles. His fame is due to the publication, in 1651, of *Le Cuisinier françois* (The French cook), the first of a new generation of cookbooks to document the changes that had taken place in French cuisine during the first half of the seventeenth century, and by far the most popular. Cooks were abandoning the use of spices that typified medieval and Renaissance cookery and replacing them with native European herbs: parsley, thyme, bay leaf, basil, etc. Many recipes, which are still popular with French chefs today—*bisque* and various *ragoûts*, for instance—are mentioned for the first time in *Le Cuisinier François*. La Varenne emphasizes the use of the *roux*, almost systematically employs a *bouquet garni* (a bundle of herbs) in stews and soups, and is the first to publish a recipe for *Oeufs à la neige* (snow eggs). His was also the first French cookbook to be translated into English (1653).

Although some have attributed other works to La Varenne, most notably *Le Pâtissier françois* (The French pastry chef) and *Le Confiturier françois* (The French confectioner), recent scholarship has shown that there is little reason to believe that he is the author of these texts.

See also **Chef; Cookbooks; France.**

BIBLIOGRAPHY

Flandrin, Jean-Louis, Philip Hyman, and Mary Hyman. Introduction to *Le Cuisinier françois* by La Varenne. Paris: Editions Montalba, 1983.

Hyman, Philip, and Mary Hyman. Introduction to *The French Cook* by La Varenne. Southover, Lewes, England: Southover Press, 2001.

Mary Hyman
Philip Hyman

LEAF VEGETABLES. Leaf vegetables are a diverse and eclectic group of plants comprising several different taxonomic plant families: Aizoaceae, Amaranthaceae, Asteraceae (Compositae), Basellaceae, Boraginaceae, Brassicaceae (Cruciferae), Chenopodiaceae, Convolvulaceae, Cucurbitaceae, Euphorbiaceae, Malvaceae, Phytolaccaceae, Polygonaceae, Portulacaceae, and Tetragoniaceae. In the literature, leaf vegetables are commonly known as "greens" and "potherbs." They are grown for their tender, succulent, and normally green leaves, and are usually cooked before eating, thus the name "potherb." Alternatively, the salad greens, for example, lettuce, radicchio, and endive, are usually eaten uncooked. Nevertheless, the leaf vegetables can be added fresh to tossed salads, giving the salad color and novel flavors. Not included in the group are those plants with leaves that serve as an important herb or flavoring ingredient, but do not constitute the main ingredient in the dish, such as cilantro, parsley, rosemary, etc.

Additionally, there are a large number of plants the leaves of which are eaten in certain parts of the world although the leaves are actually a secondary crop. For example, in Southeast Asia, chili pepper (capsicum) leaves are eaten, but it is the fruit that Americans usually consume. Other examples of plants whose fruits or roots are the primary crop but whose leaves are also consumed are peas and beans, plantain, cassava, cucumber, radish, and sweet potato.

Leaf vegetables may be cool-season or warm-season crops and can be grown as annuals or as perennials. In addition, some leaf vegetables are adapted to the tropics, while others are adapted to the temperate climates. Depending on location, leaf vegetables are either a main crop or treated as a minor crop. The more important leaf vegetables, based on dollar value, are spinach, kale, collards, mustard greens, and Swiss chard. Other leaf vegetables such as New Zealand spinach and dandelion are popular with home gardeners and are grown on a limited scale by market gardeners.

Leaf vegetables are among the most nutritious vegetables on a fresh weight basis and are also among the world's most productive plants in terms of nutritional value per unit area, in part because they grow rapidly, allowing several crops or harvests in a season. Although some of the constituents are lost during cooking, they still contribute significant amounts of provitamins A and C and several minerals. Leafy vegetables are also good for the eyes. Age-related macular degeneration is a leading cause of blindness among individuals over the age of 50. A research study in Massachusetts found that people who ate spinach, collards, and other dark green, leafy vegetables five or six times a week had about a 43 percent lower risk of the disease than those who ate it less than once a month. The typical shelf life for most leaf vegetables is ten to fourteen days.

Major Leaf Vegetables

Spinach. Spinach (*Spinacia oleracea* var. *inermis*) is a member of the Chenopodiaceae family, which also includes table beet, Swiss chard, sugar beet, and amaranth. Spinach is native to an area near present-day Iran and was first cultivated by the Persians more than 2,000 years ago. Records of its use are meager, but it is believed that cultivation of the crop developed during the period of the Greek and Roman civilizations. It was introduced to China in 647 C.E. and apparently was transported across North Africa to Spain by the Moors by 1100. Two seed types exist, one having a smooth, round shape and the other an irregular, prickly shape. The crop was known in Germany in the thirteenth century only in the prickly-seeded form. Smooth-seeded spinach, which is used exclusively in today's commercial production, was not described until 1552. The colonists introduced spinach to the Western Hemisphere, and it was listed in American seed catalogs by 1806.

SPINACH

Apparently the time of the introduction of spinach into China is well-recorded in Tang Dynasty history (618–907 C.E.) because it marked the flow of many new food offerings of grain and seed from Tibet. Also, the trade routes to the West went through Tibet, and presumably spinach may have been traded from its origins in Persia. One story is that it was included as a part of the bridal offerings that were carried into China with the marriage of Princess Wencheng to the Tang Emperor Taizong sometime before 641 C.E. This marriage was well recorded in both Han and Tibetan writings and folklore. It is also known that during this same period many other food products flowed (such as pepper and cardamom) into China. This trade resulted from the extensive connections Emperor Taizong had established with the western Asian region. While it is possible that spinach came into China through the marriage, it was also likely that it could have come anytime during the later reign of this emperor after establishing all of these connections. It is also relevant to note that this period (618–641 C.E.) also marks the time when both tea and porcelain were first extensively traded with the west.

Solomon H. Katz

Spinach is the most important leaf vegetable in the United States. The edible portion of the plant is the compact rosette of fleshy leaves attached to a short stem. Leaves vary from ovate or nearly triangular to long and narrow arrowhead shapes; the latter are a characteristic of more primitive types. Leaf margins may be smooth or wavy, and surfaces are smooth, semisavoyed to heavily savoyed (crinkled). The crinkled appearance of the savoy tissue results from differential growth of parenchyma tissues between leaf veins.

When plants have attained marketable size, which, depending on the season, can be 30 to 80 days, and when overwintered as much as 150 days, they are pulled or undercut below the stem. Each plant will have five to eight fully developed leaves. Intact plants are trimmed, and several are tied together in bunches and packaged. Not all hand-cut spinach is bunched. Some are bulked into harvest baskets and sold in that manner. Savoy types are preferred for the fresh market because the leaves are dark green and resist compression during packing, thus allowing for better aeration, cooling, and postharvest life. Most of the commercial frozen spinach is machine-harvested. The machines have cutting blades adjusted to cut

four to six inches above ground level to reduce the amount of petioles harvested with the leaves. The smooth or semisavoyed leaf types are generally used for machine harvesting because they yield more and are easier to clean. A limited amount of greenhouse spinach is produced in northern Europe during the winter.

Because spinach has a high leaf-surface area and a high respiration rate, it must be cooled rapidly to prevent weight loss and decay. Overheating will destroy quality. Thus, rapid cooling is essential to reduce wilting and weight loss. Vacuum cooling can give satisfactory cooling within ten minutes, usually applied after bulk packing and washing. Hydrocooling (cold water application) takes longer than vacuum cooling but is more feasible for small market operations. Following hydrocooling, excess water must be removed by centrifuging; otherwise postharvest diseases begin to develop. The product can then be stored under shaved ice to preserve freshness.

A serving (1½ cups) of cooked spinach has forty calories and provides 70 percent of the recommended daily allowance (RDA) for adults of vitamin A, 25 percent of the RDA of vitamin C, and 20 percent of the RDA of iron (see Table 1). Spinach also contains high levels of calcium, phosphorus, and potassium. It has moderate levels of protein. However, not all constituents of spinach are nutritionally beneficial. Oxalic acid in spinach reacts with calcium to form calcium oxalates. Excessive oxalic acid may interfere with calcium absorption in humans, a condition particularly serious for infants. Levels of oxalic acid are substantial in all spinach cultivars, although apparently less in savoy types than in smooth leaf types. Oxalic acid is also found in many of the other leaf vegetables, including chard and, especially, rhubarb. The leaves of rhubarb are toxic and should never be consumed. The stalks should be fresh when eaten.

An additional problem relates to the accumulation of nitrogen in the nitrate form, especially in spinach fertilized heavily with ammonium nitrate and grown under high temperatures and low light intensity. Nitrates convert to nitrites in digestion, and nitrites will oxidize hemoglobin to form methemoglobin. This substance can lead to methemoglobinemia, a disorder of humans and ruminants. Nitrates can also form carcinogenic nitrosamines. These toxic constituents in spinach do not present a risk when the crop is grown with proper fertilization and is consumed as part of a balanced diet.

Swiss Chard. Swiss chard (*Beta vulgaris* var. *cicla*) is a type of beet developed for its large crisp leaves and fleshy leafstalks rather than for its roots. Early civilizations utilized the roots as a medicine. The first records of cultivation indicate that the Eastern Mediterranean region, not Switzerland, was the place of origin. Aristotle wrote of seeing a red chard in 350 B.C.E. From this leaf plant was selected the swollen root form, the table beet. Although large acreages are not common, it is grown widely to supply local markets.

Swiss chard leaves are of best quality just when fully expanded or slightly earlier but remain succulent throughout the season as long as the leaves are harvested at the proper size. The succulent, glossy, dark green leaves are usually slightly crinkled or savoyed. Sometimes the fleshy white leaf midribs are separated from the leaf blade and prepared much like celery or asparagus. The midrib color can be white, red, yellow, pink, or green. Swiss chard is prepared for the market by washing thoroughly, grading, and bunching. Storage is not recommended, but it can be kept for short periods.

A serving of Swiss chard (3½ oz.) provides 130 percent of the adult RDA of vitamin A and 25 percent of the adult RDA of vitamin C (see Table 1). Like spinach, which is related, Swiss chard has high levels of oxalates.

Kale and Collards. Members of the Cruciferae family, kale and collards (both *Brassica oleracea* var. *acephala*) are known as "greens" and "soul food" in the southern United States, where they are most popular. Unlike cabbage (*Brassica oleracea* var. *capitata*), neither kale nor collards forms a head—thus the name "acephala" which means 'forming no head'. Kale and collards are the oldest forms of cabbage and are native to the eastern Mediterranean region of Europe or to Asia Minor. The use of kale as a food dates to 2000 B.C.E. or earlier. The Greek philosopher Theophrastus described a savoyed form of kale in 350 B.C.E. Traders and nomads introduced these leaf vegetables to other parts of the world, and they were introduced to the United States from Europe in the seventeenth century.

Both kale and collards have dark green leaves that form a rosette-like whorl toward the apex of erect unbranched stems. Even though collards and kale belong to the same taxonomic group, they are quite distinct. Collards differ from kale mainly in leaf shape and flavor. Collards have large, broad, flat, smooth leaves with smooth leaf margins; kale has a greater variability of leaf types. Most kales have largely upright heavily curled leaves. The decorative leaves of kale have given rise to its use as an ornamental plant. Flowering kale is very attractive for landscape plantings and is edible though not very palatable. The term "flowering" derives from the shape and coloration of the plant, which resembles a flower, and does not refer to actual flowers.

Kale is also called borecole ("winter cabbage"). The name "collard" is a corruption of *colewort* or *colewyrt*, Anglo-Saxon terms meaning young cabbage plants. Curly leaf forms of kale occur because of disproportionate growth along leaf margins, whereas the savoy (crinkled) appearance is due to nonuniform growth of portions of the leaf laminae. Kales and collards are the hardiest of the cole corps; when properly acclimated, they can tolerate temperatures to 0°F or lower and they are often overwintered. In addition, kale and collards have good tolerance to high temperatures (80° to 85°F), although growth stops at about 85°F. However, the best-quality

kale collards are grown in the cooler part of the year. In general, collards are more heat tolerant, while kale is better adapted to cooler weather.

Both kale and collards are biennial, meaning that they will flower after an extended exposure to cold weather. A vigorous collard plant may reach a height of three to four feet. Kale is somewhat smaller. Two general types of kale are grown for the market: curly leaf (the most widely grown) and smooth leaf. Of the curly leaf forms, Scotch kale is rather light green, with very ruffled, finely divided leaves; it may be dwarf or tall, with the dwarf form preferred. Because of the curly leaves, one of the commercial production problems is removing sand from the leaves.

Collards can be harvested by cutting young plants. Large plants can be cut off, or the lower leaves can be removed during the season. Leaves of both crops should be young and tender. The flavor of kale is sweeter after a frost, and many prefer to harvest at that time. After harvest, the leaves or small plants should be washed, graded, and bunched or packed. Shipments are made with an ice covering to preserve freshness. When necessary, kale and collards can be stored for ten to fourteen days at 32°F at 90 to 95 percent relative humidity.

Both kale and collards excel in food value, with kale superior to most vegetables in protein, vitamin, and mineral content. On a fresh weight basis, kale is among our most nutritious vegetables. One serving (3½ oz.) provides 200 percent of the adult RDA of vitamins A and C and 13 percent of the calcium RDA for adults.

Siberian kale (*Brassica napus*) has other common names such as Hanover kale, Hanover salad, spring kale, and Hanover turnip. It is a cool-season crop that belongs to the Brassicaceae family. Siberian kale cultivars vary considerably in appearance. The plant might best be described as resembling the ordinary collard, but it is not as curly as kale. The leaves form a rosette, and are usually smooth like collards rather than hairy like turnip leaves. The petioles vary from purple to white. Although it is sometimes compared to the turnip in growth habits, it does not form a fleshy root like turnips. Young tender leaves are used in cooking.

Amaranth. Within the genus *Amaranthus*, more than fifty species, including both cultivated and weedy species, are eaten as greens. The cultivated species are collectively called "amaranth." Another crop of the amaranth family grown in tropical Asia for its edible leaves is *Celosia argentea*. In Southeast Asia, the many cultivars of this species are usually classified by leaf color and shape. Common names for Amaranthus include bush greens, Chinese spinach, hon-toi-moi, pigweed, and tampala. Because of the large number of species used, there is considerable variability in growth habit, leaf shape, color, inflorescence characteristics, and utilization. Leaf shape and color also vary considerably among the different seed accessions. Some are red, others are green, while others

TABLE 1

Nutritional constituents of leaf vegetables

Crop	Water (%)	Energy (cal)	Protein (g)	Fat (g)	Carbohydrate (g)	Vitamins A (IU)	C (mg)	Thiamin (mg)	Riboflavin (mg)	Folate (mcg)	Niacin (mg)	Ca (mg)	P (mg)	Fe (mg)	Na (mg)	K (mg)
Amaranth	92	23	2.5	0.3	4.0	2,900	43	0.03	0.16	85	0.7	215	50	2.3	20	611
Broccoli Raab	92	18	1.8	0.2	2.0	2,700	70	0.05	0.07	71	0.5	125	45	1.5	40	250
Chaya	80	64	6.2	0.6	10.7	–	194	0.2	0.20	–	1.6	234	76	2.8	58	270
Collard	91	30	2.5	0.4	5.7	3,800	35	0.05	0.13	166	0.7	145	10	0.2	20	169
Dandelion	86	45	2.7	0.7	9.2	14,000	35	0.19	0.26	27	0.8	187	66	3.1	76	397
Garland Chrys.	93	21	1.6	0.2	4.4	14,675	37	0.03	0.22	77	0.9	56	32	3.1	52	571
Ice Plant	94	05	0.7	0.2	0.3	2,000	23	0.04	0.06	–	0.3	90	26	0.6	–	–
Indian Mustard	91	27	2.7	0.4	4.9	6,000	93	0.11	0.19	187	0.8	181	46	2.0	33	374
Kale	84	50	3.3	0.7	10.0	8,900	120	0.11	0.13	29	1.0	135	56	1.7	43	447
Malabar Spinach	93	19	1.8	0.3	3.4	8,000	102	0.05	0.16	140	0.5	109	52	1.2	24	510
Mustard Greens	91	26	2.7	0.2	4.9	5,300	70	0.08	0.11	159	0.8	103	43	1.5	25	354
N. Zealand Sp.	94	14	1.5	0.2	2.5	4,400	30	0.04	0.13	15	0.5	58	28	0.8	130	130
Pokeweed	92	23	2.6	0.4	3.7	8,700	136	0.08	0.33	–	1.2	53	44	1.7	23	242
Purslane	94	16	1.3	0.1	3.4	1,320	21	0.05	0.11	12	0.5	65	44	2.0	45	494
Sorrel	93	25	0.74	0.1	3.8	010	10	0.03	0.04	–	0.3	130	21	0.9	6	360
Siberian kale	87	42	2.8	0.6	8.3	3,100	130	0.07	0.06	28	1.3	205	62	3.0	70	450
Spinach	92	22	2.7	0.4	3.5	6,700	28	0.08	0.19	194	0.7	99	49	2.7	79	558
Swiss Chard	93	19	1.8	0.2	3.7	3,300	30	0.04	0.09	14	0.4	59	46	1.8	213	379
Turnip Greens	91	27	1.5	0.3	5.7	7,600	60	0.07	0.10	194	0.6	190	42	1.1	40	296
Water Spinach	91	26	3.1	0.4	4.6	4,600	50	0.07	0.17	–	1.1	84	49	2.7	43	385

Data per 100g raw sample. 1 IU = 0.3 µg vitamin A alcohol. Vitamin C = Ascorbic acid

SOURCE: U.S. Department of Agriculture, Agricultural Research Service, 1999. USDA Nutrient Database for Standard Reference, Release 13. Nutrient Data Laboratory. Available at, http://www.nal.usda.gov/fnic/foodcomp; V. Rubatzky, and M. Yamaguchi, *World Vegetables*, 2nd ed., International Thomas Publishing, 1997; H. D. Tindall, *Vegetables in the Tropics*, AVI Publishing, 1978.

may be variegated, usually with purplish patterns on a green background. Major leaf vegetable amaranth species are *Amaranthus tricolor*, *A. lividus*, *A. dubius*, *A. gangeticus*, *A. blitum*, and *A. hybridus*. *A. spinosus*, known as uray, is a vegetable of some importance in the Philippines. Amaranth is grown not only as a leaf vegetable, but as a grain (*A. caudatus*) in subtropical and tropical climates of Africa.

The green-leafed variety of vegetable amaranth (*A. tricolor*) has been offered in the United States as the cultivar tampala. It is as acceptable as spinach when cooked, but not raw. *A. lividus*, known as bondue, is grown for vegetable uses in tropical Africa. Young plants of *A. leucocarpus* are a leaf vegetable in Algeria; in addition, the seed is made into candy. The green form of *A. gangeticus*, Chinese spinach, is most commonly cultivated for use as boiled greens in Asia.

For many of the leaf vegetable *Amaranthus* species, centers of diversity are Central and South America, India, and Southeast Asia, with secondary domestication in western and eastern Africa. The greatest diversity of leaf amaranths is found in India. The leaf amaranths are popular, low-cost, and a good protein source for the populations of many tropical, subtropical, and temperate regions.

Most leaf-type amaranth plants are erect, about one foot to three feet high, and produce numerous small flowers on terminal and axillary spikes. When harvested, plants are pulled with the roots left on to facilitate bunching. In another method, partial leaf removal is made with regrowth permitted for successive harvesting. Frequent harvesting, every seven to ten days, tends to delay flowering and encourage new shoot and leaf growth. Postharvest life is relatively short because of rapid wilting of the tender foliage.

Some general disadvantages of amaranths are the early, short-day flowering response and low-temperature sensitivity of some species and the high calcium oxalate content in leaf tissues. Nevertheless, these plants supply large amounts of provitamin A, vitamin C, protein, and fiber. Amaranth is not as high in vitamin A as spinach, but other constituents are comparable.

Mustard Greens. Mustard is often used in a generic sense to identify somewhat morphologically similar brassicas even though they are different species. All belong to the Crucifer family and are native to Central Asia and the Himalayas. For instance, black mustard (*Brassica nigra*), white mustard (*Sinapis alba*), and Ethiopian mustard (*B. carinata* and *B. juncea*) are all called mustard greens. However, in the United States "mustard greens" normally refers to *Brassica juncea* var. *crispifolia*. When *Brassica juncea* seeds are ground, they produce the famous Dijon mustard. Mustard greens are strong flavored and pungent although the inner leaves are relatively mild and quite suitable for raw salad use. It is an annual cool-season plant with its early growth in a basal rosette. Leaf

AMARANTH

Amaranth is one of the most ancient crops of the Aztecs of Mexico, who domesticated it about 5000 B.C.E.; it appears to have been independently domesticated also among the Inca of Peru. Among the Aztecs amaranth was cultivated first in the *chinampa* system; fertile algae-rich mud from their garden canals was made into seed beds, and the amaranth was allowed to grow to about eight to ten inches in height and was then transplanted to fields in the higher ground, where it was usually intercropped with maize. After the Spanish conquest, the continued use of amaranth was prohibited because the red color of the seeds reminded the Spanish of blood and its connection to traditional Aztec religious practices.

Solomon H. Katz

form can vary among cultivars. Some cultivars have large leaves while others have leaves that are broad toward the apex. Within both forms are cultivars with curled or smooth leaf margins. The young tender leaves are harvested approximately seven weeks after sowing when they reach six to eight inches in height and before they become tough and woody. Plants are cut by hand, washed, and packed. They are packed for transit in the same way as spinach.

Minor Leaf Vegetables

Several leaf vegetables are grown to a very limited extent on commercial acreage to meet a small but steady demand. One may find these leaf vegetables growing more frequently in home gardens. Some of these crops are normally thought of as weeds; however, they are grown because they feature some prominent characteristic that is favored among specific ethnic groups. These crops include broccoli raab, chaya, dandelion, garland chrysanthemum, garden sorrel, ice plant, kangkong, Malabar spinach, New Zealand spinach, orach, pokeweed, and purslane.

Broccoli raab (*Brassica campestris*) is also known by such names as raab, rapa, rapini, broccoli turnip, spring broccoli, cima di rapa, taitcat, Italian turnip, and Italian mustard. It is a highly regarded leaf green in Italy and other Mediterranean countries. The plant resembles turnip tops and sprouting broccoli but develops a much smaller, less compact inflorescence. The leaves are cut with the seed stalks before the flower buds open. There are two forms of broccoli raab: rapine, or spring raab, and rappone, or fall raab. Other than the season of maturity, there is no difference in appearance or flavor.

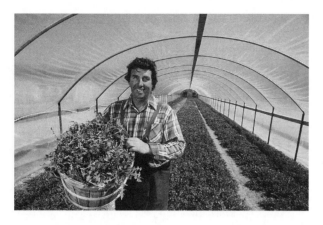

Leaf vegetables are ideal for greenhouse horticulture since many species can be forced during the winter months for early spring harvest. Angelo Favoretto, a Vineland, New Jersey, wine maker, supplements his income from grapes with an early crop of dandelion greens, a leaf vegetable rich in vitamins and minerals. © BOB KRIST/CORBIS.

Both go to seed very rapidly. In areas with a moderate climate, raab may be planted in the fall and overwintered to produce an early spring crop. Rappone seems superior to rapine for these fall plantings. In most areas, both are spring planted for early or late summer harvest. The harvest system is similar to that used for collards and turnips; the leaves and the flower stalks are tied together and sold as bunches. Raab is very perishable and must be marketed immediately.

Chaya (*Cnidoscolus chayamansa*) is a little-known leaf vegetable of dry regions of the tropics. The leaves are used as a green vegetable in many Latin American countries. The name "chaya" comes from the Mayan word for the plant, *ixchay* or *chay*. Other common names are tree spinach, chaya col, kikilchay, and chaykeken. Chaya is a large leafy shrub reaching a height of about six to eight feet. It somewhat resembles a vigorous hibiscus or cassava plant. The dark green leaves resemble okra leaves. The domesticated cultivars have little to none of the offending features—stem spines and leaf hairs—found in wild chaya. It is reported that "pig chaya" is one of the very best eating varieties. Plants are continuously harvested. Large leaves are cut into manageable pieces before cooking. Chaya is a good source of protein, vitamins, calcium, and iron. However, raw chaya leaves are highly toxic because they contain hydrocyanic glucosides. One minute of boiling destroys most of the glucosides.

Dandelion (*Taraxacum officinale*) has been encountered by almost everyone as a weed in lawns and gardens. However, there are cultivated varieties of dandelion that make excellent cooking greens. The dandelion is a European native with low-spreading deeply notched leaves forming a rosette pattern as they emerge from a central tap root. The varieties used as a leaf vegetable have been selected for their leafiness and freedom from bitterness.

The three major cultivars are Thick Leaf, Improved Thick Leaf, and Arlington Thick Leaf. The leaves are an excellent source of provitamin A, vitamin C, calcium, and several other minerals. Given that the plant is a perennial, the leaves are harvested by cutting below the whorl to keep the plant intact. The leaves are then washed, graded, and cooled.

Garland Chrysanthemum (*Chrysanthemum coronarium*) is also called edible chrysanthemum, chop suey greens, *shungiku* in Japan, and *tong hao cai* in China. It looks very much like a leaf version of the flowering ornamental chrysanthemum. A native of the Mediterranean region, it was introduced to Asia via contact with European traders. It is now a popular cooked green in Korea, Japan, and China. Leaf shape varies from lobed to highly indented. Daisy-like flower heads are yellow or yellowish white and are also eaten. All plant parts have aromatic flavor qualities, becoming most pronounced in older foliage.

Garden sorrel (*Rumex acetosa*) is a perennial plant that is closely related to rhubarb and buckwheat and is sometimes referred to as dock. However, the term "dock" has been used in Great Britain to include all members of the family Polygonaceae. Owing to its tart flavor, it is sometimes called sour dock and sour grass. In fact, sorrel derives from the Old French *surele*, meaning 'sour'. Garden sorrel is of Eurasian origin with long, thin light green or reddish green, slightly crinkled, arrow-shaped leaves. Other *Rumex* species similar to garden sorrel are French sorrel (*R. scutatus*), spinach rhubarb (*R. abyssinicus*), patience dock (*R. patientia*), and Indian sorrel (*R. vescarius*). French sorrel differs in being a short plant with branched stems that exhibit a semireclining growth habit. Leaves are arrow- or fiddle-shaped, more succulent, and smaller than garden sorrel. French sorrel is used like garden sorrel but has a milder taste. Spinach rhubarb is eaten like spinach, and the petioles are like rhubarb. Patience dock looks similar to garden sorrel although the plant is stouter and taller and has larger leaves and a noticeably stronger taproot than garden sorrel.

Ice plant (*Mesembryanthemum crystallinum*) is a little-known vegetable of the southern hemisphere. Ice plant is so named because of the shimmering silvery dots that cover the leaves. It has also been called fig marigold, frost plant, diamond plant, midday flower, and dew plant. This is not to be confused with New Zealand spinach, which is sometimes referred to in gardening books as New Zealand ice plants. Ice plant is a perennial that does best in hot, dry climates. It is grown as an annual when used as a green vegetable. The leaves are picked as wanted once the plant has several leaves and is well-established. The slightly acidic, fleshy leaves are boiled and served like spinach.

Malabar spinach (*Basella alba* & *B. rubra*) is also known as Ceylon spinach, climbing spinach, gui, acelga trepadora, bretana, libato, vine spinach, Indian spinach, and Malabar nightshade. The red leaf form belongs to the *rubra* species, while the green form is classified in the *alba* species. *Basella alba* has an African or Southeast Asian origin, while *Basella rubra* is thought to have originated in India or Indonesia. Malabar is not a true spinach, but its leaves, which form on a vine, resemble spinach and are used in the same way. Malabar spinach can be grown from seeds or cuttings. The vine is normally trellised. Two vines are sufficient to supply a small family all summer and fall. The thick, fleshy leaves are cut off together with some length of the stem to keep the plant pruned to a desired shape. When cooked, Malabar spinach is not as slick in texture as many greens such as spinach. The Bengalis cook it with chopped onions, spicy chilis, and a little mustard oil. The mucilaginous texture is especially useful as a thickener in soups and stews.

Mizuna (*Brassica juncea* var. *japonica*) is an Oriental cooking green also known as potherb mustard, kyona, Japanese greens, and sometimes California peppergrass. It is widely grown in Japan but is found only occasionally in gardens in the United States. Mizuna is twelve to eighteen inches tall with yellow-green leaves that are smooth and a bit fuzzy, similar to curly mustard, but with a different leaf shape. Leaves of mizuna are deeply notched, narrow, feathery, and quite attractive. A single plant may have as many as 180 leaves clustered together in a compact, twelve-inch diameter bunch. It withstands frost and light freezes and is not quick to seed even in periods of warm weather that occur during the winter months. Leaves are ready for use any time after three weeks of growth. Leaves are removed as needed, keeping enough young foliage to continue the regrowth.

New Zealand spinach (*Tetragonia expansa*) is indigenous to New Zealand and became widely cultivated after it was introduced to Europe. It was introduced to England by Captain Cook in 1771 and was used on his voyages as a source of vitamin C. Presently, little is grown commercially in the United States, but it is popular with many home gardeners. Not a true spinach, it does somewhat resemble spinach in appearance and is used similarly. The plant is large, growing to a height of two or more feet in a spreading and branching habit of growth, and has thick succulent leaves. The young tops are harvested for boiling, and each harvest encourages new branching. Unlike many of the leaf vegetables, New Zealand spinach is a warm-season crop with very wide adaptation. It is an excellent source of fresh greens throughout the summer and is also frost-sensitive. Its flavor is comparable to that of spinach, but milder and without the astringency. In its early growth, New Zealand spinach is entirely vegetative. As it begins to develop, however, it soon produces flowers from the leaf axils. The flowers are considered undesirable for the market. Like spinach, tissues contain oxalates that render calcium nutritionally unavailable.

Orach (*Atriplex hortensis*) is a hardy branching monoecious annual of the Chenopodiaceae family that is a substitute for spinach. It is also commonly known as mountain spinach, French spinach, and sea purslane. Some variations of the name are orache, arache, and orage. The name derives from the Old French *arrache*, a corruption of the Vulgar Latin *atripica*, from Latin *atriplex*; these in turn were from the Greek word for orach, *atraphaxus*. It is sometimes called salt bush because of its tolerance of alkaline soils. The plants have a tolerance to drought and salinity and are adapted to a broad temperature range. Orach is considered to have originated in northern India and has been used as a medicinal and food plant for more than 2,000 years, making it one of the oldest cultivated plants. It was widely grown until the eighteenth century but is of little commercial importance today although it is returning in popularity as an ingredient in mesclun salads. It is grown as a substitute for spinach in Europe and in the northern plains of the United States. It is seldom seen in the tropics. Its leaves are slightly crimped, soft, and pliable and are shaped like arrows that are four to five inches long and two to three inches wide. Plants can attain a height of five to six feet. A rosette of leaves first develops, followed by a seed stalk that can grow to a height of six to nine feet. There are four common varieties of orach. White orach is most often grown because it is the most tender and best flavored. The leaves are very pale green, almost yellow. Red orach has dark-red stems and leaves. Green orach, also called Lee's Giant orach, is very vigorous, with a stout, angular, branching stem. The leaves are rounder, less toothed, and darker green than those of the other varieties. The fourth is a copper-colored variety that is now much sought after by specialty growers.

Orach is a cool-season vegetable and is grown much like garden spinach. It is quick to bolt in summer. Although stems quickly elongate, flowering is slow, and plants tolerate growing temperatures too high for spinach. Young leaves may be harvested and the plants will continue growing for multiple harvests. Orach has a mild flavor much like that of spinach, but it contains less oxalic acid. Even when the plant goes to seed, young leaves are usable. However, old leaves are not palatable and are not harvested.

Pokeweed (*Phytolacca americana*) is a native plant throughout eastern North America. Other common names are inkberry, pigeon berry, coakun, pocan bush, scoke, garget, and poke salad. The branches bear clusters of flowers and dark red fruits that resemble the berries of a nightshade; pokeweed is therefore sometimes called American nightshade. It is a large-rooted perennial with a strong-growing tip, reaching up to ten or more feet in height. The top dies down in cold weather. There is little cultivation of pokeweed in the United States or elsewhere because it is gathered from the wild. All plant parts are poisonous. The young tender shoots and the older leaves may be eaten if boiled. The bitterness, and by association the poisonous compound, is removed by boiling and pouring off the cooking water until all the bitterness is removed.

PURSLANE

Purslane has very high levels of the linoleic omega 3 fatty acid, which is essential and relatively low in the U.S. diet as compared with the higher levels of the omega 6 fatty acids. This imbalance of the ratio between the two classes of fatty acids may be the basis of an important nutritional imbalance.

Solomon H. Katz

Purslane (*Portulaca oleracea*) is known by various names such as kitchen purslane, garden purslane, and in Spanish, *verdolaga*. One of the more descriptive names for this plant is in Malawi, where it translates to "the buttocks of the wife of a chief," because of the shape of the leaf. The exact origin of purslane is not known, but it is reported to have been used more than 2,000 years ago in Iran or India. Purslane is a popular vegetable in France, several other European countries, and Africa, especially in Egypt and Sudan. It was introduced to the United States from Europe. The name "purslane" derives through Old French *porcelaine* from Pliny's Latin *porcilaca*. The cultivated forms are upright and more vigorous than the weedy form. It is a summer annual with small, oval, juicy leaves clustered at the ends of smooth, purplish-red, prostrate stems that arise from a single taproot. The leaves are usually stripped from the stems and are prepared like spinach. The taste is a cross between watercress and spinach. An undesirable quality of purslane is that its foliage, like that of spinach, contains oxalic acid and tends to accumulate nitrates.

Water spinach (*Ipomoea aquatica*), also known as kangkong, water glorybind, water spinach, water convolvulus, and swamp cabbage, is an important green leaf vegetable in Southeast Asia, Taiwan, Ceylon, and Malaysia. It is speculated to have originated in India but is now widely grown throughout the tropics. Water spinach can become an undesirable weed. The Florida Department of Natural Resources must issue a special permit to anyone wanting to grow it in Florida. There are two major forms (cultivars) that are cultivated in two ways, either upland (dry) or swamp (wet). Ching Quat, an upland variety, has narrow leaves, while Pak Quat, a swamp variety, has arrowhead-shaped leaves. The plants produce a trailing hollow vine that is adapted to floating in aquatic environments. The leaves are light green and look somewhat like sweet potato leaves. The upland types are started from seed or cuttings and are grown on trellises. Plants are often grown in nursery beds for transplanting later to the garden. Taking cuttings from plants in the nursery beds is the usual method. Harvest may start six weeks after planting. The swamp types are usually planted with twelve-inch-long cuttings planted in mud and kept moist. As the vines grow, the area is flooded to a depth of six inches, and a continuous flow of water is maintained through the field, similar to the way watercress is grown. Harvest begins four weeks after planting. When the succulent tips of the vines are removed, lateral and upright branches are encouraged. These branches are harvested every seven to ten days. All parts of the young plants are eaten. The crop is fragile and requires rapid and careful handling to minimize damage and wilting. It is eaten like cooked spinach. A canned product is often available in ethnic markets.

Conclusions

Leafy vegetables are consumed in most cultures and regions of the world. They consist of a wide range of different plants, yet no matter which leaf vegetable is used, it is usually prepared like spinach. The leafy vegetables contribute significantly to a nutritious diet. As a food source, the leafy vegetables are some of the best sources of provitamin A and vitamin C and supply good amounts of iron, folate, and other essential minerals. They are also an excellent source of phytochemicals, which aid in fighting heart disease and cancer.

See also **Cabbage and Crucifer Plants**; **Herbs and Spices**; **Lettuce**; **Vegetables**.

BIBLIOGRAPHY

Bose, T. K., and M. G. Som, eds. *Vegetable Crops of India.* Calcutta: Naya Prokash, 1986.

Chan, Harvey T., Jr., ed. *Handbook of Tropical Foods.* New York: M. Dekker, 1983.

Daloz, C. R., and H. M. Munger. "Amaranth: An Unexploited Vegetable Crop." *HortScience* 15 (1980): 383.

Duke, James A. *Handbook of Phytochemical Constituents of GRAS Herbs and Other Economic Plants.* Boca Raton, Fla.: CRC Press, 1992.

Herklots, Geoffrey Alton Craig. *Vegetables in South-East Asia.* London: Allen & Unwin, 1972.

Larkcom, Joy. *Oriental Vegetables: The Complete Guide for Garden and Kitchen.* Tokyo and New York: Kodansha International, 1991.

Maynard, Donald N., and George J. Hochmuth. *Knott's Handbook for Vegetable Growers.* 4th ed. New York: Wiley, 1997.

National Academy of Sciences. *Underexploited Tropical Plants with Promising Economic Value.* Washington, D.C.: National Academy of Sciences, 1975.

Rubatzky, Vincent E., and Mas Yamaguchi. *World Vegetables: Principles, Production, and Nutritive Values.* 2nd ed. New York: Chapman & Hall, 1997.

Ryder, Edward J. *Leafy Salad Vegetables.* Westport, Conn.: AVI, 1979.

Stephens, James M. *Manual of Minor Vegetables.* Gainesville, Fla.: University of Florida Press, 1988.

Tindall, H. D. *Vegetables in the Tropics*. Westport, Conn.: AVI, 1983.

Weaver, William Woys. *Heirloom Vegetable Gardening: A Master Gardener's Guide to Planting, Seed Saving, and Cultural History*. New York: Henry Holt, 1997.

Yeager, Selene. *New Foods for Healing*. Emmaus, Pa.: Rodale Press, 1998.

Paul W. Bosland

LEEK. *See* Onions and Other *Allium* Plants.

LEGUMES. Legumes are members of a family of flowering plants known as Leguminosae. It is one of the three largest families of flowering plants, with approximately 690 genera and about 18,000 species. Legumes are a significant component of nearly all terrestrial biomes on all continents except Antarctica. Some are fresh water aquatics, but no truly marine species exist. The species within the family range from dwarf herbs among arctic and alpine vegetation to massive trees in tropical forests.

The leaves usually occur alternately on the stem and are compound, meaning each leaf is divided into separate leaflets. Both pinnate and trifoliate leaves exist. Legumes are easily recognized by the structure of the flower. The flowers are hermaphroditic with male (stamens) and female (pistils) parts in the same flower and usually with five sepals and five petals. The ovary has a single carpel, cavity, and style. The principal unifying feature of the family is the fruit, a pod technically known as a legume. The legume pod is modified in many ways, including flat, winged, thick, thin, straight, coiled, short, long, woody, fleshy, splitting open, or indehiscent to facilitate dispersal by animals, wind, and water.

The family is divided into three subfamilies: Papilionoideae, Caesalpinioideae, and Mimosoideae, identified by their flowers. The Papilionoideae is the largest of the three subfamilies and the most widespread, extending farther into temperate regions. This subfamily can be easily recognized by its butterfly-like flowers. Most of the important legume crop species consumed by humans, including soybean, field pea, chickpea, field bean, and peanut, are in this group.

The subfamily Caesalpinioideae is comprised of tropical or subtropical trees and shrubs. The useful products derived from this subfamily include edible fruits (*Tamarindus indica*), senna medicine (*Senna* spp.), hematoxylon red dye from the logwood tree (*Haematoxylon campechianum*), and resins used in paints, varnishes, inks, plastics, adhesives, and fireworks derived from the copal (*Copaifera* spp.) tree.

The subfamily Mimosoideae includes species of industrial, forage, browsing, and fodder importance, such as *Acacia* spp. (Bisby et al., 2000). The Australian black-wood (*Acacia melanoxylon*) tree provides useful timber, and gum arabic from the tree of that name (*Acacia senegal*) is used in an array of industrial processes.

Nitrogen Fixation

Most legumes convert atmospheric nitrogen into nitrogenous compounds useful to plants. Root nodules containing *Rhizobium* bacteria fix free nitrogen for the plants. In return, legumes supply the bacteria with carbon produced by photosynthesis. This symbiosis provides the nitrogen needed by the plants for survival. Root nodules form in all subfamilies except in rare cases among the Caesalpinioideae.

The basic process of nitrogen fixation involves penetration by the *Rhizobium* through the root hairs into the cortex, where cell division occurs. These tetraploid cells produce the nodules that appear on the root surface. The nodule growth and efficiency are influenced by the carbon-nitrogen ratio of the plant and by the presence in the soil of phosphate, calcium, magnesium, molybdenum, and boron. If the nodules are ineffective, the bacteria may be parasitic on the host plant. Effective nodules contain red leghemoglobin, which can be seen when the nodules are cut. Ineffective nodules are usually small, hard, spherical, and a greenish color inside. Legumes produce more nodules in the tropics in acid soils and soils deficient in phosphorus, calcium, and other nutrients than in temperate areas. Many strains of *Rhizobium* occur in nature with multiple hosts, and several *Rhizobium* species occur with one host (Purseglove, 1981). Many scientists suggest inoculating legume seeds with the appropriate strain of *Rhizobium* for best agricultural results. This inoculation technique is accomplished by mixing the *Rhizobium* in water to form a slurry and then adding it to the seed.

Origin

The primary temperate legumes used for human food include garden pea (*Pisum sativum*), field pea (*Pisum arvense*), winged pea (*Tetragonolobus purpureus*), green bean (*Phaseolus vulgaris*), runner bean (*Phaseolus coccineus*), butter bean (*Phaseolus lunatus*), lima bean (*Phaseolus limensis*), soybean (*Glycine max*), lentil (*Lens culinaris*), and broad bean (*Vicia faba*). These legumes originated in humid, subhumid, cool season, subtropical, semiarid, and temperate areas in diverse regions ranging from Southwest Asia and East Asia to the Mediterranean, Peru, Mexico, and Guatemala (Muehlbauer, 1993).

Common tropical legumes consumed by humans include winged bean (*Psophocarpus tetragonolobus*), jicama (*Pachyrhizus erosus* and *Pachyrhizus tuberosus*), chickpea (*Cicer arietinum*), black-eyed pea (*Vigna unguiculata unguiculata*), and peanut (*Arachis hypogaea*). These tropical legumes originated in areas characterized by humid, semiarid, cool season, subtropical, and tropical climates, primarily including South America, Southwest Asia, Ethiopia, India, Japan, China, and West Africa (Hymowitz, 1990).

History. Soybean, one of the most popular legumes, is one of the oldest cultivated crops. Cultivated soybeans probably arose from a wild type in Asia and moved to Europe and North America in the eighteenth century. Soybean soon became the third most important agronomic crop in the United States. Cowpeas were introduced to the West Indies and ultimately spread throughout the southern United States after the seventeenth century. Field beans (*Phaseolus* spp.) were cultivated by American Indians at the time of the European discovery of North America and soon were introduced to Europe. The popular peanut, introduced into the United States from Brazil when the colonies were established, was commercially developed in the mid-eighteenth century.

Peas, including garden peas, field peas, broad beans, lentils, and chickpeas, were introduced into the Americas from Europe and the Near East. Jicama is grown in Southeast Asia, Mexico, and Central America. Winged beans were introduced into more than sixty countries, primarily subtropical and tropical, after the mid-1970s.

Primary Food Legumes

Soybean **(Glycine max).** Soybean is the most important legume produced in the agricultural industry worldwide. It is an annual crop, is easy to grow, and is adapted to a temperate climate. A hot weather crop, soybean requires a minimum of 59°F (15°C) for seed germination and mean temperatures of 68–77°F (20°–25°C) for crop growth. Only moderate soil moisture is needed for germination and seedling establishment, but dry weather is essential for dry seed production. Soybeans suffer when the soil is waterlogged, and established plants tolerate drought.

Soybeans should be fertilized with phosphorous, potassium, and micronutrients, and they require typical agricultural field preparation. The important differences among soybean cultivars are day-length response, pest resistance, and production. These varieties are subdivided into groups according to tropical, subtropical, or temperate climate adaptation (Martin, 1988).

Several major obstacles obstruct optimum soybean production. Diseases cause one-eighth of all soybean losses. Noteworthy diseases and their causal agents include bacterial blight *(Pseudomonas glycinea)*, bacterial pustule *(Xanthomonas phaseoli* var. *sojense)*, and wildfire *(Pseudomonas tabaci)*. However, the most devastating diseases are caused by fungi, including brown stem rot *(Cephalosporium gregatum)*, stem canker *(Diaporthe phaseolorum* var. *batatatis)*, pod and stem blight *(Diaporthe phaseolorum* var. *sojae)*, brown spot *(Septoria glycines)*, and sclerotial blight *(Sclerotium rolfsii)*. Mosaic virus disease, root knot nematode *(Meloidogyne* spp.), and cyst nematode *(Heterodera glycines)* also cause significant soybean losses.

The chemical composition of mature soybeans varies with the cultivar plus the soil and climate conditions.

Generally, the black-seeded cultivars are protein rich with low oil content, and the yellow-seeded types are oil rich with low protein. The nutritional components of dried seeds are 5.0 percent to 9.4 percent water, 29.6 percent to 50.3 percent protein, 13.5 percent to 24.2 percent fat, 14.0 percent to 23.9 percent carbohydrate, 2.8 percent to 6.3 percent fiber, and a large amount of vitamin B. Soybean seeds contain a higher amount of protein than any other pulse and most other foodstuffs.

Soybean oil is about 51 percent linoleic acid, 30 percent oleic acid, and 6.5 percent linolenic acid and is used as a cooking oil, salad oil, shortening, and margarine. Soybean flour is mixed with wheat flour in baked products, such as bread, cakes, cookies, and crackers, and it is also used in ice cream, candy, and pudding. In Asia soybeans are consumed as soybean milk, soy sauce, soups, drinks, breakfast foods, and vegetables. People in eastern Asia eat unripe seeds and dried seeds, and elsewhere these large seeds are consumed as shelled green beans or as dry beans. Both the Bansei and the Green Giant cultivars are among the more popular soybeans. In the West soybeans are a primary ingredient of Worcestershire sauce, made by mixing boiled beans with wheat flour and salt, then fermenting the mixture with the fungus *Aspergillus oryzae* for up to one week. The fermented beans are submerged in brine and exposed to the sun for several months to extract the flavor. In Indonesia boiled beans are fermented with *Aspergillus* and formed into cakes.

Soybeans are used industrially in paints, linoleum, inks, soaps, insecticides, and disinfectants. Soy meal, the residue of oil extraction, is a healthy livestock feed (Purseglove, 1981). Soybeans are also used in the pharmaceutical and nutraceutical industries. For example, Ensure glucerna, a dietary aid for diabetics, includes soybeans, and Estroven, marketed as a dietary supplement with natural phytoestrogens, contains isoflavones, a group of antioxidants found in both humans and legumes, extracted from soybeans. While isoflavones do not show antioxidant activity in legumes, they serve various roles as protectants, attractants, and repellents. Because of their antioxidant characteristics, it is possible that isoflavones make a healthy contribution to the human diet.

Groceries and other retail stores sell products that contain soybeans in some form, and American and Oriental restaurants offer foods with soybean constituents. In addition, many products sold as dietary supplements or nutraceuticals in health food stores include soybeans.

Field peas **(Pisum arvense and Pisum sativum).** The green pea type of field pea became a food source in the sixteenth century. Field peas grow during the cool season and develop flowers and seeds as the days become longer. Field peas have a variety of uses, and production has increased worldwide. At the beginning of the twenty-first century, U.S. production was estimated at 200,000 hectares, and Canadian production exceeded that threefold. Major diseases include Ascochyta blight (*Ascochyta*

GLOSSARY

Biome—The world's major communities classified according to the predominant vegetation and characterized by adaptations of organisms to that particular environment

Carpel—A single member of a compound seed-bearing flower organ.

Cortex—The primary plant tissue between the vascular system and the epidermis of the stem and the root.

Cover crop—A crop grown between orchard trees or on fields between cropping seasons to protect the land from leaching of nutrients and erosion.

Diversity—Variety of life on the planet.

Fodder—Coarse plants harvested whole and cured in an erect position.

Forage—Plant matter, fresh or preserved, gathered and fed to animals.

Green manure—Any crop or plant grown and incorporated into the soil.

Hay—Fine-stemmed plants cut and cured for forage.

Heme—Iron-protoporphyrin IX, a ubiquitous prosthetic group structurally associated to many enzymatic, regulatory, transport, and binding proteins.

Herbivorous—Animals that consume only plant material.

Indehiscent—Remaining persistently closed.

Lectin—Proteins or glycoproteins of nonimmune origin that agglutinate cells and precipitate complex carbohydrates. They are valuable for blood grouping and erythrocyte polyagglutination, mitogenic stimulation of lymphocytes, lymphocyte subpopulation studies, fractionation of cells and other particles, and histochemical studies of normal and pathological conditions.

Leghemoglobin—Heme-containing, oxygen-binding protein found in plants.

Ovary—The part of the pistil (the seed-bearing flower organ) that contains the ovules.

Parasitic—An organism living or feeding on another organism to the detriment of the host organism.

Pasture—Land with forage plants used for grazing animals.

Petal—A division of the corolla (the inner floral envelope).

Pinnate leaf—Compound leaf with leaflets arranged on each side of a common axis.

Pulse—Legume plants or seeds used for food.

Sepal—A division of a calyx (the outer floral envelope).

Silage—Forage preserved in a succulent condition by partial fermentation in a tight container.

Style—The portion of the seed-bearing flower organ that connects the stigma and the ovary.

Tetraploid—An organism whose cells contain four haploid (4n) sets of chromosomes or genomes.

Trifoliate—Having three leaflets.

---

pisi and *Ascochyta pinodella*), bacterial blight (*Pseudomonas pisi*), and fusarium wilt (*Fusarium oxysporum* f. *pisi*). Significant insect pests are the pea weevil (*Bruchus pisorum*), the pea aphid (*Illinoia pisi*), and particularly the root knot nematode (*Meloidogyne incognita*). The wrinkled-seed types of field peas are canned in the immature stage, and the smooth-seed types are eaten as dried peas.

Field peas are usually grown as winter annuals in regions receiving 450 to 500 millimeters of rainfall annually. Generally, field peas perform best on well-drained soils with pH between 6.0 and 7.5. Nitrogen fertilization is not needed, but phosphorus, potassium, and sulfur are required (Muehlbauer, 1993).

The nutritional components of dried seeds are 10.6 percent water, 22.5 percent protein, 1 percent fat, 58.5 percent carbohydrate, and 4.4 percent fiber. Fresh green peas are about 74.3 percent water, 6.7 percent protein, 0.4 percent fat, 15.5 percent carbohydrate, and 2.2 percent fiber. These legumes are a major source of human dietary protein worldwide but are of minor importance in the United States. The seeds are consumed as a fresh vegetable and are canned, frozen, and dried. Field pea pods are also edible. Worldwide field pea plants are used for forage, hay, silage, and green manure (Purseglove, 1981).

Field beans **(Phaeolus *spp.*).** Brazil, the United States, Mexico, and Italy are the leading producers of field beans. In the United States the common field bean is grown primarily in New York, Michigan, and west of the Mississippi River. Suitable for a variety of soil types, beans are a warm season annual crop. The optimum temperature is 63–77°F (17–25°C), and the beans need 120 to 130 days without frost.

Field bean crops require fertilization with phosphorus and potassium, and zinc is often needed in residual amounts. Because beans are planted in warm soil after all danger of frost is past, planting dates vary from early April to early July according to geographic location. Dry beans are harvested after the pods turn yellow and prior to seed scattering (Martin and Leonard, 1967). Field beans are

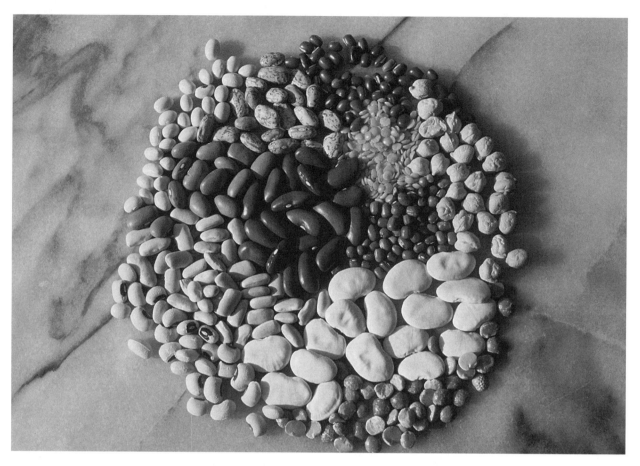

Legumes are not only a nutritious addition to the diet, they are also attractive as decorative seeds, as this artistic arrangement of lentils and beans demonstrates. © MICHELLE GARRETT/CORBIS.

subject to a wide array of diseases, including bacterial blight (*Xanthomonas phaseoli*), anthracnose (*Colletotrichum lindemuthianum*), and common bean mosaic virus. Insect pests that cause substantial damage and loss are the bean weevil (*Acanthoscelides obtectus*) and the Mexican bean beetle (*Ephilachna varivestris*).

Rich in the amino acids lysine and tryptophane, field beans are one of the most important sources of human dietary protein. Dried adzuki beans (*Phaseolus angularis*), consumed in Japan and China in soups and cakes, are about 21 percent to 23 percent protein, 0.3 percent fat, and 65 percent carbohydrate. Mung beans (*Phaseolus aureus*) are about 9.7 percent water, 23.6 percent protein, 1.2 percent fat, 58.2 percent carbohydrate, and 3.3 percent fiber. The green mung bean pods are edible, and the fried seeds are popular in India (Purseglove, 1981). Flour from the seeds is used in Indian and Chinese foods, and in the United States grocery chains and restaurants offer mung bean sprouts. Rice beans (*Phaseolus calcaratus*) are consumed in India, Burma, Malaysia, China, Fiji, and the Philippines. The beans are usually boiled, and the young

pods and leaves are also eaten. Rice beans are about 10.5 percent water, 21.7 percent protein, 0.6 percent fat, 58.1 percent carbohydrate, and 5.2 percent fiber.

Central Americans consume the green and dried seeds of the scarlet runner bean (*Phaseolus coccineus*). Lima or butter beans (*Phaseolus lunatus*) are eaten fresh, canned, or frozen in the United States. Dried lima beans are 12.6 percent water, 20.7 percent protein, 1.3 percent fat, 57.3 percent carbohydrate, and 4.3 percent fiber. However, the green beans contain about 66.5 percent water, 7.5 percent protein, 0.8 percent fat, 22.0 percent carbohydrate, and 1.5 percent fiber. The mature beans contain the glucoside phaseolutanin, which gives them their characteristic taste. Because the seeds contain hydrocyanic acid, the cooking water should be boiled and changed during preparation to dissipate the acid.

Black grams (*Phaseolus mungo*) are highly prized in vegetarian diets in India. They can be boiled or eaten whole, and they are ground into a flour used to make porridge or baked into bread and biscuits. The green pods

368

are also edible. Dried black grams are about 9.7 percent water, 23.4 percent protein, 1.0 percent fat, 57.3 percent carbohydrate, and 3.8 percent fiber (Purseglove, 1981).

The most popular and most widely used beans are known as French beans, kidney beans, runner beans, snap beans, and string beans and are sold throughout the world in grocery stores and restaurants. These are the primary protein food in Latin American and tropical Africa, and in Europe and the United States they are grown for the immature pods, which are consumed fresh, canned, and frozen. The popular baked beans are made with any of these types of whole dried beans cooked with tomato sauce.

Winged bean **(Psophocarpus tetragonolobus).** The winged bean is a perennial vine that climbs by twining. Usually grown as annuals, the plants flower during short days. Scarifying winged bean seeds induces better germination. Seeds are planted anytime during the year and germinate within five to fifteen days. The plants tolerate various soil types, including heavy, poorly drained, riverbank, sandy, and infertile soils. Organic material in soil promotes successful winged bean growth; otherwise a small amount of mineral fertilizer is generally recommended. While few pests attack winged beans, geese and chickens consume the plants, and damage by cowpea aphids and root knot nematodes has been reported (Martin and Delpin, 1978).

Winged bean leaves, flowers, shoots, immature pods, mature dried seeds, and tubers, which are highly nutritious, are primarily consumed in Papua New Guinea, South Asia, and Southwest Asia. The young, tender pods, sliced or chopped, are eaten raw. The mature dried seeds are especially nutritious because of their high protein content, 30 to 42 percent. These mature seeds can be steamed, boiled, fried, roasted, or made into milk or tofu. The beans contain some antinutritional substances, thus the seeds should always be soaked overnight and then boiled in water until tender. Oil derived from winged beans contains behenic acid, linoleic acid, and tocopherols (vitamin E). Behenic acid reduces the digestibility of winged beans. Tocopherols are antioxidants that improve the utilization of vitamin A in the human body.

Winged bean tubers, which have a protein content of 8 to 20 percent, are eaten boiled, steamed, fried, or baked in Burma and Papua New Guinea. Winged bean sprouts and shoots are consumed raw or cooked. Usually only the top three leaves are eaten. The flowers, steamed or fried, taste similar to mushrooms. The seeds contain several antinutritional phytochemicals, such as trypsin and chymotrypsin inhibitors, amylase inhibitors, phytohemagglutinins, and cyanogenic glycosides. The seed inhibitor activity can be safely eliminated only by moist heat, that is, by soaking the seeds for ten hours and then boiling them for thirty minutes. Both vanilla- and chocolate-flavored milks have been produced from the seeds in Thailand. Scientists have developed snacks of the

USES FOR LEGUMES

Senna occidentalis—Potential bactericidal, pesticidal, and viricidal plant. It also contains tannin, which is an antidiarrhetic, an antioxidant, and an antiviral agent and has cancer preventive potential.

Crotalaria juncea—Sunn hemp, known as a multiple-use small-tree crop. It is used in paper making and as green manure and has bactericidal qualities. Sunn hemp contains pectin, which has antidiabetic, antidiarrhetic, antitumor, antiulcer, and cancer preventive potential. Sunn hemp has been used in Iraq to treat psoriasis.

Mucuna pruriens—Velvet bean, a green manure crop and a nutraceutical in the United States. The seeds contain L-dopa, which is used in the treatment of Parkinson's disease, beta-sitosterol, a potential anti-inflammatory, antileukemic, antitumor, cancer preventive, and estrogenic agent; gallic acid, a potential antioxidant, antiseptic, antiviral agent, and cancer preventive; and lecithin, a potential Alzheimer's preventive. Velvet bean is also used in India, Venezuela, and Mexico to treat asthma, snake bites, cancer, coughs, diarrhea, mumps, ringworm, syphilis, and tumors and as a scorpion antidote.

tubers sliced thin, fried, and salted or softened in sugar syrup. Immature winged bean pods are pickled in southern India (Martin and Delpin, 1978). *Psophocarpus tetragonolobus* lectin is derived from winged bean seeds and is used commercially in medical diagnostics.

Jicama **(Pachyrhizus erosus *and* Pachyrhizus tuberosus).** Jicama is a tuberous legume commonly grown in Mexico on commercial farms and intercropped with maize and beans on smaller farms. It is also monocropped in Thailand, Malaysia, and Hawaii. Jicamas are usually grown from seeds, however, sprouted tubers are occasionally used. In Mexico tuber yields are highest when planted in March and harvested from September to November, and in Hawaii maximum tuber yields occur when planted in September or October and harvested five months later. Thus jicamas require a hot subtropical to tropical climate with moderate rainfall. They tolerate some drought but are sensitive to frost. They attract few pests but occasionally are attacked by the rose beetle *(Adoretus versutus)* and the bean common mosaic virus (Grum, 1990).

The edible portion of jicamas are about 87.1 percent water, 1.2 percent protein, 0.1 percent fat, 10.6 percent carbohydrate, and 0.7 percent fiber. The tubers are eaten raw or cooked. The young pods from *Pachyrhizus erosus* are prepared like French beans, but the mature seeds and roots of that plant contain a toxic substance known as rotenone. Young pods of *Pachyrhizus tuberosus* are avoided because they have irritant hairs (Purseglove, 1981).

***Chickpea* (Cicer arietinum).** Chickpea is the major pulse crop in India, where production reaches 7 million hectares. In the United States, chickpeas are primarily grown in California, Washington, and Idaho. These legumes have a high phosphorus requirement, and both potassium and sulfur should be added if the soil is deficient in either. Chickpeas are adapted to dry conditions and generally flourish on well-drained soils of pH 6.0 to 7.5. The major chickpea pests include gram blight (*Mycosphaerella rabiei*), rust (*Uromyces ciceris-arietini*), wilt (*Rhizoctonia bataticola* and *Fusarium orthoceras*), and gram caterpillar (*Heliothis armigera*).

Chickpeas are important in India, where the dried seeds are boiled and the green pods and shoots are prepared in a variety of ways. Flour made from chickpeas is used in many Indian confections. The common chickpea, also called garbanzo bean, is used in the United States primarily in salads and as a vegetable side dish. Dried chickpeas are about 9.8 percent water, 17.1 percent protein, 5.3 percent fat, 61.2 percent carbohydrate, and 3.9 percent fiber (Purseglove, 1981).

***Peanut* (Arachis hypogaea).** Peanuts, called groundnuts in other parts of the world, are one of the most important crops in the southern United States, primarily in Georgia, Texas, Oklahoma, North Carolina, Alabama, and Virginia. Other leading production countries include India, China, Nigeria, Senegal, Indonesia, and Brazil. An annual crop with a growing season from 1 May to 1 November in the United States, the peanut prefers sandy loam soils. Adequate soil moisture and high temperatures are necessities for seed germination and plant growth. Peanuts respond best when the pH is above 5. The American peanut is classified into three botanical types based on the shape of the nut and growth characteristics: Virginia (bunch and runner growth types), Spanish (bunch growth type), and Valencia (bunch growth type). Crop rotation is recommended because peanut yields are good following cotton or other nonleguminous crops, and applications of lime and potash usually increase yields. Peanuts suffer from cercospora leaf spots (*Cercospora arachidicola* and *Cercospora personata*), stem and peg rots (*Sclerotium rolfsii*), and tomato spotted wilt virus.

Peanuts are consumed by humans throughout the world as peanut butter, in candies, and as cooking oil. Peanut oil is about 53 percent oleic acid and 25 percent linoleic acid. The Virginia peanut is 38 percent to 47 percent oil, and the Spanish peanut is 47 percent to 50 percent oil. Shelled peanuts are about 5.4 percent water, 30.4 percent protein, 47.7 percent fat, 11.7 percent carbohy-

drate, and 2.5 percent fiber. The primary proteins in peanuts are arachin and conarachin, and peanuts are rich in vitamins B and E (Pattee and Young, 1982). Some people have allergenic reactions to certain types of peanuts. The peanut allergens designated as Ara h 1, Ara h 2, and Ara h 3 are glycoproteins with a molecular mass of 63 kilodaltons and are present in raw and roasted peanuts since they are heat stable and may be found in any peanut type. Peanut proteins, including arachin, conarachin, peanut agglutinin, and peanut phospholipase, can also be allergens. Other important phytochemicals in peanuts are protocatechuic acid, which has shown potential antioxidant and pesticidal qualities, and lecithin, which has shown antioxidant activity (Beckstrom-Sternberg and Duke, 1994). A lectin derived from peanuts is used commercially in medical diagnostics.

***Cowpea* (Vigna spp.).** Cowpeas led U.S. legume production until about 1941, when they were replaced by soybeans, clovers, and other special-purpose legumes. Cowpeas are produced in California on a fairly large scale, and they are cultivated in Africa, southern Asia, and the Mediterranean region of Europe. A short-day, warm-weather crop, they should be planted in warm soil after all danger of frost has passed. However, severe drought will prevent seed formation. Cowpeas grow well in sandy or clay soils with good water drainage. The common black-eyed pea (*Vigna unguiculata*) is by far the most important cowpea variety.

Common diseases include cowpea wilt (*Fusarium oxysporum* var. *tracheiphilum*), cowpea root knot nematode (*Meloidogyne* spp.), charcoal rot (*Macrophomina phaseoli*), and viral diseases. The chief insect problems are the cowpea weevil (*Callosobruchus maculatus*) and the southern cowpea weevil or four-spotted bean weevil (*Mylabris quadrimaculatus*).

Legumes Cultivated for Phytochemicals

Jack beans (*Canavalia ensiformis*) are cultivated primarily for their phytochemicals. The ripe, dried seeds are about 11.0 percent water, 23.4 percent protein, 1.2 percent fat, 55.3 percent carbohydrate, and 4.9 percent fiber (Purseglove, 1981). Jack bean seeds are the only source of the lectin known as concanavaline-A, which is used in medical diagnostics. Lectins extracted from several other legumes, including sunn hemp (*Crotalaria juncea*), red kidney beans (*Phaseolus vulgaris*), and field peas (*Pisum sativum*), are used in medical diagnostics also. Guar seeds (*Cyamopsis tetragonolobus*) contain galactomannan gum, which is used in food additives; industrials; pharmaceuticals; confectionaries, including cereal, ice cream, and candy (Whistler and Hymowitz, 1979); and nutraceuticals, such as Ensure glucerna.

Kudzu (*Pueraria* spp.) produces isoflavones used in nutraceuticals for natural estrogen therapy, such as Estroven. A nutraceutical known as kudzu root is sold in powder form. Velvet bean (*Mucuna pruriens*) extract is

TABLE 1

Minor legumes with special-purpose value

Name		Use		
Scientific	Common	Agricultural	Bioactive	Phytochemical (Pharmacological)
Canavalia ensiformis (L.) DC.	Jack bean	Forage, green manure, pulse	Pesticide	Concanavalin-A (lectin) Canaline (allelochemic)
Crotalaria juncea (L.)	Sunn hemp	Paper, green manure	Bactericide, pesticide	Pectin (antidiabetic, antidiarrhetic, antitumor, antiulcer, cancer preventive)
Mucuna pruriens (L.) DC.	Velvet bean	Green manure	Bactericide, pesticide, viricide	Beta-sitosterol (anti-inflammatory, antileukemic, antitumor, cancer preventive, estrogenic) Gallic acid (antioxidant, antiseptic, antiviral, cancer preventive) Lecithin (anti-Alzheimeran, hepatoprotective)
Rhynchosia minima (L.) DC.	Snout bean	Forage	Fungicide, pesticide, viricide	Gallic acid (see above) Protocatechuic acid (antiasthmatic, antioxidant)
Senna occidentalis (L.) Link	Coffee senna		Bactericide, pesticide, viricide	Tannin (antidiarrhetic, antioxidant, antiviral, cancer preventive)
Tephrosia purpurea (L.) Pers.			Pesticide	Rutin (antidiabetic, anti-inflammatory, antioxidant, antitumor, antiviral, cancer preventive)

marketed as an antiparkinsonian herbal supplement or nutraceutical. See Table 1 for additional legume phytochemicals.

Legumes Cultivated for Animal Food

Legume species used for forage include *Aeschynomene, Desmodium, Leucaena, Macroptilium, Neonotonia, Stylosanthes, Desmanthus, Macrotyloma, Sesbania,* and *Trifolium.* Several species, including *Desmanthus virgatus, Stylosanthes scabra,* and *Stylosanthes guianensis,* have been tested in the southeastern United States for possible forage production. *Stylosanthes hamata, Stylosanthes humilis, Macroptilium atropurpureum, Macroptilium bracteatum, Neonotonia wightii,* and *Lotononis bainesii* are grown successfully as pasture legumes in Australia and show potential for use in the United States (Morris, 1997).

Other Uses for Legumes

Several legumes have multiple uses as human foods, animal feeds, ornamentals, cover crops, green manure, and erosion control plants. Minor legumes used primarily for cover crops, forage, and green manure worldwide include calopo (*Calopogonium mucunoides*), centro (*Centrosema pubescens*), and tropical kudzu (*Pueraria phaseoloides*) (Morris, 1997).

Indigofera arrecta was once cultivated in India for indigo dye, but it declined significantly with synthetic dye production. In Central Africa, however, indigo dye derived from the plant is still used. Dhaincha (*Sesbania bispinosa*) produces galactomannan gum and is grown also for soil improvement, fiber for paper pulp, fodder, and its ornamental qualities. Lead trees (*Leucaena leucocephala*), similar in growth to mimosa trees, are used for paper products and as cover crops, fodder, pastures, green manure, and ornamentals (Morris, 1997). Other legumes are important in reclamation of mined soils, polluted soils, deforested areas, and soils with poor nutritional conditions (Morris, 1997).

Legume Traditions

The expression "blackball" comes from the ancient Greek and Roman practice of using beans for voting. A white bean signifies acceptance, while a black bean means rejection. The black-eyed pea is eaten on New Year's Day in the southern United States to bring good luck for the coming year.

The Navaho-Ramah Indian tribe used an annual clover known as *Trifolium dubium* as a ceremonial medicine. For a dermatological remedy the Iroquois used a wild bean known as *Strophostyles helvola,* and the Pawnees used spider bean (*Desmodium illinoensis*). Bush clover or rabbit foot (*Lespedeza capitata*) was an antidote in the Fox tribe and an analgesic for the Omahas and Poncas. The Cherokees chewed tickseed or trefoil (*Desmodium*

TABLE 2

Ethnobotanical uses of minor legumes

Scientific name	Common name	Uses	Countries
Canavalia ensiformis (L.) DC.	Jack bean	Kidney and tonic	China
Clitoria ternatea (L.)	Butterfly pea	Arthritis	Philippines
		Scorpion bite	Sudan
		Laxative	Samoa
		Snake bite	Iraq
Crotalaria juncea (L.)	Sunn hemp	Psoriasis	Iraq
Crotalaria retusa (L.)	Rattle box	Fever	Java
Desmodium adscendens (Sw.) DC.	Tick clover	Bronchitis, colic, ringworms, wound	Africa
		Cough	Cameroon
		Laxative	Ghana
Desmodium gangeticum (L.) DC.		Dysentery, fever, tonic	India
Indigofera tinctoria (L.)	Common indigo	Fever, inflammation, laryngitis, mumps, scabies, swelling, dysentery	China
		Antiseptic, fever	Turkey
Leucaena leucocephala (Lam.) de Wit	Lead tree	Fever, typhoid	Bahamas
		Laxative	Dominican Republic
Mucuna pruriens (L.) DC.	Velvet bean	Scorpion antidote, asthma, snake bite, cancer, coffee, cough, diarrhea, mumps, ringworms, syphilis, tumor	India, Venezuela, Mexico
Psophocarpus tetragonolobus (L.) DC.	Wing bean	Boil, tumor	Java
Tephrosia candida DC.	White tephrosia	Insecticide, piscicide	India, Java
Tephrosia cinerea (L.) Pers.		Fever, piscicide, venereal, tumor	Mexico, Guiana, Brazil, Venezuela
Tephrosia purpurea (L.) Pers.		Colic, piscicide	Sudan, Guiana, Mexico
Tephrosia vogelii Hook. f.	Fish poison bean	Insecticide, insect repellant, piscicide	India, Tanzania, Sudan, Africa

perplexum) roots for sore gums and mouths. The Mohegans made a blood purifier from rattle box (*Crotalaria sagittalis*) root, and the Delawares treated venereal disease with rattle box root (Beckstrom-Sternberg, Duke, and Wain, 1994). See Table 2 for additional ethnobotanical and multicultural uses of legumes.

See also **Nuts**; **Peanut Butter**; **Peas**.

BIBLIOGRAPHY

Beckstrom-Sternberg, Stephen M., and James A. Duke. "The Phytochemical Database." Data version July 1994. Available at http://ars-genome.cornell.edu/cgi-bin/WebAce/webace?db= phytochemdb.

Beckstrom-Sternberg, Stephen M., James A. Duke, and K. K. Wain. "The Ethnobotany Database." Data version July 1994. Available at http://ars-genome.cornell.edu/cgi-bin/WebAce/webace?db=ethnobotdb.

Bisby, Frank A., James L. Zarucchi, B. D. Schrire, Y. R. Roskov, and Richard J. White, eds. *International Legume Database and Information Service.* 5th ed. Reading, U.K.: ILDIS, 2000.

"Ecology." In *The Columbia Encyclopedia*, edited by Paul Lagassé. 6th ed. New York: Columbia University Press, 2000.

Grum, Mikkel. *Breeding Pachyrhizus Rich. Ex DC.: A Review of Goals and Methods.* Copenhagen, Denmark: Royal Veterinary and Agricultural University, Department of Crop Husbandry and Plant Breeding, 1990.

Hymowitz, Theodore. "Grain Legumes." In *Advances in New Crops*, edited by Jules Janick and James E. Simon. Portland, Oreg.: Timber Press, 1990.

Martin, Franklin W. *Soybean*. Fort Myers, Fla.: Educational Concerns for Hunger Organization, ECHO Technical Note, 1988.

Martin, Franklin W., and Herminio Delpin. *Vegetables for the Hot, Humid Tropics.* Part 1: *The Winged Bean, "Psophocarpus Tetragonolobus."* New Orleans: Department of Agriculture, Science, and Education Administration, 1978.

Martin, John H., and Warren H. Leonard. "Legumes." In *Principles of Field Crop Production.* 2d ed. New York: Macmillan, 1967.

Morris, John Bradley. "Special-Purpose Legume Genetic Resources Conserved for Agricultural, Industrial, and Pharmaceutical Use." *Economic Botany* 51, no. 3 (July–September 1997): 251–263.

Muehlbauer, Fred J. "Food and Grain Legumes." In *New Crops*, edited by Jules Janick and James E. Simon. New York: Wiley, 1993.

Pattee, Harold E., and Clyde T. Young, eds. *Peanut Science and Technology.* Yoakum, Tex.: American Peanut Research and Education Society, 1982.

Purseglove, J. W. "Leguminosae." In *Tropical Crops: Dicotyledons.* 2 vols. New York: Wiley, 1987.

Whistler, Roy L., and Theodore Hymowitz. *Guar: Agronomy, Production, Industrial Use, and Nutrition.* West Lafayette, Ind.: Purdue University Press, 1979.

Brad Morris

LENT. The word "Lent" is derived from Old English *lencten*, meaning 'spring', the lengthening of days after winter is over. This was a period of spring fasting known in Old English as Lencten-Fasten, or in its abbreviated form, as Lencten or Lent. The ecclesiastical name for this once mandatory period of fasting is the Quadragesimal Fast, or the fast of the Forty Days, in imitation of the forty days of fasting performed by Jesus in the wilderness.

Like other institutions of Christianity, Lent took time to evolve into its full medieval form. Fasting was practiced in the early Christian Church and was viewed as an aid to prayer. Credence was given to the practice by a statement of Jesus: "When the bridegroom shall be taken from them, then shall they fast" (Matthew 9:15). What was called "half-fasting" was practiced very early on Wednesdays and particularly on Fridays to commemorate the passion or crucifixion of Christ. The Friday fast, as well as the Lenten fast, is still practiced by Roman Catholics, Eastern Orthodox Christians, and some Protestants.

Historically, the forty-day fast reaches back to the second century C.E., although forty days were not always required. By the fourth and fifth centuries, the fasting took place on thirty-six days representing the six weeks prior to Easter, minus six Sundays since Sundays were not fast days. Later, four extra days were added to make forty: Ash Wednesday and the three days following it.

The medieval Catholic Church in general took a middle ground on fasting. Those who put too high a value on the merit of fasting were rebuked with the words of St. Paul: "The kingdom of God is not meat and drink, but righteousness, and peace and joy in the Holy Ghost." Some extremist heretical groups, such as the Montanists in the second century, fasted frequently on bread, water, and salt.

Abstinence involves refraining from certain foods, meat in the case of Lent, and indeed, during the Middle Ages, all animal products, including butter, lard for cooking, and eggs. Many cookery books contained special recipes designed to make use of non-animal ingredients, such as olive oil, almond milk, and dried fruit. But fasting also refers to the number and fullness of the meals one partakes of on fast days. Both practices are subsumed under penance or penitence, which involves contrition and reparation for sin in human life. Since Vatican II, the rules of Lenten fasting for Roman Catholics have been modified, but earlier they were quite elaborate and even published in newspapers so that the guidelines would be clearly set forth. The following regulations were in force during the 1950s.

Everyone over the age of seven was to observe the Roman Catholic Lent with complete abstinence on all Fridays, Ash Wednesday, and Holy Saturday Morning. During these times, meat and soup, or gravy made from meat, could not be used. During days of partial abstinence, which included the Saturdays in Lent (except the last one), meat and soup, or gravy made from soup, could be taken only once a day during the main meal. For those over twenty-one and under fifty-nine, only one full meal per day was allowed during the weekdays of Lent. Other meatless meals were allowed only to maintain strength, but could not equal another full meal. Eating between meals was not permitted, except for liquids, but those people whose health or ability to work were seriously affected by fasting could be excused from the regimen. Acts of charity and of self-denial (such as abstaining from alcoholic drinks and amusements) and daily attendance at mass were encouraged.

In 1966, following Vatican II, Pope Paul VI issued his "Apostolic Constitution on Penance" (*Poenitemini*), which gave present shape to the Roman Catholic Church's practice of abstinence. This papal clarification modified the elaborate rules for Lent. Still, all Roman Catholics between the ages of eighteen and fifty-nine were required to fast on Ash Wednesday and Good Friday. Everyone over the age of fourteen had to abstain from meat on Ash Wednesday, Good Friday, and all Fridays during Lent. Fasting was defined as taking only one meal per day, but with smaller meals permitted. Abstinence for Roman Catholics does not now include meat juices, broths, consommés, soups made or flavored with meat, meat-based gravies or sauces, margarine or lard. Even bacon drippings poured over salads and meat by-products such as gelatin are now allowed. With the permission of the Episcopal Conference, many American Roman Catholics have substituted other forms of penance, such as works of charity or acts of piety, for the other meatless Fridays during the year.

By contrast, Orthodox Christians abstain from all meat products during most days of the Great Lent, and also from fish and animal products—lard, milk, butter, cheese, and eggs—together with wine and oil during Holy Week. The rigor and austerity of Orthodox fasting remains unchanged and follows the proscriptions of the early Church and its ecumenical councils. For the Orthodox, there are four main periods of fasting during the year: the Great Fast (Lent), the Fast of the Apostles (starting eight days after Pentecost), the Assumption Fast (from 1 to 14 August), and the Christmas Fast (from 15 November to 24 December). There are also a number of lesser fasts that fall outside the Lenten period.

Protestant attitudes to Lent range from complete rejection by denominations of Puritan and Pietist origin, to a rather full acceptance by Anglicans and Lutherans, who retain many practices similar to those of Catholicism. Even the Church of the Brethren, which in its sectarian, separatist beginnings opposed any celebration of the liturgical year, in the late twentieth century began, in some of its congregations, to hold special services on Ash Wednesday and the Sundays of Lent. Such services highlight repentance and prayer, but there are no special Lenten restrictions on food. There has been a movement among most of the Protestant churches to find common ground during Lent with such community-wide observances as the World Day of Prayer on the first Friday of Lent, and the One Great Hour of Sharing on the fourth Sunday of Lent with offerings dedicated to relieving world hunger.

In order to relieve the dietary austerity of Lent, and to enrich the formerly meager and restricted meals, special Lenten dishes developed in nearly all branches of Christianity. In the United States, they often appear in ethnic markets or in supermarkets catering to certain ethnic groups. One common theme is desserts, with sweet foods taking the place of meat. Recipes for Lent were once commonly published in the spring issues of women's magazines as well as in the food columns of daily newspapers. Cookbooks such as Florence S. Berger's *Cooking for Christ* (1949) and William I. Kaufman's *The Catholic Cookbook: Traditional Feast and Fast Day Recipes* (1965) generally include sections on Lenten meals and recipes that have been found acceptable under the canon law of the Roman Catholic Church.

See also **Christianity; Easter; Fasting and Abstinence: Christianity; Shrove Tuesday.**

BIBLIOGRAPHY

Apostolic Constitution on Penance (*Poenitemini*). Issued by Pope Paul VI, 17 February 1966.

Berger, Florence S. *Cooking for Christ: The Liturgical Year in the Kitchen*. Des Moines, Iowa: National Catholic Rural Life Conference, 1949.

"Bishop Publishes Roman Catholic Lent Regulations." *Altoona Mirror* (Altoona, Pa.), 18 February 1955.

The Code of Canon Law. Vatican City: Libreria Editrice Vaticana, 1983. Book 4, Chapter 2, "Days of Penance."

Franke, Hermann. *Lent and Easter: The Church's Spring*. Westminster, Md.: Hermann, 1955.

Flicoteaux, Emmanuel. *Le sense du carême*. Paris: Cerf, 1956.

Gulevich, Tanya. *Encyclopedia of Easter, Carnival, and Lent*. Detroit: Omnigraphics, 2002.

Jacobs, Henry Eyster, and John A. W. Haas. *The Lutheran Cyclopedia*. New York: Scribners, 1899. Articles on fasting, Lent, and church year.

Kaufman, William I. *The Catholic Cookbook: Traditional Feast and Fast Day Recipes*. New York: Citadel, 1965.

"Lent." *The Brethren Encyclopedia*. Vol. 2, p. 737. Philadelphia, Pa., and Oak Brook, Ill.: The Brethren Encyclopedia, 1983.

"Lent." *New Catholic Encyclopedia*. Vol. 8, pp. 634–636. New York: McGraw-Hill, 1967.

Rifkin, Ira. Religious News Service. "Catholic Bishops to Study Return to Meatless Fridays." *Mobile Register* (Mobile, Ala.), 11 November 1997.

Ware, Timothy. *The Orthodox Church*. Harmondsworth, Middlesex, U.K.: Penguin, 1963.

Don Yoder

LESLIE, ELIZA. Eliza Leslie (1787–1858) was an American cookbook writer, poet, editor, and author of fiction and nonfiction for children and adults. Although her primary literary activity focused on *belles lettres*, Eliza Leslie is remembered today mainly for the cookery books that launched her career as an author and earned her a national reputation as one of the most popular and influential American food writers prior to the Civil War.

In 1828, Leslie edited and published *Seventy-Five Receipts for Pastry, Cakes and Sweetmeats*, a collection of recipes she had compiled many years earlier while a student at the cooking school of Elizabeth Goodfellow in Philadelphia. The book was an instant success and quickly assumed its place as the first bestselling cookbook in the United States. This was followed by *Domestic French Cookery* (1832), *Directions for Cookery* (1837), *The Lady's House Book* (1840), *The Indian Meal Book* (1846), the first cookbook devoted entirely to corn recipes, *New Receipts for Cooking* (1854), and *The New Cookery Book* (1857), this last title being a massive reworking of her *New Receipts*. Many of these books popularized regional American foods (such as terrapin and okra) at a time when America was searching for a more distinct culinary identity. Of these, *Directions for Cookery* is generally considered Leslie's most influential culinary work, since it remained in print well into the 1880s.

Portrait of Eliza Leslie from a copper engraving originally published in *Godey's Ladies'* Book. The engraving is based on an undated oil portrait by Thomas Sully in the collection of the Pennsylvania Academy of the Fine Arts, Philadelphia. ROUGHWOOD COLLECTION.

OKRA SOUP

Take a large slice of ham (cold boiled ham is best) and two pounds of lean fresh beef. Cut all the meat into small pieces. Add a quarter of a pound of butter slightly melted, twelve large tomatas pared and cut small, five dozen okras cut into slices not thicker than a cent, and a little cayenne pepper to your taste. Put all these ingredients into a pot, cover them with boiling water, and let them stew slowly for an hour. Then add three quarts of *hot* water, and increase the heat so as to make the soup boil. Skim it well and stir it frequently with a wooden or silver spoon.

Boil it till the tomatas are all to pieces and the okras entirely dissolved. Strain it, and then serve it up with toasted bread cut into dice, put in after it comes out of the pot.

This soup will be improved by a pint of shelled lima beans, boiled by themselves, and put into the tureen just before you send it to table.

FROM: *Directions for Cookery*, 32–33. Philadelphia: Carey and Hart, 1837.

Eliza Leslie's success has been attributed to several factors working in tandem: improved female literacy; a growing urban middle class in need of instruction on points of cookery according to American taste and ingredients; and the proliferation of the cookstove, the technological revolution upon which all of Leslie's recipes are based.

See also **Goodfellow, Elizabeth; Maize**.

BIBLIOGRAPHY:

Dictionary of American Biography, vol. 11, pp. 185–186. New York: Scribners, 1933.

James, Edward T., ed. *Notable American Women*, vol. 2, pp. 391–393. New York: Scribners, 1971.

Manuscript Collections of the Historical Society of Pennsylvania.

William Woys Weaver

LETTUCE. Lettuce has been described as a "weedy Cinderella" by T. W. Whitaker (1974) and as the "queen of the salad plants" by Franklin W. Martin and Ruth M. Ruberté (1975). What is this plant that merits two such disparate descriptions? It is certainly the most commonly used salad vegetable, occurring in or under most salads. Many types exist, varying in size, form, leaf shape, color, and taste. All of these types may have evolved from a weedy form that was used in ancient Egypt as a source of cooking oil from pressed seeds, so both descriptions are probably justified.

Among the several lettuce types, most of which are consumed as raw leaves, one is used for its stem instead of its leaves. This lettuce is depicted on the walls of tombs dating back to about 2500 B.C.E., during the Middle Kingdom of ancient Egypt. Lettuce is shown as a long stem with marks indicating where leaves had been removed. At the top of the stem is a tuft of elongated leaves, bluish green in color. This lettuce may have been the one that first was eaten and may have been derived in turn from the type used for seed oil. The blue color is associated with the process in the growth of lettuce called bolting or stem formation. Leaves that form in the development of the head are green. As the process of bolting begins, the leaves become bluish green, signaling the elongation of the stem, which emerges from the interior of the head and eventually produces many small, yellow flowers that mature into small, narrow fruits. The fruits are less than four millimeters long. They look like seeds and usually go by that name.

Oilseed lettuce is a primitive, wild-looking plant that forms no head or rosette of leaves. It bolts early in its growth cycle, forming a thin stem with elongated, narrow leaves. The seeds produced on this stem are about 50 percent larger than those formed on cultivated lettuce. The seeds are pressed to express an oil used in cooking. This is an ancient custom still practiced in twenty-first century Egypt.

Evolution of Lettuce

One can speculate that somewhere in time ancient Egyptians selected, perhaps from oilseed lettuce, plants that bolted more slowly and formed a thick stem that was less bitter than the more primitive type and therefore edible. This new stem lettuce also had somewhat broader leaves. Later, perhaps many centuries later, further selection may have yielded a newer form with a still shorter stem and broader leaves that were appealing enough to eat, the romaine type. From Egypt, romaine lettuce moved around the Mediterranean Sea and to the Middle East. In these areas it was the most commonly grown lettuce in the twenty-first century. The original stem type traveled eastward, eventually reaching China. Numerous mentions of lettuce in ancient literature, beginning with Herodotus in 550 B.C.E., document its travels into Persia, Greece, Rome, and Sicily and later into France, Germany, and England. Use of descriptive names, such as crispa and purpurea, and place names, such as Cappadocian and Cyprian, indicate further proliferation into various distinctive types differing in color, size, leaf shape, and adaptation to specific environments. The various modern butterhead, leaf, and crisphead forms undoubtedly were selected and developed as lettuce spread through Europe. Lettuce reached the shores of the New World with the second voyage of Christopher Columbus in 1494. Many

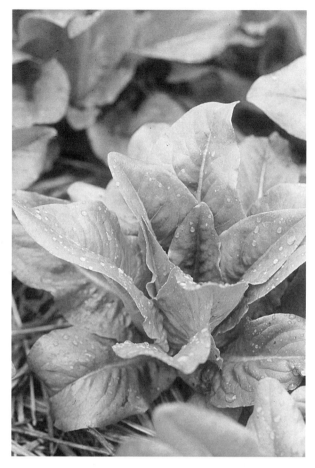

Chadwick's Rodan is a variety of lettuce developed in England for small kitchen gardens. It was created by Alan Chadwick, the "father" of organic gardening. PHOTO ROB CARDILLO.

varieties within the different types were brought to the Western Hemisphere in subsequent years.

The scientific name of lettuce is *Lactuca sativa*. *Lactuca* means 'milk forming', *sativa* means 'common'. It is related to over one hundred wild species of *Lactuca* and also to sunflower, artichoke, aster, and chrysanthemum. Among the modern types of lettuce are two crisphead forms, iceberg, which forms a large, firm head, and Batavia, which is slightly softer and smaller than iceberg and is popular in Europe. Romaine lettuce has long leaves in a loaf-shaped head. Butterhead lettuce is quite small with oily, soft textured leaves. Red and green leaf lettuces form no head and have leaves with a variety of shapes. Less commonly found are the Latin type, which looks like a small romaine, and the aforementioned stem and oilseed lettuces.

Preparing a Salad
Since lettuce is used mainly in salads, preparation methods are simple, rapid, and informal. The ubiquitous tossed salad is made of lettuce leaves cut up into various-sized pieces. To some people the use of a knife is anathema, and they tear the leaves by hand. The salad maker may use one type of lettuce alone or a mixture of two or more kinds. Depending upon the ingenuity of the salad maker and the availability of edibles, any combination of other vegetables, fruits, and even cheeses or meats can be added to the lettuce. A dressing is added, and the ingredients are mixed together. Salads are vital to many slimming diets, the effectiveness of which can be reinforced or negated by the calorie value of the chosen dressing.

In the United States head lettuce was for many years commonly cut and served as a wedge, covered with mayonnaise or another dressing, and eaten with a knife and fork. This simple salad was served less frequently by the beginning of the twenty-first century. The popular Caesar salad is made only with leaves of romaine lettuce tossed with a special dressing, including a raw egg and small pieces of anchovy. A relative newcomer to the salad scene is mesclun, a mixture of baby leaves consisting of several lettuce types and other leafy vegetables, some of which are fairly exotic. These may include arugula or rocket, actually a partially domesticated weed; a fine-leaved endive called *frisée*; mizuna, a small, dark green round leaf from Japan; spinach, beet tops, or chard; red chicory (radicchio); and romaine, butterhead, and red and green leaf lettuces. These leaves are cut in the field by hand, or mowed, when they are no more than ten centimeters long. In parts of the American Southwest wilted lettuce is a favorite salad made by pouring bacon fat over lettuce leaves.

Some salads consist primarily of other vegetables or fruits, such as sliced tomatoes or a scoop of cottage cheese. These are often arranged in a more formal manner than a tossed salad. Lettuce may find its way into these salads as whole or shredded leaves serving as a base for the main constituent.

Lettuce may also be used to make soup, as part of the filling for sandwiches, or as a wrap for holding cooked meat and vegetable mixes. Stem lettuce is consumed raw, like a stalk of celery, in Egypt or as a cooked vegetable in China.

The Biological Human Connection
Lettuce relates to human biology in several ways. The most obvious way is in its role as a food. Some less well-known relationships to human consumption also exist.

As a green vegetable, lettuce contains many of the same nutrients found in other green vegetables, although mostly in lesser amounts. These include vitamins, minerals, water, and fiber but essentially no protein or fat (Table 1). Lettuce is a low to moderate source of vitamins and minerals. Among the various types of lettuce, romaine and leaf varieties exceed crisphead and butterhead varieties for most of the common nutrients. This is directly related to the proportion of dark green leaves in the edible portion. The nutrient contribution of lettuce

TABLE 1

Selected nutritional values per 100 grams for crisp, butter, romaine, and leaf lettuces									
	Minerals (g)					Vitamins		Water	Fiber
	Ca	P	Fe	Na	K	A (IU)	C (g)	%	g
Crisp	22	26	1.5	7	166	470	7	95.5	0.5
Butter	35	26	1.8	7	260	1,065	8	95.1	0.5
Romaine	44	35	1.3	9	277	1,925	22	94.9	0.7
Leaf	68	25	1.4	9	264	1,900	18	94.0	0.7

SOURCE: Adapted from Rubatzky and Yamaguchi (1997) as compiled from several original sources.

compared to other vegetables is affected by the amount consumed. For example, a study by M. A. Stevens in 1974 showed that broccoli has considerably more vitamins and minerals than lettuce but that much more lettuce was consumed than broccoli; therefore the total contribution of nutrients to the diet by lettuce was greater than that of broccoli. This relationship may have changed somewhat as consumption habits changed. Nonetheless lettuce is important for its nutrient content, which complements its usefulness as a diet food because of its high water and fiber content.

Prevention of Cancer

Research in recent years has identified a connection between the consumption of vegetables and certain other foods and beverages and anticarcinogenic activity due to the presence of compounds known as antioxidants. These compounds inhibit the formation of carcinogenic substances in the body. Among the antioxidant compounds in lettuce are 0-beta-carotene, a precursor to Vitamin A, and anthocyanin, which gives the red color in certain lettuce varieties.

The oil pressed from large seeds of certain primitive types of lettuce contributes to a minor food use. The oil is used for cooking and is similar to other oils used for the same purpose. This practice is believed to be hundreds, perhaps thousands of years old.

Nonfood Uses of Lettuce

Turning to nonfood uses, the stems and leaves of lettuce and its wild relatives contain a milky liquid called latex. The latex contains two substances called sesquiterpene lactones, which are the active ingredients in preparations used in some western European countries as a sedative and as a sleep inducer. In folk medicine additional uses for lettuce extracts include treatment for coughs, nervousness, tension, pain, rheumatism, and even insanity. The efficacy of these treatments is not well documented, but some of these effects have been shown in mice and toads.

Another minor nonfood use is drying lettuce leaves for the production of cigarettes without tobacco. Actu-

ally leaves of a wild relative of lettuce produce a more tobacco-like appearance. These have been manufactured for use in several brands of cigarettes. Effects on health are not known.

Rarely lettuce may impact human biology in a harmful way. Green leafy vegetables are normally the standard for healthful food, providing vitamins and minerals in a fresh, tasty, and light context. Nitrogen is a vital constituent of chlorophyll, the plant substance that gives the green color and controls photosynthesis. However, green leafy vegetables, including lettuce and spinach, when grown under low light and low temperature conditions in greenhouses in the winter, may accumulate high levels of the nitrate form of nitrogen. In the body nitrate may be converted to compounds that may cause the syndrome called blue baby in infants or may be carcinogenic. Fortunately the likelihood of these consequences is remote, since nitrate accumulation in greenhouse-grown lettuce can be prevented by growing the crop with adequate heat and with supplemental light. Lettuce grown outdoors is not subject to this problem.

Symbolism: Fresh, Cool, Green

The obvious symbolism associated with lettuce is three words, "fresh," "cool," and "green." "Fresh" is a word that many think of as important to health. Lettuce is eaten fresh and raw. In the gardening months many can cut it and eat it almost immediately. It is not that fresh in the store bin of course, but it is still only a few days old. Even the leaves in a packaged salad were growing in the soil shortly before they appeared on the shelf. Lettuce is never frozen or canned.

Lettuce is kept cool. After being cut in the field it is transported to a cooler, where the temperature is quickly reduced to just one degree above freezing. It is transported in refrigerated trucks to a market, where it is kept in a cooler before being placed in a refrigerated bin. Finally, it is purchased by the consumer, taken home, and placed in the refrigerator. This sequence is called the cold chain and is designed to maintain the quality of the lettuce at the time of harvest in the field as long as possible.

Finally, lettuce comes in various shades of green. Even red lettuce contains chlorophyll, which confers the green color, though it may be hidden in the red parts of the leaf. Green means vitamins. Green is a cool color. Many also associate greenness with the health of the planet and with personal health. The process of photosynthesis produces oxygen and sugar converted from carbon dioxide and water. The absorption of carbon dioxide by green plants, from lettuce to trees, helps prevent its accumulation in the air, thus mitigating the greenhouse effect and possible global warming.

The symbolism of these words is so strong that they and similar words, such as "ice," "crisp," "winter," and "spring," have been used repeatedly in various combinations in the names of lettuce varieties. Consider the names Green Ice, Iceberg, Crisp as Ice, Coolguard, Green Towers, Valverde, Valspring, and Winterset.

In ancient Egypt lettuce had sexual symbolism. After completing its vegetative development with the formation of a head or a rosette of leaves, the plant goes into its reproductive phase with the formation of an erect seed stalk bearing flowers. The amount of latex in the plant increases and is under pressure, so if the top of the flowering stalk is cut off, the latex spurts out in a manner reminiscent of ejaculation. The same tomb paintings portraying the ancient stem lettuce also picture the god Min with an erect phallus. Consumption of lettuce may therefore have been thought to increase sexual prowess.

Commercial Production and Marketing

Lettuce has become a major player in commercial production and marketing. Total production worldwide does not compare with the major cereal crops, especially rice, corn, and wheat, or with other commodities, such as sugar crops, beans, and potatoes, but among the vegetables it ranks high. In the United States it is in the top three with tomatoes and potatoes. The key word in contemporary use of lettuce is change: in use of the various types, in development of world markets, in methods of marketing, and in methods of production.

The primary markets for lettuce were, until the late twentieth century, in western Europe and North America, the consequence of its first appearance in the Mediterranean basin followed by movement into northern Europe and then to the New World. In the late twentieth century lettuce became important in Japan, China, Hong Kong, Australia, and some countries of South America and Africa. In the different regions where lettuce was consumed, one type was usually more popular than the others. In northern Europe, for example, the butterhead type predominated. Until the 1970s about 80 percent of the lettuce consumed in England was butterhead, and the other 20 percent was divided among the other major types. In the countries surrounding the Mediterranean nearly all the lettuce was romaine. Stem lettuce was the main type in Egypt and China. In the United States, until the early part of the twentieth century, no one type was strongly

dominant. At that time crisphead lettuce began to increase in popularity at the expense of the other types. After the modern iceberg lettuce was developed in the 1940s, 95 percent of the production and consumption was of this type. The first modern iceberg variety was created by T. W. Whitaker of the United States Department of Agriculture and was named Great Lakes, although it was actually bred in California.

Changes in Consumption Patterns

In the late 1970s and early 1980s changes in consumption patterns began. In Britain and Scandinavia iceberg lettuce increased in popularity until it became the dominant type. Iceberg lettuce also made inroads into the butterhead and romaine domains in other western European countries. In the United States, where the iceberg type reigned supreme for most of the twentieth century, romaine, butterhead, and leaf lettuces regained popularity and comprised about one-third of the total production at the end of the twentieth century.

The construction of a home-cooked meal has become a casualty of the modern fast-paced lifestyle. People either eat out more frequently or rely on food packages that are partially processed and therefore can be prepared quickly. Salads are included in this drive for efficiency and speed. Modern supermarkets have dedicated extensive shelf space to packaged salads containing what appears to be an infinite number of combinations of leaves (lettuce, cabbage, radicchio, spinach), cut vegetables (carrots, broccoli, cauliflower), dressings, bacon bits, shredded cheeses, croutons, cut fruits, and more.

Changes have also occurred in production methods. Growing, harvesting, and marketing of lettuce is mainly on a large scale, from planting, with significant inputs of water, chemical fertilizers, and appropriate pesticides, to harvesting, cooling, and shipment to market. Production of food with organic methods has become a rapidly growing industry although it is still a small part of the production picture. Lettuce is included in this cultural change. Most of the change has been in the production of nonheading types, such as romaine and leaf lettuce, but some iceberg lettuce is grown in this way. Organic production emphasizes nonuse of chemical fertilizers and pesticides. This type of production began with small-scale growers, but has been included by growers in large-scale production systems.

Where Lettuce is Grown

The need for coolness is a key factor in the location and magnitude of lettuce production areas. In the early twenty-first century the United States was by far the largest producer of lettuce in the world (Table 2). However, few of the fifty states produce lettuce commercially, and of the ones that do California and Arizona are responsible for over 90 percent of the production in the country. California alone accounts for over 70 percent and actually grows lettuce year-round. In the summer let-

TABLE 2

Commercial production of lettuce in the United States and the European Union

Area in hectares (1 hectare = 2.47 acres), production in millions of metric tons.

	Area	Production
United States (1997)	82,150	3,116
California	57,090	2,243
Arizona	21,900	765
European Union (1996)	90,200	2,351
Spain	33,600	925
Italy	21,300	420
France	13,500	366
United Kingdom	7,500	231
Germany	5,900	144
Greece	3,600	70
Belgium	2,500	85
Netherlands	2,300	110

SOURCE: Compiled from U.S. Department of Agriculture and Eurostat statistics for the years shown.

tuce is produced in coastal valleys near the Pacific Ocean, particularly in the Salinas Valley, which is the most important production region in the world. In the winter lettuce is produced in the desert regions of California and Arizona. For short periods in the spring and fall lettuce is grown in the great Central Valley of California. The coolness of the season is the reason for the movement from location to location. Lettuce grows best when the daytime temperature rarely exceeds 70 to 75°F (21 to 24°C). The desert and inland areas are too hot in summer, while the coastal areas are too cold in winter. Those locations and others with similar seasonal climates in other countries, such as eastern portions of England, the Mediterranean Coast, the Negev Desert in Israel, and the southeastern portions of Australia, produce nearly all the commercially grown lettuce in the world.

Lettuce is grown in home gardens worldwide. In warm climates lettuce growing is usually restricted to the spring and fall, when temperatures are more moderate than in summer or winter. Lettuce grows fast and is easy to grow, especially leaf lettuces, which are the ones most commonly found in the backyard garden.

See also **Oil; Organic Farming and Gardening; Salad.**

BIBLIOGRAPHY

Cao, G., E. Sofic, and R. L. Prior. "Antioxidant Capacity of Tea and Common Vegetables." *Journal of Agricultural and Food Chemistry* 44 (1996): 3426–3431.

Gonzalez-Lima, F., A. Veledon, and W. L. Stiehil. "Depressant Pharmacological Effects of a Component Isolated from Lettuce, *Lactuca sativa* L." *International Journal of Crude Drug Research* 24 (1986): 154–166.

Harlan, J. "Lettuce and the Sycomore: Sex and Romance in Ancient Egypt." *Economic Botany* 40 (1986): 4–15.

Martin, Franklin W., and Ruth M. Ruberté. *Edible Leaves of the Tropics.* Mayagüez, Puerto Rico: Agency for International Development, Department of State, and Department of Agriculture–Agricultural Research Service, 1975.

Reinink, K., and R. Groenwold. "The Inheritance of Nitrate Content in Lettuce (*Lactuca sativa* L.)." *Euphytica* 36 (1987): 733–744.

Rubatzky, Vincent E., and Mas Yamaguchi. *World Vegetables: Principles, Production, and Nutritive Values.* 2d ed. New York: Chapman and Hall, 1997.

Ryder, E. J. *Lettuce, Endive, and Chicory.* New York: CABI, 1999.

Said, S. A., H. A. El Kashef, M. M. El Mayar, and O. Salama. "Phytochemical and Pharmacological Studies in *Lactuca sativa* Seed Oil." *Fitoterapia* 67 (1996): 215–219.

Stevens, M. A. "Varietal Influence on Nutritional Value." In *Nutritional Qualities of Fresh Fruits and Vegetables*, edited by Philip I. White and Nancy Selvey. Mount Kisco, N.Y.: Futura, 1974.

Sturtevant, E. Lewis. *Sturtevant's Edible Plants of the World*, edited by U. P. Hedrick. New York: Dover, 1972.

Whitaker, T. W. "Lettuce: Evolution of a Weedy Cinderella." *Hortscience* 9 (1974): 512–514.

Edward J. Ryder

LIPIDS. Lipids (fats and oils) have borne the brunt of the blame for the degenerative diseases (heart disease and cancer) that are the major causes of death in the developed world. The negative view of lipids has obscured their essentiality for human health. If a problem exists, it is one of quantity, in general, and specific lipids in particular.

Lipids are important for maintenance of human health and well-being in a number of ways. Probably the most important function of lipids is provision of an efficient energy source. Fat provides 9 calories of energy per gram or 2.25 times as much as either carbohydrate or protein. Carbohydrate is not stored in the body and protein stores are predominantly muscle, whose breakdown entails serious health consequences. Fat is stored as such and can be easily mobilized if needed. In primitive times survival may have been possible because of energy provided by metabolic use of stored fat (Gurr and Harwood, 1991).

Lipids are a group of substances of diverse structures that share the common trait of being soluble in solvents such as ether or benzene. The major lipids of the body are triglycerides, which comprise a molecule of glycerol to which three fatty acids are bonded. Phospholipids are substances in which glycerol carries only two fatty acids plus phosphoric acid and an organic base such as choline or serine. Cholesterol is a member of the family of large complex molecules generically called steroids. It has the capacity to carry one molecule of fatty acids (cholesteryl ester). Cell membranes are predominantly composed of phospholipids and cholesterol. Cell membranes confer stability to cells and control entry or release of chemicals into or from the cell. Lipids serve as effective insulators and help in maintaining body temperature. Important organs such as the heart, kidneys, and reproductive organs are cushioned by fat. Nerves are protected by a sheath (myelin) that contains cholesterol, phospholipids, and other lipids. The animal organism carries a number of essential substances that catalyze chemical reactions in cells. These are called vitamins and are designated by letters. The B and C vitamins are soluble in water; the others, vitamins A, D, E, and K, are insoluble in water but soluble in fats. They are transported in lipids in the blood and stored in fat in the body.

Chemistry

Cholesterol is a molecule that is found in the membrane of every cell. About 0.2 percent of the average body weight is cholesterol. Most of this cholesterol is present in the muscle (cell membrane) or brain (as insulation against trauma). The functions of cholesterol in the brain are still poorly understood. Most of the cholesterol in the body is manufactured in the liver, and the diet makes a relatively small contribution to this pool. Cholesterol, in turn, is the parent substance of a number of vital compounds. Among these are the bile acids that are necessary for proper absorption and digestion of fat; the corticosteroids such as cortisol and hydrocortisone that are essential to life; progesterone which is required for normal reproduction, and the male and female sex hormones. The involvement of cholesterol in the etiology of coronary heart disease will be discussed below.

Fatty acids are chains of carbon acids that culminate in an acidic group called a carboxyl group. Each carbon atom has the capacity to bind four other atoms. In the fatty acid chain, two of those binding elements are bound to the carbon atoms on either side, and the other two are bound to hydrogen atoms. If the hydrogen atoms on adjacent carbon atoms are missing, the two carbons (which are already bound by one bond) form a second bond, and these are called double bonds. A fatty acid lacking the maximum number of hydrogen atoms is called an unsaturated fatty acid. The most common fatty acid in the human body is palmitic acid (16:0, which designates sixteen carbon atoms and no double bonds). Oleic acid (18:1) is the next common fatty acid. The diet provides linoleic (18:2) and linolenic (18:3) acids, which are called "essential fatty acids," meaning fatty acids that are essential to life and health and cannot be synthesized by the human body. Linoleic acid is converted via arachidonic acid to a series of compounds with hormonal activity called prostaglandins. The prostaglandins are usually made within the tissue in which they act and are involved in diverse functions such as control of inflammation, uterine contraction during labor, and blood platelet aggregation. An important group of long-chain polyunsaturated acids (polyunsaturated fatty acids [PUFAs]) occur in the fats of cold-water fish such as salmon and cod. The two principal PUFAs are eicosapentaenoic acid (20:5) and docosahexaenoic acid (22:6). While these fatty acids do not necessarily affect blood cholesterol levels, their presence in the diet has been associated with a reduced risk of cardiovascular disease. They have been shown to be essential to development of normal vision and also to influence brain development in newborns (Innis, 1991).

Phospholipids are glycerol derivatives in which two of the hydroxyls are esterified to fatty acids and the third to phosphoric acid, which is, in turn, esterified to a base. In lecithin, the most abundant phospholipid, the base is choline. The fatty acid in the 2 position of a phospholipid is usually polyunsaturated. It is often arachidonic acid (20:4), a product of metabolism of essential fatty acid, and a direct precursor of prostaglandins.

Biochemistry

Blood is an aqueous medium that contains an appreciable amount of lipid. Normal blood serum or plasma appears as a pale yellow, clear liquid, because the fat has been emulsified to give water-soluble fat-protein aggregates. These aggregates are designated as lipoproteins and have a lipid core and a protein coat. Fat enters the lymph in the form of chylomicrons, which are large triglyceride-rich particles. In the course of circulation the triglyceride is deposited in or metabolized by cells and the particles become smaller in size. The lipoproteins can be separated physically on the basis of their hydrated density and are designated as very low-density lipoproteins (VLDL), low-density lipoproteins (LDL), and high-density lipoproteins (HDL). Although estimations of the lipid composition of the various lipoproteins are available, their size and shape may vary.

The proteins surrounding the lipid core (apoproteins) have been characterized and their biological functions catalogued. Thus, apolipoprotein AI (ApoAI) and apolipoprotein AII (ApoAII) are present only in HDL and are required for metabolism of the lipid portion of HDL. ApoAI activates lecithin-cholesterol acyltransferase, which is active in the synthesis of cholesterol esters, and ApoII is required for breakdown of the triglycerides by lipoprotein lipase.

Apolipoprotein B (ApoB) occurs only in LDL and is required for secretion of the triglyceride-rich lipoproteins. The exclusivity of ApoA and ApoB to HDL and LDL, respectively, is often used for determination of LDL/HDL ratios. Apolipoprotein E (ApoE) is present in both VLDL and HDL. It occurs in several modifications (isoforms), which may determine level of success in treatment of hypercholesterolemia and which have been hypothesized to influence susceptibility to Alzheimer's disease. An LDL variant, Lp(a), appears to confer increased susceptibility to atherosclerosis, and its presence in serum is often used as an additional diagnostic indicator. The principal lipoproteins, LDL and HDL, are known popularly as the "bad" and the "good" cholesterol.

TABLE 1

Functions of human plasma lipoproteins		
Lipoprotein class	Origin	Function
Chylomicrons	Intestine	Transport lipids from intestine to liver and tissues
Very low density (VLDL)	Liver	Transport lipid from tissues to liver
Intermediate density (IDL)	VLDL	Precursor of LDL
High density (HDL 2 and 3)	Intestine	Remove cholesterol from tissues

Elevated levels of LDL are a risk factor for heart disease, hence LDL is considered to be a "bad" lipoprotein. Elevated HDL levels lower the risk of heart disease, hence the designation "'good" cholesterol. LDL is rich in cholesterol and delivers cholesterol into cells, whereas HDL, which is about 50 percent protein, aids in cholesterol egress from cells.

Heart Disease

There is a roster of risk factors that are associated with an increased chance of succumbing to heart disease, but none of these factors is an unequivocal risk. Risk in places like Las Vegas is called "odds." There are a number of well-documented risk factors for development of coronary heart disease. Heredity and age are beyond control. The others are elevated blood pressure, elevated blood cholesterol, smoking, obesity, diabetes, physical inactivity, and stress. Each factor exerts its effects differently in each individual. These factors may also interact. It is now becoming accepted that the initial injury in atherosclerosis may be inflammation, which complicates the risk picture (Ross, 1993). There are suggestions that infection in some way prepares the arterial tissue for the subsequent metabolic events. At present we must monitor the various controllable risk factors, bearing in mind the possibility that a prior event may determine the extent to which the risk factors affect risk. In the United States, deaths from heart disease (cases per 100,000, adjusted for age) peaked in 1968 and have been falling since then. Between 1960 and 1998 mortality from all causes in men fell by 33.8 percent and coronary heart disease mortality by 51.0 percent. In women the reductions were 33.7 and 50.1 percent, respectively. Incidence of the disease may be rising as population increases and other modes of demise diminish or disappear. A century ago the major causes of death were related to infection, while a half-century ago the average age of victims of coronary disease was considerably below what it is today. This is a public health triumph due to improved diagnosis and treatment. The aim now should be to achieve productive and healthy aging.

Of the risk factors cited above none has received more attention than blood cholesterol. Dietary studies related to atherogenesis were conducted early in the twentieth century; they usually involved a combination of dietary alterations plus physical stress. The earliest purely nutritional study was carried out by Ignatowski in 1909. He observed aortic atherosclerosis when weanling rabbits were fed milk and egg yolk or when adult rabbits were fed meat. A few years later Anitschkow (1913) fed rabbits cholesterol and reported atherosclerotic lesions and fat deposition. Anitschkow's work established dietary cholesterol as the modality for establishment of atherosclerotic-like lesions, and this was carried over to human nutrition; consequently dietary cholesterol was presumed to be the principal contributor to cardiovascular disease. Relatively mild interest in cholesterol and atherosclerosis was evinced in the research and medical communities for the few decades after Anitschkow's publications. In the late 1940s and early 1950s interest in cholesterol intensified. The reasons for this renewed interest were an increase in death from coronary disease, as death from infectious causes waned and new research findings, especially Gofman's demonstration of the separation of different lipoprotein classes, which differed in their chemistry (Gofman et al., 1950). The cholesterol-rich lipoproteins were associated with greater susceptibility to heart disease. Subsequently the research area developed the concept of risk factors, of which elevated blood cholesterol was the first clearly defined one. At about the same time epidemiological studies, many conducted by Ancel Keys, began to show that populations whose diets were rich in cholesterol and fat demonstrated high death rates from heart disease.

At this point it might be important to distinguish between the effects of dietary cholesterol and dietary fat. While there is no argument that blood cholesterol is a risk factor for coronary disease, the connection with dietary cholesterol is not strong. The connection between dietary cholesterol and blood cholesterol is controversial. The data show that the amount of dietary cholesterol plays a lesser role in affecting blood cholesterol than does the type of dietary fat. Dietary cholesterol plus saturated fat is much more cholesterolemic than the same amount of cholesterol plus unsaturated fat (McNamara, 1987). Since dietary cholesterol is often accompanied by saturated fat, it is considered prudent to limit its intake. Gertler et al. (1950) reported a study in which they had segregated from a large cohort of coronary patients and controls four groups of ten men each, those who ate the most cholesterol and those who ate the least, and those with highest or lowest plasma cholesterol levels. In every subgroup the coronary patients exhibited significantly higher plasma cholesterol levels than did the controls—thus confirming the role of cholesterol as a risk factor. However, in no group did the investigators find any correlation between dietary cholesterol intake and blood cholesterol level. Thirty years later an attempt was made to correlate diet with coronary disease in three large populations under continuous study. The populations were in Framingham, Massachusetts; Puerto Rico; and Hawaii. Diets of men who had had a coronary event and those who had not differed significantly in total calories (lower in cases), complex carbohydrate (lower in cases), and alcohol intake (lower in cases). Intake of fat or cholesterol was the same in cases and controls (Gordon et al., 1981).

Type of dietary fat affects atherogenesis in rabbits and cholesterolemia in humans. Keys (1965) and Hegsted (1965) and their colleagues showed that fats rich in saturated fatty acids promoted cholesterolemia. They developed formulas to predict changes in blood cholesterol based on dietary saturated and/or unsaturated fatty acids. Since the publication of the original formulas many revised and refined versions have appeared. The new formulas provide coefficients for specific fatty acids, but none has proved to be more serviceable or useful than the originals. It should be pointed out that even the most saturated dietary fat, coconut oil, contains oleic (about 7 percent) and linoleic (about 2 percent) acids, and that one of the most unsaturated fats, safflower oil, contains about 7 percent palmitic acid and 2 percent stearic acid. In the Keys and Hegsted formulas stearic acid is viewed as "neutral" because it has no effect on blood cholesterol.

An issue that has been debated for several decades is the role of trans-fatty acids. In most naturally occurring unsaturated fatty acids the hydrogen atoms attached to the carbons that constitute the double bond are spatially on the same side of the molecule (*cis*); when they are on opposite sides, they are designated as "trans." There are many trans fats in nature but not many in our usual diet. However, trans double bonds may be formed during hydrogenation of fat used for margarines. The major source of trans fat in the diet is margarine and baked goods made with margarines or margarine stock. Concerns over diets high in trans fats were aired in the 1940s and 1950s. It was found then that in rabbits fed atherogenic diets trans fat elevated cholesterol levels but did not increase severity of atherosclerosis (McMillan et al., 1963). The question of trans fat effects is complicated because hydrogenation may provide fats with double bonds anywhere from carbon 4 to carbon 14 of the fatty acid. Recent research shows that trans fat lowers levels of HDL-cholesterol in humans. It has also been demonstrated that trans fats have little effect in diets containing high levels of polyunsaturated fat. Because of health concerns margarine manufacturers have begun to produce products containing little or no trans-unsaturated fat (Kritchevsky, 1999b).

Ingestion of cholesterol per se appears to have little effect on cholesterolemia. Numerous studies have shown that eggs, the richest source of cholesterol, have little effect on blood cholesterol (McNamara, 2000). However, most cholesterol in the diet is associated with animal fats, which are more saturated than plant fats.

Hence the admonition to exercise prudence in ingestion of cholesterol.

The field of fat and cholesterol is still active and as new fats and new facts emerge dietary suggestions will be modified. At one time we were admonished to eat a virtually fat-free diet, but fat is a necessary nutrient. Very low-fat diets present their own problems, since diets too high in carbohydrate may affect insulin metabolism and can lead to triglyceridemia (Lichtenstein and Van Horn, 1998). In the 1950s high plasma triglyceride levels were considered to be an independent risk factor for coronary disease. For a long while triglyceride levels were virtually ignored, but they are beginning to reassume importance as new clinical and epidemiological data appear. Similarly, the appreciation of specific aspects of fatty acid effects has led to changes in recommendations regarding their intake. At one time the entire emphasis was on polyunsaturated fat, but it was shown that this type of fat lowered both LDL and HDL cholesterol whereas monounsaturated fat (olive oil, for instance) reduced only the "bad" lipoprotein (LDL), leading to a more acceptable LDL-cholesterol/HDL-cholesterol ratio (Mattson and Grundy, 1985). These observations have led to support of the "Mediterranean diet," which is rich in monounsaturated fat but also contains more vegetables and fruit than does the present American diet.

In general terms, current recommendations suggest a diet containing 30 to 35 percent calories from fat with no more than 7 to 10 percent being saturated fat and about 30 to 40 percent carbohydrate, with adequate levels of dietary fiber. Liberal intakes of vegetables and fruit (five to seven servings per day) are also recommended as we begin to find that various plant constituents (carotenoids, flavonoids, phytosterols) may contribute to cardiovascular health. The role of caloric intake is not always addressed directly, but obesity is looked upon as a risk, and daily physical activity is encouraged (Krauss et al., 1996, 2001).

Our view of coronary disease keeps changing with new research findings. Whereas it was originally thought to be simply fat deposition, we now view it as an inflammatory process that can be stimulated by oxidized cholesterol and specific growth factors (Ross, 1993). The initial inflammation may be caused by viral or bacterial infection. The size of the LDL particle may be important; thus small, dense LDL particles may indicate increased risk even in the face of normal lipid levels (Krauss and Burke, 1982). Lipoprotein (a), a slightly altered LDL, affects blood clotting and may be an independent risk factor (Loscalzo, 1990).

The question of established and emerging risk factors has been addressed. The well-established, major risk factors continue to be cigarette smoking, hypertension, elevated serum cholesterol, elevated LDL cholesterol, low-HDL cholesterol, diabetes, and aging. Additional factors that predispose to coronary disease are family history of premature coronary disease (genetics), obesity, physical inactivity, and psychosocial factors (stress, for instance). Other risk factors are also beginning to appear—some are general and the causative actions of some are not clear. Among these are elevated serum homocysteine levels, first suggested over thirty years ago and possibly connected with metabolism of folic acid and vitamins B_6 and B_{12} (Malinow et al., 1999). C-reactive protein (CRP) is a general marker of inflammation produced in the liver in response to bacterial infection or physical trauma. The risk of coronary events is elevated in subjects with elevated levels of cholesterol and CRP (Ridker et al., 1999).Coronary heart disease is related to elevated serum lipids, diabetes, and obesity. All may be influenced by diet but the view of diet becomes more sophisticated and goes beyond dietary fat, although fat still plays a significant role. There is a plethora of risk factors of varying significance, and we still have no unequivocal indication of which subject's risk is affected by which particular factor.

Cancer

The role of fat in cancer has also been the subject of much research inquiry. In a classic study, Armstrong and Doll (1975) investigated the effects of diet on a number of cancers. Positive associations were found between total fat consumption and colorectal or breast tumors. Animal studies showed that a high-fat diet was more co-carcinogenic than a low-fat diet and that unsaturated fat was more co-carcinogenic than saturated fat. The latter result were due to the fact that linoleic acid is a growth factor for tumors (Carroll and Khor, 1971).

The data concerning fat and cancer risk are inconsistent. High intake of fat is a marker for a high-calorie diet and it is possible that it is the caloric contribution of fat rather than fat itself that is the culprit. Hoffman (1913) suggested that "erroneous diet" was a factor in the etiology of cancer. Excess body weight has been correlated with cancer mortality (Garfinkel, 1985). Animal studies dating to 1909 show that caloric restriction leads to reduced tumor growth. Lavik and Baumann (1943) showed that the incidence of methylcholanthrene-induced skin tumors in mice fed a diet high in fat but low in calories was 52 percent lower than that seen in mice fed a diet high in calories but low in fat. It has also been shown that incidence of dimethylbenz(a)anthracene induced mammary tumors in rats fed 5 percent fat ad libitum is lower than in rats fed a diet containing 20 percent fat but whose energy intake is restricted by 20 percent (Klurfeld et al., 1989).

Epidemiological studies have shown a positive correlation between energy intake and breast or colon cancer risk. The factors underlying the cancer-inhibiting effects of energy restriction are under study. Energy restriction leads to reduction in circulating insulin, and insulin is a growth factor for tumors. Energy restriction also reduced oncogene expression and leads to enhanced DNA repair (Kritchevsky, 1999a).

Diet

When all of the above has been said, the question each of us must answer remains, "What should I eat?" Dietary suggestions have ranged from the four food groups (meat, carbohydrates, dairy, and fruits and vegetables) to the United States Department of Agriculture (USDA) pyramid. The USDA pyramid is an attempt to illustrate which foods should be eaten in which amounts. The broad base of the pyramid represents large quantitites of grains and starches, and the narrow peak represents small quantities of fats and oils. Other dietary components are displayed between the peak and the base and their position in the pyramid represents the relative suggested levels of intake. The idea is to incorporate the best dietary information of the day into a healthful eating pattern. The "Dietary Guidelines for Americans" are written by select committees appointed by the United States Departments of Agriculture and Health and Human Services, and the publication is disseminated under their joint sponsorship. The guideline recommendations have changed relatively little in the past few decades, but the changes that appear reflect current findings and opinion. We are told to maintain ideal weight, although nobody is certain what that means. Originally we were advised to eat a diet that would provide protection against the ravages of infection, but now we are intent on protection against degenerative diseases, heart disease, and cancer, for which we have developed a catalog of risk factors but have no unequivocal diagnoses. Another general factor that we did not have to deal with in the past is the rise in obesity.

Vegetables and fruits provide chemicals that, in the laboratory, protect against cancer and heart disease and provide little or no fat. Grains are part of a healthful diet because they provide complex carbohydrate and fiber. Meat provides high-grade protein, necessary trace minerals (zinc, manganese, iron) and vitamin B_{12}, but fear of its fat content is reflected in advice to limit its consumption. Dietary fats are limited because of their caloric content, but they contain the essential fatty acids. Advice about dietary components is presented with the implied view that they are metabolized in a similar manner despite their quantity or presence of other nutrients in the diet. There is virtually no information concerning interaction of individual nutrients.

Fat is feared because of its caloric density and its connection with the risk of heart disease or cancer. The food industry is capable of producing foods that address current concerns. We have available a host of fat-free snacks, but their caloric content is rarely different from the fat-rich food they are replacing. Thus, influence on a risk may be diminished but there is no effect on body weight. Very low-fat diets are criticized as unhealthy. Diets high in carbohydrate may affect insulin metabolism, and there are some investigators who believe that insulin resistance may underlie both cancer and coronary disease.

General dietary advice—enough essential nutrients to maintain health—is constant but the specifics are distributed on an ad hoc basis depending on current knowledge. A case in point is the avocado. Thirty or so years ago this fruit was not recommended because of its fat content. Today we know the fat is monounsaturated ("good") and the avocado also contains generous quantities of various carotenoids. The avocado is now recommended by nutritionists everywhere. Fat content?—well, just don't eat too much of it. Carotenoids are a family of chemicals that occur in highly colored fruits and vegetables. Some may be precursors of vitamin A. The most common carotenoid is lycopene, which occurs in tomatoes.

To return to the specifics—namely, what we should eat—we still mean a "well-rounded" diet, to be taken in quantities that do not influence body weight. Suggestions to exercise regularly are also becoming part of dietary advice, again for purposes of weight control. Sugary snacks and sugar-rich beverages should be kept to a minimum. The ideal diet, in addition to its content, requires input from the consumer—namely, a measure of discipline.

Healthful diets go beyond "one size fits all." Growing children have different requirements than adults. The elderly may require different levels of various nutrients, and the active elderly have different needs than do the infirm elderly.

So we come down to the general advice of a little of everything but not too much of anything. The advice has to consider age, activity, and health status. Eating should be a pleasurable, social activity and not feared as the specific arbiter of life and death. The best advice for the average healthy person is variety, balance, and moderation. The watchword should be: Moderation, not Martyrdom.

See also **Assessment of Nutritional Status; Dietary Assessment; Dietary Guidelines; Disease: Metabolic Diseases; Fats; Intake; Mediterranean Diet; Nutrition; Vitamins**.

BIBLIOGRAPHY

Anitschkow, N. "Über die Veränderungen der Kaninchen Aorta bei experimenteller Cholesterinsteatose." *Beitrag Pathologische Anatomie und Allgemeine Pathologie* 56 (1913): 379–404.

Armstrong, B., and R. Doll. "Environmental Factors and Cancer Incidence and Mortality in Different Countries with Special Reference to Dietary Practice." *International Journal of Cancer* 15 (1975): 617–631.

Carroll, Kenneth K., and H. T. Khor. "Effect of Level and Type of Dietary Fat on Incidence of Mammary Tumors Induced in Female Sprague-Dawley Rats by 7,12-Dimethylbenz(a)anthracene." *Lipids* 6 (1971): 415–420.

Garfinkel, L. "Overweight and Cancer." *Annals of Internal Medicine* 103 (1985): 1034–1036.

Gertler, M. M., S. M. Garn, and P. D. White. "Serum Cholesterol and Coronary Artery Disease." *Circulation* 2 (1950): 696–702.

Gofman, J. W., et al. "The Role of Lipids and Lipoproteins in Atherosclerosis." *Science* 111 (1950): 155–171.

Gordon, T., et al. "Diet and Its Relation to Coronary Heart Disease in Three Populations." *Circulation* 63 (1981): 500–515.

Gurr, M. I., and J. L. Harwood. *Lipids Biochemistry: An Introduction*, 4th ed. London: Chapman and Hall, 1991.

Hegsted, D. M., R. B. McGandy, M. L. Myers, and F. J. Stare. "Quantitative Effects of Dietary Fat on Serum Cholesterol in Man." *American Journal of Clinical Nutrition* 17 (1965): 281–295.

Hoffman, F. L. "The Menace of Cancer." *American Journal of Obstetrics and Diseases of Women and Children* 68 (1913): 88–91.

Ignatowski, A. "Über die Wirkung des tierischen Eiweisses auf die Aorta und die parenchymatösen Organe der Kaninchen." *Virchow's Archiv für pathologische Anatomie und Physiologie und für Klinische Medizin* 198 (1909): 248–270.

Innis, S. M. "Essential Fatty Acids in Growth and Development." *Progress in Lipid Research* 30 (1991): 39–103.

Keys, A., J. T. Anderson, and F. Grande. "Serum Cholesterol Response to Changes in the Diet IV. Particular Saturated Fatty Acids in the Diet." *Metabolism* 14 (1965): 776–787.

Klurfeld, D. M., C. B. Welch, L. M. Lloyd, and D. Kritchevsky. "Inhibition of DMBA-Induced Mammary Tumorigenesis by Caloric Restriction in Rats Fed High Fat Diets." *International Journal of Cancer* 43 (1989): 922–925.

Krauss, R. M., and B. J. Burke. "Identification of Multiple Subclasses of Plasma Low Density Lipoproteins in Normal Humans." *Journal of Lipid Research* 23 (1982): 97–104.

Krauss, R. M., et al. "Dietary Guidelines for Healthy American Adults. A Statement for Health Professionals from the Nutrition Committee, American Heart Association." *Circulation* 94 (1996): 1795–1800.

Krauss, R. M., et al. "Revision 2000: A Statement for Healthcare Professionals from the Nutrition Committee of the American Heart Association." *Journal of Nutrition* 131 (2001): 132–146.

Kritchevsky, D. "Caloric Restriction and Experimental Carcinogenesis." *Toxicological Sciences* 52 (Suppl.) (1999a): 13–19.

Kritchevsky, D. "Trans Unsaturated Fat in Health and Disease." In *Lipids in Health and Nutrition*, edited by J. H. P. Tynan. Cambridge, U.K.: The Royal Society of Chemistry, 1999b, pp. 32–46.

Lavik, P. S., and C. A. Baumann. "Further Studies on the Tumor-Promoting Action of Fat." *Cancer Research* 3 (1943): 739–756.

Lichtenstein, A. H., and L. Van Horn. "Very Low Fat Diets." *Circulation* 98 (1998): 935–939.

Loscalzo, J. "Lipoprotein(a). A Unique Risk Factor for Atherothrombotic Disease." *Arteriosclerosis* 10 (1990): 672–679.

Malinow, M. R., A. G. Bostom, and R. M. Krauss. "Homocyst(e)ine, Diet, and Cardiovascular Diseases: A Statement for Healthcare Professionals from the Nutrition Committee, American Heart Association." *Circulation* 99 (1999): 178–182.

Mattson, F. H., and S. M. Grundy. "Comparison of Effects of Dietary Saturated, Monounsaturated, and Polyunsaturated Fatty Acids on Plasma Lipids and Lipoproteins in Man." *Journal of Lipid Research* 26 (1985): 194–202.

McMillan, G. C., M. D. Silver, and B. I. Weigensberg. "Elaidinized Olive Oil and Cholesterol Atherosclerosis." *Archives of Pathology* 76 (1963): 106–112.

Mcnamara, D. J., et al. "Heterogeneity of Cholesterol Homeostasis in Man: Responses to Changes in Dietary Fat Quality and Cholesterol Quantity." *Journal of Clinical Investigation* 79 (1987): 1729–1739.

McNamara, D. J. "Dietary Cholesterol and Atherosclerosis." *Biochimica et Biophysica Acta* 1529 (2000): 310–320.

Ridker, P. M., R. J. Glynn, and C. H. Hennekens. "C-reactive Protein Adds to the Predictive Value of Total and HDL Cholesterol in Determining Risk of First Myocardial Infarction." *Circulation* 97 (1998): 2007–2011.

Ross, R. "The Pathogenesis of Atherosclerosis: A Perspective for the 1990s." *Nature* 362 (1993): 801–809.

David Kritchevsky

LIQUOR. *See* **Alcohol; Cocktails; Spirits.**

LIVESTOCK PRODUCTION. Domesticated livestock have played a pivotal role in the development of human civilizations around the world and continues to be an integral part of human culture, society, and the local and global economy. Domestic livestock has contributed to the rise of human societies and civilizations by increasing the amount of food and nutrition available to people in four ways: by providing sources of meat, milk, and fertilizer, and by pulling plows. Throughout history livestock have also provided leather, wool, other raw materials, and transport.

Livestock furnish high quality protein and energy foods, and function as part of integrated, renewable systems of plant and animal agriculture. The digestive systems of ruminant animals such as cattle, sheep, goats, llamas, and camels are specially adapted to convert plant materials that humans cannot utilize into proteins of high biological availability to humans.

Livestock and the Origins of Civilization

In his Pulitzer-prize winning book *Guns, Germs, and Steel*, Jared Diamond describes how the availability and husbandry of domesticated plants and animals enabled prehistoric peoples to produce and store sufficient food supplies to develop large, dense societies that did not have to wander in search of food. Agriculture generated the ample, dependable food supply needed to develop specialized, stratified societies, political organization, writing, and technology. Diamond argues that through close coexistence with domestic animals, people in these societies acquired some immunity to epidemic diseases that devastated other populations. His examples include the Spanish conquest of the Inca and other Native American populations, and the near extermination of the Aboriginal peoples of Australia and other regions by British and other European settlers.

DEFINITION OF DOMESTICATED ANIMALS

Domesticated animals have been modified from their wild ancestors through being kept and selectively bred for use by humans who control the animals' breeding and feeding.

Just five major species of large, plant-eating mammals have been widely domesticated by people for use around the world: sheep, goat, cattle, pig, and horse. Another nine minor species have been domesticated for use in smaller numbers or in restricted geographical areas. These minor species include the Arabian and Bactrian camels, llama, alpaca, donkey, reindeer, water buffalo, yak, Bali cattle of Southeast Asia, and mithan (another bovine descended from the wild gaur) of India and Burma. Under domestication cows, sheep, and pigs have become smaller in size than their wild ancestors. Sheep and alpacas have been selectively bred for fleece characteristics, while cows have been bred to increase milk production. Pigs, cattle, and some sheep have been bred for meat quantity and characteristics. Horses have been bred for specialized purposes including work, war, speed, and riding. Breeds or strains of all the major species have been developed and adapted for specific climatic, physical, and cultural conditions and needs.

Many questions remain about the origins of agriculture, but in most regions archaeologists have found evidence that domestication of plants preceded that of animals by several hundred years. Yet the herding of sheep and goats had become integral to the local economy in areas of the central Levant between eight and nine thousand years ago.

The pastoral societies of Central Asia and reindeer-herding Lapps and Samoyeds of the Arctic are examples of cultures that domesticated livestock, but engaged in little or no cultivation of plants. Augustin Holl, a specialist on western Africa and the advent of food economies, believes pastoralism—herding of animals for food without cultivating plants—was the first form of food production developed by post-Paleolithic groups in regions of the Sahara. Cattle may have been domesticated around ten thousand years ago in Northern Africa.

Evolution of Domestic Livestock through Animal Husbandry

The ancient Romans developed sophisticated agricultural systems that integrated livestock and crop production, with particular attention to use of animal manures and

DID AN EARLY SYMBIOSIS OF COWS AND PEOPLE LEAD TO THE CIVILIZATION OF ANCIENT EGYPT?

Anthropologists Angela Close and Fred Wendorf (in *Transitions to Agriculture in Prehistory*) have uncovered a story—of humans and cattle surviving together where neither could likely have survived alone, in the harsh conditions of early Holocene Southeastern Sahara—that illustrates mutually beneficial relationships between humans and cattle. The cattle needed people to find and dig water sources in a region with no standing water. The humans could not have survived without the protein provided by the cattle. Archaeological evidence suggests the cattle were not kept for meat. The authors point out that wild or tame, animals do not have to cooperate with their slaughter for meat, but animals must cooperate for humans to collect animal milk or blood.

People and cattle were able to migrate together to a new area with more resources. Close and University of Rome anthropologist Barbara Barich maintain, as outlined in the January 2000 issue of *Discover*, that these Neolithic Saharans fleeing the desert brought the rudiments of agriculture and of organized, hierarchical society to the Nile Valley, giving rise to one of the earliest great world civilizations. This theory challenges old assumptions about the source of Ancient Egyptian culture and development, and has sparked considerable discussion among scholars in the field.

composts. They developed the art of animal husbandry and selectively bred well-determined breeds of livestock. Their capacity for food production enabled the building of the Roman Empire. Cattle were a significant source of wealth and prestige to the early Romans and to early Germanic peoples. *Pecunia*, the Latin word for money, comes from *pecus*, the word for cattle. The English word "fief" derives from the Old High German word for cattle, *fehu*, denoting the value of cattle for medieval noblemen. Life in the Middle Ages revolved around farming, as the majority of people lived off the land. When hunting became a privilege reserved for the nobility in medieval Europe, livestock became even more important as food sources. But compared to Roman practices, animal husbandry suffered decline during the fifth through the thirteenth centuries. Animals became smaller and less productive with the loss of Roman breeds and selective breeding techniques. Still, the lasting effects of Roman breeding kept medieval stock in the areas of the former Roman Empire superior to those in neighboring regions.

Bökönyi suggests deteriorating climate and crop conditions, changing lifestyles, and devastation of cattle populations by frequent wars as likely causes for the widespread dwarfing of livestock, most pronounced in cattle, which lost 20 centimeters in height at the withers. Beef was the primary meat consumed by the armies of Europe—the origin of the name Beefeaters for the king's guard. Soldiers drove off any cattle they did not eat.

Bökönyi notes that cattle typical of the early medieval era—small, slender, long-legged, and short-horned—are still found in areas of the Balkans, Anatolia, and the Near and Middle East where animal husbandry largely remains at a medieval level. Early medieval pigs were small, long-legged, and primitive, with skulls similar to the wild boar, with which they could interbreed since domestic pigs roamed freely, foraging in the forests. This approach to pig husbandry continued for centuries, and was common practice in colonial North America. Early medieval horses were more variable, with descendants of Roman horses mixed with large numbers of horses from the East. Horses were similar to modern Asian horses, with slender legs and light trunks. The first coldblood (heavy) horses were selectively bred in Central Europe to carry the weight of a knight in heavy armor.

The Renaissance of Animal Husbandry

The demographic expansion and rise of urban centers in the Middle Ages could not have happened without an increasingly productive agricultural base, Sweeney argues in his introduction to *Agriculture in the Middle Ages*. The Renaissance in Europe brought the reintroduction of intentional, conscious animal husbandry and breeding, based on classical sources. Farmers and scholars also began to rediscover the value of manure—well documented and practiced by the classical Romans—in fertilizing and rebuilding soils.

Livestock animals grew in size, and increased in productivity, efficiency, and quality. From the fourteenth century to the early modern era (later in Eastern Europe) cattle regained the twenty centimeters in height lost in the early Middle Ages. New breeds of lasting economic consequence were developed, and growth in trade, migration, and exploration brought new domestic species and breeds to various regions around the world. Improved breeds of sheep and cattle yielded higher quality wool and more milk. The excellent meat and stamina for long drives of Hungarian gray steppe cattle, the standard breed in Hungary and neighboring territories by the fourteenth and fifteenth centuries, gained the breed quick popularity through Central and Western Europe, Bökönyi reports.

Livestock and the Agricultural Revolution 1750–1880

The growth of animal husbandry—including greater use of manure from livestock as fertilizer, was the first of four factors contributing to the Agricultural Revolution that

TABLE 1

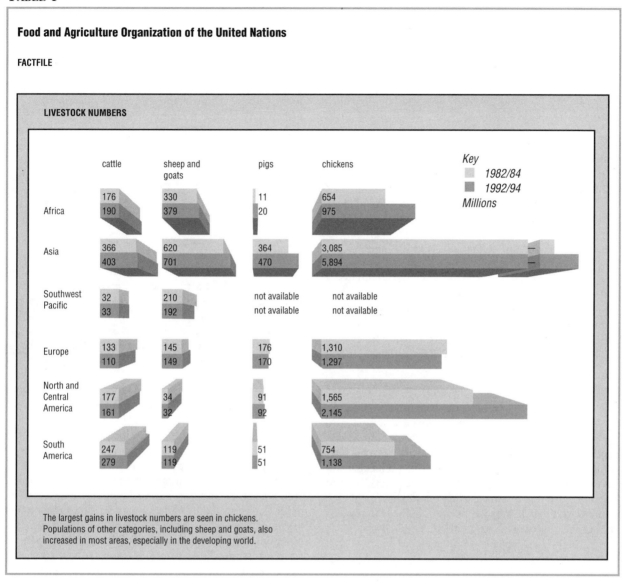

Food and Agriculture Organization of the United Nations

FACTFILE

LIVESTOCK NUMBERS

	cattle	sheep and goats	pigs	chickens
Africa	176 / 190	330 / 379	11 / 20	654 / 975
Asia	366 / 403	620 / 701	364 / 470	3,085 / 5,894
Southwest Pacific	32 / 33	210 / 192	not available / not available	not available / not available
Europe	133 / 110	145 / 149	176 / 170	1,310 / 1,297
North and Central America	177 / 161	34 / 32	91 / 92	1,565 / 2,145
South America	247 / 279	119 / 119	51 / 51	754 / 1,138

Key
1982/84
1992/94
Millions

The largest gains in livestock numbers are seen in chickens. Populations of other categories, including sheep and goats, also increased in most areas, especially in the developing world.

ended the cycles of dearth and hunger that had afflicted Europe for centuries (Chambers and Mingay, *The Agricultural Revolution*, p. 4). The Renaissance openness to scientific discoveries, new crops, improved animals, and the resulting productivity gains in agriculture, set the stage for the Agricultural and Industrial Revolutions and the rise of the great cities.

The spread of Merino sheep from Spain is an example. Before the end of the 1700s, Merinos were found throughout the sheep-breeding centers of Western and Central Europe. The first Merinos were brought to New England in 1811. Within two decades the Merino and related Saxony imports, prized for their long-fiber wool, dominated the rising New England woolen industry. Howard S. Russell describes how skilled breeders increased fleeces from only 6 percent of a sheep's live weight in 1812, to 21 percent by 1865 (*A Long Deep Furrow*, p. 352). Prize breeding stock from Vermont sold for prices in the thousands of dollars. Russell describes how the kinds and populations of domestic animals changed over time in response to market, economic, technological, and social trends and needs in a specific geographical region.

New fodder crops—legumes such as clover, and root vegetables such as turnips—greatly increased the supply and nutritive value of livestock feed. Improved feeding and selective breeding accelerated gains in meat, milk, and wool production. As late as the early 1700s, cattle and sheep—even castrated steers and wethers—took four to five years to fatten, or put meat on their bones. Improved feeding and breeding cut fattening time in half, and by 1800 progressive farmers recognized the value of quality breeding in livestock.

TWENTIETH CENTURY BRINGS BONANZA IN PRODUCTIVITY GAINS

The twentieth century brought stunning productivity gains, perhaps best illustrated by dairy farming. In 1905 New England was a center of dairy farming, with nearly one million dairy cows on farms throughout the six-state region (Russell, p. 496). In that era, cows produced an average 5,354 pounds of milk in a year. By 2001, the New England milk cow population had declined to 265,800 cows, just 3.1 percent of total U.S. dairy herd. But at over 17,500 pounds of milk per cow per year, the modern cows averaged more than three times the production of their ancestors a century earlier. In the 10 years from 1992 to 2001, milk per cow increased 16 percent in the U.S., while cow numbers declined 6 percent, resulting in a ten-percent increase in total milk production. Over this same ten-year period, the number of dairy farms in the United States decreased by 43 percent, from over 170,000 to fewer than 100,000 dairy farms. (See USDA graphics)

Progress in knowledge and husbandry skills led to specialization in livestock types and breeds, crops, and products. In the 1720s Daniel Defoe described in his *Tour of England and Wales* how farmers in different locales specialized in particular crops such as cereal grains, fruit or hops, on fattening livestock, or dairying. He reported on how the cow-herders of the village of Cheddar cooperated in making their already famous Cheddar cheese.

By 1800 agriculture had become specialized in areas of the United States. Southern New England and eastern New York were already dedicated to dairying, and Connecticut was a center of butter and cheese production and export. Progressive farmers and their associations began importing prize breeding stock from Europe in the early 1800s. Feeding and shelter for livestock improved, especially for milk cows.

Livestock in the Modern Era

Trends established by the late 1880s continue into the twenty-first century. Lower-priced imports of grain, dairy products, and meat kept prices low, even in times of crop failure, as in 1870s Britain. Yet escalating demand for meat, cheese, and other dairy products encouraged investment and expansion in livestock enterprises. Progress in the art and science of breeding, feeding, health, and care of livestock continues to bring gains in livestock productivity and efficiency. Transportation improvements allow the raising of food-producing animals at greater distances from population centers. Sheep, cattle,

and hog numbers have fluctuated in response to market demand changes and regional comparative advantages.

Government Protection of Animal and Human Health

To combat severe outbreaks of sheep-rot and of cattle plague (rinderpest) brought by infected cattle imported from Europe in the 1860s and 1870s, the British government restricted the movement of animals and compensated owners for animals slaughtered to control the spread of the diseases, programs first tried in the mid 1700s. In the first half of the 1900s the United States intervened to eradicate livestock diseases such as hog cholera, tuberculosis, and brucellosis in cattle that were transmissible to humans. These tactics remain mainstays of animal disease control efforts.

Commercial pasteurization, introduced in 1895, greatly increased the safety of milk. Improvements in refrigeration and containers further enhanced milk's safety and shelf-life. The serial publication in 1905 of *The Jungle*, Upton Sinclair's muckraking novel about the meat-packing industry, helped lead to government regulation of the food industry. The U.S. Congress passed both the Pure Food and Drug Act and the Meat Inspection Act in 1906, the beginning of federal food safety inspection and regulatory programs.

Modern Agricultural Trends and the Environment

In response to market demands for lower-cost production, livestock agriculture continues the trend to fewer and larger operations. The U.S. poultry industry became highly intensive and vertically integrated in the last quarter of the twentieth century, with a handful of companies dominating the industry and contracting with growers to raise flocks owned by the companies. The swine industry is experiencing similar restructuring and vertical integration. Intensification and specialization has separated crop production from livestock-raising in many regions, resulting in heightened concerns about environmental impacts, primarily related to manure runoff into water bodies in some areas of Europe and North America. Soil fertility, health, and structure have deteriorated in some crop-intensive areas from lack of livestock manure.

The United States and Europe have increased technical assistance and environmental regulation of livestock operations in response to these concerns. The Clean Water Act legislation of 1972 and 1977 set higher standards of water quality. Less-developed countries have not evolved regulatory or technical assistance programs to address livestock-related pollution.

Sustainable agriculture advocates have sought ways to reintegrate and balance animals and crops to promote soil health and protect natural resources, and have promoted the environmental benefits of practices such as intensively managed grazing. Some dairy, beef, sheep, and other livestock producers have adopted these scientific grazing systems in major livestock-producing regions including North America, Europe, Australia, and New Zealand. Government farm programs and subsidies have been increasingly linked to plans and practices to protect soil, water, and wetlands.

Global Livestock Expansion and Trade

World meat production including poultry totaled 236,991,142 metric tons in 2001, according to the Food and Agriculture Organization of the United Nations. The United States produced 16 percent of the world supply, and the European Union produced 15 percent, while the nations of the Far East produced 35 percent. World milk production in 2001 was 584,651,111 metric tons. The European Union produced over one-fifth, and the United States produced one-eighth of the world milk supply.

China is one of the world's top producers of hogs, beef, poultry, corn, and soybeans. The U.S. Department of Agriculture's February 2002 Agricultural Baseline Projections projected strong growth for the next decade in world beef production, especially in China, Mexico, Canada, and the countries of the former Soviet Union. Brazil, Mexico, China, and Canada are expected to expand pork production. In 2001 Russia was the world's top volume importer of poultry meat, second-highest of pork, and third-highest importer of beef. But Russia, Ukraine, and Kazakhstan have the resource potential to develop into agricultural powerhouses once they establish market economies.

Australia's small population offers a limited market, but its low-cost production capacity limited only by water gives it a competitive advantage in export markets. Australia's herds and flocks fluctuate dramatically in response to world markets.

Brazil and Argentina are major livestock and feed producers. Argentina's exports were temporarily set back by a foot and mouth disease outbreak in 2001. Brazil is expanding livestock production capacity and adopting new technology to increase yields.

Saudi Arabia, Egypt, and Iran import grain to support expanding livestock production. Most Moslem countries prefer meat from home-grown livestock to ensure animals are slaughtered in accordance with Islamic rites.

The U.S. Department of Agriculture expects global trade in livestock products will continue to expand, based on ample global supplies and steady growth in demand. Livestock production is expanding globally to meet demand for meat and dairy products in the growing economies of Asia and Latin America. Livestock development will continue to be a part of economic progress in the developing world.

See also **Cattle**; **Goat**; **Mammals**; **Meat**; **Pig**; **Sheep**.

BIBLIOGRAPHY

Chambers, J. D., and George E. Mingay. *The Agricultural Revolution 1750–1880*. New York: Schocken Books, 1966.

Dal Maso, Cinzia. "Stonehenge in the Desert," *Galileo*, April 18, 1998. Found at galileonet.it/galileo_eng/archivio/mag/980418/2_art.html.

Defoe, Daniel. *A Tour through England and Wales*. London: Everyman's Library, 1928.

Diamond, Jared. *Guns, Germs, and Steel: The Fates of Human Societies*. New York and London: Norton, 1997.

Gebauer, Anne Birgitte, and T. Douglas Price., eds. *Transitions to Agriculture in Prehistory*. Madison, Wis.: Prehistory Press, 1992.

Holl, Augustin. "The Dawn of African Pastoralisms," Special Issue – *Journal of Anthropological Archaeology* 17, no. 2 (1998).

Kunzig, Robert. "Exit from Eden," *Discover* 21, no. 1 (January 2000): 84-96.

Russell, Howard S. *A Long, Deep Furrow: Three Centuries of Farming in New England*. Hanover, N.H.: University Press of New England, 1976.

Sweeney, Del, ed. *Agriculture in the Middle Ages: Technology, Practice, and Representation*. Philadelphia: University of Pennsylvania Press, 1995.

United Nations Food and Agriculture Organization, FAOSTAT Agriculture Data, Agricultural Production: Livestock Primary. Found at: http://apps.fao.org/cgi-bin/nph-db.pl?subset=agriculture.

Westcott, Paul. Agricultural Baseline Projections February 2002, U.S. Department of Agriculture Economic Research Service, Staff Report WAOB-2002–1. Washington, D.C.: U.S. Department of Agriculture Economic Research Service, 2002.

Lorraine Stuart Merrill

LOW COUNTRIES, THE. At the beginning of the twenty-first century, twelve Belgian restaurants operated in New York City, but only one Dutch restaurant planned an opening. Historically tied together, Belgium and the Netherlands nevertheless developed dissimilar cuisines. During the fifteenth century the area subsequently divided between the two countries became part of the holdings of the powerful duke of Burgundy. With the death of Charles V in 1555, Belgium became a possession of the Spanish Crown. It was part of the Habsburg Empire from the beginning of the seventeenth century until the Napoleonic age. After the revolution of 1578 the Netherlands was an independent republic, confirmed as such in 1648 by the Treaty of Westphalia. In 1813 the two countries were united under King Willem I, which lasted until 1831, when the Netherlands and Belgium, where Flemish, a Dutch dialect, and French are spoken, became separate monarchies. Although the two countries share the Dutch language, they have made different culinary contributions. Belgium's kitchen, akin to the French, is known for its exuberant bistro-style foods that became popular in the United States. The Netherlands' cuisine is more staid, but the country exports fine food products, such as vegetables and cheeses, sought all over the world.

The Middle Ages and the Renaissance

The first printed cookbook in the Dutch language was *Een Notabel Boecxken van Cokeryen* (A notable little book of cookery). It was published circa 1514, during the time the Low Countries were part of the Burgundian Empire under the reign of Maximilian of Habsburg. The presumed author and publisher is Thomas van der Noot, who belonged to one of the prominent Brussels families.

The book was meant for the well-to-do, the nobility and the high-placed clergy, who could afford the expensive foodstuffs called for in the recipes. As was common for cookbooks at that time, many of the 170 or so recipes were copied from other authors. In this case they were copied especially from the famous French cookbook of the period, Taillevent's *Le Viandier*. The Dutch book includes sauces; fish dishes; ways to prepare meat, poultry, and game, including peacock and pheasant; raised pies; tarts; sweets; and eggs. The recipes are clearly divided into dishes for everyday and those for the church-ordained days of fasting and abstinence, when meat, dairy products, and eggs were forbidden. This prohibition encompassed altogether about 150 days in a year, when only fish, vegetables, and bread were permitted.

Eggs were particularly popular. Said to be the poor person's supper, they often were barely cooked and were slurped from the shell. Milk was cooked in porridges or custards, some of which were given a pastry base. Milk was preserved as cheese and butter. Unlike in southern Europe, in the Low Countries butter rather than oil was used as a cooking medium.

Several kinds of cheese made of cow's and sheep's milk were marketed in the fourteenth and fifteenth centuries. Cheeses were usually named for the places they came from. The Netherlands is known for its cheeses from the cities of Gouda and Edam. Gouda cheese is made from milk with cream, while Edam-style cheeses are made from skimmed milk and are sometimes flavored with cumin, as in Leyden cheese. By the end of the eighteenth century cumin was replaced in the north by cloves to create Frisian *nagelkaas*. Sheep cheeses were popular early on. Often colored green with sheep feces, these cheeses came from the island of Texel or from 's-Gravenzande. As breeding improved and cows produced more milk, more recipes called for milk products, including homemade ricottalike cheeses.

Pork, particularly the fatty parts, was the favorite meat of all classes. Pigs were kept everywhere and generally roamed free. In the fall families who could afford it would purchase a cow that was slaughtered and preserved for winter through salting and smoking.

Cattle, particularly oxen, were imported from Denmark and Schleswig-Holstein in northern Germany. They were herded or transported by ship to Holland for grazing and fattening for slaughter in the grassy meadows of that province. Chickens, ducks, and geese were the common poultry, although songbirds were eaten as well. Deer, goats, and wild boars were among the large game animals hunted, whereas rabbits, pheasants, bitterns, cranes, swans, herons, and ducks were considered small game. The hunt was the privilege of nobility. Falcons and sparrow hawks were trained to catch partridge, geese, ducks, kites, doves, or any other fowl. By the fifteenth century game was reserved more for special occasions than for the daily table of the nobility.

It is often implied that medieval people strongly seasoned their foods because the meats were generally spoiled. That is an unlikely premise. People knew how to preserve foods by drying, smoking, and salting and many regulations concerned the sale of meat. Seasoning was instead more a matter of taste. Spices from the Orient, such as pepper, nutmeg, cloves, and cinnamon, were introduced by way of Venice and became a status symbol for the well-to-do. These spices were mixed with sour verjuice (juice from unripe grapes) or apple juice and some locally grown herbs such as parsley, sage, or savory. They gave the dishes a sharply spiced and sour taste that was popular.

Little is known about the food of the masses. Much of what is known about the food of the period comes from records of the elaborate banquets of the nobility on the occasions of weddings, victories, or coronations. These extravagant medieval feasts consisted of several courses, each with ten or more dishes, and were known for their between-course happenings. For example, at one of Philips of Burgundy's banquets, an entire orchestra stepped out of a raised pie and started to play.

Fishery was as important to the food supply as to the economy. In the fifteenth century, when the schools of herring moved from the Sont, the strait between Denmark and Sweden, to near the English coast, the Dutch herring fishery bloomed. The development of cleaning and salting herring onboard ship made the fish less perishable. Consequently herring became not only a folk food but also another major trade good for the Low Countries. The salt, which was needed in large quantities not only for preserving herring but also for preserving meat, was imported from France and Portugal. Dried cod, imported from Bergen, Norway, was the main fish eaten by all classes and an important food for the days of fasting and abstinence.

From the rivers the abundant eel were harvested, as were carp, pike, and bream. These were the fish for the more affluent, while the poor and the working classes ate dried plaice, flounder, or whiting. Among its forty or so fish recipes, *Een Notabel Boecxken* describes how to make a brown sauce for a freshly boiled carp. The cooking liquid is mixed with *lebkuchen* (a chewy honey cake), vinegar, and wine and seasoned with ginger, cinnamon, rosemary, quite a bit of sugar, and a little salt.

Castles and cloisters were the centers of horticulture during the Middle Ages. Their gardens provided vegetables, herbs, fruits, and nuts. When, in the second half of the fifteenth century, the sand dunes near Haarlem were removed, fertile grounds became available for horticulture. Through the increased mercantile influence of the large towns, such as Antwerp and Amsterdam, with their expanding markets, horticulture started to flourish beyond castles and cloisters, and by the sixteenth century the Netherlands was known all over Europe for its vegetables. Seeds were cultivated under glass to extend the growth period. Gheeraert Vorselman's *Eenen Nyeuwen Coock Boeck* (A new cookbook) of 1560 was the first to publish salad and vegetable recipes in the Low Countries.

In the Middle Ages, wheat, rye, barley, oats, peas, and beans were grown, but even in the beginning of the period the Netherlands did not grow enough grain to supply its inhabitants. The grain trade developed early on, and by the fifteenth century it was concentrated in Amsterdam. Bread was the mainstay of the diet. It was prepared by bakers, who were organized in powerful guilds. As early as 1341 the government set regulations on bread content, weight, and price. The more expensive wheat bread (called white bread) was eaten by the affluent. Rye bread (called black bread) was the common food for the poor until the second half of the nineteenth century, when through improved transportation methods American wheat, cheaper than the local rye, was imported. At that time wheat bread became the common bread for all.

Beer was the common drink, wine was for the well-to-do, and buttermilk was popular on farms. Beer was brewed at home, but by the fourteenth century the cities of Haarlem and Amersfoort had famous breweries. Cloisters were often known for their brews, and some of the famous Belgian beers hail back to that tradition. The sweeter and less-perishable wines from the Mediterranean countries were popular with the upper classes. The mostly young and white wines, imported from France and Germany, were at that time sour, so they were mixed with honey and spices, such as cloves, coriander, cinnamon, and ginger, to make a drink like hippocras that was enjoyed at the end of a large meal.

Abundant feasts at times of plenty contrasted with the famines of the Middle Ages that wiped out large parts of the population. The Dutch were true trencherpeople who ate and drank immoderately at parties and banquets for guild celebrations; weddings; births, where they would "drown the child"; or funerals, called in jest "grave weddings." Paintings by Brueghel and others depict such events. But the regular meal pattern consisted at most of two meals a day. The main meal, two dishes, was served around eleven in the morning, and the evening meal was one dish. Bread; cheese; root vegetables, like parsnips, carrots, and turnips; cabbage; garlic; onions; peas and beans; fruit in season; porridge; eggs; and a little meat or fish when available were the main foodstuffs.

Mealtimes shifted toward the end of the Middle Ages, when increasingly people ate breakfast. Before meals a water pitcher, a bowl, and a towel or napkin were provided for washing the hands. The plates were first made of bread, then wood, and later tin. The table was covered with a cloth, and bread and salt were placed upon it. The fingers, spoons, or knives were used for eating as the fork was not yet in fashion.

A major change in eating habits came after the Protestant Reformation in the middle of the sixteenth century, when the northern Netherlands largely embraced the Protestant faith as preached by John Calvin and the southern Netherlands remained Catholic. It may be assumed that the Calvinists stopped the days of abstinence immediately, though they continued to eat fish on Friday. Meeting the obligation not to eat meat and dairy products on many days of the year was difficult and expensive. Some medievalists hold that this might be one of the contributing causes of the Reformation's success.

The Seventeenth Century
The seventeenth century brought prosperity. Both the East India and the West India Companies were founded in its first quarter. Dutch ships brought spices from the Dutch East Indies (now Indonesia) and sugar first from Brazil and then from plantations in the West Indies. Exotic plants, like the pineapple, arrived from every port where Dutch ships docked. With more food available, consumption increased, and the common meal pattern grew to four meals a day. Breakfast consisted of bread

NEW NETHERLAND

The history of the colony New Netherland begins in 1609. In that year Henry Hudson explored the river that bears his name on behalf of the Dutch East India Company with the aim of finding a northern passage to the Orient. Hudson's explorations established the Dutch claim to a vast area from the Connecticut River to the Delaware Bay. In 1621 the Dutch States General granted a charter with exclusive trading rights in the Western Hemisphere to the Dutch West India Company. In 1626 the island of Manhattan was purchased and settlement began. In 1664 the English took over New Netherland, and with the exception of a brief interlude in 1673–1674, the area remained in British hands until the American Revolution. Yet in only seven brief decades the persistent Dutch settlers entrenched their culture in the country.

Americans eat dishes that can be traced back to the foodways brought by early Dutch settlers. The practical merchants who formed the West India Company intended that the colony should be not only self-sufficient but also able to provision the company's officials and ships engaged in the fur trade and in trade with the West Indies. The settlers brought fruit trees, such as apples, pears, and peaches; vegetables, such as lettuces, cabbages, parsnips, carrots, and beets; and herbs, such as parsley, rosemary, chives, and tarragon. In addition they brought farm animals, such as horses, pigs, and cows. Aboard ship the animals had their own stalls, and often each had an attendant, who would get a bonus when the animal arrived safely.

The new land was fertile. Jacob Steendam, one of the three major Dutch-American poets of New Netherland, called the colony "a land of milk and honey." Adriaen van der Donck, who wrote *A Description of the New Netherlands* (1655) to entice his fellow citizens to settle in the new colony, also was impressed with its fertility. He reports that by the middle of the seventeenth century all sorts of European fruits and vegetables "thrive well" and marvels at the native fish, fowl, and other wildlife available in great abundance.

Trade with the Indians was an important aspect of life in New Netherland. The Dutch traded cloth, beads, and ironware, such as axes and cooking kettles, for beaver skins. The Dutch also used their baking skills to produce breads, sweet breads, and cookies to trade with the Native Americans. The Indians valued the wheat bread of the Dutch, which previously had been unknown to them. Harmen Meyndertsz van den Bogaert relates in his diary of 1634–1635 that, when he was more than a day's walk away from Fort Orange, a Mohawk Indian who had just come from the fort offered him a piece of wheat bread. An ordinance for Fort Orange and the village of Beverwijck (now Albany) forbade further baking of bread and cookies for the Indians. Evidently the bakers were using so much flour for this Indian trade that not enough was left to bake bread for the Dutch community. A record survives of a court case in which a baker was fined because "a certain savage" was seen coming out of his house "carrying an oblong sugar bun."

In their new country the colonists continued to prepare the dishes they were used to. Ship records confirm that the West India Company ships brought them kitchen tools, such as frying pans for pancakes or irons for hard and soft waffles. The settlers tried to duplicate life in the Netherlands in New Netherland. However, while they continued their own foodways, they incorporated native foods into their daily diets but in ways that were familiar to them. For instance, they made pumpkin cornmeal pancakes, made pumpkin sweetmeat, or put cranberries instead of the usual raisins and apples in their favorite *oliekoecken.* For lovers of porridge, it was easy to get used to *sappaen,* Indian cornmeal mush, but the Dutch added milk to it. This dish became such an integral part of the Dutch-American diet that it is mentioned on an 1830 menu for the Saint Nicholas Society at the American Hotel in Albany under the heading of "National Dishes." Although many descendants forgot the native tongue, they did not forget the foods of their forebears, and they continued to enjoy the pastries and other dishes connected with feasts and holidays into the twenty-first century. Cookies; pancakes; waffles; *oliekoecken,* a forerunner of doughnuts; pretzels; and coleslaw are among the items the Dutch colonists imported into to America. Vestiges from those original foodways remained in the American kitchen.

and butter or cheese. The noon meal became a stew of meat and vegetables or fish with a dish of fruit, cooked vegetables, honey cake, or raised pie. The afternoon meal of bread and butter or cheese was served a few hours later. Just before people went to bed they ate leftovers from noon, bread and butter or cheese, or a porridge. The poor had a more meager diet.

With the fortunes made in the overseas trade, well-to-do families built country houses away from their city houses, which were usually their places of business also. Country houses had gardens with fruits and vegetables for home consumption and plants from far-away lands. For example, corn was grown as an ornamental and was used in flower bouquets, as still lifes testify. The definitive cookbook of the seventeenth century, *De Verstandige Kock* (The sensible cook), published by an anonymous author in 1667, gives recipes for the homegrown bounty. The book starts with recipes for salads, which were eaten before the meal "to open the stomach." It gives a full range of recipes for greens; meat; game; poultry; salted, smoked, and dried fish; fresh saltwater and freshwater fish; baked goods; raised pies; and tarts. Separate chapters on preserving meat and fruits end the volume. This was a cookbook for the rapidly developing, affluent burgher class, which, since the nobility had comparatively little influence, was the leading segment of Dutch society. While the peasant diet consisted mostly of bread, milk dishes, vegetables, and meat, the middle classes ate a plentiful diet of varied foods.

The people of the Low Countries were known for their love of sweets. Such treats as sweet breads, like honey cake or gingerbread; or confections, like marzipan, candied almonds, or cinnamon bark, were consumed in addition to the daily fare. Like cheese, Dutch *koek* (*Kuchen* in German) or honey cake was named for its city of origin. By the fourteenth and fifteenth centuries Deventer *koek* from the town of Deventer in the eastern part of the country was famous all over the Netherlands. An important component of the Saint Nicholas celebration on 6 December was another special kind of *koek* named for its chewy texture, *taai taai* or tough dough. All of these cakes were made by professional bakers, who protected their recipes and were united in guilds. Waffles, wafers, and *olie-koecken*, deep-fried balls of dough with raisins, apples, and almonds, were some of the celebratory foods prepared at home, but they were also sold on the streets, as the contemporary artists portrayed.

In the second half of the seventeenth century tea and coffee were introduced, and they had a significant impact on meal patterns and social customs. The East India Company brought tea to the Netherlands first from Japan, then from China through Chinese merchants situated in Batavia. An early shipment in 1610 was considered a curiosity, but as shipments gradually increased, domestic markets developed. Preparing tea required its own paraphernalia, such as small porcelain teacups and small teapots, which were also imported from the Orient. Using a small teapot, an extract of tea was brewed that was diluted with boiling water when served. The small teapots remained in fashion until the nineteenth century, when, according to the English custom, tea was brewed at the required strength directly in a large teapot. Teacups did not have handles until the eighteenth century. Many humorous tales relate the enormous number of cups drunk at the popular late-century tea parties. One woman, admonished by her husband that it was time to go home, told him she could not leave yet because she had only had twenty cups. Tea was served with sweets, like hard candies, marzipan, cookies, and particularly an Utrecht specialty called *theerandjes* (tea cookies), which were strongly spiced

small gingerbread slices. The third meal of the day, which earlier in the century had consisted of bread and butter, was incorporated into the tea ritual and was moved to a later time in the afternoon.

While tea drinking, for which women would gather in the afternoon, had a certain air of high society and snob appeal, coffee was the more public drink. Coffee was consumed in coffeehouses, where men stopped in to have a cup, smoke a pipe, and read the paper. Stefanus Blankaert, an Amsterdam physician and author of a 1686 book on diet, commented on the crowds visiting the coffeehouses in his city. At the end of the century it became the custom of the wealthy to furnish their guests with eating implements, not only a knife and spoon but also a fork. However, it took several decades for the fork to be accepted generally. As late as 1733 a leading journalist argued against its use because, according to a contemporary saying, "God has given us fingers."

The Eighteenth Century

The eighteenth century marked greater sophistication in recipes and more variety in dishes offered at one meal. *De Volmaakte Hollandse Keuken Meid* (The perfect Dutch kitchen maid) of 1761 describes in detail how to serve the customary succession of three courses, each consisting of at least ten dishes, and how to place each dish on the table. It was so popular that in 1838 it was reprinted as *De Volmaakte Belgische Keuken Meid* (The perfect Belgian kitchen maid), an updated version that included a section on potato recipes. With some twenty editions spanning the second half of the century, *La Cuisine bourgeoise* (1753) by Menon is an important part of Belgian culinary history.

Fish rather than meat was an important food for the common folk, but oysters and mussels were foods of the rich except in those areas with ready access, such as the Belgian provinces and Zeeland. Game was still the food for nobility, but rabbits became more commonly available.

The more affluent kitchens increased their use of vegetables, including nettles and watercress, abundantly available in rivers and streams. The Italian broccoli was cultivated and was preferred over white cauliflower. Although Carolus Clusius, the founder of the extant botanical garden of Leiden, mentioned the potato plant as early as 1601, potatoes did not enter the popular cuisine until the second half of the eighteenth century. At that time crop failures had made grain expensive and scarce, and cattle diseases had created a lack of milk products. The potato took up the slack and became the most important foodstuff of the poor person's diet. Not until the Napoleonic age, when the economy was failing, did the upper classes include potatoes in their main meals. That was also when the custom developed of not eating bread when potatoes were served. In Dutch restaurants the bread is removed when the main course is served.

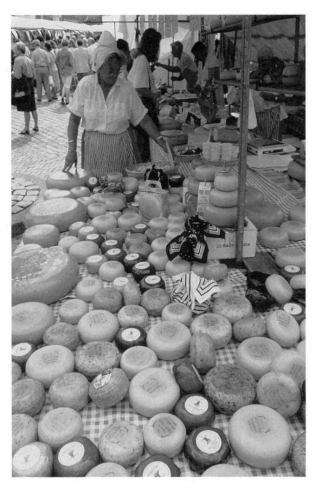

Market stall selling traditional Dutch cheeses in Gouda, the Netherlands. © OWEN FRANKEN/CORBIS.

Desserts and treats were presented in even greater variety in the eighteenth century. *De Volmaakte Hollandse Keuken Meid* offers a recipe for a luxurious double-crust pie filled with sliced oranges, sprinkled with sugar and cinnamon, and topped with a layer of chopped pistachio nuts. The same volume includes a vast assortment of cookies and sweets, presumably served with tea. The first famous version of the centuries-old *koek* was a simple mixture of rye, honey, spices, and the secret addition of leavening potash made from wood ash imported from the Baltic to make the heavy dough rise. By the seventeenth century *koek* was made all over the Netherlands. The northern parts of Groningen and Friesland were known particularly for their spiced honey cakes with candied citrus fruit peel. But in 1751 the first pastry book, Gerrit van den Brenk's *T'Zaamenspraaken Tusschen een Mevrouw, Banket-bakker en Confiturier* (A dialogue between a lady, a pastry baker, and a confectioner), finally revealed a professional baker's secrets and gave helpful insights into its preparation. By 1750 sugar had overtaken honey as the general sweetener. By that time chocolate had become a

popular drink at home, especially on Saturday and Sunday evenings. Fruit, though seasonal, was eaten by all classes.

The Nineteenth Century

An even wider difference between the diets of the middle classes and the poor is evident in the nineteenth century. By the end of the century the well-to-do ate meat once or twice a week; only rarely did the worker have meat or, for that matter, fish. An 1869 peat worker's family ate mainly potatoes, rye bread, buckwheat flour, barley, rice, some melted fat, oil, and butter and went without wheat bread, meat, eggs, cheese, or vegetables. They drank a little milk and some coffee. Such unhealthy conditions raised enough concern by midcentury that charitable groups began to establish soup kitchens to provide food for the poor.

The nineteenth century also produced mechanical inventions and a wider selection of cookbooks. Cheese and butter making had been the province of women, but in the 1860s machines took over the work. A machine was invented for kneading rye bread, which up to then, because of its heavy structure, had been kneaded with the feet. While Belgium's most important cookbook of the time, *L'économie culinaire*, written by a Ghent caterer in 1861, enjoyed multiple editions, the main cookbook in the Netherlands, Philippe-Édouard Cauderlier's *Aaltje, de Volmaakte en Zuinige Keukenmeid* (Aaltje, the perfect and frugal kitchen maid), spanned the entire nineteenth century. First published in 1803, it was reissued in 1893. This book presented for the first time the mashed one-pot dishes and the typically Dutch menus of meat, vegetable, and potatoes followed by a dessert made with milk.

Until the nineteenth century the sugar beet was used as cattle feed. But during the Napoleonic age, when the supply of sugar cane was interrupted, the emperor encouraged the fabrication of sugar from sugar beets. By 1812 fourteen such factories operated, but after Napoleon's defeat they disappeared until later in the century.

Changes occurred as well in the general use of beverages. Beer lost its popularity and was replaced with coffee, particularly in the eastern and southern provinces. Tea was more popular in the west, where both beverages were served. The use of *jenever* (juniper-flavored gin) increased dramatically among the working classes, and even hospital personnel received a daily ration of *jenever*. The affluent still drank wine.

The Twentieth Century

After the industrial revolution and two world wars, the customary meal pattern changed to three meals a day, including breakfast and lunch, of which bread was the major component, and one hot meal in the evening. Coffee breaks in the morning and tea breaks in the afternoon became the common interruptions of the workday. Snack foods, especially French fries and soda, readily available from corner snack shops or street carts, were consumed anytime. Holiday foods still included *taai taai* and *oliekoecken* (*oliebollen* in modern Dutch). Indonesian restaurants, serving the well-known *rijsttafel* (rice table), became especially popular after World War II. In the year 2000 cosmopolitan restaurants, including America's McDonald's and Pizza Hut, reflected the Dutch trade interests in most countries in the world.

At the end of the nineteenth century and the beginning of the twentieth century, the interest in wholesome foods and the plight of the masses prompted the founding of so-called household schools in both the Netherlands and Belgium. Household schools were intended to instruct working-class housewives in a proper family diet. A better-fed worker could produce more work. But because working-class women had to work, daughters of the middle classes, who were expected to stay home and tend their families as adults, attended these institutions. The teachers did not adjust their curricula or their recipes to the new, higher-class audience. With the goal to simplify and improve, they took away much of the charm, the joy, and some say the taste of the good, centuries-old Dutch burgher kitchen described above. The aim was to create recipes that were considered nutritious and healthful with the right combination of protein, fat, and carbohydrates. Martine Wittop Koning's *Eenvoudige Berekende Recepten* (Simple calculated recipes, 1901), which went through sixty-two editions, is a prime example. In addition, rather than instructing their students in home cooking from scratch, the teachers encouraged and popularized time-saving, factory-made products in both their classrooms and their cookbooks. The influence of the household schools lasted through several generations, until at least the 1960s. These developments coupled with ever increasing agricultural mechanization and industrialization of food production might explain the demise of the Dutch burgher kitchen. The Netherlands' renowned and outspoken food writer Johannes van Dam also cited them as the explanation for the Netherlands' lesser status as a culinary power. Others look to the lingering trend to think that "one eats to live" coupled with the Calvinist spirit, which frowns on earthly pleasures. Yet others indicate the Dutch commercial inclinations to sell the best products and keep the lesser quality for use at home. The fact remains that, while Dutch foodstuffs are highly sought after and are sold all over the world, its restaurants are not well known.

In contrast, the Belgian kitchen remained true to its French-inspired original. Belgian restaurants have achieved the coveted three-star Michelin status on more than one occasion. Nika Hazelton in *The Belgian Cookbook* (1970) lauds home cooking from scratch. She savors the fish soup from Ghent called waterzooi and marvels at mussels *marinière* with white wine, butter, lemon, and parsley. She cannot stop talking about the *friture* or deep-fried foods, particularly French fries, and she toasts the cuisine with a smooth Bruges wheat beer or a Brussels *geuze lambiek*.

The generous custom of treating friends on a person's own birthday rather than being treated is the origin of the expression "Dutch treat." Both countries, Belgium with its restaurants, artisan-made beers, and melt-in-the-mouth chocolates, and the Netherlands with its horticultural products, beers, cocoa, and cheeses, bring the world a true Dutch treat.

BIBLIOGRAPHY

Aaltje, de Volmaakte en Zuinige Keukenmeid [Aaltje, the perfect and frugal kitchen maid]. Amsterdam: J. B. Elwe and J. R. Werlingshoff, 1803.

Bogaert, Harmen Meyndertsz van den. *A Journey into Mohawk and Oneida Country, 1634–1635*. Edited and translated by Charles T. Gehring and William A. Starna. Syracuse, N.Y.: Syracuse University Press, 1991.

Burema, Lambertus. *De Voeding in Nederland van de Middeleeuwen tot de Twintigste Eeuw* [Food in the Netherlands from the Middle Ages to the twentieth century]. Assen, Netherlands: Van Gorcum, 1953.

Cauderlier, Philippe-Édouard. *L'économie culinaire* [The culinary economy]. Ghent, Belgium: De Busscher Frères, 1861.

Dagelijks Leven op Limburgse Kastelen (1350–1600): Voeding en Voedselbereiding [Daily life in Limburg castles (1350–1600): food and food preparation]. Limburg: Limburgs Museum, 1995.

Hazelton, Nika. *The Belgian Cookbook*. New York: Atheneum, 1970.

Holland and Belgium at the Table. Round the World Cooking Library. Amsterdam: Meijer Pers B.V., 1974.

Jansen-Sieben, Ria, and Johanna Maria van Winter, eds. *De keuken van de Late Middeleeuwen* [The kitchen of the late Middle Ages]. Amsterdam: B. Bakker, 1989.

Jobse-van Putten, Jozien. *Eenvoudig Maar Voedzaam* [Simple but nourishing]. Amsterdam: P. J. Meertens-Instituut, 1995.

Kalm, Pehr. *Peter Kalm's Travels in North America: The English Version of 1770*. Edited by Adolph B. Benson. 2 vols. New York: Dover, 1966.

Menon. *La Cuisine bourgeoise* [The burgher kitchen]. Brussels: Francois Foppens, 1753.

Molen, J. R. ter. *Thema Thee: De Geschiedenis van de Thee en het Theegebruik in Nederland* [Theme tea: the history of tea and the use of tea in the Netherlands]. Rotterdam: Museum Boymans–Van Beuningen, 1978.

Rose, Peter G. *Foods of the Hudson*. Woodstock, N.Y.: Overlook Press, 1993.

Rose, Peter G., trans. and ed. *The Sensible Cook: Dutch Foodways in the Old and the New World*. Syracuse, N.Y.: Syracuse University Press, 1989.

Schama, Simon. *The Embarrassment of Riches*. New York: Knopf, 1987.

Van den Brenk, Gerrit. *T'Zaamenspraken Tusschen een Mevrouw, Banket-bakker en Confiturier* [A dialogue between a lady, a pastry baker, and a confectioner]. Amsterdam: Wed. J. van Egmont, op de Reguliers Breestraat, 1752.

Van der Donck, Adriaen. *A Description of the New Netherlands*. Edited with an introduction by Thomas F. O'Donnell. Syracuse, N.Y.: Syracuse University Press, 1968.

Van der Noot, Thomas. *Een Notabel Boecxken van Cokeryen* [A notable book of cookery]. Annotated by Ria Jansen-Sieben and Marleen van der Molen-Willebrands. Amsterdam: De KANS Katernen, 1994. Originally published in Brussels in 1514.

Van Waerebeek, Ruth, with Maria Robbins. *Everybody Eats Well in Belgium Cookbook*. New York: Workman, 1996.

De Volmaakte Hollandse Keuken Meid [The perfect Dutch kitchen maid]. Facsimile of 2nd ed. Leiden: A. W. Sijthoff's Uitgeversmaatschappij N. V., 1965.

Vorselman, Gheeraert. *Eenen Nyeuwen Coock Boeck* [A new cookbook]. Annotated by Elly Cockx-Indestege. Wiesbaden: G. Pressler, 1971. Originally published in Antwerp in 1560.

Winter, Johanna Maria van. "The Consumption of Dairy Products in the Netherlands in the 15th and 16th Centuries." Proceedings of the Ninth International Conference on Ethnological Food Research, Ireland, 1992. Part 1, 3–13.

Winter, Johanna Maria van. *Van Soeter Cokene* [Of delicious cooking]. Haarlem: Fibula Van Dishoeck, 1976.

Witteveen, J. "Introduction." In *De Verstandige Kock, of Sorghvuldige Huishoudster* [The sensible cook, or careful housekeeper]. 1670. Kans Katernen 2. N.p. Amsterdam: De Kan, 1993.

Witteveen, J. "Van Trinolet tot Ragout: Kookboeken in Nederland in de 17e en 18e eeuw." [From *trinolet* to *ragout*: cookbooks in the Netherlands in the 17th and 18th centuries]. *Nederlands Tijdschrift voor Dietisten* [Dutch magazine for dieticians] 36 (May 1981): 170–175.

Witteveen, J., and Bart Cuperus. *Bibliotheca Gastronomica* [Gastronomic library]. 2 vols. Amsterdam: Linnaeus Press, 1998.

Wittop Koning, Martine. *Eenvoudige Berekende Recepten* [Simple calculated recipes]. Almelo, Netherlands: W. Hilarius Wzn., 1901.

Peter G. Rose

LUNCH. Lunch, the most informal and unassuming of meals, defies easy definition. A relatively late entry into the cycle of dining, it is replete with socioeconomic forms and meanings. Though the notion of the lunch or luncheon is most often attributed to nineteenth-century Britain, the terms had long been in use in England, albeit in slightly different form. Descended from the Spanish *lonja*, referring to a slice of ham, as the *Oxford English Dictionary* notes, the term has been in use since the Middle Ages as a word for a small snack, often eaten in the fields during the workday and sometimes called *nunchin*. Dr. Johnson's 1755 *Dictionary* defines "luncheon" as "as much food as one's hand can hold." For many centuries, lunch or luncheon was precisely this: a hunk of food, a few hurried bites of sustenance, a snack.

The Evolution of Meals

The reason for this minor version of the contemporary lunch was simple: For many centuries, the cycle of meals in England was considerably foreshortened. Breakfast was taken when one rose with the dawn to begin work in an economy that remained largely agrarian and rural. The day's first meal, however, was not originally the elaborate affair that we now identify as the classic British breakfast, and by midday, the medievals were ready for a more substantial repast. This was dinner, the most serious meal of the day for rich and poor alike, involving as much elaboration as one's pocket could afford. For the worker, dinner was meant to help the body recover from the exertions of the morning and to power it through the afternoon's remaining labors. For the rich landowner, it was a marker of ease and privilege and often occupied quite a large portion of the afternoon.

Dinner was generally taken between 11 A.M. and 1 P.M. Dining hours in the medieval period were proscribed both by science and religion. Doctors determined when food might be taken, in what manner and quantity, and in what form. The church also played a role in determining dining hours. In the monasteries of the age, as in contemporary contemplative communities, the hours of the day were divided up according to cycles of prayer; and the monks restricted their dining to the period after prayers at the hour of none, nine hours after dawn. The dining hour in the monasteries moved about, depending on the hour of dawn across the year's cycle. It is from this habit of taking the meal at the ninth hour that the term "noon" is derived, and, thus, the concept of "nooning." Noun or verb, nooning was not unlike *nuncheon*: Though the meaning of the term shifted about, it referred to a small meal taken at or around the noon hour and was in use in this sense, according to the *Oxford English Dictionary*, as early as 1652.

Not everyone in medieval society adhered to the edicts of doctors or priests, however, and the earliest manifestations of the meal we now call lunch seem to have appeared among the rich and idle. Erasmus's *In Praise of Folly* (published in 1511) describes hard-partying courtiers who slept late but observed the religious forms of the day by having "a wretched little hired priest waiting at their bedside [who] runs quickly through the mass before they're hardly out of bed. Then they go to breakfast, which is scarcely over before there's a summons for lunch." The accumulation of meals is telling: The notion of eating while one was still full from the meal before was thought to be particularly unhealthy, and meals were few and far between in part because the pleasures of dining were, in proper thinking, subordinate to the real occupation of the day—that is, work. By noting that his courtier eats a full meal for this snack, and eats it directly after breakfast, Erasmus emphasizes the morally and physiologically uncertain nature of the lives of the idle rich—and their distance from the strictures of the working world.

Urbanization and Industrialization

Over time, the hours of dining became increasingly flexible. Urbanization, industrialization, and technology all

396

played roles in changing the dinner hour. Like much related to the English Industrial Revolution, the transformation of the noon-hour meal progressed at a glacial pace through the eighteenth century and then abruptly picked up speed at the turn of the nineteenth century. In the mid-eighteenth century, dinner was still eaten in the middle of the day. As Horace Walpole wrote in a letter to Richard Bentley in 1753, "[a]ll I will tell you more of Oxford is, that Fashion has so far prevailed over her collegiate sister Custom, that they have altered the hour of dinner from twelve to one. Does it not put one in mind of religion? One don't abolish Mahommedanism; one only brings it back to where the imposter left it." But after James Watt's invention of the steam engine, in 1765, life in England picked up speed in every possible way, and gastronomy was hardly excepted.

One of the most apparent—and arguably most abrupt—of many changes in the socioeconomic landscape of the nation was urbanization. As northern rural land rented for centuries by tenant-farmers was transformed into factories and mines, as families of farmers who had worked common land for generations found themselves without means of support, and as the factory towns offered ever-growing possibilities for employment, a wholesale and unprecedented move to the cities took place across the nation. The mass migration affected every aspect of life, and meals were no exception. Men and women who had lived their lives according to the rhythms of the fields and livestock—rising early to feed animals and work the land before the heat of the afternoon set in, dining heartily in the middle of the day, and taking a small supper (often indistinguishable from breakfast) in the early evening before retiring—found themselves faced with the artificial hours of the factory. In this age before any meaningful regulation of labor, men, women, and children commonly worked twelve- to fifteen-hour shifts on the great factory floors and in smaller, artisanal assembly works. Working days began and ended in darkness, and regularly scheduled breaks were unimaginable. Instead, workers took their food when they could—buying breakfast from a cart on the way to work to maximize their sleeping time (and thus marking the dawn of fast-food culture), and eating a snack—a nuncheon or luncheon—brought from home or bought on the street, in the brief breaks between stretches of work. The abbreviated meal might consist of bread and cheese, boiled bacon, or a bit of pie or oatcake. Like the monks of old, the workers often took this break during the none or noon hour, in the middle of their extended workday.

Urbanization, of course, was not limited to the poor, and the middle class, too, found its meal schedules profoundly affected by the rhythms of the city. The growth of middle management through industrialization brought legions of men into the factory towns of the north as well as into London: men of the newly reimagined middle classes, strivers seeking to better themselves and climb the social ladder by dint of hard work of the mind. Such men were also deeply involved in the labor of buying, selling, and transport. Britain's seemingly ever-expanding empire, Parliament's simultaneous embrace of laissez-faire capitalism and tariff laws, and such new technologies as canning created possibilities for widespread international import and export, so that London's docks teemed with firms promoting the buying, selling, and shipping of wholesale goods. In these firms, middle-class men sat on upper floors with ink and paper, working columns of figures and making deals in a new kind of labor of the mind, while working-class men dirtied their hands with the work of moving actual product around. Similarly, the eighteenth and nineteenth centuries saw the rise to new prominence of "Change Alley," home of the stock exchange—the near mythic locus where, then as now, where fortunes might be made or lost in an instant, and place of irresistible temptation for men of little fortune and much ambition. These, then, were the new proving grounds of the middle class: the spaces where strivers might push themselves into the upper echelons, by dint of hard work, good luck, and vast infusions of filthy lucre. The laborers were driven by coffee, often consumed in the coffeehouses of the city: Once the bases for political radicals of the Reformation, these purveyors of speediness and drive were the meeting grounds for movers and shakers. Coffee helped to distance the worker from his body: Divorced from physical fatigue, the entrepreneur and the city man were able to work efficiently and quickly, laboring entirely with the head, not the hand.

The world of the middle-class striver, then, was utterly distanced from the sun-dictated realm of the rural worker: Dawn and dusk became nothing more than markers for those who could work as easily by candlelight as they could by daylight. And as the striver rushed through his businesslike day, urgently buying and selling in the fast-paced world of commerce, he was increasingly unwilling to stop work for a heavy, mind-dulling dinner; nor was he willing to afford his clerks, rising young men themselves, the opportunity to eat and drink themselves into uselessness. Accordingly, the striver began to take his dinner after the workday was done, when the markets were closed and nothing more could be earned. Since coffee alone often proved insufficient fuel for the workday, he grew accustomed to taking a bite of something: a small meal at the coffeehouse or cookshop, a snack from a food vendor in the street, or a bite of bread and cheese, brought from home and eaten at his desk—a luncheon, or, as it was vulgarly known, a lunch.

Urbanization, industrialism, and class mobility, then, all played central roles in the development of a small, relatively casual noontime meal, taken at the once accustomed hour for dining, yet distinct from the more formal and substantial dinner. But the nineteenth-century trend toward lunching was not limited to the laboring classes, and the changing habits of the workingman, ironically, were the driving force behind the changing habits of the man and woman of leisure. In the country manors and fine town houses, too, the dining hour moved further and further up the clock, creating a substantial alimentary gap in the middle of the day. In some great families, of course, this move reflected the changing working hours of their own city men, lawyers and legislators (and, as the middle classes moved into the realm of the upper crust, the waiting of dinner for the arrival of the great man became increasingly common—hence the late and formal dinners held in the home of Charles Dickens's businessman Mr. Merdle in his 1854 *Little Dorrit*). For others, however, the late dinner hour was a marker not of labor but of excessive leisure—and, thus, of privilege.

City men, after all, dined late because they came home late from work; they swallowed their dinners and retired to bed soon afterward, ready to do it all again the next day. The elder sons of aristocracy and moneyed gentry, on the other hand, had no such demands on their time, and their schedules, like the fare on their tables, reflected this. For the rich, coffee was consumed at breakfast as an aid to recover from the depredations of the night before; similarly, it was swallowed after a period of after-dinner drinking, with only men present, so that card-playing, dancing, and other entertainments might go on until the wee hours. Dinner, a leisurely meal involving many dishes and, later in the century, many courses, was held late as a marker of sophistication and of wealth. An extensive dinner consumed in the hours of darkness, illuminated by expensive wax candles, was an occasion of glamour for those whose bodies were not bound by the demands of the clock. Let the ordinary working folk dine in full daylight and retire to bed early; those who need not work might gossip and intrigue round the table in the intimacy of candlelight, sup at midnight, and retire to bed in the wee hours—practices that were especially prized during the Regency period, from 1811 to 1820. Technology played a role here as well: While candlelight was certainly adequate for dining, it was hardly ideal for the labor of cooking and cleaning, and so dining at night was difficult for those not equipped with a large staff to deal with the work effectively and the means to light a kitchen well with many candles (or, later in the century, with gaslight). Dining late, then, was in and of itself a marker of means.

Because dinners were relatively public events, at which the rich (nouveau and old alike) displayed their wealth with quantities of heavy, preferably imported food and drink, they were, like every public display of wealth, competitive. The constantly shifting markers of true class necessitated ever-increasing demonstrations of deep pockets and cultural currency, one sign of which was the lateness of the hour. Accordingly, "half-gentlemen," as Jane Austen terms strivers, with pretensions to true gentility, held their dinners late as a means of classing themselves with the sophisticates of the upper echelons, and every time the hour of dining for such ordinary folk moved up, the sophisticates themselves, feeling the com-

petition close in, felt the need to assert their class distinction by pushing their dinner hour later still.

The result of all this, of course, was a need for more meals to fill in the stomach-rumbling spaces between breakfast and dinner—often a gap of some twelve hours or more. The English afternoon or "high" tea evolved around the middle of the nineteenth century, as a genteel late-afternoon sop to the appetite (and, probably, a much-needed dose of restorative caffeine). In the noontime hour or a little afterward, the gentle classes began to take a refreshment that was more formal and more substantial than a tea, but considerably less extensive than a dinner. In the kitchens and servants' halls, this meal was referred to as lunch, and was taken as a snack, as it was in the factories. In the dining room, the repast was luncheon.

The French Influence on Lunch

The prestige of this upper-crust version of the British luncheon was helped along by French cachet. Though gentle Britain was extremely uneasy about the revolutionary developments across the channel, where the aristocracy had been jailed or beheaded, fashionable moneyed Britons nevertheless coveted all things French, and particularly all things French and gastronomic. Gallic chefs, sauces, and dishes were all perceived as both foreign and dangerous, and, thus, as the crucial markers of chic, up-to-the-minute elegance. Luncheon was no exception. Prosper Montagné's bible of all things gastronomic and French, *Larousse gastronomique*, attributes the development of *dejeuner*, the French precursor to the genteel English luncheon, to the Revolution itself, claiming that the long hours of the new Constituent Assembly, which sat from noon to six, brought about a particular alimentary transformation. According to Montagné, the members of the Assembly obligingly moved their dinner hour (*diner* in French) from one o'clock or so to six o'clock or later, but they soon found that they were unable to work effectively without food from breakfast (*dejeuner*), eaten first thing in the morning, to dinner. To stave off hunger, the members made it a practice to eat a "second breakfast" before their sessions began, around 11:00 A.M. "This second dejeuner," Montagné notes, "was more substantial than the first and included eggs and cold meat." The practice caught on, and the first *dejeuner* (a meal of soup or coffee with milk) was soon relegated to the status of *petit dejeuner*. The term "lunch" or "luncheon" was introduced into France in the nineteenth century, generally referring to a cold buffet for a large group of people, eaten standing up.

While the French *dejeuner* was driven by the lofty labor of hard-thinking men, the genteel English version was originally a ladies' amusement: The twentieth-century "lady who lunches" had her cultural birth in nineteenth-century England. Women of fashion and leisure, left at home while their husbands tended to business or pleasure, soon found that delaying their dinner to eight o'clock or later left them hungry in the afternoons; they began taking a midday repast, generally at the same time that the servants and children had their dinner. This small luncheon soon turned into an occasion for entertaining, reserved nearly exclusively for women. Arnold Palmer in *Moveable Feasts* cites such luncheons, served at one o'clock in the afternoon, occurring as early as 1818, but notes that this is an aberration. By the 1830s, however, luncheons were increasingly common. The meal was dainty. By the 1850s the practice had spread to the relatively financially stable members of the striving classes, as women who were freed from the real labor of the home by servants filled their afternoons with visiting and eating. The middle-class meal was not always as elaborate as the luncheon of the rich, however: Frugal housewives might make a lunch of leftovers from the last night's dinner or the children's meals, though only when no company was expected. When guests were present, luncheon foods were lighter than the fare of other meals, and because visitors generally retained their bonnets and shawls throughout the meal, the food could not be cumbersome or messy. It was served elegantly but simply. Sara Paston-Williams writes in *The Art of Dining* that by the close of the century, the fashionable table was quite bare: All food except fruit was served from the sideboard by the butler, so that the meal was at the crossroads between utter formality of service and utter informality of appearance. Less dressed-up luncheons featured hot meats on the sideboard, cold sweets in a row in the middle of the table, and other dishes served by the hostess. By the late 1800s, formal luncheons as celebrations and special occasion meals were not uncommon.

As Palmer makes clear, this form of luncheon was generally shunned by men, viewed as a despicable product of daintiness, trendiness, and boredom, a bastion of gossip and irrelevancy. While women's luncheons developed into a full-fledged meal, men tenaciously clung to the original sense of the term, downing a bite or two of wine and a swallow of biscuit, with or without a bit of meat, in a chophouse, at a club, at work, or on the street. For city men in particular, luncheon was public, and thus associated with business; there was nothing of indulgence or leisure about it. As the middle class grew more stable toward the end of the century, however, the practice of the lengthy business lunch, generally held at gentlemen's clubs, gradually caught on.

Gentlemen of leisure, on the other hand, incorporated luncheon into their days in more relaxed ways. They may well, for instance, have taken their cues from French epicureans. Jean-Anthelme Brillat-Savarin, in *The Physiology of Taste*, describes the great pleasures of the "hunting-luncheon," a snack of bread and cheese, chicken, and wine taken beneath the trees, as the epitome of leisure, and thus brings the notion of the courtier's lunch back to the leisured classes, while retaining its implications as a light, unmeal-like meal.

LUNCH MENUS

Arnold Palmer quotes Edgeworth's satisfying luncheon of 1823 thusly:

"First course, cold; two roast chickens, better never were; a ham, finer never seen, even at my mother'[s] luncheons; pickled salmon, and cold boiled round. Second course, hot; a large dish of little trout from the river; new potatoes and . . . a dish of mashed potatoes for me; fresh greens, with toast over, and poached eggs. Then, a custard pudding, a gooseberry tart, and plenty of Highland cream—highly superior to lowland—and butter, ditto." He adds, "[f]or this, she was charged six shillings." (Quoted in Allen, p. 180)

Edward and Lorna Bunyard's *The Epicure's Companion* cites a day of ladies' meals in a great house, recorded in the 1857 *Country Hospitality*, or *Lord and Lady Harcourt,* thusly:

Lady Axminster and Lady Rachel had that morning breakfasted on a first course of fish-curry, followed by meat pies, preserves, eggs, chocolate, tea, coffee, and muffins. At luncheon they had reveled on hashed venison, stewed mushrooms, an immeasurable apricot tart drenched in cream, and a bottle of soda water with sherry, but both ladies now declared they felt "quite faint"—a mountain of bread and butter now vanished rapidly, and numberless cups of tea were drained off (p. 422).

A luncheon (probably catered) held by Theodore Mander, a self-made industrialist, to celebrate the opening of the Higher Grade School in Wolverhampton, included the following (Paston-Williams):

Consommé
Saumon et mayonnaise
Soufflés de homard à la Montglas
Dindonneau froid à la Grande Duchesse
Soufflé à la Marguérite
Aloyau de boeuf rôti
Cotelettes de mouton en aspic
Galantine de volaille
Pâté de gibier
Jambon glacé, Langues
Dindon rôti
Pièce de boeuf braisée à la Napolitaine
Faisans, perdreaux
Gâteau d'abricots
Gelée à la Russe, gelée à la Française
Charlotte à l'Alexandra
Pommes à la Princesse Maud
Créme à la Munich
Fruits

The Acceptance of Lunch

By the middle of the nineteenth century, the regular luncheon meal had become, if not commonplace, at least commonly accepted among the fashionable. But the trajectory of the meal was by no means clear. Benjamin Disraeli, in his collected *Letters*, refers to luncheon as "my principal meal," at once marking his own sense of distinction by referring to luncheon and demonstrating his old-fashioned bent, by turning his luncheon, as it were, into dinner. Palmer describes writer Maria Edgeworth's oscillation between meal cycles as she moves from country house to country house, enjoying a full-fledged lunch of two courses and dessert one day, and reverting to the old-fashioned habit of midday dinner on the next. Lunch was sometimes amalgamated with tea, and taken in the middle of the afternoon. Sarah Freeman declares in *Mutton and Oysters* that "[l]unch as an occasion for entertaining was introduced in the late 1850s," but the first edition of Isabella Beeton's *Book of Household Management*, published in 1861, wastes little time on the meal. In her all-purpose guide for the up-to-date housewife, she makes mention of a light, sweet dessert known as a "luncheon cake" but declares it "seasonable at any time." And though she refers to luncheons in her survey of the well-bred lady's day as "a very necessary meal between an early breakfast and a late dinner, as a healthy person, with good exercise, should have a fresh supply of food once in four hours," she devotes scant space to its forms. In a brief section at the end of the book, she advises women to take

> [t]he remains of cold joints, nicely garnished, a few sweets, or a little hashed meat, poultry or game . . . with bread and cheese, biscuits, butter, &c. If a substantial meal is desired, rump-steaks or mutton chops may be served, as also veal cutlets, kidneys, or any dish of that kind. In families where there is a nursery, the mistress of the house often partakes of the meal with the children, and makes it her luncheon. In the summer, a few dishes of fresh fruit should be added to the luncheon, or, instead of this, a compote of fruit or fruit tart, or pudding.

For Beeton, in other words, luncheon remained a meal for fuel, rather than an occasion for entertaining and social niceties, and leftovers or nursery food were more than sufficient. This easy dismissal of luncheon may be due, in part, to her focus on helping women become useful helpmates and mothers, rather than fashionable figures: Since luncheon was patently a women's meal in the home, it could occupy little space in the husband-centered Beetonian oeuvre. Breakfast, on the other hand, warranted a great deal of ink in Beeton's work, since this was a meal over which men did business, and at which the men and women of the household ate together. And it was substantial: It is easy to imagine that anyone who ate a breakfast of cold meats, broiled fish, chops or sausage, kidneys, eggs, fruit in season, and toast might find themselves not exactly hungry when the luncheon hour came around. Indeed, it is not unthinkable that the

ladies' luncheon evolved in tandem with the lady of genteel appetites. As women's eating habits came under increasing scrutiny in tandem with the development of the medicalized and rigorously controlled female body of the nineteenth century (the precursor to our own cultural preoccupation with women's bodily shapes), any self-respecting lady would restrain her appetites, particularly for strong meats and organ foods, at a meal at which men were present. Thus, it is conceivable that the woman who ate breakfast with becoming propriety would find herself hungry by noon, while her husband, free to eat whatever was before him, could not conceive of such alimentary weakness.

However, Beeton's neglect of the meal also signals its still-precarious position in the pantheon of meals at midcentury. In mealtimes, as in the realms of work and fashion, nineteenth-century England seemed to exist in several periods at once: The old-fashioned dinner sat alongside the newfangled luncheon, and the two meals were sometimes taken, as Beeton notes, at the same moment by members of various echelons of the household (servants and children dined while ladies lunched). Participation in one regime or the other marked the eater: The luncher was urban or, at least, in touch with the latest London fashions; female; young or progressive in her style; and wealthy, or hoping to be taken as such.

By the end of the nineteenth century, the luncheon was well-established in English society; the 1899 edition of Beeton's *Book*, for example, gives a full seven pages to luncheon forms, etiquette, and menus. Even at this late date, however, confusion remained. Beeton introduces her section on luncheon by remarking that "[u]nder the above name come a very great variety of meals; for we have no other name for the one that comes between breakfast and dinner. It may be a crust of bread and butter or cheese, or an elaborate meal of four or five courses; it is still 'luncheon.' Also it may take place at any time. The lower classes lunch between 10 and 11; the upper, some three or four hours later." Everyone, it seems, found a lunch of some sort necessary by the close of the century: the chasms between rich and poor, man and woman, urban and rural had more or less closed on this point. And despite the confusion over the hour and contents of luncheon, the meal remained an informal one, generally lighter than either breakfast or dinner. Through the Edwardian period, lunch became a lighter meal, similar to contemporary imaginings of the repast, and more generally indulged in by both men and women.

The end of the century also saw the advent of brunch, a meal closely associated with the Oscar Wilde-esque dandies of the period. The *Oxford English Dictionary* notes that the word was originally university slang; *Punch* magazine attributes the term to Guy Beringer, writing in *Hunter's Weekly* about a meal that combined breakfast and lunch—and was presumably indulged in by university rakes and other men about town who slept through breakfast, exhausted by the exertions of the night

MRS. BEETON'S INSTRUCTIONS FOR A PROPER LUNCHEON

The 1899 edition of Mrs. Beeton's *Book of Household Management* includes instructions for laying a proper luncheon table, guidelines for menu construction, and a warning to avoid extravagance at this most informal of meals. The book offers a number of menus for luncheons with guests, picnic luncheons, and "family luncheons."

On a Monday in summer, a family might lunch on "[m]utton cutlets and peas, cold chicken, ham, salad.—Gooseberry fool, cold milk pudding.—Bread, cheese, butter, biscuits." On a Saturday, the menu might include "Minced beef or any other cold meat, Russian salad.—Macaroni cheese.—Cake, fruit, bread, butter, biscuits." A winter family menu might consist of "Curried cold fish, steak fried, mashed potatoes.—Tinned pine.—Custard.—Bread, butter, cheese, biscuits." (Note the marks of technology and of Empire: curries from India, generally stripped of much of their spiciness, became standard fare on British tables during the nineteenth century, and canned goods were at once economical and alluring in their factory-stamped newness.) A Thursday winter family lunch, on the other hand, might be based around a "[j]oint from servants' table with vegetables"—incorporating both economy and good old English style, as the plain joint—a well-cooked piece of meat without fancy foreign sauces—was the epitome of old-fashioned English fare. It could be accompanied by "[a]ny cold pudding.—Cake, preserve.—Bread, butter, cheese, biscuits." (p. 246)

An "economical luncheon" was much more limited, incorporating one main course, one simple dessert, and bread with butter, cheese, or marmalade; the main course might consist of "rissoles of cold meat" or "potato pie made from remains of cold meat" (p. 247). The inclusion of such recipes demonstrates the reach of luncheon through every class.

*

A luncheon for guests was somewhat more elaborate. The 1899 edition of Beeton lists the following menu for a summer repast for ten:

Cold salmon, tartar sauce, cucumber
Roast chicken, potatoes, green peas
Cold lamb, salad
Raspberry and current tart (cold), custard
Maraschino jelly
Strawberries and cream
Bread, butter, cheese, biscuits, &c. (p. 245)

In winter, Beeton's *Guide* suggests the following:

Clear soup
Fried soles, caper sauce
Hashed turkey, cold roast beef, beetroot, mashed potatoes
Pheasants
Sweet Omelette, stewed prunes and rice (cold), cheese, celery
Pears, oranges
Bread, butter, &c. (p. 245)

In 1934 Florence B. Jack's *Cookery for Every Household* offered a series of seasonal menus for "the luncheon proper, which resembles the French déjeuner in style" (p. 674). While noting that dishes might be added or subtracted depending on appetite and occasion, she generally proposes menus of four courses, including the following:

For spring: spring soup, mayonnaise of halibut, stewed pigeons, and French pancakes or eggs on spinach, cold beef with mixed salad, orange soufflé, and cheese cakes. For summer, fish salad, French beans à la maitre d'hotel, roast lab, and compote of cherries with custard sauce; for fall, grilled mackerel, minced chicken with spinach, bread-crumb pudding, and stewed prunes; and for winter, stuffed fillets of fish, Russian steaks, apple charlotte, and coffee eclairs.

---

before. In this, the brunchers improved on the medieval courtiers who ran from one meal to the next. A meal of absolute leisure, brunch obliterated the need for form and attention to hours, trumpeting the freedom of the brunchers from the tyrannies of the workday. It was an excellent means of marking the dandy as a creature entirely divorced from the middle class, and only when it was taken up as a weekend form, largely in the United States in the 1930s and 1940s, did it transform itself into the respite from the workweek that we know it as today.

Lunch in America

Though the process through which lunch developed in America closely mirrored that of England, the timetable was much slower, as the country moved more gradually from rural to urban economies. The working classes began eating a quick meal known as lunch—usually a brown-bag affair brought from home—in the nineteenth century, but the practice of referring to the midday meal as dinner persisted in many rural areas through the 1940s. The development of the upper-class lunch also occurred much later. Harvey A. Levenstein in *Revolution at the Table* places that transition in the 1880s and attributes the later dinner hour not only to fashion, but also to the American work ethic. Even men who did not work, he claims, liked to be seen as busy during working hours, and so were loathe to sit down to dinner in daylight. Particularly, but not exclusively, among the privileged, "nooning" persisted in America through the nineteenth century as a term referring to a light midday meal taken at leisure, often in less than formal circumstances.

By the early years of the new century, the ladies' luncheon was common, and home-based luncheon clubs for ladies were proliferating. But since many men of the middle and upper classes ate their midday meal at home, luncheon in America had much less of a gendered character than the British variety. Through the twentieth century, as children came home from school to eat lunch, the meal was made to bear the weight of America's great nutritional edicts, so that homemade meals and the women who cooked them shouldered the responsibility for the emotional, physical, and intellectual well-being of the nation's children. Women of leisure took their midday sustenance in public restaurants, marking their distance from the labor of the home by combining lunching or luncheon, as they termed it, with shopping and other wealth-driven pursuits of pleasure.

In the public world of work, lunch in America was driven by the nation's speedy, progress-obsessed business culture. As Daniel Boorstin notes in *The Americans*, soon after the Civil War, the notion of the lunch counter evolved, modeled on the horrible "refreshment rooms" in railroad stations, where commuters in a hurry downed worse than mediocre food at top speed. The lunch counter, like the refreshment room, was based on the premise of moving patrons in and out quickly; the setting and the seating were less than luxurious, and the food was served up extremely quickly, encouraging rapid turnover (a business practice that Ray Kroc, the entrepreneur behind McDonald's, elevated to an American art form). Unsurprisingly, innovation- and efficiency-driven Americans also developed the concept of the lunch box, complete with divisions for various types of food and eating implements, for which patents were applied in 1864.

In its contemporary American incarnation, lunch continues to incorporate many of the class- and gender-driven connotations of its nineteenth-century manifestations. Office workers may eat a quick lunch—brought from home or ordered from a take-out or delivery restaurant, contemporary versions of nineteenth-century food carts and chophouses—at their desks, or they may use their lunch hour, a sacred American twentieth-century institution, for leisure activities, shopping, exercising, or eating out at restaurants that devote themselves in some way to fast noontime service. People of real leisure and means eat lunches in restaurants, and the notion of the salad-eating "lady who lunches" still holds considerable currency. Though the notion of the business lunch, an-

other midcentury American institution, has declined somewhat (and the legendary three-martini lunch has more or less disappeared, as a faster, meaner working world has evolved), lunch remains an important public meal for executives, who often use it as an opportunity for doing business, just as eighteenth- and nineteenth-century "Change Alley" businessmen once made deals in the coffeehouses of London. Business luncheons are more formal affairs, held for a larger number of people, and often involving a speaker. The term "luncheon" in general now refers, in the United States, to a formal affair involving a substantial number of participants, though in Britain it may also refer to a relatively formal repast for one person or a small group of people. For children, lunch is still seen as a particularly important source of nutrition, as the hot lunch programs in the schools attest, but as women have moved out of the home and into the workplace, the responsibility for this all-important feeding now rests with the schools and the public domain. Perhaps most tellingly, in the go-go American business environment of the early twenty-first century, the most important lunch is the one that is not eaten: As businesspeople seek to mark themselves as serious, driven, busy, they have come to see lunch as a sign of indulgence, even of weakness. Like their nineteenth-century London counterparts, ambitious workers often scorn lunch as a meal reserved for the weak, the slow, the unambitious, and the overly leisured. The best kind of lunch for the upwardly mobile entrepreneur is the one he or she has forgotten to eat.

See also **Art, Food in: Literature; Beeton, Isabella Mary; Breakfast; Brillat-Savarin, Anthelme; Dinner; England; Etiquette and Eating Habits; Fast Food; Gender and Food; Household;** *Larousse gastronomique;* **Places of Consumption; Restaurants.**

BIBLIOGRAPHY

Allen, Brigid. *Food: An Oxford Anthology.* Oxford; New York: Oxford University Press, 1994.

Aron, Jean-Paul. *The Art of Eating in France: Manners and Menus in the Nineteenth Century.* Translated by Nina Rootes. London: Owen, 1975.

Barer-Stein, Thelma. *You Are What You Eat: A Study of Canadian Ethnic Food Traditions.* Toronto: McClelland and Stewart, 1979.

Bédarida, François. *A Social History of England, 1851–1990.* 2d ed. Translated by A. S. Forster and Jeffrey Hodgkinson. London; New York: Routledge, 1991.

Beeton, Mrs. (Isabella Mary). *The Book of Household Management.* London: S. O. Beeton, 1861.

Beeton, Mrs. (Isabella Mary). *The Book of Household Management.* London: Ward, Lock & Co., 1899.

Boorstin, Daniel. *The Americans: The National Experience.* New York: Random House, 1965.

Brett, Gerard. *Dinner Is Served: A Study in Manners.* Hamden, Conn.: Archon, 1969.

Brillat-Savarin, Jean Anthelme. *The Physiology of Taste, or Meditations on Transcendental Gastronomy.* 1825. Translated by M. F. K. Fisher. San Francisco: North Point Press, 1986.

Bunyard, Edward Ashdown, and Lorna Bunyard. *The Epicure's Companion*. London: J. M. Dent & Sons, 1937.

Burnett, John. *Plenty and Want: A Social History of Diet in England from 1815 to the Present Day*. London: Nelson, 1966.

Cannadine, David. *The Decline and Fall of the British Aristocracy*. New Haven, Conn.: Yale University Press, 1990.

Dallas, E. S. *Kettner's Book of the Table: A Manual of Cookery, Practical, Theoretical, Historical*. London: Dulau, 1877.

De Rochemont, Richard, and Waverly Root. *Eating in America: A History*. New York: Echo Press, 1981.

Drummond, Jack C., and Anne Wilbraham. *The Englishman's Food: A History of Five Centuries of English Diet*. London: J. Cape, 1939.

Freeman, Sarah. *Mutton and Oysters: The Victorians and Their Food*. London: Victor Gollancz, 1989.

Goody, Jack. *Cooking, Cuisine, and Class: A Study in Comparative Sociology*. Cambridge; New York: Cambridge University Press, 1982.

Henisch, Bridget Ann. *Feast and Fast: Food in Medieval Society*. University Park, Penn.: Pennsylvania State University Press, 1976.

Hooker, Richard James. *Food and Drink in America: A History*. Indianapolis, Ind.: Bobbs-Merrill, 1981.

Jack, Florence B. *Cookery for Every Household*. London: Jack, 1914.

Jeaffreson, John Cordy. *A Book about the Table*. London: Hurst and Blackett, 1875.

Kasson, John F. In *Dining in America, 1850–1900*, edited by Kathryn Grover. Amherst, Mass.: University of Massachusetts Press; Rochester, N.Y.: Margaret Woodbury Strong Museum, 1987.

Kittler, Pamela Goyan, and Kathryn Sucher. *Food and Culture in America: A Nutrition Handbook*. New York: Van Nostrand Reinhold, 1989.

Levenstein, Harvey A. *Revolution at the Table: The Transformation of the American Diet*. New York and Oxford: Oxford University Press, 1988.

Lupton, Deborah. *Food, the Body, and the Self*. London; Thousand Oaks, Calif.: Sage, 1996.

Mariani, John F. *The Dictionary of American Food and Drink*. New Haven, Conn.: Ticknor & Fields, 1983.

McIntosh, Elaine N. *American Food Habits in Historical Perspective*. Westport, Conn.: Praeger, 1995.

Mead, William Edward. *The English Medieval Feast*. New York: Barnes & Noble, 1967.

Mennell, Stephen. *All Manners of Food: Eating and Taste in England and France from the Middle Ages to the Present*. 2d ed. Urbana, Ill.: University of Illinois Press, 1996.

Montagné, Prosper. *The New Larousse Gastronomique: The Encyclopedia of Food, Wine & Cookery*. Translated by Marion Hunter, edited by Charlotte Turgeon. New York: Crown, 1977.

Palmer, Arnold. *Moveable Feasts: A Reconnaissance of the Origins and Consequences of Fluctuations in Meal-Times with Special Attention to the Introduction of Luncheon and Afternoon Tea*. London; New York: Oxford University Press, 1952.

Paston-Williams, Sara. *The Art of Dining: A History of Cooking & Eating*. London: National Trust, 1993.

Pollard, Sidney. *Britain's Prime and Britain's Decline: The British Economy, 1870–1914*. London; New York: Edward Arnold, 1989.

Schivelbusch, Wolfgang. *Tastes of Paradise: A Social History of Spices, Stimulants, and Intoxicants*. Translated by David Jacobson. New York: Pantheon, 1992.

Scully, Terence. *The Art of Cookery in the Middle Ages*. Woodbridge, Suffolk, U.K.; Rochester, N.Y.: Boydell Press, 1995.

Tannahill, Reay. *Food in History*. 2d ed., revised. London: Penguin, 1988.

Thompson, F. M. L. *English Landed Society in the Nineteenth Century*. London: Routledge and Kegan Paul, 1963.

Wilson, C. Anne. *Food and Drink in Britain: From the Stone Age to Recent Times*. London: Constable, 1973.

Wilson, C. Anne, ed. *Luncheon, Nuncheon, and Other Meals: Eating with the Victorians*. Stroud: Sutton, 1994.

Gwen Hyman

LUTEIN AND LYCOPENE. *See* Antioxidants.

LUXURY.

Luxury means spending more than one needs to, and, in the view of some who concern themselves with the matter, more than one ought to, on comforts and pleasures. Since eating and drinking are (to most people) pleasures, luxury may take the form of lavish spending on eating and drinking, which is the form relevant to this encyclopedia.

Consider the possibilities. You can eat more than would be necessary to stay alive and healthy. You can drink more wine than is consistent with sobriety. You can choose foods and drinks for their flavor, their appearance, their rarity, their cost, their reputation, or their brand name, rather than because they are handy and nourishing. You can also make choices of dining companions and of ambience that others consider luxurious. If you entertain friends in a Michelin three-star restaurant, you and your guests are probably doing all these things. With a focus on different individual aspects of your pursuit of pleasure, you may thus earn specialized epithets such as glutton, gourmand, gastronome, connoisseur of fine wine, bon vivant. All of these, along with the nonfood pleasures that you enjoy before and after your visit to the restaurant, are subsumed in the general term "luxury."

Can we manage without it? *Le superflu, chose si nécessaire*: "The superfluous, a very necessary thing" is the paradoxical definition with which Voltaire approaches the topic of luxury in *Le Mondain*, a poem published in 1736. Whether or not luxury is necessary to individuals, we may still see it as playing a crucial role in human society, making the distinction between haves and have nots, identifying social classes, setting targets for the upwardly mobile.

At any rate, luxury exists in most cultures in which some people have superfluous wealth, power, or leisure to expend on its pursuit. In ancient Greece, even the Spartans (who were proverbial for their frugal way of life) found that some fellow citizens brought better game and finer delicacies to the communal meal than others. In the twentieth century, even among the Russian Communists there was a distinction between the Nomenklatura, who could afford—and were authorized—to buy luxury imported produce, and the others, who could not. It seems that to bring full satisfaction to those who practice it, luxury must not be shared too widely. Thus the list of luxuries changes continually. In the early twentieth century, fresh fruits that were not in season locally, hothouse peaches, for example, were costly luxuries, available to few. Thanks to refrigeration, air freight, and cheap gasoline, fresh exotic fruit is now no luxury—but the number of food luxuries, costly products that only some people can afford, is somehow no smaller than it was before.

The practices of luxury extend worldwide. In China, there have been costly, exotic luxury foods for more than two millennia. Beginning with the Emperor and the Court, there have been people who have spent lavishly on fine foods, enjoying banquets that might number hundreds of dishes. In India and Southeast Asia, too, it is possible to read descriptions of luxury feasts and entertainments dating back nearly two thousand years. In all these countries, there have been many people who could afford none of this. Thus the necessary contrast has existed between those who want and those who command luxury. Throughout the world, there have been philosophers and hermits who have consciously renounced the pursuit of luxury in favor of meditation; among them was the Buddha, who lived in India in the 6th century B.C.E. and whose life and teaching have influenced the whole region deeply. However, Buddhism and the other ascetic traditions stopped short of criticizing those who chose to live a life of luxury. To the Buddha himself this statement is attributed: "I do not despise sensuality: I know that is what this world is. I also know it to be transitory; therefore it does not seduce my mind" (Aśvaghoṣa, *Buddhacarita* 4.85). Thus his renunciation of luxury was a personal matter; it was not enjoined on all. In this sense, in traditional southern and eastern Asia, the pleasures of luxury were not a problem: simply, some people abstained.

The great Near Eastern civilizations, Sumerian, Babylonian, Assyrian, Egyptian (fourth to first millennia B.C.E.), as they grew in wealth, grew also in their appetite for luxury. Of the Persian Empire (sixth to fourth centuries B.C.E.), which swallowed up all of these, it was said that the best foods and luxuries, and even the best drinking water, were brought from every province to the Persian king's table. Classical Greek travelers and historians reported with awe on the vast quantities of fine produce (four hundred fatted geese and thirty pounds of anise are just two items in a very long list) that were supplied every day to the Persian court for the so-called "King's Dinner." At the courts of the Hellenistic kingdoms of the Near East, ruled by Greek monarchs in the third to first centuries B.C.E., lavish and costly banquets followed the patterns already established by the Persians. The biblical legends of King Solomon's wealthy court and of Belshazzar's feast are inspired by Persian and Hellenistic royal feasting.

Rome's conquests in the East, particularly in Anatolia (modern Turkey) in the second and first centuries B.C.E., brought the wealth and skills that enabled Rome to enjoy luxury on an imperial scale. The Roman general Lucullus, who served in Anatolia, is proverbial for his luxurious lifestyle: one may speak still of a "Lucullan" feast that offers the finest food and entertainment at astronomical cost. Several of the Roman emperors (first to fifth centuries C.E.), unmatched in wealth and power, fully demonstrated a capacity for luxury and gluttony. Among these emperors, Claudius (ruled 41–54 C.E.) is famous for his practice of vomiting after a big dinner to make room for another. Arabs and Byzantines continued these Roman traditions. At the marriage of the emperor Maurice, in 582, "the city celebrated for seven days and was garlanded with silver: deep platters, basins, goblets, bowls, plates and baskets. Roman wealth was spent; a luxury of golden display, the secret riches of the imperial household, formed a theatre for all who wished to feast upon visions" (Theophylact Simocatta, *History*, Book 1, section 10). There are equally breathtaking anecdotes of luxury from late medieval, Renaissance, and modern European royal courts.

The Western literary tradition of sensuous description and lavish praise for the pleasures of gastronomy and luxury has been paralleled, for more than two thousand years, by an opposing tradition urging renunciation of luxury and of the wealth that pays for it. This tradition may be traced to Greek philosophers, including Plato (c. 428–348 B.C.E.) and his contemporary Diogenes the Cynic. The pronouncement of Jesus, "It is easier for a camel to go through the eye of a needle, than for a rich man to enter into the kingdom of God" (Matthew 19:24.10) foreshadows the early Christian thinkers' fierce criticism of the usages of luxury. Such philosophers and religious teachers were reflecting popular views and also helping to shape them. Many people, ancient and modern, have believed that overspending on food, wine, entertainment, and other luxuries is morally wrong. These views have influenced government policies. Some Greek and Roman governments imposed direct restrictions on luxury spending or legislated to cap the prices charged for fashionable products. For example, in 89 B.C.E. the Censors at Rome decreed that Greek wine should not be sold at more than one copper per gallon; a few years later, Julius Caesar (it was said) authorized officials to enter private dining rooms to confiscate dishes whose ingredients contravened the antiluxury laws. Many modern govern-

A luxurious dinner was used as tool for teaching humility and tolerance in the 1987 movie *Babette's Feast*. The story on which this film was based was a critical attack on a puritanical religious movement in Denmark called the Holy Danes. © THE KOBAL COLLECTION/BETZER-PANORAMA FILM/DANISH FILM INSTITUTE.

ments impose differential taxes on luxury purchases. In France, for example, sales tax on fast food is levied at the reduced rate for "essentials" of 5.5 percent while on restaurant meals it is levied at the standard 19.6 percent.

Those who oppose luxury tend to complain that the businesslike satisfaction of hunger, which ought to be the purpose of food and drink, is progressively overshadowed by the pleasurable satisfaction of the senses. To satisfy the sense of taste is natural enough, but it is wrong to put flavor above nourishment in one's selection of food. The same applies to the sense of smell, and are we distracted from the proper business of the meal by scents and perfumes around us? As for the sense of sound, serious conversation is quite appropriate, if only conversation were always serious and never seductive. And must the senses of sound and sight be distracted by artists employed to dance and make music at a meal? Finally, the sense of touch: must these entertainers also mix with the guests and seduce them to promiscuous sexual pleasures? Thus, at some times and in some places, luxurious meals have turned into orgies. All of this comprises "luxury," a term that in Christian moral thinking came to be characterized as a sin. In the canonical list of mortal sins as

catalogued by Pope Gregory in the sixth century, five sins are subsumed under Pride, leaving two, gluttony and lust, to belong to the classification of Luxuria, or sins of the flesh. These Seven Deadly Sins have been a recurrent theme of art and literature ever since, woven in the mid-twentieth century into Anthony Powell's novel sequence *A Dance to the Music of Time* (*A Buyer's Market* [1952] and *The Kindly Ones* [1962]).

Examples in this article are taken from many cultures at many periods, to show how widespread is the appreciation of luxury in food and dining. In each case, therefore, the date and place are specified.

Luxury in Detail

The simplest characterizations of gastronomic luxury are those that focus on the quantity of food and wine and on the convivial pleasures that surround them. In the *Odyssey*, one of the two early Greek epics (c. 700 B.C.E.), the hero Odysseus, addressing his host Alcinous on the magical island of Scherie, sets out what later Greek readers considered to be the quintessence of ancient *tryphe* (Greek for luxury): "I believe there is no more delightful pleasure than when there is happiness among all the people;

when feasters in the house, sitting in rows, can listen to a singer, while beside them tables are full of bread and meat, and a waiter brings wine from brimming bowls and fills their cups: this seems to me in my heart to be the best of all." Such descriptions can be found in oral literature of other times and places. Modern Americans, if recommending a barbecue, are likely to paint a similar picture, and to emphasize, like Odysseus, the quantity of meat available.

If tastes become more sophisticated, one will find that emphasis is placed on the quality rather than the quantity of food. This leaves room either for encyclopedic listing or for mouth-watering details.

The wine will perhaps be of varied kinds; Julius Caesar (100–44 B.C.E.) made his gastronomic mark by being the first politician in Rome to serve four wines in sequence at his public banquets. Or it will be from a good vineyard: the vogue of Chateau Haut-Brion, still a noted name among the Bordeaux vineyards, can be dated from the April 1663 dinner at which the London diarist Samuel Pepys "drank a sort of French wine called Ho Bryen that hath a good and most particular taste I never met with." Or it will be from a renowned region: the luxury banquet laid out in the famous tomb of King Tutankhamen of Egypt (died 1352 B.C.E.), intended for the monarch to enjoy in the afterlife, included a gourmet selection of wines inscribed with names of wine districts—appellations, one may call them—in the Nile Valley, the Nile Delta, and the Oases. Or it will be a well-aged vintage wine: in the fictional Dinner of Trimalchio, an episode in Petronius's novel *Satyricon* (Italy, first century C.E.), the boastful host presents a wine labeled with a truly great vintage, the consulship of Opimius in 121 B.C.E., and spoils the effect by adding, "I didn't serve such good stuff yesterday, and my guests then were much better class." Or it will be of a special style, like the so-called East Indian Madeira favored in eighteenth-century England: loaded in casks at the Portuguese island of Madeira, this wine took the long sea journey to the East Indies (modern Indonesia) and back again to Europe, crossing the equator ten times, rapidly developing a toasty maturity, and just as rapidly increasing its price. Or, if nothing else, it will be expensive: witness the strange early-twenty-first century vogue for Beaujolais Nouveau, harvested, vinified, and bottled in indecent haste. Wines and liqueurs that claim to belong to the luxury class may sometimes be as boastful as Trimalchio. The sweet wine of Tokay, in Hungary, is labeled in Latin *Vinum regum—rex vinorum* (the wine of kings—the king of wines). Bénédictine, a commercial liqueur from Fécamp in northern France, carries the dedication *D.O.M.* (to God, best and greatest) on every bottle.

The food will be notable in various similar ways. The meat may perhaps be that of a suckling animal, suckingpig or baby lamb or kid; these are always expensive, because economic sense dictates slaughtering animals when full-grown. Or it may be game, from wild hare to wild boar to grouse. In many cultures, game reflects glamour on a male host by implying that he is the huntsman; in others, including the modern West, serving boar or venison is simply a sign that serious money has been spent. As far back as the Assyrian and Persian empires, the wealthy have kept private hunting parks stocked with "wild" animals such as boar and deer; for example, thirty gazelles were supplied each day to the Persian King's Dinner mentioned above. Or the food may be taken at the precise time of year when it is known to be at its best, its tenderest, or its most flavorsome; Archestratus, Europe's first gastronomic writer, insists on this point continually in his instructions for selecting Mediterranean fish. Like an appellation wine, the food may come from the very region where it is said to reach its peak of quality or from the producer who has the best reputation; this emphasis found fashion in restaurant menus in the United States in the early twenty-first century. It may be of very distant origin—which in earlier times would mean that it had necessarily made a slow voyage across dangerous seas, had passed through the hands of many traders, and would fetch a vast price at journey's end. This helps to explain certain strange and lavish uses of spices: true camphor (from Borneo) in medieval Chinese tea, nutmeg and cloves (from eastern Indonesia) in modern European cakes and puddings, myrrh (from southern Arabia) in classical Roman spiced wine, cinnamon in medieval Byzantine porridge. Cinnamon, which came to early Europe from Southeast Asia across the stormy Indian Ocean, fetched three times the price of gold.

Above such tastes as these lie the higher levels of luxury, those at which a host will pay fabulous prices to make the desired statement. Notice in the examples that follow, and in some of those already given, that the high price and reputation of the food and wine matter more than their effect on the taste buds. The visual effect of the display of wealth in tableware, decoration, service, and entertainment matters more than the (often minimal) contribution of these things to the participants' pleasure.

At these levels the wine will be of the highest reputation and of the most expensive vintage. "What kind of champagne is it?" "I'm afraid to look." "Suffering Pete—Bollinger 1911," said Guy Bolton to P. G. Wodehouse (New York, 1920s) in awed contemplation of a luxury buffet, ordered in their name, that they could not pay for (Bolton and Wodehouse, *Bring on the Girls*, chapter 5, section 6). The food must also be at the top of its class. It may be perennially rare, as is caviar (it will become rarer each year). It may be costly to produce, as hothouse peaches used to be and as foie gras still is. Foie gras and caviar are not bad, but are they really a hundred times as good as pork liver and cod roe? It is easy to name other foods that are neither as tasty nor as nourishing as their price might lead one to suppose. The ordinary eater can do little with truffles, yet their rarity and reputation ensure that the price fetched by the truffles of Périgord and

Tuscany remains extremely high. Bird's nest soup is said to be almost tasteless, yet the difficulty of obtaining it and its reputation ensure that its price is still fabulously high in China. There have through the centuries been many delicacies whose price owed more to fashion than to flavor and food value. Rome's second emperor, Tiberius (ruled 14–37 C.E.), considered legislating when the market price of red mullet, in response to fashion, rose to ten thousand sestertii each. (Note that it was Tiberius on one occasion who demanded luxury of a non-gastronomic kind by insisting, when accepting an invitation to dinner, that the waitresses be nude.) Three of this emperor's successors—Caligula (37–41), Vitellius (69), and Elagabalus (218–222)—were famed for their use of ridiculously costly ingredients. Vitellius's triumph (shortly before his assassination) was the recipe "Shield of Minerva," his personal invention. It included parrot-wrasse livers, pheasant and peacock brains, flamingoes' tongues, and the milt of moray eels, all these supplies specially fetched for him by Roman naval commanders from both ends of the Mediterranean and even beyond.

Once-exotic foods are available across the world; spices that were once fabulously costly are ridiculously cheap; philosophers and religious thinkers have ceased to decry luxury. Luxury has a past; the difficult question is whether luxury has a future.

See also **Art, Food in: Literature· Class, Social; Feasts, Festivals, and Fasts; Greece, Ancient; Medieval Banquet; Pleasure and Food; Renaissance Banquet; Rome and the Roman Empire.**

BIBLIOGRAPHY

A readable collection of historical episodes and anecdotes of luxury in ancient Greece and the Near East is to be found in *Athenaeus*, the Deipnosophists sections 510b–554f; see vol. 5, 293–521 of Charles Burton Gulick's translation (London: Heinemann, 1927–1941). On the Persian King's Dinner see David Malcolm Lewis, "The King's Dinner (Polyaenus IV 3.32)" in H. Sancisi-Weerdenburg and A. Kuhrt, eds., *Achaemenid History II: The Greek Sources* (Leiden: Nederlands Instituut voor het Nabije Oosten, 1987), 79–87. On the Deadly Sins in medieval Christianity see John T. McNeill, Helena M. Gamer, eds, *Medieval Handbooks of Penance: A Translation of the Principal Libri Poenitentiales and Selections from Related Documents* (New York: Columbia University Press, 1938). The following works focus on luxury in general or luxury in specific cultures:

Berg, Maxine, and Helen Clifford, eds., *Consumers and Luxury: Consumer Culture in Europe, 1650–1850*. Manchester, U.K.: Manchester University Press, 1999.

Coe, Sophie. *America's First Cuisines*. Austin: University of Texas Press, 1994.

Dalby, Andrew. *Empire of Pleasures: Luxury and Indulgence in the Roman World*. London and New York: Routledge, 2000.

Davidson, James N. *Courtesans and Fishcakes: The Consuming Passions of Classical Athens*. Hammersmith, London: Harper Collins, 1997.

Schafer, Edward H. *The Golden Peaches of Samarkand: A Study of T'ang Exotics*. Berkeley: University of California Press, 1963. [Early China.]

Twitchell, James B. *Living It Up: Our Love Affair with Luxury*. New York: Columbia University Press, 2002.

Andrew Dalby

M

MACROBIOTIC FOOD.   Macrobiotics is a way of eating and living in accordance with the natural order of the universe. This simple way of life has been practiced for thousands of years, originating with the ancient Far Eastern theory of yin and yang energies, a never-ending continuum where opposites change into one another to complement, balance, and form a union; for example, the sun (yang) and moon (yin), night (yin) and day (yang); summer and spring (yang), winter and fall (yin). All things on earth are created and held in balance by these two complementary forces, a fundamental understanding that governs the whole universe. The human body is included in the universal cycle of the endless harmonious motion of change. All the major organs and functions within the body have a cycle of yin and yang movement. For example, when we inhale (yin), we must also exhale (yang); the body needs both rest (yin) and activity (yang). Foods and liquids restore and maintain the body. Therefore, the macrobiotic way of living and eating is about understanding how to live simply and choose and prepare food in conjunction with the natural order of the universe, creating physical, mental, and spiritual well-being. The sidebar at right lists yin and yang characteristics.

The History and Development of Macrobiotics

The word "macrobiotics" comes from the Greek *makros* meaning 'large', 'a great' and *bios* meaning 'life'. Hippocrates first used the term in the fifth century B.C.E. in his essay "Air, Water, Places," about a group of people who lived long and healthy lives. Even to this day, his famous quote, "Let food be thy medicine and medicine thy food," continues to be acknowledged and respected. Hippocrates emphasized that life itself depends upon what foods are consumed and how they are prepared. He suggested that healing takes place when foods are eaten in their most natural form.

While Hippocrates coined the term, macrobiotics was practiced hundreds of years earlier in the Far East. Around 500 B.C.E. one of the world's oldest medical books was written, *The Yellow Emperor's Classic of Internal Medicine*, a compilation of the medical wisdom of ancient China. The book states that people who lived in harmony according to the laws of nature, balancing yin and yang energies, lived long and healthy lives. This wisdom is be-

lieved to go back even several thousand years earlier. "Macrobiotics" became a common term used in early Western literature, including the Bible, to describe patriarchs such as Abraham as "Macrobiotic people." In 1797 Dr. Christopher W. Hufeland, a German philosopher and physician, challenged medical practices by becoming a macrobiotic spokesman in Europe. His publication of *Macrobiotics or the Art of Prolonging Life* warned against popular foods like meat as well as foods containing refined sugars in favor of a simple vegetable and grain diet.

The development of macrobiotics as it is known today is credited to George Ohsawa (1893–1966; formerly Yukikazu Sakurazawa), who overcame tuberculosis in 1909 by rejecting Western medical treatment in favor of a simple diet of whole cooked grains such as brown rice, earth and sea vegetables, beans, seeds and nuts, and miso soup. The source of the information that relieved his illness was *A Method for Nourishing Life Through Food: A Unique Chemical Food-Nourishment Theory of Body and Mind*, written by Japan's Sagen Ishizuka in 1897. Ishizuka's vision consisted of eliminating a diet of meat, dairy products, potatoes, eggs, white bread, simple sugars, and the other highly refined foods of modern civilization. He contended that eating this way goes against the natural order of the universe and humans' immediate environment, thus causing people to lose their physical, psychological, and spiritual

CHARACTERISTICS OF YIN AND YANG

Yin	*Yang*
Colder	Hotter
Darker	Brighter
Longer	Shorter
Larger	Smaller
Softer	Harder
More inactive, slower	More active, faster
More expansive, hollow	More contractive, solid

Food Classification According to Yin and Yang

Extreme Yang Foods

Some Chemicals, Drugs, and Roots
- Refined salt
- Iodized salt
- Crude gray sea salt
- Ginseng
- Insulin
- Thyroxin
- Various others

Eggs
- Chicken eggs
- Duck eggs
- Caviar
- Other eggs from poultry or fish

Meat
- Beef
- Lamb
- Pork
- Ham
- Sausage
- Bacon
- Veal
- Wild game

Poultry
- Chicken
- Duck
- Goose
- Pheasant
- Turkey

Fish and Seafood
- Carp
- Clams
- Crab
- Cod
- Flounder
- Haddock
- Herring
- Iriko
- Lobster
- Octopus
- Oysters
- Red Snapper
- Scallops
- Scrod
- Shrimp
- Smelt
- Sole
- Trout
- Other white-meat fish and seafood

Condiments
- Gomashio
- Sea vegetable powders
- Tekka
- Umeboshi plum
- Shio kombu
- Shiso leaves
- Green nori
- Yellow mustard
- Green mustard

Moderate Foods

Whole Grains and Grain Products
- Brown rice
- Millet
- Barley
- Whole wheat
- Oats
- Rye
- Buckwheat
- Corn
- Sorghum
- Wild rice
- Amaranth
- Quinoa
- Other cereal grains
- Sweet rice
- Mochi
- Bread
- Chapatis
- Tortillas
- Soba
- Udon
- Somen
- Noodles and pasta
- Couscous
- Bulghur
- Fu
- Seitan
- Oatmeal
- Corn grits
- Cornmeal
- Arepas
- Popcorn

Beans and Bean Products
- Azuki beans
- Black-eyed peas
- Black soybeans
- Black turtle beans
- Broad beans
- Chickpeas
- Great Northern beans
- Kidney beans
- Lentils
- Lima beans
- Mung beans
- Navy beans
- Pinto beans
- Soybeans
- Split peas
- Whole dried peas
- Other beans
- Miso
- Natto
- Okara
- Tamari soy sauce
- Tempeh
- Tofu
- Other bean products

Pickles
- Bran
- Brine
- Miso
- Pressed
- Rice flour

Sea Vegetables
- Agar-agar
- Alaria
- Arame
- Dulse
- Hijiki
- Irish moss
- Kelp
- Kombu
- Mekabu
- Nekabu
- Nori
- Wakame
- Others

Seasonings
- Unrefined sea salt
- Tamari soy sauce
- Real tamari
- Miso
- Rice vinegar
- Brown rice vinegar
- Umeboshi vinegar
- Sauerkraut brine
- Mirin
- Amazake
- Barley malt
- Rice malt
- Grated gingerroot
- Grated gingerroot
- Grated daikon
- Grated horseradish

Vegetables

Root:
- Beets
- Burdock
- Carrots
- Daikon
- Dandelion roots
- Jinenjo
- Jerusalem artichoke
- Lotus root
- Parsnip
- Radish
- Rutabaga
- Taro
- Turnip
- Others

Round/Ground:
- Acorn squash
- Broccoli
- Brussels sprouts
- Buttercup squash
- Butternut squash
- Cabbage
- Cauliflower
- Cucumber
- Green beans
- Green peas
- Hubbard squash
- Hokkaido pumpkin
- Mushrooms
- Onions

Fruits

Fresh and Dried:
- Apricots
- Blackberries
- Blueberries
- Cantaloupe
- Grapes
- Honeydew melon
- Lemon
- Mulberries
- Nectarines
- Olives
- Oranges
- Peaches
- Pears
- Plums
- Raisins
- Raspberries
- Strawberries
- Tangerines
- Watermelon
- Wild berries
- Other temperate-climate varieties

Garnishes
- Grated daikon
- Grated radish
- Grated horseradish
- Chopped scallions
- Grated ginger
- Red pepper

Beverages

Regular use:
- Bancha twig tea
- Bancha stem tea
- Roasted rice tea
- Roasted barley tea
- Roasted grain tea
- Kombu tea
- Spring water
- Well water

Occasional Use:
- 100% grain coffee
- Amazake
- Dandelion tea
- Lotus root tea
- Burdock root tea
- Other traditional, nonstimulant, nonaromatic natural herbal teas

Infrequent Use:
- Fruit juice
- Cider
- Dyed foods
- Soy milk
- Vegetable juice
- Barley green juice
- Sake
- Beer, natural Fermented

Extreme Yin Foods

Tropical Foods
- Asparagus
- Avocado
- Bananas
- Brazil nuts
- Cashews
- Coconut
- Coconut oil
- Dates
- Eggplant
- Figs
- Grapefruit
- Green peppers
- Kiwi fruit
- Mango
- Palm oil
- Papaya
- Plantain
- Potato
- Red peppers
- Spinach
- Sweet potato
- Tomato
- Yams

Dairy Foods[1]
- Butter
- Cheese
- Cream
- Ice cream
- Kefir
- Milk

Stimulants
- Black tea
- Green tea
- Mint tea
- Other stimulating aromatic teas
- Coffee
- Decaffeinated coffee
- Cola
- Soft drinks
- Chocolate
- Cinnamon
- Curry
- Nutmeg
- Other spices

Processed Foods
- White rice
- White flour
- Refined grains
- Instant foods
- Canned Foods
- Frozen foods
- Sprayed foods
- Dyed Foods
- Irradiated foods
- Foods produced with chemicals, additives, artificial coloring, flavoring, emulsifiers, preservatives, stabilizer
- Vitamin pills

[CONTINUED]

Food Classification According to Yin and Yang

Extreme Yang Foods

Some Chemicals, Drugs, and Roots

Fish and Seafood
Bluefish
Salmon
Swordfish
Tuna
Other red-meat and blue-skinned varieties

Fish and Seafood
Cooked nori
Roasted sesame seeds
Other traditional condiments

Moderate Foods

Whole Grains and Grain Products
Other grain products

Seeds and Nuts
Almonds
Chestnuts
Filberts
Peanuts
Pecans
Pinenuts
Pistachios
Poppy seeds
Pumpkin seeds
Sesame seeds
Squash seeds
Sunflower seeds
Walnuts
Other temperate-climate varieties

Beans and Bean Products
Salt
Salt and water
Sauerkraut
Takuan
Tamari soy sauce
Umeboshi
Other traditional types

Sea Vegetables
Horseradish
Umeboshi plum
Umeboshi paste
Lemon juice
Tangerine juice
Orange juice
Fresh black pepper
Red pepper
Green mustard
Yellow mustard
Sesame oil
Corn oil
Safflower Oil
Mustard seed oil
Olive oil
Sake
Sake lees
Other natural seasonings

Fruits
Other traditional garnishes

Vegetables
Patty pan squash
Pumpkin
Red cabbage
Shiitake mushrooms
Snap beans
Summer squash
Swiss chard
Wax beans
Zucchini
Others

White/Green Leafy:
Bok choy
Carrot tops
Celery
Chinese cabbage
Chives
Daikon greens
Dandelion greens
Endive
Escarole
Kale
Leeks
Lettuce
Mustard Seeds
Scallians
Sprouts
Turnip Greens
Watercress
Wild Grasses
Others

Beverages
Wine, natural
Fermented
Other grain- and fruit-based mild alcoholic beverages of natural quality

Sweeteners
Amazake
Barley malt
Rice syrup
Maple syrup
Fruit juice
Cooked fruit
Dried fruit

Extreme Yin Foods

Tropical Foods
Sour cream
Whipped cream
Yogurt

Sweeteners [2]
Aspartame
Blond sugar
Brown sugar
Cane sugar
Carob
Corn syrup
Chocolate
Dextrose
Fructose
Glucose
Honey
Molasses
Nutra-Sweet
Raw sugar
Saccharin
Sorbitol
Turbinado sugar
White sugar
Xylitol

Stimulants
Mineral supplements
Other food capsules, tablets, and similar products

Some Chemicals and drugs
Amphetamines
Antibiotics
Aspirin
Cortisone
Cocaine
LSD
Marijuana
Others

Seasonings
Margarine
Soy margarine
Lard
Shortening
Animal fats
Refined vegetable oils
Herbs
Spices
Wine Vinegar
Mayonnaise
Hot Pepper

[1] Brie, Roquefort, and several other salted cheeses that have aged for a long time are classified as yang rather than yin.
[2] Soft drinks, candy, pastries, desserts, and other items containing these sweeteners should also be avoided.

vitality and harmony. According to Ishizuka, the ability to experience the highest levels of spirituality is controlled by food. He emphasized that the great sages and saints all lived on whole cooked grains and vegetables cooked with salt. Ishizuka was also concerned with the way eating patterns determined how families and societies functioned. His philosophy and scientific studies echo the macrobiotic way of living and eating in the early twenty-first century. He emphasized balancing Na-dominance (sodium) and K-dominance (potassium) in foods, which is also known as the acid-alkaline balance. Ohsawa amended Iskizuka's theory by imposing yin and yang forces onto the acid-alkaline balance, contending that these energies make up the mystery of life. Iskizuka's work sparked Ohsawa's passion to study, write, and extend his own version of macrobiotic practice and teachings to American, Asia, and Europe.

Macrobiotic Foods

A macrobiotic diet is defined as eating in balance between extreme yin and yang energies. For example, animal meat is considered an extreme yang food and creates natural strong cravings for extreme yin foods, such as refined sugar in cookies and cakes. Extreme foods create sickness and are the body's warning that there is an imbalance. The imbalance causes the blood to become too acidic, creating an environment in which diseases can thrive. Human organs, especially the kidneys, need to work harder to buffer the acids and maintain a normal pH alkaline blood condition of 7.35–7.45. Scientific studies have shown how a sustained acidic condition can cause normal cells to change to cancer cells. (The sidebar below illustrates foods in relation to acid and alkaline.) If extreme foods continue to be consumed, the body starts accumulating and storing toxins in the form of mucus, fats, cysts, and tumors.

To avoid these undesirable conditions, the consumption of whole, unprocessed foods grown without pesticides and other chemicals is recommended. These consist of earth and sea vegetables, whole cooked grains such as brown rice and millet, bean products, seitan (a

wheat-based food), nuts, seeds, and occasionally fish. Seasonings and condiments are used to add nutritional value and to enhance flavor. These include miso, made from soybeans and sea salt commonly flavored with fermented barley or brown rice, which strengthens the blood; *umeboshi*, a salty plum that neutralizes extreme foods and conditions; sea vegetable flakes, which are high in minerals such as *dulse* and nori; tekka, a powder made from *hatcho* miso, sesame oil, burdock, lotus root, carrots, and gingerroot that is simmered for several hours and gives strength; *gomoshio*, a mixture of sesame seeds and sea salt high in calcium; and shoyu soy sauce to help with digestion. *Kuzu*, a white starch made from the deep root of a wild vine that helps digestion, thickens sauces. These condiments and seasonings have a variety of medicinal uses and can also maintain normal levels of blood alkaline. Eating these foods, seasonings, and condiments balances the body without causing cravings for extreme foods; thus, the transition of foods from yin to yang and vice versa is smoother, thereby creating internal balance and promoting health.

In a temperate climate, macrobiotic foods do not include nightshade vegetables such as tomatoes, potatoes, peppers, and eggplant. These foods are high in alkaloid content and contrary to the healing process. By eating nonpollutant food, the body has a chance to clean out stored chemicals, increase nutrient absorption, and improved health.

Cooking Techniques

Cooking processes also have a yin and yang quality. For example, cooking meals, such as beans, longer involves more heat, which indicates yang energy, and this way of cooking complements cooler seasons such as winter, which is yin. In contrast, lighter meals, such as salads, and quicker cooking methods are yin, which complements warmer seasons such as summer, which is yang. This style of cooking and eating promotes remaining in balance with the changing seasons, supporting the natural order of the universe.

A gas stove is recommended for cooking macrobiotic foods because the heat comes from natural energy. Also urged are cooking with natural spring water when needed and using stainless steel, glass, cast iron, and porcelain cookware to keep the food away from possible contamination that may occur with aluminum and synthetic coatings. Ideally, foods are locally grown in season to promote internal balance and harmony with the environment.

Food and Behavior

There is also a cause and effect relationship between food and behavior. For example, eating mostly extreme yang foods usually leads to irritability and anger, while eating mostly extreme yin foods usually leads to depression and reduced energy; however, soon after eating extreme yin foods, such behavior as explosive anger has been noted.

ACID AND ALKALINE IN FOODS

Too much alkaline	*Too much acid*	
Refined salt	Meat, eggs, fruits, sugars	

Lower alkaline	*More Balanced*	*Lower acid*
Miso/shoyu soy sauce	Sea/land vegetables	Grains, beans

Eating foods that are balanced with yin and yang energies without extremes maintains a normal alkaline blood level and leads to vitality and a peaceful, more comfortable state of mind. Table 1 illustrates foods associated with certain behaviors and moods.

TABLE 1

Yin and Yang foods associated with behaviors

	Foods	Behaviors
Extreme Yang	Refined salt	Aggressive
	Meats	Overactive
	Poultry	Angry, irritable
	Fish (blue and red skin)	Attacking, intolerant
	Hard salty cheese	Self pride
		Voice too loud, tense
		Tense muscles
		Dry skin
Balanced	Grains	Assertive
	Vegetables	Active
	Sea vegetables	Content, patient
	Miso	Positive outlook
	Beans	Satisfied with life
	Seeds	Voice pleasant
	Nuts	Relaxed muscles
		Smooth, clear skin
Extreme Yin	Sugar	Passive
	Honey	Overly relaxed
	Molasses	Depressed, sad
	Coffee, caffeine	Negative, retreating
	Milk	Self-pity
	Ice cream	Voice too soft, timid
	Yogurt	Loose muscles
		Moist skin

The standard macrobiotic diet consists of 30 to 50 percent whole cooked grains and whole grain products, such as sourdough bread and pasta (including *udon* noodles made with wheat flour, brown rice, and sea salt and *soba* noodles made from buckwheat flour); 20 to 30 percent locally grown organic vegetables; 5 to 10 percent beans such as adzuki and lentil (including tofu made from soybeans, *nigari*, and water and tempeh made from split soybeans, vinegar, and water); 5 to 10 percent soups, including miso and vegetable; and 5 percent condiments, such as *umeboshi* plum, *gomashio*, and sea vegetables, including *wakame* and *kombu*. Macrobiotic foods are high in complex carbohydrates, fiber, vitamins, and minerals that provide the balance of proper nutrition that the body needs.

A very basic balanced macrobiotic meal may consist of: one cup of miso soup made with onions, carrots, and sea vegetables such as *wakame;* one cup of whole cooked grains, such as brown rice seasoned with a pinch of sea salt; one-quarter cup of cooked beans, such as adzuki mixed with a small amount of the sea vegetable *kombu* and a sweet vegetable such as butternut squash seasoned with shoyu soy sauce; one cup of cooked green and yel-

low root and leafy vegetables; a pickled vegetable; and a garden salad. Fish can be eaten occasionally along with soy products such as tofu and tempeh to substitute for beans to provide protein. For dessert, a recommended dish may be couscous cooked with apple juice and apples. Also used for sweeteners are barley malt and brown rice syrup. In addition, *kukicha bancha* tea, which has a pleasing taste, is used as a daily beverage that has virtually no caffeine, alkalizes the blood, has a beneficial effect on digestion, and relieves fatigue.

Recommended macrobiotic foods and their portions vary according to a person's physical and mental condition, climate, and age. For example, someone with a slower metabolism may benefit from eating fewer grains and more vegetables. Macrobiotic counselors throughout the United States help people adjust the diet to their specific needs.

The Spread of Macrobiotics

Macrobiotics owes much of its contemporary popularity to George Ohsawa and his wife, Lima. His students Aveline and Michio Kushi developed the Kushi Institute in Brookline, Massachusetts, which helped spread macrobiotic teachings and practices in the eastern United States. Cornelia and Herman Aihara, also Ohsawa's students, developed the study and practice of macrobiotics in the western United States. Macrobiotic food may be found in health-food stores, and macrobiotic cookbooks are available there and in major bookstores throughout the United States. In the early twenty-first century, there are over five hundred macrobiotic centers throughout the United States whose advocates stress the advantages of this way of eating and living. The more common benefits experienced are increased vitality, better sleep, a stronger immune system, reduced fatigue, and improved memory. There are also scientific and medical studies which indicate that following a macrobiotic diet can prevent or relieve cancer and other terminal illnesses. These benefits are said to result from a body cleared of chemicals and toxins. Practicing the macrobiotic way of life moves beyond physical health to also revitalize the true nature of mental and spiritual well-being.

See also **Eating: Anatomy and Physiology of Eating; Health and Disease; Health Foods; Natural Foods; Organic Food; Preparation of Food; Soy.**

BIBLIOGRAPHY

Aihara, Herman. *Basic Macrobiotics.* Tokyo and New York: Japan Publications, 1985.

Esko, Edward, and Wendy Esko. *Macrobiotic Cooking for Everyone.* Tokyo: Japan Publications, 1980.

Kushi, Aveline, and Wendy Esko. *The Changing Seasons Macrobiotic Cookbook.* Wayne, N.J., Avery Publishing Group, 1985.

Kushi, Michio. *Doctors Look at Macrobiotics.* Edited by Edward Esko. Tokyo and New York: Japan Publications, 1988. See the forward by Lawrence H. Kushi.

Kushi, Michio. *How to See Your Health: The Book of Oriental Diagnosis*. Tokyo and New York: Japan Publications, 1980.

Kushi, Michio. *Macrobiotic Home Remedies*, edited by Marc Van Cauwenberghe. Tokyo and New York: Japan Publications, 1985.

Kushi, Michio. *Natural Healing through Macrobiotics*. Tokyo and New York: Japan Publications, 1979.

Kushi, Michio, with Stephen Blauer. *The Macrobiotic Way: The Complete Macrobiotic Diet and Exercise Book*. Wayne, N.J.: Avery Publishing Group, 1985.

Kushi, Michio, with Alex Jack. *The Book of Macrobiotics: The Universal Way of Health, Happiness, and Peace*. Tokyo and New York: Japan Publications, 1986.

Kushi, Michio, with Alex Jack. *The Cancer Prevention Diet*. New York: St. Martin's Press, 1993.

Roberta Bloom

MAGIC. The English term "magic" (*magie* in French, *Magie* in German, and *magija* in Russian) comes from the Greek *magikos*, a term that referred to a class of priests in ancient Persia and Greece. Later the word was taken over by Christianity and applied to the kings ("magi") who traveled to pay their respects to the infant Jesus. It was not until the Middle Ages that the word "magic" took on negative connotations. In modern times, magic refers to witchcraft, sorcery, and the casting of spells. Magic is also part of rites and ceremonies that are connected with the belief in a supernatural influence on nature, animals, and human beings. The field of ethnology uses the term "magic" very widely, but the meaning of the term is not always clear. Witchcraft was opposed by official religions from ancient times, as, for example, the Indian "Laws of Manu" (sixth to fifth centuries B.C.E.) and the Roman "Laws of 12 Tables" (mid-fifth century B.C.E.). The position of Christianity was shown in the Codex of the Emperor Justinian (529). Among the East Slavs, witchcraft was considered a superstition and a relic of paganism and therefore a sin. There is a tradition of identifying magic with witchcraft and distinguishing "white magic" from "black magic." Around the turn of the twentieth century, A. Lemann and others associated magic with sorcery. Lemann formulated the most popular definition of magic: "Magic or witchcraft is every action provoked by superstitions." B. Malinovsky wrote that magic was from ancient times the province of specialists and that witchcraft or healing was the first profession.

The connection of magic with religion and religious rites has also been interpreted in many ways. Sir James George Frazer thought that magic was founded on men and women's belief in their own potential to influence nature; this stands in contrast to the concept of religion, which is built on a belief in supernatural beings (gods, spirits, ghosts) that control natural phenomena. Other theories assert that religion is inseparably linked with magic. S. A. Tokarev gave a description of religious rites

that can be classified as magic rites, depending on their form and function. The division of magic by form proceeds from the psychological mechanism behind the use of magic forces, including establishing contact, initial (beginning), imitative magic, apotropaic magic (to avert evil), cleansing, and verbal magic. The division of magic according to function is linked to real-world or practical roots of magical beliefs: for example, medical magic is connected with folk medicine, love magic is connected with courting, trade magic is associated with hunting techniques, and agrarian magic is linked to primitive agronomics.

Food is associated with almost every kind of magic. Magic rites connected with food production, processing, and presentation reflected ancient beliefs and motifs that had lost their primary mythological meanings over time and had become inalienable elements of different religions. For example, it is no coincidence that figures from Slavic mythology were identified with Christian saints, such as Peroun, the god of rain, or in India Pardjanja, Pirva (Hettish), Perkons (Lettish), with St. Eliash; Veles, the god of cattle and wealth, with St. Vlasij; and Yarila, the god of fertility, with St. George. The roles of these figures are reflected in folklore, and especially in demonology. Traces of this type of folklore can still be found in modern times. For example, the Orthodox Church does not deny the presence of evil and other evil spirits in everyday life, but it does not support the spreading of superstitions among its followers. Nevertheless, such beliefs still exist and are reflected in ceremonies surrounding food production.

Beyond its main role of satisfying one of the vital requirements of the human organism, food plays a large symbolic role in every culture. Group meals and specific types of food are obligatory components of any festivity or event in most cultures. Depending on the societal and cultural context, food can be viewed as ritualistic, festive, sacred, funeral, prestigious, and non-prestigious. For example, many sacred rites are connected with the production of bread. It was common in many cultures to bless and to pray during bread baking and to put a cross on the bread before it was eaten. In Georgian beliefs, bread protected a child from evil spirits. Depending on the situation, a different number of loaves (accounts tell of anywhere from three to twenty-nine) could be used during magic actions. In Armenia, in order to protect her child from evil, a mother collected flour from seven families, baked bread (*lavash* in Armenian) in the shape of human being, put it under the pillow of the child, and on a certain day buried the bread. If a child became ill during the first forty days of life, he or she was passed through the hole made in a large loaf of bread. In Armenia bread was also seen as a form of sustenance in the afterlife: this belief was observed in a ceremony where fresh bread was offered for the deceased. The Udmurts often used similar magic. To return her child to health a mother baked bread three times in a day: the first time

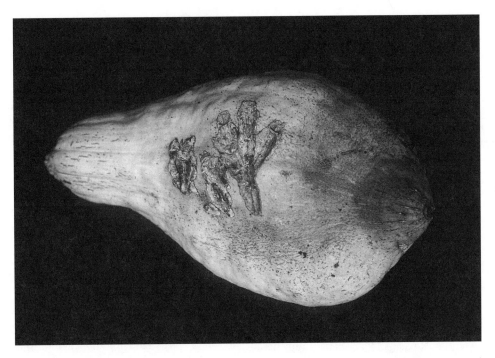

Hexefuss (witch track) on a Hubbard squash. The mark, which resembles a goosefoot, was viewed as an omen of bad luck or impending disaster among the Pennsylvania Dutch. It appears on both fruit and vegetables and is thought to be caused by a fungus, although folk belief explains it otherwise. PHOTO BY WILLIAM WOYS WEAVER.

she baked five small loaves; the second time she baked seven loaves; and the third time, nine loaves. To strengthen the magic influence she formed dough on a kneading trough and hid herself from the daylight under a shawl.

In some rituals, bread was used to protect the human world from another one. Among eastern Slavs it was a custom to keep bread on the table that was in the "red" corner (red in Russia means beautiful) or iconostasis, a shelf on which icons were kept, regarded as a sacred place. Bread has upper and bottom sections; thus, turning bread over was forbidden, as it was believed that the bread could be "offended" by that act. Bread and salt were the obligatory foodstuffs involved in the Russian ritual of entering a new house. Among Russians, Ukrainians, and Belorussians (White Russians), only men could first enter a new house, with icons and bread in their arms as the main symbols of a new living space. They might also carry a pot of porridge or kneading trough with dough, which symbolized prosperity, abundance, and fertility. Over time these items were supplemented with such cultural symbols as poppy seeds, thistle, burdock, garlic, and religious texts, which were supposed to protect a house from evil spirits and witches. In northern Russia, peasants invited friends and neighbors to enter a new home and treated them to a good meal to protect the house from undesirable people.

Magic and magical acts, such as the casting of spells, have traditionally been connected with health. Thus, many rites included actions and language that were supposed to help maintain or attain a state of good health. Rites such as these stood in opposition to illness, death, and misfortune. The main elements of water, fire, earth, plants, and animals were considered symbols of health and played a prominent role in different magical ceremonies.

World folklore provides evidence of a close correlation between the universe and human beings. According to the the cosmological beliefs of the people of the Caucasian region, there is a Tree of Life at the back of beyond that connects with three vertical levels: a sky (the upper world), Earth (the middle world), and an underground kingdom (the lower world). The upper world is populated with gods, deities, birds, and fantastic beings. Earth is populated with people, animals, and plants, and the underground kingdom is a world of the dead, as well as devils, dragons, and deep waters. Fantastic horses, eagles, devils, dragons, animals, birds, and others beings were seen as means of communication among different levels or worlds. For example, in Caucasian-Iberian mythology there is an image of a deer with a large antler that holds up or supports the upper world.

Baking rituals in different countries reflected some of the beliefs about communication between the lower world, the human (middle) world, and the upper world. In one ritual, the Belorussians baked three pies as symbols of the three parts of the structure of the world; in modern times, these pies have taken on different religious significance. These pies can be either round, three-cornered, or oval in shape. One never cuts three-cornered and oval pies with a knife; rather, one divides them by hand into arbitrarily sized parts. Only the round pie, which in more recent times is dedicated to the Christian savior, is cut into sections with a knife in accordance with ancient rules. The final form or figure of the sliced pie is a circle divided into an eight-segment circle or *mandala*—a cosmological symbol of the universe. Thus, these three pies reflect in a symbolic form the vertical structure of mythological space.

Religious symbolism very often stems from magic practice, which supposed a transfer of symbolic qualities from one object to another. For example, eggs, rice, and pomegranates are traditional symbols of fertility and prosperity. An egg, as a symbol of life, was used for Easter festivities and also for many other ceremonies connected with food production. Russians, Ukrainians, and Belorussians prepared special pies or chicken with an egg inside for weddings. In Daghestan, women always baked fancy cakes with eggs inside in the springtime as a symbol of the revival of life. There is a tradition among the Crimean Karaims (Karais) of putting magic patterns of sun, moon, stars, and fish on Easter bread, which is made in the form of a sun.

Magic stemming from the upper world was thought to provide a possibility of survival in difficult situations, such as finding food when one is faced with starvation. An example is the fairy tale "Jack and the Beanstalk," which tells a story of the magical properties of three fava beans (*Vicia faba*). A. C. Andrews pointed out an abundance of bean stories and superstitions and attempted to explain these as being an adjunct of an original Indo-European totemism. He drew almost exclusively on classical sources from the Greeks, Romans, and other closely related Mediterranean peoples.

The earliest and most abundant mentions of bean superstitions came from Greek city-states. Literature from ancient Rome contains similar references. R. Rowlett and J. Mori analyzed the work of their predecessors, including A. C. Andrews, and discovered that "favistic" folktales about beans were not always connected with favism (1971, pp. 98–100).

The motif of communication with the upper world can be seen in the calendar ceremonies of eastern Slavs, who bake special bread with forty stripes, which recall Jesus's footsteps on the Day of Ascension (forty days after Easter). The eastern Slavs bake another type of bread—*onoochkee*—that represents the cloth wrapped around Jesus' feet. Russian peasants put such bread in the rye field, believing that grain would provide strength. People in southern Russia baked similar bread on the fortieth day after an individual's death. Mourners put bread on the bench by the gate of the house, and people later ate it with honey. On that day some people ate pancakes at the nearest crossroads to prevent the deceased from returning home.

Magical food has been involved in many burial customs and rites that confirm a constant link between the living and the dead. For example, in many cultures magic rituals involved feeding deceased people, or more specifically, feeding their souls. Such symbolic actions were often performed on the stove in the home. Food was thrown about the house near the body of the deceased. Sometimes people placed food in the deceased's mouth, such as in the traditions of the Nganasans of Taymyr, Russia. Closely associated with these rites are the ceremonies that occurred after burial, because they include the same feeding of the souls. In addition to traditional funereal meals, many religions have ceremonies on special days that involve food and the deceased. Such celebrations are popular in Latin America. Mexicans have celebrations in August and November that involve the notion of spirits enjoying the smell of food. Persians put food on houses and roofs in the middle of March to encourage prosperity in the next year. B. Propp retraced the great role of the cult of ancestors in Russian agrarian festivals. Eastern Slavs celebrate "Parents' Saturdays" in accordance with the Orthodox calendar (*Dzjady* in White Russia) and the Japanese celebrate a Bon' Day. Russians always put out a glass of spirits with a piece of bread on the day of a funeral and on subsequent anniversaries. It is still a rule in Ukraine to have breakfast together with the deceased at the cemetery on the next morning after the funeral and to eat bread, sweets, and cakes and drink spirits. In Russia, visiting the cemetery on the second day after Easter (*radunitsa*) and sharing a meal with the deceased also became a custom: the meal was a painted Easter egg and sweet bread that were placed in the tomb.

Eastern Slav celebrations at Shrovetide and at Christmas were both devoted to the memory of the deceased. These days were observed by the preparation of such obligatory ritual dishes as bliny (pancakes) and *kissel*, made from oat, fruits, or berries. This tradition still exists among Russians. Ukrainians have a custom of preparing compote and small sweet pies with jam at funerals.

An example of using verbal cliché with magic purpose can be found in the texts of the Apocrypha, biblical books of dubious authenticity that are excluded from the Jewish and Protestant versions of the Old Testament. Nevertheless, apart from the fasts on Fridays established by the Orthodox Church, there was a tradition of fasting on the twelve "Temporary" Fridays, or "Vow" or "Big" Fridays, that were very popular among Orthodox adherents. Fasting on Fridays was a well-known practice of the use of the apocryphal texts as amulets, which was widespread in many cultures. The main role of the Apocrypha was to protect people from different troubles but only under the condition of fasting. Orthodox Christians kept fasts on these days to prevent unexpected misfortunes such as drought, bad harvests, infestations, and diseases.

The apocryphal Twelve Fridays were widespread in Russia in the guise of legends, spiritual verses, and tales dating from the eleventh century. Wandering (usually blind) minstrels sang the verses and advised followers to respect Fridays by "saint fasting and praying, faith and love, gentleness and humility." The verses warned that anybody who committed a breach of Fridays would be punished for generations to come.

In Russia the texts about the Twelve Fridays (as the texts "Dream of Our Lady") were also used for magical purposes and were worn on the body and used as amulets. However, such texts were not just magical; they were manifestations of piety in many provinces where they were distributed in the form of manuscript copies, apocryphas, and spiritual songs.

In the nineteenth and twentieth centuries, the texts of the Twelve Fridays could be found in many Russian provinces. They were dedicated to the main feasts of the Church calendar, and people fasted on Fridays before these holidays. Every Friday had a special grace and promised special preferences. The Twelve Fridays manuscript is still popular. People still believe that keeping fasts on these Fridays protects them against diseases and disasters.

See also **Feasts, Festivals, and Fasts; Folklore, Food in; Religion and Food; Russia.**

BIBLIOGRAPHY

Afanasjev, Alexander N. *Poeticheskiye vozzreniya slavjan na prirodu* [Poetical views of Slavs on nature]. 3 vols. Moscow, 1865–1869.

Afanasjev, Alexander N. *Narodnye russkie skazkee* [Russian folk tales]. 3 vols., edited by E. V. Pomerantseva and K. V. Chistov. Moscow: Nauka, 1984–1985.

Andrews, A. C. "The Bean and Indo-European Totemism." *American Anthropologist* 51 (1949): 274–292.

Anikin, V. P. *Russkaya narodnaya skazka* [Russian folk tales]. Moscow: Prosveshcheniye, 1978.

Domotor, Tekla. *Hungarian Folk Beliefs.* Budapest: Athenaeum Printing House, 1982.

Frazer, J. G. *The Golden Bough. A Study in Magic and Religion.* London: 1925.

Gerber, A. *Great Russian Animal Tales.* Baltimore, Md.: 1891.

Ivanitsky, Nickolaj A. "Materials on Ethnography of Vologda Province." *News of the Society of Amateurs of Natural History, Archeology, Ethnography* LXIX (1980).

Kalinsky, J. A. "Tserkovno-Narodny mesjatseslov na Rusi [A church-folk monthly calendar in Russia]." *Notes of the Imperial Russian Geographical Society, Ethnographical Department* 7 (1877).

Lemann, A. *Illustrirovannaya istorija sueverij i volshebstva ot drevnosti do nashih dney* [Illustrated history of superstitions and sorcery from ancient times to the present]. Moscow, 1900; Kiev, 1991.

Maksimov, S. V. *Nechistaya, Nevedomaya i Krestnaya sila* [Evil spirit, mysterious and christened forces]. Saint Petersburg: 1994.

Malinovsky, Boris. *Magic, Science, and Religion and Other Essays.* Boston, 1948.

Pomerantseva, Erna V. *Myfologicheskye Personazhy v russkom folklore* [Mythological personages in Russian folklore]. Moscow, 1975.

Rowlett, Ralph M., and Joyce Mori. "The Fava Bean in English Folklore." In *Ethnologia Europaea.* vol. 4, pp. 98–102. Arnhem, 1971.

Ryan, W. F. *The Bathhouse: A Historical Survey of Magic and Divination in Russia.* London: Sutton Publishing, 1999.

Rybakov, Boris A. *Yazychestvo drevnyh Slavjan* [Paganism of the ancient Slavs]. Moscow: Science, 1987.

Thompson, Stith, trans. *The Types of the Folktales. A Classification and Bibliography/Antti Aarne's Verzeichnis der Märchentypen.* 2d rev. Helsinki, 1964.

Tokarev, Sergej A. *Religioznye vozzrenija vostochnyh Slavjan* [Religious beliefs of the East Slavs in the 19th and early 20th centuries]. Moscow: Nauka, 1957.

Tokarev, Sergej A. "Suchshnost i proishozhdeniye magii" [The nature and origin of magic]. In *The Studies and Materials on Religious Beliefs in Primitive Society. The Works of the Institute of Ethnography.* Moscow: Nauka, 1959.

Tokarev, Sergej A., ed. *Mify Narodov Mira* [Myths of the peoples of the world]. Vols. I–II. Moscow: Sovetskaya Encyclopedia, 1987–1988.

Veselovsky, A. "Opyty po istotii razvitija Christianskoj legendy. IV. skazanie o 12 pjatnitsah. [The essays on the history of the evolution of the Christian legend, part IV, A story about 12 Fridays]." *Magazine of the Ministry of Folk Population* Part 185, department X, 1876.

Zelenin, Dmitry K. *Russische (ostslavische) Volkskunde.* Berlin: Walter de Gruyter, 1927.

Tatiana Voronina

MAGNESIUM. *See* **Minerals.**

MAIZE.

This entry includes two subentries:
The Natural History of Maize
Maize as a Food

THE NATURAL HISTORY OF MAIZE

Maize, also referred to as corn or Indian corn in the United States and Great Britain, respectively, is a cereal plant of the Gramineae family of grasses that today constitutes the most widely distributed food plant in the world. Accordingly, maize—from the Arawak *mahiz*—is grown in diverse regions and climates, from 58 degrees north latitude in Canada and Russia to 40 degrees south latitude in South America. Maize cultivation and processing are driven by the production of food and livestock feed, fermentation, and raw materials for industry.

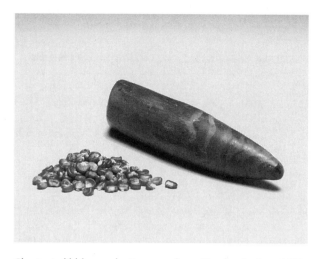

Chestnut dibble or planting peg from Maryland, circa 1850. The top of the dibble is cut to fit the thumb. Farmers planted maize by stabbing the plowed ground with the dibble and dropping a seed into each hole. Beside the dibble are seeds of King Philip Flint Corn, a variety that emerged in New Hampshire during the 1830s. ROUGHWOOD COLLECTION. PHOTO CHEW & COMPANY.

Given its many uses, maize is likely to be found in over 1,000 products in a well-stocked U.S. supermarket. The specifics of maize production, reproduction, cultivation, processing, and consumption—its resiliency, mutability, as well as the intractability of cultural and botanical constraints—continue to provide science with insights into the past and possible future of the species. Not surprisingly, maize is the most studied plant species on the planet.

The Ethnobotany of Maize

Ethnobotany, the study of symbiotic relationships between human cultures and the plants on which they rely, is one of the many fields of study fueling investigations into the earliest domesticated maize and its subsequent global diffusion. Ethnobotanists, archaeologists, anthropologists, taxonomists, food and horticultural scientists, nutritionists, geneticists, biotechnicians, art historians, and many others are all trying to find answers to the numerous questions posed by the evolution and proliferation of maize. This diverse body of scientific sources provides information about the natural and cultural history of maize.

The Quintessential Maize Plant

Experts have established that modern maize evolved from *teosinte* (God's corn), or *Zea mays* ssp. *Mexicana*, although some botanists continue to argue that it evolved from an early Mesoamerican maize variety called *Chapalote*. Even the timing of maize origins has been questioned. A review of the botanical characteristics of both maize and *teosinte* will distinguish them and provide some idea of how maize developed into the fully domesticated cultigen it is today.

According to plant geneticist John Doebley, maize (*Zea mays* L. ssp. *mays*) and the teosintes (*Zea* spp.) differ profoundly in terms of vegetative characteristics and "inflorescence architecture" (1996, p. 66). That is, differences are specific to the form of the plant and its reproductive architecture, including variation in the mode of development and arrangement of the flowers or blooms along the axis of the plant.

In this instance, the distinctions are most notable in the forms of the male tassel, or spikelet, that sprouts at the summit of the maize or teosinte stalk, as well as in the form and development of the female inflorescence or maize ear. Despite these distinctions, Doebley acknowledges that maize and the Mexican teosintes are essentially variants of the same biological species. As such, they form fully fertile hybrids and cross-pollinate; the inherent differences in chromosome structure and other genetic aspects between teosinte and maize are no greater than those observed among the diverse races of maize (p. 66). Experiments distinguishing genes of teosinte from maize have been replicated in recent years through the use of molecular analysis.

The characteristic reproductive pattern of maize is a very ancient and primitive one. Maize includes both male and female reproductive characteristics and constitutes an Andropogonoid grass that bears a spike-like axis or tassel on which flowers or blooms are attached and from which pollen is dispersed; it is a self-pollinating plant that disperses pollen from the tassels to the "style" or "silk" of the maize ears (female inflorescences), where it is absorbed in the reproductive process. Whereas each tassel contains some 25 million pollen grains, each female inflorescence or maize ear contains upwards of 1,000 ovules or potential kernels. Each pollinated silk is thereby transformed into an individual kernel of maize that grows to contain a single ovule necessary for the reproduction of the plant itself. Maize leaves track the sun's light and absorb its energy; a field of maize is optimally designed for producing high yields from solar energy.

Maize Variation and Race

There are some twenty-five "primary" races of maize found in Mesoamerica, and none of these is pure. The proliferation of hybrid variants and recent advances in bioengineered or genetically modified varieties of maize has seemingly sealed the fate of this most ancient foodstuff. In fact, the global proliferation of genetically engineered foods is poised to completely displace or replace existing strains of the primary grain crops with biologically engineered substitutes.

The evolutionary history and inherent mutability of maize are so complex that scientists continue to debate and question the taxonomic identification of all the extant races of maize in both wild and domestic contexts.

418

There is no agreement about the taxonomic names or numbers of races that may exist in any single world region. Since maize is so easily hybridized, the number of varieties far exceeds any other crop species on record. Botanical taxonomists have loosely grouped these varieties into some 300 races for the Western Hemisphere alone. Early textbook taxonomies, on the other hand, once identified only six races, including dent, flint, flour, sweet, pop, and waxy varieties. Of these, two dominate American commercial agriculture and include the Flint (*Zea indurata*) and Dent (*Zea indentata*) varieties. The nine major types cultivated in the United States include the Southwestern Semidents, Southwestern twelve-row, Pima-Papago, Great Plains Flints and Flours, Corn Belt Dents, Southeastern Flints, Southern Dents, Derived Southern Dents, and Northern Flints.

Of those races of maize indigenous to Mesoamerica, four main groups of maize have been identified. Their respective taxonomic classifications are based on the vegetative characteristics of the plant, characteristics of the spike or spikelet, characteristics of the cob, and the physiological, genetic, and cytological characteristics of the plants studied. These primary maize groups are (1) antique indigenous, (2) exotic pre-Columbian, (3) prehistorical mestiza, and the (4) not well-defined or modern races. To this latter category may be added the proliferation of genetically engineered strains.

The antique indigenous group consists of those races that originated in Mesoamerica with the primitive earliest races of maize. Variations within this group are thought to be evidence of multiple independent origins in diverse areas of Mesoamerica. The races specifically identified with this group include Palomero Toluqueño, Arrociclo Amarillo, Chapolote, and Nal-Tel.

Maize in the New World
The history of maize and its domestication may be traced back some 8,000 years. Maize spread across the length and breadth of the Americas, and subsequently to Europe, Africa, and Asia. Teosinte (*Zea mexicana*) has been linked with the earliest maize in Mesoamerica and was first harvested as early as 10,000 years ago.

The origins of maize begin on the Pacific slope of the modern Mexican states of Oaxaca, Tehuacán, and the Valley of Mexico. The earliest primitive corncobs discovered in Mesoamerica were obtained from specimens recovered within a cave near Oaxaca. From there maize diffused rapidly into Central America and then into South America by way of the eastern slopes of the Andes approximately 4,000 years ago. Guatemala may have served as the source or conduit for the adoption of the earliest strains of maize in Andean South America and Peru. In fact, the initial appearance of maize in Peru has been dated to 6070 B.C.E. Ecuador, Chile, and Argentina, with Andean Peru, form a likely corridor for the transmission of maize from Guatemalan sources into coastal valleys. Some nineteen races of maize from ten Latin American coun-

tries have been identified with the Classic period of 300 to 900 C.E. Six of these evidenced interactions between Mesoamerican and Peruvian societies from the most remote periods of pre-Columbian cultural development.

New World dispersals. Walton C. Galinat has traced the diffusion of maize into North America to a Northern Flint Pathway established by 700 C.E. in the Rio Grande valley. From there maize spread northward along both the eastern and western flanks of the Rocky Mountains, and eastward along major river courses—including those of the Arkansas, Mississippi, Platte, and Ohio Rivers—permitting its continued cultivation and dispersal eastward. By 1200 C.E., maize cultivation was established in upstate New York and New England. While the eight-rowed variety of maize was cultivated in the southeastern United States in pre-Columbian times, the Southern Dent Pathway accounts for the distributions of other varieties of maize after 1500 C.E., subsequent to Spanish contact in those regions. Ultimately, the hybrid vigor identified with the larger and more robust forms of maize can be traced back to the merging of the Northern Flint varieties with the Southern Dent varieties by U.S. farmers of the Midwest in the mid-nineteenth century. According to Galinat, this hybrid fusion can be characterized as having resulted in an "inadvertent evolutionary explosion" that ultimately transformed maize into a highly productive and important foodstuff.

Maize in the Old World
Even before the Wampanoag Indians presented the early Plymouth colonists with maize at the first Thanksgiving celebration in 1621, enabling this early English colony in present-day Massachusetts to survive, maize had already made its way back to the Old World and was rapidly being incorporated into the agricultural economies of sixteenth- and seventeenth-century Europe and the Middle East, the Balkans, Africa, India, and Asia. In fact, according to Sylvia Johnson, as early as the mid-sixteenth century, maize had been introduced to Europe, western Asia, Africa, and China. These early Old World encounters with maize were ambivalent toward the exotic grain then known as Turkish wheat, Turkish grain, Spanish wheat, or Indian corn. In fact, negative reactions to maize in the Old World largely focused on the belief that maize was less nourishing than extant European grain products such as the wheat, barley, or oat cereals used in the production of bread and related by-products.

Despite its considerable productivity in comparison with wheat, its shorter growing season, and its considerable adaptive potential to marginal environments, maize was initially seen as a foodstuff fit only for animals or the poorest of the peasantry, who ground it up with water and ate it as a finely ground mush or porridge. This came to be known as "polenta" to the peoples of northern Italy, which has since been incorporated into European and American cuisines. Beginning in Italy, a variety of toppings and additives, including cheese and pasta, have diversified the ingredients of this poor persons' food and transformed it into an international favorite.

In China and Southeast Asia, maize is cultivated in rotation with other, more traditional crops like rice or millet, and sequential cropping (relay cropping) strategies permit a form of multiple-cropping that overlaps the life cycles of two or more crops. These methods made possible the generation of crop surpluses in Asia beyond those originally identified with the exclusive or traditional reliance on rice as a primary cultigen. In fact, maize is being used throughout Asia to supplement more traditional crops by extending the growing season and expanding production potentials throughout the year. In addition, the production of maize fodder and feed for livestock has fueled the adoption of maize agriculture throughout the developing countries of Asia and Africa. Maize provides the world's most cost-effective and highest yield plant resource currently available for the production of livestock forage, fodder, and feed (Dowswell et al., 1996, pp. 27–28).

Old World dispersals. The cultural, economic, and political impacts of the European discovery of maize were evident in the ensuing population boom that followed its introduction into the Old World. After 1492, maize rapidly diffused into Europe, Africa, and Asia and was successful in large part because it did not directly compete with existing grain crops such as rice, wheat, oats, millet, and barley. Maize was also suited to cultivation in otherwise poor growing conditions related to topography, soils, climates, aridity, and elevation. Significantly, maize also prospers in exceptionally wet climates unsuited to wheat or relatively arid regions unsuited to rice cultivation. Moreover, maize has the additional advantage of rapid returns and twice the productive yield per unit of land of wheat.

The adoption of maize in Africa and China heralded a dramatic social and cultural transformation. Maize provided a level of food surplus that permitted the exponential growth of populations. Whereas in Europe maize was seen as a substandard cereal grain, fit only for feeding the poor and hungry and livestock, in many areas of Africa and Asia maize came to dominate the agricultural economies of many nation-states. The productivity and efficiency of maize horticulture and its low production and transportation costs made it a cheap food for slaves captured and held by European and Arabic slave traders. Maize made possible the efficient and economical transport and exchange of horrific numbers of sub-Saharan Africans destined for the markets of Europe, the Middle East, and the Americas.

The African Connection

Although it remains unclear who first introduced maize to Europe, Africa, and the Old World more generally, a number of scholars now argue that the Portuguese colonies of Africa served as the initial conduit to the dif-

fusion of maize in that hemisphere. Jean Andrews claims that maize, beans, peppers, squash, and turkeys diffused into the Balkans, or southeastern Europe, by way of Portuguese Africa, India, and the Ottoman Empire in the period following the voyages of Columbus (1993, pp. 194–204). So profound was the impact of maize on the African economy that, like Mesoamerica, culture and society, subsistence and settlement, political economy and gender relations, and the respective cuisines and culinary technologies of each of these vast regions were rapidly transformed to accommodate the adoption of maize and those human diasporas with which it was associated. The unique maize-based cultural complex of agricultural practices, extensive settlement patterns, and storage, distribution, and food processing technologies identified with maize cultivation in fact fueled much of the transformation in question. In *Africa's Emerging Maize Revolution*, Derek Byerlee and Carl Eicher acknowledge that the adoption of maize has been the primary engine driving the transformation of the African social, political, and economic landscape for the many societies that have been swept up in this new agricultural revolution.

More specifically, it is becoming increasingly evident that those agricultural practices identified with maize, such as swidden cultivation, extensive or shifting settlement patterns that are, in turn, identified with swidden systems, the processing of maize with basalt grinding slabs, the female domination of these labor-intensive food processing and storage traditions, and the emerging role of women in the maize-dominated marketplace have all played significant roles in the transformation of the African political economy. Moreover, given the fact that in many areas of Africa, much of the traditional African agricultural complex—centered on such crops as millet—has been displaced by maize has much to do with the changing face of African cuisine at the most fundamental level of analysis, and more generally, at the interface of cultural change and transformation.

Africans prepare a maize porridge—called *kpekple* in Ghana, *bidia* in Zaire, *sadza* in Zimbabwe, *putu* in Zululand, *mealie* in South Africa, and *posho* or *ugali* in East Africa—consumed by millions. Virtually no African country has remained untouched by the diffusion and exchange of maize, and the agricultural practices on the African continent range from the simple sowing of maize kernels along rivers and streams to the cultivation of maize in household gardens. While widespread, these traditional practices are primitive compared to the magnitude and intensity of agribusiness development and investment in commercially viable maize agricultural field systems.

Maize Procurement and Processing

Maize is seldom described outside of the so-called Mesoamerican triumvirate of maize, beans, and squash. Early Mesoamerican peoples planted these food crops together, often planting beans and squash adjacent to maize so as to provide the former plants stalks on which to ex-

MAIZE-TORTILLA TECHNOLOGIES

Neolithic maize-tortilla technology persisted well into the late nineteenth and early twentieth centuries throughout Mesoamerica, and the Americas more generally. It did so in large part due to the unique lime processing of the soaked and softened maize kernels for *nixtamal* used in Mesoamerica. This maize dough by-product was then washed so as to remove the pericarp, or outer skin of the individual kernels, and was ground on metate grinding platforms. Apparently, the resulting mix of moist flour (*masa*) was then processed into tortillas.

The use of metate grinding slabs and the pestle (*metlapilli* or *tejolote*) provided a range of nutritive and socioeconomic benefits: (1) reduction, fractionation, and mineral supplementation of maize kernels, (2) lime treatment, (3) the shearing stroke used to process maize kernels, (4) craft specialization and the appearance of markets oriented to the production and exchange of maize-tortilla technologies, (5) nutritional and subsistence economics of maize preparation, (6) the social and economic reorganization of maize preparation, including cooperative production among households and the appearance of specialists such as tortilla vendors, and (7) the emergence of maize-tortilla technology and equipment—including *comalli* or *comal* ceramic griddles—that were indicators of social or economic status.

As for the persistence of maize-tortilla technologies specific to the metate and *tejolote*, because tortillas require a very finely ground *masa*, the adoption of power milling (*molinos de nixtamal*) of maize flour for the production of tortillas was not generally adopted until the improvement of power milling technologies in the 1940s and 1950s. Male heads of household resisted the adoption of power milling technologies because the thirty-five to forty hours per week required to hand mill *masa* on the traditional metate grinding slab was construed as women's work. Women, however, generally favored the adoption of the new *molinos de nixtamal*, and between the years of 1935 and 1940 the number of *molinos* (power mills) in Mexico increased from 927 to almost 6,000. The efficiency of the power mills freed women for other household tasks, including those pertaining to their newfound roles, industries traditionally reserved for males, in the marketplace and arts and crafts. Similar patterns affecting the displacement of men and or the relegation of women to maize-processing industries have been identified with the adoption of maize agriculture in Africa, Europe, and other regions of the Old World. In fact, the metate identified with Mesoamerica is now a familiar feature of that material culture associated with both women's daily activities and the African kitchen more generally.

---

tend their vines. Mesoamerican cuisine similarly combined the products of these plants in a culinary mix that reinforced and supplemented the otherwise niacin-poor composition of maize-dominant dietary practices. Without these supplements, or the lime processing inherent in the production of *masa* (maize flour) used in the production of tortillas and related foodstuffs, maize-dominant diets have the potential to result in the spread of the skin disease pellagra. Pellagra spread rapidly and in epidemic proportions throughout all the European and African countries that first adopted maize consumption without similarly adopting the critically important *nixtamalización* process necessary for the production of *nixtamal* or lime-treated *masa*. The source of the disease remained a medical mystery until it was studied in the context of maize consumption in the southern United States. It was ultimately determined that the niacin-deficient nature of maize-dominant diets played a key nutritional role in the onset of those symptoms identified with pellagra.

Traditional Maize Agricultural Systems

In Latin America, maize is the central foodstuff of the hearth and household. Because of the broad range of cli-mates, soils, and topographic and hydrological conditions under which maize may be cultivated, diverse agricultural methods have evolved to accommodate its cultivation and processing. Maize environments in the Third World have been classified into four major types: tropical, subtropical, temperate, and highlands. As of 1996, tropical environments accounted for 90.6 million acres, or 45 percent of the total area under maize cultivation in developing countries; temperate environments accounted for 55.1 million acres, or 27 percent of the total; subtropical environments accounted for 42 million acres, or 21 percent of the total; and highland environments constituted 15.3 million acres, or 8 percent of the total area under maize cultivation in the developing world (Dowswell, Paliwal, and Cantrell, pp. 38–46).

In the tropical forests of Mexico and Central America, maize agriculture is predominantly associated with swidden (slash-and-burn or shifting) agricultural systems and the development of *milpas* (maize fields). Swidden cultivation entails the scoring or felling of trees and the subsequent torching of dry foliage and timber left in the wake of the clearance operation. Once the forest parcel has been cleared, dibble sticks are used to pierce the soil

CUITLACOCHE: AKA "CORN SMUT"

Of the many ancient and traditional food by-products of maize, "corn smut" (*Ustilago maydis*), a fungus called *huitlacoche* or *cuitlacoche* by the Mexican Aztecs, continues to hold its own as one of the more popular delicacies of Mexican cuisine on the U.S market. *Huitlacoche*, comparable to the Portobello mushroom in some respects, is a soil-borne fungal growth that affects the internodes, the base and midrib of leaves, and immature ears of maize. This fungus is but one more in a constellation of foodstuffs not previously considered for the modern marketplace. In fact, it has been surmised that corn smut may soon become a part of the nouvelle cuisine in the United States. Like the skepticism that greeted the initial introduction of maize in Europe, it may take time before corn smut becomes popular with consumers.

Corn smut accounts for some 3 to 5 percent of maize crop losses or damage in the United States alone. As such, it will likely provide a continuing source of economic incentives to U.S. farmers prepared to define a market niche for the maize-based fungal growth.

for the sowing of maize kernels in the charred timbers of the *milpa*. In contrast, in highland Guatemala maize is cultivated on the steepest of mountain slopes and under the most challenging topographical and hydrological conditions. In highland central Mexico, on the other hand, maize cultivation took the form of *chinampas* (floating gardens)—perhaps the most unique agricultural system devoted to maize—that rapidly evolved and proliferated in the Basin of Mexico in pre-Columbian times. In fact, *chinampas* were a fundamentally important aspect of agricultural development in the highly populated Basin in the precontact period from the thirteenth to sixteenth centuries C.E. Earlier forms of agricultural intensification associated with both *chinampas* and maize cultivation have similarly been identified with the ancient metropolis of Teotihuacan, Mexico. This ancient city, which contained a population of some 150,000 people within an area of just under 8.5 square miles, was sustained through such productive systems of agricultural intensification during the period from 100 to 650 C.E. The only remaining Mesoamerican examples of this form of agricultural intensification are found in Xochimilco, Mexico.

In essence, *chinampas* entailed the creation of new agricultural parcels of land built atop floating islands or enclosures created within the shallow margins of Lake Texcoco. *Chinampas* plantations were framed within long, narrow rectangular enclosures formed from willow branches staked into the depths of the shallow lake bed—part of a system of lakes identified with Lake Texcoco—that once dominated the Basin of Mexico. Earth and mud gathered from the shallow lake bottom were dumped into these enclosures and used to form the agriculturally viable portion of those *chinampas* that were eventually anchored to the shallow lake bottom through the growth of those willow shoots and branches used to stake the plots. The recurring introduction of nutrients for maize grown atop *chinampa* parcels entailed the use of lake bottom mud, silt, vegetation, and excrement in an otherwise effective and ecologically sound practice. In this way, the Mexican Aztecs and their predecessors increased their ability to feed a rapidly growing Basin population by expanding the amount of cultivable lands devoted to maize and related crop systems. The area identified with the lakeside community of Xochimilco in the southern Basin of Mexico continues the practice of *chinampa* cultivation and floating gardens, and such parcels enable Mexican farmers to excel at the production of maize, beans, squash, flowers, and a variety of other Mesoamerican crops.

In the Maya lowlands and along the coastal margins of the Yucatan peninsula, the ancient Maya devoted considerable resources to the production of maize and related crops in raised or ridged field systems. These massive ridged field systems are among the largest and most extensive earthworks ever produced by the Maya or other societies of ancient America. Created within swamps, flooded *bajos*, or water-filled shallow limestone sinks or coastal estuaries, raised fields (or ridged islands or embankments) were formed into elongated, roughly rectangular agricultural parcels by piling soils or upcast scooped from drained areas immediately adjacent to the embankment or island. The overall appearance of such fields resembles massive waffle-like garden grids. These individual islands, however, were broad enough to accommodate the passage of a tractor-trailer rig. Pollen studies from these large earthen constructions have determined that, while maize was the major product of these systems, a variety of other Mesoamerican foodstuffs were also cultivated. In fact, the quantity of foods produced by such systems far exceeded the amount projected for swidden agricultural systems (once thought to be the predominant means by which food was grown in the tropical landscapes of the Maya heartland).

Whether produced by the indigenous systems of *milpa* or *chinampa* agriculture, maize cultivation in much of the Third World, and in more traditional contexts, has been dominated by the use of the "dibble stick" since pre-Columbian times. Consisting of a shaft of wood with a pointed tip used to pierce the soil for the sowing of maize kernels, the dibble stick has persisted for thousands of years and has been adopted by subsistence farmers throughout developing countries that have adopted maize agriculture. Nineteenth-century American maize farmers

422

adopted both the cylindrical silo or "corn crib" and the "dibble stick" from American Indian prototypes (Fussell, p. 152). Improvements on the dibble stick developed in the 1850s ranged from the Randall and Jones Double Hand Planter to the long-lived "Stabber" or "Jobber." Both of these variations "stab" the soil and simultaneously dispense maize kernels into the holes (Fussell, pp. 144–146). Such early efforts ultimately led to the evolution of the automated maize planters of today. Unlike commercial systems of mass production identified with the technology of maize planting and cultivation, the dibble stick has weathered the introduction of new techniques and continues to dominate more traditional, nontechnological farming practices around the world.

The Maize Harvest of the Machine Age

One need only travel to places like the state of Nebraska to realize that maize agriculture dominates the agricultural traditions of some societies. In fact, a drive through Nebraska during the growing season might leave some outsiders with the impression that it consists of a seamless, seemingly endless, and very dense field of maize. For the past two hundred years, farmers and agricultural scientists in such areas have developed a variety of means, technologies, and hybrids suitable for the continuing propagation of maize. In *The Story of Corn* (1992), Fussell summarizes the many agricultural technologies, cropping and harvesting methods, hybrids, commercial products, and cultural and religious values identified with maize agriculture in the Americas and other parts of the world.

Methods of harvesting of maize range from the hand culling of hybrid maize cobs from home gardens to towering high-tech combines or harvesting machines and tractors rigged—in the largest combines—to cull maize ears or cobs at the rate of twelve rows at a time and thousands of bushels per day. Even an older combine or harvester can harvest some 10,000 bushels of maize per day, yielding 150 to 200 bushels per acre. On the other hand, the maintenance and upkeep of such machines easily runs into the thousands of dollars per year, an amount likely to double or triple in the Third World. A new combine harvester can cost from $100,000 to $200,000 or more in the United States. Whereas subsistence farmers throughout much of the Third World continue to thresh maize by hand without specialized equipment or resources, this task is left to agribusiness giants and commercial agricultural concerns in industrialized nations.

An array of farm machinery patents for the harvesting and processing of maize appeared shortly after the industrialization of farms. The U.S. Patent Office Report of 1860 lists hundreds of patents for corn planters, cultivators, harvesters, cornhuskers, corn shellers, cornstalk cutters, corn-shock binders, cornstalk shocking machines, corn cleaners, seed drills, rotary harrows, smut machines, corn and cob crushers and mills, and seed drills (Fussell, p. 144). The advent of the canning industry in 1862 and the proliferation of new land-grant colleges de-

Maize has become an important agricultural crop throughout Africa. These farm workers in Zimbabwe are harvesting maize on a cooperative. © HULTON-DEUTSCH COLLECTION/CORBIS.

voted to science, agriculture, and industry helped fuel the industrialization and modernization of maize procurement, processing, storage, distribution, and hybridization. In time, the industrialized farming operations and agricultural cooperatives of the Corn Belt adopted many mechanized methods for harvesting and threshing maize. Soon thereafter the towering grain silos and high-rise grain elevators of the Midwest replaced the humble corncribs adopted from the North American Indians. Despite this, traditional household corncribs survived the onslaught of the Industrial Age, and survivals include the Mesoamerican *cuezcomatl* (thatch-roofed adobe brick granary), the crib-logged granaries of the Sierra Tarahumara Indians of northern Mexico, and the clay-lined maize grain silos of Africa. In each instance, subsistence farmers and agribusiness giants alike must take into account the difficulties of storing maize at optimal conditions and balance humidity, the moisture content of the kernels, and the potential for pest infestations.

The Future of Maize

Maize is processed into a dizzying array of consumer products ranging from corn on the cob and popcorn to cornstarch, corn oils, automotive fuels, such as ethanol and gasohol, and alcoholic beverages, including corn beer (*chicbi*) and whiskey. In addition to the more than 1,000 maize-based products that one is likely to find in the local supermarket, the genetically modified by-products of maize are creating their own culinary diversity and potentials, pitfalls, controversies, and complications for the world of food production and biotech industries. Beyond the diversity inherent in the production and distribution of maize in the marketplace, the reality is that maize remains the most important agricultural crop for over 70 million farm families worldwide. Eighty percent of the world's farmers who cultivate maize are in developing nations of the Third World. This reality, coupled with the "genetic erosion" of the crop, has prompted some to ask whether maize can be bred so as to assure the sustainable evolution of the crop (Sevilla, p. 221). If the lawsuits for patent infringements against farmers by agribusiness corporations and biotechnology firms for the unlicensed use of their patented hybrids are any indication, the potentials of genetic diversity and hybrid vigor once identified with maize may be constrained to ever fewer and increasingly more vulnerable hybrid offspring.

See also **Africa; Central America; Columbian Exchange; Mexico; Mexico and Central America, Pre-Columbian; Niacin Deficiency (Pellagra); Swidden.**

BIBLIOGRAPHY

Ackerman, Jennifer. "Food: How Safe? How Altered?" *National Geographic* 201 (2002): 2–51.

Andrews, Jean. "Diffusion of the Mesoamerican Food Complex to Southeastern Europe." *Geographical Review* 83 (1993): 194–204.

Bauer, A. J. "Millers and Grinders: Technology and Household Economy in Meso-America." *Agricultural History* 64 (1990): 1–17.

Beadle, G. W. "Teosinte and the Origin of Maize." *Journal of Heredity* 30 (1939): 245–247.

Benz, Bruce F. "Reconstructing the Racial Phylogeny of Mexican Maize: Where Do We Stand?" In *Corn and Culture in the Prehistoric New World*, edited by Sissel Johannessen and Christine A. Hastorf, pp. 157–179. Boulder, Colo.: Westview, 1994.

Benz, Bruce F. "Maize: Origin, Domestication, and Development." In *The Oxford Encyclopedia of Mesoamerican Cultures: The Civilizations of Mexico and Central America*, edited by David Carrasco, vol. 2, pp. 147–150. New York: Oxford University Press, 2001.

Biskowski, M. "Grinding Implements." In *The Oxford Encyclopedia of Mesoamerican Cultures: The Civilizations of Mexico and Central America*, edited by David Carrasco, vol. 1, pp. 441–442. New York: Oxford University Press, 2001.

Brandes, Stanley. "Maize as a Culinary Mystery." *Ethnology* 31 (1992): 331–336.

Brenneman, Dale S. "The Verdict Is In: Corn Is the Direct Descendant of Teosinte." *Southwestern Mission Research Center Newsletter* 35 (2001): 52.

Byerlee, Derek, and Carl K. Eicher, eds. *Africa's Emerging Maize Revolution*. Boulder, Colo.: Lynne Rienner, 1997.

Cowan, R. "Amazing Gastronomy: Sup or Smut?" *Science News* 137 (1990): 207.

Doebley, J. A. "Genetics and the Morphological Evolution of Maize." In *The Maize Handbook*, edited by Michael Freeling and Virginia Walbot, pp. 66–77. New York: Springer-Verlag, 1996.

Doebley, J., A. Stec, J. Wendel, and M. Edwards. "Genetic and Morphological Analysis of a Maize-Teosinte F2 Population: Implications for the Origin of Maize." *Proceedings of the National Academy of Sciences* 87 (1990): 9888–9892.

Dowswell, Christopher R., R. L. Paliwal, and Ronald P. Cantrell. *Maize in the Third World*. New York: Westview, 1996.

Eubanks, Mary W. *Corn in Clay: Maize Paleoethnobotany in Pre-Columbian Art*. Gainesville, Fla.: University Press of Florida, 1999.

Fussell, Betty. *The Story of Corn*. New York: North Point, 1992.

Galinat, Walton C. "Maize: Gift from America's First Peoples." In *Chiles to Chocolate: Food the Americas Gave the World*, edited by Nelson Foster and Linda S. Cordell, pp. 47–60. Tucson: University of Arizona Press, 1992.

Galinat, Walton C. "The Patterns of Plant Structures in Maize." In *The Maize Handbook*, edited by Michael Freeling and Virginia Walbot, pp. 61–65. New York: Springer-Verlag, 1996.

González, Roberto F. *Zapotec Science: Farming and Food in the Northern Sierra of Oaxaca*. Austin: University of Texas Press, 2001.

Hammond, Norman. *Ancient Maya Civilization*. New Brunswick, N.J.: Rutgers University Press, 1990.

Johnson, Sylvia A. *Tomatoes, Potatoes, Corn, and Beans: How the Foods of the Americas Changed Eating around the World*. New York: Atheneum, 1997.

MacNeish, Richard S. *The Science of Archaeology?* North Scituate, Mass.: Duxbury, 1978.

Maiti, Ratikanta, and Pedro Wesche-Ebeling. "Origin, Evolution, and Domestication of Maize: Recent Approaches." In *Maize Science*, edited by Ratikanta Maiti and Pedro Wesche-Ebeling, pp. 1–36. Enfield, N.H.: Science, 1998.

Mendoza, Ruben G. "Plant and Animal Domestication: Direct versus Indirect Evidence." *Antiquity* (St. John's College, Cambridge) 60 (1986): 1–14.

Roe, Keith. *Corncribs: History, Folklife, and Architecture*. Ames: Iowa State University Press, 1988.

Sánchez González, José Jesús. "Modern Variability and Patterns of Maize Movement in Mesoamerica." In *Corn and Culture in the Prehistoric New World*, edited by Sissel Johannessen and Christine A. Hastorf, pp. 135–156. Boulder, Colo.: Westview, 1994.

Sevilla, Ricardo. "Variation in Modern Andean Maize and Its Implications for Prehistoric Patterns." In *Corn and Culture in the Prehistoric New World*, edited by Sissel Johannessen and Christine A. Hastorf, pp. 219–244. Boulder, Colo.: Westview, 1994.

Ruben G. Mendoza

MAIZE AS A FOOD

The evolution, dispersal, and consumption of maize span the better part of the past eight thousand years of human cultural development. Until European exploration in the Americas began in 1492, maize was a New World domesticate with an exclusively American distribution and consumption. After 1492, maize rapidly diffused throughout the Old World of Europe by way of ships returning from the New World. In fact, by 1498 cultivation of maize had begun in Seville, Spain. With its subsequent adoption in Africa for the purpose of feeding the growing numbers of African slaves destined for southwest Asia and the Americas, consumers throughout Africa, Europe, and Asia began to use maize as food and as fodder. According to Sophie D. Coe's review of America's first cuisines, maize constitutes the third most important food crop in the world, following on the heels of wheat and rice (p. 10). It is no accident, therefore, that maize constitutes a fundamental ingredient in many of the world's cuisines, ranging from Mexican enchiladas and Chinese baby-corn, to African-American grits, corn flakes, popcorn, Italian polenta or gruel, corn meal, maize-based alcoholic beverages (such as whiskey and bourbon), mayonnaise, and corn oil. Thus, maize has more than demonstrated its cross-cultural adaptability, gastronomic significance, and culinary versatility.

Maize Preparation and Consumption

The preparation of maize into food and beverages subsumes a world of food and beverage variations. Maize-based foods and beverages in Mesoamerica—the place where maize originated—are many and diverse, and many of these are quite old. In Mexico alone, food and beverage varieties range from those by-products of maize that derive from the food process known as *nixtamalización* (or nixtamalization) to the fermentation of processed maize into alcoholic beverages and the creation of a very broad variety of foods. The oldest and most enduring method for processing cereal grains is one that originated in ancient Mesoamerica long before the Common Era.

Nixtamal Production

In order to produce any one or more of the aforementioned maize-based foods or beverages, maize must be reduced to a paste or flour. The resulting by-product was known to the Mexica-Aztecs as *nixtamal*, and the process for rendering the maize kernels into a paste has since come to be known as *nixtamalización*. According to Sebastián Verdi, *nixtamalización* entails the fundamental process of rendering maize kernels into a paste that is treated with lime and heat in order to incorporate calcium and digestible iron into the *masa*, or maize dough. Ultimately, *nixtamalización* enhances the nutrient content of tortillas and related maize food by-products in such a way that maize is rendered superior in nutrient value to other grain-based foods such as white bread (p. 9).

In their study of the physiochemical, structural, and textural properties of tortillas and the *nixtamal* process, G. Arámbula-Villa and colleagues provide a detailed overview of the distinctions inherent in the methods and mechanics of the *nixtamalización* process. In comparing the efficacy and mechanics of traditional methods of dry-*masa* flour production versus modern methods of instant-*masa* flour production, these researchers present two detailed diagrams (p. 246). The traditional dry-*masa* production method entails several distinct steps, including cooking, steeping, *nixtamalización*, washing, *nixtamal*, milling with a hammer mill, drying, re-milling with the hammer mill, classification, and product collection. The modern production of instant masa entails dry milling, the mixing of water and lime with ground maize, extru-

TARAHUMARA INDIAN *TESGÜINO* PRODUCTION

Anthropologist Bernard Fontana has documented the process identified with the production and fermentation of the maize beverage known as *tesgüino* to the Tarahumara Indians of Chihuahua, Mexico. This fermented maize drink may be processed from newly sprouted maize or malt, even though other variants of *tesgüino* may be processed from roasting maize ears or the fruit of the nopal cactus, shrubs, and selected fruit trees. The Tarahumara recipe for *tesgüino* is as follows: Maize kernels are distributed along the bottom of shallow baskets. The baskets are then covered with grasses and placed in a darkened location where they are sprinkled with water daily for four or five days, so as to stimulate the sprouting of the maize kernels contained therein. When the maize sprouts are approximately one inch in height, they are ground on a ground stone slab or metate and placed into pottery jars or metal bowls containing water. These are set to boil for approximately eight hours. Once the liquid acquires a yellowish hue, it is left to cool. The liquid is then strained into another bowl and mixed with other herbs to produce a paste into which more water is added. The mixture is then placed into specialized fermenting vessels that are stored in a warm location for the evening. The watery paste is then mixed with the strained maize broth and allowed to ferment for three to four days. Ultimately, *tesgüino* is intended for festive occasions such as the *rarajipari* kick-ball game and related rituals, and it should be consumed immediately since it begins to spoil within twelve hours of completing the recipe (p. 54).

sion or *nixtamalización*, fresh *masa*, drying, milling with a hammer mill, and product collection.

Nixtamalización often involves the use of a lime or alkaline bath or pre-soak that results in the softening and "shelling" of maize kernels. Once softened, the maize kernels are rendered or ground by way of basalt-stone grinding technologies, such as the ancient metate grinding slab or the modern automated *molinos*, or maize grinding mills, that pulverize maize for preparation into such by-products as *masa* or maize dough. *Masa* is used predominantly in the production of the pancake-like maize cakes or flat breads known as tortillas. *Masa* is also used in the production of a broad variety of foods and beverages, including the ever-popular corn-husk encased Mexican *tamale*, *totopos*, or *tostaditas*. *Masa* is also used in the Mexica-Aztec ground maize drink or gruel known as *atolli*

A frontier settler in Potter County, Pennsylvania, is shown using a hominy block for crushing corn to make grits. The pestle is attached to a sapling, which allows for easier pounding. Woodcut, circa 1840. ROUGHWOOD COLLECTION.

or *atole*, in *champurrado*, which consists of a rich broth of *atole* mixed with chocolate, and in the alcoholic beverage known to the Tarahumara Indians of northern Mexico as *tesguino*. Many of these indigenous Mexican foods and beverages have been adopted or reinterpreted by agribusiness, nutritional scientists, the general public, and the food industry. Such foods are distributed internationally under such brand and trade names as Quaker *masa harina* (dough flour), Fritos, Taco Bell, Corn Chex, Kellogg's Corn Flakes, Doritos, and many others.

Maize Nutritional Composition

Scientists from several disciplines have studied the tortilla and its counterpart the tamale as examples of the nutritional value or mineral composition of processed maize products. In one such study conducted in 1988 and 1989, nutritional scientist Charles Weber and colleagues studied commercially produced tortillas and tamales from food chain stores. The tamales in this study included both green corn and stuffed beef and pork varieties. The researchers contrasted those tortillas and tamales with others produced in neighborhood factories or outlets and homes in the Mexican-American barrio communities of Tucson, Arizona. Thus, the results of these studies provided one basis for understanding the nutritive values of processed maize as represented by both commercial and domestic by-products. The study demonstrated that there was little variation in the size, composition, and mineral content in the commercially milled tortillas obtained from different commercial outlets.

The findings also demonstrated that the average size and weight of the maize or corn tortilla were 5.7 inches and 0.71 ounces, respectively. Average moisture content

was 42.9 percent; protein content was 5.9 percent; lipid values were 2.3 percent; and acid detergent fiber and ash values were 1.8 percent and 1.3 percent, respectively. Carbohydrate content averaged 49 percent, while energy values averaged 240 kcal/100 grams (pp. 326–327). In contrast, tamales averaged 4 ounces in weight; moisture content averaged 59 percent; protein values averaged 5.4 percent; and lipid concentrations varied considerably but averaged 11 percent. This latter variation was thought to be the result of the wide variety of recipes used to produce tamales, and the variable use of fat sources such as lard versus hydrogenated vegetable oil. Also, it should be noted that whereas beef tamales averaged 4.2 ounces in weight, green corn tamales averaged 3.5 ounces in weight (pp. 330–331). Finally, in regard to mineral content, Charles Weber and his colleagues found that maize or corn tortillas contain calcium, phosphorous, iron, zinc, copper, and magnesium in variable amounts. Their study also noted that the calcium content of tortillas produced from lime-processed *nixtamal* was ten to twenty times higher than that of the original grain source (pp. 331–332). These studies demonstrate that the dry milling and lime processing of maize at the most fundamental level have a profound effect on the inherent nutritive values of maize.

Pellagra and the Indian Triad

Because of the inherent nutritional values and mineral composition of maize grain, the lime processing of *nixtamal* and the evolution of the so-called "Indian triad" or "Mesoamerican triumvirate" were critical innovations that were directly attributable to the ancient Native Americans who nurtured maize through much of its evolutionary history. The triad or triumvirate in this instance refers to the American Indian horticultural heritage and/or tendency to cultivate maize, beans, and squash together in the same agricultural plots and, subsequently, to mix these ingredients into their culinary repertoire in a nutritionally balanced and sophisticated way. The combination of maize with both beans and squash is culturally and biologically critical in that the nutritional value of maize is significantly enhanced by the addition of these two fundamental foods. While maize lacks the amino acid niacin, common beans (*Phaseolus vulgaris*) are a significant source of amino acids, including niacin, tryptophan, and lysine. In her account of the *nixtamalización* or lime processing of maize developed in ancient Native America, Betty Fussell documents the means by which this process transforms maize's inherent protein structures (mainly albumins, globulins, glutelin, and zein) into the metabolically and nutritionally critical amino acids niacin, tryptophan, and lysine (pp. 203–204).

The maize-dominant diets of some European, Egyptian, and other African peoples at the end of the nineteenth century lacked the aforementioned essential amino acids. This lack resulted in the spread of pellagra in epidemic proportions. Kwashiorkor—a severe form of malnutrition identified with infants and children dependent on high-carbohydrate and low-protein diets—also appeared among African and other peoples whose diets were maize-dominant. In her book on the culture and agriculture of tomatoes, potatoes, corn, and beans, Sylvia Johnson notes that those afflicted with pellagra suffered skin rashes, dizziness, sore muscles, and in the worse-case scenario, insanity and death (pp. 24–25). According to Betty Fussell, to Europeans pellagra was widely known as "corn sickness" until it was renamed pellagra by an Italian in 1771 (p. 202). Even so, the specific causes of pellagra remained a mystery until after 1915, when the U.S. National Institute of Health commissioned a pellagra investigation headed by Dr. Joseph Goldberger, whose findings ultimately led to the effective treatment of the disease in the United States by the 1930s. These deficiencies and the epidemics with which they were associated might have been averted with the adoption of the "Indian triad" and the alkaline or lime processing of maize into *nixtamal*. According to Betty Fussell, this variety of maize processing can be documented to as early as 100 B.C.E. through the discovery of lime-soaking pots at the ancient site of Teotihuacan. She concludes that such discoveries have led many to believe that "corn is the oldest chemically processed grain in the world" (p. 176).

The Primordial Maize Tortilla

The maize flat breads or tortillas of Mexico are ancient and ubiquitous in the Americas. These breads are a fundamental staple of Mexican and other Latin American cuisine and have inspired the creation of a wealth of pre-Columbian or indigenous American foods, including en-

FROM *AREPAS* TO BLUE CORN *PIKI*

Arepas are to Venezuelans, Colombians, and Peruvians what tortillas are to the Mexican people. In order to prepare *arepas*, dry white maize kernels are ground into flour, which is then mixed with water, oil, and salt, and then prepared in much the same way that tortillas are formed, except in this instance, the flat breads are smaller but much thicker in shape than tortillas. The larger and thicker tortillas, which characterize the maize flat breads of the Nicaraguans, allow for larger servings of beef or other ingredients to be placed in the tortilla-like container. The *pupusas* of El Salvador, prepared from lime-treated maize with the addition of cheese, are essentially smaller tortillas that are used primarily for burritos or taco-like containers of beef or chicken and legumes and vegetables. The *humitas* of Bolivia and Chile are yet another form of tamale consumed in South America. Invariably, pre-cooked maize flour similar to lime-treated *masa* is mixed with other regional ingredients to produce *humitas*.

The Hopi Indians of Northern Arizona have processed maize into a particularly unique food known as *piki* bread for the past eleven centuries. *Piki* bread consists of a very thin, gray, and ashy maize tortilla or wafer created from blue corn meal by way of hand-coating a very hot and finely polished stone griddle with a watery maize dough paste. In *The Story of Corn*, Betty Fussell cites Hopi matriarch Helen Sekaquaptewa's acknowledgement that "*Piki* are the original cornflakes," thereby noting that these otherwise paper-thin, flaky, and quite tasty *piki* blue-corn wafers inspired the subsequent development of flaked corn (pp. 167–168).

chiladas, tacos, tostadas, *sopes, flautas, chilaquiles,* and *sopa de tortilla.* The principal distinctions in these foods evolve from the treatment of the tortilla. In these Mexican food examples, tortillas are rolled, folded, flattened, thickened, and or fried. In the case of *chilaquiles* and *sopa de tortilla,* old, hardened, or otherwise stale tortillas are broken up or cut into strips and used in the preparation of casseroles and soups. In most of the aforementioned examples, the tortilla serves as the container, packet, or flat bread into or upon which varying types and quantities of meats and vegetables are placed. Alternately, the tortilla becomes but one additional, albeit important, ingredient in the preparation of casseroles and soups. Sophie D. Coe acknowledges that late-fifteenth and early-sixteenth-century Mexica-Aztec peoples of the Valley of Mexico

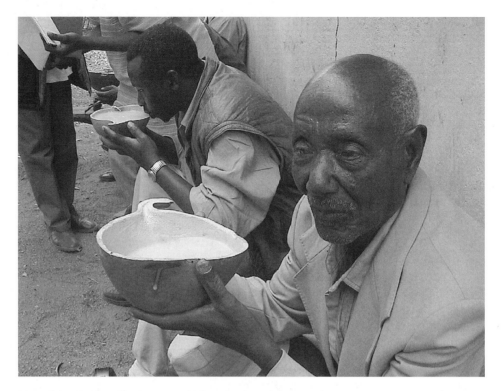

Men of the Kamba tribe in Kenya drink maize beer from gourds. It was common in earlier times for the men to drink the beer with straws from a common gourd. PHOTO BY Y. MORIMOTO.

used tortillas and steamed maize-dough tamales as containers or packets for an incredible variety of foodstuffs, including beans, squash, tomatoes, mushrooms, avocados, worms, rabbit, deer, turkey, and many other items (pp. 112–119). Heriberto García Rivas has also investigated the extraordinary wealth and variety inherent in the maize-based pre-Columbian cuisines of Mexico.

In addition to its status as the premier Mexican foodstuff, the tortilla is also part of indigenous and Catholic religious traditions and rituals in Mesoamerica and beyond. Aside from their status as the gastronomic and culinary archetype of maize-based foods, tortillas also serve a practical need in their role as edible utensils (spoons or spatulas) used for scooping up beans, rice, and meats served in Mexican cuisine. In fact, legend has it that Motecuhzoma Ilhuicamina—the illustrious penultimate emperor of the Mexica Aztec—never used the same eating utensils more than once. This was due in large part to the fact that the emperor used tortillas in the same way that the Spanish used spoons and other utensils in the Old World. In many areas outside of Mexico (including the southwestern United States) tortillas have taken on a culinary predominance: they are regularly substituted for breads and other carbohydrates. This phenomenon was unheard of in colonial times. For example, in New Spain or Spanish colonial Mexico (c. 1521–1821), those who believed maize to be an inferior food fit only for the feeding of swine often substituted wheat for maize in the pro-

duction of tortillas. From that point forward, wheat or flour tortillas took on a status as the flat bread food of choice for Spanish colonials in Mexico, whereas tortillas prepared from maize continued to be perceived as the primary foodstuff of Mexican Indians and the poor. Ironically, what were once called *totopos* or *tostaditas* in Mexico are today called "corn chips," such as Doritos, Fritos, and nachos, which are a widely consumed snack food in the United States and elsewhere.

Other Traditional Maize Foods

Once maize was introduced into the Old World of Europe, foods containing maize as a main ingredient were created for a variety of distinctive dishes and regional palettes across that vast cultural region. Italians adopted maize into a dish today known as polenta, which consists of a finely ground maize mixed with water in order to produce a porridge or mush. Sylvia Johnson describes polenta as a maize mush cooked in a pot, poured onto a wooden board, and allowed to cool for a few minutes until ready to consume. Eventually, polenta was mixed with other ingredients typical of Italian cuisine including grated cheese, mushrooms, tomatoes, and peppers, or it was served with pasta. When mixed with sugar or honey, polenta took on one other food use: as breakfast porridge (p. 21). In Rumania, *mamaliga* is prepared from sweet cornmeal and consists of a food akin to polenta that is sometimes referred to as "cornmeal mush." Cornmeal remains a primary staple of Rumanians and Hungarians alike, with *puliszka* being the staple food of Hungarians. *Puliszka* is prepared in much the same way as either polenta or *mamaliga*; however, it is often topped with feta cheese, butter, and other ingredients lightly blended into the cornmeal mush before the meal has been thoroughly cooked. Also popular in Romania and Hungary is *malderash*, which consists of maize cakes seasoned with cumin and coriander.

African Maize Cuisine

In the sixteenth century, maize rapidly diffused across the African continent as a result of the slave trade. By the end of the nineteenth century, a maize meal called *posho* was among the most popular foods of eastern Africa. Sylvia Johnson notes that the primary African use of maize as a food is in mush or porridge. Africans grind and boil maize in water in much the same way Europeans and Americans have done for many years (pp. 236–237). Maize porridge is known as *kpekple* in Ghana and *bidia* in Zaire. In Zimbabwe, people consume *sadza*, whereas East Africans eat *posho* or *ugali*. Zulu-speaking people consume *putu* as a primary source of nutrition. One African dish called *coo-coo* contains maize mush with okra, an African vegetable that slaves introduced in the Caribbean as fungi (pp. 22–23). In Nigeria, maize is boiled and roasted in different forms. For example, *adalu* consists of maize kernels or cornmeal boiled with beans, while *ogi* and *tuwo* consist of ground and boiled maize flour. *Ogi* is a breakfast dish prepared from maize flour that is boiled until it attains a smooth consistency. *Tuwo* also consists of maize flour that is boiled until it acquires a thick consistency. Nigerians generally consume *tuwo* with soup dishes. Similarly, *kokoro* is a Nigerian snack food comprised of ground maize dough rolled together with other ingredients and then fried in vegetable oil. Finally, *aadun* consists of a cooked or baked snack prepared from ground maize, red pepper, and oil. Invariably, many of those maize foods developed in Africa found their way back to the New World by way of the Caribbean and have lasted in the African-American culinary tradition. Grits can also be added to this list of African maize culinary concoctions. Grits consists of coarsely ground dried corn and is used as an ingredient in any number of other maize-based recipes, ranging from cracklin' cornbread to corn chowder, fried catfish basted with yellow corn meal, and a host of cornbread stuffings and hominy-based recipes.

Maize as a Fermented Beverage

According to a Food and Agriculture Organization report, the fermentation of maize by indigenous Latin American peoples provides the basis for virtually all indigenously produced alcoholic beverages in the Americas. *Chicha de jora*, or maize beer, is perhaps the most important and popular beverage produced in South America, including the countries of Argentina, Bolivia, Brazil, Colombia, Ecuador, and Peru. In fact, according to Betty Fussell, *chicha* was the critically important nu-

MAIZE: MYTH AND SYMBOL

The *Popol Vuh*, the sacred book of the ancient Quiche Maya, relates an origin myth that illustrates the role of maize as the hearth and source of Mayan culture and civilization itself. According to the Maya, the ancestors were fashioned from maize and bitter water. Thus depictions of maize plants and foods in the form of human–maize anthropomorphs in Mesoamerican ceremonial and ritual contexts are common. The seventh-century polychrome murals of Cacaxtla, Mexico, present depictions of maize stalks with cobs in the form of human heads bearing Maya-like features and hair consisting of maize silks. Dennis Tedlock's translation of the *Popol Vuh* notes that in order to create the first human ancestors, it was necessary for the female deity and midwife Xmucane—"the Bearer, Begetter, Sovereign Plumed Serpent"—to grind the yellow and white maize nine times in order to render whole the flesh of the earliest ancestors (pp. 145–146). Through this most ancient of legends and cultural lenses, the Maya continue to interpret their world, and in turn, be interpreted by the world about them. According to anthropologist Evon Z. Vogt, the Zinacanteco Indian healers and shaman of Chiapas, Mexico, conduct ancient and traditional rituals that make use of maize kernels, which are still viewed as a model for the structure of the human soul (pp. 94–95). In addition to the spiritual and divinatory place of maize in both ancient and modern Maya cosmology and worldview, Zinacanteco and other Mayan healers prescribe maize in a variety of forms as a remedy for any and all spiritual and physical conflicts.

According to the Food and Agriculture Organization, the Lacandon Maya used *pozol* with water and honey to reduce fevers. At the same time, *pozol* was used as cataplasm to heal minor wounds and to counter the effects of diarrhea. According to Jorge Fernandez Chiti, a tea was blended from *barbas de elote* (corn silk or maize tassels) and this concoction remains a popular Latin American diuretic used in natural healing and medicine in this day and age. *Barbas de elote* continues to be used by Latin American *curanderos* or "curers" for the treatment of kidney and bladder problems, as well as a remedy for hepatitis and edema (p. 59).

tritional counterpart to the *nixtamalización* and ash-and-lime-processed maize products used in other areas of the Americas (but unknown in Andean South America) in pre-Columbian times (p. 249). Other alcoholic beverages

ATOLE: AN AZTEC BREW

According to Heriberto García Rivas, *atole*, from the Aztec term *atolli*, signifies watery or watered-down liquid or beverage. *Atole* is one of the preferred maize-based drinks of the indigenous peoples of Meso-america. Since remote antiquity, atole has been prepared from boiled fresh maize ground into *nixta-mal*. Once rendered into *nixtamal*, this by-product is boiled with a variety of ingredients including sugar, milk, and water to produce *atole*. In Mexico, when *atole* is mixed with chocolate it is called *champurrado*. The sixteenth-century Franciscan chronicler Bernar-dino de Sahagún documented information from his Mexican Aztec informants regarding the different kinds of atoles available in New Spain since pre-Columbian times. Heriberto García Rivas adds that beverages identified by Aztec-era chronicler Sahagún included *totonquiatulli* or hot *atole*, *necuatolli* or *atole* with syrup or honey, *chinecuahtolli* or atole with syrup and yellow chili, *guanexatolli* or *atole* processed from a thick or pasty *nixtamal* mix (p. 46). *Atole* is available from street-based food vendors and Mexican restau-rants that serve traditional specialty food items in Mex-ico, Central America, and in many areas of the southwestern United States.

---

fermented from maize dough or flour include *abati*, consumed primarily in Paraguay and Argentina; and *chica*, *charagua*, *ostoche*, *sendechó*, *zambumbia*, and *tesgüino*, all consumed in Mexico. *Sora*, or maize beer, is also consumed primarily in Peru. For Latin America, maize-based non-alcoholic beverages and porridges include *acupe* from Venezuela; *cachiri* and *fubá* from Brazil; *champuz* and *napú* from Colombia and Peru; and *pozol*, *sendechó*, and *atole* from Mexico. When producing *pozol*, a mixture of water and lime is mixed in a suitable container and maize is added to the aforementioned mixture and boiled. Once *nixtamal* has been prepared, the by-product is washed and ground into maize dough, which is then shaped into small balls and covered with banana leaves. The fermentation of *nixtamal* is necessary for the production of *pozol*, which ultimately requires one to fourteen days to produce.

Whereas maize is a primary staple of American Indian maize-beer production, in North America its use is best known from the Prohibition-period exploits of "bootleggers" who produced moonshine or corn liquor, or whiskey, and the like. Both Kentucky bourbon and Tennessee whiskey variously make use of no less than 51 percent cornmeal mash. The primary distinction between mash and malt liquors is that mash is derived from corn-

Fermented maize-based cereal products eaten in Latin America

Name	Description	Country
Abati	Alcoholic beverage produced from maize	Paraguay, Argentina
Acupe	Beverage produced from germinated maize that has been both fermented and sweetened	Venezuela
Agua-agria	Non-alcoholic beverage produced from ground maize and water.	Mexico
Atole	Non-alcoholic porridge produced from maize dough	Mexico
Atole agrio	Non-alcoholic porridge produced from black maize dough fermented 4 to 5 days	Mexico
Cachiri	Fermented beverage produced in clay pots from maize and manihot or fruit	Brazil
Champuz	Fermented beverage produced from maize or rice	Colombia, Peru
Charagua	Alcoholic beverage produced from pulque syrup, chili, and toasted maize leaves heated slowly and fermented.	Mexico
Chica	Alcoholic beverage produced from pineapple, barley steep liquor, and black maize dough. Beverage is fermented for 4 days, after which brown sugar, cinnamon, and cloves are added	Mexico
Fubá	Germinated maize grains fermented in water	Brazil
Jamin-bang	Bread produced from maize fermented for 3 to 6 days and cooked as a cake.	Brazil
Napú	Beverage consisting of germinated, ground, and fermented maize.	Peru
Ostoche	Alcoholic beverage concocted from maize juice and pulque or brown sugar	Mexico
Pozol	Non-alcoholic, albeit acidic, beverage produced as maize liquor. Balls of dough prepared from fermented masa are enveloped in banana leaves	Mexico
Quebranta huesos	Alcoholic beverage consisting of maize juice, toasted maize, and pirú fruits (*Schinus molle*)	Mexico
Sendechó	Alcoholic beverage fermented from germinated maize and red chili. Maize dough is resuspended in water, boiled, bestowed, cooled, and inoculated with *Sendechó*	Mexico
Sora	Alcoholic beverage produced from germinated, ground, cooked and fermented maize	Peru
Tepache	Alcoholic beverage fermented from maize grains, brown sugar, and water.	Mexico
Tesgüino	Alcoholic beverage produced from germinated maize, both ground and cooked with fragments of plants that serve as enzyme sources	Mexico
Tocos	Dessert produced from maize fermented for 2 to 3 months and then cooked.	Peru
Zarzaparrilla bark wine	Alcoholic beverage consisting of maize beer and zarzaparrilla bark	Mexico

SOURCE: Argelia Lorence-Quiñones, Carmen Wacher-Rodarte, and Rodolfo Quintero-Ramírez, 1999, with modifications and deletions).

meal made from ground and unsprouted maize kernels, whereas the malt liquors make use of cornmeal ground from sprouted and dried maize kernels. Betty Fussell provides a detailed overview of the history and culture of moonshine, as well as first-hand accounts concerning the methods, ingredients, participants, and paraphernalia involved in bootlegging (pp. 252–264).

The Globalization of Maize

Although the United States is the leading maize producer in the world, maize remains the primary staple for much of Latin America, which is why that region is the leading consumer of maize as a food for humans (as opposed to its consumption as a fodder for livestock and poultry). Since the days of its earliest evolution and domestication in Mexico, maize has been adopted as a primary staple or supplement in virtually every world region. Thus it has become the stuff of cross-cultural traditions and, more often than not, has taken center stage as the primordial embodiment of myth, ritual, legend, folklore, and ultimately multinational commerce and globalization. Apart from its many traditional uses and its consumption as whole maize kernels or as corn-on-the-cob, maize is key to an incredible variety of foods and products. One need only review Diane Kennedy's *The Cuisines of Mexico* to recognize the totality and dominance of maize and its by-products in the whole of Mexican cuisine. Similarly, any superficial review of Julia Child's recipes in her book *The Way to Cook* will provide an encyclopedic retrospective on the place of maize as culinary ingredient and staple foodstuff in the most popular and trendy of American and international favorites.

See also **Africa; Agriculture, Origins of; Combination of Proteins; Mexico and Central America, Pre-Columbian.**

BIBLIOGRAPHY

Amador Naranjo, Ascensión. *Los tarahumaras*. México: Agualarga Ediciones, 1995.

Arámbula-Villa, G., J. González-Hernández, and C. A. Ordorica-Falomir. "Physicochemical, Structural and Textural Properties of Tortillas from Extruded Instant Corn Flour Supplemented with Various Types of Corn Lipids." *Journal of Cereal Science* 33 (2001): 245–252.

Child, Julia. *The Way to Cook*. New York: Alfred A. Knopf, 1989.

Coe, Sophie D. *America's First Cuisines*. Austin: University of Texas Press, 1994.

Eubanks, Mary W. *Corn in Clay: Maize Paleoethnobotany in Pre-Columbian Art*. Gainesville: University Press of Florida, 1999.

Fernandez Chiti, Jorge. *Hierbas y plantas curativas*. Argentina: Ediciones Condorhuasi, 1999.

Fontana, Bernard L. *Tarahumara: Where Night Is the Day of the Moon*. Flagstaff, Ariz.: Northland Publishing, 1979.

Fussell, Betty. *The Story of Corn*. New York: North Point Press, 1992.

García Rivas, Heriberto. *Cocina prehispánica mexicana: la comida de los antiguos mexicanos*. México: Panorama Editorial, 1991.

Irigoyen Rascon, Fructuoso. *Rarajipari: The Kick-Ball Race of the Tarahumara Indians*. Mexico: Centro Librero La Prensa, 1995.

Iturriaga de la Fuente, José N. *De tacos, tamales y tortas*. México: Editorial Diana, 1987.

Johnson, Sylvia A. *Tomatoes, Potatoes, Corn, and Beans: How the Foods of the Americas Changed Eating around the World*. New York: Atheneum Books for Young Readers, 1997.

Kennedy, Diana. *The Cuisines of Mexico*. Revised ed. Foreword by Craig Claiborne. New York: Harper & Row, 1986.

Lorence-Quiñones, Argelia, Carmen Wacher-Rodarte, and Rodolfo Quintero-Ramírez. *Cereal Fermentations in Latin American Countries*. Rome, Italy: Food and Agriculture Organization of the United Nations, 1992. Available online at http://www.fao.org/docrep/x2184e/x2184e10.htm.

Orozco H., Maria Elena. *Tarahumara, una antigua sociedad futura*. Torreón, México: Impresora Colorama, 1992.

Pindell, Terry, with Lourdes Ramirez Mallis. *Yesterday's Train, A Rail Odyssey Through Mexican History*. New York: Henry Holt, 1997.

Preet, Edythe. "Thanks for the Miracle of Corn." *Los Angeles Times* Syndicate. 8 September 2000. Available online at http://www.cnn.com/2000/FOOD/news/09/08/corn.lat/index.html.

Tedlock, Dennis. *Popol Vuh: The Mayan Book of the Dawn of Life*. Revised ed. Translated by Dennis Tedlock. New York: Simon and Schuster, 1996.

Verdi, Sebastián. *Esplendor y grandeza de la cocina mexicana*. México: Editorial Diana, 1994.

Vogt, Evon Z. *Tortillas for the Gods: A Symbolic Analysis of Zinacanteco Rituals*. Cambridge, Mass.: Harvard University Press, 1976.

Weber, Charles W., Edwin A. Kohlhepp, Ahmed Idouraine, and Luisa J. Ochoa. "Nutritional Composition of Tamales and Corn and Wheat Tortillas." *Journal of Food Composition and Analysis* 6 (1993): 324–335.

Ruben G. Mendoza
Irene Casas

MALNUTRITION. Malnutrition results from the chronic dietary intake of nutrients or energy that provides considerably less or more than is required to be considered adequate or appropriate to support the everyday needs of the human body. Such adverse nutrient intakes are detrimental to human health and may lead to a state of deficiency, dependency, toxicity, or obesity. Malnutrition includes undernutrition, which means the body is not receiving nearly enough nutrients, and overnutrition, which means the intake of nutrients is grossly excessive.

Undernutrition

Undernutrition continues to be a significant cause of malnutrition in developing countries, although it is relatively rare in developed countries. Poverty in developing countries contributes more to undernutrition than a lack of global food production and is considered the chief cause of malnutrition. Families that are poor do not have the economic, social, or environmental resources to purchase or produce enough food. Poor soil conditions may also contribute to a family's inability to grow enough food to prevent malnutrition and the accompanying complications to health. Additionally, for the urban poor, low wages, underemployment, and food prices beyond the reach of families also contribute to undernutrition.

Prolonged dietary intakes deficient in energy or calories, protein, fat, vitamins, and minerals lead to illness and eventually death if not corrected. Undernutrition may also be the result of psychological disorders, such as anorexia nervosa, which manifests as an unwillingness to eat enough food to sustain life. Elderly adults often have a decrease both in appetite and intestinal function and are at an increased risk for undernutrition. Children, particularly infants and those under five years of age are also at an increased risk for undernutrition due to a greater need for energy and nutrients during periods of rapid growth and development. Infants born to undernourished mothers are more likely to be low birth weight infants. Addiction to alcohol or drugs may also lead to undernutrition when the addicted individuals favor alcohol and/or drug intake over adequate food intake. Severe, prolonged diarrhea, renal failure, infection, or diseases that cause the malabsorption of nutrients in the small intestine also may cause undernutrition even if dietary intake is adequate. It is obvious that the causes of undernutrition are varied and complex, requiring solutions that may also be complex.

Nutrients Required to Prevent Undernutrition

The nutrients required in adequate amounts by the body to prevent undernutrition are carbohydrates, fat or lipids, protein, vitamins, minerals, and water. Carbohydrates provide the body with energy (about 4 kilocalories per gram of carbohydrate consumed). Carbohydrates also protect protein stores in the body. A minimal intake of 50 to 100 grams (1.8 to 3.5 oz.) of carbohydrates is required to prevent the development of ketones that the brain can use somewhat inefficiently for energy. The brain optimally uses carbohydrate for energy, but when carbohydrate intake is inadequate for several weeks, the body does not metabolize fatty acids completely in order to produce ketones for energy. In addition to ketone formation resulting from insufficient carbohydrate consumption, body protein will also be lost, and the body will generally become weakened.

Fats or lipids provide essential fatty acids upon metabolism following consumption. Essential fatty acids are obtained from dietary lipids and are termed essential because the human body cannot synthesize them. Essential fatty acids are important for human health because they participate in immune processes, vision, are an integral part of cell structures, and participate in hormone-like compound production. If an inadequate intake of lipids is routinely consumed, the body becomes deficient in essential fatty acids. This results in skin problems, diarrhea, and an increase in infections with a corresponding decrease in the ability of the body to heal wounds. Lipids also provide energy for the body (about 9 kilocalories per gram (28 kilocalories per ounce of fat consumed), can be stored for future use as energy, insulate the body and protect body organs, and aid in the absorption and transport of fat-soluble vitamins (vitamins A, D, E, and K) throughout the body. The fat-soluble vitamins are important for vision (vitamin A), bone metabolism (vitamin D), providing antioxidant protection from free radicals (vitamin E), and blood coagulation (vitamin K), among other functions.

Protein is a very important nutrient because so many substances in the body are made from it. Proteins are made when amino acids are combined in specific sequences to form specific proteins. The sequence of the amino acids determines the shape of the protein, and the shape of the protein, in turn, determines the function of the protein. Amino acids can be obtained from plant or animal sources. There are nine essential amino acids: histidine, isoleucine, leucine, lysine, methionine, phenylalanine, threonine, tryptophan, and valine. The human body is not able to synthesize these amino acids, so they must be derived from the foods we eat. There are eleven nonessential amino acids that the human body is able to make: alanine, arginine, asparagine, aspartic acid, cysteine, glutamic acid, glutamine, glycine, proline, serine, and tyrosine. As stated previously, amino acids are necessary for protein synthesis, but they are also important because they provide the body with a special form of nitrogen that the body cannot get from carbohydrates or lipids. Protein, like carbohydrate, provides approximately 4 kilocalories per gram of protein consumed, but requires much more metabolizing and processing by the liver and kidneys to put the energy from protein to use. Protein is a part of every cell in the human body. Blood proteins enable the body to maintain the right balance of fluid inside and outside of cells. When adequate protein is not consumed, there is a lower concentration of blood proteins in the bloodstream, which causes the balance of fluids inside and outside of cells in tissues to be thrown off, resulting in swelling of tissues or edema, which can lead to serious medical problems. Proteins also help regulate the pH, or acid-base balance, in the blood, are necessary for the synthesis of many hormones and enzymes, and participate in important cell formation for cells vital for the immune system. Amino acids from protein can also be used to produce glucose, which is a positive thing for providing glucose after an overnight fast. But in the case of starvation, excessive muscle tissue is wasted and results in diminished health. Protein-energy malnutrition results from near starvation and may be seen in the body tissues in either a wet, dry, or combined form. The dry form, marasmus, is caused by deficiency of protein and nonprotein nutrients, with the individual being very thin from the loss of muscle and body fat. The wet form, kwashiorkor, is caused primarily by protein deficiency, with energy deficiency being secondary, and is accompanied by edema. The combined form, marasmic kwashiorkor, results from protein and energy deficiency with edema and more body fat than is seen in marasmus.

There are also water-soluble vitamins in addition to the fat-soluble vitamins. Because water-soluble vitamins are not stored in any appreciable amounts in the body, but are excreted readily in urine, it is relatively easy to become depleted of them. Fat-soluble, in contrast, are stored in adipose tissue and the liver, and consequently it is more difficult to become deficient of them. The water-soluble vitamins are the B vitamins and vitamin C. The B vitamins are thiamin, riboflavin, niacin, pantothenic acid, biotin, pyridoxine, folate, and vitamin B_{12}. All of the water-soluble vitamins except vitamin C have coenzyme functions and are involved in a variety of reactions including energy metabolism, DNA synthesis, nerve function, protein and carbohydrate metabolism, and fat synthesis. Vitamin C is involved in protecting the body from oxidative damage caused by substances called free radicals. It also functions in connective tissue synthesis, hormone synthesis, and neurotransmitter synthesis. Physiological consequences of deficiency include inflammation of the mouth and tongue (riboflavin deficiency); diarrhea, dermatitis (niacin deficiency); edema, weakness (thiamin deficiency); tongue soreness, anemia (biotin deficiency); fatigue, tingling in hands (pantothenic acid deficiency); poor growth, inflammation of the tongue (folate deficiency); poor nerve function, macrocytic anemia (vitamin B_{12} deficiency); and poor wound healing, bleeding gums (vitamin C deficiency).

Minerals are important nutrients that must be obtained from foods consumed, as the human body is unable to synthesize them. Some factors that influence mineral bioavailability (the extent to which minerals in food consumed is available for the body to put to use) are the amount of mineral content in the soil in which the food providing the mineral was grown; dietary fiber consumed in the same meal as a food containing the minerals; mineral-mineral interactions; and vitamin-mineral interactions. Sodium, potassium, chloride, calcium, phosphorus, magnesium, and sulfur are the major minerals. Deficiencies of these minerals lead to such symptoms as muscle cramps (sodium), irregular heartbeat (potassium), convulsions in infants (chloride), an increased risk for osteoporosis (calcium), diminished bone support (phosphorus), and poor heart function (magnesium). There are also so-called trace minerals that are only required in very small amounts to contribute to optimal health. These trace minerals are iron, zinc, selenium, iodide, copper, fluoride, chromium, manganese, and molybdenum. When inadequate amounts of foods containing the trace minerals are consumed, symptoms begin to appear. These symptoms include low blood iron (iron), skin rash/poor growth and development (zinc), muscle weakness (selenium), goiter (iodide), anemia/poor growth (copper), increased risk for dental cavities (fluoride), and high blood glucose after eating (chromium).

Developed countries typically have water supplies that are monitored for safety by government agencies and are provided in large enough quantities that a lack of drinking water is not the norm. Developing countries, however, may not have water that is free from contamination, or because of drought or other natural disasters do not have a large enough water supply for human consumption or to provide water for livestock or crops. Water is vital for life and, without it, an adult can survive only a few days because the human body does not have the ability to store water. Water is found inside of cells as intracellular fluid and outside of cells as extracellular fluid. A proper balance between intracellular and extracellular water is necessary to prevent complications such as edema. Water also is responsible for regulating body temperature, most notably through the cooling-off process accomplished by perspiration. Water is necessary to provide lubrication for joints such as the knees. Without adequate water in the form of amniotic fluid in the womb of a pregnant woman, the growing fetus does not have sufficient support to prevent injury should the mother fall or be otherwise jarred abruptly. Water is also the primary avenue utilized by the body to rid itself of waste products. While water does not supply energy as carbohydrates, protein, and fats are able to do, it is still a very important nutrient necessary to prevent malnutrition.

Overnutrition

Overnutrition results when energy expenditure is grossly exceeded by energy intake and leads to overweight and obesity. Developed countries, with their abundant food supplies and processed foods, are most afflicted with overnutrition and the medical complications associated with it. Due to the excessive intake of food products, the amount of fat-soluble vitamins and minerals in the body can rise to toxic levels because they are stored in the body. Developed countries have greater incidences of cardiovascular disease, blood lipids, diabetes mellitus, hypertension, respiratory problems, gallbladder disease, arthritis, and cancer, all of which are connected to complications stemming directly from overnutrition.

Methods of Evaluating Malnutrition

Malnutrition is diagnosed based on the findings of a medical and diet history, physical examination, and laboratory tests. The results are then compared with norms of weight for height, body mass index (body weight in kilograms divided by height in meters squared), dietary intake, physical findings, and plasma levels of nutrients and nutrient-dependent substances such as hemoglobin. The physical examination would necessarily include anthropometric measurements, as well as close examination of the skin, hair, and mouth for symptoms of malnutrition.

For example, depigmentation of the hair is indicative of undernutrition, and a body weight that is 20 percent above the average desirable body weight as determined by insurance company standardized charts would indicate overnutrition. A triceps skinfold test may be utilized to determine the body's energy stores. Laboratory tests are used to reveal the extent to which amino acid nutrition is meeting the body's needs to determine undernutrition, or plasma lipids in the diagnosis of overnutrition. In the field when assessing nutritional status, the medical and diet history and physical examination may be the only tools accessible to the physician or nurse, particularly in developing countries.

Who is at Increased Risk for Malnutrition?

The risk for malnutrition is increased for a variety of reasons. Increased nutritional needs during growth, pregnancy, lactation, old age, infection, certain cancer therapies, or immune deficiency disorders increase the risk of malnutrition. Diets that focus on a narrow range of foods may not provide the variety of nutrients required and lead to deficiencies. Those experiencing famine, with the accompanying reduction in available food, are at great risk for malnutrition in the form of undernutrition. Lack of money to purchase an adequate diet or cultural practices that dictate which members in the family get a large or small amount of food may also lead to malnutrition. Any medical condition that effects the absorption of nutrients from foods, or requires medication that has adverse consequences on appetite, may cause malnutrition if the condition is long term. Taking megadoses of vitamin/mineral supplements may result in toxic levels of the substances taken in the body with the outcome being a state of overnutrition.

Correcting Malnutrition in the United States

Since the Great Depression of the 1930s, the federal government of the United States has undertaken the task of alleviating and/or preventing malnutrition. In the 1960s, President John F. Kennedy reestablished the federal government's efforts to end debilitating hunger. Individuals and families who have low incomes may take advantage of several federally sponsored programs to ensure a better quality of nutrient intake. Food stamps are available to those who are usually employed but having difficulty purchasing an adequate food supply by using coupons to purchase food from grocery stores. The Commodity Supplemental Food Program distributes U. S. Department of Agriculture surplus foods through county agencies to such low-income populations as pregnant women and families with young children. The School Lunch and Breakfast Programs offer free or reduced-priced meals based on the Food Guide Pyramid to children of low-income families, with the cost of the reduced-priced meals being based on family income. The Summer Food Service Program offers free, nutritious meals and snacks to low-income children and distributes the meals from a central location during lower and secondary school vacations. There are also programs targeted specifically at different age groups. Preschool children enrolled in organized child-care programs receive meals at no cost, and the child-care program receives reimbursement for the meals through participation in the Child-Care Food Program. For individuals 60 years or older, a free noon meal is provided at centralized sites as part of the Congregate Meals for the Elderly Program. Homebound individuals over 60 years of age can take advantage of home-delivered meals at no cost or for a fee, depending on income, at least five days per week.

World Hunger: Addressing a Global Problem

In 1798 the English clergyman and political economist Thomas Malthus suggested that the world's population was growing at a rate faster than the food supply. The year 2002 finds world population growth exceeding economic growth, and poverty on the rise. Globally less than one-half of 1 percent of the world's yearly production of goods and services goes exclusively to economic development assistance, yet 6 percent goes to support the world's military operations. Civil wars in some countries have substantially retarded progress of the poor and continue to contribute to massive undernutrition. Environmental factors such as soil erosion or lack of fresh water for irrigation of crops exacerbate the problem of providing sufficient quantities of foods for many countries. What is being done to overcome all of these detriments to feeding the world's hungry? Since the 1960s, an American program, the Peace Corps, has been instrumental in providing education, distributing food and medical supplies, and building structures for locals to use in developing nations. National surveys such as the National Family Health Survey conducted in India are valuable tools in the determination of whether any progress is being made to improve the nutritional status of the nation. Advances in biotechnology to genetically alter plants and animals to improve the nutritive quality of the foods produced from them may help to meet increasing food needs both now and in the future. The United Nations and the World Health Organization cry out for governments in developed countries to facilitate greater strides in improvements in malnutrition in undeveloped countries by financial, educational, and scientific interventions. What will be required to eradicate malnutrition in this world is a coming together of the leaders of rich and poor nations to the same degree. Globally, there is an adequate food supply and the technical expertise necessary to address the problems and complications of malnutrition. All that is lacking is the political cooperation to address this devastating situation.

See also **Anorexia, Bulimia; Aversion to Food; Body Composition; Caloric Intake; Disease: Metabolic Diseases; Eating: Anatomy and Physiology of Eating; Fasting and Abstinence; Fluoride; Food Politics: United States; Hunger, Physiology of.**

BIBLIOGRAPHY

Agarwal, S., et al. "Birth Weight Patterns in Rural Under-nourished Pregnant Women." *Indian Pediatrics* 39, no. 3 (2002): 244–253.

Berkman, D. S., et al. "Effects of Stunting, Diarrhoeal Disease, and Parasitic Infection during Infancy on Cognition in Late Childhood: A Follow-Up Study." *Lancet* 359, no. 9306 (2002): 564–571.

Bouis, H. E. "Plant Breeding: A New Tool for Fighting Micronutrient Malnutrition." *Journal of Nutrition* 132, sup. 3 (2002): 491S–494S.

Charlton, K. E., et al. "Poor Nutritional Status in Older Black South Africans." *Asia Pacific Journal of Clinical Nutrition* 10, no. 1 (2001): 31–38.

Chen, C. C., L. S. Schilling, and C. H. Lyder. "A Concept Analysis of Malnutrition in the Elderly." *Journal of Advanced Nursing* 36, no. 1 (2001): 131–142.

Fenton, M., and S. Simon. "Legislating Good Sense: It's Time for Medical Nutrition Therapy to be Part of Standard Care for People with HIV/AIDS." *Positive Living* 11, no. 1 (2002): 44–45.

Gillet, R. M., and P. V. Tobias. "Human Growth in Southern Zambia: A First Study of Tonga Children Predating the Kariba Dam (1957–1958)." *American Journal of Human Biology* 14, no. 1 (2002): 50–60.

Griffiths, P. L., and M. E. Bentley. "The Nutrition Transition Is Underway in India." *Journal of Nutrition* 131, no. 10 (2001): 2692–2700.

Hunt, J. M. "The Agricultural-Industrial Partnership for Eliminating Micronutrient Malnutrition: The Investment Bargain of the Decade." *Biomedical and Environmental Sciences* 14, no. 1–2 (2001): 104–123.

Ke-You, G. and F. Da-Wei. The Magnitude and Trends of Under- and Over-Nutrition in Asian Countries. *Biomedical and Environmental Sciences* 14, no. 1–2 (2001): 53–60.

Krishnaswamy, K. "Perspectives on Nutrition Needs for the New Millennium for South Asian Regions." *Biomedical and Environmental Sciences* 14, no. 1–2 (2001): 66–74.

Leube, M. G., and I. Fernandez-Abad. "The Applied Nutrition Project of Eastern Kenya: An Initiative for Reducing Hunger and Malnutrition." *Collegium Antropologicum* 25, no. 2 (2001): 665–672.

Lipton, M. "Challenges to Meet: Food and Nutrition Security in the New Millennium." *Proceedings of the Nutrition Society* 60, no. 2 (2001): 203–214.

Malekafzali, H., et al. "Community-Based Nutritional Intervention for Reducing Malnutrition among Children under Five Years of Age in Islamic Republic of Iran." *Eastern Mediterranean Health Journal* 6, no. 2–3 (2000): 238–245.

Nantel, G., and K. Tontisirin. "Functional Consequences of Adult Malnutrition in Developing Countries: A Review." *Journal of Physiological Anthropology and Applied Human Science* 21, no. 1 (2002): 1–9.

Nantel, G., and K. Tontisirin. "Policy and Sustainability Issues." *Journal of Nutrition* 132, sup. 4 (2002): 839S–844S.

Salomon, J., T. P. De, and J. C. Melchior. "Nutrition and HIV Infection." *British Journal of Nutrition* 87, sup. 1 (2002): S111–110.

Shils, Maurice E., et al. *Modern Nutrition in Health and Disease.* 9th ed. Baltimore, Md.: Williams and Wilkins, 1999.

Wardlaw, Gordon M., and Margaret W. Kessel. *Perspectives in Nutrition.* 5th ed. Boston, Mass.: McGraw-Hill, 2002.

Rebecca J. (Bryant) McMillian

MALNUTRITION: PROTEIN-ENERGY MALNUTRITION.

Protein-energy malnutrition (PEM) may be present at any time during the life cycle, but it is more common in the extreme ages, that is, during infancy/childhood and in the elderly. The present review will be restricted mostly to the condition present during infancy and childhood.

Protein-energy malnutrition is a syndrome characterized by its progressive onset and a series of symptoms and signs that encompass a continuum, ranging from clinically undetected manifestations to the full-blown clinical picture of marasmus or kwashiorkor. A syndrome is defined in clinical practice as a set of symptoms and signs that may be caused by different etiologies.

In the case of PEM, the earliest symptoms include subtle changes in the mood of the child, which may be described by the mother as saying that the child is not as playful as he/she used to be. Further changes include a loss of appetite and a loss of interest in the surroundings, which lead to decreased social interaction with peers or siblings and adults (parents or other caregivers). When PEM becomes more severe, there are adverse effects on the child's cognitive and behavioral development, evident in both the short and the long term.

In relation to signs, the earliest clinical sign of PEM is the lack of adequate weight gain. Also common in the early stages are mild episodes of common acute infectious diseases, such as acute diarrhea or acute respiratory infections. As the condition advances, the child will show signs of body wasting, progressing to an extreme thinness. If the syndrome becomes chronic, there are small or no increases in length. When the condition becomes more severe, the child may show the clinical pictures of marasmus or kwashiorkor, which will be defined later in this article.

The etiology of protein-energy malnutrition as a syndrome may be classified as primary or secondary. Although in practice most cases of PEM are caused by a combination of both, the concept may be useful for targeting interventions. Primary PEM refers to a deficit of available food. This, in turn, may be because of biological conditions, such as maternal malnutrition prior to or during pregnancy and lactation, or to social conditions, such as poverty; to a limited or selective unavailability of food; to war; to ecological disasters leading to famine, or, more often, as a result of profound social inequalities, either at the individual level (discrimination, refugees, prisoners) or at the community or country level. The largest prevalences of protein-energy malnutrition are found in socioeconomically deprived areas of the world, as will be reviewed further on in this article. Secondary causes of PEM include several conditions that impair food intake, absorption, or utilization, or that increase energy and/or protein requirements or losses. Secondary causes of PEM may be biological or social conditions.

Biological conditions may interfere with food intake, such as congenital anomalies (for example, harelip); with absorption, such as any of several malabsorption syndromes (for example, tropical sprue); or with utilization, such as inherited metabolic diseases (for example, phenylketonuria). Biological conditions that increase the need for energy include all infectious diseases accompanied by fever, and other diseases that increase catabolism, such as tuberculosis, or that are accompanied by an increased nutrient loss, such as intestinal parasitism.

On the other hand, social causes that affect food intake, whether it be in quantity or quality (protein-energy or micronutrient content), include several conditions associated with poverty, such as ignorance, inadequate weaning practices, child abuse, alcoholism or other drug addictions, and others.

Different conceptual frameworks for the study of malnutrition have been proposed and adopted throughout the years; one of the most widely accepted ones was developed during the WHO/UNICEF Joint Nutrition Programme in Iringe, Tanzania (B. Jonsson et al., 1993) (UNICEF 1990), from where it has been extended to many parts of the world. An appealing feature of this conceptual framework is that it may be adapted to describe causes of the major nutritional deficiencies present in the world, including vitamin A, iron, and iodine deficiency.

Clinical Picture of Marasmus and Kwashiorkor

Marasmus is characterized by a chronic and severe restriction of both energy and protein to the body. Marasmus is more frequently found at a younger age than kwashiorkor, usually in children under one year of age. A marasmic child presents severe wasting, with a very low weight-for-age and reduced length-for-age, often below −3 standard deviation of the reference population values. The clinical history of a marasmic child may reveal poverty or famine affecting the family; inadequate child-rearing practices, like starvation wrongly prescribed as part of the management of diarrhea; an early stopping of breast-feeding; over-dilution of formula; a history of repeated and/or chronic infections, such as diarrhea or tuberculosis; or some physical condition that affected the child's growth and development, such as prematurity, mental defects, or a malabsorption syndrome. The mother or caregiver will often report that the child is hungry. On a first appreciation, the child may be interested in the environment, with an active cry and reaching for food if offered, or else he/she may be depressed to the point of coma. The typical clinical picture is that of a striking loss of subcutaneous fat and muscle wasting, observed as markedly thin limbs, an evident rib cage,

sunken cheeks and eyes that give the child a "monkey-like" or gaunt appearance, a prominent abdomen (although with no evidence of an enlarged liver), and a relatively big head. The hair is often thin and dry, and comes off easily. However, skin rashes or dermatosis are not usually present. Common micronutrient deficiencies include vitamins A and D, zinc, and iron, although anemia is less common in marasmus than in kwashiorkor.

The clinical picture of kwashiorkor is not as striking in appearance, as this syndrome often affects slightly older children, i.e., between one and three years of age. The clinical onset of kwashiorkor usually takes place in a shorter period of time as compared to marasmus, and is characterized by a relative, though severe, limitation in protein intake, with a lesser involvement of energy deficit. A child affected with kwashiorkor is often apathetic to external stimuli, is irritable, and gives the impression of misery, rejecting or crying when cared for. The most salient clinical characteristic of this syndrome is the presence of edema, which may mask the evidence of body weight loss and reduced length in relation to age. It is also common to find skin lesions that range from a flaky, pink dermatosis with skin dryness and depigmentation to deep ulcerations. Also common are petechiae and ecchymoses, as well as clinical signs of anemia. The hair presents discoloration with bands of dark and light hair (described by clinicians as the "flag sign"). An enlarged, fatty liver is also characteristic of kwashiorkor, palpable as a soft mass under the right rib cage. Co-occurring micronutrient deficiencies are common, so clinical signs of deficiencies of specific vitamins, including A, B, C, D, iron, or others, also may be present.

Classification of Protein-Energy Malnutrition

The clinical signs of severe PEM are so impressive that, for several years, they drew the attention of pediatricians and other physicians interested in furthering the understanding of the clinical syndromes and their treatment. Therefore, the study of PEM was long confined to the hospital setting. Actually, the first classification of PEM came from Mexican observers, who ranked the severity of malnutrition based on the risk of death for children with a clinical diagnosis of PEM. This group, led by Gomez, proposed that children with a weight-for-age deficit greater than 40 percent in relation to a reference population were in the greatest risk of dying, and thus labeled them as having third-degree malnutrition. Further, children with 25–40 percent weight-for-age deficit were labeled as having second degree malnutrition, and children with 10–25 percent weight-for-age deficit were classified as having first degree malnutrition (Gómez-Santos, 1946).

This classification had a high predictive value for the risk of death, and therefore had important implications for clinical practice. It was further abused, however, when its use was extended to the classification of malnutrition at a population level. In other words, children with no evidence of clinical malnutrition who have low weight-for-age should not be classified as malnourished; doing so may not only misdiagnose an individual, but may overestimate the prevalence of malnutrition in a population. Also, the Gomez classification has been criticized because a single measure of a child's weight referred to age gives no idea about the nutritional history of the child. That is, an underweight child may be growing according to his/her normal growth channel, may be recovering from a recent episode of weight loss ("catch-up growth"), or may be deteriorating in relation to the recent past.

In order to overcome these caveats, Waterlow proposed combining weight-for-height, as an indicator of an acute episode of malnutrition, with height-for-age, as an indicator of chronic nutritional deficits that would be reflected in growth stunting (Waterlow, 1972).

Although these classifications have been used for several years, they have two important disadvantages that often are overlooked. To illustrate the first disadvantage, it is important to highlight the concept of Z-scores as a means of describing an individual child's anthropometric indicators in a normal distribution. The normal distribution of a reference population has been published by the World Health Organization (WHO) and is most often accepted worldwide as the standard for comparison. Eighty percent of the median weight-for-age might be above or below -2 Z-scores, depending on the child's age. The second disadvantage is that, to approximate a fixed point in the normal distribution, say, -2 Z-score, different percents of median have to be used depending on the anthropometric index used—for example, 90 percent for low height-for-age, or 80 percent of low weight-for-height.

In consequence, the World Health Organization Expert Committee on Physical Status has recommended the use of Z-scores to express weight-for-age, weight-for-height, or height-for-age relative to values reported in a reference population (WHO Expert Committee on Physical Status, 1995). The use of this system has several advantages; i.e., when applied at a population level, it allows the mean and standard deviation to be calculated for a group of Z-scores, and it allows the use of fixed cut-off points (i.e., -1, -2, or -3 Z-scores) to classify mild, moderate, or severe deficits for any anthropometric indicator. Although the use of Z-scores may be difficult to grasp for those who have been accustomed to classifying nutritional deficits based on the percent of median, the advantages of Z-scores outweigh their disadvantages.

Global Prevalence of Protein-Energy Malnutrition

The most recent estimates about the distribution of PEM at a worldwide level were compiled by the World Health Organization (WHO) Programme of Nutrition, available in its Global Database on Child Growth and Malnutrition (de Onis and Blössner, 1997). This database covered 95 percent of the total population of children under 5 years of age who lived in 103 developing nations in 1995,

as was reported in nationally representative surveys available at the time. According to these data, an estimated 206.2 million children, who represent 38 percent of all children under 5 years old, were stunted (low height-for-age); 167.3 million children (31 percent) were underweight (low weight-for-age), and 48.8 million children (9 percent) were wasted (low weight-for-height). PEM is most often found in the poor regions known as the "developing world." The largest number of affected children were found in Asia, where 41 percent of all under 5 years old were stunted, 35 percent were underweight, and 10.3 percent were wasted. Africa had 38.6 percent stunted, 28.4 percent underweight, and 8 percent wasted children of all those under 5 years old; Latin America and the Caribbean showed 17.9 percent stunted, 9.5 percent underweight, and 3 percent wasted children of all those under 5 years old. The proportion of children under 5 years of age affected in Oceania was 31.4 percent, 22.8 percent, and 5 percent, respectively, but the total number of children living in this region is much lower, so in reality, these percentages translate into many fewer children affected than in the other regions.

Since the mid-1980s, the Administrative Committee on Coordination/Sub-Committee on Nutrition (ACC/SCN) of the United Nations periodically has examined the trends of malnutrition in the world's children. In its Third Report on the World Nutrition Situation (ACC/SCN, 1997), this Committee (from data from 61 countries) estimated the trends in stunting with two or more nationally representative surveys. In the period from 1980 to 1995, stunting declined globally at a rate of 0.54 percentage points per year. Sub-Saharan Africa had an increase of 0.130 percentage points per year in the average prevalence of stunting; the remaining regions of the world showed statistically significant decreases that ranged from -0.26 in Middle-America and the Caribbean to -0.90 in Southeast Asia (Table 1).

The same Committee was able to use data from 95 countries that had data from at least one national survey to estimate the prevalence of undernutrition; underweight and stunting showed a consistent 11.5 percentage point difference. The higher prevalence was for the underweight classification. During the 1980–1995 period studied, only sub-Saharan Africa had an increase in the prevalences of both stunting and underweight; all the other regions showed decreasing trends in these two indicators (Table 1).

Acute and Long-Term Consequences of Protein-Energy Malnutrition

PEM results from a relative deficiency of protein (essential amino acids and/or total nitrogen) and energy substrates (carbohydrates, fats, or proteins). However, these deficiencies are almost always accompanied by micronutrient (minerals and vitamins) deficits. Manifestations of PEM differ depending on the duration, the severity, and the combination of these deficiencies. In the early stages,

TABLE 1

Estimated prevalence of stunting (%) and numbers of children affected for 1980, 1985, 1990, and 1995 and by region

Region	Prevalence stunting				Numbers stunted (in millions)				% Increase/ decrease in numbers from 1980 to 1985
	1980	1985	1990	1995	1980	1985	1990	1995	
Sub-Saharan Africa	37.4	38.1	38.7	39.4	26.255	30.832	36.248	42.590	+62
Near East/North Africa	30.8	25.9	23.0	22.2	11.397	10.991	10.865	10.913	-4
South Asia	66.1	61.9	57.7	53.5	88.873	93.237	91.520	89.877	+1
South East Asia	51.9	47.3	42.8	38.3	35.581	32.862	30.119	30.206	-15
Middle America/Caribbean	31.6	30.4	29.1	27.8	5.398	5.467	5.631	5.626	+4
South America	25.0	21.0	16.9	12.9	8.285	7.309	5.965	4.644	-44
China(1982)			31.4				36.068		
Across all regions (excluding China)	48.8	45.6	42.5	39.9	175.789	180.698	180.348	183.856	+5

Note: These estimates were derived assuming a linear relationship between stunting and year. The only region for which there was evidence of a nonlinear relationship was Near East/North Africa. For this region, a quadratic model was used to approximate the nonlinear relationship . The estimated prevalence values for this region were from this model.

there are functional impairments, which are later followed by biochemical and physical damage.

The identification, understanding, and treatment of the full-blown clinical syndromes characteristic of severe PEM began in the mid-1930s with the description of kwashiorkor (Williams, 1933). On the other hand, the identification and understanding of the functional manifestations of malnutrition have only come about during the last three decades of the twentieth century, with the launching of two large-scale, community-based research projects: the first one, known as the INCAP Longitudinal Study, was based in Guatemala (Habicht and Martorell, 1992). The second took place simultaneously in three countries—Egypt, Kenya, and Mexico—and was known as the CRSP study (Calloway, Murphy, et al., 1988).

Functional consequences of protein-energy malnutrition. As described earlier, the functional consequences of PEM were recognized and studied only relatively recently (Allen, 1993). Among the most well documented functional consequences of PEM are growth impairment, a reduced immune response, and a disruption in cognitive ability.

Growth impairment. Growth failure because of PEM usually starts to manifest very early in life. Information from the INCAP longitudinal study, as well as from the CRSP studies, coincides in showing that growth stunting begins at about 3 to 4 months of age and is complete before 18 months (Allen, 1995). A further contribution from the INCAP study was provided by a long-term follow-up of the same populations that showed not only that growth stunting present during infancy carried on until adolescence, but also that length at 3 years of age was a strong predictor of adolescent size (Martorell, Schroeder, et al., 1995). It also seems as if stunting in

early life is correlated significantly with reduced physical performance (Haas, Martinez, et al., 1995) and reduced psychomotor and mental performance, both during late childhood (Mendez and Adair, 1999) and even until adolescence (Grantham-McGregor, 1995; Pollit, Gorman, et al., 1995).

Two more relevant issues related to growth failure are that there is a window of opportunity for intervention from the ages of 3 to 6 months, when response to the intervention may be greatest (Lutter, Mora, et al., 1990), and that most of the growth deficit found at later ages accumulated during the first months of life (Rivera, Cortes, et al., 1998).

Immune response. It has been recognized that malnutrition is the most common cause of immunodeficiency worldwide (Chandra, 1991). Actually, malnutrition and infection interact in a vicious cycle: the presence of one more easily leads to the development of the other (Scrimshaw, Taylor, et al., 1968). There are several mechanisms involved in this relationship. PEM impairs cell-mediated immunity, phagocitic function, and the complement system. It also diminishes immunoglobulin (IgA, IgM, and IgG) concentrations, and cytokine production (Chandra, 1991). Micronutrient deficiencies associated with PEM also adversely effect the immune response. For example, iron plays an important role in several metabolic functions, including both the host and invasive bacteria. Several microorganisms that infect the human body only achieve their full infectious activity in the presence of iron. Such is the case of bacteria that cause diarrheal disease, such as *Escherichia coli, Yersinia septica, Salmonella sp.,* and *Vibrio cholerae*; and others responsible for lower respiratory infections, such as *Mycobacterium tuberculosis, Klebsiella pneumoniae, Pseudomona aeruginosa*, and *Listeria monocytogenes*. These microorganisms actively seek iron in their host during infection, uptaking it from destroyed

438

THE IMPORTANCE OF MARGINAL MALNUTRITION

The borderline between normal nutrition and malnutrition is so thin that, in clinical practice, there is no foolproof way to distinguish them. This is at least one of the reasons why so little attention was given to marginal malnutrition (i.e., malnutrition that borders normal limits). A further reason, though, obeyed a misconstruct that prevailed for a long time; that is, that only children with severe malnutrition had an increased risk of dying. This concept was probably triggered by the initial clinical observations on the increased risk of death in hospitalized children with third degree malnutrition (Gomez, Ramos-Galvan, et al., 1956), and was reinforced further by epidemiological observations in the field.

In a classic study, Chen and colleagues reported their findings on 2,019 Bangladeshi children between the ages of 13 and 23 months, who were followed for a period of 24 months, assessing death rate (Chen, Chowdhury, et al., 1980). The study team had precise information on the age of these children and had performed a cross-sectional nutritional assessment at baseline. Further, a demographic surveillance team identified all deaths occurring during the study period, recording age and probable cause of death. Child mortality rates were analyzed stratifying by percentage weight-for-age, weight-for-height, and height-for-age. The authors found that severely malnourished children experienced about a twofold higher mortality risk over the first twelve months of the study, and fourfold during the second twelve months of the study, as compared to normally nourished and mildly and moderately malnourished children, who shared the same level of mortality risk. The nutritional index with the strongest discriminative power to identify risk of death was weight-for-age.

This article, and others that followed in the literature (Trowbridge and Sommer, 1981; Heywood, 1982; Bairagi, Chowdhury, et al., 1985), seemed to find a threshold effect for mortality at the cutoff corresponding to third-degree malnutrition, below which the risk of death increased sharply. It was not until 1993 that Pelletier, Frongillo, and Habicht questioned this model (Pelletier, Frongillo, et al., 1993). Following their reasoning, the threshold effect reflects a model in which a popula-

tion's mortality rate increases as a linear function of malnutrition.

An alternative model is a quadratic one that accounts for the sharp increase in mortality found beyond the threshold. Pelletier et al., however, sustained that a synergistic or multiplicative model, in accordance with the clinical observations that child mortality is a function of the adverse synergism between malnutrition and morbidity (Scrimshaw 1970), provides a much better explanation of the relationship. When testing their multiplicative (i.e., synergistic or exponential) model on a set of available data from several large-scale population studies, they found that an exponential model fit the available data best. Based on the best fit of the exponential model, they calculated that the odds of dying increased at a compound rate of 7.3 percent for each percentage point deterioration in weight-for-age.

In summary, these authors provided strong evidence that a threshold effect does not exist. Their model is consistent with the view that because of the greater number of affected children, mild to moderate malnutrition is associated with a greater absolute risk of dying. The policy implications of this conclusion are striking. Considering that the majority of malnourished children fall in the mild to moderate category, and that their risk of dying is higher than that of non-malnourished children, the attention of health-care programs should be immediately drawn to this population.

Certainly, a larger number of childhood deaths would be prevented if efforts were directed to improve the nutritional status of this group and to lower morbidity burden of all malnourished children, and not just for the ones who are in the worst condition. Therefore, the authors estimate that 45 percent to 83 percent of all malnutrition-related deaths occur in children who present mild to moderate malnutrition, a group that is usually excluded from direct interventions based on the impression that their risk of dying is small. Also, it highlights that either reducing morbidity or reducing malnutrition would reduce child mortality, but a much larger effect (actually, a synergistic effect) would be achieved if both conditions were addressed simultaneously (Pelletier, 1994).

red cells (erythrocytes) and body stores (liver). On the other hand, the host tries to make iron less available to invasive microorganisms, sequestering it through different mechanisms—referred to as nutritional immunity—that include the binding of iron to transferrin and lactoferrin, and the increase in ferritin saturation in the liver (Kochan, 1976). Other micronutrients that play ac-

tive roles in modulating immunity include zinc, selenium, copper, vitamins A, C, E, B_6, and folic acid (Nezu and Nakahara, 1994).

Conversely, infectious diseases lead to malnutrition by several mechanisms that often interact with each other. Almost every malnourished child will sooner or later present with diarrhea. Many of the interactions between malnutrition and infection are understood because of studies of diarrheal disease (Chen, 1983); hence the illustration of the mechanisms by which these two morbid conditions interact is particularly useful. One of the first symptoms of diarrheal disease is anorexia, as a result of vomiting and abdominal discomfort. Also, fever, dehydration, and electrolyte imbalances contribute to it (Martorell, Yarbrough, et al., 1980). Anorexia leads to a restricted intake, which is often reinforced by erroneous caregiver practices. In part, it is culturally engrained in different societies to withhold food from a diarrhea-affected child (Bentley, 1988), and it is also quite common to find physicians who still think that it is necessary to "put the bowel to rest" during the acute stage of the illness (Brown and MacLean, 1984). The deleterious effect of decreased food intake is worsened by increased catabolic losses of nitrogen that occur as a result of increased metabolic rates and structural damage to the intestine (Powanda, 1977). Another consequence of intestinal damage is the transient loss of absorptive surface and absorptive function as a result of villous atrophy (Davidson and Barnes, 1979). This condition leads to a decreased absorption of macronutrients (fat and carbohydrates) and micronutrients (particularly fat-soluble vitamins). The presence of unabsorbed carbohydrates in the intestinal lumen increases the osmolarity of the intestinal content, thus causing an hyperosmolar diarrhea (Wapnir, 1982). It also subjects these substrates to bacterial fermentation, which produces gas and intestinal bloating, worsening gastrointestinal symptoms. Catabolic losses also are increased by the presence of fever. In cases of parasitic infestations, the child's nutritional status is impaired by blood losses that are secondary to colitis or direct intestinal mucosal damage (common in cases of roundworm [*Ascaris lulmbricoides*], hookworm [*Ancylostoma duodenale* and *Necator americanus*], or whipworm [*Trichuris trichiura*]). Parasitic infestations also are associated with respiratory symptoms (particularly in case of *Ascaris* infestations) and anorexia (Lunn and Northrop-Clewes, 1993).

Disrupted cognition. PEM can disrupt cognition in several ways. Following the lessons learned from the effect of PEM on the body during infections, the classic explanation was that malnutrition caused physical damage to the brain, particularly during sensitive periods of development, namely, during the first two years of life, when about 80 percent of the brain's growth is achieved (Guilarte, 1993; Levitsky and Strupp, 1995). At present, however, it is clear that there are several other mechanisms, aside from organic damage, by which malnutrition can impair intellectual development. There is also evidence that at least part of this damage may be reversible, even in the presence of structural damage to the brain (Levitsky and Strupp, 1995).

Malnutrition may affect brain growth and development, which will be reflected in cognitive disabilities, mo-

tor impairment, or lower intelligent quotient (IQ), by means of micronutrient deficiencies such as vitamin B_6 or iron, both of which are vital for normal brain function (Guilarte, 1993; Pollitt, 1997). Malnutrition also may affect these functions because of energy deficiency, which limits activity and social interaction with peers and caregivers. This mechanism was explored first in the early 1970s by Levitsky and coworkers in a rat model. They showed that energy-deprived rats scored lower on such tests as maze running—a proxy for mental ability—because they were so feeble that they withdrew from contact with their peers and the objects in their surroundings (Levitsky and Strupp, 1995). Similar findings were shown to be present in children living in deprived third-world communities (Chávez and Martínez, 1982).

The extent to which PEM affects intellectual potential has been explored by studying the effect of protein-energy supplementation on behavioral development. In spite of different study designs that focused on prenatal supplementation (Rush, Stein, et al., 1980), on postnatal supplementation (Grantham-McGregor, Meeks Gardner, et al., 1990; Husaini, Karyadi, et al., 1991), or in both (Waber, Vuori-Chirstiansen, et al., 1981; Chávez and Martínez, 1982), results from these studies are consistent in showing that a significant proportion of the variability in mental and motor developmental scales during the first two years of life may be accounted for by nutritional supplementation.

The extent to which the differences in intellectual performance found at early ages in children affected by PEM carries on to later stages in life has been addressed by Pollitt et al. in a long-term follow-up study of Guatemalan children, who received supplements during the prenatal period and the first 2 years of life and were later followed up between the ages of 13 and 19 years old (Pollitt, Gorman, et al., 1995). This study found that children who had received a protein-energy supplement had significantly higher scores on tests of knowledge, numeracy, reading, and vocabulary, as well as a faster reaction time in information-processing tasks compared with children who had received only an energy supplement. This effect was particularly strong for protein-energy supplemented children at the lowest end of the socioeconomic distribution, an interesting finding when compared to only energy supplemented children, in whom the higher cognition test scores varied as a positive function of socioeconomic status, as expected. The authors interpretation is that the protein-energy supplement acted as a social equalizer in relation to the differences in performance usually found in populations as a function of differences in socioeconomic status.

Another long-term supplementation study was carried out in a Mexican village, where women received nutritional supplements during pregnancy and their offspring continued to receive micronutrient supplements from 12 weeks until 10 years of age. Compared to a control group (mothers and children from the same village, recruited two years before supplementation began), children who received supplements showed significantly better IQs, school performance, and behavior (Chávez, Martínez, et al., 1995).

The studies of the effects of iron deficiency on intellectual and motor abilities were addressed specifically during the 1980s and 1990s. Several well-designed intervention-control studies have shown that, before treatment, average mental scores on the Bayley Scales of Infant Development of infants with anemia were 6 to 14 points lower than the scores of non-anemic controls (Lozoff, Brittenham, et al., 1982; Grindulis, Scott, et al., 1986; Lozoff, Brittenham, et al., 1988; Walter, De Andraca, et al., 1989), and average motor development scores were 9 to 11 points lower, differences of statistical and clinical significance. No significant improvement on the test scores of initially iron-deficient children were noted following iron supplements for two to three months (Aukett, Parks, et al., 1986; Lozoff, Brittenham, et al., 1988; Walter, De Andraca, et al., 1989). Fewer studies have addressed whether these deficits prevail in later ages. In a long-term follow-up study of Costa Rican children at age 5 years whose iron status had been documented and consequently treated in infancy under careful supervision, Lozoff et al. found that at five years of age, all children had excellent iron status. However, those children who had been severely iron deficient during infancy (hemoglobin ≥100 g per liter) showed lower mental and motor functioning scores at school entry than did the rest of the children, even after controlling for background factors that were potential confounders (Lozoff, Jimenez, et al., 1991). Further, even anemic children with hemoglobin levels > 100 g per liter before and after treatment also had poorer outcomes at five years of age, compared to non-anemic children. Strong as this evidence may be, it is relevant to point out that, to date, there is no definite proof that iron deficiency is the cause of children's lower test scores. For obvious ethical reasons, the gold standard of experimental designs, the double-blind placebo-control study, has not been carried out.

Protein-energy malnutrition also may affect children's performance on cognitive tests by other, indirect mechanisms (often conceptualized as confounding variables in studies that attempt to establish links between PEM and impaired cognition). These include social and economical disadvantages (Johnston, Low, et al., 1987), differences in parental education (LeVine, LeVine, et al., 1991), years of schooling (Ceci, 1991), inadequate attention or affection from caregivers (Engle and Ricciuti, 1995), and other environmental factors, which may include peer interaction, parental presence in the home, etc. (Engle and Lhotska, 1999).

Recent research has addressed the role of breast-feeding (the gold-standard of good nutrition during the first months of life) on cognitive development, adjusting for the aforementioned variables. The results of a meta-analysis that included 11 studies that controlled for ≥ 5 covariates on the effect of breast-feeding on cognitive function, a statistically significant increment in cognitive function of 3.16 points was seen in breast-fed infants, consistent through all the studies, at 6 to 23 months of age. This study found a greater benefit of breast-feeding for cognitive development of premature babies (an adjusted benefit of 5.18 points), and a larger benefit in relation to duration of breast-feeding (an increase of the weighted mean benefit of 1.68 points with 8–11 weeks of breast-feeding to 2.91 points with ≥28 weeks) (Anderson, Johnstone, et al., 1999).

Concluding Remarks

Over the years, much has been learned about protein-energy malnutrition, its causes, and its effects. Without pretending that all is known, available knowledge can alleviate this burden on human development and social inequalities. Although the treatment of malnourished children all over the world is a clear imperative, the key to solving the problem is to focus on prevention. Preventive actions should be interdisciplinary. These actions should encompass a broad focus on education, particularly directed to women; they should include actions to improve sanitary conditions, schooling opportunities, employment, agricultural produce, and access to diverse food sources, particularly those rich in micronutrients. All sectors of society, including government and non-government organizations, should work together toward a common end. The opportunities to make a substantial improvement in the nutritional status of children all over the world are here, as never before in history. We have studied the causes of malnutrition, its mechanisms, and its consequences. It is now time to study the impact of specific interventions tailored to solve persistent problems.

BIBLIOGRAPHY

ACC/SCN. *Third Report on the World Nutrition Situation*. Geneva, Switzerland, 1997.

Allen, Lindsay H. "Malnutrition and Human Function: A Comparison of Conclusions from the INCAP and Nutrition CRSP Studies." *Journal of Nutrition* 125 (1995): 1119S–1126S.

Allen, Lindsay H. "The Nutrition CRSP: What is Marginal Malnutrition and Does It Affect Human Function?" *Nutrition Reviews* 51 (1993): 255–267.

Anderson, James W., Bryan M. Johnstone, et al. "Breast-feeding and Cognitive Development: A Meta-analysis." *American Journal of Clinical Nutrition* 70 (1999): 525–535.

Aukett, M. A., Y. A. Parks, et al. "Treatment with Iron Increases Weight Gain and Psychomotor Development." *Archive of Disease in Childhood* 61 (1986): 849–857.

Bairagi, R., M. K. Chowdhury, et al. "Alternative Anthropometric Indicators of Mortality." *American Journal of Clinical Nutrition* 42 (1985): 296–306.

Bentley, Margaret. "The Household Management of Childhood Diarrhea in Rural North India." *Social Sciences and Medicine* 27 (1988): 75–85.

Brown, Kenneth. H., and William C. MacLean, Jr. "Nutritional Management of Acute Diarrhea: An Appraisal of the Alternatives." *Pediatrics* 73 (1984): 119–125.

Ceci, S. J. "How Much Does Schooling Influence General Intelligence and Its Cognitive Components? A Reassessment of the Evidence." *Developmental Psychology* 27 (1991): 703–722.

Chandra, Ranjit. "Nutrition and Immunity: Lessons from the Past and New Insights into the Future." *American Journal of Clinical Nutrition* 53 (1991): 1087–1101.

Chávez Adolfo, Celia Martínez, et al. "The Effect of Malnutrition on Human Development. A 24-year study of well-nourished and malnourished children living in a poor Mexican village." In *Community-Based Longitudinal Nutrition and Health Studies: Classic Examples from Guatemala, Haiti, and Mexico*, edited by N. S. Scrimshaw. Boston, International Nutrition Foundation for Developing Countries, (1995).

Chen, Lincoln. "Interactions of Diarrhea and Malnutrition: Mechanisms and Intervention." In *Diarrhea and Malnutrition*, edited by L. C. Chen and N. S. Scrimshaw pp. 3–19. New York: Plenum Press, 1983.

Chen, Lincoln C., A. Chowdhury, et al. "Anthropometric Assessment of Energy-Protein Malnutrition and Subsequent Risk of Mortality among Preschool Aged Children." *American Journal of Clinical Nutrition* 33 (1980): 1836–1845.

de Onis, Mercedes and Monika Blössner, *WHO Global Database on Child Growth and Malnutrition*. Geneva, Switzerland: World Health Organization Programme of Nutrition, 1997.

Engle, Patrice L. and Henry N. Ricciuti "Psychosocial Aspects of Care and Nutrition." *Food and Nutrition Bulletin* 16 (1995): 356–377.

Gomez, Federico, Rafael Ramos-Galvan, et al. "Mortality in Second and Third Degree Malnutrition." *Journal of Tropical Pediatrics* 2 (1956): 77–83.

Gómez-Santos, Federico. "Desnutrición." *Boletin Medico del Hospital Infantil de Mexico* 3 (1946): 543–551.

Grantham-McGregor, Sally. "A Review of Studies of the Effect of Severe Malnutrition on Mental Development." *Journal of Nutrition* 125 (1995): 2233S–2238S.

Grindulis, H., P. H. Scott, et al. "Combined Deficiency of Iron and Vitamin D in Asian Toddlers." *Archives of Diseases in Childhood* 61 (1986): 843-848.

Haas, Jeree D., E. J. Martinez, et al. "Nutritional Supplementation During the Preschool Years and Physical Work Capacity in Adolescent and Young Adult Guatemalans." *Journal of Nutrition* 125 (1995): 1078S–1089S.

Habicht, Jean-Pierre, and Reynaldo Martorell "Objectives, Research Design and Implementation of the INCAP Longitudinal Study." *Food and Nutrition Bulletin* 14 (1992): 176–190.

Heywood, Peter. "The Functional Significance of Malnutrition: Growth and Prospective Risk of Death in the Highlands of Papua New Guinea." *Journal of Food and Nutrition* 39 (1982): 13–19.

Husaini, M., L. Karyadi, et al. "Developmental Effects of Short-term Supplementary Feeding in Nutritionally-at-risk Indonesian Infants." *American Journal of Clinical Nutrition* 54 (1991): 799–804.

Johnston, R. E., W. M. Low, et al. "Interaction of Nutritional and Socioeconomic Status as Determinants of Cognitive Development in Disadvantaged Urban Guatemalan Children." *American Journal of Physical Anthropology* 73 (1987): 501–506.

Kochan, I. "Role of Iron in the Regulation of Nutritional Immunity." Advanced Chemistry Series No. 162. Washington, D.C.: American Chemical Society (1977): 55–62.

LeVine, R. A., S. E. LeVine, et al. "Women's Schooling and Child Care in the Demographic Transition: A Mexican Case Study." *Population Development Reviews* 17 (1991): 459–496.

Levitsky, D., and B. Strupp "Malnutrition and the Brain: Changing Concepts, Changing Concerns." *Journal of Nutrition* 125 (1995): 2212S–2220S.

Lozoff, B., G. M. Brittenham, et al. "The Effects of Short-term Oral Iron Therapy on Developmental Deficits in Iron-deficient Anemic Infants." *Journal of Pediatrics* 100 (1982): 351–357.

Lozoff, B., G. Brittenham, et al. "Iron Deficiency Anemia and Iron Therapy Effects on Infant Developmental Test Performance." *Pediatrics* 79 (1987): 981–995.

Lozoff, B., E. Jimenez, et al. "Long-term Developmental Outcome of Infants with Iron Deficiency." *New England Journal of Medicine* 325 (1991): 687–694.

Lunn, P., and C. A. Northrop-Clewes. "The Impact of Gastrointestinal Parasites on Protein-energy Malnutrition in Man." *Proceedings of the Nutrition Society* 52 (1993): 101–111.

Lutter, C. K., J. O. Mora, et al. "Age-specific Responsiveness of Weight and Length to Nutritional Supplementation." *American Journal of Clinical Nutrition* 51 (1990): 359–364.

Martorell, Reynaldo, Dirk G. Schroeder, et al. "Patterns of Linear Growth in Rural Guatemalan Adolescents and Children." *Journal of Nutrition* 125 (1995): 1060S–1067S.

Mendez, Michelle A., and Linda S. Adair "Severity and Timing of Stunting in the First Two Years of Life Affect Performance on Cognitive Tests in Late Childhood." *Journal of Nutrition* 129 (1999): 1555–1562.

Pelletier, David. "The Relationship between Child Anthropometry and Mortality in Developing Countries: Implications for Policy, Programs and Future Research." *Journal of Nutrition* 124 (1994): 2047S–2081S.

Pelletier, David, Ed Frongillo, Jr., et al. "Epidemiologic Evidence for a Potentiating Effect of Malnutrition on Child Mortality." *American Journal of Public Health* 83 (1993): 1130–1133.

Pollitt, Ernesto. "Iron Deficiency and Educational Deficiency." *Nutrition Reviews* 55 (1997): 133–141.

Pollitt, Ernesto, K. S. Gorman, et al. "Nutrition in Early Life and the Fulfillment of Intellectual Potential." *Journal of Nutrition* 125 (1995): 1111S–1118S.

Rivera, Juan A., Cecilia Cortés, et al. "Capacidad de peso para edad y longitud para edad para predecir desmedro a los tres años de vida." *Salud Publica de Mexico* 40 (1998): 127–132.

Scrimshaw, Nevin S. "Synergism of Malnutrition and Infection. Evidence from Field Studies in Guatemala." *Journal of the American Medical Association* 212(10) (1970): 1685–1692.

Scrimshaw, Nevin, C. Taylor, et al. *Interactions of Nutrition and Infection*. Geneva: World Health Organization, 1968.

Trowbridge, Frederick L., and Alfred Sommer. "Nutritional Anthropometry and Mortality Risk." *American Journal of Clinical Nutrition* 34 (1981): 2591–2592.

UNICEF *Strategies of Improving Nutrition of Children and Women in Developing Countries*. New York: United Nations Children's Fund, 1990.

Waber, D. P., L. Vuori-Christiansen, et al. "Nutritional Supplementation, Maternal Education, and Cognitive Development of Infants at Risk of Malnutrition." *American Journal of Clinical Nutrition* 34 (1990): 807–813.

Walter, T., I. De Andraca, et al. "Iron Deficiency Anemia: Adverse Effects on Infant Psychomotor Development." *Pediatrics* 84 (1989): 7–17.

Waterlow, John C. "Classification and Definition of Protein-calorie Malnutrition." *British Medical Journal* 3 (1972): 566–569.

WHO Expert Committee *Physical Status: The Use and Interpretation of Anthropometry*. Geneva: World Health Organization, 1995.

Williams, Cicely D. "A Nutritional Disease of Childhood Associated with a Maize Diet. " *Archives of Diseases in Childhood* 8 (1933): 423–433.

Homero Martínez

MAMMALS.

Mammals—warm-blooded, milk-producing animals—have provided meat protein, milk protein, collagen, hides for leather and shelter, and bones and sinew for various tools since humans began to hunt. Mammals also have provided the power for transportation (still called horsepower) and for heavy lifting or pulling. They have often been regarded as companion animals. Indeed, the existence and progress of humanity have depended heavily on mammals. As human societies became more complex and some took up the settled practices of farming and animal husbandry, certain mammalian species were selected to provide sustainable supplies of meat protein. Bovine (cattle), porcine (swine), ovine (sheep), and caprine (goat) species became valued livestock. Domestic animals, whether raised for food, work, or companionship, were selectively bred by controlling the animals' breeding and food supply to ensure desired traits in the next generation.

Types of Mammals

The three main classes of mammals, based on food preference, are herbivores, omnivores, and carnivores. Herbivores are strict plant eaters (sheep, goats); omnivores are opportunistic meat and plant eaters (humans, pigs); carnivores are almost exclusively meat eaters (wolves, cats). Mammals, thus, are both prey and predator in any food chain, depending on their size and aggressive behavior.

Herbivores. Plant-eating mammals provide most of the world's protein. Virtually every culture around the world tends one of the grazing (herbivorous) species of mammals as a protein source. Dairy cattle, water buffalo, sheep and goats, camels, yaks, reindeer, and llamas and alpacas all provide dairy products such as yogurt, cheese, butter, and milk in various societies.

Cattle originated in northern Europe and were domesticated by the northern Germanic and Celtic tribes in approximately 4000 B.C.E. Romans then brought them into southern Europe in the first century B.C.E. From the upper reaches of the Nile to the plains of southern and eastern Africa, cattle herding was common. Cattle became the basis of wealth for warrior-dominated societies in southern Africa. During the Middle Ages in Europe, cattle represented real wealth as milk providers and as work animals, not as meat animals. Cattle were slaughtered only when they could no longer work. Beef was not widely eaten, as cattle and oxen (castrated dairy bulls) had tough, dry flesh.

Water buffalo, valuable for hauling, transportation, and other work, were also used for milk, and buffalo milk mozzarella is still enjoyed as a table cheese in Italy.

Sheep and goats, small ruminants, are kept for their fleece, hides, meat, and milk. Both are docile and socially inclined mammals, and were herded beginning in 8000 B.C.E. in southwest Asia. Camel, yak, and reindeer are herding animals that provide meat, milk, and hides for the nomadic tribes of Asia and the Arctic Circle, respectively. Reindeer herding developed in the northern latitudes even before herds were kept on the Eurasian steppes. Camel herding became common in Arabia and the Sudan of Africa, and camels were critical to the maintenance of trade routes that crossed the great deserts of Africa and Asia. The yak, a large, long-haired ox with a bushy tail, is native to the Tibetan plateau. It provides dairy products and is used for transport. Llamas and alpacas have provided the peoples of Peru and Bolivia with hides, fleece, meat, and milk since at least 3500 B.C.E.

The American bison, the largest land mammal of North America, is believed to have migrated from the steppes of Central Asia into what is now Alaska by crossing the narrow strip of land (Beringia) that existed during the last Ice Age. Native Americans revered bison for the wealth it provided in clothing, food, and tools made from sinew and bone.

Deer, along with their cousins—elk, moose, and caribou—are antlered, hoofed ruminants. These grazing animals supplied food and clothing to both Native Americans and, later, the European invaders of the North American continent. Antelope are the surviving members of an ancient family of grazing animals native to North America. Lewis and Clark, on their long exploratory trip across the continental United States, found large herds of antelope on the Great Plains. Gazelles and other wild grazing animals of Central Africa and Central Asia are hunted by native peoples for their meat.

Many species of small game have provided meat and fur when large game was not available. Wild hares and some rabbits, both native to Europe and the Americas,

Traditional bowl made of grass fibers for milking camels. Oman, twentieth century. The handle and exterior covering are goat hide. ROUGHWOOD COLLECTION. PHOTO CHEW & COMPANY.

are hunted, while other breeds of rabbit are reared specifically for consumption. Muskrats, sometimes called "marsh rabbits," and squirrels are rodents found throughout North America; both have supplemented the human diet. Squirrels are still hunted today in many parts of the United States and are usually served in a stew. Guinea pigs are popular in many Peruvian dishes, especially in the Andes, where these herbivorous rodents (much larger than the guinea pigs kept as pets or laboratory animals) are raised in many households, like rabbits elsewhere. Rats and mice are rarely eaten, though both have provided meat for people in times of famine.

The beauty of its fur led to the beaver's being overhunted by British, French, and Russian trappers in the northern territories of the North American continent in the sixteenth and seventeenth centuries. Beaver pelts were in great demand in Europe, especially for men's top hats. The fatty tail of the beaver was also prized for food. In the Middle Ages, the tail was declared "fish" by the Catholic Church, since the animal lived in water, making it acceptable as a meal on meatless days. Because its meat is very strong, only farm-raised beavers are recommended for cooking.

Kangaroos and opossums, both marsupials, are not consumed widely, though in Australia a cottage industry has developed around the production of kangaroo meat. Opossums, though not farm-raised, are hunted in the southern states of the United States for their meat.

Omnivores. Pigs are descended from a distant ancestor in southern Asia. Domesticated pigs brought to North America by the Spanish occasionally escaped captivity and multiplied, increasing the populations of wild pigs in the southeastern United States. Other breeds subsequently brought to the United States also occasionally escaped and bred with feral pigs, further mongrelizing the pig population.

Peccaries, known also as javelinas, North America's native wild pig, are not related to domesticated pigs and wild boars. Peccaries belong to a separate genus indigenous only to North America. They favor a warm climate and are hunted in New Mexico, Arizona, and Texas.

Raccoons range widely throughout the United States. Although valued primarily for their fur, their meat was commonly eaten during colonial times, and raccoons are still hunted for their fur and meat in the southern states of the United States.

Archeological evidence suggests that bear meat was consumed by native peoples in North America following ritual hunts. Bear meat was prized by European colonists and Native Americans, mainly for its fat for cooking. Though not a widely popular meat, bear are culled from game reserves and the meat is sometimes available frozen.

Carnivores. The small Asiatic wolf, a social animal and meat eater—the ancestor of our canine companions—was reportedly domesticated as early as 11,000 B.C.E., probably because it was more useful for herding and hunting than as a source of food. This is not to say that the dog was not a source of meat. Dog meat has been eaten and enjoyed in Asian cultures, and is still commonly consumed in both China and Korea.

Domestication

Although the history of domestication of mammals by humans is not recorded, archeological evidence suggests that it occurred on all continents between 7000 and 10,000 B.C.E. Each human group chose local migrating herbivores for domestication on the basis of their availability and docility. The first mammals to live with people were likely wolves and small ruminants such as sheep and goats. By the end of the second millennium B.C.E., civilizations based on livestock domestication and agriculture had emerged in Asia, Europe, and Africa. Small grazing animals like deer and sheep, which could provide meat, milk, and fiber, were probably herded by humans as they roamed the broad landscapes of western Asia. No evidence exists that early humans domesticated the numerous grazing animals of Africa.

Goats and sheep. Besides being docile and adaptable, goats and sheep breed successfully in the company of humans, and in time each generation gradually lost more of its feral nature. It is widely believed that the goat was the first herding animal to be domesticated, due to its gregarious nature. As the Romans moved north through Europe during the first century B.C.E., sheep and goats accompanied them, becoming sources for the wool industry, and mutton became a readily available meat. Sheep store fat well and so are efficient animals to maintain.

Goats are browsers, able to digest not only grasses but also woody shrubs and less desirable plants. Goats are even more adaptive and less choosy about their diet than sheep and can graze in arid climates. Goats continue to be prized for their milk and the resulting fermented dairy products. Goat meat, particularly the tender and milder flavor of kid, was enjoyed throughout the Mediterranean and the Asian continent and is also eaten in some regions of the Americas.

Cattle. The ancestor of today's domestic cattle, the aurochs (*Bos primigenius*), is extinct. Members of the bovine genus inhabited most of the world's continents and were introduced into the Western Hemisphere during the European conquests of the late fifteenth and early sixteenth centuries.

Asian cattle, also known as humped back cattle (*Bos indicus*), have provided meat and motive power on the Asian subcontinent. Religious and cultural beliefs in India prevent cattle from being consumed as food, although the milk can be used. In Africa, cattle are probably descended from European and Indian breeds introduced by traders, probably in the first millennium B.C.E.

Veal, meat from castrated young dairy bulls, was a choice dish even in ancient times. Just-weaned calves produce veal, which still brings a handsome price, more per pound than beef. Veal is a light-colored meat because the animals are fed milk or milk-replacer diets and are never permitted to graze.

The distinction between beef and dairy cattle breeds began in eighteenth-century Europe. Breeds that were best for beef and those best for milk production were identified and cultivated. Among the dairy-consuming peoples of northern Europe, the dairy breeds of cattle were selected for the high butterfat content of their milk.

It is generally believed that cattle first came to the North American continent with the Spanish. Columbus carried cattle to Santo Domingo in 1493, and in 1519 Cortés brought long-horned Andalusian cattle to Mexico. In the early seventeenth century, Spanish missionaries were raising cattle throughout the southwest United States.

Pigs. The ancestors of domestic swine were dispersed throughout Europe, Asia, and North Africa. The nomadic lifestyle of early peoples precluded their domestication. They were probably first encountered as pillagers of crops and therefore hunted, but young pigs might have been taken into early settlements and raised for meat. The omnivorous habits of the pig meant that it could thrive on the scraps from humans combined with its own rooting and foraging.

Pigs have evolved gradually over a period of ten million years with a few minor variations. Early pigs were taller than six feet, with an elongated wedge-shaped head, lacking a modern pig's snout, and a body shape similar to that of the European boar. This ancestor of the pig ranged from Europe to Asia and became the ancestor of the European wild boar.

Columbus is credited with bringing the pig to the Americas in 1493. These hogs ran wild throughout the Spanish West Indies, and were later joined by a load of pigs that arrived in Mexico with Cortés in 1521. On his trek west to the Mississippi Delta in 1539, Hernando de Soto brought pigs from the West Indies to Florida.

Dogs. Evidence suggests that early canine-human interactions may have occurred over the kills of larger wild herbivores, leading dogs and humans to be wary competitors at first but ultimately to become allies. Bones of dogs are common in campsites of the late Stone Age from around 7000 to 6000 B.C.E. The Asian wolf was probably the first wild animal domesticated by humans, and it is believed to be the ancestor of all domestic dogs. Until the eighteenth or nineteenth centuries, most of the breeds of dog were described by their purpose (wolfhound, sheepdog), and it was not until the nineteenth century that many breeds were developed.

Horses. The earliest fossil examples, Eohippus, are found in northwestern North America. This wild ancestor of the horse was not much larger than a cat and had four toes on its forefeet and three on its hind feet. It was probably very widely distributed across the globe. Around 4000 B.C.E. the horse was domesticated in eastern Europe, and played a significant role in transportation, draft power, and warfare. Mounted soldiers were important military weapons until the twentieth century. Modern horses were reintroduced to the Americas by the Spanish conquistadors and were quickly adopted by native peoples for transport.

Game mammals and hunting. Those mammals not domesticated were hunted. Hunting animals for food or sport, or to rid a locale of animals that are seen as pests, is a human activity that spans the centuries and the globe. As early as the Late Paleolithic period, successful hunts required methods to preserve meat after slaughter. Meat was dried, smoked, or frozen in pits dug in the earth, or carcasses were weighted down with stones and sunk in cold lakes that froze during the winter. Meat stored was eaten dry, boiled, or grilled.

Hunting still provides some animal protein for the human diet; amounts vary depending upon the culture and region. In developed countries, hunting is largely a sport, while in less developed countries it remains, with fishing, an important source of dietary protein.

Nutrition

Meat. Meat is a popular high-quality protein food that satisfies the appetite and taste of people around the world. With the exception of organ meats, which tend to have concentrated nutrients, all of the cuts of meat from an animal are equally nutritious, providing roughly equivalent amounts of protein, minerals, and vitamins. Nutrition experts recognize meat as a food that also contributes varying amounts of fat to the diet. Meat supplies complete protein (all essential amino acids), essential minerals such as iron and phosphorus, significant B-complex vitamins (for example, thiamin), and trace minerals such as zinc. The protein of meat is comparable to that of fish, poultry, eggs, and milk.

The consumption of organ meats is sometimes encouraged because of the extremely rich vitamin and mineral content contained in edible glands and organs, including the liver, heart, kidneys, brain, sweetbread (thymus gland), tongue, tripe (stomach), and testicles, as well as the lungs and spleen in some cultures.

Dairy. Dishes prepared with milk or cheese are sometimes called "meat alternates" because of the similarity of the nutrient profiles, particularly when it comes to complete protein. The most significant milk products are:

- Yogurt: A fermented milk product made from whole, low-fat, or skim milk, providing all the food value of the milk from which it was made.

- Cultured cream: A product similar to yogurt but made with cream and so higher in butterfat. Sour cream is used widely in eastern European cooking; crème fraîche is more popular in France.

- Butter: A concentrated milk fat that provides fat in the diet and fat-soluble vitamin A.

- Cheese: A concentrated form of milk, fermented and often aged, that loses some of its protein in the cheese-making process but remains a high-protein food.

Mammals and Human Societies

Mammals have long played an important role in human mythology, religion, and social customs. As an act of reverence, humans have sacrificed animals, drunk their blood, and eaten their flesh. There are also taboos against certain relationships between humans and some animals, from the kosher prohibitions on eating pork and certain cuts of other animals to sexual taboos concerning congress between man and beast. Animals have been believed to be the habitat of both evil spirits and the souls of deceased human beings. Superstitions abound about animals, from bad luck brought by a black cat crossing one's path to good luck brought by carrying a rabbit's foot.

Culture, religion, symbolism, tradition, and taboos. Animal worship figures in many cultures and religions, including the cow among Hindus and the cat in ancient Egypt, and involves the role of reincarnation in some Asian religions. In many cultures, the spirits of important food animals were appeased to ensure their continued fertility, or ceremonies were performed to propitiate predators that threatened human survival. Stone Age art, cave drawings dating from 20,000 to 40,000 B.C.E., shows the animals and activities most important to the peoples of those cultures. The archeological evidence strongly suggests that these early people hunted and killed wild animals. Anthropologists believe the caves in which these drawings are found were not dwellings but served a religious or ritual function because food animals and hunting scenes predominate.

The earliest records of meat consumption indicate that animals were ritually slaughtered and the meat distributed to members of the community on the basis of an individual's place in the social hierarchy. Such practices required settled groups engaged in crop and pasture production. With farming and the formation of population clusters came the division of labor necessary to support specific food practices—grain milling, baking, meat processing, leather tanning, and so on. In some societies, meat processing emerged as part of sacrificial offerings to the deities for atonement, appeasement, supplication, or thanksgiving.

Meat eating and religious practices. In ancient times, sacrifices to the gods and goddesses often consisted of roasted sheep, goats, and lambs. Homer, Virgil, and the authors of the Old Testament all give accounts of roasted meat being offered to please the gods or the Lord. The biblical Book of Leviticus stipulates that the sacrificial animal be perfect, without any physical flaws; thus, a castrated animal was forbidden as a sacrifice.

The story of Adam and Eve in the Book of Genesis suggests that humans were created essentially vegetarian. Meat eating followed Eve's transgression. Under the laws of Kashrut, which govern kosher practices, Jews are forbidden to eat pork and shellfish ("tref"). In addition, certain parts of an animal, such as the hindquarters (unless butchered in a special fashion) as well as some organ meats, are forbidden. Another dietary restriction is that meat and milk may not be eaten together. These limits have resulted in fewer choices when it comes to meat for Jews than for others.

Muslims also do not eat pork, and, like Jews, they slaughter their meat according to religious guidelines. Such meat is called *halal*, or lawful. The month-long fast of Ramadan, while strict, is more of a joyful occasion than the Christian Lent, a forty-day period of abstinence and penitence.

The Roman Catholic Church established many restrictions on eating meat on certain days during the year, particularly during Lent and on specified fast days. Until the reforms of Vatican II (1962), meat eating was traditionally forbidden on Fridays. For generations, fish on Fridays was the rule in Roman Catholic communities. Meat, broth, and fat from warm-blooded animals were forbidden, while meat from waterfowl and from coldwater fish was considered acceptable.

Given the Church calendar—abstaining from meat on Fridays, on the eve of certain feast days, and on other days as well—meat eating was forbidden almost every other day: 180 days a year. The Orthodox Church was even stricter. This refusal to eat meat and fat (including butter in some times and places) had an ascetic aspect as well as a penitential one in its denial of human desire. In

India cattle are not consumed because of the religious proscriptions of the Hindu faith. Since pigs, goats, and sheep are raised for meat and milk, however, India is not entirely vegetarian. Butter from the milk of sacred Indian cows was made for religious ceremonies, and ghee, a kind of clarified butter, is used for cooking.

Meat eating and vegetarianism. Meat, whether from mammals, poultry, or fish, provides a concentrated, easily digestible source of protein and fat. Ruminants in particular are able to convert herbaceous material into muscle more efficiently than monogastric animals, such as pigs or poultry, and are therefore better suited as sources of meat protein.

A vegetarian diet—eschewing meat or any animal food products—is undertaken by individuals for many reasons: health reasons and concern for the environment, ecology, and world hunger issues. Vegetarians often also cite economic reasons and ethical considerations as reasons. For some, religious beliefs dictate following a diet that avoids animal products. In India, for example, many are vegetarians because they find the taking of life abhorrent; in addition, many believe in reincarnation and fear that a living soul could be inhabiting a living creature.

Significant scientific data suggest links between a vegetarian diet and reduced risk of developing several chronic degenerative diseases and conditions, including heart disease, high blood pressure, diabetes, obesity, and some types of cancer.

The eating patterns of vegetarians vary considerably. The lacto-ovo-vegetarian diet is based on grains, vegetables, fruits, legumes, seeds, nuts, dairy products, and eggs, and excludes meat, fish, and fowl. The vegan, or total vegetarian, eating pattern is similar with the additional exclusion of eggs, dairy, and other animal products, even honey. Even within these patterns, considerable variation exists in the extent to which animal products are avoided.

Human beings, however, have been omnivorous since before recorded history. It seems unlikely that they will turn en masse to vegetarianism. In fact, arguments from the 1968 Rome conferences of the Food and Agriculture Organization of the United Nations suggest that humans could not abandon the consumption of meat in favor of a solely vegetarian diet. There was not, nor is there now, sufficient arable land to produce adequate protein or calories for the world's population.

Global Issues

While some of the problems discussed here primarily reflect events and situations in Europe and the United States, their repercussions will almost certainly have global consequences as impoverished regions of the world struggle to provide a nutritious diet for their increasing populations. What began as animal husbandry in prehistory threatens worldwide disaster. As the human population has increased beyond the capacity of the planet to feed its numbers, the practice of high-intensity animal

ANIMAL RIGHTS

The animal rights movement is a loose-knit coalition of groups who oppose abusing, mutilating, or killing animals to serve human purposes, including inhumane "farming" methods to raise animals for high-status luxury items like fur and leather. Most visible in North America and Europe, the movement includes benign meat eaters and farmers who want to ensure that livestock are treated humanely to vegetarians to activists who smear blood on fur coats and urge supermarkets to remove their lobster tanks. The politically and ideologically motivated efforts have had an impact on mainstream economics, although those with a financial interest dismiss their efforts as romantic or as malicious and dangerous, especially if they still believe that humans are superior to other animals and, therefore, that they have the "right" to do whatever they wish to them in the name of some "grander" (human) purpose. Research has demonstrated that the humane treatment of animals actually improves production and meat quality. Some of the results of that research have been incorporated into animal raising practices. In addition, some major food companies have adopted policies for their meat suppliers that stipulate humane handling practices, and some retail food packages— for example, chicken sausage—bear labels declaring such policies. As people grasp the "radical" idea that animals feel pain and, like humans, have the right not to suffer, whatever the rationale, the animal rights movement grows.

production has caused numerous environmental problems that endanger humans as well as the animals bred for food.

The risks and costs of high-intensity animal production. Since World War II, agricultural production has striven to produce more from less without, some critics say, thought of the consequences. With high-intensity animal production, because animals are kept in close quarters they are more susceptible to the various diseases and parasites afflicting livestock. To counter disease and parasitism, scientists developed inexpensive pharmaceuticals to protect and treat animals. Surprisingly, many of these drugs actually improved livestock feed conversion performance faster than breeding and breed selection. As a consequence, livestock producers adopted these products widely, and meat production operations grew and consolidated in rural areas near feed grain sources.

Feedlots and large poultry operations, however, though extraordinarily efficient, are smelly and environmentally risky as well. Also, starting in the early 1970s, mounting public concern about the residues of pharmaceutical products in meat used for human consumption entered the debate about the wisdom of intensive livestock production. The food supply seemed to be contaminated with unnecessary, and perhaps toxic, chemical substances, and the methods of raising animals that required their use became targets of public protests. One result of these concerns has been the increase in sustainable livestock production, sometimes called "natural" or "organic" production. In natural production the animals are raised without performance-enhancing chemicals or feed additives. Livestock living in herds are as susceptible to disease as those raised in close quarters, and the effects of disease are devastating to herds. However, ranchers claim that it is more expensive to raise pigs or cattle without the aid of drugs or additives and so justify the higher prices charged for such meat.

Organic livestock production is stricter still, involving the feeding of grains and oil seeds produced under National Organic Standards. As adopted by the U.S. Department of Agriculture (USDA), the National Organic Standards specify that livestock and poultry may not be treated with antibiotics or any medicine and must be fed grains and rations that derive from organic crop production.

Intensive livestock production systems are based on concentrating large numbers of animals (housed or not) on small parcels of land and feeding them high-energy diets that guarantee the fastest weight gain in the least time. While feed efficiency (pounds of gain per pounds of feed) is important to the owners of such systems, intensified livestock production also results in large-scale animal waste. The concentration of live animals in a total confinement unit rivals a small city in terms of the annual waste output. Cities of such size are required by law to maintain tertiary water treatment facilities to handle their wastewater outfall. No such provision has yet forced pig or cattle feeders to treat their production wastes in a similar manner.

Among mammals, pigs represent the biggest waste threat to the environment because of the very large confinement units used to raise them. The most efficient pig will convert two pounds of feed into one pound of additional body mass, not all of which is edible protein. In order to acquire that pound, the animal produces one pound of feces and urine. Cattle are even less efficient, converting twelve to eighteen pounds of feed to one pound of body weight during the last weeks of feeding. This waste presents a considerable disposal problem.

With the animals living in such limited space, the waste must be stored for later treatment or use. In the past, this meant applying the manure as fertilizer to agricultural land, but this method of handling manure is no longer sound. Lagoons that hold animal waste often leak

or break, with disastrous consequences for local streams and lakes. The open pools of raw waste also fill the surrounding countryside with a prevailing stench. The recent history of such environmental disasters and resulting legal battles is a complex story about shifting the costs of production to others, including future generations. Moreover, the available solutions cost money, so are unacceptable to those watching the bottom line. Steel holding tanks or glass-lined tanks, for example, clearly better containment choices, are prohibitively expensive, usually more than the average pork or beef production operation can, or is willing to, pay. With the infusion of new capital into pork production in the late 1980s, more attention was given to waste management, but the disposal problem has not yet been solved.

Intensive livestock production poses other risks to the environment and human health, for example, pollution of surface and ground water by animal waste. Such spills contaminate water, cause loss of property values for residential land, and harm recreational areas. The frequent and periodic contamination of ground and surface water from manure spills has become a familiar headline, reminding the public that profit-driven production methods endanger their health and the welfare of future generations.

With the appearance in the 1990s of bovine spongiform encephalopathy (BSE; more familiar to the public as "mad cow disease") in England and France, and the deaths caused by its spread to humans who ate meat from diseased cows, vigilance with respect to safe meat production became even more critical. In spite of research demonstrating that the disease had been spread in herds that had eaten feed that contained meat products, some feed suppliers in the United States were found continuing the practice in 2001, and, without enough USDA inspectors to monitor meat production from start to finish, the public cannot be sure that the meat they eat does not come from cows infected with BSE.

Facing continual pressure from environmentalists, real estate developers, and non-farm landowners, livestock producers struggle with presenting a responsible image. This reality applies both to producers managing large, intensified operations and to those who pasture their livestock. In terms of the stocking capacity of open land, whether for cattle, pigs, or small ruminants, it is now being argued that small ruminants (sheep and goats) can provide as much meat per acre as cattle or pigs without the subsequent environmental risks. Raising dual-purpose sheep or goats (those that provide both food and fiber) can be a more efficient use of limited land resources than the typical practices of cattle ranching.

This issue will become more pressing in the future as residential suburbs push into traditionally rural areas. The resolution will need to be political because of the constituencies involved. Technological advances have made the cost of farming too expensive for family farmers. As they are forced to sell their land to the giants of agribusiness or go into bankruptcy, farmers are becoming a smaller and smaller percentage of the population, and their real voice in legislatures will continue to diminish. City dwellers will demand that a fairer burden of the cost of farming be placed on those who profit from it than has been the practice since the New Deal under Franklin D. Roosevelt's administration in 1932–1940.

Another aspect of the urban-rural confrontation involves the cropping practices needed to support the intensified meat-production industry. Of the more than 70 million acres of corn grown annually in the United States, more than 65 percent is used for animal feed, and the price of corn drives all other commodity prices. Federal farm policies during the twentieth century resulted in overproduction of corn and soy relative to world market demands, depressed world prices, and significant loss of farm income. Add to this the loss of agricultural diversity and soil productivity caused by producing the same crop or the same rotation of crops on the same land year in and year out. Such farming practices had forced farmers to use more and more chemical pesticides and fertilizers in order to achieve uniform yields. Biotech crops may be a solution, because they permit more intensified cultivation and higher yields. However, controversy remains within the scientific community about the sustainability of high yields from biotech seed crops. This concern is added to the ongoing problems of groundwater contaminated with fertilizer runoff and pesticides.

Bioengineering. Unlike plant biotechnology, which has quickly introduced numerous varieties of common plants genetically reengineered to include certain traits, such as resistance to common pests for corn, animal biotechnology has had little success in changing the basic properties of livestock or poultry. A few applications of genetic manipulation may eventually prove useful in producing meat protein for human consumption. Of these, cloning is the most obvious and most likely to succeed, if public opposition fails to halt such research. Cloning livestock requires the nuclear transfer from an animal with the most desired traits (for example, efficient feed conversion, muscling, and tenderness) to eggs from the same species. One application would be the cloning of highly desirable boar and sow lines to be used in creating market pigs with specific, repeatable characteristics.

The technology for cloning livestock at this time is prohibitively expensive compared to conventional breeding or artificial insemination. For this reason, cloning is not expected to make a significant contribution to meat production for years. Such genetic manipulation also arouses considerable controversy in public and scientific discourse regarding the ultimate safety of food derived from such genetically modified organisms.

As populations continue to expand and the food crisis intensifies, the twenty-first century will witness societies worldwide struggling with the multitude of social, environmental, economic, and health issues that surround the production of livestock.

See also **Aversion to Food; Cattle; Christianity; Dairy Products; Disgust; FAO (Food and Agriculture Organization); Food Safety; Goat; Government Agencies; High-Technology Farming; Horse; Hunting and Gathering; Inspection; Judaism; Mammals, Sea; Meat; Organic Agriculture; Pig; Prehistoric Societies; Sheep; Vegetarianism.**

BIBLIOGRAPHY

Budiansky, Stephen. *The Covenant of the Wild: Why Animals Chose Domestication.* New York: Morrow, 1992.

Caras, Roger A. *A Perfect Harmony: The Intertwining Lives of Animals and Humans throughout History.* New York: Simon and Schuster, 1996.

Cheeke, Peter R. *Contemporary Issues in Animal Agriculture.* Danville, Ill.: Interstate, 1999.

Conlin, Joseph R. *Bacon, Beans, and Galantines: Food and Foodways on the Western Mining Frontier.* Reno: University of Nevada Press, 1986.

Deutsch-Renner, Hans. *The Origin of Food Habits.* London: Faber and Faber, 1944.

Diamond, Jared M. *Guns, Germs, and Steel: The Fates of Human Societies.* New York: Norton, 1997.

Drury, John. *Rare and Well Done: Some Historical Notes on Meats and Meatmen.* Chicago: Quadrangle, 1966.

Duyff, Roberta Larson. *The American Dietetic Association's Complete Food and Nutrition Guide.* Philadelphia: Wiley, 1998.

Ellis, Merle. *The Great American Meat Book.* New York: Knopf, 1996.

Ensminger, M. E. *Beef Cattle Science.* 6th ed. Danville, Ill.: Interstate, 1987.

Ensminger, M. E *Sheep and Goat Science.* Danville, Ill.: Interstate, 1986.

Ensminger, M. E *Swine Science.* 5th ed. Danville, Ill.: Interstate, 1984.

Flandrin, Jean-Louis, and Massimo Montanari. *Food: A Culinary History from Antiquity to the Present.* (English edition by Albert Sonnenfeld; translated by Clarissa Botsford.) New York: Columbia University Press, 1999.

Haber, Barbara. *From Hardtack to Home Fries.* New York: Free Press, 2002.

Harris, Marvin. *The Sacred Cow and Abominable Pig: The Riddle of Food and Culture.* New York: Touchstone, 1987.

Hemmer, Helmut. *Domestication: The Decline of Environmental Appreciation.* Translated by Neil Beckhaus. Cambridge, England: Cambridge University Press, 1990.

Hibler, Jane. *Wild about Game.* New York: Broadway Books, 1998.

Kittler, Pamela G., and Kathryn Sucher. *Food and Culture in America: A Nutrition Handbook.* New York: Van Nostrand Reinhold, 1989.

Knutson, Ronald, J. B. Penn, and Barry L. Flinchbaugh. *Agricultural and Food Policy.* 4th ed. Upper Saddle River, N.J.: Prentice-Hall, 1998.

Levenstein, Harvey A. *Revolution at the Table: The Transformation of the American Diet*. New York: Oxford University Press, 1988.

Lobel, Leon, and Stanley Lobel. *The Lobel Brothers' Complete Guide to Meat*. Philadelphia: Running Press, 1990.

Lovegren, Sylvia. *Fashionable Food: Seven Decades of Food Fads*. New York: Macmillan, 1995.

McHughen, Alan. *Pandora's Picnic Basket: The Potentials and Hazards of Genetically Modified Foods*. Oxford: Oxford University Press, 2000.

National Research Council (U.S.). *Agricultural Biotechnology: Strategies for National Competitiveness*. Washington, D.C.: National Academy Press, 1987.

Nelson, Gerald C. *Genetically Modified Organisms in Agriculture: Economics and Politics*. San Diego, Calif.: Academic, 2001.

Paul, Roland, J. Marvin Garner, and Orville K. Sweet. *The Pork Story: Legend and Legacy*. Kansas City, Mo.: Lowell, 1991.

Rifkin, Jeremy. *Beyond Beef: The Rise and Fall of the Cattle Culture*. New York: Dutton, 1992.

Robbins, John. *Diet for a New America*. Toronto, Ontario: Publishers Group West, 1987.

Romans, John R. *The Meat We Eat*. 14th ed. Danville, Ill.: Interstate, 2001.

Rorabacher, Albert J. *The American Buffalo in Transition: An Historical and Economical Survey of the Bison in America*. St. Cloud, Minn.: North Star, 1970.

Sanderson, Fred H., ed. *Agricultural Protectionism in the Industrialized World: Resources for the Future*. Baltimore, Md.: Johns Hopkins University Press, 1990.

Schlosser, Eric. *Fast Food Nation: The Dark Side of the All-American Meal*. New York: Houghton Mifflin, 2001.

Simoons, Frederick J. *Eat Not This Flesh: Food Avoidances in the Old World*. Madison, Wis.: University of Wisconsin Press, 1961.

Sokolov, Raymond. *Fading Feast*. New York: Dutton, 1979.

Stevens, Patricia Bunning. *Rare Bits: Unusual Originals of Popular Recipes*. Athens, Ohio: Ohio University Press, 1998.

Swatland, H. J. *Structure and Development of Meat Animals*. Englewood Cliffs, N.J.: Prentice Hall, 1984.

Toussaint-Samat, Maguelonne. *History of Food*. (English translation by Anthea Bell.) Cambridge, Mass.: Blackwell, 1993.

"Vegetarian Diets." Position paper of the American Dietetic Association. *Journal of the American Dietetic Association* 97 (1997): 1317–1321.

Visser, Margaret. *Much Depends on Dinner*. New York: Collier, 1986.

Visser, Margaret. *The Rituals of Dinner*. New York: Grove, 1991.

Wason, Betty. *The Language of Cookery: An Informal Dictionary*. New York: World, 1968.

Willett, Walter, with P. J. Skerrett, Edward L. Giovanucci, and Maureen Callahan. *Eat Drink and Be Healthy: The Harvard Medical School Guide to Healthy Eating*. New York: Simon and Schuster, 2001.

Robin Kline

MAMMALS, SEA. Sea mammals provide meat and fat in the diet of cold-climate–dwelling hunters living primarily in the Northern, but also the Southern, Hemisphere. The skins and fur from sea mammals provide clothing and shelter, while the bones and ivory tusks are carved for tools, talismans, and objects to be sold as art. The fat may be processed for oil to eat or to be used for heat and light. Offal, fat, and less desirable meat products are often fed to dogs.

The most common sea mammals in the human diet are the many species of *Phocidae*, seals. Other sea mammals commonly eaten include walrus, *Odobenus rosmarus*; whales, *Cetacea*; polar bears, *Ursus maritimus*; the bearded seal, *Ergnathus barbatus*; porpoises, *Phocena*; narwhals, *Monodon nanuk*; sea lions, *Eumentiapias jubata* and *Otaria jubata*; and fur seals, *Callorhinus ursinus alsacensis* and *Arctocephalus australis*. Seals, walrus, polar bears, bearded seals, sea lions, fur seals, and porpoise feed on fish, but seals also eat krill. The most commonly hunted and consumed whale is the baleen whale, which filter-feeds on plankton. Polar bears, considered by Arctic native people to be a sea mammal, eat seal, fish, and other land mammals, but are known to be omnivorous. The livers of the meat-eating sea mammals are never eaten.

Arctic coastal-dwelling Canadian Inuit, Alaskan Aleut and Yu'pik, and Siberian Eskimos are best known for hunting seals. Northern Alaskan Inuit, for example, who live on the North Slope and Point Hope, are famous for hunting whales. All Sikumiut (sea-ice–dwelling) peoples share histories of hunting all sea mammals. North Baffin Inuit, for example, begin the spring with hunting seals through breathing holes; infant seals are stomped in their mother's dens in late spring; juvenile ring seals, prized for their silver coats and tender meat, are hunted in late spring, while the adults are hunted as they bask near open water leads. Dangerous trips are taken to the pack ice to hunt migrating narwhals, and summer brings open-water seal hunting from cargo canoes. Freeze-up in the fall brings the return of breathing-hole seal hunting, which extends through the winter months. Polar bear season begins in the late fall and continues through the winter months. Summer bear hunting is not possible due to Canadian conservation laws. The large baleen whale species in the eastern Arctic were overhunted by European whalers in the nineteenth and early twentieth centuries. Since then, eastern Arctic Inuit rarely have hunted whales.

A complex set of skills is required to hunt sea mammals. Cooperative hunting requires an adaptive social organization specific to each sea mammal species. Cultural rules and rituals ensure that the values of sharing, patience, cooperation, stoicism, and emotional containment prevail among Arctic social groups. The social organization used by peoples in northern Alaska for hunting large whales surpasses the complexity of all Arctic groups, but does not need to be maintained intensely for subsistence hunting of other sea mammals. Lone hunters can hunt polar bears and seals, but it is difficult. Breathing-hole hunting is better done with at least two hunters and/or families, and polar bears are less dangerous to hunt with a group. Bear are pursued with a .306 rifle, but have been harpooned or shot with bow and arrow. Walrus, because they are dangerous, are hunted by groups armed with harpoons or large-caliber rifles. In general, the larger or more dangerous the sea mammal, the greater the need for a complex social organization when hunting.

In the Subarctic, seacoast-dwelling native people depend on sea mammals, with those closest to the Arctic being most dependent on them for food, clothing, and shelter. The Tlingit, who live in southeastern Alaska and northwestern coastal Canada, follow an annual cycle of hunting that includes summer sealing camps when harbor seals, fur seals, and sea lions are hunted. There are two sea otter hunts in the fall, another sea otter hunt in the early spring, and late spring concludes with both seal and sea otter hunting. The Tlingit use bows and arrows to hunt small sea mammals and harpoons for open sea hunting, while the Quinault, who live in the state of Washington, use bows and arrows to hunt sea lions and hair seals, which they dry and boil, during the summer. Both of these societies have developed social structures that make cooperative hunting and food sharing possible.

The Eastern Woodland seacoast-dwelling Micmac occasionally hunt seals, but focus primarily on land mammals. At the other end of the earth, the Selk'nam of Tierra del Fuego feast on the flesh of beached whales and seals, but do not actively hunt them because they lack the kind of social organization necessary for actively hunting sea mammals.

The meat, skin, fat, bones, and specific organs of sea mammals are consumed both cooked and raw. Uncooked seal, bearded seal, walrus, whale, and polar bear are relished by Inuit from Siberia across the circumpolar region to Greenland. Inuit also prepare the flesh of sea mammals by boiling, frying fresh meat slices, freezing, aging it in caches, freeze-drying, and cooking it over a heather fire. Although the Inuit once ate polar bear and walrus meat raw, they no longer do because of the risk of Arctic trichinosis, which can survive freezing conditions and infect human hosts. Other meats are safe to eat raw due to the low temperatures and the lack of food-borne pathogens when meat is traditionally processed. The introduction and use of airtight plastic bags for meat storage in the second half of the twentieth century caused deaths from botulism. For this reason, traditional food storage and handling methods are recommended for people who live on the ice.

Subarctic populations cook meat in stews and soups or bake, roast, or fry it. Mixed meat and vegetable dishes are also prepared. Meat strips are dried or smoked and stored. Sea mammal meat was not as important among the Subarctic populations as in the Arctic because of the abundance of other food resources.

Seal and whale oil are significant in the diet of both Arctic and Subarctic hunters. The oil, which provides an excellent source of energy during periods of hunger, such as at break-up and freeze-up, is rendered by pounding fat on a hard surface. Plants and raw or dried fish, meat, or skin are dipped in either fresh or aged oil. Both Arctic and Subarctic peoples will whip seal or whale blubber and add bits of meat and/or plants for flavor.

Seal blood is consumed by Inuit and considered a powerful tonic that improves their mental and physical health. Strong beliefs are held among Inuit concerning the need to eat traditional foods, especially seal, to maintain the health of individuals as well as that of their communities.

The meat of whales, seals, bearded seals, walrus, narwhals, and polar bears is divided and shared according to cultural rules at the end of the hunt among both Arctic and Subarctic groups. Meat and all the edible parts of killed animals is distributed at feasts after large organized hunts. Furs are usually retained as the property of the hunter but can be shared as needed in the community. Families meet at the feast to collect their share but return home to further distribute and consume the food.

Cooperative hunting and food sharing define Arctic and Subarctic hunting populations socially. Sea mammals have an essential role in the diet of all circumpolar and some Subarctic groups. Human exploitation of sea mammals has allowed hunters to flourish in regions under frigid environmental conditions.

See also **Arctic**; **Canada: Native Peoples**; **Fish**; **Fishing**; **Hunting and Gathering**; **Inuit**; **Lapps**; **Mammals**; **Siberia**.

BIBLIOGRAPHY

Borré, Kristen. *A Biocultural Model of Dietary Decision Making among the North Baffin Island Inuit: Explaining the Economy of Food Consumption by Native Canadians.* Ann Arbor, Mich.: University Microfilms, 1990.

Borré, Kristen. "The Healing Power of the Seal: The Meaning of Inuit Health Practice and Belief." *Arctic Anthropology* 31 (1994): 1–15.

Chapman, Anne M. *Drama and Power in a Hunting Society: The Selk'nam of Tierra del Fuego.* New York: Cambridge University Press, 1982.

Damas, David, ed. *Arctic.* Vol. 5 *Handbook of the North American Indians,* edited by William C. Sturtevant. Washington, D.C.: Smithsonian Institution, 1984.

De Laguna, Frederica. *Under Mt. Elias: The History and Culture of the Yakutat Tlingit.* Washington, D.C.: Smithsonian Institution, 1972.

Helm, June, ed. *Subarctic.* Vol. 6. *Handbook of the North American Indians,* edited by William C. Sturtevant. Washington, D.C.: Smithsonian Institution, 1981.

Nowak, Michael. "Sea Mammals in a Mixed Economy: A Southwestern Alaskan Case." *Arctic Anthropology* 25 (1988): 44–51.

Schaefer, Otto, and Jean Steckle. *Dietary Habits and Nutritional Base of Native Populations of the Northwest Territories.* Yellowknife, Northwest Territories: Science Advisory Board of the Northwest Territories, 1980.

Smith, Eric Alden. *Inujjuamuit Foraging Strategies: Evolutionary Ecology of an Arctic Hunting Economy.* New York: Aldine de Gruyter, 1991.

Spencer, Robert F., and Jesse D. Jennings, et. al. *The Native Americans: Ethnology and Background of the North American Indians.* 2d ed. New York: HarperCollins, 1977.

Wenzel, George W. *Clyde River Adaptation and Ecology: The Organization of Subsistence.* Canadian Ethnology Service Paper No. 77. Ottawa, Ont.: National Museums of Canada, 1981.

Wenzel, George W. "Resource Harvesting and the Social Structure of Native Communities." In *Native People and Renewable Resource Management*, edited by J. Green and J. Dahl, pp. 10–22. Edmonton: Alberta Society of Professional Biologists, 1986.

Wolfe, Robert J. *Food Production in a Western Eskimo Population.* Ann Arbor, Mich.: University Microfilms, 1979.

Kristen Borré

MANNERS. *See* **Etiquette and Eating Habits; Table Talk.**

MARDI GRAS. *See* **Shrove Tuesday.**

MARGARINE. Margarine was invented by Hippolyte Megè-Mouriès in 1869 in response to an order from Napoleon III to produce a cheap and stable substitute for butter. The product had a pearly luster, and Megè-Mouriès named it margarine after the Greek word meaning 'pearl-like'. The process of manufacture entailed churning oleo oil (obtained from beef tallow) at 77 to 86°F (25 to 30°C) with water or milk. The product was flavored with salt. Over time margarine has been used in baked goods, to improve the palatability and quality of butter, to improve heat transfer during frying, and to add to the flavor of foods. Margarines may contain about 80 percent fat (animal or vegetable), milk solids, emulsifying agents, and salt.

The U.S. Food and Drug Administration (FDA) established a standard of identity for margarine. It must contain not less than 80 percent edible fat of animal or vegetable origin; water, milk, or milk products; suitable edible protein, and vitamin A. Optional ingredients include vitamin D, salt or potassium chloride, nutritive carbohydrate sweeteners, emulsifiers, preservatives, colorants, flavorants, acidulants, and alkalizers. Fat-free and low-fat spreads are available commercially. While it is convenient to describe them as margarines, they do not conform to the FDA standard of identity. Early in the

twentieth century the texture of margarine was improved by replacing animal fat with coconut oil. In the 1930s hydrogenated vegetable oils became available, and these became the basic ingredient of margarine. Hydrogenated vegetable fat provided a uniform base for margarine, and control of the extent of hydrogenation gave a series of fats of varying hardness that could be used for specific products.

The hydrogenation process causes migration of the double bonds of vegetable oils and provides both cis and trans double bonds, whereas the double bonds in most vegetable oils are in the cis configuration. A cis double bond is one in which the hydrogen atoms attached to the carbons that form the double bond are on the same side of the carbon chain, and the molecule "bends" at the site of the double bond. In trans double bonds the hydrogen atoms are on opposite sides of the carbon chain, and the molecule has a more linear configuration, similar to that of a saturated fatty acid. Trans double bonds are not unknown in nature, occurring in many plant fats and some animal fats. Where most of the vegetable fats contain eighteen carbon atoms or more, the trans animal fats are generally shorter than eighteen carbon atoms.

Concern regarding the biological effects of trans double bonds was voiced in the 1940s. Studies of effects of trans fats on growth and reproduction in rats show that they have no untoward effects when the diet is replete in essential fatty acids, but when fed as the sole source of fat, they exaggerate symptoms of essential fatty acid deficiency. In this they resemble saturated fatty acids, as they do in many other biological processes.

The effects of trans fats in experimental atherosclerosis were first examined in the 1950s by Gardner McMillan and his colleagues. They found that, while trans fats raised blood cholesterol levels in cholesterol-fed rabbits, their presence in the diet did not lead to more severe atherosclerosis. Studies of rabbits fed cholesterol-free diets, of pigs, and of vervet monkeys have yielded similar results. One six-year study of the effects of partially hydrogenated soybean oil yielded atherosclerosis at a level of severity seen in rabbits fed coconut oil and less than that seen in rabbits fed soybean oil.

In humans the effects of trans fats on cardiovascular disease can only be assessed by effects on risk factors. Early studies yielded variable results of trans fat–rich diets on serum cholesterol. It was observed that the level of hypercholesterolemia varied inversely with the amount of linoleic acid in the diet. Trans fat was not hypercholesterolemic in diets that were also rich in linoleic acid. No differences were found when tissue levels of trans fats in human subjects who had died of cardiovascular disease were compared with that in human controls.

Analysis of human studies in which energy from carbohydrates was replaced by trans–18:1 fat shows that this exchange leads to increases in levels of LDL cholesterol and decreases in levels of HDL cholesterol, which increases the risk of cardiovascular disease. Serum levels of lipoprotein(a), another risk factor, are also increased.

Epidemiological studies of the effects of dietary trans fat on coronary heart disease yield variable results. One study (239 cases and 282 controls) shows a positive association between high intake of trans fat and coronary heart disease (CHD) risk but an inverse association at moderate intake, whereas another study carried out in nine European countries (671 cases and 717 controls) found no association between intake of trans fat and CHD risk. Cohort studies found positive associations between intake and risk only at the highest level of intake. Two studies found the lowest risk at the third quintile of intake. The Seven Countries Study revealed a significant positive association between 18:1 trans fatty acid intake and twenty-five-year CHD mortality rates.

The overall findings concerning intake of trans fat and risk of CHD are not consistent. These disparities are complicated because the data regarding effects of specific trans fatty acids are sparse and differences between populations and interactions with other dietary ingredients are not considered. The trend to consider dietary patterns rather than individual dietary ingredients may help organize the findings. Nevertheless the sum of the experimental data suggests that high intake of fats containing trans fatty acids may pose an increased risk of CHD. The industry response to these findings has been a major effort to produce margarines that are either low in trans-unsaturated fat or devoid of it.

Much is unknown about the balance of dietary fats–trans fat, saturated fat, and polyunsaturated fat and their interactions with other components of the diet. The attitude should be one of prudence, not panic.

See also **Baking**; **Butter**; **Cholesterol**; **Fats**.

BIBLIOGRAPHY

Kritchevsky, David. "Trans Unsaturated Fat in Health and Disease." In *Lipids in Health and Nutrition*. Edited by J. H. P. Tynan. Cambridge, U.K.: Royal Society of Chemistry, 1999.

Sebedio, J. L., and W. W. Christie, eds. *Trans Fatty Acids in Human Nutrition*. Dundee, Scotland: Oily Press, 1998.

Shirley C. Chen
David Kritchevsky

MARINATING AND MARINADES. Marinades are used to enhance the flavors of grilled meats, seafood, and fruits and vegetables. Seemingly simple concoctions of acids, fats, and aromatics, marinades are used around the world; for example, Jamaican jerk, Indian *tandoor*, and Texas barbecue are marinades that form the basis of particular cuisines.

Simply put, tradition or a creative chef dictates the combination of flavors that compose the marinade, in which selected meats, seafood, or fruits are macerated for a period of time. This technique allows the marinade to transfer some of its flavors to the outer layers of the food. When the food is grilled, the marinade blend imparts a new flavor to the food being cooked.

For delicate seafood, such as a teriyaki-glazed grilled salmon, marinades baste the outer surfaces with a soy-sweet flavor. The taste of briefly marinated fruits and vegetables (i.e., pineapple briefly soaked in light vegetable oil, rum, and brown sugar) improves greatly.

More practically, marinades tenderize the tougher fibers of inexpensive cuts of meat. Acid causes the denaturation of the long proteins in meat, rendering the meat tender as well.

Cooking and Safety Precautions
Any excess marinade must be first boiled or reduced before being used as a side sauce, to completely kill any bacteria associated with the raw meat or seafood. Never reuse marinades unless they are cooked first.

Marinades should be mixed in a nonreactive container, such as stainless steel, porcelain, clay, or plastic—cast iron and aluminum are not acceptable choices. Plastic containers may pick up residual flavors, of the marinade, and should be reserved only for the making of marinade in the future. Although food does not need to be completely submerged in the marinade, it needs to be turned often so its surface area comes into contact with the marinade. Food may be marinated far in advance, but after three to six hours there is no perceivable difference in penetration of the marinade into the food. Generally, marinades coat only the outer few layers of the meat. Immersion of foods for an overly long period results in an overly broken down piece of meat, cooked seafood, or macerated fermenting fruit.

Components of Marinades
Marinades have three main components, acids, aromatics, and fats. The combination of the three can show a distinct ethnic profile.

Acids. Acids include all types of vinegar, fruit juices, and cultured milk products, such as yogurt. Flavored vinegars such as balsamic from Italy are used sparingly, adding top notes of flavor, while a hearty apple cider vinegar will add a robust flavor to a pork roast marinade. Wine and wine vinegar are common for European marinades, while rice vinegar is common in Asia for simple fish marinades. Citrus juices shine in marinades; the souring agents of lemon juice or pomegranate juice are common in the Middle East. Lime juice in Latin America is the base for *seviche*. In this case, the marinade actually "cooks" the fish or scallops, transforming the proteins in the fish to a cooked state while still retaining the texture of uncooked fish. Orange or grapefruit juice may be used for variation. Dairy-based marinades include well-known yogurt and spice mixtures for lamb in the Middle East, yogurt and cayenne for India's *tandoor*, and buttermilk for catfish in the American South. Even Coca-Cola is a common marinade base for some barbeque sauces.

Aromatics. Aromatics add a distinctive character, with spicy, hot, sour, or sweet flavors. Chopped ginger will dominate in an Asian-influenced teriyaki marinade, along with lemongrass and soy sauce. Chinese-style marinades use ginger, green onion, and garlic. A *mirepoix* (finely minced onions, carrots, celery, and leeks in red wine vinegar) flavors French-style marinades. Herbs may be fresh or dried, such as parsley, bay leaf, oregano, allspice, and peppercorns; juniper berries are typical ingredients for game marinades. Strongly flavored condiments such as Tabasco, Dijon mustard, fish sauces, or Worcestershire sauces add intense bursts of flavor to the marinade. Chilies are the foundation for many Latin marinades, including ground chili powder, or the smoky *ancho adobo* chile. Latin marinades also feature large proportions of garlic, cumin, and lime juice.

Fats. The fats in a marinade seal in flavor and help to keep foods moist during grilling. Olive oil or oils with mono- and diglycerides penetrate deeper and faster. As with other recipes, the oils provide a clue to the regional and ethnic profile for the recipe. Olive oil is preferred in the Mediterranean and in the western United States. Heavy fruity olive oils are best. Flavored nut oils such as hazelnut or sesame oil provide a balance to the acids and aromatics.

Yogurt, which has an acid component, also provides fat; it is one of the simplest marinades to create and use. More complex marinades will consider the balance between the right acid, aromatic, and fat. A heavy fruity olive oil will not balance light rice vinegar. Nor should the cook use strongly flavored oil such as sesame oil in large quantities. Sesame oil, like balsamic vinegar, is used lightly.

Since marinated foods are grilled over heat, the combination of fat and acid is needed when grilling to prevent the food from burning off the marinade combination before the food is properly cooked. During grilling, a chef will often use a basting brush to continue to coat the grilled food with reserved marinade as it cooks. Even the brush can be part of the art of marinade; rosemary sprigs can become a basting brush while adding additional flavor. As the marinades cook on the surface of the meats, carmelization and a slight glazing of flavors is produced on the surface as well.

Consistency of Marinade

Marinades may be quite liquid, as in the classic red wine, olive oil, and rosemary-garlic marinade. They may also be thick and viscous, as in spiced cumin yogurt. Drier pastes are also marinades, and somewhat easier to spread over large pieces of meat. Jamaican jerk seasoning is thick, textured, and often features the intense heat of a scotch bonnet pepper. Blended with allspice, cinnamon, nutmeg,

brown sugar, and vinegar, jerk is a memorable marinade now used by gourmets. *Chimichurri* is a famous thick sauce-paste from Argentina, using cayenne, parsley, sherry vinegar, and lemon. Indonesian *sambals* grill strips of meat covered in a thick peanut and chili marinade. North Africans are familiar with Berber spice paste, with top notes of cumin, cinnamon, lemon, and olive oil.

Dry rubs are another marinade version. Rubs are a combination of spices, sugars, and salts spread onto the meat. The meat then basted with oil before grilling.

As long as the three components of marinades are kept in mind, many marinades are possible. A simple marinated chicken breast can transport the diner's palate to desert India with the use of *tandoor* marinade; to sultry Jamaica with Caribbean jerk; to sunny and sophisticated Provence, with garlic and rosemary; or to a down-home Texas barbecue, with chilies. Marinades can enhance the simplest ingredients, elevating them to a novel dining experience.

See also **Barbecue; Caramelization; Caribbean; France; Fruit: Citrus Fruit; Grilling; Herbs and Spices; India; Italy; Meat; Mexico; Middle East; Oil; Proteins and Amino Acids; Sauces; South America.**

BIBLIOGRAPHY

Barnard, Melanie. *Marinades: The Secret of Great Grilling.* New York: HarperCollins, 1997.

Corriher, Shirley O. *Cookwise: The Hows and Whys of Successful Cooking.* New York: Morrow, 1997.

France, Christine, ed. *The Complete Book of Sauces: Salsas, Dips, Relishes, Marinades, and Dressings.* New York: Lorenz Books, 2000.

Raichlen, Steven. "The Magic of Marinades." *Los Angeles Times,* 12 July 2000.

Terrie Wright Chrones

MARKETING OF FOOD.

MARKETING OF FOOD. In order to understand how food is marketed in grocery stores or in restaurants or other food outlets, it is important to understand how consumers make choices among food options. It is generally believed that, although consumers sometimes have strong, stable preferences for some foods—for example, one may have a clear, unambiguous preference for sardines over and above any other food—more often than not, consumers' preferences are constructed on the spot and are contingent on a variety of factors, such as the social context, the other choices available, or the decision-maker's consumption goals. Therefore consumers do not always choose the same brands, or the same products, each time they go to the store. In this kind of decision context, marketing stimuli can be very effective at persuading consumers to buy one brand over another. In particular, the packaging and the branding of foods can be influential in how consumers choose among food items.

Packaging Strategies

There has been a great deal of research done on how packaging influences consumers' perceptions of products. The first research in packaging was done in the 1930s when self-service supermarkets were becoming more popular. At this time, marketers placed *identical* detergents in two different packages: one had circles on the outside and the other had triangles. The marketers asked consumers which product they preferred and why. Eighty percent of the consumers preferred the product in the box with circles because they believed it had "higher quality." Even when the consumers took the two boxes of detergent home and used both products, the belief that the one in the box with circles was of higher quality persisted. This example points out an important aspect of the marketing of food: it is the perception of quality, not the actual quality, that influences consumers' decision making.

The packaging can influence a consumer's decision about what foods to choose even more than the taste of the product in some cases. One aspect of packaging that is very influential is the package shape. One of the most successful campaigns has been the Absolut Vodka campaign in which the shape of the distinctive Absolut Vodka bottle is featured in all of its advertising. Whereas some people may not be able to differentiate among the tastes of vodka in a blind taste test, they can easily differentiate between the different packages. Coca-Cola has also been successful in creating a distinctive bottle shape that influences perceptions about the taste of their product. One of the most famous bottle shapes is the Heinz ketchup bottle, which has been called the "best-known bottle in the world." The irony in this shape is that it is not really conducive to the use of ketchup as it is difficult to get the product out of the bottle. Heinz however used this difficulty as a positive feature in their advertising by promoting "ketchup races" in which being the last one to come out of the bottle was perceived as an advantage because it indicated the ketchup was very thick.

During the 1990s, Campbell's was concerned about decreasing sales of the company's soup. The marketing department did research to try and discover how to increase consumers' interest in their soup. Their research indicated that new soup in the old package would taste the same, but familiar soup in a new can would taste different. So Campbell's redesigned the label on their soup cans. The familiar red and white Campbell's soup can (made famous by Andy Warhol) was changed so that the red banner was thinner and a photograph of the soup in a bowl was placed on the white banner on the can. In fact, Campbell's was so convinced that the new labeling, rather than a change in the soup, would be a decisive factor in persuading consumers to buy their soup again that they declared right on the can, "New Look, Same Great Soup."

GROCERY SHOPPING ON THE INTERNET?

Although there has been a great deal of interest in the United States in trying to make grocery shopping on the Internet a viable concern (for example, Webvan, HomeGrocer.com), few companies have been able to make it profitable. Part of the problem is the delivery of the groceries. In most residential areas in the United States, delivery locations are too far apart, meaning a truck can waste a great deal of time driving from one neighborhood to another. In order to make this kind of arrangement profitable, grocers will need a 25 to 30 percent gross profit on each order as well as average orders over $100. This just has not occurred yet in the United States, and the firms such as Peapod and Webvan that have tried to make it work have not been profitable so far.

One retailer that has made it work is Tesco in Britain. Tesco is Britain's biggest grocer with more than 650 sites; they have said that their online grocery site, tesco.com, was profitable in 2000. Tesco allows its consumers to make their decisions online, and these orders are then sent to the store nearest the customer, where a store employee picks out the items ordered. Once the order is assembled, vans carry it to the customer's house. Orders average sixty items, and perhaps surprisingly, the most popular items purchased in this way include fresh fruit and vegetables (*not* bulk items such as laundry detergent). Tesco reports that in 2000, its online business represented one percent of its total grocery business.

If a model does become viable in the United States, we can probably expect online shopping to differ from shopping in a physical locale. Online consumers can sort their purchases much more easily and are not constrained by the physical layout of the store. For example, when shopping online, consumers can sort by price or nutritional information or create a list of products that were bought last time. These conveniences could potentially make grocery shopping a more efficient and more enjoyable endeavor. On the other hand, the flexibility of layout on the Internet can also help marketers to position their products in such a way as to increase the likelihood of consumers' purchasing them. For example, more packaging or advertising information could potentially be made available online.

Framing Strategies

Another aspect of marketing that influences consumers' perceptions about the food, which in turn affects consumers' choices, is how the product is positioned or

GROCERY CART

The grocery cart was invented in 1937 by Sylvan N. Goldman for his Standard Food Stores in Oklahoma City, after he noticed that shoppers would quit shopping when their hand-carried baskets became too heavy. The grocery cart on wheels was a stroke of genius in food marketing: It promoted greater sales, led to greater efficiency, and saved on labor costs. It was the start of self-service.

Before the grocery cart, food store merchants kept food on floor-to-ceiling shelves behind counters; a clerk was needed to assist customers with each purchase. Using the shopping cart, customers could select food items directly from "gondola shelves" set across the floor space, lowered so they could reach the top shelf and set just far enough apart for two shopping carts to pass between them, and fill their basket themselves. The width of the carts determined the width of the aisles in supermarkets.

The first cart was a folding cart with two baskets one above the other. Initially, the carts reminded women of pushing baby buggies; men eschewed them thinking they were strong enough to carry groceries by themselves. One of the early models of a shopping cart is enshrined at the Smithsonian Institute.

Once shopping carts caught on, they changed forever the way people shop and the way stores are laid out. By the late twentieth century grocery carts had increased in size and took on various configurations. They came in metal and plastic, some with special seats for children and some motorized for handicapped shoppers. Grocery stores on two or more floors have carts with locking wheels to allow them to be taken up or down moving ramps between floors. Some department stores are experimenting with nylon mesh carts.

In 2001, a cart cost around $100 apiece in the United States and an average supermarket owned about 300 carts; at least 9.6 million grocery carts were in service (Weir, p. 37). In urban neighborhoods people would use them to transport their purchase home. Shopping carts are also commonly seen on the streets of big cities being used by homeless people as "portable households." Strategies to prevent the loss of carts include imposing fines on anyone found with a cart off the store premises, locking carts together with a small device that releases a cart when the customer inserts a coin, and installing electronic sensors around the perimeter of store parking lots or at the store's exit doors. These sensors detect when a cart is about to leave the premises and lock the wheels, making the cart impossible to remove.

The shopping cart is a symbol of a consumer-led economy that is fueled by an affluent and mobile society. It is a piece of equipment that has become part of the distribution system of goods between manufacturers and consumers. It allows consumers to expand their purchases until the cart is full, wheel them in the cart to their cars, and drive them home. It also changed the need for labor in stores and allowed mass merchandising to the masses. As Terry Wilson wrote in 1978, it is "the cart that changed the world."

BIBLIOGRAPHY

Cahill, Joseph B. "Hot Wheels: the Secret Weapon of Big Discounters: Lowly Shopping Cart—It Encourages More Buying: Now Department Stores Jump on the Bandwagon—Sweating it Out at Sears." *Wall Street Journal*, 24 November 1999.

Mayo, James M. *The American Grocery Store: The Business Evolution of an Architectural Space.* Westport, Conn.: Greenwood, 1993.

Weir, Tom. "Shopping Carts Hold Unending Expenses," *Supermarket Business Magazine* 55, no. 4 (15 April 2000): p. 37.

Wilson, Terry P. *The Cart That Changed the World.* Norman: University of Oklahoma Press, 1978.

Jean D. Kinsey

framed. Ground beef that is 75 percent lean beef and 25 percent fat can be labeled either way: as 75 percent lean or 25 percent fat. Although these alternative labels convey the same information, however, they will not affect consumers' perceptions about the product equally. Studies showed that labeling the beef as 75 percent lean as opposed to 25 percent fat increases sales. The framing of the product can even be implicit. For example, the placement of a product in a certain aisle in the supermarket can affect the framing of the product. Consider Guiltless Gourmet Tortilla Chips. Placing this item in the regular chip aisle suggests that the product is a low-fat, perhaps worse-tasting, alternative, compared to the other chips. Placing the same product in the health food aisle suggests that the product is a better-tasting snack as compared to other alternatives.

Supermarket Layout

In general, the physical layout of the supermarket can also affect consumers' food-shopping decisions. Everyone knows that many supermarkets place high-demand items such as milk in the back of the store so that consumers are required to walk through the entire store and perhaps purchase extra items. Similarly, marketers can

456

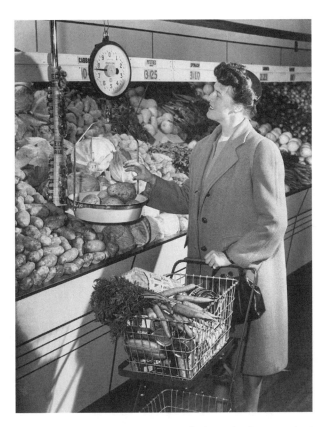

The original shopping cart consisted of two baskets attached to a frame with a handle and wheels. This woman is seen using one of the early models in a self-service store in the 1950s. © BETTMANN/CORBIS.

use cross-merchandising techniques in the supermarket to try to influence decisions. Cross merchandising is a promotional technique that ties a promotion for one product to the promotion of another. For example, Duncan Hines might include a coupon for its frosting in a cake mix box, or Rice Krispies might include a coupon for Marshmallow Fluff in its cereal box. Similarly, in the physical store, marketers can link together certain items to encourage purchase. For example, higher-priced salad dressing might be located closer to the fresh produce, or a coupon for one product might be located on the shelf of another, higher-traffic product category. In another example, an in-store coupon for a health and beauty aid product could be located in the high-traffic bathroom tissue aisle. Some of these cross-merchandising strategies might be even more effective if consumers begin shopping for groceries on the Internet.

Branding Strategies

Another aspect of food marketing that can very much affect consumers' decisions is branding. From the consumer's point of view, a brand name is generally a strong influence on purchase if three elements of the brand name are in place. First, the consumer must have a positive evaluation of the brand name. Second, the brand name must be easy to remember and strongly associated with the product category. The ease with which the name is remembered when a consumer thinks of a category will depend on the frequency with which the consumer has seen the brand associated with the category, how recently the consumer has seen the brand, and the salience of these connections for the consumer. In addition, a strong association with the category will depend on how similar the brand is to others in the category and also how prototypical the brand is to the category. For example, Coke is seen as a prototypical soft drink and thus will easily come to mind when the category "soft drinks" is evoked. Finally, the brand image and evaluation must be consistent over time. In particular, a very strong brand name is one in which a consumer holds favorable associations that are unique to that brand and that imply some kind of differential advantage over other brands.

One of the strongest brand names in food marketing is the Coca-Cola brand name. After years of advertising and marketing, Coke also has a very strong, clear, consistent brand image—therefore, consumers form clear associations with it. For example, consumers may recall the packaging (the distinctive bottle or the red can), the taste of the product, or the current advertising appeals—for example, "Coke is the real thing." It is thought of as a "fun drink." Coke is also positioned as a different drink than Pepsi or its other competitors. Finally, and perhaps most importantly, Coke has a clear emotional bond and relationship with its customers. Coke learned just how important that brand name was in 1985 when they considered taking the old Coca-Cola product off the grocery shelves and replacing it with "New Coke." This prompted strong consumer reaction. Consumers felt that Coke violated something that was "theirs"—they felt that the Coke brand name belonged to its consumers and that Coca-Cola could not remove this classic icon from the market. Coke eventually returned "Classic Coke" to the marketplace to the delight of its customers.

Brand names can also influence consumers' perceptions of new products. If a marketer puts a familiar brand name on a new product, for example, Oreo cookie ice cream sandwiches, the consumer immediately knows something about the product even if she has never seen it before. Marketers are usually very careful about which new products they support with existing brand names as sometimes these brand extensions can backfire. For example, although Miller Lite was a very successful brand extension because the new light beer was instantly recognized and adopted in the marketplace, the new light brand had a negative effect on the main Miller High Life brand by causing consumers to think the original brand was less hearty.

In conclusion, sometimes when consumers go into the supermarket or into a restaurant to buy food, they have clear preferences for the foods they are buying and are not influenced by the food packaging, merchandising, branding, or promotion. However, more often than not, food preferences are not that stable and are constructed on the spot. In these cases, what consumers end up buying can be swayed by marketing cues in the environment such as labeling, branding, and packaging.

See also **Advertising of Food; Food Cooperatives; Food Politics: United States; Food Supply, Food Shortages.**

BIBLIOGRAPHY

Aaker, David A. *Building Strong Brands.* New York: Free Press, 1995.

Aaker, David A. *Managing Brand Equity: Capitalizing on the Value of a Brand Name.* New York: Free Press, 1991.

Kahn, Barbara E., and Leigh McAlister. *Grocery Revolution: The New Focus on the Consumer.* Reading, Mass.: Addison-Wesley, 1997.

Schmitt, Bernd H., and Alex Simonson. *Marketing Aesthetics: The Strategic Management of Brands, Identity and Image.* New York: Free Press, 1997.

Staten, Vince. *Can You Trust a Tomato in January?* New York: Simon and Shuster, 1993.

Stepankowsky, Paula L. "Safeway, Albertson's Market Retooled Web Grocery Concept." *Wall Street Journal,* 4 April 2002.

Barbara E. Kahn

MARKETING OF FOOD.

ALTERNATIVE (DIRECT) STRATEGIES

Direct marketing refers to the strategy in which the producer of a commodity sells that commodity retail, directly to the consumer or end-user, rather than through a broker, distributor, or wholesaler. Direct markets for producers of food commodities include roadside stands, pick-your-own, farmers' markets, community-supported agriculture, mobile marketing, and mail-order sales. The supply of many food products through direct channels will fluctuate in accordance with the local harvest calendar. This is particularly true for fresh fruits and vegetables and less so for other foods, such as milk and milk products, eggs, meats, fish and poultry, grains, beans, and cereals.

In the United States, direct marketing continues to grow as a method for small- and medium-sized producers to increase their profits. Several forms of direct marketing—farmers' markets, roadside stands, Community Supported Agriculture (CSA) farms, and pick-your-own operations—have accounted for most alternative marketing strategies. Newer forms, such as "farm-to-school" connections and Internet marketing, are also being developed and piloted in many locations through the United States. Direct marketing data from the Census of Agriculture showed that between 1992 and 1997, the

SENIORS FARMERS MARKET NUTRITION PROGRAM

The Seniors Farmers Market Nutrition Program (SFM-NPP) is a new program established by USDA's Commodity Credit Corporation (CCC). Under the program, CCC makes grants to states and to Indian tribal governments to provide coupons to low-income seniors that may be exchanged for eligible foods at farmers' markets, roadside stands, and community-supported agriculture programs. USDA CCC awarded almost $15 million in grants to thirty-one states and five Indian Tribal Organizations for the new program. State departments of agriculture, aging, and health and tribal governments administering the grants have developed creative partnerships. They are utilizing existing infrastructure to offer farmers' markets the opportunity to expand to serve seniors and to certify and distribute benefits to the estimated 370,000 low-income seniors this pilot is expected to serve.

number of farms involved in direct marketing increased 7.8 percent to 93,140 farms. The total value of direct-marketing sales and direct-marketing sales per farm also increased.

"Alternative" or direct-marketing opportunities are part of a new agriculture that is being referred to as civic agriculture. The name suggests a locally based agricultural and food production system that is tightly linked to a community's social and economic development and to enhancing social capital. While civic agriculture may not represent a challenge to the conventional agriculture and food industry, it does include some innovative ways to produce, process, and distribute food. Additionally, the connections and relationships that are possible between producers and consumers from these marketing channels are unique to community-based food systems and civic agriculture.

Several factors have led to a growing consumer interest in purchasing directly from farmers: desire for fresh, high-quality products, the ability to personally interact directly with farmers who grew/raised the food, and interest in supporting local, small farms. Availability of product information such as growing method, instructions about use, recipes, and taste samples also draw customers to direct-marketing outlets.

Farmers' Markets

Farmers' markets, now an integral part of the urban/farm linkage, have continued to rise in popularity, mostly due

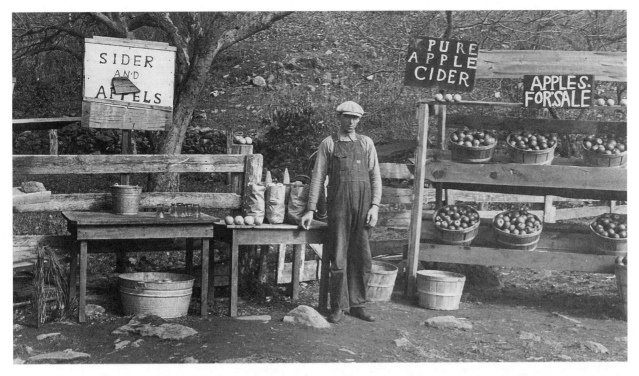

Apple vendor along the Lee Highway in Shenandoah National Park, Virginia, 1935. Courtesy of the Library of Congress.

to growing consumer interest. The number of farmers' markets in the United States has grown dramatically, increasing 63 percent from 1994 to 2000. According to the 2000 National Farmers' Market Directory, nearly 3,000 farmers' markets now operate in the United States. This growth indicates that farmers' markets are meeting the needs of an increasing number of farmers with small- to medium-sized operations. Small farm operators benefit most from farmers markets—those with less than $250,000 in annual receipts who work and manage their own operations meet this definition (94 percent of all farms). Farmers' markets are also an important source of revenue. In the 2000 USDA Farmers' Market Study, 19,000 farmers reported selling their produce only at farmers markets. Communities also benefit from farmers' markets. Dollars spent on food are recycled several times within the community and thereby help boost the local economy.

Farmers' markets also serve an important role in increasing community food security. In many urban centers where fresh, nutritious foods are scarce, farmers markets increase the availability and access of these options for segments of the population that need them most. Farmers' markets also help to provide nutrition education, focusing on selection, storage, and preparation of a wide diversity of fruits and vegetables. Nearly 60 percent of markets participate in WIC Farmers' Market Nutrition Program, most accept food stamps (although the development of electronic benefit transfer [EBT] will make

this difficult at many markets) as well as other local and/or state nutrition programs. A quarter of all farmers' markets participate in gleaning programs aiding food recovery organizations in the distribution of food and food products to needy families.

USDA's Women, Infants, and Children (WIC) Farmers' Market Nutrition Program (FMNP), established in 1992, provides additional coupons to WIC participants that they can use to purchase fresh fruits and vegetables at participating farmers' markets. The program has two goals: To provide fresh, nutritious, unprepared, locally grown fruits and vegetables from farmers' markets to WIC participants who are at nutritional risk; and to expand consumers' awareness and use of farmers' markets. Fiscal Year 2000 federal funding for the WIC Farmers' Market Nutrition Program was $15 million. The FMNP operates in thirty-nine state agencies, including four Indian tribes, one territory, and the District of Columbia.

Roadside Stands

Roadside stands or markets are a type of direct marketing system where a grower establishes a selling place (stand) near a roadway and sells produce directly to consumers. Often a stand is located on a farm or orchard. Produce sold in a roadside stand may be grown exclusively on the farm or may be purchased from outside sources. A roadside stand may be open only during harvest periods or throughout the year, depending on produce supply sources.

Direct marketing of food products is an age-old practice designed to eliminate middlemen. This Persian illumination from 1540 shows an Iranian butcher selling his cuts of meat from a stand along the street. © BURSTEIN COLLECTION/CORBIS.

increase, so too will stand size, operating costs, and management time.

Pick-Your-Own Operations
This type of direct marketing, where customers come to the farm and harvest produce directly, is most common at fruit farms in the northeastern United States. As fewer families now "put up" (can, freeze, or otherwise preserve) large quantities of food, the "farm experience" has become a more important reason for people to pick produce at a farm.

Farm-to-School Connections
Through the school meals programs during the school year and summer programs, schools, colleges, and universities represent a largely untapped opportunity to strengthen the market for farmers and increase access to locally grown, high-quality foods for young people. Such direct purchases are increasing through an expanding number of farm-to-school projects throughout the country.

Direct Marketing as a Way to Build Civic Agriculture
Increasingly, alternative or direct-marketing channels are seen as engines for growth in civic agriculture. Since over 80 percent of the consumer food dollar currently goes to pay for the marketing bill, leaving less than 20 cents for every dollar for the farmer, direct marketing may be critical to the economic survival of agriculture.

See also **Farmers' Markets; Food Cooperatives; Marketing of Food; Retailing of Food; WIC (Women, Infants, and Children) Program.**

BIBLIOGRAPHY

Beus, Curtis, and Riley Dunlap. "Conventional Versus Alternative Agriculture: The Paradigmatic Roots of the Debate." *Rural Sociology* 55, 4 (1990): 590–616.

DeLind, Laura B. "Market Niches, 'Cul de Sacs,' and Social Context: Alternative Food Systems of Production." *Culture and Agriculture: Bulletin of the Culture and Agriculture Group of the American Anthropological Association*, no. 47 (1993).

Feenstra, Gail W. "Local Food Systems and Sustainable Communities." *American Journal of Alternative Agriculture* 12, 1 (1997): 28–36.

Fieldhouse, Paul. "Community Shared Agriculture." *Agriculture and Human Values* 13, 3 (1996): 43–47.

Friedmann, Harriet. "After Midas' Feast: Alternative Food Regimes for the Future." In *Food for the Future: The Conditions and Contradictions of Sustainability*, edited by Patricia Allen, pp. 213–233. New York: Wiley, 1993.

Kloppenburg, Jack Jr., John Hendrickson, and G. W. Stevenson. "Coming into the Foodshed." *Agriculture and Human Values* 13, 3 (1996): 33–42.

Koc, Mustafa, and Kenneth A. Dahlberg. "The Restructuring of Food Systems: Trends, Research, and Policy Issues." *Agriculture and Human Values* 16, 2 (1999): 109–116.

To producers, a roadside stand often represents a supplemental source of income, additional employment for family members, and a way to market surplus produce. Besides measurable financial benefits, producers establish relationships through direct exchange with customers. These relationships provide critical feedback to farmers when making planting decisions, developing customer education, and developing marketing strategies.

Roadside stands allow direct market sales without off-farm transportation costs, although some stands are located off the farm to get closer to traffic volume or population centers. Generally, marketing costs depend on the size of the retail outlet. These range from self-serve tables at the end of a driveway to pseudo-supermarkets with a huge selection of off-farm merchandise in addition of farm products. As volume, traffic, and product selection

Lyson, Thomas A., and Judy Green. "The Agricultural Marketscape: A Framework for Sustaining Agriculture and Communities in the Northeast U.S." *Journal of Sustainable Agriculture*, 1999.

Whatmore, Sarah, and Lorraine Thorne. "Nourishing Networks: Alternative Geographies of Food." In *Globalising Food: Agrarian Questions and Global Restructuring*, edited by David Goodman and Michael Watts, pp. 287–304. London: Routledge, 1997.

Jennifer L Wilkins

MARKETS. *See* **Farmers' Markets; Food Cooperatives; Food Marketing: Alternative (Direct) Strategies; Retailing of Food.**

MAYAS. *See* **Mexico and Central America, Pre-Columbian.**

McDONALD'S. *See* **Fast Food; Hamburger.**

MEAL. Academic interest in meals, while crossing many disciplines, is concentrated mostly in the fields of social anthropology and sociology. The premise of much of this research is that whatever broader historical and social influences on food and eating may be identified in any cultural milieu, the taking of food is more often than not organized around some concept of the meal.

Historical Aspects
There is a modest literature that, while not focusing precisely on the meal, offers insights into the history of meals. Of undoubted importance is the reduction in the size of meals in Western civilizations. From the Roman poet Petronius's account of Trimalchio's feast in *The Satyricon*, through medieval banquets, to the gluttony of restaurant dining in France, the size of a meal in terms of the varieties and number of courses has declined, at least for the affluent social classes. One difficulty with historical studies of food and eating is their focus on aristocratic and bourgeois habits. This is perhaps unsurprising, as the diet of the poor appears to hold in variety and content less fascination, although John Burnett's *Plenty and Want* (1979) elegantly counters this view. Sociologist-historians like Norbert Elias maintain that the diminution in the number of courses represents a trend to civilizing taste through self-restraint such that the epitome of "good taste" is, crudely put, reflected in a "less is more" philosophy, and gluttony and excess is associated with the bestial side of human nature.

A second theme of interest is the impact on meal taking of industrialization, whose main consequences in the food arena include "improvements" in food production, preservation, and transportation, and the exploitation and creation of markets for existing and previously unavailable foods. The growth of agribusiness and subsequent opposition to it has cast doubts on these supposed benefits of industrialized society.

What is perhaps less appreciated about the industrialization of food is the extent to which it has created and supported the embedding of male and female roles in the home and elsewhere. This leads, thirdly, to the profound effects of industrialization on patterns of family life. In the last quarter of the twentieth century, the demands of industrialization have seen greater female participation in the labor force in much of the developed world that, taken together with the increasing application of technology to the culinary sphere, has had implications for food consumption. This is reflected in debates about the decline of the meal and the rise of snacking, or grazing, which, in recent years, have been linked to broader ideas about the "McDonaldization" of food and eating.

Functions of the Meal
No account of the role of the meal in society can ignore efforts to explain the apparent human need to dine communally. In a popular approach to understanding the nature of meal-taking, scholars have delineated five general functions of the meal and of feeding more generally. First, meals demonstrate much about the nature of status differences in society. The display and distribution of food as a means of demonstrating social status is common to many societies. The giving of food can be an act designed to heighten the status of donors by emphasizing the difference between them and the recipients of their largesse.

Second, whom one dines with and what one eats define social and status group membership and the closeness or distance of relationships between individuals. For example, a hot meal generally reflects closeness and intimacy and can be confined to immediate family and intimates (Douglas, 1972). Within the family, status and power differences determined by gender can be reflected in the distribution of food. Several researchers have demonstrated that high meat consumption is associated with men, and that women often give priority to male food preferences at the expense of their own tastes. In the workplace, class and status differences can be mirrored in a separate provision of food for managerial and related grade staff, and for "blue collar" workers (Murcott, pp. 45–53). Third, food has symbolic functions and meanings. Various forms of feasting serve to link individuals to the wider social fabric through shared understandings of cultural conventions (as, for example, with Christmas or Thanksgiving). Meals also offer opportunities for status symbolism, where food is a form of currency either literally (whereby animals are exchanged for goods and services), or through the medium of gift-giving (intended to elicit some reciprocal gift or service). Status symbolism is also conveyed in the case of dining out, in the selection by the host of a meal environment appropriate in its level of excellence and expense.

461

Fourth, meals give opportunities to demonstrate role performance. For a host, the meal allows demonstration of good taste and knowledge of what is relevant to particular dining situations. For all individuals, mistakes over etiquette and the actual eating of food can be embarrassing, discrediting a person in the eyes of others (for example, using the "wrong" knife or fork or employing the "wrong" terminology). Fifth, control of role performance is closely related to the role played by food in socialization. Meal times, as occasions when social groups are normally together, provide opportunities for the uninitiated—particularly the young—to observe what is acceptable in terms of food-related behavior. For children, meal times allow observation of what foods are routinely available for consumption and how these should be consumed; in other words, children are inculcated both formally and informally into matters of etiquette.

Structures of the Meal

The observation that in many societies, food consumption is organized around some concept of the meal led much early sociological research to focus on the nature and meaning of meal structure. The pioneering work of Mary Douglas offers theoretical grounding of the study of food and eating in localized empirical studies of dining. In her article "Deciphering a Meal" (1975), she identifies two contrasted food categories—meals and drinks. Meals are structured and named events (for example, lunch, dinner) whereas drinks are not. Meals are taken against a background of rituals and assumptions that include the use of at least one mouth-entering utensil per head; a table; a seating order; and cultural restrictions on the pursuit of alternative activities (such as reading) while seated at table. A meal also incorporates a series of contrasts: hot and cold, bland and spiced, liquid and semi-liquid. Both meals and drinks reflect the quality of social relationships. Drinks are generally available to strangers, acquaintances, and family. Meals, by way of contrast, are reserved for family, close friends, and honored guests.

Douglas's key empirical study with colleague Michael Nicod relates meal structure to meal content. Nicod recorded over various periods the dining patterns of four English working-class families, whose diet of the time centered on two staple carbohydrates—potatoes and cereals, in contrast to upper- and middle-class diets, which made greater use of a range of cereals, beans, and roots. Focusing on the type and cycle of meals within the domestic economy, Nicod identified three types of meal: Meal A, a major meal, served around 6:00 P.M. on weekdays and in the early afternoon on weekends; Meal B, a minor meal taken at 9:00 P.M. or 10:00 P.M. on weekdays and 5:00 P.M. on weekends; and Meal C, consisting of a biscuit and a hot drink. This last meal was a flexible component available at any time in the daily dietary cycle but most often taken both in late afternoon, on the return home of the principal wage earner, and before retiring for the night.

Meal Content and Cycles

Of the three types, Meal A is accorded the greatest analytic importance by Douglas and Nicod. A strong correspondence between the weekday evening meal and the Sunday meal was apparent. In both instances, the first course was the main course, always hot and savory and based on a tripartite structure of potato, centerpiece (meat, fish, eggs, with one or more additional vegetables), and dressing—usually gravy. The second course repeated these rules of combination except that it was sweet. The staple took a cereal form (pastry, sponge), the centerpiece was often fruit, and the dressing custard or cream. On Sundays and other special occasions, the second course was often followed by a third consisting of a hot drink and biscuit(s). This third course maintained similarities in rules of combination in that a biscuit has a cereal staple form enclosing a fruit or cream-type filling. In one respect, however, the pattern differed, in that liquids and solids were totally separated, in contrast to other courses, and the structure was reversed in so far as the hot drink appeared in a cup or similar receptacle, whereas the cold biscuit was on a plate.

Thus, according to Douglas and Nicod, meals possess the following elements. First, they have rules of non-reversibility in the archetypal meal. Second, the order of food runs from savory to sweet and from hot to cold in terms of the principal food items consumed. Third, quantity decreases with each course as formal patterning of foodstuffs increases. Regarding the latter, Douglas sees the first course as fairly amorphous, but as a meal progresses, this gives way to increasing geometric precision and structure (Douglas, 1982; Wood, 2000).

The "Cooked Dinner"

Whereas Douglas places equal emphasis on meal structure and meal content, it is the latter that has driven many subsequent and empirical studies of meal taking. Murcott's (1982) study of thirty-seven pregnant women in South Wales is almost as important as Douglas's work for the elaboration of a research tradition. Murcott found that the "cooked dinner," an elaborated model of Douglas's principal Meal A type, comprising meat, potatoes, at least one additional vegetable, and gravy, was regarded as a "proper meal," and perceived as essential to family feelings of health and well-being. Structurally, the cooked dinner was thought of as a meal in itself, was heavy and large rather than small and light, and hot, never cold. Thus, although a succession of courses was permissible, the cooked dinner as centerpiece could, in contrast to sweet-based items, stand in its own right as a meal. Fresh meat was a priority, and potatoes were always specified and itemized separately from other vegetables. Certain meats had common circulation—beef, lamb, pork, chicken—whereas others, notably turkey, were reserved for special occasions. Fish was not regarded as an acceptable substitute for meat in the cooked dinner form. While potatoes were invariably a constant (roast on Sunday, usually boiled at other times), slightly more flexibility was evident in the choice of additional vegetables. Even here, however, certain rules appeared to operate. First, additional vegetables were almost invariably green and from "above ground" (typically peas, beans, sprouts, cabbage, and occasionally broccoli and cauliflower). Second, additional vegetables were prepared only in addition to these and were generally from "below ground" (for example, carrots and parsnips). Together with meat and potatoes, the final ingredient necessary to the structural integrity of the cooked dinner was gravy, last in the cooking and serving sequence, and poured onto the plate after other items had been assembled, an action Murcott sees as linking and transforming items in the cooked dinner into a coordinated whole. Cyclically, the importance of the cooked dinner to Murcott's sample was emphasized in the fact that it was eaten on only three or four days of the week (including, invariably, on a Sunday) and thus had relative scarcity in the family dietary system.

The "Cooked Dinner" in America

The British work of Douglas and others is echoed in various American studies, which generally support a view of meals as central to domestic dining systems. In a 1942 study of food habits in Southern Illinois, researchers found that food consumption centered on three staples: potatoes, beans, and pork. The authors term this the "core diet" and note that around the core was, first, a secondary core, consisting of many foodstuffs that had recently become available for purchase from local stores; and, second, a peripheral diet of infrequently used foods outside of the core and secondary core (Bennett et al., 1943). All three of these concepts are used in similar form by Norge Jerome, who charts content variations found in meals and snacks for all of "normal" weekday meals, "Sunday dinner" and festive meals (for example, Thanksgiving). Jerome argues that the dietary order consists of core and staple items; secondary core items, which are added to or substituted for items in the core as circumstances and contexts vary; and peripheral dietary items, which are those items used infrequently, including ceremonial foods.

In a much more complex series of studies of Italian-American diet in Philadelphia, Judith Goode and various colleagues relate variations in the selection of different meal formats to meal cycles (food consumption patterns over time), community values, and activity patterns of households, building up a many-layered picture of the interrelationships between the role of food in people's lives and other aspects of the social order (Brown, pp. 66–68).

Gender and the Meaning of Meal Structure

For Douglas, the meaning of meal structure lies in its implications for family constitution. The patterning of food performs a regulatory function, encouraging family stability, a view with clear policy implications for dietary and nutritional intervention . For Murcott, an important

The construct or format of a meal varies greatly from one culture to the next. In this meal at Île de Gorée, Senegal, a family partakes of its food from a common bowl. © CORBIS (BELLEVUE).

symbolic feature of cooked dinners is the extent to which their preparation validates women's roles in family and marital contexts: "If a job defines how a man occupies his time during the working day, to which the wage packet provides regular testimony, proper provision of a cooked dinner testifies that the woman has spent her time in correspondingly suitable fashion . . . the cooked dinner in the end symbolizes the home itself, a man's relation to that home and a woman's place in it." According to Murcott, the overall responsibility for domestic affairs falls to the woman of the house, whose responsibility for the cooked dinner includes the process of accommodating family food preferences, especially those of the husband or male partner. Most women choose what food is purchased for family consumption, but, because of the need to balance factors such as family tastes and preferences, food cost, variety, and nutrition, this is often considered a burden rather than bestowal of authority to determine the domestic dietary cycle.

Second, women frequently subordinate their own food preferences to those of male partners. Men, especially if employed, are regarded as requiring food in quantity, and male energy needs are regarded as exceeding those of other family members and, in particular, of women. Researchers Nickie Charles and Marion Kerr found that very high consumption of meat was almost totally confined to men, while very low meat consumption was associated primarily with women and children. Several other studies have shown that women often go without food, particularly in families where there is financial hardship. Women's voluntary denial is further reinforced by societal pressures to maintain "ideal" body weight and image.

Third, the "absence" of cooked dinners or a female to cook for men can disrupt the social fabric. Two very different examples of this are found in instances of domestic violence and of "womanless men." Researchers have observed that the centrality of food in marital relationships can often lead to violence as men turn on

In contrast to the family scene from Africa, this image from Biedermeier Austria depicts the essentials of a midday meal during the 1840s. Nanny with baby, the kitchen maid bringing in a pudding, father carving the roast—all of these are visual clues that tell us that this meal in a well-off household is being eaten in several courses and that there is probably a pecking order in terms of who eats what. COURTESY OF THE ROUGHWOOD COLLECTION.

women for perceived failures in the performance of those tasks that are accorded them and that men usually learn domestic cooking and practice that skill only when they have no woman to cook for them (Murcott, pp. 164–171, 172–177).

The Limitations of Structure

The investigations alluded to thus far are highly ethnocentric, useful for elaborating the parameters of the structural model of meal-based food consumption but limited in geographical scope. These studies also suffer from criticism of their over-reliance on evidence from studies of traditional working-class/blue-collar communities and families; an exaggeration of the extent to which women are the main providers and preparers of food, as these activities become much more democratically organized; and a failure to analyze the decline in meal taking and rise in snacking, or grazing.

"McDonaldization"

Arguments supporting the decline of the meal have received impetus in the thesis of George Ritzer that the global fast-food franchise McDonald's has been in the vanguard of the rationalization both of cuisine and of social life more generally. For Ritzer, the interplay between technology and food production has led to fragmentation of private and public food consumption. In fact, Ritzer's early work on McDonald's and "McDonaldization" is the

summation of an extensive literature on fast food arguing similar themes (Leidner, 1993). Implicit in Ritzer's analysis is a view of American domestic cuisine at odds with research on the British experience. The relative absence, however, of parallel detailed studies of food in American domestic life makes it difficult to assess uniformity and diversity of the meal-taking experience in the United States.

Restaurant Meals

It was noted earlier that social scientific study of food and eating is a relatively young and under-researched field. Nowhere is this more true than in the study of dining out. The early work of Campbell-Smith (1967) promulgated the concept of the "meal experience" whereby customer satisfaction in dining out was attributed to multiple environmental factors and not food choice and quality alone. This view is probably no longer tenable. Studies of the restaurant "meal experience" suggest that consumers prioritize available food choice, price, and quality when dining out. According to researcher Joanne Finkelstein, dining out is a mannered act in which the participants rarely derive much enjoyment, since the very act of engaging in restaurant dining entails consumers subordinating themselves to the rituals and imperatives of the establishment, a condition Finkelstein calls "uncivilised sociality." Her analysis has attracted supporters (see Wood, 1995), but also detractors, whose own multimethod studies emphatically show consumer control and enjoyment of dining out. They also reject the arguments of theorists who argue that domestic dining and dining out have increasingly converged.

This convergence takes the form of public menus reflecting more and more the structured dining of the home with greater similarity of offerings and a concomitant overall reduction in the choices available to consumers. This "interpenetration" of private and public dining is supported by advances in technology, which have increasingly allowed foods eaten in the public domain to be purchased at the supermarket and consumed at home. Warde and Martens (2000) at least partially reject this view, instead concurring with Mennell (1985) that increasing variety is indeed a feature of public and private dining and claiming that writers such as Wood have exaggerated trends in convergence and the reduction of choice. This is despite finding some evidence of considerable similarities with domestic food consumption in the structure of meals taken outside the home.

Public to Private Again

Warde and Martens's arguments are often contentious but they set the pattern for future explorations of Western public food consumption in empirically grounded studies of actual consumer behavior. At the same time, a note of caution can usefully be sounded. The concept of meal and related structures as described in this article have for the most part been empirically demonstrated by reference to Anglo-American standards. Yet, similar structures (such as the centerpiece, carbohydrate staple, and dressing) compose many meal formats around the world even if they do not precisely mirror the "cooked dinner." Variation may not, in fact, be so great, since many cultures follow the stew or "ragout" model, combining centerpiece and dressing, and sometimes combining these with a carbohydrate staple (such as curries or certain pasta dishes), while others observe the carbohydrate "base" model (as found in pizzas, tacos, fajitas), where food is placed on the staple or enclosed within it.

Through the work of theorists of the latter half of the twentieth century, a social scientific study of the meal has emerged and, employing various models of structure, has advanced considerably. But many more diverse empirical studies remain to be done before we can gain confidence in any assertions about this fascinating and fundamental aspect of human existence.

See also **British Isles; Carbohydrates; Class, Social; Combination of Proteins; Custard and Puddings; Dinner; Etiquette and Eating Habits; Fast Food; Food Studies; Gender and Food; Gravy; Holidays; Household; Lunch; Meat; Petronius; Potato; Restaurants; Sociology; Table Talk; Take-out Food; Tea (Meal).**

BIBLIOGRAPHY

Alfino, Mark, John S. Caputo, and Robin Wynyard, eds. *McDonaldization Revisited: Critical Essays on Consumer Culture*. Westport, Conn.: Praeger, 1998.

Bennett, J. W., H. L. Smith, and H. Passin. "Food and Culture in Southern Illinois: A Preliminary Report." *American Sociological Review* 8, no. 5 (1943): 561–569.

Brown, Linda Keller, and Kay Mussell, eds. *Ethnic and Regional Foodways in the United States: The Performance of Group Identity*. Knoxville: University of Tennessee Press, 1984.

Burnett, John. *Plenty and Want: A Social History of Diet in England from 1815 to the Present Day*. London: Scolar Press, 1979.

Campbell-Smith, Graham. *The Marketing of the Meal Experience*. London: Surrey University Press, 1967.

Charles, Nickie, and Marion Kerr. *Women, Food, and Families*. Manchester, U.K.: Manchester University Press, 1988.

Douglas, Mary, ed. *Implicit Meanings*. London: Routledge and Kegan Paul, 1972.

Elias, Norbert. *The Civilising Process, Volume 1: The History of Manners*. Oxford: Basil Blackwell, 1982.

Finkelstein, Joanne. *Dining Out: A Sociology of Modern Manners*. New York: New York University Press, 1989.

Jerome, Norge W., Randy F. Kandel, and Gretel H. Pelto, eds. *Nutritional Anthropology*. Pleasantville, N.Y.: Redgrave, 1980.

Leidner, Robin. *Fast Food, Fast Talk: Service Work and the Routinization of Everyday Life*. Berkeley: University of California Press, 1993.

Mennell, Stephen. *All Manners of Food: Eating and Taste in England and France from the Middle Ages to the Present*. Oxford: Basil Blackwell, 1985.

Murcott, Anne, ed. *The Sociology of Food and Eating*. Aldershot: Gower, 1983.

Petronius, Arbiter. *The Satyricon*. Translated by P. G. Walsh. Oxford: Oxford University Press, 1997.

Ritzer, George. *The McDonaldization of Society*. Newbury Park, Calif.: Pine Forge Press, 1993.

Spang, Rebecca L. *The Invention of the Restaurant: Paris and Modern Gastronomic Culture*. Cambridge, Mass.: Harvard University Press, 2000.

Visser, Margaret. *The Rituals of Dinner*. New York: Grove Weidenfeld, 1991.

Warde, Alan, and Lydia Martens. *Eating Out: Social Differentiation, Consumption and Pleasure*. Cambridge: Cambridge University Press, 2000.

Wood, Roy C. *The Sociology of the Meal*. Edinburgh: Edinburgh University Press, 1995.

Wood, Roy C., ed. *Strategic Questions in Food and Beverage Management*. Oxford: Butterworth-Heinemann, 2000.

Roy C. Wood

MEALS ON WHEELS. A change in the 1965 Older Americans Act (OAA) allowed prepared meals to be delivered to qualified individuals assessed to be homebound or otherwise isolated. In 1972 the OAA, which initially addressed the needs of the elderly to promote independence and successful aging, was amended to include nutrition. Federal funds were allocated for local

Meals on Wheels specializes in providing daily meals for shut-ins, especially the elderly. PHOTO COURTESY OF AP/WIDE WORLD PHOTOS.

communities to provide hot meals in group dining situations for persons over sixty years of age and their spouses, regardless of the spouse's age.

For those senior citizens who were unable to prepare adequate meals for themselves or attend the congregate nutrition centers because of ill health or physical incapacity, the first so-called meals-on-wheels program was established in Pennsylvania. Volunteers dubbed "Platter Angels" prepared, packaged, and delivered meals to homebound elderly in the community.

As the demand for the service continued to grow, additional neighborhood meals-on-wheels programs sprung up across the country. Volunteers organized programs and delivered meals. A fee was charged to cover the cost of food and preparation. Charitable institutions such as churches and civic organizations were called upon to subsidize costs for those unable to pay.

Although limited federal funds were available to the volunteer programs, Congress recognized that a major federal effort was needed. Another change to the OAA in 1978 (Title IIIC-2, Home-delivered nutrition services) provided for the home-delivered meals for those assessed as unable to participate in the congregate meal program. Administered by the U.S. Department of Health and Human Services Administration on Aging, the program focuses on those in greatest economic and/or social need.

By requirement, each home-delivered meal must supply at least one-third of the Recommended Dietary Allowances for this age group. It is estimated that 40 to 50 percent of most required nutrients are supplied in practice. Guidelines developed to assist in menu planning indicate both the types and the amounts of food to be included in each meal. Some state programs have chosen

to offer additional services such as offering medical nutrition supplement products. Delivery packaging materials for the meals should be safe and acceptable for both hot and cold foods, they should prevent contamination, and be reasonable in cost. Improper handling by recipients leading to food safety issues has been raised as a concern. Evaluation studies of program effectiveness affirm that the nutrient-dense meals improve the status of the homebound.

Thirty percent of the cost of the home-delivered meals is met through OAA funds. Public and private partnerships leverage additional resources. Every $1 in federal funds leverages an additional $3.35 in the home delivered meals program. The demand for homebound meals has dramatically increased in concert with the growing number of frail and homebound elderly who want to remain independent. Based on the most recent figures, about 135 million home-delivered meals are served annually. From the program's inception more applicants were attracted than could be accommodated, and waiting lists in many areas are not uncommon.

A separate but similar national organization that complements the federally supported home-delivered meal service is the Meals-on-Wheels America (MOWA) program. Their additional home-delivered meal service is seamlessly integrated into existing meals on wheels programs. Meals-on-Wheels America helps local communities raise funds and expand their nutrition programs for homebound elderly.

With the elderly population expected to double by 2030, senior feeding programs such as meals on wheels will continue to provide much-needed ongoing services.

See also **Government Agencies**; **Government Agencies, U.S.**; **Poverty**; **WIC (Women, Infants, and Children's) Program**.

BIBLIOGRAPHY

Meals on Wheels Association of America. Available at http://www.mowaa.org/mowaa.html.

Owen, Anita L., Patricia L. Splett, and George M. Owen. *Nutrition in the Community: The Art and Science of Delivering Services*, 4th ed. Boston, Mass.: McGraw-Hill, 1999.

Wellman, Nancy S., Lester Y. Rosenzweig, and Jean L. Lloyd. "Thirty Years of the Older Americans Nutrition Program." *Journal of The American Dietetic Association* 102 (2002): 348-350.

Connie E. Vickery

MEAT. For most human beings, meat is a highly desired food, but it is more of a treat than a staple. Meat, whether obtained from hunted or domesticated animals, is more expensive than staple carbohydrate-rich foods because of the investment in land and labor required to produce it. This reality is often the justification for reserving meat, or the best parts of it, for those with higher status.

In a majority of the world's cultures, this elite is men and, sometimes, the women and children attached to them. Furthermore, when there is enough meat to go around, the preferred parts, usually the muscle, go to these same individuals.

It is this special status of meat that makes it of particular interest in human culture, psychology, and cuisine. Meat is also the only class of food that is frequently formally proscribed by certain religions, cultures, or cultural subgroups.

Ambivalence and the Psychology of Meat

The stakes are high with meat. Meat is both the most tabooed—and the most favored—food across the human race, in both developed and traditional cultures. Meat is a magnet of ambivalence for human beings. It is meaningful, in both the positive and negative sense. Eating meat is both attractive and repulsive. Hunting, too, is problematic. It is a skilled accomplishment at the same time that it is a destructive act. Meat provides a food for humans that is more similar to humans than any other type of food. The similarity means that the biochemical composition of meat is much like that of humans, so that, by eating it, humans get all the nutrients they need. The meat of any mammal is a complete, or almost complete, food, in contrast to vegetable foods. But this similarity means that microorganisms living in the meat are also likely to find a happy home in humans. Meat is thus the most nutritive and most infective food humans eat.

You Are What You Eat

It is quite natural and sensible to believe that a person takes on the properties of the food he or she eats. In general, when A and B are mixed, the resulting product shows properties of both A and B, so why should this not occur when A eats B? The problem, of course, as understood through the lens of biochemistry, is that after digestion the components of various foods, foods as different as beef and bananas, are the same molecules: amino acids, sugars, and so on. From this perspective, the identity of an eaten food is lost by the time it is digested. Nonetheless, the belief remains, and it is present in the thinking of almost every traditional culture. This "principle" is behind such notions as eating owls improves vision, eating swift animals increases running speed, eating rapidly growing plants speeds up growth, and the appearance of foods, including their color, can influence humans' appearance. "You are what you eat" is not just a primitive superstition; it is believed, implicitly, by educated people in technologically advanced cultures.

It follows from "you are what you eat" that the consumption of animals will impart some of their animal properties to the person consuming them. Although many animals have desirable attributes, they all share the property of not being human. And it is a major theme, across cultures, that humans are superior to, and qualitatively different from, animals. Yet, consumption of an-

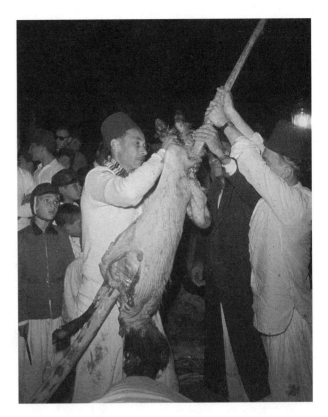

Samaritans sacrificing and roasting lamb at Passover on Mount Gerisim near Nabulus, Israel. © DEAN CONGER/CORBIS.

imals, according to the "you are what you eat" principle, would render humans more animal-like, that is, less distinctively human. This belief contributes to human ambivalence about eating meat, and may partially account for the disgust aroused by animal foods in some people.

Meat and the Human Primate

Primates show substantial variation in the types of diets they consume; however, there is a general focus on fruits. Some, particularly large primates, move to a more folivorous (leaf-eating) diet, and some consume a moderate amount of small animals, including insects. The larger stomachs and colons that characterize folivorous animals contrast with the smaller colons and stomachs of the carnivores. Frugivores (fruit eaters) typically have a gut that lies between the carnivore and the folivore extremes, and this is what humans have. This type of gut, and the associated general-purpose set of teeth, are well suited to generalist or omnivorous feeding habits, which characterize humans and chimpanzees. Humans can be distinguished from other primates, including chimpanzees, in their ability to hunt animals larger than themselves. This hunting capacity, related to the movement from the forest to savannah environment, has major implications for human nature and human evolution. First, it introduces the possibility of a substantial amount of meat in the diet.

Native American method of drying meat on racks. PHOTOGRAPH BY EDWARD S. CURTIS, 1908. COURTESY OF THE LIBRARY OF CONGRESS.

In addition, the demands of hunting encourage elaborate communication and cooperative effort as well as the creation of weapons and the technology that goes with them. The yield that results from killing a large animal encourages sharing, communal eating, and preservation technologies. It is fair to say that the shift to a diet with more meat in it, with the inclusion of large animal hunting, was a major force in human evolution. In an important sense, meat as food has shaped human nature.

Meat in Traditional Society

It is presumed that the hunter-gatherer mode of existence, with varying degrees of reliance on vegetable and animal products, was the situation of Homo sapiens prior to the appearance of domestication and agriculture. However, this should be recognized as a presumption. Studies of the diverse range of existing cultures that rely to a large degree on hunting and gathering suggest that meat, even at this stage of human cultural and biological evolution, assumed a central role. Meat is generally the favored food, the center of celebrations and social gatherings, and the food selectively available to adult males, the most powerful and high-status members of most hunter-gatherer societies. This situation probably results from a combination of the caloric density of meat and the fact that meat, unlike any particular vegetable, is a complete food. On the other hand, the relative rarity of meat, which usually constitutes much less than half of the diet, encourages rules for its selective distribution.

Even among hunter-gatherers, however, there are signs of ambivalence to meat. Most food taboos of hunter-gatherers, and they are extensive, are about meat. Taboos are sometimes general, namely that certain types of animals are forbidden as food. On the other hand, most taboos are conditional, restricting the eating of meat, or certain parts (muscle, innards) to particular groups. Generally, the adult males get the greater amount of meat, get to eat the preferred animals, and get the preferred parts (usually muscle). But there are many exceptions to this general rule. Meat or animal taboos, whether in hunter-gatherer or technologically developed cultures, seem to have a few general characteristics. In what has been referred to as "zones of edibility," tabooed creatures tend to be those very close to humans (humans themselves, primates, or companion animals), those very different from humans, and/or those that are rarely encountered.

Domestication

Meat figures prominently in what might be called the two most important transitions in human evolution: the development of complex cultures and sophisticated technologies. Just as hunting had a major influence in shaping human nature, the combination of agriculture and domestication laid the foundation for high densities of humans and the subsequent elaboration of culture. By making the human food supply more independent of the seasons and of short-term extremes in weather, agriculture and domestication set the stage for major changes in human life. Domestication made it possible for humans to be the only mammals that could have continued access to the almost perfect mammal food of infancy, milk; it also frequently made meat a less scarce resource. Just as hunting helped encourage the upright posture, the development of hand skills, and major cognitive developments, agriculture and domestication of animals freed humans to develop a wide range of impressive technologies.

Meat in Developed Societies

The tables have begun to turn on meat in today's affluent, developed world. The excitement of meat hunting has given way to factory farming. The butchering of the carcass takes place out of sight of almost everyone, so that the skills involved in butchering as well as hunting are almost gone. The caloric density of meat has lost much of its appeal because the threat to human health is too many calories, rather than too few. Similarly, the nutritional completeness of meat is a less salient virtue, what with the great variety of plant foods available in any neighborhood supermarket. The epidemiological revolution has shifted health risks from minimal diets, unbalanced diets, and infections spread by humans through food and other products, to degenerative diseases like heart disease and cancer. And animal fat has been implicated as a risk factor for heart disease. Finally, the affluence of modern societies permits the development of great sensitivities to nature and the morality of using animals as food; with many options available, it is possible to allow moral concerns to influence diet. Vegetarianism is on the rise, for both moral and health reasons, and many of the nonvegetarians in the urban developed world are queasy about the actual process of killing animals. This attitude appears even in the slaughterhouse itself, where responsibility for killing the animals is diffused across a number of different people and roles. In Britain, the United States, and Canada, the human approach to meat has become increasingly ambivalent. The human primate still loves the taste and smell of meat, while cultural knowledge and sensitivities argue against it.

Disgust

Disgust is a powerful emotion, and animal products often arouse it. Almost all foods that are labeled as disgusting in a number of cultures are of animal origin. It is odd, because "dis-gust" means 'bad taste', and meat is one of the best-tasting foods to humans. It is odd also because, given the superior nutritional properties of meat, it should not be the target of the strongest negative food-related emotion.

Meat preference may be a human predisposition, but it is probably not present in infants. Ironically, there may be some predisposition to find meat disgusting, but this as well is not present in the first few years of life. Human infants eat, or at least try to eat, everything they can get into their mouth. Feces, the universal core of disgust, and itself an animal product, is attractive as a food to human infants, as it is to other young and adult mammals. Presumably the odor of decay, associated as it is with microorganism-infested meat, would be innately repugnant, but there is no evidence for an infant aversion to this odor. Nor is there evidence for such an aversion in other primates or mammals. By age two or three, in Western developed cultures (which have provided all of the data up to this time), children have a clear aversion to feces, and a variety of other animal products, especially those that are decayed. This is probably the result of toilet training, although there is no account available of the actual process through which this aversion to feces and decay is aroused.

The foods that are disgusting to adults, cross-culturally, are almost entirely of animal origin, beginning with feces and, for Americans, extending widely to many of the edible parts of animals. Indeed, considering all of the possible animal foods (insects, mollusks, reptiles, amphibians), it is quite remarkable that Americans consume only four or five species of mammals, a few species of birds, no amphibians and reptiles, a moderate number of the many species of fish, only a few types of shellfish, and no insects. Furthermore, the meats eaten by Americans exclude many parts of edible animals; consumption is almost exclusively limited to muscle, and, in general, not the heart or tongue, although these are muscles. So far as is known, this idiosyncratic selection of animals and animal parts as acceptable food has no nutritional or health basis.

These facts lead to the conclusion that disgust at animal products, and the avoidance of most animal products, has an ideational base; it is based neither on taste (most of the "disgusting" types of meat have never been tried) or actual health risks. It is the *idea* of eating lizards, cow eyes or intestines, or insects that is upsetting and expressed as disgust, somewhat parallel to the formal taboos in other cultures against the consumption of many types of animals or animal parts.

Humans are clearly adapted to a partial meat diet and to liking the taste of meat, especially when it is cooked. But there are some negative sides to meat eating. Perhaps most important is the threat of microbial contamination; because animals are more like humans than plants are, animals are more likely to harbor microorganisms that can afflict humans. This microbial load also makes animal flesh vulnerable to decay after death. Many have argued that the use of many spices originated as a culinary means of discouraging spoilage of meat. During the twentieth century most of the microbial risks were overcome with controlled raising, preparation, and storage of meats. However, as feeding a population of billions a diet with substantial amounts of meat became the goal, a new problem arose: it takes much more out of the environment to make a pound of meat than a pound of vegetable starch or fruits and vegetables. This was not much of a problem when there were fewer humans, and when animals were hunted rather than herded. For some it has become a serious issue that threatens the welfare of our planet.

Plants, of course, as the alternative food source, have their own problems. They are more likely to contain toxins, and they are less calorie dense and less complete nutritionally. As with the minimization of the microbial risks of meat consumption by technological rearing and preparation techniques, the risk of plant toxins can be reduced both by a culture-based selection of appropriate plant products to eat and by the development, through agriculture, of staple plant-based starches that are essentially toxin-free.

Meat and Vegetarianism

Most people in the Third World eat relatively little meat, mostly because of its cost and rarity. They would eat more if they could. On the other hand, in some religious groups, such as orthodox Hindus, all meat is prohibited. And within some meat-eating cultures, individuals or groups of individuals reject meat as food. This type of vegetarianism has a history that goes back at least to ancient Greece. Historically, this type of elective vegetarianism has been motivated primarily by moral or religious concerns, often having to do with negative reactions to the killing of animals or the psychological effects of consuming animals. Within many developed cultures, vege-

tarians invoke, in addition to moral, religious, or aesthetic concerns, worries about the long-term health effects of eating meat. Some vegetarians can be classified as either health or moral vegetarians, though most long-time vegetarians express a little of both motivations. Interestingly, moral vegetarians are more likely to find meat disgusting than are health vegetarians. When meat becomes disgusting, it is much easier to avoid it.

Vegetarianism seems to be growing in the Western world, impelled by health and moral motivations. For most people who choose this path, it is usually a long development over time, frequently a movement from rejection of a small category of animal products (for example, baby mammals or red meat) through larger and larger spheres of rejection (adding poultry, fish and shellfish, eggs and dairy products, and nonfood animal products). For many, the sequence stops at some point along this trajectory. People also often slide backwards, either abandoning a particular level of rejection for a less stringent set of prohibitions or completely abandoning the vegetarian style.

Mad Cow Disease

Although in general Americans seemed to be the most concerned group about the diet-health link as the twentieth century ended, the advent of mad cow disease engaged Europeans more than Americans. Mad cow disease (bovine spongiform encephalopathy [BSE]) is quintessentially about meat. Mad cow is doubly animal: it involves not only animal meat—beef—but also feed consumed by cows, animals that are normally vegetarian, that contains animal parts. Studies of risk perception by psychologists indicate that people tend to exaggerate risks when they are catastrophic, hidden, delayed, and not understood. Mad cow disease meets all of these conditions and adds the predisposition to be emotionally involved with foods of an animal nature. It is hard to believe that as much fuss would be made if this were mad broccoli disease. It is also just as likely that "mad broccoli disease," because it would not originate with diseased animals, would not lead to a delayed, unexpected, hideous, and certain, death.

See also **Aversion to Food; Cannibalism; Cattle; Disgust; Game; Goat; Hinduism; Horse; Hunting and Gathering; Mammals; Pig; Sheep**.

BIBLIOGRAPHY

Billing, J., and P. W. Sherman. "Antimicrobial Functions of Spices: Why Some Like It Hot." *Quarterly Review of Biology* 73 (1998): 3–49.

Chivers, D. J. "Diets and Guts." In *The Cambridge Encyclopedia of Human Evolution*, edited by Ed S. Jones, R. Martin, and D. Pilbeam, pp. 60–64. Cambridge, England: Cambridge University Press, 1992.

Diamond, J. *Guns, Germs, and Steel: The Fates of Human Societies.* New York: Norton, 1997.

Douglas, M. *Purity and Danger: An Analysis of Concepts of Pollution and Taboo.* London: Routledge, 1966.

Fiddes, N. *Meat: A Natural Symbol*. London: Routledge, 1991.

Kass, L. *The Hungry Soul: Eating and the Perfecting of Our Nature*. New York: Free Press, 1994.

Kelly, R. L. *The Foraging Spectrum: Diversity in Hunter-Gatherer Lifeways*. Washington, D.C.: Smithsonian Institution Press, 1995.

Miller, W. I. *The Anatomy of Disgust*. Cambridge, Mass.: Harvard University Press, 1997.

Nemeroff, C., and P. Rozin. "The Makings of the Magical Mind." In *Imagining the Impossible: Magical, Scientific, and Religious Thinking in Children*, edited by K. S. Rosengren, C. N. Johnson, and P. L. Harris, pp. 1–34. New York: Cambridge University Press, 2000.

Rhodes, R. *Deadly Feasts: Tracking the Secrets of a Deadly New Plague*. New York: Simon and Schuster, 1997.

Rozin, P., and A. E. Fallon. "A Perspective on Disgust." *Psychological Review* 94 (1987): 23–41.

Rozin, P., J. Haidt, and C. R. McCauley. "Disgust." In *Handbook of Emotions*, edited by M. Lewis and J. Haviland, 2d ed., pp. 637–653. New York: Guilford, 2000.

Simoons, F. J. *Eat Not This Flesh: Food Avoidances from Prehistory to the Present*. 2d ed., rev. and enl. Madison: University of Wisconsin Press.

Tambiah, S. J. "Animals Are Good to Think and Good to Prohibit." *Ethnology* 8 (1969): 423–459.

Twigg, J. "Food for Thought: Purity and Vegetarianism." *Religion* 9 (1979): 13–35.

Vialles, N. *Animal to Edible*. Translated by J. A. Underwood. Cambridge: Cambridge University Press, 1994. (Original edition: *Le Sang et la chair: Les Abatoirs des pays de l'adour*. Paris: Fondation de la Maison des Sciences et l'Homme, 1987.)

Washburn, S. L., and C. S. Lancaster. "The Evolution of Hunting." In *Man the Hunter*, edited by R. B. Lee and I. Devore, pp. 293–303. Chicago: Aldine, 1968.

Whitehead, H. *Food Rules: Hunting, Sharing, and Tabooing Game in Papua New Guinea*. Ann Arbor: University of Michigan Press, 2000.

Paul Rozin

MEAT, SALTED. The food industry incorporates sodium chloride (NaCl) in preservation, processing, and manufacturing operations for vegetables, poultry, fish, seafood, and meat. Although a number of food preservation techniques have been used for many years, including drying, freezing, heating, canning, filtration, enzyme treatment, high-energy irradiation, and chemicals such as organic acids, nitrate, and liquid smoke, salt remains one of the common methods of meat preservation with a long history. Salt is used to preserve meat in its dry form, as a brine, or in solution pumped into tissues (Doyle and Roman, 1982). Researchers still are examining the beneficial functional properties of NaCl in meats and other food commodities (Hajmeer, Marsden, Crozier-Dodson, Basheer, and Higgins, 1999; Pszczola, 1997).

Use of Salt in Meat and Meat Products

Sodium contents of unprocessed meat are about 55 mg/100 g of beef fiber, and 65 mg/100 g of pork fiber (Institute of Food Technologists, 1980). The level is increased when NaCl is added to the meat during processing. Salt has been used by the meat industry as a dry application and in the formulation of fermented, processed (cured or uncured), and restructured meats. Salt added to a meat system serves three main functions: extracting salt-soluble proteins, enhancing flavor, and extending the shelf life (Claus, Jhung-Won, and Flick, 1994).

Originally, in the absence of refrigeration, meat was dry-salted for extended periods of time to preserve it from microbial deterioration. Excessive salting and extended storage increased water loss, and dehydration removed water from the tissues by osmosis, lowering the water activity in the system to conditions unsuitable for microbial growth and leading to cellular plasmolysis, shrinking of cytoplasm away from the cell wall. In addition to dry-salting, NaCl is incorporated in fermented meats such as semi-dry sausage during preparation. Adding NaCl prevents growth of undesirable spoilage or pathogenic microorganisms by favoring the growth of acid-producing, salt-tolerant bacteria, such as lactobacilli and micrococci. Production of acid by these microorganisms gives the meat a desirable tangy flavor and lowers the pH of the system, which adds another safeguard against the growth of undesirable microorganisms.

In processed comminuted meats, for example, bologna, frankfurters, and summer sausage, and non-comminuted meats, for example, ham, bacon, and pastrami, NaCl is one of the basic ingredients, after the meat itself. Other ingredients include water, spices, nonfat dry milk, sweeteners, phosphates, and nitrite. Salt and nitrite are the main ingredients used to cure meats and are applied dry, by immersion, or by injection methods. Salt added to processed meats helps to extract NaCl-soluble proteins, increases the gel strength of the emulsion or batter, enhances the flavor, inhibits or minimizes microbial growth, and enhances antimicrobial activity of other compounds in the system. Salt-soluble proteins coat the fat molecules in the system and provide a stable emulsion, which is important in improving moisture retention and texture of the final product (Claus et al., 1994). Salting prerigor hot-boned meat to be further processed, for example, when making sausage, helps maintain its water-holding capacity (WHC) and fat-emulsifying properties (Hamm, 1981).

Salt, in conjunction with sodium tripolyphosphate, is used for protein extraction in the preparation of restructured meats, which are sectioned and formed noncured products. Restructuring meats makes it feasible to use lower-grade, less expensive cuts and, similar to the concept of processing meats, restructuring them provides more diversified products that are flavorful, nutritious, affordable, and convenient.

Salt can be encapsulated with partially hydrogenated vegetable oil to prevent excess extraction of salt-soluble proteins during meat processing. This eliminates undesirable changes in meat texture and viscosity. Encapsulated salt used in sausage preparation produces desirable qualities such as high moisture, crumbly and tender texture, and good flavor (Pszczola, 1997). Normally, 2 to 3 percent NaCl is added during the chopping or emulsifying process to help extract the proteins, but this amount may range from as little as 1.5 to 5.0 percent (Claus et al., 1994).

Advantages, Disadvantages, and Limitations of NaCl

Salt enhances the flavor of meat by suppressing undesirable or unpalatable savors. It extends the shelf life by retarding microbial growth because it exerts both bactericidal and bacteriostatic effects on many microbes found in meat (Marsden, 1980). This might be associated with changes in water activity and ionic strength that render water unavailable to microorganisms (Hajmeer et al., 1999). Other factors include dehydration, the direct effect of chlorine ions, removal of oxygen from the medium, sensitization of microorganisms to carbon dioxide, and interference with the rapid action of proteolytic enzymes (Polymenidis, 1978).

Spoilage and pathogenic bacteria such as *Escherichia coli* O157:H7, *Listeria monocytogenes*, *Salmonella* spp., *Staphylococcus aureus*, *Clostridium botulinum*, and lactic acid bacteria have various tolerances and differ in their responses to salt. Among other factors, these depend on microbial tolerance to NaCl, type and concentration of NaCl, exposure time, pH, and temperature. *Salmonella* spp., *S. aureus*, and *C. botulinum* have the ability to grow in brine solutions with high salt concentrations and at low temperatures (Marsden, 1980). Therefore, using a combination of ingredients and processing methods, such as the curing process, that employ both NaCl and nitrite is important in controlling microbial growth.

Excess use of NaCl has undesirable effects on the flavor, color, and appearance of meat. Application of dry NaCl, for example, can result in an unattractive and darker color of lean (Pearson and Gillett, 1999). As a powerful prooxidant, NaCl has undesirable oxidative effects on meats. Processed frozen products containing salt become rancid and produce unacceptable flavors during extended storage (Claus et al., 1994). Incorporation of other ingredients in the meat system, such as sugar, nitrite, and antioxidants, for example, butylated hydroxyanisole (BHA) helps minimize or control these negative effects by masking adverse flavors, preventing color degradation, and reducing oxidative properties. Salt can have a synergistic effect and enhance the activity of other preservatives such as BHA (Stern, Smoot, and Pierson, 1979). However, impurities in NaCl can reduce its effectiveness in extracting NaCl-soluble proteins because they interfere with the WHC and emulsifying properties of the meats. Therefore, it is important to use a purified grade of NaCl.

Because of increased concerns regarding high salt intake and its role relative to hypertension, high blood pressure, and potential heart disease, public health authorities recommend reduction in NaCl intake (IFT, 1980). Intake can be reduced by lowering its levels during processing or by substituting potassium chloride (KCl) for part of the NaCl (Pearson and Gillett, 1999). Unfortunately, reduction of NaCl in meat products weakens its preservative capacity and the binding and WHC of the systems. Furthermore, complete replacement of NaCl with KCl is undesirable because of the aftertaste left by KCl. Polyphosphates and other chloride salts also can be used to replace NaCl.

NaCl levels in the diet have been of some concern, and maintaining public health is a priority. Salt use cannot be eliminated completely in the meat industry to reduce health risks because of the important technological functions it performs. It is important to determine the minimum levels of NaCl necessary to maintain its functionality while addressing the health concerns of consumers.

See also **Fish, Salted; Game; Hunting and Gathering; Iodine; Mammals; Meat; Military Rations; Preserving; Salt; Sodium.**

BIBLIOGRAPHY

Claus, J. R., C. Jhung-Won, and G. J. Flick. "Processed Meats/Poultry/Seafood." In *Muscle Foods: Meat, Poultry, and Seafood Technology*, edited by D. M. Kinsman, A. W. Kotula, and B. C. Breidenstein. New York: Chapman and Hall, 1994.

Doyle, M. P., and D. J. Roman. "Response of *Campylobacter jejuni* to Sodium Chloride." *Journal of Applied and Environmental Microbiology* 43 (1982): 561–565.

Hajmeer, M. N., J. L. Marsden, B. A. Crozier-Dodson, I. A. Basheer, and J. J. Higgins. "Reduction of Microbial Counts in a Commercial Beef Koshering Facility." *Journal of Food Science* 64 (1999): 719–723.

Hamm, R. *Development in Meat Science*. Barking, England: Elsevier, 1981.

Institute of Food Technologists. "Dietary Salt: A Scientific Status Summary." *Food Technology* 33 (1980): 85–91.

Marsden, J. L. "Sodium Containing Additives in Processed Meats: A Technological Overview." In *Proceedings of the Sodium and Potassium in Foods and Drugs Conference*, edited by P. L. White and S. C. Crocco. Chicago, Ill.: American Medical Association, 1980.

Pearson, A. M., and T. A. Gillett. *Processed Meats*. Gaithersburg, Md.: Aspen, 1999.

Polymenidis, A. "Salting, Curing, and Reddening of Meat and Meat Products." *Die Fleischwirtschaft* 4 (1978): 585–591.

Pszczola, D. E. "Salty Developments in Food." *Food Technology* 51 (1997): 79–90.

Stern, N. J., L. A. Smoot, and M. D. Pierson. "Inhibition of *Staphylococcus aureus* Growth by Combinations of Butylated

Hydroxyanisole, Sodium Chloride, and pH." *Journal of Food Science* 44 (1979): 710–712.

Maha N. Hajmeer
James L. Marsden

MEAT, SMOKED.

Smoking is an ancient method of food preservation that is still practiced because it adds an interesting flavor to meat, fish, poultry, and other foods; allows foods such as hams to be stored at room temperature; and slightly dries and preserves some foods, such as sliced salmon, that are eaten raw.

Smoking dates back centuries, especially for fish, which is highly perishable. Archeological evidence suggests that ninth-century residents of Poland smoked large quantities of fish (Shephard, p. 117). In medieval Europe, the religious practice of avoiding meat on certain days created a tremendous demand for fish, and enormous quantities of salmon and herring were salted and smoked in seaside towns before being shipped to the interior. Pork was also a popular meat for smoking since pigs were slaughtered in the fall and their meat could be preserved on the farm to last through the winter. Smoked pork was found in China as well as Europe. In South America, long strips of dried meat are called *charqui*, which has come into English as "jerky" as the name for a snack made from beef or turkey.

Smoking is a preservative because smoke contains chemical compounds that retard the growth of harmful bacteria. More than three hundred components of smoke have been identified. Carbonyl compounds in smoke contribute to the distinctive flavor and aroma of smoked meat, while the carbon dioxide and carbon monoxide help produce the bright red pigment. Phenolic compounds in smoke play a role in protecting fat from oxidizing and turning rancid, which is no doubt a major reason why fatty foods, such as herring or pork, were (and are) so often smoked. The composition of the smoke changes as the temperature of the fire rises, with the best quality smoke produced at a temperature of 650° to 750°F. Control of humidity in the smokehouse is also important since high humidity favors deposition of smoke on the surface of the food and absorption of the flavor. High humidity also assists in the rendering of fat.

Smoking operations fall into two categories: hot-smoking and cold-smoking. In hot-smoking, the temperature in the smoke chamber ranges from 120° to 180°F, which produces a strong smoky flavor. However, the meat is usually only partially cooked and must be finished in a conventional oven. In cold-smoking, the smoke is produced in a firebox but allowed to cool before being passed into the smoking chamber, where the temperature is a mere 70° to 90°F. The food is hardly cooked at all, but long exposure to cool smoke gives the food a mild, smoky flavor and dries it to some extent. Cold-smoking is used largely for foods that will be eaten raw, such as smoked salmon or smoked fillet of beef. The temperature range from 90° to 120°F is considered too hot for cold-smoking and too cool for hot-smoking. A temperature over 180°F is considered "cooking with smoke" rather than smoking as such; pork barbecue and regional dishes such as Texas beef brisket are in this category. A great variety of foods can be successfully cold-smoked or hot-smoked, ranging from fish to pork, poultry, and beef to wild game.

Many foods are cured before smoking, especially cold-smoking, to draw out the moisture, which would otherwise promote spoilage. The cure is a mixture of salt, sodium nitrate, nitrites, sometimes sugar, spices, and other seasonings, and additives such as phosphates or ascorbates. Nitrate and nitrites contribute to the flavor and coloration of products such as ham. Nitrite and salt inhibit the growth of *Clostridium botulinum*, the bacterium that causes botulism.

A dry cure can be applied by rubbing the meat with the mixture or packing the food in a container of the cure mix and letting it sit for several days or weeks. A wet cure can be applied through a brine of water or other liquid containing the cure ingredients; brine can also be injected into the food in order to impregnate its center and speed up the curing process. Once cured, the food is dried and smoked.

Some items, such as hams, are hung for weeks or months under conditions of controlled temperature and humidity to develop flavor. Humidity is controlled by the addition of steam or water vapor as well as the use of dampers. Air movement is also critical to uniform heating, curing, and flavor in the final product. High air velocities tend to produce more rapid drying and a firm consistency.

Home units for hot-smoking are typically upright cylinders with an electric hot plate, charcoal grate, or gas range at the bottom to produce heat; wood is placed over the heat source to create smoke, and the food is placed on a rack above the wood. A pan of water is often placed in the smoker to catch the drippings from the food so that they do not fall into the heat source and cause flare-ups. The more elaborate units include adjustable baffles and other controls to allow the cook to control the smoke. Double-chamber units for both hot- and cold-smoking are usually horizontal and tend to be rather large and heavy.

Different types of wood are used to produce different flavors in the smoke. Hickory is a great favorite in the eastern United States, while alder is popular in the Pacific Northwest. Maple, oak, and pecan are also used in the United States. In Scotland, peat fires were once used to smoke fish. Beech, oak, and chestnut are the most popular woods in Europe. Commercial operations use sawdust or logs, while most home smokers use wood chips set in a pan on the heating element; the large, dual-chamber home smokers can use small logs. Evergreens are usually avoided because they contain resins that can produce a sticky smoke and impart a bitter flavor to the food. However, resinous wood is sometimes used at the end of the smoking process to give the outside of the food a protective coating. No matter what fuel is used, a smoldering fire is preferred to an open flame because it produces abundant smoke and avoids very high temperatures.

Smoked salmon, usually sliced very thin, is an elegant dish. It is cold-smoked and eaten raw. Lox (from the Yiddish word for smoked salmon) is usually more heavily cured than other types and is often eaten on a bagel with cream cheese. Kippers are cured and smoked herrings, still very popular in Britain at breakfast, lunch, or tea. The village of Findon in Scotland gave its name to smoked haddock (finnan haddie), which is served hot after being broiled or poached. Halibut, sturgeon, and fish roe (eggs) are also cold-smoked. Eel, trout, and mackerel are hot-smoked and can be eaten without further cooking.

A whole ham is the hind leg of a pig. Many regions in the United States and Europe have particular styles of ham production and preparation. "Country ham" from Virginia, Tennessee, or Kentucky, for example, is heavily cured and smoked for weeks or months over smoldering fires of hickory or apple wood. The resulting ham is so dry and hard that it must be soaked overnight to get rid of some of the salt, and then boiled to soften it. Britain produces the York ham, popular for boiling, the Suffolk ham, cured with spices and honey, and the Bradenham, which is cured with molasses. Prague ham (from Czechoslovakia) is lightly smoked over beechwood coals and is said to be among the sweetest of hams. Many hams are smoked but eaten raw, such as Westphalian ham from Germany. (Prosciutto ham from Parma, Italy, is also raw but is not smoked).

Smoking also gives meat its distinctive reddish color. Sausages are often smoked, as are frankfurters. In the United States, bacon is usually smoked and often cured with sugar to give it a sweet taste.

Chickens, turkey, duck, and geese can be hot-smoked, usually after being cooked, and the resulting meat tastes like ham. Smoked poultry, however, is perishable and must be kept frozen or refrigerated until it is reheated or served cold. Boneless beef roast can be hot-smoked for several hours to the desired temperature and sliced very thin.

Nearly any type of game can be smoked, from squirrel meat to bear and wild boar. Hunters should ensure that game meats are properly handled and cooked to at least 180°F to eliminate the danger of botulism or trichinosis.

See also **Barbecue**; **Botulism**; **Cooking**; **Fish**; **Fish, Smoked**; **Game**; **Mammals**; **Meat**; **Pig**; **Preparation of Food**; **Salt**.

BIBLIOGRAPHY

Terence Conran, Caroline Conran, and Simon Hopkinson. *The Essential Cook Book: The Back-to-the-Basics Guide to Selecting, Preparing, Cooking, and Serving.* New York: Stewart, Tabori and Chang, 1997.

McGee, Harold. *On Food and Cooking: The Science and Lore of the Kitchen.* New York: Simon and Schuster, 1997. Originally published by Charles Scribner's Sons, 1984.

Park, Lue, and Ed Park. *The Smoked-Foods Cookbook: How to Flavor, Cure and Prepare Savory Meats, Game, Fish, Nuts, and Cheese.* Harrisburg, Pa.: Stackpole, 1992.

Shephard, Sue. *Pickled, Potted, and Canned: How the Art and Science of Food Preserving Changed the World.* New York: Simon and Schuster, 2001.

Richard L. Lobb
Francis McFadden

MEDICI, CATHERINE DE'. Orphaned soon after her birth in Florence, Catherine de' Medici (1519–1589) inherited the wealth and theatrical style of her grandfather, Lorenzo the Magnificent, the most notable of the Florentine family who made the name of Medici synonymous with quattrocento (Italian fifteenth-

Catherine de' Medici (1519–1589), wife of Henry II of France, was better known for her cruelty and political machinations than for culinary sophistication. Nineteenth-century engraving based on an original portrait. © CORBIS (BELLEVUE).

century) art and power. At age fourteen Catherine was sent to France to marry Henry of Orleans (Henry II), who inherited the French throne in 1547 at the death of his father Francis I. Catherine bore ten children. After the death of Henry II in 1559, three of Catherine's sons successively became kings of France, and Catherine served as queen regent.

The thirty-year length of her reign and the horrific religious wars of her time have given Catherine a symbolic identity that stretches historical fact. Popular myth has long named her the Italian queen mother of France's high cuisine, for she is often presumed to have imported new notions of cooking as refined as the other civilized arts reborn in the Italian Renaissance of the fifteenth century. But in fact Catherine's innovations were not culinary but theatric and were geared to politics rather than to gastronomy.

Regent of a weak government during the conflicts between Catholics and Huguenots that culminated in the St. Bartholomew's Day Massacre of 1572, Catherine used spectacle to create an image of stability and order when reality denied it. In 1564 she displayed the virtual power of monarchy in a grand tour through the countryside with her son Charles IX. Throughout her regency she staged court festivals or masques that used food as the excuse for lavish theatrical happenings, which combined drama with dance, music, sculpture, and the decorative arts. In France she created a new style for royal banqueting that achieved its apotheosis in the court of Louis XIV at Versailles.

See also **France; Italy.**

BIBLIOGRAPHY

Heritier, Jean. *Catherine de Medici.* Translated by Charlotte Haldane. London: George Allen and Unwin, 1963.

Wheaton, Barbara Ketcham. *Savoring the Past: The French Kitchen and Table from 1300 to 1789.* Philadelphia: University of Pennsylvania Press, 1983.

Betty Fussell

MEDICINE. Food plays both a causative and curative role in health and disease. Thus, its role in medicine may be as a risk factor for, protector against, or treatment of an illness. While too much food or exposure to certain foods can reduce someone's health, too little food or inadequate amounts of certain foods can be equally damaging. In the years before modern transportation, packaging, and refrigeration, medicine was primarily concerned with food deficiencies and food spoilage. The focus of medicine was on the identification of critical components of food and common pathogens and on the prevention of nutritional deficiencies and foodborne infections. The role of food in medicine has changed as food production, preservation, and preparation techniques have progressed. Today far more people in de-

veloped countries such as the United States suffer from excessive food consumption than from food deficiencies. In addition, certain components of food have been found to have therapeutic or protective properties when administered in levels greater than generally considered necessary. For instance, large quantities of vitamin A are used to treat acne, therapeutic quantities of vitamin E may be protective against heart disease, and extra fiber appears to reduce the risk of colon cancer. However, the problems of malnutrition or inadequate food intake and foodborne illness have not been eliminated. Undernutrition continues to plague developing nations, while the prevention and treatment of foodborne illness is a concern for all nations.

The Basics of Food and Health

Food is fundamental to support life. People get energy, water, and all of the building blocks for growth and proper bodily functioning from the foods they eat and the liquids they drink. The components of food necessary to life are termed "nutrients" and the study of the role of food in health is called nutrition. The goal of medicine is to ensure health, and because adequate nutrition is necessary to accomplish this, nutrition is a crucial component of medicine. Nutritional science combines food science and medical science. Nutrients include protein, fat, carbohydrates, fiber, thirteen vitamins, seventeen minerals, and more substances that are still being identified. The majority of nutrients essential to health are found in a variety of different foods. No one food is absolutely essential to support life. People with access to adequate amounts of food get all of the nutrients they need by eating a varied diet complete with fruits, vegetables, meat or meat alternatives, dairy foods, and grains. However, some people are not able to or do not choose to eat the full variety of foods available. These people may require special foods or supplements to meet their nutritional needs.

The Study of Food in Medicine

All branches of medicine, from pediatrics to geriatrics and from internal medicine to surgery, study food and its role in health and disease. Nutritional scientists in government, industry, and academia are constantly seeking to understand the role food plays in illness and well-being. Meanwhile health-care practitioners treat patients with nutritional plans and food supplements. Registered dietitians are health-care specialists who integrate food into medical treatment—this is referred to as medical nutrition therapy.

The Role of Food in Maintaining Health

Although the presence of adequate nutrition does not ensure health, it is a significant contributor. The energy contributed by the protein, carbohydrates, and fat in food provides the fuel for every element of body functioning from breathing to thinking to fighting disease to running marathons. Adequate energy intake is crucial to promote proper growth and development as well as to maintain healthy functioning once one is fully grown. Food also provides the materials necessary to build healthy bone, muscle, skin, hair, etc. For example, bone is a complex matrix of calcium, phosphorus, and collagen fibers. A person's bone strength is directly related to their nutrient intake such that inadequate calcium intake is one of the primary reasons for bone disease such as osteoporosis. Nutrients are also necessary to support proper chemical and neurological functioning. For example, fat insulates nerve fibers such that they can conduct electrical signals along the length of the body. Meanwhile, those electrical signals are generated via channeling ions such as sodium, potassium, and calcium into and out of the nerve cells. Finally, the neurotransmitters released from the nerve cells are made from amino acids contributed largely from proteins in the diet. Thus, thinking and feeling are intricately connected to food.

Food for Those Who Can't Feed Themselves

Food is generally eaten, or drunk, and swallowed. However, many people cannot obtain adequate nutritional levels by conventional ways of ingesting food. In the past, these people would suffer and die from malnutrition. Modern nutritional medicine offers people several alternatives to conventional chewing and swallowing of food so that those who cannot do so will not die. Liquid solutions have been manufactured by pharmaceutical companies that are easier to digest than solid food and provide 100 percent of nutritional needs. People who can drink but not eat rely on these formulas just as babies who cannot breast feed rely on baby formula to meet their nutritional needs. People who cannot consume anything orally are fed via a tube inserted into the stomach or intestines. Finally, those whose gastrointestinal tracts cannot absorb even liquids are fed intravenously with solutions that provide 100 percent of human nutritional needs.

Examples of Food as a Cause of Disease

Food allergies and intolerances are common medical reasons for eliminating specific foods from one's diet. An *allergy* is an immune response to proteins in food that the body identifies as foreign. The most common food allergies include those to peanuts, tree nuts, shellfish, milk, soy, corn, wheat, and eggs. Most allergies appear in childhood and require complete elimination of the offending food if the symptoms are to be eradicated. Childhood food allergies may persist for a lifetime or may resolve a few years after getting rid of the offending food. Symptoms of allergies may include rashes and other skin irritations, gastrointestinal inflammation and bleeding, and respiratory distress, which may even involve arrest of breathing.

Food intolerances are not allergies but rather uncomfortable reactions to food that are not generally considered life threatening. One well-known example is lactose intolerance. Lactose is the carbohydrate in milk and other dairy products. The body requires a specific enzyme if lactose is to be absorbed. As people age their bodies may make less of the enzyme necessary to break down lactose and as a result they may experience gastrointestinal distress, including such symptoms as gas or diarrhea, when they consume milk products containing lactose. Most people with lactose intolerance can tolerate dairy products if they accompany their meal with a lactase enzyme pill or if they consume dairy products pretreated with lactase enzyme. Thus, food technology allows people with intolerances to tolerate the offending foods but avoidance is the only option for people with food allergies.

In countries such as the United States where food is abundant, some of the greatest medical risks result from overeating rather than insufficient eating. For example, an excess intake of energy in the form of food leads to an increased risk of obesity. Obesity increases one's risk of cardiovascular disease, cancer, diabetes, and obstructive pulmonary disease—among the most common and most deadly diseases today. Medical practitioners have tried to determine how much food is adequate to support healthy living. People who consume too much food and become obese may seek medical treatment to lose weight and treat diseases resulting from obesity. Treatments may include nutritional therapy, exercise programs, drug therapy, or surgery. *Foodborne illness* results from eating contaminated food. Foodborne illness can be caused by parasites, bacteria, viruses, toxins, or other pathogens that are harmful to humans. Food is not the direct cause but rather the carrier of the problematic agent. The effects of foodborne illness can range from flulike symptoms to death depending on the type of pathogen and the amount of exposure. Foodborne illnesses are generally prevented by appropriate growing, harvesting, packaging, preparation, cooking, and storage of food. However, many countries lack the technology and resources necessary to accomplish this. Thus, assuring food safety continues to be an area of international concern.

Food as a Treatment

Food is not only necessary to sustain health but it can also help ill people regain health. Although the common advice to "feed a fever" may sound like folklore it is actually based in scientific evidence. A rise in body temperature is required in order to fight disease. People with a fever also require extra energy if they are to have adequate energy to maintain their strength while they battle illness. Likewise, the immune system uses a wide range of nutrients to combat intruders. All infectious diseases result in increased need for nutrition to strengthen the immune system as if fights against invading viruses or bacteria. People who suffer from diseases such as cancer, cystic fibrosis, and acquired immunodeficiency syndrome (AIDS) generally require extraordinarily large amounts of nutrients to battle their disease. Likewise, young children who are ill require extra food to ensure that they have adequate nutrition to ensure normal growth and development. Food is crucial in combating both minor and major illnesses.

Many specific nutrients defend against disease. Calcium, a mineral found mainly in dairy products, is critical in the promotion of bone health and protection against osteoporosis. Fluoride, now added as a supplement to most water supplies, is crucial to tooth development. Iron is most commonly found in meats and protects against anemia. Folic acid prevents neural tube defects such as spina bifida in developing fetuses and has recently been found to protect against cardiovascular disease. In fact, almost every vitamin and mineral is known to be critical to one or more life processes. Nutritional specialists and medical practitioners are constantly studying the role each nutrient plays in protecting the body and investigating further possible cures.

See also **Dietetics; Digestion; Disease: Metabolic Diseases; Enteral and Parenteral Nutrition; Health and Disease; Hunger, Physiology of; Immune System Regulation and Nutrients; Intestinal Flora; Microbiology; Nutrient-Drug Interactions; Nutrients; Nutrition; Nutritionists; Safety, Food.**

BIBLIOGRAPHY

Duyff, Roberta Larson. *The American Dietetic Association's Complete Food and Nutrition Guide.* New York: Wiley, 1998.

Mahan, Kathleen L., and Marian Arlin, eds. *Krause's Food, Nutrition and Diet Therapy.* 10th ed. Philadelphia: W.B. Saunders; Harcourt Brace Jovanovich, 2000.

Margen, Sheldon, and the editors of the University of California at Berkeley Wellness Letter. *The Wellness Encyclopedia of Food and Nutrition: How to Buy, Store, and Prepare Every Variety of Fresh Food.* New York: Health Letter Associates, 1992.

Nelson, Jennifer K., Karen E. Moxness, Michael D. Jensen, and Clifford F. Gastineau. *Mayo Clinic Diet Manual: A Handbook of Nutrition Practice,.* 7th ed. St. Louis: Mosby, 1994.

Pennington, Jean A.T., Anna De Planter Bowes, and Helen N. Church. *Church's Food Values of Portions Commonly Used.* 17th ed. Philadelphia: Lippincott, Williams & Wilkins, 1998.

Zeman, Frances J., and Denise Ney. *Applications in Medical Nutrition Therapy.* 2nd ed. Englewood Cliffs, N.J.: Prentice Hall, 1995.

Jessica Rae Donze

MEDIEVAL BANQUETS.

Banquets during the European Middle Ages were often given on such important ecclesiastical feast days as New Year and Pentecost. But the greatest ones for which we have records were given for weddings and the coronation of kings or installation of bishops. There were also banquets for funerals, the coming of age (or knighting) of a son, or such lesser occasions as a harvest, the feast day of the patron saint of the local parish guild, various civic occasions, or even a tournament. Who was invited depended on the circumstances; wedding guests were apt to be family and close friends, as today, but many people of quite humble status would be included in festivities at a manor house.

This is not to say that banquets were frequent: they were very special occasions. Of the twenty-seven menus given in the fourteenth-century *Menagier de Paris*, a work compiled by an elderly Parisian for his young wife, only three are banquet menus: two for weddings and one for a civic event (Brereton and Ferrier, *Le Menagier de Paris*, pp. 175–190). The fifteenth-century English manor house of Dame Alice de Bryene, for which we have complete records of meals served over a period of a year (28 September 1412–28 September 1413), had only one major banquet that year, serving dinner to 160 people on New Year's Day. But it also provided fairly lavish meals to many of those involved in gathering the harvest in August, with several dinners for from forty to sixty guests, about twice the number usually present at Dame Alice's table.

Menus

The food served was quite different in quantity, and in some respects nature, from everyday meals, which for most people were apt to start with (or, for the poor, consist of) vegetable pottages (soups or stews). For a banquet, vegetables, if any—in England, they rarely appear on feast menus—were vastly outnumbered by a parade of roasts or fish of all kinds, and more elaborate dishes. Even the pottages were usually ones considered as special treats, such as frumenty (a wheat or barley pottage) with venison, or a *blancmange* of chicken or fish in spiced almond milk, usually also containing rice.

What is most striking to the modern eye about the menus for important banquets is the number of dishes served. An extreme example is the banquet celebrating George Neville's installation as Archbishop of York in 1465, which had a first course containing seventeen dishes, a second with twenty, and a third with twenty-three—not counting the "subtleties," discussed below. Three was the normal number of courses for the high (head) table at an English banquet, two for lesser guests. At the coronation feast of Richard III, there were three courses for high table, two for the lords and ladies, and one for commoners—who included the Lord Mayor of London!

Usually the dishes given to those not at high table were a selection of those in the three-course menu, including the most basic dishes. A feature of the (fictional) thirteenth-century banquet of Walter of Bibbesworth (Hieatt and Butler, *Curye on Inglysche*, pp. 2–3) is that there was enough venison and frumenty for the "whole household," clearly suggesting that not everyone got a taste of all the goodies that followed.

Manuscript 279 in the British Library's Harleian collection gives two-course menus for "the lower part of the

Depictions of medieval banquets are not common in secular art, but in religious paintings, biblical stories are often shown as medieval events. In this case, the Banquet of Herod, during which Salome serves up the head of John the Baptist, appears as a medieval banquet complete with table linens and customary serving vessels. From the Convent of Saint John the Baptist. © Sandro Vannini/CORBIS.

hall" for the banquets celebrating the installation of John Stafford, Bishop of Wells, and the wedding of the Earl of Devonshire (Austin, pp. 63–64). In the first case, the two-course menu is a selection of seventeen of the forty-seven dishes on the three-course menu, but the wedding banquet has less overlap, substituting several dishes not found on the three-course menu. These are not all humbler dishes: they include Caudel Ferry, a dish of sweetened wine thickened with eggs, resembling a modern *zabaglione*, and doucetys, custard tarts.

Distribution of Dishes

Those lower in rank not only got fewer courses but also were served smaller portions. Only the host and any exceptionally high-ranking guest got an individual serving; other high-ranking guests shared dishes (messes), usually two to a mess. If there were lower-ranking guests, as there would have been at a manor house, they were more apt to dine three or four to a mess. Sometimes those of higher rank were so served, to judge by a German banquet scene showing a number of crowned ladies at the side tables being served four to a mess.

This does not mean that those at high table ate all they were offered. The lord (or lady) of the house was expected to give some of the choice dishes to others. The thirteenth-century "household rules" for the Countess of Lincoln, attributed to Bishop Robert Grosseteste, advise that her "dish be so refilled and heaped up, especially with the delicacies, that you may courteously give from your dish to right and left to all at high table and to whom else it pleases you." The fifteenth-century Latin poem *Modus Cenandi* tells us empty plates are to be brought to the host so that he may distribute delicacies to others, and many recipes tell us to allow a whole chicken for a lord but only a quarter for commoners ("The Way of Dining," Furnivall, pp. 231–257).

If the Countess of Lincoln was to offer food from her dish to others at high table, clearly even those honored guests were not served everything on the menu. Just how many they had to choose from in each course probably varied according to the wealth and generosity of the host. The fourteenth-century poem *Sir Gawain and the Green Knight* describes lavishness that is highly unlikely in real life when it states that the members of King Arthur's court at a New Year's feast had so many dishes that it was hard to find room on the table for them: "Every two had twelve dishes / Good beer and bright wine both" (translation of lines 128–129).

Order of Service

Generally there was soup or other pottage to start with, followed by meats (on a meat day), with the more commonplace boiled or roasted meat and fowl first; on a fish day, there would be salt fish. More "delicate" items, such as roasted wild birds and fresh fish, came next, along with other dishes, then sweet or richer foods including tarts and fritters. This order is already apparent in that banquet described by Walter of Bibbesworth, although there the pottages follow rather than precede substantial meats. But some fifteenth-century menus for grand occasions were so expanded that each course might run the gamut from soup to fritters.

The basic order is spelled out in *Modus Cenandi*, which calls for pottage to be followed by meat of large animals and fowls, then smaller ones, and finally "better dishes" (*fercula dant meliora*). This "natural rule" is also claimed in the *Liber Cure Cocorum*—that for a feast featuring fowl, the larger ones come first, then "bakyn mete" (mainly pies), with more dainty foods at the end. A similar order is found in continental banquet menus, with a few differences.

French banquet menus varied in the number of courses, but the basic model seems to consist of four courses. The first course was much like an English first course, except that it excluded roasts. Roasts, with some accompaniments, came in the second course, and more elaborate dishes (*entremets*) in the third. Any or all of these courses might consist of only one or two dishes, as is the case with one of the *Menagier*'s menus for wedding feasts. As in England, the French last course (*dessert*) usually included sweet dishes and/or fruit, although it might also contain meat or fish dishes we would not consider dessert today.

Italian banquets ran to more courses: eight, ten, and sometimes twenty or more courses, generally with two or more dishes in each. Sometimes they began with pasta dishes, but otherwise the order was much like the French: soups and meats in sauces preceded roasts. German banquets also ran to a good many courses, but most of them consisted of a single dish.

Setting and Protocol of the Banquet

The menu order, however, does not give the complete order of the banquet. The first thing given to all diners was water and a towel for washing hands, usually before they were seated at the table. They were seated strictly according to rank at tables which, for a large banquet, were arranged in a U-shape. The host and especially honored guests sat at the head (high) table, and the others at the side tables. The nearer a guest was placed to the host, the greater the honor. The principal salt cellar, often a very elaborate affair, was placed at the host's right hand: hence the saying that others sat "below the salt." Salt for general use was distributed in piles on pieces of bread that served as individual salt cellars.

On the table, guests would find bread, and often a knife, a spoon, and a napkin, but not a fork: fingers or pieces of bread were used to pick up food not eaten with a spoon. "Trenchers" of coarse bread were cut and placed in front of each diner to receive pieces of meat or fish. Wine and/or ale would soon be poured, but before the meal was served, grace was said. Food was brought from the (often distant) kitchen; the German banquet scene referred to above shows a servant bringing a pile of covered dishes, much like those used in restaurants today to keep food warm. Roasts were carved and served in the hall.

French banquets usually started with an aperitif, or *assiette de table* (as against the *première assiette*, first course). *Grenache*, a fairly sweet wine (compare modern French aperitifs), seems to have been usual, with such accompaniments as fresh fruits, butter, salad, or small meat or fish pastries. While English banquet menus do not mention aperitifs, John Russell's *Boke of Nurture* (Furnivall, *The Babees Book*, p. 122) advises serving soft fruits before dinner, and they would seem to be the same fruits recommended for the aperitif course in France.

It is thus possible that aperitifs may have sometimes preceded the first course in England. The English menus often omit mention of how the meal ended, although we know the custom was the same as in France: a sweetened, spiced wine was usually served with wafers, fruit and cheese being an alternative way to end the banquet. After grace and the final handwashing, the table was cleared (or removed) and more wine and candied spices followed, at least for the higher-ranking diners.

Entertainment

Anyone who has seen medieval pictures of banqueting scenes will have noticed musicians almost invariably present, blowing fanfares to herald the beginning of a course or playing to entertain the diners while they eat. Other entertainers might include minstrels, jugglers, mummers, or players putting on a pageant or interlude, a form of theatrical entertainment referred to in *Sir Gawain and the Green Knight*. This poem is also one of many sources of evidence that the guests themselves did a lot of singing and dancing. Since the banqueting in the poem takes place in the Christmas season, much of the singing and dancing consists of carols. But a major source of entertainment at a medieval banquet was apt to be culinary in nature, at least in part. This was what was known in England as a subtlety, usually a creation of sugar, marzipan, or pastry depicting one or more birds, beasts, or people, brought out at the end of every course. At the coronation feast of Henry V, the subtlety at the end of the first course was a (confectionery?) swan surrounded by cygnets, all of whom carried messages in their bills that were lines of verse. But that was not enough. Twenty-four more swans followed, each one carrying the last line of the poem. Some subtleties were considerably simpler, including foods decorated with a motto or appropriate symbol, such as a coat of arms.

In France, subtleties were known as *entremets*, indicating their placement between courses. But the situation is complicated by the fact that *entremets* were originally just interesting dishes brought out between courses: the *Menagier* considers any elaborate dish to be in this category, including jellies and frumenty. This explains why frumenty with venison, which invariably appears at or near the beginning of the first course in England, occurs in the third or fourth course in France.

Still, the French also prepared elaborate *entremets* that are certainly in the category of subtleties. One of the manuscripts of the *Viandier de Taillevent* contains a number of these, some of which are edible: for example, the "helmeted cocks" for which roasted chickens are mounted on roasted piglets, with paper helmets and lances, probably wooden but covered with foil. But the *Viandier*'s "painted entremets" are strictly decorations, made of wood and other inedible materials, depicting such subjects as a knight in a swan boat, sailing on a cloth sea.

See also **Christianity: Western Christianity; Middle Ages, European; Renaissance Banquets.**

BIBLIOGRAPHY

Austin, Thomas, ed. *Two Fifteenth-Century Cookery-Books.* Early English Text Society. London: Oxford University Press, 1888. Reprint, 1964.

Brereton, Georgine E., and Janet M. Ferrier, eds. *Le Menagier de Paris.* Oxford: Clarendon Press, 1981.

Dale, M. K., trans., and Vincent B. Redstone, ed. *The Household Book of Dame Alice de Bryene of Acton Hall, Suffolk, September 1412–September 1413.* Ipswich, U.K.: Suffolk Institute of Archeology and History, 1984.

Furnivall, Frederick J., ed. *The Babees' Book: Medieval Manners for the Young.* Early English Text Society, 1868. Reprint, New York: Greenwood Press, 1969. Includes the "Bokes of Nurture" of Hugh Rhodes and John Russell, Wynkyn de Worde's "Boke of Kervyng," courtesy books, related poems.

Hammond, P. W. *Food and Feast in Medieval England.* Stroud, Gloucestershire, U. K.: Sutton, 1993.

Hieatt, Constance B., and Sharon Butler, eds. *Curye on Inglysch: English Culinary Manuscripts of the Fourteenth Century* (Including the Forme of Curye). Early English Text Society. London: Oxford University Press, 1985.

Hieatt, Constance B., Brenda Hosington, and Sharon Butler. *Pleyn Delit: Medieval Cookery for Modern Cooks.* 2nd ed. Toronto: University of Toronto Press, 1996.

Morris, Richard, ed. *Liber Cure Cocorum.* Berlin and London: Asher, 1862.

Pichon, Jerome, and Georges Vicaire, eds. *Le Viandier de Taillevent.* Paris: Techener, 1892. Reprint, Luzarches, France: Daniel Morcrette, n.d. Those needing English translations may prefer the 1988 edition edited by Terence Scully, but it does not include the 15th-century menus.

Redon, Odile, Françoise Sabban, and Silvano Serventi. *The Medieval Kitchen: Recipes from France and Italy.* Translated by Edward Schneider. Chicago: University of Chicago Press, 1998.

Scully, Terence. *The Art of Cookery in the Middle Ages.* Woodbridge, Suffolk, U.K.: The Boydell Press, 1998.

Tolkien, J. R. R., and R. V. Gordon, eds. *Sir Gawain and the Green Knight.* Oxford: Clarendon Press, 1925. Numerous translations are available.

Constance B. Hieatt

MEDITERRANEAN DIET. The Mediterranean diet is defined variously. It sometimes refers simply to the dietary patterns and social mores surrounding eating in the countries bordering the Mediterranean Sea. In nutritional parlance the meaning is somewhat more confined. It applies to the traditional diet of European countries on the Mediterranean as characterized by foods and by patterns of nutrient intake.

Italy, Greece, France, and Spain are particularly associated with the diet because they were involved in the several ecological studies of dietary patterns, lifestyles, and coronary artery heart disease in the 1950s and 1960s led by Ancel Keys of the University of Minnesota (Keys, 1970, 1995; Keys et al., 1954). These landmark studies associated the relatively high dietary fat intake in those countries with a much lower prevalence of coronary artery disease than in the United States or northern Europe. Since dietary fat was thought to be the major culprit in coronary artery disease, this seemed remarkable at the time. Later discoveries linked saturated fat and cholesterol rather than total fat to heart disease risk. Olive oil, high in monounsaturated fat, and fish, high in polyunsaturated fat, which constituted the majority of the fat in the Mediterranean diet, were associated with lower risk. Other aspects of the food and nutrient profiles and lifestyles (for example, more physical activity, less smoking, etc.) may have contributed to low disease risk as well.

Reasons for Interest

Originally, interest in the Mediterranean diet was based on that association with decreased risk of coronary artery disease. The traditional Mediterranean diet included liberal amounts of fruits, vegetables, legumes, grains, and wine; high amounts of monounsaturated fats; moderate consumption of alcohol; liberal amounts of fish; and low amounts of meat and milk products. The diet was accompanied by a lifestyle that involved a good deal of obligatory physical activity, no smoking, and a relaxed attitude toward life. The actual diets were usually moderate in energy for physical activities. They were also relatively low in saturated fats and sugars and relatively high in most of the fat- and water-soluble nutrients and phytochemicals.

In the late twentieth century nutritional scientists attempted to examine whether or not the Mediterranean diet is associated with decreased risks of other diseases. Where traditional diets conforming to the Mediterranean pattern are eaten, health benefits seem to be present. In addition, the increased American interest in fine dining, ethnic cuisine, and food habits contributed to the popularity of the Mediterranean diet.

Evolution of the Mediterranean Diet Concept

Keys popularized the Mediterranean diet in the early 1970s, and other nutritionists, culinary experts, and commodity groups subsequently advocated it. In the early 1990s, Oldways, a group dedicated to preserving traditional eating patterns, joined members of the Harvard School of Public Health in conducting a series of conferences and other activities to popularize the Mediterranean pattern. This group published a healthy-eating Mediterranean pyramid based on the dietary traditions of the region.

Mediterranean Diet Pyramid

The Mediterranean diet pyramid is available at the website. W. C. Willett, and colleagues described it at length in "Mediterranean Diet Pyramid," published in the *American Journal of Clinical Nutrition* in 1995. The pyramid puts bread, other grain products, and potatoes at the base. The second tier is vegetables, including beans, other legumes, and nuts, and fruits. Third is a shallow tier for olive oil, and next is a cheese and yogurt tier. All of these foods should be consumed daily.

Near the top of the pyramid are small blocks for foods consumed a few times a week, including fish, poultry, eggs, and sweets. At the peak of the pyramid are foods consumed only a few times a month, including red meats, fats, oils, and sweets. The pyramid is accompanied by a wineglass to indicate "wine in moderation" and a running stick figure with the headline "regular physical activity" (Wilson, 1998).

Acceptable Alternative or Dietary Imperative?

Is consumption of a Mediterranean diet mandatory for good health? The notion of a single Mediterranean cuisine has been criticized on the grounds that no single such diet exists and that to contend one does promotes stereotypes and fails to account for the dynamic nature of dietary changes. Also, diets in the Mediterranean region and elsewhere in Europe change rapidly and no longer reflect those of yesteryear. Many healthful dietary patterns are associated with diets designed to reduce chronic disease risks. It is not necessary to consume diets similar to those traditionally eaten in the Mediter-

ranean to stay healthy, but the Mediterranean diet is one alternative that provides an appropriate and healthful nutrient pattern.

Does the inclusion of Mediterranean-type foods make contemporary American diets healthier? This depends on a number of factors, chiefly how they are used. While decreased risk is associated with traditional Mediterranean diets, the patterns in these countries have changed a great deal since the early 1950s. They may not always provide all of the health advantages their traditional counterparts did, especially if food is eaten in excess. The specific health benefits of individual foods rather than the entire Mediterranean pattern are also unclear. Although most of the traditional foods are delicious and nutritious, other foods with similar nutrient compositions would seem to be equally effective. Therefore simply adding one or more "Mediterranean" foods to American diets does not necessarily provide positive health effects. The overall pattern in moderation has been linked to positive health outcomes.

During the late twentieth century, awareness of the considerable culinary and aesthetic advantages of the Mediterranean diet grew. Many staples of traditional Mediterranean diets have become popular and are widely available in the United States and other Western countries.

The plant-based Mediterranean diets of the early and mid-twentieth century were environmentally sound and responsible in the locales in which they flourished. Whether they are exportable and feasible on a large scale in other climates in non-Mediterranean countries is a matter of debate.

Traditional food habits typical of countries bordering the Mediterranean Sea in the mid-1950s have health and nutritional advantages. Guides for eating in the Mediterranean manner are readily available, but following their advice is not mandatory for good health.

See also **Africa: North Africa; Ancient Mediterranean Religions; Greece, Ancient; Greece and Crete; Italy; Rome and the Roman Empire.**

BIBLIOGRAPHY

Crotty, P. A. "Response to K. Dun Gifford." *Nutrition Today* 33 (1998): 244–245.

Ferro-Luzzi, A., and S. Sette. "The Mediterranean Diet: An Attempt to Define Its Present and Past Composition." *European Journal of Clinical Nutrition* 43, supp. 2 (1989): 12–29.

Gifford, K. Dun. "The Mediterranean Diet as a Food Guide: The Problem of Culture and History." *Nutrition Today* 33 (1998): 233–243.

Keys, Ancel. "Coronary Disease in Seven Countries." *Circulation* 41, supp. (1970): 1–21.

Keys, Ancel. "Mediterranean Diet and Public Health: Personal Reflection." *American Journal of Clinical Nutrition* 61, supp. (1995): 1321S–1323S.

Keys, Ancel, and Margaret Keys. *How to Eat Well and Stay Well the Mediterranean Way.* Garden City, N.Y.: Doubleday, 1975.

Keys, Ancel, et al. "Studies on Serum Cholesterol and Other Characteristics of Clinically Healthy Men in Naples." *Archives of Internal Medicine* 93 (1954): 328–335.

Nestle, M. "Mediterranean Diets: Historical and Research Overview." *American Journal of Nutrition* 61, supp. 13 (1995): 135–205.

Oldways website. "Mediterranean Diet Pyramid." Available at http://www.oldwayspt.orghtml/meet.htm.

Willett, W. C., F. Sacks, A. Trichopoulou, G. Dresher, A. Ferro-Luzzi, E. Helsing, and D. Trichopoulos. "Mediterranean Diet Pyramid: A Cultural Model for Healthy Eating." *American Journal of Clinical Nutrition* 61, supp. (1995): 1402S–1406S.

Wilson, C. S. "Mediterranean Diets: Once and Future?" *Nutrition Today* 33 (1998): 246–249.

Johanna Dwyer

MELANESIA. *See* **Pacific Ocean Societies.**

MENU. *See* **Places of Consumption; Restaurants.**

MESOAMERICA. *See* **Central America; Mexico; Mexico and Central America, Pre-Columbian; South America.**

MESOPOTAMIA, ANCIENT. Cuneiform clay tablets from ancient Mesopotamia, the region between the Euphrates and Tigris Rivers (mostly present-day Iraq), preserve a few kitchen recipes dating from the eighteenth to the seventeenth centuries B.C.E. Except for these texts, the oldest recipes known, our information about food supplies and their processing is indirect: on the one hand, dictionarylike lists of foodstuffs and, on the other, administrative texts recording the acquisition and expenditures of raw staples and kitchen supplies. A few proverbs and literary passages occasionally give additional details. Although an enormous number of names of edible plants, animals, condiments, and the like is known, in too many cases their exact identification is not possible. In contrast with Egypt, food remains of ancient Mesopotamia, other than bones and seeds, are extremely rare (Ellison et al.). In Mesopotamia, cooking was considered to mark, alongside clothing, the beginning of civilization. To quote an ancient Sumerian poem ("The Debate between the Ewe and the Barley," Alster and Vanstiphout) describing prehistoric times:

> The men of those remote days
> did not have bread to eat,
> did not have clothes to wear.
> People went around with naked limbs,
> ate grass with their mouths, like sheep,
> drank water from the gullies.

The onset of historical time is metonymically described as "when bread was eaten in the shrines of the land, when the ovens of the light were burning" ("Gilgamesh and Enkidu," George).

Lexical Information

Extensive word lists covering the botany, zoology, and material culture of southern Mesopotamia are a typical element of cuneiform literature. Among the oldest intelligible tablets (c. 2900 B.C.E.) there are lists of cereal and dry meat products, vegetables and alliaceous plants, fish, and birds. These lists were expanded through the centuries, culminating after the fourteenth century B.C.E. in long classical lists that were in use until the second century B.C.E. In an encyclopedic compilation of twenty-four tablets, of an average length of three hundred lines each, there is one dedicated to domestic animals (XIIIth tablet), one to wild ones (XIV), one to meat cuts (XV), one to plants (XVII), one to birds and fish (XVIII), and two to foods and drink in general (XXIII–XXIV). In detail, Tablet XXIII has three long sections:

1. soups
2. beer and brewery products
3. flours and bread

Tablet XXIV is more varied:

1. syrups and honey (12 entries)
2. oils and fats (53)
3. spices (11, also treated elsewhere in other tablets)
4. seeds (12, also treated elsewhere)
5. dairy products (34)
6. pulses (8)
7. emmer and wheat (10)
8. barley (67)
9. straws (10)
10. fruits: figs, raisins, pomegranates (10), dates (at least 38).
11. salt and condiments (12)
12. melons and cucumbers (8)

These lists are Sumero-Akkadian bilinguals (Mesopotamian culture was bilingual from its earliest days). Sumerian is an isolated language, but Akkadian is Semitic, a sister language of Hebrew and Arabic, and thus it is helpful in the identification of some food names, although too many uncertainties still remain. For instance, the names of the two condiments more often mentioned, after salt, in the texts of the end of the third millennium, are *gazi* and *zahili*. Neither of them is unambiguously identified.

Accounting

A meticulous and detailed accounting system is another typical feature of Mesopotamian civilization. Adminis-

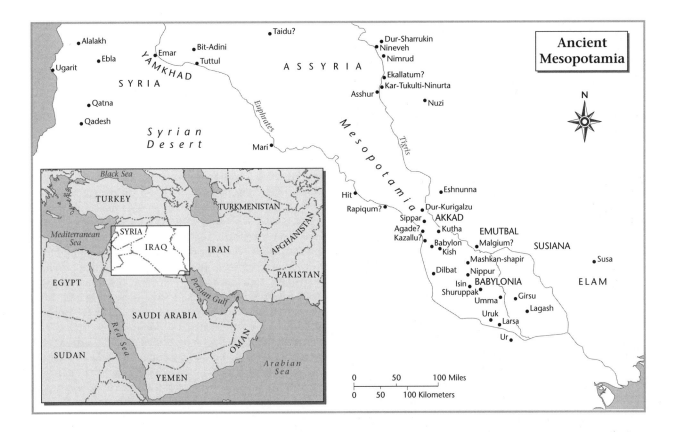

Ancient
Mesopotamia

trative tablets, found by the tens of thousands, give a general idea of the circulation of goods, of supplies, their origin, and their destination. A substantial number of these tablets deal with alimentation. Thus, for instance, an archive of c. 2400 B.C.E. from the town of Girsu gives us detailed information about the teams of fishermen, their catch classified by species, the amounts regularly provided to the governor's palace, and so on. By their nature, these accounts give better information about the tables of the upper classses, and very little about the diet of the working population. What is known about the latter comes from payment sheets that show that a workman would get about six liters of barley for a hard day's work. Women and children were given less.

Cereal Products

Locally grown cereals, mostly barley and relatively small amounts of emmer wheat and wheat, constituted the nutritional base in ancient Mesopotamia. Cereals were consumed in the form of bread, soups, and beer.

Bread. Bread (Sumerian, *ninda*; Akkadian, *akalu*) must have been made, at least in some cases, from leavened dough. There are no direct descriptions, but allusions to its bulky size and to leaving the dough overnight to rest seem to be indications of fermentation. One may assume, however, that in most cases the bread was made from unleavened dough shaped into flat, round loaves, similar to the present-day Near Eastern *khubuz*. This bread was baked in a peculiar, ubiquitous type of oven called an

öurin (Sumerian) or *tinûru* (Akkadian). It was a clay implement of cylindrical shape, tapering to a conical form in its upper part and with a side opening at its base. The whole was between 3 and 4 feet high. Once the oven was sufficiently heated, the flat, unleavened loaves were plastered to the side for baking. Salaries of the workers were often paid in bread. Roasted barley was sold in the streets and at the marketplace.

Alcoholic drinks. The Mesopotamian brewing process is relatively well known: the fermentation of a mixture of malt and barley bread, with the addition of sugar in the form of dates, produced different types of beer (Sumerian, *kaö*; Akkadian, *öikaru*) consumed by drinking with a straw from a communal jar. This beer had a short shelf life due to a certain instability caused, among other factors, by the absence of hops. Only in later periods, after the seventh century B.C.E., are there indications of the addition of an element, perhaps cuscuta, with a function similar to hops. Lists of supplies to brewers give the relative amounts of ingredients for various types of beer, but the absence of any indications about the processing does not allow any evaluation of the final product. The same ingredients can result in products of quite different taste and aspect, depending on the processing. A fermented beverage made of dates was also known. Chemical residues have identified some jars as wine containers in the late Uruk period, c. 3500 B.C.E. (Badler et al.). Wine, nevertheless, is mentioned rarely, and although there were some vineyards in the south, in the Lagash area and

This 4,000-year-old Sumerian tablet in the collection of the museum of the University of Pennsylvania is inscribed with one of the oldest known medical remedies. The ingredients are ground to a powder, then served to the patient in beer—a primitive form of medical dietetics. Other tablets in the same collection contain culinary recipes. © BETTMANN/CORBIS.

in the eastern hills toward Iran at the end of the third millennium, the climatic conditions were in general unfavorable for growing vines. The conditions were better in the north, in the hilly regions of Assyria. Some wine may have been imported from the northwest in Syria where the conditions were better. Consumption of alcoholic drinks, beer above all, seems to have been substantial. The rations given to the royal couriers and travelers consist always of bread and beer. There are lists of supplies for festive occasions, and drinking parties (*kaö-dé-a*, literally, "the pouring of beer") are mentioned. These parties—one could perhaps call them "receptions"—were celebrated for religious, social, or political reasons such as the visit of foreign ambassadors, often with the presence of the king and his court.

Animal Products

Meat, from sheep, goats, and cattle, seems to have been consumed regularly by the upper classes, only occasionally by the rest (Limet). Salted, dried strips of meat are mentioned already in the oldest texts. The use of meat must have been more extensive than sparse mentions in texts seem to suggest. The consumption of pork, initially frequent, seems to have declined after the beginning of the second millennium. The extreme south of Mesopotamia was an immense estuary with lagoons and marshes where fowl and fish were present in huge quantities. Fish is better documented for the older periods up to 3000 B.C.E. Whether the subsequent decline in fish consumption is real, for reasons of taste or availability, or apparent, due to administrative changes, is hard to say. Semitic populations seem to have held fish in low esteem. Fats for cooking were predominantly of animal origin (lard, tallow, suet); vegetable oils, presumably from sesame, were reserved mostly for cosmetic, ritual, and technical (tanning hides, cloth finishing, etc.) uses. For example, the total production of vegetable oil in the Girsu province in 2047 B.C.E. was some 14,445 liters, but none of it was earmarked for cooking. Dairy products, including clarified butter and various types of cheeses, were very important, but there are no indications about the consumption of fresh milk by adults; its preservation must have been severely limited by climatic conditions. Dairy fats were the only ones used in the confection of pastries. Hunting (enormous flocks of gazelles roamed the desert until a few centuries ago) is often described in royal commemorative texts but has left no trace in bureaucratic records and must have been a sport (lions and boars being a favorite prey) rather than a means to procure subsistence. As for more exotic foods, an Assyrian relief shows a servant carrying locusts impaled on long sticks.

Vegetables and Fruits

If close to a hundred names of green vegetables, as well as their parts and varieties, are known (from Tablet XVII of the compilation listed above), their use is poorly documented, due probably to their perishability, which made them unsuitable to be recorded by the bureaucratic administration. An exception are the alliaceous plants (onions, garlic, leeks), which are less perishable, and evidently much esteemed and consumed in large amounts by all levels of the population. There are detailed accounts of the production of onion beds. Lettuce was particularly appreciated, judging from its mention in literary texts. The names of many spices are known but, as usual, their identification is extremely difficult. The fruits more frequently mentioned are apples, figs, and pomegranates; the first two were often dried, and a ring of dried apples from the royal tombs of Ur (c. 2700 B.C.E.) has been exceptionally preserved (Ellison et al.).

The date palm occupied a place apart. It grew easily in extensive gardens on the southern plain and the tree production was the object of careful bookkeeping. Besides the fruit, which was eaten dried and was a source of a fermented drink, most parts of the palm were useful for making ropes, baskets, and ceiling beams. Date syrup seems to have been the main sweetener; beekeeping is

RECIPES FROM ANCIENT MESOPOTAMIA

Genuine cooking recipes, written about 1700 B.C.E., have been preserved on three cuneiform tablets in the collections of Yale University and are available in a professional edition and commentary by Jean Bottéro. One of them gives instructions to prepare "twenty-one meat soups and four vegetable ones" in a rather concise style. The other two are much more detailed, but the text is less well preserved. They are almost completely devoted to the preparation of fowl dishes. It is quite possible that these cuneiform tablets are survivors of a large collection of culinary works. The style of cooking described represents probably the activities of the cooks of some royal court, perhaps from the later part of the Larsa Dynasty (ended 1763 B.C.E.) since it appears from older texts that birds were a favorite dish at the queen's table. The interpretation of these recipes is hampered by the usual uncertainties in the identification of the spices and other ingredients, as well as in the meaning of some highly technical terms. Follow the translations of the recipes (adapted from Bottéro, 1995) for a simple soup and for a complicated dish of wild pigeon (additional comments in square brackets):

1. To prepare goat's kid soup. Singe the head, legs, and tail [the parts of the animal to be used], the meat will be ready. Prepare the water, add fat, onions, *samîdu* [a type of flour preparation, or a spice], leeks, and garlic bound with blood, crushed *kisimmu* [a type of cheese or coagulated milk], and an adequate amount of wild onion [*Allium desertorum*].

The addition of blood (of what animal is not specified, the kid's presumably here) as a binding and flavoring agent is frequent in these recipes. Amounts and cooking times are left to the experience of the cook.

2. To prepare wild pigeons (*amursânu*) in broth. Slaughter the wild pigeon and, after soaking it in hot water, pluck it. Once plucked, wash it with cold water and skin the neck, leaving attached to the body the skin with its meat. Cut out the ribs. Open the underbelly and remove the gizzard. Wash and soak the bird in cold water. Open and peel the membrane from the gizzard. Cut open

and chop the intestines. To cook in broth, first put in a kettle the gizzard, intestines, and head, as well as a piece of mutton [fat], and cook it. Remove from the fire. Wash well [the bird] with cold water and wipe carefully. Sprinkle with salt and assemble all the ingredients. Prepare the broth, adding a piece of fat from which the gristle has been removed, some vinegar, *samîdu* flour, leek and garlic, mashed with onion, and if needed add some water. Let simmer. When it is cooked, pound and mash together leek, garlic, *andahöu* [a kind of onion], and *kisimmu* to add to the dish [follows a damaged passage in which apparently the pigeon is disjointed and the legs are covered with dough]. When everything is cooked, remove the meat from the fire, and before the broth cools, serve it accompanied with garlic, greens, and vinegar. Carve and serve. The broth can be consumed later by itself.

The kind of wild pigeon of this recipe is known to have been regularly supplied centuries earlier to the royal kitchens for its consumption by the queen and ladies of the court. These recipes also include instructions to make a sort of bread to accompany the fowl dishes. It was made of sifted *sasku* flour, a sort of semolina, mixed with milk and condimented with *siqqu*, a salty paste made from fish and crustaceans, akin to the garum of the Romans. It was kneaded "being careful that it remains pliant," and condimented with leek and garlic. Part was formed to line the bottom of the serving plate, and part to make small loaves (*sebetu*). It was left to rise, and then baked on the bread oven already described.

These are at present the oldest known recipes. Nothing has survived from the following centuries, except for a short isolated recipe written in a small tablet probably from the fifth or fourth centuries B.C.E. It describes the preparation of a spiced liquid in which to cook meat:

The right amount of roasted *nuhurtu*, roasted [seeds of] mustard(?), roasted cuscuta, and roasted cumin. Boil slowly with [dried] cucumber in 6 quarts of water until it is reduced to 1 quart. Filter it. Kill the animal [to be cooked] and throw it [in the liquid].

This is a general-purpose cooking liquid for meat. The recipe illustrates once more the problems raised by the difficulties in identifying the ingredients.

---

not documented until very late times, and whenever the texts mention "honey," it must be generally assumed that it refers to date syrup. There are isolated allusions to mushrooms, but their consumption seems to have been considered a barbaric custom: the stereotyped ethnic description of the Bedouin nomads has them digging for truffles. Present-day Bedouins are still very fond of the

white truffle (*Tarfezia leonis*) and of a smaller red-brown one, growing in the desert after rain from February to April.

Religious and Social Uses of Food
The sacrifice of cattle and smaller animals was an essential part of many religious rites, generally accompanied

Bas-relief on the ancient Assyrian throne of Shalmaneser III depicting offering bearers carrying various items of food. Courtesy of the Iraq Museum, Baghdad. © GIANNI DAGLI ORTI/CORBIS.

by bread, pastry, and beer libations. The only food taboo mentioned is the abstinence from fish and leeks by some type of priests (and by some evil spirits). Banquets and dining halls, but with very vague information about the dishes served in them, are mentioned in the mythological and historical texts. Meat dishes (lamb mostly, rarely beef) and beer are invariably included in the menu.

In 879 B.C.E., the Assyrian king Assurnasirapli II boasts, on an inscription on a stele (Grayson, pp. 288–293), of having given a gigantic banquet, on the occasion of the inauguration of his new palace, for no fewer than 69,574 guests, from workers to dignitaries, local and foreign. The supplies for this banquet give an idea of the requirements of the Assyrian gourmet, leaving aside the question of the historical precision of the round numbers: 1,000 oxen, 1,000 calves, 14,000 sheep, 1,000 lambs, 500 deers, 500 gazelles, 1,000 large birds, 500 geese, 500 cranes, 1,000 mesukku-birds, 1,000 qaribu-birds, 10,000 pigeons, 10,000 turtle doves, 10,000 smaller birds, 10,000 fish, 10,000 akbiru (a small rodent), 10,000 eggs, 10,000 containers of beer, 10,000 goatskins of wine, 10,000 jars of a hot condiment, 1,000 boxes of fresh vegetables, and large quantities of honey, pistachios, roasted grain, pomegranates, dates, cheeses, olives, and all kinds of spices. These are the highlights of a list thirty-six lines long on the stele.

Kitchens and Utensils

Professional cooks (Sumerian, *muhaldim*; Akkadian, *nuhatimmu*), assigned to palaces, temples, and other institutions, are known from remote antiquity. The common name for the kitchen was "the cooks' house," or "the cooks' room." The most frequent type of bread oven, often encountered in the ruins, has already been described

above. The names of larger ovens, called *udun* and *kir*, are also known, but their physical features are difficult to ascertain. Although remains of large ovens and fireplaces of various types have been found in archeological excavations, there is no comprehensive study so far of their characteristics. Cooking and serving utensils, from large kettles to soup bowls, are known by name, but it is not easy to assign these names to the various types of clay and metal containers recovered by the archaeologists.

Recipes

There was a tradition according to which the kitchen recipes came from Enki, the god of wisdom and knowledge. Thus, one reads in a literary text: "King (?)ulgi will have a banquet in his pleasant palace after large beautiful dates mixed with raisins, butter from the holy sheepfold, and the sweetest (date) honey have been worked together, and the sweets have been mixed with fine flour, according to the good instructions of god Enki" (unpublished translation). This passage describes the preparation of a very traditional type of cake (Sumerian, *ninda-ì-dé-a*; Akkadian, *mirsu*). The administrative "shopping lists" give at times the ingredients for a given dish or confection. From them one can infer that this cake required, for instance, the following proportion of ingredients: fine flour: three cups; clarified butter: one-fourth cup; dates: one cup. Small amounts of cheese or raisins were occasionally added. This of course is not really a recipe; it tells what, but not how.

See also **Food Archaeology; Greece, Ancient; Middle East**.

BIBLIOGRAPHY

Alster, Bendt, and Herman L. J. Vanstiphout. "Lahar and Aönan." *Acta Sumerologica* 9 (1987) 1–43.

Badler, Virginia R., Patrick E. McGovern, and Donald L. Glusker. "Chemical Evidence for a Wine Residue from Warka (Uruk) Inside a Late Uruk Period Spouted Jar." *Baghdader Mitteilungen* 27 (1996): 39–43.

Bottéro, Jean. "Küche." In *Reallexikon für Assyriologie* 6 (1961): 227.

Bottéro, Jean. "The Culinary Tablets at Yale." *Journal of the American Oriental Society* 107 (1987): 11.

Bottéro, Jean. *Textes culinaires Mesopotamiens* (Mesopotamian culinary texts). Mesopotamian Civilizations VI. Winona Lake, Ind.: Eisenbrauns, 1995.

Ellison, Rosemary. "Methods of Food Preparation in Mesopotamia (c. 3000–600 B.C.)." *Journal of the Economic and Social History of Orient* 27 (1984): 89–98.

Ellison, Rosemary, Jane Renfrew, Don Brothwell, and Nigel Seeley. "Some Food Offerings from Ur, Excavated by Sir Leonard Woolley, and Previously Unpublished." *Journal of Archaeological Science* 5 (1978): 167–177.

George, Andrew. *The Epic of Gilgamesh*. Harmondsworth: Allen Lane, The Penguin Press, 1999.

Gomi, Tohru. "On Dairy Productivity at Ur in the Late Ur-III Period." *Journal of the Economic and Social History of Orient* 33 (1980): 1–42.

Grayson, A. Kirk. *Assyrian Rulers of the Early First Millennium B.C. (1119–859)*. Royal Inscriptions of Mesopotamia 2/I. Toronto: University of Toronto Press, 1991.

Limet, Henri. "The Cuisine of Ancient Sumer." *Biblical Archaeologist* 50 (1987) 132–141.

Limet, Henri. "La consommation de viande en Mésopotamie ancienne (vers 2000 av. J.-C.)." In *L'animal dans l'alimentation humaine: critères de choix*, Anthropologica Special No. 2, edited by Liliane Bodson, pp. 51–38. Paris: J.-D. Vigne, 1988.

Salonen, Armas. "Die Öfen der alten Mesopotamier." *Baghdader Mitteilungen* 3 (1964): 100–121.

Miguel Civil

METABOLIC IMPRINTING AND PROGRAMMING.

It has long been recognized that environmental influences during early development have profound and long-lasting effects on humans and other animals. Metabolic imprinting describes a subset of such effects, comprising subtle but persistent responses to prenatal and early postnatal nutrition. This article will describe how the term "metabolic imprinting" was conceptualized and will provide some examples of putative metabolic imprinting phenomena to illustrate the important roles they may play in human health.

Background

A growing body of human epidemiologic data suggests that the quality and quantity of nutrients available during prenatal and early postnatal development can affect susceptibility to various adult-onset chronic diseases, including cardiovascular disease, type-II diabetes, and hypertension. Some of the earliest indications of such relationships were gleaned from ecological data showing a regional correlation between infant mortality and mortality from cardiovascular disease several decades later. These data led researchers to postulate that a poor environment that causes high infant mortality could also impair the development of surviving infants, increasing their susceptibility to cardiovascular disease in adulthood.

David Barker's group in the United Kingdom bolstered the ecological data by collecting retrospective data on individuals. By linking obstetric records from the early 1900s with mortality records from several decades later, his group found that individual birth weight was related inversely to adult cardiovascular disease mortality. In numerous populations in industrialized countries, similar relations were later found between birth weight and morbidity and mortality associated with cardiovascular disease, coronary heart disease, and type-II diabetes. Viewing birth weight as a proxy for the quality of the prenatal environment, these relations were interpreted to indicate that prenatal factors (such as maternal nutrition) could "program" the development of adult chronic disease. Extensive epidemiologic research investigating this so-called "fetal origins" hypothesis is underway. However, the inherent weaknesses of human epidemiologic research in this field, including the long period of follow-up from exposure to outcome and inability to accurately adjust for various potential confounding variables, limit our ability to draw causal inferences from epidemiologic relations alone.

The Concept of Metabolic Imprinting

It remains unknown whether developmental responses to fetal and early postnatal nutrition are major determinants of chronic disease susceptibility in humans. Understanding the biological mechanisms underlying such phenomena in appropriate animal models should help to gauge their potential importance to human health. The term "metabolic imprinting" was proposed to provide a framework for the investigation of such biological mechanisms. Metabolic imprinting encompasses adaptive responses to specific nutritional conditions early in life that are characterized by 1) susceptibility limited to a critical ontogenic period early in development (the critical window), 2) a persistent effect lasting into adulthood, 3) a specific and measurable outcome, and 4) a dose-response relationship between exposure and outcome (Waterland and Garza, 1999). "Programming" has been used as a more general term to describe effects that occur when "an early stimulus or insult, operating at a critical or sensitive period, results in a permanent or long-term change in the structure or function of the organism" (Lucas, 1991; p. 39). However, imprinting, first used to describe the setting of animal attachment behavior based on early experience, more effectively conveys the important characteristics of the phenomena under consideration. As Konrad Lorenz noted, ethological imprinting occurs only during "a quite definite period" in the animal's life and the imprinted behavior "cannot be 'forgotten'" (Lorenz, pp. 126 and 127). The remainder of this section will discuss the most salient features of metabolic imprinting.

Adaptive responses are those that contribute to survivability of the organism. Limiting the scope of metabolic imprinting to adaptive responses excludes persistent effects of severe nutritional deficiencies or exposure to toxic levels of specific nutrients during critical stages of development. For example, it is well established that neural tube defects can be caused by maternal folate deficiency during early embryonic development. Also, fetal exposure to pharmacological levels of vitamin A can cause teratogenesis. Clearly, both of these examples represent persistent effects of early nutrition, but neither is adaptive. It may seem illogical to propose that adaptive responses putatively characterized as metabolic imprinting could contribute to adult chronic disease susceptibility. However, adaptive responses in early development are not necessarily beneficial throughout an individual's life. A metabolic response that increases prenatal or early postnatal survivability in one environment may prove detrimental to the individual in a different environment or at a later ontogenic stage.

The "critical window" criterion in the definition of metabolic imprinting limits consideration to effects resulting from nutritional perturbation of developmental pathways. Mammalian development occurs in stages. At each stage, specific processes must be completed in a limited time frame to enable progression to the next stage. A given nutritional stimulus may have diverse effects, depending on the developmental processes underway during the stage at which the stimulus is applied. Therefore, each specific metabolic imprinting phenomenon should have a finite critical window.

To illustrate, the fertilized mammalian egg proceeds through a series of reductive cell divisions (cleavage) to the formation of the three germ layers (gastrulation), to the establishment of organ rudiments (organogenesis), to the stage of histogenesis, when cellular differentiation results in the formation of specialized cell types and, lastly, to metabolic differentiation, during which the specialized functions of the different cell types proceed toward functional maturation. Organogenesis requires inductive interactions between adjacent germ layers. Hence, during organogenesis, localized concentrations of diverse nutrients or their metabolites could alter organ structural development by interacting with these signaling systems. As another example, the wave of rapid cell proliferation that follows cellular differentiation in various organs puts a high demand on the nutrients necessary for the synthesis of cellular components. Transient deficiencies (or excesses) of these food-derived precursors during limited periods of rapid cell proliferation could result in permanent alterations in cell number and, hence, metabolic activity.

Examples of Putative Metabolic Imprinting Phenomena

It should be emphasized that metabolic imprinting remains a theoretical construct intended to provide a framework for investigations into the biological mechanisms linking early nutrition and adult chronic disease susceptibility. Research is underway to identify candidate phenomena that satisfy the criteria of metabolic imprinting. This discussion therefore focuses on candidate phenomena that appear most consistent with metabolic imprinting.

Retrospective studies linking birth weight to adult chronic disease outcomes represent by far the most numerous class of epidemiologic data in support of metabolic imprinting. Studies of many different populations have found that individual birth weight is related to adult risk of coronary heart disease, hypertension, type-II diabetes, stroke, overweight, and other disorders. In most cases, there is a simple inverse correlation, with adult disease risk increasing as birth weight decreases. Some adult outcomes, such as type-II diabetes, appear to follow a "U-shaped" relation with birth weight, with adult risk increasing at very low and very high birth weights.

Proponents of the fetal origins hypothesis conclude that these examples demonstrate that nutritional status during critical periods of fetal life influences the development of diverse organ systems, leading to effects on adult chronic disease risk. As discussed above, however, there are many limitations to the interpretation of such long-term retrospective epidemiologic studies. Moreover, there are several reasons that birth weight is not an ideal proxy for fetal nutritional status. For example, maternal nutritional status during pregnancy is just one of many factors that determine infant birth weight. Also, an individual's genetic makeup could influence both fetal growth and adult susceptibility to a specific disease, leading to an association between birth weight and adult chronic disease that is not mediated by fetal nutritional environment. Conversely, it is likely that fetal nutrition can affect metabolic development without affecting birth weight. Hence, a misplaced focus on birth weight as the major early-life predictor of adult chronic disease susceptibility could result in a gross underestimation of the importance of metabolic imprinting to human health.

For these reasons, studies of human populations with documented exposure to extreme nutritional conditions in early life are an important source of support for the metabolic imprinting hypothesis. The best characterized of such populations comprises individuals exposed perinatally to starvation during the Dutch famine of 1944–1945. In 1976 Gian-Paolo Ravelli and co-workers published an analysis of Dutch military draft induction records of 300,000 young men and found that, compared to those born in non–famine-stricken control areas, men who were exposed to famine conditions at some time during the first six months of fetal development experienced an 80 percent higher prevalence of overweight. In contrast, those exposed to famine during the last trimester of gestation and/or the first five postnatal months experienced a 40 percent lower prevalence of overweight. Perinatal famine exposure was later related to adult glucose tolerance in several hundred individuals from the Dutch famine cohort. During standardized glucose tolerance tests, plasma glucose concentrations were higher in adults who had been exposed prenatally to famine than in individuals born before the famine. Because the timing, severity, and geographical extent of nutritional deprivation caused by the Dutch famine were well documented, these studies are not weakened by the methodological issues inherent to observational studies predicated on birth weight.

In the only large-scale experimental trial designed to investigate metabolic imprinting–like phenomena in humans, Alan Lucas and co-workers randomized preterm infants to receive standard infant formula, a special preterm formula, or banked breast milk during the first month of postnatal life. At the start of the trial, none of the feeding alternatives were clearly superior for preterm infants, allowing ethical randomization of early diet in this cohort of several hundred individuals. In this ongoing study, long-term follow-up has already shown that subtle differences in early postnatal diet affect cognitive development and bone mineralization in childhood. Conversely, childhood growth, body composition, and blood pressure were not associated with the early dietary exposure.

Controlled experimental investigations in animal models have demonstrated the biological plausibility of metabolic imprinting. Such studies have confirmed that subtle variation in prenatal and also early postnatal nutrition can affect adult outcomes including glucose-stimulated insulin secretion, blood pressure, body weight, organ structure, and lipid metabolism. Guided by the framework of metabolic imprinting, future animal studies of candidate phenomena should identify the tissues responsible for their effect persistence and characterize their critical windows to generate testable hypotheses about the effects of early nutrition on specific developmental processes.

Significance

Subtle nutritional perturbation of developmental pathways may have an important impact on human health. The immediate challenge for researchers in this field is to elucidate the specific mechanisms by which nutrition influences biological development in appropriate animal models. Doing so will suggest specific areas of focus for future research into the biological links between early nutrition and adult metabolism in humans. Clearly, the potential importance of gaining this information is great, especially in populations that continue to be at high risk for marginal nutritional status in early life.

BIBLIOGRAPHY

Barker, David J. P. *Mothers, Babies and Disease in Later Life*. London: BMJ Publishing Group, 1994. Summarizes much of the data leading to development of the fetal origins hypothesis.

Kalthoff, Klaus. *Analysis of Biological Development*. New York: McGraw-Hill, Inc., 1996.

Lucas, Alan. "Programming by Early Nutrition: An Experimental Approach." *The Journal of Nutrition* 128 (1998): 401S–406S. Describes the ongoing study of preterm infants randomized to receive normal formula, preterm formula or human milk during the first postnatal month.

Lucas, Alan. "Programming by Early Nutrition in Man." In *The Childhood Environment and Adult Disease*. CIBA Foundation Symposium 156. Chichester, U.K. and New York: Wiley, 1991.

Lorenz, Konrad. *Studies in Human and Animal Behaviour*, volume I, translated by Robert Martin. London: Methuen, 1970.

Ravelli, Gian-Paolo, Zena A. Stein, and Mervyn W. Susser. "Obesity in Young Men after Famine Exposure in Utero and Early Infancy." *The New England Journal of Medicine* 295 (1976): 349–353. Historic study describing the Dutch famine of 1944–1945 and demonstrating relationships between early famine exposure and adult overweight.

Waterland, Robert A., and Cutberto Garza. "Potential Mechanisms of Metabolic Imprinting That Lead to Chronic Disease." *The American Journal of Clinical Nutrition* 69 (1999): 179–197. Reviews data in support of metabolic imprinting and discusses potential underlying biological mechanisms.

Robert A. Waterland

METAPHOR, FOOD AS.

"The essence of metaphor is understanding and experiencing one kind of thing in terms of another" (Lakoff and Johnson, p. 5). Many aspects of social and cultural life are talked about and experienced in terms of food. This kind of comparison occurs easily because of the systematic organization of food and food habits within each culture. Through language and through daily practices, food is ordered in terms of the categorization of foods, the organization of food production and consumption, and the linguistic expressions about food and eating. Cultural systems of food and food habits form conceptual frameworks that are metaphorical in nature. In other words, food, as anthropologist Claude Lévi-Strauss tells us, is good to think with.

Food can serve as a metaphor for family, religion, sex, gender, social position, and group identity, among other things. These principal metaphors appear across cultures, but are organized locally as different peoples speak of different foods and equate them with specific elements of their lives. The following overview of food as metaphor provides explanations of the different metaphorical constructs with a variety of specific local examples.

Food as a Metaphor for Religion

Food is a powerful metaphor for sacrifice, order, obedience, self-discipline, purity, generosity, and other key values in religious and ritual life around the world. Special rules and practices concerning dietary standards and ceremonial behavior distinguish and make concrete complex values and belief systems.

For example, Jewish food practices revolve around kashruth, the dietary laws outlined in the Old Testament books of Deuteronomy and Leviticus. Kashruth prohibits the consumption of pork, shellfish, reptiles, and amphibians and calls for the strict separation of dairy and meat foods. Anthropologist Mary Douglas interprets this regulation of food as part of a larger process of ordering the natural world according to social and moral precepts. By systematizing everyday experience into categories of clean and unclean, kashruth provides a practical foundation for understanding theological classifications and the proper relationship to God. The value of order is reiterated in the Passover seder, a ritual meal that metaphorically reenacts the Jews' flight from slavery in Egypt.

In the Hindu belief system, food is a metaphor for body, mind, and spirit. Daily and ceremonial rituals of food-giving demonstrate the values of generosity and selfless service. Fasting and dietary self-control are metaphors for mental clarity and religious authority, while prohibited or improperly prepared foods are believed to cause spiritual unrest and poor health. Anthropologist R. S. Khare notes that Hindu holy people are highly sensitive to individual foods and must strictly monitor their diets in order to maintain physical, mental, and spiritual balance.

Food as a Metaphor for Sex and Gender

Ideas about "Man the Hunter" and "Woman the Gatherer" permeate understandings of gender in contemporary Western societies. The man who "brings home the bacon" is a competent provider for his family; "he's a meat and potatoes man" connotes a hearty appetite and robust character. These and other sayings connect masculine qualities such virility and strength with the provisioning and consumption of meat. After all, "real men don't eat quiche."

Among the indigenous peoples of Papua New Guinea, food production, gender relations, and human reproduction are intertwined in a metaphorical cycle of energy exchange. Men are credited with cultivating staple crops to meet the nutritional needs of the community, while women's task is to raise children, supplying the next generation of "manpower." In this context, men's agricultural practices are understood in terms of feminine procreative abilities. Watering the crops is likened to breast-feeding, and men who are actively cultivating their gardens are subject to the same food taboos as pregnant and nursing women (Meigs).

Food is not only used to communicate ideas about gender roles; it can also express overtly sexual qualities. Food acts as a visual metaphor for sex in many art forms. It can convey voluptuousness and sensuality (a lingering shot of ripe fruit), temptation and the arousal of desire (oysters as aphrodisiacs), and consummation and fulfillment (sharing food as an exchange of bodily juices). Food is also used in linguistic metaphors when food items are compared to body parts in scatological references to sexual activity, and, more generally, as terminology for sexual "appetite," "hunger," and pleasure is common also for food and eating.

Food as Metaphor for Family

Food can be used metaphorically to talk about and enact various elements of social interaction and organization, one of which is the family. Cross-culturally, the family represents many things. It is a basic form of social organization, an economic unit, and a structure for social and cultural reproduction.

In some societies, growing certain crops, distributing food, and preparing food are the responsibility of one side or another of the family—of the woman's side of the family in some societies (Richards), of the man's side in others (Weiner). Food production and preparation represent and enact the extended family networks that structure kinship-based models of social organization.

In many contemporary Western societies, the nuclear family is often the basic economic unit, in which money for food provisioning and then food preparation are centered. The way people organize their food and meal-related activities also helps define the roles of individuals in the household. These roles may be gendered or age-dependent. The pleasure of eating and serving food becomes a metaphor for the structure and emotion of family relationships (Ochs et al.). A family discussion about food preparation tasks, or about who eats what and why, may also actually be a more concrete means of addressing issues of household division of labor, family power structures, and family dynamics.

When family commensality takes place around a table, or around a cooking hearth, the place for the meal is a metaphor for family solidarity. Indeed, in many cultures the hearth is thought of as the center of the home—home in the sense of family space.

The affective and sensory aspects of food, as well as shared experiences of foods, can help cement the family unit via associations of certain foods with specific people and events. For example, the smell of a roast turkey may evoke fond memories of a time when family comes together. In this way, tasting and reminiscing about food items metaphorically bring up family members and family bonds without explicitly mentioning them. Recipes and food-related stories also provide links between generations and help ensure the transmission and reproduction of cultural practices and family, ethnic, local, and national identities.

Food as Metaphor for Social Hierarchy

Regulation of food and food habits is a persistent metaphor for social stratification. Such varied systems as class, caste, and status can all be thought of in terms of food. For example, food as class positioning arises in discussions of people and their consumption patterns. In the consumer societies of North America and Europe, eating caviar and foie gras and drinking expensive Champagne are seen as consuming luxury goods and are associated with the wealth of the upper classes. In certain Andean countries, the kind of starch eaten most frequently marks overlapping boundaries of class and ethnicity, with potatoes consumed by poor, rural farmers of Native American descent and white flour and bread consumed mainly by the more wealthy urbanites of European descent (Weismantel).

Food as Group Identity: Local and National Identities

The idea of food as metaphor for the eater's identity comes across clearly in popular parlance. For example, the expression "You are what you eat" goes beyond the physical realities of the human digestive process and nutrient absorption. It compares one's existence to one's eating habits and can extend to others' existences—and, hence, to people's perceptions of others and their ways of labeling others.

National identity. People's nationalities are sometimes spoken of in terms of the foods they eat. Not always positive, food stereotyping can be pejorative, as in the case of the French being called "frogs" by the British and the British being referred to as "roastbeefs" by the French. While food metaphors can deconstruct identities, they also construct them.

Anthropologist Emiko Ohnuki-Tierney analyzes Japan's elaborate mythic histories, rituals, and public debates about rice as attempts to define the essence of a distinctive national identity. As a central metaphor in Japanese culture, rice is surrounded by a complex system of beliefs: each grain of rice is a living being with its own soul; "the Deity of the Rice Paddies" is a benevolent, peaceful figure embedded in the agrarian landscape; the soul of the deity is manifested in the perfection of rice grains; eating rice is a religious act as the consumer ingests the spiritual energy of rice and the rice god. Rice is also a focus of artistic and literary production: writers extol the beauty of rice, and painters idealize agrarian society. In daily life, a meal is not complete without rice, women are judged by their ability to cook it, and family cohesiveness is expressed by serving rice from a communal bowl. Efforts to restrict the importation of "foreign" rice reveal the extent to which Japanese notions of self- and national-identity are intertwined with this staple food.

Local identity. Preserving local food habits both practically and metaphorically promotes the survival of a variety of local and ethnic groups because community members experience and transmit their local identity in terms of food-related experiences. For example, in some minority cultures of the southeastern United States, such as the Gullah of South Carolina and Georgia, community-centered storytelling, recipe-sharing, cooking instruction, everyday food preparation techniques, and festival rituals maintain cultural identity by preserving the specificities of rice-based foodways (Beoku-Betts).

Sometimes local identities are constructed or maintained in the face of more encompassing identities. In this sense, food is a metaphor not only for the specific local identity in question, but also for political and cultural resistance. Some French farmers promote local, artisanally produced foods against the pressures of globalization in the food industry. For example, José Bové has made headlines in the United States and in Europe by leading demonstrations against international food companies, such as McDonald's, and by promoting his locally produced Roquefort cheese outside the doors of international trade meetings.

Conclusion

Not just figures of speech, metaphors express relationships of ideas, using the terms of one conceptual system to achieve understanding of another. As frameworks for thinking about the world, metaphors are shaped by their cultural context. Yet food-based metaphors crop up around the globe. Food and food systems are "good to think," often serving as a metaphor for complex issues such as family, religion, sex and gender, social position, and group identity.

See also **Gender and Food**; **Religion and Food**; **Sex and Food**; **Women and Food**.

BIBLIOGRAPHY

Beoku-Betts, Josefine. "We Got Our Way of Cooking Things: Women, Food, and the Preservation of Cultural Identity among the Gullah." *Gender and Society* 9, no. 5 (1995): 535–555.

Bourdieu, Pierre. *Distinction: A Social Critique of the Judgement of Taste.* Cambridge, Mass.: Harvard University Press, 1984.

Douglas, Mary. *Purity and Danger: An Analysis of Concepts of Pollution and Taboo.* London: Routledge and Kegan Paul, 1966.

Feeley-Harnik, Gillian. *The Lord's Table: The Meaning of Food in Early Judaism and Christianity.* Washington, D.C.: Smithsonian Institution Press, 1994.

Khare, R. S. *The Eternal Food: Gastronomic Ideas and Experiences of Hindus and Buddhists.* SUNY Series in Hinduism. Albany: State University of New York Press, 1992.

Lakoff, George, and Mark Johnson. *Metaphors We Live By.* Chicago: University of Chicago Press, 1980.

Lévi-Strauss, Claude. *The Raw and the Cooked.* Translated by John and Doreen Weightman. New York: Harper & Row, 1969.

Meigs, Anna S. *Food, Sex, and Pollution: A New Guinea Religion.* New Brunswick, N.J.: Rutgers University Press, 1984.

Ochs, Elinor, C. Pontecorvo, and A. Fasulo. "Socializing Taste." *Ethnos* 61 (1996): 7–46.

Richards, Audrey I. *Land, Labour and Diet in Northern Rhodesia.* Oxford: Oxford University Press, 1939.

Ohnuki-Tierney, Emiko. *Rice as Self: Japanese Identities through Time.* Princeton: Princeton University Press, 1993.

Weiner, Annette B. *Women of Value, Men of Renown: New Perspectives in Trobriand Exchange.* Austin: University of Texas Press, 1976.

Weismantel, Mary J. *Food, Gender and Poverty in the Ecuadorean Andes.* Philadelphia: University of Pennsylvania Press, 1988.

Wendy Hunnewell Leynse
Ramona Lee Pérez

MEXICO. The Mexicans form a mestizo nation, born of the intermarriage of Spaniards and Native Americans, and their foods reflect this mixed heritage. Before the conquest of Mexico by the Spanish, the indigenous people created a sophisticated cuisine based on the staple grain maize (corn), which they cooked in a multitude of fashions, from everyday tortillas (griddle cakes) to festive tamales (dumplings). The conquistadors, hoping to establish a New Spain in the Americas, transplanted their familiar foods, particularly wheat bread, which was the foundation of the Mediterranean diet and the only grain accepted by the Catholic Church for the Holy Eucharist. Royal officials attempted to segregate Hispanic and native societies throughout the colonial period (1521–1821), but widespread race mixing occurred nevertheless. Ethnicity became a function more of culture than color, and eating corn or wheat, like speaking Spanish or Nahuatl, denoted a person's status. While the staple grains

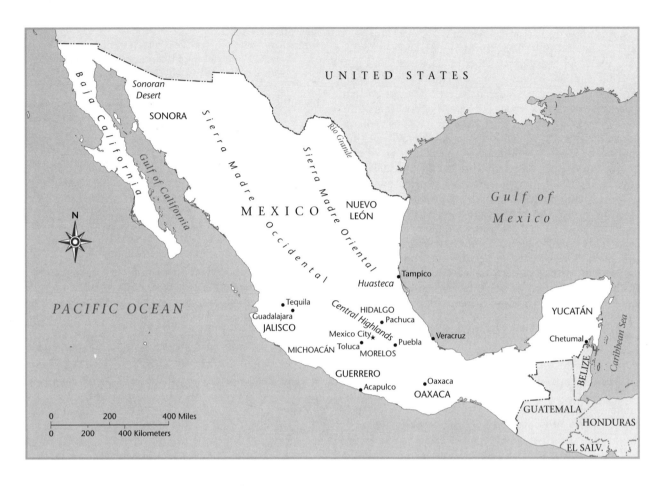

remained largely separate, culinary blending took place among the condiments, as indigenous cooks incorporated European meats into their moles (chili pepper stews) while Hispanics adopted native chilies and beans. The rejection of European doctrines of racial superiority came only after the revolution of 1910, when Mexicans accepted *mestizaje* as the national identity, and the combination of wheat bread and corn tortillas as the national cuisine.

In addition to class and ethnic divisions, Mexican cuisine contains tremendous regional variation. Perhaps the simplest classification consists of three complementary pairs: the mestizo foods of the central plateau and the indigenous center of Oaxaca in the south; foods of the frontiers of the Maya in the southeast and of Spanish settlement in the north; and the distinctive foods of the Gulf and Pacific coasts. Although Spanish influence tended to prevail in the north while the Indians better retained their culture farther south, no simple formula can capture the disparate topographies, climates, and settlement patterns that combined to produce these rich regional cuisines.

This diversity notwithstanding, a number of characteristics, common throughout Mexico, compose an identifiable national cuisine. As the original site of the chili pepper's domestication, Mexico has both the greatest botanical wealth of chilies, with some ninety different varieties, and the highest per capita consumption, since vir-

tually no Mexican considers a meal complete without some kind of peppers. The structure of the meal, with a succession of individual courses, unifies the Mexican dinner table and distinguishes it from the combination plates found in restaurants north of the Rio Grande, which jumble together the rice—properly eaten before the main course—with the beans that should follow. A common calendar also exists, combining religious feasts such as Christmas and Easter, secular holidays like Independence Day, and community and family celebrations of saints' days and weddings, each with their own traditional foods. The Mexican diet has been changing recently as a result of globalization and the spread of both junk food and haute cuisine, but these influences represent merely the latest in a long series of culinary encounters.

Cosmic Cuisine

José Vasconcelos helped define the Mexican national identity in *La raza cósmica* (*The Cosmic Race*, published in 1927), which rejected Social Darwinist views about the problems of race mixture and instead proclaimed mestizos to be the highest form of human evolution. This new nationalist ideology, called *indigenismo*, brought about the revalorization of Mexico's native heritage, including the indigenous cuisine based on corn. But embracing the pre-Hispanic past did not imply a rejection of Spanish contributions to Mexico's development, especially wheat bread and European livestock. Many other ethnic groups also contributed to Mexico's "fusion" cuisine, from African slaves and clandestine Jews in the colonial period, to European and Chinese immigrants in the nineteenth century and Lebanese and North Americans in the twentieth century.

One of the most fundamental cultural clashes between Native Americans and Spaniards in the colonial period revolved around the staple grains, corn and wheat. Maize not only provided the nutritional basis of pre-Hispanic civilizations, accounting for as much as 80 percent of the caloric intake of common people, it also served as the basis for religion and identity. Spanish missionaries therefore sought to substitute the European wheat as part of their work of extirpating the idolatry associated with indigenous corn gods, but their evangelical mission was undermined by economics as well as taste. Corn made an ideal subsistence crop, growing well in all manner of ecological niches from the tropical forests of Yucatán to the mountains of the central plateau. Wheat, by contrast, was here a fragile plant, susceptible to disease, requiring lavish irrigation, and offering comparatively low yields even under the most favorable circumstances. As a result, corn remained the staple crop of the rural masses in both native and mestizo communities, while wheat was grown as a market crop for wealthy Hispanic city dwellers. The price differential between wheat bread and corn tortillas persists to the present day, as do many of the stereotypes formed during the colonial period. Affluent Mexicans invariably keep wheat bread on the table, even when serving dishes such as mole, which is more properly eaten with corn tortillas.

The greatest European influence on Mexican cuisine came from the introduction of livestock. Before the Spanish arrived, the native inhabitants consumed a basically vegetarian diet incorporating only two domesticated animals, turkeys and dogs. The deaths of millions of Native Americans due to Old World diseases such as smallpox and measles, against which they had no natural immunities, opened up large amounts of formerly cultivated land for grazing. With no competitors, the cattle, sheep, goats, and pigs, and chickens brought by the Spanish reproduced at a fantastic rate, although their numbers soon declined through overgrazing. During the colonial period, the elite retained the Spanish preference for mutton, and only the poor consumed beef. Over the course of the nineteenth century, with the adoption of French fashions, the consumption of beef surpassed that of mutton. Mexicans also developed an elaborate art of *tocinería* (sausage and other pork products), and pork fat became the invariable cooking medium, despite European preferences for olive oil and butter. Culinary blending occurred through the incorporation of chili peppers into Spanish dishes such as chorizos (sausages) and *adobos* (marinades). Although Native Americans initially rejected the taste of lard, they eventually learned to add it to tamales and beans, improving their taste and texture.

The complexity of culinary blending can best be seen in the debate over the origins of the national dish, *mole poblano*, an elaborate festival food of turkey served in a deep brown sauce of chili peppers, diverse spices, and a small amount of chocolate. Anthropologist Margaret Park Redfield, who studied the foods of a native community near Mexico City in the 1920s, at the height of the *indigenista* movement, described mole as an essentially pre-Hispanic legacy of chili cookery. Fifty years later, disillusioned by the Mexican government's refusal to respect indigenous rights, anthropologist Judith Friedlander examined a neighboring village and reached the opposite conclusion: that mole, with its numerous Asian spices, had been imposed by Spanish missionaries. A third interpretation, based on popular legend rather than scholarly analysis, attributed the complexity of *mole poblano* to the Baroque artistry of the city of Puebla, where colonial nuns supposedly combined Old World spices with New World chilies to symbolize the mestizo "cosmic race." The lack of pre-Hispanic and colonial culinary literature makes it impossible to resolve the question definitively, but all three versions probably contain an element of truth.

Successive waves of immigrants, despite their relatively small numbers, have added significantly to the culinary blending of Spanish and Native American. Jews fleeing the Spanish Inquisition came to the colonies, par-

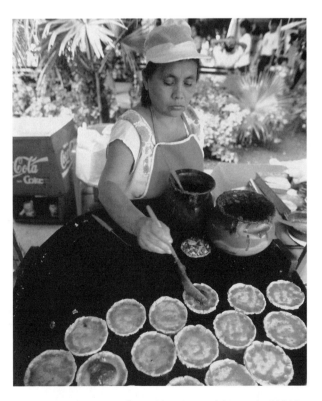

Woman preparing tortillas with salsa and beans in Mérida, Mexico. © Robert Holmes/CORBIS.

ticularly the northern province (now state) of Nuevo León, where their distinctive dish, *cabrito* (roasted kid), remains a regional specialty. African slaves meanwhile diffused their skills with rice agriculture throughout the Caribbean basin, including coastal Mexico. In the eighteenth century Italians began arriving from Naples, then part of the Spanish Bourbon empire. They had already established noodle factories in Mexico City by the 1790s, not long after the industry was founded in southern Italy. After independence in 1821, British miners brought with them a taste for meat pies, called *pastes*, around Pachuca (Hidalgo), site of the Real del Monte silver mine. German immigrants opened up breweries, and by the twentieth century their beers had supplanted the native beverage pulque, the fermented juice of the maguey (century [agave]) plant. French foods were the most fashionable among the nineteenth-century Mexican elite; nevertheless, all of these immigrant foods underwent a process of nationalization, so that Parisians today would scarcely recognize many of the dishes served under French names in Mexico City.

More recent immigrants have also left their mark on Mexican cooking, although none more so than the fast-food invasion from the United States. Large numbers of Chinese settled in northwestern Mexico in the late nineteenth century after the United States passed exclusion laws forbidding them entry. Then in the 1920s Lebanese immigrants began arriving, particularly in Puebla and Yucatán, and the gyro became the inspiration for *tacos al pastor* (shepherd's tacos). By the 1940s industrial processed foods from the United States had acquired enormous popularity among the rising middle class. Aunt Jemima pancakes became a favorite breakfast food, while Coke and Pepsi battled for the soft drink market. Moreover, these imports had to compete with domestic products such as Pan Bimbo, a Mexican clone of Wonder Bread. The spread of junk foods to even the most remote indigenous communities by the 1970s further complicated Mexico's diverse gastronomic geography.

Many Mexicos

Of the many culinary regions in Mexico, none exhibit the mestizo blending to a greater extent than the central highlands. The city of Puebla, legendary home of *mole poblano*, illustrates Iberian cooking techniques used on native ingredients through the production of *camotes* (candied sweet potatoes). Toluca is known for superb chorizo sausages combining pork with chili peppers. In the state of Hidalgo, shepherds pit-barbecue lamb wrapped in the leaves of the maguey to make a local specialty called *mixiotes*. Nahua Indians in the states of Mexico and Morelos cook *nopales* (cactus paddles), squash blossoms, and *cuitlacoche* (corn fungus) in quesadillas (corn pastries fried in pork fat). All of these different foods, and indeed the culinary traditions of the entire country, can be found in cosmopolitan Mexico City, with its countless markets, restaurants, and street vendors.

Oaxacan cuisine. In contrast to this cultural blending, indigenous communities such as the Zapotecs and Mixtecs in the southern state of Oaxaca have preserved their traditional foods. Unlike the complex blend of spices in *mole poblano*, the Oaxacan *mole verde* (green mole) derives its pristine taste from a few simple chilies and herbs, most notably the anise-flavored *hoja santa*. Oaxacan cooks wrap tamales in banana leaves instead of the corn husks common farther north, and they have raised tortilla making to a high art with the large, soft *blanditas* and *tlayudas* as well as the crisp *totopos*. The tiny grasshoppers known as *chapulines*, another local specialty, are flavored with smoky *chipotle* chilies and eaten in tacos with guacamole.

The Gulf Coast. Cooks along the Gulf Coast prepare seafood in both Mediterranean and pre-Hispanic styles. The snapper Veracruz (*huachinango a la veracruzana*) served in the eponymous port city contains olives, olive oil, tomato, capers, and only the mildest green peppers. Farther up the coast, at Tampico, one can sample the fiery hot crab soup called *chilpachole*. In the northeastern tropical forest of the Huasteca, ethnic groups such as the Totonacs make more than forty different types of tamales, including the legendary meter-long *zacahuil*, which can feed an entire village. Other seafood specialties of the region include baked pompano, *robalo al mojo de ajo* (snook cooked in garlic), and various seafood soups, cocktails, and *escabeches* (pickled seafood).

The Pacific Coast. The most typical food of Pacific Coast states is not from the sea at all, but rather *pozole*, a hominy stew made with pork. This dish comes in a number of different varieties, red in Guadalajara, green and white to the south in Guerrero, and with tripe in the northern state of Sonora. A common street food, eaten late at night, *pozole* is served with chili powder, oregano, chopped onion, sliced radishes, shredded lettuce, and limes for squeezing. In port cities such as Acapulco, the citric acid of lime juice is used to "cook" fresh seafood into *ceviche*. The Purépecha Indians of Michoacán prepare a variety of distinctive tamales, most notably the triangular *corundas* and fresh-corn *uchepos*.

Yucatán. Mexico's southeastern frontier, the Yucatán peninsula, is home to the ancient Maya civilization, whose pre-Hispanic traditions can still be found in dishes such as *papadzules*, the "food of the lords." These enchiladas, made entirely of native ingredients, require the freshest possible tortillas, to avoid the need for frying with pork fat. They are stuffed with chopped hard-boiled eggs in place of cheese, then covered in two sauces: a green *pipían* made of pumpkin seeds and a tomato sauce lightly flavored with habanero chilies. Yet the Maya have also adapted to the latest trends of globalization with the *queso relleno*, a large Dutch cheese, imported duty-free at the port of Chetumal, and stuffed with *picadillo* (chopped meat filling).

Northern cuisine. The Mexican foods best known in the United States, wheat flour tortillas and beef fajitas,

Tzotzol Maya prepare tortillas at dawn at Joigelito, Chiapas, Mexico. © DANNY LEHMAN/CORBIS.

exemplify the cuisine of northern Mexico. Wheat tortillas represent a mestizo adaptation of Native American cooking techniques to the European grain in areas where expensive milling and baking facilities were unavailable. The finest wheat tortillas are from the Sonoran desert, where settlers learned to roll them into paper-thin, eighteen-inch rounds. Fajitas illustrate how working-class Mexican Americans took an inexpensive yet flavorful cut of meat, the flank steak or diaphragm muscle, then tenderized and cooked it in thin strips. Restaurateurs devised the sizzling iron plate as a fancy way of presenting an ordinary taco—bits of meat rolled up in a soft tortilla—although Mexicans generally eat corn rather than wheat tortillas. Another Tex-Mex food, chili con carne, was the simplest of moles: just beef, chili powder, oregano, and cumin. The addition of beans to chili probably began with Anglos, because it violates Mexican ideas about the proper sequence of a meal.

Daily Bread and Tortillas

The foods eaten daily by rich and poor Mexicans differ significantly, but there is nevertheless a common structure to their meals. Work in the fields governs the eating habits of campesinos (rural laborers), who generally take two meals, a small breakfast before men set off in the morning, and a more substantial dinner when they return in the evening. To have fresh tortillas ready for breakfast, women traditionally had to awaken several hours earlier to grind corn on a basalt metate (concave grindstone) and pat it out by hand into thin disks. Because tortillas grew hard and stale after a few hours, they had to be cooked on a *comal* (earthenware griddle) before

each meal; the *nixtamal* (dough) likewise kept poorly, so the laborious grinding had to be repeated each day. One of the most significant social changes in Mexican history came in the first half of the twentieth century with the spread of mechanical mills capable of grinding the moist *nixtamal*. Freed from this onerous daily burden, women had the time to engage in commerce and craft production and thus begin to challenge the male domination of society.

In contrast to the austerity of the working class, wealthy Mexicans traditionally ate large amounts of food. The day began with *desayuno*, a simple breakfast consisting of a bread roll and coffee or hot chocolate, followed in midmorning by a substantial brunch, *almuerzo*, consisting of perhaps *mole poblano* or an omelette. The main meal, *comida*, began about two o'clock in the afternoon and progressed through an invariable sequence of four courses: a wet soup such as chicken broth, a dry soup of either rice or spaghetti, a main plate of roasted or stewed meat, and then beans. The elite accompanied their meals with imported wine, while members of the middle class drank the native pulque in the nineteenth century, and more recently beer. After awakening from an afternoon siesta, Mexicans took a *merienda* or snack of sweets, then returned to work for several hours. The *cena* or supper was taken quite late at night, often in cafés, with street foods such as enchiladas or tacos.

Class and ethnic distinctions were manifested less in the foods themselves than in their place within the daily routine. Native Americans in Oaxaca and elsewhere introduced European foods at the periphery, for example, by eating wheat bread for breakfast, while retaining the

Sor Juana, otherwise known as Juana Inés de la Cruz, was not only the most intellectual woman in 17th-century Mexico, she compiled the oldest surviving Mexican cookbook on confectionery. Consisting of 36 recipes, it is today a foundation text for the study of cloister cookery in the New World. PORTRAIT COURTESY OF THE PHILADELPHIA MUSEUM OF ART/CORBIS.

indigenous staples corn, beans, and chilies for their main daily meal. By the same token, the Hispanic elite consumed European foods for the central *comida*, and sampled lower-class foods of indigenous origin during the evening *cena*. Indeed, "slumming" at an all-night taco stand is still a favorite diversion of stylish Mexico City youth. The recent spread of an American-style workday, without the lengthy afternoon *comida* and siesta, has caused considerable loss of business for many upscale restaurants. Nevertheless, the traditional eating habits are preserved in numerous festivals throughout the year.

Celebrating Saints and Feeding the Dead

The festival foods of Mexico are as extravagant as the campesino diet is meager. Pre-Hispanic calendars contained numerous feasts dedicated to indigenous deities, which were replaced by Catholic holy days after the Spanish arrived. Each native community adopted a patron saint, and the inhabitants dedicated their meager savings to celebrating the saint's day with lavish abandon. Women worked for days with little rest to feed the entire community with dishes such as mole, tamales, and chocolate. These same elaborate foods were also prepared

for family ceremonies including weddings, christenings, and funerals. The wealthy Hispanic society also feasted on such occasions, although their foods tended to feature more imported goods from Europe. In recent years, traditional festival foods have even replaced French cuisine in the most fashionable restaurants.

The primary feasts of the Christian calendar—Christmas, Easter, and All Saints' Day—are celebrated throughout Mexico. The traditional Hispanic Christmas Eve feast includes an elaborate salad of lettuce, fruit, nuts, and beets, followed by *bacalao a la vizcaína* (Biscay-style cod), made with tomato, olive oil, olives, and capers, and served with wheat bread and wine. Indigenous and mestizo families celebrate the Nativity with tamales and mole instead of imported luxuries. Good Friday features fish, lentils, *romeritos* (dried shrimp fritters with greens) and *capirotada* (bread pudding). All Saints' Day is stretched out over three evenings, from 31 October to 2 November, known as the Days of the Dead. Families decorate the tombs of deceased relatives and construct altars incorporating salt, water, candy skulls, and *pan de muerto* (bread of the dead), decorated with strips of dough resembling human bones.

The most important civic holiday, Independence Day, celebrated on the eve of 16 September has no definite culinary traditions. There are many tricolor dishes, most notably *chiles en nogada*, stuffed green chilies with white walnut sauce and red pomegranate seeds. Nevertheless, the essence of the holiday is the *grito* or cry of independence repeated by public officials in plazas throughout the country, which lends itself not to elaborate cookery but to simple street foods: tacos, fritters, beer, and tequila.

Traditional festival foods have provided the basis for the latest trend, *la nueva cocina mexicana*, which combines Native American ingredients with the techniques of international haute cuisine. This "new Mexican cuisine" actually began in the 1950s, with dishes such as corn fungus *cuitlacoche* served in crêpes with bechamel sauce, invented by Jaime Saldívar to make a lower-class indigenous food acceptable for elite tables. By the 1990s hybrid dishes like *huauhzontle* pesto, pistachio mole, and *cuitlacoche* mousse had become ubiquitous on menus, and no fashionable Mexico City restaurant could avoid offering some version of the rose petal sauce invented by Laura Esquivel for her best-selling novel, *Like Water for Chocolate*. Many of these restaurants were owned by women, who thereby rejected the male dominance of Mexico's traditional society. Meanwhile, in the town of Tequila (Jalisco), firms such as Sauza and José Cuervo had improved their distilling technology to a level equal with that of the finest Scotch whisky and French cognac.

The *nueva cocina* represents simply another example of Mexico's ongoing gastronomic blending. Ever since the Spanish Conquest, cooks have combined native and European ingredients and techniques to create a sophisticated and original cuisine. It was only after the revolution of 1910 that Mexicans embraced their mestizo heritage, including the indigenous foods made of corn. The acceptance of diverse regional culinary dialects came, moreover, just as many rural cooking traditions began to be lost because of migration to urban areas and the arrival of mass-produced foods from the United States. Despite the spread of soft drinks and snack crackers, the elaborate tamales and moles prepared to celebrate festivals remain a vital source of identity within families, communities, and the Mexican nation.

See also **American Indians: Prehistoric Indians and Historical Overview; Chili Peppers; Day of the Dead; Iberian Peninsula; Inca Empire; Maize; Mexico and Central America, Pre-Columbian; United States,** *subentries on* **Ethnic Cuisines** *and* **Southwest.**

BIBLIOGRAPHY

Bauer, Arnold J. "Millers and Grinders: Technology and Household Economy in Meso-America." *Agricultural History* 64, no. 1 (Winter 1990): 1–17.

Esquivel, Laura. *Like Water for Chocolate: A Novel in Monthly Installments, with Recipes, Romances, and Home Remedies.* Translated by Carol Christensen and Thomas Christensen. New York: Doubleday, 1992.

Friedlander, Judith. *Being Indian in Hueyapan: A Study of Forced Identity in Contemporary Mexico.* New York: St. Martin's Press, 1975.

Juárez, José Luis. *La lenta emergencia de la comida mexicana, ambigüedades criollas, 1750–1800.* Mexico City: Editorial Porrúa, 2000.

Long-Solís, Janet. *Capsicum y cultura: La historia del chilli.* Mexico City: Fondo de Cultura Económica, 1986.

Novo, Salvador. *Cocina mexicana: Historia gastronómica de la Ciudad de México.* Mexico City: Editorial Porrúa, 1967.

Ochoa, Enrique C. *Feeding Mexico: The Political Uses of Food since 1910.* Wilmington, Del.: Scholarly Resources, 2000.

Pilcher, Jeffrey M. ¡*Que vivan los tamales! Food and the Making of Mexican Identity.* Albuquerque, N.M.: University of New Mexico Press, 1998.

Redfield, Margaret Park. "Notes on the Cookery of Tepoztlan, Morelos." *American Journal of Folklore* 42, no. 164 (April–June 1929): 167–196.

Sandstrom, Alan R. *Corn Is Our Blood: Culture and Ethnic Identity in a Contemporary Aztec Indian Village.* Norman, Okla.: University of Oklahoma Press, 1991.

Stephen, Lynn. *Zapotec Women.* Austin, Texas: University of Texas Press, 1991.

Super, John C. *Food, Conquest, and Colonization in Sixteenth-Century Spanish America.* Albuquerque, N.M.: University of New Mexico Press, 1988.

Jeffrey M. Pilcher

MEXICO AND CENTRAL AMERICA, PRE-COLUMBIAN.

When the Spanish conquistador Hernán Cortés set foot on the beach in the Mexican state of Veracruz, he encountered advanced cultures whose ex-

istence had not been previously suspected. The great Aztec empire, ruled by a people called the Mexica, had conquered much of the region, establishing a city of grand temples and causeways called Tenochtitlán, while the rainforest cities of the Maya were slowly returning to the jungle after being abandoned several centuries earlier. Cultures including the Totonac, Tlaxcalans, and Zapotec also met the Spanish at this time, some as friends, others as enemies. All, however, impressed many of the Spanish with their cities, governments, markets, and material goods that rivaled those of the Old World. The food and cuisine of these cultures of present-day Mexico and Central America, an area termed by anthropologists and archaeologists as Mesoamerica, are the subject of discussion here.

While these cultures lived in different areas, had different forms of social and political organization, and spoke a variety of languages, there were certain shared traits, including an intricate calendrical system, hieroglyphic writing, and a distinct architectural style. These cultures all made use of corn, beans, squash, chili peppers, chocolate, and domesticated dogs and turkeys. Despite some differences in preparation and availability of ingredients, many of the dishes and their style of preparation in these varied cultures were very similar.

Evidence for Pre-Columbian Cuisine

How do we know what and how ancient people ate? Fortunately Mesoamerica provides several lines of evidence. The documents written by the early Spanish conquistadors offer invaluable insight into the customs of early Mesoamerican civilizations. Many priests and nobility accompanied the explorations of Columbus and Cortés and learned and recorded the language, customs, and beliefs of the indigenous cultures. These documents reveal methods and techniques of food preparation, farming techniques, and available ingredients.

Archaeology provides a second line of evidence for reconstructing the foodways of these cultures. Whereas the colonial documents record what the Spanish witnessed or were told by their informants, archaeology, and the subdisciplines of paleoethnobotany and zooarchaeology, provide material evidence invisible in the ethnohistoric record. The Spanish did not often take note of foods eaten by the commoners, and without modern scientific nomenclature, it is sometimes difficult to determine exactly what plant or animal the Spanish were talking about. Archaeology often helps to clarify these problems.

The translation and interpretation of the writing and iconography of codices, the term for pre-Columbian and early Colonial books, pottery, and other works of private and public art, also provide evidence for pre-Columbian food use. Decipherment of Mayan hieroglyphs on ceramic vessels, for example, gives new insight into their use, and lists of tribute items demanded by the Mexica of their dependents show us what food items were kept in their central storehouses.

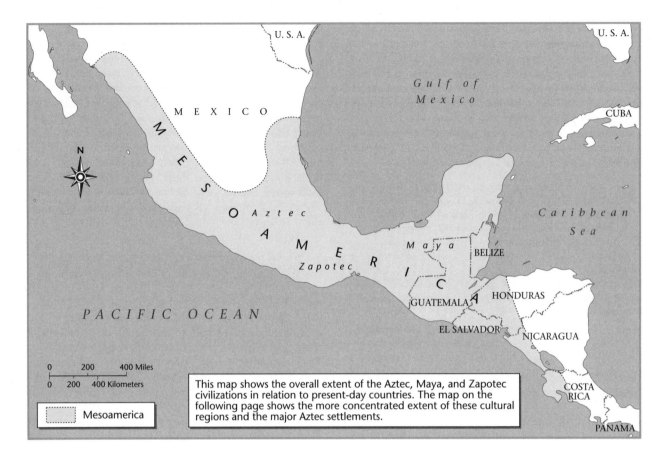

This map shows the overall extent of the Aztec, Maya, and Zapotec civilizations in relation to present-day countries. The map on the following page shows the more concentrated extent of these cultural regions and the major Aztec settlements.

Grains

All cultures utilize a staple food around which the rest of their cuisine is based; in Europe and the Middle East it is wheat, and in the Far East, rice. In Mesoamerica, the staple undoubtedly was corn, or maize (*Zea mays*). And not only was maize the primary foodstuff, forming the basis of virtually all meals, it had spiritual and religious significance as well. From birth, when the umbilical cord would be cut over a maize cob, to death, when a small piece of maize dough was placed in the mouth of the deceased, maize played a central role in the cultures of Mesoamerica. According to the *Popol Vuh*, the "bible" of the Maya, humans are not made of earth but rather were formed from maize dough.

Maize was prepared in a variety of ways, depending on the time of year, the race of maize, and the particular meal. For the most part, however, maize was prepared by a process called nixtamalization. The ripe maize grains were first soaked and then boiled in water mixed with burned and ground limestone or ash. After boiling, the maize kernels were ground to varying degrees on a *metate*, a flat grinding stone, and this resulting dough was used in all manner of preparations. The boiling in lime or ash makes the maize easier to grind, as well as creating a chemical reaction that makes it much more nutritious. Combined with beans, another important Mesoamerican crop, nixtamalization provided an almost complete nutritional package.

Once processed, maize was prepared either as a solid breadstuff or as a beverage. The term "beverage" is helpful for describing certain dishes, but these preparations could easily be called a gruel, porridge, or even a stew, especially with the addition of different foods. Maize dough was also soured by being stored in containers or wrapped in leaves used just for that purpose, much like sourdough bread.

Atolli is the Nahuatl term for a beverage made from the most finely ground maize dough mixed with water. Whole maize kernels, beans, chili pepper, marigold leaves, toasted squash seeds, and even boiled and mashed root crops, especially sweet potato, were stirred into the beverage, creating more of a stew or soup. Honey or, in the Mexica and Zapotec areas, maguey syrup, could be added for sweetness. Elite and commoner alike consumed *atolli*, although the finest, bone-white maize was reserved for the nobility, as was the addition of cacao seeds. It was generally drunk in the mornings, although it could complement a meal at any time of day.

Tortillas and tamales formed the basis of the solid breadstuffs. Tortillas are cakes of maize dough flattened to varying degrees of thickness and cooked on a ceramic griddle called a *comal*, on a hot stone, or simply over the hot ashes of a fire. *Comales* are frequently found in archaeological deposits throughout central Mexico, attesting to the importance of the tortilla in the daily diet, and

498

Spanish documents mention that many women were brought along on long journeys or during warfare to grind corn and prepare tortillas. Tortillas were generally paired with a sauce or casserole of spices, herbs, and vegetables and served both as food and as a utensil to transport the food to the mouth. There were different grades of tortillas, from paper-thin, pure white tortillas enjoyed by the elite, to thick and heavy tortillas for everyday consumption or for long journeys.

The presence of the tortilla among the Maya is less definite. We find few *comales* in the Mayan area, leading some to suggest that the tortilla was less important and tamales more prevalent. Tamales are thick maize dough, mixed with a vast array of foods—beans, chilis, eggs, meat, fish, and mushrooms were all incorporated into tamale dough—wrapped in leaves or corn husks, and steamed or baked in a fire. Mayan iconography also shows plates with round balls that resemble tamales, rather than flat cakes indicative of tortillas.

A fermented beverage called *balché* was made from maize and flavored with different fruits and spices. Fermented beverages were quite common in the New World (except for areas north of Mexico), and quite intoxicating as well. The Maya drank *balché* for the most part, whereas the drink in the more arid regions was called pulque and was fermented from the sap of the maguey,

And then the yellow corn and white corn were ground, and Xmucane did the grinding nine times. Food was used, along with the water she rinsed her hands with, for the creation of grease; it became human fat when it was worked by the Bearer, Begetter, Sovereign Plumed Serpent, as they are called.
After that, they put it into words:
the making, the modeling of our first mother-father,
with yellow corn, white corn alone for the flesh,
food alone for the human legs and arms,
for our first father, the four human works.

From Tedlock, *Popol Vuh,* p. 140

or agave. These fermented beverages were mostly used for rituals, and public drunkenness was especially frowned upon in the Aztec empire, being punishable by death.

Maize was not the only grain utilized by Mesoamerican cultures. Amaranth, a seed crop of the genus

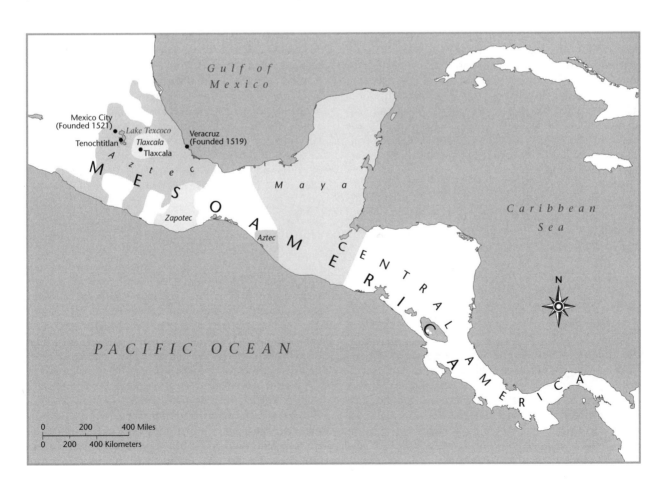

cacao

atole

tamale/bread

honey

turkey tamale

Mayan hieroglyphs showing a few of the important food terms used in pre-Columbian America. Turkey tamales were consumed by the Mayan nobility. DRAWINGS COURTESY OF THE AUTHOR.

Amaranthus, was brought under cultivation throughout central Mexico and was one of the four primary tribute items demanded by the Mexica along with maize, beans, and *chia*, a relative of sage. Called *huautli* in Nahuatl, amaranth was prepared in a similar manner to maize, ground into flour for tortillas, tamales, and *atolli*. Amaranth was also popped like popcorn and ground into a lighter flour, or incorporated into regular maize dough. It was prized as a gourmet food, and the nobility enjoyed specially prepared tamales and tortillas of amaranth, as well as a sauce from the highly nutritious greens.

But the most important use of amaranth was in religious rituals. Popped amaranth flour tamales and a mixture of popped amaranth and sweet maguey syrup, called *tzoali*, were offered to certain deities. The contemporary descendents of *tzoali* are the Mexican treats *alegrías*, popped amaranth bound with molasses, which can be found throughout Mexico City. Of special importance to the Mexica were the seeds of bright red amaranth, whose color resembled blood, the most sacred of human substances. This special ritual role of amaranth, and the desire of the Spanish to eliminate any evidence of indigenous religion, may have led to its sudden disappearance from the modern diet.

Vegetables and Fruits

The staple foods of maize and amaranth were supplemented in the daily diet by a diverse array of vegetables and fruits. Beans, although not technically a vegetable, were perhaps the most extensively cultivated crop outside of maize and amaranth. The New World beans all belong to the same genus, *Phaseolus*, and are represented by the modern-day varieties navy, wax, lima, pinto, kidney, and black, although many more were cultivated in pre-Columbian times.

Beans were not harvested green but were picked and stored dry. They were prepared generally by boiling, often with the addition of epazote, a flavorful herb that is said to reduce gassiness. The boiled beans were mashed and added to maize dough for tortillas or tamales, or made into a stew. Quite often, however, they were simply boiled in plain water, flavored with a little chili, and scooped into the mouth with tortillas.

Different types of squashes (*Lagenaria* and *Cucurbita* spp.) complemented the Mesoamerican diet in a number of ways. The cleaned and dried shells were often used as serving vessels and eating utensils. Toasted and ground, their seeds were added to tamales and tortillas, used as a flavoring for various sauces, used as a relish, or even mixed with ground beans to make a drink. The flesh was used to a lesser extent, often roasted or stewed in honey. And as is the fashion with many Mesoamerican crops, all parts of the plant were used, with the flower blossoms added to soups and stews and the greens used as wrappings for tamales or meat dishes.

A great many other vegetables were utilized by Mesoamerican cultures, including tomatoes, tomatillos, many types of greens, and a variety of root crops, such as sweet potato, manioc, and jicama. These were all commonly used in the sauces and casseroles that formed the primary part of a meal along with tortillas and tamales. Root crops have been the subject of debate in Mesoamerican archaeology. Some see their role in the diet as relatively minor, whereas others stress their importance beyond what is indicated in the ethnohistoric record. Little mention is made of them by the Spanish, yet records of explorations in the Mayan area mention large fields of root crops, interspersed with other cultigens.

Although technically a fruit, avocado (*Persea americana*) generally played the role of a vegetable. It could be eaten simply sliced and wrapped in a tortilla, added to soups, or prepared as a relish, similar to guacamole. Also eaten were the cactus pads and fruits of a variety of cactus, primarily *Opuntia* sp., as well as different parts of the succulent agave (*Agave* sp.), also known as maguey. Fruits, and especially fruit trees, play a major role in Mesoamerican cuisine, although their methods of preparation were fairly simple. Commonly known and frequently used New World cultigens include pineapple, papaya, and passion fruit, while lesser-known fruits such as chico zapote (*Manilkara zapota*), the various species of Annona including soursop and cherimoya, and hog plum (*Spondias mombin*) were also eaten. When not eaten plain, fruits were often made into intoxicating beverages used in ceremonies and rituals. The fruit tree orchards held special significance to the Maya, and when the Spanish forced them to cut them down, in large part because of the excessive drinking and intoxication from fruit beers, the Maya were devastated. Orchards were not simply locations for harvesting fruit, but were sacred sites passed down and maintained through generations.

Spices, Herbs, and Specialty Items

Fundamental to Mesoamerican cuisines is the chili pepper (*Capsicum* sp.) perhaps second in importance only to maize. It acquired the name "pepper" as it was the closest to black pepper (*Piper nigrum*) that Columbus could find in the New World, although it is not very similar at all. However, as an all-purpose spice to flavor nearly all concoctions, it fulfilled the role of black pepper quite well. It was sprinkled over sauces, ground into maize dough, and boiled with beans, providing taste as well as great quantities of vitamins A and C. Its importance is evident in the ritual fasting of the Aztec priests, who considered a "fast" an abstinence from salt and chili, as well as meat.

Chilies were also used in nonculinary fashion. Children were punished by being held over chili smoke, and during warfare, calabashes (squash shells) with coals and chilies were thrown at the enemy to create a pungent smoke.

No discussion of Mesoamerican cuisine can proceed without mentioning chocolate, or cacao (*Theobroma cacao*). Primarily used by the elite, cacao was prepared as a beverage and was served as the last course of a meal. Cacao beans were prepared by being fermented, cured, roasted, and then ground into a powder, which was added to hot water and frothed. The Aztec would create a foamy head to the drink by using a spoon or a special utensil, whereas we see from some Mayan iconography that they would pour the cacao from one vessel to another to make the foam. Creating this foam was integral to the preparation of cacao, and to be served a drink without it was a grave insult.

An innumerable array of additions flavored these cacao drinks. Honey or maguey syrup was added for sweetness, maize dough could be added to thicken the drink, and herbs, spices, and flowers provided different tastes and flavors. The Aztec and Maya frequently mixed in vanilla, the seedpod of an orchid grown on the Gulf Coast, and achiote (*Bixa orellana*), although the latter was more to impart a deep red color than for taste. Achiote, the seed of a small tree, was actually used to tint many things, including human skin.

Countless flowers also flavored cacao drinks. Marigold (*Tagetes lucida*), *Cymbopetalum penduliflorum*, and *Quararibea funebris* were all added to the cacao drink, each flower providing a different taste, ranging from cinnamon to black pepper to ripe melon. Some flowers were added to the finished beverage, whereas others were closed in a sealed container with the dried beans to impart their aroma.

Cacao was reserved solely for the elite, and generally only the males. At the great Aztec banquets, the men were served vessels of cacao at the completion of the meal, whereas the women drank a beverage of chia seeds and chili. Priests also likely drank cacao, as it was often mixed with hallucinogenic substances such as psychoactive mushrooms or peyote.

Cacao also served as a form of currency. The beans were used as a coin, and there were those who would attempt counterfeiting by filling empty cacao shells with clay, although this was a heavily punishable offense. The use of cacao as currency continued up to the twentieth century in parts of Mesoamerica.

Meat and Fish

When the Spanish arrived, they likened the diet of the inhabitants of Mesoamerica to a perpetual Lent, so little was their meat consumption. Prehistoric environmental factors left Mesoamerica with few large mammals. Among the few animals raised in Mesoamerica were the dog, the turkey (*Meleagris gallopavo*), and the Muscovy duck (*Cairina moschata*). One could also include among the domesticated animals several types of stingless honeybee and the cochineal insect, the latter used for a red dye later employed by the British for their "redcoats."

The meat of these domesticated animals was reserved for special feasts, with the exception of the nobility, who enjoyed meat on a daily basis. For any one of these feasts, a huge quantity of dogs, turkeys, and duck would be fattened and slaughtered and prepared generally in tamales or in one of the many soups and stews. Turkeys were considered a feast food, with the Maya especially reserving this bird for ceremonies related to planting and rain. After the introduction of the chicken, the role of the turkey diminished, although it was still used in the most important rituals.

At the time of European contact there were many dog breeds, including a rather large, hairless breed that has since become extinct. These breeds were separate from the dogs used as guard dogs, for hunting, or for companionship. The raising of edible breeds was a lucrative profession, and the animals were fed a rich diet of maize and even large quantities of avocado.

The New World was replete with wild game, however, and these were hunted and even somewhat "tamed." Several types of deer, while technically "wild," were kept in pens nearby the living quarters, and it was even said that Mayan women would suckle baby deer from their own breasts. Deer was probably the most commonly hunted and eaten of the wild animals; it has been found in archaeological contexts from the highest nobility to the lowest of peasants. Also utilized were two types of iguana, whose eggs and flesh were eaten, the armadillo, the peccary, the tapir, and several types of monkeys.

Food from the sea was important as well. Tropical fish, lobsters, other shellfish, and manatees were all caught and transported great distances to the major Aztec, Mayan, and Zapotec cities to be enjoyed by nobility and commoner alike. The fish were usually sun-dried or salt-dried, using the resources from the massive saltworks along the coastal regions.

From freshwater lakes and streams came turtles, crocodile, and many types of fish. The Aztec, who lived by Lake Texcoco, made perhaps the most extensive use of their lake resources, extracting a variety of fish, shrimp, insects, and insect eggs. A type of water bug called *axay-acatl* was collected, formed into balls, and cooked in maize husks, and the eggs of this same water bug, called *ahuau-til*, were eaten in tortillas and tamales. A tiny worm that lives in the lake was gathered and cooked with salt and chili until black and soft, and a type of algae was skimmed off the top of the lake, formed into bricks, and left in the sun until it turned black, when it was utilized somewhat like cheese. The Aztec were not the only ones to indulge in insects. The Maya and the Zapotec prepared and ate many insects, which apparently disgusted the Spanish, but little is known of how they were prepared.

The contact between Europe and the New World fundamentally changed the cuisines of the world. Where would Italian cuisine be without the tomato; Indian cuisine without the chili pepper; or the cuisines of northern Europe without the potato? Some of the ingredients and dishes presented here are instantly recognizable, whereas others are not, but this far from comprehensive list gives only an idea of the wealth and complexity of the pre-Columbian cuisines of Mesoamerica.

See also **Central America; Chili Peppers; Feasts, Festivals, and Fasts; Fermented Beverages other than Wine or Beer; Flowers; Game; Iberian Peninsula; Inca Empire; Legumes; Maize; Meat; Mexico; South America; Squash and Gourds.**

BIBLIOGRAPHY

Coe, Michael D. *The Maya.* 6th ed. London: Thames and Hudson, 1993.

Coe, Sophie D. *America's First Cuisines.* Austin: University of Texas Press, 1994.

Coe, Sophie D., and Michael D. Coe. *The True History of Chocolate.* New York: Thames and Hudson, 1996.

Flannery, Kent V., ed. *Maya Subsistence: Studies in Memory of Dennis E. Puleston.* New York: Academic Press, 1982.

Foster, Nelson, and Linda S. Cordell, eds. *Chilies to Chocolate: Food the Americas Gave the World.* Tucson: University of Arizona Press, 1992.

Harrison, Peter D., and B. L. Turner, II, eds. *Pre-Hispanic Maya Agriculture.* Albuquerque: University of New Mexico Press, 1978.

Lentz, David L. "Maya Diets of the Rich and Poor: Paleoeth-nobotanical Evidence from Copan." *Latin American Antiquity* 2, no. 3 (September 1991): 269–287.

Sokolov, Raymond. *Why We Eat What We Eat: How the Encounter Between the New World and the Old Changed the Way Everyone on the Planet Eats.* New York: Summit Books, 1991.

Tedlock, Dennis, trans. *Popol Vuh: The Mayan Book of the Dawn of Life.* New York: Simon and Schuster, 1996.

Townsend, Richard. *The Aztecs.* London: Thames and Hudson, 2000.

Weaver, Muriel Porter. *The Aztecs, Maya, and their Predecessors: Archaeology of Mesoamerica.* 3d ed. San Diego, Calif.: Academic Press, 1993.

White, Christine D., ed. *Reconstructing Ancient Maya Diet.* Salt Lake City: University of Utah Press, 1999.

Andrew R. Wyatt

MICROBIOLOGY.

Microbiology is the study of a diverse group of microscopic organisms, or microorganisms: bacteria, fungi, algae, protozoa, and viruses. Bacteria are prokaryotes; the other microorganisms are eukaryotes. Prokaryote cells lack a nuclear membrane and membrane-bound organelles. Recently, bacteria have been divided into eubacteria and archaebacteria, with the latter more closely related to eukaryote cells. Bacteria are mostly unicellular and range in size from tiny mycoplasmas, 200 nanometers (that is, 200 billionths of a meter, or less than 1/100,000 of an inch) in diameter, to the recently discovered *Thiomargarita namibiensis*, at one millimeter (or about 1/25 of an inch). *E. coli* cells are one to two micrometers in length (about five to ten times the diameter of the mycoplasmas). Fungi include yeasts, molds, and mushrooms. The bread, wine, and beer yeast, *Saccharomyces cerevisiae*, is ten micrometers (about 1/2,500 of an inch) in diameter. Algae are photosynthetic organisms, unicellular or multicellular. Protozoa are microscopic, unicellular, and usually motile. Viruses are not cellular organisms; they are intracellular parasites of animals, plants, or bacteria. They are composed of nucleic acid (DNA or RNA) enclosed in a protein coat. Viruses range from 18 to 450 nanometers (from less than one-millionth to almost 1/50,000 of an inch). Microorganisms, with the exception of viruses, can be observed with a compound light microscope (up to ×1,000 magnification). Electron microscopes (up to ×100,000 magnification) are used to visualize viruses.

History of Microbiology before Pasteur

Microorganisms were first visualized by Antoni van Leeuwenhoek (1632–1723), a Dutch cloth merchant and an expert lens grinder. His simple microscopes magnified up to three hundred diameters. In the eighteenth century, many people still believed that living organisms could arise spontaneously from organic matter—the doctrine of abiogenesis, or spontaneous generation.

Lazzaro Spallanzani (1729–1799), an Italian priest and physiologist, did an experiment that came close to proving that life (in this case, microorganisms) does not arise spontaneously from nonliving matter. He sealed flasks containing broth and then boiled them. No spontaneous generation or growth occurred in the flasks; however, the debate continued, as proponents of the doctrine said that air was needed for spontaneous generation. Opponents of this doctrine had a very difficult task trying to prove a negative, namely that something did not happen.

The ancient Egyptians and Romans were comfortable with the idea that organisms invisible to the naked eye could cause disease. During the Dark Ages and the medieval period of Western history, this idea virtually disappeared. In the sixteenth century, Girolamo Fracastoro (1483–1553) described disease passing from one person to another by "germs." Athanasius Kircher (1602–1680) furthered the "germ theory" by observing bacteria from plague victims.

History from Pasteur Onward

Louis Pasteur (1822–1895) was an intellectual giant who dominated science in the middle of the nineteenth century. In 1861, in the midst of a twenty-year study of microbial fermentation, Pasteur dealt the deathblow to the doctrine of spontaneous generation by demonstrating the presence of microorganisms in the air and then by showing that sterile liquid in a swan-necked flask remained sterile. Air could enter such a flask, but microorganisms could not. In 1875, Ferdinand Cohn (1828–1898) published the first classification of bacteria, and used the genus name, *Bacillus*, for a spore-forming bacterium. In 1875, Robert Koch (1843–1910), a German bacteriologist, proved that a spore-forming bacterium, *Bacillus anthracis*, caused anthrax. His experiments demonstrated four principles, now known as Koch's postulates, which are still the hallmark of disease etiology: (1) the microorganism must be present in every diseased animal studied, but not be isolated from healthy animals; (2) the microorganism must be isolated from the animal and cultivated; (3) an animal inoculated with the microorganism must develop the disease; (4) the same microorganism must be isolated from the diseased animal inoculated with the microorganism. Working independently on anthrax, Pasteur and his colleagues confirmed Koch's findings. Koch introduced three practices that allowed bacteriologists to obtain pure cultures simply: (1) a semisolid medium composed of nutrients solidified with gelatin, (2) platinum needles sterilized in a flame to pick up bacteria, (3) streaking of bacteria onto a gelatin surface to obtain single cells that would grow into colonies. In 1881, Fanny Hesse, the wife of German bacteriologist, Walther Hesse, suggested using a seaweed extract, agar, which she used to thicken jam, to solidify media in petri plates. Agar had neither of the disadvantages of gelatin: it was rarely degraded by microorganisms and it stayed solid at temperatures above 28°C (about 82°F). Agar is still the solidifying agent of choice. In 1882, Koch used the pure-culture techniques to isolate the bacterium that causes tuberculosis. In 1884, Charles Chamberland, a collaborator of Pasteur's, developed a porcelain filter that would retain all bacteria. When, in 1892, a young Russian scientist, Dmitri Iwanowski, transmitted tobacco mo-

YEAST EXTRACT

In the United Kingdom, South Africa, and Down Under, people enjoy yeast spreads—that is, spreads made from a dark-brown, extremely salty yeast extract. Oddly enough, one, Marmite, is preferred in Australia, and another, Vegemite, is preferred in New Zealand. Some say Marmite is sweeter than Vegemite; others say that Marmite has more caramel flavor. One of babies' first foods Down Under is toast fingers spread with Vegemite or Marmite. These spreads are rich in niacin, thiamine, and riboflavin. Neither of these spreads is tolerated well by North Americans.

saic disease to healthy plants using a porcelain-filtered extract, he postulated the presence of a toxin. In 1898, the Dutch microbiologist, Martinus Beijerinck, reproduced Iwanowski's results, but he postulated the existence of very small infectious agents, "filterable viruses." Thus began the field of virology, although visualization of viruses had to wait until the development of the electron microscope in the 1930s. Medical bacteriology progressed rapidly at the Pasteur Institute in Paris, where Pasteur presided, and the Koch Institute in Berlin, where Koch presided.

History of Food Preservation Microbiology

In 1810, Nicolas Appert (1750–1841) applied Spallanzani's results to develop a system of preserving food by sealing it in airtight cans and heating the cans. Without understanding that the heat treatment, or "appertization," was killing microorganisms in the canned food, Appert established the basis for the modern practice of canning. In 1852, Napoleon III asked Pasteur to study the problem of "wine diseases," particularly wine souring. In 1886, Pasteur proclaimed that the off-flavors in wine were caused by contaminating microorganisms. He suggested heating (pasteurizing) the grape juice to kill the spoilage bacteria. He discovered that some microorganisms could grow in the absence of oxygen. He used the term "anaerobic" to apply to microbial metabolism that occurs only in the absence of oxygen, and "aerobic" for metabolism that occurs under normal atmospheric conditions. Fermentation of grape juice by yeast is one kind of anaerobic metabolism. He also described the anaerobic degradation of protein, or putrefaction, by bacteria. Aerobic bacteria, namely the acetic-acid bacteria, were the cause of wine souring. Some of these bacteria metabolize ethanol to acetic acid; others metabolize the acetic acid to carbon dioxide and water. The process of pasteurization, a mild heat treatment of liquids, originated as a means of preserving the

BACTERIA AS FOOD

In the pre-European Aztec culture, people harvested the cyanobacterium, *Spirulina,* from lakes for food, and still do so in Chad. Cyanobacteria are capable of photosynthesis, and so some lakes in Chad and in Mexico develop a deep green color. *Spirulina* may be the only bacterium directly consumed by people. Today, about nine hundred tons a year of *Spirulina* is produced, mainly by the United States and Thailand. The spirulina product is 65 percent protein and amino acids, 20 percent carbohydrates, and 5 percent fats. Spirulina is rich in vitamins A, D, K, and B$_{12,}$ as well as beta carotene.

desired flavor of milk, fruit juices, beer, and wine. For example, Pasteur recommended that heating bottled wine for a short time at 122°F (50°C) would kill the lactic-acid and acetic-acid bacteria that can spoil wine. In traditional pasteurization, liquids are heated at about 145°F (63°C) for thirty minutes, then held at 50°F (10°C). Nowadays, flash or high-temperature, short-time (HTST) pasteurization is the preferred method (about 162°F [72°C] for fifteen seconds, followed by rapid cooling to 50°F [10°C]) because it has less effect on the flavor of the food being heated. Currently, milk is pasteurized to eliminate the bacteria responsible for tuberculosis, food poisoning, undulant fever, and Q fever. The treatment does not result in sterilization of milk, which can contain twenty thousand bacteria, such as lactobacilli, per ml post-pasteurization. More common in Europe than other parts of the world, is ultrahigh temperature (UHT) treatment (300°F [148.9°C] for one to two seconds), which sterilizes milk, allowing it to be stored without refrigeration for more than the limit of two to three weeks for pasteurized milk. Many brewing companies pasteurize their bottled or canned beer at 140°F (60°C) for a few minutes. Pasteurization is infrequently used, however, in modern winemaking, as it adversely affects the flavor.

Cohn and John Tyndall (1829–1893) both demonstrated that the endospores of *Bacillus subtilis* cells were far more resistant to heating than were vegetative bacteria. Tyndall developed a method of sterilizing liquids that contained bacterial spores: a medium was first incubated to allow the spores to germinate, then heated to kill most of the bacteria. This process, later termed "tyndallization," was repeated several times. This was a very important development in food science since the bacteria that form endospores include the food-borne pathogens, *Clostridium botulinum, C. perfringens* and *C. difficile.* Today, canned food is subjected to a temperature–time

treatment that ensures the death of heat-resistant bacterial endospores, particularly those of *C. botulinum.*

For hundreds of years, substances that inhibit microbial growth have been added to foods in an attempt to prevent spoilage. One of the oldest practices is the salting of meat and fish as a means of preservation. Growth of most bacteria is inhibited by the high osmotic strength generated by the salt. In a relatively dry climate, salted meat can last up to twelve months. In 1958, the United States government determined that no chemical could be added to food or beverages without having been tested for safety. Three important antifungal preservatives for acidic foods (foods with a pH of 4.6 or less) such as canned drinks, salad dressings, cheese, and wines, are benzoic acid, sorbic acid, and propionic acid (or their salts). Sodium nitrate has been used in meat in China and the Middle East since 1200 B.C.E. A bacterial conversion of nitrate to nitrite results in a reaction with the heme pigment, giving the pink color of ham. Nitrite is antibacterial and prevents the germination of *C. botulinum* and other anaerobic bacteria in meats like ham, bacon, and frankfurters. Sulfur dioxide in some form, for example as produced by sodium metabisulfite, is used to control yeast and bacteria in wines and bacteria in brewing. Sulfur dioxide or bisulfite is an unusual chemical in that it is also an extremely effective antioxidant. Fermentation is another method of preservation. A commonly held dictum is that pathogenic bacteria do not grow at pH levels below 4.5. Fermented foods are inoculated with microorganisms, which reduce the pH of the food by producing acid during their growth. Acids such as acetic or citric acid are also added to decrease the pH of foods. Heat treatments are more effective at killing microorganisms at lower pH. It appears that low pH does not ensure safety from pathogens: in 1993, *E. coli 0157:H7* in fresh-pressed apple juice caused an outbreak of diarrhea and hemolytic uremic syndrome. *Yersinia* spp. may also be able to survive in low pH foods.

Irradiation is a process that destroys microbial pathogens in food. Gamma rays from cobalt 60 or cesium 137, X rays (five million electron volts [5 MeV] maximum), and electrons (10 MeV maximum) are approved sources in the U.S. Irradiation was first used in the U.S. to ensure safe food for astronauts. Subsequently, the Food and Drug Administration (FDA) approved irradiation for wheat, wheat flour, and potatoes. Currently, irradiation is used mostly for spices, but also to disinfect cured meats, to kill *Trichinella spiralis* in pork, to control salmonella on chicken carcasses, and to reduce microbial load on fresh fruits and vegetables. There is some public resistance to irradiated foods, as the thought is that the food becomes radioactive. It does not.

Control of Microorganisms in Food

The contemporary food microbiologist has the challenges of a growing number of food pathogens and food spoilage. For example, eighty percent of commercial chickens in the U.S. are contaminated with *Campylobacter jejuni.* The food microbiologist may be involved in food manufacturing and processing, in retail food, in research in a university or government organization, such as the Agricultural Research Service of the United States Department of Agriculture (USDA), FDA, Centers for Disease Control and Prevention, and National Institutes of Health (NIH); or in food-plant inspection or the USDA's Food Safety Inspection Service (FSIS). In food plants, the food microbiologist is often a food technologist with a thorough training in chemistry as well as microbiology, who establishes a laboratory quality assurance manual (LQAM), a training program, and a statistical quality-control program. The food microbiologist must be versed in good manufacturing practices (GMP's), standard operating procedures (SOP's), sanitation, Hazard Analysis and Critical Control Points (HACCP's), rapid methods for the isolation and identification of microorganisms, as well as assays for toxins. HACCP's are designed to ensure food safety, extending beyond microbiological hazards, to chemical (for example, those from mycotoxins and pesticides) and physical (for example, from glass breakage) dangers. To generate an HACCP, the hazards in the plant's processes must be identified, the risk involved at each Critical Control Point must be established, and the critical levels of pathogens at each step in the process must be determined. The process must be monitored, and the monitoring verified. HACCP's are rapidly being required by government industries for more and more food processors. The USDA now mandates that all meat and poultry processors that are federally inspected have an HACCP in operation. The FDA now requires HACCP's for fruit-juice producers. Sanitation methods and monitoring are an extremely important part of any HACCP and a chief duty of a plant's food microbiologist. Surfaces in food-processing plants, meat carcasses, fruits, and vegetables must be kept pathogen-free. The use of simple rapid ATP detection systems (ATP—adenosine triphosphate—degrades quickly and is only found in living cells) allows a food microbiologist to involve plant workers in the sanitation effort. Workers swab sanitized surfaces, process the swab, and read the printout that has been calibrated to tell them the level of cellular contamination. They can resanitize surfaces until the results are acceptable.

In food-production and retail-food plants and in the home, good hygiene, especially hand washing, is the most effective way to eliminate the transmission of these pathogens. Another important practice is proper refrigeration of foods. Finally, proper cooking of raw meats, fish, and eggs by the consumer will destroy any remaining pathogens.

The explosion in genetic and immunological research in the 1980s resulted in many antibody-based and DNA-based methods for the identification of bacteria and toxins. These methods are rapid, reliable, sensitive, and becoming simpler daily. The time-consuming step in the assays is the necessity of initially growing or in some way enriching for the pathogen of interest. There are DNA-based assays for all the major food-borne pathogens. These assays use either DNA probes (usually of 16S rRNA genes, since there are relatively so many copies of these genes in cells) or PCR (a short DNA sequence is amplified in a thermocycler). There are also antibody-based assays for the major food-borne pathogens and toxins. These assays depend upon an antibody produced to some component of a bacterial cell or toxin. The most commonly used antibody-based assay is an ELISA, an enzyme-linked immunosorbent assay. It is described as a "sandwich assay." The test substance is added to a solid support to which the antibody to a particular pathogen is bound. The cell or toxin binds to the antibody. A secondary antibody, which is conjugated to an enzyme, binds to the primary antibody. Addition of the enzyme's substrate results in activity that can be detected. As the field of diagnostics speeds on, the food microbiologist must devote time to a continuing evaluation of newly emerging technologies aimed at reducing or eliminating pathogens as well as microorganisms that adversely affect the quality of food.

Use of Microorganisms for Various Helpful Ends
Before ancient people had any idea of microorganisms, they were using them to ferment foods. Bacteria, yeast, and molds are now used extensively to preserve foods and improve their aroma and flavor. Beer is probably the oldest fermentation product consumed by humans. Its history has been traced back to the Sumerians in 7500 B.C.E. The basic component of beer is a grain or cereal, for example, malted barley, rice, corn, or millet. The major food source in cereals is starch. Barley is germinated to produce starch-degrading enzymes, or amylases. This mixture, "malt," is used to process the starch in barley or other cereals; starch must be broken down into sugar for fermentation to take place. Strains of *Saccharomyces cerevisiae* are used for lager-style beers, and strains of *S. uvarum* for ales. Wine, also an ancient beverage, is made by inoculating fruit juice, usually grape juice, with strains of *S. cerevisiae,* fermenting the high level of sugar in the juice. Many kinds of lactic-acid bacteria (LAB) are also found during yeast fermentation: *Lactobacillus* spp., *Leuconostoc* spp., and *Pediococcus* spp. Winemakers often inoculate their wines with commercial LAB cultures to reduce overly high acidity of juice (grape juice, for example, has a pH of 3.0 to 3.8) and, through their metabolism, to add flavors or "complexity" to the wine.

The bacteria that Pasteur identified as wine spoilers, the acetic-acid bacteria, are used to make vinegar. Wine or cider is inoculated with *Acetobacter* spp., which produce acetic acid by oxidizing ethanol.

Basic bread is made by adding water and salt to wheat flour. Yeast is added to "leaven" bread. The Egyptians obtained yeast from beer vats to leaven their bread. The Greeks and Romans used yeast from wine vats. Now,

SALMON COLOR

Farmed salmon are pale in color. The color of wild salmon comes from their consumption of crustaceans in the ocean. A red yeast, *Phaffia rhodozyma,* is now fed to farmed salmon to color them red. The red pigment in the yeast, astaxanthin, is a carotenoid similar to that found in lobsters.

strains of *S. cerevisiae* are used to ferment the sugars in bread dough. LAB are also used to give special flavors to some breads: for example, *Lactobacillus sanfrancisco* for sourdough and *Lactobacillus plantarum* for rye bread.

LAB are most important in dairy products. In 1878, Joseph Lister (1827–1912) isolated, in pure culture, a bacterium that caused milk souring. LAB are used to curdle milk for cheese production, and to ripen certain cheeses (*Propionibacterium* spp., for instance, for Swiss cheese). LAB are also used in the production of yogurt, buttermilk, and kefir, an alcoholic fermented-milk product. Molds, mainly of the penicillia family, are used to break down the fats in cheese and add distinctive flavors, for example, *Penicillium roqueforti* in Roquefort cheese.

Plant material is fermented to make pickled vegetables, sauerkraut, Spanish-style olives, and soy sauce. LAB, for example, are used to ferment cabbage into sauerkraut. Several genera of bacteria, including LAB, and fungi are used to ferment olives, which are inedible before this processing.

Many fermented products are made in the Far East, often from soybean meal. A *koji,* or mixed culture of bacteria, yeast, and molds, is used to inoculate the food. For soy sauce, for example, soybean meal is inoculated with a *koji* containing *Aspergillus oryzae* and LAB such as *Lactobacillus delbrueckii.* Other common fermented-soybean foods are tempeh, miso, and *sufu* (a traditional Chinese cheeselike product). The acids these microorganisms produce, chiefly acetic, butyric, and lactic, prevent the growth of most other microorganisms. The fermentations not only favorably modify flavors and textures, but also have preservative action.

A bacterium, *Xanthomonas campestris,* produces a polymer, xanthan gum, which is used as a thickener in such foods as salad dressings, cottage cheese, yogurt, ice cream, and frostings.

Harmful Microorganisms

Bacteria, viruses, and protozoa that cause gastroenteritis are transmitted by the fecal–oral route— that is, by the consumption of food or water fecally contaminated by infected persons. The major bacteria that cause gastroenteritis are *Salmonella* spp, *E. coli, Campylobacter jejuni, Vibrio parahaemolyticus,* and *Yersinia enterocolotica.* Ingesting toxins produced by bacteria that have grown in food can also result in gastroenteritis. Bacteria that cause gastroenteritis by producing toxins are *Staphylococcus aureus, Clostridium perfringens,* and *Bacillus cereus.* Rotavirus and the Norwalk virus group are the two major viruses causing gastroenteritis.

Milk is pasteurized to eliminate *Mycobacterium tuberculosis, M. bovis, Salmonella* spp., *Listeria* spp., enteric viruses, *Brucella* spp., *Coxiella burnetii,* and *Campylobacter jejuni.*

Food-borne bacteria can cause serious diseases: *Salmonella typhi* causes typhoid fever; *Shigella* spp. cause bacillary dysentery; *E. coli* strains can cause dysentery; *M. tuberculosis* and *M. bovis* cause tuberculosis; *Vibrio cholerae* causes cholera; *Brucella* spp. cause undulant fever; and *Coxiella burnetii* causes Q fever. *Listeria monocytogenes* causes listeriosis in predisposed populations, for example, immune-compromised individuals. Hepatitis is caused by the Hepatitis A virus and the recently discovered Hepatitis E virus, which is common in Africa and India and other Asian countries, but not in Western countries. In meat and poultry products, *Salmonella, E. coli, Campylobacter jejuni, Listeria,* and *Clostridium perfringens* are the major pathogens. *Listeria monocytogenes* is the major cheese pathogen. Unlike other food-borne pathogens, its temperature growth range (from 31 to 122°F [–0.4 to 50°C]) allows it to grow under refrigeration conditions. Hepatitis viruses and *Yersinia enterocolitica* are major oyster pathogens. Some of the pathogens found on fish are of marine origin, for example, *Vibrio vulnificus, V. parahaemolyticus,* and *V. cholerae,* and others are from sewage, for example *Salmonella* spp. *and Campylobacter* spp. Nuts and grains can become contaminated with mycotoxins, aflatoxins produced by *Aspergillus flavus,* being the most dangerous.

Prions are particles, smaller than viruses, and mostly composed of protein. It has recently been proposed that prions are the cause of four diseases: Creutzfeldt-Jacob disease and kuru in humans, bovine spongiform encephalopathy (BSE or mad cow disease) in cows, and scrapie in sheep. It is now thought that several dozen people have gotten a human form of BSE by eating the meat of infected cattle. This disease has been named new variant Creutzfeldt-Jakob disease, or nvCJD.

See also **Beer; Cheese; Dairy Products; Fermentation; Fermented Beverages other than Wine or Beer; Government Agencies, U.S.; Microorganisms; Packaging and Canning; Pasteur, Louis; Safety, Food; Wine**.

BIBLIOGRAPHY

Bozoglu, T. Faruk, and Bibek Ray, eds. *Lactic Acid Bacteria: Current Advances in Metabolism, Genetics and Applications.* Berlin: NATO ASI series, Springer-Verlag, 1996.

De Kruif, Paul. *Microbe Hunters*. New York: Pocket Books, 1964.

Harrigan, Wilkie F. *Laboratory Methods in Food Microbiology*. 3d ed. London: Harcourt Brace, 1998.

Lechevalier, Hubert A., and Morris Solotorovsky. *Three Centuries of Microbiology*. New York: McGraw-Hill, 1965.

Mortimore, Sara, and Carol Wallace. *HACCP: A Practical Approach*. 2d ed. Gaithersburg, Md.: Aspen, 1998.

Postgate, John. *Microbes and Man*. 3d ed. Cambridge: Cambridge University Press, 1992.

Reed, Gerald, ed. *Prescott and Dunn's Industrial Microbiology*. 4th ed. Westport, Conn.: AVI Publishing, 1982.

Stanier, Roger Y., John L. Ingraham, Mark L. Wheelis, and Page R. Painter. *The Microbial World*. 5th ed. Englewood Cliffs, N.J.: Prentice-Hall, 1990.

U.S. Food and Drug Administration, Center for Food Safety and Applied Nutrition, *Bacteriological Analytical Manual Online*. Available at http:/vm.cfsan.fda.gov/ebam/bam-toc.html.

U.S. Food and Drug Administration, Center for Food Safety and Applied Nutrition, *Foodborne Pathogenic Microorganisms and Natural Toxins Handbook*. Available at http://vm.cfsan.fda.gov/mow/badbug.zip.

Vanderzant, C., and D. Splittstoesser, eds. *Compendium of Methods for the Microbiological Examination of Foods*. Washington, D.C.: American Public Health Association, 1992.

Wood, Brian J. B., ed. *Microbiology of Fermented Foods*. 2d ed., 2 vols. London: Blackie Academic and Professional, Thomson Science, 1998.

Susan Rodriguez
Roy Thornton

MICRONESIA. *See* **Pacific Ocean Societies.**

MICROORGANISMS. Microorganisms are organisms (forms of life) requiring magnification to see and resolve their structures. "Microorganism" is a general term that becomes more understandable if it is divided into its principal types—bacteria, yeasts, molds, protozoa, algae, and rickettsia—predominantly unicellular microbes. Viruses are also included, although they cannot live or reproduce on their own. They are particles, not cells; they consist of deoxyribonucleic acid (DNA) or ribonucleic acid (RNA), but not both. Viruses invade living cells—bacteria, algae, fungi, protozoa, plants, and animals (including humans)—and use their hosts' metabolic and genetic machinery to produce thousands of new virus particles. Some viruses can transform normal cells to cancer cells. Rickettsias and chlamydiae are very small cells that can grow and multiply only inside other living cells. Although bacteria, actinomycetes, yeasts, and molds are cells that must be magnified in order to see them, when cultured on solid media that allow their growth and multiplication, they form visible colonies consisting of millions of cells.

Many people think of microorganisms mainly in terms of "germs" causing diseases, but some "germs" are beneficial to humans and the environment. Disease-causing (pathogenic) microorganisms need to be controlled, and in many cases, beneficial microorganisms are also controlled in plant and food production.

For thousands of years, people had no concept or knowledge of organisms invisible to the naked eye. In fact, it is only within the last several hundred years that magnification systems (lenses, magnifiers, microscopes) were developed that enabled scientists to observe microorganisms. In 1673 Antoni van Leeuwenhoek, a linen merchant in Delft in the Netherlands, was the first to observe and study microorganisms, using single lenses that magnified objects fifty to three hundred times. The role played by microorganisms was not clarified until the 1830s, when Theodor Schwann in Germany demonstrated that yeasts were responsible for alcohol production in beer and wine fermentations.

In 1854, Louis Pasteur in France found that spoilage of wines was due to microorganisms (bacteria) that convert sugars to lactic acid, rather than the alcohol produced by yeasts. He developed the process of "pasteurization," in which the temperature of food materials is raised to about 140 to 158°F (60 to 70°C), thereby killing many spoilage organisms. Pasteur also discovered that certain bacteria are responsible for the souring of milk. Today, milk is generally pasteurized to reduce its content of microorganisms, to extend its keeping quality, and to protect against pathogenic microorganisms that may be present.

Pasteur also discovered that each type of fermentation, as defined by the end products, is caused by specific microorganisms and requires certain conditions of acidity or alkalinity. He discovered further that some microorganisms, the aerobes, require oxygen and others, the anaerobes, grow only in the absence of oxygen. The latter probably developed in the earliest days of the earth when there was no oxygen in the atmosphere.

Microorganisms are present in high populations in soil, and in varying numbers in the air we breathe, the water we drink, and the food we eat; they are on our skin and in our noses, throats, mouths, intestinal tracts, and other bodily cavities. They are everywhere in our environment.

Evolution of Microorganisms

Microorganisms came into being on earth over a period of about 1.2 to 1.5 billion years. Fossil microbes have been found in rocks 3.3 to 3.5 billion years old. Since then, microorganisms have had the principal task of recycling organic matter in the environment. As such they are absolutely essential to the health of the earth. Without them, the earth would be a gigantic, permanent waste dump.

Microorganisms are responsible for recycling the huge masses of organic matter synthesized by plants as

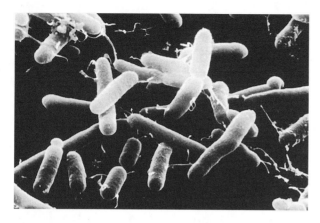

A microscopic view of *Salmonella,* the bacteria that contaminate food and cause widespread illness. COURTESY OF PHOTO RESEARCHERS, INC.

life on earth evolved. Furthermore, microorganisms—the cyanobacteria or their DNA in the chloroplasts in plant cells—were the source of most of the free oxygen in the early atmosphere. They also oxidize ammonia (the universal end product of protein metabolism) to nitrate, which is the only nitrogen source used by plants and is therefore essential for production of our plant foods. Microorganisms also are responsible for cellulose hydrolysis in the rumens (first stomach compartments) of cattle, facilitating the production of animal protein for human consumption. And, in recent times, microorganisms have been the sources of antibiotics that have enabled the cure of numerous diseases.

Blue-green algae (cyanobacteria) are prokaryotes (that is, their cells have no distinct nucleus). They are very independent nutritionally since they can perform photosynthesis using chlorophyll a. Thus they can synthesize sugars for energy from carbon dioxide using the sun's radiation. They also release oxygen. They can respire aerobically and can fix nitrogen, generating amino acids and protein. They require only water, nitrogen gas, oxygen, carbon dioxide, some minerals, and sunlight. The evidence is that they were on earth 3.2 billion years ago. The cyanobacteria are among the earliest microorganisms and very important even today.

Green algae are eukaryotes (that is, their cells have a distinct nucleus). They evolved about one billion years ago. They contain chlorophylls a and b, which enable them to convert carbon dioxide, through sunlight radiation, to sugars, and to polymerize sugars to starches, hemicelluloses, and celluloses—some of our most important sources of food energy.

Green algae are still major sources of food in the oceans. Green algae were likely the life forms that evolved into plants, which first lived primarily in the oceans but moved to the land about 450 million years ago, about the same time as the amphibians and first land animals

evolved. It is believed that the first mammals evolved about 150 million years later, along with insects and reptiles, which were dominant. Another 150 million years later, dinosaurs and the first birds evolved, along with the first flowering plants. During the entire period from 3.6 billion years ago, microorganisms were consuming and recycling the organic matter from themselves and other forms of life as they lived and died. For several billion years, bacteria, algae, and other microorganisms served as food for other microbes and for higher animals as they evolved. When plants evolved in the oceans and then subsequently moved to land, they became the major sources of food for other forms of life, including microorganisms, animals, and eventually humans.

Evolution of Plants: The Basis for Human Foods and Animal Feeds

For at least 400 million years before humans appeared on earth, plants were producing food consisting of leaves, stems, seeds, nuts, berries, fruits, tubers, etc., that made life possible for humans and animals when they evolved. Early plant evolution was essential not only for food but also for producing an oxygen environment necessary for animal and human survival. Plants introduced a very effective way of using the sun's radiation to transform carbon dioxide into food materials, such as sugars, starches, and cellulose, through the green pigment chlorophyll and the organelle that serves as the site for photosynthesis, the chloroplast.

Both plants and animals evolved in a microbial environment, where the microbes were ready and able to recycle organic matter. Plants and animals had to develop ways of resisting microbial invasion. Plants did this in part by developing a lignocellulosic body resistant to microbial breakdown. Humans also evolved in a sea of microorganisms and have a tough skin over their bodies resistant to microbial invasion. They had to develop internal immune systems against invasion by microorganisms. Human blood contains phagocytes similar to and probably derived from free-living amoebas, which search out and consume invading bacteria. Then as now, some microorganisms could invade the live animal or human, causing disease.

Microbes enter our bodies in the air we breathe into our noses and lungs, into our mouths and throats, stomachs, and intestinal tracts via the water and foods we swallow, through our eye sockets, through our skin via abrasions and punctures, and through our genitals and other mucous membranes. This intimate contact with microbes begins at birth and continues through life. Some microorganisms become regular inhabitants, parasites of our bodies; they become what can be described as our normal flora. Some microorganisms are virulent, invading our bodies and upsetting our metabolic activities and causing disease; these are the pathogenic microbes. Other microbes are normal microbial flora or pathogens on plants. Still other microbes are continuously invading plant food materials and recycling the organic matter. If this activity is controlled and stopped at the proper levels, these become our fermented foods, which include alcoholic foods and beverages; vinegars; lactic-acid-fermented cabbage and other vegetables (that is, sauerkraut and pickles); lactic-acid-fermented milks and cheeses; sourdough breads; Indian *idli* (from rice); Ethiopian *enjera* (a bread made from teff, an indigenous cereal grass); textured-vegetable-protein meat-substitutes, such as Indonesian tempeh (from soybeans or, sometimes, peanuts) and *ontjom* (from peanuts or, sometimes, soy fiber); high-salt meat-flavored amino acid/peptide soy sauces and pastes; African alkaline-fermented foods such as *dawadawa, soumbara,* and *iru* (all from locust beans *[Parkia biglobosa]* or soybeans); Indian *kenima,* Japanese *natto,* and Thai *thua-nao* (all from soybeans); and leavened yeast breads.

Microorganisms Causing Food Poisoning

Three species of bacteria cause food poisoning via preformed toxin: *Clostridium botulinum, Staphylococcus aureus,* and *Bacillus cereus.*

Clostridium botulinum is a bacterium that grows in the absence of oxygen and produces one of the most toxic, deadly chemicals known to humans. It was first isolated from sausages, but later was responsible for death in persons consuming home-canned vegetables. The symptoms are flaccid paralysis eighteen to thirty-six hours after ingestion, with respiratory paralysis and death if untreated. There are antitoxins against botulinum toxin, if the type is identified and the antitoxin is injected in time. Botulinum toxin can be inactivated by heating the food to boiling for five minutes. Interestingly enough, botulinum toxin, in spite of its great toxicity is finding a use in eliminating lines and wrinkles from human skin by preventing activity of muscles directly involving those areas of the skin that have wrinkles or expressions. This is partially a response to the fact that very toxic substances in minute quantities can become stimulants.

A second serious type of food poisoning is caused by the ingestion of staphylococcal toxin produced by *Staphylococcus aureus* in foods such as cream puffs, mayonnaise, ice cream, or other nutritious foods that become infected with staphylococci, often carried in the nasal secretions of food handlers. Staphylococcal toxin causes a rather violent nausea and vomiting thirty minutes to six hours after consuming food contaminated with the toxin. Staphylococcus toxin is not inactivated by boiling. It generally is not fatal.

Bacillus cereus also produces a food-poisoning toxin. Steamed rice held overnight at room temperature has been a typical food causing *Bacillus cereus* poisoning. There are two toxins involved—one causing nausea and vomiting, the other causing diarrhea. The toxins are not inactivated by boiling.

Microorganisms Producing Food Poisoning by Toxins Formed in the Intestinal Tract

Clostridium perfringens, an anaerobic microorganism that can cause gangrene in wounds, can also cause food poisoning if it overgrows food materials, such as gravies and meats, which are then consumed. It produces its toxin in the intestinal tract of the consumer and causes diarrhea.

Vibrio cholerae is a major cause of cholera in man; it is spread via contaminated water and food. The symptoms are profuse diarrhea, which, if not treated to replace fluids in the body, will lead to death. *Vibrio parahemolyticus,* found in contaminated shellfish, also leads to profuse diarrhea and requires fluid replacement and antibiotics.

Shiga toxin–producing *Escherichia coli* (STEC), found in contaminated water and meats such as hamburger, is a serious food pathogen leading to hemorrhagic colitis (diarrhea with blood). Bovine products are a major source, but lettuce, alfalfa sprouts, and apple cider have also been implicated.

Enterotoxigenic *E. coli* (ETEC) is frequently found in developing countries in contaminated water and food and is associated with travelers' diarrhea (diarrhea without blood).

Food-Borne Bacteria Invading Intestinal Epithelial Cells

Common causes of food-borne illness are salmonella bacteria. *Salmonella typhi* and *Salmonella paratyphi,* gram negative bacilli that invade the intestinal epithelial cells, cause typhoid and paratyphoid fever, respectively. They are generally found in water or food contaminated with fecal material from carriers of salmonella. Other salmonellae are carried by infected poultry meats and eggs.

Campylobacter spp. are now recognized as one of the most common causes of food gastroenteritis. Main vehicles are raw meats (especially poultry), milk, and water. Fever (sometimes high), headache, and myalgia (muscle pain) precede nausea, vomiting, and diarrhea. *Yersinia* spp., carried chiefly in undercooked pork but sometimes also in milk, is another serious food-borne infection.

Listeria monocytogenes is the cause of a food-borne disease that is frightening because of its high mortality (fatality is over twenty percent). Among incriminated foods are milk, cheese, raw vegetables, and undercooked meat, including frankfurters.

Viral food-borne pathogens include hepatitis A, hepatitis E, rotavirus, and Norwalk virus. Although these viruses do not reproduce in food or water, they are spread by contaminated human carriers and food handlers through such media.

Fermented Foods

Seeds for plants germinate in the soil surrounded and covered with microorganisms. A pinch of dirt can contain a billion microorganisms of many types. The plants destined as foods for humans and animals grow in soil surrounded and covered with microorganisms ready to invade any organic matter and recycle it (essentially consume the organic matter and return it to compost utilizable by new seeds and plants). When the plant materials—seeds, nuts, leaves, tubers, stems, roots—are harvested, they are contaminated or infected with the types of microbes present in the soil; the microbes immediately start to grow on any susceptible organic matter that is available, as long as there is sufficient moisture to allow growth. Dry seeds and leaves are resistant to overgrowth by microorganisms, but as soon as they absorb enough moisture, they become susceptible to microbial growth. If the products of the microbial growth have desirable or attractive aromas and flavors and if they are nontoxic and do not cause disease when consumed, they can be described as "fermented foods" and can become an accepted food in the diet. If they have unpleasant aromas or bad flavors or if they cause food poisoning or death when consumed, they are considered to be spoiled and become garbage on their way to compost or soil. From the earliest times, our food supply has been strongly affected by fermentation.

Alcoholic beverages. The earliest sweet food on earth was likely honey, produced by honeybees and stored for their future use. Humans, in competition with animals such as bears, have always striven to collect honey for their own consumption. Honey is very resistant to spoilage in its concentrated form (about eighty percent sugars), but if it is collected and stored in a container and becomes diluted by rain water, yeasts present in the environment ferment the sugar in the honey to ethyl alcohol (ethanol). The products are called mead or honey wine, one of the earliest alcoholic beverages known to humans and still consumed today.

Similarly when humans started collecting sweet fruits and berries in containers, the juices as well as the fruits and berries themselves were quickly invaded by yeasts on the surfaces of the fruits that ferment the sugars to alcohol (actually a step in recycling), producing a primitive wine. For better or worse, humans have prized alcoholic beverages and they are still consumed in large quantities throughout the world except in those populations that avoid alcohol because of religious restrictions. In some religions, wines are a component of the religious services. Humans discovered ways of producing other alcoholic beverages. For example, early man probably discovered that chewed corn when mixed with water and stored in a container produces an alcoholic beverage. The process occurs because saliva contains an enzyme, diastase, that converts starch in the corn to sugars; then yeasts in the environment ferment the sugars to alcohol. The beverage thus produced is called *chicha* in the Andes region of South America. In ancient times, an emperor in that region could hold office only as long as he delivered sufficient *chicha* to the citizens to keep them happy. Even today, among families in the Andes region, husbands will get drunk one weekend and wives will get drunk the next, ensuring that at least one parent is sober and able to look after the children.

Juices from palm trees are collected by cutting the flowers and allowing the sap to flow through bamboo tubes into a container. As the juices flow through the tubes, they become infected with yeasts and other microorganisms. The sugars are fermented to alcohol and the product, palm wine, is produced in large quantities in the tropics. It is very rich in vitamins valuable to the consumer.

When cereal grains such as rice, barley, wheat, and corn are collected and soaked, or if they become wet from rain, they start to germinate, and starch in the seeds is changed to fermentable sugars that are fermented by yeasts in the environment, yielding an alcoholic beer. It has been suggested by anthropologists that this process was an early cause of fundamental social change. To ensure the continuity of supply of fermentable sugars, people settled in permanent locations. Agriculture, in turn, was a way of ensuring the regularity of production of fermentable cereal grains.

Alcoholic beverages are major fermented foods in the diet of humans. The yeast fermentation not only leads to a highly accepted beverage, it is a safe method of preserving fruit and berry juices until they can be consumed. The yeasts also enrich the beverages with B-vitamins.

As long as the wine or beer is kept anaerobic (air is excluded), it is preserved, but if there is access to air, there is a second fermentation by bacteria (*Acetobacter*) in the environment that transforms the alcohol to acetic acid (vinegar), which is even more preservative than ethyl alcohol. Many primitive wines and beers contain both alcohol and acetic acid. The vinegar fermentation is an ancient process that is still very important today. Vinegar is used to preserve cucumbers and other vegetables as pickles, which make an important contribution to the food supply of people around the world.

Milk products. As soon as humans started milking cows, they found that milk held a few hours at room temperature became sour. They did not know why, but it was, in fact, the streptococci and lactobacilli in the environment that produce lactic acid from lactose in the milk. This is the basis for yogurts, and the souring process as practiced in the early days also led to the development of cheeses.

The principal early milks were those from sheep or goats. Milk was often collected and stored in animal stomachs or hides, which allowed for the souring process to occur, the butter to be removed, and the milk curds to accumulate. The skin of a sheep or goat was carefully removed undamaged. The openings of the limbs and neck and the natural openings were tied. The hair was removed and the skin bag was used to collect the milk. During souring, the curds separate from the whey. The curds gradually lose moisture through the porous container, and further microbial activity and chemical changes lead to a primitive cheese. Today there are more than three hundred types of milk cheeses available. They have a wide range of flavors and textures and add variety and high-quality nutrition to the diets of consumers.

In addition to the bacterial cheeses, fungal cheeses involving growth of *Penicillium roqueforti* (Roquefort cheese and blue cheese) and *Penicillium camemberti* (Camembert cheese) on or in the cheese curd led to new flavors and textures for this class of fermented foods.

The Chinese developed a cheese from soybean milk, called *sufu*. Soybeans are soaked, ground with water, filtered to obtain the fluid milk, and heated to near boiling, and the curd is precipitated with calcium or magnesium salts. The filtered and pressed curd is then inoculated and becomes overgrown with *Mucor* spp. mold, after which it is aged in a salt and alcoholic brine. It is then ready for consumption.

Lactic-acid fermentations. An ancient food-fermentation technique is found in the South Pacific, where islanders centuries ago discovered that foods such as cassava, plantains, and bananas could be preserved for long times by piercing them and packing them in pits that were sealed against oxygen entry. Lactobacilli, *leuconostocs*, and streptococci ferment sugars in the stored food materials to lactic acid, acidifying them and preserving the food against spoilage as long as the pits remain sealed. Pits opened after one hundred years of storage have revealed edible products—the result of bacterial fermentation.

In Ethiopia, pulp of the false banana, a starchy paste, is similarly stored in pits and undergoes lactic-acid fermentation, preserving the starch, which serves as a base for bread. Lactic-acid fermentations of cabbage—for example, sauerkraut and Korean kimchi (which is based upon Chinese cabbage, radishes, and red pepper)—are important processes around the world. Sauerkraut and kimchi are particularly interesting applications of bacterial fermentation. The cabbage is shredded and two to three percent common salt is added. The salt extracts nutrients from the cabbage and a series of bacterial species (*Leuconostoc, Lactobacillus, Pediococcus*) overgrow the cabbage, producing lactic acid and carbon dioxide that preserve the cabbage; and as long as the product is kept anaerobic, it remains preserved.

Soybeans, with a content of about twenty percent fat and forty percent protein, are a very nutritious food source, first cultivated in Asia. They are harvested dry and have an excellent keeping quality. However, if they are moistened or soaked in water, they become susceptible to overgrowth by bacteria that first acidify them. Then they may be boiled, as in preparation for eating. After this, they become susceptible to overgrowth by molds. In Korea and northern China, the average temperature is cool, below 86°F (30°C), and the moistened soybeans become overgrown by *Aspergillus oryzae*, a mold that is present in the environment, particularly on the soybean straw. If such soybeans are stored under the roof, as is commonly practiced, the soybeans first become white from the mold mycelium (a mass of filamentous growth). Then they become green from the mold spores. During this time, the mold is producing many kinds of digestive enzymes. If such mold-covered soybeans are then mixed with water and salt to form a paste, it will be found that the paste has a meatlike flavor because of the amino acids and peptides released by the mold as it digests the soybean proteins. The end product of this process, called miso in Japan and *chiang* (soybean paste) in China, is used extensively as an ingredient for soup. If the mold-covered soybeans are placed in salt water, especially concentrated salt brine, it is found that the soybeans, which are initially bland in flavor, become meat-flavored, as in the miso process. The product, when filtered, is soy sauce. Today, soy sauces are used to season and marinate foods, not only in Asia but around the world.

Soybeans are also used in Southeast Asia—in Indonesia, Malaysia, and Vietnam. However, the average temperature is generally higher, about 90 to 100°F (32 to 38°C). *Aspergillus* molds grow optimally at about 77 to 86°F (25 to 38°C), so they tend to invade the soybeans in North Asia. In Southeast Asia, other molds such as *Rhizopus oryzae* and *Mucor* spp. grow faster and better at the higher temperature. Thus the environment becomes infected with spores of these molds. When soybeans are soaked or moistened in Southeast Asia and are then cooked and cooled, they become overgrown with molds of the *Rhizopus* or *Mucor* types. If allowed to digest as a paste or in salt brine, they also can lead to a soy-sauce or miso flavor, but the Indonesians and Malaysians allow the mold-covered soybeans to become knitted into a cake that can be sliced and deep-fat fried or used in soups as a substitute for meat, which is generally in short supply in the diet. The product is called *tempeh kedelee* when made from soybeans. The Indonesians have developed other products using peanut and coconut press cakes (from the production of oil) as substrates. The pulverized, soaked press cakes are re–formed into cakes and steamed. They then become overgrown with *Rhizopus* or *Neurospora* molds to produce foods called *ontjom* (peanut) and *bongkrek* (coconut) that like tempeh have a texture that allows them to be sliced and used as a substitute for meat in soups.

Fermented foods have been consumed by humans for centuries and are generally safe, but it should be cautioned that some molds produce toxic, even carcinogenic, products (for example, aflatoxins) and should not be consumed.

There are numerous other fermented foods that utilize edible microorganisms in their production and add variety and nutritive value to our diets.

The Role of Microorganisms in Soil

Plant life, our basic food supply, is dependent upon the trillions and trillions of microbes that exist in the soil, degrading organic matter, recycling nitrogen and carbon, and producing new soil in forms plants can use directly. Thus, good soil, far from being dead, should be described as "living soil," because of its content of living microorganisms. In fact, the rhizosphere, the area surrounding the roots of most plants, contains a wide variety of microorganisms that help the plant to absorb minerals and other plant nutrients. Some plants, such as legumes, have nodules on their roots that contain nitrogen-fixing bacteria, which take nitrogen from the air and produce nitrogen compounds the plants use in the synthesis of amino acids and protein; these are an important protein source in the human diet.

Microorganisms as Food

Blue-green algae of the genus *Spirulina* have been harvested from ponds and eaten for centuries by the ancient Aztecs in Mexico and Africans in the region of Lake Chad.

Mushrooms, the fruiting bodies of microorganisms that live on decaying lignocellulosic compounds in soil, are highly prized as food by nearly all human societies, as well as by many animals, including insects.

Fermentation plays several roles: (1) enrichment of the human diet through development of a wide diversity of flavors, aromas, and textures in food; (2) preservation of substantial amounts of food through lactic acid, alcoholic, acetic acid, and alkaline fermentations; (3) enrichment of food substrates biologically with protein, essential amino acids, essential fatty acids, and vitamins. Protein content is often increased, as for example in Malaysian *tape ketan* and *tape ketella* by utilization of the carbohydrates, lowering their percentage and raising the percentage of protein in the food. Protein quality is also increased by the synthesis of essential amino acids such as lysine, first limiting amino acid in rice. In the Malaysian *tape* fermentation the content of lysine is raised, improving its protein quality. In the Indian *idli* fermentation, it has been reported that methionine, the first limiting amino acid in many legumes, is increased from 10.6 to 60 percent. Highly polished rice is deficient in thiamine (vitamin B_1), and consumption can lead to beriberi, a disease characterized by muscular weakness. In the Malaysian *tape* fermentation, thiamine content is raised to that of the original unpolished rice. In the Indonesian *tempeh* fermentation the content of riboflavin doubles, niacin increases seven-fold, and vitamin B_{12}, which generally absent in vegetarian foods, is synthesized. In the African kafir beer fermentation, riboflavin doubles and niacin/nicotinic acid concentration nearly doubles. Mexican *pulque*, the oldest alcoholic beverage on the American continent, contains thiamine, riboflavin, niacin, pantothenic acid, pyridoxine, and biotin that are of particular importance to the low income children of Mexico.

There is much hunger, starvation, and malnutrition in parts of the world today, and the world population is predicted to reach eight to twelve billion by the year 2050. As world population increases, the supply of meat and other animal products available per person is likely to decrease. A large, capable research institute in England has developed a process in which edible mold mycelium is grown and used to provide protein and texture for meat analogues (substitutes) for the human diet. Microbial protein can also be extracted from cells, and then concentrated, isolated, and spun or extruded to make meat substitutes.

Although this would appear to be very advanced technology, the Indonesians for centuries have overgrown soaked, partially cooked soybean cotyledons with the mold *Rhizopus oligosporus* (as mentioned above), which knits the soybean cotyledons into a firm cake that can be sliced and deep-fat fried or used in chunks as a substitute for meat in soups. The protein content rivals that of meat and the cost is very low, within the means of the average Indonesian. Also, the microorganisms involved enrich the food with vitamin B_{12}, increase niacin by a factor of seven, and double the riboflavin content.

Among plants, the grasses are the most efficient fixers and utilizers of carbon dioxide, producing sugars, starches, and cellulose; they are also synthesizers of protein, using nitrogen from the soil. Grasses can double their cell-mass in two to three weeks. A 1000 kg harvest of grass can be repeated every two to three weeks. However, yeasts are much more efficient in this regard. A yeast (1000 kg) grown in tanks on limited land space can produce 168,000 kg of cells containing 84,000 kg of protein every two weeks.

Bacteria are even more efficient: whereas yeasts can double their cell mass in about two hours, some bacteria can double their cell mass in twenty minutes. Still, 1000 kg of yeast growing in a suitable fermentor can produce 1000 kg of new cells for harvesting every two hours, with a daily production of 12,000 kg of cells containing 50 percent or 6000 kg of protein. (Molds generally grow more slowly, doubling their cell mass in four to six hours.) Since the protein content of bacterial cells may reach 80 percent (compared with 40 to 45 percent in soybeans, for example), there is no method of producing protein that can compete with microbial cells. Except for algae, microbes require energy sources such as sugars, starches, cellulose, or hydrocarbons—all derived originally from the sun's radiation. But they can utilize energy sources that humans cannot digest, such as cellulose and lignocellulose found in straw. As described earlier, mushrooms are a good example of such microorganisms: they produce delicious, edible food directly from straw and sugarcane bagasse.

Only about twenty-five species of more than two thousand edible fungi are widely accepted as human food. The four most important mushrooms are the commonly cultivated white mushroom or button mushroom (*Agaricus campestris*), the black forest mushroom shiitake (*Lentinus edodes*), the straw mushroom (*Volvariella volvacea*), and the oyster mushroom (*Pleurotus ostreatus*).

Mushrooms can be grown on a wide variety of inexpensive, inedible substrates such as cereal straws, sugarcane bagasse, banana leaves, sawdust, cotton wastes, and animal manure. World production of straw is estimated to be about two billion tons. One kg of dry straw compost material can yield one kg of fresh mushrooms. Thus, straw, if all were used for production of mushrooms worldwide, could provide eight billion consumers with 250 grams of fresh mushrooms daily. Mushrooms are high in essential amino acids and nutritional value. They also appeal to almost all consumers for their flavors and flavor-enhancing capabilities. Mushrooms, a microbial product, are thus likely to play an important role in feeding the world in the future. And straw, after serving as a substrate for mushroom production, is nutritionally superior to raw straw for feeding cattle. The straw has been partially recycled and made more digestible in the process.

As world population rises in the twenty-first century, microbes may be used to a much greater extent to feed mankind, or at least feed animals that, in turn, will yield meat for the human diet. Humans, plants, and animals have been intimately involved with microorganisms ever since they evolved. While some of the microorganisms cause serious diseases, there are also many that provide foods and feeds and are beneficial to other life on earth.

See also **Cheese**; **Fungi**; **Microbiology**; **Packaging and Canning**; **Pasteur, Louis**; **Safety, Food**; **Southeast Asia**; **Soy**.

BIBLIOGRAPHY

Jay, James M. *Modern Food Microbiology.* 6th ed. Westport, Conn.: AVI Publishing, 2000.

Kosikowski, Frank V. *Cheese and Fermented Milk Foods.* 2d ed. Brooktondale, N.Y.: F. V. Kosikowski, 1982.

Readers Digest Association, Ltd. *The Last Two Million Years.* London: Readers Digest, 1974.

Schopf, J. W., and B. M. Packer. "Early Archean (3.3 billion-to 3.5 billion-year-old) Microfossils from the Warrawoona Group, Australia." *Science* 237 (1987): 70–73.

Singleton, Paul. *Bacteria in Biology, Biotechnology, and Medicine.* 5th ed. New York: Wiley, 1999.

Steinkraus, Keith H. "Bio-Enrichment: Production of Vitamins in Fermented Foods." In *Microbiology of Fermented Foods,* edited by B. J. B. Wood, pp. 603–621. London: Blackie Academic and Professional, 1998.

Steinkraus, Keith H. "Classification of Fermented Foods: Worldwide Review of Household Fermentation Techniques." *Food Control* 8, no. 5–6 (1997): 311–317.

Steinkraus, Keith H., ed. *Handbook of Indigenous Fermented Foods.* 2d ed. New York: M. Dekker, 1996.

Steinkraus, Keith H., ed. *Industrialization of Indigenous Fermented Foods.* New York: M. Dekker, 1989.

Steinkraus, Keith H. "Nutritional Significance of Fermented Foods." *Food Research International* 27 (1994): 259–267.

Tortora, Gerard J., Berdell R. Funke, and Christine L. Case. *Microbiology: An Introduction.* 7th ed. San Francisco: Benjamin Cummings, 2001.

Toussaint-Samat, Marguellonne. Trans. Anthea Bell. *History of Food.* Cambridge, Mass.: Blackwell, 1993.

Wilson, Edward O., et al. *Life on Earth.* 2d ed. Sunderland, Mass.: Sinauer, 1978.

Keith H. Steinkraus

MICROWAVE OVEN.

While experimenting with radar during World War II, Percy Spencer of Raytheon Corporation in Waltham, Massachusetts, discovered the heating properties of microwaves. With a candy bar in his pocket, he leaned in front of the microwave tube and the candy bar promptly melted. This event led to the birth of microwave ovens.

In 1945 Spencer submitted his first patent application for heating food with microwaves. The patent described two parallel magnetrons that heat food that passes by on a conveyor belt. Two years later, William M. Hall and Fritz A. Gross, Spencer's co-workers, applied for a patent for a microwave-heating device enclosed in an oven. This device consisted of two microwave-generating magnetron tubes packed in a metallic box. The oven included a timer and a means of controlling power.

Raytheon's president, Laurence Marshall, was interested in Spencer's patent. A prototype microwave oven was constructed in 1946 costing an estimated $100,000. Marshall was also enthusiastic about the prototype and ordered engineers to develop an oven in which cold sandwiches could be heated. A contest was held to name the new oven—the winner was "Radarange."

Commercial Microwaves

The first commercial Radarange model was a freestanding white-enamel unit operating at 220 volts of electricity and with an internal water-cooling system. The first Raytheon microwave oven was sold to a restaurant in Cleveland, Ohio, in 1947. Subsequent Radaranges incorporated sliding vertical doors. With a price tag of $3,000, sales were mainly limited to restaurants, railroads, cruise ships, and vending-machine companies.

Development of the microwave oven continued during the 1950s. Raytheon dominated the field of commercial microwave ovens and heating applications: It was the only manufacturer of ovens for restaurants and was the principal magnetron manufacturer. Raytheon licensed other companies, such as Hotpoint, Westinghouse, Kelvinator, Whirlpool, and Tappan, to manufacture the ovens. Raytheon furnished power supplies, magnetrons, and basic-oven design data to each company. The Tappan Company began experimenting with a Radarange installed in their lab. Tappan engineers, who were experts in cooking, teamed up with the Raytheon microwave engineers. In January 1952 the Tappan Company developed the first domestic commercial Radarange. It was powered by a 1,400- to 1,700-watt magnetron that was water cooled and required plumbing connections. The unit was five and a half feet high and weighed 750 pounds.

Domestic Microwaves

The experimental unit developed by Tappan was impractical for domestic use. What was needed was a magnetron requiring less power and a heat dislocation system that could replace the water cooling mechanism. Tappan engineers designed a cabinet with an air-cooled system. Eventually, the magnetron and related components, which had fed microwaves directly into the cavity, were relocated behind the oven. In October 1955, Tappan introduced the first domestic microwave oven for the consumer market. Designed to fit a standard forty-inch range or for built-in use, the unit had a stainless-steel exterior and aluminum oven cavity with a glass shelf. The oven featured two cooking speeds (500 or 800 watts), a browning element, timer, and a recipe-card file drawer. It retailed for $1,295. The unit was marketed as an "electric range." Its advertised advantages were cooking speed, a cool oven, and a unique reheating capability.

General Electric's Hotpoint division, which also had been researching microwave cooking, unveiled its electronic oven the following year. Both the Tappan and Hotpoint oven generated unprecedented enthusiasm and interest in 1956, but sales were dismal. The price was high for the average consumer, and food-processing techniques for the microwave were not well understood. Few food processors took the technology seriously, thus few microwaveable foods were produced.

Breakthroughs

Tappan continued to improve its product. By 1965 Tappan had introduced the first "microwave cooking center," which consisted of a microwave oven mounted above a conventional range. This unit still retailed for well over $1,000. Despite these advances, only ten thousand households in the United States owned microwaves by 1966.

Two events revolutionized the microwave industry. The first was the invention by Keisha Ogura of the New Japan Radio Company—40 percent of which was owned by Raytheon—of a compact, low-cost magnetron. The second was Raytheon's acquisition of Amana Refrigeration, Inc. George Forestner, Amana's president, was a microwave visionary. Amana appliance engineers teamed up with Raytheon experts to develop and design a household Radarange. In August 1967, Amana released its first microwave oven, the Amana RR-1. It operated at 115 volts and sold for $495. The unit was well received. The Amana RR-1 set off a revolution in microwave oven technology, and Amana's success encouraged other appliance manufacturers to produce microwave ovens.

Another important microwave oven manufacturer was Litton, which acquired a small microwave manufacturer called Heat & Eat in 1964. Previously, Litton had manufactured commercial microwave ovens for restaurants. Its newly named Microwave Cooking Products Division in Minneapolis targeted the home market. Litton's Model 500 used 115 volts and was compact. These ovens were installed on TWA planes in 1965, and Litton dominated the restaurant business by 1970.

Microwave Challenges

Despite the initial successes, there were still problems to overcome before the microwave oven would be generally accepted. Manufacturers needed to convince the public that microwave ovens were safe. This fear began with the U.S. Congress's passage of the Radiation Control for Health and Safety Act in 1968. On 4 January 1970, the U.S. Department of Health, Education, and Welfare published the results of microwave oven radiation tests. The tests showed that microwave ovens leaked microwaves. Thus the federal government developed new standards and required changes in the construction of ovens beginning on 6 October 1971. These new regulations required design changes that would result in safer microwave ovens. Public apprehension slowly abated.

Another crucial challenge was convincing food processors to repackage their products. Foods packed in foil blocked microwaves and damaged ovens. Also, frozen foods contained too much water for microwave use. At first, food processors were not interested in working with microwave manufacturers. By the 1970s, however, more than 10 percent of all U.S. homes possessed microwaves, many microwave ovens were in use in vending businesses, and numbers were steadily increasing. Major food processors quickly reversed their direction and invested in microwaveable food products, and specialized microwave cookware was introduced. By 1975 microwave ovens outsold gas ranges, with sales of over one million units. In the early twenty-first century, the primary use of microwave ovens in the United States was to reheat food.

See also **Fast Food; Frozen Food; Kitchen Gadgets; Kitchens, Restaurant; Popcorn; Preparation of Food; Storage of Food**.

BIBLIOGRAPHY

Behrens, Charles W. "The Development of the Microwave Oven." *Appliance Manufacturer* 24 (November 1976): 72.

Buderi, Robert. *The Invention That Changed the World: How a Small Group of Radar Pioneers Won the Second World War and Launched a Technological Revolution.* New York: Simon & Schuster, 1997.

Osepchuk, John. "A History of Microwave Applications." *IEEE Transactions on Microwave Theory and Technique* 32 (September 1984): 1211.

Smith, Andrew F. *Popped Culture: A Social History of Popcorn in America.* Columbia: University of South Carolina Press, 1999.

Andrew F. Smith

MIDDLE AGES, EUROPEAN. To understand medieval cuisine, we have to start with Roman culinary practice, which probably kept its influence long after the decline of the Roman Empire. Two ingredients were of particular importance here: the liquid salt called *garum* or *liquamen* and the granular gum *asa foetida* or *laser Parthicum*. *Liquamen* or *garum* was the liquid salt of Roman high cuisine; it was usually made not by the cooks themselves but in factories, notably in Pompeii. For this purpose a vessel holding about thirty liters was filled with layers of fish, salt, and dried herbs, and then covered. This mixture stayed in the sun for a week and was then stirred well daily for twenty days until the fish and herbs were fully pulverized by fermentation and blended into a liquid. This was strained and sold in amphorae. Often it was combined with olive oil and wine, sometimes with honey or sweet wine and with pepper, lovage, and sweet marjoram as well. Some of the herbs for the *garum* were dill, coriander, fennel, celery, savory, sage, rue, mint, lovage, thyme, and sweet marjoram. These herbs are available today in dried or fresh form, and we can more or less imitate the *garum* ourselves. We also can make use of a Vietnamese product, called *nuoc mam*, which is prepared in the same way and has the same function. The advantage of liquid salt in comparison with solid salt is that the liquid keeps the meat succulent, whereas the solid salt extracts the juices.

The Romans also made a cheaper version with fewer herbs by not putting the fish, salt, and herbs in the sun for fermentation, but boiling them for a short time. In this way, the fish quickly becomes pulverized and releases its liquid, which, depending on the quality of the bones, tends to become a jelly. Just before this happens, the liquid is strained and kept as a substitute for *garum*. The Romans called this salty juice *allec*, which in the Middle Ages became the word for (salted) herring.

Besides *garum*, the Romans used another favorite product now called *asa foetida*. This gum, derived from the roots of a Near Eastern umbellifer, not only smells bad but also tastes bad; nevertheless, it seems to have been consumed lavishly by the Romans. Originally, the Romans had used not this plant, which they called *laser Parthicum*, but the *silphium* or *laserpicium* from North Africa, a plant they consumed so recklessly that it was nearly extinct at the beginning of our era. The Romans then started to import *laser Parthicum*, which is called "ferula asafetida" by modern pharmacists, as a substitute. In large quantities it is hardly digestible for our stomachs and soon gives one a feeling of satiation and even nausea, but in small quantities it is not disagreeable.

From these two products, *liquamen* or *garum* and *asa foetida*, we may conclude a lot about the taste preferences of the Romans: savory with herbs from the Mediterranean region, which were grown partly in their own gardens. They favored East Asian spices like ginger and cardamom much less, although these were well known. Only the peppers, both black and white, were commonly

used. As for sweeteners, sugar was still unknown; it was not imported from Ceylon and Asia Minor until the seventh century. Sugar cane was grown by the Arabs in Sicily starting in the tenth century, but it was only after the Crusades that it found its way to Europe as a very expensive kind of spice. Instead of sugar, the Romans used honey or reduced wine (*defrutum*) and raisins, dates, and figs. For the rest, their victuals consisted of fish, fowl, a bit of pork, beef, or mutton, many legumes such as chickpeas and lentils, fruits, vegetables, olive oil, eggs, cheese, and various kinds of grain.

Pasta already existed, if we may translate the word *tracta* this way; however, it was not pasta in strands like spaghetti but in sheets like lasagna. These were used as dividers between wet fillings to make layers within a pie. The very thin, round sheets, called *tracta*, were rubbed between the fingers and used as a binding agent for stews, a practice which survives as *Reible* in South German cooking.

The Early Middle Ages
How long this kind of nourishment held the stage in Western Europe during the Middle Ages is hard to say because detailed information is lacking. We can only conclude that there must have been a certain continuity in the taste for herbs and spices, at least until the Carolingian era of the ninth century. This can be deduced from a 716 charter of the Merovingian king Chilperic II for the abbey of Corbie in Northern France that was, in turn, a confirmation of a charter of King Chlotar III from the third quarter of the seventh century. In the charter, freedom from duties at the toll in Fos near Marseilles was granted for the following imported foodstuffs: olive oil, *garum*, pepper, cumin, cloves, cinnamon, spikenard, *costum* (an aromatic root from India), dates, figs, almonds, olives, peas, and rice. So *garum* was still in use in that period together with a few Indian spices, but *asa foetida* is no longer mentioned.

Not only some of the spices, but also the garden herbs must have remained in favor, judging from the last chapter of the *Capitulare de Villis* (Ordinance in chapters about the demesnes) of Charlemagne, in which the cultivation of about seventy kinds of herbs and vegetables in the gardens of every demesne in his empire was enumerated. There we find most of the herbs needed for the making of *garum*, as well as several other plants like beans, peas, onions, chives and garlic, cucumbers, watermelons, gourds, beets, endive, and lettuce, as well as fruit trees. The Carolingian population could be assured of a healthy diet if it lived according to the prescriptions of Charlemagne.

The same holds true for the monks at St. Gall in Switzerland, provided that they actually grew and used all the plants that are shown on the map of their monastery from about 817. There we find three gardens with edible plants: the *hortus* or vegetable garden, the *herbularius* or herb garden, and the orchard. The species, however, were not strictly separated, for in the *hortus* there were not only vegetables like onions, garlic, leeks, celery, beets, black radishes, lettuce, parsnips, and cabbage, but also herbs like coriander, dill, parsley, chervil, and savory, and, for medical use, poppy and corn-cockle. In the *herbularius* we not only find roses, lilies, and iris, but also beans, next to herbs like savory, costmary, goat's horn, rosemary, peppermint and water-mint, sage, rue, cumin, lovage, and fennel. In the orchard we come across apple, pear, prune, mountain ash, quince, medlar, fig, chestnut, peach, hazelnut, walnut, almond, mulberry, and bay.

Monks were allowed to eat vegetables and fruits, for the Rule of St. Benedict states that at every meal, fresh vegetable or fruit, when available, were to be served in addition to two cooked dishes (which were probably made of fish, dairy products, and grains). Walafrid Strabo, ninth-century abbot of the Benedictine monastery at Reichenau on Lake Constance in Switzerland, celebrated in his poem "De cultura hortorum" (About the cultivation of gardens) the plants in his abbey's garden, such as sage, rue, lemon herb, gourd, water-melon, fennel, lovage, chervil, mint, celery, catnip, and black radish, along with poppy, rose, lily, and iris. For the most part we find these plants as well in the *Capitulare de villis* and on the map of St. Gall, from which we may conclude that they were widespread in the Carolingian period. But recipes for preparing them are not known, and nothing can be said about the refinement of the dishes served. The same holds true for the eleventh-century food prescriptions from the abbey of Werden on the Ruhr River in Germany, according to which the monks alternately had fish, cheese, and eggs, or cheese with vegetables for dinner, with wine and ale for drinks and mead on Sundays.

It must have been possible to compose quite delicate menus with simple ingredients that were permissible for the monks; this is indicated by the ironic words of Bernard of Clairvaux in 1124 in his *Apologia ad Guillelmum* (Apology to the Abbot William [of Saint Thierry near Reims]) about the eating habits of the abbey of Cluny in Burgundy. In this treatise he ridiculed the many ways of preparing a simple ingredient like eggs and reproached the abbot for the manner of serving one dish after another when the stomach had already been fully satisfied, but the eye remained curious about new colors and shapes. In this way, he condemned exactly those characteristics that would later become the glory of French cuisine, especially the refined sequence of the courses, in which the former dishes did not give a feeling of satiation but on the contrary stimulated the appetite for the latter ones.

The Later Middle Ages

In the meantime, however, this refined sequence of courses was far from common if we judge from the existing menus of the meals of princes and other nobles in the later Middle Ages. These menus contained in England in the fourteenth and fifteenth centuries no more than two or three courses—each course, however, consisting of at least ten dishes without any specific sequence of sweet, savory, sour and sharp, fish or fowl or meat, boiled, baked or roasted. In France the dishes at a festive dinner were divided among five or six courses, but there was also no fixed sequence like that of later ages. A common feature of aristocratic foodways all over Europe was the accent on meat, fowl, and fish (sometimes game, although less than one would expect), in contrast to the rather vegetarian eating habits of former centuries.

It is possible to study late-medieval recipes and to imitate them more or less exactly. By the late Middle Ages, tastes had changed rather drastically from those of the Carolingian period; new spices from East Asia with vinegar or sour grape juice, called *vertjus*, had taken over the role of primary seasonings, replacing the many herbs and vegetables with *garum* that had been favored earlier. Parsley, savory, sage, and hyssop were still used, but other herbs had become rare. Salt, when it was used at all, was added after cooking. This was due not to the presumed expensiveness of salt—the Asiatic spices were much more expensive—nor to the fact that much salted fish and meat was used, but probably to the dominant role of spices like ginger, cinnamon, cloves, mace, nutmeg, galingale, cardamom, and pepper. These ingredients provide enough flavor that the absence of salt is not noticeable, even in dishes that are prepared with fresh meat, game, fish, or fowl.

In this context, another critical point must be made. We sometimes hear or read that people in the Middle Ages needed so many sharp spices because their meat was always spoiled, and they had to hide the bad smell and taste. But although their means of controlling the quality of their food was less elaborate than in the modern Western world, it is nonsense to pretend that they were always balanced on the edge of food poisoning and tried to conceal this with heavy seasonings. They certainly had other medical conceptions than today, but in practice they understood very well how to combine these theories with wisdom gained from long experience. People knew quite well what was healthy and what was not and were on their guard not only against really spoiled meat but also against unsafe water: instead of water, they used wine or broth or boiling liquid from peas (*purée de pois*) in the kitchen. They drank beer and ale in Northern Europe, wine in Southern Europe, and cider in a narrow strip from England to Normandy and Brittany. So the difference in our eating habits is not in the lack of hygiene, but in the fact that they dined less frequently but in bigger quantities with more calories at the same time, and, in the case of the strict rules and regulations in the monasteries, no more than twice a day.

The change in taste after the Carolingian era was caused not by the consumption of half-spoiled meat or fish, but by other factors, largely economic ones. The merchants of the tenth and eleventh centuries had a keen eye for the fact that the small ships and simple harbor equipment of their time meant that the best gains were to be expected from articles that took little space and at the same time were very expensive because they were rare. The Asian spices fit these requirements exactly. They were transported through Asia along land routes and brought to the Levantine harbors of the Mediterranean, and then taken by Venetian ships to Italy. From there they were traded along rivers and land routes to the North, where in the fairs of Champagne in France there were middlemen who exchanged the spices for the products of Flanders and Scandinavia, such as woolen cloth and timber.

Included were not only the spices that had been known and favored in antiquity, such as pepper, ginger, and cardamom, but also cinnamon, nutmeg, mace, cloves, and galingale. Added to these was an article from Asia Minor and the Balkans that was and still is even more expensive than the Asiatic spices—saffron, the dark-yellow stigmas of the stamen of the *Crocus sativus*. In antiquity, saffron was mainly used as a dye and a medicinal drug, but in the Middle Ages it became obligatory in high cuisine and primarily served the purpose of coloring the food yellow. Pure, genuine saffron was as expensive as gold. Adulteration of the stigmas, mainly in the shape of powder and mixed with other yellow stuff had already been the nightmare of physicians in antiquity and was punished with heavy fines or mutilation.

Fasting Prescriptions

Colors played an important role in medieval cookery because the cooks not only tried to make dishes as attractive as possible, but also very often to disguise their real nature. This tendency was connected with the impediments the Christian Church imposed on the foodways with strict rules about fasting and abstinence. People had to abstain two days a week—for example, Wednesday and Friday, or Friday and Saturday—from the meat of quadrupeds. However, fish and other aquatic animals were permitted on those days, as were chicken eggs and dairy products. During some periods of the year, however, not only the meat, but also the milk, butter, and cheese of quadrupeds were forbidden, together with fowl and its eggs. Only fish, snails, and aquatics like mussels and oysters remained outside these prescriptions: they were always allowed as long as they were not prepared with butter or lard.

There were periods of the year in which not only a two-days-a-week abstinence but a full fast was ordered; this meant that dairy products and eggs, in addition to meat, were forbidden. The most important of these periods was the forty days of Lent from Ash Wednesday to Easter (not including Sundays, which were never fast days). The so-called Ember days were also a time of fasting. These days, whose name is a corruption of *quatuor tempora* (four seasons), coincided more or less with the change of the seasons. They were the Wednesday, Friday, and Saturday following the Feast of Saint Lucia (December 13), Ash Wednesday, Whitsunday (Pentecost),

Fifteenth-century woodcut depicting a medieval banquet where both the king and queen are shown with their tasters. Tasters were nobles who generally came from the royal entourage. Their purpose was to ensure that the food was not poisoned. Before each of the diners is a slice of bread called a trencher. It served as a plate and was changed often during the course of the meal. ROUGHWOOD COLLECTION.

and Holy Cross Day (September 14). Religious were required to fast during the four weeks of Advent, but this was not obligatory for laymen.

Fish was always permitted, for the Church did not promote pure vegetarianism, and the regulations were not made out of compassion for the suffering of animals. It is possible that the fasting cycle was not a Christian invention at all, but an adaptation of medical conceptions about the need for refraining from food during a short period in order to prepare the body for a new season. The physical meaning of the four seasons with their various qualities, derived from the humoral system, was already implicit in the writings of the physician Galen of Pergamon in the second century C.E. The Christian Church adopted this concept and interpreted it by applying it to the avoidance of the capital sins and the devout observance of Lent. The forty days before Easter required a total change-over of the kitchen, especially in those regions that did not have good vegetable oils (like olive oil in Greece, Italy, and Spain) but used butter, bacon, and lard, as was the case in England, Scandinavia, and large parts of Germany and the Netherlands.

Food Imitations

During fasting weeks, wealthy people ate a lot of fish, salted like herring or dried unsalted like "stockfish" (i.e., cod that has been split and then unfolded and dried hanging on a stick), but also fresh fish from the sea, the rivers, and the lakes or ponds. Fresh fish was very expensive because of the difficulty of transporting it without ice to keep it cool. Ordinary people who lived far from the water had to be satisfied with salted herring, a popular food of which, however, people tired. Anyone who could afford it tried to stimulate the appetite not only with fresh fish, but also with imitation eggs and meat. Eggs were imitated by mashing white almonds with a mock-yolk that was colored with saffron. Meat could be imitated by forming dough into the shape of an oxshank, like the Dutch *duvekater*, which is seen in seventeenth-century paintings but must have been much older. The marzipan sausages that are still sold in Germany and the Netherlands in December are relics of this medieval custom. Such meat substitutes were common during the Ember days around the Feast of Saint Lucia in December. Other ingredients that were typically used during periods of fasting, especially in Lent, were dried fruits like figs, raisins, dates, and currants, as well as nuts, particularly almonds. Colors were very important in medieval cuisine, not only in these imitation dishes, but in other recipes as well; litmus was used to color sauces flaming red, sandalwood (*Pterocarpus santalinus*) was used for a reddish brown, the juice of parsley and other garden herbs for green, and saffron for a goldish yellow. As mentioned, saffron was originally meant not for the kitchen but for the pharmacist's shop because of its stimulating influence. Especially in combination with wine, it makes one feel high, an effect that soon turns into a deep fatigue. The Greek pharmacy knew of more remedies that were recommended for their medicinal effects but might at the same time be used as delicacies as well. For example, confitures, prepared with fruit juice and honey, had a laxative effect but were enjoyed by people with normal bowels, too. The best known of these confitures are marmalade or quince jelly (derived from Greek *melon kudonion*, which means 'quince') and the *diamoron* or mulberry jelly. These recipes from the Greek pharmacy reached medieval Latin medical books, such as the *Antidotarium Nicolai* (Nicholas's book of antidotes) and the *Regimen sanitatis Salernitanum* (A Salternitan regimen of health) through Syrian and Arabic translations. Greek medical science from the time of Hippocrates (fifth century B.C.E.) and Galen (second century C.E.) had been studied at the School of Salerno since the late eleventh and twelfth centuries.

Medical Theory

The medical science of the Greeks developed the theory of the four humors or fluids (blood, yellow bile, black bile, and phlegm), which corresponded with the four human temperaments (sanguine, choleric, melancholic, and phlegmatic). Each fluid belonged to a distinct season and a distinct period of life and had two qualities: blood was humid and warm and belonged to spring and youth; yellow bile was warm and dry like summer and adolescence; black bile was dry and cold like autumn and midlife; and phlegm was cold and humid like winter and old age. In the course of life, a person slowly changed his or her temperament, although some dominant characteristics remained the same. One's mood also changed a bit with the seasons, in such a way that an adaptation of the body in the Ember days was necessary from a medical viewpoint.

Food played a crucial role in this adaptation because it was held that illness depended not on internal factors but on external ones, mainly on foodstuffs that were contrary to the temperament and age of the patient. The balance between the fluids was disturbed, and the physician had the duty to restore it. An example that still appeals to us is the "hippocras," a beverage of wine with spices and honey, named after the Greek physician Hippocrates, that was supposed to be warm and dry and for that reason to counterbalance the cold and humid phlegm of a flu. Wine and spices like ginger, cinnamon, cloves, and nutmeg were regarded as "warm" and "dry" and were therefore held in high esteem. Moreover, they were expensive, a fact that may have contributed to their use in high society.

In this way the exotic spices found an expanding market in Europe to such an extent that they altered the dominant taste quite strongly. Alas, cookbooks are lacking for the period between late antiquity and the end of the thirteenth century, so that we cannot tell exactly how and when the use of the many spices became fashionable in monastic and courtly circles. The Crusades and pilgrimages to the Holy Land presumably played a role in this process because more people found their way to the Near East and told about their adventures on their return. Another product of this contact was cane sugar, which was grown in Syria and Egypt and became a major cash crop for the kingdom of Cyprus. It appeared in Western Europe around the twelfth century. Sugar was much more expensive than honey and, like the Asian spices, was only available to the very wealthy.

Ordinary People

How the mass of the population was fed in these periods is difficult to ascertain because of the lack of documentation. We can suppose that rye bread, grain porridge, lard, sausages, and salted herring belonged to their food supply, together with vegetables like onions, leeks, cabbage, and white parsnips. Certainly some kinds of fruit were consumed, like apples, pears, and prunes, but they were probably processed in pies or stews, not eaten raw. Raw fruits, being humid and cold, were not considered to be healthy.

An illumination from a fifteenth-century French manuscript based on the *Tractatus de Herbis* by the ancient Greek physician Dioskorides. The woman is making fry-bread, round slabs of sweet dough pan-fried in lard or butter. This type of food was eaten only on feast days. © ARCHIVO ICONOGRAFICO, S.A./CORBIS.

Cookery Books

Our knowledge of medieval kitchen recipes is derived from fourteenth- and fifteenth-century cookery books, of which more are extant than most people think. The most famous cookbook was the *Viandier* of Guillaume Tirel dit Taillevent (c. 1310–1395), who was the chief cook of the French king Charles V. This manuscript was copied several times in the fourteenth century and influenced the other famous French cookbook of the fourteenth century, which is called *Le Ménagier de Paris* (The goodman of Paris) after its anonymous author. The *Viandier* of Taillevent appeared around 1490 in a printed edition that includes not only the fourteenth-century recipes, but also quite a few newer ones that might have originated in the court of the dukes of Burgundy.

The capacity of cookbooks to become bestsellers is also proven by the many printed editions from 1475 onward of the Latin work by the Vatican librarian Bartolomeo Platina, titled *De honesta voluptate et valitudine* (On right pleasure and good health). His book was based on the handwritten cookbook by Maestro Martino, chief cook of the patriarch of Aquileia, who lived in Rome in

the middle of the fifteenth century. Actually, Platina did nothing more than translate Maestro Martino's Italian recipes into Latin and add some medical remarks about their qualities as related to the humoral theory. Maestro Martino's recipes, although more often than not qualified by Platina as unhealthy, can be easily imitated and enjoyed today. They were derived partly from Byzantine as well as Spanish-Catalan cuisine, of which a fourteenth-century cookbook, *El libre de Sent Sovi* (The book of Sent Sovi), is known. There the Armenian Arabic influence is notable, for example in the use of mashed almonds stirred with cooking liquid for the binding of sauces and stews, and of pasta in strands like spaghetti. The use of ground almonds became common practice in high cuisine all over Europe, but pasta in strands remained limited to the Mediterranean regions: in Italy several varieties were developed, like vermicelli and macaroni, along with pasta in sheets like lasagna, which was probably known already by the Romans.

No less professional a cook than Maestro Martino was Maistre Chiquart, who wrote his book *Du fait de cuisine* (On cookery) while in the service of the Duke of

Savoy around 1420. A little bit earlier, around 1390, a collection of recipes from the English royal household was composed under the title *The Forme of Curye* (The way of cookery). Several other English collections of recipes date from the fifteenth century. In the German language the oldest known collection of recipes is *Daz Buoch von guoter spise* (The book of goodly fare), which was composed in Würzburg around 1350 by a high official of the bishop and, therefore, probably reflected the food served in an ecclesiastical household. But there are also some recipe collections from secular German courts, for example, the cookbook of Maister Eberhard, cook of the duke of Bavaria-Landshut in the fifteenth century. All of these handwritten texts are now available in modern editions. The earliest printed German cookbook is the *Küchenmeisterey* (Mastery of the kitchen), which was published in Nürnberg by Peter Wagner around 1490.

As for the Netherlands, the series starts rather late with some fifteenth-century written recipe collections and a cookbook printed in Brussels around 1514 by Thomas van der Noot, called *Een notabel boecxken van cokeryen* (A notable book of cookery). Why this occurred so late is difficult to tell: Is it because older texts are lost or because Dutch courts mainly used foreign cookbooks? Certainly the bourgeois cuisine of the Low Countries, for which the *Notabel boecxken* was intended, was deeply influenced by French and German as well as English sources.

In general, we should realize that handwritten and printed cookbooks in the Middle Ages were only accessible to educated people, who were able to either read themselves or have the books read to them: ecclesiastics, noble ladies, and wealthy bourgeois. The foodways of the average population in towns and villages can therefore not be learned from cookbooks.

With the invention of printing and the advance of teaching in town and chapter schools, the number of people who could read and write increased, as did the readership for cookbooks. Could a book like Platina's *De honesta voluptate* even be counted among the bestsellers? We must ask, however, whether these books were meant for use in the kitchen or rather as showpieces in the owner's library. A Latin collection of recipes with medical remarks like Platina's is more conceivable in the latter case. Innovations in culinary practice are not to be found there but rather in sixteenth-century handwritten household collections that were sometimes later printed.

The Renaissance

A remarkable innovation of the Renaissance was the return to the natural taste and shape of the ingredients, which came about under Italian influence in reaction to the medieval predilection for faux preparations and spiced stews. Certainly, the sausages made of marzipan did not disappear—on the contrary, as cane sugar became cheaper, people could indulge in the luxury of more imitated animals and other sweets—but such items were driven to the edge of the dinner instead of being the main course. Fish was now allowed to taste like fish with a simple sauce of boiling liquid and vinegar. A novelty was the consumption of raw salads with a dressing of oil, vinegar, pepper, and salt. Salad comes from *insalata*—'salted'. In Italy the habit of eating green leaves with *garum* or salt had never been dropped, and although it was contrary to the medical theory about the humid and cold qualities of raw vegetables, this practice slowly reached the regions north of the Alps as well. By way of concession, however, the physicians advised placing the salads at the beginning of the meal, in order that the warm and dry dishes that would follow them could correct their injurious qualities.

Under the influence of the Protestant Reformation, the fasting prescriptions of the Roman Catholic Church were gradually mitigated, so that the strict prohibition of animal fats like butter and lard during Lent was dropped. It was in precisely those countries that did not possess good vegetable oils and had therefore always experienced the greatest impediments during periods of fasting, that the Reformation gained its staunchest adherents—perhaps not by accident. So dairy products became more important in the kitchen, and in the coastal regions along the North Sea a remarkable increase in the number of dairy cattle can be observed in the sixteenth and the beginning of the seventeenth centuries, in comparison with former ages, when horned cattle had been raised mainly for their meat. A larger output of butter and cheese was the result, together with more recipes for sour and curdled milk.

Through the discovery of America, many new plants became known that were more or less successfully introduced in Europe. Travels to India over the sea made the Asian spices available to many more people: they became cheaper and ceased to be a status symbol. This fact certainly played a role in the change of tastes back to the natural flavors of foods and away from the camouflage of sharp sauces and stews.

In this way, the mainstream of history always has exercised its influence upon our civilization and upon our eating habits as well. Next to long waves and secular trends in our foodways, those habits always have been moving and changing.

See also **Christianity: Western Christianity; Fasting and Abstinence: Christianity; Medieval Banquet; Poisoning; Renaissance Banquet; Rome and the Roman Empire.**

BIBLIOGRAPHY

André, Jacques. *L'Alimentaion et la cuisine à Rome* [Nourishment and the kitchen in Rome]. Paris: Librairie C.Klincksieck, 1961.

Chiquart's "On Cookery": A Fifteenth-Century Savoyard Culinary Treatise. Edited and translated by Terence Scully. New York: P. Lang, 1986.

Curye on Inglysch: English Culinary Manuscripts of the Fourteenth Century (Including the *Forme of Cury*), edited by Constance

B. Hieatt and Sharon Butler. New York: Oxford University Press, 1985.

Henish, Bridget Ann. *Fast and Feast: Food in Medieval Society.* University Park London: Pennsylvania State University Press, 1976.

Lambert, Carole ed., *Du Manuscrit à la table: Essais sur la cuisine au Moyen Age et Répertoire des manuscrits médiévaux contenant des recettes culinaires* [From the manuscript to the table: Essays on the kitchen in the Middle Ages and the repertoire of medieval manuscripts containing culinary recipes]. Montreal: Les Presses de l'Université de Montréal et Champion-Slatkine, 1992.

Laurioux, Bruno. *Le Moyen Age à table* [The Middle Ages at the table]. Paris: Adam Biro, 1989.

Laurioux, Bruno. *Le règne de Taillevent: Livres et pratiques culinaires à la fin du Moyen Age* [The reign of Taillevent: Culinary books and practices at the end of the Middle Ages]. Paris: Publications de la Sorbonne, 1997.

Libellus de arte coquinaria: An Early Northern Cookery Book. Edited and translated by Rudolf Grewe and Constance B. Hieatt. Tempe: Arizona Center for Medieval and Renaissance Studies, 2001.

Le Ménagier de Paris [The goodman of Paris]. Edited by Georgine E. Brereton and Janet M. Ferrier. Oxford: Clarendon Press, 1981.

Platina: On Right Pleasure and Good Health. A critical edition and translation of *De Honesta Voluptate et Valetudine* by Mary Ella Milham. Tempe: Arizona Center for Medieval and Renaissance Studies at Arizona State University, 1998.

Rodinson, Maxime, A. J. Arberry, and Charles Perry. *Medieval Arab Cookery: Essays and Translations.* Devon, U.K.: Prospect Books, 2001.

Scully, Terence. *The Art of Cookery in the Middle Ages.* Woodbridge: Boydell Press, 1995.

Taillevent. *Le Viandier de Guillaume Tirel dit Taillevent.* Introduction and notes by Jérôme Pichon and Georges Vicaire. Geneva: Slatkine Reprints, 1967.

Taillevent. *Le Viandier of Taillevent: An Edition of All Extant Manuscripts.* Edited by Terence Scully. University of Ottawa Press, 1988.

Weiss Adamson, Melitta, ed. *Food in the Middle Ages: A Book of Essays.* New York: Garland, 1995.

Weiss Adamson, Melitta, ed. *Regional Cuisines of Medieval Europe: A Book of Essays.* New York and London: Routledge, 2002.

Winter, Johanna Maria van. "Kochbücher" [Cookbooks]. In *Lexikon des Mittelalters,* edited by Robert Auty et al., vol. 5, pp. 1245–1246. Munich and Zurich: Artemis, 1991.

Johanna Maria van Winter

MIDDLE EAST. The Middle East is that part of Western Asia extending from the eastern Mediterranean coast of Turkey and Syria, through the desert to Iraq and Arabia, and to the East through Iran to the Caspian, the Caucasus, and the Black Sea. Into Africa, it includes Egypt, and, by some accounts, Arab North Africa. This area comprises mountains, deserts, fertile plains irrigated by grand rivers, and seacoasts. Climatically, the Middle East ranges from the temperate Mediterranean coast, to the extreme heat of the arid desert areas, to snowy mountains. This variety of terrain produces a wide range of food ingredients.

The Population

The ecology of these lands fosters different modes of adaptation. Nomadism was a prevalent form of existence for much of the history of the region, and remains so on the margins. Equally, the region saw the earliest agricultural settlements and the first cities in human history. Indeed, the contrast and conflict between nomad and city dweller is an ever-present theme in the culture, lore, and politics of the region from earliest times. Ethnically, it embraces Arabs, Persians, Turks, Kurds, Armenians, and, until recently, Greeks, as well as many pockets of ancient ethnicities and religions. Jewish communities, many of ancient ancestry in the region, partook in this ethnic diversity, most of them now settled in the state of Israel, which also includes many European and African Jews, creating a melting pot of diverse cultures and cuisines.

Islam is the majority religion in the Middle East and enters into the constitution of many of its cultural elements, including food and drink. There are many Christian communities, of diverse denominations, and their religious prescriptions of feasting and fasting have also left their mark on food culture. Ancient religions and sects persist in some quarters, notably the Zoroastrians of Iran, as well as many sects, such as Baha'i, professing syncretistic combinations of old Persian religion with Islam and Christianity.

History and Culture

Successive conquests and rule of different empires have shaped the civilizations and cultures of the region, and led to the common themes in its culture that we find today. The ancient civilizations of Mesopotamia and Egypt were subject to subsequent conquests and incorporation in wider empires, starting with the Persians and the Greeks, then the Romans, including Byzantines, which Hellenized much of the region. The Muslim Arab conquests established a vast political entity, soon fragmented, but retaining common cultural elements. The Islamization of much of Iran and the Byzantine Empire brought these elements of older cultures to shape the emergent civilization, notably its culinary elements. The last empire to rule the region (before European colonial rule) was the Ottoman, which also included much of southeast Europe, creating a wide cultural synthesis of Turkish statecraft, Arab religion, Persian culture, and many elements from the territories under its control. This synthesis included the food cultures. An important epoch in the history of the region, which also affected food culture, was that of Arab Spain, from the eighth to the fifteenth centuries. Moorish Spain created its own cultural

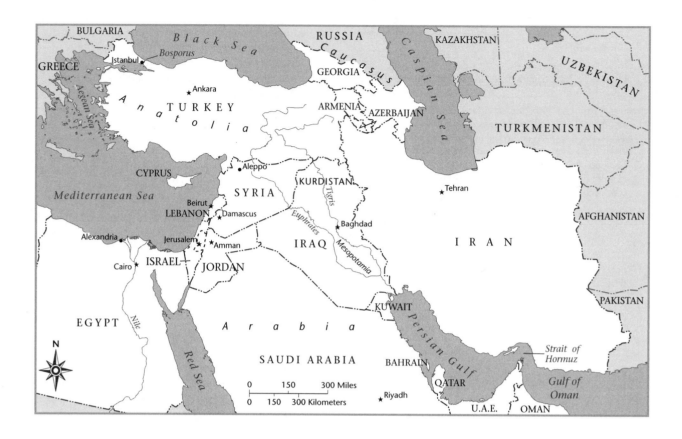

synthesis, which is evident in Spain and North Africa to the present day. Spain and Morocco never came under Ottoman rule, and this exclusion, as well as distance from Ottoman lands, has left its traces in the distinction of Moroccan food culture.

Ingredients, Techniques, and Cooking Media

Cereals and breads. Cereals constitute the bases of the Middle Eastern diet, historically and today. Wheat and rice are the major and preferred sources of staple foods. Barley is common in the region and is an ingredient in cheaper bread, and millet and sorghum are used in a few places to make porridge and gruel. Maize became common in some areas, notably the Black Sea coast of Turkey, as well as in parts of Egypt. It is made into a kind of cake and eaten as bread. A wide range of breads are baked, mostly from wheat, but also in combination with barley. Bread is generally leavened. Flat breads are the most common. Naan in Iran, *pide* in Turkey, *khubz* or *'aysh* (more of a generic term for bread) are all similar forms of flat bread made from leavened and risen dough in an oven. In Iran and many Arab lands as well as in Anatolia, a *tannour* or *tandir* is the most common oven: an earthenware pot built into a wall or freestanding, is fired with wood or charcoal, and disks of dough are stuck to its sides until baked, usually soft with crisp edges and a bubbly surface. Modern, industrial ovens are becoming more common for large-scale commercial production, which include both flat breads and European style loaves. Another kind of flat bread, called *lavash* in Iran and Turkey, or *khubz saj* in Arabic (also *saj ekmegi* in Turkish), is cooked over a concave iron pot, a *saj*, much like Indian chapati. Bread is a universal staple in the region, eaten, in one form or another, by all classes and groups, practically at every meal.

Another common use of wheat is in the forms of bulgur (Turkish; in Arabic, *burghul*) and couscous. *Burghul* is cracked wheat, made by partially cooking the wheat grains in water, drying it in an oven or in the sun, then breaking it into pieces, in different grades of size. It is used as a staple in a wide area covering Anatolia, Syria, and northern Iraq. Typically, it is cooked in water, with flavorings, much like rice. It is also used in making meat pies, *kibbe/kubba* (see below), and as an ingredient in salads, notably in tabbouleh, with chopped parsley, tomato, lemon, and oil. Couscous, almost exclusive to North Africa, where it is a staple, is made from rolling semolina grains (mostly durum wheat, but it can be barley) in flour, to make a kind of cross between grain and pasta. This is typically steamed and served as a base to meat and vegetable sauces. Another wheat product is *firik* or *frik*, cracked green wheat, sometimes from burned fields, to give a smoky flavor. It is used much like *burghul*, but considered finer.

Rice

Rice is produced in particular parts of the region with suitable climate, soil, and water. Notable rice-producing areas include the Caspian provinces of Iran, the delta of Egypt, and the marsh area of southern Iraq (before its recent drainage). In the areas where it is produced, rice can be a staple, to the extent of making bread from its flour in southern Iraq. Elsewhere in the region, rice was considered a luxury item to be eaten on special and festive occasions. *Burghul*/bulgur in wheat-producing areas was considered a cheaper substitute for rice, such as the *bulgur pilavi* of Anatolia (*pilav* originally referred to rice).

There are many types of rice produced and consumed in the region. Varieties that cook into separate grains (*ruz mufalfel*) are the most valued, and aromatic varieties are also prized. Traditional varieties in Egypt and Turkey were mostly round or boat-shaped grains, much like Italian rice, while in Iran and Iraq, mostly slender, long grains were grown. In recent years, however, much of the rice consumed in the region is imported from North America or the Far East. Basmati rice from India-Pakistan is highly valued: it is aromatic and produces the desired separate grains. Cheaper long-grain varieties are common.

There are a number of different cooking procedures for rice. Iran boasts the most elaborate and refined rice cookery. The standard procedure there is for the rice to be washed in several changes of water, ostensibly to remove the starch (it is not clear that this operation is necessary with modern rice varieties), then it is soaked in water for at least one hour, but preferably for much longer. It is then drained and thrown into boiling salted water for a few minutes, until grains are just cooked, at which point it is drained (much like cooking pasta), then returned to the pot over some fat, oil, or melted butter; the pot then is covered with a cloth and a lid, and left over a low flame for at least half an hour. Known in Iran as *chelow*, this plain rice is served under grilled meats (*chelow kebab*) or with meat/vegetable stews (*khoresht*). More complex rice dishes are called *polow* (*pilaf*, used in Turkish for all rice dishes). When the rice is drained after boiling, it is then layered in the pot with meats and/or vegetables and/or sauces, as well as nuts, currants, or other dried fruit in some dishes, and always with some fat or oil, then covered and steamed as with *chelow*. These methods of cooking are also followed in some communities in Iraq and in Anatolia. More typical methods of cooking in Turkey and the Arab world involve covering the raw rice (sometimes after washing and soaking) with just enough water to cook it, adding salt, and perhaps aromatics, as well as oil, then boiling until the water is absorbed, at which point it is covered and allowed to steam. More complex rice dishes are prepared by first frying the raw rice in oil or butter, sometimes with onions or other aromatics, then adding water or stock, sometimes with meat or vegetables, and allowing it to cook in the same way.

Oils and Fats

Butter and clarified butter (called ghee in India) are, traditionally, the preferred medium of cooking for those who can afford them. Olive oil is prevalent in the Mediterranean coastal areas. It has many nonculinary uses, such as in making soap and as a lighting oil (which is how it is mentioned in the Qur'an). It was used for cooking predominantly by Christians and Jews. Christians use it during Lent, when meat and dairy products are excluded, and Jews use it in place of animal fats such as butter to avoid mixing meat and dairy products. In regions where olive oil was not prevalent, as in Iraq, Iran, and most of Egypt, Christians and Jews used other oils, mainly sesame.

In Turkish cookery a whole class of vegetable dishes is labeled *zeytinyagli*, a reference to olive oil. These are usually eaten cold. In the refined cookery of the urban upper classes, butter was used for cooking meat, poultry and rice, while oil would be used for cooking or dressing vegetables or salads.

Another cooking medium is rendered meat fat, especially that derived from the fat tail of a local breed of sheep. Traditionally much appreciated and featured in historical recipe books and manuals of the princes and the upper strata, it is now largely avoided on account of its strong odor and the health worries of consumers. In recent times, modern industrially produced vegetable oils predominate in the region, and seem to have replaced butter and olive oil in cooking. Cheapness and convenience, as well as perceived health benefits, are involved. The use of olive oil persists in particular regions, such as coastal Tunisia and parts of Aegean Turkey, where there are strong traditions of its consumption, although even there, cost diminishes its accessibility to the poorer sectors.

Spices and Herbs

Most regions in the Middle East use spices. Typically, a stew will include a small amount of a spice mixture called *baharat*, which includes cinnamon, clove, cumin, and coriander. Black pepper is common, and chili peppers are used occasionally, especially as a separate sauce, or as a pickle. Some dishes require specific spices, such as *kamouniya*, a meat stew with cumin, or the Egyptian *molokhiya* (see below), with coriander. Iranian cookery features a more extensive use of spices, including the pungent fenugreek leaves and whole dried limes.

Parsley is commonly used in cooking and in salads, and so is mint. Varieties of thyme are common in Syria, Lebanon, and Palestine, and a mixture of dried thyme and sumac, crushed sour berries, is a common breakfast item with oil and bread. Sumac is also sprinkled over grilled meat. Garlic is common to many dishes and salads.

Meat, Poultry, and Fish

Lamb and mutton have always been the favored meats of the region, with veal as a subsidiary choice in some instances, and, in other places, goat. Pork, prohibited in the religions of Islam—though there are accounts of wild boar being hunted and eaten by some Bedouins—and

Judaism, was also largely avoided by the Christians of the region. Beef was generally considered to be an inferior meat, consumed, if at all, by the poorer classes. This may reflect the quality of the beef it was possible to produce on the sparse pastures of the region. Beef, however, was considered suitable for certain dishes, such as *harissa*, a porridge of pounded grain and meat. Camel meat was consumed in some parts, but is not so commonly now.

Prominent among the meat preparations were the grilled meats, kebabs, which distinguish the region. There is a wide variety of these grills, with many regional specialties and styles. The most common are the cubed cuts on skewers, known as shish kebab in most places, but *tikka* in Iraq (and India). Chicken may also be grilled in the same fashion. Another common variety is *kofta kebab* (*kebab kobedeh* in Iran, or just *kebab* in Iraq), made from ground meat, sometimes with onions and spices, shaped around the skewer like a long sausage and grilled. A popular kebab of recent origin is the *doner kebab*, also known as *shawarma* in much of the Arab world (*gass* in Iraq). It is either layers of meat and fat or a shaped ground meat loaf, placed on a large skewer that rotates vertically next to a strong heat source that cooks the outside crisp. The cooked outside pieces are then sliced off and served with bread and salad. There are many other types of kebab: ribs, thin slices of meat wrapped around a skewer; small cubes of liver, kidney, and sweetbreads, sometimes alternating on a skewer with cubes of fat (*kofte* or liver); wrapped in caul fat, like a sausage, and many others.

Kebab is typically a street or restaurant food, served with bread (rice in Iran), salad, and pickles. It is not usually prepared in domestic kitchens. In recent years, kebab, and especially the *doner/shawarma* variety, have become regular features of fast-food joints in European and American cities.

Meat and vegetable stews, served with rice, bulgur, or bread, are the other genre of typical meat preparation in the region. A typical domestic meal for those who can afford meat would be a stew of lamb in butter or oil, with onion, tomato (usually as paste), and spices with one vegetable, such as okra, beans, or aubergine (eggplant). Often poorer families would use little meat, usually on a large bone, to flavor the stew. There are many variations on this theme, including the distinguished Iranian stew of *korma sabzi*, of lamb in butter and a mixture of green herbs minced fine, as well as whole dried limes, often with the addition of red kidney beans or split peas.

Offal, tripe, heads, and feet are much appreciated in many quarters. A typical broth found in practically all parts of the region is *kelle pacha*, made with sheep heads and feet. This is typically found at a street or specialized restaurant, which is often open all night or very early in the morning, catering to early-rising workers for breakfast, and to revelers after a night of partying and drinking.

Kibbe (Syria) or *kubba* (Iraq) is a genre of pie or dumpling made with meat and cereal. The most common

are made with ground meat (typically lamb) and *burghul*, worked together like a dough, then stuffed with minced meat that has been fried with onion, aromatics, and, sometimes, pine nuts or almonds and raisins. This can either be in the form of individual small dumplings (usually shaped like a torpedo), or in slices like a cake, baked on an oven tray with the stuffing placed between two layers of the dough. In the form of small dumplings, this can also be cooked in a sauce with vegetables. One striking variation is a *kibbe niyye*, raw *kibbe*, made by pounding lean meat and *burghul* together with seasoning, which is then served as small dumplings, sometimes with dips of lemon juice and chili sauce. In Anatolia this genre is known as *kofte*, in common with other ground meat *rissoles*: the stuffed version is called *icli kofte*, and the raw one is *cig kofte*. In Iraq and Iran, there are versions of this dumpling made with rice instead of *burghul*.

Poultry. Chicken is ubiquitous in the region. Squab pigeon is eaten in some parts, notably Egypt and Morocco. Wild fowl, especially duck, quail, and pheasant, are appreciated by some, especially in the Caspian region of Iran, but also in many other parts where there is a tradition of hunting.

In the past, before the introduction of industrial production of chicken, these birds were tough, and were generally boiled and stewed, often in sauces and vegetables, just like meat. If they were to be fried, they would be boiled first (in pieces), then finished in a frying pan in oil or butter. A banquet dish would be chicken stuffed with rice or some other grain with meats, nuts, and aromatics, then stewed or baked in butter and further aromatics. Modern battery hens are tender and do not require boiling or long cooking. But old habits persist, especially in domestic kitchens, though many cooks are now roasting and frying their chickens.

In Egypt, pigeon is served grilled (after being spatchcocked, or opened flat) or stuffed, typically with rice or *firik*, and baked or stewed.

Wild fowl are cooked in a similar fashion as chicken. One unique dish of wild duck comes from Caspian Iran and is called *faisanjoun*. The pieces of duck are stewed in a sauce of pomegranate syrup and walnuts. This dish has now become popular all over Iran and in parts of Iraq, but chicken is substituted for the duck. Iranians regard it as one of their foremost national dishes.

Fish cookery and consumption tend to follow specific local tastes and styles, depending on local varieties, forms of fishery, and, sometimes, religious beliefs. Even the names given to the same fish vary widely, and in Mediterranean regions, often follow Greek or Italian derivations. Fried or grilled fish are the most common, as indeed elsewhere in the world. However, local styles are important even for simple grilling. In Baghdad, for instance, Tigris fisherman developed a method of grilling the local carp and barble (called *shabbout*, and highly valued, now almost extinct), by opening the fish flat, like a kipper, and skewering it on robust sticks, which are then erected around an open wood fire on the ground. This is called *masgouf*, and Iraqis came to consider it as a national dish.

Istanbul and the Aegean region of Turkey have a rich and varied fish culture, as does the Black Sea region. There are numerous fish restaurants and bars (known as *meyhane*) along the shores of the Bosphorous, serving varieties from the Mediterranean and the Black Sea. A notable fish from the latter is *kalkan*, a kind of turbot that is much appreciated. They also feature sea bass, different types of bream, a kind of bonito, and mackerel. These are fried or grilled, or sealed in paper, foil, or a salt crust and baked. A typical Turkish dish is *buglama*, a kind of fish broth. Any of these fish or *hamsi*, the small anchovy-like fish from the Black Sea, are boiled in a broth of vegetables and aromatics, with oil or butter, and served in the pot. Fish stews are common elsewhere, such as the *salona* of Iraq, in which fillets are stewed in onions, tomato, tamarind, and other spices.

In many regions, fish is cooked or served with rice. In Iran, fried fillet of fish is served over *sabzi polow*, "green" rice, cooked with a herb mixture. *Sayyadiya*, "fisherman's dish," is typical of the Syrian coast, in which pieces of fish are fried with onions and spices, then cooked with rice. In the Black Sea region of Turkey they have *hamsi pilavi*, combining rice with the fried small fish. Similar dishes are found all over the region.

Seafood, in the sense of crustaceans and mollusks, such as shrimp, crab, squid, and mussels, are available in the coastal region, but not always consumed. There is a widespread religious taboo against this genre, similar to the Jewish prohibitions. It is not, however, common to all Muslims, but confined to particular interpretations of religious law. These foods are widely appreciated in Istanbul, the Aegean, Alexandria, and parts of Syria and Iraq. A typical street and bar food in Istanbul is mussels stuffed with rice, pine nuts, and raisins.

Vegetables and Pulses

Vegetables and pulses are the predominant everyday food of the great majority of the people of the Middle East. They are boiled, stewed, grilled, stuffed, and cooked with meat and with rice. Among the green leaf vegetables, many varieties of cabbage, spinach, and chard are widely used. Root and bulb vegetables, such as onion and garlic, as well as carrot, turnip, and beet are equally common. Fruit vegetables include marrow or squash, tomato, and eggplant. *Bamia* (okra or gumbo) is a distinctive element in the cookery of the region, appreciated for the peculiar consistency of the stews made in combination with meat, tomato, and spices, often with a sour flavoring. A similar consistency is achieved with *molokhiya* (mallow), a green leaf, used fresh or dried, chopped up fine and cooked in a broth with chicken or meat. This is most common in Egypt, where, traditionally, it was cooked with rabbit. Aubergine or eggplant is perhaps the most

distinctive vegetable of the region, cooked and served in diverse fashions. It is fried in slices and dressed in yogurt and garlic; or roasted over an open fire, then pulped and dressed with tahini (sesame paste), lemon juice, garlic, and cumin, a dish known as *mutabbal* or *baba ghannoush*; stuffed with various ingredients and roasted in the oven, as in the famous Turkish dish of *imam bayeldi* ("the imam fainted!"); pulped into a sauce for meat in the Turkish *hunkar begendi* ("the king liked it"); or combined with meat in various stews. Tomato, a relatively recent import from the New World (it arrived in most places in the nineteenth century), is now the most ubiquitous ingredient in Middle Eastern cookery. It is used fresh in a variety of salads, cooked, either from fresh tomatoes or as a preserved paste, in almost every stew and broth, and grilled with kebab.

Beans and pulses are crucial to the diet of the region, second only to cereals. The fava bean (broad bean in England) is original, indeed ancient, to the region. Known as *foul* in Egypt and Syria, and *baqilla'/baqelli/bakla*, in Iraq, Iran, and Turkey, they are eaten green and dried. Dried, they are boiled in one of the most popular Egyptian foods of *foul medames*, a domestic and street food, eaten for breakfast or any other meal, mashed and dressed in oil, lemon, and chili. Similar dishes are found in all other parts of the region. The famous *ta'miyya* or falafel, now popular in Europe and America, was originally made from dried fava, crushed and formed into a *rissole* with herbs and spices, then fried. It is also made from chickpeas, or a mixture of the two. Green fava are cooked like other green beans, boiled and dressed in oil, or stewed with meat. A famous Iranian dish is *baghelli polow*, green fava with rice and dill, often with meat; versions of this combination are found elsewhere. The haricot bean (*fasoulya*) is used fresh or dried, boiled and dressed, sometimes as an accompaniment to grilled meats, or stewed with meat. Black-eyed beans (various names, mostly *loubia*) are typically used dried, boiled, often with green leaves, and dressed in oil and lemon.

Lentils, split peas, and chickpeas are widely used in soups, with rice, in salads, or with meat. *Homous bi-tahina*, made from chickpeas and sesame paste, is now common throughout the world, but originated in Syria/Lebanon. Lentils are cooked with rice in various dishes, notably *mujadarra*, found in many parts of the Arab world, as well as in adaptations of the Indian *kichri*. This latter, in the form of *kushari*, is the most popular street food in Egypt. Macaroni is added to the rice and lentils to extend its bulk with a cheaper ingredient, and the taste is enhanced with fried onions and a chili sauce.

Stuffed vegetables are a dish most associated with the Middle East in the popular mind. They are commonly called *dolma*, the Turkish word meaning "stuffed," but also the Arabic *mahshi*. *Yaprak*, "leaves" in Turkish, often vine leaves, but also chard and cabbage, are stuffed with rice, ground meat, pine nuts, and spices, then stewed in oil and tomato, and, less commonly, with a small amount of rich meat such as sheep's feet or breast. There is a version without meat, cooked in oil and served cold, known as *yalinci dolma*, or "false dolma." Many vegetables are similarly stuffed and stewed or baked, such as squash, onion, tomato, eggplant, peppers, and even carrots. There are many regional and local variations of ingredients and flavorings, such as the use or not of tomato or lemon, or the addition of sugar.

Dairy Products

Milk, fresh or soured, was commonly consumed by Arabs, with camel milk predominating in Bedouin regions. Yogurt, a Turkish contribution, is commonly consumed plain, used in cooking, used in salad dressing, or diluted as a drink (Turkish, *aryan*). Butter, as we have seen, was the favored cooking medium. White cheese, like the Greek feta, is the most common in the region, the best made from sheep or goat milk, as is the much valued *halim* or *haloumi*. There are many local and little known cheeses, especially in the mountainous regions of Anatolia, Kurdistan, and Lebanon, which offer rich pastures.

Meals

Patterns of consumption depend, of course, on class, region, and communal affiliation. Desert nomads, for instance, consumed milk, fresh or soured, butter, if affordable, and dates with bread at most meals. Meat was a luxury eaten on festive occasions when a camel or a sheep was slaughtered, boiled in great cauldrons, and served on rice with copious quantities of butter, a rare delight. Rural inhabitants had similarly limited diets. Egyptian peasants, as well as the urban poor, eat a great quantity of bread (often at subsidized prices) combined with a little salted cheese and onion. Anatolian and Syrian peasants eat much cooked *burghul*/bulgur, sometimes with yogurt, in season with tomato. Many urban workers purchase many meals in the street from vendors of *kushari* (rice, lentils, and macaroni) in Egypt, *foul/baqella'*, in that country and Iraq, boiled turnips and beets, roasted corn, kebab, and bread with everything, in many parts of the region depending on income and season.

Historically, meal patterns varied greatly, and the one feature that seems to be common to all regions and classes was a large midday meal. Most people also ate something in the evening, usually a lighter meal. Now the daily three-meal pattern is common among the urban classes, especially the more prosperous.

Breakfast, if eaten, was not usually a distinctive set of foods, but items and leftovers from other meals. Balls of boiled rice washed down with tea in Caspian Iran, for instance, or the ubiquitous foul or *kushari* in Egypt. Prosperous households would serve grilled meats or stews for breakfast. Over the course of the twentieth century, many of the urban prosperous and middle classes have come to regard breakfast as a specific meal, influenced by Western models. Breads or pancakes of various kinds with butter, yogurt, and preserves are often served, as well as eggs in various forms.

Lunch and supper are not distinct from one another. Which one is more substantial depends on work patterns and lifestyle, mostly now tending to the Western pattern of emphasis on an evening meal after work, at least for the upper and middle classes. Except, that is, on weekends, holidays, and festivals, when larger lunches are eaten. A typical Middle Eastern meal would consist of a stew of meat (or chicken) with a vegetable, such as beans or *bamia*, served with rice and bread, and perhaps a salad. Soup, fried fish, roast chicken, or grilled meat are possible additions or variations. The meal finishes with fruit, and sometimes other sweets or pastries. Historically, however, pastries and sweets were not eaten at the end of the meal, but as a separate snack or as a meal in itself. To this day, poorer people lunch on pastries as a special treat.

Eating Out

Restaurants are not traditional to the region, but have developed over the course of the twentieth century. Vendors of cooked food, however, are traditional, and continue to do good business in Middle Eastern cities. The central market areas of cities are redolent with the smells of grilling meat and onion from the kebab stalls, of *kibbe* or falafel frying, displays of pastries, sweet and savory. Tales of the *Thousand and One Nights* feature many of these cook shops and their wares. You see people standing, sitting on stools, or crouching around these stalls, sampling their wares. Historically, many urban people did not have domestic kitchens and sent out for their cooked food, as did market people in their shops and workshops, and many still do. The vendors also cater to the customers of surrounding teahouses, taking food to their tables where they are drinking tea, smoking, and playing games. Now, of course, pizza and hamburgers are added to the repertoire of street food.

The Tavern and the Meze

A type of food specifically related to drink is the meze. Drinking alcohol and drink cultures are widespread, especially in the Mediterranean regions. Historically, wine was the most common alcoholic drink, but during the twentieth century, distilled liquor (typically *arak* or *raki*) became common, and more recently beer. Historically, most "respectable" people who drank did so at home, with friends. Taverns were rough and low-class. The making, distribution and serving of alcohol were carried out predominantly by Christians—in Turkey mostly by Greeks and Armenians—and they were usually the tavern keepers. This picture changed over the course of the twentieth century. An increasingly cosmopolitan, modern, and educated middle class patronized public places of entertainment and association, including cafes, bars, and restaurants that served alcohol. That is where the distinctive meze developed into a kind of convivial meal around the drink table. It consists of a number of small dishes (*mezze* is a Persian word meaning "taste"), picked at leisure: cheese, melon, nuts, various salads and dips, such as *tabboule* (chopped parsley, tomato, and a few grains of

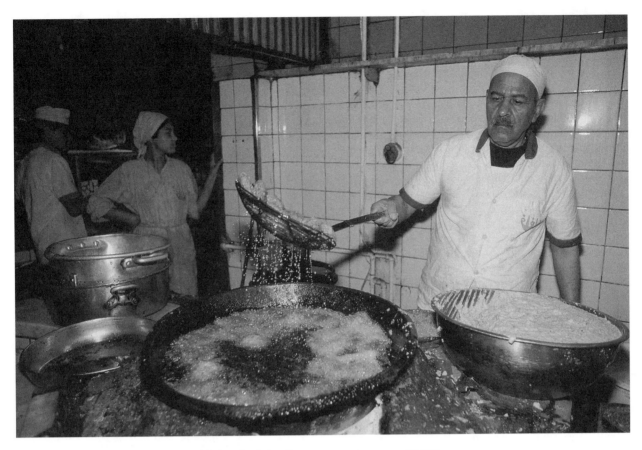

A chef prepares falafel in a restaurant kitchen in Cairo, Egypt. © HANS GEORG ROTH/CORBIS.

burghul), *homous* and *mutabbal*, pickles, and also more substantial items, such as grilled meat, *kibbe*, and sausage. The centers of excellence of meze preparations were initially the Middle Eastern cities with a strong Christian presence, such as Istanbul, Beirut, and Aleppo, but it later became more general, and meze is now widespread in Europe and America, primarily through Lebanese restaurants.

Feasting and Fasting

Festivals and fasts, mostly religious, are celebrated with particular foods, which vary by community and region.

Ramadan, the fasting month for Muslims, is the most important occasion in this respect. Paradoxically, it is the month during which food consumption increases dramatically throughout Muslim communities. Fasting is prescribed for the daylight hours, to be broken at sunset of each day, then people can eat and drink through the night, until daybreak. Breaking the fast becomes a banquet, with exchanges of invitation between kin and friends, and public banquets held by charities and associations. The cafes and pastry shops are open at night, and a carnival atmosphere prevails in the streets. Many Muslims, following the reported example of the Prophet,

break their fast with a date, followed by a variety of dishes. A common Ramadan dish in many regions is *harisa* (Arabic), *keshke* (Turkish), or *halim* (Persian), a porridge of meat (often beef) and wheat, boiled then pounded to a paste, spiced with cinnamon and sometimes sugar, or fried onions and strong spices. Lentil and other substantial soups of meat broth and pulses are common items. Otherwise, the Ramadan table consists of a selection of the popular local foods, of rice dishes, fava beans, salads, and dips, and so on. Sweet pastries and puddings are ubiquitous on Ramadan nights everywhere, and the large-scale consumption of dates is common. A common drink for breaking the fast is that made from *qamareddin*, dried apricots pulped and dried in sheets, like paper, which is found throughout the Arab world.

The end of Ramadan is marked by a festival, Id 'al-Fitr, a feast that breaks the fast, during which a great quantity and variety of sweets and pastries are consumed. The other major Muslim feast is that of 'Id al-Adha , feast of the sacrifice, which occurs during the pilgrimage month, and at which an animal, usually a sheep or a goat, is slaughtered in every household that can afford it, and great banquets are prepared, with an obligation to give food to the poor.

Lent, the Christian fasting period before Easter, is distinguished by its own foods, dishes that avoid meat and dairy products. This generates a great many dishes made with vegetables, pulses, and oil, many of them described above.

Jewish Saturday meals. Every Jewish community has its typical Saturday dish, one that is prepared on Friday (Cholent) and cooks overnight for Saturday, preferably with the means to keep it hot, but with an extinguished fire. Iraqi Jews, for instance, prepared a dish of stuffed chicken with rice called *tebit*, "overnight." The chicken is stuffed with rice and aromatics, boiled in a broth with tomato paste and spices, then more rice is added to the broth; the whole ensemble, in a large pot, is then put over a wood fire, covered with old blankets and cushions (to keep the heat), and allowed to cook slowly overnight. At Saturday lunch, the fire will have been extinguished, allowing the handling of the food without fear of breaking the Saturday rules. Eggs were placed over the rim of the pot to cook slowly, and these were eaten for breakfast.

Ancient festivals, pre-Islamic and unrelated to the existing religions, are also celebrated with food. *Nowrouz* is the Persian New Year and spring festival, falling at the spring equinox in March. It is celebrated in Iran, Kurdistan, and some parts of Anatolia and Iraq. The *haft-I sin* (seven S's) is a tray on which seven symbolic items, all of whose names begin with the letter "S," are displayed in every household: these include apple, garlic, and vinegar. Part of the ritual of this feast is eating in the open air, which engenders many picnics in parks, gardens, and in the countryside. Another spring festival is the Egyptian Shamm al-Nasim, "the breathing of the breeze," which also requires eating outdoors and having picnics. *Fasikh*, the traditional dish for this festival, is best eaten outdoors, as it consists of rotted fish (usually mullet) eaten with raw onions.

Globalization

Global commerce, travel, tourism, and the new media have affected Middle Eastern food patterns in diverse ways. Most commentators note the spread of Western fast foods, such as hamburgers, pizzas, and fried chicken—in what has been dubbed "McDonaldization." But this is only one part of the story. Another is the region's development of standard restaurant repertoires, based largely on Lebanese styles, and the spread of these styles to Europe and America: McDonald's in Cairo and *shawarma* in New York. Another element has been the "invention of tradition": placed on the global stage through tourism and communications, caterers and cooks responding creatively to the demand for "authentic" national and local cuisines. Many hotels and restaurants in Istanbul are reviving a so-called Ottoman cuisine, and grand hotels in Cairo are serving *foul* and *ta'miya*, as well as obscure village dishes, to tourists. Globalization, then, does not necessarily lead to uniformity in cuisine, but to diversity, and hopefully, to creativity.

See also **Africa: North Africa; Fasting and Abstinence; India: Moghul India; Iran; Islam; Judaism; Passover; Ramadan.**

BIBLIOGRAPHY

Basan, Ghillie. *Classic Turkish Cookery*. London: Tauris Parke, 1997.

Batmangalij, Najmieh. *Food for Life: A Book of Ancient Persian and Modern Iranian Cooking and Ceremonies*. Washington, D.C.: Mage Publishers, 1986.

Halici, Nevin. *From Sini to the Tray: Classical Turkish Cuisine*. Istanbul: Basim, 1999.

Helou, Anissa. *Lebanese Cuisine*. London: Grubb Street, 1994.

Mallos, Tess. *The Complete Middle East Cookbook*. New York: McGraw-Hill, 1979.

Roden, Claudia. *A New Book of Middle Eastern Food*, Harmondsworth, U.K.: Viking, 1985.

Rodinson, Maxime, A. J. Arberry, and Charles Perry. *Medieval Arab Cookery*. Blackawton, U.K.: Prospect Books, 2001.

Shaida, Margaret. *The Legendary Cuisine of Persia*. Henley-on-Thames, U.K.: Lieuse Publications, 1992.

Watson, Andrew. *Agricultural Innovation in the Early Islamic World: The Diffusion of Crops and Farming Techniques, 700–1100*. Cambridge, U.K.: Cambridge University Press, 1983.

Wolfert, Paula. *The Cooking of the Eastern Mediterranean: 215 Healthy, Vibrant, and Inspired Recipes*. New York: Harper Collins, 1994.

Wright, Clifford A. *A Mediterranean Feast*. New York: William Morrow, 1999.

Zubaida, Sami, and Richard Tapper, eds. *A Taste of Thyme: Culinary Cultures of the Middle East*. London: I. B.Tauris, 2000.

Sami Zubaida

MIDWEST. *See* **United States.**

MILITARY RATIONS. Rations are the foods issued to soldiers, particularly those given when they are engaged in field operations. Since rations are often carried over long distances, they have to be as nonperishable as possible. Dry bread and salted meat were the mainstay of soldier's fare until modern preservation techniques were developed.

In the days of the Roman Empire, soldiers on active service were supposed to get two pounds of bread per day, plus meat, olive oil, and wine. If baker's bread was not available, the soldiers were given grain that could be mixed with water to produce a gruel or porridge, or baked into flat (unleavened) bread. In the Byzantine army, the soldiers were given *paximadion*, a biscuit baked twice to make it light and, more importantly, very dry, since it would keep better that way than bread with any moisture in it.

From the fall of Rome to early modern time, armies in Europe were typically small and temporary. They collected grain for bread and animals for meat; when on the march, they depended largely on supplies purchased or simply taken from civilian populations. Before setting off on an expedition to France in 1294, for example, Edward I of England procured cattle and swine to be slaughtered for meat, and salt to preserve it. Bread, flour, and wheat were also issued to the units for the soldiers to eat. Records indicate that while some of these supplies were purchased on the open market, others were requisitioned from apparently unwilling sellers. Forces heading off on longer trips, such as Crusaders, carried hard money to buy provisions along the way.

When more permanent armies were established, the problem of sustaining them on the march was again solved with bread and salted beef or pork, plus dried peas or beans. The Continental Congress decreed in 1775 that the daily ration for soldiers was to consist of a pound of beef, three quarters of a pound of pork, or a pound of salted fish, plus a pound of bread or flour, along with a pint of milk and a quart of spruce beer or cider to wash it down. Quantities of peas, beans, and rice or cornmeal were also allotted. Unfortunately, these generous rations were often not available, the Continental supply system not being up to the task.

In the American Civil War (1861–1865), soldiers on both sides ate salted beef or pork and made johnnycakes out of flour and fried them in bacon grease, or kneaded the dough into a long roll, wrapped it around a ramrod, and roasted it over a fire. They became accustomed to hard bread, or hardtack, so hard that the best thing to do with it was to smash it with a musket butt and soak it in the soup or coffee. The federal army attempted to provide a more balanced meal through a concoction of dehydrated potatoes, cabbage, turnips, carrots, parsnips, beets, tomatoes, onions, peas, beans, lentils, and celery called "desiccated vegetables." The soldiers had little luck trying to cook the newfangled product and called it "desecrated vegetables."

The process of preserving food by sealing it in tin cans and heating it to high temperatures was invented by the Frenchman Nicholas Appert around 1800. The French army and navy were the first to adopt canned rations. Other armies adopted "iron rations" as the technology was perfected and industrialized. Quality control was critical, however: inadequate canning led to death by food poisoning for some U.S. soldiers in the Spanish-American War.

Canned corned beef—"bully beef"—became the mainstay of British army rations in World War I, along with the usual dry bread, called "dog biscuits" by the soldiers. "Maconochie rations"—a canned soup of turnips and carrots—provided men in the trenches with some variety, but was unappealing when eaten cold, as it often had to be.

In World War II, the U.S. Army's "C" rations were individual canned items such as beef and beans or corned

NAVAL RATIONS

Soldiers' food in times past was bad enough. Sailors on long voyages had it even worse, subsisting mainly on ship's biscuit (similar to soldiers' hard bread) and salted beef or pork. The meat often stayed in casks for years before being opened, and was distinctly unappetizing: "It was of a stony hardness, fibrous, shrunken, dark, gristly, and glistening with salt crystals," as the British poet and historian John Masefield put it. A sailor handy with a knife could turn a chunk of salt beef into a box or other useful item. The lack of vegetables and fresh food led to scurvy, a disease caused by vitamin C deficiency that could decimate crews on long voyages. The British eventually solved the scurvy problem by issuing sailors lemon or lime juice. The juice ration gave rise to the nickname "limeys" for British seamen.

beef hash. "K" rations—said to be named after Dr. Ancel Keys, the nutritionist who helped develop them—were complete meals in a water-resistant package, such as a breakfast of canned hash, biscuits, a compressed cereal bar, instant coffee, a fruit bar, and chewing gum. They were intended for short-term use and became monotonous when eaten for days or weeks on end. K rations were discontinued in 1948, although C rations remained in use through the Vietnam War.

The concept of a complete, packaged meal was obviously sound, and armed forces have developed new versions with the food sealed in plastic pouches. The U.S. "Meal, Ready To Eat," or MRE, comes in twenty-four varieties reflecting the range of tastes in the United States, from grilled beefsteak to pasta with alfredo sauce and chicken with Thai sauce. Side dishes such as beans or noodles, fruit, crackers, and dessert round out the meal. The meals provide an average of thirteen hundred calories each. Other armies have similar ration packs, with the British version heavy on tea and puddings while the French version offers duck or salmon appetizers and veal or stewed lamb among the entrees. None of them are particularly popular with the troops, and American soldiers say "MRE" stands for "Meals Rejected by Everyone."

BIBLIOGRAPHY

Fox, David. "Army Rat Packs Keep Afghanistan Forces Fighting Fit." *Reuters*, 27 January 2002.

Gragg, Rod. *The Illustrated Confederate Reader*. New York: Gramercy, 1998.

Keegan, John. *A History of Warfare*. New York: Vintage, 1994.

Kislinger, Ewald. "Christians of the East: Rules and Realities of the Byzantine Diet." In *Food: A Culinary History*, edited by Jean-Louis Flandrin and Massimo Montanari, pp. 194–206. New York: Penguin, 2000.

Koehler, Franz A. *Army Operational Rations—Historical Background*. Washington, D.C.: Office of the Quartermaster General, 1958.

Lynn, John A. *Feeding Mars: Logistics in Western Warfare from the Middle Ages to the Present*. Boulder, Colo.: Westview Press, 1993.

Masefield, John. *Sea Life in Nelson's Time*. Annapolis: U.S. Naval Institute, 1971.

Montanari, Massimo. "Food Systems and Models of Civilization." In *Food: A Culinary History*, edited by Jean-Louis Flandrin and Massimo Montanari, pp. 69–78. New York: Penguin, 2000.

Pedrocco, Giorgio. "The Food Industry and New Preservation Techniques." In *Food: A Culinary History*, edited by Jean-Louis Flandrin and Massimo Montanari, pp. 481–491. New York: Penguin, 2000.

Prell, Patricia. "Giving Thanks for Better Rations." Available at http://www.natick.army.mil. The army laboratory at Natick, Massachusetts, developed Meals, Ready to Eat (MREs).

Tannahill, Reay. *Food in History*. New York: Three Rivers Press, 1989.

Vaughn, Mark Kennedy. "'Mount Your War-Horses, Take Your Lances in Your Grip' . . . Logistics Preparations for the Gascon Campaign of 1294." In *Thirteenth Century England*, vol. 8, pp. 97–111. Suffolk, U.K.: Boydell and Brewer, 2001.

Ward, Christopher. *The War of the Revolution*. New York: Macmillan, 1952.

Ward, Geoffrey C. *The Civil War: An Illustrated History*. New York: Knopf, 1990.

Richard L. Lobb

MILK. *See* **Dairy Products.**

MILK, HUMAN. Human milk is a food that evolved to ensure optimal growth, development, and survival of human infants and young children. All female mammals are uniquely equipped to provide species-specific nourishment and immunity through the provision of milk to their newborns.

Lactation refers to the physiological process of producing milk and its removal by an infant. Women produce breast milk as a response to the baby's suckling in an efficient system of supply and demand. Two hormones, prolactin and oxytocin, play important roles in this process. Prolactin is essential for both the initiation and the maintenance of milk production, while oxytocin stimulates milk ejection. Both hormones play complementary roles in breast-feeding, helping the mother relax and easing the infant into sleep. Oxytocin is particularly intriguing because it controls milk letdown, which can be affected by fear, pain, stress, and anxiety. The oxytocin reflex is more complex than the prolactin reflex. The mother's thoughts and fears may hinder the letdown reflex, and thinking about her baby may trigger the production of oxytocin and milk ejection.

Colostrum, the first milk mothers produce after giving birth, meets all the nutritional needs of the newborn. It has strong antiviral properties, strengthens the newborn's immune system, and acts as a laxative to remove meconium (first feces) from the digestive tract. It is thicker and richer in minerals and protein than mature milk. Colostrum is particularly rich in vitamins E and A. Infants usually consume only a small amount of this first milk. Within one or two days colostrum becomes transitional milk, and the supply increases greatly. The rate at which colostrum changes to mature milk varies from woman to woman, however, mature milk is present within two weeks.

Human milk is a living substance, changing constantly and adapting to meet the changing needs of the infant. For example, it changes from the beginning to the end of a feed. The fore milk has more protein, vitamins, minerals, and water and the hind milk has more fat to signal the end of the feed. Human milk has the highest fat content in the morning and the least at night. It even changes by season, age of the infant, and according to the baby's demand. Human milk reflects the environment, the diet, and the germs of the mother. Ultimately the infant determines the composition of the feed in an interactive process. Although breast pumps are available to many women in urban settings, a breast-feeding infant is the most efficient remover of human milk.

Human milk contains the right mixture of proteins, carbohydrates, fats, vitamins, and minerals to meet all the nutritional needs of infants for about the first six months of life. After the addition of other foods, breast milk continues to offer important nutritional benefits. In May 2001 the World Health Assembly confirmed by unanimous resolution that infants should be exclusively breast-fed for six months and continue to be breast-fed to age two and beyond.

One liter of human milk provides approximately 750 calories and contains 70 grams of carbohydrate, 46 grams of fat, and 13 grams of protein in addition to vitamins and minerals. Breast milk composition is remarkably stable around the world and changes only slightly with different maternal diets and under different environmental conditions. Fat is the most variable component, since maternal diet can modify the fat content of milk. Milk fat provides essential fatty acids and fat-soluble vitamins. The fats in human milk are in forms appropriate for the age of the infant and are readily bioavailable. Lactose is the primary carbohydrate in human milk. Human milk contains both casein and whey protein, but with more whey than casein, human milk is easier for human infants to digest than cow's milk.

The variety of vitamins and minerals produced in breast milk meets the needs of a full-term healthy infant. Water soluble vitamins, however, are influenced by maternal diet. Minerals in breast milk are highest in the first few days after birth. Infants build up iron reserves in utero, and the iron in breast milk is easily absorbed. As a result breast-fed babies are rarely iron deficient. Breast milk contains enough water for a baby, even in hot climates.

The amount of milk produced by a breast-feeding mother varies from around five hundred milliliters a day at day five to around eight hundred milliliters a day at six months, with a slow decline in volume as other foods are added to the diet. Women exhibit differences in the rate of milk synthesis, although the nutritional status of the mother does not significantly affect milk volume or quality. Current research suggests that differences in breast milk storage capacity among women may exist.

Knowledge about the properties of human milk is accumulating rapidly but remained incomplete at the beginning of the twenty-first century. Debates about how human milk is affected by drugs and chemical contaminants center on health consequences for infants and on the ethics of raising concerns when evidence is inconclusive and new mothers are most vulnerable to negative suggestions about the quality of their milk.

Mother's milk has also been recognized as a medium for early flavor experiences, since it is flavored by the mother's ingestion of foods such as garlic, mint, and vanilla. Human milk provides an opportunity for infants to become familiar with the flavors that they will encounter in the household cuisine.

Breast milk is a living substance. It contains living white blood cells that fight infection. Maternal antibodies are passed to the fetus through the placenta before birth and through breast milk after birth, providing temporary immunological protection for newborns. Milk proteins, such as lactoferrin, play an important immunological role, as do enzymes, immunoglobulins, and leukocytes. Human milk is clean and free of bacteria. Unlike artificial milk substitutes, human milk contains nonnutrient substances with the capacity to enhance immunity and destroy pathogens. Human milk has antibacterial, antifungal, and anti-infective properties that have been recognized for centuries. For example, expressed human milk has been used as a folk remedy for conjunctivitis. The protective effect of human milk is strongest for gastroenteritis and respiratory infections. However, the beneficial and protective effects of human milk include lowering the risk of allergies, multiple sclerosis, Crohn's disease, and sudden infant death syndrome (SIDS).

Human milk is seldom considered as a food resource or recorded in food composition tables. It has been suggested that it should be included in the calculations of a country's food supply and food balance sheets. Norway calculated the national production of breast milk to be

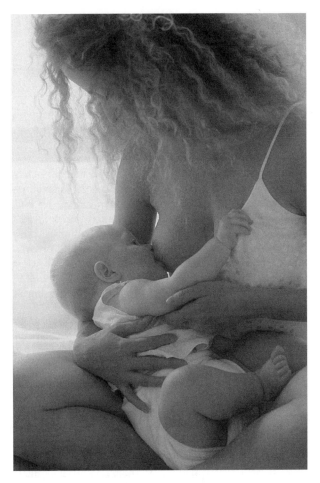

Woman nursing her baby. PHOTO BY KARIN GOZZANO. © PICTURE PRESS/CORBIS.

8.2 million kilograms in 1992, valued at U.S. $410 million (at U.S. $50 per liter). Norway has subsequently included human milk in calculating national food balance sheets.

It is impossible to put a precise economic value on human milk because it is seldom sold in the marketplace. Attempts to calculate its value include estimating the costs of breast milk substitutes or replacements or more rarely from the price charged for donated breast milk in milk banks. As a unique, incomparable product, its value to human survival is beyond calculation.

See also **Baby Food; Lactation; Nutrient Bioavailability.**

BIBLIOGRAPHY

Jelliffe, Derrick B., and E. F. Patrice Jelliffe. *Human Milk in the Modern World*. Oxford and New York: Oxford University Press, 1978.

Riordan, Jan, and Kathleen G. Auerbach, eds. *Breastfeeding and Human Lactation*. Boston: Jones and Bartlett, 1993.

Stuart-Macadam, Patricia, and Katherine A. Dettwyler, eds. *Breastfeeding: Biocultural Perspectives.* New York: Aldine de Gruyter, 1995.

Penny Van Esterik

MINERALS. Living organisms appear to selectively concentrate certain elements from the environment while rejecting others. The adult human body contains approximately thirty-five elements. Four of these (hydrogen, oxygen, carbon, and nitrogen) constitute 99 percent of the atoms in the body. As a comparison, the most abundant elements in the Earth's crust are oxygen (67 percent), silicon (28 percent), and aluminum (8 percent). The remaining 1 percent of the elements in the human body (with the exception of sulfur) are the inorganic or mineral constituents of the body and thus form the ash when the body is "burned." Seven of the remaining elements, sodium, potassium, calcium, magnesium, phosphorus, sulfur, and chloride, together represent about 0.9 percent of the body's weight. The seventeen others make up the remaining 0.1 percent, some of which, but not all, are considered nutritionally essential. These elements appear in the body at measurable concentrations but may not perform an essential biological function. Cadmium is one such example. The newborn infant is virtually free of this element, but gradually accumulates cadmium by ingestion and inhalation, such that over a lifetime an average person living in an industrial society accumulates milligrams of this element. Not only does cadmium appear to serve no essential function in the body, it is also likely to be undesirable and potentially detrimental.

Most experts agree that thirteen mineral elements are nutritionally essential. These are minerals that when deficient consistently result in an impairment of a function that is prevented or cured by supplementation. There still is some question about seven others (Table 1).

The functions of mineral elements are structural, osmotic, catalytic, and signaling. Calcium plays the most obvious role as structural component of bone but also participates in many examples of cell signaling. Sodium, chloride, and potassium constitute the majority of minerals whose function is to maintain osmotic and water balance and membrane electrical potentials. The micromineral elements listed in Table 1 have historically been classified as "trace" elements primarily because they occurred at levels below past methods for detection. In general, these minerals function as biocatalysts. Iron is the most prominent example because a deficiency of iron is probably the most common nutritional deficiency on earth (anemia afflicts more than 15 percent of the world's population). Copper and zinc are the prototypical biocatalysts because virtually all of their known functions involve either catalytic or structural roles in many different enzymes. Copper is unique in that all of the known deficiency symptoms in experimental animal models can be explained on the basis of failure of known enzymes. Zinc

deficiency, on the other hand, presents symptoms that are not directly attributable to any of the fifty or more enzymes in which it is found. Selenium, manganese, and molybdenum are also constituents of enzymes. Deficiency symptoms for selenium and manganese have been well characterized but a nutritional deficiency of molybdenum has not been satisfactorily demonstrated. The most compelling reason to include molybdenum among the thirteen nutritionally essential elements is because of its presence (and thus function) in several important enzymes. Some microminerals serve a very narrow range of biological functions. Iodine and cobalt are exclusively constituents of thyroid hormones and vitamin B_{12}, respectively. No other role has been identified for these el-

TABLE 1

Known nutritionally essential minerals

Element	Amount in 70-kg Human (g)	Function
Macrominerals		
Calcium	1,200	Component of bones; signal transduction in hormonal action, muscle contraction, blood clotting; and structural role in proteins
Phosphorus	700	Component of bone Necessary for activation of high energy intermediates
Potassium	240	Osmotic, electrolyte, and water balance
Chloride	120	Osmotic, electrolyte, and water balance
Sodium	120	Osmotic, electrolyte, and water balance
Magnesium	35	Activation of ATPases, kinases, and other enzymes
Microminerals		
Iron	4.0	Catalytic redox reactions, oxygenation, and O_2-carrying proteins
Zinc	2.0	Catalytic as a Lewis acid and structural function for some metalloenzymes
Copper	0.1	Catalytic in redox reactions some involving iron
Selenium	0.020	Structural and catalytic component of peroxidases, especially glutathione peroxidase. Provides antioxidant protection
Iodine	0.015	Component of thyroid hormones
Molybdenum[a]	0.012	Structural component of enzymes, especially xanthine oxidase and sulfite oxidase
Manganese	0.015	Catalytic role in enzymes involved in cartilage formation
Co[b]	0.001	Structural component of vitamin B_{12}

Abbreviations: ATPase, adenosine triphosphatase.
[a]Biochemical evidence only that it is essential.
[b]Essential only as a component of vitamin B_{12}.

532

ements. The remaining mineral elements are those that occur in significant concentrations in the human body and most probably serve an important biological function. However, consistent findings regarding deficiency symptoms and specific biochemical functions have not been reported. Fluorine is a unique example of a mineral that currently has no definitive biological function but because it appears beneficial to dental health, it is a recommended nutrient.

Calcium and Phosphorus

Approximately 99 and 85 percent of the total calcium and phosphorus, respectively, in the human body are found in bone. Both ions leave the bone and are deposited back each day representing normal metabolic activity or "turnover" of bone. The remaining 1 percent of calcium is found in both extracellular and intracellular pools and is absolutely critical for normal body function such as muscle contraction and nerve activity. Although very rare, a sudden drop in extracellular concentrations of calcium (>50 percent) can lead to an emergency situation such as tetany or convulsions. Nerve cells bathed in hypocalcemic fluid spontaneously "fire," leading to uncontrolled nerve activation and muscle spasm. The majority of the extracellular calcium is in chemical equilibrium with bone. Approximately 30 percent is under hormonal control by several hormones, parathyroid hormone, vitamin D, and thyrocalcitonin. As a result, the concentration of extracellular calcium is remarkably constant. Blood levels of phosphorus fluctuate much more and appear to be determined in large part by urinary excretion.

The absorption of calcium from the diet is dependent on a number of dietary and physiological factors. Vitamin D is synthesized in skin when exposed to ultraviolet irradiation [290 to 315 nanometers of ultraviolet (UV) light]. Sunscreen lotions [Sun Protection Factor (SPF) 8] can reduce this synthesis as much as 90 percent. Inadequate sunlight exposure was most likely the cause of calcium deficiency rickets observed at the turn of the century in countries at northern latitudes. A change in dietary calcium absorption in humans appears to take several weeks to accomplish but accounts for the ability of humans to tolerate diets that provide relatively little calcium (200 to 400 mg/day). This activation process becomes less potent with age and may account in part for the increased calcium requirements with age.

Dietary factors affecting the absorption of calcium are well known. They include chelating organic acids such as oxalic and phytic acid. The former is the most potent and is responsible for the markedly diminished "availability" of calcium found in spinach. The amount of calcium contained by a food is only an approximation of the amount of calcium that is ultimately "available." Estimated fractional absorption (percent of intake absorbed into the body) of calcium from these foods ranges from 5 percent for spinach to 61 percent for broccoli. Vegetables of the Brassica family such as broccoli and cab-

CALCIUM AND OSTEOPOROSIS

The relationship between dietary calcium and osteoporosis has been studied for many years. Early indications suggested that dietary calcium intake was not correlated with bone density (a indicator of bone strength) or the bone loss that naturally occurs with aging. The complexity of the issue is illustrated by observations that many people consume relatively low calcium diets and yet show little evidence of osteoporosis. The genetic contribution to bone density is well established. Studies of identical twins demonstrate that a considerable proportion of the variation in bone density is attributable to inheritance. Mothers with osteoporosis have daughters (thirty years of age) who possess bone density that is significantly less than age-matched controls. Dietary intervention with calcium has been attempted in many different studies. Those in the past decade suggest that some changes may be effected by increased calcium intake but they are relatively minor and perhaps short-lived. For example, calcium supplements of 500 mg/day over three years were found to affect bone density of some bones significantly only in older women whose habitual calcium intakes were relatively low (<400 mg/day). Supplements had no effect in older women who had higher habitual calcium intakes. This study seemed to indicate that there might be a subset of elderly women who may benefit from increased calcium intake. Because vitamin D has such a critical role in the absorption of calcium, some workers have examined both vitamin D status and calcium supplementation. Overall, the results not surprisingly support the idea that vitamin D may be a limiting factor in the absorption of dietary calcium. Many other dietary variables may also be important in optimizing the effectiveness of dietary calcium. Dietary acidity, which is promoted by protein intake and ameliorated by the consumption of fruits and vegetables, may contribute. Alkaline diets rich in potassium appear to reduce the loss of body calcium and thus preserve bones. Elevated sodium intake also appears to increase urinary calcium losses. Therefore, the development of osteoporosis is unlikely to be a simple matter of too little dietary calcium consumption, especially in the later years of life, but more of an effect of total dietary conditions superimposed on a particular genetic background.

bage appear to contain little oxalate and thus contain calcium that exhibits higher bioavailability than dairy products. Milk and dairy products have relatively high calcium content as well as relatively high fractional absorption (30 percent), resulting in the highest amount of calcium per serving. Lactose in milk enhances the absorption of calcium in infants but its effect in adults is less clear. Other dietary factors affect the retention of dietary calcium but have little impact on its absorption. For example, high intakes of either sodium or protein are thought to result in increased urinary losses of calcium. Protein increases renal calcium loss by increasing acid load while sodium increases losses via shared renal transporters. Both of these conditions may affect calcium balance and ultimately the requirements for this nutrient. The bone loss associated with chronic calcium losses or negative calcium balance may ultimately lead to weakened bones or osteoporosis. Calcium supplements may adversely affect the bioavailability of iron.

Calcium deficiency occurs primarily as rickets or osteomalacia in young children. Bones are deformed (bowed legs) and weak due to inadequate calcification of the protein matrix of bone. This deficiency can arise as a result of too little dietary calcium (relatively rare) or inadequate vitamin D synthesis. Historically, the latter has been the major cause brought about primarily because of reduced exposure to sunlight. It is conceivable, however, that dietary factors such as oxalates and cultural customs (clothing) may interact to play a role in the development of rickets especially since recent cases have been reported in areas of the world near the equator where sunlight should not be limiting. Calcium deficiency does not appear to be a primary cause of osteoporosis. This condition is characterized not by inadequate bone mineralization but by a loss of total bone both protein matrix and mineral. Bones weaken and become susceptible to fracture.

Sodium and Chloride

Total body sodium is approximately one-tenth of that of calcium. One-third of body sodium is found in bone but its metabolic significance is unknown. Sodium and chloride constitute the major cation and anion, respectively, in the extracellular fluid of humans. Sodium is the primary determinant of the osmotic pressure of the extracellular fluid and as such is the main determinant of extracellular fluid volume. The sodium ion concentration changes less than 3 percent day in and day out despite dramatic fluctuations in sodium intake. This is a reflection of a very tightly controlled and highly regulated system to maintain constant osmotic pressure. Through most of human evolution, the availability of dietary salt has been very highly restricted. Much of dietary sodium (and chloride) were derived from sources such as meat and vegetables, which contain very low levels. Consequently, humans and other mammals have evolved physiological mechanisms that permit sodium conservation under extreme conditions. This physiological conservation system comprised of pressure receptors, renal renin, lung angiotensinogen, adrenal aldosterone, and vasso-pression all makes dietary requirements extremely diffi-

cult to assess. For example, the Yanomamo Indians in Northern Brazil have been found to excrete as little as 1 mEq/day of sodium (Na) per day. This reflects a dietary consumption of approximately 60 mg salt per day (over 100 times less than that which is normally consumed in Western populations). At the other extreme are the northern Japanese, who consume nearly 26 grams of salt each day. These regions of Japan have unusually high incidences of cerebral hemorrhage, most likely related to the high incidence of hypertension. Other areas of the world such as Northern Europe and the United States consume approximately 10 g/day or less of salt. The sodium and potassium contents of some selected foods are shown in Figure 1. It is apparent that many "unprocessed" foods contain very little sodium. Estimates of sodium intake suggest that over 85 percent of the sodium consumed in Western diets is sodium added during processing. This is clearly illustrated by the progressively higher sodium content of peas (fresh, frozen, and canned) and perhaps more important, the dramatic reduction in potassium content. The net result is a reversal of the naturally low sodium to potassium ratio found in all fresh plants.

A deficiency of sodium normally does not occur even in areas where salt is scarce. The abnormal loss of sodium and other electrolytes, however, could occur under conditions of extreme sweat loss, chronic diarrhea and vomiting, or renal disease, all of which produce an inability to retain sodium. Acute episodes of diarrhea or vomiting resulting in a loss of 5 percent of body weight could lead to shock. The most important therapy under these circumstances is to restore sodium and water or circulatory volume. Chloride deficiency has been reported in infants consuming low-sodium chloride formulas. They show signs of metabolic alkalosis, dehydration, anorexia, and growth failure. Potassium depletion most notably affects cardiac function where either elevations or reductions in serum potassium can cause arrythmias.

FIGURE 1

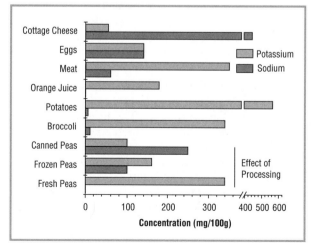

Magnesium

Magnesium is an important intracellular ion involved in many enzymatic reactions of food oxidation and cell constituent synthesis. Approximately 60 percent of total body magnesium is found in bone, where approximately half can be released during bone resorption. Magnesium food sources are widely distributed in plant and animal products with the highest content found in whole grains and green (high chlorophyll) leafy vegetables. Refining wheat with the removal of the germ and outer layers may remove nearly 80 percent of the magnesium from wheat. Meats and most fruits and vegetables are poor sources of magnesium. The absorption of magnesium appears to be unrelated to the absorption of calcium (that is, is independent of vitamin D) and is relatively unaffected by food constituents. Phytate and phosphates, however, may adversely affect magnesium availability by forming insoluble products although their practical significance is unclear. Experimental magnesium deficiency has been produced in humans. Urinary magnesium drops virtually to zero while plasma levels are relatively well preserved. The change in urinary excretion reflects a "urinary threshold" for magnesium. After continued deficiency, however, neuromuscular activity is affected, ultimately leading to tremors and convulsions. Serum and urinary calcium levels are profoundly reduced and not restored by parathyroid hormone administration. It was concluded that magnesium is essential for the mobilization of calcium from bone. A deficiency of magnesium under normal conditions is unlikely but may occur with the presence of other illnesses such as alcoholism or renal disease.

Iron

Over 65 percent of body iron is found in hemoglobin, the respiratory pigment used to transport oxygen within and between tissues. One-third of body iron is a "storage" form that can be mobilized during times of need. The amount of "storage" iron may vary greatly with age and gender. Food sources of iron are complicated by numerous factors that affect the bioavailability of dietary iron. Non-heme sources of iron are found in plant and vegetable products and the absorption from these sources (versus heme found in meat products) is generally lower and influenced to a greater extent by total diet composition. Vitamin C is probably the most signficant enhancer of non-heme iron absorption, while plant phenolics such as tannins found in teas and phytates found in cereals are some of the most potent inhibitors. None of these factors, however, affect the absorption of heme iron found in meats. Iron status can markedly affect the amount of iron absorbed from a meal—low status increases iron absorption. The effect is most pronounced for non-heme iron, changing over fourfold compared to 50 percent for heme iron. Although iron status can influence absorption, the most important determinant of iron availability is the composition of the diet. It is clear that non-heme iron absorption is markedly affected by the characteristics of the food with which it is eaten and that there are

SODIUM AND POTASSIUM

In the early 1950s, scientists found that experimental animals could be selected genetically to be susceptible to dietary salt-induced hypertension. Lewis K. Dahl and colleagues established a genetic strain of rat that was sensitive to high dietary salt. These rats showed remarkably elevated blood pressure when dietary salt was increased approximately ten times above normal. The rats' kidneys appeared to have a genetically programmed sensitivity to salt-induced hypertension. However, in the absence of high dietary salt, these animals were normal. Dietary potassium was also recognized as an important factor since high concentrations could ameliorate the effect of sodium chloride. Establishing a direct link between high dietary salt intake and hypertension in humans has been difficult to prove. The problem has been that not all individuals within a population are equally sensitive. Much evidence has come from studies of populations with widely differing salt intake. Populations whose sodium intake is low (less than 100 milligrams of salt) do not appear to develop elevated blood pressure with age. Those whose intake is relatively high do show increased blood pressure with age and evidence of increased incidence of essential hypertension. Recent studies with nonhuman primates have clearly shown that changes in salt intake alone are sufficient to induce changes in blood pressure. Many other studies suggest that lower potassium intake may also be important in the etiology of elevated blood pressure. Certain individuals may be more susceptible or sensitive to sodium-induced changes in blood pressure (similar to experimental animals). All of the known mutations resulting in a phenotype of hypertension involve some aspect of sodium renal excretion and/or retention. It is likely, then, that genetic sodium sensitivity will be a prerequisite to an environmentally induced development of hypertension.

clear differences in the nature of absorption of heme and non-heme iron. Iron deficiency is seldom related to iron intake per se. Major causes of anemia (too little hemoglobin) include blood loss and/or diets containing either no enhancers (such as meat or ascorbic acid) or high levels of inhibitors. Infection can also change iron metabolism significantly such that much of the anemia in the world is due to chronic infection. The losses for iron for both men and women are known precisely but the amount of dietary iron requirement depends on the overall diet.

Zinc

Zinc is present in all tissues and performs both structural and catalytic functions in many different enzymes. Unfortunately, changes in the activities of these enzymes are not sufficient to explain the pathological effects of experimental zinc deficiency. Experimental animals refuse to eat experimental diets that are very low in zinc. Human zinc deficiency was demonstrated nearly two decades ago in the United States. Young children from 6 months to 5 years of age showed low amounts of zinc in the hair relative to other groups. Hair zinc and taste acuity were restored after three to five months of zinc supplementation. Earlier studies also revealed zinc deficiency in regions of Iran and Egypt. It is very difficult to assess zinc status in humans. Serum zinc is not adequate to assess nutritional status. In experimental situations, serum zinc falls remarkably (>50 percent) following a low zinc intake without immediate (or apparent) ill effects. In 1974, a Recommended Dietary Allowance (RDA) of 15 mg/day was established for zinc. (It was not until 1974 that we had enough information to estimate an RDA for zinc, at which time the value was established at 15 mg. The RDA presented in 1989 gives 15 mg per day for adults. The 2001 Institute of Medicine value is 11 mg per day.) Approximately 70 percent of zinc consumed by most people is derived from animal products. Cereals contain appreciable zinc but the availability varies considerably. Several plant compounds interfere with the absorption of zinc. The most prominent of these is phytates (inositol hexa- and pentaphosphate). These inhibitors most likely contribute to the natural incidence of dietary zinc deficiency observed in humans.

Copper

Although the importance of copper deficiency in animals has been recognized since the 1930s, it is still not possible to establish an RDA for copper in humans because of the uncertainty regarding the quantitative requirements. There is no doubt that copper is an essential nutrient for humans. Current estimates of the minimum copper requirement are between 0.4 and 0.8 mg/day. Copper is critical for the function of several enzymes, especially blood ceruloplasmin. The activity of this enzyme in blood falls dramatically in experimental animals soon after giving copper-deficient diets and is thought to be a good indicator of copper depletion even in humans. Ceruloplasmin is essential for iron absorption (it catylizes the oxidation of Fe^{2+} to Fe^{3+} required for binding of iron to the blood transport protein, transferrin) and explains the anemia observed in copper deficiency. In contrast to zinc, all of the symptoms of a copper defeciency under experimental conditions can be explained by changes in various enzymes that require copper. Two inherited diseases associated with abnormal copper metabolism have been observed—one (Menkes' disease) is associated with copper deficiency, while the other (Wilson's disease) is a disease of excessive copper accumulation. Excessive intake of zinc can precipitate a copper deficiency. An example of zinc-induced copper deficiency has been reported in humans and is attributed to a reduction in the absorption of copper. Excessive zinc may induce intestinal proteins that bind copper and thereby prevent its transfer from the intestine into the body.

Iodine

Approximately 80 percent of total body iodine (20 milligrams) is found in the thyroid gland. All of the iodine that leaves this gland does so as a component of the thyroid hormones—thyroxine and triiodothyronine. In fact, all of the functional significance of iodine is as a component of these hormones. Iodine deficiency represents the most common cause of preventable mental deficits in the world's population. Since most of the world's iodine is found in the oceans, coastal areas are not deficient. However, mountainous areas such as the Himalayas, European Alps, and the mountains of China, as well as the flooded river valleys of Asia, areas where leaching of iodine from soils has occurred for eons, produce iodine-deficient crops and plants. Iodine deficiency during pregnancy causes cretinism, a diet-related birth defect that is characterized by permanent mental retardation and severe growth stunting. In young children and adults, iodine deficiency results in enlarged thyroid glands or goiter. Although various foods such as cassava, cabbage, and turnips contain goitrogens, substances that interfer with iodine metabolism, their practical signficance is not clear. Cassava, the dietary staple in regions of Africa and other areas, may be the exception, especially when not well cooked. The cyanide released by the ingestion of this plant is transformed and ulitmately leads to an inhibition of the uptake of iodine by the thyroid. Goiter was once common in areas of the United States near the Great Lakes and westward to Washington State, but the introduction of iodized salt almost competely eliminated goiter in these areas by the 1950s. The minimum requirement for iodine to prevent goiter is approximately 1 μg/kg/day whereas the recommended intake is nearly twice this amount.

Selenium

Although selenium was first recognized as a toxic trace element for livestock, it is now clear that selenium is an essential nutrient for all animals. During the 1930s, livestock grazing in parts of the Great Plains of North America were found to contract a disease characterized by hair loss, lameness, and death by starvation. The cause of this disease was excess selenium obtained from the plants grown in soils containing high selenium concentration. In fact, selenium, more than any other essential trace element, varies greatly in its concentration in soils throughout the world. Plants accumulate selenium from soils but are not thought to require selenium for growth. Although human toxicity was not observed in affected regions in the United States, endemic selenium poisoning has been observed in high-selenium regions of China where the symptoms included loss of hair and nails. China also possesses regions of very low selenium where, in fact, humans have been diagnosed with selenium deficiency—Keshan disease (cardiomyopathy) and Keshan–Beck disease (degenerative joint disease). Although other factors may be involved, selenium deficiency is clearly a predisposing factor. Selenium functions as part of several important enzymes. The most prominent is a soluble enzyme, glutathione peroxidase, whose function is to reduce hydrogen peroxide and organic (lipid) peroxides, thus preventing the oxidative destruction of cell membranes. Selenium is incorporated into the enzyme as the amino acid selenocysteine by reactions that are unique to selenium. Together with vitamin E, selenium, as a structural component of glutathione peroxidase, forms an antioxidant defense against oxidative stress. The requirement for selenium has been estimated by various methods. On the basis of intakes in regions of China with and without deficiency disease, approximately 20 μg/day is considered an adequate amount to prevent deficiency. The estimated safe and adequate selenium intake suggested by the U.S. National Research Council ranged from 50 to 200 μg/day in 1980. An amount to maintain the highest serum glutathione peroxidase activity appears to be 70 and 55 μg/day for an average man or woman, respectively, which became the Recommended Dietary Allowance (RDA) in 1989. In 1996, the World Health Organization recommended 40 and 30 μg/day for men and women, respectively. Intakes greater that 400 μg/day are considered to be the maximum safe level. Selenium is thus an example of a nutrient that possesses a relatively narrow range of intakes that are safe and that meet requirements.

Manganese

Normal body content of manganese is very low—approximately 15 milligrams or very similar to iodine. In contrast to iodine, manganese deficiency has not been observed in humans but has occurred naturally in chickens and experimentally in many other species. Manganese is required by several enzymes, which may or may not be inolved in the symptoms of a manganese deficiency. Symptoms include impaired growth, skeletal abnormalities, and defects in lipid and carbohydrate metabolism. The role of manganese in the synthesis of the mucopolysaccharide component of bone and cartilage is the most crucial whereas mineralization of bone appears to be independent of manganese. Excessive manganese will interfere with iron absorption. Under conditions of iron deficiency, manganese absorption is increased. Both iron and manganese appear to share a common site for absorption. The recommendations for manganese intake are based on estimates of normal dietary intakes of 2 to 5 mg/day. This amount is thought to be sufficient to replace the 50 percent of body manganese that is lost every 3 to 10 weeks.

Chromium

Chromium is one of the most intriguing and potentially important trace elements because it appears to influence the action of a critical hormone, insulin. Unfortunately, the definitive role of chromium in this regard awaits further study. Decreased sensitivity of peripheral tissues to insulin appears to be the primary biochemical lesion in experimental chromium deficiency. Impaired glucose tolerance has been attributed to chromium deficiency in several experimental models. Also, several patients receiving total parenteral nutrition have responded to chromium supplementation in the predicted manner, that is, improved glucose tolerance. These findings have established chromium as an essential nutrient for humans but the specific deficiency symptoms in those who receive enteral feeding have not emerged. Overt chromium deficiency is very unlikely under normal conditions due to the small amounts of chromium needed. Moreover, a marginal deficiency is very difficult to identify due to the lack of reliable markers for diagnoses concerning chromium. Currently, there is little or no evidence that chromium supplements are either warranted or effective. Even the recommended intakes for adults (50 to 200 μg/day) are uncertain due to the lack of reliable methods for assessment.

Fluoride

Fluoride is not generally considered to be an essential element for humans. It is, however, considered beneficial in that normal intakes appear to reduce the incidence of dental caries. The mechanism of this benefit is thought to be due to incorporation of fluoride into the mineral matrix of tooth enamel, thus producing a more resistant mineral apatite crystal. Over 99 percent of the fluoride found in the body is found in bones and teeth as a component of this mineral apatite crystal. An unusually high intake of fluoride causes permanently discolored or mottled teeth, a condition identified in children drinking water with 2 to 3 parts of fluoride per million. The level of fluoride commonly maintained in municipal water supplies is 1 part per million.

Silicon and Nickel

Silicon is the most abundant mineral in the Earth's crust. It is thus surprising that a need for silicon in biological systems has not been more prominent. Limited research conducted since 1974 has indicated a role for silicon in the development of mature bones in chickens and rats. A human requirement has not been established but estimates in the range of 10 to 20 mg/day have been suggested. Most likely intakes of this magnitude occur under normal conditions. Nickel deficiency has been experimentally produced in several species. Growth depression and changes in iron metabolism have been described. Nickel has been discovered in the enzyme urease from bacteria, fungi, yeasts, algae, plants, and invertebrates. Many other enzymes exist for which nickel is apparently a component. Thus, it is likely that nickel plays an essential functional role in higher organisms, including humans.

Molybdenum

Molybdenum is an essential component of at least three important enzymes found in animals and humans. A deficiency of one of these enzymes, sulfite oxidase, can have severe consequences—seizures and severe mental retardation in infancy. This deficiency has arisen in patients with genetic mutations in cofactor synthesis but not as a primary molybdenum deficiency. The dietary requirements of molybdenum cannot be given, or even approximated, for any animal species including humans. A deficiency of molybdenum has not been observed under natural conditions for any species. Despite this, the biochemical role of molybdenum as a component of several enzymes establishes it as an essential nutrient for humans.

See also **Assessment of Nutritional Status; Calcium; Dietary Assessment; Dietary Guidelines; Fluoride; Food, Composition of; Fruit; Iodine; Iron; Malnutrition; Nutrients; Nutrition; Sodium; Trace Elements; Vegetables; Vitamins.**

BIBLIOGRAPHY

Brody, Tom. *Nutritional Biochemistry*. San Diego, Calif.: Academic Press, 1994.

da Silva, J. J. R. Frausto, and R. J. P. Williams. *The Biological Chemistry of the Elements*. Oxford: Oxford University Press, 1991.

Gillooly, M., T. H. Bothwell, J. D. Torrance, P. MacPhail, D. P. Derman, W. R. Bezwoda, W. Mills, and R. W. Charlton. "The Effects of Organic Acids, Phytates and Polyphenols on the Absorption of Iron from Vegetables." *British Journal of Nutrition* 49 (1983): 331–342.

Groff, James L., Sareen S. Gropper, and Sara M. Hunt. *Advanced Nutrition and Human Metabolism*. Minneapolis/St. Paul, Minn.: West, 1995.

Hallberg, L., L. Hulten, and E. Gramatkovski. "Iron Absorption from the Whole Diet in Men: How Effective Is the Regulation of Iron Absorption?" *American Journal of Clinical Nutrition* 66 (1997): 347–356.

Institute of Medicine. *Dietary Reference Intakes*. Washington D.C., National Academy Press, 2001.

Layrisse, M., C. Martinez-Torres, J. D. Cook, R. Walker, and C. A. Finch. "Iron Fortification of Food: Its Measurement by the Extrinsic Tag Method." *Blood* 41 (1973): 333–352.

Linder, Maria C., ed. *Nutritional Biochemistry and Metabolism*. New York: Elsevier, 1985.

MacGregor, Graham A., and Hugh E. de Wardner. *Salt, Diet and Health*. Cambridge, U.K.: Cambridge University Press, 1998.

Odell, Boyd L., and R. A. Sunde, eds. *Handbook of Nutritionally Essential Mineral Elements*. New York: Marcel Dekker, 1997.

Schrauzer, Gerhard N. "The Discovery of the Essential Trace Elements: An Outline of the History of Biological Trace Element Research." In *Biochemistry of the Essential Ultratrace Elements*, edited by Earl Frieden, pp. 17–31. New York: Plenum, 1984.

Shils, Maurice E., James A. Olson, Moshe Shike, and A. Catherine Ross, eds. *Modern Nutrition in Health and Disease*, 9th ed. Baltimore: Williams and Wilkins, 1999.

Stipanuk, M. H., ed. *Biochemical and Physiological Aspects of Human Nutrition*. Philadelphia: W. B. Saunders, 2000.

Underwood, E. J., ed. *Trace Elements in Human and Animal Nutrition*, 4th ed. New York: Academic Press, 1977.

Weaver, C. M., and R. P. Heaney. "Calcium." In *Modern Nutrition in Health and Disease.*, 9th ed., edited by M. E. Shils, J. A. Olson, M. Shike, and A. C. Ross, pp. 141–156. Baltimore: Williams and Wilkins. 1999.

Ziegler, Ekhard E., and L. J. Filer, Jr., eds. *Present Knowledge in Nutrition*, 7th. ed. Washington, D.C.: ILSI, 1996.

Charles Chipley W. McCormick

MOLLUSKS. Mollusks exist in diverse forms, and although a mollusk is easily recognizable as such to a scientist who studies them, there is no obvious relationship between, say, an oyster and a flying squid. In fact people with no specialist knowledge are more likely to think of them as comprising separate groups: the gastropods (single shells), such as abalone or whelk, inhabiting single shells; the bivalves, such as clams and oysters, which have double shells; and the cephalopods (the name literally means "head-feet," referring to their strange configuration), which include cuttlefish, squid, and octopus.

The number of species in each of these groups is huge. The biodiversity of mollusks is far greater than that of fish and is exceeded only by the vast armies of insects. Three-quarters of the species of mollusks are gastropods, the category that is on the whole of least interest to human consumers. Next come bivalves. Third in numbers but greatest in size are the cephalopods. In relation to the human diet, the bivalves were probably the most important in prehistoric times, because most of them do not move around and many of them exist in the intertidal zones, or in very shallow waters, and are therefore easily gathered. Excavations at Skara Bray in the Shetlands have uncovered huge middens (a term used by archaeologists for a prehistoric refuse-heap of shells and bones) of bivalve shells, indicating very heavy consumption of them during the Stone Age. Evidence from coastal areas in many other parts of the world, including Japan, confirms this. Although consumption of clams and oysters and mussels and scallops is considerable today, especially in Europe and North America, it is the cephalopods that have become most important globally. The fishery for squid is conducted on a huge scale, and squid are a major source of protein for people in the Indo-Pacific area, as well as elsewhere.

In very ancient times, only people living near the coasts could benefit from eating marine mollusks ("marine" is specified in order to distinguish this group from terrestrial mollusks such as edible snails). Even if transport had been available to take mollusks far inland to other communities, the perishability of most of them (still a major factor today, despite the advent of refrigeration and freezing) would have ruled out such traffic. However, there may have been some exceptions. Preservation by drying is a method that is not applicable to many mollusks but can be used for cephalopods. The Greek practice of drying octopus is probably of great antiquity.

In developed countries where modern techniques are available, the transport of even delicate mollusks such as oysters (which have to be kept alive until consumption) is well assured and there is hardly anywhere in these countries where customers cannot enjoy the full range of mollusks. Availability accounts for increased demand, as does the dramatic increase in the size of human populations. However, the factor that has done most to make mollusks almost ubiquitous on dining tables is undoubtedly the great advances made in fishing techniques since medieval times. The huge resources of oceanic squid were simply not accessible in earlier times, whereas today there are few parts of any of the oceans where squid are relatively safe from capture. The sophistication of the equipment used by the vessels that fish for them, especially those from Japan, is extraordinary.

Before considering the three groups of mollusks in more detail, there is one question of nomenclature to consider, and another of classification.

The term "shellfish" is defined in the *New Shorter Oxford English Dictionary* as "any aquatic invertebrate animal whose outer covering is a shell, usually a mollusc (as an oyster, a winkle, a mussel, etc.) or a crustacean (as a crab, a prawn, a shrimp, etc.), especially one regarded as edible." The term is commonly used for crustaceans and for any mollusk living in an exterior shell. Thus it would apply to the single shells and bivalves but not to cephalopods, with one exception: the so-called chambered nautilus shells, which count as cephalopods but do inhabit shells. A few species of nautilus have value as food in the Indo-Pacific area. It is also relevant to point out that the other cephalopods tend to have what might be called "internal" shells, for example, the "cuttlebone" found in the cuttlefish. These constitute traces of external shells that have disappeared in the course of evolution. The chambered nautilus is, so to speak, poised to take a further step in evolution and abandon its shell, whereupon it would bear some resemblance to a small squid. The question of classification referred to above is this: does the term mollusk include miscellaneous sea creatures such as the sea cucumbers and sea anemones that are eaten in some parts of the world and that are neither fish nor crustaceans but, owing to their general appearance, might be taken to be mollusks? The answer is no; they belong to separate orders. For example, the sea cucumbers belong to the order Holothurian. Furthermore, if a creature is not a fish but does have a shell, must it be either a crustacean or a mollusk? Again the answer is negative. The sea urchin, whose ovaries are a prized delicacy, has what would normally be called a shell (cov-

Seafood merchant selling octopus in Tokyo, 1986. © ROBERT HOLMES/CORBIS.

ered usually with spines to repel predators), but it belongs to the phylum Echinodermata.

Having thus cleared what might otherwise be muddy waters for some readers it is time to look more closely at the three main groups of edible mollusks.

Single Shells

The gastropods, or single shell mollusks, have contributed less to human nutrition than either the bivalves or the cephalods. This is not because the single shells are too small. Some, such as whelks, attain a considerable size, up to 90 cm (35 inches) in the case of the species *Melongena pugilina*, which is eaten in Malaysia and the Philippines. Large whelk, often called conch, are eaten in the Caribbean, where they are known locally as *lambis* or *lambie*. One speciality is the conch stew of Martinique and Guadaloupe while another is soused conch, (*lambie souse*). In *Life and Food*, Cristine Mackie describes this specialty as well as other food of the region, and makes one particularly interesting observation. She believes that the native inhabitants, who are known to have consumed conch in large quantities and whose experience preparing it stretches back over many centuries, probably showed early white settlers how to extract the meat and clean it, a special skill requiring instruction.

Even very small single shells are eaten, for example, the little top-shell of the Mediterranean (*Monodonta turbinata*, of the family Trochidae) or the equally small periwinkle (*Littorina littorea*, family Lacunidae), known locally as winkles and found on North Atlantic shores, both east and west, but mostly appreciated in Europe. In general, however, the appetite for single shells has diminished in many parts of the world, largely because they are fished locally and few of the edible species have more than minimal gastronomic merit.

Nevertheless, one family among the single shells, Haliotidae, to which the abalone belong, certainly does merit attention for human consumption. There are species all round the world. In California, for example, the red abalone (*H. rufescens*), is probably the best known although *H. tuberculata* has been famous since classical times in the Mediterranean and on the European Atlantic coast as far north as the Channel Islands (where it is known as ormer in English and *ormeau* in French). However, supplies are not abundant. Indeed, along much of the northwest coast of the United States the fishery is either closed outright or subject to severe restrictions. In Japan there is a tradition that stretches back to antiquity of husband-and-wife teams fishing for abalone; the wife dives while the husband tends the boat and the lifeline. Depending on the quality of the various species, the Japanese may eat them raw, diced and iced and furnished with a dipping sauce, or grilled and steamed. Generally, abalone is tough and must be tenderized before being cooked.

Although some abalone can reach a size of up to 25 cm (10–11 in.), they may be regarded as a sophisticated descendant of the ordinary limpet. Limpets, seen clinging tenaciously to seaside rocks, are much smaller and biologically less complicated creatures, but are edible and utilized in interesting local recipes; for example, in some parts of Scotland people were known to mix limpet juice with oatmeal.

Bivalves

The aristocrat of bivalves, in the western world, is the oyster. This is odd because in the nineteenth century oysters were so plentiful and cheap that they were considered to be a food of the poor. Today virtually all the oysters brought to market are cultured. In France especially, there are complex systems followed by oyster farmers, from the initial seeding (planting on special tiles) of the spat of existing oysters through various changes of environment designed to afford protection from predators and to encourage growth. Oysters thrive in the "parks" created for them, and are carefully graded before being transported live to markets. The district of Marennes-Oléron accounts for well over half the French production, but other place names such as Arcachon indicate other famous oyster areas. In England the oysters of Colchester in Essex and of Whitstable in Kent were once of great renown, but nowadays most of the oysters reaching British markets come from the south of Ireland.

What is said above relates in part to the European oyster, *Ostrea edulis*. However, populations of this species have been very seriously depleted, in some places to vanishing point, and 90 percent of the oysters now consumed in Europe belong to the species *Crassostrea angulata*, popularly known as the Portuguese oyster. It is a native of Portugal and Spain and also known in the Indo-Pacific as the Giant Pacific oyster.

In North America, the American oyster, *Crassostrea virginica*, holds sway. Like the Portuguese, it is larger than the European. American oysters are marketed under many names, indicating the place of origin, for example, Cape oysters from Cape Cod (notably Wellfleet and Chatham); Long Island (Bluepoint, Gardiners Bay), and the Chesapeake Bay area (Chincoteague Bay). Of the other American species of oyster, the best is probably the Olympia oyster, a subspecies of the Californian oyster, *Ostrea lurida*.

Australasian oysters include the Sydney rock oyster, *Crassostrea commercialis*, which is perhaps the most esteemed of all seafoods for Australians.

Whereas oysters are always visible, many bivalves are not. They burrow into the sand and all one can see is perhaps their "siphon" protruding, or a little hole left by the siphon. Some species are remarkably adept at burying themselves quickly and deeply. The razor shells (so-called because they resemble old cut-throat razors) are among the champions in this art. They are known in Orkney as "spoots," and "spooting" by hand is a pastime that calls for great expertise. There are many other clams in both hemispheres that live closer to the surface of the sand and are gathered more easily. Consumption is highest in North America, where they play a leading role in the traditional clambake, which is an important feature of the seafood cultures of many coastal areas, especially New England. Kathy Neustadt explains the cultural and social importance of clams in *We Gather Together: Food and Festival in American Life*. A purely practical description is found in the classic cookbook by Mrs. Lincoln, *Mrs. Lincoln's Boston Cookbook* (1891).

Mussels dominate the European market, at least in terms of quantities sold. The waters surrounding Galicia in the north of Spain include bays that are ideal for the culture of mussels on big ropes suspended from the surface of the sea. By the end of the twentieth century, Spanish exports of mussels had grown to such an extent that they dominated the market, although there is a smaller but substantial industry in the Netherlands, providing mussels mainly for consumption in Belgium. Mussels with french fries (*moules et frites*) is counted by some as the national dish of the Belgians; it enjoys popularity there which is without a parallel anywhere else in the world. However, there are many other ways of preparing mussels including the famous French dish *moules à la marinière* (mussels steamed open in a large covered pot with chopped shallots, herbs, white wine, vinegar, and butter). Mussels are also a useful ingredient in seafood stews and kindred dishes. Mussels can be steamed or fried, and it is also possible to dry mussels (after a boiling). In Thailand dried mussels are coated with sugar and then fried, producing an intriguing dish that might seem strange to western palates.

Those familiar with Irish culture know the song about Sweet Molly Malone who, in the streets of Dublin (where she is commemorated by a charming statue), would cry her wares: "Cockles and mussels alive alive o'." Cockles constitute a large and important group of bivalves, with the European *Cerastoderma edule* being the most important. In some places it is quite remarkably abundant; densities of over ten thousand individuals per square meter have been recorded. With a maximum measurement around 6 cm (2 inches), this is not the largest cockle; that distinction goes to the spiny cockle of the Mediterranean, *Acanthocardia aculeata*, whose body inside the shell is blood red, may reach 10 cm (4 in.). One of the cockles of the Pacific coast of North America, *Clinocardium nuttalli*, may be slightly larger still. Cockles resemble clams in their burrowing down into the sand.

Like oysters, mussels are visible wherever they grow. Another visible bivalve of gastronomic importance is the scallop, who for most of its life is not attached to anything but swims freely, using the rapid opening and shutting of its two shells as a means of propulsion. The muscle connecting the two shells is therefore particularly large and strong, a feature welcome to consumers since this white muscle is the principal edible part. (The orange-yellow coral is also eaten and the "mantle" or "frill" more rarely.)

Of the many species, *Pecten maximus*, the Great Scallop, and *Pecten jacobaeus*, the Pilgrim scallop, are the best known in Europe. The former may measure 16 cm (6 in.) across, while the latter is smaller. It is, however, the latter which has a special religious significance, since its shell has for very many centuries been the badge worn by pilgrims to the shrine of St. James at Santiago de Compostela in Galicia. Indeed, the French name Coquille Saint-Jacques is sometimes applied to scallops in a more general way, as in the famous dish *Coquilles Saint-Jacques à la provençale*. Besides being a badge for pilgrims, scallops have a cultural significance in many other contexts, a point that is well brought out by Cox (1957).

The so-called bay scallop, *Argopecten irradians*, is the common commercial scallop of the American Atlantic coast. Its muscle, which is usually the only part sold, is a great delicacy. If really fresh, it may be eaten raw, flavored by its own juices. There is also a growing North American fishery for the Atlantic deep-sea scallop, *Placopecten magellicanus*.

The scallop is well provided with eyes. About fifty of these, green ringed prettily with blue, are set in the frill. These do not show the scallops where they are going, since they are necessarily always going in the other direction, but they do warn them of any danger approaching from behind.

Edible bivalves can be very small, such as the little wedge shells. Other bivalves, of which parts only can be eaten, are huge, notably the giant clam of the Indo-Pacific, *Tridacna gigas*, which can measure 1 meter (40 in.) across and weigh several hundred kilos; the shells from one of these can provide two washbasins or church fonts.

Because bivalves have two shells joined together, they symbolize in Chinese and other cultures a married couple. Although many of them are plain in color, some have very striking patterns on the outside of their shells, such as zig-zag markings.

Cephalopods

A comprehensive reference book published by the Food and Agriculture Organization, or FAO (by Clyde F. E. Roper, Michael J. Sweeney, and Cornelia E. Nauen), provides a good overview of the cephalopod fisheries, offering information on over two hundred species. Although confined to species "of interest to fisheries," this work does include some which are utilized at the subsistence and artisanal levels only and some which at present have only a potential value in commerce. A few cephalopods are of outstanding importance in commerce: squid of the genus *Loligo* and *Todarodes pacificus*, the Japanese flying squid, are outstanding examples. Squid account for approximately 70 percent of the world catch, while cuttlefish represent between 10 and 15 percent and octopus between 10 and 20 percent.

The "flying squid" do not really fly but can propel themselves out of the water and glide. They have longer and thinner bodies than other squid, which makes them less suitable for being stuffed. All squid have eight short and two long tentacles. The long ones can be shot out to catch prey. The size of adult squid varies greatly from little more than 20 cm (8 in.) to 20 m (67 ft.) overall.

Cuttlefish also have eight short and two long tentacles, but they are more compact than the squids, having a broader body. Their "ink," like that of squid, is contained in sacs but may be expelled in large clouds to facilitate evasive action. Cuttlefish ink was used historically to make the color sepia, and the Chinese have called the cuttlefish "the clerk of the sea-gods," in a reference to the ink (Read, 1939). Generally, Chinese names for cephalopods are far more descriptive than English ones. For example, the Chinese call one small squid "shallow water soft fish," indicating where it is found, while the cuttlefish may be known as "tiger-blotched black thief." This highly specific nomenclature is in line with the fact that cephalopods play a larger part in food culture in China than in most other countries. While it is true that

Palestinian refugees washing squid in a courtyard in the Gaza Strip. © ED KASHI/CORBIS.

cephalopods, especially squid, have now reached the market in almost all important countries of the world, it is only in certain regions, including the whole of the Mediterranean, that there is a long tradition of eating them. Full acceptance in North America is still to come, although the influence of Americans from a Mediterranean background has done much to show the way to others.

Those repelled by the appearance of cephalopods might be especially upset by the octopus. The name octopus refers to its eight arms, each armed with suckers for grasping prey. The best octopus for eating have arms with a twin row of suckers on each. The most common octopus of the Mediterranean, *Octopus vulgaris*, has been important since classical times in many of the cultures of the region, and has figured frequently in art, as on Greek vases of the late classical period.

The flesh of the octopus is notorious for being tough and requiring treatment to soften it before cooking. This does not apply to tiny baby octopus, but the larger specimens are beaten against rocks by fishermen, or struck with mallets, to tenderize them. Delicious and flavorful octopus dishes include the Spanish *pulpos con papas*, the French *poulpe à la niçoise*, and the Neapolitan *polpetielli alla Luciana*.

In connection with the last-named dish, a Neapolitan author, Signora Jeanne Caròla Francesconi (1965), has given a vivid description of methods of fishing based on the fact that the true octopus (the kind with two rows of suckers on each arm) is especially attracted by the color white. Thus a piece of white rag may be placed in the center of a five-pronged hook and lowered down to ensnare the octopus. "It is also fished with a pottery amphora (called a 'mummarella') which is likewise painted white and contains white stones; this is lowered to the bottom on the end of a rope, near a rock. The 'true' octopus, if he sees it, will empty the pebbles out and instal himself inside as though in a nest. The fisherman, alerted by seeing the white pebbles scattered outside the amphora, pulls it up and thus catches the octopus." Although the octopus is thus outwitted, it is fair to add that of all mollusks it possesses the most intelligence. Experiments conducted at an aquarium in Naples established that an octopus is capable of learning, for example, how to move from one tank to another, when there are several apparent exits of which only one allows passage.

BIBLIOGRAPHY

Clark, Eleanor. *The Oysters of Locmariaquer.* New York: Pantheon, 1964.

Cox, Ian, ed. *The Scallop: Studies of a Shell and Its Influences on Humankind.* London: Shell Transport and Trading Co., 1957.

Francesconi, Jeanne Caròla. *La Cucina Napoletana.* Naples: Fausto Fiorentino Editore, 1965.

Lincoln, Mrs. D. A. *Mrs. Lincoln's Boston Cook Book.* Boston: Roberts Brothers, 1891.

Mackie, Cristine. *Life and Food in the Caribbean.* London: Weidenfeld & Nicolson, 1991.

Neustadt, Kathy. "'Born among the Shells': The Quakers of Allen's Neck and Their Clambake." In *We Gather Together: Food and Festival in American Life,* edited by Theodore C. Humphrey and Lin T. Humphey. Ann Arbor: UMI Research Press, 1988.

Read, Bernard E. *Chinese Materia Medica: Fish Drugs.* Peking: Peking Natural History Bulletin, 1939.

Roper, C. F. E., M. J. Sweeney, and C. E. Nauen. *FAO Species Catalogue.* Vol. 3. *Cephalopods of the World.* Rome: Food and Agriculture Organization of the United Nations, 1984.

Warner, William W. *Beautiful Swimmers—Watermen, Crabs, and the Chesapeake Bay.* Boston and Toronto: Little, Brown, 1976.

Alan Davidson

MONTAGNÉ, PROSPER. *See Larousse gastronomique.*

MOOD. Eating and drinking affect, sometimes markedly, people's moods. The interaction runs the other way, too, so that depressed, manic, or anxious states lower or sometimes heighten appetite, or a particular mood can affect food choices. The connections between food and mood have implications for advertisers of snack foods, for those seeking to lift their spirits through binge eating or drinking, and for gourmands planning successful dinners.

Alcohol can manipulate mood by affecting the release of certain chemicals in the brain called neurotransmitters. The caffeine in coffee and other drinks is another stimulant whose overuse has detrimental health effects. Herbs have a range of medical effects, and some mushrooms are mind-altering. But while a variety of foods contain chemicals with known psychotropic properties, they are generally in such minuscule quantities as to have little discernible effect on human consumers.

More noticeable changes occur through a combination of cognitive, sensory, cultural, social, and environmental factors. For example, chocolate contains chemicals that alter mood, such as caffeine, theobromine, and phenylethylamine, in quantities too small to account for the cravings of so-called "chocoholics." Instead, people value chocolate's sweet taste and voluptuousness, be-

cause it melts just below body temperature, and so coats the tongue. The pleasurable sensations release chemicals, called opioid peptides, in the brain that lift mood. Chocolate has long been advertised as a luxury, and parents and others choose it to reward good behavior. All these uses reinforce chocolate's reputation as an "indulgence," "temptation," and even "sin."

Likewise, some acclaimed aphrodisiacs contain traces of chemicals that might stimulate sexual activity (suggestions include the zinc in oysters and a chemical related to the male hormone testosterone in truffles). But the pleasures associated with their consumption can be more striking than any actual chemical effect. One of these foods is extraordinarily slippery and the other headily aromatic. In addition, the seducer may offer them in a mood-inducing setting, such as a comfortable, candlelit room filled with "mood music."

Even the psychological response to alcohol is dependent on numerous factors, not the least of which are the experience and existing mood of the drinker, the setting, and the organoleptic or sense-stimulating properties of, perhaps, a fine wine. As such, the same drink can make people feel euphoric, merry, riotous, bored, or maudlin. Some researchers have found that high-carbohydrate foods reduce tension and cheer people up, while high fat foods have the opposite effect, but this theory is not supported by the English writer Charles Lamb's paean to pork crackling, "Dissertation on Roast Pig," published in the 1820s. With mock seriousness, Lamb attributes the discovery of cooking to the "oleaginous . . . ambrosian" deliciousness of pork fat.

An angry remark, an overlong gap between courses, a disturbing location, or the overdoing of food and drink can destroy the pleasant mood of a meal. But an enticing plate of food placed in front of a willing guest can be entrancing. An experienced waiter can guide indecisive diners, turning their entire evening around. The right foods, company, and circumstances cast a positive spell, whether of gaiety, carefreeness, reverie, or joy.

The New Testament refers often to "joy" (in Greek, *charà*), frequently experienced at meals. A blissful state is encapsulated in many of the brief *Rubáiyát* of Omar Khayyám, written nearly one thousand years ago, and most famously in Edward FitzGerald's translation: "Here with a Loaf of Bread beneath the Bough, / A Flask of Wine, a Book of Verse—and Thou."

Jean-Anthelme Brillat-Savarin analyzed the special mood attainable at the table in his gastronomical classic, *The Physiology of Taste* (published in 1826). Reporting on a lifetime of dinners, closely observed, he consistently suggests that a meal's greatness depends less on particular foods than on achieving an overall mood. His term, *le plaisir de la table,* has often been translated in the plural as the "pleasures of the table." However, the book's "Meditation 14" discusses a composite "table-pleasure" that one might call "mood." Table-pleasure is "the reflective sensation" (*la sensation réfléchie*) generated by the thoughtful assembling of foods and people in an appropriate setting. This manifold pleasure of the table is known only to the human race and is largely independent of the drive for food, he writes.

While Brillat-Savarin precludes from table-pleasure ravishments, ecstasies, or transports, the experience, as he sees it, gains in duration what it loses in intensity. Physically, a diner's brain awakens, face grows animated, color heightens, eyes shine, and a "gentle warmth" creeps over the whole body. Morally, the diner's spirit grows more perceptive, the imagination flowers, and clever phrases fly from the lips. At the end of good meal, "body and soul both enjoy a special well-being" (p. 189). Table-pleasure is so powerful that "all human industry" has concentrated on increasing its intensity and duration, he writes. Stomachs may have had limits, but people could improve the accessories. So, they ornamented goblets and vases, ate under the open sky and in gardens and woods, invented the charms of music, and sprayed exquisite perfumes. Dancers, clowns, and other entertainers amused the eyes of diners. To all of these ancient gratifications, his recent contemporaries had contributed exquisite food, dishes so delicate that people would never get up from table if other business did not intrude.

Preferring simplicity to embellishment, Brillat-Savarin asked only four necessities—at least passable food, good wine, agreeable companions, and plenty of time (p. 191). Passing on a recipe for fondue, he recommends memorably: serve the fondue on a gently heated platter, call for the best wine, "and you will see miracles" (p. 417).

At odds with Brillat-Savarin's suggestion that the many elements of a meal generate a composite pleasure is a modern tendency to associate mood with particular foods, drinks, or diets. This view represents a somewhat "medical model" of dining rather than a convivial model, and some food scientists even speak of "functional foods," with druglike uses.

The food and drink industries implicitly market many products as improving mood. Alcoholic drink advertisements appeal to an elevated, "party" mood. The soft drink Coca-Cola is named after two traditional drugs, coca and cola, revealing its origins as an early proprietary "functional food" that still contains caffeine. Cereals manufacturer Kellogg has sold its Strawberry Pop-Tarts—pastries heated in a toaster and aimed at pre-teens—as a "mood food" by linking the snack to a social setting and a color suggestive of a particular mood (*Brandweek* [18 March 2002], p. 6). Television commercials showed girls and boys dancing, and the color red predominating, such as a red garland of lights and a girl in a red dress. The product also received placement in the television series *Gilmore Girls*, in which characters are depicted regularly eating Pop-Tarts for breakfast, suggesting that a single item can summon up a complex social setting.

Meanwhile, other researchers seek to understand why young women in particular crave and binge on sweet snacks in attempts to improve depressed moods. Many get into bulimic cycles of binge-eating and compensating, with accompanying mood swings.

Researchers led by Wesley C. Lynch found in a survey, contrary to expectations, binge eating did not lift depressed and anxious feelings but worsened them. However, moods did improve immediately before and after "compensatory activities," which included not just vomiting, but also fasting, exercise, and the use of laxatives and diuretics that did not decrease, but instead increased significantly following binge episodes and decreased immediately before and after compensatory activities" (Lynch et al., pp. 310–311). One possible interpretation of these findings is that binge eating is not the "problem" except as the prelude to self-punishing or ascetic behavior.

As the advertisers of "mood food" implicitly accept, the product does not act alone but within wider circumstances. A positive mood results most often from a satisfying meal, rich in social interactions. The aim might be to avoid solitary snacking in favor of Brillat-Savarin's nineteenth-century formula of honest viands, good company, and reduced time pressures.

See also **Anorexia, Bulimia; Brillat-Savarin, Jean Anthelme; Coffee; Marketing of Food; Pleasure and Food; Presentation of Food; Sensation and the Senses**.

BIBLIOGRAPHY

Brillat-Savarin, Jean-Anthelme. *The Physiology of Taste: Or, Meditations in Transcendental Gastronomy*. Translated by M. F. K. Fisher. New York: Heritage Press, 1949. Originally published in Paris as *La Physiologie du gout*, 1826.

Khayyám, Omar. *The Rubáiyát of Omar Khayyám, the Astronomer-Poet of Persia*. "Rendered" into English verse by Edward FitzGerald. New York: Grosset and Dunlap, 1946. Originally translated in 1859.

Lamb, Charles. "Dissertation on Roast Pig." In *The Essays of Elia*. 1st ser. London: Harrap, 1909. Collection originally published in 1823.

Lynch, Wesley C., et al. "Does Binge Eating Play a Role in the Self-regulation of Moods?" *Integrative Physiological and Behavioral Science* 35, no. 4 (Oct.–Dec. 2000): 298–313.

Somer, Elizabeth. *Food and Mood: The Complete Guide to Eating Well and Feeling Your Best*. 2nd ed. New York: Henry Holt, 1999.

Michael Symons

MOVIES AND FOOD. *See* Art, Food in.

MUSHROOMS. *See* Fungi.

MUSLIMS. *See* Islam.

MUSTARD. Mustard is the world's third most important spice after salt and pepper, and in temperate regions it is the most important native spice. The term "mustard" is believed to be derived from the practice of mixing the sweet must of old wine with crushed mustard seed to form a paste, *mustum ardeus* (hot must), hence mustard. The condiment is made from seeds of annual plants of the family Cruciferae, so named for the flower's four yellow petals, which form a cross. The mustard family includes the cole vegetables, radishes, turnips, cress, and horseradish, as well as many important weedy species, such as wild mustard or charlock (*Sinapis arvensis* L.).

Black mustard (*Brassica nigra* [L.] Koch), although later considered a weed, was likely the first mustard species harvested as a spice as it grew in the wild or was cocultivated with cereal crops. Its use predates recorded history with seeds, ready for sowing, found in a Bronze Age lake dwelling at the Bielersee (Lake of Bienne) in Switzerland and in vessels in northwest China dating to 5000–4000 B.C. The spice was well known to the earliest Egyptian dynasties and was spread by spice traders and conquering armies throughout Europe and Asia. The Spaniards introduced mustard to the Americas, and in California, Father Junipero Serra scattered black mustard seeds along the routes from monastery to monastery to mark the way in 1768. The bright yellow spring blooms, which mark the old trail, can be seen from the main north-south highway.

The Mustard Species
Black mustard plants are tall (up to 3 meters) and sparsely branched, and they produce many short pods (sliques). As the pod matures, the highly pungent, small (1.5 grams per 1,000 seeds), round dark brown seeds are shed, necessitating frequent hand harvesting or cutting and stacking immature plants on the threshing floor.

The characteristic seed shedding and seed dormancy of black mustard made it unsuited to monoculture and mechanized agriculture, and the spice trade turned to the production of a closely related species, *Brassica juncea* (L.) Czern and Coss. Plants of *B. juncea*, when compared to black mustard, are shorter (1 to 2 meters) and have many upright, heavily podded branches with longer pods that retain their seeds when ripe. The seed is larger (3 grams per 1,000 seeds) but produces the same pungency. The seed color is either brown (brown mustard) or yellow (Oriental mustard).

The species originated from a natural cross between *B. nigra* and *Brassica rapa* L. (turnip rape) followed by chromosome doubling to produce a vigorous and productive interspecific hybrid. This interspecific cross is believed to have occurred more than once where the two species occupied the same region. Possible centers of origin are believed to be North Africa, northern India and Pakistan, and western China.

The third condiment mustard species, *Sinapis alba* L., is called yellow or white mustard and produces a different pungency from both *B. nigra* and *B. juncea* seeds. From its Mediterranean center of origin, it has been widely disseminated throughout the temperate regions where day lengths (hours of sunshine) were sufficient to stimulate flowering. When moistened, the ripe seed will exude a mucilage from its yellow seed coat to form a whitish coating when dry. This may explain why white mustard is the common name in Europe, while in North America it is called yellow mustard.

Plants of yellow mustard are shorter (0.6 meters) than either *B. nigra* or *B. juncea* and have deeply lobed leaves. The short, hairy pods, with flat beaks, contain and retain 5 to 6 seeds when ripe. The seed is significantly larger than the other mustard species (6 grams per 1,000 seeds), which aids in rapid seedling establishment. In Europe the crop is frequently sown and ploughed under as a green manure crop.

The Chemistry of Mustard
All three mustard species contain a significant amount of edible oil and high quality protein. Indeed on the Indian subcontinent *B. juncea* seeds are the second most important source of edible vegetable oil, and the residual high protein meal, after it is soaked in water, is fed to cattle. However, for the spice trade the important ingredient is the presence and concentration in the seeds of sulphur compounds called glucosinolates. Over forty such compounds are known, and their presence and quantity determines the flavor and odor of the cole vegetables as well as the taste and heat of the mustards. The glucosinolate that imparts the pungency and flavor to black and *B. juncea* mustards is called "sinigrin," while in *Sinapis alba* it is "sinalbin." When the seeds are stored whole and dry, they retain their quality for several years. However, when the cells of a mustard seed are broken and moisture is present, the enzyme myrosinase, also present in the seed, breaks down the glucosinolates to release sugar, sulphur, and the hot principles called isothiocynates. Black and *B. juncea* mustard seeds release the pungent, volatile, biting allyl isothiocynate found in powdered and Dijon mustards. Yellow mustard, on the other hand, releases the milder, nonvolatile para-hydroxybenzyl isothiocynate characteristic of hot dog or cream salad mustard.

Making Mustard
English powdered mustard is made from brown or Oriental (yellow seeded) *B. juncea* seeds using a dry milling

Mustard flour and oil have strong antioxidant and antibacterial properties.

In addition to the American-style hot dog mustard and the well-known Dijon style, there exists a multitude of "specialty" mustards as well as such variations as the Russian (hot and sweet), the Chinese (extra hot), the English (smooth and hot), the German (hot, smooth, and horseradishy), and the Italian *mostarda di frutla* (a thin, sweet, very hot mustard syrup containing large pieces of various fruits).

Modern Mustard

Mustard was a common spice in ancient Greek and Egyptian civilizations, where it was often eaten raw, chewed with meat to mask off flavors, to aid digestion, and for its antimicrobial properties. However, the Romans recognized mustard's potential by grinding and mixing mustard flours with unfermented grape juice, vinegar, and honey. They introduced mustard manufacture into Dijon and other regions of France and later into England. They recorded its application as a preservative and its use in sauces with meat, fish, and vegetables. In medieval times mustard making was primarily done by the monasteries, but by the thirteenth century French family firms supplied quality mustard to French royalty. In England large-scale mustard manufacture did not flourish until the sixteenth century, when large dried balls of mustard infused with horseradish were manufactured in Tewkesbury and were sold by peddlers throughout the country. Later Mrs. Clements in Durham began to mill and distribute mustard flour, a product later made famous by the competing firms of Keen's and Colman's. In the United States, R. T. French, seeking a milder mustard in the 1800s, introduced cream salad and hot dog mustard, thereby adding a new dimension to the mustard industry.

In the second half of the twentieth century, world usage of mustard more than doubled, from 75,000 tons to over 170,000 tons. Originally most countries grew their own supplies, but by the twenty-first century the predominant supplier was Canada. The United States and central Europe also are important producers. Yellow mustard has become more important with the popularity of fast-food outlets. In addition, a strong demand developed for deheated yellow mustard because of its high protein content and excellent emulsifying, water-holding, and stabilizing characteristics. It is also widely used as a meat extender in prepared meats. The hulls of yellow mustard are also in demand for the unique properties of the mucilage (vegetable gum) they contain.

Specialty mustards, which include almost every possible blend of added flavors and range of textures, have grown dramatically. Popular formulations include ingredients such as honey, beer, wines, whiskey, garlic, horseradish, lemon peel, ginger, onion, peppers, tarragon, and so forth (see Man and Weir for a more extensive list). The Mount Horeb Mustard Museum in Wisconsin boasts a collection of 3,341 different prepared mustards. The use of mustard in restaurants and in home cooking has expanded and become more subtle and more adventurous.

process in which the seeds are passed through a series of rollers and sieves to produce a fine flour. The seed coats, which are cracked off by the first roller, may be used in food preparation or sent to an oil extraction mill. The pure mustard flour is then blended with some yellow mustard flour, prepared separately in the same way, plus a certain amount of wheat flour to give the desired level of heat when mixed with water.

French or Dijon-style mustard is made with only brown mustard seeds using a wet milling process in which whole seeds are ground to a fine paste and the hulls or seed coats are separated with centrifuges. Some of the hulls may be added back to the paste along with vinegar, herbs, and spices. Since the hot principle allyl isothiocynate is volatile, much of the heat is lost in the process, resulting in less pungency than might be expected from *B. juncea* seeds.

Hot dog or cream salad mustard is made from yellow mustard seeds using a wet milling process that creates a fine paste. However, the hulls are usually separated from the embryos by passing the seeds through a set of break rollers prior to grinding. The paste is then mixed with cereal flours, spices, and vinegar according to the recipe being followed.

Mustard seeds and leaves have also been harvested as a food and for medicinal purposes. The medical applications, such as mustard plasters, baths, and treatments for chilblains, are largely a thing of the past, but mustard greens and mustard seed oil are still household staples in parts of China and on the Indian subcontinent.

BIBLIOGRAPHY

Antol, M. N., and B. Levenson. *The Incredible Secrets of Mustard.* Garden City Park, N.Y.: Avery, 1999.

Holder, K., and J. Newdick. *A Dash of Mustard.* Willowdale, Ont.: Firefly Books, 1995.

Man, R., and R. Weir. *The Compleat Mustard.* London: Constable, 1988.

Four major mustard millers supply flour of various grades to processors the world over, largely replacing small local mustard millers.

Mount Horeb Mustard Museum. Available at http://www .mustardmuseum.com.

Vaughan, J. G., and J. S. Hemingway. "The Utilization of Mustards." *Economic Botany* 13 (1959): 196–204.

R. Keith Downey

MYTH AND LEGEND, FOOD IN.

MYTH AND LEGEND, FOOD IN. Food imagery appears in the myths and legends of many cultures worldwide; for example, in the concept of the earth as a life-giving mother and as an explanation for agricultural innovation. Gifts of food were thought proper to propitiate the gods and ensure success in food production.

Across cultures, the germination of plants and their ripening and dying are identified with the cycle of human life—the regeneration of the cosmos. The juxtaposition of life with death, fertility with infertility, and order with chaos is interwoven with the ideas of salvation and revival, of which woman is a symbol and the incarnation. For example, the Aztecs believed that the earth was female and called their goddess of fertility Tlazolteotl, Mother-Earth; similarly, other examples are the Celtic goddesses Aine and Anu (Danu, Dana), the Greek Demeter, the Hindu goddess Devi, and the Aboriginal deity Gunabibi, who was called the First Mother.

Egyptian myths about eternal forces of nature center on the male deity Osiris. His death at the hand of his brother Set and his resurrection, brought about by his wife Isis and his sister Nephtida, is associated with the cycle of plant vegetation and with the cereals that are sown after the harvest and regenerate with the coming of spring. The snake goddess Renenutet has custody over the harvest and field crops.

In ancient mythologies, everything is a gift of the gods' generosity, even the knowledge needed to improve food production. Examples appear cross-culturally: the Sumerian god Enlil makes a hoe and gives it to man so that he can cultivate land; the Chinese are taught how to cultivate land by the Divine Farmer, Shen-nung, who is the first to plow and sow grain, which rained from the sky or was dropped by the Purple Bird. A Hindu who sincerely worships goddess Devi is rewarded with rice by the household goddess, Annapurna; Indian bees make honey because of the divine intervention of the twin brothers Avins; and the Greek goddess Athena creates the olive tree from the depths of Attica's barren earth. The short poem in honor of Ninkasi, the Mesopotamian goddess of strong liquors, relates that it is due to her grace the dough rises when beer leaven is added to it, and that it is she who inspires bakers add sesame seed and herbs to bread.

In the epic of Gilgamesh, the goddess Ishtar asks her father, the god Anu, to use the heavenly bull to punish Gilgamesh. When Anu replies that the bull would not leave a single wheat grain on the earth for people, the

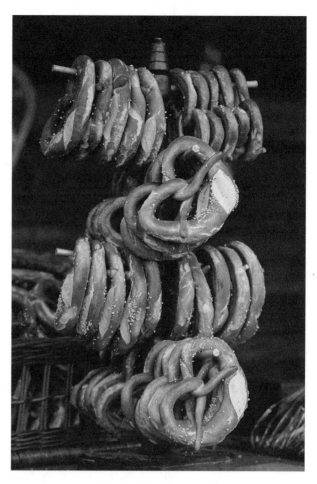

Many foods play a significant role in old myths and legends, such as the pomegranate in the Greek myth of Persephone. Other foods are themselves the subject of complex mythologies, and one of these is the pretzel. The commonly told story (at least in America) of the invention of the pretzel by an Italian priest to signify crossed arms in the act of blessing was created in the early 1900s to dilute the association of pretzels with beer drinking during Prohibition. In fact, the twisted pretzel traces to pre-Christian cult foods in the Rhine Valley, although its name derives from *bracellus* (an arm band or bracelet). The pretzels shown here were displayed in the Alsatian town of Wissembourg, France, during Christmas 1998. © DAVE BARTRUFF/ CORBIS.

goddess assures him that the grain reserves stored in the granaries of Uruk were sufficient to last for seven successive years of crop failure, and that they could sustain both people and cattle.

The association between humans and the gods endows food with a sacred quality, a mystical solidarity of man with plants and animals. When humans consume votive food they are in a way convinced that ultimately they consume a divine being. Offering food is a common practice in mythologies, and in order to prevent the wrath of the gods, priests were obliged to procure food for the sanctuaries.

TEA AND COFFEE IN MYTHOLOGY

In Chinese and Japanese cultures, tea is a frequent subject matter of legends. The tea plant was created from eyelids of a certain Buddhist monk, or sage, who, wanting to punish himself for falling asleep during meditation, cuts them off and discards them with contempt. Each eyelid gives rise to one tea shrub. According to the Japanese version of this legend, the eyelids belong to Bodhidharma (Daruma), who cuts them off as a preventive measure, since he wants to be unable to ever close his eyes.

The discovery of coffee is sometimes ascribed to goats. Coptic monks, who are compelled to observe a strict religious order of overnight prayers, notice that goats that had nibbled the leaves and fruit of wild coffee shrubs became excited and could not sleep at night. Thus, the monks follow the goats and, although they do not really like the taste of the leaves and bean, they are greatly satisfied with their unusual effect. Another, more poetic legend has Arabic origins: the first cup of this beverage was served to Muhammad by the Archangel Gabriel. The drink has an amazing effect. Right away Muhammad mounts his stallion, defeats forty knights in tournament, and lets forty Arabic ladies "taste the sweetness of love."

Each deity has a liking for a particular food; for example, lettuce is the favorite vegetable of the Egyptian god Set. In Hindu mythology, the god Dharmathakur accepts only white offerings (rice, milk, poultry), while the demonic and semi-divine female Dakini acquires strength from raw meat. As a child, Krishna goes into peasants' houses and pinches butter from them as he is very fond of it. The Hindu made offerings of boiled rice mixed with sesame seed, milk, ghee, and honey to their mystical ancestors residing in the other world.

Before any undertaking, a Greek promised the gods he would make some offering to them in order to gain their support. If someone could not afford to buy a sacrificial animal, he made a cake baked in the shape of an ox, a cow, or a sheep. Replacement offerings were made to gods when cities were besieged by enemies, or when meat was in short supply.

Beer is a food product most frequently referred to in mythologies of Mesopotamia, Egypt, and Scandinavia.

Mesopotamian mythology in particular abounds in episodes with beer in the background. The goddess Inana makes the god Enki drunk with beer in order to steal the heavenly secrets away from him. In turn, in Greek mythology wine plays the most prominent role. On a holiday celebrated in December, when the new wine was stowed in granaries, the Greeks would kill a goat and sprinkle vine roots with its blood. Liquors were even thought to make the horrid existence in the underworld more pleasant; for example, in the Welsh underworld, in Annwn, there is a spring from which wine was flowing.

After his exhausting journey in search of the "herb of life" Gilgamesh falls into a deep sleep that lasts seven days. The host of that place, Ut-napishtim, says to his wife: "Start [to] bake bread and every day put one loaf next to his head and make a sign on wall so that you know how many times you have baked." The ritual meal in praise of Aboriginal deity Djanggawul was composed exclusively of fresh bread made of sago nut flour. Eating it formed a sacred bond of friendship between the participants of the feast.

In Greek mythology, ambrosia is the food that gives the Olympian gods eternal youth and beauty. Unlike nectar, which is a drink, ambrosia is probably a dish. It was believed to make even an ordinary person immortal. The Indian counterparts of ambrosia are *amryta*, the nectar found at the ocean bottom, and *soma*, a heavenly elixir that ensures immortality on earth. The Australian Aborigines told tales about an elixir of immortality, though this elixir had no name.

See also **Art, Food in: Literature; Ancient Mediterranean Religions; Australian Aborigines; Beer; Bible, Food in the; Buddhism; Christianity; Coffee; Folklore, Food in; Greece, Ancient; Herodotus; Hinduism; Inca Empire; Islam; Judaism; Mesopotamia, Ancient; Religion and Food; Symbol, Food as; Tea; Wine in the Ancient World.**

BIBLIOGRAPHY

Black, Jeremy, and Anthony Green. *Gods, Demons and Symbols of Ancient Mesopotamia: An Illustrated Dictionary.* British Museum Press, 1992.

Campbell, John R., and Robert T. Marshall. *The Science of Providing Milk for Man.* New York: McGraw-Hill, 1975.

Cotterell, Arthur. *Mythology: An Encyclopedia of Gods and Legends from Ancient Greece and Rome, the Celts, and the Norselands.* London: Southwater, 2000.

Hart, George. *Egyptian Myths. The Legendary Past.* British Museum Press, 1990.

Mudrooroo, Nyoongah. *Aboriginal Mythology.* New York: Aquarian, HarperCollins, 1994.

Michael Abdalla

N

NAMING OF FOOD. Foods are named primarily according to their origins. Foods from the plant kingdom usually have the same name as the plant, such as *carrot*, *potato*, *peas*, and *spinach*. Sometimes the name of the food is from the fruit (the seed-bearing part of the plant), such as *apple*, from apple trees, and *raspberry* from raspberry bushes.

Food from animals usually has the same name as the animal: *lamb, chicken, rabbit, quail, salmon, Dungeness crab, snails*. The exceptions are words such as *calf* and *veal* or *pig* and *pork* or *sheep* and *mutton*, where the former word is of Anglo Saxon origin and the latter of French origin. A few remnants of Anglo-Saxon names remain, as in *oxtail soup* or *pigs' feet*. The names of animal parts when cooked and eaten often refer to the common anatomical names, such as *wing, breast*, or *leg* of birds and *rib* and *tongue* of mammals. However, most cuts of meat have their own special names: *sirloin, strip steak, lamb chop. Bacon* and *ham* denote that the meat is from a pig and that it is smoked. Innards like liver and kidneys are the same as the organ name. However, some interior parts have better-sounding food names, such as *sweetbreads* for *pancreas*, *tripe* for the *stomach* of a ruminant, *roe* or *caviar* for *fish eggs*, and *mountain oysters* for *testicles*.

Names of Dishes

Names for prepared foods follow several patterns. The commonest is a phrase with the main ingredients: *chicken almond, beef and mushrooms, creamed tuna casserole*, or with the cooking method as well as the food: *poached eggs on toast, pork and vegetable stir-fry*.

Another common pattern is to name foods after places. The meaning only indicates an origin and/or style. Sometimes the meaning is transparent, as in *Polish sausage, Belgian waffle*, or *Spanish omelet*, but often additional knowledge is required. *Florentine* (named for Florence, Italy) is for dishes with spinach, *Bolognese* (from Bologna) is with a meat sauce, and *Bologna* is a sausage. *Veal Milanese* (Milan) or *Wiener Schnitzel* (Vienna) is breaded and fried veal cutlet. *Provençal* (Provence) means made with tomato, garlic and olive oil, and *chicken Kiev* is chicken breast wrapped around butter, breaded, and fried, *Salad Niçoise* (Nice), *Mongolian hot pot*, *Peking duck, Buffalo wings*, and *baked Alaska* are other examples.

Chicken Marengo was named in honor of Napoleon's victory at Marengo. Occasionally the name is misleading. French toast is an American dish, while *homard à l'americain* 'lobster American style' is a French dish. French-fried potatoes are common in France under the name *pommes frites* 'fried potatoes'.

A small number of words derived from place names have been resegmented and reanalyzed. Hamburger and Frankfurter were named after the German cities of Hamburg and Frankfurt, and Wiener is from Wien, the German name for Vienna. Hamburger was resegmented as ham + burger, although the food is made with chopped beef. Burger became a combining form to be added to any food served with ground beef (*cheeseburger, baconburger*) or some meat instead of beef (*chickenburger, fishburger*), or for a particular style (*California burger*). Vegetarian versions are *veggie burgers* or *garden burgers*. Subsequently, *burger* has become an independent word. *Frankfurter*, often shortened to *frank*, has also become a combining form, yielding new words like *turkeyfurter* or *turkeyfrank*, with each part of the word combining with new parts. *Hot dog*, an informal term for frankfurters, has generated *Tofu Pup*, a vegetarian sausage. It also illustrates the trendiness of wordplay.

Some dishes are named after people, either for the inventor or in honor of some famous person. *Sandwiches* were invented by the Earl of Sandwich, and *Beef Wellington* honors the Duke of Wellington. *Beef Stroganoff* is a French dish created to honor the Russian diplomat Stroganov. Other examples are *Oysters Rockefeller*, *Pavlova*, a meringue dessert created to honor the dancer Anna Pavlova, and the pastries named for Napoleon and Bismarck.

French has had an especially strong influence on English names for food and dishes. The phrase *à la* appears in several dishes. One phrase taken from French is *à la reine* 'to the queen' or 'in honor of the queen' for creamed foods often served on a puffed pastry. This has led to *à la king*, a mixture of French and English that violates French grammar, since "la" is the feminine definite article, and king by virtue of its meaning would be masculine (if English still had grammatical gender in its definite articles). Other examples are *riz à l'impératrice* 'rice pudding' literally 'to the empress' and *à la mode* 'with ice cream' (literally 'in the style').

English speakers have borrowed freely from other languages for hundreds of years, taking the original spelling (if that language uses Roman letters) as well as an anglicized pronunciation. (This phenomenon is part of the reason for the irregular spelling of English.) Food names have been heavily borrowed along with the dish: *sauerkraut* and *strudel* (German); *soufflé, mousse, crêpes, meringue,* and *fondue* (French); *spaghetti* and other pasta names as well as *pizza* and *spumoni* (Italian); *souvlaki* (Greek); *goulash* (Hungarian); *tortilla* (Spanish); *paella* (Catalan); *guacamole* (Nahuatl, a native Mexican language); *blini* (Russian); *cole slaw* (Dutch); *curry* (Tamil, a language of South India); *chutney* (Hindi); *shish kabob* and *baklava* (Turkish); *couscous* (Arabic); *sushi* and *tempura* (Japanese); *won ton* (Chinese); *succotash* (Narragansett, a North American Indian language); and *matzoh* (Hebrew).

Marketing Strategies

In selling foods, whether in stores or restaurants, attractive names are selected for the product or the dish. Often foreign-language equivalents are used, sometimes along with the English equivalent. For example, spaghetti in tomato sauce might be labeled pasta in marinara sauce. In addition to the euphemisms for innards described above, the names of pet foods are especially interesting since the names are intended to appeal to the owners. One popular brand of cat food has names like "country-style dinner," "mariner's catch," and "prime entree." The ingredients listed in small print on the label do not sound so nice.

Zwicky and Zwicky (1980) in their investigation of menus in American restaurants show that names both inform and advertise. Two examples they present are "Entrecôte au Poivre Madagascar–sirloin steak topped with green peppercorns, served with cream sauce and cognac" (Zwicky and Zwicky, p. 86) and "sautéed shrimp in garlic butter–the zesty garlic butter brings out the best in this epicurean treat from the sea" (Zwicky and Zwicky, p. 87). The first example describes and the second advertises. Zwicky and Zwicky observe that French is used on menus frequently because of the traditional association of French with fine food. The restaurant need not be French, and the French is often ungrammatical or mixed with English. Therefore, one finds *Cuisine de Holland* and *Stuffed Tomato aux Herbs, Shoreham Style* (Zwicky and Zwicky, pp. 89–90).

Since many people are on diets for reason of health and/or weight control, there is concern with calories and with fat. The food industry has responded by offering products with less fat and fewer calories. One word for referring to these products is "light," sometimes spelled "lite." The Miller Brewing Company used the word to denote a beer with fewer calories than regular beer. Since a light beer is ambiguous—it can be light in color (pale vs. amber or dark)—the spelling difference can disambiguate the two senses. Although other beer companies have been prevented from using this spelling, lite has spread to many other foods with fewer calories than the normal counterpart. More recently, "free," a clipping of "fat free," has emerged to denote foods without fat.

See also **Etymology of Food; Sandwich.**

BIBLIOGRAPHY

Cook's and Diner's Dictionary: A Lexicon of Food, Wine, and Culinary Terms. New York: Funk & Wagnall's, 1968.

Lehrer, Adrienne. "As American as Apple Pie–and Sushi and Bagels: The Semiotics of Food and Drink." In *Recent Developments in Theory and History: The Semiotic Web 1990,* edited by Thomas A. Sebeok and Jean Umiker-Sebeok, pp. 389–402. Berlin and New York: Mouton de Gruyter, 1991.

Zwicky, Ann, and Arnold Zwicky. "America's National Dish: The Style of Restaurant Menus." *American Speech* 55 (1980): 83–92.

Adrienne Lehrer

NATIONAL CUISINES, IDEA OF. Cuisines and nations are artifacts of human enterprise, will, and imagination. They refer ostensibly to material things: to the earth, to the natural world, to particular geographical locales and the products of these places. In this sense, cuisines tell one something about food, and nations tell one something about places. Cuisines, too, are made up of earthly products, such as butter, beef, saffron, and garlic, much as nations inhabit physical localities, whether protruding landmasses, landlocked mountains, or chains of islands. In the modern period, however, foods have become associated with cuisines and places with nations to such an extent that one does not perceive any difference between them. National cuisines are a product of the modern emphasis on nationalism and the nation-state.

In fact, the coining of "national cuisines" has become an almost exclusive means of organizing the link between food and place. One talks with ease of Germany and German cuisine and India and Indian cuisine, as if German cuisine and Indian cuisine have existed as long as the mountains, valleys, and lakes that define their namesakes' topographies. If the history of the subcontinent, and the food practices of people there, are reviewed, the limits of the term "Indian cuisine" will be fast apparent. The food habits of the Punjabi Sikh and the Kerala Christian, for instance, have little in common, though both groups occupy India and eat its food products. While a handy moniker to grasp onto the food habits of a group of people, "Indian cuisine" is not a product of nature. Classifying a cuisine helps mark a geographical locale as a nation; it allows people to imagine national unity and to create convenient categories for understanding food practices. The convenient shorthand of "German cuisine" and "Indian cuisine" belies the complex historical formation of national cuisines, and their link to nationalism, a way of speaking about place, identity, and sovereignty.

Because of the tangible and visceral nature of food, nationalists have long used food to help solidify claims and gain legitimacy. This can clearly be seen in the shift from food to cuisine as a way to mark ownership over ingredients and practices understood to come from a certain place. For at least two hundred years, France has been a geographical region where arguments have been made for the authenticity of national cuisines by citizens, the state, and culinary professionals. The arguments concern the natural, authentic nature of "French cuisine" as a national cuisine. The French also often argue for the superiority of French cuisine in general. A historical examination of cookbooks from this region reveals a shift in the assumptions about audience and organization away from noble patrons toward fellow citizens. This shift occurred from the sixteenth century to the early part of the nineteenth century. By the 1880s, almost all cookbooks were aimed toward national citizens.

More recently, newer nation-states such as Mexico and Israel have promoted their national cuisines as a means of legitimizing their claims to nationhood. But, according to anthropologist Sidney Mintz, "a national cuisine is a contradiction in terms. . . . for the most part, a national cuisine is simply a holistic artifice based on the foods of the people who live inside some political system, such as France or Spain" (Mintz, p. 104) Yet this "holistic artifice" has become a very successful enterprise. All manner of food ways, now packaged as "national cuisines," are promoted in restaurants, cookbooks, tourist guides, and television shows. In particular, cookbooks have been very effective at creating and promoting such assumptions; contemporary cookbooks include such titles as *A Taste of India*, *Mastering the Art of French Cooking*, and *The Art of Mexican Cooking*. The discourse of food writing has largely become bounded by the notion of national cuisines: National cuisines are seen as natural occurrences and the culinary discourse reflects that very assumption.

To really comprehend the tremendous complexity and diversity of human food practices, it is necessary to move beyond the discourse of national cuisines. Food—the raw ingredients, the cooking techniques, the ritual practices, the social significance—is ultimately more fluid, varied, meaningful, and powerful than the reliance on national cuisine as a category of explanation allows for in exploring it. Perhaps the twenty-first century, if significant in demonstrating the limited control of any sovereign nation-state, will be the period when food is removed from the nationalist agenda.

See also **Foodways; France: Tradition and Change in French Cuisine; Fusion Cuisine; Geography; United States: Ethnic Cuisines**.

BIBLIOGRAPHY

Mintz, Sidney. *Tasting Food, Tasting Freedom: Excursions into Eating, Culture and the Past*. Boston: Beacon Press, 1996.

Pilcher, Jeffrey. *Que Vivan Los Tamales!: Food and Drinking and the Making of Mexican Identity*. Albuquerque, N.M.: University of New Mexico Press, 1998.

Trubek, Amy. *Haute Cuisine: How the French Invented the Culinary Profession*. Philadelphia: University of Pennsylvania Press, 2000.

Zubaida, Sami, and Richard Tapper, eds. *Culinary Cultures of the Middle East*. London: I. B. Tauris, 1994.

Amy B. Trubek

NATIVE AMERICANS. *See* **American Indians.**

NATURAL FOODS. The concept of natural foods is obscure from many perspectives. Although international literature offers no clear definition, the term is used in food surveys, in the food industry, in the marketing of foods, and in modern discourses surrounding food choice. "Natural" is defined as 'produced by nature, that is, not produced artificially' in *Funk and Wagnalls Standard Dictionary*. Since all food can be said to be produced by nature, the term "natural foods" becomes even more unclear unless one considers the meaning Felipe Fernández-Armesto has proposed: "the oyster is eaten uncooked and unkilled. It is the nearest thing we have to 'natural' food—the only dish which deserves to be called 'au naturel' without irony" (p. 2).

If the concept of natural foods originates from the French phrase *au naturel*, that is, eating something uncooked and alive, it would relate first to modes of processing. An "unkilled" food like the oyster is a food uncooked and is, by that definition, a food that has not been altered by human hand. Thus natural foods are foods not deliberately altered in the course of production and processing. Asked in a study how they perceived naturalness in relation to food production, respondents in England and Denmark said they perceived organic food and free-range livestock products as the most natural foods and genetically modified foods as the most unnatural foods (Von Alvensleben).

Furthermore, natural foods can be interpreted in terms of connections to nostalgic rural life (Lupton). Yet regional foods, products that are not imported from exotic, faraway lands and not distributed in ways injurious to the environment are also representations of natural foods. Moreover, the concept of natural foods is related more to some groups in society than to others. Some associate natural foods with specific food choice ideologies, such as vegetarianism, and thus exclude certain animal products while including plants, cereals, fruits, and berries, preferably produced in an organic or ecological way (Lindeman and Sirelius).

The marketing strategies for natural foods may be understood on two levels. First: natural foods are considered unprocessed foods in the sense that they are not influenced by industry for mass production. Second: natural foods are seen as originating in the vegetable kingdom. Both dimensions are marketed as healthy for people and the environment.

Contradictions in Health and Purity

The marketing of natural foods actually refers to health issues. Natural foods are projected as guaranteeing a long, healthy life since they are portrayed as foods that can prevent diseases and aging. In this concept lies the belief that natural foods are pure and free from harmful and unwholesome components. Pure food is perceived as natural, simple, unspoiled, and earthy, but at the same time it is expected to be germ-free, biologically cleansed, and scientifically aseptic (Mintz).

Natural foods in fact can include more harmful and naturally occurring toxic substances than highly processed food. The latter, thanks to modern developments in biotechnology, (i.e., genetic manipulation) can be more "healthy" and can more effectively prevent diseases than the so-called natural foods (Coveney and Santich). Advances in biotechnology have produced foods that are much safer from a hygienic perspective with the same tastes, appearances, textures, and colors as foods produced in the conventional way. This is the ultimate goal for the modern food industry, and these are the foods modern consumers actually demand and look for even though they are not always aware of it.

Quality Aspects of Natural Food

The concept of natural foods is closely related to quality aspects of food. Adulteration of food has been evident since the growth of towns and the development of food distribution in medieval Europe. Adulteration became more prevalent in the late nineteenth century, a period also characterized by the food scientists' obsession with purity (Tannahill). This obsession was mainly a reaction to the development of the food industry and the loss of control over local food production, but it can also be linked to the development of food science per se. New scientific methods enabled scientists to measure and detect impurities in food. Thus the quality aspects of food were seen under the microscope, that is, scientists could actually see with their own eyes the bacteria, microorganisms, and chemical residues in the food; therefore, food was determined chemically clean or not. However, as Sidney W. Mintz emphasizes, this state is not the same as a natural one. Nature is not chemically clean.

At the same time a new genre of books with advice and guidelines on how to shop for safe, unaltered foods was published widely in Europe. The consumers, mostly women, were told what foods they should be suspicious of, what foods to avoid, how to detect adulterations in food, and so on. In these books and in the general debate in the newspapers, the development of food industries and fast-growing global trade was much criticized. Foods produced in the consumer's own country and sold by local, well-known salespeople were recommended

(Fjellström). The debate continued in the twenty-first century within the European Union (EU) despite the fact that most states in the EU have effective measures to control quality in food production and distribution. Consumers in Europe and the United States fear unnatural foods produced outside national and regional borders.

The Ideology about Nature and Food

The vision of the foods eaten by humankind in prehistory is one of natural and healthy foods from a nutritional point of view (Jenkens et al.). This diet is perceived as plant-based; high in vegetable protein, dietary fiber, and antioxidants; and low in saturated fat. It is considered the best alternative for modern people forced to eat the food of the supermarket, which is characterized as bottled, canned, refined, preserved, and frozen.

The ideology and attitudes toward the wild and natural landscape on the one hand and the domesticated and cultivated landscape on the other shifted back and forth throughout the first millennium B.C.E. (Montanari). For example, in Greek and the Roman cultures the untilled, uncultivated landscape or nature was seen as something negative, the opposite of the civilized and human world. Only unfortunate people obtained food in wild nature. Although the vegetarian diet, as opposed to the animal one, appealed more to both the Greeks and the Romans, it had to derive from land cultivated by people. During the seventh and eighth centuries C.E. in Europe the preference for nature and for the wild landscape as a source of a daily food supply became more dominant among the lay nobility, while domestically produced foods were preferred by groups within the church and in monasteries. In the early part of the second millennium C.E., the dominant ideas supported an effective medieval agricultural system. Foods obtained from the wild or naturally grown were regarded as unsuitable for human consumption (Montanari).

In eighteenth-century Scotland the physician George Cheney won a reputation for his ideas on health and illness. Natural foods were once again in favor. Cheney saw natural foods as those that remained unaltered by strange preparation techniques and ingredients, although he was not a vegetarian (Beardsworth and Keil). The development of organicism in mid-twentieth-century England preceded the ideology of natural foods (Matless). Important symbols within this movement were the earth and the soil. Values such as nature and wholeness were seen as the right kind of values for the survival of humankind, just as production methods and geographies of foods were emphasized as important for people's health. Organicists were critical of the global food production and distribution industries, thus their approach can be understood as a critique of modernity.

Natural Foods and a Critique of Modernity

The choice of natural foods could be interpreted in terms of Anthony Giddens's theories about people's calculations of risk elements in modern everyday life. Health issues, fear of diseases, and ultimately existential questions, such as the fear of death, are the underlying reasons that people began to examine what foods they could trust in a global society, where multinational food industries control food production and distribution and where experts have commandeered the knowledge of what is safe and healthy food. In his well-known culinary triangle Claude Lévi-Strauss emphasized that raw food was related to nature, while cooked food handled in vessels made by people had become culture. At the beginning of the twenty-first century the discourses surrounding food, especially so-called natural foods, involve new and different meanings and symbols. In some groups, particularly those who favor natural foods, nature and rural living are favored before culture and urban living (Lupton). Thus Lévi-Strauss's ideas about the the raw and cooked have changed place. Raw food rather than processed and cooked food is considered culture among some groups.

See also **Green Revolution; Health Foods; Organic Agriculture; Organic Farming and Gardening; Organic Food.**

BIBLIOGRAPHY

Beardsworth, Alan, and Teresa Keil. *Sociology on the Menu: An Invitation to the Study of Food and Society.* London: Routledge, 1997.

Coveney, John, and Barbara Santich. "A Question of Balance: Nutrition, Health, and Gastronomy." *Appetite* 28 (1997): 267–277.

Fernández-Armesto, Felipe. *Food: A History.* London: Macmillan, 2001.

Fjellström, Christina. "Safe Food and Consumer Attitudes of Yesterday and Today." Paper presented at the Annual Swedish Food Industry Conference, Halmstad, September 2001.

Jenkens, David J. A., et al. "The Garden of Eden: Implications for Cardiovascular Disease Prevention." *Asia Pacific Journal of Clinical Nutrition* 9 (October 2000): S1–S3.

Letarte, Anick, Laurette Dubé, and Viviane Troche. "Similarities and Differences in Affective and Cognitive Origins of Food Likings and Dislikes." *Appetite* 28 (1997): 115–129.

Lévi-Strauss, Claude. *The Raw and the Cooked: Introduction to a Science of Mythology.* Translated from the French by John and Doreen Weightman. New York: Harper and Row, 1969.

Lindeman, Marjaana, and Minna Sirelius. "Food Choice Ideologies: The Modern Manifestations of Normative and Humanist Views of the World." *Appetite* 37 (2001): 175–184.

Lupton, Deborah. *Food, the Body, and the Self.* London: Sage, 1996.

Matless, David. "Bodies Made of Grass Made of Earth of Bodies: Organicism, Diet, and National Health in Mid-Twentieth-Century England." *Journal of Historical Geography* 27, no. 3 (2001): 355–376.

Mintz, Sidney W. *Tasting Food, Tasting Freedom: Excursion into Eating, Culture, and the Past.* Boston: Beacon Press, 1996.

Montanari, Massimo. *The Culture of Food.* Oxford: Blackwell, 1994.

Tannahill, Reay. *Food in History.* London: Eyre Methuen, 1973.

Von Alvensleben, Reimar. "Beliefs Associated with Food Production Methods." In *Food, People, and Society: A European Perspective of Consumers' Food Choices,* edited by Lynn J. Frewer, Einar Risvik, and Hendrik Schifferstein. Berlin: Springer, 2001.

Christina Maria Fjellström

NETHERLANDS. *See* **Low Countries.**

NEW ENGLAND. *See* **United States.**

NIACIN DEFICIENCY (PELLAGRA). Deficiency of the vitamin niacin can result in the disease pellagra. This illness is characterized by the appearance of severe dermatitis on the parts of the skin that have been exposed to the sun, with deep cracking and flaking. Sufferers also have diarrhea and, in many cases, some kind of dementia. The condition typically flares up during spring, as sunshine becomes stronger. In practice, patients were often found to be deficient in the vitamin riboflavin in addition to niacin. Both in the Old and New Worlds, the condition has almost always been confined to people consuming corn (that is, maize) as their staple grain. The explanation is complex. We can synthesize niacin for ourselves to some extent if our diet contains a good supply of the amino acid tryptophan because we have enzymes that can, in a series of steps, turn a portion of any excess tryptophan molecules into niacin. The problem with corn is that the proteins that it contains have an unusually low proportion of tryptophan, and this is insufficient to provide a second source of the vitamin. Mature corn, like the mature grains of other cereals, does contain niacin, but it is mostly present in linkage with other compounds that make it essentially indigestible, because the digestive enzymes in the gut cannot break these linkages. In Central America and Mexico, where corn has been the staple grain for millennia, the populations have learned to soften the grains by soaking them with lime (calcium hydroxide) before grinding them to a paste. It is now realized that, in addition to its softening action, the alkaline lime liberates the niacin from its linkages, so that it is now nutritionally available. This is, at least, a partial explanation for the freedom of these peoples from pellagra. In addition, if a diet rich in maize is supplemented with a diet that also uses beans as a stable, as is the case among the traditional natives of Mexico, then the low level of tryptophan in maize is compensated by the higher tryptophan level in beans. Many types of long-established diets have this type of essential amino acid complementarity among the foods consumed.

However, when corn was brought back to the Old World, and gradually came to be adopted as a staple food in Southern Europe, but without the use of lime in its preparation, pellagra became a serious problem. In the nineteenth century it was suspected that corn developed toxic molds during storage. In France its use as a food crop was made illegal, and in Italy a special class of "pellagra hospitals" was established. In the southern regions of the United States, pellagra became a serious problem from about 1910 onward. There had been no obvious change in dietary habits to explain this, but it is now realized that corn processors had introduced a new method of milling corn that separated the germ. This was advantageous in reducing the oil content of the cornmeal and increasing its storage life, but it further halved the tryptophan content of the meal. The average consumer in the South was using approximately equal parts of cornmeal and of white wheaten flour that was somewhat richer in tryptophan. It appears that the change in milling was just enough to tip the balance toward the appearance of pellagra in those with only low intakes of good supplementary foods such as meat and milk. Niacin is now one of the synthetic vitamins included in the supplements routinely used to enrich flours in many Western countries.

See also **Assessment of Nutritional Status; Dietary Assessment; Dietary Guidelines; Food, Composition of; Maize; Malnutrition; Mexico; Nutrients; Nutrition; United States: The South; Vitamins: Overview.**

BIBLIOGRAPHY

Carpenter, Kenneth J., ed. *Pellagra*. Stroudsburg, Pa.: Hutchinson Ross, 1981.

McDowell, L. R. *Vitamins in Human and Animal Nutrition*. Ames: Iowa State University Press, 2000.

Kenneth John Carpenter

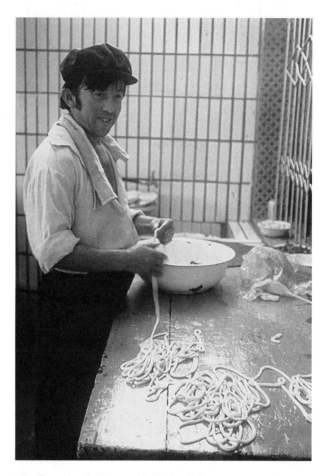

Noodle maker in Turpan, Xinjiang, China. PHOTO BY GLENN MACK.

NOODLE IN ASIA, THE. Noodles originated in northern China during the last half of the Han Dynasty (206 B.C.E.–220 C.E.) when large-scale wheat grinding became available, providing flour to make *mian, mein,* or *mi,* the Chinese word for noodle. We learn about the earliest noodles from Shu Hsi, one of China's most learned men, who in 300 B.C.E. wrote a *fu* or rhapsody on noodles, in which he provided detailed recordings of noodle making. For centuries, *la mian* or hand-pulled or hand-swung noodles were popular. The chef grasped a length of dough between two hands, stretched it with a toss of several feet, and repeated the tossing and extending until the dough divided into thinner and thinner strands, resulting in soft, smooth, and chewy noodles.

In the centuries that followed, variations of noodle making were introduced. In the Tang Dynasty (618–907 C.E.), noodles were first cut into strips. Then, in the Yuan Dynasty (1271–1368 C.E.) the making of dried noodles began (Ang, p. 46).

With travel and trade, noodles migrated into the rest of Asia. Noodles moved from China to Japan to Korea and to Southeast Asia. The Chinese influence is first evident in the name for noodle. The Chinese word for noodle, *mian* or *mien* or *mi* became *men* or *menrui* in Japan, *myun* in Korea, and *mee* in Thailand. It was even believed that Chinese noodles moved into Europe. According to legend, Marco Polo discovered pasta in China and took the idea home. But it was misinterpretation of his records that started this story because pasta was known to the ancient Greeks and Romans—a culinary evolution independent of China.

Asian noodles are distinctive because of the assortment of flours used. The notion that rice is the dietary staple in China is misleading as the majority of China eats wheat products. Southern China with its monsoon rains provides perfect rice-cultivating conditions while the large area north of the Yangtze River is excellent for wheat. Northern China, Korea, and Japan use wheat flour. Buckwheat noodles are found in Japan and Korea. Southern China uses wheat flour with the addition of egg as well as rice flour. Southeast Asia uses mostly rice flour, but also mung bean flour. Other Asian noodles are made from potato starch, sweet potato, soy bean, yam, and dried shrimp. They come dried, fresh, thin, thick, coarse, flat, round, and in broken sheets. Each country has similar yet distinctive ways of making noodles.

China

In China, the most popular noodle is the regular *gan mian* or *mian*, made of wheat flour and water. Salt is sometimes added, and cornstarch is sprinkled on fresh noodles to keep them from sticking together. Dried wheat noodles are either 12-inch lengths or, in the case of thinner noodles, nest-like swirls. Egg noodles or *dan mian*, occasionally flavored with shrimp and yellowish in color, are popular in southern China. *Chow mian*, or stir-fried noodles, is perhaps the most popular noodle dish.

Other noodles eaten in China are made with rice flour or mung bean flour. Dried rice noodles, *mi fen*, or rice sticks or rice vermicelli come in different widths, but in China, the thin, white opaque white noodles are most popular; they are softened in hot water or immediately puffed up when tossed in hot oil. *Sha He fen* or rice noodles from the southern village of Sha He, or vermicelli sheets, are wide, slippery, rice noodles sold in large squares. These fresh noodles made from rice flour, cornstarch, and potato starch are used in soups and stir-fried in a dish called *chow fen*. At other times, the sheets are filled with beef or shrimp and then rolled and steamed. Mung bean noodles or *fen si* (literally translated 'powdered silk') or cellophane noodles, bean threads, glass noodles, or vermicelli are from the starch of mung beans. They rehydrate in hot water to a slippery, translucent noodle, or puff up when fried in hot oil.

Japan and Korea

Japan is the most noodle- or *menrui*-consuming nation on earth. Japanese noodles include wheat-based noodles found in Osaka or southern Japan, and buckwheat-based noodles associated with old Edo, now Tokyo, and the north country. Wheat noodles include *udon*, which are thick round, square, or flat noodles; *kishimen*, which are also wide and flat; *hiyamugi*, which are round, very slender and served cold; *somen*, which are even more slender and slightly moistened with cottonseed or sesame oil, and also made with tea powder, *cha somen*; egg yolk, *tomago somen*; or tinted with red perilla oil, *ume somen*. Buckwheat-based noodles, or *soba*, are mixed with wheat flour. These noodles are long, thin, and gray-brown in color. A variation of this noodle, made with green tea, is *cha soba*.

Ramen, the most popular noodle in Japan, is of Chinese origin. These noodles are steamed and dried, making them easily rehydrated for quick eating. *Harusame* or 'spring rain' or cellophane noodles are made from Japanese potato starch or Chinese style from mung beans. Finally, *shirataki* or 'white waterfall' is made from the starch of the devil's tongue or *Amorphophalus konjac*.

TABLE 1

Asian Noodles

Name	Ingredients	Use
Chinese Noodles		
wheat noodles (mian, gan mian, mien, mi)	wheat flour and water	stir-fries, soups
egg noodles (dan mian)	wheat flour, egg, and water	stir-fries, soups
mung bean noodles (cellophane noodles, bean threads, glass noodles, fen si)	mung bean starch and water deep-fried	stir-fries, soups,
rice noodles (rice sticks, rice vermicelli, mi fen)	rice flour and water	stir-fries, soups, deep-fried
vermicelli sheets (Sha He fen)	rice flour, cornstarch, potato starch, and water	soups, stir-fries
Japanese Noodles		
ramen noodles	wheat flour, egg, and water	soups, stews, stir-fries
devil's tongue starch noodles (shirataki)	devil's tongue starch or Amorphophalus konjac starch with milk of lime	soups
soba noodles	buckwheat flour, wheat flour, and water	soups, stews, salads
somen noodles	wheat flour and water	soups, salads
udon noodles	wheat flour and water	soups, stews, salads
Korean Noodles		
buckwheat noodles (naeng myon)	buckwheat flour, wheat flour, and water	salads, soups
sweet potato noodles (vermicelli, tang myon)	sweet potato flour and cornstarch and water	salads, stir-fries
Thai Noodles		
thin rice noodles (rice sticks, rice vermicelli, sen mee)	rice flour and water	soups, stir-fries, salad
flat rice noodles (flat rice sticks, rice vermicelli, dried gway tio, banh pho)	rice flour and water	soups, stir-fries, salad
vermicelli sheets (Sha He fen, gway tio)	rice flour, cornstarch, potato starch, and water	soups, stir-fries
mung bean noodles (cellophane noodles, bean threads, glass noodles, woon sen)	mung bean starch and water salads	soups, stir-fries,
Vietnamese Noodles		
thin rice noodles fillings (rice sticks, rice vermicelli, bun)	rice flour and water	salads, soups,
flat rice noodles (flat rice sticks, rice vermicelli, banh pho)	rice flour and water	soups, stir-fries
mung bean noodles (cellophane noodles, bean threads, glass noodles, bun tau)	mung bean starch and water	salads, soups, fillings

Udon is usually served in broth with chopped scallions or *shichimi* or a seven-spice mixture consisting of red pepper, *sansho* or Japanese prickly ash pepper pods, dried mandarin orange peel, black hemp seeds, dark green nori seaweed bits, and white sesame seeds. *Soba* is traditionally served on bamboo slats inside a square wooden box with a dipping sauce made of *dashi* or a bonito flake-*kombu* seaweed broth. If the noodles are presented cold, then the dipping sauce may be accompanied by sliced scallions, wasabi or Japanese horseradish, and grated daikon or Japanese white turnip. *Somen* is usually served cold. *Shirataki* comes packed in lime water and needs to be parboiled before using in sukiyaki, a popular beef dish made in a shallow cast-iron pan.

Korea's proximity to Japan and China is reflected in the noodles eaten there. Koreans enjoy buckwheat noodles or *naeng myon* cold, much as the Japanese do, but with some unique variations. The Korean version of the Chinese mung bean noodle is *tang myon*, which is made with sweet potato and cornstarch. These grayish, rubbery noodles are used in stir-fries.

Southeast Asia

Vietnamese noodles come in various sizes and are prepared in different ways. *Bun* or rice vermicelli comes in small and thin sizes, and in much wider widths. Small or thin noodles are used in salads, *bun bo*, while the much wider noodles are found in soups. *Banh pho* is a flat rice noodle that looks like linguine and comes in widths of small, medium, and large, and is used in soups and stir-fries. Vietnam's most popular soup is *pho bac*, or rice noodles in beef soup served with slices of beef and fresh herbs. *Mi soi*, thin egg noodles, is of Chinese origin. *Bun tau* or mung bean noodles, cellophane noodles, bean threads, or glass noodles are made from mung bean starch. After these thin, wiry white sticks are softened in hot water, they are used in soups, stir-fries, and fillings.

In Thailand, noodles also come in every size and shape, from flat white rice noodles or *gway tio*, to brittle white rice stick noodles or *sen mee*, to glass-like bean thread noodles or *woon sen*. *Gway tio* can be served in stir-fries or soups. *Sen mee* is served fried, stir-fried, or in soups. *Woon sen* is used in soups and stuffings for its slippery texture. Popular dishes in Thailand are the *pad thai* noodle, which uses thicker-width rice noodles, and *mee krob*, which uses a thin rice vermicelli that is fried.

In other parts of Southeast Asia, variations of the noodles found in China, Vietnam, and Thailand are eaten. In Malaysia, rice vermicelli noodles are combined with a tamarind mackerel sauce for *laksa asam*. In the Phillipines, rice vermicelli is stir-fried with meats and vegetables to make *pancit*. In Singapore, *char kway teow* or flat white rice noodles are stir-fried with seafood, while egg noodles or *Hokkien*, yellow noodles, and rice vermicelli are stir-fried in the same dish with meat, seafood, and vegetables for *Hokkien mee*. Though there may be similarities in preparation of the noodle dishes, the flavors are distinctive of each region because of the indigenous ingredients used.

Ceremony and Symbolism

Noodles not only play an important role in Asian daily eating, but contribute to rituals in honoring the dead, celebrating birthdays of the living, and marking other special occasions. They are brought to the grave of a deceased family member or friend on the twenty-fourth day after the first of each lunar month. It was Emperor Chu Yuan-Chang of the Ming Dynasty (1368–1644) who built a *t'ai miao* or shrine to the imperial ancestors where he placed spiritual tablets of his paternal relatives for four generations. Offerings of foods, including noodles with sesame oil, were brought to the shrine on the appropriate day.

After the birth of a child, especially a son, the mother's family sends over gifts for the new mother of wheat flour or wheat flour noodles, chickens, and a basket of eggs. For the birthday celebrant, a plate of long thin noodles expresses a wish of long life. Long-life and happiness wishes with noodles continue with the New Year feast.

In Japan, *soba* is usually the final item eaten on New Year's Eve. This dish is called *toshi-koshi* which means 'year-passing' and symbolizes the old year passing. It is customary for a person who moves into a new neighborhood to make gifts of *soba* to households next to and in front of one's new house. The word for *soba* is a homonym of the word *soba* meaning 'near' or 'next to'.

Summary

One cannot think of Asia without thinking of noodles. Noodles, the symbol for longevity, play important roles in everyday eating as well as for special occasions and celebrations. Consumed at home or on the streets, noodles originated in China but are a permanent presence in all of Asia.

See also **China; Japan; Korea; Rice; Southeast Asia; Wheat.**

BIBLIOGRAPHY

Ang, Catharina Y.W., Keshun Liu, and Yao-Wen Huang, eds. *Asian Foods, Science and Technology.* Lancaster, Pa.: Technomic, 1999.

Chang, Kwang-chih, ed. *Food in Chinese Culture: Anthropological and Historical Perspectives.* Binghamton, N.Y.: Vail-Ballou Press, 1979. New Haven: Yale University Press, 1977.

Cost, Bruce. *Asian Ingredients, A Guide to the Foodstuffs of China, Japan, Korea, Thailand, and Vietnam.* New York: Harper-Collins, 2000.

Gelle, Gerry G. *Filipino Cuisine: Recipes from the Islands.* Santa Fe: Red Crane Books, 1997.

Jue, Joyce. *Savoring Southeast Asia: Recipes and Reflections on Southeast Asian Cooking.* San Francisco: Time-Life Books, 2000.

Laudan, Rachel. "The Origins of Chinese Pasta." *Flavor and Fortune* 7, 2 (Summer 2000): 5, 20.

Loha-Unchit, Kasma. *It Rains Fishes: Legends, Traditions, and the Joys of Thai Cooking.* Rohnert Park, Calif.: Pomegranate Artbooks, 1995.

Marks, Copeland. *The Korean Kitchen: Classic Recipes from the Land of the Morning Calm.* San Francisco: Chronicle Books, 1993.

Pham, Mai. *Pleasures of the Vietnamese Table: Recipes and Reminiscences from Vietnam's Best Market Kitchens, Street Cafes, and Home Cooks.* New York: HarperCollins, 2001.

Routhier, Nicole. *The Foods of Vietnam.* New York: Stewart, Tabori and Chang, 1989.

Simmons, Nina. *Asian Noodles: Deliciously Simple Dishes to Twirl, Slurp, and Savor.* New York: William Morrow, 1997.

Solomon, Charmaine. *Charmaine Solomon's Encyclopedia of Asian Food: The Complete Cookbook with Ingredients, Techniques, and Over 500 Recipes.* Boston and Singapore: Periplus Editions (HK) Ltd., 1998.

Tannahill, Reay. *Food in History.* New York: Three Rivers Press-Crown, 1988.

Trager, James. *The Food Chronology, A Food Lover's Compendium of Events and Anecdotes, From Prehistory to the Present.* New York: Henry Holt, 1995.

Tsuji, Shizuo. *Japanese Cooking, A Simple Art.* Bunkyo-ku, Tokyo: Kodansha International, America, 1980.

Stella Fong

Three examples of a *Nudelholz*, an old tool for cutting pasta into thin strips by means of a ridged rolling pin. Made in southwest Germany, circa 1850 to 1870. This very ancient tool dating to Roman times was used in traditional culture to cut pasta or pastry into strands resembling modern linguini. ROUGHWOOD COLLECTION. PHOTO CHEW & COMPANY.

NOODLE IN NORTHERN EUROPE, THE.

The word "noodle" is German in origin. By the mid-1400s, it appeared as *Nudel* in connection with *composita*, layered dishes employing cabbage, dried fruits, some form of meat (usually ham), and dumplings. There is no firm agreement among German food historians about the origin of the term *Nudel* even though it can be found in German- and Yiddish-speaking communities in Middle Europe by the 1500s. For example, in the 1581 cookbook of Hungarian-born Marcus Rumpolt, there is a recipe for *Nudeln aus der Grafschaft Tyrol* (Noodles from the county of Tyrol), evidence of the fact that, by the 1580s, there were already many regional variations in methods of preparation and serving contexts. Furthermore, the plural form of the word passed into French as *nouilles*, probably via Alsace. The original meaning, however, was *Teigwerk*, anything made of dough regardless of shape. Even to this day, the *Nudel* falls under the broad category of *Teigwerk* in most German-language cookbooks. The distinguishing difference between *Teigwerk* for pie crusts and doughs for noodles is that the latter are boiled or in some manner cooked with steam or water.

The most commonly accepted explanation for the origin of *Nudel* is that it derives from *Knödel*, or, as the word appeared in a number of old German dialects, *Nutel*, a dumpling (literally, a ball or turd). Recipes mentioning noodles appear in German as early as 1480, but at that time, the term applied to any sort of doughy addition to a boiled or baked dish, whether a shaped dumpling or thinly sliced noodles. The dough could be rolled, pressed, shredded, cut, chopped, stretched, or shaped into small "buttons"—all of this was included in the word *Nudel*. The oldest German lexicons define *Nudel*

as a dough dish composed of wheat flour, butter, and milk. This paste is then boiled in water. There is no mention of eggs—eggs do not appear in noodle recipes until the 1600s. However, because the dough was made with white wheat flour (a luxury), the *Nudel* was at one time a food denoting high economic status.

Conceptually, the *Nudel* of Northern Europe differs from Italian pasta in that the enriched dough is not dried for later use, but rather cooked the same day it is made. The high fat content would probably preclude long storage because noodles are generally made with egg yolks, butter, and other unstable ingredients. Because of these rich ingredients, the German *Nudel* was not viewed as appropriate fasting food by strict Roman Catholics, although noodles of all sorts were indeed treated as meat substitutes. The cost of the ingredients alone set noodle dishes apart as special occasion or festive fare even in the late eighteenth century.

Earlier medieval sources are consistently clear in categorizing this type of food as something found in the invalid cookery of hospices operated by nunneries or monasteries. As a branch of invalid cookery, noodles were generally served with hot milk or cream depending on the patient's condition. Otherwise, noodles were a special-occasion food eaten only by the well-to-do as part of a larger menu, such as a side dish with a roast of meat. The concept of the noodle as health food survived in the once popular recipe for *Nürnberger Nudlen*, one of the most commonly cited sickroom recipes in old German medical literature.

By the seventeenth century, the noodle had evolved into three broad types in German cookery: flat noodles rolled thin and cut into various shapes (most often thin strips), shaped noodles or dumplings, and yeast-raised noodles as in the case of South German *Dampfnudeln*. This last dish is prepared by steam-baking balls of yeast-leavened dough in a heavy iron skillet.

There are also a large number of specialized terms associated with noodle making. Among these are *Nudelteig* (the dough from which any sort of noodle is made), *Nudelholz* (a special rolling pin for cutting the dough into strips), and *Nudelspritze* (a press for squeezing noodle dough into strips or strands, especially for *Nürnberger Nudeln*). Cristoforo Messisbugo illustrated a *Nudelholz* under the rubric *ferro da maccaroni* in his 1549 work on Italian Renaissance cookery. This tool was widespread in Europe, and its origin cannot be pinpointed.

The general presumption among German food scholars is that noodles (under a wide variety of names) were present in northern Europe during the early Middle Ages. Various methods of preparation, such as serving them with fried bread crumbs, may also be quite old. There is no evidence suggesting that the idea came from medieval Italy. In fact, the German noodle can be traced to the pre-Christian era, since pastry wheels and rolling pins for making noodles have been found in numerous Roman archeological sites north of the Alps. Yet the question remains whether these tools were used for making dried pasta as known to the Italians, or the richer noodle known later to German-speaking countries. It is quite possible that the Romans knew both types.

The *Nudel* appears to have entered English during the Georgian period, perhaps owing to the fact that the Hanoverian monarchs were German. The word was transliterated into English as *newdel* and noodle. The latter spelling is now the accepted form. In eighteenth-century England and America, the noodle was associated primarily with one dish: noodle soup. This is a preparation in which strands of freshly made noodles are boiled in meat stock, sometimes with the addition of small meat dumplings. This became a ubiquitous working-class dish by the nineteenth century.

The center of noodle cookery in America was the region settled by the Pennsylvania Dutch and the thickly settled German districts of the upper Midwest. In the German-American community, noodle dishes were generally reserved for Sunday dinners due to the amount of work required to make the dough. Additionally, the egg whites left over from noodle making were normally turned into sponge cakes—another special occasion dish. The Pennsylvania Dutch developed a number of interesting noodle recipes, including saffron noodles for boiled Sunday chicken, and a noodle dessert made with walnuts, sugar, and cinnamon.

By the mid-nineteenth century, noodle cookery became associated with regional peasant fare in Germany. German Romanticism elevated the noodle to an icon of German ethnicity, with the result that we see it everywhere today as a symbol of German cooking.

See also **Compote**; **Noodle in Asia**; **Pasta**; **United States: Pennsylvania Dutch Food**.

BIBLIOGRAPHY

Benker, Gertrud. *Kuchlgschirr und Essensbräuch* [Cooking utensils and eating habits]. Regensburg: Friedrich Pustet, 1977.

Birlinger, Anton. "Älteres Küchen-und Kellerdeutsch" [Old-time kitchen and cellar German]. *Alemannia* 18 (1890): 244–266.

Borst, Otto. *Alltagsleben im Mittelalter* [Daily life in the Middle Ages]. Frankfurt: Insel, 1983.

Gérard, Charles. *L'Ancienne Alsace à table* [Old Alsace at the table]. Paris: Berger-Levrault, 1877.

Grimm, Jacob, and Wilhelm Grimm. *Deutsches Wörterbuch*, vol. 7, pp. 975–977. Leipzig: S. Hirzel, 1889.

Messisbugo, Cristoforo di. *Banchetti, Composizioni di Vivande et Apparecchio Generale*. Ferrara: Giovanni de Bughalt ed Antonio Hucher, 1549.

Rumpolt, Marcus. *Ein New Kochbuch* [A new cookery book]. Frankfurt: Sigmund Feyerabend, 1581.

Schlemmer, Fridolin. *Alemannisch angerichtet* [Served up in Alemannic style]. Freiburg: Badischer Verlag, 1976.

Troll, Thaddäus. *Kochen wie die Schwaben* [Cooking like Swabians]. Munich: Mosaik, 1982.

Wiswe, Hans. *Kulturgeschichte der Kochkunst* [A cultural history of cookery]. Munich: H. Moos, 1970.

William Woys Weaver

NORDIC COUNTRIES. The Nordic countries—members of the Nordic Council—are Finland, Iceland, and the Scandinavian countries (in a strict sense Norway and Sweden—the Scandinavian Peninsula—but generally this group includes Denmark as well). Finland is in many ways different from the other Nordic countries because its language is of the Finno-Ugric group (related to Estonian and Hungarian). The languages in the other countries belong to the Germanic group, and Swedes, Danes, and Norwegians understand each other when they talk together. The Icelandic language has closer ties with Old Norse. In the circumpolar areas there is an ethnic group of about around 50,000 people called Samis (often called Lapps, a designation they consider derogatory) who use a Uralic language, in addition to the language of their state (Norwegian, Swedish, and Finnish).

Many parts of Norway and Sweden consist of mountains, valleys, and enormous forests, while Denmark's highest point is less than two hundred meters above sea level. Denmark is smaller than Norway and Sweden, but comparatively it has much more cultivated land. Iceland, with its glaciers, hot springs, volcanoes, and large areas of barren land, is only populated along the coast, and fishing has always been important there. Finland, "the land of a thousand lakes," is a country of forests crisscrossed by rivers and lakes.

Sweden and Denmark are old independent kingdoms that historically have had strong aristocratic cultures. Both Norway (independent since 1905) and Iceland (independent since 1945) were ruled by Denmark for centuries, and the culture imposed by Danish or Danish-educated civil servants is still a part of the heritage in those countries. Finland, first under Swedish and then under Russian rule, gained its independence in 1919 and is also marked by the traditions of its former rulers.

The Nordic countries were mainly agricultural societies (although fishing was also important) until the last part of the nineteenth century, when industrialization marked a shift from rural to urban dominance.

The Lutheran religion was introduced in the middle of the sixteenth century, and this is still the religion of the majority of Nordic people, even though church attendance is relatively low and secular ideas dominate most fields. A Greek orthodox minority lives in Finland.

It is possible to draw a line between a northern area, which comprises Iceland, Norway, and the north of Sweden, and a southern area, including Denmark and the south of Sweden, which has ties to northern Germany and the Baltic. The west (in particular, the southwest) of Finland has strong ties to Sweden, while in parts of eastern Finland there are many similarities with Russian traditions.

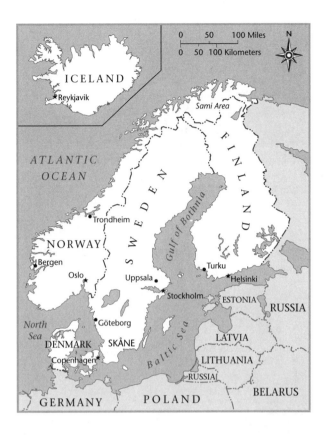

Nordic Diet and Food Distribution—Sell the Best, Use the Rest

In general, diet in a region depends on what kind of food a region produces. For example, in the Nordic countries people along the coast eat more fish, people in the mountains eat more milk and cheese from sheep and goats, and people in the lowland plains eat more meat and bread. Yet a little more than one hundred years ago, many agricultural products were not only seen as food but also as money. Social conditions were such that much of what the farmers and peasants cultivated and caught was used in a barter economy to obtain other necessary goods (such as salt, spices, and special tools).

The Nordic elite had strong ties to their counterparts abroad. The aristocracy in Sweden and Denmark, the civil and ecclesiastic administrators in Norway, and merchants in the many ports along the Atlantic and Baltic coasts followed European habits and fashions and wanted fresh and exclusive food. Many of these people were rich landowners with lots of livestock; thus they could afford to have fresh meat at all times. They slaughtered animals regularly and had cooks to prepare different dishes at their request. The wealthy also had poultry, geese, turkeys, and sometimes fish ponds on their estates. They also had regular delivery of game, fish, and wild berries from the forests. Poor people picked lingonberries (*Vaccinium vitis-idaea*), bilberries (*Vaccinium myrtillus*), and in the north the yellow cloudberries (*Rubus chamaemorus*), which they sold to the upper classes, who used them for

fruit drinks or for jams and jellies to go with roasts. Game was a privilege of the aristocracy in Denmark, as it was in most of Europe, but in the big forests of northern Scandinavia, hunting was free for everyone. Among the European nobility, the prestige of using wild animals as food was very high; this was also true in the upper classes in the Nordic countries, and very often the wealthy in these countries would buy game sold by poorer countrymen. When the smaller farmers and peasants slaughtered their domestic animals, they put aside the best cuts of meat and sold them to the manors, to the butchers in the towns, or to the ironworks where there were many foreign engineers and specialists who preferred this kind of food. In this way farmers received a certain amount of necessary cash. If a farmer had a goose or two, he would sell them, and if he had hens, he would sell the eggs. One of the most important dairy products, butter, was a means of payment as well as food.

The Food of the Elite—More European than Nordic

Even if the Nordic countries were sometimes considered the Ultima Thule (the northernmost part of the world fit for human habitation) by people farther south, they were never isolated from the European continent. The well-known Viking raids during the Middle Ages were quickly followed by diversified commerce. Luxury products began to be imported, and there are even two Danish cookbooks from about 1300, among the earliest manuscripts of this kind in Europe, that exhibit clear

A Swedish breakfast buffet at Grinda, Sweden, featuring a variety of flat breads, pickled fish, cold cuts, and cheeses. © Bo Zaunders/CORBIS.

influences from Mediterranean cuisine. German and French cookbooks were translated into Nordic languages in the seventeenth century: a Swedish edition of the famous *Le cuisinier françois* was published in 1664. This means that many of the dishes consumed in the Nordic countries were not too different from what was being eaten elsewhere in Europe. However, certain national specialities were still popular. In the eighteenth century, Swedes served the hors d'oeuvres at a so-called brandy table, which was often placed in a separate room from the dining room. Many foreign travelers in Sweden reported a habit of eating bread, butter, and salt fish before the meal and swallowing it down with glasses of brandy. The similarities with the Russian *zakuski* tradition seemed evident, but no one has resolved the issue of which tradition influenced the other.

Some of the game was unique to the Nordic region, particularly reindeer, but also elk, capercaillie, hazel hen, and black grouse. The upper classes valued fresh fish very highly, but they also consumed lots of dried, salted, and smoked fish. Salmon was considered a great delicacy, as were oysters, mussels, lobsters, and eels.

Fresh fruit and vegetables were granted much prestige in upper-class circles, and many different species of produce were imported or grown on experimental farms in the eighteenth century. Menus from that time indicate that asparagus, artichokes, and pineapples were popular items. In general, people stuck with cabbage, onion, carrots, and other roots, but they generally considered vegetables an "animal food" and not proper nourishment for manual workers. A study from the 1890s by Amund Helland that compared food habits in Norway with those in Paris showed that the Norwegians ate 10 kilograms of vegetables per head per year, while Parisians ate 118 kilograms.

The Food of the Lower Classes—"Humble Pie"
Since the best cuts were generally sold, offal and the less desirable parts of the animal were the most-used cuts of meat, especially among poor farmers. People always used the offal efficiently, for example, it was often minced and put into sausages or similar casings. Blood was used to make puddings, sausages, and other dishes. When making sausages, people also put grain or flour, salt and pepper, and sometimes onion in the casings. These blood dishes were in use in all the Nordic countries, but not in the eastern part of Finland, where many people belonged to the Orthodox Church.

Newborn calves were a special case. Calves were born at different times throughout the year, and the elite fattened them for some weeks and used them as roasts. However, there are accounts of a more popular and simple preparation dating from seventeenth- and eighteenth-century Norway. Ordinary people would not have the means to feed a calf in winter, so the whole newborn animal was boiled, the bones and hairs sifted away, and the remaining substance, a sort of jelly, eaten at once or kept for later use. The fat meat from the head of pigs and sheep was used in dishes such as *sylte*, which was more in keeping with the German tradition (*Sülze*) than in the French (*fromage de tête*) or English (brawn). *Sylte* was spiced with pepper and clove.

Different kinds of fat were also important ingredients in very simple, popular dishes. Some of them were dumplings, where the fat from the slaughtered animals and poultry was mixed with flour. They had many local names (*klubb, kams, klot, palt, kumle, kumpe, ball*) and corresponded roughly to the Central European *Knödeln* and *Klösse*. The flour was mixed with leaf fat from domestic animals, as well as with fat from seabirds, seal blubber, and roe and liver from fish. The fishermen in the north mixed cod liver and roe with flour, spices, and raisins and put this mixture into the cod's head or sound (air bladder) and boiled it in water. In some cases parts of the fish itself, fresh or salted, were added to this mixture, and potatoes were partly substituted for the flour. Before the use of forks and plates, slices of the ball were cut with a knife and placed between two bits of crisp flat bread, similar to the way one eats hamburgers today. A special type of ball was made from the blood of domestic animals, but more often this mixture of flour, blood, and some spices was made into sausages or baked into a soft flat bread.

Another way of combining fat and cereals was the *mölje* (jumble): crisp flat bread was broken into small pieces and put into a bowl with the liquid from boiling meat liver. Fishermen ate a *mölje* with crisp flat bread and cod liver. All these examples show an efficient use of all the parts of animal or fish products that were not sold or saved for important occasions.

In Finland there were and are examples of a special combination of flour with fish or meat, pies, and pasties. In the east they are called *piiras* or *piirakka* (Russian *pirog*) and *kukko*, which is a big pie with dough all around. *Pirog* is normally smaller than *kukko*, and if it is big, the filling is exposed with no crust on top. The filling in *kukko* may be meat, potatoes, cabbage, and turnips, but it was originally fish. In the west, along the coast, a similar pie had the name "herring cake."

Meat and Status

As in most societies, meat held more prestige than other food in Nordic countries, but there were also differences in the evaluation of different kinds of meat. The importance of pork in older times could be seen in the Swedish and Danish terms used for it, *fläsk/flaesk*, which are similar to the German *Fleisch*, which is a generic word for "meat." Today beef is more expensive than pork, but in the Middle Ages pork was much more expensive than beef and mutton if one calculated its average price by weight.

As a general rule, it is possible to say that swine dominated the meats of the south for a very long time, while cattle were more important in the north for several reasons, not least of which was that they provided hides and milk products. The tough meat from old and worn out cows and oxen was not used in steaks and roasts; rather, it was boiled in a pot with cabbage, groats, roots, and available herbs and spices. This meat was normally salted and put into water before it was boiled, so the salt could be extracted and the meat would soften. Mutton was also boiled this way. One common word for these dishes was *kål* (cabbage), which was used whether they contained cabbage or not. The Old Norse word, however, was *sodd*, which simply means "boiled." The use of this word is probably a sign of how old this dish is.

Mutton had played a very important role in Nordic countries, but the number of sheep—and goats, the even less prestigious domestic animals—has gradually diminished in Nordic countries during the last few centuries. Mutton was often eaten uncooked, since it had been dried, salted, and occasionally smoked. In general the meat was very seldom eaten fresh, except among the elite—a fact often commented upon by foreign visitors. This was, especially in the northern regions, a result of the climatic conditions. The summer season during which animals could graze was very short. During a winter with deep snow, feeding animals required a lot of fodder. Animals that were raised only for meat production were slaughtered after the summer, when they were at their fattest. In order to preserve the meat, the farmers had to dry, salt, or smoke it. Pork was often kept in brine.

This preserved meat could be kept for years: it was considered a symbol of wealth to have stocks of meat at the *stabbur*, a special storehouse built on pillars. From Denmark we know of the tradition of *gammelmadsfad* (plate of old food) or *saltmadsfad* (plate of salt food), which involved a big platter with all sorts of smoked and salted meat that could stand on the table for weeks. In Norway reports from wedding feasts in the eighteenth century tell about plates with old food that were put on the table but not eaten—they were only used as a decoration year after year.

Fish Consumption and Preservation

In the United States, especially in the Midwest, the Scandinavian population identifies with a peculiar dish: *lutefisk*. This dish has a jelly-like consistency and often a yellowish color. The dish is generally unpopular among people who have never tried it. The same holds true in Sweden, where *lutefisk* is considered a national dish.

The best raw material for *lutefisk* is the dried cod from the northern coast of Norway, where the air is rather cool. The *tørrfisk*, or stokfish, holds almost no humidity, lasts for years, and has been exported to Europe since before the year 1000. The fish had to be beaten or softened in water before they were cooked. In the late Middle Ages a special method emerged for the preparation of this dish: a potash lye or soda was put in the water to help soften the fish, and the result was *lutefisk* (lye fish). The oldest sources for this method are found in Sweden and Germany, but there are also recipes in early Spanish and French cookbooks, so the dish may have existed elsewhere.

Drying is probably the oldest method for fish preservation in Scandinavia, where all sorts of fish were cleaned and hung up to air dry. Even herring was dried, but it did not last as long as other fish because of its high fat content. In the north of Sweden and Finland, pike and other freshwater fish were dried. Salmon that could be dried, salted, and/or smoked held the most prestige.

Cod and other white fish were also salted in brine. This was the most common way to preserve herring, and salted herring has been an important part of Scandinavian diet for centuries. It was either eaten cold or grilled, normally with bread or porridge, and later with potatoes.

High-quality salt was expensive, but necessary for a good product. Among ordinary people who had little money for salt, a special method of preservation developed for herring and some freshwater fish. The Swedish term *gravlaks* (buried salmon) dates back to the Middle

Fresh salmon on display in the fish market at Bergen, Norway. © Wolfgang Kaehler/CORBIS.

Ages, when the fish, sometimes lightly salted, was buried in the ground or in a barrel. It could be kept for months because of the slow fermentation that occurred. The result was soft flesh, but also a sour taste and a strong, unpleasant smell. In Sweden this method is still used to make the sour *strömming*, a herring from the north of the Baltic Sea (the Gulf of Bothnia). People in Norway also used herring, but today they mainly use trout from inland rivers and lakes. Icelanders use the flesh of the *hákarl*, a species of shark. The same fermentation technique exists in other circumpolar areas, and it is related to the old Roman *garum/liquamen* process.

In the modern version of *gravlaks*, the salmon has only gone through the early stage of the chemical process, where enzymes soften the flesh. Filets of salmon, with salt, sugar, pepper, and fresh dill spread between them, are placed under heavy weights for a couple of days in a cool place. This method of fermentation probably developed within the upper classes at a later time than the original method.

Milk—A Way of Life

Milk was extremely important in the northern part of Scandinavia, Iceland, and parts of Finland. In this area's tough climatic conditions, sheep and cattle were raised partly for hides, partly for food, but first and foremost for milk. In Iceland *skýr*, a curdled milk from sheep or cows, is considered a national dish.

One of the most important dairy products, butter, was so important in the northern countryside that it was used for hundreds of years as a symbol of wealth, partic-

ularly at weddings, where pyramids of sculptured butter were raised at each end of the table. The butter was formed in special wooden cases with patterns of flowers or animals. Folk museums display these butter sculptures as examples of popular art.

For the past several centuries, the elite of the Nordic countries have imported cheeses from Holland and Switzerland. These cheeses are made in the general European fashion by adding rennet to the milk. This was a different tradition from the one in the northern regions, where the milk was coagulated in a process caused by lactic acid. Some of these cheeses were sweet, a little like puddings or desserts, and others were made from sour milk, usually from a cow, but also from sheep and goats. One of the most famous and prestigious cheeses was the *gammalost* (old cheese), which was dark brown and rather hard with a grainy texture.

Milk was almost never drunk sweet; rather, it was made into different sour-milk varieties. A very special type was the "long milk" or "thick milk" that would stay fresh during the summer. It was also called *tettemjølk* in Norway and *tätmjölk* in Sweden after an herb (*Pinguicula vulgaris*) that was put into the milk that was said to cause the souring process. Today many people dispute the role of the herb: the process also starts when a little old milk, containing certain bacteria, is put in the kettle with the new milk.

In the northern areas, milk had to be substituted for beer as a common drink because of the low production of grains. The daily drink of ordinary people was *blanda*, which was sour whey blended with water. The inventive use of whey, the substance remaining after cheeses are made, is specific to the northern regions. It might be boiled into a sort of soup and eaten together with bread (sour milk was also used this way). Whey might also be boiled for hours until it became a thick substance. This was then put into wooden cases to cool and, when finished, looked like brown bricks. This "cheese" was either made from the whey of sweet or sour milk (the sour being the cheapest) and was spread on flat bread instead of butter by the poor and servants.

Bread—Flat, Soft, Hard, Sweet, Dark, White

The cold climate and the meager soil in the north made it difficult to grow grains other than oats and barley; since these do not contain gluten, they could not be used for leavened bread. The result was different sorts of flat, thin bread, specialties of the northern regions. These stood in contrast to the leavened rye bread in the southern part of Scandinavia, Denmark, and the Swedish region Skåne (which was part of Denmark until the seventeenth century). In Finland a dividing line can be drawn between the west and north, where different sorts of hard breads were baked, and the east, where soft rye bread was common.

The Danes, like the German and Dutch, had *smørrebrød* (butter bread), a dark rye bread served with butter and cheese, cold meat, sausage, liver paste, or other delicacies (internationally known as "open sandwiches"). While the flat bread in the north was baked on griddles (iron plates), bakery ovens were more widespread in the south, and the Danes often bought their bread from the baker. The Danish bakers, organized in guilds with strict rules, were obliged to have certain products ready at all times: white bread, coarse rye bread, and *skonrogger* (from sifted rye), in other words, alternatives for all classes of society. The status of bread had to do with the kind of flour used: for example, during festivals, the elite would eat only white bread made from wheat flour. This bread was best when fresh, but most people would let their bread dry out, which made it more economical since it would last longer.

The Swedes are especially known for their sweet and spiced breads. One French diplomat remarked as early as 1634: "The bread had a terrible taste, made as it was with wort and sweet fennel." This was the dark *vörtbröd*, made with beer wort, molasses, spices, citrus peel, and raisins. These sweet breads were earlier a luxury or used only for festive situations. The expression "sweet bread days" meant (and still means) good times.

Porridge—For Hunger and Luxury

Porridge is an old dish, perhaps more ancient than bread, and it has been used in many cultures. Flour mixed with water ("water porridge") was the simplest variety and was long thought to be a synonym for poverty. Scandinavians also mixed the grains with milk, cream, or whey. As was already mentioned, whey soup was eaten with bread. Milk

made the porridge more attractive, and during annual festivals and rites of passage it turned into a luxury dish, *rømmegrøt* (sour cream porridge), with the addition of cream or butter. In modern times, porridge is more like a pudding made from rice and milk and is often sprinkled with sugar and cinnamon, but the *butterye* (a lump of butter in the middle) is still a relic from the past.

In early modern times and up until the nineteenth century, rice was a luxury that very few could enjoy. It was more common in Denmark, where they also ate porridge from *maiz* (corn), buckwheat, and pearl sago. Oats were not popular in Denmark unless they were made into groats, which were easier to digest. Danish porridges were often boiled with sweet milk, but in Skåne (southern Sweden) there is also a tradition of serving beer on porridge. In Denmark they have *øllebrød* (beer bread), which is rye bread that is diced and boiled in beer with sugar and lemon peel. In characteristically Norwegian style, when *øllebrød* was introduced there it was made with a mixture of beer and milk.

Nordic Drinks

Blanda, sour whey or milk mixed with water, was previously mentioned as a daily drink in northern regions. But beer production occurred everywhere: a very light and simple beer for daily use, and stronger brands for festivals and special occasions. Since the Middle Ages, more exclusive beers were imported from Germany, and the more affluent of society imported mead (made from honey). Grapes have never been grown in the Nordic countries, but wine has been imported since the time of the Vikings, especially after clergy with southern European roots established churches and monasteries in the region.

Ever since the eighteenth century, *akevitt*—brandy made from grain—has become more and more common. It is considered good for health and physical strength. Farm hands received a shot of *akevitt* when they started work at around 5:00 A.M. and when they began to tire in the afternoon. *Akevitt* was also used with sugar and spices in drinks, but imported brandy was preferred for this use. The introduction of potatoes in Nordic countries offered new and cheaper possibilities for *akevitt*, and the production and consumption led to widespread alcoholism in the countryside in the early nineteenth century. However, things began to change when popular temperance and abstinence movements emerged in the second half of the nineteenth century. The government introduced restrictions on distillation of alcohol, and coffee gradually replaced beer and brandy as the daily restorative drink.

The Sami Diet

A portion of the Sami people lived as nomads with their flocks of domesticated reindeer, but some also lived on the coast (the sea Samis) and were more residential in nature. Their diet placed an emphasis on meat and milk. The Samis ate meat from many wild animals: bear, otter, hare, marten, and wolverine, but never fox and wolf. Contrary to the rest of the Nordic population, they had no prejudice against horseflesh, which they ate dried. Their main source of food was reindeer, and they used every bit of it: the head, heart, and tongue were delicacies of great value. They never roasted fresh meat, but always boiled it. They preserved much meat for future use by drying—they never used brine. Dried meat was easier to transport. Also, blood was freeze-dried and then ground into a powder. Fat was appreciated, especially the rich rectum fat that was dried and used as cream in coffee, when this drink was introduced.

Among the Samis there were strict rules as to who could eat what. The heart and the genitals of the buck were reserved for men. Men also had the responsibility of preparing meals, particularly if the meal involved meat from reindeer and bear.

Fish was important for the Samis along the coast, but people also fished in the rivers of the great plains. The fish was boiled or dried for later use, and the roe was considered a special delicacy.

In general, bread has no tradition among the Samis, the exception being the sea Samis. For the nomads, carrying bread or flour and purchasing flour was no easy task. When bread finally was introduced, it was almost always unleavened.

Butter, cheese, and boiled dishes were made from milk. Herbs and berries were used instead of spices. The usual drink before coffee was water, sometimes mixed with male (sap from birch trees). The main meal was in the evening, and it always consisted of meat or fish. For lunch a lighter meal was common, such as soup or reindeer meat or, in summer, a cheese gruel.

A New Diet in an Urban Society

During the late nineteenth and the early twentieth centuries, the Nordic countries went through a process of urbanization, industrialization, democratization, and the emergence of stronger commercial links to the world outside. Many of the old traditions in meat preparation were changing. For example, the introduction of meat grinders made it possible for most social groups to mince meat. In earlier times, this was a privilege of rich houses, because it demanded servants who worked for hours with knives. Now everybody could make the meatballs that were and still are extremely popular national, everyday dishes in several of the Nordic countries, where they are referred to as "mother's meat balls."

A special dish that is less common today because it demands so much work to prepare is stuffed cabbage—minced meat in cabbage leaves (instead of the Mediterranean version with grape leaves). An unsubstantiated legend claims that the Swedish recipe, called *dolma* (a Turkish word), was brought to Sweden by King Charles XII, who spent several years in Turkey after his defeat at Poltava.

In general, with the advent of urbanization, the tendency went in the direction of more fresh food than before. In addition to the balls made of minced meat, cutlets of pork, sausages, chicken or veal fricassees, roasts, and steaks also became very popular. In Denmark the "old food platters" were replaced by "roast platters." The introduction of the kitchen stove was instrumental in this change.

In Norway, where there was no local tradition of leavened bread, the spread of bakeries and bakery ovens in the late nineteenth century led to the emergence of a great variety of breads. Apart from the wheat and rye bread known in Denmark, healthy new alternatives were offered, such as *kneippbrød* (after the German doctor Sebastian Kneipp), *grahambrød* (after the American dietician Sylvester Graham), and later whole-meal breads of different recipes.

As in so many countries, butter faced competition from the new artificial substitute, margarine. Many farmers replaced butter with margarine and received extra money to buy salt, spices, coffee, sugar, and other foreign products. This happened at about the same time that the entire system of dairy production went through a fundamental change. Instead of making different dairy products on the farm, farmers started to sell their milk to the new factories where butter and cheese were produced with modern techniques. This practice also followed a shift in cheese preferences. During the nineteenth century, Swiss and Dutch cheeses grew more popular, and the Nordic countries imported both cheese and dairy specialists from Gouda, Edam, Leiden, and Switzerland. The specialists trained local dairymen to make cheese a new way, and one of these cheeses, the Norwegian Jarlsberg, has been a success in the world market.

During the nineteenth century, coffee became the daily drink everywhere. It spread from the big cities to the countryside and from the elite down through all the other levels of society.

Potatoes represented the most extraordinary shift in food consumption, with a complete breakthrough occurring during the Napoleonic Wars. After that time, preparing the main hot meal was barely possible without boiled potatoes, the basis of Scandinavian cuisine. The nineteenth century was also a great time for herring catches, and the low price of these two products led to the expression "salted herring and potatoes," meaning a poor man's food or *husmannskost*. Also roast fresh herring was a very common dish among ordinary people. However, herring was also present in the *smörgåsbord*, which has been popular in Swedish restaurants and hotels since the late nineteenth century. Around a big brandy pot with taps for different brandies and *akevitts* were several sorts of cured herring, sardines, marinated sprats, smoked eel, grilled eel, eel in jelly, pig trotters, brawn, sausages, and later also *gravlaks* and smoked salmon. Today the *smörgåsbord* is not only an introduction to a meal, but it can be a full buffet lunch or din-

Danish painting on wood panels from 1836 showing the interior of a local bakery. Courtesy of the Københavns Bymuseum, Copenhagen. © ARCHIVO ICONOGRAFICO, S. A./CORBIS.

ner, complete with hot dishes (such as meatballs and steaks with onion). Dessert consists of different kinds of fruits, sweets, and cakes.

Food and Feast

Special occasions in life and rites of passage have always involved special dishes. The main objective has been to serve something special that sets that day apart from the rest. In rural societies, where resources were not always abundant and cash flow was low, a system of gifts emerged. Guests brought food to weddings and funerals, often butter and rich cheeses, which were all put on the table and then brought back if they were not finished. In the twentieth century, this custom changed with the advent of a more urban society and smaller families. New habits spread gradually from the aristocracy to the middle classes and then to the whole population. The *pièce de résistance* at special occasions, in most cases, was a roast.

Different regional traditions have developed around religious holidays. Among the many old traditions tied to the long Lenten period before Easter, only the sweet rolls with whipped cream still exist. A special Easter dish in Finland originated as a Lenten dish among Catholics in the southwest, but it has since spread to the whole country. *Mämmi*, a dark brown porridge-like substance made from malted rye and baked in the oven in boxes of birchbark (today cardboard), is served with thick cream and sugar.

Feasts for saints were much more important in earlier times, but the roast goose of St. Martinmas in November has survived in Denmark and in southern Sweden, where it is accompanied by *svartsoppa* (black soup) made from goose blood and giblets. On the thirteenth of December the Swedes celebrate Sancta Lucia with elements from an ancient regional feast. Young girls in white robes and candles on their heads march through the streets singing an Italian song and handing out *lussekatter* (Lucia cats), which are small saffron cakes. A special feast without any connection to religious traditions is held every August when crayfish are in season. Crayfish parties are merry events that involve paper hats, special plates, and lots of singing and drinking. The crayfish are boiled in dill and served cold. Swedes eat more crayfish than most people in the world. Most of the crayfish are wild, but there is an increasing farming industry in addition to the importation of about 3,000 tons of crayfish every year.

The Icelandic Thórablót in January is named after the Norse god Thor (Thunder). *Blót* was a religious ceremony that involved offerings to the gods and reputedly much eating and drinking. The food is *hákarl* (sour buck's balls), boiled sheepheads, and *hangikjöt* (smoked meat of lamb).

Christmas Celebrations

The one occasion in which the Nordic population as a whole still maintains traditions is Christmas. At this time people eat large quantities of meat. Many baked items are prepared exclusively for Christmas and are called Christmas cakes, of which there are seven required types.

The traditional Christmas meal is generally served on Christmas Eve, but the food is very different from country to country. In Denmark the traditional main dish was goose, as in Hans Christian Andersen's story "The Little Match Girl." In recent times, duck has been substituted for goose, but the stuffing is the same: apples and prunes. Dessert is a sweet rice pudding made from rice boiled in milk, with almonds and whipped cream added. Christmas Day in Denmark involves different traditions, but very often roast pork is served.

In Norway there are regional differences: roast rib of pork with sauerkraut is served on Christmas in the east, boiled cod is served in the south, and *lutefisk* is served in the north. The specialty of the west is *pinnekjøtt* (stick meat), a dried, salted, and sometimes smoked rib of lamb, which is put in water during the night so some of the salt is extracted and placed above steam for several hours. Tradition says that during the steaming process the long ribs should rest on sticks of birchwood. It is served with mashed turnips. Boiled potatoes accompany all the aforementioned dishes.

In Sweden *julskinka* (Christmas ham) is obligatory, but it is only one of the dishes served at an expanded *smörgåsbord*. Swedes eat *lutefisk* and rice porridge during the Christmas period. Another traditional element of this feast is the *vörtbröd*, which is dipped in the broth where the Christmas ham has been boiled, and a special hard Christmas bread that is a little softer than the crisp rye *knäckebröd*.

Julskinka is also a main dish in Finland on Christmas Eve, but there it is often smoked in the sauna. In addition, the table holds sausages and the traditional oven-baked dishes in earthenware, called "boxes." These boxes contain liver, potatoes, turnips, and so forth. This kind of meal is also typical for weddings and other big events, although the *julskinka* is then often replaced by a roast of elk or other game. Dessert is a thick soup of dried fruits, also a very popular dish in Finland. Before this rich meal the Finns eat a hot lunch with *lutefisk* and rice porridge. In the southeastern part of the country, the *pirogs* will be on the table for Christmas.

On Christmas Day in Iceland the traditional dish *hangikjöt* is served and eaten cold. On Christmas Eve in Iceland people have no set tradition, but loin of pork and grouse are fairly common dishes.

Toward an International Cuisine?

Since the start of the twenty-first century, many old Nordic traditions have begun to change. Food consumption and food habits in Nordic countries today have been strongly influenced by international trends such as fast food, ethnic cuisine, and gourmet-restaurant culture. This development is a break from what was, until the late twentieth century, the general fare for the majority of the people in this region.

The use of minced meat is no longer limited to meatballs, as it is eaten with spaghetti, in lasagna, on pizzas, in tacos, and in pita breads. This trend also implies a reduction in the consumption of boiled potatoes. However, there has been an increase in consumption of *pommes frites* (fried potatoes) and potato-based snacks. This has partly to do with the strong increase in fast food (so-called "street kitchens"), where earlier only hot dogs were sold, but which now offer hamburgers, grilled chicken, and other dishes.

Different types of fast food or ready-made dishes are also being used for the main hot meal, served in the afternoon after parents come from work and children from school. In Sweden and Finland they also eat hot meals for lunch, either in cantinas, cafeterias, or street kitchens. Many Danes and Norwegians, who earlier enjoyed their lunches of open sandwiches, are now choosing hot fast food or cold salads for lunch. Open sandwiches are also being challenged by new varieties made from French baguettes or Italian ciabatta. Whereas the extravagant open sandwich had to be eaten on a plate with a fork and knife, the baguette and ciabatta sandwiches, with fillings of ham, cheese, or shrimp, can be taken away and eaten while standing or walking; at the same time, these sandwiches have more substance than the original, less substantial English sandwiches.

Drinking habits are changing in the direction of a more southern European style. Alcohol is still important for festive situations, but wine consumption is increasing rapidly compared to consumption of beer and strong liquor. Coffee is still brewed and drunk in the same way (what is often called American coffee), but new coffee bars are growing up all over, offering cappuccino, cafe latte, and espresso.

Important factors behind these changes are increased wealth and prosperity, travel by Nordic people to Mediterranean countries, an influx of new products from southern Europe, Africa, Asia, and the Americas, and the new urban lifestyle promoted through mass media. However, the break with tradition is not complete, because the new trends are mainly affecting smaller groups, such as urban, educated young people with relatively good financial freedom. This probably indicates that more pronounced changes will take place in coming generations.

See also **Germany, Austria, Switzerland**; **Lapps**; **Low Countries**; **Russia**.

BIBLIOGRAPHY

Becker, Wulf, ed. *Befolkningens kostvanor och näringsintag i Sverige 1989*. Uppsala, Sweden: Livsmedelsverkets förlag, 1994.

Bringeus, Nils Arvid. *Mat och måltid. Studier i svensk matkultur*. Stockholm: Carlsson Bokförlag, 1988.

Bringéus, Nils-Arvid. *Man, Food and Milieu. A Swedish Approach to Food Ethnology*. East Linton, Scotland: Tuckwell Press, 2001.

Fagerli, Rønnaug Aarflot. *Endringer i nordmenns matvaner på 80- og 90-tallet*. Lysaker, Norway: Statens Institutt for Forbruksforskning, 1999.

Fagt, Sisse, Margit Velsing Groth, and Niels Lyhne Andersen, eds. *Danskernes kostvaner 1995*. Copenhagen: Fødevaredirektoratet, 1999.

Gísladottir, Hallgerður. *Íslensk matarhefð*. Reykjavik: Mál og menning, 1999.

Grøn, Fredrik. *Om kostholdet i Norge fra omkring 1500-tallet og op til vår tid*. Oslo: Det Norske Videnskaps-Akademi/ Jacob Dybwad, 1941.

Grøn, Fredrik. *Om kostholdet i Norge indtil aar 1500*. Oslo: Det Norske Videnskaps-Akademi/Jacob Dybwad, 1927.

Notaker, Henry. *Ganens makt*. Oslo: Aschehoug, 1993.

Olsson, Alfa. *Om allmogens kosthåll: studier med utgångspunkt från västnordiska matvanor*. Lund, Sweden: Gleerup, 1958.

Riddervold, Astri. *Lutefisk, Rakefisk and Herring in Norwegian Tradition*. Oslo: Novus, 1990.

Roos, Eva. *Social Patterning of Food Behaviour among Finnish Men and Women*. Helsinki: National Public Health Institute, 1998.

Siggaard, Niels. *Fødemidlerne i ernærings-historisk Belysning*. Copenhagen: Nielsen and Lydiche, 1945.

Swedish IBP Committee. *Food and Nutrition Research in Denmark, Finland, Norway, Sweden*. Stockholm: The Swedish IBP Committee, 1970.

Talve, Ilmar. *Folkligt kosthåll i Finland*. Lund, Sweden: CKW Gleerup, 1977.

Henry Notaker

NOSTALGIA. The elusive word "nostalgia" is formed from two Greek roots: *nostos* ("return home") and *algia* ("pain"). The *Oxford English Dictionary* defines nostalgia as "a form of melancholia caused by prolonged absence from one's home or country; severe homesickness." In her remarkable book *The Future of Nostalgia*, Harvard professor Svetlana Boym says that the word was coined in 1688 by the Swiss doctor Johannes Hofer to identify the homesickness of Swiss soldiers who reacted physically to the hearing of certain folk melodies and the eating of rustic soups while on missions away from home. She centers her study on the effects of leaving one culture and residing in another, and of exploring cities rich in archaeological layers of memory. She also distinguishes nostalgia as either being restorative, as in recovering a lost home, or reflective, as in shaping a certain way of thinking about a particular time and place. In the latter, memory becomes a transformative and a reconstructive power.

The Idiom of Exile
In politics, art, music, literature, psychology, and even pop culture, nostalgia is the idiom of exile with, as Boym says, Adam and Eve as prototypes. While it may be a stretch to imagine their longing for the prelapserian apple after they left the Garden of Eden, it is certainly true that through the years the exiles and emigrants that followed their path from their native land to another country either tried to replicate the foods of their homeland or the taste sensations of their childhoods. Almost without exception French chefs, especially when transplanted to America, nostalgically craved the simple soups, daubes, and *pot-au-feux* of their childhood. The four-star chef Fernand Point believed that his mother's cooking was the best kind of cooking, and his disciples Paul Bocuse and Alain Chapel also went back to the simpler foods of the countryside in a movement called nouveau cuisine that captured immediate attention in France and abroad. Known as *cuisine de meres*, these ancestral cooking ideas perpetuated in their respective provinces fed their souls as well as their bodies. Nostalgia proved to be a powerful force.

Nostalgia in Literature
Literature, moreover, abounds with powerful nostalgic works like Jean Jacques Rousseau's *Confessions* and Henry David Thoreau's *Journal*—both motivated by early memories of a purer, more innocent, psychological, as well as physical, place to which there is no possible return except through memory. It was Marcel Proust, however, who irrevocably linked the subjective and often unreliable vagaries of memory with the particularity, sensory modality, and physical presence of food. In pursuit of vanished time, he found a transfiguring moment in the taste of a madeleine dipped in a cup of lime flower tea. Although he frequently had passed the golden shell-shaped French cookies in patisseries, it was not the sight or taste of the madeleine itself or even the tea, but the sensation, or Baudelairean correspondence, that immediately took him back to those Sunday mornings in Combray with his Aunt Leonie when he was a treasured child and not the world-weary adult he had become. The remembrance of

The old New England kitchen is evoked in this circa 1900 photograph of Quaker women gathered around a Nantucket hearth. Nostalgia for old-time foodways is everywhere evident in this picture, although distorted by Victorian notions about the past. A foot warmer is prominently displayed on the tea table instead of under the feet of the elderly woman facing the hearth. Spinning wheels abound, and the woman on the left is wearing a bonnet, which was only worn in public, not in the house. Finally, in spite of the clutter of utensils on the hearth, there is no fire. ROUGHWOOD COLLECTION.

food and, more specifically, the eating of a meal became a trigger point to his self-discovery.

Memories of a wistfully longed for earlier time exist not only in novels, but also in the various autobiographical forms. In *Memories of My Life*, Auguste Escoffier remembered his childhood in Villeneuve-Loubet and wrote about watching his grandfather toast bread and spread it with a particularly strong local cheese called *brousse*. One Sunday, when the young Escoffier tended the fire while his grandfather went to church, he prepared the same cheese toasts, which he then savored with a glass of sweet wine. Seen from the perspective of the mature and successful chef he had become, the incident was but one example of how easy it had been for him to satisfy both his curiosity and his gourmandise. In other personal narratives, odors rekindled memories of other kitchens. Writing about growing up in his mother's boarding house in a *Feast Made for Laughter*, Craig Claiborne described the smell of chopped onions, celery, green sweet peppers, and garlic sautéing together in butter or oil. The smell pervaded the kitchen and in his memory seemed the basis for seemingly hundreds of dishes his mother prepared and that he always identified with "southern cooking" and home. And in James Beard's *Delights and Prejudices*, beach breakfasts of sautéed razor clams gathered along the Oregon coast vie with the Welsh rabbit of the family's Chinese cook to epitomize all that was wonderful about his childhood in Portland.

The sights, smells, and tastes of the holidays almost without exception also evoke nostalgia. In his testament to childhood, *My Father's Glory; and, My Mother's Castle: Memories of Childhood*, Marcel Pagnol recreated his Provençal childhood through the eyes of an aging and successful filmmaker. In this autobiography there are scenes about a small boy exploring the streets of Marseille, and about the family's trips to their rented vacation home in the hills where the young Pagnol learned to hunt, trap, and explore the caves and the forest. Neither before nor since was the Christmas holiday in that place so exciting and memorable. Thrushes that he and his friend had trapped "tumbled from branch to spit," a small pine tree from the forest occupied the corner of the room, and on its branches hung hastily assembled presents, and after the Christmas Eve meal, the family feasted on dates, crystallized fruit, whipped cream, and the *marrons glaces* that his uncle had brought from the city. Seeing his father and uncle greet each other, Pagnol felt a new emotion and as a child recognized real friendship for the first time while savoring the *marrons glaces*.

Autobiographies and memoirs that are driven by taste, by memory, and by real life communicate reality in a basic way. When asked about why she wrote about food rather than love, war, sorrow, and death, M. F. K. Fisher simply said that our human hungers for security, warmth, love, and sustenance were inseparable. And she, more than any other American gastronomical writer, combined autobiography and her philosophy of the art of eating to create a hybrid genre called the culinary memoir. Whether she gently folded recipes into her narratives or simply explored the bliss or misfortune of family feasts, vegetable snobbism, the best oyster stew she ever ate, or learning to dine alone, she established the familiar "I myself" pattern that echoes through contemporary culinary food writing. The note of nostalgia or longing for an ideal past that can only be repossessed symbolically by familiar foods—a note that pervades the most memorable memoirs—has been given a voice in her distinctive first-person style. And the unremitting use of gastronomy as a kind of surrogate to ease all human longings has found a varied expression in her narratives.

M. F. K. Fisher has had many imitators because the act of remembering has become a dominant part of how writers—especially cookbook authors—thought about food in the last decade of the twentieth century and continue to do so. Some memoirs have been straightforward records of the author's life and his experience of memorable meals, and recipes have been either abundant or completely absent. In the best of these memoirs, however, the recipes have become an extension of the text. They function as a kind of chart of the emotions evoked by meals or certain moments frozen in time. Other memory-plus-recipe books have been plainly cookbooks in which nostalgia functions as a stylistic devise. Headers tout Aunt Tillie's doughnuts and Uncle Jerry's barbecue, or evoke quaint breadboxes lined along Formica counters or that exciting aperitif sipped in a café along the Boulevard St. Germaine. Unfortunately, their authors often lack the authentic voice of M. F. K. Fisher, and their work does not resonate with the depth of continuous reminiscence.

Whether it is a once-in-a-lifetime Reine de Saba, a comforting Toad-in-the Hole, or an ordinary macaroni and cheese meal, the pleasures of the table need a writer to transcribe them, and a writer needs a sensibility that is shaped by empathy with the conditions of time past as well as time present. Nostalgia is a powerful motivator.

See also **Art, Food in,** *subentries on* **Literature** *and* **Poetry; Beard, James; Comfort Food; Cookbooks; Escoffier, Georges-Auguste; Fisher, M. F. K.; Sensation and the Senses.**

BIBLIOGRAPHY

Beard, James. *Delights and Prejudices.* New York: Atheneum, 1964.

Beck, Simone. *Food and Friends: Recipes and Memories from Simca's Cuisine.* New York: Viking, 1991.

Boym, Svetlana. *The Future of Nostalgia.* New York: Basic Books, 2001.

Claiborne, Craig. *A Feast Made for Laughter.* New York: Doubleday, 1982.

Colwin, Laurie. *More Home Cooking: A Writer Returns to the Kitchen.* New York: HarperCollins, 1993.

Ehrlich, Elizabeth. *Miriam's Kitchen: A Memoir.* New York: Viking, 1997.

Escoffier, Auguste. *Memories of My Life.* Translated by Laurence Escoffier. New York: Van Nostrand Reinhold, 1997.

Field, Carol. *In Nonna's Kitchen: Recipes and Traditions from Italy's Grandmothers.* New York: HarperCollins, 1997.

Fisher, M. F. K. *The Art of Eating.* New York: Macmillan, 1954.

Franey, Pierre, with Richard Flaste and Bryan Miller. *A Memoir of Food, France, and America.* New York: Knopf, 1998.

Fussell, Betty. *My Kitchen Wars.* New York: North Point Press, 1999.

Grammatico, Maria, Simeti Grammatico, and Mary Taylor. *Bitter Almonds: Recollections and Recipes from a Sicilian Girlhood.* New York: Morrow, 1994.

Hazelton, Nika. *Ups and Downs: Memoirs of Another Time.* New York: HarperCollins, 1989.

Kamman, Madeleine. *When French Women Cook: A Gastronomic Memoir.* New York: Atheneum, 1976.

Knopf, Mildred O. *Memoirs of a Cook: Yesterday and Today.* New York: Atheneum, 1986.

Kotre, John. *White Gloves: How We Create Ourselves Through Memory.* New York: The Free Press. 1995.

Lang, George. *Nobody Knows the Truffles I've Seen.* New York: Knopf, 1998.

Olney, Richard. *Reflections.* New York: Brick Tower Press, 1999.

Pagnol, Marcel. *My Father's Glory; and, My Mother's Castle: Memories of Childhood.* Translated by Rita Barisse. San Francisco: North Point Press, 1986.

Proust, Marcel. *A la recherche du temps perdu.* Edited by Pierre Clarac and Andre Ferre. Paris: Gallimard, 1954. The authoritative edition.

Reichl, Ruth. *Tender at the Bone: Growing Up at the Table.* New York: Random House, 1998.

Schiavelli, Vincent. *Bruculinu, America: Remembrances of Sicilian-American Brooklyn, Told in Stories and Recipes.* Boston: Houghton Mifflin Company, 1998.

Thompson, Sylvia. *Feasts and Friends: Recipes from a Lifetime.* San Francisco: North Point Press, 1988.

Joan Reardon

NOUVELLE CUISINE. The expression "nouvelle cuisine" has been used several times in the course of the history of cooking, particularly in France in the middle of the eighteenth century. It was introduced to subordinate the practice of cooking to principles of chemistry that were to be established by Lavoisier later on. People had mixed feelings about it: for instance, Voltaire wrote "I must say that my stomach does not at all agree with the 'nouvelle cuisine.'"

Origin

Today nouvelle cuisine refers to a trend of opinion that appeared in France in the 1960s. At the time, it caught on rapidly and was a great international success. Yet, as it got tangled up in its contradiction, it stopped being fashionable, and nowadays it has a negative connotation. In spite of that, it was an innovative and quite important movement, which brought about a revolution within the "grande cuisine" whose lessons are still present in the grand chefs' minds.

Among the precursors of the movement were Fernand Point, Alex Humbert (who first made the *petits legumes*), André Guillot, and Jean Delaveyne, former chef at Buckingham Palace; they were those who questioned Auguste Escoffier's heavy heritage. They rejected the overused *fonds de sauce* as well as the so-called Allemande (German) sauce, a light one, and Espagnole sauce (Spanish), a dark one, gravies that were the basis of all kinds of rich and little refined dishes whose taste was almost always the same, since the products lost their specificity when cooked. They made their sauces less rich, highlighting the freshness and the quality of the products, thus paving the way for a revolutionary generation who was to shake up the tradition.

One has to bear in mind that at the beginning, the chefs of the nouvelle cuisine were not outsiders to French cooking. On the contrary, they were the brilliant pupils of the greatest traditional chefs. The revolution in cooking came from within the Michelin-starred restaurants. Paul Bocuse, Alain Senderens, Jean and Pierre Troigros, Alain Chapel, Michel Guerard, when very young, all started studying the traditional way, a painstaking, difficult time of apprenticeship, moving from one place to another almost in the same way as the students who graduate from different universities. An important characteristic of the movement was friendship. Although French chefs are usually individualistic, even selfish, these young chefs were always in contact, telling one another of their discoveries, discussing their problems, and so on. Today, they still do it, although they themselves have become the symbols of a new tradition.

Characteristics of Nouvelle Cuisine

Nouvelle cuisine has several characteristics. Most important were the quality and the freshness of the products chefs used. They went shopping to the market every morning and looked for the best products, and never used any preservatives, deep-frozen food, or any product that was not absolutely fresh. They did not offer a menu card with a long list of dishes that never changed, the reason being that such a long list required having a great quantity of products available. As a result the leftovers would necessarily lose their freshness and thus could not be used. Instead, they offered a reduced number of recipes that kept changing every day according to their market shopping. At the time, in Paris, this was made easier thanks to Les Halles, a huge market right in the heart of the city, within walking distance of every restaurant. Because they were looking for quality, the chefs became more and more attracted by unusual, exotic products. Foreign influences prevailed, particularly those of North Africa (Morocco,

especially), Italy, China, and Japan. In 1960 Shizuo Tsujui opened the first school of French cuisine in Japan, which multiplied the cultural exchanges between the two countries. So much so that in 2000, Alain Senderens remarked "the nouvelle cuisine is now Japanese."

In the new style of preparations, there were no *fonds de sauces* used in the dishes any more. Sometimes, short juices, quickly made, were turned into a small quantity of sauce, which was to be served on fresh, only lightly cooked products.

The spices banished from the French cuisine since the seventeenth century were now back in use; contrary to the Middle Ages, they were no longer used in large quantities, but in small touches and only to rouse the flavors that would blend with those of the products. The effect they aimed at was to enhance the quintessence of the product, that is to say that sauces or spices were only used to bring out the product's taste and qualities, not as a substitute for them.

The approach was similar to that of previous cuisine movements. The new chefs stressed the importance of nutrition and its consequence for people's health. They wanted to change the image of an obese gastronome into that of the slim, smart dilettante so much in vogue in the magazines of the 1960s. For their female clients, always anxious to watch their figures, the chefs felt urged to contrive new recipes that could be delightful without being rich. Indeed, it is significant to note that the first book written in 1976 by Michel Guerard was *La cuisine minceur*.

As a result, less food was served; of course what each dish lacked in quantity had to be replaced by better quality and a better esthetic presentation. It is true that the grande cuisine had always included an element of display and ceremony: As the dishes were prepared for all the guests present, the dinners were organized as a ceremony for the whole party, to such an extent that, at the beginning of the nineteenth century, Antonin Carême defined the *patisserie* (pastry cooking) as a branch of architecture. Instead, the new chefs replaced the presentation of entire dishes with that of individual plates; what was considered beautiful and attractive was not the whole chicken, the whole *pate en croute*, or *baba*, but the layout of the food on each plate that the guest was about to eat. To serve the dishes, the chefs no longer enacted their ritual at the pedestal tables on which they used to carve the meat or flambé the basses. They brought each guest their own plates, with the food previously prepared. Sometimes, it was hidden under shining dish covers the waiter would take off as a surprise, once the plate was set in front of the guest. Then the guests would appraise the esthetic aspect of the layout and enjoy the all-pervading fragrances of the food.

The chefs were always in search of new products and new aromas. Similarly they also kept looking for new techniques. As they were the best technicians of their generation, they began using all the new tools available:

cutter blenders, food processors, nonstick materials, and so forth. The relationship between food and fire had become a central problem, so they started experimenting with new methods such as cooking under vacuum, microwave ovens, and steam ovens. Yet this did not mean that they ignored some of the old methods; in fact quite a number of them were brought back into fashion, for instance, the *cuisson en croute de sel* and steam cooking. Moreover the fact that they had learned how to control the use of refrigeration enabled them to use new ways of preparing the food or carving the meats, which otherwise would not have been possible.

A Cultural Phenomenon

First and foremost, the nouvelle cuisine was a genuine revolution accomplished by the chefs themselves, more precisely the best of them. However, the newspapers and other media played an important part in the overall outcome. Raymond Oliver was the first to appear on a weekly TV show, which lasted for fourteen years and made him a star. Other chefs also became stars, which was seldom the case before that.

The expression "nouvelle cuisine" owes a great part of its success to two journalists, Henri Gault and Christian Millau (who for the first time in 1969 published the *Nouveau Guide*, followed in 1971 by the *Guide Gault et Millau*, a monthly magazine which soon became popular and had a great influence on the chefs as well as on their clients). Besides, at the time, the expression itself fitted nicely into a whole set of new trends of thought, of things or events which had appeared after World War II, for instance *la nouvelle critique litteraire* (the new literacy criticism), *le nouveau roman* (the new novel, with Alain Robbe-Grillet, Nathalie Sarraute, and Nobel Prize winner Claude Simon), and *la nouvelle vague* (the new wave) in the cinema with Alain Resnais, Jean-Luc Godard, François Truffaut, and Claude Chabrol. Traditional guides, the *Michelin* in particular, had already acknowledged the worthy chefs by giving them one to three stars: for example, Paul Bocuse was awarded three stars in 1965, Haberlin, in 1967, and Troigros and Barrier, in 1968. The new *Gault et Millau Guide* quite cleverly introduced a new distinction between the nouvelle cuisine chefs and the traditional ones. Later on the distinction was noted by a printed symbol, the former having a red one and the latter a black one.

Heyday and Demise

In 1973, in number fifty-four of their guide, Gaut and Millau published the ten commandants of nouvelle cuisine, among which they advocated that one should reduce cooking time, use best-quality products and products fresh from the market, offer a shorter menu, limit the use of modern technical tools, while keeping open to new developments, do away with marinades and game hanging, cook sauces that were less rich, respect dietary rules, use a simple estheticism, and be creative. To these commandments, they added another one: friendship.

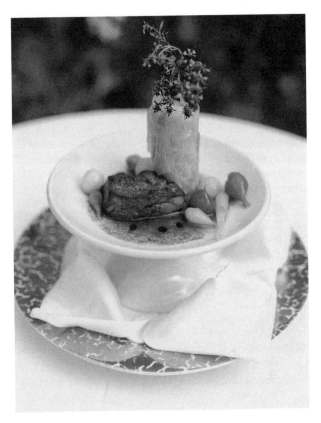

Nouvelle cuisine has been described as a blending of Japanese food presentation with French cooking techniques. The concept has taken on a life of its own in the hands of its imitators. In this interpretive study, a tiny piece of meat is served with miniature vegetables ("bonsai" vegetables to food critics), while an upended pastry serves as a vertical element topped with sprigs of blooming thyme. Is it art, or campy novelty? PHOTO BY ANDRÉ BARANOWSKI.

From then on, nouvelle cuisine became quite fashionable. It was everywhere, on television, on the radio, in the newspapers; people talked about it and held controversial discussions. The chefs who had become real stars were rich enough to purchase their own restaurants and become their own masters. The economic boom of the 1960s and the 1970s boosted the careers of the chefs, providing them with much money, which of course incited other less-gifted chefs to follow suit. Unfortunately for several of them, what ought to have been simple, original, or healthy food became approximate, ridiculous, meager food. The journalists who had praised the best chefs, now did the same with drudges, and gave the seal of quality to poor, ridiculous, and botched dishes. As a result, the movement was quite discredited though the greatest chefs were never criticized by those who blamed their imitators. By the 1980s, nouvelle cuisine had lost its appeal and today it is no longer used; it even has turned into a pejorative connotation.

The concepts used by the chefs who inspired them predominate within today's grande cuisine, not only in France, but the world over. Products must be selected with a ruthless eye on quality, wines and dishes matched with flair, cooking times short and accurate, and sauces lighter. Judicious blending of foreign trends and customs is a major element. An attractive plate is served, the food displayed simply and esthetically. An open mindedness and a concern for nutrition and diet are the essential ingredients binding the whole approach. Today, there cannot be a grand chef in the world who has not in some way or other been influenced by the nouvelle cuisine ethos.

See also **Carême, Marie Antoine; Cuisine, Evolution of; Escoffier, Georges-Auguste; Fads in Food; France; Icon Foods.**

BIBLIOGRAPHY

Beauge, Benedict. *Aventures de la cuisine française.* Paris: Nil, 1999.

Brousse, Jean, and Thibault Leclerc. *Les Étoiles de la gastronomie française.* Bottin Gourmand, 1998.

Gault, Henri, and Christian Millau. "Vive la nouvelle cuisine française. *Nouveau guide Gault et Millau* 54 (1973).

Gault, Henri, and Christian Millau. *Gault et Millau se mettent a table.* Paris: Stock, 1976.

Guerard, Michel. *La Cuisine minceur.* Translated by Narcisse Chamberlain with Fanny Brennan. New York: Morrow, 1976. Originally published by Laffont in 1976.

La Nouvelle cuisine, avec de nouveaux dessins de table et vingt quatre menus-Paris. Paulus du Mesnill, 1738.

Marin, François. *Les dons de comus.* Paris, 1739.

Jean-Philippe Derenne

NUTRACEUTICALS. There are many ways to think about food. In the simplest sense, food is fuel. Food provides the energy needed to perform daily functions and maintain normal metabolic processes. But we all know that food is more than fuel. Food contains nutrients that are essential to prevent diseases. For example, scurvy will occur if vitamin C is not continually present in the human diet. Similarly, blindness can occur where diets are deficient in vitamin A. The "essential nutrients"—those that are needed to prevent specific diseases—have been a major focus of human nutrition research for the past century. Through this research we have determined the amount of each essential nutrient required to prevent disease in populations of various ages, cultures, and genetic predispositions. What is interesting, however, is that the link between diet and disease, or more important, diet and health, cannot be entirely explained by the absence or presence of the various essential nutrients in our diets. And so today, a multitude of components that are found in foods are being investigated to determine what, if any, role they play in maintaining health and reducing the risk of disease. Numerous phytochemicals (plant chemicals)

that occur in fruits and vegetables are taking center stage in this research, as more evidence accumulates regarding their health-promoting properties (Beecher, 1999).

Human Nutrition Research

Concurrent with these new activities in nutrition research is a reevaluation of the medicinal practices of past and present cultures. These traditional medicines are based largely on the use of plant materials. Chinese medicine, which predates modern medicine by thousands of years, employs a vast array of botanical materials for the treatment of disease and the maintenance of health. Similarly, East Indian Ayurvedic medicine, early European folk medicine, and native North American medicine are based largely on the use of plant materials.

Health-Promoting Foods

Today the exploration and exploitation of the disease-fighting properties of a multitude of phytochemicals found in both food and nonfood plants have created a renaissance in human health and nutrition research. At the same time, many opportunities for the development of novel dietary products have been created. With all new fields of study come new terms. "Nutraceuticals" and "functional foods" are two new terms used to describe health-promoting foods or their extracted components. Although debate continues regarding the exact meaning of these terms, it is convenient to consider nutraceuticals as healthful products that are formulated and taken in dosage form (for example, capsules, tinctures, or tablets). Functional foods, on the other hand, are products that are consumed as foods, and not in dosage form.

The beneficial role of many nutraceuticals and functional foods may relate to their protective effects against degenerative diseases, such as cancer and cardiovascular disease. Typically the active ingredient(s) in the food or supplement is believed to help the body combat metabolic processes that lead to degenerative conditions. In this way, supplementing the diet with beneficial phytonutrients may reduce the risk of degenerative diseases

NEURODEGENERATIVE PROCESSES

Foods and supplements are also being examined for their effects on neurodegenerative processes. Blueberries have recently been shown to reverse some of the losses in memory and motor skills that occur during aging (Joseph et al., 1999). Gingko biloba supplementation may be effective in the prevention and treatment of Alzheimer's disease.

ANTICANCER AND CARDIOPROTECTIVE PROPERTIES

The anticancer and cardioprotective properties of plant flavonoids and isoflavonoids are being investigated in human health and nutrition research. In the field of biotechnology, genetic techniques are being developed to control the synthesis of flavonoids and isoflavonoids in various food crops (Dixon and Steele, 1999).

during aging. These concepts are well illustrated by the example of dietary antioxidants.

There is overwhelming evidence to suggest that oxygen and its highly reactive by-products are responsible for oxidative damage ("rust") to biomolecules in our bodies. Oxidative damage to biomolecules is believed by many to be a significant factor in the etiology of many degenerative diseases and the aging process itself. Oxidative damage to cellular DNA is an underlying element in the initiation of cancer. Similarly, oxidative damage to low-density lipoprotein in the blood is a causal agent in the development of atherosclerotic plaque in cardiovascular disease. It has been suggested and supported by various types of evidence that consuming antioxidants may provide greater protection against the deleterious effects of oxidative damage (Ames et al., 1993).

Several groups of plant phytochemicals, including carotenoids, tocopherols, and polyphenolics, are extremely effective antioxidants; these antioxidants are found at various levels in fruits, vegetables, and nonfood plants. Thus, with respect to the terms "nutraceutical" and "functional foods," a fresh or processed fruit or vegetable that is particularly high in antioxidant phytochemicals could be considered a functional food. The high antioxidant level may be a normal characteristic of the plant, or may be due to phytochemical fortification during manufacture of a processed food product. A nutraceutical may be an antioxidant phytochemical concentrate, having been extracted from raw materials and formulated as a standardized capsule or tablet (Hasler, 1998).

Challenges and Opportunities

The field of nutraceuticals and functional foods is new, and many gaps exist in the knowledge base. For example, it is widely accepted that the health-promoting properties of foods are not necessarily due to single components, but rather a few or several active ingredients. This creates a significant paradigm shift from the pharmaceutical model, which is based on the efficacy of

single agents. Many of the bioactive phytochemicals under investigation have long been ignored, thus methods for their handling and measurement are lacking. Manufacturers wish to make specific claims of health benefits on their product labels. Clearly such claims must be based on solid scientific evidence, which to date is often lacking. Government regulatory bodies also face challenges in this new category of health products, which lies between foods and drugs. However, all parties share the desire to improve personal and public health through diet modification, to reap the consequent social and economic benefits.

The field of nutraceuticals and functional foods is at times confused, or at least lumped together with the field of biotechnology and genetic modification. The two areas are distinctly different, although there is some potential for overlap. Techniques in genetic modification may be applied to enhance the phytochemical content of food and nonfood plants. Although the complex series of biochemical reactions used by plants to synthesize specific phytochemicals is often not well understood, there is tremendous potential to harness the plant's sophisticated biochemical machinery to synthesize valuable compounds and ultimately enhance human health.

See also **Antioxidants; Biotechnology; Crop Improvement; Dietary Assessment; Dietary Guidelines; Ethnobotany; Ethnopharmacology; Functional Foods; Genetic Engineering; Vitamins.**

BIBLIOGRAPHY

Ames, Bruce N., Mark K. Shigenaga, and Tory M. Hagen. "Oxidants, Antioxidants and the Degenerative Disease of Aging." *Proceedings of the National Academy of Science USA* 90 (1993): 7915–7922.

Beecher, Gary R. "Phytonutrients' Role in Metabolism: Effect on Resistance to Degenerative Processes." *Nutrition Reviews* 57, no. 9 (1999): S3–S6.

Dixon, Richard A., and Christopher L. Steele. "Flavonoids and Isoflavonoids—A Gold Mine for Metabolic Engineering." *Trends in Plant Science* 4, no. 1 (1999): 394–400.

Hasler, Clare M. "Functional Foods: Their Role in Disease Prevention and Health Promotion." *Food Technology* 52, no. 11 (1998): 63–70.

Joseph, James A., Barbara Shukitt-Hale, Natalia A. Denisova, Donna Bielinski, Antonio Martin, John J. McEwan, and Paula C. Bickford. "Reversals in Age-Related Declines in Neuronal Signal Transduction Cognitive, and Motor Behavioral Deficits with Blueberry, Spinach, or Strawberry Dietary Supplementation." *Journal of Neuroscience* 19, no. 18 (1999): 8114–8121.

Wilhelmina Kalt

NUTRIENT BIOAVAILABILITY. The chemical analysis of a food gives us values for the total amounts of particular nutrients that are present. Commonly, when a food is to be analyzed, it is first treated with a strong acid, or an enzyme, that breaks up complex materials into simpler, soluble products. Thus, the starch content of a food may be measured as the amount of additional sugar found after the treatment of the food with an enzyme that acts specifically on starch, and nothing else, to break the large molecules down to glucose. Usually, if different analytical methods are compared, the one giving the highest values is chosen, on the grounds that it has extracted the nutrient in question most completely.

However, from a nutritional point of view our interest is in how much our digestive system will be able to extract in a form that can be absorbed into the bloodstream. The term "digestibility" was formerly used to designate this, but nowadays it is becoming more common to use the term "bioavailability." It must be remembered that, after a period of preliminary storage and preparatory digestion in the stomach, ingested food passes into the small intestine and it is there that final digestion occurs and the smaller, digestible molecules are absorbed. The residual gut contents are then passed into the large intestine, whose major function is the removal of water, though the presence of a large bacterial population ferments some of the otherwise indigestible components of food. Since the fermented material is not recovered in the feces it may, wrongly, be considered to have been digested, even though it is not "bioavailable."

The final measure of bioavailability must therefore be some overall response of the subject to a test dose of the food in question. If the subject is a human "guinea pig," this might be the increased level in the blood of the nutrient in question; if young, growing animals are used, it could be their rate of growth when receiving a supplement of the test food, compared with that of other animals receiving the pure nutrient. We will cite some examples below to illustrate why the subject has some importance, and how it can be studied with different nutrients.

Protein

Proteins are enormous molecules composed of chains of hundreds of amino acids. Our bodies can only build up their own proteins from single amino acids, and the absorptive system of the gut will only allow single amino acids to pass into the bloodstream. This breakdown, which is very efficient for most of the protein in ordinary foods, requires a complex series of enzymes, beginning with pepsin, which is secreted into the stomach. It is only very resistant proteins, like those in hair, that fail to be digested by the combined attacks of digestive enzymes.

In general, cooking makes proteins more digestible by loosening and breaking up some of their natural coatings. However, there is one exception—the so-called Maillard (or Browning) reaction, which occurs when a reducing sugar is heated in contact with protein under conditions of relatively low moisture. These reactions are limited to a subset of amino groups. This reaction is not very common but can occur, for example, if dried skim milk is used to fortify cookies intended for undernourished toddlers. During the baking the reactive group of the lactose in the dried milk combines with reactive groups on the surface of the protein molecules present. One of these reactive groups is attached to the essential amino acid lysine and the resulting compound is resistant to digestion, so that the protein has lost much of its nutritional value.

Niacin

The disease associated with a deficiency of the vitamin niacin (also called nicotinic acid) is pellagra, which is characterized by terrible dermatitis on parts of the skin exposed to the sun and by mental deterioration. The disease has nearly always been associated with poor people eating a diet based on corn (that is, maize) and little in the way of meat or milk. It is now known that, as the grain matures, the niacin combines with structural materials to form a complex that is not readily broken down by digestive enzymes. This gives the vitamin a very low bioavailabilty, and ordinary cooking in boiling water does not liberate it. Corn is also lower in the amino acid tryptophan than are other grains (and also lower in tryptophan than meat and milk). By means of a series of chemical reactions in the body, tryptophan can provide an indirect source of niacin.

These two characteristics of corn serve to explain its association with pellagra, which began to be seen in southern Europe when corn first became the staple food of many low-income peasant communities. However, this seemed inconsistent with the fact that pellagra was not a problem among low-income communities in Central America where corn had been the staple food for very long periods. It is now realized that a difference in the way that corn is prepared for cooking in the two geographic areas was at least partly responsible for the differing rates of pellagra. In Central America, corn is traditionally soaked in lime water, which is strongly alkaline, before being cooked and made into tortillas. This treatment, which softens the hard grains, also has the effect of releasing the niacin from its B vitamin complex and making it bioavailable. This is an interesting example of a traditional folk custom having a beneficial effect in addition to the obvious one of softening the grain. It has also been recorded that Native American groups in North America who relied on corn as their staple food, but did not have access to lime, used infusions of wood ash, which is also alkaline, for the same purpose.

Maize came from the New World. One could say, therefore, that the thousands of Europeans who suffered and died from pellagra in the 1800s did so because the first explorers who brought maize to Europe failed to bring with them the cooking instructions that had been adopted from long experience where it had been a staple food for many centuries. Furthermore, people of European origin and habits, but living in the American South, were again subject to the disease in the early 1900s.

Other Vitamins

Pernicious anemia results from a long-term deficiency of vitamin B$_{12}$. A normal mixed diet provides enough of this vitamin. However, its absorption requires the secretion of a specific "intrinsic factor" by cells in the stomach wall. These cells may atrophy, particularly in some older people, and then the vitamin in the food remains unabsorbed so that, when the tissue reserves are used up, the result is a macrocytic (large cell) anemia and progressive neurological damage. After the problem has been detected, the vitamin can be supplied by intramuscular injection.

Vitamin A is found naturally only in animal products. Many people, for lack of purchasing power or other reasons, eat little or no animal products and meet their need for vitamin A by ingesting carotene and related compounds (carotenoids) that provide the coloring of carrots and are present in all green leafy material. Carotene can be hydrolyzed by enzymes within the gut wall to form active vitamin A. However, it has very limited solubility and can be absorbed only in conjunction with fats. Unfortunately, low-income children in Third World countries who rely on carotenoids as their source of vitamin A also commonly have diets that are very low in fat, so that even a reasonable intake of carotenoids does not save them from blindness and other effects of vitamin deficiency.

Iron

Deficiency of iron and the resulting anemia is a major nutritional problem in many parts of the world. This metallic element is, of course, an essential component of hemoglobin, the oxygen-carrying chemical in our red blood corpuscles, as well as having other functions. However, iron can also be toxic if the body absorbs much more than it needs, because we have no mechanism for excreting the excess. Our bodies therefore have to regulate the absorption of iron so that very little is absorbed when we already have enough, but that we do absorb more after blood loss, or during pregnancy when the growing fetus has to be provided with its hemoglobin. It appears that there is a feedback system that informs the cells on the inner surface of the small intestine how much iron is required to be absorbed.

However, there are limits to this control, and children may die from acute iron poisoning as a result of finding iron pills and eating them as candy. A small proportion of people also absorb more iron than they need even from a normal diet and suffer from a serious disease (hemachromatosis) as a consequence. Iron, therefore, is a nutrient for which a relative low bioavailability is normal, and in fact essential.

It is estimated that adult men need to absorb about 1 milligram of iron per day to replace their losses from rubbed-off skin, and so forth, and that premenopausal women need to absorb some 50 percent more in order to compensate for losses of menstrual blood. It is commonly recommended that people consume 10 times these

levels each day, on the assumption that there will be about 10 percent bioavailability. In general, "heme iron" from meat is best absorbed, with a typical value of about 20 percent. The absorption of the iron compounds present in vegetable foods is lower and variable, but is increased if vitamin C is present in the same meal. It is particularly low from green vegetables like spinach that are relatively rich in iron but also in another compound called phytic acid or phytate. This compound can form insoluble salts with iron that inhibit its absorption. Legumes (that is, beans, lentils, and peas) are generally richer sources than the grains, but the iron compounds they contain are also less well absorbed than those in meat.

Wheat fully milled to "white flour," and used to make white bread, is particularly low in iron, and yet it can form a large portion of the diet of many people. Because of this, many technically developed countries legally required that millers add a source of iron, as part of a micronutrient supplement, to all the white flour that they produce. This is a problem for millers because the addition of ferrous sulfate, the common iron salt with relatively high availability, can catalyze the oxidation of fat in foods, producing rancid off-flavors. That can be avoided by adding the actual metal in very fine form. On chemical analysis, this form of iron is fully measured and meets the legislative standard for the iron content of white flour. However, its bioavailability is more doubtful and depends on whether the gastric acid, which it meets in the stomach, is sufficient to react with it to produce soluble salts. Even iron with the finest particle size seems to have only 20 percent of the bioavailability of the iron in ferrous sulfate.

Other Trace Minerals

Zinc provides the best example of deficiency of a trace mineral occurring in practice as the result of low bioavailability, rather than as a result of an absolute deficiency of the mineral in the diet. In the Middle East, cases were observed of young men who had failed both to grow to normal height and to reach puberty. Tests showed that these subjects did respond to dietary supplements of zinc; even though their diet was low in zinc they were not really deficient in the element. The traditional diet in the area was based on wheat, but it was not customary there when cooking wheat flour to first "raise," or leaven the dough by fermenting the flour with yeast, as in Western baking. We now realize that yeast, in addition to producing bubbles of carbon dioxide that "raise" the dough, secretes enzymes that hydrolyze the phytate present in the flour. Unfermented products, like "falafel," still contain a significant amount of phytate and, when they are eaten, the phytate binds with zinc present in the same meal to make it largely unavailable. When a diet includes more meat or fish, which are richer sources of zinc, enough remains uncombined to provide what is required for normal functions; but the young men who had failed to mature and grow were typically from poor families who ate little in the way of animal products.

Another problem with trace minerals is that they share absorption pathways and are, in a sense, in competition with each other. As a consequence, very high intakes of one element can reduce the bioavailability of another. Thus, if one were to take a high supplement of an iron salt, in order to avoid any risk of an iron deficiency, one could precipitate a deficiency of zinc since that element would no longer be so well absorbed. Equally, a particularly high intake of zinc could reduce one's absorption of copper, and so on.

There is no one "ideal diet." Our bodies can tolerate and adapt to considerable differences in the intake of nutrients, but there are limits, and it is clearly dangerous to supplement the diet with a very large amount of a single nutrient. The simplest way to maintain a reasonable balance in one's diet is to follow the traditional advice of eating a wide variety of foods.

See also **Assessment of Nutritional Status; Cooking; Disease: Metabolic Diseases; Dietary Guidelines; Ecology and Food; Functional Foods; Iron; Maize: Maize as a Food; Nutraceuticals; Nutrition; Nutritional Biochemistry; Trace Elements; Vitamins.**

Kenneth John Carpenter

BIBLIOGRAPHY

Fairweather-Tait, S. J. "Trace Element Bioavailability." *Bibliotheca Nutritio et Dieta* 54 (1998): 29–39.

Hallberg, Leif. "Perspectives on Nutritional Iron Deficiency." *Annual Review of Nutrition* 21 (2001): 1–21.

Southgate, D. A. T., I. T. Johnson, and G. R. Fenwick, eds. *Nutrient Availability: Chemical and Biological Aspects.* Royal Society of Chemistry Special Publications 72. Cambridge, U.K.: Royal Society of Chemistry, 1988.

World Health Organization. *Trace Elements in Human Nutrition and Health.* Geneva: World Health Organization, 1996.

NUTRIENT–DRUG INTERACTIONS.

The terms "nutrient-drug interaction" and "diet-drug interaction" refer to the process whereby the consumption of a food affects the absorption, metabolism, action, retention, and/or excretion of a drug, or conversely the process whereby taking a drug affects the absorption, metabolism, action, retention, and/or excretion of a nutrient.

Adverse consequences of nutrient-drug and diet-drug interactions are so common that in their 1996 accreditation standards, the Joint Commission on Accreditation of Healthcare Organizations began requiring hospitals to ensure that "patients are educated about the potential for drug-food interactions" by "[i]nstruction on potential drug-food interactions and counseling on nutrition intervention and/or modified diets, as appropriate" before they are discharged.

In the following discussion, we will first address the effects of diet and nutritional status on drug absorption, disposition, metabolism, and action; thereafter, we will address the effects of drugs on nutrient absorption, disposition, metabolism, and action, with attention to certain specific food/nutrient/drug interactions.

Terminology Used in Describing Nutrient-Drug Interactions

The following terms are useful when discussing nutrient-drug interactions:

- *Pharmacokinetics:* the characteristics of a drug's absorption, distribution, metabolic transformation (biotransformation), and excretion. Interactions affecting pharmacokinetics are the most common form of nutrient-drug interactions.

- *Pharmacodynamics:* the mechanisms of drug action and the relationships between a drug's concentration at the active site and its pharmacological effects. Interactions affecting pharmacodynamics are less common, and certainly less well-studied, forms of nutrient-drug interaction.

- *Absorption:* the rate at which, and the extent to which, a drug leaves its site of administration. Sites of drug absorption can include all surfaces of the body, and for drugs given by injection, the bloodstream. Specifically, drugs taken orally are absorbed to some extent in the mouth and stomach (if the formulation is designed for this purpose), but predominantly in the small intestine, the organ that is specifically designed for absorption. In order to be absorbed, drug particles must be broken down and dissolved in liquid, for example, by both stomach juices and the fluid you swallow when taking the pill, so that they can reach the cells of their absorption site successfully. Note, however, that there are some drugs that may be destroyed in the stomach—therefore many preparations are coated in order to pass through the stomach intact, and only be broken down when they reach the small intestine.

- *Bioavailability:* the extent to which a drug reaches its site of pharmacological action. In practice, bioavailability is measured as the extent to which the drug reaches the bodily fluid that bathes the tissue site where the drug should act. The bioavailability of a drug increases with increased absorption and distribution of the drug to its site of action, and decreases with increased metabolism and excretion of the drug before it can reach the site of action.

- *Biotransformation:* the process through which drugs, nutrients, and hormones can be metabolized, and thereby either activated or inactivated.

Host Factors Affecting the Development of Adverse Interactions between Foods and Drugs

The likelihood of adverse interactions between foods and drugs is affected by the following factors: (1) age, because older people have less metabolic reserve; (2) medical conditions, such as diabetes mellitus, that lead to abnormalities in both food and drug handling; (3) conditions, such as arthritis, that increase the likelihood that the person will be taking over-the-counter medications; (4) sex; (5) size and fat mass, which are related to a person's diet and nutritional status; (6) exclusionary diets, for example, diets from which all animal products are excluded (vegan diets); (7) the use of substances of abuse, such as alcohol, which alter the handling of both drugs and nutrients; and finally, (8) medical conditions that require the care of different specialists and multiple medications.

Effects of Foods and Food Components on Drug Absorption and Bioavailability

There are at least four ways in which foods and their components can affect the absorption and bioavailability of a drug:

- *Physicochemical binding:* The food component and the drug can bind to each other physicochemically, so that neither the drug nor the component can be absorbed. For example, the antibiotic tetracycline binds with calcium, magnesium, iron, and zinc; once bound, the antibiotic becomes unavailable—that is why this drug should not be taken with dairy products, which contain high amounts of these minerals.

- *Stability:* The food can alter the stability of the drug preparation in the stomach, so that it breaks down before it can be absorbed.

- *Gastric emptying:* The drug or food can change the rate at which the stomach empties, and therefore the rate at which the drug arrives in the small intestine. Gastric emptying is normally a three-phase process. When you begin to eat, a small amount of food mixed with stomach juices enters the small intestine. The presence of this mixture makes the small intestine send a signal to slow down gastric emptying. This slow-down allows the stomach time to thoroughly mix the food with the stomach juices, and to break down the food into small particles. Fatty foods are highly effective in slowing stomach emptying, while erythromycin, an antibiotic, increases the speed of gastric emptying.

A drug taken on an empty stomach is likely to be dumped rapidly into the small intestine. As a result, there will be only one peak in the curve describing the concentration of the drug in the blood across time. By contrast, a drug taken with food will arrive in the small intestine more slowly, and in small spurts (via the second phase of gastric emptying), so that there may be two or more peaks in this curve. Remember, though, that one job of the stomach is to break down pills into particles. If you take a pill on an empty stomach, it may arrive in the small intestine more quickly, but it may not be absorbed if the pill is not sufficiently broken up. Furthermore, a drug taken on an empty stomach will pass more rapidly through the small intestine, with the result that the time for absorption is shorter and less of the drug

may be absorbed. Finally, in the third phase of gastric emptying, approximately every 24 hours, the normal stomach has a massive series of contractions that propel larger particles and any remaining material in the stomach into the small intestine. If there are any large drug particles left behind in the stomach, this "housekeeping" emptying may lead to a sudden dumping of a large quantity of the drug into the small intestine, with a corresponding sharp peak in the blood concentration of the drug. The duration and extent of the phases of gastric emptying in response to food vary considerably from individual to individual, but is longer in women than in men, and is much longer in chronic alcoholics. Smoking while eating also delays stomach emptying.

The fourth way in which foods can affect the absorption and bioavailability of a drug is by:

- *Competition for absorption:* Many drugs use the intestine's natural transport systems—which normally transport food components—to cross the intestinal wall. They therefore compete with food components for transport. For example, L-dopa and methyldopa (drugs used to control Parkinson's disease) use the same transporter mechanism as aromatic amino acids from proteins, so absorption of these drugs is decreased if you eat a high-protein meal at the same time you take the drug.

In general, we can divide drugs into those that are best absorbed on an empty stomach (for example, most but not all antibiotics, digitalis preparations, captopril, and sucralfate); those absorbed best with food (for example, some hypertension medications such as chlorothiazide and spironolactone, and drugs for blood lipid abnormalities such as lovastatin and gemfibrozil), and those for which absorption varies by the type of preparation or formulation. For example, drugs that are enterically coated (so that they are not destroyed by stomach acid) may be more easily absorbed if they are taken with food, because a long stay in the stomach may weaken the coating just enough that it disintegrates more easily in the small intestine.

The examples given above are general rules and may not be true for the specific preparation you may be taking. Therefore, it is critical to check the package insert for your drug and to consult with your pharmacist. For example, theophylline, a commonly used asthma drug, comes in several different formulations, depending on the manufacturer. One version of theophylline is best absorbed when accompanied by a high-fat meal, while another is poorly absorbed. The rate of absorption of theophylline is extremely important because it is one of the many drugs that has a narrow therapeutic window; in other words, there is a very small difference between the concentration of drug that you need in your bloodstream for it to be effective, and the concentration at which the drug becomes toxic. For the drug to work properly, it is critical to maintain a steady level of the drug in the bloodstream—neither too little nor too much. Therefore, switching from one formulation to another has to be done carefully.

Effects of Foods and Food Components on Drug Biotransformation

Biotransformation can be divided into two phases: Phase I, in which compounds are transformed by enzymes (proteins that transform the structure of other molecules such as drugs to make them either inactive or more active), and Phase II, in which compounds are prepared for excretion in the urine by attaching a molecule that makes them soluble in water. The small intestine has some capacity for drug biotransformation, but the major site of biotransformation is the liver. Because blood from the small intestine must pass through the liver before it goes on to the rest of the body, some drugs that are readily absorbed may not be bioavailable, because they are inactivated by the liver before they can get to the site of action. Blood flow through the liver, and the size of the liver itself, decrease as people age, so some drugs may be effective at lower doses in the elderly than in the young.

The dietary factors that activate the liver enzymes are just beginning to be elucidated. These include both nutritive factors (protein, carbohydrate, and fat) and nonnutritive factors, compounds in charbroiled meat, in cruciferous vegetables such as cabbage, turnip, and broccoli, and in citrus fruits, especially grapefruit. If you are taking a drug that is activated or inactivated by liver enzymes, it is important to maintain a diet that does not vary much from day to day in order to assure a steady level of the active drug in your bloodstream. Note that large changes in macronutrient composition of your diet, for example, adoption of a low-protein diet, can also affect Phase II biotransformation, and therefore drug excretion.

Effects of Drugs on Food and Nutrient Intake and Function

Drugs can affect food and nutrient intake, either as a desired effect or as a side effect. They can alter appetite; cause nausea and vomiting; cause food aversions; alter the taste of food, decrease taste sensations, or cause the mouth to be painful; cause gastric irritation; and alter intestinal function. One class of drugs that can cause all of these problems consists of the anticancer drugs, which can potentially cause malnutrition because they can decrease food intake dramatically.

Specific Diet/Food-Drug Interactions

There is a large number of well-known food-drug interactions in which the drug's action is altered by specific dietary components. Common examples are diuretics used for hypertension, digoxin used for cardiovascular disease, coumarin anticoagulants used for blood thinning, and monoamine oxidase (MAO) inhibitors used for depression. Similarly, there are a number of drugs, such as

the drugs designed to reduce stomach acidity, that affect vitamin and mineral status, requirements, and activity.

Drugs can inhibit enzymes that may be critical for the metabolism of toxic substances in food. In the case of disulfiram, a drug used to curb alcohol consumption, the enzyme inhibition is the desired therapeutic effect. This drug inhibits aldehyde dehydrogenase, the enzyme that breaks down the aldehyde derived from alcohol consumption. As a result, people taking the drug become ill when they drink alcohol, and thus learn to avoid alcohol. For most drugs, however, food-drug incompatibility is an undesirable side effect.

General Principles

The considerations we have discussed bring us to enunciate two important general principles:

1. First, if you are taking any drug, either prescription or over-the-counter, be sure to consult your pharmacist concerning any nutrient-drug interaction for that drug.

2. Second, be sure to take both drug and food on a regular basis, so that drug absorption, action, metabolism, and excretion are consistent and predictable.

See also **Assessment of Nutritional Status; Disease: Metabolic Diseases; Enteral and Parenteral Nutrition; Health and Disease; Immune System Regulation and Nutrients; Intestinal Flora; Nutrients; Nutrition.**

BIBLIOGRAPHY

Joint Commission on Accreditation of Healthcare Organizations. *1996 Comprehensive Accreditation for Hospitals.* Regulation PF2.2.3. Oakbrook Terrace, Ill., 1995.

Utermohlen, V. "Diet, Nutrition, and Drug Interactions." In *Modern Nutrition in Health and Disease,* edited by M. E. Shils, J. A. Olson, M. Shike, and C. A. Ross, pp. 1619–1641. 9th ed. Baltimore: Williams and Wilkins, 1999.

Virginia Utermohlen

NUTRIENTS. Nutrients are those organic and inorganic compounds that a living organism must acquire from the environment to support essential life processes, including basal metabolism, growth and maintenance of body tissues, activity, reproduction, and maintenance of general health. Nutrients are normally obtained by the ingestion of foods. Organic nutrients include carbohydrates, proteins or amino acids, lipids, and vitamins. Inorganic nutrients include minerals. Water is sometimes included in a listing of nutrients.

Classification of Nutrients

Nutrients often are classified as essential or nonessential. Essential nutrients are those that cannot be synthesized in the body at all or in sufficient amounts to meet needs and, thus, must be obtained preformed in the diet. These include the essential (indispensable) amino acids, the essential fatty acids, the vitamins, and the minerals. Two amino acids are classified as semi-essential because, although they can be synthesized in sufficient quantities in the body, their synthesis depends upon a supply of an essential amino acid. Other nutrients are considered conditionally essential, meaning that they are not normally required by a healthy adult but may be required in certain disease states or at certain stages of life because of increased demand or impaired synthesis. Nonessential nutrients include those that are oxidized as fuels and those that provide carbon skeletons and amino groups for endogenous synthesis of body constituents. The term "dispensable" is sometimes used to describe these nutrients, as the nutrients are not truly nonessential: an adequate amount of carbohydrate, protein, and fat must be taken in to supply the substrates required for maintenance of blood glucose, as fuel for oxidative metabolism and synthesis of ATP, and as substrate for synthesis of body components. They are "nonessential" only in the sense that carbohydrate, fat, or protein, as well as ethanol, can be used as fuels; in that either carbohydrate or protein or even the glycerol backbone of triacylglycerols (fat) can be a source of glucose; in that any fuel potentially can be used for synthesis of most lipids; and in that amino groups from most amino acids can be used for synthesis of indispensable amino acids. Also, some food components that have health benefits and are considered important parts of healthy diets, such as fiber and phytochemicals, are not required and are not considered nutrients per se.

The following table summarizes the nutrient classes, the essential compounds in each class, and the basic functions of these nutrients in the body.

Additional information about some of these nutrients can be found below. Additional information for the other nutrients can be found under separate entries in this volume.

Niacin
The term "niacin" is used to refer to either nicotinic acid (pyridine-3-carboxylic acid) or nicotinamide (pyridine-3-carboxamide). Niacin is widely distributed in foods of both plant and animal origin. Good sources of niacin include meats, poultry, fish, legumes, peanuts, some cereals (mainly in the bran), and enriched or whole grain products. Much of the niacin in cereals is not readily available because it is esterified to complex carbohydrates or peptides.

The amino acid tryptophan also is an important precursor for synthesis of pyridine nucleotide coenzymes (see below). The estimated conversion factor for adults is 60 mg of tryptophan to 1 mg of niacin. The term "niacin equivalent" (NE) is used for expression of niacin intakes and requirements, with either 1 mg of nicotinic acid, 1 mg of nicotinamide, or 60 mg of tryptophan equal to 1 NE.

The adult recommended daily (or dietary) allowance (RDA) for NEs is 14 mg per day for females and 16 mg

per day for males (Institute of Medicine, 1998). Most mixed diets in the United States provide more than 5 mg of preformed niacin. However, for individuals consuming typical Western diets, most NEs are derived from tryptophan rather than from preformed niacin. The tryptophan content of proteins ranges from about 0.6 percent for corn to 1.5 percent for animal products. Assuming that the average tryptophan content of protein is about 1 percent, a diet for adults that contains 100 g or more of protein provides about 16 mg NEs and would by itself meet the RDA for niacin. One should note that food composition tables do not take into account the bioavailability of niacin (from plant foods) and do not include an estimate of the NE available from tryptophan in the food. The adult male RDA for NEs would be supplied by ¼ cup peanut butter, 3½ slices roast beef, 4½ cups green peas, or 15 slices enriched wheat bread.

Nicotinic acid and nicotinamide are actively absorbed from the small intestine as well as from the renal filtrate. Niacin metabolites are excreted in the urine. Defects in tryptophan absorption or reabsorption from the renal filtrate have been associated with cases of niacin deficiency (pellagra).

Niacin is essential for the formation of the pyridine nucleotide coenzymes, nicotinamide adenine dinucleotide (NAD), and nicotinamide adenine dinucleotide phosphate (NADP). Reduced forms of these coenzymes are indicated as NADH and NADPH. NAD and NADP function in oxidation-reduction reactions that are involved in the catabolism of glucose, fatty acids, ketone bodies, and amino acids. These coenzymes ultimately funnel electrons to electron-to-oxygen transfer systems, including the mitochondrial electron transport chain. These coenzymes also are essential for reductive biosynthetic reactions. In addition, NAD has a non-coenzyme function: NAD serves as the donor of adenosine diphosphate-ribose moieties for ADP-ribosylation reactions. Poly-ADP-ribosylated proteins appear to function in DNA repair, DNA replication, and cell differentiation.

Symptoms of pellagra, or niacin deficiency, include functional changes in the gastrointestinal tract and nonspecific lesions of the central nervous system. Early symptoms include weakness, lassitude, anorexia, and indigestion. Later symptoms include various gastrointestinal and mental symptoms and a bilaterally symmetrical dermatitis that affects parts of the body exposed to sunlight, heat, or mild trauma. Pharmaceutical doses of nicotinic acid cause vasodilation, and long-term use can cause gastrointestinal irritation and possibly liver damage. The tolerable upper intake level (UL) set by the Institute of Medicine (1997) is 35 mg of niacin per day for adults.

Riboflavin
Riboflavin is the common name for 7,8-dimethyl-10-(1'-D-ribityl)isoalloxazine, which also is known as vitamin B_2. Much of the riboflavin in the American diet is supplied by dairy products. Meats, especially organ meats,

TABLE 1

Summary of nutrients and their functions		*(See Appendix for complete chart of vitamins.)*
Nutrient class	**Essential compounds in class**	**Function in body**
Carbohydrates (composed of glucose, galactose, fructose, and other sugars)	None	Fuel—oxidation or storage as glycogen; Source of carbon skeletons for synthesis of various organic compounds
Proteins (composed of amino acids)	Histidine Isoleucine Leucine Lysine Methionine (and Cysteine) Phenylalanine (and Tyrosine) Threonine Tryptophan Valine	Protein synthesis; Substrate for synthesis of essential nonprotein compounds; Source of amino groups for synthesis of nonessential amino acids; Source of carbon skeletons for synthesis of various organic compounds including glucose and nonessential amino acids; Fuel—oxidation or conversion to carbohydrate or fat for storage
	Sufficient total amino acids to supply amino groups for synthesis of nonessential amino acids	
Lipids	n-6 Essential fatty acids (e.g., linoleic acid) n-3 Essential fatty acids (e.g., α-linolenicacid)	Fuel—oxidation or storage; Carbon skeletons for synthesis of various organic compounds in body; Polyunsaturated (n-6 and n-3) fatty acids are required for synthesis of eicosanoids, inositol phosphoglycerides, sphingolipids, and membrane phospholipids
	Sufficient dietary lipids to ensure adequate absorption of fat-soluble vitamins	
Vitamins B vitamins	Niacin	Synthesis of coenzymes NAD(H) and NADP(H) that participate in oxidation-reduction reactions; Substrate for ADP-ribosylation of macromolecules
	Thiamin	Synthesis of coenzyme thiamin pyrophosphate (TPP) that is required by transketolase and α-ketoacid dehydrogenase complexes
	Riboflavin	Synthesis of coenzymes FAD and FMN that participate in oxidation-reduction reactions
	Vitamin B_{12}	Synthesis of coenzymes deoxyadenosylcobalamin and methylcobalamin that participate in the metabolism of methionine and of propionyl/methylmalonyl CoA, respectively
	Folate	Synthesis of folate coenzymes, including tetrahydrofolate, methyl-tetrahydrofolate, methylene-tetrahydrofolate, and 10-formyl-tetrahydrofolate; the coenzymes are required for the metabolism of glycine, serine, methionine, and histidine, and the synthesis of purines and dTMP
	Vitamin B_6	Synthesis of coenzymes pyridoxal 5'-phosphate (PLP) and pyridoximine 5'-phosphate (PMP) that are involved in amino acid metabolism
	Pantothenic Acid	Synthesis of coenzyme A; Synthesis of acyl carrier protein domain of fatty acid synthase
Other Vitamins	Biotin	Coenzyme for synthesis of holocarboxylases
	Vitamin C	Electron donor for enzymatic and nonenzymatic reactions
	Vitamin A	Precursor of 11-*cis*-retinal required for visual function; Precursor of all-*trans* retinoic acid and other metabolites that bind retinoid nuclear receptors
	Vitamin D	Precursor of vitamin D hormone
	Vitamin E	Lipid-soluble antioxidant
	Vitamin K	Substrate for γ-glutamylcarboxylase

[continued]

TABLE 1 (CONTINUED)

Summary of nutrients and their functions

Nutrient class	Essential compounds in class	Function in body
Minerals		
Macroelements	Calcium	Regulation of cellular activities by intracellular Ca^{2+} (2^d messenger function); Activation of certain proteins; Effects on excitability of nerve and muscle tissues; Component of mineralized tissue
	Phosphorus	Substrate for synthesis of nucleotides, DNA and RNA, phospholipids, signaling molecules, creatine phosphate, and other phosphoesters; Regulation of protein function via phosphorylation of tyrosyl, seryl, or threonyl residues of proteins; Substrate for oxidative phosphorylation (ATP synthesis); Component of mineralized tissue; Acid-base buffer system
	Magnesium	Anion charge neutralization (e.g., $Mg^{2+}.ATP^{4-}$); Essential for function of certain proteins; Stabilization of DNA and RNA structures
	Sodium	Membrane potentials of all cells and excitability of nerve and muscle tissues; Major extracellular cation; Generation and maintenance of electrical and osmotic gradients; Nutrient transport
	Potassium	Major intracellular cation; Membrane potential and excitability of nerve and muscle tissues
	Chloride	Major inorganic anion in body fluids
	(Sulfur)	Not essential as sulfur because sufficient inorganic sulfur is formed from catabolism of methionine and cysteine; Synthesis of Fe-S cluster proteins, various sulfo-esters, including those in glycosaminoglycans
Microelements	Iron	Synthesis of heme proteins, iron-sulfur cluster proteins, Fe-containing metalloenzymes
	Zinc	Conformation of zinc-finger proteins; Metalloenzymes—catalytic and noncatalytic roles
	Copper	Metalloenzymes—catalytic role
	Manganese	Metalloenzymes—catalytic and regulatory roles
	Iodine	Synthesis of thyroid hormone
	Molybdenum	Synthesis of Mo-containing coenyzme
	Selenium	Synthesis of selenocysteinyl residues of selenoproteins
	Boron and Chromium?	Probably are essential
	Nickel, Vanadium, Silicon, Arsenic, and Fluorine?	Possibly are essential (Although fluorine is not known to be nutritionally essential, its health benefits in prevention of dental caries are significant and fluoride intake, mainly from water, is recommended.)
	(Cobalt)	Vitamin B_{12} contains cobalt, but inorganic cobalt is not required

eggs, and vegetables such as broccoli, spinach, and mushrooms are also good sources. Enriched flour and enriched breakfast cereals also contribute significantly to riboflavin intakes. The RDA for riboflavin is 1.3 mg for men and 1.1 mg for women (Institute of Medicine, 1998). Some amounts of common foods that would need to be consumed to supply 1.3 mg of riboflavin (assuming they were the sole dietary source of this vitamin) are 3 cups milk, 1¼ pounds beef round, 8 large eggs, 4⅓ cups broccoli, or 65 slices whole wheat bread. Daily intakes of riboflavin in the United States average about 1.5 to 2 mg for adults (Institute of Medicine, 1998).

Following ingestion, flavin coenzymes are released from noncovalent attachment to proteins by gastric acidification and subsequent proteolysis. Nonspecific pyrophosphatases and phosphatases act on coenzyme forms to release riboflavin. Covalently bound flavin coenzymes make up about 5 percent to 10 percent of the riboflavin naturally occurring in foods, and the 8α-(amino acid)-riboflavins obtained from their digestion cannot by used for resynthesis of coenzymes. Free riboflavin is actively taken up from the small intestine. Riboflavin and small amounts of riboflavin catabolites are excreted in urine.

Riboflavin is required for synthesis of flavin mononucleotide (FMN), which is riboflavin 5′-phosphate, and flavin-adenine dinucleotide (FAD). Fully reduced forms of these coenzymes are indicated by $FMNH_2$ and $FADH_2$. Riboflavin coenzymes are involved in oxidation-reduction reactions in which the ring portion of the coenzyme undergoes sequential addition or loss of hydrogens and electrons. Flavoproteins function in either one- or two-electron transfer reactions.

The flavin coenyzmes, FAD and FMN, function indispensably in oxidation-reduction reactions involved in the catabolism of glucose, fatty acids, ketone bodies, and amino acids, as well as in energy production via the respiratory chain and in reductive biosynthetic reactions.

Inadequate dietary intake of riboflavin can result in stunting of growth, a variety of lesions involving the skin and the epithelium of the gastrointestinal tract, anemia, and neuropathy. Riboflavin has a low toxicity, perhaps because of its low solubility or ready excretion in the urine. No tolerable upper intake level has been established because of a lack of suitable data.

Thiamin

Thiamin, also known as vitamin B_1, is 3-(2-methyl-4-aminopyrimidinyl)methyl-4-methyl-5-(β-hydroxyethyl)thiazole. Excellent sources of thiamin include unrefined cereal germs and whole grains, meats (especially pork), nuts, and legumes. Enriched flours and grain products in the United States contain thiamin, as well as niacin, riboflavin, iron, and folic acid.

The RDAs for thiamin are 1.2 mg of thiamin for men and 1.1 mg for women (Institute of Medicine, 1998). Typical intakes of thiamin in the United States average 1.2 to 2.0 mg per day for adults (Institute of Medicine, 1998). The recommended 1.2 mg of thiamin per day is provided by a 3½-ounce pork chop, 20 slices of whole wheat bread, 1⅔ cups of pecan halves, or 17 ounces of roasted peanuts.

Thiamin is released from its phosphate ester forms in which it is found in most natural foods by the action of pyrophosphatases and phosphatases in the small intestine. Free thiamin is absorbed by an active transport process that is probably carrier mediated. Trapping of thiamin as thiamin pyrophosphate in the mucosal cells appears to facilitate the uptake by metabolic trapping. Excess thiamin is excreted in the urine as various metabolites.

Raw fish may contain microbial thiaminases, which hydrolyze and, thus, destroy thiamin in the gastrointestinal tract. Certain thiamin antagonists that are found in coffee, tea, rice bran, and heme-containing animal products can impair thiamin uptake or utilization. Chronic alcoholism results in impaired thiamin absorption, which may be secondary to a folate deficiency. Thiamin requirements also appear to be elevated in individuals with high caloric intakes, especially when calories are derived primarily from carbohydrates, in renal patients undergoing long-term dialysis, in patients fed intravenously for long periods, and in patients with chronic febrile infections.

Thiamin is required for synthesis of thiamin pyrophosphate (TPP), which is also known as thiamin diphosphate (TDP); this may be the sole coenzyme form of thiamin. However, monophosphate and triphosphate esters occur naturally, and thiamin triphosphate has been implicated in nerve function. TPP functions in two general types of reactions in which TPP functions as a Mg^{2+}-coordinated coenzyme for "active aldehyde transfers." First, TTP is a coenzyme for the oxidative decarboxylation of α-keto acids (catalyzed by the pyruvate, α-ketoglutarate, and branched-chain keto acid dehydrogenase complexes). Second, TPP is required as a coenzyme for transketolase, which catalyzes sugar rearrangements in the pentose phosphate pathway of glucose metabolism.

Thiamin deficiency, or beriberi, affects the nervous and cardiovascular systems. Clinical symptoms include mental confusion, anorexia, muscular weakness, ataxia, peripheral paralysis, paralysis of the motor nerves of the eye, edema, muscle wasting, tachycardia, and an enlarged heart. In Western countries, symptomatic thiamin deficiency is usually observed only in association with alcoholism.

No toxic effects of thiamin administered by mouth have been reported in humans, and thiamin is readily cleared by the kidneys. Injection of doses of thiamin that are more than 200 times those required for optimal nutrition produces a variety of pharmacological effects and can even induce death because of depression of the respiratory center. No tolerable upper intake level has been established for thiamin because of a lack of sufficient data.

Vitamin B_{12}

Vitamin B_{12}, or cobalamin, consists of a central cobalt atom coordinately linked to the four pyrrole nitrogens of a heme-like planar corrin ring structure. The 5th coordinate bond of cobalt is to one of the nitrogens in a phosphoribo-5,6-dimethylbenzimidazolyl side group of the corrin ring structure, and the 6th coordinate bond of cobalt can be occupied by a number of ligands. In vitamin B_{12} preparations, this ligand is typically a cyano group that is formed by trace amounts of cyanide during purification of the vitamin from natural sources.

Vitamin B_{12} is synthesized by some anaerobic microorganisms and by some algae, such as seaweed. Most

582

plants and higher organisms do not use vitamin B_{12} as a coenzyme, and they do not synthesize it. Vitamin B_{12} is found in meat, dairy products, some seafoods, and in fortified cereals. A strictly vegetarian diet contains low levels of vitamin B_{12}, most of which come from algal sources or possibly microbial contamination associated with plant roots.

The RDA for vitamin B_{12} is 2.4 micrograms for adults (Institute of Medicine, 1998). This amount of vitamin B_{12} can be obtained from $1/10$ ounce of beef liver, 1 egg, or $2^{2}/_{3}$ ounces of canned tuna. Typical intake of vitamin B_{12} in the United States averages 3.3 to 5.6 micrograms per day for adults (Institute of Medicine, 1998).

Absorption of vitamin B_{12} is a complex process. Vitamin B_{12} in food must be released from proteins to which it is naturally bound; this is accomplished in the stomach by the acid environment and by proteolysis of proteins by pepsin. The vitamin B_{12} then binds to other proteins that have affinity for vitamin B_{12}, but these binding proteins are hydrolyzed by pancreatic proteases in the small intestine. The free vitamin B_{12} then binds to an intrinsic factor, which is a high-affinity vitamin B_{12}-binding protein secreted by the gastric glands. The vitamin B_{12}-intrinsic factor complex binds to receptors located near the end of the small intestine, and the complex is taken up by endocytosis. The intrinsic factor is degraded by lysosomal enzymes, and free vitamin B_{12} is released into the cytosol of the mucosal cells. The vitamin B_{12} is released from the intestinal mucosal cells into the plasma as a complex with another protein, transcobalamin II. The transcobalamin II-B_{12} complex is transported into tissues by receptor-mediated endocytosis; the complex is degraded in the lysosome, and the free vitamin B_{12} is transported out of the lysosome into the cytosol.

Vitamin B_{12} is excreted from the body in the urine. It is also secreted in the bile, but vitamin B_{12} secreted in the bile is normally reabsorbed via the enterohepatic circulation. Vitamin B_{12} is needed for synthesis of two coenzymes: methylcobalamin, which is a cofactor for cytosolic methionine synthase, and 5'-deoxyadenosylcobalamin, which is a cofactor for mitochondrial methylmalonyl CoA mutase.

Vitamin B_{12} deficiency seldom is caused by a dietary lack of the vitamin and most commonly is because of a defect in vitamin B_{12} absorption. Malabsorption of vitamin B_{12} can result from a lack of intrinsic factor secretion, decreased gastric acid production, or pancreatic enzyme insufficiency. Food vitamin B_{12} is malabsorbed by many elderly individuals, and it is recommended that adults older than 50 years ingest adequate vitamin B_{12} from supplements or fortified foods. Symptoms of vitamin B_{12} deficiency include megaloblastic anemia and a severe, and often irreversible, neurological disease called subacute combined degeneration.

No toxicity of vitamin B_{12} has been reported. Absorption is limited by the amount of intrinsic factor secreted. No tolerable upper intake level has been established for vitamin B_{12} because of lack of suitable data.

Vitamin B_6

Vitamin B_6 refers to several 4-substituted 2-methyl-3-hydroxyl-5-hydroxymethylpyridine compounds, which include pyridoxal, pyridoxine, pyridoxamine, and their respective 5'-phosphate derivatives. Good sources of vitamin B_6 include cereals, meat, especially organ meats, poultry, fish, starchy vegetables, and noncitrus fruits and juices.

The RDA for vitamin B_6 is 1.3 mg for adults (Institute of Medicine, 1998). The median intake of vitamin B_6 from food sources (i.e., not including supplements) is about 2 mg for men and about 1.5 mg for women. Amounts of some foods that would by themselves supply the daily RDA for vitamin B_6 include $1^{1}/_{3}$ whole chicken breasts, 2 bananas, $1^{1}/_{3}$ cups of oatmeal, 12 cups of milk, or 22 large eggs.

Phosphate derivatives of vitamin B_6 are hydrolyzed by phosphatase prior to uptake from the small intestine. Some plants contain pyridoxine as a glucoside derivative; these normally are deconjugated by a mucosal glucosidase before the pyridoxine is absorbed. Vitamin B_6 in a mixed diet is about 75 percent bioavailable, whereas the vitamin B_6 in supplements is about 90 percent bioavailable. Vitamin B_6 is absorbed by a nonsaturable passive diffusion mechanism with metabolic trapping of the vitamers by formation of the phosphate derivatives. Excess vitamin B_6 is excreted in the urine. The major excretory form of vitamin B_6 is the 4-carboxylate derivative 4-pyridoxic acid, but unmetabolized vitamin also is excreted and may be the major excretory form when very high doses of vitamin B_6 are ingested.

Vitamin B_6 is used to form pyridoxal phosphate (PLP), this vitamin's major coenzyme form. PLP binds to proteins and PLP-dependent enzymes via Schiff base formation with the ε-amino group of specific lysyl residues in the proteins. PLP serves as a coenzyme for many enzymes involved in amino acid metabolism, including aminotransferases, decarboxylases, aldolases, racemases, and dehydratases. Aminotransferase reactions convert the coenzyme between the PLP and pyridoxamine phosphate forms.

Vitamin B_6 deficiency can result in seborrheic dermatitis, microcytic anemia (because of decreased hemoglobin synthesis), convulsions, depression, and confusion. Low vitamin B_6, folate, or vitamin B_{12} intakes can lead to an elevated plasma homocysteine level. Alcoholics tend to have low vitamin B_6 status.

Some subjects taking very large pharmaceutical doses of pyridoxine have developed severe sensory neuropathy. There is some evidence for toxicity at daily doses of 500 mg or more, and a safe upper level of intake is thought to be 100 mg/day. The tolerable upper intake level set for vitamin B_6 by the Institute of Medicine (1998) is 100 mg/day for adults.

Pantothenic Acid

Pantothenic acid, also known as vitamin B_5, consists of a β-alanine moiety condensed with pantoic acid. Pantothenic acid is distributed widely in plant and animal sources. Meat (especially liver), fish, poultry, milk, yogurt, legumes, and whole-grain cereals are good sources of pantothenic acid. Pantothenic acid is present in foods in the free form and in various bound forms, including coenzyme A, coenzyme A esters, acyl carrier protein, and glucosides.

The Adequate Intake established for pantothenic acid by the Institute of Medicine (1998) is 5 mg per day for adults. This amount of pantothenic acid can be obtained by eating 2½ cups of peanuts, 6 eggs, 3 whole chicken breasts, 6½ cups of milk, or 19 slices of whole wheat bread. The average dietary intake of pantothenic acid in the United States is about 5 to 6 mg, with somewhat lower average intakes in the elderly and young children.

Dietary coenzyme A, coenzyme A esters, and acyl carrier protein are degraded enzymatically in the small intestine to release free pantothenic acid. Pantothenic acid is taken up by active transport. Approximately 50 percent of dietary pantothenic acid is available. Pantothenic acid is excreted unchanged in the urine. The kidneys regulate excretion of pantothenic acid, secreting it when plasma concentrations are high and largely reabsorbing it when plasma concentrations are in the physiological range.

Cells use pantothenic acid to synthesize coenzyme A, which consists of pantothenate linked to cysteamine by a peptide bond and to a 3′-phospho-ADP moiety via a phosphoester linkage. Coenzyme A contains a reactive sulfhydryl group that is involved in the formation of thioesters with fatty acids and other carboxylic acids. Coenzyme A plays a major role in fatty acid metabolism and in the final oxidative steps in the catabolism of all fuels. Much of the metabolism of fatty acids and certain amino acid derivatives, as well as a numerous amphibolic steps in metabolism, use coenzyme A thioester substrates and produce coenzyme A thioester products. Coenzyme A also is used for the synthesis of the acyl carrier protein domain of fatty acid synthase, a multifunctional enzyme that catalyzes palmitate synthesis. Coenzyme A is involved in oxidative decarboxylation reactions catalyzed by α-keto acid dehydrogenase complexes, β-oxidation of fatty acids, ketone body synthesis, fatty acid and triacylglycerol synthesis, amino acid and organic acid catabolism, and in synthesis of isoprenoids, cholesterol, and steroids.

A naturally occurring deficiency of pantothenic acid has not been documented reliably and is undoubtedly rare because of the wide distribution of pantothenic acid in foods. Pantothenic acid deficiency has been produced experimentally in a small number of volunteers via a pantothenic acid-free diet; these volunteers appeared listless and complained of fatigue after nine weeks on the pan-

tothenic acid-free diet. A "burning feet" syndrome that was observed among prisoners of war and among malnourished individuals in Asia may have been because of pantothenic acid deficiency, as symptoms appeared to be reduced by pantothenic acid.

Pantothenic acid is relatively nontoxic. Doses below 10 g of pantothenic acid per day do not seem to be associated with any toxic symptoms. No tolerable upper intake limit was set by the Institute of Medicine (1998) because of insufficient data.

Biotin

Biotin contains a ureido group attached to a tetrahydrothiophene ring and has a valeric acid side chain extending from the tetrahydrothiophene ring. Biotin is synthesized by bacteria, yeast, algae, and some plant species. Biotin is distributed widely in foods, existing both as free biotin and as biotin covalently bound to lysyl residues in biotinyl-proteins. Liver, whole-grain cereals, nuts, legumes, yeast, and egg yolks are relatively high in biotin. Biotin is synthesized by microflora in the large intestine, but biotin produced at that site appears to be excreted mainly in the feces.

The Adequate Intake for biotin, as set by the Institute of Medicine (1998), is 30 micrograms per day for adults. About 3 ounces roasted peanuts, 3 medium eggs, 5 cups of milk, ⅓ cup of peanut butter, or 1⅓ cups of oatmeal will provide 30 micrograms of biotin. The daily intake of biotin in Western countries is estimated to be about 60 micrograms per day.

Digestion of proteins releases biotinyl-lysine (biocytin) and small lysine-containing peptides with biotin attached covalently. These are hydrolyzed to release free biotin by a specific hydrolase called biotinidase that is present in the pancreatic digestive secretions. Free biotin is transported into the mucosal cells of the small intestine by a carrier-mediated, sodium-dependent process.

Biotin is excreted as such and as several degradation products. Degradation products include bisnorbiotin, in which the 5-carbon valerate side chain has been shortened by two carbons, and biotin sulfoxide, in which the thiophene ring sulfur has been oxidized to a sulfoxide.

The only known function of biotin in humans and other mammals is as a prosthetic group for four carboxylases: pyruvate carboxylase, acetyl CoA carboxylase, propionyl CoA carboxylase, and 3-methylcrotonyl CoA carboxylase (in the pathway of leucine catabolism). Holocarboxylase synthetase attaches biotin to the apocarboxylases in an ATP-requiring reaction; the biotin is attached by an amide bond to an ε-amino group of a specific lysyl residue in the enzyme protein. In the holocarboxylases, biotin serves as a CO_2 carrier and carboxyl donor to substrates.

A dietary deficiency of biotin is very rare because of the wide distribution of biotin in foods. Biotin deficiency with clinical symptoms of hair loss, dermatitis, and neurological symptoms has occurred in individuals consuming an abnormal diet that is low in biotin and high in raw egg white. Raw egg white contains avidin, a protein that binds biotin with a very high affinity and prevents its uptake from the intestine. Biotin deficiency may occur in individuals who routinely take certain anticonvulsants or in individuals with severe protein-energy malnutrition. 3-Hydroxyisovalerate is elevated in the urine of biotin-deficient subjects.

Intakes of biotin up to 10 mg per day have not been reported to be associated with toxicity. No tolerable upper intake level has been set for biotin because of lack of data. Inborn errors of biotin metabolism, biotinidase deficiency and holocarboxylase synthetase deficiency, can both be treated with pharmacological doses of biotin.

Vitamin C

Ascorbic acid or vitamin C is a 6-carbon lactone synthesized from glucose by plants and many animals. Humans, as well as nonhuman primates and several other species, are unable to synthesize ascorbic acid because of a lack of gulonolactone oxidase, the terminal enzyme in the biosynthetic pathway.

Ascorbic acid is found in many fruits and vegetables. Some dietary vitamin C is present as an oxidized form, dehydroascorbic acid. Cantaloupe, kiwi, oranges, lemons, strawberries, and watermelon are especially high in vitamin C. Vegetables that are rich sources of vitamin C include broccoli, red peppers, cauliflower, brussels sprouts, asparagus, potatoes, cabbage, spinach, collard greens, green peas, and carrots. Citrus juices and tomato juice are good sources of vitamin C. Many foods, such as fruit drinks and breakfast cereals, are fortified with vitamin C.

The current RDA for vitamin C is 75 mg for women and 90 mg for men (Institute of Medicine, 2000). An additional 35 mg per day is recommended for smokers. The adult female RDA is contained in $\frac{3}{4}$ cup orange juice, 1 orange, 1 kiwi, $\frac{1}{3}$ cantaloupe, 1 small sweet pepper, 2 cups broccoli, or 3 baked potatoes. Typical intake of vitamin C by adults is 70 to 100 micrograms per day.

Ascorbic acid absorption probably occurs by a Na^+-dependent system in the intestine. Bioavailability is close to 100 percent for vitamin C at doses between 15 and 200 mg but declines at higher doses. Ascorbic acid and its metabolites are excreted mainly in the urine.

Ascorbic acid acts as an electron donor, or reducing agent. Two electrons are lost, probably sequentially, with formation of semidehydroascorbic acid (free radical) and dehydroascorbic acid. Dehydroascorbic acid can be enzymatically or nonenzymatically reduced back to ascorbate or hydrolyzed irreversibly to 2,3-diketogulonic acid, which is converted to other products, including oxalate.

Vitamin C acts as an electron donor for eight mammalian enzymes: three dioxygenases that are involved in collagen hydroxylation (prolyl 4-hydroxylase, prolyl 3-hydroxylase, and lysyl hydroxylase), two dioxygenases

that are involved in carnitine synthesis (6-N-trimethyl-L-lysine hydroxylase and γ-butyrobetaine hydroxylase), 4-hydroxyphenylpyruvate dioxygenase, dopamine β-hydroxylase, and peptidylglycine α-amidating monooxygenase. Ascorbic acid may also function in nonenzymatic reduction reactions and thus acts as a water-soluble antioxidant.

An early sign of vitamin C deficiency is fatigue. With more severe deficiency, petechial hemorrhage, coiled hairs, ecchymoses, bleeding and tenderness of the gums, hyperkeratosis, joint pain, and shortness of breath may occur.

Vitamin C is relatively nontoxic. Excess vitamin C may promote the formation of oxalate kidney stones. The tolerable upper intake level, or maximum intake level likely to pose no risk of adverse health effects in most individuals, was set at 2000 mg ascorbic acid per day from food plus supplements (Institute of Medicine, 1998).

Vitamin K

Vitamin K refers to a group of compounds that are 2-methyl-1,4-napthoquinones with a hydrophobic substituent at the 3-position. Phylloquinone (vitamin K_1), which is synthesized by plants, has a 20-carbon phytyl substituent at the 3-position of the napthoquinone ring. Menaquinones (vitamin K_2) are synthesized by bacteria and have an unsaturated side chain, made up of four to thirteen isoprenyl units, instead of the saturated phytyl chain present in phylloquinone. Animal tissues contain both phylloquinone and menaquinones. In addition to these naturally occurring compounds with vitamin K activity, a synthetic form of vitamin K called menadione can be alkylated to an active form in the liver and is used in animal feeds. Human vitamin K supplements are phylloquinone.

Green vegetables are the major dietary source of phylloquinone: kale, spinach, broccoli, brussels sprouts, cabbage, and lettuce are rich sources. Some vegetable oils, especially soybean oil and rapeseed (canola) oil, are good sources. Menaquinones, which are obtained especially from liver, provide only a minor portion of the vitamin K needed to meet the requirement. The nutritional significance of menaquinones synthesized by bacteria in the lower bowel is uncertain.

The RDA for vitamin K for adults who are age twenty-five years and older is 65 and 80 micrograms for women and men, respectively (National Research Council, 1989). The RDA for males is provided by $\frac{1}{3}$ ounce of spinach or kale, $\frac{1}{3}$ cup of broccoli, $\frac{2}{3}$ cup of shredded cabbage, or $2\frac{1}{4}$ ounces of lettuce. Typical intake of vitamin K by adults is 70 to 100 micrograms per day.

Absorption of dietary vitamin K depends upon adequate lipid absorption. Vitamin K is incorporated into chylomicrons, along with other lipids, and ultimately is taken up by the liver as part of the chylomicron remnants. Vitamin K is stored in liver; the hepatic phylloquinone pool turns over more rapidly than that of menaquinones. Vitamin K is excreted predominantly as metabolites and glucuronides; these are excreted primarily in feces via the bile, but significant amounts are also excreted in urine.

The hydroquinone form of vitamin K is required for the posttranslational modification (γ-glutamylcarboxylation) of a group of proteins (referred to as Gla proteins or vitamin K-dependent proteins) during their synthesis. Vitamin K serves as substrate, or coenzyme, for an enzyme that converts targeted glutamyl residues to γ-carboxyglutamyl (Gla) residues in these proteins. This posttranslational modification of glutamyl residues is essential for the normal physiological function of vitamin K-dependent proteins. Continued function of vitamin K in γ-glutamylcarboxylation reactions is dependent upon the recycling of oxidized vitamin K (vitamin K epoxide) back to the hydroquinone form (vitamin KH_2).

Vitamin K-dependent proteins include four plasma clotting proteins (prothrombin, factor VII, Factor IX, and factor X), two plasma proteins involved in thrombin-initiated inactivation of factor V (protein C and protein S), plasma protein Z of uncertain function, and two bone proteins (osteocalcin, or bone Gla protein, and matrix Gla protein). At physiological pH, both carboxyl groups of each Gla residue are negatively charged, and these anionic residues are involved in the association of Gla proteins with Ca^{2+}.

Primary vitamin K deficiency is rare. Vitamin K-responsive hemorrhagic disease of the newborn can occur because of low vitamin K stores in the liver of the newborn and the low vitamin K content of human milk, along with other factors. In developed countries, commercial infant formulas are supplemented routinely with phylloquinone, and the practice of oral or intramuscular administration of phylloquinone to the newborn is almost universal. Vitamin K deficiency also has been reported in adults with low intakes of vitamin K who are receiving antibiotics and in patients subjected to long-term total parenteral nutrition without vitamin K supplementation. Vitamin K status should be of concern in disorders of lipid digestion or absorption and in persons treated with anticoagulant drugs that act by blocking reduction of oxidized vitamin K.

Toxic manifestations from ingestion of large amounts of vitamin K have not been reported. Menadione administration to infants has been associated with hemolytic anemia and liver toxicity, and should not be used for human supplements.

Vitamin E

Vitamin E is the term used for all tocopherols and tocotrienols and their derivatives that exhibit vitamin E activity. Tocopherols are more important sources of vitamin E. Both the tocopherols and tocotrienols consist of a chromanol head and a phytyl tail. The side chain of tocopherols is saturated, whereas that of tocotrienols con-

tains double bonds at the 3′, 7′, and 11′ positions. Four tocopherols and four tocotrienols occur naturally; they differ in the number and position of the methyl groups on the chromanol ring. The naturally occurring isomer of α-tocopherol is the 2′R, 4′R, 8′R isomer, whereas synthetic tocopherols are mixtures of all eight possible stereoisomers.

Tocopherols in foods exist primarily as the free or unesterified forms. Ester forms (e.g., α-tocopheryl acetate or α-tocopheryl succinate) are less susceptible to oxidation and are used for food fortification and for supplements. The 6-hydroxyl group on the phenolic ring is the site for esterification of fatty acids.

A variety of naturally occurring RRR-α-tocopherols and tocotrienols are supplied by foods. Tocopherols differ in their antioxidant and biological activities. Currently, the biological activity of various forms of vitamin E are expressed as units of activity in relation to that of all-rac-α-tocopheryl acetate, which is a common pharmaceutical or synthetic form of vitamin E. The unit used to express vitamin E activity is the α-tocopherol equivalent (α-TE) with 1 equivalent equal to 1.49 mg of all-rac-α-tocopheryl acetate or 1.0 mg of RRR-α-tocopherol. The majority of the tocopherols consumed in the diet are not α-tocopherol, and γ-tocopherol accounts for more than half the estimated total tocopherol intake. Rich sources of vitamin E include vegetable oils, vegetable shortenings, margarines, mayonnaise, salad dressings, wheat germ, rice bran, nuts, seeds, peanut butter, eggs, potato chips, whole milk, and tomato products.

The RDA for vitamin E is 15 mg α-TEs for adults. This amount of vitamin E could be provided by 4 teaspoons of soybean oil, ⅔ cup of margarine, 2 cups of whole milk, 4½ cups of green peas, or 2 pounds of salmon. The average intake of vitamin E from American diets is 11 to 13 mg α-TEs daily in adults not taking vitamin E supplements.

Tocopheryl esters are hydrolyzed to free tocopherol in the small intestinal lumen, presumably by pancreatic esterases. Vitamin E is absorbed with other lipids, and the majority of the vitamin E is incorporated into chylomicrons in the mucosal cells of the small intestine. The chylomicrons are secreted into the lymph and then enter the circulation. Vitamin E is taken up by the liver in the chylomicron remnants and is then either stored in the parenchymal cells of the liver, incorporated into nascent very low density lipoproteins (VLDL) that are secreted into the blood stream, or excreted via the bile. Both vitamin E and its metabolites are primarily excreted in the feces via biliary secretion from the liver. Some metabolites are excreted in the urine.

Vitamin E is the major lipid-soluble, chain-breaking antioxidant found in plasma, red cells, and tissues, and it plays an essential role in maintaining the integrity of biological membranes. Among the biological functions proposed for vitamin E, the reaction of α-tocopherol with lipid peroxyl radicals to prevent uncontrolled free radical-initiated lipid peroxidaion is the best understood. Whether other tocopherols have other roles is uncertain.

Patients with familial isolated vitamin E deficiency have clear signs of vitamin E deficiency (extremely low plasma vitamin E levels and neurological abnormalities—spinocerebellar dysfunction with progressive ataxia) but do not have fat malabsorption or lipoprotein abnormalities. Absence of hepatic α-tocopherol transfer protein impairs secretion of α-tocopherol into hepatic lipoproteins (VLDL) and appears to be responsible for the low plasma vitamin E status of patients with familial isolated vitamin E deficiency and the low delivery of vitamin E to tissues. In humans, low plasma levels of vitamin E are associated with shorter lifespans of red blood cells because of their increased susceptibility to hemolysis. Vitamin E deficiency is rarely associated with lipid malabsorption syndromes or lipoprotein abnormalities. Neurological symptoms occur in individuals with malabsorption syndromes as well as in individuals with familial isolated vitamin E deficiency.

Vitamin E is relatively nontoxic when taken by mouth. The upper tolerable intake level set by the Institute of Medicine (2000) is 1000 mg of α-TEs per day from vitamin E supplements in addition to dietary intake. Consumption of more than this increases risk of hemorrhagic damage because vitamin E can act as an anticoagulant.

Potassium

Potassium (K^+) is distributed widely in the body and is the principal cation in intracellular fluids. Like sodium and chloride ions, potassium ions exist as free hydrated ions that bind only weakly to organic molecules. Potassium functions in the maintenance of electrolytic and osmotic balances or gradients. The distribution of potassium between the intracellular and extracellular fluids is the result of ion pumps and of the permeability characteristics of cell membranes. The Na^+, K^+-ATPase pump, which moves 3 Na^+ out of the cell in exchange for 2 K^+ that are moved into the cell, is of particular importance.

Potassium is widely distributed in foods, especially in fruits and vegetables. Rich sources of potassium include fruits such as avocado, banana, cantaloupe, orange juice, and watermelon; vegetables such as lima beans, potatoes, tomatoes, spinach, and winter squash; and fresh meats.

Obligatory losses of potassium, which must be replaced, average about 800 mg of potassium per day. The estimated minimum requirement for potassium established by the National Research Council (1989) is 2 g per day for adults. Two grams of potassium are provided by 4 cups of fresh orange juice, 5½ small bananas, 5 medium potatoes, or ⁹/₁₀ pound of beef chuck. Typical Western diets provide about 3 g of potassium per day.

Over 90 percent of the potassium in the diet is absorbed from the gut into the circulation. However, although nearly all of the dietary K^+ is absorbed in the small intestine, there is normally some net secretion of K^+ in the colon that results in loss of potassium in the feces. Absorption of dietary K^+ causes a rise in the concentration of K^+ in the plasma, and this immediately stimulates physiological mechanisms to promote rapid entry of K^+ into cells so that a rapid rise in the plasma K^+ concentration is prevented. Uptake of K^+ by cells is essential in preventing life-threatening hyperkalemia. Nevertheless, in the long-term, to maintain K^+ balance, the excess K^+ from the diet must be excreted by the kidneys.

At typical potassium intakes, renal tubular secretion of K^+ is required to maintain potassium balance. Renal secretion of K^+ is under the control of various homeostatic regulatory mechanisms. The most important hormone regulating secretion of K^+ is aldosterone, the release of which is triggered by a high concentration of K^+ in plasma (or a low concentration of Na^+ or by angiotensin II). When potassium intake is high, secretion of K^+ by the colon as well as the kidney is increased to eliminate the excess potassium.

During potassium depletion, the kidney reabsorbs most of the filtered K^+, and essentially no K^+ is secreted. The small amount of K^+ excreted in the urine under these circumstances comes from the filtered K^+ that escaped reabsorption.

The high concentration gradient of K^+ between the intracellular fluid and the extracellular fluid is important for generation and maintenance of the normal resting membrane potentials across cell membranes and for excitability of nerves and muscles. Higher intakes of potassium may have beneficial effects in preventing hypertension.

Dietary deficiency of potassium does not occur under normal circumstances. Large losses can occur, by either gastrointestinal or renal routes, in cases of prolonged vomiting, chronic diarrhea, use of diuretic agents, some forms of chronic renal disease, and in some metabolic disturbances such as metabolic acidosis. Hypokalemia causes membrane hyperpolarization, and this can interfere with the normal functioning of nerves and muscles, resulting in muscle weakness and decreased smooth muscle contractility. Deficiency symptoms include weakness, anorexia, nausea, drowsiness, and irrational behavior.

Acute hyperkalemia can result from sudden enteral or parenteral increases in potassium intake to amounts of about 18 g per day for an adult. Hyperkalemia causes membrane depolarization, causing muscular weakness, flaccid paralysis, and cardiac arrhythmias. Severe hyperkalemia can cause cardiac arrest and death.

Chloride

Chloride is the principal inorganic anion in the extracellular fluids of the body. Dietary chloride comes almost entirely from sodium chloride, and a small amount comes from potassium chloride. Thus, table salt and foods or beverages that contain NaCl added during food processing or preparation are the major sources of chloride in the diet. The amount of chloride contributed by water is low compared to that contributed by salt.

The estimated minimum requirement for chloride is 750 mg/day for adults, which corresponds to about 1.3 g of sodium chloride per ¼ teaspoon of table salt). Typical salt intake in the United States is higher than this. It is recommended that daily salt intake should not exceed 6 g because of the association of high intake with hypertension.

Loss of fluids through the skin, feces, and urine cause loss of both sodium and chloride. Chloride movement tends to parallel that of sodium, and loss of sodium usually is accompanied by a similar molar loss of chloride. Thus, conditions that cause loss of sodium (e.g., heavy losses through sweating, chronic diarrhea or vomiting, trauma, or renal disease) also cause loss of chloride and can result in hypochloremic metabolic alkalosis.

Chloride is essential for maintenance of fluid and electrolyte balance. Hydrochloric acid is an essential component of the gastric juice secreted by the stomach.

Deficiency of chloride does not occur under normal circumstances. Toxicity from excess intake of chloride is not known to occur, but water-deficiency dehydration can cause hyperchloremia.

See also **Choline, Inositol, and Related Nutrients; Gene Expression, Nutrient Regulation of; Immune System Regulation and Nutrients; Malnutrition; Malnutrition: Protein-Energy Malnutrition; Nutrition; Vitamin C; Vitamins; Appendix.**

BIBLIOGRAPHY

Chow, Ching K. "Vitamin E." In *Biochemical and Physiological Aspects of Human Nutrition*, edited by Martha H. Stipanuk. Philadelphia: Saunders, 2000.

Church, Charles F., and Helen N. Church. *Food Values of Portions Commonly Used—Bowes and Church*, 11th ed. Philadelphia: Lippincott, 1970.

Institute of Medicine. *Dietary Reference Intakes for Thiamin, Riboflavin, Niacin, Vitamin B₆, Folate, Vitamin B₁₂, Pantothenic Acid, Biotin, and Choline*. Washington, D.C.: National Academy Press, 1998.

Institute of Medicine. *Dietary Reference Intakes for Vitamin C, Vitamin E, Selenium, and Carotenoids*. Washington, D.C.: National Academy Press, 2000.

Levine, Mark, et al. "Vitamin C." In *Biochemical and Physiological Aspects of Human Nutrition*, edited by Martha H. Stipanuk. Philadelphia: Saunders, 2000.

Mahan, L. Kathleen, and Sylvia Escott-Stump. *Krause's Food, Nutrition, and Diet Therapy*, 9th ed. Philadelphia: Saunders, 1996.

McCormick, Donald B. "Niacin, Riboflavin, and Thiamin." In *Biochemical and Physiological Aspects of Human Nutrition*, edited by Martha H. Stipanuk. Philadelphia: Saunders, 2000.

National Research Council. *Recommended Dietary Allowances*, 10th ed. Washington, D.C.: National Academy Press, 1989.

Shane, Barry. "Folic Acid, Vitamin B₁₂, and Vitamin B₆." In *Biochemical and Physiological Aspects of Human Nutrition*, edited by Martha H. Stipanuk. Philadelphia: Saunders, 2000.

Sheng, Hwai-Ping. "Sodium, Chloride, and Potassium." In *Biochemical and Physiological Aspects of Human Nutrition*, edited by Martha H. Stipanuk. Philadelphia: Saunders, 2000.

Suttie, John W. "Vitamin K." In *Biochemical and Physiological Aspects of Human Nutrition*, edited by Martha H. Stipanuk. Philadelphia: Saunders, 2000.

Sweetman, Lawrence. "Pantothenic Acid and Biotin." In *Biochemical and Physiological Aspects of Human Nutrition*, edited by Martha H. Stipanuk. Philadelphia: Saunders, 2000.

Martha H. Stipanuk

NUTRITION. Food is comprised of nutrients that are classified by their role in the body: the energy-yielding macronutrients (carbohydrates, protein, and fat), the essential micronutrients (vitamins, minerals, and water), and numerous other components. Although micronutrients do not supply energy to fuel the body, they are indispensable for the proper functioning of the metabolic and regulatory activities in the body. Other nonessential nutrients, such as flavonoids, phytoestrogens, carotenoids, and probiotics, also may have important health-promoting properties, and investigations are ongoing. The daily intake of a variety of foods provides energy and nutrients that are essential to the health and well-being of an individual. The relationships among food intake, nutrition, and health define the field of nutrition. More fully, nutrition is the study of food, its nutrients and chemical components, and how these constituents act and interact within the body to affect health and disease.

The scope of the field has grown in recent years and the boundaries between the science of nutrition and many other biological sciences have blurred. For example, the science of nutrition includes chemistry to study how food ingredients interact with each other; physiology to investigate how nutrients within food are assimilated into body tissues; engineering to design new fortified foods; anthropology to explore why we chose to eat certain foods in centuries past; and psychology to determine what attitudes and behaviors influence our dietary patterns today. Nutritionists often have either a college or advanced degree in nutrition or a related field, whereas clinical (human) nutrition specialists will have graduate degrees, which may include medicine, and have completed an examination for certification. Registered dietitians are nutrition professionals who are often responsible for applying nutritional science to clinical practice to promote health and treat disease. Dietitians frequently work in hospitals but also may be employed in universities, public health departments, restaurants, the food industry, and exercise facilities. Similarly, given the broad

PROFESSIONAL NUTRITION CREDENTIALS IN THE UNITED STATES

Certification Board	Type of Certification*
Commission on Dietetic Registration	*DTR:* Dietetic Technician (A.A., B.S., B.A.)
	RD: Registered dietitian (B.S.)
	CSP or *CRD:* Board certified specialist in pediatric or renal nutrition
	FADA: Fellow of the ADA (R.D. and Ph.D., M.S.)
American Board of Nutrition	Clinical Nutrition Specialist (M.D.)
	Human Nutrition Specialist (Ph.D.)
National Board of Nutrition Support Certification	*CNSP:* Certified Nutrition Support Physician (M.D.)
	CNSD: Certified Nutrition Support Dietitian (R.D.)
Certification Board for Nutrition Specialists	*CNS:* Certified Nutrition Specialist (Ph.D., M.S.)

* Type of education required for certification indicated in parentheses.
Italicized acronyms denote the professional credentials required for certification.

scope of the field, other nutrition professionals include but are not limited to physicians, biochemists, anthropologists, epidemiologists, geneticists, food scientists, and engineers.

For this review, the field of nutrition is divided into three major categories: (1) nutrition in research, (2) nutrition in clinical practice, and (3) nutrition in policy and education. An overview of nutritional research is presented, from how nutrients interact within the body and among themselves (nutritional biochemistry), to the investigation of the relationships between specific foods or food groups and the health status of populations (nutritional epidemiology). Research findings in the field provide the information needed to guide nutrition practice for the care of individuals as well as large groups of people. The development of nutrition policy comes from both research and clinical practice advances. Concise descriptions of each are given and a brief history of the field and projected directions of the future of the field are offered.

Nutrition: A Historical Perspective

Numerous advances in the field of nutrition have occurred within the last century. The major focus of nutrition research and practice shifted from concern over which foods are required to avoid nutritional deficiencies and overt illness, to what foods and supplements may be consumed to promote optimal health. Functional foods are a part of the vocabulary, and energy bars, herbal remedies, and nutritional supplement products are now widely available.

In biblical times certain foods were understood to have special healing properties; however, the concept of nutrients as essential for health is relatively new. Recent discoveries in the field have been dependent on the development of scientific methods to analyze nutrient con-

tent and interactions. Therefore, though some vitamins were understood to be essential in the early part of the twentieth century, trace elements such as zinc and selenium were not considered essential for humans until the 1970s.

As the field of nutrition has developed, it has also expanded. In 1950 the history of nutrition science during the two previous centuries was summarized by Dr. Elmer McCollum in just under five hundred pages. It would likely take ten volumes of such texts to encapsulate the nutrition-related findings and proceedings from the latter half of the twentieth century. Accomplishments in the field of nutrition over the last century are highlighted in five major eras: (1) food as energy, (2) micronutrient deficiency diseases, (3) nutrition in public policy, (4) nutrition and chronic disease, and (5) nutrition for optimal health.

Food as energy (1880–1920). By the end of the nineteenth century the major, energy-yielding components of food—protein, fat, and carbohydrate—had been identified, and nutrition research, especially concerning the metabolism of proteins and the energy composition of foods, was flourishing. Much of this work had been conducted in animals; therefore, the human nutrition experiments performed by Dr. W. O. Atwater (1844–1907) and colleagues were particularly novel. From their studies, the energy yield of carbohydrate, protein, and fat was derived (4, 4, and 9 kcal per gram, respectively), values that are still used today. Dr. Atwater also developed the first human calorimeter in the United States to measure energy expenditure. However, it was a pair of medical doctors, James Harris and Francis Gano Benedict, who perfected this methodology to establish standards for the energy needs of healthy individuals. Energy expenditure was measured in approximately 250 healthy men and women at the Carnegie Institute Laboratory in Washington, D.C., and equations were derived from the data. The Harris-Benedict energy expenditure prediction equations for men and women, published in 1919, remain some of the most useful tools in clinical nutrition assessment today.

Micronutrient deficiency diseases (1920–1940). The period between 1920 and 1940 brought about a paradigm shift in the understanding of the etiology of some common diseases. Until this time it was thought that all disease resulted from poor sanitation and hygiene; therefore, bacteria, mold, and toxins were identified as the likely cause of disease. As Alfred Harper has suggested, "the concept that a disease might be caused by a deficit of a substance that was nutritionally essential was beyond the grasp even of most nineteenth-century physicians and scientists" (p. 217). In order to combat disease as well as increase shelf life, food was sterilized, milled, and polished to reduce the danger of ingesting bacteria, mold, and toxins. Despite these efforts, pellagra, beriberi, and infantile scurvy actually increased in prevalence. In a number of studies conducted by Dr. Joseph Goldberger from 1914 to the 1920s, where the diets of individuals suffering from pellagra were compared to those of healthy individuals, foods that decreased the presence of diarrhea and dementia in pellagrous individuals were identified. From his work it was later determined that pellagra was due to a diet poor in the vitamin niacin and not infection. At approximately the same time, Dr. Christiaan Eijkman (1858–1930) won a Nobel Prize in medicine (1929) for the discovery of the "antineuritic" vitamin thought to be responsible for curing beriberi. Through his experiments, in which chickens were fed human hospital diets, combined with studies of beriberi in prisoners who survived on polished rice, he hypothesized that the hull of the rice grain contained an antidote to the neurological disorder. Although not completely correct, his observations led to the discovery of the essential vitamin thiamin.

As Kenneth J. Carpenter summarized, "new technologies of food processing that have obvious advantages may also have a downside" (p. 227). While technology decreased infectious disease and increased the shelf life of food products, it inadvertently led to nutritional deficiencies. The heat-sterilization of cow's milk, which destroyed vitamin C, was related to the outbreak of infantile scurvy in well-to-do families. The practices of polishing rice and degerming corn to increase grain stability also led to increased prevalence of beriberi (thiamin deficiency) and pellagra (niacin deficiency), respectively.

Nutrition in public policy (1920–1964). One of the most fruitful periods in the history of public health nutrition followed on the coattails of World War I. It became possible to manufacture the micronutrients that had been identified by chemists as essential for health cheaply and efficiently. In 1922 the first of a series of public health efforts at eradicating nutrient deficiency in the United

States was initiated by the voluntary addition of iodine to salt (see Table 1). The fortification of other foods was used to address rampant public health problems such as rickets (vitamin D), beriberi (thiamin), pellagra (niacin), and dental caries (fluoride). Since the initiation of fortification policies in the United States, clinically evident nutritional deficiencies have been virtually eliminated.

The first attempt at defining nutritional requirements was directed toward the prevention of nutrient deficiencies in military personnel during World War II. In the early 1940s the Food and Nutrition Board of the National Academy of Sciences reviewed the scientific evidence and developed the Recommended Dietary Allowances for energy, protein, and eight essential vitamins and minerals. The first national food supplementation program was initiated in 1946 (National School Lunch Act) to improve the dietary intake of children from economically disadvantaged families. Other national food assistance programs were added over the next fifty years.

Nutrition and chronic disease (1960–1990). The last forty years of the twentieth century saw continued discovery in the field of nutritional biochemistry and a new research emphasis on the role of nutrition in the cause of and treatment for chronic disease. Disease patterns shifted from infectious and nutrient deficiency diseases to increasing rates of cardiovascular disease, diabetes, cancer, and osteoporosis. Nutrient deficiencies, when present, were often secondary to restrictive dietary habits, economic deprivation, or the presence of another disease that altered nutrient metabolism. The more pressing problem now was the change in the American lifestyle and a dietary shift from too little to too much. Modern household technologies increased productivity in housework but decreased physical activity, and the home-cooked family meal became a thing of the past. Varied diets consisting of whole grains, fruits, and vegetables gave way to convenience foods resulting in a much higher consumption of fat and sugar. Results from the Framingham Heart Study were perhaps the first glimpse into the relationship between fat intake and cardiovascular disease and the realization that each type of fat plays a specific role in health and disease. During this era, links among fat intake, serum cholesterol, and cardiovascular disease were studied thoroughly, and the reasons for the increasing prevalence of obesity in the United States were explored. In 1985 Michael Brown and Joseph Goldstein were awarded the Nobel Prize in medicine for their work on the regulation of cholesterol metabolism and its influence on arteriosclerosis.

The essentiality of macrominerals (e.g., calcium, phosphorus, sodium) was understood in the 1850s. However, it was not until technological advances triggered an explosion of new research that trace and ultra-trace elements were identified as essential for humans. Working together, nutritionists, biochemists, biologists, immunologists, geneticists, and epidemiologists uncovered the mysteries behind minerals such as zinc, selenium,

TABLE 1

Significant policies and recommendations in nutrition (1901–2001)

Date	Nutrition policies and recommendations	Description
1917	Food Guide, "5 Food Groups"	Food groups included flesh foods, breads/cereals, butter/fats, fruits and vegetables, and sweets (USDA).
1922	Iodine fortification	Iodized salt was initially added to salt (60 mg/g salt) in Michigan, goiter virtually eradicated by 1927.
1932	Vitamin D fortification	Vitamin D was added to milk at a minimum of 400 IU/quart. Was also added to some margarine.
1941	Enrichment with iron, niacin, riboflavin, and thiamin	Iron, niacin, riboflavin, and thiamin were added to refined wheat flour, and eventually to bread, pasta, rice, and cereal grain products.
1943	Recommended Dietary Allowances, 1st edition (United States)	Purpose: "To serve as a guide for planning an adequate diet for every normal person." (FNB/NRC)
1945	Fluoride fortification	Voluntary artificial fluoridation of municipal water supply in the United States; currently, 62 percent of U.S. population drinks fluoridated water.
1946	Food Guide, "Basic 7"	Food groups included milk, meat, green/yellow vegetables, citrus fruits, potatoes/other vegetables, bread/cereal, and butter/margarine (USDA).
1946	National School Lunch Act	It provides nutritionally balanced, low-cost, or free lunches to nearly 27 million children each school day. The program was established under the National School Lunch Act, signed by President Harry S Truman.
1958	Daily Food Guide, "Basic 4"	Food groups included meat/eggs/fish, milk/dairy, fruit/vegetables, and bread/cereals (USDA).
1964	Food Stamp Act	The first Food Stamp Act was started as a pilot project in 1961. The current law was enacted in 1977 and is amended regularly by the Congress. Purpose is to end hunger and improve nutrition and health. It helps low-income households buy food for a nutritionally adequate diet.
1975	National School Breakfast Program	The School Breakfast program began as a pilot project in 1966 under the Child Nutrition Act. The purpose was to ensure that all children have access to a healthy breakfast at school to promote learning readiness and healthy eating behaviors. It provides nutritionally balanced, low-cost, or free breakfasts to 7.4 million children each school day.
1971–1974	National Health and Nutrition Examination Survey (NHANES)	The first of a series of surveys to assess the health and nutritional status of the U.S. population (NCHS/CDC).
1974	Special Supplementary Nutrition Program for Women, Infants, and Children (WIC)	Nonentitlement program designed to improve the intake of protein, vitamins A and C, calcium, and iron, to low-income, pregnant, and lactating women and children less than 5 years old.
1980	Dietary Guidelines for Americans: Nutrition and Your Health	First set of recommendations for individuals to guide food choices without specifying amounts (USDA/DHHS).
1985	Continuing Survey of Food Intakes of Individuals (CSFII)	The first of a series of surveys to provide information on the dietary status of the U.S. population and monitor changes in dietary intakes (ARS).
1988–1994	NHANES III	National Health and Nutrition Examination Survey, noted the significant increase in obesity in the United States (NCHS/CDC).
1989	RDA, 10th edition	Definition: the level of intake of essential nutrients that . . . meet the known nutrient needs of practically all healthy persons.
1989	VI. Diet and Health: Implications for Reducing Chronic Disease Risk	Thorough review of the evidence on which dietary guidelines are based. Specific evidence provided on intake of fat, fruit and vegetables, protein, salt, alcohol, calcium, fluoride, and physical activity (FNB).
1990	VII. Nutrition Labeling and Education Act (NLEA)	This act made standardized nutrition labeling on food products in the United States mandatory. There are now 11 health-related claims that are approved to be used in advertising on food packages (FDA).
1992	Food Guide Pyramid	Eating guide based on the RDA that also considered salt, fat, and sugar intake (USDA/HNIS).
1994	Dietary Supplement Health and Education Act (DSHEA)	Exempts any product labeled as a dietary supplement from FDA regulatory approval. Permits structure/function claims without prior FDA authorization.
1997	Dietary Reference Intakes (DRI)	This was the first in a series of revised recommendations now called DRI, which replaces the RDA. This report included recommendations for calcium, phosphorus, magnesium, vitamin D, and fluoride.
1998	Folate fortification	Fortification of all breads, pasta, rice, flour, and breakfast cereals with folate to decrease the risk of neural tube defects in women of childbearing age. Program initiated in United States, Mexico, and Canada.
1998	Dietary Reference Intakes (DRI)	Second series of the DRI for thiamin, riboflavin, niacin, vitamins B_6 and B_{12}, folate, pantothenic acid, biotin, and choline.
2000	Dietary Guidelines for Americans, 4th edition	The dietary guidelines are updated about every 5 years. They provide nontechnical suggestions for healthy dietary patterns and activity (USDA/DHHS).
2001	Dietary Reference Intakes (DRI)	Third series of the DRI for vitamins A and K, arsenic, boron, chromium, copper, iodine, iron, manganese, molybdemum, nickel, silicon, vanadium, and zinc.

copper, molybdenum, and chromium. Scientists first recognized human zinc deficiency in the mid-1960s. Severely growth-retarded, young Middle Eastern men were anemic, extremely lethargic, and hypogonadal. Their diet consisted mainly of wheat bread with little animal protein. When their diets were supplemented with zinc, their lethargy, growth, and genital development improved.

Nutrition for optimal health (1990–present). In the understanding of nutrition, the American public experienced yet another paradigm shift in the 1990s. They wondered if all nutrients that provided a health benefit needed to fit the traditional definition of "essential nutrient." As a result of this question, herbal and botanical extracts, phytochemicals, and other alternative nutritional therapies to promote optimum health were explored. In 1999 the U.S. market for functional foods alone was estimated to be $6 billion (Hasler, p. 504) and it continues to grow by approximately 12 percent each year. The explosion of this market is likely due to the increase in social acceptance, changes in regulations, the booming economy of the 1990s, and the targeting of products to particular populations. The scientific validation of some therapies also is of increasing interest.

Pharmacological uses (larger amounts than required to prevent deficiencies) of essential nutrients are being explored. Although much of the current interest in megavitamin supplementation began in the 1990s, the work of Dr. Linus Pauling in the 1970s initiated the movement. Pauling was the only individual to be awarded two unshared Nobel prizes for his work in chemistry (1954) and peace (1962). In the field of nutrition, however, he is noted most for his unproven theories regarding the potential protective role of vitamin C on the common cold, cancer, and heart disease. Pauling himself reportedly took up to six hundred times the recommended daily amount of vitamin C. Given that many individuals also practice a "more must be better" approach, the national recommendations for nutrient intake now include guidelines for safe upper limits for individual nutrient intakes.

Nutrition in Research

Experimental nutrition research is one aspect of the science of nutrition. Nutrition research is conducted to answer questions raised both in clinical practice and policy. Research in nutrition can focus on individual cells, whole animals or humans, or entire populations, and often overlaps with research in genetics, biochemistry, molecular biology, toxicology, immunology, physiology, and pharmacology.

Nutritional biochemistry. Nutritional biochemistry is the backbone to the understanding of the structure and function of nutrients within food and the body. Nutrients serve as cofactors for enzymes, components of hormones, and participants in oxidation/reduction reactions through metabolic processes. Though required in small amounts,

nutrients are essential for body growth, sexual development and reproduction, psychological well-being, energy level, and the normal functioning of most organ systems in the body. Nutritional biochemists study the functional roles of vitamins and minerals in the body, metabolic blocks that occur from deficiencies, the effects of hormones on nutrient metabolism, and interactions among nutrients within the body. In the 1990s a whole new area of research emerged that focuses on relationships between nutrition and genetics. An example of this type of study includes the identification of a genetic defect in folate metabolism (C677T), which increases a woman's risk of delivering a baby with a neural tube defect.

Food science. Food science is the study of the composition of food materials and the reaction of food to processing, cooking, packaging, and storage. Food science integrates knowledge of the chemical composition of food materials; their physical, biological, and biochemical behavior; the interaction of food components with each other and their environment; pharmacology and toxicology of food materials, additives, and contaminants; and the effects of manufacturing operations, processes, and storage conditions.

The potential beneficial role of functional foods in the American diet has gained attention and recent food science research focuses on the development of such foods. Functional foods are generally defined as those that provide health benefits beyond basic nutrition, and include fortified, enriched, or enhanced foods, and whole foods, which have high levels of protective nutrient components. Examples of these foods include orange juice with added calcium or echinacea, or snack foods with antioxidants, fruit-flavored candy with vitamin C, various soy products, and margarine with added plant sterols. Factors that drive the market for such foods include a growing general public interest in nutrition and its impact on health, an aging population that is more concerned with health, research findings receiving media attention, and an increasingly unregulated consumer food market.

Human nutrition. Human nutrition, or clinical nutrition, research is that which focuses on the study of nutrients within the living human body. Although biochemical studies are extremely informative, until the nutrient is added to or depleted from the diet, the effects on individuals can only be hypothesized. Human nutrition research includes the study of individual nutrient requirements (e.g., nutrient intake assessment, energy expenditure assessment, nutrient turnover balance studies, and nutrient bioavailability), the effects of nutrients on body growth (e.g., body composition techniques, anthropometry, pubertal assessment), and the dietary, physiological, or disease factors that influence nutrient requirements. In the 1990s one important human nutrition study found that increasing folic acid intake in young women reduces the incidence of neural tube defects (spina bifida) in their babies.

Nutritional epidemiology. Nutritional epidemiology is the science of systematically studying the relationships between food choices and health status. Epidemiological studies are particularly valuable in understanding complex relationships between food intake (dietary exposure) and determinants of diseases with multiple etiologies and long latent periods. Examples of such studies include the relationships between low folic acid intake and increased incidence of spina bifida, and elevated saturated fat intake and elevated risk of arteriosclerosis. There are, however, limitations to these studies in that they describe relationships rather than prove cause and effect. Frequently, clinical trials and intervention studies are used as follow-up studies to evaluate more fully the questions raised by epidemiological evidence.

Nutrition in Clinical Practice

Scientific evidence continues to mount regarding the key roles that nutrients and their metabolism play in the prevention of the most common chronic diseases. Half of the leading causes of death in the United States (heart disease, cancer, stroke, and diabetes) are associated strongly with unhealthy eating habits. Clinical nutrition is the practice of applying research evidence to aid in the care of individuals with or at risk for diet-related diseases. These principles are used to develop individualized nutrition care plans. Generally, diseases may affect nutritional status by (a) decreasing the intake of nutrients, (b) altering the metabolism of nutrients (or unusual losses), or (c) altering energy expenditure. Alternatively, as mentioned briefly above, poor nutritional status can lead to disease. For example, zinc deficiency can decrease the function of the immune system that in turn leads to increased risk for diarrhea and infectious diseases.

Assessment of nutritional status is essential for identifying undernourished and overnourished states (obesity is now a major health problem) and estimating the optimum intake to promote normal growth and well-being. Nutritional assessment has several components, including the evaluation of dietary intake, growth status, body composition, energy expenditure, and biochemical measures of nutritional status in the context of a medical history, diagnoses, and current therapy. These data are used to develop individualized nutritional care plans, which may include recommendations for total energy intake, adjustments in the diet to increase or decrease the consumption of certain foods, and possibly the inclusion of nutrient supplements. For patients who cannot be fed orally, more technology-based nutritional support is used to maintain or improve nutrient intakes and nutritional status. This involves either feeding the patient through a tube directly into the stomach or intestine (enteral) or through an intravenous line directly into the bloodstream (parenteral). Because malnutrition will add to complications of illness and prolong the illnesses and hospitalization, appropriate assessment of the patient is extremely important. In the complex and rapidly changing context

DEFINITION OF TERMS

Nutrition: the study of foods, their nutrients, and other chemical components; their actions and interactions in the body; and their influence on health and disease.

Nutritional Science: the body of scientific knowledge that relates to the processes involved in nutrition.

Health: a state of optimal well-being—physical, mental, and social; relative freedom from disease.

Functional Foods: foods that provide a health benefit beyond basic nutrition.

Essential Nutrient: a substance that must be obtained from the diet because the body either cannot make it or cannot make adequate amounts.

Enteral Nutrition: nutrient solutions delivered into the gastrointestinal tract (e.g., stomach, small intestine) through a tube inserted through the nose or directly into the stomach.

Parenteral Nutrition: nutrient solutions delivered directly into the bloodstream through an intravenous catheter.

of critical illness, individualized nutrition assessments are crucial and require the sequential monitoring of all patients to maintain appropriate nutritional care plans.

It is unlikely that individuals who have not been seriously ill have had the opportunity to seek the counsel of a trained nutritional professional for developing an individualized diet plan. The average American displays a keen interest in how nutrition affects his or her health, and is disappointed with the information physicians are able to provide because traditional medical training has limited nutrition content. Therefore, greater numbers of individuals are seeking nutrition information for themselves, and using the information to self-diagnose and self-prescribe. The advances in communications technology, particularly the explosion of information on the World Wide Web, allow the ready accessibility of sound nutritional advice, and substantial amounts of quackery. Without training and a significant amount of time dedicated to the task, it is difficult to decipher truth from fraud. Future directions in nutritional education likely will include tools to aid Americans in deciphering information, particularly from the Internet, in order to make educated choices to optimize their diets and live healthier lives (see Table 2).

Nutrition in Public Policy: Monitoring and Education

Nutrition in public health or nutrition policy generally is regarded as the combined efforts taken toward im-

TABLE 2

Credible sources of nutrition information on the World Wide Web

Professional Organizations
American Dietetic Association: www.eatright.org
American Society for Clinical Nutrition: www.faseb.org/ascn
Society for Nutrition Education: www.sne.org
American College of Sports Medicine: www.acsm.org
Institute of Food Technologists: www.ift.org

Government Organizations
Centers for Disease Control: www.cdc.org
Office of Food Labeling: www.cfsan.gda.gov
Center of Food Safety and Applied Nutrition: www.vm.cfsan.fda.gov/
 list.html
Food and Nutrition Information Center: www.nal.usda.gov/fnic
Center for Nutrition Policy and Promotion: www.usda.gov/fcs/cnpp.htm
International Food Information Council: www.ificinfo.health.org
National Center for Complementary and Alternative Medicine: http://
 nccam.nih.gov/
Office of Dietary Supplements of NIH: http://odp.od.nih.gov/ods/

Private Organizations
Quack Watch: http://www.quackwatch.com/
Gatorade Sports Science Institute: www.gssiweb.com
National Dairy Council: www.dairyinfo.com
The Dannon Company: www.dannon.com
United Fresh Fruit and Vegetable Association: www.uffva.org

---

proving nutrition and health status of populations. With increasing emphasis on health promotion and disease prevention, there is a proliferation of nutrition-related disease prevention, screening, and education programs targeted at increasing fiber, fruit, and vegetable intake, and reducing saturated fat intake. Additionally, a number of food assistance programs and mandated food fortification programs have been instituted, all promoting a healthy diet and lifestyle.

Nutrition research, public policy programs, and nutrition surveillance systems work synergistically like spokes on a wheel. Evidence obtained from scientific research is used to set nutritional recommendations such as the Dietary Reference Intakes and the Dietary Guidelines for Americans. These standards are used to judge the adequacy of the American diet, provide the basis for nutrition labeling of foods, formulate special diets, and guide the development of food fortification and nutrition policy developed to assist those who are at nutritional risk. Specific food assistance programs (such as, food stamps, Special Supplementary Nutrition Program for Women, Infants, and Children) are targeted at specific economically disadvantaged and nutritionally at-risk populations. Fortification programs generally are less specific, but some target at-risk populations through specific foods, for example, vitamin D–fortified milk to prevent rickets in young children. Finally, the wheel is completed by nutrition monitoring programs that are used to evaluate the effectiveness of instituted policies. The National Health and Nutrition Examination Survey (NHANES) and the Continuing Survey of Food Intake of Individu-

als (CSFII) are ongoing monitoring tools used to assess the population's nutrient intakes, nutrition and health status, and knowledge and attitudes about health.

Perhaps most important, public health nutrition includes the dissemination of scientific findings, the explanation of dietary recommendations, and outreach of federal assistance programs. The responsibility of communicating experimental findings in an understandable form falls on nutrition scientists, journalists, educators, and the public. The scientists are responsible for interpreting the research findings into a form that is understandable to the general public. Journalists are responsible for communicating the scientific message in an objective way, and the public is responsible for pursuing an accurate understanding of the issues. Various government agencies have the responsibility to organize and administrate the myriad of nutritional policies and programs, and to communicate information regarding these programs to the public.

The Future of Nutrition and Food Science

In the twentieth century nutrition research, practice, and public policy shifted from a focus on the quantitative aspects—to ensure food security and eradicate nutritional deficiencies—to a greater attention on the qualitative aspects—to achieve optimal, balanced, dietary intakes. In the twenty-first century nutrition research, practice, and policy will likely explore the following areas:

relationships between human genetics and nutrition,
the role of genetically modified foods in human health,
the relationship of nonfood substances in the promotion of health and the bioengineering of functional foods,
the promotion of economic growth and food security in developing nations to prevent or delay the undesirable health effects of malnutrition, and
the prevention and treatment of the obesity epidemic in children and adults.

Relationships between food intake and human health will continue to be of great public interest, and nutrition and food scientists will face new challenges in a faster-changing environment.

See also **Assessment of Nutritional Status; Dietary Assessment; Dietary Guidelines; Dietary Systems: A Historical Perspective; Dietetics; Enteral and Parenteral Nutrition; Food Stamps; Functional Foods; Malnutrition; Nutrients; Nutritionists; Nutrition Transition: Worldwide Diet Change; Obesity; Physical Activity and Nutrition; Vitamins; WIC (Women, Infants, and Children's) Program.**

BIBLIOGRAPHY

American Dietetic Association. "Position of the American Dietetic Association: Domestic Food and Nutrition Security." *Journal of the American Dietetic Association* 98 (1998): 337–342.

American Dietetic Association. *Nutrition and You: Trends 2000.* Chicago, Ill.: American Dietetic Association, 2000.

Carpenter, Kenneth J. "Vitamin Deficiencies in North America in the 20th Century." *Nutrition Today* 34 (1999): 223–228.

Committee on Diet and Health, Food and Nutrition Board, National Research Council. *Diet and Health: Implications for Reducing Chronic Disease Risk.* Washington, D.C.: National Academy Press, 1989.

Dupont, Jacqueline. "The Third Century of Nutrition Research Policy—Shared Responsibility." *Nutrition Today* 34 (1999): 234–241.

Food and Nutrition Board. *Recommended Dietary Allowances.* National Research Council Reprint and Circular Series No. 115. Washington, D.C.: National Research Council, 1943.

Food and Nutrition Board, Institute of Medicine. *Dietary Reference Intakes.* Washington, D.C.: National Academy Press, 1997. Studies on calcium, phosphorus, magnesium, vitamin D, and fluoride.

Food and Nutrition Board, Institute of Medicine. *Dietary Reference Intakes.* Washington, D.C.: National Academy Press, 1988. Studies on thiamin, riboflavin, niacin, vitamin B$_6$, folate, vitamin B$_{12}$, pantothenic acid, biotin, and choline.

Food and Nutrition Board, Institute of Medicine. *Dietary Reference Intakes.* Washington, D.C.: National Academy Press, 2001. Studies on vitamins A and K, arsenic, boron, chromium, copper, iodine, iron, manganese, molybdenum, nickel, silicon, vanadium, and zinc.

Harper, Alfred E. "Nutritional Essentiality: Evolution of the Concept." *Nutrition Today* 34 (1999): 216–222.

Hasler, Clare M. "The Changing Face of Functional Foods." *Journal of the American College of Nutrition* 19 (2000): 499S–506S.

Intersociety Professional Nutrition Education Consortium. "Bringing Physician Nutrition Specialists into the Mainstream: Rationale for the Intersociety Professional Nutrition Education Consortium." *American Journal of Clinical Nutrition* 68 (1998): 894–898.

McCollum, Elmer V. *A History of Nutrition.* Boston, Mass.: Houghton Mifflin, 1957.

Mertz, Walter. "Food Fortification in the United States." *Nutrition Reviews* 55 (1997): 44–49.

Parascandola, Mark. "The History of Clinical Research." *Journal of Clinical Research Practice* 1 (1999): 7–20.

Shils, Maurice E, James A. Olson, Moshe Shike, and A. Catherine Ross. *Modern Nutrition in Health and Disease,* 9th ed. Philadelphia: Lippincott, Williams, and Wilkins, 2000.

Walker, W. A., and J. B. Watkins. *Nutrition in Pediatrics,* 2d ed. London: Decker, 1997.

Willett, Walter. *Nutritional Epidemiology,* 2d ed. Oxford: Oxford University Press, 1998.

Ellen B. Fung
Virginia A. Stallings

NUTRITIONAL ANTHROPOLOGY. Many cultural anthropologists and sociologists who are interested in food and food systems examine the interrelationships of social, cultural, and economic factors as they relate to food use. In contrast, nutritional anthropology refers to a field of study at the interface of anthropology and nutritional sciences focused particularly on understanding how the interactions of social and biological factors affect the nutritional status of individuals and populations. This does not mean that all research in nutritional anthropology involves measurement of nutritional status, and many studies in this field do not include biological outcomes in their research design. However, they differ from studies in the "anthropology of food" because their basic aim is to understand how the physical well-being of humans is affected by their food systems, while cultural anthropologists and sociologists analyze food use in order to understand how social and cultural systems work.

In their investigations, nutritional anthropologists use methods from both the social and biological sciences, which they also draw on in developing theories and testing hypotheses. Occasionally, they turn to humanistic scholarship as a source of insights into the cultural and historical aspects of food. The field can be characterized, therefore, as a biocultural discipline, which emphasizes the importance of integrating multiple perspectives on human behavior and experience in explaining nutrition.

The types of research undertaken by nutritional anthropologists can be classified into the following main categories: (1) sociocultural processes and nutrition; (2) social epidemiology of nutrition; (3) cultural and ideational systems and nutrition; (4) physiological adaptation, population genetics, and nutrition; and (5) applied research for nutrition programs.

Investigations in the category of sociocultural processes and nutrition are often focused on large-scale processes of change, such as globalization, modernization, urbanization, changing women's roles, and technological change in order to understand how these processes affect food and nutrition. While many investigators conduct studies in which they examine the effects in a specific location of a particular manifestation of change (for example, rural to urban migration in a particular developing country), others are concerned with understanding how large-scale changes have affected nutritional conditions across many populations. For example, nutritional anthropologists have studied the consequences for nutrition of a shift from foraging-hunting to agriculture. Studies of the effects on nutrition of a shift from subsistence farming to cash cropping are another example.

Nutritional anthropological research that falls into the category of social epidemiology and nutrition includes a range of topics, for example, describing how particular social and cultural factors place people at risk for nutritional problems or identifying health problems related to nutrition. Among the topics that have attracted attention are the social and ecological determinants of vitamin A deficiency and other micronutrient deficiencies, interactions of socioeconomic and cultural factors that adversely affect growth in infants and young children, and the functional consequences of malnutrition in childhood and adulthood.

Studies in the area of cultural and ideational systems and nutrition are often aimed at understanding how particular beliefs relate to food selection, including food prescriptions and proscriptions. Among the topics investigated by nutritional anthropologists who link their work to public health issues are the ways culturally structured food avoidances during pregnancy or childhood illness affect health outcomes. For example, studies have been conducted on how beliefs about illness and food affect the treatment and household management of children with diarrhea.

There has been a long-standing interest among biocultural anthropologists in the interactions of cultural, physiological, and genetic adaptations in relation to food systems and nutritional patterns. One type of research that falls within this general category includes studies of behavioral adaptations that permit people to create and sustain diets that, over the long run, would be untenable biologically without such adaptations. For example, in Central America, ancient cultures developed the technique of soaking maize kernels in an alkaline solution, which improves its amino acid composition and the bioavailability of the B vitamin, niacin. Without these improvements, a population that subsisted on maize as its primary staple food would be at risk of serious malnutrition.

Another area of research in nutritional anthropology is the relationship between genetic variability in populations and food consumption patterns. A specific topic that falls within this area is the matter of lactose tolerance. Anthropologists have sought to understand how it is possible for adults in some populations to consume milk when the common pattern is for humans to lose their capacity to digest lactose after childhood. The role of this genetic trait has been explored in relation to the development of dairy-based food economies in northern Europe and some regions in Africa. It is likely that there will be an expansion of this type of research with the development of new techniques and knowledge in nutritional genomics.

In addition to conducting basic research, some nutritional anthropologists also engage in applied research, undertaken in direct support of public health activities. Often, investigations in this category involve community-level investigations, although applied nutritional anthropology may also be carried out for the purpose of informing national or international nutrition policy and planning. Studies at the community level may focus on identifying the sociocultural factors to be taken into account in instituting intervention activities (formative research) or in process evaluations to see how these factors are affecting the utilization of programs.

Applied anthropological studies in nutrition and health have been facilitated by the development of man-

uals for Rapid Assessment Procedures (RAP) or Focused Ethnographic Studies (FES). For example, with the aid of manuals, short-term qualitative studies have been conducted in planning interventions to improve vitamin A status in deficient populations and for interventions intended to improve the feeding of infants and young children.

As would be anticipated for a field that cuts across the disciplinary boundaries of the biological and social sciences, nutritional anthropology is eclectic in the scope of its theories and methods. Within that broad scope, however, one can identify a number of commonalities, including: (1) a focus on populations rather than studying individuals without consideration of the larger group of which they are a part; (2) a focus on communities and households as key social units that affect nutrition; and (3) a mixed method approach that utilizes both qualitative and quantitative techniques for data collection and analysis.

See also **Anthropology and Food; Food Archaeology; Nutrition; Prehistoric Societies.**

BIBLIOGRAPHY

Counihan, Carole, and Penny van Esterik, eds. *Food and Culture: A Reader*. New York and London: Routledge, 1997.

Goody, Jack. *Cooking, Cuisine, and Class: A Study in Comparative Sociology*. New York and Cambridge: Cambridge University Press, 1982.

Messer, Ellen. "Anthropological Perspectives on Diet." *Annual Review of Anthropology* 13 (1984): 205–249.

Stinson, Sara. "Nutritional Adaptation." *Annual Review of Anthropology* 21 (1992): 143–170.

Gretel Pelto

NUTRITIONAL BIOCHEMISTRY. Nutritional biochemistry is one of the academic foundations that make up nutritional sciences, a discipline that encompasses the knowledge of nutrients and other food components with emphasis on their range of function and influence on mammalian physiology, health, and behavior. Nutritional biochemistry is a subdiscipline that is made up of the core knowledge, concepts, and methodology related to the chemical properties of nutrients and other dietary constituents and to their biochemical, metabolic, physiological, and epigenetic functions. A primary focus of research in nutritional biochemistry is the scientific establishment of optimal dietary intakes (Dietary Reference Intakes or DRIs) for every nutrient and food component throughout the life cycle (Thomas and Earl, 1994; Standing Committee, 1998).

Nutritional biochemistry is an integrative science whose foundation is derived from knowledge of other biological, chemical, and physical sciences, but it is distinguished in its application of this knowledge to understanding the interactive relationships among diet, health, and disease susceptibility. For example, nutritional biochemistry is rooted in analytical methodology that permits the purification of individual nutrients and the determination of their structures, as well as in classical biochemical approaches that identify metabolic pathways and elucidate the role of dietary components in regulating metabolism and gene expression. Additionally, human genetic studies of inherited inborn errors of metabolism, such as phenylketonuria, have contributed to core nutritional biochemical knowledge by revealing important interrelationships among nutrition, metabolism, and genotype and their interactions during normal and abnormal human development.

Knowledge generated from nutritional biochemistry research forms the foundation upon which nutrition-based public health interventions are designed and implemented. Many common diseases and disabilities afflicting human populations in both developing and developed countries result from general malnutrition, deficiencies of specific nutrients, or overnutrition. Inadequate diets or poor dietary habits are associated with increased risk for morbidity and mortality, including birth defects, diabetes, cardiovascular disease, obesity, and certain cancers. Specific nutrients, food components, or metabolites, singularly or in combination, can contribute to risk for disease or, alternatively, can be protective by preventing disease. Furthermore, associations among dietary components and diseases are strongly influenced by subtle genetic variation, such as single nucleotide polymorphisms, which are prevalent in all human populations. Research-based diet therapies and strategies to decrease the incidence of nutrition-related diseases have a successful history of improving public health and individual quality of life. Such strategies include (1) the fortification of grain products with folic acid to decrease the incidence of common birth defects (spina bifida), (2) the iodinization of table salt to prevent cretinism, a developmental disorder associated with severe neurological and cognitive deficits in children, and (3) the promotion of diets low in cholesterol to prevent and to manage cardiovascular disease. These nutrition-based interventions have impacted the quality of life for individuals, and the monetary effects associated with the amelioration of these disorders have significantly benefited health care systems and national economies.

Current research and discovery in nutritional biochemistry is focused broadly in several areas, including nutritional genomics and metabolomics. Nutritional genomics is the study of genome–nutrient interactions and includes (1) the role of nutrients and dietary components in regulating genome structure, expression, and stability, and (2) the role of genetic variation on individual nutrient requirements. Nutritional metabolomics is the study of metabolic pathways and networks and includes (1) the regulation of metabolic pathways and networks, by nutrients and other food components, and (2) the establishment of analytical methods that "profile" human

CORE KNOWLEDGE THAT DEFINES NUTRITIONAL BIOCHEMISTRY

- Structure and function of nutrients and other dietary constituents
- Chemical structure and metabolic functions of essential and nonessential nutrients
- Physiological and biochemical basis for nutrient requirements
- Motifs of absorption and transport of nutrients
- Integration, coordination, and regulation of macro- and micronutrient metabolism
- Regulation of nutrient metabolism and nutritional needs by hormones and growth factors
- Interaction of nutrients with the genome; nutrient control of gene expression; DNA stability
- Dietary bioactive components (functional foods)—nontraditional roles of nutrients
- Food, diets, and supplements
- Food sources of nutrients and factors affecting nutrient bioavailability
- Effect of food processing and handling on nutrient content and bioavailability
- Nutritional toxicology—upper limits of intake; nutrient–nutrient and drug–nutrient interactions
- Dietary Reference Intakes (DRIs); Food Guide Pyramid
- Nutrient supplements—risks/benefits, life stage, bioavailability
- Molecular markers of nutrient intake—gene arrays and analytical chips
- Nutrition and disease
- Impact of disease and genetics on nutrient function and requirements
- Genetic basis of inherited metabolic disease

SOURCE: Allen, Lindsay H., Margaret E. Bentley, Sharon M. Donovan, Denise M. Ney, and Patrick J. Stover, "Securing the Future of Nutritional Sciences through Integrative Graduate Education." *Journal of Nutrition* 132 (2002): 779–784.

serum and urinary metabolites to assess nutritional imbalances and disease risk. It is anticipated that knowledge derived from these new approaches will enable nutrient requirements to be tailored to an individual's genetic profile for optimal health throughout the life cycle. In addition, information obtained from these new technologies will inform efforts (1) to improve or to enhance the food supply through the targeted introduction of traditional or novel foods, (2) to fortify food chemically with specific nutrients, or (3) to enhance crops genetically for higher nutrient content or quality.

Nutritional sciences academic training programs with a strong emphasis in nutritional biochemistry reside in medical colleges (e.g., Columbia University), schools of public health (e.g., Harvard University), and land grant universities (e.g., Cornell University). Nutritional sciences training programs can be independent units, jointly administered or affiliated with programs of toxicology, biochemistry, animal sciences, food sciences, and various medical programs. Academic faculty in nutritional biochemistry can be expert in many disciplines, including chemistry, biochemistry, genetics, and physiology. Therefore, individual nutritional sciences programs with distinct nutritional biochemistry concentrations are highly unique. Nutritional biochemists establish careers in teaching and research within universities, governmental and regulatory agencies, and the food, pharmaceutical, or biotechnology industries. Nutritional biochemists may also work in fields related to public policy, health care, or product development and marketing in the food industry.

See also **Dietary Guidelines; Nutraceuticals; Nutrient Bioavailability; Nutrients.**

BIBLIOGRAPHY

Allen, Lindsay H., Margaret E. Bentley, Sharon M. Donovan, Denise M. Ney, and Patrick J. Stover. "Securing the Future of Nutritional Sciences through Integrative Graduate Education." *Journal of Nutrition* 132 (2002): 779–784.

Standing Committee on the Scientific Evaluation of Dietary Reference Intakes, Food and Nutrition Board, Institute of Medicine. *Dietary Reference Intakes for Thiamin, Riboflavin, Niacin, Vitamin B6, Folate, Vitamin B12, Pantothenic Acid, Biotin, and Choline.* Washington, D.C.: National Academy Press, 1998.

Thomas, Paul R., and Robert Earl, eds. *Opportunities in the Nutrition and Food Sciences.* Washington, D.C.: National Academy Press, 1994.

Patrick J. Stover

NUTRITIONISTS.

The field of nutrition is a broad one and has a wide variety of individuals working in it. Self-styled experts abound—based on the premise that they have eaten all of their lives, have grown, and are healthy adults, they regard themselves as nutrition experts. Unfortunately, it is not quite this easy to become a nutritionist. Cooks, chefs, science teachers, and many allied health professionals may have taken a course or two in nutrition during their training, but this does not qualify them as nutritionists either. Nutritionists have undergone rigorous educational programs in the sciences and have studied nutrients and other components of food in depth.

For the purpose of this discussion, four different types of nutritionists will be described along with the educational pathways needed to qualify for each position. These include the nutrition scientist, the public health nutritionist, the dietitian (known in the United States as the registered dietitian or RD) and the dietetic technician (known as the dietetic technician, registered, or DTR in the United States). Each of these groups develops different skill sets, and each group is responsible for carrying out different functions in the broader field that is nutrition.

Nutrition Scientists

Nutrition scientists are those individuals who use the scientific method to study nutrients, both as individual compounds and as they interact in food and nutrition. The role of the nutrition scientist is to develop new knowledge related to nutrients or nutrition or to develop new processes or techniques to apply existing knowledge. For example, nutrition scientists have been involved in developing food preservation processes, determining nutrient requirements for various animal species, describing how individual nutrients function within the cells of the human body, and identifying nutrition-related problems in various populations.

Nutritionist scientists may have their basic training in nutrition or in a related field such as biochemistry, microbiology, cell biology, epidemiology, toxicology, agriculture, or food science. In most cases, they hold a PhD in their respective field of study. Sometimes, they hold another terminal degree such as an MD or a doctorate in public health (DrPH). Other nutrition scientists do not hold a terminal degree but are trained at the master's degree level and may assist in laboratories or in fieldwork. The characteristic that defines the nutrition scientist is not the field in which the training occurred, but the area in which the person is working. If scientists are conducting research with food, nutrients, or the nutritional status of groups, individuals, or animals, it is appropriate for them to be known as nutrition scientists. In the United States, the universities that train individuals to be nutrition scientists are regionally accredited, but the discipline-specific programs are not.

Public Health Nutritionists

Public health nutritionists are professionals who view the community as their client. They specialize in diagnosing the nutritional problems of communities and in finding solutions to those problems. Some classic examples of public health nutrition interventions include the fortification of salt with iodine to prevent goiter or the enrichment of grain products with B vitamins to prevent deficiency diseases like pellegra or beriberi.

Public health nutritionists are often dietitians who hold a bachelor's degree in applied nutrition. In addition, they study public health theory and practice at the master's degree level, earning a master's degree in public health (MPH). The curriculum for the MPH includes coursework in epidemiology, advocacy, public policy, program management, grant writing, and social marketing. Programs in public health nutrition may accept students whose bachelor's degree is in a field other than nutrition; in that case, they also do graduate work in nutrition. In the United States, there is an organization known as the Association of Graduate Programs in Public Health Nutrition, Inc. that establishes voluntary guidelines for knowledge, skills, and competencies for public health nutritionists.

Dietitians

Dietitians, RDs in the United States, are practitioners who translate the science of nutrition into practice for individuals and groups. Though dietitians may work in a variety of settings, they traditionally practice in the areas of clinical nutrition, food service, or community nutrition. RDs hold bachelor's degrees and have completed a supervised practice program known as a dietetic internship.

The profession of dietetics is self-regulating. Undergraduate dietetics programs in the United States are known as didactic programs in dietetics (DPDs) and are accredited by the Commission on Accreditation for Dietetics Education (CADE). DPDs are required to provide a curriculum that includes "foundation knowledge and skills" which are mandated by CADE for entry-level dietetic education programs.

Students who successfully complete a DPD may apply for entry into a supervised practice program. These dietetic internships, also accredited by CADE, are designed to meet the "competency statements" for the supervised practice component of entry-level dietetic education programs. Dietetic internships provide a minimum of 900 hours of supervised practice experience. Curricula for these programs include core competencies but also allow programs to train generalists or specialists in a particular practice area, such as nutrition therapy or foodservice systems management.

An alternate training route for dietitians is the Coordinated Program in Dietetics (CP). Coordinated programs provide the student with both the didactic and the supervised practice components of dietetics education in a single program. CPs may be offered in conjunction with either a bachelor's or master's degree.

After completion of both the didactic and supervised practice components of dietetics education, graduates sit for a national registration examination, which is administered under the auspices of the Commission on Dietetics Registration (CDR). Individuals who pass the examination may practice as RDs. Licensing is also required in some states; the same examination may be used for both purposes.

Dietitians who have completed their education in other countries may sit for the RD examination in the United States if their country has established reciprocity with CDR. Reciprocity requires that the course of study include both didactic and practice components. Some of the countries that have reciprocal agreements

with the United States include Canada, Denmark, and the Philippines.

The RD credential is used to protect the public from practitioners whose educational and professional credentials are below published and accepted standards. In addition, that credential must be maintained to ensure that dietetics practitioners do not allow their knowledge base to become outdated. Every five years, the RD credential must be renewed by demonstrating that a program of planned learning activities has been undertaken to allow for continued competence. Dietitians who allow their credentials to lapse must retake the registration examination in order to reestablish their level of competence.

Dietetic Technicians

Dietetic technicians, DTRs in the United States, are dietetics practitioners who work with dietitians in all three areas of dietetics practice, clinical, foodservice, and community. They may work independently, if the expertise of a dietitian is not required for the specific task that is being done. For example, the dietetic technician could counsel a new mother on infant feeding practices but would not recommend a parenteral formula for the recipient of an organ transplant. DTRs hold at least an associate's degree and have attended a program that includes a supervised practice component.

In the United States, CADE accredits dietetic technician programs (DTs). The curriculum for these programs must include didactic content in the eight "foundation knowledge and skills." The specific requirements for DTs differ from those for DPDs in the depth involved. DTs include a supervised practice component of at least 450 hours, during which students develop the practice competencies set by CADE for DTRs.

Like RDs, DTRs are required to pass a national registration examination established by CDR. Passing the examination provides them with the credential to practice as dietetics professionals. DTRs are also required to demonstrate continued competence by engaging in planned learning activities and renewing their credential every five years.

BIBLIOGRAPHY

Commission on Accreditation for Dietetics Education. *CADE Accreditation Handbook.* Chicago, Ill.: American Dietetic Association, 2002.

Competency Assurance Panel of the Commission on Dietetics Registration. "The Professional Development 2001 Portfolio." *Journal of the American Dietetic Association* 99 (1999): 612–614.

Owen, Anita L., Patricia L. Splett, and George M. Owen. *Nutrition in the Community: The Art and Science of Delivering Services.* 4th ed. Boston: WCB McGraw Hill, 1999.

Winterfeldt, Esther A., Margaret L. Bogle, and Lea L Ebro. *Dietetics: Practice and Future Trends.* Gaithersburg, Md.: Aspen, 1998.

Nancy R. Hudson

NUTRITION TRANSITION: WORLDWIDE DIET CHANGE.

The world is witnessing rapid shifts in diet and body composition, with resultant important changes in health profiles. In many ways, these shifts are a continuation of large-scale changes that have occurred repeatedly over time; the changes facing low- and moderate-income countries today, however, appear to be occurring very rapidly. Broad shifts in population size and its age composition; in disease patterns; and in dietary and physical-activity patterns are occurring around the world. The former two sets of dynamic shifts are termed the demographic and epidemiological transitions. Dietary and physical-activity changes, reflected in nutritional outcomes such as changes in average stature and body composition, are referred to as the nutrition transition.

Historical Nutrition Patterns

Human diet and activity patterns and nutritional status have undergone a sequence of major shifts, which can be defined as broad patterns of food use and of corresponding nutrition-related diseases. Since the eighteenth century, the pace of dietary and activity change appears to have accelerated, albeit to varying degrees in different regions of the world. Dietary and activity changes have been paralleled by major changes in health status, as well as by major demographic and socioeconomic changes. Obesity emerges early among these shifting conditions, as does the level and age composition of morbidity and mortality. Five broad nutrition patterns have been identified, going back to the origins of modern man. The two "earlier" patterns continue to characterize certain geographic and socioeconomic subpopulations, but much of the modern world is experiencing one or more of three later patterns: receding famine; the appearance of nutrition-related noncommunicable diseases (NR–NCDs); and, in response to these, behavioral change.

Receding famine. In this stage, the consumption of fruits, vegetables, and animal protein increases, and starchy staples become less important in the diet. Many earlier civilizations had made great progress in reducing chronic hunger and famines, but only in the last third of the last millennium did these changes become widespread, leading to marked shifts in diet. Famines continued well into the eighteenth century in parts of Europe, however, and they remain common in some regions of the world. Activity patterns start to shift in this stage, and inactivity and leisure become a part of the lives of more people.

Nutrition-related noncommunicable diseases (NR–NCDs). A diet high in total fat, cholesterol, sugar, and other refined carbohydrates, and low in polyunsaturated fatty acids and fiber, and often accompanied by an increasingly sedentary life, is characteristic of most richer societies (and of increasing portions of the population in poorer societies) in this stage. These characteristics result in increased prevalence of obesity and degenerative diseases that characterize Omran's final epidemiological stage.

Behavioral change. A new pattern appears to be emerging in this stage as a result of changes in diet, evidently associated with the desire to prevent or delay degenerative diseases and prolong health. Whether these changes, instituted in some countries by consumers and prodded in others by government policy, will constitute a large-scale transition in dietary structure and body composition remains to be seen.

Nutrition science is increasingly focusing on these three later stages, in particular on the rapid shift in much of the world's low- and moderate-income countries from the stage of receding famine to the stage of nutrition-related noncommunicable diseases. The concern about this change is so great that, for many, the term "the nutrition transition" is synonymous with it.

Apparent Increasing Rapidity of Shifts in Dietary and Activity Patterns and Body Composition

The pace of nutrition-transition shifts from the receding-famine period to that dominated by nutrition-related noncommunicable diseases seems to be accelerating in poor and developing countries. As use of the term "nutrition" rather than "diet" suggests, the category "nutriton-related noncommunicable disease" incorporates the effects of diet, physical activity, and body composition, rather than dietary patterns and their effects alone. This usage is based partly on incomplete information, which seems to indicate that the prevalence of obesity and a number of other NR–NCDs is increasing much faster in the poor and developing world than it has in the West. Rapid growth in urban populations there is much greater than that experienced less than a century ago in the West. Another element is the shift in occupation structure and the rapid introduction of mass media.

Clearly, there are both quantitative and qualitative dimensions to these changes. On the one hand, changes toward a high-density diet with reduced complex carbohydrates and other important elements, and toward increasing inactivity, may be proceeding faster than in the past. The shift from labor-intensive occupations and physically demanding leisure activities toward less strenuous work and leisure is also occurring faster. On the other hand, qualitative dimensions related to multidimensional aspects of the diet, activity, body composition, and disease shifts may exist. For example, the human diet and every one of these other factors are composed of many components, each of which will affect a person in a range of ways. Eating meat, for instance, will provide humans with many valuable nutrients such as bioavailable iron and vitamin B_{12} or B_6 not found in plant foods, but also with others such as saturated fat that, when consumed in excess, may harm human health. Social and economic stresses people face and feel as these changes occur might also be included.

At the start of the new millennium, the pace and complexity of life seem to be increasing exponentially. While the penetration and influence of modern communications, technology, and economic systems (related to what is termed "globalization") have been a dominant theme since the late twentieth century, there seems to have been a confluence of changes in these factors that have led to a major global concern about the rapid globalization of the world economy and its impact on various subpopulations.

Increasing access to Western media and the removal of communication barriers enhanced by the World Wide Web, cable television, mobile telephone systems, and other technology are important. The accelerated introduction of Western technology into manufacturing, basic sectors of agriculture, mining, and services is also a key element.

Globalization and China: an example. The types of changes the developing world is facing can be seen in considering life in China in two different periods. During the 1970s food-supply concerns still existed. There was no television, limited bus and other mass transportation, and little food trade. Minimal processed food existed, and most rural and urban occupations were very labor-intensive.

By the end of the twentieth century, work and life in China had changed. Small gas-powered tractors were available, modern industrial techniques were multiplying, offices were quite automated, soft drinks and processed foods were consumed everywhere, televisions were found in about 89 percent of households (at least a fifth of whom received Hong Kong and Western advertising and programming), younger children did not ride bicycles, and mass transit had become heavily used.

Add to such changes similar ones occurring in much of Asia, North Africa, the Middle East, Latin America, and many areas (particularly cities) in sub-Saharan Africa, and it is evident that the shift from a subsistence economy to a modern, industrialized one occurred in a span of ten to twenty years, whereas in Europe and other richer industrialized societies, it took place over many decades or centuries.

To effectively examine the nutrition aspects of these changes, one would need to compare changes in poorer countries in the period from 1980 to 2000 with changes that occurred a half century earlier in the developed world. However, data on diet and activity patterns are not available, and there is only minimal data on nutrition-related noncommunicable diseases and on obesity.

The negative elements of the nutrition transition known to be linked with nutrition-related noncommunicable diseases are obesity, adverse dietary changes (for example, shifts in the structure of diet toward a greater role for higher fat and added sugar contents, reduced fruit and vegetable intake, reduced fiber intake, greater energy density, and greater saturated fat intake), and reduced physical activity in work and leisure. The causes of these elements are not as well understood as are the trends in each of them. In fact, there are few studies attempting to examine the causes of such changes, and there are only a few data sets that are equipped to allow such crucial policy analyses to be undertaken.

Obesity Trends

The most commonly measured health outcome due to shifts in the structure of diet is obesity. Increases in overweight and obese adults in the developing world since the 1970s have occurred much faster than in richer countries. Shifts in body composition among Chinese adults have been examined (Bell et al., 2001) over an eight-year period. Not only did the average BMI (body mass index, which is the common measure for overweight status and measures weight in kilograms divided by height in square meters) level increase, but the shape of the BMI distribution curve changed over the eight-year period of the study so that there was a large proportion of high BMI adults. From 1989 to 1997 the proportion of underweight men and women dropped considerably, and the prevalence of both overweight and obesity increased greatly, the proportion of overweight or obese men more than doubling and the proportion of overweight or obese women increasing by 50 percent.

China's changes are not unique. Annual increases in the prevalence of overweight and obese adults in selected poor and middle-income countries can be compared with those in the United States. Elsewhere we present data that illustrate the annualized increases from richer countries with comparable data from poorer countries (Popkin, 2002). We also show how quickly overweight status and obesity have emerged in Mexico as a major public-health problem. Compared with the United States and European countries, where annual prevalence increases in overweight and obesity are about 0.25 percent each, rates of change are very high in Latin America. Similar shifts in the prevalence of obesity are found for North Africa and the Middle East and Asia. In each of these countries the annual rate of increase in the prevalence of overweight plus obesity is between 1 and 2.5 (Popkin, 2002).

What is important to note is that increases in the proportion of the adult population who are overweight are far greater in all of these poorer countries than in the United States or most European countries. Only Spain, with its large growth in overweight population in the last decade, is similar, in speed of change, to these countries.

Dietary Changes: Shift in the Overall Structure over Time

The diets of the developing world are shifting rapidly. Good data for most countries on total energy intake are not available, but shifts in the structure of the diet can

601

be examined. Thus, the shift in diet, over time, in the proportion of energy derived from fat has been explored (Guo et al., 2000).

The dramatic changes in the aggregate income–fat relationship from 1962 to 1990 are found in China. Most significantly, by 1990 even poor nations (having a gross national product [GNP] of only $750 per capita) had access to a relatively high-fat diet, which derived 20 percent of its energy from fat; in 1962 the same diet was associated with countries having a GNP of $1,475 (both GNP values in 1993 dollars). This dramatic change arose from a major increase (from 10 to 13 percent) in the consumption of vegetable fats by poor and rich nations alike. Increases (of 3 to 6 percent) also occurred in middle- and high-income nations.

At the same time, there were decreases in the consumption of fat from animal sources for all except the low-income countries. The availability of animal fats continued to be linked to income, though less strongly in 1990 than in 1962. These decreases, combined with the increase in vegetable-fat intake for countries rich and poor, resulted in an overall decrease in fat intake for moderate-income countries of about 3 percent, but an increase of about 4 to 5 percent for low- and high-income countries.

In 1990 vegetable fats accounted for a greater proportion of dietary energy than animal fats for the poorest 75 percent of countries (all of whom had incomes below approximately $5,800 per capita). The absolute level of vegetable-fat consumption increased, but there remained, at most, a weak association of GNP and vegetable-fat intake. Changes in vegetable-fat prices, supply, and consumption equally affected rich and poor countries, but the net impact was much greater on lower-income countries.

There has been an equally large and important shift in the proportion of energy from added sugar in the diets of lower-income countries (Drewnowski and Popkin, 1997).

Examination of the combined effect of these various shifts in the structure of rural and urban Chinese diets reveals an upward shift in the energy density of the foods consumed. Energy intake from foods and alcohol in both urban and rural Chinese adult diets increased over 10 percent between 1989 and 1997. These numbers represent a very rapid shift in energy density. (It is important to note that the Chinese Food Composition Table, from which these data were extracted, measures only a few beverages [milk, coconut juice, sugarcane juice, spirits, beer, wine, champagne, and brandy] and excludes many beverages, in particular tea and coffee, included in normal measures.) Other clinical studies have found that the consumption of higher-density diets is associated with increased total energy intake. Energy density changes in the diet of China, and most likely in other developing countries, are critical components to be monitored.

The Importance of Rapid Social Change, Including Urbanization, Demographic Change, and Behavioral Changes

Diets have shifted far more dramatically in urban than in rural areas. Some critical sociodemographic issues include:

- rapid reductions in fertility that have speeded shifts in age distribution;

- unabated urbanization in Asia and Africa that will leave more of the poor residing in urban than rural areas in future decades;

- economic changes, in particular increased income and income inequality, that appear to define changes in many regions of the developing world;

- globalization of mass media that faces countries at an earlier stage of economic development than in the past.

Urbanization. The structure of diet has shifted markedly as populations have urbanized (Drewnowski and Popkin, 1997). This relationship will, by itself, shift the structure of national diets significantly as the proportion of the population in urban areas grows.

Structural shifts in income-diet relationships. Economists speak of two types of behavioral change. One relates to shifts in the "population composition" of society toward the educated, rich, or urban. The other is "behavioral" and relates to the way people with different characteristics behave, particularly their economic behavior. At the same level of education or income, a person might buy different amounts or types of commodities at different points in time. Research conducted in China shows there have been profound behavioral shifts since the 1980s. For each extra dollar of income, additional high-fat foods are being purchased, when compared with previous years (Guo et al., 2000). This suggests that the demand pattern for food has changed, so that for the same income level patterns of demand are significantly different from those in earlier periods. The explosion in access to goods and exposure to mass media may well have created this situation.

Mass media. There is no doubt that access to modern mass media has grown very rapidly. It is most useful to look at the proportion of households in a country that own television sets. Overall, 88.5 percent of Chinese households owned televisions in 1997. Not only the proportion of people with access to television but also the types of programs and access to Western influences were shifting. In the 1980s cable systems in China did not provide outside programming; by 1997 many provinces provided access to China Star, a Hong Kong system that relies heavily on U.S. and British programming and modern advertising.

While there are not extensive data on the proportions of Chinese households with access to mass media more than thirty years ago, research has shown a marked increase in television ownership and viewing and indicates that media's penetration into Chinese households in 1997 is far greater than into American households fifty years ago, when television was in its infancy.

Health effects. The BMI-disease relationships have been found to vary between major Asian and other subpopulation groups and those of European background. Are these related to differences in the distribution of fat in a body (e.g. fat distributed around the heart and livers in the abdomen versus in the hips and buttocks), or are there underlying equally important genetic factors that account for these differences?

There are a number of different ways these questions could be answered in the affirmative. One is if body composition and other unmeasured racial and ethnic factors affect susceptibility to nutrition-related noncommunicable diseases. Another might be if previous disease patterns (such as the presence of malaria or other tropical diseases) have predisposed the population to certain problems. One component of this might be the fetal insult syndrome hypothesized and popularized by Barker.

A growing body of research shows that international standards used to delineate who is overweight and obese are not appropriate for many large subpopulations. For instance, a BMI of 25 appears to have a far greater adverse metabolic effect in an Asian adult than in a Caucasian adult (Deurenberg et al., 1998). In fact, the World Health Organization (WHO) and the International Obesity Task Force (IOTF) have formed a group of scientists and agencies in Asia to review this topic. This group has held international meetings and has proposed a lower BMI cutoff for Asians, of 23 for overweight and 25 for obesity (International Diabetes Institute, 2000). In one paper comparing China, the Philippines, and U.S. Hispanics, African Americans, and whites, the odds of being hypertensive were higher for Chinese men and women in the 23–25 BMI range than for other subpopulation groups (Bell et al., 2001). Ethnic differences in the strength of the association between BMI and disease outcomes warrant further consideration.

Zimmet and others who have focused on this issue as it relates to lower-income countries have felt that the highest genetic susceptibility for adult-onset diabetes was for Pacific Islanders, American Indians, Mexican Americans and other Hispanics, and Asian Indians. Those groups with modest genetic susceptibility include Africans, Japanese, and Chinese. The age of onset (usually after fifty) of non-insulin-dependent diabetes mellitus (NIDDM) is much lower for these susceptible populations, and it appears that the prevalence is higher for a given level of obesity and waist-hip ratio.

What is not clear is how much of this difference between subpopulations' BMI-diabetes or other BMI-morbidity relationships is a function of differences of body composition, of metabolic or genetic factors, or

of social causes. Part of the apparent race-hypertension relationship may also be explained by socioeconomic status (Bell et al., 2001).

There is possibly another factor related to the role of exposure to poor health in this population, for which there is less understanding and no real documentation of its impact (e.g., malnutrition that causes a virus to mutate, parasitic infections that affect long-term absorption patterns, or a parasite that is linked with an unknown genotype—comparable to sickle-cell anemia and its evolutionary linkage with malaria). There is no basis for speculation about the importance of this factor.

The effect of fetal and infant insults on subsequent metabolic function, however, appears to be a critical area. If rapid shifts toward obesity are occurring among those who earlier faced higher levels of low birthweight in a population, then this becomes a much more salient aspect of this argument. In the developing world, where intrauterine malnutrition rates have been and continue to remain high, and nutrition insults during infancy are highly prevalent, research suggests important potential effects on the prevalence of nutrition-related noncommunicable diseases in coming decades (Barker, 2001; Adair et al., 2001). There is an emerging consensus that fetal insults, in particular with regard to thin, low-birthweight infants who subsequently become overweight, are linked with increased risk of these diseases. Infancy itself, however, may equally be a period of high vulnerability. Three further studies by Hoffman and collaborators (2000) suggest that fat metabolism of stunted infants is impaired to the extent that it could lead to increased obesity and other metabolic shifts. Other work on the role of stunting and obesity (Popkin et al., 1996) had suggested such an effect; Hoffman's work offers the mechanism.

The Coming Cardiovascular Disease Epidemic

Evidence from many developing countries shows that nutrition-related chronic diseases prematurely disable and even kill a large number of economically productive people, a preventable loss of precious human capital. Four out of five deaths from nutrition-related chronic diseases occur in middle- and low-income countries. Reddy (2002) has pointed out that these low- and middle-income countries now account for over three-quarters of global mortality and over 40 percent of the global burden of disease, measured as disability adjusted life years (DALYs) lost, that is attributable to noncommunicable diseases. Among the low- and moderate-income developing countries, the burden of cardiovascular disease alone is now far greater in India and China. Together these two countries account for over half of all new cases of diabetes in the world. Lower-income communities are especially vulnerable to nutrition-related chronic diseases, which are not only diseases of affluence. Such nutrition-related chronic diseases as cardiovascular diseases (CVDs), cancers, and diabetes are becoming major contributors to the burden of disease, even as infections and nutritional deficiencies are receding as leading contributors to death and disability.

Furthermore, cardiovascular diseases in the developing world emerge at an earlier age. Over 45 percent of heart disease–related deaths in low- and moderate-income countries occur under the age of 70 (compared with about 20 percent in high-income countries) (Reddy, 2002).

There are large differences in the profiles of the CVD epidemic across the developing world. Hypertension and stroke, for instance, are more likely to emerge in East Asia, whereas diabetes comes earlier in South Asia.

As would be expected from the dietary and obesity data noted above, CVD levels are far greater in urban areas of the developing world; the opposite is often true in the higher-income developed countries.

The Social Burden of Changes in Diet, Body Composition, and Health

In the richer countries of the world, higher-income groups increasingly follow a more healthful lifestyle when compared to poorer groups. Higher-income Americans consume a more healthful diet, exercise more, and smoke less; similar patterns are found in other high-income countries (Popkin et al., 1996). The prevailing opinion has been that the opposite is found in the developing world, namely, that the poor are less likely to have a heavy burden of nutrition-related noncommunicable diseases than the rich. This statistic is changing rapidly. Monteiro and his collaborators have shown that obesity has gone down among the better-educated, and increased among the less-well-educated, in southeastern Brazil. Soowon Kim and collaborators have shown that not only are less healthful dietary patterns common among higher-income Chinese; so are other harmful dimensions of lifestyle (inactivity, smoking, drinking). Other Chinese scholars have shown a rapid shift in food-consumption patterns among different income groups, which seems to indicate a shift in the burden of unhealthy diets toward poor Chinese (Guo et al., 2000).

The Future

Consuming a more tasteful and richer diet is a goal of most of the world's population. Dietary change is universal; rapid change, though, is now seen especially in the poorest areas of the world. The challenge is to learn how to continue to improve the palatability and quality of our diet, while discovering ways to accomplish this task in a more healthful manner.

See also **Food Politics: United States; Food Supply and the Global Food Market; Health and Disease; Nutrients; Nutrition; Obesity; Political Economy**.

BIBLIOGRAPHY

Adair, L. S., C. W. Kuzawa, and J. Borja. "Maternal Energy Stores and Diet Composition During Pregnancy Program Adolescent Blood Pressure." *Circulation* 104 (2001): 1034–1039.

Barker, D. J. P. *Fetal Origins of Cardiovascular and Lung Disease.* New York: Marcel Dekker, 2001.

Bell, C., K. Ge, and B. M. Popkin. "Weight Gain and Its Predictors in Chinese Adults." *International Journal of Obesity* 25 (2001): 1079–1086.

Bell, E. A., V. H. Castellanos, C. L. Pelkman, M. L. Thorwart, and B. J. Rolls. "Energy Density of Foods Affects Energy Intake in Normal-weight Women." *American Journal of Clinical Nutrition* 67 (1998): 412–420.

Caballero, Benjamin, and B. M. Popkin, eds. *The Nutrition Transition: Diet and Disease in the Developing World.* London: Academic Press, 2002.

Deurenberg, P., M. Yap, and W. A. Staveren. "Body Mass Index and Percent Body Fat: A Meta Analysis among Different Ethnic Groups." *International Journal of Obesity* 22, no. 12 (1998): 1164–1171.

Drewnowski, A. "Energy Density, Palatability, and Satiety: Implications for Weight Control." *Nutrition Reviews* 56 (1998): 347–353.

Drewnowski, A., and B. M. Popkin. "The Nutrition Transition: New Trends in the Global Diet." *Nutrition Reviews* 55 (1997): 31–43.

Guo, X., T. A. Mroz, B. M. Popkin, and F. Zhai. "Structural Changes in the Impact of Income on Food Consumption in China, 1989–93." *Economic Development and Cultural Changes* 48 (2000): 737–760.

Hoffman, D. J., S. B. Roberts, I. Verreschi, P. A. Martins, C. de Nascimento, K. L. Tucker, and A. L. Sawaya. "Regulation of Energy Intake May Be Impaired in Nutritionally Stunted Children from the Shantytowns of Sao Paulo, Brazil." *American Journal of Clinical Nutrition* 130, no. 9 (2000): 2265–2270.

International Diabetes Institute. *The Asia-Pacific Perspective: Redefining Obesity and Its Treatment.* Australia: Health Communications Australia Pty Limited, 2000.

Lee, Min-June, Barry M. Popkin, and Soowon Kim. "The Unique Aspects of the Nutrition Transition in South Korea: The Retention of Healthful Elements in Their Traditional Diet." *Public Health Nutrition* 5, no. 1A (2002): 197–203.

Milio, N. *Nutrition Policy for Food-Rich Countries: A Strategic Analysis.* Baltimore, Md.: Johns Hopkins University Press, 1990.

Monteiro, C. A., M. H. D'A Benicio, W. L. Conde, and B. M. Popkin. "Shifting Obesity Trends in Brazil." *European Journal of Clinical Nutrition* 54 (2000): 342–346.

Nielsen, Samara Joy, A. M. Siega-Riz, and Abdel R. Omran. "The Epidemiologic Transition: A Theory of the Epidemiology of Population Change." *Milbank Memorial Quarterly* 49 (1971): 590–638.

Popkin, Barry M. "An Overview on the Nutrition Transition and Its Health Implications: The Bellagio Meeting." *Public Health Nutrition* 5 (2002): 93–103.

Popkin, B. M., A. M. Siega-Riz, and P. S. Haines. "A Comparison of Dietary Trends among Racial and Socioeconomic Groups in the United States." *New England Journal of Medicine* 335 (1996): 716–720.

604

Reddy, K. Srinath. "Cardiovascular Diseases in the Developing Countries: Dimensions, Determinants, Dynamics, and Directions for Public Health Action." *Public Health Nutrition* 5, no. 1A (2002): 231–237.

Watkins, S. C. "The Fertility Transition: Europe and the Third World Compared." *Sociological Forum* 2 (1987): 645–673.

Zimmet, P. Z., D. J. McCarty, and M. P. de Courten. "The Global Epidemiology of Non-insulin-dependent Diabetes Mellitus and the Metabolic Syndrome." *Journal of Diabetes Complications* 11, no. 2 (1997): 60–68.

Barry M. Popkin

NUTS. Botanically, a nut is a hard, one-seeded fruit that is indehiscent, which means it does not split open on its own at maturity. Many commercial nuts, however, do not meet the strict botanical definition. One common characteristic of nuts is a hard outer covering or shell. The shell is a natural package that protects the inner seed, usually very high in food value, from animal predation. To overcome thick nutshells, humans (and other primates) developed tools. The most primitive tools are rocks used by chimpanzees for cracking nuts. Some scientists speculate that the shards broken from such primitive nutcrackers may have been the first scraping and cutting tools used by early humans as they gradually developed and improved technology.

Nuts may have helped spark early humans' technological creativity by coupling a challenge with a nutritious reward. The hard nutshell is a challenge that must be overcome to gain the reward of the kernel and has become a metaphor for a challenging puzzle, "a hard nut to crack." The names given to nuts by indigenous people sometimes reflect the effort of cracking. The word *pacan*, for example, was used by Native Americans to refer to all hard-shelled nuts that required an instrument (stone or hammer) to crack. The folds, wrinkles, and lobes of walnut kernels bear a resemblance to the brain, and are similarly encased in a skull-like protective case. Under the "Doctrine of Signatures," a medical system used in the sixteenth and seventeenth centuries, that similarity was considered meaningful so walnuts were prescribed for maladies related to the head. It may be from such visual, verbal, and historical connections that the term "nut" came to be associated with the head, as well as with an idiosyncratic personality.

Modern technology has provided global access to a wide range of nut crops, at the same time threatening the maintenance of the genetic and ethnobotanical diversity that produced them. Perhaps exploring the variety of nut crops within the context of their usefulness to humanity will contribute to improved stewardship.

Almonds (*Prunus dulcis* [Miller] D. A. Webb)

Plant biology. The almond is a deciduous tree of the arid temperate zone. It grows to a height of twenty-five to thirty feet and has white to pink solitary flowers, 1–1.5 inches across, that develop with or before the early foliage. The flowers of most almond cultivars are self-incompatible, although there is selection for self-compatibility, especially in Europe. Honeybees typically transfer the heavy pollen. The flower has a single pistil with two ovules. If both develop, an undesirable "double kernel" is produced. The fruit is a compressed, pubescent, oblong-ovoid drupe that splits at maturity to reveal the shallow pitted stone containing the seed (the edible kernel).

Almonds are a concentrated source of energy, being relatively high in fat (54 percent, see Table 1). The fatty acid in highest concentration is oleic acid (70–78 percent), a monounsaturated fatty acid that can contribute to lowered cholesterol levels. Kernels are also relatively

TABLE 1

Nutritive value and composition of major nut crops

Crop	% water	% protein	% fat	fat composition % sat	% oleic	% linoleic	% carb	minerals	cal/g
almond	4.70	18.59	54.23	8.05	67.01	20.00	19.51	0.48	5.98
brazil nuts	4.60	14.30	66.85	20.00	48.01	26.00	10.88	1.60	6.54
cashews	5.20	17.18	45.66	16.98	70.00	6.99	29.27	0.90	5.61
chestnuts	52.50	2.91	1.50				42.07	0.60	1.94
coconut	50.90	3.56	35.33	86.16	6.92	.	9.33	0.04	3.47
hazelnuts	5.80	12.60	62.33	4.99	54.04	16.03	16.70	1.25	6.33
peanuts	1.80	26.18	48.68	21.97	43.08	28.96	20.63	0.38	5.82
pecans	3.40	9.19	71.15	7.00	63.00	20.00	14.58	0.97	6.86
pine nuts	3.10	13.21	61.43				20.71	0.04	6.43
pistachios	5.30	19.27	53.66	10.02	64.98	19.01	18.99	1.61	5.93
walnuts	3.50	14.78	63.94	6.99	14.98	62.00	15.79	0.93	6.50

high in protein (18 percent). Seedlings vary in kernel quality, with some producing bitter kernels due to high levels of the glucoside amygdalin. Amygdalin is hydrolyzed by the enzyme emulsin to form benzaldehyde and cyanide, which cause the bitter taste. Substrate and enzyme are both present in the seed and are united when cells are injured, as occurs during consumption. The trait has adaptive value as a protection against predation.

History. Almonds originated in Asia and moved with the migrations of peoples, which were often impelled by the upheavals of famine and warfare. In Genesis 43:11, the patriarch Jacob instructed his sons to carry almonds and pistachio nuts from their home in Palestine to Egypt when the family had to relocate during a period of extreme famine (c. nineteenth century B.C.E.).

The almond may have been introduced in Greece during the conquests of Alexander the Great (c.320 B.C.E.). From Greece, almonds spread into Italy and the Mediterranean region, a movement that can be traced in the etymology of the English word. "Almond" is derived from the French *amande*, from the Latin *amygdala*, which came from the Greek.

The Arab conquest of North Africa in the sixth and seventh centuries started another wave of almond introductions. The Moors took almonds with them when they conquered southern Spain. Almonds were then transported from Spain to California during the Spanish Mission Period (1800). The warm, dry climate of California, coupled with intensive agricultural systems, led to the preeminence of California in world almond production.

Almonds are currently grown in regions characterized by a subtropical Mediterranean climate. Primary production centers are the central valleys of California, the Mediterranean region, and Central to Southwestern Asia.

Procurement. In California, culture is intensive. Cultivars are selected for high production of soft-shelled kernels. Grafted trees of improved cultivars are propagated on rootstocks selected for the constraints of particular sites. Trees are planted in irrigated orchard configurations with densities of up to 134 per acre. Two rows of the main cultivar to one row of a pollinizer are planted and hives of bees are maintained to aid pollination. Trees are heavily fertilized and protected with chemical pesticides, and yields of over 3,000 pounds of kernels per acre are achieved. Harvest operations are heavily mechanized, with specialized machines to shake nuts from the tree and others to collect them from the orchard floor.

In the Mediterranean region of production, culture is not as intensive, and many orchards are composed of selected seedlings rather than grafted trees. Furthermore, most classes and cultivars are hard- or semi-hard-shelled. Orchards contain fewer trees than in California, with only fifty to seventy trees per acre being typical. Selection has occurred within particular regions that have become

identifiable for the class of almonds produced, despite heterogeneity. For instance, the Spanish island Majorca is known for the Farmer Majorca class, composed of a multitude of related seedling trees. Recent selection has been for late-blooming cultivars that avoid frost damage, for self-compatibility, and for adaptation to the environmental stresses that are not as completely controlled as in California.

Global and contemporary issues. Standardization accompanying globalization puts pressure on diversity. Increased uniformity allows increased mechanization, and may contribute to marketability and even profitability, but at the cost of genetic diversity. Small areas in the Mediterranean once comprised distinct land races of selected seedlings. The diversity of those local populations is being reduced as grafted culture increases. Maintenance of ex situ germ plasm collections cannot substitute for the continued selection of desirable seedlings by multiple local growers.

Brazil Nuts (*Bertholletia excelsa* Humbl. & Bonpl.)

Plant biology. Brazil nuts are produced by giant evergreen trees indigenous to the Amazon forest of South America. Trees may reach heights of over 160 feet, and form part of the upper forest canopy. Cream-colored flowers are borne in racemes at the ends of shoots, and have both male and female parts. Female *Euglossine* bees accomplish pollination, while males of that species primarily visit orchids. Flowers mature and drop quickly, within a single day. Fruit matures in fourteen months, falling from the tree from January to June. The fruit is a four- to six-inch spherical pod with a thick outer shell encasing twelve to twenty-four wedge-shaped nuts, each in its own dark brown rough shell. Each nut is two inches long or more and has a single solid kernel. Kernels are about 66 percent fat, 20 percent of which is saturated (see Table 1). The high oil content makes the nuts valuable as a source of oil for cosmetics and soap making, as well as for consumption. The nuts are about 14 percent protein and are a concentrated source of selenium, which is being studied for its role in preventing some forms of cancer.

History. Although Brazil nuts have been used by indigenous people of the Amazon for millennia, they were "discovered" by the outside world in 1569 when Juan Alvarez Maldonado was directed to the nuts by the Cayanpuxes Indians on the Madre de Dios River. The Spanish called the nuts "almendras de los Andes" or "almonds of the Andes." Dutch merchants began trading for Brazil nuts in the early 1600s, but it was not until the beginning of the nineteenth century that the tree was given its botanical name. The German botanist Alexander von Humboldt and his French colleague Aime Bonpland went on an expedition to Brazil in 1799; following their return to Paris about five years later, the men named the nut after von Humboldt's friend Claude Louis Berthollet.

Brazil nuts became a traditional Christmas delicacy in England in the nineteenth century, and the market for the nuts soared as rubber exports increased in the last half of the century: the settlers who ventured into the forest to harvest rubber also harvested the Brazil nuts. When the market for rubber dropped, the demand for Brazil nuts remained consistent and has continued to support the *castaneros* who make their living harvesting the wild trees. The value of the nuts is dependable enough to serve as a type of currency in the area where they are grown.

Procurement. Brazil nuts are the only globally distributed nut crop produced almost entirely from wild trees. The long time required to establish a bearing tree, and low yields related to problems with pollination in established orchards, have made plantations of the trees economically unattractive. Most nuts come from the Brazilian states of Para, Amazonas, and Acre. Brazil nuts are also produced in Bolivia, Peru, Colombia, the Guianas, and Venezuela. A single tree may produce over 300 of the heavy, nut-filled pods. *Castaneros* do not stand under the trees in windy conditions to avoid being hit and possibly killed by the falling pods. Most collecting is done in the morning, and an experienced worker can collect close to a thousand pods in a day. Pods are opened with a machete, and nuts are carried to the river in sacks often weighing over one hundred pounds. They are taken by canoe or raft to marketing centers, where a few exporters accumulate and market the crop and receive the majority of the profit.

Global and contemporary issues. Increased attention has focused on Brazil nuts as a "keystone species," a species critical to the intricately interwoven web of life for many organisms. Studies in the wild have revealed the role of specialized bees for pollination, a factor that may be missing in planted orchards. The agouti, a large rodent, is unique in its ability to open the pods and to scatter-hoard the nuts, contributing to seedling establishment. Other organisms rely on the empty pods as a substrate for development. In recognition of their value to local people, laws in several countries prevent cutting down Brazil nut trees. Creative efforts are being made by local people to market the valuable crop directly and establish a sustainable ecological and economic system centered on this valuable nut tree.

Cashew Nuts (*Anacardium occidentale* L.)

Plant biology. The cashew tree is a medium-sized (up to forty feet tall), spreading evergreen tree that originated on the dry, salty coastal beaches of northeast Brazil. Trees have a deep taproot and extensive lateral roots that adapt them to their habitat. Leaves are simple and alternate, with entire margins. Flowers may be unisexual or perfect and are borne in terminal-branching panicles. The fruit is composed of a greatly enlarged receptacle, sometimes called the "cashew apple," at the base of which develops a thick-shelled, single-seeded, kidney-shaped nut. Inside the nut is the edible kernel, covered with another, thinner shell. Between the outer and inner shells is a thick, caustic oil called "cardol" that can cause blisters and must be removed. The kernels are roasted to remove toxins. Cashews are lower in oil than many nuts, having only 45 percent. The primary oil is oleic acid. Kernels are relatively high in carbohydrates (see Table 1). In addition to the edible nuts, the peduncle (or apple) can be eaten, pressed for juice, or used to make wine. The caustic nutshell liquid (CNSL) has heat-absorbing properties that make it useful in several industrial applications, from clutch facings to waterproof paints. Other plant parts are also useful: sap is used as insect repellent and varnish, and leaves and bark are used medicinally.

History. Indigenous people of Brazil were using cashew nuts and apples when the first Europeans visited in the mid-1500s. The Portuguese introduced trees to India in the 1560s, from which the species spread to other tropical parts of Asia. India was the source of the first international trade in cashews in 1907, exporting 430 tons of kernels to Britain and importing unshelled nuts from East Africa.

Procurement. The World Bank estimates that 97 percent of world cashew production is from "wild trees" (self-sown rather than systematically planted in orchards), although research on crop improvement is proceeding in Brazil, India, and Africa. Seedlings are capable of producing nuts only three years after planting. The vast majority of the very perishable cashew apples are allowed to rot rather than being processed. Yield from a mature cashew tree is estimated at between 100 and 150 pounds of fruit (apples and nuts), from which twenty pounds of hulled, unshelled nuts can be obtained, yielding about six pounds of kernels. Nuts are dried immediately after harvest, and then must be roasted to remove the caustic nutshell liquid, which complicates processing. Traditional methods of roasting result in the loss of the CNSL, as well as causing hazardous working conditions due to spurting oils and toxic smoke. More modern extraction methods salvage the CNSL, but require expensive solvents and technical expertise.

Chestnuts (*Castanea* spp.)

Plant biology. Chestnuts are deciduous trees with simple, alternate leaves that have serrate to dentate margins. Chestnuts are monoecious, with separate male and female flowers on the same tree. Male flowers are borne as unisexual catkins at the terminal end of shoots and as bisexual catkins on the lower shoots. Female flowers appear singly or in clusters of two or three at the base of the bisexual catkins and become the nut-bearing burrs. Male flowers tend to shed pollen prior to female receptivity, creating a tendency to cross-pollination. Pollen is primarily wind disseminated. The fruit is a spiny burr that dehisces into four valves at maturity to reveal three nuts. Chestnuts are rich reddish brown with a conspicuous pale oval scar at the base. The shell is relatively thin and is not as protective as the burr is. When the shell is removed, a hairy pellicle (seed coat) covers the embryo and two irregular cotyledons. Chestnuts have the highest water content, the lowest fat content, and the highest carbohydrate (starch) content of any nut crop (see Table 1). If chestnuts dry after harvesting, some of the starch converts to sugar and viability of the seed is lost. As a result, postharvest handling dramatically affects both the edible quality of the product as well as its viability for seed.

Three species account for the majority of world production: the Chinese chestnut (*Castanea mollissima* [Bl.]), the European chestnut (*C. sativa* [Mill.]), and the Japanese chestnut (*C. crenata* [Sieb & Zucc.]). All species have a somatic chromosome number of 2n=24 and hybridize freely.

History. Seven species of *Castanea* are found around the world in the temperate zone, and each has a long history of utilization. The Japanese chestnut is native to the Japanese islands and Korea and has been cultivated for over 2,000 years, with some cultivars being maintained since 750 C.E. The species is considered the most domesticated, with the largest fruit, the most precocious seedlings, and the smallest mature tree size. Unfortunately, some of them produce nuts that are not very palatable until they have been cooked.

Most chestnuts consumed in Europe and the United States are derived from the European chestnut, which has been cultivated in southern Europe and Asia Minor since the Roman Empire. Increasingly, hybrids between the European and Japanese chestnuts are grown commercially because the latter species is resistant to ink disease.

American chestnuts (*C. dentata* [Marsh.] Borkh) were a dominant tree in the eastern forests of North America until ink disease (*Phytophthora cinnamomi*) eliminated them from the Gulf states in the early 1800s, and chestnut blight disease (*Cryphonectria parasitica* [Murr.] Barr) developed in the United States in the late 1800s. Ink disease probably came in on cork oak trees from Portugal, which were planted in the south before 1823. Blight disease was introduced in the 1880s, with Japanese chestnut planting stock. It spread up and down the eastern seaboard with nursery stock, and then moved into the forest by other vectors, until by 1950 almost all large chestnut trees were infected. Ink disease is lethal to chestnuts, but the blight fungus does not kill roots, so trees continue to sprout, are reinfected, and die back. There is good evidence that, in the southern United States, heavy shading, competition, grazing, and continued infections often kill the trees completely, but this is not the case in northern forests, where canopy type, competition, and predation are quite different.

In addition to the two diseases, chestnuts in the United States are also threatened by the Oriental Chestnut Gall Wasp (*Dryocosmus kuriphilus*), another introduced pest that has become established and is damaging native chestnut species. The Gall Wasp is believed to have been introduced from Asia into Georgia in 1974 on scion wood that did not pass through proper quarantine. It infested orchards of Chinese chestnuts in Georgia and has also been found in wild trees of the American chestnut along the Appalachian Trail.

Procurement. Chestnuts are exported in large numbers from Italy, Spain, Australia, China, and Korea. Japan and the United States are primarily importers, although these markets are partially satisfied by locally grown chestnuts. New cultivars are being registered at an increasing rate, and interest in the crop is increasing.

Global and contemporary issues. The chestnut exemplifies both the dangers and benefits of globalization. The devastation of the North American forest by introduced diseases and insects argues in favor of the careful regulation of genetic materials moving between countries. Breeding programs are succeeding in developing resistance to these pests by the use of interspecific hybrids that were created using introduced germ plasm, illustrating the value of carefully sharing genetic resources.

Coconut (*Cocos nucifera* L.)

Plant biology. The coconut is a tall, tropical palm tree that reaches reproductive maturity six to ten years from planting and may live one hundred years. Tall varieties may reach heights of one hundred feet and have a single, usually curved or leaning, trunk with smooth gray bark marked by the ringed scars left by fallen leaf bases. A many-leafed crown tops the trunk, with each pinnately compound leaf being fifteen to twenty feet long. Male and female flowers are borne on a fleshy spike (spadix) enclosed within a leaflike sheath (spathe) arising from the leaf axils. Female flowers are in the basal position and male flowers are at the apex. Pollination may be either anemophilous (wind-distributed) or entomophilous (insect-distributed). The fruit is a large drupe eight to nine inches in diameter. The coconut has a thin, smooth, grayish brown epicarp, a one-to-three-inch-thick, fibrous mesocarp (yielding coir, a fiber used in thatching), and a woody endocarp (the shell). Inside the shell the endosperm comprises the single seed. A portion of the endosperm is solid (the flesh) and a portion is liquid (the milk). The coconut is light in relation to its volume, which allows it to float and be transported by water for long distances. Eventually it washes up on sandy, saline, tropical beaches where it is well adapted to survive. When the embryo germinates, the radicle emerges through one of three germinating pores visible on the outside of the shell. The three pores give the head-sized coconut the appearance of a monkey face. The genus name *Cocos* is derived from the Portuguese word for "monkey."

Coconut oil is extracted from the dried flesh, or copra, and is rich in lauric acid, a valuable antifungal, antiviral, and antiprotozoal compound. As a food, coconut oil is very high (86 percent) in saturated fats, which occur as medium-chain triglycerides that do not raise serum cholesterol or contribute to heart disease as much as long-chain triglycerides. Coconut oil is also a component of soaps and other health products.

History. Coconut fossils from the Tertiary period have been found in the Indo-Pacific Ocean region where the plant originated, and charred coconuts have been found in Western Melanesian archeological sites dated to 3000 B.C.E. The plant is a valuable source of food (the flesh), drink (the milk), and shelter (leaves, shell fibers, and trunk). In Sanskrit, the coconut palm is called "the tree which provides all the necessities of life." As a valued source of life's requirements, the coconut was spread by seafaring people throughout the Pacific, possibly as far as the Pacific coast of Central America, and west to India and East Africa. The first written mention of the tree was by an Egyptian monk in 545 C.E., and Marco Polo described coconuts growing in Sumatra, India, in 1280 C.E.

Procurement. Coconuts were first established in large-scale commercial plantations in the mid-nineteenth century, many from the seeds of local wild palms along the seashore. Planted coconuts now greatly outnumber wild palms, and coconut products form the main export of Ceylon, the Philippines, and other Indian and Pacific Ocean islands.

Hazelnuts (*Corylus avellana* L.)

Plant biology. Hazelnuts, also known as filberts, are produced on small, shrubby, often multitrunked trees that usually grow to heights of fifteen to twenty-four feet. They have simple, alternate, round-oval leaves with toothed margins. Hazelnuts are monoecious, with both male and female flowers on the same plant, but they are not self-fruitful. Flowers appear before the leaves. Male flowers are borne in catkins at nodes on one-year-old wood, and their wind-disseminated pollen is shed in midwinter. Female flowers are inconspicuous clusters of tiny flowers enclosed within bud scales, visible at the time of pollination as bright red stigmas extending from buds. Fruit matures from early September to October, with the ovoid or oblong nut inside a leafy husk. There is wide diversity in fruit and husk shape, and that diversity is reflected in the common names: "hazel" is from the Old English word for hood or bonnet (*hæsel*), which referred to a nut whose husk was shorter than the nut. "Filbert" is probably derived from the name of St. Philibert, a Frankish abbot whose feast day falls in the season when the nuts ripen; it has also been said that the name comes from "full beard," which referred to a long husk. In some countries long nuts are called "filberts," while shorter, round nuts are called "hazels."

The nuts are composed of a shell that has variable amounts of pubescence, especially at the tip. Inside the shell, the kernel is encased in a more-or-less-fibrous seed coat (pellicle) that is usually removed by blanching. Kernels are high in fat (62 percent), with the predominant

being oleic acid (see Table 1). Hazelnut kernels are also high in Vitamin E, averaging 400 mg/100 g.

History. The European hazelnut was the first plant of the temperate deciduous forest to move into areas vacated by receding glaciers at the close of the last ice age, due primarily to its great climatic tolerance. Nuts are recovered at European archeological sites in conjunction with prehistoric human settlements, indicating a long history of food usage. Hazelnuts are one of Europe's oldest cultivated plants. They have been grown for centuries in Turkey, Italy, Spain, France, Germany, and England, although different conventions have arisen for their culture in each country. Hazelnuts were introduced in North America by shipments of seed sent in 1629 to the Massachusetts Company. Due to the eastern filbert blight (*Anisogramma anomala* [Peck] E. Muller), the culture of hazelnuts in the United States is concentrated in the coastal valleys of Oregon and Washington.

Procurement. In Turkey, the leader in world hazelnut production (65 percent), hazelnuts are cultured in traditional systems that rely on hand labor. Multitrunk seedling trees are planted in clumps of four or five bushes, often arranged irregularly on steep hillsides. Stems are progressively removed as they grow too old, allowing younger shoots to come into production. Nuts in the husk are hand harvested before the crop drops.

Italy follows Turkey in hazelnut production, accounting for about 23 percent of world production. Hazelnut culture in Italy is similar to that in Turkey, using clumps of multitrunk seedling trees, but with more uniform spacing. In Spain, where about 5 percent of world production originates, orchards are planted in still more regular rows, with a single bush at each location rather than a clump of separate bushes as in Turkey and Italy.

The United States produces about 3 percent of the world hazelnuts. In the United States, hazelnuts are grown in systems that facilitate mechanization and maximize nut size and yield per acre. Grafted trees of selected cultivars (mostly "Barcelona") are grown as single-trunk trees in evenly spaced rows, with about 200 trees per acre. Trees are sprayed with chemicals to accelerate and concentrate ripening. Nuts fall to the ground and are mechanically windrowed and harvested.

Global and contemporary issues. The European hazelnut, *Corylus avellana*, hybridizes with other species of *Corylus* that occur from China to the United States and that are largely untapped resources. The genetic diversity of the European hazelnut is well established, based on diverse seedling culture in the primary production centers. The potential is excellent for continued genetic improvement of hazelnuts through selection and breeding.

Peanuts (*Arachis hypogaea* L.)

Plant biology. The peanut (or groundnut) probably originated in South America although it was also cultivated in ancient China. It is a low-growing annual legume with subterranean fruits. Its leaves are stipulate and even-pinnate, mostly with two pairs of oval leaflets and no tendril. Flowers are formed in the axils of leaves and have a very long pedicel. Flowers are self-pollinated and usually do not open. After pollination, cell division in the pedicel drives the pod below ground, where it ripens. The fruit is an indehiscent, fibrous, constricted pod containing one to three dry edible seeds, each encased in a papery integument. The seeds are 20 to 25 percent carbohydrate, 25 to 30 percent protein, and 45 to 50 percent oil (see Table 1).

History. Peanuts may have been domesticated by selection from the related species *Arachis monticola*, found in northwest Argentina, and the only other member of the genus with the same chromosome number ($4x = 40$), although other candidates are possible. Peanuts have been found in archeological sites in Peruvian desert oases dated to 2000 B.C.E. and were mentioned in Spanish historical records in 1550. Four major varieties of peanut form the foundations of world trade. "Virginia" prostrate peanuts were reported in the West Indies by the Spanish, and introduced from there into Mexico, as well as to West Africa via slaving ships. This variety was introduced to eastern North America from both the West Indies and West Africa in the seventeenth century. The Spanish took "Peruvian" prostrate peanuts from Peru to the Philippines and into southeastern China before 1600, with subsequent transport by Chinese traders. "Spanish" peanuts are an erect variety that is very high in oil. They were taken from Brazil to Africa in early introductions, and were established in Spain in the late eighteenth century. From Spain the "Spanish" peanuts were taken to southern France and were introduced in the United States in 1871. The "Valencia" was named for a location in Spain and introduced in the United States from that region about 1910. However, it had been introduced in Spain from Cordoba, Argentina, about 1900.

Procurement. Peanuts are grown worldwide in areas that have hot summers, alternating wet and dry seasons, and sandy soils. The plant is capable of fixing nitrogen in root nodules via symbiosis with the *Rhizobium* bacterium. Plants are harvested by digging and are piled to dry. In the United States, yields of over two tons per acre are often achieved. The major world producers of peanuts are China, India, and the United States (USDA–National Agricultural Statistics Service, 2001). The primary use for peanuts is as a source of edible oil, but they are also eaten as a food either boiled or dried. The tops of plants, as well as the residual protein-rich cake from oil extraction, can be fed to cattle.

Pecans (*Carya illinoinensis* [Wangenh.] K. Koch)

Plant biology. The pecan is a deciduous, temperate tree species native to North America. It is found in well-drained alluvial soils of the Mississippi River and its tributaries from Illinois and Iowa south to the Gulf Coast of Louisiana and west to the Edwards Plateau of Texas. Isolated populations are found as far east as southwestern Ohio, as far west as Chihuahua, Mexico, and as far south as Oaxaca, Mexico. In modern times, the distribution of pecans has been extended from the Atlantic seaboard west to California, with major commercial production in the non-native states of Georgia and New Mexico.

Trees are long-lived (to 300 years) and grow to heights of over 120 feet. Leaves are alternate, odd-pinnately compound, with nine to fifteen serrate leaflets. Trees are monoecious (male and female flowers are borne on the same tree) and dichogamous (male and female flowers mature at different times), a system that encourages out-crossing with other trees of a complementary bloom period. Male flowers are borne on pairs of three stalked catkins that arise from buds of the previous season. Female flowers are borne as spikes at the tip of the current season's shoots, usually with two to four flowers per spike. Pollen is disseminated by wind (anemophily). The fruit is a "drupelike nut," with the dehiscent husk splitting at maturity (usually September to December) to expose the elongated, relatively thin-shelled nut. Kernels are two-lobed, separated in the shell by an internal partition or septum. Kernels are high in oil (70 percent), with the predominant oil being oleic acid (60 to 70 percent).

History. Some scientists think that early people carried pecan nuts north as the Laurentide ice sheet retreated at the close of the last ice age. Nuts have been found in Illinois in association with the artifacts of early people dated to around 8900 B.C.E. There is a rich history of pecan use by Native American tribes recorded in the writings of Hernando de Soto, Cabeza de Vaca, and Oviedo. Dense groves of native pecan trees growing along the Guadalupe River of Texas were visited every other year, due to the alternate-bearing cycle. In years of heavy production, pecans were a major component of people's diet.

Shell thickness and nut size were probably the two most important criteria of selection by early foragers, just as they are for modern pecan collectors. Trees producing large, thin-shelled nuts are more highly valued, more regularly visited, more extensively harvested, and (probably) more widely dispersed over time. About 1882, Edwin E. Risien of San Saba, Texas, offered a prize for the best native pecan. His intention was to obtain nuts from the prize-winning tree and plant them to establish an orchard of superior seedlings. The tree that won the competition came to be known as the "San Saba" pecan. Seedlings of that tree were selected and propagated, producing the "Western," "San Saba Improved," and "Onliwon" pecans, among others.

The first report of successful asexual propagation was by Abner Landrum in 1822. However, it was the gardener Antoine, a slave, who first established a commercially viable orchard by asexual propagation by grafting "Centennial" pecan on the Oak Alley Plantation in

610

Nuts have always provided a dimension of humor in cookery. From left to right: Folk art serving basket for walnuts constructed of sliced walnut shells and wire, American circa 1870. Cast-iron nutcracker in the form of a dog, American, circa 1930 (press the tail and crack the nut). Austrian marzipan mold of carved boxwood, circa 1840. Marzipan (almond paste) is used here to make faux walnuts and walnut shells. ROUGHWOOD COLLECTION. PHOTO CHEW & COMPANY.

Louisiana in 1846. In the late 1800s several nurseries sold grafted trees, providing material for the first great boom in pecan orchard establishment, which occurred in Georgia in the early 1900s. The extensive acreage established at that time, largely using the "Stuart" cultivar, quickly moved Georgia to the lead in production of improved pecans.

Procurement. Native pecans are harvested from wild trees. Trees are often unmanaged except at harvest and yield less per acre and have lower-quality pecans than improved orchards. As a result, native pecans sell for less on the market. Land clearing for other crops greatly reduced native pecans during the last quarter of the twentieth century. Efforts to characterize and conserve the diversity of native pecans are being pursued.

Commercial pecans are grown in orchards of variable numbers of selected cultivars, grafted onto regionally adapted seedling rootstocks, in configurations that vary by geographic region. Tree density tends to increase from the East to the West, with many orchards planted on 50′ × 50′ spacings in the East, with 35′ × 35′ spacings common in Texas, and 30′ × 30′ spacing common in New Mexico and farther west. Cultivar diversity tends to be greatest in the Southeast, while many western orchards contain large blocks of a single cultivar, usually "Western." Grafted trees begin to bear between the

fourth to eighth leaf, but may not achieve a positive cash flow until the twelfth to fifteenth leaf. Cost of culture varies by region, with increased cost for pesticide application in the Southeast, but increased irrigation expense in the arid West.

Pecans are the most important nut crop in Mexico, which has native as well as grafted orchards. Pecans are also grown to some extent in Israel, South Africa, Australia, Egypt, Peru, Argentina, Brazil, and China.

Global and contemporary issues. The United States is the world center of diversity for the pecan. As native trees are cleared, much of that diversity may be lost. Efforts are being made to collect and characterize the diversity of the pecan across its range and to establish appropriate in situ reserves.

Pine Nuts (*Pinus cembroides* Zucc.)

Plant biology. Pine nuts are produced by the *piñon* pine tree, a small- to medium-sized tree found at high elevations in the arid North American Southwest. *Piñon* is found from west Texas to California, north to Wyoming, and south into Chihuahua, Baja California, and Hidalgo, Mexico. Trees form broad pyramidal crowns and become round-topped with age. Trunks are often twisted and gnarled, with rough, irregularly furrowed bark. Typically there are two needles per fascicle, with needles being one to two inches long, sharp-pointed, and fragrant. Trees are monoecious, with male flowers produced as short staminate cones. Female cones are lateral or subterminal, about one to two inches long and almost as wide, and brown at maturity. Cones mature the second year, in August to September. The brown to black edible seeds are one-half to three-quarters of an inch long, triangular to ovate in shape, and often rounded at the base. They have a thin, brittle shell. The kernels are aromatic and flavorful, are rich in fat (61 percent), and have about 13 percent protein (see Table 1).

History. Pine nuts have been found in excavations at Gatecliff Shelter, Nevada, and dated at 6,000 years B.C.E. Nuts were used by Native Americans in the Southwest as an important component of their diet, both medicinally and ritualistically. The terminal buds, inner bark, and the core of green cones can be eaten in the spring. Several parts of the plant were used medicinally: crushed nuts for treatment of burns; pitch for treatment of wounds; smoke from burning branches for treatment of coughs, colds, and rheumatism; fumes of burning pitch for head colds, coughs, and earaches. Wood was used as fuel and in construction. Pitch was used for waterproofing, as a black dye, and as an adhesive. Ritualistically, the pitch was used by the Navajo to prepare corpses for burial, and by the Hopi, who painted it on their foreheads to protect them from sorcery.

Procurement. Most nuts are harvested from wild trees when the crop presents itself, which is irregularly. Traditionally, nuts are collected from the ground after the cones have opened. Piñon nuts have become regionally popular as an ingredient in specialty recipes, and the demand for nuts has been met by harvest practices that damage the tree, such as breaking off cone-bearing limbs. Once harvested, nuts store well and may be kept for up to three years without becoming rancid.

Pistachios (*Pistacia vera* L.)

Plant biology. Pistachios are members of the same family as the cashew nut, the Anacardiaceae (which also includes mango and poison ivy). Commercial pistachio nuts are produced by *Pistacia vera*, a deciduous tree that grows to a height of twenty-five to thirty feet, with alternate, pinnately compound leaves, each with three to five leaflets. Trees are dioecious, producing male flowers on some trees and female flowers on others. Both male and female flowers are borne on panicles in the axils of the previous year's growth. Pollen is spread by the wind to the apetalous female flowers. The fruit is a dry drupe with an outer hull and a dry, thin shell that splits upon drying to expose the greenish kernels, each usually about one inch long by one-half inch wide. Kernels have about 20 percent protein and over 50 percent fat, 65 percent of which is the monounsaturated fat oleic acid.

History. The pistachio tree probably originated in western Asia and Asia Minor, but grows wild eastward to Pakistan and India. Pistachios have been recovered from archeological excavations in Jordan, dated to 6760 B.C.E. The Jewish patriarch Jacob instructed his sons to carry pistachio nuts and almonds with them from their home in Palestine to Egypt, as gifts for their brother Joseph, when the family had to move during a period of extreme famine (*New International Version Study Bible*, Genesis 43:11). Pliny reported that pistachios were introduced to Italy from Syria during the first century B.C.E., and spread from there throughout the Mediterranean area.

Pistachios were first introduced to the United States around 1853–1854 by the commissioner of patents, who distributed seed for experimental purposes. The crop did not gain much interest until later introductions began to fruit, in about 1881. The cultivar "Kerman" was introduced in Chico, California, by USDA (United States Department of Agriculture) plant explorer W. E. Whitehouse in 1929, from collections made near Kerman, Iran. That cultivar is the basis of the California pistachio industry.

Procurement. The major pistachio-producing areas are Iran, Turkey, and the San Joaquin Valley of California. In Iran and Turkey, nuts are harvested from trees of improved cultivars growing in established orchards, but harvesting and processing methods are primitive. Nuts are harvested by hand and many are allowed to dry in the hull, which can stain portions of the shell red, making them unattractive. As a result, many imported nuts are dyed with a red vegetable dye to camouflage the stains. Pistachios produced in California are mechanically harvested, hulled, and dried, and are unstained. Technology ensures that they can usually be marketed in natural condition. Small, wild nuts with desirable green color are still harvested in Afghanistan, although destruction of forests by clearing, overgrazing, and producing charcoal has reduced wild populations.

Global and contemporary issues. International political issues have resulted in barriers to marketing pistachios, which has influenced domestic crop value and acreage planted.

Walnuts (*Juglans regia* L.)

Plant biology. Nuts from several species of the genus *Juglans* are consumed worldwide, but the most horticulturally important is the Persian walnut. Persian walnut trees grow to heights of seventy-five feet and have trunks with tight, silvery bark. Shoots have chambered pith, distinguishing *Juglans* from its sister genus *Carya* (which has a solid pith). Leaves are odd pinnately compound, with five to nine elliptic-ovate to long elliptic leaflets with entire margins, while black walnuts have more leaflets (fifteen to nineteen) that have serrate margins. Male flowers are borne laterally as single catkins on shoots of the previous season. Female flowers are borne terminally on current season shoots and usually have one to three nuts.

Flowers are wind pollinated, and male and female flowers mature at different times of the season, promoting cross-pollination, which results in increased heterozygosity. Despite the predisposition to cross-pollinate, walnuts are self-fruitful. The fruit is a drupelike nut with a thick, irregularly dehiscent husk covering a shallowly fissured shell that encases the two kernels, each of which is deeply divided at the base.

Walnut kernels are rich in oils (64 percent), making them a high-energy food. The primary fatty acid is linoleic (62 percent), a polyunsaturated oil (see Table 1).

History. Progenitor trees were originally distributed across mountainous regions of central Asia, from eastern Turkey to Xin-jiang Province of western China. Walnuts have a long association with humans and have been found in archeological excavations of caves inhabited by prehistoric groups in China and the United States. Initial selection for large nut size and thin shell could have been unconscious, as seeds from unconsumed caches of preferred seed germinated and established seedlings near habitations. Over time, and in association with people, walnuts having large, relatively thin-shelled nuts were developed.

Improved walnuts were sent to Greece from Persia "by the kings," according to the Roman historian Pliny. From Greece, walnuts were introduced to Rome, where they were given the Latin name *Jovis glans* ('nut of Jupiter'), which was contracted to provide the genus name *Juglans*. The connection to Persian royalty is reflected in the specific epithet *regia*, meaning 'royal'. Romans spread walnuts throughout the Mediterranean, where the trees readily adapted to the warm, dry climate. The trees spread across Europe and into England where they became known in Old English as *wealhhnutu* (*wealh* means 'foreign' or 'strange', and *hnutu* means 'nut'). Although the tree is not capable of bearing profitable crops in the cool, wet English climate, it was esteemed for its high-quality wood. Walnuts were carried around the world in English ships, and came to be known in commerce as "English walnuts." Walnuts came to the United States with the first settlers in New England, although the first established production was from Spanish materials introduced in California.

Procurement. Walnuts are intensively cultured in California, with improved cultivars selected for high production and quality grafted onto hybrid rootstocks. Pollinizer cultivars are included to provide adequate cross-pollination. Orchards are irrigated, with up to five acre-feet of water per acre being required to mature a crop. Trees are chemically protected from pests, and mechanically harvested and processed.

In Europe and Asia, much production comes from seedling trees, with use of grafted cultivars increasing in Western Europe. Over centuries of cultivation, the selection of horticulturally valuable individuals and continued propagation by seed have resulted in distinct landraces in different regions.

Global and contemporary issues. In Europe, the economic incentive to increase production and quality by establishing monocultures of a few genotypes is being balanced by the awareness that regionally distinct land races provide a valuable source of genetic diversity. As more seedling trees are harvested for their valuable lumber, the need for conservation by in situ reserves has increased.

See also **Fruit; Horticulture; Legumes; Vegetables.**

BIBLIOGRAPHY

Adams, Catherine F. *Nutritive Value of American Foods in Common Units.* Agricultural Research Service, Agriculture Handbook No. 456. Washington, D.C.: U.S. Department of Agriculture, 1975.

Amazon Conservation Association. Brazil Nut Homepage, 2002. Available at www.bertholletia.org/bertholletia/.

Anagnostakis, Sandra. "The Effect of Multiple Importations of Pests and Pathogens on a Native Tree." In *Biological Invasions* 3 (2001): 245–254.

Bailey, Liberty Hyde. *Manual of Cultivated Plants.* Rev. ed. New York: Macmillan, 1974.

Barker, Kenneth, Donald Burdick, John Stek, Walter Wessel, and Ronald Youngblood, eds. *The New International Version Study Bible.* Grand Rapids, Mich.: Zondervan, 1985.

Clay, Jason H. "Brazil Nuts." In *Harvesting Wild Species,* edited by Curtis H. Freese, Chapter 7, pp. 246–282. Baltimore, Md.: Johns Hopkins University Press, 1997.

Crane, H. L., C. A. Reed, and M. N. Wood. "Nut Breeding." In *USDA Yearbook Separate No. 1590,* pp. 827–890. Washington, D.C.: U.S. Department of Agriculture, 1937.

Duke, James A. *Handbook of Nuts.* New York: CRC, 2001.

Forde, Harold I., and Gale H. McGranahan. "Walnuts." In *Fruit Breeding,* edited by Jules Janick and James N. Moore. Nuts, vol. 3. New York: Wiley, 1996.

Grauke, L. J., and Tommy E. Thompson. "Pecans and Hickories." In *Fruit Breeding,* Nuts, vol. 3 edited by Jules Janick and James N. Moore, vol. 3. New York: Wiley, 1996.

Harris, W. T., and Sturges Allen, eds. *Webster's New International Dictionary of the English Language.* Springfield, Mass.: Merriam, 1927.

Kester, Dale E. "Almonds." In *Nut Tree Culture in North America,* edited by Richard Jaynes, pp. 148–162. Hamden, Conn.: Northern Nut Growers Association, 1979.

Kester, Dale E., and Thomas M. Gradziel. "Almonds." In *Fruit Breeding,* edited by Jules Janick and James N. Moore. Nuts, vol. 3. New York: Wiley, 1996.

Kester, Dale E., Thomas M. Gradziel, and Charles Grasselly. "Almonds (*Prunus*)." In *Genetic Resources of Temperate Fruit and Nut Crops,* vol. 2, edited by J. N. Moore and J. R. Ballington, Jr., vol. 2. Wageningen, Netherlands: International Society for Horticultural Science, 1990.

Lu, Anmin, Donald E. Stone, and L. J. Grauke. "*Juglandaceae.*" In *Flora of China, Cycadaceae* through *Fagaceae,* vol. 4, edited by Wu Zheng-yi and Peter Raven. St. Louis, Mo: Missouri Botanical Garden, 1999.

Manchester, Stephen R. "The Fossil History of the *Juglandaceae*." *Monographs in Systematic Botany. Missouri Botanical Garden* 21 (1987): 1–137.

McGranahan, Gale, and Charles Leslie. "Walnuts (*Juglans*)." In *Genetic Resources of Temperate Fruit and Nut Crops*, vol. 2, edited by J. N. Moore and J. R. Ballington, Jr. Wageningen, Netherlands: International Society for Horticultural Science, 1990.

Mehlenbacher, Shawn A. "Hazelnuts (*Corylus*)." In *Genetic Resources of Temperate Fruit and Nut Crops*, vol. 2, edited by J. N. Moore and J. R. Ballington, Jr. Wageningen, Netherlands: International Society for Horticultural Science, 1990.

Mercader, Julio, Melissa Panger, and Christophe Boesch. "Excavation of a Chimpanzee Stone Tool Site in the African Rainforest." *Science* 296 (2002): 1452–1455.

Miller, Gregory, Diane D. Miller, and Richard A. Jaynes. "Chestnuts." In *Fruit Breeding*, Nuts, vol. 3, edited by Jules Janick and James N. Moore. New York: Wiley, 1996.

Rosengarten, Frederic, Jr. *The Book of Edible Nuts*. New York: Walker, 1984.

Rutter, Philip A., Gregory Miller, and Jerry A. Payne. "Chestnuts (*Castanea*)." In *Genetic Resources of Temperate Fruit and Nut Crops*, vol. 2, edited by J. N. Moore and J. R. Ballington, Jr., Wageningen, Netherlands: International Society for Horticultural Science, 1990.

Sauer, Jonathan D. *Historical Geography of Crop Plants: A Select Roster*. Ann Arbor, Mich.: CRC, 1993.

Thompson, Maxine M., Harry B. Lagerstedt, and Shawn A. Mehlenbacher. "Hazelnuts." In *Fruit Breeding*, Nuts, vol. 3, edited by Jules Janick and James N. Moore. New York: Wiley, 1996.

Thompson, Tommy E., and L. J. Grauke. "Pecans and Other Hickories (*Carya*)." In *Genetic Resources of Temperate Fruit and Nut Crops*, vol. 2, edited by J. N. Moore and J. R. Ballington, Jr. Wageningen, Netherlands: International Society for Horticultural Science, 1990.

True, R. H. "Notes on the Early History of the Pecan in America." *Smithsonian Institute Annual Report* (1917): 435–448.

Trumbull, J. Hammond. "Words Derived from Indian Languages of North America." *Transactions of the American Philological Association* 4 (1872): 19–32.

U.S. Department of Agriculture, National Agricultural Statistics Service. *Agricultural Statistics 2001*. Washington, D.C.: U.S. Government Printing Office, 2001.

Vines, Robert A. *Trees, Shrubs, and Woody Vines of the Southwest*. Austin: University of Texas Press, 1960.

L. J. Grauke